THE

INTERNATIONAL ENCYCLOPEDIA

OF

# EDUCATIONAL EVALUATION

## Advances in Education

This is an internationally acclaimed series of Pergamon education reference works. Each volume in the series is thematically organized and aims to provide comprehensive and up-to-date coverage of its own specialist subject area. The series is being developed primarily from the well-received *International Encyclopedia of Education* using the latest electronic publishing technology for data capture, manipulation, and storage of text in a form which allows fast and easy modification and updating of copy. Where appropriate a number of other volumes have been specially commissioned for the series. Volumes that are not derived from *The International Encyclopedia of Education* are indicated by an asterisk.

DUNKIN (ed.)
The International Encyclopedia of Teaching and Teacher Education

ERAUT (ed.)
The International Encyclopedia of Educational Technology

KEEVES (ed.)
Educational Research, Methodology, and Measurement: An International Handbook

LEWY (ed.)
The International Encyclopedia of Curriculum

POSTLETHWAITE (ed.)
The Encyclopedia of Comparative Education and National Systems of Education

PSACHAROPOULOS (ed.)
Economics of Education: Research and Studies

REYNOLDS (ed.)*
Knowledge Base for the Beginning Teacher

THOMAS (ed.)
The Encyclopedia of Human Development and Education: Theory, Research, and Studies

TITMUS (ed.)
Lifelong Education for Adults: An International Handbook

WANG, REYNOLDS & WALBERG (eds.)* (3 volumes)
Handbook of Special Education: Research and Practice

## A Related Pergamon Journal[†]

Studies in Educational Evaluation

*Editor:* Arieh Lewy, Tel Aviv University, Tel Aviv, Israel

[†]Free Specimen copy available on request.

# THE
# INTERNATIONAL ENCYCLOPEDIA
## OF
# EDUCATIONAL EVALUATION

Edited by

### HERBERT J WALBERG

*University of Illinois at Chicago, Illinois, USA*

and

### GENEVA D HAERTEL

*Palo Alto, California, USA*

## PERGAMON PRESS

Member of Maxwell Macmillan Pergamon Publishing Corporation

OXFORD · NEW YORK · BEIJING · FRANKFURT
SÃO PAULO · SYDNEY · TOKYO · TORONTO

| U.K. | Pergamon Press plc, Headington Hill Hall, Oxford OX3 0BW, England |
| U.S.A. | Pergamon Press, Inc., Maxwell House, Fairview Park, Elmsford, New York 10523, U.S.A. |
| PEOPLE'S REPUBLIC OF CHINA | Pergamon Press, Room 4037, Qianmen Hotel, Beijing, People's Republic of China |
| FEDERAL REPUBLIC OF GERMANY | Pergamon Press GmbH, Hammerweg 6, D-6242 Kronberg, Federal Republic of Germany |
| BRAZIL | Pergamon Editora Ltda, Rua Eça de Queiros, 346, CEP 04011, Paraiso, São Paulo, Brazil |
| AUSTRALIA | Pergamon Press Australia Pty Ltd., P.O. Box 544, Potts Point, N.S.W. 2011, Australia |
| JAPAN | Pergamon Press, 5th Floor, Matsuoka Central Building, 1-7-1 Nishishinjuku, Shinjuku-ku, Tokyo 160, Japan |
| CANADA | Pergamon Press Canada Ltd., Suite No 271, 253 College Street, Toronto, Ontario, Canada M5T 1R5 |

First edition 1990

**Library of Congress Cataloging-in-Publication Data**
The International encyclopedia of educational evaluation/edited by Herbert J. Walberg and Geneva D. Haertel.—1st ed.
p.    cm.—(Advances in education)
1. Educational evaluation—Handbooks, manuals, etc. I. Walberg, Herbert J. 1937–    II. Haertel, Geneva D. III. Series.
LB2822.75.I57   1990
379.1'54—dc19 90-3853

**British Library Cataloguing in Publication Data**
The international encyclopedia of educational evaluation.—
(Advances in education)
I. Walberg, Herbert J. II. Haertel, Geneva D.
371.2'64

ISBN 0-08-037269-4

*Computer data file designed and computer typeset by Page Bros (Norwich) Ltd.*

*Printed in Great Britain by BPCC Wheatons Ltd, Exeter*

# Contents

† deceased

**PART 2**      **CONDUCT OF AND ISSUES IN EVALUATION STUDIES**

## PART 3    CURRICULUM EVALUATION

**PART 4**      **MEASUREMENT THEORY**

## PART 5    MEASUREMENT APPLICATIONS

† deceased

## (a) Creation, Scoring, and Interpretation of Tests

## (b) Using Tests in Evaluation Contexts

† deceased

## PART 6     TYPES OF TESTS AND EXAMINATIONS

**(b) Testing Formats Used in Evaluation**

**(c) Testing in Educational Settings**

† deceased

## PART 8    EDUCATIONAL POLICY AND PLANNING

† deceased

# Preface

Over the past two decades, evaluation has become well-established as a distinctive field of research and practice. The potential of evaluation studies to serve a range of purposes has been clarified, consensus has been reached about key terms and distinctions, and clearly differentiated perspectives and approaches have emerged. Today, the field of evaluation has its own conferences, professional organizations, and journals; and an increasing cadre of professionals identify themselves primarily as evaluators. Formal evaluations of programs and policies are accepted as routine in medicine and the allied health professions, in business, in social programs, and perhaps most of all, in education.

The accumulated knowledge of evaluation theory and practice may be found scattered in journal articles, textbooks, review annuals, and innumerable evaluation reports, but to date there has been no single, definitive source for such information. The *International Encyclopedia of Educational Evaluation* provides a current and comprehensive treatment of evaluation theories and practices, focusing especially on evaluation in education. It is organized for effective use by both the beginning student of evaluation and the advanced practitioner, both as a reference work and as a set of guiding articles for planning and conducting evaluation studies. The emphasis throughout is on practicality. Over 150 signed articles represent the major evaluation approaches and methods, ranging from rigorous experiments to ethnographic case studies, and focusing on educational needs assessment, measurement, evaluation design, decision making, and educational policy. Broad, philosophical issues of evaluation are addressed, but always in the context of their potential relevance to the actual conduct of evaluation studies. The *Encyclopedia* is international in scope as many nations are represented among the article authors and among the educational programs and evaluation studies chosen as examples.

## 1. Definition of Evaluation

Throughout this volume, the term *evaluation* refers to a careful, rigorous examination of an educational curriculum, program, institution, organizational variable, or policy. The primary purpose of this examination is to learn about the particular entity studied, although more generalizable knowledge may also be obtained. The focus is on understanding and improving the thing evaluated (formative evaluation), on summarizing, describing, or judging its planned and unplanned outcomes (summative evaluation), or both. Evaluation pertains to the study of programs, practices, or materials that are ongoing or in current use. These may range in duration from an hour-long television program to a multi-year curriculum, and in scope from a program within a single school to one installed in a nationally representative sample of hundreds of schools.

Evaluation is also characterized by a plurality of methods and approaches. The traditional, goal-driven model sometimes attributed to Tyler (1949) focuses on pre-specified curriculum or program objectives, relies on tests to quantify these objectives, and aspires to rigorous experimental designs to determine their attainment. Further examples of this quantitative approach are presented by Riecken and Boruch (1974). In contrast to this experimentalist perspective, proponents of naturalistic or illuminative evaluations may embrace a case study approach, in which program goals and even research questions emerge in the course of the evaluator's immersion or the program's operation. Narrative descriptions are likely to form a major part of the data collected, although objective tests and other more readily quantifiable data may also be used. The naturalistic approach is illustrated in studies by Stake (1975) and Patton (1980). A third evaluation research perspective, in some sense intermediate between the quantitative and the naturalistic, is espoused by Cronbach et al. (1980). Advocates of this pragmatic approach place substantial emphasis on quantitative methods and strong designs where feasible, but also stress the importance of process and contextual data. They attend to a program's stated goals, but also advocate the examination of other significant outcomes that might plausibly be affected, for better or for worse, by the curriculum or program implementation. A fourth approach to evaluation is cost-benefit or cost-effectiveness analysis, as described by Levin (1983). Cost-benefit or cost-effectiveness approaches seek to quantify the resources consumed by a program, and to relate these resource expenditures to the monetary benefits or program effects obtained. Of course, the relatively narrow perspective of cost accounting methods may be subsumed as one component of evaluation studies is carried out according to some other approach.

The field of evaluation is distinguished from research methodology both by its applied focus and by the range of concerns it embraces. Evaluators must not only be familiar with one or more traditions of research methodology, but may also utilize their expertise in educational and psychological measurement, organizational theory, the dynamics of interpersonal interactions, effective oral and written communication, and other realms. Evaluators also need to be familiar with the substantive dimensions of the fields in which they are engaged. An intimate connection between substance and methodology is one hallmark of the best evaluation practice. The evaluator must not only be able to design and conduct sound research studies under difficult field conditions, but must also choose or create appropriate measurement instruments to represent the often poorly specified intended and probable outcomes of the entity under examination.

## 2. An Historical Overview

An understanding of educational evaluation as a profession should begin with a consideration of its historical roots. There has not as yet been extensive scholarship on the history of evaluation, but an excellent, brief treatment is provided by Madaus et al. (1983). Although their work focuses on program evaluation, its historical review touches on the evaluation of policies, curricula, institutions, and other kinds of entities. Educational evaluation was not clearly differentiated from other problems of educational research until the early part of this century. Thus, general treatments of the history of educational research prior to that time are also informative with regard to the history of educational evaluation.

Madaus et al. divide the period from the early nineteenth century to the present into six stages, beginning with the Age of Reform (1800–1900); followed by the Age of Efficiency and Testing (1900–30); the Tylerian Age (1930–1945); the Age of Innocence (1946–57); the Age of Expansion (1958–72); and finally, the Age of Professionalization (1973–90). The following characterizations of these six periods are outlined below.

*2.1 The Age of Reform (1800–1900)*

The nineteenth century was the time of the Industrial Revolution, a period marked by dramatic economic and technological change. Throughout this period rapid change was accompanied by increasing concern for the improvement of educational and social programs, especially in the United Kingdom and the United States. In the United Kingdom, attempts were made to reform social institutions, including hospitals, orphanages, and schools, often through the mechanism of government-appointed commissions charged with evaluating their efficacy and practices.

Educational research, or experimental pedagogy, may also be traced back to the latter part of the nineteenth century. Its philosophy and methods began in the psychological laboratory of Wundt and other German psychologists who began the precise observation and recording of human behavior. Several major figures in twentieth-century education studied with Wundt in his laboratory at Leipzig, including Cattell, Hall, Judd, and Meumann, and his work influenced scholars around the world. In 1890 Cattell first used the term *mental test*, and a decade later in Germany, Lay and Meumann explicitly distinguished experimental pedagogy from experimental psychology. By the turn of the century Binet in France, Galton in the United Kingdom, and Cattell in the United States were all deeply involved in problems of psychological or psychophysical measurement.

Another important form of educational evaluation during this period was the use of external school inspectors. Kellaghan and Madaus (1982) describe a system of school inspectors required to provide annual reports on school conditions and pupil attainments—a system that continues in some form today in a number of nations. The model of evaluation through external inspectors has also been implemented by state and federal agencies in the United States, an example of which is illustrated by inspections conducted by the Occupational Safety and Health Administration in the workplace.

In the United States, Madaus et al. (1983 p. 5) chronicle one of the earliest formal evaluations of a school, conducted in Boston in 1845. Oral examinations were replaced by written examinations at that time, in part to facilitate comparisons among schools. Objective data on standardized essay examinations could also be used in making decisions about the annual appointment of headmasters. Madaus et al. note that an attempt was made to use these data "to establish differential school effects and . . . to eliminate headmasters who opposed . . . abolition of corporal punishment" (p. 6).

In the late 1800s, Rice conducted an important, large-scale comparative study of education, devising a spelling test and administering it to thousands of pupils throughout the eastern and southern United States. He found little difference between spelling outcomes for schools with widely varying amounts of spelling drill, and his findings led to reconsideration and reform of instructional approaches.

These early evaluations of schools and other social institutions raised many of the same issues as evaluators are grappling with today, including the nature of evidence, the challenge of fashioning trustworthy evaluation designs for ongoing programs in natural settings, the potential tension between the evaluator roles of facilitating and improving versus documenting or judging outcomes, and the responsible use of evaluation results to inform social policy. Following the turn of the century, all of these issues took on heightened importance with the advent of the Age of Efficiency and Testing.

*2.2 The Age of Efficiency and Testing (1900–30)*

The early part of this century brought the rise of scientific management in the United

States, and what came to be referred to as the *school survey movement*, as a number of larger school districts throughout the country undertook studies of all phases of educational life. The centerpiece of these surveys was generally a battery of the "new-type" examinations (Paterson 1925), employing a relatively large number of objective items rather than a handful of essay questions. In Europe, the scientific study of pedagogy advanced with the 1905 publication of Lay's *Experimentelle Didaktik* and Meumann's *Einführung in die Experimentelle Pädogogik* published in 1911. In Switzerland Claparède founded his Laboratory for Experimental Psychology and published his *Psychologie de l'enfant et Pédagogie Expérimentale* in 1911.

In the United States, the use of objective tests of all kinds increased dramatically during this time, especially in education (Ayers 1918). The broad use of the Army Alpha examination for military recruits as the United States prepared to enter the First World War encouraged the expansion of testing programs of all kinds, and soon after the war standardized achievement test batteries made their first appearance (Kelley et al. 1922). Thorndike, who had studied under Cattell at Columbia, became a leading figure in the development and use of educational tests. Standardization in testing brought norm referencing of test performance on a scale never possible before, but gains in comparability across districts had their price. National tests could no longer be as closely tied as they once were to the specific curricula and objectives of individual schools and school districts.

With respect to the history of evaluation, the principal developments during the Age of Efficiency and Testing were increasing acceptance of systematic, empirical studies of program effectiveness, and an increasingly close identification of evaluation with the use of standardized tests. Toward the end of this period, centers specializing in school evaluation were established at a number of universities (Madaus et al. p. 8). Despite the increasing availability and use of standardized tests permitting comparisons across districts, evaluation throughout this period was addressed almost exclusively to local information needs and questions. This emphasis in the design of evaluations upon local questions was to continue into the 1960s (Madaus et al. p. 8).

## 2.3 The Tylerian Age (1930–45)

The work of Tyler has had an enormous influence on several areas of educational research and practice, including educational evaluation. In fact modern evaluation research is often dated from Tyler's evaluation of the Eight-year Study which ran from 1932 to 1940 (Smith and Tyler 1942). The Eight-year Study evaluation was notable for its scale (nearly 1500 matched pairs of students from thirty schools), its sophisticated experimental design, and its use of a broad range of outcome measures, many specially designed for the evaluation. The conception of evaluation it introduced was both broader in scope and more practical in execution than were those of earlier comparative studies. The Tylerian model is goal-driven, beginning with a broad consideration of intended learning outcomes, then proceeding to the operationalization of these outcomes, and finally an evaluation focused on the degree to which a program is attaining its objectives. Tyler brought a focus on outcomes rather than inputs to the educational system, and in a sense introduced a criterion-referenced as opposed to norm-referenced basis of comparison for the interpretation of program outcomes. Rather than comparisons among schools, districts, curricula, or programs, evaluation turned to comparisons between actual and intended outcomes. The findings of the Eight-year Study were overshadowed by the advent of the Second World War, but Tyler's conceptions of curriculum, measurement, and evaluation had great influence for decades to come.

## 2.4 The Age of Innocence (1946–57)

The period following the Second World War brought a significant expansion in standardized testing, and substantial technical improvements in test design and in scoring technology. Educational evaluation continued to focus on local needs and local questions, and a goal-driven, Tylerian approach was dominant (Madaus et al. 1983). A number of major technical contributions appeared during this period, including books by Tyler (1949), setting forth his rationale for curriculum design and evaluation; by Gulliksen (1950), consolidating and systematizing classical measurement theory; by Lindquist (1953), extending and applying principles of experimental design; and by Bloom et al. (1956), organizing cognitive learning outcomes in a systematic taxonomy, and calling attention to higher-level learning outcomes that had received relatively little attention in many evaluation and curriculum development efforts.

## 2.5 The Age of Expansion (1958–72)

From the late 1950s through the 1960s, the United States saw a dramatically increased federal role in social policy and programs, especially in education. The launching of Sputnik by the Soviet Union in 1957 shocked the American public, and lent impetus to large, federally funded curriculum development efforts. The civil rights movement brought school desegregation, and an increasing awareness of the problems of the poor. These changes, together with a largely untested belief in the efficacy of early childhood intervention programs, led to Project Headstart and to the Elementary and Secondary Education Act of 1964 (ESEA). As a result of these massive federal expenditures, there was legitimate concern that programs should be held accountable for their use of the monies received, and so an evaluation requirement was written into "Title I" of the ESEA, including the examination of learning outcomes. The very large number of local "Title I" programs, each required to submit a yearly evaluation report, greatly accelerated the development of evaluation theory, the growth of evaluation as a professional specialization, and the acceptance of program evaluation as a normal and expected activity.

As program evaluation moved from the realm of theory into practice, serious weaknesses were found in the models and methods of earlier times. Experimental designs could not be implemented under realistic field conditions, standardized tests proved insensitive to the effects of specific curricula in specific settings, and evaluations aimed at serving local needs and answering local questions were ill-suited to judging the overall effectiveness of programs on a national scale.

There was clearly a need for evaluation models that went well-beyond the collection of objective test data and the comparison of measured outcomes to stated goals. In response, a number of new evaluation models were developed (for example, Caro 1971, Cronbach 1963, Provus 1971, Stake 1967, Stufflebeam et al. 1971, Tyler 1969, Weiss 1972, Worthen and Sanders 1973) taking account of a wider range of intended and unintended outcomes, attending more carefully to the needs of multiple evaluation purposes and the constituencies served, and permitting a more refined differentiation among the many activities going under the name of evaluation. Campbell and Stanley's (1966) *Experimental and Quasi-experimental Designs for Research* called attention to the limitations of rigorous experimental designs in field settings, and led to a more serious consideration of practical alternatives.

## 2.6 The Age of Professionalization (1973–90)

Since the mid-1970s evaluation has emerged as a profession distinct from research.

Professional journals have appeared (e.g., *Educational Evaluation and Policy Analysis, Evaluation Review, New Directions for Program Evaluation, and Studies in Evaluation*), the American Evaluation Association has been founded, courses in evaluation are widely available, and degree programs in evaluation are available at a number of universities. There is increasing recognition that a sound, maximally useful evaluation may have to draw on a plurality of models and methods, including both quantitative and naturalistic approaches, but also an acceptance of fundamental philosophical differences that will continue to divide the profession (Cronbach et al. 1980, Cronbach 1982, Guba 1987). This *Encyclopedia* is intended to provide a comprehensive, state-of-the-art perspective on this complex and important field as it exists today.

## 3. Organization of this Volume

The *Encyclopedia* is organized into eight major parts. The first Part provides a broad overview of evaluation as a field of research and practice, including its purposes and goals, and the major models and approaches it encompasses. This is extended in the second Part, which examines the role of the evaluator and normative dimensions of evaluation practice, major issues in test use and interpretation, as well as other forms of evidence used in evaluation research. Part 3 offers a perspective on curriculum and school settings as they shape and constrain the design and execution of educational evaluation studies. Different educational philosophies and curriculum theories comport most easily with different evaluation models, and so Part 3 addresses both goal-driven evaluation models and ethnographic approaches to curriculum evaluation. Major components and applications of curriculum evaluation are also addressed. Taken together, the first three parts provide the reader with a thorough grounding in evaluation issues and approaches as they are manifested in educational settings.

The next four parts, which are the longest in the *Encyclopedia*, are directly concerned with the practice of evaluation research. Because tests and measurements of different kinds play such a critical role in most evaluation studies, Parts 4 and 5 are devoted to Measurement Theory and Measurement Applications respectively. Part 6 presents more specific information about different Types of Tests and Examinations, and Part 7 discusses evaluation Research Methodology, once more encompassing both quantitative and qualitative approaches. The practical emphasis of the *Encyclopedia* is maintained throughout these parts.

Part 8 of the *Encyclopedia*, on Educational Policy and Planning, returns to a more macroscopic level, and complements the broad introduction to Part 1. This concluding part once more considers the purposes and impacts of evaluation research, especially its relation to educational policy, planning, and decision making, and its dissemination and utilization. Thus, the reader is taken from Evaluation as a Field of Inquiry in Part 1 through important evaluation issues and curriculum considerations, and then through the specifics of evaluation research studies, and returned at the end of the volume to a reconsideration of evaluation as a field of inquiry and practice, placing it now in its broad societal context and considering its utility in guiding educational policy and practice.

## 4. Contents of the Individual Parts of the Encyclopedia

Part 1, Evaluation Approaches and Strategies, provides an introduction to the remainder of the volume. It is divided into three sections. The first, Evaluation as a Field of Inquiry, consists of five articles which address the nature of the field of evaluation, distinguishing evaluation from measurement and assessment, broadly considering the nature of evaluation models, and developing the critical distinction between formative and summative evaluation. Several distinctive purposes of evaluation are considered in the second section, Purposes and Goals of Evaluation Studies. A series of eight articles cover topics including *Needs Assessment Studies*, decision making, *Goal-free Evaluation, Program Evaluation, School Inspectors and Advisers, Evaluation of National Comparisons*, and *Meta-evaluation*. The final section of Part 1, Evaluation Models and Approaches, presents eight articles on specific evaluation approaches, ranging from naturalistic, illuminative, or transactional evaluation approaches through intrinsic and responsive evaluation to adversary and judicial evaluation models. The section concludes with an article on the *Delphi technique*.

Part 2, Conduct of and Issues in Evaluation Studies, begins with a section entitled Normative Dimensions of Evaluation Practice. This section comprises four articles covering the several roles that the evaluator must assume, including the *Role of the Evaluator, Ethics of Evaluation Studies, Professional Standards for Educational Evaluation,* and the *Impact of Evaluation Studies*. Part 2(b) deals with Issues in Test Use and Interpretation and other forms of data collection common to evaluation studies. The articles on testing issues begin with a consideration of the two major bases for interpreting and using tests, *Norm-referenced Assessment* and *Criterion-referenced Assessment in Evaluation*. These are followed by a series of more specific articles on issues in *Test Administration, Coaching for Tests and Examinations, Test-wiseness, Student Evaluation and Examination Anxiety, Test Bias, Item Bias,* and *Unintended Effects in Educational Research*, together with an article on *a Guide to Sources and Reviews of Tests*. The concluding section of Part 2 examines Issues Affecting Sources of Evaluation Evidence. These include *Handwriting Legibility*—an issue whenever written responses are elicited—*Self-report* and *Interviewing*.

The curriculum is close to the heart of an educational program, prescribing the content, organization, and delivery of school instruction. Thus, curriculum evaluation is the major evaluation application in educational settings. In Part 3 of this *Encyclopedia* entitled Curriculum Evaluation, the approaches in Part 1 and the issue perspectives in Part 2 are brought to bear on this important area. The first of two sections in Part 3, Models and Philosophies, moves from a broad consideration of curriculum evaluation philosophies and definitions through traditional and more recent evaluation models. It begins with three articles that successively focus on the problem of curriculum evaluation in the context of other kinds of curriculum study. These articles address *Alternative Paradigms in Curriculum Inquiry, Curriculum Validation,* and *Curriculum Evaluation*. They serve as a background for the next two articles on *Curriculum Evaluation Models* and *Curriculum Evaluation Research*. The sixth article in this section provides a specific case of great historical importance, describing the *Eight-year Study*, which, in the author's words "spawned the field of evaluation." The *Eight-year Study* article leads naturally into treatments of Tyler's evaluation model, *Educational Objectives, Taxonomies of Educational Objectives,* and *A Twenty-year Perspective on Educational Objectives*. The classic, objectives-driven evaluation approach is contrasted with more naturalistic, qualitative approaches in the section's concluding articles on *Qualitative Curriculum Evaluation*, and on the *Curricular Implications of Educational Connoisseurship and Criticism*. The second section of Part 3 focuses on specific Components and Applications of Curriculum Evaluation, beginning with feasibility studies and curriculum tryout, analysis of textbooks and other learning resources, evaluation in distance education, analysis of student learning outcomes (error analysis), and finally, curriculum impact analysis and retrospective evaluation.

Part 4, Measurement Theory, is comprised of two sections: General Principles, Models, and Theories; and Specialized Measurement Models and Methods. The first section begins with two articles offering an overview of *Measurement in Educational Research*, and of *Future Developments in Educational Measurement*. These articles are followed by discussions of the fundamental concerns of *Validity* and *Reliability*. The article on *Reliability* is followed by a brief treatment of the effect of reliability on obtained correlations, (*Attenuation*). The basic concepts of classical test theory and extensions to that theory are reviewed next, including *Generalizability Theory* and a variety of *True-score Models*. This section concludes with a general introduction to *Latent Trait Measurement Models* including the *Rasch Measurement Models*. The second section turns to more specific topics, beginning with specialized models and methods for rating scales and for achievement tests, two of the most widely used forms of instruments in educational evaluation. The next two articles, on *Item Analysis* and on *Validation of Individual Test Response Patterns*, address classical and item response theoretical approaches to test construction and validation. These are followed by eight articles, all dealing with specific models or approaches for specialized measurement applications. Most of these have implications for test design and format, as well as analysis. The areas covered include Thurstone, Guttman, and Likert scales; semantic differential and *Repertory Grid Techniques*; diagnostic assessment, *Confidence Marking*, and *Correction for Guessing*.

Part 5, Measurement Applications, presents practical information about a variety of paper-and-pencil instruments used in evaluation research. The first section addresses the Creation, Scoring, and Interpretation of Tests and other paper-and-pencil measures. It begins with three articles setting down general principles of item development, including *Item Writing Techniques*, *Item Bank*, and *Readability and Reading Levels*. These are followed by four articles on particular types of measuring instruments, including *Domain-referenced Tests*, *Culture-fair Assessment*, *Attitudes and their Measurement*, and *Questionnaires*. An additional five articles on scaling, norming, and scoring tests complete this section. The second section covers Using Tests in Evaluation Contexts and begins with five articles on the use of tests for selection and prediction, including selection for entry into secondary and higher education, *Prediction of Success in Higher Education*, *Credentialing*, and a final article on *Interviews for Selection*. Six articles on the use of tests for description conclude this section. These begin with the description of individuals via *Educational Profiles* or *School Records and Reports*, then proceed through increasingly global levels of description with articles on *Environmental Measures*, evaluation of compensatory categorical programs, *Monitoring National Standards*, and finally, the United States National Assessment of Educational Progress.

Part 6, Types of Tests and Examinations, is organized into four sections, beginning with a section considering practical issues cutting across a range of test types and testing situations. This section discusses the uses of computers in maintaining item pools, preparing test materials and administering tests, scoring, and data processing, as well as adaptive testing, in which the items presented are selected on the basis of an examinee's previous responses. It also addresses issues of test security, group versus individual test administration, and power and speed tests.

The second section of Part 6, entitled Testing Formats Used in Evaluation, begins with discussions of *Cloze Tests*, which may be used to measure readability, and *Cognitive Preference Tests*, which were developed to measure certain affective or attitudinal outcomes in educational evaluations. Consideration is then given to *Objective Tests*, *Sentence Completion Tests*, and *Oral Examinations*, which are generally useful in measuring cognitive learning outcomes across a range of subject matters, and to more specialized *Nonverbal Tests*. The section concludes with treatments of *Performance Tests*, *Practical Examinations*, and *Written Simulation in the Assessment of Problem Solving*.

The third section of Part 6 focuses on Testing in Educational Settings. Distinctive types of tests and examinations have been developed for different educational purposes, known by such names as *Achievement Tests*, *Criterion-referenced Tests*, *Standardized Tests*, and *Minimum Competency Tests*. *Placement Tests*, *External Examinations*, and *Differential Test Batteries Omnibus and Tests* are also considered. The final section of Part 6 is devoted to testing in specific knowledge, ability, and interest domains. It begins with a group of five articles focusing on language and literacy assessment, including *Reading Comprehension Assessment*, *Assessing Communication Skills*, *Essay Examinations*, *Vocabulary Measures*, and *Foreign Language Performance Tests*. These are followed by a second group of five articles on the testing of cognitive abilities, including *Models of Intelligence*, *Cognitive Style*, *Verbal Reasoning Tests*, *Learning Ability Tests*, and so-called *Culture-free Tests*. The final two articles address the testing of *Vocational Aptitude* and *Vocational Interest Measures*.

Part 7, on Research Methodology, is divided into three sections presenting Basic Principles of Design and Analysis in Evaluation Research, Issues in the Design of Quantitative Evaluation Studies, and Issues in Qualitative Evaluation Research. The first section provides a balanced overview of both quantitative and qualitative evaluation research methods, beginning with a general overview of design for evaluation studies and continuing with articles on basic principles of design and analysis in evaluation research, including *Experimental Design* and *Statistical Analysis in Educational Research*. *Multilevel Analysis* and the important area of *Regression Analysis* methods are treated in the next two articles—multilevel data are ubiquitous in educational settings where children are nested within classrooms within schools within larger educational authorities, and sophisticated multiple regression models have become a mainstay of educational research and evaluation. The section continues with an article on the fundamental qualitative research principle of *Triangulation*—a principle of using multiple sources of evidence which pertains to quantitative research methodology as well, of course, where the multiple sources of evidence may include multiple indicators and prior studies. The final article in the first section examines *Data Banks and Data Archives*, through which data from earlier studies can be extracted, and new data can be preserved and disseminated for future use. Following the presentation of these seven articles on basic principles, Part 7 continues with a section of four articles on design issues in quantitative studies, and a concluding section of three articles on issues in qualitative evaluation research. The quantitative articles address *Sample Design*, *Cross-sectional Survey Studies*, *Longitudinal Research Methods*, and the measurement of change. The qualitative articles address *Observation Techniques*, *Case-study Methods*, and *Analysis of Evidence in Humanistic Studies*.

The final Part of the *Encyclopedia*, Educational Policy and Planning, is concerned with the application of evaluation studies in educational decision making and in the formulation and evaluation of social policy. It is divided into two sections: Evaluation Research, Decision Making, Social Policy and Planning; and Dissemination and Utilization of Evaluation Research. The first of these two sections places evaluation in a broader context of social inquiry, and considers some specific purposes and contexts of evaluation studies. It begins with an article on *Social Theory and Educational Research*, followed by four articles on *Educational Research and Policy Making*, *Legitimatory Research*, *Policy-oriented Research*, and *Policy Analysis*. Two more articles address educational planning. The second section, covering the Dissemination and Utilization of Evaluation

Research includes six articles. The first three of these concern *Knowledge Diffusion in Education*, *Dissemination of Educational Research*, and *Knowledge Utilization*. The last three articles examine local information needs and the reporting of evaluations.

## 5. Suggestions for Using the Encyclopedia

The primary purpose of this *Encyclopedia* is to provide an easily accessible, practical, yet scholarly source of information about a broad array of significant topics in educational evaluation. Each article is followed by an up-to-date bibliography, which can be consulted for further information. These bibliographies offer access to a range of expert commentaries, and many include sources from a variety of countries and continents.

The introductions to the eight Parts explain the organization of the articles included, and provide brief synopses relating each article to others within the Part. It is recommended that the reader consult these introductions for an overview of the topics covered before reading specific articles of interest.

This *Encyclopedia* is enhanced by the provision of a complete Name Index, as well as a Subject Index. Together with the Contents, these indexes provide multiple points of entry according to readers' specific needs and preferences.

## 6. Acknowledgements

We are grateful to the many individuals who provided encouragement and expertise as we prepared this *Encyclopedia* for publication. We begin by acknowledging the support of Robert Maxwell, who provided the impetus for the parent encyclopedia, *The International Encyclopedia of Education: Research and Studies*, and encouraged the production of this *Encyclopedia*. We are also grateful to Torsten Husén and Neville Postlethwaite, the Editors-in-Chief of the parent encyclopedia. Their interest and suggestions provided guidance as we proceeded toward publication. Professors John P. Keeves, Richard M. Wolf, and Edward H. Haertel lent their expertise to assist in the final selection of content, technical accuracy, and organization of the *Encyclopedia*. The authors of the articles used their own broad knowledge of the different aspects of evaluation theory and practice to provide the variety of information in this *Encyclopedia*. Finally, the staff at Pergamon Press require special mention, in particular the efforts of Barbara Barrett, Editorial Director, Joan Burks, Editorial Manager, Debra Rosen, Editor, and Kate Sharp, Editorial Assistant, who provided superb encouragement and services throughout the preparation of this *Encyclopedia*. For all their efforts, we are grateful.

## 7. Bibliography

Ayers L P 1918 History and present status of educational measurements. In: Whipple G M (ed.) 1918 *The Seventeenth Yearbook of the National Society for the Study of Education*, Part II: *The Measurement of Educational Products*. Public School Publishing, Bloomington, Illinois

Bloom B S, Engelhart M D, Furst E J, Hill W H, Krathwohl D R 1956 *Taxonomy of Educational Objectives*, Handbook I: *Cognitive Domain*. David McKay, New York

Campbell D T, Stanley J C 1966 *Experimental and Quasi-experimental Designs for Research*. Rand-McNally, Chicago, Illinois

Caro F G (ed.) 1971 *Readings in Evaluation Research*. Russel Sage, New York

Claparède E 1911 *Psychologie de l'enfant et Pédagogie Expérimentale*, Vol. 2, *Les Méthodes*. Delachaux and Niestlé, Neuchâtel

Cronbach L J 1963 Course improvement through evaluation. *Teach. Coll. Rec.* 64: 672–83

Cronbach L J 1982 *Designing Evaluations of Educational and Social Programs*. Jossey-Bass, San Francisco, California

Cronbach L J, Ambron S R, Dornbusch S M, Hess R D, Hornik R C, Phillips D C, Walker D F, Weiner S S 1980 *Toward Reform of Program Evaluation*. Jossey-Bass, San Francisco, California

Guba E G 1987 Naturalistic evaluation. In: Cordray D S, Bloom H S, Light R J (eds.) 1987 *New Directions for Program Evaluation*, No. 34: *Evaluation Practice in Review*. Jossey-Bass, San Francisco, California, pp 23–43

Gulliksen H 1950 *Theory of Mental Tests*. Wiley, New York

Kellaghan T, Madaus G F 1982 Trends in educational standards in Great Britain and Ireland. In: Austin G R, Garber H (eds.) 1982 *The Rise and Fall of National Test Scores*. Academic Press, New York, pp. 195–214

Kelley T L, Ruch G M, Terman L M 1923 *Stanford Achievement Test, Manual of Directions for Primary Examination and Advanced Examination*. World Book Company, Yonkers-on-Hudson, New York

Lay W A 1905 *Experimentelle Didaktik*. Nemnich, Leipzig.

Levin H M 1983 *Cost-effectiveness: A Primer*. Sage, Beverly Hills, California

Lindquist E F 1953 *Design and Analysis of Experiments in Psychology and Education*. Houghton Mifflin, Boston, Massachusetts

Madaus G F, Scriven M S, Stufflebeam D L 1983 *Evaluation Models: Viewpoints on Educational and Human Services Evaluation*. Kluwer-Nijhoff, Boston, Massachusetts

Meumann E 1911 *Vorlesungen zu Einführung in die Experimentelle Pädagogik*, Vols. 1, 2. Wilhelm Engelmann, Leipzig

Paterson D G 1925 *Preparation and Use of New-type Examinations: A Manual for Teachers*. World Book Company, Yonkers-on-Hudson, New York

Patton M Q 1980 *Qualitative Evaluation Methods*. Sage, Beverly Hills, California

Provus M 1971 *Discrepancy Evaluation*. McCutchan, Berkeley, California

Riecken H W, Boruch R F 1974 *Social Experimentation: A Method for Planning and Evaluating Social Intervention*. Academic Press, New York

Smith E R, Tyler R W 1942 *Appraising and Recording Student Progress*. Harper, New York

Stake R E 1967 The countenance of educational evaluation. *Teach. Coll. Rec.* 68: 523–40

Stake R E 1975 *Evaluating the Arts in Education: A Responsive Approach*. Merrill, Columbus, Ohio

Stufflebeam D L, Foley W J, Gephart W J, Guba E G, Hammond R L, Merriman H O, Provus M 1971 *Educational Evaluation and Decision-making*. Peacock, Itasca, Illinois

Tyler R W 1949 *Basic Principles of Curriculum and Instruction*. University of Chicago Press, Chicago, Illinois

Tyler R W (ed.) 1969 *Sixty-eighth Yearbook of the National Society for the Study of Education*, Part II: *Educational Evaluation: New Roles, New Means*. University of Chicago Press, Chicago, Illinois

Weiss C H 1972 *Evaluation Research*. Prentice-Hall, Englewood Cliffs, New Jersey

Worthen B R, Sanders J R 1973 *Educational Evaluation: Theory and Practice*. C A Jones, Worthington, Ohio

January 1990

HERBERT J. WALBERG
*Chicago, Illinois, USA*
GENEVA D. HAERTEL
*Palo Alto, California, USA*

**Part 1**

# Evaluation Approaches and Strategies

# Part 1

# Evaluation Approaches and Strategies

## Introduction

The first Part of the *Encyclopedia* introduces evaluation as a field of research and practice, discusses the range of purposes and goals of evaluation studies, and presents selected evaluation models and approaches.

In Part 1(a), Evaluation as a Field of Inquiry, evaluation is distinguished from measurement and assessment in the first article entitled *Evaluation, Assessment, and Measurement*, and the nature of educational evaluation is described. Measurement refers to the quantification of some attribute of the persons or objects measured—an assignment of numbers to objects. Assessment refers to the grading, examining, or certifying of individuals; it is a term restricted to persons as objects of measurement. Evaluation refers to a process applied to abstract entities, such as programs, curricula, policies, or organizational variables. The article on *The Nature of Educational Evaluation* provides an overview of the role of evaluation, comparing it with measurement, research, and learner appraisal. The importance of evaluation for improving instructional programs is stressed, and limitations are pointed out.

As will become clear in subsequent articles, measurement and assessment results may play an important part in evaluation research studies, but evaluation itself seeks information about the value or worth of some abstract entity, the thing evaluated. Evaluation as a field of inquiry may be understood as a collection of distinct approaches embodied in evaluation models. The third article in this section discusses the *Development of Evaluation Models*, including the range of underlying principles or value orientations for the major models in use. This article provides a broad organizing framework encompassing both prescriptive, purposive approaches, and the more recently emergent area of descriptive evaluation models. The fourth article, on *Program Theory in Evaluation*, complements the treatment of evaluation models, highlighting the importance of a model for the effective functioning of the program being evaluated. Such a conception cannot only guide the evaluator in formulating questions and selecting instrumentation, but can serve as a basis for generalizations to other contexts, and can help discover possibly unintended program effects. The last of these introductory articles addresses the important distinction between *Formative and Summative Evaluation*. The formative–summative dichotomy is one of the most fundamental distinctions in the evaluation literature, and one of the earliest. In brief, formative studies are more informal, short-term, and intended primarily for internal use to guide improvement of the entity evaluated, while summative evaluations are more formal, longer-term studies intended for external audiences, summarizing the overall success or effectiveness of the entity examined.

Part 1(b), Purposes and Goals of Evaluation Studies, discusses a series of distinctive purposes of evaluation, beginning with an article on *Needs Assessment Studies*. Needs assessment refers to the processes of information gathering and analysis required to identify the concerns of individuals, groups, institutions, communities, or societies. The article describes a variety of approaches, focusing on methods of educational needs assessment, and considering needs assessment as a component of more comprehensive evaluation models. *Decision-oriented Evaluation* looks at those evaluative processes intended to produce information for selecting among alternative courses of action. This is an historically important perspective. The early evaluation literature often characterized evaluation as a technical process of collecting information and summarizing it for use by some "decision maker," and decision-making contexts are still an important locus of evaluation research and practice. However, as discussed in the next article, entitled *Beyond Decision-oriented Evaluation*, the evaluator should sometimes share the responsibility of determining what information administrators ought to have. This article stresses the active role the evaluator must play in determining not only the design and technical aspects of the evaluation but also its relevance. The article on *Goal-free Evaluation* presents an argument for even greater latitude in the evaluator's role. Goal-free evaluation is a term introduced in 1972 by Michael Scriven to refer to an evaluation approach that seeks to avoid program-based bias. It can happen that a program with one set of ostensible intents is in fact better justified by its success in serving some other function. Conversely, a program may serve its stated purposes, but may at the same time engender unintended negative effects. In either case, an evaluation focused narrowly on the stated goals may not give an accurate rendition of its value.

The next three articles, on *Program Evaluation, School Inspectors and Advisers*, and *Evaluation of National Comparisons*, deal with evaluation at successively broader levels of the educational system. The purposes entailed in program evaluation are of historical importance, and most consonant with early conceptions of the evaluator's role. In the United States, the evaluation of federally funded programs at the level of local education agencies greatly accelerated the development of program evaluation theory, training programs for evaluators, and evaluation as a profession. The article on *Program Evaluation* introduces the component parts of a program as conceived for evaluation purposes, and offers an organizational framework for the major program evaluation approaches.

The article on *School Inspectors and Advisers* turns from programs to schools as institutions, and distinguishes the functions of inspection and advisement, roughly paralleling the summative–formative distinction. It describes the role conflicts created when these two evaluation purposes are combined, and discusses the organization of these evaluative processes in the United Kingdom, France, and the Federal Republic of Germany.

Turning to the broadest level of educational evaluation, the article on *Evaluation of National Comparisons* takes up the history of cross-national comparative evaluations in education. It describes the history of the International Association for the Evaluation of Educational Achievement (IEA), and discusses issues such as sampling, preparation of comparable items in different languages, and the problem of fairly representing different national curricula using a single test. The article also discusses cross-national achievement comparisons that were not IEA studies, and clearly indicates that problems of sampling and instrumentation can threaten the interpretability of cross-national evaluation research.

The final article of this section dealing with evaluation purposes introduces the concept and practices of *Meta-evaluation*. Seven distinct approaches to meta-evaluation are described, all designed to identify potential biases in the original evaluations that meta-evaluation treats as its objects of study. Issues and recent developments in meta-evaluation are also presented.

As suggested by the range of purposes just described, the term *evaluation* covers a host of distinctly different kinds of studies. One of the first tasks in conducting an evaluation is to select a type of study that is suited to the purposes of the evaluation, as well as the philosophies of both the client and the evaluator. To organize these approaches, the last section of Part 1, Evaluation Models and Approaches, begins with the article *A Framework for Evaluation*. This article focuses attention not on formal models of evaluation, but rather on the different types of information used. In order to conduct a comprehensive evaluation, five types of information are identified as necessary. They include (a) initial status of the learners; (b) learner performance after a period of treatment; (c) program implementation; (d) costs; and (e) supplementary information.

The remainder of Part 1(c) introduces a broad range of approaches, all methods of evaluation research, and all quite distinct from one another. This discussion begins with those approaches in some sense closest to the manner in which we understand and interpret our day-to-day experience, termed *Naturalistic Evaluation*, then moves through the related perspectives of *Illuminative Evaluation* and *Transactional Evaluation* approaches. Illuminative evaluation is characterized by an eclectic, holistic "systems" approach to evaluation, taking its direction largely from the perceptions and understandings of the participants in an educational setting; whereas transactional evaluation focuses on the participants themselves, seeking to understand an educational setting through an examination of the ways in which persons in the setting contend with the tension between personal needs and aspirations, and institutional demands and sanctions. The next two evaluation approaches described, *Intrinsic Evaluation* and *Responsive Evaluation*, are more narrowly focused. Intrinsic evaluation entails a direct examination of the materials or products of an educational program using, for example, content analysis, or methods of curriculum criticism. Responsive evaluation shares with illuminative evaluation a concern for the participants' perspectives, but in contrast to the holistic focus of the illuminative approach, it is characterized by a responsiveness to key issues as perceived by the multiple stakeholders. The models of adversary and judicial evaluation are still more focused, typically seeking to resolve a small number of specific questions by guiding the development and comparison of arguments for and against. The article on *Adversary Evaluation* sets forth this general approach, and the one on *Judicial Evaluation* illustrates the range of adversarial approaches with a specific example. The section concludes with a brief article on the *Delphi Technique*.

# Evaluation as a Field of Inquiry

## Evaluation, Assessment, and Measurement

### B. H. Choppin

These three topics are treated in numerous articles scattered throughout the Encyclopedia. They are, however, interpreted separately and differently. The purpose of this article is to draw as clear a distinction as possible between the different terms and to provide some guidance as to where to look for a treatment of a particular problem or issue.

In the United States during the 1970s, and now increasingly in other parts of the English-speaking world, evaluation is being used with less and less regard to its original meaning. In the minds of many educational practitioners the words evaluation, testing, and measurement appear to be used interchangeably.

In this Encyclopedia an attempt has been made to maintain the semantic distinctions that are embedded, for example, in the writings of Ralph Tyler who may be appropriately regarded as the founding father of educational evaluation (Tyler 1950). What evaluation, assessment, and measurement have in common is testing. Each frequently (but not always) makes use of tests; but none of them is synonymous with testing, and the types of tests required for each of the three processes may be different. Keeping the ultimate objective, whether evaluation, assessment, or measurement, in mind will help the practitioner determine the type of test that will optimally serve his or her purpose. The three areas of application are considered in reverse order.

## 1. Measurement

The regular dictionary definition of "assigning a numerical quantity to . . . ." will serve in most educational applications. While instruments such as rulers and stopwatches can be used to determine height, speed, and so on, many intellectual capacities or other quantities of educational interest must be measured indirectly. Thus tests are typically used to measure such dimensions as level of intelligence, the ability to apply a given principle in a variety of situations, the proportion of material learned or forgotten.

Measurement is rarely carried out for its own sake.

It may be included in an assessment or evaluation (see below), but is more to be regarded as a basic research procedure. Because of this, a complete miniscience of psychological measurement, psychometrics, has developed to describe the different approaches to "mental" measurement and some of their properties. A number of basic psychometric concepts are relevant for users of tests for evaluation or assessment.

In many applications, raw scores on tests are unsatisfactory as measures (because of their nonlinear nature, and the uncertainty as to the meaning of zero and perfect scores) so the reader will find several references to the topic of scaling. There are also more general treatments of measurement theory.

## 2. Assessment

As far as possible the term assessment should be reserved for application to people. It covers activities included in grading (formal and nonformal), examining, certifying, and so on. Student achievement on a particular course may be assessed. An applicant's attitude for a particular job may be assessed. A teacher's competence may be assessed. Note that the large monitoring program within the United States, the National Assessment of Educational Progress (NAEP), is not an assessment within this definition. Although individual students are given tests, no interest is attached to their individual results. Data are aggregated before analysis, interpretation, and reporting (e.g., "Performance levels of 17-year-olds are declining," or "The gap in standards between the South Eastern states and the Far West is decreasing"). NAEP is an example of evaluation rather than assessment.

Throughout the world, most educational systems find it appropriate to record student achievement in some way, whether with a number, a letter code, or a comment such as "satisfactory" or "needs improvement." Such assessments are based on the informal synthesis of a wide variety of evidence, and although they often include test results, they rarely have much in common with scientific measurement. These procedures are increasingly being labeled "student evaluation" in the

United States, perhaps because of the legitimacy accorded educational evaluation by the United States Congress when it passed the Elementary and Secondary Education Act in 1965. However, neither the purposes served by grading students, nor the procedures used, match the compilation of evidence regarding program quality that Congress had in mind.

## 3. Evaluation

In general, it would seem preferable to reserve the term educational evaluation for application to abstract entities such as programs, curricula, and organizational variables. Its use implies a general weighing of the value or worth of something, and, as Scriven pointed out in an important article (1967), it usually involves making comparison to other programs, curricula, or organizational schemes.

Just as assessment may be characterized as a routine activity in which most educators will be involved, evaluation is an activity primarily for those engaged in research and development. Its potential importance in the improvement of educational systems has been accorded almost universal recognition, but fierce controversy surrounds the issue of evaluation methods.

### Bibliography

Scriven M 1967 The methodology of evaluation. In: Tyler R W, Gagné R M, Scriven M (eds.) 1967 *Perspectives of Curriculum Evaluation*. Rand McNally, Chicago, Illinois
Tyler R W 1950 *Basic Principles of Curriculum and Instruction*. University of Chicago Press, Chicago, Illinois

# The Nature of Educational Evaluation[1]

## R. M. Wolf

Any work that sets out to deal with a relatively new aspect of education is obliged to furnish the reader with a definition, description, and discussion of that aspect. This is particularly true of the burgeoning field of educational evaluation where there is considerable confusion. This confusion stems partly from the fact that many of the techniques and procedures used in evaluating educational enterprises are rather technical, and educators are often not knowledgeable about such matters. A more basic reason for the confusion, however, is that different authors have different notions of what educational evaluation is or should be. These dissimilar views often stem from the training and background of the writers, the particular professional concerns with different aspects of the educational process, specific subject-matter concerns, and even from differences in temperament. One result is that a reader unfamiliar with the field is all too often exposed to written works that not only differ but are even contradictory. Such writings are not just expressions of honest differences about what evaluation is about and how it should be carried out. They are often reflections of a deeper confusion which attends the development of a relatively new field of inquiry.

### 1. Toward a Definition of Evaluation

There are several definitions of educational evaluation. They differ in level of abstraction and often reflect the specific concerns of the person who formulated them. Perhaps the most extended definition of evaluation has been supplied by C E Beeby, who described evaluation

as "the systematic collection and interpretation of evidence, leading, as part of the process, to a judgment of value with a view to action" (Beeby 1977). There are four key elements to this definition. First, the use of the term *systematic* implies that what information is needed will be defined with some degree of precision and that efforts to secure such information will be planned. This does not mean that only information which can be gathered through the use of standardized tests and other related measures will be obtained. Information gathered by means of observational procedures, questionnaires, and interviews can also contribute to an evaluation enterprise. The important point is that whatever kind of information is gathered should be acquired in a systematic way. This does not exclude, a priori, any kind of information.

The second element in Beeby's definition, *interpretation of evidence*, introduces a critical consideration sometimes overlooked in evaluation. The mere collection of evidence does not, by itself, constitute evaluation work. Yet uninterpreted evidence is often presented to indicate the presence (or absence) of quality in an educational venture. High dropout rates, for example, are frequently cited as indications of the failure of educational programs; doubtless, they are indicators of failure in some cases, but not all. There may be very good reasons why people drop out of educational programs. Personal problems, acceptance into higher level educational programs, and finding a good job are reasons for dropping out which may in no way reflect on the program. In some cases, dropping out of an educational program may indicate that a program has

---

1   This article is adapted from material presented in Wolf R 1984 *Evaluation in Education*, (2nd edn.) Praeger, New York, and was originally published in *The International Journal of Educational Research*, Vol. 11, No. 1. It appears here with permission from Pergamon Press plc © 1987.

been successful. For example, a few years ago, the director of a program that was engaged in training people for positions in the computer field observed that almost two-thirds of each entering class failed to complete the two-year program. On closer examination it was found that the great majority of "drop outs" had left the program at the end of the first year to take well-paying jobs in the computer departments of various companies (usually ones they had worked with while receiving their training). The personnel officers and supervisors of these companies felt that the one year of training was not only more than adequate for entry- and second-level positions but provided the foundation on which to acquire the additional specialized knowledge and skill required for further advancement. Under such circumstances, a two-thirds dropout rate before program completion was no indication of a program failure or deficiency.

Clearly, information gathered in connection with the evaluation of an educational program must be interpreted with great care. Evaluation workers who cannot make such interpretations themselves should enlist the aid of others who can, otherwise their information can seriously mislead. In the above example, the problem of interpretation was rather simple. Dropout statistics are easily gathered, and one can usually have confidence in the numbers. More complex situations arise when one uses various tests, scales, or observational and self-report devices such as questionnaires and opinionnaires. In these situations the interpretation of evaluation information can be extremely difficult. Unfortunately, the interpretation of information has too often been neglected. Specific mention of it in a definition is welcome since it focuses attention on this critical aspect of the evaluation process.

The third element of Beeby's definition, *judgment of value*, takes evaluation far beyond the level of mere description of what is happening in an educational enterprise. It casts the evaluation worker, or the group of persons responsible for conducting the evaluation, in a role that not only permits but requires that judgments about the worth of an educational endeavor be made. Evaluation not only involves gathering and interpreting information about how well an educational program is succeeding in reaching its goals, but judgments about the goals themselves. It involves questions about how well a program is helping to meet larger educational and social goals. Given Beeby's definition, an evaluation worker who does not make a judgment of value—or if, for political or other reasons, an openly harsh judgment is inexpedient, does not strongly imply one—is not, in the full sense of the term, an evaluation worker. Whoever does make such a judgment, after the systematic groundwork has been laid, is completing an evaluation.

A distinction needs to be made between two types of judgments. The first is the judgment of value of the program, curriculum, or institution being evaluated. This is the type described above which is clearly within the scope of the evaluation worker's professional func-

tion. The second type of judgment is taken in light of the first and, along with other relevant factors, is the decision on future policy and action. This is clearly in the domain of administrators, governing boards, and other policy makers. If these decision makers make both kinds of judgments, they are taking over an essential part of the professional evaluation functions, and this is to be avoided.

It is quite possible that a decision will be made to retain a marginally effective program. It may be that the political or public-relations value of a program is deemed important enough to continue it despite low effectiveness. It is also possible that funds are available to operate a program of marginal quality which would not be available for other more worthwhile endeavors. It is the decision maker's job to determine whether to fund it or not. The point remains: the evaluation workers, or those charged with the evaluation of a program, will render a judgment of value; it is the responsibility of decision makers to decide on future policy and action. Each has their area of responsibility, and each must be respected within their domain. This point must be understood at the outset. If it is not, there is a danger that evaluation workers may become frustrated or cynical when they learn that policy decisions have been made contrary to what the results of their evaluation would suggest.

The last element of Beeby's definition, "with a view to action", introduces the distinction between an undertaking that results in a judgment of value with no specific reference to action and one that is deliberately undertaken for the sake of future action. The same distinction is made by Cronbach and Suppes (1969) although the terms *conclusion-oriented* and *decision-oriented* are used. Educational evaluation is clearly decision-oriented. It is intended to lead to better policies and practices in education. If this intention is in any way lacking, evaluation probably should be dispensed with. Evaluation workers can use their time to better advantage.

So far no mention has been made about what kinds of actions might be undertaken as the result of an evaluation study. The range is considerable. A conscious decision to make no changes at all could result from a carefully conducted evaluation study; or a decision to abolish a program altogether could be made although the latter case is not very likely. In fact, this writer has not heard of a single instance where a decision to terminate a program was based solely on the results of an evaluation study. Between these extremes, modifications on content, organization, and time allocation could occur, as well as decisions about additions, deletions, and revisions in instructional materials, learning activities, and criteria for staff selection. Such decisions come under the general heading for course improvement and are discussed in some detail by Cronbach (1963). M Scriven (1967) uses the term *formative evaluation* to characterize many of these kinds of decisions. In contrast, decisions about which of several alternative programs to select for adoption or whether to retain or eliminate a particular program are *summative* in nature to use Scriven's terminology. Scriven's distinction between formative and summative evaluation has achieved a fair measure of popular acceptance although the number of clearly summative studies is small. The basic point is that evaluation studies are undertaken with the intention that some action will take place as a result.

## 2. Differences between Evaluation, Measurement, Research, and Learner Appraisal

Beeby's definition of evaluation goes some distance towards specifying what evaluation is. However, in order to function effectively, a definition must not only say what something is, it should also say what it is not. This is particularly important with regard to evaluation. Three activities that are related to evaluation are *measurement, research*, and *learner appraisal*. Evaluation shares some similarities with each. The differences, however, are considerable and need to be examined so that evaluation can be brought more sharply into focus.

### 2.1 Evaluation and Measurement

Measurement is the act or process of measuring. It is essentially an amoral process in that there is no value placed on what is being measured. Measurements of physical properties of objects such as length and mass do not imply that they have value; they are simply attributes that are being studied. Similarly, in the behavioral sciences, measurement of psychological characteristics such as neuroticism, attitudes toward various phenomena, problem-solving, and mechanical reasoning do not, themselves, confer value on these characteristics.

In evaluation, quite the opposite is the case. The major attributes studied are chosen precisely because they represent educational values. Objectives are educational values which define what we seek to develop in learners as a result of exposing them to a set of educational experiences. They can include achievements, attitudes toward what is learned, self-esteem, and a host of other prized outcomes. Such outcomes are not merely of interest; they are educational values. Thus, while evaluation and measurement specialists often engage in similar acts, such as systematically gathering information about learner performance, there is a fundamental difference between the two in the value that is placed on what is being measured.

A second important distinction between evaluation and measurement inheres in the object of attention of each. By tradition and history, measurement in education is undertaken for the purpose of making comparisons between individuals with regard to some characteristic. For example, two learners may be compared with regard to their reading comprehension. This

is accomplished by administering the same reading comprehension test to the two learners and seeing how many questions each has answered correctly. Since they have been given the same test, a basis for comparison exists. This is the traditional measurement approach. In evaluation, on the other hand, it is often neither necessary nor even desirable to make such comparisons between individual learners. What is of interest is the effectivenesss of a program. In such a situation, there is no requirement that the learners be presented with the same test. In fact, under some circumstances, it may be prudent to have them answer different sets of questions. The resulting information can then be combined with that obtained from other learners and summarized in order to describe the performance for an entire group. Such a procedure introduces efficiencies into the process of information gathering. The point to be made here is that evaluation and measurement are typically directed towards different ends: evaluation toward describing effects of *treatments*; measurement toward description and comparison of *individuals*. In evaluation, it is not necessary that different learners respond to the same questions or tasks.

### 2.2 Learner Appraisal

Closely related to the notion of measurement is learner appraisal. Appraising the proficiencies of learners for purposes of diagnoses, classification, marking, and grading is usually considered the prerogative of those charged with the instructional function, typically teachers. The introduction of systematic evaluation procedures has been viewed in some cases as an intrusion on this traditional teacher function. Nothing could be further from the truth. Evaluation is directed toward judging the worth of a total program and, sometimes, for judging the effectiveness of a program for particular groups of learners. Evaluation is not an external testing program that is intended to supplant teacher responsibility for learner appraisal. In fact, it is more often than not, simply not possible to do so. For example, if in the course of evaluating a program, it is decided to have different groups of learners answer different sets of questions, the resulting evaluative information will contribute nothing to the process of learner appraisal. Measurements of individual learner proficiencies will still have to be made to fulfill the appraisal function. Thus, teachers need not fear that systematic evaluation of educational programs will intrude on the appraisal role of their professional function. Quite the opposite may occur. Teachers wishing to use evaluative information to assist them in appraising learner performance may find themselves frustrated when they learn that evaluative information does not help them in this regard.

### 2.3 Evaluation and Research

Evaluation and research share a number of common characteristics. There are some notable differences, however. Research typically aims at producing new knowledge which may have no specific reference to any practical decision, while evaluation is deliberately undertaken as a guide to action. This distinction is highlighted in the last phrase of Beeby's definition of evaluation—"with a view to action". Any distinction based on motivation is obviously fragile, and one operation can shade into another; but in practice there is usually a marked difference in content, presentation, and often method between research inspired by scholarly interest or an academic requirement, and an investigation undertaken with a definite practical problem in mind. To be sure, scholarly research has often led to highly practical payoffs—the work of atomic physicists in the 1930s is a dramatic case in point. A basic difference in motivation, however, remains.

A more basic distinction between evaluation and research lies in the *generalizability* of results that each type of activity produces. Research is concerned with the production knowledge that seeks to be generalizable. For example, a research worker may undertake an investigation to determine the relationship between student aspiration and achievement. The study will be designed and carried out in such a way as to ensure results that are as generalizable as possible. They will obtain over a wide geographic area, apply to a broad range of ages, and be as true in several years as now. Generalizability of results is critical in research. Little or no interest may attach to knowledge that is specific to a particular sample of individuals, in a single location, studied at a particular point in time. In fact, if a researcher's results cannot be duplicated elsewhere, they are apt to be dismissed. In their now famous chapter on designs for research in teaching, D T Campbell and J Stanley (1966) drew attention to the notion of generalizability, when they discussed threats to the integrity of various designs under two broad headings—internal validity and external validity. External validity was their term of generalizability.

Evaluation, in contrast, seeks to produce knowledge specific to a particular setting. Evaluators, concerned with the evaluation of a reading improvement program for third graders in a single school or school district, will direct their efforts toward ascertaining the effectiveness of the program in that locality. The resulting evaluative information should have high local relevance for teachers and administrators in that school district. The results may have no relevance for any other school in any other locality; well-intentioned educators, interested in such a program, will have to determine its effectiveness elsewhere in a separate enterprise.

Another important distinction between evaluation and research lies in the area of method. In research there are fairly well-developed canons, principles, procedures, and techniques for the conduct of studies, which have been explicated in various works (Kerlingera 1986, Kaplan 1964, Campbell and Stanley 1966). These methods serve to ensure the production of dependable and generalizable knowledge. While the methods of research frequently serve as a guide to evaluation endeavors, there are a number of occasions when such methods are neither necessary nor practicable. Evaluation is not research, and the methods of the latter do not need to dictate the activities of the former.

Some writers assert that any evaluative effort must rigorously employ the methods of experimental research and that anything less is apt to be a waste of time and money. This is an extreme position. While research methods are often useful in planning evaluation studies, they should not be too limiting. Meaningful evaluative activity that does not follow a research model can be carried on. For example, a program intended to train people in a particular set of skills, for example welding, could be undertaken with a single select group of learners and their proficiency ascertained at the conclusion of the training program. Such an enterprise would violate most, if not all, of the precepts of scientific research, for example lack of randomization, absence of a control group, and so on. However, it could yield highly pertinent evaluative information that could be used for a variety of purposes. An inability to follow research prescriptions for the design and conduct of studies need not be fatal for evaluation work. There are occasions when departures from a strict research orientation are necessary and appropriate. The important point is that substantial and important work can be done in evaluation that does not require the use of formal research methods. This must be done extremely carefully.

## 3. The Role of Evaluation in the Educational Process

The prominence given to educational evaluation in the United States can be traced to the mid-1960s. The United States Congress passed the Elementary and Secondary Education Act (ESEA) of 1965 which provided massive amounts of funds for the improvement of educational programs. The ESEA also contained a requirement that programs funded under Titles I and III of the Act be evaluated annually and that reports of the evaluation be forwarded to the federal government. Failure to comply with this requirement could result in a loss of funding for programs.

It was unfortunate that what came to be known as the *evaluation requirement* was introduced in the way that it was. Still, it seems unlikely that the need to evaluate the worth of educational programs would have been taken so seriously or so quickly without such a spur. One unfortunate aspect of the requirement to evaluate arose from the fact that evaluation, initially, was viewed by many as an activity engaged in to satisfy an external funding agency, i.e., the federal government, rather than as an integral part of the educational enterprise. It was also unfortunate that only externally funded programs were, in fact, evaluated. Resources were often not available for evaluating conventional programs.

The view that developed in the mid- and late-1960s regarding the evaluation requirement was, to say the least, lamentable. It was also in marked contrast to the view that evaluation was an integral part of the educational process, which had been developing since the late 1920s and early 1930s, principally under the advocacy of Ralph Tyler. Briefly, Tyler originally used the term *evaluation* to denote those procedures used to appraise learner progress toward the attainment of objectives. He saw such procedures as being critical for furnishing information about the extent to which objectives were being attained and about the appropriateness and efficacy of the learning experiences. Tyler's rationale postulated three major elements in the educational process: *objectives, learning experiences*, and *appraisal procedures*. Objectives refer to one's intentions for an educational endeavor; they represent the desired, or valued performances or behaviors that individuals in a program are supposed to acquire. An educational program's purposes may range from having learners (whatever their age or other characteristics) acquire a narrowly specified set of skills to reorganization of an entire life style. The nature of the objectives is not significant at this point. What is important is that an educational program is undertaken with some intentions in mind and that these intentions refer to desired changes in the learners served by the program.

The term *learning experiences* refers to those activities and experiences that learners undergo in order to acquire the desired behaviors. For example, if a program in nutrition education is concerned with learners acquiring information about the importance of including various food groups in a diet, the learning experiences designed to help students acquire this information might include reading, lectures, audio visual presentations, and the like. *Learning experiences* is a broad term that includes both individual and group activities carried on in and out of class at the instigation of educators for the sake of attaining the objectives of the program. Thus, if a teacher requires that learners visit a museum to view a particular exhibit, this would be classified as a learning experience, provided it is intended to help attain a particular objective. Correspondingly, homework assignments, individual projects, and term papers, completed outside of school, would also be classed as learning experiences. According to Tyler, learner appraisal in the educational process is critical because it is concerned with ascertaining the extent to which the objectives of the program have been met.

Tyler's representation of the educational process is presented in Fig. 1. The representation is a dynamic one as signified by the two directional arrows, linking each element with each of the others. Beginning with objectives, the arrow pointing to learning experiences indicates that objectives serve as a guide for the selection or creation of learning experiences. For example, if a geometry course is supposed to develop deductive thinking abilities in learners, then learning experiences

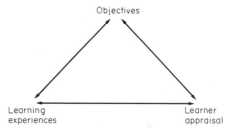

*Figure 1*
Representation of educational process. Adapted from Tyler (1969)

that require work with other than geometry content, such as newspaper editorials, advertisements, and the like, will have to be included in the program. Other examples could easily be cited. The central point is that the nature of one's objectives will be an important determinant of the learning experiences that constitute the operational program. The arrow pointing from objectives to learner appraisal indicates that the primary (some would maintain the exclusive) focus of appraisal is on gathering evidence on the extent to which the objectives of a program have been attained. Just as the objectives provide specifications for the establishment of learning experiences, they also furnish specifications for learner appraisal. To return to the previous example, a program that seeks to have students develop and use deductive thinking in life-situations might require, in its appraisal of learning, evidence regarding student proficiency to apply deductive principles to the analysis of a variety of material outside the realm of geometry.

The two arrows stemming from objectives in Fig. 1 are easily explained. The meaning of the other arrows is less apparent but no less important. The arrow pointing from learning experiences to learner appraisal is indicative of the fact that learning experiences can provide exemplars for the development of appraisal tasks. The activities that students engage in during the learning phase of a program should furnish ideas for appraisal situations. In fact, there should be a fundamental consistency between learning experiences and appraisal tasks for learners. If there is not, something is amiss in the program. This is not to say learning experiences and appraisal tasks must be identical. Appraisal tasks may contain an element of novelty for the learner. This novelty may appear in the content of the evaluation task, the form of it, or both. If there is no element of novelty, one does not have an educational program but, rather, a training program where learning experiences are designed to develop relatively narrow behaviors in the learner, and appraisals procedures are expected to ascertain only whether the narrow set of behaviors has been acquired. Education, on the other hand, involves the acquisition of fairly broad classes of behaviors. Thus, the arrow pointing from learning experiences to learner appraisal indicates that learning experiences furnish ideas and suggestions for learner appraisal; but there should not be an overspecification of appraisal procedures.

The two arrows pointing from learner appraisal to objectives and to learning experiences are especially important. In the case of the former, the arrow signifies that appraisal procedures should furnish information about the extent to which the objectives are being attained. This is an important function of learner appraisal. In addition, appraisal information can furnish valuable information that may result in the modification of some objectives and the elimination of others. Particular objectives may have been included as a result of noble intentions on the part of a group of educators, but appraisal activities may yield information that indicates the goals were not attained. This should cause the educators to reconsider the objectives. Should the objectives be modified or perhaps eliminated? Are the objectives realistic for the group of learners served by the program? Are the resources necessary for achieving the objectives available? Such questions will, of course, have to be answered within the context of a particular situation.

The arrow pointing from learner appraisal to learning experiences is suggestive of two important notions. First, just as appraisal activities can furnish information as to which objectives are being successfully attained and which are not, learner appraisal can also provide information bearing on which learning experiences appear to be working well and which ones are not. In any educational enterprise there will be a variety of learning experiences. It is unreasonable to expect that all will be equally effective. Appraisal procedures can furnish information as to which learning experiences are succeeding, which ones may be in need of modification, and which ones should, perhaps, be eliminated. This is the notion of formative evaluation described by M Scriven (1967) and discussed in some detail by Cronbach (1963). A second important idea suggested by the arrow pointing from appraisal to learning experiences is that tasks, exercises, and problems, developed by evaluation specialists may be suggestive of new learning experiences. The incorporation of novel and imaginative appraisal materials into the learning phase of a program has, on occasion, contributed significantly to the improvement of learning. Of course, the appropriation of such materials for the improvement of the quality of the learning experiences renders the materials unusable for appraisal purposes. However, this is usually considered a small price to pay for the improvement of the quality of the learning experiences.

The last arrow, which points from learning experiences to objectives, denotes that learning activities can result in encounters involving teachers, learners, and learning materials which can suggest new objectives. Alert and sensitive teachers can identify potentially new objectives. A teacher, for example, may be conducting a discussion with a group of learners and, as happens, the discussion will take a turn in an unexpected direction. The teacher may allow the discussion to follow this new course with considerable benefit to all. Such a development may lead the teacher to ask that specific provisions be made to ensure such benefits by incorporating one of more new objectives into the program. If formal provision is not made for such activities, then they may not occur in the future—the basis limitation of incidental learning being that if it is not formally provided for, it may not take place. For this reason the arrow, pointing from learning experiences to objectives, has been included.

The above characterization of the educational process is attributed to Tyler (1949); its roots can be seen in his earlier work (1934). The important point to note is that Tyler saw evaluation as central to the educational process and not as an appendage to be carried out merely to satisfy the demands of an outside funding agency. All serious writers about evaluation share Tyler's view about the critical role evaluation has to play in the educational process, although there is considerable variance as to how this role should be fulfilled. Unfortunately, the view about the centrality of evaluation in the educational process is neither universally shared by educational practitioners nor, when it is held, necessarily applied. For example, a number of writers in the field of curriculum development exhort practitioners to engage in the systematic evaluation of educational programs but furnish little guidance as to how this function should be carried out. Even practitioners will often give lip service to the importance of evaluation but will do little or nothing about it.

While Tyler's view of education and the role of evaluation in the educational process has been of enormous value to persons in curriculum development as well as to those in educational evaluation, it provides only a foundation for current evaluation thought and practice. Technical developments in the methods of evaluation, measurement, research, decision theory, information sciences, and other related areas, as well as new demands for educational planning, have resulted in additions and modifications to Tyler's original formulation.

There has been a notable shift in thinking about the role of evaluation in the educational process since Tyler's original work. Tyler viewed evaluation primarily as the assessment of learner performance in terms of program objectives. For Tyler, evaluation was virtually synonymous with what was previously defined as learner appraisal. There was good reason for this. At the time that Tyler formulated his rationale, evaluation work was largely haphazard. Tyler sought to make evaluation a more systematic and rational process. Accordingly, Tyler urged that clear objectives be formulated and that they serve as the basis for the development of evaluation instruments. The results from the use of such instruments would permit people to determine how well program objectives were being attained and thus enable them to judge program success. Given the level of educational thought and practice at the time that Tyler formulated his rationale, it was clearly a great leap forward.

A number of recent writers have argued for an expanded role for evaluation. Their reasoning is that strict fidelity to a program's objectives can place an evaluation worker in a very difficult position. What if a program is pursuing worthless or unrealistic objectives? Must evaluation workers restrict their activities to assessing the extent of attainment of those objectives or are they to be allowed to question or even challenge the objectives themselves? Opinion and practice are divided on this issue. The emerging consensus is that evaluation workers should be free to question and challenge dubious objectives when there is a real basis for doing so. This begs the issue, however, since one needs to know what constitutes a "real basis" for challenging or even questioning a program's objectives especially if the evaluation worker had no part in developing the program.

There appear to be two valid bases for challenging a program's objectives, the first more obvious than the second. If an evaluation worker has had considerable experience in evaluating the types of programs that he or she has been called on to study, then the evaluation worker might be able to question or challenge a program's objectives in light of this experience. For example, an evaluation worker who is also a specialist in elementary school mathematics might be in a strong position to question the appropriateness and even the worth of a particular set of objectives for an elementary school mathematics program. The second basis for questioning or challenging a program's objectives is the need which a program was designed to meet. Programs are established to meet some need, as Tyler clearly pointed out in his classic monograph (Tyler 1949). It is one thing to determine whether a program is achieving its objectives, it is another to say whether the objectives, even if they were achieved, meet the need that gave rise to the program. Thus, the need furnishes a basis for reviewing a program's objectives. More important, it frees an evaluation worker from having to simply accept a program's stated objectives. This does not mean that one can freely criticize program objectives. One should question or challenge program objectives only after careful study of the relationship between a program's objectives and the need the program was designed to meet, or on the basis of sufficient expertise about the nature of the program and the learners to be served.

The inclusion of objectives as part of an educational enterprise to be evaluated rather than as an external set of specifications that are beyond question is part of the contemporary view of educational evaluation. An attempt has been made to represent this view of the role of evaluation in Fig. 2. Evaluation has as its province objectives, learning experiences, learner appraisal, and the relationships between the three. Note, however, that the need on which the program is based is not included. The reason for this is that evaluation workers, because of their background, training, experience, and

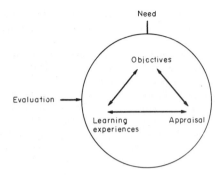

*Figure 2*
Representation of the role of evaluation in the educational process

limited view of an educational enterprise, are usually not in a good position to say whether particular needs are valid, or which of several needs should be addressed. Such matters are usually left to a group of professional workers called policy analysts working closely with decision makers.

## 4. The Limitations of Evaluation

It is common in education to make strong claims for one thing or another, whether it be a teaching method, a form of organization, or the like. In fact, one function of evaluation is to test such claims. It seems fitting, therefore, to identify limitations of evaluation lest the reader develop the mistaken notion that there are no limitations in educational evaluation.

One limitation of educational evaluation was suggested earlier. Educational evaluations, typically, do not produce generalizable results. The evaluation of a particular program in a given location can provide useful information about that program in that place, but such information may not apply to any other locale. Separate studies would have to be conducted in different sites to estimate the effects of programs in those sites.

A second limitation of educational evaluation stems from the fact that educational programs are rarely, if ever, static. Programs are continuously changing. Thus, any evaluation is at least partially out of date by the time data are gathered and analyzed. The report of an evaluation study is probably best seen as a historical document since the program that was evaluated has undoubtedly undergone some change in the period from when information was gathered until the report was produced. Some of these changes are quite natural and represent normal processes of growth and change in an educational enterprise. An evaluation study, in contrast, is a snapshot or a series of snapshots at a particular time. Readers of evaluation reports need to keep this point in mind as they seek to understand and improve educational programs.

A third limitation of evaluation studies centers on the distinction between diagnosis and prescription. Educational evaluations are often similar to medical diagnoses. That is, they can indicate the presence or absence of a fever and what particular set of symptoms are exhibited. Such information can be quite useful. However, it may not provide a prescription as to how to remedy identified deficiencies. For example, an evaluation study may indicate that students are failing to make an expected amount of progress in a particular school subject and even furnish some reasons for the lack of progress. Deciding what to do to improve the program is a different matter. An evaluation study may not be able to provide recommendations on how to improve a program that is found to be deficient.

The limitations of educational evaluation are important to recognize. Just as strong claims are made for various educational ventures, evaluation has been seen, by some, to be a panacea. It is not. Thoughtful evaluation workers recognize this. Other educators and policy makers should recognize this also.

*Bibliography*

Beeby C E 1977 The meaning of evaluation. In: *Current Issues in Education*, No. 4: *Evaluation*. Department of Education, Wellington, pp 68–78

Campbell D T, Stanley J C 1966 *Experimental and Quasi-experimental Designs for Research*. Rand McNally, Chicago, Illinois

Cook T D, Campbell D T 1979 *Quasi-experimentation: Design and Analysis Issues for Field Settings*. Rand McNally, Chicago, Illinois

Cronbach L J 1963 Course improvement through evaluation. *Teach. Coll. Rec.* 64: 672–83

Cronbach L J, Snow R E 1977 *Aptitudes and Instructional Methods*. Irvington, New York

Cronbach L J, Suppes P (eds.) 1969 *Research for Tomorrow's Schools: Disciplined Inquiry for Education*. Macmillan, New York

Cronbach L J, Ambron S R, Dornbusch S M, Hess R D, Hornik R C, Phillips D C, Walker D F, Weiner S S 1980 *Toward Reform of Program Evaluation*. Jossey-Bass, San Francisco, California

House E R 1980 *Evaluating with Validity*. Sage, Beverly Hills, California

Kaplan A 1964 *The Conduct of Inquiry*. Crowell, New York

Kerlinger F N 1986 *Foundations of Behavioural Research*, 3rd edn. Holt, Rinehart and Winston, New York

Popham W J 1975 *Educational Evaluation*. Prentice Hall, Englewood Cliffs, New Jersey

Scriven M 1967 The methodology of evaluation. In: Stake R E (ed.). 1967 *Curriculum Evaluation*, AERA Monograph Series in Education No. 1. Rand McNally, Chicago, Illinois

Scriven M 1973 Goal-free evaluation. In: House E R (ed.) 1973 *School Evaluation: The Politics and Process*. McCutchan, New York

Tyler R W 1934 *Constructing Achievement Tests*. Ohio State University, Columbus, Ohio

Tyler R W 1949 *Basic Principles of Curriculum and Instruction*. University of Chicago Press, Chicago, Illinois

Tyler R W (ed.) 1969 *Educational Evaluation: New Roles, New Means*, Yearbook of the National Society for the Study of Education. University of Chicago Press, Chicago, Illinois

Wolf R M 1984 *Evaluation in Education*, 2nd edn. Praeger, New York

# Development of Evaluation Models

**M. C. Alkin and F. S. Ellett Jr.**

Evaluation models either describe what evaluators do or prescribe what they should do. Generally, evaluators are concerned with determining the value or current status of objects or states of affairs. The term "model" is used in two general ways. (a) A prescriptive model, the most common type, is a set of rules, prescriptions, prohibitions, and guiding frameworks which specify what a good or proper evaluation is and how evaluation should be carried out. Such models serve as exemplars. (b) A descriptive model is a set of statements and generalizations which describes, predicts, or explains evaluation activities. Such models are designed to offer an empirical theory.

The importance of studying evaluation models is shown in a number of ways. For example, understanding the various evaluation models provides insights and a framework for conducting evaluations in a more defensible way. Prescriptive models provide consistent frameworks and strategies for performing evaluations, and descriptive models present a range of validated possibilities for conducting evaluation. Further insights for practice are gained from the dynamics of model development itself.

Before examining differences among model types, it is appropriate to present some areas of common concern. Most often, educational evaluation models direct their attention to evaluating teaching, learning, and curriculum efficacy. However, some evaluation models also consider those activities, practices, and policies designed to facilitate teaching, learning, and curriculum efficacy. For example, evaluation might focus on the decision-making process which manages education. Hence, evaluation models are often concerned with the financing, the administration, and in general, the sociopolitical organization of education.

The scope and depth of issues and problems which fall under the rubric of educational evaluation are surprisingly extensive. For example, the evaluation might be primarily directed towards problems of statistical inference and empirical generalization, but might also involve problems of how one can and how one should arrange the decision-making structures of a community. The topics range from specific and important problems in epistemology and scientific inquiry to specific and important problems in a political and ethical theory.

The wide disparity of topics and issues included in evaluation models is attributable to two factors. First, evaluation is still an emerging field seeking to bring definition and description both to its activities and to the way these activities might be conducted. Second, individual model builders have restricted the purposes or goals for developing their models.

There are a number of things that will not be explicitly examined within this article—primarily because they do not precisely come within the domain of evaluation models as currently conceived. Since evaluation models have tended to focus on program evaluation, this article will not be concerned with evaluation of students or teachers (assessment). Nor will it consider personnel evaluations (appraisal).

Similarly, some theories or models relate to the various tools or components of evaluation. For example, evaluation often requires the use of measurement procedures, statistical analyses, financial analyses, and so on. Modeling activities related to these kinds of matters are also not to be included within the discussion of curriculum/program/system evaluation.

Before turning, however, to an examination of the further distinctions between prescriptive and descriptive models and to a closer view of the variety of prescriptive models in particular, it is appropriate to examine the logical thought progression of the rationales which underlie the development of evaluation models.

## 1. Principles Underlying Evaluation Models

In this section the set of principles which underlie the dominant evaluation models will be analyzed.

When considering whether a program is a good or worthwhile one, it seems reasonable to determine whether it achieved its intended objectives. One of the earliest and most dominant prescriptive views of evaluation has this determination as its ultimate purpose. It is often called the Tylerian approach.

For those using this approach, the important questions ask how the objectives are to be determined, classified, behaviorally defined, and measured. In large studies, such as the National Assessment Project, the sampling of the various objectives becomes an important issue. Other important areas include the consideration of short-term and long-term objectives and the use of traditional and nontraditional forms of measurement.

One example of a situation where being guided by considerations of this type would provide useful information is the characterization of the status of student learning in the population. This approach also prescribes activities which appear to be central to any evaluation activity: (a) formulating the objectives clearly and finding reliable measures for them, and (b) using learning achievement information to judge the program.

In summary, the Tylerian view suggests the following as a basic principle: principle (a)—*the evaluation should judge that a program is good if, and only if, its objectives are achieved.*

There are limitations, however, to this basic principle. Suppose it is found that the program's objectives are not achieved? Does it follow that the program is not a good one? On the other hand, if it is found that the program's objectives are achieved, does it follow that it is a good one? Not necessarily. In the former case, it may turn out, for example, that the program is generally effective, but it did poorly because the student population was atypical. Perhaps the program was never implemented properly. In the latter case, it may turn out that something else caused the student achievement.

Thus, whether a program is a good one or worthwhile depends not only on the achievement of its objectives, but also on the degree to which such achievements are caused directly by the program. In the 1950s and the early 1960s, the causal efficacy of a program was assumed but never tested.

The recognition that the evaluation of a program should determine its causal efficacy gave rise to a cluster of evaluation approaches which took as their sole purpose, or the ultimate purpose, the determination of causation. Those who view evaluation in this way generally prescribed randomized controlled experiments as the method, or the ideal method, of establishing causation. Some prescribed quasi-experimental or "causal modeling" procedures.

A principle, then, derived from the "evaluation as an experiment" point of view is the following: principle (b)—*the evaluation should judge that a program is good if, and only if, it causes the achievement of its objectives.*

Both of these principles (practices to the exclusivity of other concerns) soon came under criticism. It was argued that the evaluation activity is typically comparative. Seldom is it shown that a program achieved all of its objectives or that a program was completely efficacious in causing the achievements. Thus, it was recommended that principles (a) and (b) be replaced by: principle (c)—*the evaluation should judge that program X is better than program Y if, all other things being equal, programs X and Y meet all of the intended objectives while program X meets others as well*; and principle (d)—*the evaluation should judge that program X is better than program Y if, all other things being equal, program X is causally more effective with respect to the objectives than program Y.*

Among those who accept principle (d) there is a dispute about whether an evaluation should provide a causal explanation of how the program produces the achievements or whether it is sufficient to show that the program *does* produce the outcomes. Prominent evaluation theorists have long maintained the former position, thereby prescribing the extensive use of randomized controlled experiments whenever possible. Others have defended the latter position, thereby recommending less structure in the experiment. Both sides agree, however, on the relevance of causal efficacy.

When one program is achieving some of the objectives while another program is achieving others, principle (c) does not apply—because weighing of the two programs is required. In order to accomplish a relative weighing of programs, it seems the objectives or the ends of the programs themselves must be evaluated. If the objectives of a program are trivial or worthless, then it seems unimportant that the program can achieve its objectives. This position recommends adding the following: principle (e)—*the evaluation should judge that program X is better than program Y if, all other things being equal, program X's objectives are better or more valuable than program Y's.*

Different positions are held, however, concerning who should make the various judgments about "better" and "more valuable" and how they should be done. In essence, each of these viewpoints represents a different corollary of principle (e), with authors disagreeing about who determines intrinsic value (see Sect. 3). Scriven has argued that the evaluator should make the judgments; Stake has at one time argued that the evaluator should collect data relevant to the values of all the various groups in the community and then make the overall judgment. Because Scriven and Stake recommend that the evaluator make this judgment, their models are often called judgmental models. Some writers doubt whether a single evaluator can fairly present the views of all sides. They have argued that each side of the dispute must have its own "advocate" and these advocates must present the arguments to a jury or a judge. Here the evaluation model is likened to judicial (or legal) proceedings. Stufflebeam argued that the evaluator should collect data relevant to the values or criteria of the decision maker who has "charge" of the evaluation; others argued that the evaluator should collect and provide information to each of the various audiences so that they may judge (Cronbach et al. 1980).

It has also been argued that evaluating a program only in terms of its intended objectives is likely to be quite misleading. For the program is also likely to have unintended consequences and such unintended consequences should be used in evaluating the impact of the program. Thus, it has been argued that evaluation should look at the unspecified outcomes, and that the evaluation should be "goal free." Of course, the unintended consequences can be good or worthwhile as well as being bad. However, the "side effects" may be so bad that they outweigh the good the program is bringing about. Such a view recommends the following principle: principle (f)—*the evaluation should judge that program X is better than program Y if, all other things being equal, program X's total consequences are on balance better than program Y's total consequences.*

In order for evaluators to follow principle (f), they must discover or identify the unintended consequences. Furthermore, they must have procedures for weighing the various consequences of the two programs. These are two sizable and difficult tasks.

Another comparative principle is often recommended for evaluating programs: principle (g)—*the evaluation should judge that program X is better than program Y if, all other things being equal, program X is less costly than program Y.*

Often, however, an expensive program may bring about very valuable learnings while an inexpensive program may only bring about somewhat less valuable learnings. In such situations, financial considerations must be weighed against the value of achieving certain educational outcomes. Principles (f) and (g) evolve naturally into the following: principle (h)—*the evaluation should judge that program X is better than program Y if, after considering both the financial aspects and the total consequences on balance of the two programs, program X outweighs program Y.*

With the elucidation of principle (h), and with the growing concern for large state-funded and federally funded programs, many evaluation theorists have attempted to deal with a new level of complexity. For often, in order to apply (h), the party making the judgments would not only have to consider the total consequences and costs of achieving the intended educational objectives A; he or she would also have to weigh the importance of objectives A against the importance of different educational objectives B. For example, it might be necessary to evaluate "new mathematics" versus "old mathematics," or the new mathematics program versus a new writing program. In some situations it might be necessary to evaluate an educational program versus a noneducational program, for example, a new reading program versus a new healthcare program. Communities and legislatures often face such choices.

Evaluators concerned about the choices that are faced by the various audiences or potential users of the report dictate yet another principle: principle (i)—*the evaluation should judge programs based upon information needs of particular audiences.*

Although most evaluation theorists have said that their models are intended to influence and assist audiences, for the most part the nature and the role of these audiences has been given little or no special emphasis.

Early attention to audiences as a major determinant in the way that evaluation should be conducted focused on decision makers. Such theorists generally believed that evaluations should be performed in the service of individuals or groups responsible for making decisions, and should provide information which is useful to them. It was held that useful information is that which satisfies predetermined criteria evolved through the initial interaction of the evaluator and the decision maker. The incorporation of the decision makers' perceptions and values determines in large part the questions to be asked and the range of possible answers.

A further extension of the principle that evaluations should be relevant to the audience is to be found in those who advocate a broader role for the evaluator. This role acknowledges the various ways an evaluator can be useful to a potential user, whether or not that user is an immediate decision maker. This point of view recognizes that all "uses" of evaluation need not eventuate in immediate decisions and that decision making is incremental (Patton 1978, Alkin et al. 1979). It is recommended that evaluators seek out potential users and engage the users in active and continuing interaction. It is held that an important result of this interaction is reflected in changes in the users' perceptions and understanding (see next section).

In this section, the development of evaluation principles has been discussed. It has also been shown that these principles provide insight into the proper purposes of evaluation activities and the methods for achieving those purposes, and it has been indicated that the prevalent evaluation models are guided by individual principles or combinations of these principles. Consideration of the underlying principles of evaluation provides a way of understanding evaluation models and the relationships between them.

## 2. Prescriptive Evaluation Models

A prescriptive evaluation model prescribes which evaluation activities are good or bad, right or wrong, adequate or inadequate, rational or irrational, just or unjust. It implicitly claims that evaluation activities should be conducted in certain ways; it talks about the evaluator's obligations, responsibilities, and duties. A model is prescriptive because it gives advice, recommendations, warnings, and guidance about doing evaluations. The recommendations appear as recipes, flow diagrams, maxims, priority rules, strategies, and general guidelines. Often, a prescriptive model points out problems, pitfalls, demands, and restrictions in doing an evaluation. In developing an evaluation model, a theorist is implicitly (or explicitly) specifying which standards, criteria, principles, and guidelines are the proper or appropriate ones to regulate the activities of an evaluator.

Almost everyone who has written about educational evaluation has, one way or another, made prescriptions. Some have spent more time systemizing their standards, criteria, and principles. A few have tried to defend or justify their prescriptions.

All prescriptive evaluation models have three aspects: empirical (methodology), valuational (values), and purposive (uses). The empirical aspect is concerned with describing or explaining various properties of an educational phenomenon which the model builder perceives as important. The valuational aspect is concerned with ascribing or determining the value of the object, given that it has such properties. Third, the purposive aspect pertains to the evaluation purposes or functions. An examination of the various prescriptive evaluation models shows that all have these three aspects stated or implied, but controversy and disagreement arise about each aspect.

"Methodology," "values," and "uses" are considered to be the major bases for categorizing the various evaluation models. These concepts emerged in the generation and discussion of evaluation principles. All evaluations involve some kind of methodology for description and explanation; all necessitate the valuing of data acquired; and all evaluations are conducted with some use in mind. Thus, the distinction between evaluation models based upon these three dimensions is not one based on exclusivity—for example, that one model only believes in the use of methodology and others do not. Rather, the category system is based upon relative emphasis within the various models. It might then be possible to ask this question: when evaluators must make concessions, what do they most easily give up and what do they most tenaciously defend?

A number of evaluation model builders are strong advocates of a particular methodology or methodological approach which dominates the way in which they think about evaluation. There are a variety of "types" within this category. Some perceive evaluation as nearly synonymous with experimental research methods. Others advocate an emphasis on the richness of qualitative data as the sine qua non of evaluation. As noted above, many insist that proper measurement is the essence of quality evaluation—failure to measure well nearly abrogates the evaluation findings. A slight variation of this theme may be found among those whose erstwhile belief is that only the use of criterion-referenced testing procedures can lead to appropriate evaluation. Other major positions to be found within this general category include those whose concern for causal modeling, quasi-experimental procedures, and so forth dominate their approach to evaluation.

Another group of evaluation model builders are best categorized as having values as their primary concern. We have alluded to several of them in the discussion of principle (e) in the previous section. When looking at the issue of making judgments, it was noted that some model builders recommend that the evaluator make the valuational judgment. In some instances the evaluator is to benefit from data collected from a variety of relevant groups; in other instances the evaluator's personal background, knowledge, and experience serves to ground the valuing process.

The final category, use, includes those evaluation model builders who advocate that the primary emphasis within evaluation must be the concerns of decision makers and other users. Thus, even though they recognize the necessity for employing diverse methodology and for valuing data, they would make compromises on these dimensions in order to produce valid data relevant for decision/user audiences. (Note that their definition of "valid" would differ from those in the methodology category.) As previously indicated, early emphasis within this category revolved around decision makers and the explication of questions of concern to this group. A more recent thrust within the category has focused on users and recognized the dynamic relationship between evaluators and users—a relationship in which decision concerns have been replaced by interaction attuned to decisions in a more incremental sense (e.g. knowledge acquisition, and attitude change). Though it might be said that some evaluation model builders who view "evaluation" as nearly synonymous with "research" are governed to a large extent by *their* intended use and user audience (the research community), this article has generally tended to classify these individuals within the methodology category.

## 3. General Features of Prescriptive Evaluation Models and their Justification

In the previous sections some principles underlying evaluation models and a way of categorizing the models were discussed. Implicit within this discussion has been the meaning of "model" as exemplified by current work. It is important to note the way that the term "evaluation model" has been used. A consideration of Michael Scriven's work best illustrates the point in question. Scriven was among the first to clearly articulate and argue for principles (c), (d), (e), and (f) (in Sect. 1). Such principles in the aggregate are often taken to constitute the essence of Scriven's evaluation model. As Scriven has often said, evaluation consists simply of the gathering and combining of performance data with a weighted set of criterial scales to yield either comparative or numerical ratings, and in the justification of (a) the data-gathering instruments, (b) the weighings, and (c) the selection of criteria. Sometimes, however, Scriven's "model" of evaluation is depicted simply as his views on goal-free evaluation. At issue is whether an individual's "model" of evaluation consists of a particular writing or, more generally, of an individual's full body of writing over time. This confusion is, of course, further complicated by the fact that many model builder's views (and thus perceptions) change over time. (This point will be discussed more fully in Sect. 5.) In this article, an attempt has been made to refer to "models" as the largest coherent set of ideas put forward by a particular model builder at a particular time. Thus, authors' models would be differentiated if they changed over time (e.g. "early Cronbach" and "recent Cronbach").

Items referred to as "models" also differ with respect to yet another dimension—their level of specificity and detailed prescription. Here it is possible to contrast a single idea (conceptualized but not fully described) portrayed as a model (Scriven's goal-free evaluation) against a step-by-step kit intended as a detailed recipe for the beginning evaluator.

General issues concerning the justification of prescriptive models will now be discussed, and the valuational and empirical aspects of evaluation models will be examined. Similar remarks pertain to the purposive aspect. The following distinctions will be helpful in examining the valuational aspect of evaluation models: (a) extrinsic value: properties which render a program instrumental as a means to something desirable or good;

(b) intrinsic value: properties which are desirable or good as an end in themselves. Intrinsic value is presupposed by extrinsic value. (c) "Value" refers to what is valued, judged to have value, thought to be good, or desired. The expression "one's values" refers to what a person thinks to be good. Many people assume that nothing has objective value, that "value" means only being valued and "good" means being thought to be good. However, there is a related sense: (d) "value" refers to what *has* value or is valuable, or good, as opposed to what is regarded as good or valuable. What certain people regard or think is good or desirable is, of course, a question empirical science can answer. Whether anything has *objective* value is a question which belongs primarily to moral or political philosophy.

In general, the cluster of models within the decision maker/user category view the evaluator (the evaluation group) as an advisor to the decision-making body, or an educator of the affected audiences, in much the same way as lawyers interact with their clients. These models make the assumption that intrinsic value refers to what some decision maker, manager, or group thinks of or regards as valuable. Many of these evaluation models assume that the society's legal and political structures are in compliance with a justifiable democratic theory. Hence, they are anxious to forbid the evaluator from preempting the legitimate roles of such people in their decision making. It is plausible that evaluation should not take on a decision-making role. However, it is possible that evaluation models within this cluster might provide for the role of critic of the system and its structure (Benn and Mortimore 1976).

Some models have an air of impartiality because they recommend that it be determined what all parties or all sides think is good, or each person thinks is good. But such models offer few or no principles for selecting the appropriate reference groups. House (1978) has tried to develop criteria for group selection by using the work of a social political philosopher, John Rawls. House argues that the least advantaged group of society should always be a reference group. Overall, model builders have yet to clarify and defend their sociopolitical assumptions and commitments.

The empirical aspects of evaluation models also require validation. Many evaluation theorists see themselves as social scientists and urge that their work have the objectivity appropriate to such sciences. This is particularly true for those within the methodology category. Many of the global prescriptions within these models are defended by appeals to the philosophy of science. For example, the requirement for "operational" and for "behavioral" definitions were defended on the grounds that that is the way proper science is conducted. Another issue illustrating proper science methodology involves causation. A large number of evaluation theorists hold that the causal efficacy of the program must be shown in the evaluation. They hold that randomized, controlled experiments are the best way to establish causation. But what is causation? Are there causal laws in the social sciences? Indeed, these are questions pertaining to the philosophy of social science, and whose answers are still controversial.

In the previous discussion, the controversies related to the nature of social science principles have been considered as a justification of evaluation models. Beyond the validation of models using these principles, a related concern associated with the social sciences is the extent to which evaluation models may draw upon presumed models from other disciplines. For example, many current educational evaluation models focus on problems and issues in management and organizational theory. Whatever the value of such inquiries, it is debatable whether these areas have achieved status as a science.

There is, therefore, much disagreement among the evaluation models as to the kind and level of precision and objectivity appropriate to the evaluation tasks being carried out. There is the realization that the imposition of unrealistic standards and criteria can only retard model development and limit the value of models in practice.

## 4. Descriptive Educational Evaluation Models

A descriptive model is a "theory." An evaluation theory (a descriptive model) is a general set of empirical statements containing generalizations (or laws) for describing, predicting, or explaining evaluation activities. Since the early 1970s, there has been no single global study which was directed towards the development of a comprehensive theory of evaluation. Most of the research has been directed at particular aspects of evaluation.

A good example of research on evaluation directed at particular aspects is provided by the recent studies of evaluation utilization. While these studies constitute attempts at evaluation theory building, they are limited by their focus and their points of view. Determination of factors influencing the use of evaluation findings provide the first steps in what might ultimately be a well-confirmed theory (Alkin et al. 1979). In all but one instance, these researchers have used case studies of educational evaluations to produce their generalizations. Thus, their theory formulations are directly grounded in field data.

Findings from the evaluation utilization research provide the evidence upon which ultimate elements of an evaluation theory might be constructed. For example, Patton's findings suggest the likely importance of the "personal factor" in a complete theory of those factors which influence evaluation use. Again, several researchers suggest that a single database may not be useful to all audiences of the evaluation. However, even if well-confirmed theoretical formulations are developed, a theory of evaluation utilization would be only a part of a possible comprehensive theory of evaluation. For as was noted earlier, evaluation oriented towards utilization is but one of many dimensions of evaluation.

Other attempts at building descriptive models have drawn on general social science studies. The implication is that the generalizations produced by social scientists pertaining to institutions in general apply to educational institutions in particular. Most notable are the attempts to describe and explain the educational decision-making process in this way (Cronbach et al. 1980). These researchers use social science generalizations to ground their theoretical formulations.

Although the development of descriptive evaluation models is in but a preliminary stage, its importance should not be underemphasized. Not only is theory useful in the understanding of evaluation activities but, more importantly, descriptive evaluation models should undergird prescriptive models. Descriptive models provide the limitations and possibilities for the prescriptive models.

## 5. Evaluation Model Development

Since the early 1970s, evaluation theorists have been increasingly aware of the need for systematization and the defense of their purposes and methods for carrying out educational evaluations. This has led to an increasing amount of literature on the articulation and the contrast and comparison of various evaluation models. Some attention has also been given to understanding the process of evaluation model development itself.

Much of the work on articulation and systematization has resulted in the development and refinement of category systems of the various evaluation prescriptive models. These categorizations have generally been in terms of the model's ultimate purposes and related procedures and methods. Such category systems serve model development by identifying hidden commonalities and related possibilities or tasks among the models. The category systems developed by Worthen and Sanders (1973) and House (1978) are illustrative of this work.

As in jurisprudence, such systematization and codification do not seek an absolute and final category system. Rather, such efforts are part of the dialectical process of developing new models and methods which will fulfill more of the pressing needs and demands for evaluations in our society.

Empirical studies investigating the comparative merit of various descriptive evaluation models have been few. Such studies might contribute both to an understanding of how the prescriptive models actually work (an alternative basis for generating data for descriptive theory) and provide grounds for preferring one prescriptive model over another.

A few works have examined the process of evaluation model development. Given that a model builder is at least trying to develop a coherent and realistic set of prescriptions for evaluation, evidence suggests that theorists' views of the key problems and their prescriptions change dynamically over time. Often these changes are brought about by renewed reflection on a person's own writings. Surprisingly enough, it seems that even the most articulate writers formulate only some of the more salient points of their models. Often key assumptions and presuppositions remain hidden in the background. These matters have been investigated by Alkin and Ellett (1979).

## Bibliography

Alkin M C, Ellett F S Jr. 1979 An inquiry into the nature of evaluation theorizing. *Stud. Educ. Eval.* 5: 151–56

Alkin M C, Daillak R, White P 1979 *Using Evaluations: Does Evaluation Make a Difference?* Sage, Beverly Hills, California

Benn S I, Mortimore G W (eds.) 1976 *Rationality and the Social Sciences: Contributions to the Philosophy and Meth-odology of the Social Sciences.* Routledge and Kegan Paul, London

Cronbach L J et al. 1980 *Toward Reform of Program Evaluation: Aims, Methods, and Institutional Arrangements.* Jossey-Bass, San Francisco, California

Glass G V, Ellett F S Jr 1980 Evaluation research. *Ann. Rev. Psychol.* 31: 211-28

House E R 1978 Assumptions underlying evaluation models. *Educ. Res.* AERA 7(3): 4–12

Patton M Q 1978 *Utilization-focused Evaluation.* Sage, Beverly Hills, California

Raizen S A, Rossi P H (eds.) 1981 *Program Evaluation in Education: When? How? To What Ends?* National Academy Press, Washington, DC

Worthen B R, Sanders J R 1973 *Educational Evaluation: Theory and Practice.* Wadsworth, Belmont, California

# Program Theory in Evaluation

**A. J. Reynolds and H. J. Walberg**

Recent interest in program theory evolves from the view that in order to enhance the quality and use of evaluation results, a comprehensive understanding of a program is needed. The growth of this perspective is, to a large extent, attributable to the limitations of the traditional experimental methods of evaluation dating back to the 1960s and Campbell's (1969) "experimenting society." This experimental or manipulative approach considers the extent to which programs work, but not why or how they work. As Cook and Shadish (1986) note, evaluators have learned in the past 20 years of experience "that analyses of implementation and causal mediation are crucial in evaluation for they promote explanation, and explanation may be crucial for the transfer of evaluation findings to new settings and populations" (p. 226). Program theory seeks to provide this greater understanding. This article describes the increasing role of program theory in evaluation. Drawing on Bickman (1987b) and Wang and Walberg (1983), the conceptualization and uses of program theory are reviewed. Two examples utilizing the approaches are discussed.

## 1. Program Theory Defined

Program theory is a conception of how and why a program works. Although it is often implicit in evaluation by the assumptions a program manager or evaluator makes, program theory generally refers to the explicit formulation of the way in which a program operates. Scheirer (1987) defines program theory as "the set of cause-and-effect relationships that provide the rationale for the nature of the treatment" (p. 60). Bickman (1987b) defines it as "the construction of a plausible and sensible model of how a program is supposed to work" (p. 5). Whatever its definition, the theory of the program is specified in relation to purposes and means as defined by planners and evaluators in order to clarify what can be expected from the pro-gram and as a guide to selecting measures to assess the inputs, processes and outcomes.

## 2. Recent Developments in Program Theory

Cook and Shadish (1986) identified two alternatives to the traditional paradigm of evaluation research ("manipulative solutions"), one concerned with providing "stakeholder services" (for example, to interested parties, Patton 1978, Stake 1975), and the other focused on seeking "generalizable explanations" (Cronbach 1982, Chen and Rossi 1983). While the stakeholder approach strives to make evaluation more responsive to programs, the explanatory approach makes greater use of program theory in constructing models of the evaluation process.

A volume edited by Bickman (1987b) entitled *Using Program Theory in Evaluation* provides a comprehensive introduction of program theory and its uses. In this volume, Bickman (1987a) describes a number of uses of program theory in the context of evaluation, including: (a) contributions to social science knowledge, (b) assisting policymakers, (c) discrimination between program failure and theory failure, (d) identification of the problem and target group, (e) facilitating a description of program implementation, (f) uncovering unintended program effects, (g) specification of intervening variables, (h) improving the formative use of evaluation, (i) clarifying measurement issues, and (j) improving consensus formation.

Given these uses, it is surprising that evaluators have not paid more attention to program theory. For example, Lipsey et al. (1985) reviewed 119 evaluation studies and found that two-thirds exemplified the use of program analysis at no higher than the subtheoretical level (that is, vague theoretical descriptions), while only nine percent displayed integrated theoretical frameworks. As a result of the dearth of program theory in evaluation, a number of techniques and conceptions have been developed.

Conrad and Miller (1987) describe a technique for testing program philosophy as a means of incorporating program theory in evaluation. *Program philosophy* refers to both the values and theories embodied in a program. Conrad and Miller describe five stages to an evaluation utilizing program philosophy. First, the philosophy of the program is measured by the evaluator through a variety of means including literature review, observation of pilot implementation, and survey of project administrators and staff. Second, means testing is accomplished to see if the avowed program philosophy is consistent with program delivery (for example, the appropriateness of target population, staff, and materials). Third, the implementation of the program is tested by the degree to which services were delivered to the target population. Fourth, the philosophy of the program is evaluated by assessing program effects. Testing effectiveness of the program philosophy is accomplished through statistical analysis such as regression or structural equation modeling. A fifth stage, reflection, is the reexamination of the philosophy and the methodology for assessing effectiveness in the light of evaluation findings.

McClintock (1987) emphasized conceptual and action heuristics to measure program theory and to identify policy alternatives as a product of formative evaluation activities. Conceptual heuristics "elucidate the subjective program theories held by various program 'stakeholders' and the definitions of the situations that underlie the choices and commitments these stakeholders make" (p. 46). Such theories include metaphors through conversation, argument, logical analysis, and conceptual maps mentioned by developers. Action heuristics "are used to simplify program theory so that decisions can be made about implementing, expanding, altering, or terminating specific programs and activities" (p. 50). In McClintock's approach, causal modeling, decision analysis, and cost-benefit studies, evaluability and implementation assessment may also be employed. A causal modeling technique could be used as a heuristic device to describe the complex network of the evaluation process by mapping of relevant input, intervening, and output variables. Such causal modeling could be either qualitative or quantitative in design and execution.

Scheirer (1987) discussed the relationship between program theory and implementation theory. Program theory is used to guide the measurement of the extent of program implementation at the micro-organizational and macro-organizational levels. According to Scheirer, "the evaluator must be able to specify the range of possible program components . . . then provide data on the extent and types of program implementation" (p. 63). In this view, a program theory must be identified and defined from a micro-organizational perspective as a series of cause and effect relationships. Scheirer indicated that an "evaluation design focused primarily on outcomes is likely to overlook the diversity of underlying program theories" (p. 62).

These theories should be operationalized as a set of observable behaviors. Data sources can include existing records, surveys, telephone interviews, direct observation, and unobtrusive measures. The extent of implementation at the macro-organizational level would focus on the degree of linkages between program components across levels. Implementation process theory addresses the questions of why there are variations in the delivery of evaluation treatments. Social systems theory would be one such approach and would include program and participant inputs, characteristics of program deliverers, operational characteristics, organizational structure, and environmental pressures. Both qualitative (i.e., case studies) and quantitative research techniques may be employed to develop implementation theory.

Wholey (1987) addresses the question of evaluability assessment as the key to program theory. It is an attempt to clarify program intent, and its feasibility and likelihood of improving program performance from the point of view of policymakers and interest groups. Developing program theory, for example, includes the participation of policymakers and managerial staff to clarify the program theory, test and refine the theory, and discuss the collection of evaluation information.

An example of evaluability assessment is given of evaluation consultants working with the Tennessee Department of Public Health to develop program theory and evaluation of a prenatal program. The program was designed to increase the number of low-income women entering early prenatal care and to reduce the number of low-birthweight infants. The collaborative nature of the evaluation and its subsequent positive findings justified continued funding. The theory development process, which took five weeks, promoted understanding of the nature and uses of the program. Wholey's perspective is closely aligned with stakeholder services evaluation.

Shadish (1987) described the importance of program microtheory in evaluation and its relationship to macrotheory. Microtheory identifies program characteristics that can be altered relatively easily by program managers. Macrotheory deals with the forces that influence change both within and outside of the program. Shadish shows how macrotheory since the late 1960s has had less than optimal results for program evaluation and social change. For example, a number of obstacles have restricted the use of evaluation findings including (a) its dependence on other aspects of the policy-making process, (b) multiple stakeholders, (c) heterogeneous social programs, (d) programs permanence fixtures, which result in (e) the paradox that programs that have the greatest likelihood of helping the most people are also the ones most resistant to change in response to evaluation information.

To correct these difficulties, Shadish indicated that evaluators have begun to focus on incremental program improvement and short-term change rather than providing social criticism and advocating social change. It was also in view of these difficulties that alternative evaluation theories were developed (Cook and Shadish 1986). Shadish concluded that macrotheory can be used to encourage summative evaluations and to promote program change. A central challenge for evaluation researchers, he argues, is to become more knowledgeable in the social change literature and establish a broader disciplinary perspective.

Thus, program theory is accomplished through a theoretical description of the program developed from a review of literature, extant theories, discussion with program administrators, and observations of implementation. Techniques to formulate and assess the theory include surveying managers, conducting evaluability assessments, designing heuristic approaches, testing program philosophy, using implementation process theory, and developing micro- and macrotheoretical perspectives.

## 3. A Discipline-based Causal Modeling Approach

Extending the above developments, Wang and Walberg (1983) presented a case for the use of causal models derived from a substantive knowledge base of theory and research in evaluation of educational programs. Such evaluation, they hold, can be based on a synthesis of theory, empirical research, and program evaluations that are often disparate and unrelated. Included among the inquiries on which evaluation can be based are substantive research in academic disciplines such as anthropology, psychology, and sociology; case, correlational, and experimental studies; and needs assessment, implementation, process, and outcome evaluations.

Wang and Walberg analyzed eight classificatory typologies of evaluation as follows:

(a) Forms of Inquiry (Guba 1978)

(b) Types of Evaluation (Glass and Ellett 1980)

(c) Evaluation Models (House 1980)

(d) Philosophical Value Questions (Gowin and Green 1980)

(e) Alternative Approaches (Stufflebeam and Webster 1980)

(f) Evaluation Standards (Joint Committee 1981)

(g) Basic Questions (Cronbach 1982)

(h) Methodologies (Talmage 1982)

These representative typologies include a total of 47 different categories: two forms of inquiry, seven types, eight models, five philosophical questions, 13 alternative approaches, four groups of standards, four basic questions, and four methodologies. Examination of these sets of categories reveals that, although they are useful in pointing out important distinctions and trends

in the field of evaluation, little consensus can be found among recent major efforts at classification. For example, the jurisprudence and adversary models, which appear to be similar, are subsumed by the Glass and Ellett (1980) and House (1980) typologies, yet they are excluded from the six other classifications. Similarly, what might be called "qualitative inquiry" constitutes a category in the Guba (1978), Glass and Ellett, and Talmage (1982) classifications but not in the others.

The primary literature cited by these classifiers encompasses numerous positions and procedures, none of which appears to be without merit and utility. Two features, however, seem worthy of stronger integration or reintegration into the field of evaluation: causal modeling and substantive research from disciplines such as psychology and sociology. These are explicitly represented in three of the 47 categories: Glass and Ellett's (1980) first and last categories, applied science and rational empiricism, and Cronbach's (1982) first category, causal conclusions.

## 4. Relinking Research and Evaluation

Wang and Walberg argued that the link between evaluation and substantive research in academic disciplines may have been weakened in the late 1960s and early 1970s by influential writings that emphasized their different purposes. Hemphill (1969), for example, distinguished evaluation and research with respect to the type of problem selected and how it is defined, the use of hypotheses, the role of value judgments, the replicability of findings, the specification of data to be collected, and the randomization of study samples. Worthen and Sanders (1973) added other distinguishing features: laws versus description, autonomy of inquiry, criteria for judging activities, disciplinary base, and training. Suchman (1967) also cited many of these distinctions in earlier writing.

Removing evaluation from the mainstream of substantive research, however, may weaken both fields. Without theory, parsimony, generalizability, and other research canons, evaluation may lose its substantive validity and practical utility. Uninformed of current developments in educational and disciplinary research, evaluation also would tend to overlook new constructs from topics such as motivation, time-on-task, and teaching that have important bearings on the success of educational innovations.

Conversely, substantive research in psychology and other disciplines stands to lose its relevance to educational policy and practice, unless it is stimulated by the puzzles and findings of needs assessments as well as by evaluations of program implementations, processes, and outcomes. Several authorities have pointed out the need for a close connection between substantive theory and methodological and utilitarian research (for example, Anastasi 1967, Glaser 1973). In an analysis of the relationship between psychological science and testing, Anastasi concluded that "psychological testing today places too much emphasis on testing and too little on psychology. As a result, outdated interpretations of test performance may remain insulated from the impact of subsequent behavior research" (p. 297). She further pointed out the tendency of "test theory" to focus on the psychometric property or the mechanics of test construction rather than psychological theory about behavior.

A widely recognized prerequisite for maintaining the theoretical and practical utility of research is sufficient concern for causal relations among means and ends. Perhaps because many believe that causality can only be inferred from experiments, which may be difficult to execute in natural settings, recent evaluations and commentaries have tended to give short shrift to causal questions. Nevertheless, the most obvious question about new programs from both the scientific and practical perspectives is: Do they work? (Florio et al. 1979).

Cook and Campbell (1979) described many practical ways to execute experiments, pointing out that a reasonable indication of causality may be inferred from quasi-experiments and correlational studies, particularly if they are repeated in varying circumstances. The statisticians Mosteller and Tukey (1977) insisted that an approximate answer to the right question is more valuable than an exact answer to the wrong question; and they offered reasonable hope that regression and related correlational techniques can be helpful in coming closer to answering the right questions.

In further consideration of this issue, Murray and Smith (1979) argued that, even in cases where relatively few units, occasions, and variables are observed, simple correlations, particularly across time intervals, can be informative about the results of training and other programs. They recommended that evaluators work with program developers and practitioners to make their implicit or latent causal models of the program explicit and testable. According to the authors, such models should include identification of program components, depiction of the presumed chains of causality, measurement of the components, and calculation of the correlations among them. Correlations that are small, insignificant, or wrong in hypothesized sign may yield formative insights and clues about areas in which a program is less efficient, encountering difficulties, or contrary to expectations. On the other hand, correlations that are large and in the hypothesized direction hardly prove causality, but they do lend some degree of confidence and plausibility to the validity of the presumed and portrayed causal model of the program.

Both simple and elaborate causal models of evaluation may be derived from disciplines such as psychology and from research on teaching and learning (Bentler 1980, Maruyama and Walberg 1982). Program evaluations guided by a combination of substantive research findings and practitioners' wisdom are likely to lead to findings that remain robust across settings, conditions, and subjects. Accumulation and synthesis of evidence from extensive or multiple evaluations can yield useful generalizations that extend beyond the immediate programs and studies. Because subsequent evaluations may merely check, rather than exhaustively probe, the efficacy of local implementation, such smaller scale evaluations can be less critical and demanding of educational and evaluation resources.

Thus, as Wang and Walberg argued, an integrative, causal modeling approach can build on theory and research from academic disciplines such as psychology; from educational research findings; from wisdom and experience of practitioners and program developers; and from various research methodologies such as quasi-experiments, correlational analyses, and case studies. Rather than oppose existing models and techniques of evaluation like those outlined above, this approach attempts to incorporate more fully and explicitly the standards and procedures of the mainstream research on education, particularly those related to causal questions of means and ends, into the emerging evaluation canon.

## 5. Examples from Educational Evaluation Research

### 5.1 The Effects of Coaching on Test Performance

Reynolds et al. (1988) evaluated the effects of a six-week Preliminary Scholastic Aptitude Test (PSAT) (a criterion for awarding college scholarships) coaching program on urban gifted students in a large metropolitan school district. The goal of the program was to increase the number of National Merit scholars. The theory of the program, derived from traditional learning theory, stated that test performance can be enhanced by consistent review, practice, drill, and feedback on appropriate content. Consequently, the evaluation was set up to monitor and test this theory through extensive observation of the implementation process. Although results of the quasi-experimental comparison group design showed an average program effect of about half of a standard deviation (47 SAT points), there was a negligible increase in the number of National Merit scholars and mixed effects in the three sites. The site that most conformed to the underlying theory had the highest gains in the program. The evaluation had a number of features consistent with the functions of program theory: (a) the program's underlying theory was made explicit, (b) the evaluation included measures of the extent of implementation, and (c) the outcome measures were well-matched to the theory.

But the theory itself was unrealistic because it did not take into account the difficulty of raising test scores of an already atypical group to an even higher level. By most other criteria, it had achieved its short-term effects. As discussed by Wholey (1987), collaboration between program staff and the evaluators before the design of the program might have made the theory more realistic. It is worth noting that understanding why the program worked came from knowledge of the implementation process rather than the quasi-experimental design.

### 5.2 *Prekindergarten Experience and Disadvantaged Students*

Demonstrative of Wang and Walberg's (1983) and McClintock's (1987) causal modeling perspective, the effects of prekindergarten experience on cognitive and affective outcomes were evaluated for children in government-funded prekindergarten programs (Reynolds, in press). Using a social-context structural equation model, input (including prekindergarten experience), intervening, and outcome variables were specified based on the research literature and the time sequence of variables. The hypothesized effects of prekindergarten experience were based on the notion that early schooling may have lasting effects on cognitive and affective outcomes, especially for disadvantaged students. The results showed that prekindergarten experience was significantly related to entering kindergarten composite achievement and end-of-kindergarten achievement, after controlling for other variables (gender, socio-economic status, and prior achievement). However, results for first grade outcomes (reading achievement, mathematics achievement, and maturity ratings) were negligible after additional variables were entered in the model (i.e., motivation, parent involvement, and peer achievement).

Although the model had conceptual clarity (action heuristics), was based on longitudinal research in educational attainment, and included intervening variables, it was not clear from the program theory what kind of outcomes were expected and over which particular time period. Consequently, the evaluation was exploratory. It is possible, for example, that outcomes not measured in the evaluation (for example, grade retention, referral to special education, social competence), may have been more appropriate. Longitudinal studies of prekindergarten have shown just such effects (Lazar and Darlington 1982, White 1985–86). A clearer program theory would have clarified this problem. However, the overall strategy did demonstrate an effective approach for conceptualizing and testing program effects, especially from a longitudinal perspective.

### 6. *Conclusion*

The examples above highlight the importance of specifying program theory before and during the implementation of an evaluation. In one case (test preparation), the theory of the program was unrealistic given the stated goal of increasing the number of National Merit scholars. In the other instance, the theory appeared too exploratory to guide the evaluation in a productive manner. In these cases and many others, programs not fulfilling expectations may reflect theory failure rather than program failure. The techniques discussed (i.e., tests of program philosophy, evaluability assessment,

heuristics, and causal modeling) help avoid this problem.

Program theory is an attempt to understand the nature of a program and what can be expected from it. It suggests which methods are most appropriate for testing theory, how to guide the implementation process, why particular outcomes are reached, and how findings can be used. These features do not imply that other related evaluation practices are obsolete, but that they should be integrated in an explicit formulation to test implementation and outcomes of the program. Indeed, the explanatory approach rests on the optimistic assumption that complex program theories can be readily identified and their results meaningfully interpreted (Cook and Shadish 1986). Clearly, more evidence is needed in this regard.

Thus, the emergence of program theory leaves evaluators with better ideas and means. It reveals the further growth of the field. As with the traditional experimental perspective, it would be short-sighted to view theoretical evaluation as the only approach to conducting evaluation, or even the best. In conjunction with other practices, program theory may further bridge the gap between social science theory and evaluation practice.

### *Bibliography*

Anastasi A 1967 Psychology, psychologists, and psychological testing. *Am. Psychol.* 22: 297–306

Bentler P M 1980 Multivariate analysis with latent variables: Causal modeling. *Ann. Rev. Psychol.* 31: 419–56

Bickman L 1987a The functions of program theory. In: Bickman L (ed.) 1987 *Using Program Theory in Evaluation:* Jossey-Bass, San Francisco, California, pp. 5–18

Bickman L (ed.) 1987b *Using Program Theory in Evaluation.* Jossey-Bass, San Francisco, California

Campbell D T 1969 Reforms as experiments. *Am. Psychol.* 24: 409–29

Chen H-T, Rossi P H 1983 Evaluating with sense: The theory-driven approach. *Eval. Rev.* 7: 283–302

Conrad K J, Miller T Q 1987 Measuring and testing program philosophy. In: Bickman L (ed.) 1987 *Using Program Theory in Evaluation.* Jossey-Bass, San Francisco, California, pp. 19–42

Cook T D, Campbell D T 1979 *Quasi-Experimentation: Design and Analysis Issues for Field Settings.* Rand McNally, Chicago, Illinois

Cook T D, Shadish W R 1986 Program evaluation: The worldly science. *Ann. Rev. Psychol.* 37: 193–232

Cronbach L J 1982 *Designing Evaluations of Educational and Social Programs.* Jossey-Bass, San Francisco, California

Florio D H, Behrmann M M, Mason G D, Goltz L 1979 What do policy makers think of educational research and evaluation? Or do they? *Educ. Eval. Policy Analysis* 1(6): 61–87

Glaser R 1973 Educational psychology and education. *Am. Psychol.* 28: 557–66

Glass G V, Ellett F S Jr. 1980 Evaluation research. *Ann. Rev. Psychol.* 31: 211–28

Gowin D B, Green T F 1980 Two philosophers view education. *Educ. Eval. Policy Analysis* 2(2): 67–70

Guba E G 1978 *Toward a Methodology of Naturalistic Inquiry in Educational Evaluation.* Center for the Study of Evaluation, Los Angeles, California

Hemphill J K 1969 The relationship between research and evaluation studies. In: Tyler R W (ed.) 1969 *Educational Evaluation: New Roles, New Means.* University of Chicago Press, Chicago, Illinois, pp. 189–220

House E R 1980 *Evaluation with Validity.* Sage, Beverly Hills, California

Joint Committee on Standards for Educational Evaluation 1981 *Standards for Evaluation of Educational Programs, Projects, and Materials.* McGraw-Hill, New York

Lazar L, Darlington R 1982 Lasting effects of early education: A report from the consortium for longitudinal studies. *Monographs of the Society for Research in Child Development.* 47 (2/3 Serial No. 195)

Lipsey M W, Crosse S, Dunkle J, Pollard J, Stobart G 1985 The state of the art and the sorry state of science. In: Cordray D S (ed.) 1985 *Utilizing Prior Research in Evaluation Planning.* Jossey-Bass, San Francisco, California, pp. 7–28

McClintock C 1987 Conceptual and action heuristics: Tools for the evaluator. In: Bickman L (ed.) 1987 *Using Program Theory in Evaluation.* Jossey-Bass, San Francisco, California, pp. 43–57

Maruyama G, Walberg H J 1982 Causal modeling. In: Mitzel H M (ed.) 1982 *Encyclopedia of Educational Research.* Macmillan, New York, pp. 248–52

Mosteller F, Tukey J W 1977 *Data Analysis and Regression: A Second Course in Statistics.* Addison-Wesley, Reading, Massachusetts

Murray S L, Smith N L 1979 Causal research on teacher training. In: Walberg H J (ed.) 1979 *Educational Environments and Effects.* McCutchan, Berkeley, California, pp. 386–401

Patton M Q 1978 *Utilization-Focused Evaluation.* Sage, Beverly Hills, California

Reynolds A J A structural model of first grade outcomes for an urban, low economic, black population. *J. Educ. Psychol.,* in press

Reynolds A J, Oberman G L, Perlman C 1988 An analysis of a PSAT coaching program for urban gifted students. *J. Educ. Res.* 81: 155–64

Scheirer M A 1987 Program theory and implementation theory: Implications for evaluators. In: Bickman L (ed.) 1987 *Using Program Theory in Evaluation.* Jossey-Bass, San Francisco, California, pp. 59–76

Shadish W R 1987 Program micro- and macrotheories: A guide for social change. In: Bickman L (ed.) 1987 *Using Program Theory in Evaluation.* Jossey-Bass, San Francisco, California, pp. 93–109

Stake R E (ed.) 1975 *Evaluating the Arts in Education: A Responsive Approach.* Charles E. Merrill, Columbus, Ohio

Stufflebeam D L, Webster W J 1980 An analysis of alternative approaches to evaluation. *Educ. Eval. Policy Analysis* 2(3): 5–20

Suchman E A 1967 *Evaluative Research.* Russell Sage Foundation, New York

Talmage H 1982 Evaluation of programs. In: Mitzel H M (ed.) 1982 *Encyclopedia of Educational Research.* Macmillan, New York, pp. 592–611

Wang M C, Walberg H J 1983 Evaluating educational programs: An integrative, causal-modeling approach. *Educ. Eval. Policy Analysis* 5: 347–66

White K R 1985–1986 Efficacy of early intervention. *Journal of Special Education* 19: 401–16

Wholey J S 1987 Evaluability assessment: Developing program theory. In: Bickman L (ed.) 1987 *Using Program Theory in Evaluation.* Jossey-Bass, San Francisco, California, pp. 77–92

Worthen B R, Sanders J R 1973 *Educational Evaluation: Theory and Practice.* Charles A. Jones, Worthington, Ohio

# Formative and Summative Evaluation

## A. Lewy

The terms formative and summative appeared first in the context of curriculum evaluation. Scriven (1967), who coined these terms, specified the differences between them, and stated that both formative and summative evaluation may examine the worth of a variety of entities such as products, processes, personnel, or learners. Nevertheless, for several years these terms were uniquely applied to describing various types of curriculum evaluation activities. Only later did they become generalized and employed in the context of learner evaluation (Bloom et al. 1971) and educational actions other than curricula (Cronbach et al. 1980). The distinction between formative and summative evaluation contributed to broadening the range of disciplined inquiries recognized as evaluation studies, by attributing scholarly significance and professional status to evaluation activities conducted in the course of program development. Prior to the emergence of these terms, program evaluation, insofar as it was carried out, typically meant the comparison of the outcomes of

competing programs for the sake of advising the decision maker about selecting or continuing educational programs. The evaluators, taking a stance of impartial aloofness and employing some legitimate form of experimental design, made an attempt to compare the relative merits of neatly packaged or fully structured competing programs. The failure of studies of this type to provide conclusive results on the one hand, and the conviction of evaluators that they can, and should, contribute to the improvement of education programs at various stages of their development on the other hand, gave issue to relatively small-scaled studies focusing on particular aspects of programs in the course of their development. Such studies, which in many cases waived the demanding patterns of experimental design and frequently revealed little interest in comparisons, came to be labelled formative evaluation studies. At the same time, comparative studies examining the outcomes of finished programs, with the aim of providing recommendations about program selection and continuation, which up to that time had been considered the sole permissible genre of evaluation, were redefined as a particular type of evaluation study within the framework of a variety of summative evaluation studies.

Attempts at conducting evaluation studies of instructional programs in the course of their development had been made before the emergence of the formative–summative distinction (Markele 1967). But the introduction of these terms constituted a point of departure for systematically exploring and conceptualizing the differences between the two types, and for disseminating the idea that it is both permissible and highly desirable to conduct evaluation studies in the course of program development, with a design deviating from that of the classical comparison studies.

## 1. The Formative–Summative Dichotomy

Two decades after the emergence of these innovative terms, a full consensus had not been reached as to their precise meaning. Therefore some experts tend to disregard the summative–formative distinction and focus on other, in their view, more clearly defined evaluation study dichotomies, such as prospective versus retrospective, responsive versus preordinate, naturalistic versus experimental, holistic versus analytic, process versus outcome, and so on. Some of these have been erroneously interpreted as parallel to (if not fully identical with) the formative–summative distinction. In response to this confusion Scriven, the originator of these terms, provided definitions of formative and summative evaluations, which emphasize their orthogonality to the dichotomies mentioned above. According to Scriven (1980), formative evaluation is conducted during the development or improvement of a program or product (or person). It is an evaluation conducted for in-house staff and normally remains in house, but it may be done by an internal or external evaluator, or (preferably) a combination. Summative evaluation, on the other hand, is conducted after completion of a program (or a course of study) and for the benefit of some external audience or decision maker (e.g., funding agency or future possible users), though it too may be done either by an internal or an external evaluator or by a combination.

Scriven adheres to the view that there are no basic logical and methodological differences between formative and summative evaluation. Both are intended to examine the worth of a particular entity. Only timing, the audience requesting it, and the way its results are used can indicate whether a study is formative or summative. Moreover, the same study may be viewed by one client as formative and by another one as summative.

## 2. The Relative Importance of Formative and Summative Studies

While the scholarly status of formative evaluation studies was established only recently, they have swiftly dominated the field of program evaluation. Cronbach et al. (1980) claim that formative evaluation is more impactful and therefore more significant than summative evaluation. In their opinion, evaluation employed to improve a program while it is still fluid contributes more to the improvement of education than evaluation used to appraise a product already placed on the market. To be influential in course improvement, evidence must become available midway through program development and not in the home stretch, when the developer is naturally reluctant to tear apart a supposedly finished body of materials and techniques. Similarly, providing feedback to the teacher and learner about success or failure in mastering specific skills or components of the program constitutes an essential part of the teaching–learning process. It makes it possible to spot weak points of the program and to identify those learners who need corrective teaching. Formative information of this type contributes more to the improvement of learning than do results of end-of-course testing.

The superior usefulness of formative evaluation is so stressed in the writings of numerous evaluation experts that people dealing with specific programs often display no interest in conducting summative evaluation studies. Scriven deplores this attitude and points out that both types of study have unique and essential roles. Summative evaluation is an inescapable obligation of the project director, an obvious requirement of the sponsoring agency and a desideratum for schools.

## 3. Characteristics of Formative and Summative Studies

Despite the tremendous growth in the number of formative and summative evaluation studies published in the 1960s and 1970s, theoreticians have not produced rules as to the procedures appropriate for either type of study. An exception is within the field of formative and summative evaluation of students' learning. As to other targets of evaluation, Scriven plays down the differences between formative and summative studies. Nevertheless, several reviews of empirical studies have pointed out systematic differences.

Stake (1977) provides a series of terms which characterize differences in information sought by users of formative and summative evaluation. Formative evaluation focuses on relatively molecular analyses, is cause seeking, is interested in the broader experiences of the program users, and tends to ignore the local effect of a particular program, while summative evaluation focuses on molar analyses, provides descriptive information, is interested in efficiency statements, and tends to emphasize local effects.

Alkin (1974), analysing 42 evaluation reports, and questionnaires completed by the 42 project directors, lists additional characteristics of formative evaluation studies. Their design is characterized as exploratory, flexible, focusing on individual components of the program, and as emphasizing iterative processes. While not comparative, it seeks to identify influential variables. A formative evaluation study uses a great variety of instruments which are either locally developed or standardized; it relies on observation and informal data collection devices, mostly locally chosen. In contrast, summative evaluation studies tend to use well-defined evaluation designs, as unobtrusive and nonreactive as possible; they are comparative and concerned with a broad range of issues, for example, implications, politics, costs, competing options. The instruments used in summative evaluation are publicly accepted, reliable, and valid instruments, reflecting concerns of the sponsor and of the decision-maker.

The rules provided by Bloom et al. (1971) for conducting formative and summative evaluation of students' learning are more specific. For formative evaluation, it is first necessary to analyze the instructional materials, to map the hierarchical structure of the learning tasks, and to administer achievement tests after completing a short learning unit covering study materials for 6 to 10 periods of study. A sample of test items appearing in the formative tests, or equivalent items, should constitute the summative evaluation test to be administered at the end of the course, with the aim of providing a basis for grading or certifying the learner.

## 4. The Consequences of the Formative and Summative Distinction

The formative–summative distinction has increased the range of evaluation studies and contributed to the improvement of educational planning. But two decades of utilizing these terms produced little consensus concerning their distinct features. The allegation that they differ only from the point of view of decisions they are supposed to support, and that no distinction should be made between them from the point of view of design, methodology, etc., has been endorsed by many evaluators without its veracity having been empirically examined. At the same time, other evaluators have asserted that methodological rigor is required only in summative studies, while in formative ones the evaluator may rely on less rigorously validated data and analysis procedures. This claim has never been confirmed by evaluation experts, but nevertheless it, unfortunately, has lead to the burgeoning of sloppily designed formative evaluation studies.

To avoid such theoretical and empirical pitfalls, there is a need to conduct empirical studies to ascertain the characteristic method and design features of formative and summative evaluation. Such studies might facilitate the use of formative and summative evaluation, and enhance their quality.

## Bibliography

Alkin M C 1974 *Evaluation and Decision Making: The Title VII Experience.* Center for Study of Evaluation, University of California, Los Angeles, California
Bloom B S, Hastings J T, Madaus G F 1971 *Handbook on Formative and Summative Evaluation of Students' Learning.* McGraw-Hill, New York
Cronbach L J et al. 1980 *Toward a Reform of Program Evaluation.* Jossey-Bass, San Francisco, California
Markele S M 1967 Empirical testing of programs. *Sixty-sixth Yearbook of the National Society for the Study of Education.* University of Chicago Press, Chicago, Illinois
Sanders J R, Cunningham D J 1973 A structure for formative evaluation in product development. *Rev. Educ. Res.* 43: 217–36
Scriven M 1967 The methodology of evaluation. In: Tyler R W (ed.) 1967 *Perspectives of Curriculum Evaluation.* Rand McNally, Chicago, Illinois
Scriven M 1980 *Evaluation Thesaurus*, 2nd edn. Edgepress, Inverness, California
Stake R 1977 Formative and summative evaluation. In: Hamilton D et al. (eds.) 1977 *Beyond the Numbers Game: A Reader in Educational Evaluation.* MacMillan, London, pp. 156–57

# Purposes and Goals of Evaluation Studies

## Needs Assessment Studies

### T. M. Suarez

Needs assessment is an information-gathering and analysis process which results in the identification of the needs of individuals, groups, institutions, communities, or societies. In education the process of needs assessment has been used, for example, to identify the needs of students for instruction in a given subject area; to determine weaknesses in students' overall academic achievement; to determine the needs of teachers for additional training; and to determine the future needs of local, regional, and national educational systems. It is the intent of needs assessments to identify areas in which deficits exist or desired performance has not been attained. The results of needs assessments are then used for further action such as planning or remediation to improve the situation.

Educational needs have been assessed and analyzed for centuries. However, formalized assessments of educational needs were not conducted on a widespread basis until the middle of the twentieth century (Suarez 1981). At that time, public and professional demands for more systematic and accountable processes of providing education led to the emergence of information-based models for educational planning and evaluation. This was particularly true in the United States where widespread federal aid to education with accompanying accountability requirements was instituted in the mid-1960s. Among the information-based processes which emerged during that time was the systematic determination of needs as a basis for program planning and development. This process was called needs assessment.

Since then development and activity regarding needs assessment have been intense. Many educational needs assessments have been conducted to meet an array of intents using a wide variety of designs and procedures. Because of the wide range of situations in which needs assessments have been found to be appropriate, there does not appear to be a single set of concepts that can be used to describe the process. Instead, needs assessments are described or designed on the basis of their purpose and the types of needs that are identified.

## 1. The Purposes of Needs Assessments

Providing information for planning is the most common reason given for conducting needs assessments. Needs assessments for planning may result in the identification of goals, the determination of the extent to which desired goals are being achieved, or the specification of areas in which efforts and resources should be placed. Such assessments may be used to develop plans for immediate action or to develop long-range plans for the future.

The diagnosis or identification of problems or weaknesses is another common purpose for needs assessments. Needs assessments for this purpose focus on identifying the areas in which the educational process or system is ineffective so that remedial actions may be taken.

Needs assessments are components of several evaluation models. These assessments are part of the evaluation process and may have as their purpose determining areas of weakness prior to the implementation of a given form of instruction or treatment, determining gaps in implementation, or determining the status of performance at intervals during the development or implementation of a treatment. The results of these assessments become part of the evaluation findings or, in the case of needs assessments prior to treatment, the basis upon which the evaluation criteria for judging the effectiveness of treatments are determined.

Needs assessments are also conducted to hold educational institutions accountable for their efforts. The most common forms of these types of needs assessments are mandated large-scale assessments of student educational outcomes. Results of these assessments are used to determine if the educational efforts of schools or school systems are effective and to identify subject areas or locations in which educational achievements are less than desired.

## 2. The Concept of Need

To understand a needs assessment it is necessary to understand the concept of need upon which the process is based. This requires an understanding of the definition used in the study for the term "need," a specification of whose needs are of interest and the type of need that is to be identified.

A variety of concepts of the term "need" are used in

both the discussions and practice of needs assessment. Controversy regarding the definition of "need" for needs assessments, together with a proliferation of studies using different definitions, has limited the development of universally accepted conceptual or theoretical models of the process. The majority of needs assessment studies, however, has been based on a variation of one of three definitions of the term "need."

The most widely used definition of "need" for needs assessments is that of a discrepancy. This definition, introduced by Kaufman (1972), suggests that needs are areas in which actual status is less than targeted status. Targeted status has come to encompass ideals, norms, preferences, expectations, and perceptions of what ought to be. Needs assessments based on this definition require procedures for selecting or determining targeted status, gathering information to determine current status relative to the target status, and comparing the two to discover discrepancies and identify needs.

Another commonly used definition of need is that of a want or preference. Identification of needs does not require the determination of a discrepancy. Instead, it requires determining the perceptions of needs of selected individuals or groups. Although there are writers who oppose the use of this definition, many needs assessments are based on this definition, particularly in those situations where public and professional opinion regarding needs are used as a basis for establishing educational goals or policy.

A more stringent and less used concept of need for needs assessment studies is that of a deficit. A need is said to exist if the absence or a deficiency in the area of interest is harmful. Scriven has expanded this definition to describe a need as a state in which a minimum satisfactory level has not been reached or cannot be maintained. Few needs assessment studies have been conducted using this definition due to the difficulty in determining the point at which a deficit or minimum satisfactory level can be said to exist.

In addition to understanding the definition of need that is used, it is also necessary to know whose needs or what needs are to be identified. When conducting needs assessments in education the needs of participants (individuals, subgroups, or groups), the educational institution, or society at large may be of interest. Needs may also be determined in relation to such aspects of the educational process as implementation, availability of resources, or facilities. Related to the target of the needs assessments are the types of needs that will be determined. Needs are usually described as those which are of an outcome nature, for example, performance or basic needs, and those which contribute to outcomes, for example, treatment or incremental needs.

## 3. Needs Assessment Strategies and Procedures

Because needs assessments are conducted for a variety of reasons in many different settings and to identify many types of needs, the strategies and procedures used

to conduct such assessments also vary a great deal. There are, however, several procedures or stages which are common to many needs assessment studies.

### 3.1 Preparing to Conduct a Needs Assessment

Like other forms of inquiry, preparing to conduct a needs assessment requires decisions to conduct such a study, determining the purposes the assessment is to serve, and delimiting the areas in which the study is to concentrate. In addition, because educational needs are based to a large extent on the values of the institution or society in which they are to be determined, procedures must be incorporated into the process to ensure that these values are represented. This is most often accomplished by involving a variety of interested or involved individuals or groups in the process. A preparation activity for these assessments is the identification of those who will be involved in or affected by the study and the procurement of their commitment to participate.

### 3.2 Determining the Standards by which Needs will be Identified

When planning is the purpose of a needs assessment, educational goals are often the standards against which status is compared to determine needs. A common practice for these types of needs assessments is the determination of goals prior to the assessment of needs. When goals have been determined, the needs assessment is then conducted to determine if there are discrepancies between identified goals and current status. The process of goal determination involves identifying the individuals and/or groups who should participate in the determination of goals and involving them in the process. Two major procedures for goal determination are usually used: (a) generating the set of goals, and (b) selecting goals from present lists of goal statements. When goals already exist in the area of interest, this step is omitted and current status is compared to the existing goals.

Norms are another standard often used in the determination of educational needs. The norms most often used are those associated with standardized tests. Needs are determined by comparing performance on the tests with existing norms, that is, the performance of the population upon which the test was standardized. Other norms used for needs assessments are previous behaviors of similar groups, for example, number of graduates entering college in previous years.

Minimum satisfactory level is a standard not often used but widely advocated for needs assessments. Determining minimum satisfactory levels of performance requires determining the level of performance at which goals cannot be met or harm due to educational deficits will be the result. These types of standards are most often applied in biological and medical situations and are based on research evidence or experience. There is little research evidence regarding the minimum level of education that is needed to predict future achievement with certainty. Most minimum educational levels are therefore determined on the basis of experience as represented by public and professional opinion.

Other standards used to determine needs are desires or wants, perceptions of what should be the status of performance, and requirements. The first two are determined by public or professional opinion. Requirements are found in existing laws, policies, and regulating procedures.

### 3.3 Designing the Needs Assessment

Good designs for needs assessments begin with a clear specification of the focus of the study. This includes a delineation of the specific purposes of the study, the areas in which needs are to be assessed, and the type of needs to be identified.

A clear focus for the assessment will dictate most of the data collection, analysis, and reporting procedures. Needs assessments designed to gather community opinions of educational needs, for example, would require the methods of opinion-survey research. Procedures such as selecting appropriate sampling methods would be of prime importance. Data collection procedures might include the administration of surveys or the use of ranking procedures such as card sorts or budget allocation simulations. To conduct assessments designed to determine student performance needs, one might administer tests, analyze school work, survey teachers, or examine existing records. Still other assessments, designed to determine needs and their cause, would require the use of experimental research techniques.

Complete designs would include procedures for analyzing data and reporting results. For many needs assessments it is necessary to conduct discrepancy analyses to identify needs. These may be conducted by determining differences among two sets of data, combining analyses of several sets and types of data, and developing criticality indices or functions (Witkin 1977).

### 3.4 Assigning Priorities to Needs

Needs assessment studies may result in the identification of many needs. To be of maximum use, identified needs should be placed in order from most to least crucial. Procedures for setting priorities include ordering needs by the strength of their ratings of importance, by the extent of the discrepancy between targeted and actual status, by the importance ratings and extent of discrepancy, and using previously established decision rules (Witkin 1977).

### 3.5 Using the Results

A particular characteristic of needs assessment studies is the intended utility of the results. Whether for planning, problem solving, setting criteria for evaluation results, or praising or censuring education efforts, the final stage in the process is intended to be one of active use of the findings.

### Bibliography

Kaufman R A 1972 *Educational System Planning*. Prentice-Hall, Englewood Cliffs, New Jersey

Kaufman R A, English F W 1979 *Needs Assessment: Concept and Application*. Educational Technology Publications, Englewood Cliffs, New Jersey

Scriven M, Roth J 1978 Needs assessment: Concept and practice. *Exploring Purposes and Dimensions: New Directions for Program Evaluation* 1: 1–11

Suarez T M 1981 Needs assessment. In: Lewy A, Devo D (eds.) 1981 *Evaluation Roles in Education*. Gordon and Breach, London

Witkin B R 1977 Needs assessment kits, models and tools. *Educ. Technol.* 17(11): 5–18

# Decision-oriented Evaluation

G. D. Borich

Decision-oriented evaluation is a process that produces information for selecting among alternative courses of action. An evaluation is decision oriented if it (a) services a decision, (b) implies a choice among alternatives, and (c) is used in committing resources for the next interval of time before another decision is to be made. Properly conceptualized, decision-oriented evaluation is a perspective for organizing and focusing the concepts of evaluation toward the broadly defined requirements of decision making rather than a specific method or technique by which decisions are made.

## 1. Some Decision-oriented Definitions and Concepts

The Phi Delta Kappa National Study Committee on Evaluation (Stufflebeam et al. 1971) represented one of the first attempts to consider evaluation from a decision-making perspective. They defined educational evaluation as "the process of delineating, obtaining, and providing useful information for judging decision alternatives" and divided evaluation into four distinct activities, each with its own decision-making purpose. Similarly, Hagedorn and co-workers (1976), writing to mental-health professionals, defined evaluation as "a systematic set of data collection and analysis activities undertaken to determine the value of a program to aid management, program planning, staff training, public accountability, and promotion." This definition reflects the same view of evaluation as that which prevailed in education, that of an information feedback process to aid administrators and project management.

The primary impetus for the development of decision-oriented evaluation was a desire to maximize the utilization of evaluation results. For the Phi Delta Kappa National Study Committee on Evaluation utilization was to be fostered by having the evaluator serve "as an extension of the decision maker's mind." The Commission suggested that the evaluator must assume, in addition to a technical role, an interface role in which he/she interacts with the decision maker for the purpose of delineating decision alternatives and providing information for selecting among alternative courses of action. This role requires the evaluator to work with the decision maker in creating an awareness of the decisions to be made, spelling out the decision alternatives, and identifying the evaluative criteria to be utilized in the evaluation.

A similar decision-oriented view of evaluation can be found in the work of Alkin (1969). Alkin's definition of evaluation advanced the notion that evaluation is a process of ascertaining decision areas of concern, selecting appropriate information, and collecting and analyzing information in order to report summary data useful to decision makers. This definition, while affirming that evaluation should be an information-collection process used to make decisions about alternatives, goes further to suggest that "the manner in which the information is collected, as well as the analysis procedures, must be appropriate to the needs of the decision maker or a potential decision involved public." This definition laid the groundwork for a broad distinction between the decision-oriented evaluator whose role it was to delineate decision alternatives and to provide information for selecting among them, and the researcher whose role it was to discover or explain theoretical phenomena. Emphasized was the notion that the most important function that an evaluator can perform is to report summary data to the decision maker in the form of practical and unambiguous statements about what alternative course of action should be taken.

## 2. Decision-oriented Evaluation Paradigms

Given the diversity of evaluation contexts within any particular field, there is considerable diversity in the specific decision-oriented approaches and procedures utilized. Different decision makers have different values, priorities, and political presses on their activities. Other influences which may vary from setting to setting include administrative levels and leadership styles of decision makers, variety of organizational goals, and disparity in the communication networks that both form and inform decisions. Each context and information need places different constraints on the activity of evaluation. Some evaluation approaches and procedures will be inadequate or inappropriate in some contexts and perfectly matched with the decision-oriented information needs in others. From these practical considerations have emerged different procedural frameworks for conducting decision-oriented evaluations. Although varied in their explicit references to decisions, these frameworks—or models—are decision

oriented in that they are devoted almost exclusively to the gathering and reporting of information relevant to the needs of decision makers for the purpose of selecting among alternative courses of action.

### 2.1 Educational Psychology Models

When applied in the context of a specific program or intervention, decision-oriented evaluation often takes the form of an evaluation of the objectives of that program or intervention. The decision is usually one of adopting or revising the program based on the degree to which the program did or did not meet its objectives. Generally these evaluation models employ the following steps: (a) identifying objectives, (b) stating objectives in measurable behavioral terms, (c) devising and administering measurement instruments, (d) comparing obtained results with the objectives prespecified in step (a), and (e) reporting to decision makers discrepancies between obtained results and objectives for the purpose of program revision or adoption. Common features of educational psychology models include (a) their almost exclusive application to the evaluation of curriculum and instruction, (b) the high priority they place on defining objectives, and (c) their limited focus on comparisions of "what is" with "what should be," with discrepancy information constituting the bulk of evaluation results. One educational psychology model commonly used for the purpose of gathering and reporting information relevant to the needs of decision makers was that developed by Provus (1971). Provus proposed a five-stage evaluation process: design, installation, process, product, and program comparison.

The design stage has as its objective a description of all intended program inputs, processes, and outcomes. The installation stage is concerned with field operations and the discrepancy between the intended and actual manner in which the program was installed. The process stage has as its objective the measurement of enabling or short-term outcomes. In the product stage the evaluator determines if terminal or long-term outcomes have been attained at the level specified by the objectives. In the final program comparison stage, the evaluator compares the experimental program with some competing program to show that benefit is commensurate with cost.

At each stage of this process there are three activities: (a) agreeing on program standards (usually program goals or objectives), (b) determining if a discrepancy exists between aspects of a program, and (c) using discrepancy information to identify program weaknesses. Discrepancy information at each stage is used to inform decision makers whether or not to proceed to the next stage or to revise program standards or operations.

Although the evaluator's role as an information provider is not as explicit in the educational psychology models as in the following set of models, these models identify the decision areas of concern, select appropriate information, and collect and analyze information in order to report summary data useful to decision makers.

As is the case with other decision-oriented approaches, these models limit the evaluator's freedom in an evaluative context to activities that are congruent with the information needs of the decision maker.

## 2.2 Educational Decision Models

Some writers in the field of evaluation have explicitly put forth the notion that the role of evaluation is to provide decision makers with information. The following premises characterize this notion of evaluation: (a) the decision maker determines what is to be evaluated and may even choose the measures to be used, (b) the evaluator's role is that of an advisor to the decision maker, (c) the work of evaluation consists almost exclusively of information gathering and reporting, (d) the information gathered must be relevant to the decision maker's needs, and (e) the information that is important is dictated by the decision to be made.

The CIPP evaluation model (Stufflebeam et al. 1971) is particularly representative of this approach. This model divides evaluation into four distinct stages—context, input, process, and product evaluation, thus the acronym CIPP. Each of these stages are intended to represent a cluster of decisions to be served by the information provided within them. Context evaluation has as its objective to specify the operational context and to identify problems and underlying needs within the decision maker's domain. Input evaluation is concerned with identifying and assessing alternative means of achieving specified ends. Process evaluation has as its objective to inform decisions pertaining to procedural design or implementation and to make adjustments and refinements that seem to be called for from monitoring the program. The goal of product evaluation is to relate outcome information to objectives and to context, input and process data, eventually leading to a series of decisions (e.g., to terminate, revise, or recycle the program as is). At each stage outcomes are compared to stated objectives and differences between expected and actual results are reported to decision makers.

## 2.3 Educational Science Models

In this third view of the decision-oriented perspective, evaluative inquiry is conducted in much the same manner as in the previous models, except that the decisions to be made pertain almost exclusively to choices among alternative courses of action representing competing programs. The terms evaluative research and applied research reflect this attempt to use experimental design and the tools of classical research methodology for making practical choices among programs.

This evaluation process proposes a causal model consisting of three components: inputs (usually client or student characteristics or attributes), the programs (those experiences to which clients or students are exposed), and outcomes (certain targeted skills and abilities measured at program completion). The purpose of educational science models is to establish causal connections between these components. Regression or linear model techniques are used to compute predicted outcome scores on the basis of various input data. Then groups of students, subjected to various program alternatives, are tested to determine whether those in each program exceed, match, or fall short of what would be expected from input data alone. Program impact is inferred if outcome variance cannot be explained by input data alone and if the performance of clients or students in the experimental program represents a statistically significant improvement over the performance of those in a comparison program.

Although educational science models have not proliferated, a sorting through of evaluation studies reveals a strong reliance on the scientific method and an even heavier emphasis on the experimental designs and statistical tools of research. In this model statistical decision rules (e.g., $p < .05$) unequivocally determine program effectiveness and, hence, identify which alternative course of action (program) should be selected. Implicit in this paradigm is the translation of decisions about programs into notions of cause and effect.

Other quantitative approaches to decision-oriented evaluation can be found in the decision-theoretic work of Guttentag (1973) and the Bayesian statistics of Thompson, Schnelle, and Willemian (reviewed in Larson and Kaplan 1981). These highly quantitative procedures for informing decisions about programs attempt to bridge the gap between the complex multivariate world in which programs operate and unambiguous "go/no-go" decisions that are envisioned by decision makers who operate within it.

## 3. Other Perspectives

Some authors have taken exception to the decision-oriented perspective and, in particular, to the applied research model. The primary criticism of the decision-oriented definition of evaluation is that evaluator and decision maker share the function of evaluation unequally. The role of the evaluator is to provide the decision maker with meaningful information; the decision maker defines the information that is needed and makes the actual judgment of value or merit. The criticism of the applied research model is that all of the contextual and moderating factors that can affect a program's performance are covaried or randomized out of the evaluation, reducing the evaluation to a theoretical statement about program impact in a statistically sterilized environment. The role of the evaluator is to provide a "clean" interpretation of program effectiveness for the decision maker, sometimes at the expense of a more complex but more valid interpretation.

One approach to evaluation which is at variance with the decision-oriented notion is value-oriented evaluation. A value-oriented definition of evaluation stresses the value judgments made in evaluating programs and describes the act of judging merit or worth as central to the role of the evaluator. Scriven (1983) has argued that value judgments are a crucial part of all sciences, particularly methodological value judgments, and there appear to be no reasons to dismiss them in the evaluation of programs. He calls for goal-free evaluation, insisting that all aspects of a program should come under the scrutiny of an evaluator and that nothing should be taken as given, including the decisions to be made and the alternative courses of action to be taken.

A value-oriented definition of evaluation begins with the premise that evaluators or decision makers seldom know all of the decisions and alternative courses of action with which they or others will make a judgment of program merit. A value-oriented conception assumes that programs operate in environments characterized not by value consensus, but by value pluralism, and that different value positions should be objectively examined for the decisions and alternatives they hold. Thus, people gain from this definition the notion that evaluation includes not only the collection of data from which judgments of merit can be rendered, but also the objective determination of criteria upon which these judgements should be based. In essence, a value-oriented definition of evaluation implies that the program being evaluated ultimately must be justified in terms of the values of those it is to serve. These values should, but may not always, coincide with those values that are perceived to be important by the decision maker.

Another competing notion of evaluation is systems-oriented evaluation. The systems-oriented definition of evaluation assumes a view of programs as systems and reflects a theoretical/philosophical stance in the sciences called general systems theory. While traditional scientific inquiry attempts to understand humans within their environment by isolating the effects of single variables, holding everything else constant, the general systems paradigm posits that it is impossible to understand complex events by reducing them to their individual elements. Hence, a basic tenet of general systems theory is the often-heard exhortation of the Gestalt school of psychology that the whole is more than the sum of its parts; to understand the whole it is necessary to study the whole.

General systems theory holds that the complexity of any system, including programs, cannot be understood through analytical reduction and experimental control. Rather, programs are viewed as organismic entities that evolve and decay, depending on their relationship to other programs and the larger context to which they contribute. Furthermore, because all programs are ultimately seen as interrelated, changes in any program will have implications throughout the larger system of which the changed program is a part. This viewpoint differs from the decision-oriented perspective in which the immediate context is the focus of inquiry and the limits of the evaluation are bounded by the decision maker's information requirements and prescribed alternative courses of action.

Still other notions pertaining to the relevance of decision-oriented evaluation have emerged from the work of Cronbach et al. (1980) and from Guba and Lincoln (1981). Departing from an earlier distinction between decision-oriented and conclusion-oriented inquiry, Cronbach and co-workers question the appropriateness of an inquiry that focuses exclusively on decisions. Cronbach and co-workers point out that the theory of evaluation has been developed almost wholly around the image of command. By "image of command" these authors refer to a mistaken belief that there is a clearly identifiable decision maker on the horizon who makes decisions on the basis of informative input, including that provided by the evaluator. These writers point out that the actual context in which evaluation occurs is not consistent with the context of command assumed to exist in virtually all program settings. Their point is that only when a large confluence of data becomes available is a "decision" actually made, and even then, the decision is made interactively over a long period of time by a large number of persons (policy makers, bureaucrats, program monitors, project personnel, vested-interests, and others) who make up what constitute a "policy-shaping community." These authors advance the notion that the process of decision making does not terminate in a clearly defined decision but is a cumulative, never-ending process characterized by negotiation and accommodation among members of the policy shaping community (PSC) who continually reassess and modify the decisions to be made and the alternative courses of action to be taken. Cronbach and his colleagues describe the evolution of decisions in the policy shaping community this way:

> Most action is determined by a pluralistic community, not by a lone decision maker. Parties having divergent perceptions and aims bear down on lawmakers and administrators. Information can change perceptions but is unlikely to bring all parties to agree on which facts are relevant or even on what the facts are. If the term *decision* is understood to mean formal choice at a particular time between discrete alternatives, decision making is rarely to be observed. When there are multiple participants with multiple views, it is meaningless to speak of one action as the rational or correct action. The active parties jockey toward a politically acceptable accommodation.

Hence, these authors suggest that the proper role of evaluation is not to service decisions but to participate in and contribute to the negotiation and accommodation process by raising new issues, stimulating new debate and illuminating the complexities of the problem at hand. For these reasons evaluations should focus on programs as implementations of policy and not on specific alternative courses of action to be taken in a particular context. Their reasoning is that by the time decisions are about to be made, the alternative courses of action to which they relate will have lost their significance, while the policy which underlies these alternative actions will have remained a relevant social issue.

Guba, one of the original founders of the CIPP decision-oriented model, also has recently voiced some changed views on the relevance of decision-oriented evaluation. Although acknowledging that the decision maker or client is entitled to issue directives to the evaluator, Guba and Lincoln (1981) warn that:

> . . . the evaluator need not be naive. He must recognize that the client may have many covert reasons for putting the charge in a particular way. He may, for example, select for evaluation only those program aspects that appear to be successful, cover up program failure by focusing on partisan testimonials, make evaluation gestures designed to promote a favorable public image, respond to government mandates that he does not take seriously but must be complied with overtly and the like. Sheer ignorance may also shape the client's directives.

Looking retrospectively at the CIPP model itself, Guba and Lincoln's views essentially echo those of Cronbach and co-workers ". . . it made what are probably unwarranted assumptions about the rationality of decisions, about the openness of the decision-making process (essentially political) and about the ease with which operational decision makers can be identified (in complex organizations or loosely coupled organizations decisions appear to "bubble up" rather than be made explicitly at some particular time and place)."

The assumption of a context of command or the notion that evaluation is or should be decision-oriented has not been a result of accident or serendipity. Rather, the evolution of decision-oriented evaluation has resulted from the belief that evaluation's central role is to respond to the pragmatic needs of the decision maker and to the information requirements of those in most immediate control of the program. Hence, more complex decision making patterns involving negotiation and accommodation within a larger network of stake holders as well as more holistic and value-based criteria for program effectiveness, generally, are not assumed to be characteristic of the decision-oriented perspective.

## Bibliography

Alkin M C 1969 Evaluation theory development. *Eval. Comment* 2(1): 2–7

Cronbach L, Ambron S, Dornbusch S, Hess R, Hornik R, Phillips D, Walker D, Weiner S 1980 *Toward Reform of Program Evaluation: Aims, Methods and Institutional Arrangements.* Jossey-Bass, San Francisco, California

Guba E G, Lincoln Y S 1981 *Effective Evaluation: Improving the Usefulness of Evaluation Results Through Responsive and Naturalistic Approaches.* Jossey-Bass, San Francisco, California

Guttentag M 1973 Subjectivity and its use in evaluation research. *Eval.* 1(2): 60–65

Hagedorn H J, Beck K J, Neubert S F, Werlin S H 1976 *A Working Manual of Simple Program Evaluation Techniques for Community Mental Health Centers.* National Institute of Mental Health, Rockville, Maryland

Larson R C, Kaplan E H 1981 Decision-oriented approaches to program evaluation. In: Wooldridge R (ed.) 1981 *New Directions for Program Evaluation: Evaluation of Complex Systems.* Jossey-Bass, San Francisco, California

Provus M M 1971 *Discrepancy Evaluation for Educational Program Improvement and Assessment.* McCutchan, Berkeley, California

Scriven M 1983 The evaluation taboo. In: House E (ed.) 1983 *New Directions for Program Evaluation: Philosophy of Evaluation.* Jossey-Bass, San Francisco, California

Stufflebeam D L, Foley W J, Gephart W J, Guba E G, Hammond H D, Merriman H O, Provus M M 1971 *Educational Evaluation and Decision Making.* Peacock, Itasca, Illinois

# Beyond Decision-oriented Evaluation[1]

## J. Scheerens

The idea that evaluations should eventually support administrative or political decision-making can almost be considered as a defining characteristic of the evaluation discipline. This is apparent from classical texts such as Suchman's (Suchman 1967), Stufflebeam's well-known book on educational evaluation and decision-making (Stufflebeam et al. 1971) and Campbell's notion of "reforms as experiments" (Campbell 1969). It also applies to the more recent literature on utilization focused evaluation, such as Alkin et al. (1979) and Patton (1978).

In this article the principal ways of looking at the relation between evaluation and decision-making will be discussed. This will be done by examining the "decisional contexts" of evaluation projects in terms of a comparison between two models of organizational decision-making, the rational model and the incremental model, and by analyzing certain remedies that have been prescribed for the problems arising when an attempt is made to enhance the "decisional relevance" of evaluation. In the process, the concept of decision-oriented evaluation will be widened while at the same time its prescriptive usefulness will be regarded in an increasingly relative light.

## 1. The Rational Model

When organizational decision-making is seen as a deliberate choice between clear-cut alternatives that have to be assessed in terms of their effect on pre-established

1 This article was originally published in the *International Journal of Educational Research*, Vol. 11, No. 1. It appears here with permission from Pergamon Press plc © 1987.

goals, evaluation has a "natural place" in the process. The core task of evaluation will then be to discover, by empirical testing, which alternative is most effective. The sequence of activities corresponds to the problem-solving model: statement of the problem; development of feasible courses of action (for example, program variants); evaluation of the alternatives, and choice of the optimum or "most satisfying" solution. The most likely research designs in such a sequence of activities would be experimental or quasi-experimental (Campbell 1969). Although this model of organizational decision-making is often referred to as the rational model, it should be noted that in reality it is only a weaker modification of the "pure rationality" model (Dror 1968). The pure rationality model assumes full information on all available alternatives, all desirable end-states and on the functions that characterize relation between actions and states. In the problem-solving model of organizational decision-making probably only a few feasible alternatives will be considered, so that in actual practice the decision-making process will be more like Simon's "bounded rationality" model (Simon 1945), but this article will follow common usage in continuing to speak of the rational model. In this section the assumptions underlying evaluation within the context of rational decision-making will be examined, first by summarizing the characteristics of the decision-model itself and then by looking at how evaluation functions within this model.

The most important characteristics of the decision-model itself are as follows.

(a) *Clear statement of goals.* The assumption is that goals are stated in advance, preferably specified as operational objectives.

(b) *Distinction of goals and means.* The means are supposed to be devised after the goals have been declared.

(c) *Causal hypotheses.* There is supposed to be some kind of causal theory about means-to-end relations. The idea is that this theory is comprehensive, and that every relevant factor can be taken into account.

(d) *A long-term perspective.* There is a strong belief in long-term overall-planning.

(e) *Relatively stable programs.* The causal theory must be empirically tested. The test of a good program or policy is that it can be shown to comprise the best means of reaching the desired ends. One implication of this assumption is that program implementation is not seen as a major problem. An aspect of the rational model is its optimistic view of the ability and the willingness of the various parties concerned (i.e., teachers) to carry out programs as they are planned. Another implication is that a certain stability is presupposed during the "try-out" of program variants; goals and means are assumed not to change during the course of the program.

(f) *Identifiability of decision-makers.* The rational model usually assumes a single group of people who are authorized to make decisions, in spite of the fact that there are multi-actor variants of the rational model, such as game theory.

The well-structured and coherent nature of the rational decision-making context, as well as its long-term perspective can be seen to have the following consequences for evaluations.

(a) *Evaluation as a means-to-end analysis.* The core evaluation question is whether the means (program variants) are effective. This means that there will usually be an emphasis on performance measures (product evaluation) and that experimental, quasiexperimental, or nonexperimental causal designs will predominate.

(b) *A "safe place" for program evaluators.* The assumption is that evaluation researchers will be able to carry out their tasks relatively independently according to professional norms. Evaluation itself is seen as rational and impartial activity and not as "political".

(c) *Large-scale evaluation studies.* The most likely responses to comprehensive, long-term plans are large-scale evaluations.

(d) *Use follows evaluation in a linear sequence.* The idea is that decision-making takes place after the evaluation results have been made public. According to the rational ideal, the evaluation results will speak for themselves and will be the major basis for administrative decision-making.

The inevitable danger with characterizations such as these is that they tend to be overstylized and to emphasize extremes. This means that they make ideal material for setting up straw men who can then be destroyed with great ease as soon as a better alternative model is presented. Therefore, it should be emphasized here that there are all kinds of modifications of the rational model depicted above. In fact one could even see rationalism and incrementalism (the model to be discussed in the next section) as discrete points on several continua (see, for example, Scheerens 1985a).

The major criticism of the rational model has arisen out of meta-evaluations of large-scale evaluation projects and empirical and analytical studies on the use of evaluation-results (see, for example, Caplan 1982, Weiss 1982, Weiss 1983, Cronbach et al. 1980, Cronbach 1982, Lindblom and Cohen 1979, Patton 1978, Alkin et al. 1979, Berke 1983, De Young and Conner 1982). Discussion of these criticisms will be postponed until the alternative model that has emerged from the work of these authors has been presented in the next section. However, an important distinction for the ensuing discussion should be mentioned here. There are two ways of looking at the rational model: as a descriptive model appropriate to describing organizational decision-making or as a prescriptive model representing an ideal. It will be argued that even if there is is justifiable criticism of its descriptive validity, the rational model is nevertheless of great importance for prescriptive purposes.

## 2. *The Incremental Model*

In many practical situations the assumptions underlying the rational model do not hold. Organizational decision-making frequently fails to follow the clear-cut logic of articulated means-to-end analysis. The alternative model, in which Lindblom tried to capture "real" organizational decision-making, emphasizes a different *formal* structure for the decision-making process, summarized in terms like "successive limited comparisons", or "muddling through". Other studies of political and administrative decision-making have focused on the *context* of decision-making and the organizational background of decision-makers (see, for example, Allison 1971).

In many cases the official program goals—if they are clear at all—are mixed with other motives, like the pursuit of political careers and the self-maintenance or "imperialism" of organizational units. Since the recognition that there are often more interests at play, and that they are related to the organizational affiliation of the parties concerned, fits in well with the formal characteristics of pluralistic, "small step" decision-making, these two aspects will be dealt with together in the interpretation of "incrementalism" used here.

As in the preceding section, the main characteristics of the incremental decision-making model are summarized below, followed by an overview of the way in which this kind of organizational decision-making may affect evaluation. To facilitate comparison of the two models, the same categories will be used in the same order.

(a) *Ambiguous goal statements.* "Overall" goals, if stated at all, are formulated in vague terms. While there are usually several parties with disparate interests in a program, the relations between these individual interests and the "overall goal" are not spelt out. Vagueness of overall goals is often seen as a political advantage since it allows politicians to dissemble differences among their own adherents and because noncommitment leaves them more freedom of action.

(b) *Goals and means cannot be distinguished.* Means may function as ends in themselves. According to the incremental model, selection of means may precede the attribution of goals.

(c) *Interpolation of the past.* Since overall means-to-end planning is seen as unrealistic, the incremental model assumes that progress consists of "small steps", in which the history of an organization plays an important role. It is also recognized that proceedings will vary across sites. The consequence is, that even when large-scale programs are envisaged, they will present a fragmented pattern of local diver-

gences. This will have obvious drawbacks for overall causal analysis.

(d) *A short-time perspective.* Incrementalism is strongly associated with a conservative outlook and a distrust of detailed overall planning.

(e) *Programs are seen as fuzzy and fleeting.* Incrementalism places no reliance in the idea that a program might be carried out according to plan. In the unlikely event of a general overall-plan it will be recognized that there are still many different ways of implementing it. In terms of a well-known distinction culled from educational innovation literature, an incremental decisional context is associated more with a "mutual adjustment perspective" than with a "fidelity perspective" (Fullan and Pomfret 1977). It is also recognized that the goals, and political priority of a program may change while it is being carried out.

(f) *Diffuse decision-making.* It is seen as uncertain which decisions will be taken and by whom (see, for example, Weiss, 1982); different stakeholders are confidently expected to draw their own conclusions from the evaluation results.

Although the question of how evaluation can function within a context of incremental decision-making will be dealt with in more detail in subsequent sections of this article, some of the main observations that have been made in the literature are summarized below.

(a) *Evaluation as descriptive research.* Because of the lack of articulation of means-to-end relations, the changing character of programs, local variations and the short-time perspective, evaluation as overall means-to-end analysis will usually seem impossible (Cronbach et al. 1980). Instead, the emphasis will tend to be on descriptive case-studies of local implementation variants. The "qualitative" movement in the evaluation literature in the United States coincides with this view of the nature of decision-making and innovation processes (Weiss and Rein 1971, Berman and McLaughlin 1976).

(b) *Evaluators as pawns in a political game.* From the incremental perspective, the differences in interest between evaluators and practitioners or site workers are recognized (see, for example, Caro 1971; De Young and Conner 1982, Cohen 1983). Sometimes evaluators only obtain access to data after lengthy negotiations with practitioners (Scheerens 1985b). Other stakeholders too may try to influence the way evaluations are carried out in order to get their view of the program accepted, or to protect their interests. Some authors even state that current evaluation approaches are bound to be politically biased (Ross and Cronbach 1976, Berk and Rossi 1976, Campbell and Erlebacher 1972).

(c) *Several small-scale studies.* The lack of coherence in programs makes overall-designs risky affairs.

Cronbach et al. (1980) in this respect strongly condemn "blockbuster studies" and advocate a number of smaller studies done by different research-teams.

(d) *Use of evaluation results as a gradual process of enlightenment.* According to the incremental model, organizational decision-making is not a matter of making all-or-none decisions, but rather a slow process of "accretion" (Weiss 1980). Nor can evaluation results be expected to have the dramatic effect of forcing such important comprehensive decisions. According to Patton "research impacts in ripples, not in waves" (Patton 1978). Weiss and Caplan conclude from their studies in knowledge use that evaluation results may gradually change the way societal problems are conceptualized in decision-making communities (Caplan 1982, Weiss 1982). They refer to this view on the use of policy-research results as the "enlightenment" model. It is recognized that evaluation results will simply number among the information sources used by decision-makers. This accounts for the many instances of program-continuation after negative evaluation findings (and the opposite).

After comparing these two models of organizational decision-making, and their most likely consequences for the ·"position" of evaluation, the most interesting question seems to be to find realistic ways of saving as much as possible of the rational ideal, while recognizing at the same time that the political and organizational context will be more or less in line with the incremental model. This question will be addressed in the next section, by comparing several solutions, two of which can be seen as more or less "succumbing" to incrementalism, while the other two, in a sense, try to resurrect the rational model.

## 3. Approaches that Seek to Enhance the Relevance of Evaluations

The four approaches to be discussed in this section are: utilization-focused evaluation, stakeholder-based evaluation, evaluation according to a betting model, and the idea of rational reconstruction of diffuse decision-making contexts.

### 3.1 Utilization-focused Evaluation

The term *utilization-focused evaluation* was coined by Patton (Patton 1978). On the basis of a study on the actual use of evaluation results, Patton formulated a set of practical recommendations for evaluators. Alkin et al. (1979) took a similar approach. According to Patton, the main factors enhancing utilization are as follows.

(a) Evaluators should try to identify decision-makers. It is considered of great importance for the evaluator to know the decision-makers personally.

(b) The evaluator should try actively to identify and focus on the relevant evaluation question. This may involve trying to commit decision-makers to evaluation questions, for instance by means of public statements in the press.

(c) Evaluators should have an "active/reactive/adaptive" attitude; they should be as flexible as possible in the face of changes in program goals and political priorities.

(d) Evaluators should not be preoccupied with quantitative outcome measures and experimental designs. Attention should be given instead to the description of program variants and implementation processes. Qualitative or "naturalistic" methods can play an important role.

(e) Evaluators should try to construct the program's theory of action in terms of means-to-end relationships.

(f) Evaluators should stimulate the participation of decision-makers and practitioners in methodological choices so that they "understand the strengths and weaknesses of the data—and believe in the data" (Patton 1978 p. 202). Decision-makers should also be actively involved in the way the evaluation findings are reported. Both Patton and Alkin concluded from their research that decision-makers do not see research quality as an important factor when they decide whether or not to use evaluation findings.

Some of the findings and recommendations of Patton and Alkin are refuted by other investigations of knowledge use. Weiss's (1980) conclusion that it was hardly ever possible to identify decision-makers, stands in strong contrast to Patton's focus on the evaluators getting to know the decision-makers personally. Patton's and Alkin's findings that decision-makers do not pay much attention to research quality is contradicted by Weiss and Bucuvalas (1980) who found that decision-makers do scrutinize research quality when they do not like the evaluation outcomes.

### 3.2 Stakeholder-based Evaluation

The stakeholder approach to evaluation not only recognizes the fact that there are different parties with an interest in research outcomes but also tries to make active use of this phenomenon. The idea is that giving the various parties more proprietary feeling for the evaluation process and its outcomes will increase the chances of the evaluation results being used. Two groups of stakeholders are recognized: those involved in decision-making and those otherwise affected by the evaluation (for example, teachers, pupils, parents). The assumptions of the stakeholder approach are critically examined by Weiss (1983) and Cohen (1983). Weiss questions the assumption that stakeholders have specific information needs and that evaluators have the skills to respond adequately to these (possibly divergent) needs. According to Cohen, the orientations of contractors and evaluators on the one hand and site-workers on the other cannot be reconciled and integrated in one evaluation study. He also observes that power is unequally divided between stakeholders (to the disadvantage of site-workers). Cohen concludes that it would be better if all stakeholders had their own evaluation study.

The relativity inherent in the way these approaches (both utilization-focused and stakeholder-based evaluation) regard research quality and technique is a serious point for discussion. Both put professional evaluators, as far as research–technical know-how and objectivity is concerned, on the same level as directly interested parties with no formal training in social science research methodology. Critics of these approaches argue that these approaches overemphasize the degree to which evaluation can be "participatory", and that invalid and unreliable results would be useless even if all the stakeholders were happy.

### 3.3 Evaluation According to a Betting Model

Assuming that different stakeholders tend to have conflicting expectations of the outcomes of a program, Hofstee (1985) applies an approach to evaluation which he calls a betting model. According to this model, stakeholders indicate in advance which outcomes they expect and also the the probability of the occurrence of the expected outcomes. After thus having specified predictive probability distributions (the "bets" of the stakeholders) the outcomes are measured and finally the scores are compared with the expectations. This is done by applying a logistic scoring-rule which results in the establishment of the degree to which each of the betting parties has been right in his or her predictions. An important assumption relied on by the betting model is that stakeholders can reach agreement on an outcome operationalization. Although this may be seen as the Achilles-heel of the approach, the model has been successfully applied in the field of curriculum evaluation, with commercial educational publishers as the betting parties (Van den Berg 1985).

### 3.4 Active "Rational Reconstruction" by Evaluators

A basic stipulation in decision-oriented and utilization-focused evaluation is that evaluators should appeal to others for guidance in establishing the structure of an evaluation project. The obvious reason for doing so is to increase the relevance of evaluations, by committing the parties concerned to the evaluation as much as possible. Yet studies of evaluation-use seem to show that evaluators can only expect limited help from external sources. It is often impossible to identify an authoritative decision-maker at all. Instead, for every program there are usually several parties whose interests in the program and its evaluation often conflict. If there

is no-one "out there" waiting for evaluation results in order to make "important" decisions, and evaluation-use consists of the gradual percolation of knowledge and the gradual shaping of conceptual outlooks, then evaluators would seem all the more bound to choose a more active approach to designing program evaluation. Hofstee's betting model is a good example because the external stakeholders participate according to a set of rather strict rules already established by the evaluator. In a more general approach evaluators would use whatever information was available—including stakeholders' viewpoints—to make rational constructions of fuzzy programs and diffuse decision-making contexts (see, for example, Rossi and McLaughlin 1979). The focus should be on the causal structure relating program variants to desired outcomes. In choosing dimensions for outcome measures, evaluators should look for those criteria on which the expectations of stakeholders differ most. If evaluations succeed in providing empirical evidence on controversial issues, it is hard to imagine politicians failing to make use of it in ensuing debate.

### 4. Beyond Decision Oriented Evaluation

Decision-oriented evaluation is to be seen as an approach that attempts to increase the relevance of evaluations by taking into account the context and structure of the administrative or political decision-making to which the evaluation results are assumed to contribute. Utilization-focused and "stakeholder-based" evaluation go a long way to attaching evaluation design more closely to the decision-making context. Since decision-making contexts are often diffuse and it is hard to reconcile the demands of all stakeholders, this road reaches its natural end when evaluators find themselves forced to make their own final design-choices anyway. Also, letting stakeholders participate in every aspect of the structuring of evaluations, including the technical aspects, may well lead to the loss of a vital prerequisite of evaluation use: research quality. This realization implies that decision-oriented evaluation is to be looked upon with a certain amount of relativity. In approaches like the "betting model" and with the idea that evaluators themselves should rationally structure diffuse decision-making contexts, a counter-movement can be discerned, emphasizing a more active role for evaluators. But such a movement does not simply end up back at square one with scientific evaluators in ivory towers, neglecting the external relevance of their work, for both approaches start by gathering information on the decisional context.

There are two more reasons for thinking beyond decision-oriented evaluation. The first reason rests on the assumption that when it is established whether or not the program has succeeded in fulfilling the basic needs for which it was designed and implemented, it will be difficult for anyone to ignore the evaluation data. Although one can never be absolutely certain that decision-makers use evaluators' recommendations, they would seem more likely to, had the ultimate effectiveness of a program been assessed. The implication is that it should not be overlooked that there are other "internal" criteria for increasing evaluation relevance besides adaptation to the decision-making context.

The third reason for going beyond the concept of decision-oriented evaluation is of a different nature. Rather than expressing the relativity of the concept, it has to do with enlarging it to a more comprehensive conceptualization of the contextual analysis of evaluation projects (Scheerens, 1985b). According to this enlarged concept of contextual analysis, organizational and institutional arrangements should be taken into account too. For instance, the degree to which evaluators can cooperate with decision-makers will depend on the structure of the interorganizational network in which the various parties are located. The influence of practitioners and site-workers on evaluations depends on the autonomy of schools within a district or within a national educational system. And the independence of researchers willing to play an active role in structuring evaluations depends on their institutional location, the resources available and the management philosophy of the research-contractor. Such organizational issues should be included in the very first assessment of feasibility for any evaluation program, in order to find the optimum balance between evaluation aspirations and the contextual intricacies of a particular setting.

## Bibliography

Alkin M C, Daillak R, White P 1979 *Using Evaluations: Does Evaluation make a Difference?* Sage, Beverly Hills, California

Allison G T 1971 *Essence of Decision*. Little, Brown and Company, Boston, Massachusetts

Berk R A, Rossi P H 1976 Doing good or worse: Evaluation research politically re-examined. *Soc. Probl.* 23: 337–49

Berke I P 1983 Evaluation and incrementalism: The AIR Report and ESEA Title VII. *Educ. Eval. Pol. Anal.* 5: 249–56

Berman P, McLaughlin M W 1976 Implementation of educational innovation. *Educ. Forum* 40: 345–70

Campbell D T 1969 Reforms as experiments. In: Struening E L, Guttentag M (eds.) 1975 *Handbook of Evaluation Research*, Vol. I. Sage, Beverly Hills, California, pp. 71–100

Campbell D T, Erlebacher A 1970 How regression artifacts in quasi-experimental evaluations can mistakenly make compensatory evaluation look harmful. In: Hellmuth J (ed.) 1970 *Compensatory Education: A National Debate*, Vol. 3 of *The Disadvantaged Child*. Brunner/Mazel, New York, pp. 185–210

Caplan N 1982 Social research and public policy at the national level. In: Kallen D B P, Kosse G B, Wagenaar H C, Kloprogge J J J, Vorbeck M (eds.) 1982 *Social Science Research and Public Policy-Making: A Reappraisal*. NFER-Nelson, Windsor

Caro F G 1971 *Readings in Evaluation Research*. Russell Sage Foundation, New York

Cohen D K 1983 Evaluation and reform. In: Bryk A S (ed.) 1983 *Stakeholder-based Evaluation*, New Directions for Program Evaluation No. 17, Jossey-Bass, San Francisco, California, pp. 73–81

Cronbach L J 1982 *Designing Evaluations of Educational and Social Programs*. Jossey-Bass, San Francisco, California

Cronbach L J, Ambron S R, Dornbusch S M, Hess R D, Hornik R C, Phillips D C, Walker D F, Weiner S S 1980 *Toward Reform of Program Evaluation*. Jossey-Bass, San Francisco, California

DeYoung D J, Conner R F 1982 Evaluator preconceptions about organizational decision making. *Eval. Rev.* 6: 431–40

Dror Y 1968 *Public Policy-making Reexamined*. Chandler, San Francisco, California

Fullan M, Pomfret A 1977 Research on curriculum and instruction implementation. *Rev. Educ. Res.* 47: 335–97

Hofstee W K B 1985 A betting model of evaluation research. In: Creemers B P M (ed.) 1985 *Evaluation Research in Education: Reflections and Studies.* SVO, The Hague

Lindblom C E, Cohen D K 1979 *Usable Knowledge*. Yale University Press, New Haven, Connecticut

Patton M Q 1978 *Utilization-focused Evaluation*. Sage, Beverly Hills, California

Ross L, Cronbach L J 1976 Handbook of evaluation research (review). *Educ. Res.* 5(10): 9–19

Rossi R J, McLaughlin D H 1979 Establishing evaluation objectives. *Eval. Q.* 3: 331–46

Scheerens J 1985a A systems approach to the analysis and management of large-scale evaluations. *Stud. Educ. Eval.* 11: 83–93

Scheerens J 1985b Contextual influences on evaluations: The case of innovative programs in Dutch education. *Educ. Eval. Pol. Anal.* 7: 309–17

Simon H A 1945 *Administrative Behavior*, 2nd edn. Macmillan, New York

Stufflebeam D L, Foley W J, Gephart W J, Guba E G, Hammond R L, Merriman H O, Provus M M 1971 *Educational Evaluation and Decision-making in Education*. Peacock, Itasca, Illinois

Suchman E A 1968 *Evaluative Research*. Russell Sage Foundation, New York

Van den Berg G 1985 Curriculum evaluation as comparative product evaluation. In: Creemers B P M (ed.) 1985 *Evaluation Research in Education: Reflections and Studies.* SVO, The Hague

Weiss R S, Rein M 1971 The evaluation of broad-aim programs: A cautionary case and a moral. In: Caro F G (ed.) 1971 *Readings in Evaluation Research*. Russell Sage Foundation, New York

Weiss C H 1978 Improving the linkage between social research and public policy. In: Lynon L E (ed.) 1978 *Knowledge and Policy: The Uncertain Connection*. Study project on social research and development, Vol. 5, NRC, pp. 287–96

Weiss C H 1980 Knowledge creep and decision accretion. *Know. Creat. Diff. Utiliz.* 1: 381–404

Weiss C H, Bucuvalas M J 1980 Truth tests and utility tests: Decision-makers' frames of reference for social science research. *Am. Soc. Rev.* 45: 302–13

Weiss C H 1982 Policy research in the context of diffuse decision-making. In: Kallen D B P, Kosse G B, Wagenaar H C, Kloprogge J J J, Vorbeck M (eds.) 1982 *Social Science Research and Public Policy-making: A Reappraisal*. NFER-Nelson, Windsor, pp. 288–321

Weiss C H 1983 Toward the future of stakeholder approaches in evaluation. In: Bryk A S (ed.) 1983 *Stakeholder-based Evaluation*, New Directions for Program Evaluation No. 17. Jossey-Bass, San Francisco, California, pp. 83–96

# Goal-free Evaluation

## B. Stecher

Goal-free evaluation is an approach to evaluation in which merit is determined from an examination of program effects without reference to goals or objectives. This focus on results rather than intentions was proposed by Michael Scriven to counteract the bias that can result when attention to stated program goals narrows the range of potential outcomes that are investigated by an evaluator. In contrast, the goal-free evaluator is charged to examine all program outcomes— staunchly ignorant of project objectives—and make no distinctions between "anticipated outcomes" and "side effects."

The notion of goal-free evaluation evolved out of a concern that evaluation was too easily circumscribed by program goals and thus too strongly influenced by program managers and planners. "The rhetoric of intent was being used as a substitute for evidence of success" (Scriven 1972). Moreover, official goals are often narrow, vague, purposefully overstated, or purposefully understated. Thus, adherence to goals severely limits the scope and meaningfulness of an evaluation. By changing the focus from "what the program was trying to do" to what it was actually doing, Scriven's goal-free evaluator is free to determine merit without such program-based bias.

This is somewhat analogous to the double-blind technique used in scientific experiments. In a double-blind medical study, for example, neither the subject nor the administering physician knows who is receiving the treatment drug and who is receiving the placebo. This eliminates many potential confounding explanations for the observed effects. Scriven referred to goal-free evaluation as triple-blind, for, in addition, the evaluator does not even know the intentions of the intervention.

Goal-free evaluation is not a fully realized evaluation model with formal definitions, specification of structural relationships, frameworks for data collection and reporting, operating procedures, and so on. It is primarily a philosophical principle for guiding the evaluation process. For the most part, the goal-free evaluator must use his or her best professional skill to discover and document program effects. However, Scriven did offer some additional suggestions about how it is possible to determine which observed effects can be attributed to the program under investigation. Likening goal-free evaluation to criminal investigation, he called the process the modus operandi method. The name refers to the manner in which investigators try to establish causal connections. The method consists of a careful examination of all potential causes for observed effects and the establishment of solid connections, link by link, to prior program activities or rival influences.

There have been numerous criticisms of goal-free evaluation; the most frequent is that it simply substitutes the goals of the evaluator for those of the program manager. After all, the evaluator must have some criteria for making favorable or unfavorable judgments. Advocates of goal-free evaluation would argue that this is merely a misunderstanding. It derives, in part, from a failure to recognize that the important criterion in an evaluation is not the degree to which the program meets its goals, but the degree to which it meets demonstrated needs. Merit is derived from the congruence between program effects and the needs of the affected population, not from the correspondence between effects and goals. Consequently, the critical task for the evaluator is to determine the needs of the affected population, and these become the basis for judgments about program effects. In fact, Scriven (1981) referred to goal-free evaluation as "needs-based evaluation."

Another way in which Scriven addressed the concern about the role of goals in program evaluation is to note the similarity between goal-free evaluation and consumer product testing. A product—be it automobile or copying machine—should be evaluated from the perspective of the consumer and the society, not the producer. It would be incorrect to use the goals of Nissan Motors or Xerox as the basis for the evaluation of their products. It would also be improper to substitute the evaluator's goals. Instead, a good product evaluator determines the functional needs of the consuming audience and uses these as the criteria for assessing the merits of the product. The goal-free evaluator takes a similar approach to program evaluation; in fact, Scriven (1981) also referred to goal-free evaluation as "consumer-based evaluation."

Despite its interesting philosophical basis, goal-free evaluation has not enjoyed wide popularity as a practical evaluation approach. This is due to many factors, including the resistance of program personnel to such uncontrolled examination of their actions, the reluctance of most evaluators to accept such large responsibility, and important disagreements with Scriven about the appropriate role for evaluation. Many evaluators place greater emphasis on the provision of information to decision makers and less on abstract judgment of merit.

Yet, proponents of goal-free evaluation have had some impact on the practice of evaluation. By emphasizing the independence of the evaluator, the importance of examining all program effects, and the need to subject program goals themselves to scrutiny (when conducting a goal-based evaluation), goal-free evaluation has affected the actions of many evaluators. Though not widely employed as a practical evaluation approach, goal-free evaluation has caused evaluators to be more attentive to a wider range of program outcomes, and the ideas embodied in this approach are mentioned frequently in other scholarly writing about evaluation.

## Bibliography

Alkin M C 1972 Wider context goals and goal-based evaluators. *Eval. Comment* 3(4)

Popham W J 1975 *Educational Evaluation*. Prentice-Hall, Englewood Cliffs, New Jersey

Scriven M 1972 Pros and cons about goal-free evaluation. *Eval. Comment* 3(4): 1–4 Reprinted in Hamilton D, Jenkins D, King C, MacDonald B, Parlett M (eds.) 1977 *Beyond the Numbers Game: A Reader in Educational Evaluation*. Macmillan, London, pp. 130–1

Scriven M 1981 *Evaluation Thesaurus*, 3rd edn. Edgepress, Point Reyes, California

Stufflebeam D L 1972 Should or can evaluation be goal-free? *Eval. Comment* 3(4)

# Program Evaluation

## B. R. Worthen

Educational programs (and other publicly funded programs) have continued to increase in size and expense. Not surprisingly, taxpayers and public officials have increasingly urged that these programs be made more accountable to their publics. Indeed, "accountability" for expenditures of public funds has become the hue and cry of an ever-increasing number of economy-minded social reformers. In several countries, policy makers at both national and local levels now routinely authorize funds to be used for the express purpose of evaluating educational programs to determine their effectiveness. Thus, "program evaluation" has come into being as both a formal educational activity and as a frequently mandated instrument of public policy. Many private educational enterprises have similarly turned to program evaluation as a means of answering questions about the benefits received from monies expended on various educational programs.

To define program evaluation, it is necessary to define its component parts. In an educational context, a program can be thought of as any educational enterprise aimed at the solution of a particular educational problem or the improvement of some aspect of an educational system. Such a program would typically be sponsored by public or private funds, possess specified goals, and exhibit some structure for managing the procedures, materials, facilities, and/or personnel involved in the program.

Evaluation can be defined most simply as the determination of the worth of a thing. In its simplest form, therefore, program evaluation consists of those activities undertaken to judge the worth or utility of a program (or alternative programs) in improving some specified aspect of an educational system. Examples of program evaluations might include evaluation of a national bilingual education program, a university's preservice program for training urban administrators, a ministry of education's staff development program, or a local parent education resource center. Evaluations may be conducted for programs of any size or scope, ranging from an arithmetic program in a particular school to an international consortium on metric education.

A curriculum evaluation may qualify as a program evaluation if the curriculum is focused on change or improvement, as implied in the previous definition of "program." Program evaluations, however, often do not involve appraisal of curricula (e.g., evaluation of a computerized student recordkeeping system or evaluation of the extent to which funds from a national program for the hearing impaired are actually used to provide services to children with hearing impairments). For this reason, the closely related but more specialized topic of curriculum evaluation is not discussed further in this section (see *Curriculum Evaluation*).

## 1. Purposes of Program Evaluation

Most program evaluators agree that program evaluation can play either a formative purpose (helping to improve the program) or a summative purpose (deciding whether a program should be continued). Anderson and Ball (1978) further describe the capabilities of program evaluation in terms of six major purposes (which are not necessarily mutually exclusive). They are:

(a) to contribute to decisions about program installation;

(b) to contribute to decisions about program continuation, expansion, or "certification";

(c) to contribute to decisions about program modifications;

(d) to obtain evidence to rally support for a program;

(e) to obtain evidence to rally opposition to a program;

(f) to contribute to the understanding of basic psychological, social, and other processes (only rarely can this purpose be achieved in a program evaluation without compromising more basic evaluation purposes).

## 2. The History of Program Evaluation

The informal practice of program evaluation is not new, dating back at least to 2000 BC, when Chinese officials were conducting civil-service examinations, and continuing down through the centuries to the beginnings of school accreditation in the late 1800s. The first clear evidence of formal program evaluation, however, appears to be Joseph Rice's 1897–1898 comparative study of spelling performance of 33,000 students in a large United States school system. Few formal evaluations of educational programs were conducted in the next few decades, with Tyler and Smith's Eight-year Study of the 1930s being the next notable effort to evaluate the outcomes of an educational program. During the late 1950s and early 1960s (the post-Sputnik years), cries for curriculum reform led to major new curriculum development programs and to subsequent calls for their evaluation. The relatively few evaluation studies that resulted revealed the conceptual and methodological impoverishment of the field—or perhaps more accurately, the "nonfield"—of evaluation in that era. In many cases, the designs were inadequate, the data invalid, the analyses inaccurate, and the reports irrelevant to the important evaluation questions which should have been posed. Most of the studies depended on idiosyncratic combinations and applications of concepts and techniques from experimental design, psychometrics, curriculum development and, to a lesser extent, survey research. Theoretical work related to educational evaluation, per se, was almost nonexistent. Few scholars had yet turned their attention to the development of generalizable evaluation plans which could be adopted or adapted specifically to educational evaluation studies. In the absence of a "formal subject matter" or educational evaluation, evaluators of educational programs were left to glean what they could from other fields to help them in their work.

Since a large number of persons serving in evaluation roles during the late 1950s and 1960s were educational and psychological researchers, it is not surprising that the experimental tradition quickly became the most generally accepted evaluation approach. The work of Campbell and Stanley gave enormous impetus to predominance of experimental or quasiexperimental approaches to program evaluation. Although some evaluators cautioned that correct use of the experimental model may not be feasible, the elegance and precision of this model led most program evaluators to view the experimental method as the ideal model for program evaluations.

Not all program evaluators were enamored with the use of traditional quantitative methods for program evaluations, however, and their dissatisfaction led to a search for alternatives. Qualitative and naturalistic methods, largely shunned by program evaluators during the 1960s as unacceptably "soft," gained wider acceptance in the 1970s and thereafter as proposals for their application to program evaluations were made by Parlett and Hamilton, Stake, Eisner, Guba and Lincoln, and others. Sharp disagreements developed between proponents of the newer qualitative approaches and adherents to the more broadly accepted quantitative methods and the 1970s were marked by polemics as the

two schools of thought struggled for ascendancy. The late 1970s and the early 1980s saw the dialogue begin to move beyond this debate as analysts accelerated their discussions of the benefits of integrating both types of methods within a program evaluation (for instance see Cook and Reichardt 1979, Worthen 1981, and the especially useful summary by Madey 1982).

Concurrent with program evaluators' struggle to sort out the relative utility of quantitative and qualitative methods, a separate but closely related development was taking place. Beginning in the late 1960s, several evaluation writers began to develop and circulate their notions about how one should conduct educational evaluations; these efforts resulted in several new evaluation "models" being proposed to help the practicing program evaluator. Although these seminal writings in educational evaluation (discussed in Sect. 3) were doubtlessly influenced by the quantitative–qualitative controversy and some proved more comfortable companions with one or the other methodological persuasion, several were broader in conceptualization, providing guidelines for conducting program evaluations that could use either quantitative or qualitative data. As these frameworks for planning evaluation studies were applied and refined, program evaluators began to turn to them as promising sources of guidance. Collectively, these writings, the so-called evaluation models, represent the formal content of program evaluation and are discussed in the following section.

## 3. Alternative Approaches to Program Evaluation

Because of space restrictions, only some of the more popular current approaches used in conducting program evaluations can be presented in this section. Many of these (and other) approaches to program evaluation are summarized in Worthen and Sanders (1987) and the work of authors mentioned but not referenced herein (and in other sections of this entry) can be found in that source. For convenience, these conceptual frameworks for evaluation are clustered into five categories, although some of the frameworks are sufficiently multifaceted that they could appear in more than one category. Most of these "models" have focused broadly on program evaluation, although some are focused more specifically on curriculum evaluation. It should be noted that these frameworks deal with methods, not techniques; discussion of the many techniques which might be used in program evaluations is beyond the scope of this article.

### 3.1 Performance–Objectives Congruence Approaches

This approach to program evaluation was originally formulated by Ralph Tyler, who conceived of evaluation as the process of determining the extent to which the educational objectives of a school program or curriculum are actually being attained. He proposed a process in which broad goals or objectives would be established or identified, defined in behavioral terms, and relevant student behaviors would be measured against this yardstick, using either standardized or evaluator-constructed instruments. These outcome data were then to be compared with the behavioral objectives to determine the extent to which performance was congruent with expectations. Discrepancies between performance and objectives would lead to modifications intended to correct the deficiency, and the evaluation cycle would be repeated.

Tyler's rationale was logical, scientifically acceptable, readily adoptable by program evaluators (most of whose methodological upbringing was very compatible with the pretest–posttest measurement of student behaviors stressed by Tyler), and had great influence on subsequent evaluation theorists. Hammond's EPIC evaluation model followed Tyler's model closely, adding only a useful program-description "cube" which elaborates instructional and institutional variables often overlooked in previous evaluations. Provus' discrepancy model of program evaluation is clearly Tylerian and gains its name from the constant setting and juxtaposition of program standards against program performance to yield "discrepancy information" needed for program improvements. Popham's instructional objectives approach also clearly stems from Tyler's earlier conceptions.

Useful as this approach to evaluation is viewed by its many adherents, critics such as Guba and Lincoln (1981) have noted that it lacks a real evaluative component (facilitating measurement and assessment of objectives rather than resulting in explicit judgments of worth), lacks standards to judge the importance of observed discrepancies between objectives and performance levels, and depends on a highly utilitarian philosophy, promoting a linear, inflexible approach to evaluation.

### 3.2 Decision–Management Approaches

The most important contributions to a decision-oriented approach to program evaluation are Stufflebeam's Context, Input, Process, and Product (CIPP) evaluation model and Alkin's Center for the Study of Evaluation model, which follows a similar logic to the Context, Input, Process, and Product model but distinguishes between program implementation and program improvement, two subdivisions of what Stufflebeam terms process evaluation. In both models, objectives are eschewed as the organizer for the study and the decision to be made by program managers becomes pivotal. Stufflebeam has provided an analysis of types of decisions program managers are required to make and proposes a different type of evaluation for each type of decision. In both of these decision-oriented models, the evaluator, working closely with the program manager, would identify the decisions the latter must make and collect sufficient information about the relative advantages and disadvantages of each decision alternative to enable the decision maker to make a

judgment about which is best in terms of specified criteria. Thus, evaluation became an explicitly shared function dependent on good teamwork between evaluators and decision makers.

This approach has proved appealing to many evaluators and program managers, particularly those at home with the rational and orderly systems approach, to which it is clearly related. It was viewed by others, however, as failing to determine explicitly the program's worth and being dependent on somewhat unrealistic assumptions about the orderliness and predictability of the decision-making process.

### 3.3 Judgment-oriented Approaches

This general approach to evaluation, which historically has been the most widely used evaluation approach, is dependent upon experts' application of professional expertise to yield judgments about a program being observed. For example, the worth of a program would be assessed by experts (in the view of the evaluation's sponsor) who would observe the program in action, examine its products or, in some other way, glean sufficient information to render their considered judgment about the program. Site visits initiated by funding agencies to evaluate programs they support and visits by accrediting agencies to secondary schools and universities are examples of judgment-oriented program evaluations. Scriven, in his article *The Methodology of Evaluation* (Worthen and Sanders 1973), stressed judgment as the sine qua non of evaluation and, in his insightful examination of educational evaluation, did much to rescue this approach from the disrepute into which it had fallen in evaluation's headlong rush to gain respectability as a science. He stunned orthodox objectives-oriented evaluators by his suggestion that evaluators might go beyond measuring a program's performance to also evaluate the program's goals and later compounded the shock still further with his suggestion that evaluators should do "goal-free" evaluations, in which they not only ignore the program's goals but actually make every effort to avoid learning what those goals are. Thus, judgments about programs were based on the actual outcomes of the program, intended or not, rather than on the program's objectives or on decisions faced by program managers.

Another important judgement-oriented evaluation model is Robert Stake's Countenance Model, in which he suggests that the two major activities of formal evaluation studies are description and judgment (the "two countenances") of the program being evaluated. Within the description phase, Stake follows Tyler's rationale of comparing intended and actual outcomes of the program. However, he argued that in the judgment phase standards and procedures for making judgmental statements must be explicated to ensure the publicness of evaluative statements, although he failed to provide any suggestions as to how to weight or combine individual standards into overall judgments about the program.

Eisner's "connoisseurship model" casts program evaluators as educational critics whose refined perceptual capabilities (based on knowledge of what to look for and a backlog of relevant experience) enable them to give a public rendering of the quality and significance of that which is evaluated. In this model, the evaluator is the "instrument," and the data collecting, analyzing, and judging that Stake tried to make more public are largely hidden within the evaluator's mind, analogous to the evaluative processes of art criticism or wine tasting.

Collectively, these judgment-oriented approaches to evaluation have emphasized the central role of judgment and human wisdom in the evaluative process and have focused attention on the important issues of whose standards (and what degree of publicness) should be used in rendering judgments about educational programs. Conversely, critics of this approach suggest that it often permits evaluators to render judgments that reflect little more than figments of fertile imaginations. Others have noted that the presumed expertise of the evaluators is a potential weakness and worse, strong arguments can be made that serious disadvantages can accrue if a program is evaluated only by content experts (Worthen and Sanders 1987). Finally, many program evaluators are disinclined to play the single-handed role of educational judge (which they feel smacks of arrogance and elitism) proposed by some of these approaches.

### 3.4 Adversarial Approaches

Adversarial evaluation is a rubric that encompasses a collection of divergent evaluation practices which might loosely be referred to as adversarial in nature. In its broad sense, the term refers to all evaluations in which there is planned opposition in the points of view of different evaluators or evaluation teams—a planned effort to generate opposing points of view within the overall evaluation. One evaluator (or team) would serve as the program's advocate, presenting the most positive view of the program possible from the data, while another evaluator (or team) would play an adversarial role, highlighting any extant deficiencies in the program. Incorporation of these opposing views within a single evaluation reflects a conscious effort to assume fairness and balance and illuminate both strengths and weaknesses of the program.

Several types of adversarial proceedings have been invoked as models for adversary evaluations in education, including judicial, congressional hearings, and debate models. Of these, most of the sparse literature in this area has focused on adaptations of the legal paradigm, providing insights into how concepts from the legal system (for instance, taking and cross-examination of human testimony) could be used in educational evaluations. Owens, Wolf, and others have adapted the legal model to educational evaluations, while Worthen and Rogers have described use of the debate model in an adversary evaluation and have discussed pitfalls and potentials of the legal and other forensic paradigms in conducting program evaluations.

Despite the publicity given this approach to evaluation, as yet there is little beyond personal preference to determine whether program evaluations will profit most from being patterned after jury trials, congressional hearings, debates, or other arrangements.

### 3.5 Pluralist–Intuitionist Approaches

Ernest House has used this descriptor to characterize several evaluation models, contrasting them with more "utilitarian" models. In this approach to evaluation, the evaluator is a portrayer of different values and needs of all the individuals and groups served by the program, weighing and balancing this plurality of judgments and criteria in a largely intuitive fashion. Thus, the "best program" is largely decided by the values and perspectives of whomever is judging (an obvious fact nonetheless ignored in most other evaluation approaches). Examples of pluralist–intuitionist evaluation "models" are those proposed by Stake, Parlett and Hamilton, Rippey, and MacDonald's democratic evaluation. There are unique contributions of each of these proposals. Stake urges program evaluators to respond to the audience's concerns and requirements for information, in terms of their value perspectives, and argues that the evaluation framework and focus should emerge only after considerable interaction with those audiences. Parlett and Hamilton draw on the social anthropology paradigm (and psychiatry and sociology participant observation research) in proposing progressive focusing of an evaluation whose purpose is to describe and interpret (not measure and predict) that which exists within an educational system. Rippey focuses on the effects of programs on the program operators and views evaluation as a strategy for conflict management. MacDonald views evaluation as primarily a political activity whose only justification is the "right to know" of a broad range of audiences. Yet a common thread runs through all these evaluation approaches—value pluralism is recognized, accommodated, and protected, even though the effort to summarize the frequently disparate judgments and preferences of such groups is left as an intuitive process which depends heavily on the sagacity and impartiality of the evaluator.

Critics of this approach to program evaluation discount it as hopelessly "soft headed" and argue that few if any program evaluators are such paragons of virtue and wisdom as to be skillful in wielding the seductively simple, yet slippery and subtle tools this approach requires. Champions of pluralistic, responsive approaches reply that they can be readily used by any sensitive individual and that they are infinitely richer and more powerful than other approaches and, indeed, can subsume them, since they are flexible and do not preclude the use of other approaches within them, should that be desired by the evaluator's sponsor.

## 4. An Appraisal of Current Program Evaluation Models

Collectively, the writings reviewed briefly in Sect. 3, the so-called evaluation models, represent the formal content on which educational program evaluators draw. It is, therefore, appropriate to ask how useful they are.

The answer is "very useful, indeed," even though they collectively have not moved evaluation very far toward becoming a science or discipline in its own right (a dubious aspiration, nonetheless sought by many evaluators). In a recent analysis, Worthen and Sanders (1987) suggested that (a) the so-called evaluation models fail to meet standard criteria for scientific models, or even less rigorous definitions of models, and (b) that which has come to be referred to as the theoretical underpinnings of evaluation lack important characteristics of most theories, being neither axiomatic nor deductive, having no real predictive power, and being untested and unvalidated in any empirical sense. That same analysis, however, suggested that these conceptions about how evaluations should be conducted—the accompanying sets of categories, lists of things to think about, descriptions of different evaluation strategies, and exhortations to which one might choose to attend—influence the practice of program evaluation in sometimes subtle, sometimes direct, but always significant ways. Some program evaluators design evaluations which adopt or adapt proposed models of evaluation. Many evaluators, however, conduct evaluations without strict adherence (or even intentional attention) to any "model" of evaluation, yet draw unconsciously in their evaluation philosophy, plans, and procedures on that which they have internalized through exposure to the literature of program evaluation. So the value of the "models" lies in their ability to help us to think, to provide sources of new ideas and techniques, to serve as mental checklists of things we ought to consider, or remember, or worry about. Their value as prescriptive guidelines for doing evaluation studies seems much less.

## 5. Impediments to Improving Program Evaluation

Despite the advances made in program evaluation, there is obviously room for a great deal of improvement. In this section, four areas that need improvement for educational evaluation to reach its full potential are discussed briefly.

### 5.1 Evaluation Lacks an Adequate Knowledge Base

Since the early 1970s, Stufflebeam, Worthen and Sanders, Smith, and others have issued a call for evaluation to be researched to develop an adequate knowledge base to guide evaluation practice. That call is still largely unanswered, despite some promising research which has been launched on evaluation methods and techniques. A program of research aimed at drawing from other disciplines new methodological metaphors and techniques for use in educational evaluation existed at the Northwest Regional Educational Laboratory for nearly a decade and has introduced program evaluators to promising new metaphors and techniques drawn from areas such as architecture, philosophic analysis, investigative journalism, and literary and film criticism. A second National Institute of Education-sponsored research effort at the University of California at Los Angeles focused largely on descriptive studies of evaluation practices in educational agencies. In addition, a few research studies aimed at generating knowledge about either particular evaluation strategies and procedures or factors affecting evaluation utilization have begun to appear.

These positive developments notwithstanding, there is still little empirical information about the relative efficacy of alternative evaluation plans or techniques or many evaluation components germane to almost any model. For example, virtually no empirical information exists about the most effective way to conduct a needs assessment or weight criteria in reaching a summative judgment. Little is known about the extent to which various data collection techniques interfere with ongoing educational phenomena. Techniques for identifying goals are developed anew with every evaluation, since there is no evidence that any one way of conducting these activities is more effective than any other. Elaborate systems are developed for providing evaluative feedback, but there is little research evidence (as opposed to rhetoric and position statements) about the relative effectiveness of feedback under differing conditions and scheduling. One could go on to create an exhaustive list of phenomena and procedures in evaluation which badly need to be systematically studied, but the above should suffice to make the point. Smith (1981) has summarized the needs for research on evaluation as requiring more knowledge about (a) the contexts within which evaluation is practiced, (b) the nature of evaluation utility, and (c) the effectiveness of specific evaluation methods. Nearly a decade later those needs still remain largely unmet.

### 5.2 Evaluation Studies are Seldom Evaluated

The necessity of "meta-evaluation" has long been apparent to evaluators and completion of the *Standards for Evaluations of Educational Programs, Projects, and Materials* (Joint Committee on Standards 1981) marked a welcome milestone. Although many evaluation writers had proposed their own sets of meta-evaluation criteria, none carried the profession-wide weight reflected in the comprehensive standards so carefully prepared by the Joint Committee. These standards include criteria within each of the following categories: utility standards; feasibility standards; propriety standards; and accuracy standards.

Despite the wide acceptance and availability of these standards, however, there is no evidence that program evaluations are being subjected to any closer scrutiny than was the case before their publication. Even casual inspection reveals that only a small proportion of evaluation studies are ever evaluated, even in the most perfunctory fashion. Of the few meta-evaluations which do occur, most are internal evaluations done by the evaluator who produced the evaluation in the first place. It is rare indeed to see evaluators call in an outside expert to evaluate their evaluation efforts. Perhaps the reasons are many and complex why this is so, but one seems particularly compelling—evaluators are human and are no more ecstatic about having their work critiqued than are professionals in other areas of endeavor. Indeed, it can be a profoundly unnerving experience to swallow one's own prescriptions. Although the infrequency of good meta-evaluation might thus be understandable, it is not easily forgivable, for it enables shoddy evaluation practices to go undetected and worse, to be repeated again and again, to the detriment of the profession.

### 5.3 Program Evaluators Fail to Understand the Political Nature of Evaluation

Cronbach and co-workers (1980) have presented the view that evaluation is essentially a political activity. They describe evaluation as a "novel political institution" that is part of governance of social programs. They assert that evaluators and their patrons pursue unrealistic goals of finding "truth" or facilitating "right" decisions, rather than the more pertinent task of simply enlightening all participants so as to facilitate a democratic, pluralist decision-making process. While some may reject this view as overstated, it underscores the fact that program evaluation is inextricably intertwined with public policy formulation and all of the political forces involved in that process. Evaluators who fail to understand this basic fact expend unacceptably large amounts of human and financial resources conducting evaluations that are largely irrelevant, however impeccably they are designed and conducted.

### 5.4 Program Evaluators are too Narrow in their Choice of Evaluation Approaches and Techniques

It may be that innocence about the political nature of the evaluation enterprise contributes to the naive hope that evaluation will one day grow into a scientific discipline. That day, if attainable, would seem far off. Education itself is not a discipline but rather a social process field which draws its content from several disciplines. It seems unlikely that educational program evaluation, which also borrows its methods and techniques from many disciplines will gain the coherence that would result in it becoming a discipline in its own right. Perhaps

that is just as well, for much of the richness and potential of educational program evaluation lies in the depth and breadth of the strategies and tools it can employ and in the possibility of selectively combining them into stronger approaches than when used singly (Worthen 1981). Yet eclectic use of the evaluator's tools is a lamentably infrequent occurrence in program evaluations. Disciple-prone evaluators tend to cluster around their respective evaluation banners like vassals in a form of provincial bondage. For program evaluation to reach its potential, such intellectual bondage must give way to more mature and sophisticated approaches that draw appropriately on the richness and diversity of the many approaches, models, and techniques that characterize program evaluation today.

### Bibliography

Anderson S B, Ball S 1978 *The Profession and Practice of Program Evaluation*. Jossey-Bass, San Francisco, California

Cook T D, Reichardt C T 1979 *Qualitative and Quantitative Methods in Evaluation Research*. Sage, Beverly Hills, California

Cronbach L J, Ambron S, Dornbusch S, Hess R, Hornik R, Phillips D, Walker D, Weiner S 1980 *Toward Reform of Program Evaluation: Aims, Methods and Institutional Arrangements*. Jossey-Bass, San Francisco, California

Guba E G, Lincoln Y S 1981 *Effective Evaluation: Improving the Usefulness of Evaluation Results through Responsive and Naturalistic Approaches*. Jossey-Bass, San Francisco, California

Joint Committee on Standards for Educational Evaluation 1981 *Standards for Evaluations of Educational Programs, Projects, and Materials*. McGraw-Hill, New York

Madey D L 1982 Some benefits of integrating qualitative and quantitative methods in program evaluation, with illustrations. *Educ. Eval. Policy Anal.* 4(2): 223–36

Smith N L 1981 Developing evaluation methods. In: Smith N L (ed.) 1981 *Metaphors for Evaluation: Sources for New Methods*. Sage, Beverly Hills, California

Worthen B R 1981 Journal entries of an eclectic evaluator. In: Brandt R S, Modrak N (eds.) 1981 *Applied Strategies for Curriculum Evaluation*. Association for Supervision and Curriculum Development, Alexandria, Virginia

Worthen B R, Sanders J R 1973 *Educational Evaluation: Theory and Practice*. Jones, Worthington, Ohio

Worthen B R, Sanders J R 1984 Content specialization and educational evaluation: A necessary marriage? Occasional Paper No. 14. Western Michigan University Evaluation Center, Kalamazoo, Michigan

Worthen B R, Sanders J R 1987 *Educational Evaluation: Alternative Approaches and Practical Guidelines*. Longman, New York

# School Inspectors and Advisers

**R. Bolam**

All education authorities face the two tasks of controlling and improving their schools. Many authorities have appointed inspectors or advisers to carry out both

tasks; others have tried to allocate the two functions to separate role holders; still others have concentrated on the control function. Unfortunately, nomenclature is no guide. It should not be assumed, for example, that inspectors exclusively carry out the control task or that advisers exclusively carry out the improvement task: each could be responsible for either or both tasks. Moreover, other titles, for example, organizer, administrative education officer, supervisor, are frequently used for overlapping roles. The actual tasks, status, responsibilities, authority, and power of such role holders can only be understood in the specific conditions of the national or local system within which they work. Accordingly, this article analyses the role of school inspectors and advisers in England and Wales. The discussion is based largely upon a study of 14 local education authorities (Bolam et al. 1978). The term adviser is used to simplify the presentation and it should be understood to refer to inspectors and others who experience the role conflict discussed in relation to Fig. 1.

Local education authority (l.e.a.) advisers in England and Wales have to be distinguished from several other analogous or overlapping roles. Between 400 and 500 of Her Majesty's Inspectors (HMI) have a national role: visiting schools and colleges throughout the country offering them professional advice and periodically inspecting their work; carrying out national surveys of current practice, for example, of recent trends in primary and secondary education; using this knowledge and experience as the basis for their professional advice to national government ministers and administrators as they plan policy changes. Local education authority advisers have predominantly local responsibilities but they must also be distinguished from other local support agents: for example, from advisory teachers, who are released from their school-teaching duties for specified periods (e.g., three years) to provide specialist professional advice to other teachers in the l.e.a.; from teachers' centre leaders, who organize inservice education and training (INSET) and curriculum development activities at the l.e.a. teachers' centres; and from both educational psychologists and administrative education officers who are also employed by the l.e.a. and sometimes carry out advisory-type tasks, especially in smaller authorities.

Advisers are employed in each of the 104 local education authorities in England and Wales (different conditions exist in Scotland and Northern Ireland) on the Soulbury salary scale which is comparable with that of headteachers in large schools. The position is widely regarded by teachers as one of high status though senior-secondary-school teachers, especially headteachers, often regard advisers as equals. As a group, however, advisers are generally better qualified and have had more varied experience, and at a higher level, than their age-range peers in schools. Women are significantly underrepresented in advisers' positions.

The size and structure of advisory teams varies considerably across the country, largely for historical reasons and because the chief education officers in each l.e.a. differ in the value they attach to advisers. Certainly the overall population in an l.e.a. area is no guide: only a minority of local education authorities have one adviser per 20,000 population—the ratio recommended by the advisers' professional association. In any case, this ratio is probably too crude since it ignores both the population's age profile (some authorities contain relatively few children) and geographical size (urban schools can be visited much more easily and regularly than rural schools). A formula based upon the number of teachers, appropriately weighted to take account of geographical factors would make more sense. The term "advisory team" appears often to be more a term of administrative convenience than a working reality. One index of this is the concern expressed by some advisers over repeat and duplicate visits to schools because of inadequate internal liaison procedures. This, in turn, raised a series of questions. How do advisory teams formulate their policies and priorities? What self-monitoring procedures do they employ? What criteria do they use to evaluate their effectiveness?

Advisers are normally appointed with two sorts of responsibilities: subject (e.g., mathematics) or specialist (e.g., educational technology) responsibilities related to the relevant teachers throughout the l.e.a.; and general or pastoral responsibilities in relation to all teachers in a particular geographical area or district of the l.e.a. The tasks in which they are mainly involved include: the appointment and placement of teachers, including headteachers; the redeployment and retraining of teachers; advising the governing bodies of schools; giving professional and career advice to individual teachers, heads of department, and headteachers; the, usually unstructured, evaluative appraisal of beginning

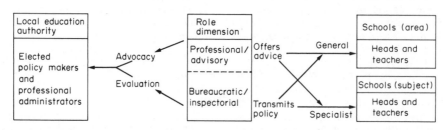

**Figure 1**
Critical features of the advisers' role

and experienced teachers; curriculum development; inservice education and training; advising on schoolwide changes; general inspection of a whole school; advising on or implementing l.e.a. wide changes, for example, in relation to curriculum guidelines; advising on the design of school-building work and the purchase of equipment; advising l.e.a. administrators and politicians about policy developments.

Most advisers see themselves as external facilitators of needed improvements in schools. Indeed, this is probably why most come into the job in the first place. On the other hand, most also operate in a "defender" role for some of the time, acting as a check on over-hasty or ill-thought-through innovations at subject, school, and l.e.a. levels. Inservice education and training is the favoured method for bringing about change and most advisers are very committed to it, many seeing it as their main task, especially in relation to their specialist subjects. Virtually all advisers spend a considerable proportion of their time planning, organizing, and actually running various types of inservice course: induction courses for beginning teachers; general professional courses; specialist subject courses; follow-up activities in schools and classrooms. This latter activity is indicative of the increasing emphasis being placed by advisers on school-based or school-focused INSET, a change brought about because of growing disenchantment with the conventional course as a means of promoting change. Other favoured improvement strategies include influencing staff appointment processes, the provision of funds and other resources, and the facilitation of interteacher and interschool communication and visiting.

Advisers encounter several difficulties and barriers in adopting an improvement–facilitator role. They lack necessary time and secretarial support. They lack the change skills needed for instance, to carry out a consultancy role. Their administrative and inspectorial responsibilities prevent some, possibly many, teachers from seeing them in a supportive role. As a result of these and other factors advisers frequently "adopt" certain schools where they have achieved success or satisfaction and spend a disproportionate amount of time in them. They also tend to adopt an initiating or pump-priming role in innovation, stepping into the background during the implementation phase, and rely on informal and unsystematic monitoring methods.

Most advisers are reluctant to embrace an inspectorial function. In the expansionist 1960s and the early 1970s the trend was for local education authorities to change the titles of inspectors to advisers and to soften or jettison their policies of regular, general inspections of individual schools. The notorious William Tyndale School affair in the Inner London Education Authority (Auld 1976) heralded a significant change in public and professional thinking, emphasizing as it did the advisers' crucially important inspectorial function as a means of ensuring the public accountability of teachers and headteachers. Subsequently, many authorities have

readopted the term "inspector", at least for the senior "advisers" and have strengthened their inspection and evaluation procedures.

Underlying these shifts in fashion and fortune is the central professional dilemma illustrated in Fig. 1. Figure 1 highlights three critical features of the advisers' role. First, advisers simultaneously face, Janus-like, in two directions: towards the local authority's elected policy makers and permanent professional administrators and towards the heads and teachers in schools. Second, they are, simultaneously, members both of the teaching profession and of the l.e.a. bureaucracy. Third, they are frequently responsible for advising a group of schools in a geographical area and for advising all the teachers of their specialist subject.

This is a perfect recipe for role conflict. In relation to the l.e.a., advisers are torn between the need to represent the views of professionals to, often uncomprehending, lay politicians (the advocacy role) and to submit inspection reports in order to ensure the social accountability of the schools (the evaluation role). In relation to schools, they are torn between the need to offer support and advice to teachers and heads, who they like to regard as professional colleagues and the requirement to assess them, sometimes for potential dismissal. This complex nexus of responsibilities, expectations, and mutual behaviours is compounded further because they have responsibilities for the staffs of perhaps 20 primary and secondary schools in their area and to every teacher of "their" subject in the l.e.a. These tensions are experienced and reacted to in various ways. Most advisers undoubtedly spend much more time on "advisory" tasks, like INSET, and advising individual teachers, than they do on "inspectorial" tasks like school inspection and teacher assessment. Moreover, and very significantly, they are more likely to want to spend more time on these "advisory" tasks than they are on the inspectorial tasks. The main exceptions are senior advisers who are generally more likely to attach importance to inspectorial tasks than their junior colleagues. It may be concluded that many advisers would react unfavourably to demands that they should extend their inspectorial work. This conclusion also finds support in the reasons given by many respondents for joining the advisory service in the first place: these were largely to do with a desire to improve the system through the advisory role.

Ironically enough, and as has been indicated, recent developments in England and Wales have pressured advisers into spending much more time on these bureaucratic/inspectorial aspects. Public concern over standards, coupled with economic cutbacks, have led to demands for cost effectiveness in schools, to which many local education authorities have responded by reemphasizing the advisers' inspectorial functions and their involvement in self-evaluation by schools. Declining pupil enrolments and economic cutbacks have led to the closure of some schools and to drastic cuts in teacher numbers: most authorities have given the job of redeploying teachers to their advisers. Economic cutbacks have led to a freezing of, and sometimes to substantial cuts in, the number of advisers and supporting clerical staff and thus to additional work loads for those remaining; in consequence, there are undoubtedly serious shortcomings in the advisory services of certain local education authorities. Meanwhile, pressures to innovate, for example in INSET, microtechnology, improved curricula for the 16–19 age group, and responsiveness of schools to the community, continue unabated. In short, l.e.a. advisory services appear to be severely underpowered and overloaded.

If these developments were simply due to the peculiar socioeconomic circumstances currently prevailing in England and Wales, they would be of little wider interest. However, if, as the present writer believes, they are due to difficulties inherent in the l.e.a. adviser's role, they are worthy of more general scrutiny. Policy makers in each country should consider how the dilemmas caused by the conflicting demands made upon advisers (Fig. 1) can be resolved. Possible technical solutions include ensuring that the number of advisers and clear support staff is adequate and that advisers' roles are clarified in relation to those of advisory teachers, consultants, and administrators. Their professional skills and status could also be strengthened: hardly any of the advisers presently in posts in England and Wales have received specific training but this is slowly being remedied as their professional association disseminates good practice through its conferences and publications. Topics for organized training programmes could include teacher evaluation; institutional evaluation; INSET methods, particularly for school-focused INSET; clinical supervision; adult counselling; microteaching; the management of innovation; organization development; team training; role workshops; administrative and curriculum theory; action research methods.

It would be particularly important for these ideas to be explored in the context of the French and Federal Republic of Germany systems for two reasons: first, because they are very different from the English and Welsh educational system; and second, because they have strongly influenced the nature and functions of inspectorates in other countries, notably in Africa. In both the Federal Republic of Germany and France the inspectorates are more like the English HMI than the English l.e.a. adviser. Nevertheless there are significant differences. In the Federal Republic of Germany the *Schulaufsichtsbeamten* are, as their name indicates, civil servants but they are employed by the Federal Länder or states. Inspection is usually organized at three levels: lower level schools inspectorates covering urban and rural administrative areas; medium-level schools inspectorates covering government administrative areas; higher schools inspectorates from the ministry of education in each Länder. In France, the inspectors operate at three principal levels: the *Inspecteurs Généraux* are high status professionals who operate at high levels and

as civil servants are much more closely involved in policy making than their English equivalents. They normally have both specialist (e.g., subject) and area responsibilities and although they were formerly very involved in the inspection of individual teachers, they now spend some time on curriculum development. The *Inspecteur Pedagogique Régionaux* operates at the regional level and the *Inspecteur Départmentaux* operates at the department level, the latter concentrating more upon the inspection of certificated teachers. Two further features of the French inspectorate are worth noting. First that they have to pass an examination in order to achieve this promotion from schools, and secondly, that, because school principals have much less authority in French schools than in English and Welsh schools, French teachers tend to see their inspectors as having more authority than do their English equivalents.

There is an urgent need for better comparative information about the work of inspectors. This is especially true of the French and Federal Republic of Germany systems about which little accessible research knowledge exists (at least in English), but this is also true of inspectorates elsewhere. The few publications about inspectors and advisers which exist are descriptive and analytic rather than research based (Dodd 1968, Lyons and Pritchard 1976). Exceptions include work done in Finland (Tuomola 1969), in Australia (MacLaine 1973, England 1973), and an Asia/Pacific survey (Commonwealth Secretariat 1975). One urgent priority for future research is to survey the roles and training needs of advisers in specific national contexts. The perceptions of advisers held by teachers, heads, administrators, teacher trainers, curriculum developers, and elected policy makers should also be researched. Action and development research related to particular aspects of advisers' work especially on teacher and school inspection and school-focused INSET, should also be pursued alongside various forms of training programmes for advisers. Comparative or experimental studies could also clarify the relative effectiveness of various combinations of national, regional, and local advisers.

## Bibliography

Auld R 1976 *William Tyndale Junior and Infants Schools Public Inquiry: A Report to the Inner London Education Authority.* Inner London Education Authority (ILEA), London

Bolam R, Smith G, Canter H 1978 *Local Education Authority Advisers and the Mechanisms of Innovation.* NFER/Nelson, Windsor

Commonwealth Secretariat 1975 *Background Paper 3: Report on the Questionnaire Survey of Inspectors and Supervisors in the Asia/Pacific Region.* Commonwealth Secretariat, London

Dodd W A 1968 *Primary School Inspection in New Countries.* Oxford University Press, Oxford

England G C 1973 Impact of the inspectorial system: A pro-

fession demeaned? *J. Educ. Adm.* 11: 43–59
Lyons R F, Pritchard M W 1976 *Primary School Inspection: A Supporting Service for Education.* International Institute for Educational Planning, Paris
MacLaine A G 1973 An evaluation of the system of inspection

in Australian state schools. *J. Educ. Adm.* 11: 22–32
Tuomola U 1969 On role-expectations applied to school inspectors. *Jyväskylä Studies in Education, Psychology and Social Research 18* (English summary). Jyväskylän Yliopisto, Jyväskylä, Finland

# Evaluation of National Comparisons

## D. Spearritt

The comparison of student achievement and attitudes in different countries, and of factors influencing achievement and attitudes, has been the subject of a large body of research since the 1960s. The fairness of cross-national comparisons, in respect of the tests and instruments employed and the comparability of the target populations and samples, is examined in this article. Methods of data analysis are evaluated, and the major findings of both large-scale surveys and small-scale intensive studies are presented. An assessment is also made of the impact of the research.

Prior to the 1960s, comparative studies of education systems tended to be descriptive, showing the variety of contexts and approaches to education in different countries. They were concerned with such matters as the organization and administration of education, the level and sources of economic support, enrolments, educational structures, curriculum patterns, and teaching methods. They took little account, except perhaps in an impressionistic way, of a crucial outcome of these systems, that is, the achievement and attitudes of the students in those countries.

The establishment in 1959 of a Council for the International Evaluation of Educational Achievement, subsequently known as the International Association for the Evaluation of Educational Achievement, or IEA, signalled a major advance in the comparative study of education systems in different countries. This body organized large-scale cross-national surveys of student achievement and attitude, made possible by the development of tests and instruments suitable for use in different countries. This provided a much sounder basis for making national comparisons than previously existed.

Since the 1960s a vast amount of comparative data about student achievement, attitude and background factors in different countries has been collected, mainly through the large-scale IEA survey studies. These comprise international studies of achievement in mathematics in from 12 to 20 countries in 1964 and 1980; the IEA Six-Subject Survey in 1970–71 (Walker 1976), involving between 8 and 19 countries and encompassing science education, reading comprehension, literature education, civic education, and the teaching of English and French as foreign languages; and a study of written composition and a second international study of science education during the period 1981 to 1986. A study of the classroom environment has been completed but

has not yet been published. IEA studies of preprimary education, reading literacy, and computers in education are in progress.

In recent years, empirically-based data on student achievement have also been provided by small-scale surveys of the achievement of selected groups of students in two or three countries, coupled with more intensive case-study approaches. For example, comparisons have been made of the mathematics achievement of Chinese, Japanese, and American students (Stevenson et al. 1986).

In both types of study, cross-national comparisons are made of student achievement and attitudes. Are these comparisons fair to the different countries?

## 1. Fairness of Cross-national Comparisons

There are three important questions to be considered in evaluating the "fairness" of cross-national comparisons:

(a) Is the test or instrument being used for this purpose equally valid for the countries being compared?

(b) Are the target populations, to which results are to be generalized, comparable?

(c) Have comparable samples of schools and students been obtained in each country?

### 1.1 Validity of Tests

It is considerably more difficult to ensure that a test is valid, that is, that it measures what it is intended to measure, when it is designed for use in different countries rather than in one country. Within any one linguistically homogeneous country it is assumed that students are competent in the language in which the items are couched and that they will perceive the relevance of items and being tested in roughly similar ways. In cross-country comparisons, test validity has to take account of the different languages in which the test is presented and possible student motivation differences in different countries, as well as differences in curriculum and even in definitions of achievement.

The validity of tests designed for cross-country comparisons can be considered under three headings: (a) item validity, (b) test validity, and (c) motivational validity.

*Item validity* is concerned with the question of whether items can be developed which test the same abilities or skills in different countries. (This concept of item validity is to be distinguished from the psychometric concept, which refers to the correlation between an item score and the total test score.) In any one country, it is assumed that there is an identifiable skill (or understanding or piece of knowledge), and an item is valid if it taps this skill. Cross-nationally, it is assumed that this skill or understanding can be identified across countries. But does the item continue to measure the same skill when it is expressed in different languages, with their different vocabulary connotations, idioms and constructions?

Test items in IEA studies have mostly been written in English and translated as necessary into other languages. Normally two independent translations are undertaken and checked against each other. If the translators cannot then agree on a specific translation, the resolution is made by the National Committee. The aim in translation has been to keep the task as nearly uniform as possible from country to country (Husén 1967). Tasks in mathematics were to be phrased as they would normally be stated in the country concerned, not as literal translations of the English. Equivalence of tests across countries is more difficult to establish with tests of various aspects of language. On the basis of content analyses by the National Research Centres in the surveys, and item analysis data, it was possible to develop comparable reading comprehension tests in the different languages. But it proved to be difficult to develop a word knowledge test which was equivalent across languages. In other IEA surveys, difficulties were experienced in identifying comparable poems in different languages, in testing sensitivity to language and appreciation of literature in the study of French as a foreign language, and in ensuring that items assessing student attitudes to democratic values and citizenship values, for instance, had the same meaning across countries.

Back translation of items originally written in English is often applied to help ensure that items measure the same skills or attitudes in different countries. Items also have to be shown to be of appropriate difficulty and discriminating power in different countries. The major source of assurance that an item is testing the same skill or attitude when expressed in different languages, however, lies in the expert judgment of the National Committees in each country that the item as expressed is measuring the skill or attitude it is intended to measure.

*Test validity*—the validity of the test itself—as a measure of achievement in subject areas such as science and reading comprehension in the different countries is also of critical importance for cross-country comparisons of achievement. Within countries, the content validity of a test is usually established with the aid of two-way grids, with content areas of a curriculum on one axis and intellectual processes on the other. Items are prepared to fill the cells in these grids, taking account of the emphasis to be given to different content areas; this enables the various content areas and objectives of a curriculum to be represented in the appropriate proportions.

Developing tests designed for making cross-national comparisons is a more complex task, as the content areas studied by students of a given age or school grade level are likely to differ in some degree from country to country. IEA committees work from the set of national statements of the objectives and content areas of a course to set up their grids. National Committees are asked to rate the importance of each cell in the grid on a three-point scale: 0 if the topic is not normally studied at the particular grade level, 1 if the topic is in the curriculum but is regarded as of slight to moderate importance, and 2 if the topic is in the curriculum and is regarded as of major importance.

In effect, this approach to test development establishes a common curriculum in the subject area, which includes all content areas specified by the participating countries except those listed by very few countries. This common curriculum is not necessarily identical with the actual curriculum followed in any of the participating countries. Nevertheless, the pooled judgment of subject experts in the various countries as to what should be in the subject curriculum for all countries seems to provide the most satisfactory basis for developing tests for cross-national comparisons.

It follows that a test may have at least two different validities in any one country, for example, its validity as a measure of the common curriculum, and its validity as a measure of that country's curriculum. These different validities are a matter of some consequence if comparisons are to be made among countries on the basis of their mean scores on the test. A country with a relatively low mean score may feel aggrieved if the score were based on a set of items which were largely outside its curriculum. A country's mean score, however, not only provides information about the achievement of its students on a test based on content areas common to most countries, but about the degree to which the curriculum of that country diverges from the common curriculum.

These distinctions between test validity indices have been made much more explicit in the more recent IEA studies. In the Second International Science Study (SISS), three indices of test validities were developed: a curriculum relevance index, a test relevance index, and a curriculum coverage index (IEA 1988).

The curriculum relevance index, which is regarded as the most important index of the test's validity, answers the question: "To what extent does the test cover the planned or intended curriculum or syllabus?" (IEA 1988). As it indicates the extent to which the topics covered in the test match the topics and their emphases in the curriculum, rather than vice versa, it could appropriately be described as the test coverage index.

The test relevance index answers the question: "To what extent are the items in the test relevant to the curriculum of a country?" (IEA 1988). Clearly, the test items could all be relevant to a country's curriculum, while the test topics covered only a small part of the country's curriculum. This index might be better described as the test items relevance index.

The curriculum coverage index answers the question: "To what extent does the curriculum of a system match the total curriculum of all systems together?" (IEA 1988). This index is independent of the test.

In the SISS, the curriculum relevance index indicated that test topics matched the intended curriculum topics for science students in the final year of secondary school quite closely in most countries, but less closely for 14-year-old students and 10-year-old students (IEA 1988). Cross-national comparisons of mean scores on the tests are still justifiable, however, if the test for each age level has approximately equal validity for the different countries, as it has in the SISS.

All of these test validity indices, however, relate to a country's intended curriculum. If, as is often the case, the implemented curriculum falls short of the intended curriculum, the estimate of student achievement on the intended curriculum may be depressed. IEA studies have adopted the practice of securing teacher ratings of whether the "opportunity to learn" the specific content involved in the test items was available to all or most of their students, to some of their students, or to few or none of their students, and relating the teachers' ratings to student achievement (Husén 1967, Garden 1987).

With less structured curricula, the problems of developing tests or tasks for cross-national comparisons are multiplied. The analysis of writing samples and curricula for the IEA studies of written composition showed that the types of writing and writing skills emphasized differ somewhat across educational systems and programmes (Gorman et al. 1988). The researchers found it necessary to establish a domain of tasks in school writing, covering all the relevant purposes and types of writing, as a basis for test development. Preliminary analyses showed that compositions within a culture could be ranked on an international scale, but there was as yet insufficient agreement about their absolute placement to justify direct comparisons of mean scores from different countries.

The question of *motivational validity* arises because cross-national comparisons of student achievement may be affected by differences in the motivation of students towards the test. Within countries, a similar cultural approach and response to testing is usually assumed. In different countries, there may be differences in the general response of students to being tested; there may be a more competitive attitude towards tests in some cultures. In comparing mean achievement test scores in IEA studies, it is assumed that students in the various countries have similar attitudes to the perceived relevance of the skills being tested, and to the IEA testing itself. The correctness of this assumption does not seem to have been explored, although much care is taken in the IEA studies to ensure that procedures for testing are carried out in the same way in each country. Some observational checks on the equivalence of conditions of testing and students' approach to the tests in different countries by international observers would be useful.

### 1.2 Comparability of Target Populations

The IEA studies have generally chosen to test students at three stages of schooling, whose significance is clearly evident. One point occurs towards the end of primary or elementary schooling, where most students are still taught by one teacher. The second point is the last year of compulsory schooling. The third point is the final year of secondary school. In this article, the student populations corresponding to these points are referred to as Population 1, Population 2, and Population 3 respectively.

For "fair" comparisons of student achievement across countries, the target populations at these levels should be comparable in each country. A target population could be defined, for instance, as all Grade 5 students in the participating countries or all students who had completed five years of schooling, but such definitions do not take account of the variations among countries in age of entry to school (from 5 years to 7 years) or varying practices in progression policy from grade to grade. Equivalence of student populations can be most clearly defined in terms of age, such as all 10-year-olds in the participating countries. Age is a common metric from country to country. If 10-year-old students in Country A have lower achievement test scores than those in Country B, it may be because of a later age of school entry or a higher incidence of grade repetition or the later introduction of a curriculum topic in Country A. If Country A is concerned about its lower scores, it may be prepared to make structural changes in any or all of these factors.

In the IEA Six Subject Survey in the early 1970s, Population 1 was an age population (all students aged 10.0 to 10.11 at the time of testing), as was Population 2 (all students aged 14.0 to 14.11 at the time of testing). Testing age populations in schools is much more inconvenient than testing whole classes, so the latter approach has been adopted in later surveys to secure the co-operation of schools. In the 1983–86 Science Survey, Population 1 consists of either all 10-year-old students or all students in the grade in which most 10-year-olds are enrolled. Population 2 is similarly defined for 14-year-olds. For Population 1, the grades were typically Grades 4 or 5, and for Population 2, Grades 8 or 9. As a result of the alternative definitions there is some variation in the ages of the samples in different countries; mean ages range from 10.3 to 11.3 for Population 1 and from 14.2 to 16.1 for Population 2. The target populations are only approximately comparable in terms of age. Population 3 not only varies in age across countries, but represents marked differences in the percentages of the relevant age group in each country enrolled in Grade 12 or 13. While the target populations are probably about as comparable as it is feasible to attain, their differences need to be kept in mind in comparing student achievement levels.

### 1.3 Comparability of National Samples

Since it is usually impracticable to apply a test to all members of large target populations, a sample of students is drawn from each population, and the mean score of these students is taken as an estimate of the mean score of all students in the population. Sampling introduces a further source of variation into cross-national comparisons, since the sample estimate for a country will mostly differ from one sample to another. The standard deviation of the various sample estimates is known as the *standard error* of the mean (or of other statistics being estimated, such as a correlation), but can be estimated from the sample itself. In order to attain relatively precise estimates of the population mean and other statistics, the IEA studies have mostly made use of two-stage stratified probability samples.

At the first stage of sampling, schools are randomly selected within strata such as size of school and type of school (for example government versus non-government) with a probability proportional to the size of the target population. At the second stage, students are selected at random from the schools chosen at the first stage. In the SISS, either a whole class or up to 24 students were selected at the second stage. As students within schools tend to be more homogeneous in performance than students across a range of schools, it is desirable to include a larger number of schools in the sample and only limited numbers of students from each school. In calculating standard errors from samples of this type, the IEA studies take into account the design effect of the sample, as compared with a simple random sample, and make use of jack-knife procedures, which involve estimates obtained by omitting each school or primary sampling unit in turn.

Cross-national comparisons of mean test scores are more difficult to interpret if the standard error of sampling differs appreciably from country to country. Fortunately, IEA samples have mostly been sufficiently well-designed and executed to provide reasonably similar standard errors.

Regardless of how well the samples are designed, comparisons of country mean scores are likely to be impaired unless there are high response rates from the schools and students selected to participate in a survey. A low response rate could mean that poorer-achieving schools in a country had chosen not to participate, resulting in an inflated estimate of that country's mean score. In the SISS, response rates for schools were above 90 percent in many countries, but as low as 49 percent for Population 3 in England. This is yet another factor which indicates the need for caution in comparing the mean test scores of students from different countries.

### 2. Analysis of Data from Cross-national Studies

Two major forms of data analysis have been applied in IEA cross-national comparisons. The first relates to the average performance of students (or of schools) on the tests or test items administered in the different countries. The second involves the analysis of factors influencing achievement in these countries.

Item analysis data typically include useful information about the percentage of students in the sample in each country selecting the correct answer to a multiple-choice item, the relative attractiveness of the incorrect options, and the percentage omitting the item. Sometimes item discrimination indices are also presented.

The analyses which attract the most immediate attention in IEA studies are presented in tables which show the mean scores of the different countries. Table 1, representing an extract for Population 2 on the 30-item core science test in the SISS, shows, for five of the seventeen countries concerned, the range of information presented in these tables.

In each country, the mean score for students and for schools is identical, as sample size is taken as equivalent from school to school. Only 60 percent of the age group was at school in the Philippines compared with over 98 percent in the other four countries. *Roh*, representing the intraclass correlation, shows the proportion of test variance attributable to differences between schools; the remaining variances arises from differences between students within schools. There are considerable differences between schools in the Philippines in their average level of science achievement, but very small

*Table 1*

Achievement data for selected countries for Population 2 (30-item core science test) (IEA 1988)

| Country | Mean | Students | | Schools | | Mean age | Roh | Percent of school means below 14.8[a] |
|---------|------|----------|-----|---------|-----|----------|------|----------------------------|
| | | N | SD | N | SD | | | |
| Australia | 17.8 | 4917 | 4.9 | 233 | 2.2 | 14.5 | 0.17 | 8 |
| England | 16.7 | 3118 | 4.9 | 147 | 2.4 | 14.3 | 0.19 | 19 |
| Hungary | 21.7 | 2515 | 4.7 | 99 | 2.5 | 14.3 | 0.26 | 0 |
| Japan | 20.2 | 7610 | 5.0 | 199 | 1.3 | 14.7 | 0.04 | 1 |
| Philippines | 11.5 | 10874 | 4.6 | 269 | 3.2 | 16.1 | 0.48 | 87 |

a Lowest school mean for Hungary was 14.8

differences in Japan. The last column indicates the percentage of schools in each country with mean scores below the mean score of the lowest performing school in the country with the highest mean score, namely Hungary. For Population 3, information is also provided about the percentage of an age group taking the course, as this is relevant to the interpretation of country mean scores; 1 percent of the age group study physics in the final year of secondary school in the United States as against 24 percent in Norway.

There has been some ambivalence in the attitudes of authors of IEA reports to tables which list the countries and their mean scores. It has been indicated that the IEA tests were not primarily designed for making comparisons between countries, or providing Olympic tables for student achievement. Unfortunately, this type of table has been, and will continue to be, interpreted in just this way by the media, by less enlightened politicians and business leaders, and probably by the public at large. The tables themselves present valuable information, but are subject to various qualifications in their interpretation. Differences between means may be entirely explainable in terms of sampling error, the varying relevance of the test to differing national curricula, varying opportunities to learn the material and so on. IEA authors mostly take due account of such factors in interpreting the data, but their cautions are often likely to go unheeded by others. Rank ordering of country means may be useful in demonstrating change in relative position over time (for example for Population 2, the Netherlands ranked 12th in the 1970–71 science study and 3rd in the SISS), but it can be misleading when differences between means are not statistically significant. The allocation of countries to groups whose means do not differ significantly, following statistical procedures such as Newman–Keuls or Scheffé comparisons, would not only reflect the differences more faithfully but would help to discourage the Olympic contest interpretation.

Correlational indices have been used to relate achievement in the different countries with variables such as mean age of students, test relevance and opportunity to learn. Correlations between achievement and each of the three curriculum indices—curriculum relevance, test relevance, and curriculum coverage—are computed across countries. In the SISS these showed that achievement levels tended to be higher in countries where the tests were more relevant to the curriculum. Achievement has been found to be substantially positively correlated with student opportunity to learn the material, and negatively with the percentage of an age group studying subjects such as biology, chemistry, and physics in the final secondary year.

In keeping with a major objective of IEA studies, much of the data analysis has been directed at identifying those home and background factors, and school-related factors, which influence student achievement and attitudes. There have been notable methodological advances in the procedures employed since the 1960s.

Correlational and stepwise regression analysis of mathematics achievement on a selection of parental, teacher, school, and student variables were used in the 1964 mathematics study (Husén 1967). In the Six-Subject Survey of 1970–71, independent variables were grouped into major blocks of variables, comprising home and student background, type of school/programme, learning conditions in the school, and kindred variables such as interests and attitudes. Achievement scores were regressed on these blocks of variables using both schools and students as the unit of analysis. The blocks were entered into the regression equation in the order indicated, in accordance with the model that earlier events may influence later events, but not conversely (Walker 1976). The importance of each block of variables was judged in terms of the additional proportion of criterion variance which it explained. This analytic approach to determining the relative importance of variables has been criticized by Pedhazur (1982), and has been largely superseded by path analysis approaches. More recently developed analytic approaches such as the structural equation models of LISREL (Jöreskog and Sörbom 1978) and the partial least squares path analysis model (Wold 1982) should contribute to a better understanding of the complex ways in which various factors interact in their relationship with student achievement and attitude. Munck (1979) has demonstrated how the LISREL model can be applied to cross-national survey data to test international path models which include country-specific measurement parameters but invariant structural parameters.

Despite their explanatory power, these analytic approaches are based on correlations or covariances between variables to which students have not been randomly assigned. Experimental studies will be needed to determine whether manipulation of factors presumed to cause differences in achievement actually brings about such differences. Recent studies, though not experimental in character, have shown some interest in tracing effects over time. The 1980 mathematics study included a longitudinal component to clarify the relation of particular outcomes to antecedent teacher practices and classroom processes (Garden 1987), while the Classroom Environment Study (Anderson 1987) set out to identify the particular aspects of the classroom environment which were likely to affect student achievement and attitudes.

Secondary analyses of data from IEA studies have been undertaken to investigate ways of improving the productivity of education systems. Using the IEA data bank from the 1964 mathematics study, Walberg et al. (1986) regressed the achievement test scores of 28,274 13-year-old students in 12 countries on independent variables such as parental socioeconomic status, highest mathematics course taken, weekly hours of homework and the like. In each country, the influence of each variable was assessed after the effects of all other variables had been controlled. Of the variables which could be altered, the amount and quality of instruction, together with homework, were found to influence achievement most strongly. Analysis of the same data bank, this time with a sample of 41,042 13-year-olds, revealed small differences in mathematics achievement and attitude, mostly in favour of males, and attributable in considerable measure to psychosocial conditions (Steinkamp et al. 1985).

## 3. Small-scale Cross-national Studies of Achievement

In both the first and second international studies of mathematics and science achievement, the mean score for Japan at the Population 2 level was much higher than that for many other countries, and similarly at the Population 3 level when the much larger percentage of students at that level in Japan was taken into account. In particular, mean scores for Japan were very much higher than they were for the United States. This finding, together with evidence of declining score levels on various types of aptitude and achievement tests in the United States and a public demand for greater accountability, stimulated interest in investigating the reasons for differing achievement levels in the two countries. This led to more intensive studies of these differences, including case study approaches.

In a study of mathematics productivity in Japan and Illinois, Harnisch et al. (1985) analysed student background factors and their achievement scores on the Educational Testing Service's High School Mathematics Test. The test was administered in 1981 to a random sample of 9,582 high-school students in Illinois and to a nationally representative sample of 1,700 high-school students tested in Japan by the Nippon Electric Company. The mean scores of the Japanese students were found to be more than two standard deviations higher than those of the Illinois students. The amount of instruction in mathematics, and student motivation, were found to be the stronger statistically controlled correlates of mathematics achievement in both samples. In a cross-national context, these findings can be taken as suggestive only, as there is some doubt about the comparability of the samples (80 percent of the Illinois sample were 16 years-of-age as against 36 percent of the Japanese sample) and most of the background factors were measured by just one questionnaire item.

Important information about student achievement and its correlates has emerged from the type of small-scale cross-national study conducted by Stevenson and his associates. In an exceptionally careful study (Stevenson et al. 1986), they compared the performance of American, Chinese, and Japanese children in kindergarten and Grades 1 and 5 on specially designed tests of mathematics, reading, and cognitive abilities. The common achievement tests were based on the content of textbooks and readers used in the three cities involved in the study: Minneapolis, Sendai, and Taiwan. Tests and other instruments were checked by bilingual researchers from each country to eliminate cultural bias.

Tests were administered to one child at a time. Interviews were conducted with the children and their mothers and teachers, and structured observations were made in the classrooms. The study indicated that the American children's scores in mathematics were substantially lower than those of Japanese children in kindergarten, and showed a consistent relative decline through to Grade 5 in comparison with the performance of Chinese and Japanese children. In the reading test the average scores of the American children at all three grade levels were slightly lower than those of the Chinese children, but higher than those of the Japanese children. On cognitive tasks of intellectual functioning, there was little difference between the three groups. Much less time was given to mathematics instruction for the American children than for the Chinese and Japanese children. Yet American mothers appeared to be rather more satisfied with their children's academic performance than did the Chinese and Japanese mothers. The significance of this research is that cross-national differences in achievement levels appear to develop in the early years of schooling, and are related to cultural expectations and outlooks. In that the study relates to one city only in each country, its generalizability must remain in doubt, despite the great care taken with the sampling. Studies of this kind nevertheless form a valuable complement to the large-scale cross-national comparisons of the IEA surveys.

In the search for reasons for the differences in achievement of American and Japanese children, sociologists have emphasized the contrasts between child socialization practices adopted at home and in school in the two countries. Fuller et al. (1986) point to the importance which Japanese mothers place on raising children capable of contributing to group social harmony, and on preparing their children to do well in school. American mothers, by contrast, placed more emphasis on self-expression and leadership skills. Socialization practices, together with the greater amount of time given to instruction in Japan and the operation of a national curriculum, may well contribute towards the Japanese superiority in mathematics and science, but it is possible that this may be at the expense of lower achievement in the language arts, as hinted at in the data from the Stevenson et al. (1986) study. The point has not been tested at the large-scale level, as Japan has not participated in the IEA studies of reading comprehension, literature, or written composition.

## 4. Evaluation of Cross-national Studies of Achievement

Despite the formidable problems involved in organizing studies covering a wide range of developed and less-developed countries, the quality of the IEA studies has been of a high standard. Great care has been taken to ensure that tests and other instruments are valid for use in the different countries, that target populations are as comparable as possible, and that sampling procedures in each country are properly designed and executed. It is recognized that complete comparability may be unattainable in all respects, but the necessary qualifications which need to be applied to the presentation and interpretation of data are clearly specified. The intensive small-scale studies of Stevenson and his associates (1986) have also been conducted with exemplary care. Their main shortcoming is their limited generalizability arising out of restricted sampling, a problem which can best be addressed through replications of such studies.

Several important findings have emerged from the IEA studies. They have revealed a remarkable range in the mean scores of countries in all of the subject areas surveyed, and some consistency over the years in the performance of the high-scoring and low-scoring countries. Japan and Hungary have been consistently high-scoring countries in mathematics and science, while low-scoring countries have included the United States in mathematics and the less-developed countries in science. There are much greater differences in school means in some countries than in others. Considerable differences occur among countries in the extent of the gap between the implemented and the intended curriculum. Not surprisingly, student achievement is affected not only by the time devoted to a subject area (including homework), but by what is taught and by how well it is taught. Other consistent predictors of achievement include student interest in the subject area, student attitude towards school learning, and home background factors. The influence of these factors on student achievement is generally confirmed by the more intensive analyses of the small-scale studies.

Are the above factors sufficient to account for the extreme differences in the mean scores of the different countries on achievement tests? This seems unlikely. More data would be useful on the range of teaching methods and learning methods employed in the specific subject areas, both within countries and between countries, notwithstanding the evidence from the Classroom Environment Study (Anderson 1987) of inconsistency in teachers' behaviour from day to day, and of similarity of classroom teaching practices across countries.

For good reason, IEA studies have mostly been concerned with surveying one subject area at a time. The results may well reflect whether that subject is emphasized in a particular country or not. Educational administrators would usually be interested in knowing what the effect would be on other subjects of allocating more time to one particular subject. The collection of data on a number of subject areas for the same sample of students, as in the 1970–71 survey, would no doubt make it more difficult to secure the cooperation of education systems in IEA studies, but would provide valuable information about the balance of the curriculum in different countries.

IEA cross-national comparisons of achievement and attitude have had a substantial impact in the field of educational research. Researchers in the participating countries have been kept abreast of modern developments in curriculum analysis, test and scale construction, research design and statistical methodology which might have been otherwise overlooked. Through their curriculum phase, IEA studies have had a significant impact on curricula in the participating countries, and also in some other countries. Some studies, such as the IEA study of written composition, have made important contributions to curriculum development.

The impact of IEA studies on educational policy is more difficult to discern, though Garden (1987) gives instances of how the Second International Mathematics Study influenced policy in Japan, New Zealand, and Sweden. There has been some resistance on the part of some educational administrators to participating in cross-national studies of student achievement. Some would regard the studies as being irrelevant to their own systems. Many would have some anxieties about how a poorer performance rating for their system would be exploited by the media and politicians to the detriment of support for education in their own country. The best defence against the latter criticism, if it is unjustified, would lie in adequate publicization of counter-arguments including restatement of the facts and the qualifications attached to their interpretation. The "irrelevance" argument is rather inward-looking if other countries are attaining higher achievement scores by adopting alternative approaches to the study of a subject area. Administrators need to consider whether they wish to improve achievement levels in particular subjects, and with or without a tradeoff in other subject areas. The IEA studies have pointed to those factors influencing achievement which can be changed within the education system. The recent succinct preliminary report on Science Achievement in Seventeen Countries (IEA 1988) brings to the attention of administrators the issues they need to look at in their own systems in a most commendable way.

Some of the cross-national research results, and particularly those arising from the small-scale studies, suggest that the values instilled in the home and accepted by the society have a major influence on student achievement. Even if acceptable to a society, changes in values will be much more difficult to bring about than changes in the malleable factors of quality and quantity of instruction.

*Bibliography*

Anderson L W 1987 The classroom environment study: Teaching for learning. *Comp. Educ. Rev.* 31: 69–87

Comber L C, Keeves J P 1973 *Science Education in Nineteen Countries.* Almquist and Wiksell, Stockholm; and Wiley, New York

Fuller B, Holloway S D, Azuma H, Hess R D, Kashiwagi K 1986 Contrasting achievement rules: Socialization of Japanese children at home and in school. *Res. Soc. Educ. Socialization* 6: 165–201

Garden R A 1987 The second IEA mathematics study. *Comp. Educ. Rev.* 31: 47–68

Gorman T P, Purves A C, Degenhart R E (eds.) 1988 *The IEA Study of Written Composition I: The International Writing Tasks and Scoring Scales*. Pergamon Press, Oxford

Harnisch D L, Walberg H J, Tsai S-L, Sato T, Fyans L J 1985 Mathematics productivity in Japan and Illinois. *Eval. Educ.* 9: 277–84

Husén T (ed.) 1967 *International Study of Achievement in Mathematics*, Vols. 1 and 2. Almquist and Wiksell, Stockholm; and Wiley, New York

International Association for the Evaluation of Educational Achievement 1988 *Science Achievement in Seventeen Countries: A Preliminary Report*. Pergamon Press, Oxford

Jöreskog K G, Sörbom D 1978 LISREL *IV: Analysis of Linear Structural Relationships by the Method of Maximum Likelihood*. National Educational Resources, Chicago, Illinois

Munck I M E 1979 *Model Building in Comparative Education: Applications of the LISREL Method to Cross-national Survey Data*. Almquist and Wiksell, Stockholm

Pedhazur E J 1982 *Multiple Regression in Behavioral Research: Explanation and Prediction*, 2nd edn. Holt, Rinehart and Winston, New York

Steinkamp M W, Harnisch D L, Walberg H J, Tsai S-L 1985 Cross-national gender differences in mathematics-attitude and achievement among 13-year-olds. *J. Math. Behav.* 4: 259–77

Stevenson H W, Lee S Y, Stigler J W 1986 Mathematics achievement of Chinese, Japanese and American children. *Science* 231: 693–99

Walberg H J, Harnisch D L, Tsai S-L 1986 Elementary school mathematics productivity in twelve countries. *Br. Educ. Res. J.* 12: 237–48

Walker D A 1976 *The IEA Six Subject Survey: An Empirical Study of Education in Twenty-One Countries*. Almquist and Wiksell, Stockholm; and Wiley, New York

Wold H 1982 Soft modelling: The basic design and some extensions. In: Jöreskog K G, Wold H (eds.) 1982 *Systems under Indirect Observation*. North-Holland, Amsterdam

# Meta-evaluation

## R. B. Straw and T. D. Cook

The term meta-evaluation has traditionally been used to describe a variety of activities intended to evaluate both the technical quality of evaluations and the conclusions drawn from them. Meta-evaluation refers to the evaluation of evaluations for the purpose of providing primary evaluators with feedback about technical matters and any restricted perspectives that may be implicit in their work. Cook and Gruder especially stressed the role of meta-evaluation in summative evaluations of an empirical nature, while Stufflebeam and Scriven have included evaluations of formative research and nonempirical evaluations which are meta-evaluative in their conceptualizations.

## 1. Purpose of Meta-evaluation

The purpose of meta-evaluation is to identify potential biases of any type that there might be in an evaluation and to use a variety of methods, statistical and otherwise, to estimate their importance. While there has been considerable emphasis on technical factors which might produce a biased estimate of the program's effect, the meaning of bias has not been restricted to statistical criteria. Bias that may arise from oversimplistic or inaccurate interpretations of the results, misunderstandings over the relative importance of evaluation questions, and the like is also important.

Meta-evaluation is, therefore, tied to a critical perspective in which no single evaluation or evaluation report should be considered definitive. The most technically competent evaluation in terms of methodology may still be flawed when broader issues of interpretations or policy implications are discussed. The goal of meta-evaluation is to obtain a broader range of views by soliciting heterogeneous perspectives on a study or group of studies. The synthesis of these various perspectives is intended to raise the reader's consciousness about all issues relevant to the program being evaluated.

## 2. Approaches to Meta-evaluation

Cook and Gruder (1978) discuss seven approaches to meta-evaluation which were derived from an analogy to a three-factor analysis of variance model (see Table 1). The three factors were timing, degree of data manipulation, and the number of studies examined. First, the meta-evaluation may take place at the same time as the primary evaluation or after it. A simultaneous meta-evaluation is obviously more timely than a subsequent one—an important consideration in evaluation research. Second, data may or may not be manipulated. Often the re-analysis of data by independent analysts can increase the credibility and validity of the original results. Finally, the number of studies included in the meta-evaluation may vary. The use of multiple, and hopefully, independent studies allows the meta-evaluator to search for a convergence of results across studies. Such convergence may indicate broader generalizability than any single evaluation can show and increase the validity of conclusions about program effectiveness. The titles in the final column of Table 1 are fairly descriptive of the various models.

A meta-evaluation obviously must be carried out by a party other than the primary evaluation team. The audience for the meta-evaluation will usually determine the most suitable group to conduct the meta-evaluation. If technical evaluation issues are considered most important, a group of independent evaluators might be given

**Table 1**
Models of meta-evaluation[a]

| | | | |
|---|---|---|---|
| Subsequent to primary evaluation | Data not manipulated | Single data set | Essay review of an evaluation report |
| | | Multiple data sets | Review of the literature about a specific program |
| | Data manipulated | Single data set | Empirical re-evaluation of an evaluation or program |
| | | Multiple data sets | Empirical re-evaluation of multiple data sets about the same program |
| Simultaneous with primary evaluation | Data not manipulated | Single or multiple data sets | Consultant meta-evaluation |
| | Data manipulated | Single data set | Simultaneous secondary analysis of raw data |
| | | Multiple data sets | Multiple independent replication |

a Source: Cook T D and Gruder C L (1978), *Eval. Q*. 2(1): 5–51 © 1978 Sage Publications, Inc. Reprinted with permission from Sage Publications Inc.

the original data and asked to re-analyze it and point out potential problems. On the other hand, if the issues to be addressed concern the policy implications of the findings, the meta-evaluators might be either the persons being evaluated or other interested audiences such as special interest groups. Regardless of who does a meta-evaluation, whenever possible the original evaluators should be given the opportunity to incorporate valid criticisms into their final report in the interest of producing higher quality evaluations. The meta-evaluators should, of course, have the opportunity to submit final comments on the revised report as well.

## 3. Issues and Recent Developments

Timing is one of the most important issues which must be considered in planning for a meta-evaluation. If the primary evaluation is important enough, some form of meta-evaluation is inevitable. However, meta-evaluation subsequent to the primary evaluation may come too late to inform and influence the policy-making process and thus serve primarily to increase the quality of later evaluations, if any are conducted. On the other hand, planning for meta-evaluations from the beginning of an evaluation project is likely to increase the time and cost necessary to provide final results. Given the political and budgetary climate in the United States in the early 1980s, possibilities for the increased use of preplanned meta-evaluations seem limited.

On the other hand, the authors believe that the ex post facto use of meta-evaluation can and will continue

to serve important functions for the evaluation community. Because of their training, scientists will continue to be constructively critical of their own and other's work. Interest groups will continue to question evaluation results and to offer alternative explanations for findings. The net effect should be more informed and reasoned public policy and higher quality evaluations in the future.

Meta-analysis (that is, quantitative literature review) is a form of meta-evaluation which readily lends itself to multiple independent analyses of the same set of evaluations without large investments of time or money beyond the initial costs of coding information in the primary studies. However, the initial costs of locating and coding the primary studies can be quite high. The costs rise with the number of studies coded and with the depth of explanatory analyses planned.

Finally, meta-evaluation has traditionally been thought of as a tool for evaluating evaluations. Recently, two additional topics, the evaluation of evaluation systems and evaluation research as an enterprise have been presented as forms of meta-evaluation. In these contexts, the meta-evaluator is posing questions not about the methodology of a particular evaluation and its effects on outcomes but about the organizational and managerial structure of evaluation and its impact on the generation of evaluative information. These developments are an indication that evaluators are beginning to take a step back from the day-to-day grind of evaluation and trying to understand some of the reasons for criticisms of the field of evaluation, including issues of quality, timeliness, and usefulness.

## 4. Summary

In its earliest usage, meta-evaluation referred to evaluating the technical quality of evaluations and to offering novel perspectives on the findings in terms of the questions asked, the cogency of any suggested policy implications, and the fit between the evaluation results and prior knowledge. The concept has now been significantly extended to include the evaluation of evaluation systems and evaluation research. The conceptualization of meta-evaluation presented here suggests that the different approaches vary along three dimensions: (a) timing; (b) degree of data manipulation; and (c) number of studies examined. The parties who do the meta-evaluation should also vary, depending on the types of information desired. The goal in conducting any meta-evaluation should be to obtain heterogeneous perspectives which serve to increase the credibility and validity of the results and raise our consciousness about the important questions and policy implications.

## Bibliography

Cook T D, Gruder C L 1978 Metaevaluation research. *Eval. Q.* 2(1): 5–51

Cook T D, Shadish W R 1981 Metaevaluation: An evaluation of the CMHC congressionally-mandated evaluation system. In: Stahler G, Tash W R (eds.) 1981 *Innovative Approaches to Mental Health Evaluation.* Academic Press, New York

Scriven M 1976 Evaluation bias and its control. In: Glass G V (ed.) 1976 *Evaluation Studies Review Annual,* Vol. 1. Sage Publications, Beverly Hills, California

Stufflebeam D L 1975 Meta-evaluation. Evaluation Center, Occasional Paper Series, No. 3. Western Michigan University, Kalamazoo, Michigan

# Evaluation Models and Approaches

## A Framework for Evaluation[1]

### R. M. Wolf

The formulation of a view of evaluation that is comprehensive is no easy task. It is not that there are no guides to help one. On the contrary, there are at least nine classes of models and, counting conservatively, 20 specific models of educational evaluation (Stake 1975 p. 33). It is not within the preview of this article to attempt to describe and compare all or even some of the models here; that would probably be more confusing than enlightening. Fortunately, descriptions and comparisons of a number of these models already exist and the interested reader is referred to those sources (Worthen and Sanders 1973, Popham 1975, Stake 1975).

Some of the ways in which evaluation models differ can be noted in order to assist in formulating a view of evaluation that attempts to transcend, take account of, and, in some way, accommodate these differences. One way in which evaluation models differ is in terms of what is considered to be the major purposes of educational evaluation. One group of writers, perhaps best exemplified by Cronbach (1963), sees improvement of instructional programs as the chief aim of evaluation. Educational programs are developed, tried out, modified, tried out again, and eventually accepted for adoption on a broad scale. Whether one holds a linear view of the process of research, development, and dissemination, characteristic of much of the curriculum development work of the early and mid-1960s, or some alternate view of the process of improvement of education, is not important here. Evaluation in any case is seen as supplying the information that will lead to improvement of the instructional endeavor. Evaluative information provides feedback to curriculum workers, teachers, and administrators so that intelligent decisions regarding program improvement can be made. Such a feedback and quality control role for evaluation, if carefully planned and carried out, is supposed to ensure success for every curriculum development enterprise.

In contrast to this view is the position that evaluation efforts should be directed toward formal, experimental comparative studies. In such instances evaluation efforts are directed at producing educational analogues of environmental-impact reports. Just as an environmental-impact report estimates the likely effects of adopting a particular educational program, educational evaluation in such cases should be able to inform educators about the likely effects of adopting a particular educational program. The methods used to arrive at such estimates center around planned, comparative studies. In well-conducted research studies, it should be possible to conclude that one program outperforms another (or fails to) in terms of various criteria, usually some collection of measures of student performance. Advocates of such a role for educational evaluation are often concerned with overall judgments about educational programs based on a comparison with one or more alternative programs.

The difference in views of the major purposes to be served by evaluation, presented above, has been drawn as sharply as possible. In reality, there is general acknowledgement of the validity of alternative purposes to be served by educational evaluation by writers holding different views. Unfortunately, the acknowledgement is often not translated into a modification of one's model so as to accommodate alternative viewpoints. This is not to say that a particular purpose for educational evaluation is, necessarily, wrong. In many instances it may be correct and highly appropriate. The point is that most models of evaluation are generally limited in terms of the purposes envisaged for educational evaluation, each tending to emphasize a limited set of purposes.

### 1. A Framework

In formulating a framework for evaluation studies, a conscious effort has been made to accommodate a variety of viewpoints about educational evaluation. Obviously the framework cannot be all-inclusive; some approaches are mutually exclusive and contradictory. When the purposes of evaluation differ, different parts of the framework will receive different emphasis. The framework presented here should not be regarded as a

1 This article was originally published in the *International Journal of Educational Research*, Vol. 11, No. 1. It appears here with permission from Pergamon Press plc © 1987.

model. While various writers have proposed different models of evaluation, what is presented here does not claim to be a model. It is hoped that it will be helpful to the reader in thinking about educational evaluation and will be useful in planning and conducting evaluation studies.

Comprehensive evaluation of educational treatments, whether they be units of instruction, courses, programs, or entire institutions, requires the collection of five major classes of information. Each class of information is necessary although not sufficient for a comprehensive evaluation of an educational enterprise. In setting forth these five major divisions, it is recognized that some may be of little or no interest in a particular evaluation undertaking. What is to be avoided is the possibility of omitting any important class of information for determining the worth of a program. Thus, the framework allows for possible errors of commission—for example, collecting information that will have little bearing on the determination of the merit·of a program—while avoiding errors of omission: failing to gather information that may be important. There are two reasons for this position. First, if a particular class of information turns out to be unimportant, it can simply be disregarded. Also, if it is known in advance that a particular class of information will have little bearing on the outcome for the evaluation, it simply need not be gathered. This does not reflect on the framework *per se* but only on the inappropriateness of a part of it in a particular situation. Second, failure to gather information about particular relevant aspects of an education venture indicates a faulty evaluation effort; this should be avoided.

### 1.1 Initial Status of Learners

The first class of information relates to the initial status of learners. It is important to know two things about the learners at the time they enter the program: who they are, and how proficient they are with regard to what they are supposed to learn. The first subclass of information—who the learners are—is descriptive in nature and is usually easily obtained. Routinely one wants to know the age, sex, previous educational background, and other status and experiential variables that might be useful in describing or characterizing the learners. Strictly speaking, such information is not evaluative. It should be useful in interpreting the results of an evaluation study and, more important, serve as a baseline description of the learner population. If it is found that subsequent cohorts of learners differ from the one that received the program when it was evaluated, then it may be necessary to modify the program to accommodate the new groups. The second subclass of information—how proficient the learners are with regard to what they are supposed to learn—is more central to the evaluation. Learning is generally defined as a change in behavior or proficiency. If learning is to be demonstrated, it is necessary to gather evidence of performance at, at least two points in time: at the beginning of a set of learning experiences, and at some later time. Gathering evidence about the initial proficiencies of learners furnishes the necessary baseline information for estimating, however crudely, the extent to which learning occurs during the treatment period. A related reason for determining the initial proficiency level of learners stems from the fact that some educational enterprises may seriously underestimate initial learner status with regard to what is to be learned. Consequently, considerable resources may be wasted in teaching learners who are already proficient. Mere end-of-program evidence gathering could lead one to the erroneous conclusion of program effectiveness when what had actually happened was that already developed proficiencies had been maintained.

It is important that a determination of the initial level of proficiencies of learners be undertaken before an educational enterprise gets seriously under way. Only then can one be sure that the learners are assessed independently of the effects of the program. Studying learners *after* they have had some period of instruction makes it impossible to determine what the learners were like before instruction began. While the point seems self-evident, it has been violated so often in recent years that several methodologists have published articles in professional journals about this to sensitize workers in the field.

The one instance in which gathering data about the initial proficiencies of learners can safely be omitted is when what is to be learned is so specialized in nature that one can reasonably presume the initial status of learners is virtually nil. Examples where such a presumption could be reasonably made would include entry-level educational programs in computer programming, welding, and cytotechnology. Outside of such specialized fields, however, it is worth the relatively small investment of time, energy, and expense to ascertain the initial status of learner proficiency.

### 1.2 Learner Performance after a Period of Instruction

The second major class of information required in evaluation studies relates to learner proficiency and status *after* a period of instruction. The basic notion here is that educational ventures are intended to bring about changes in learners. Hence, it is critical to determine whether the learners have changed in the desired ways. Changes could include increased knowledge, ability to solve various classes of problems, ability to deal with various kinds of issues in a field, proficiencies in certain kinds of skills, changes in attitudes, interests and preferences, and so on. The changes sought depend on the nature of the program, the age- and ability-levels of the learners and a host of other factors. Whatever changes a program, curriculum, or institution seeks to effect in learners must be studied to determine whether they have occurred and to what extent. The only way this can be done is through a study of learner performance. Whether the particular changes in learner behavior can be attributed to the effects of the educational experiences is another matter. Before such a determination can be made, however, it should be ascertained whether learning has occurred and, if so, to what extent.

The notion that information about what has been learned should be obtained after a period of instruction has often been interpreted to mean that learners must be examined at the end of a program or course. This is not quite correct. When information should be gathered is a function of the purposes of those who will be the major consumers of the evaluation. The developer of a program, for example, might be keenly interested in finding out how effective particular units of instruction are in bringing about particular changes in learners and also in the effectiveness of specific lessons. Such information may enable the developer to detect flaws in the program and make appropriate modifications. The same program developer might be relatively uninterested in learner performance at the end of the program. Moreover, summative information may be at such a general level as to be virtually useless in helping the developer detect where the program is working, and where it is not. On the other hand, someone who is considering the adoption of a program, may have little interest about how learners are performing at various points in the program; his or her interest lies chiefly in the final status of the learners. That is, have they learned what was expected by the conclusion of the program? A positive answer could lead to a decision to adopt the program; a negative one, to possible rejection. Different persons will approach an evaluation enterprise with different questions, and such differences should be reflected in decisions concerning *what* information should be gathered and *when* it should be gathered.

The above distinction closely parallels the one between formative and summative evaluation noted earlier. It is not, however, the only distinction that can be made. What is important is that a schedule of information-gathering with regard to learner performance should be consistent with the purposes for undertaking the evaluation and that the phrase "after a period of instruction" should not be restricted to end-of-course information gathering.

### 1.3 Execution of Treatment

The third class of information to be collected in an evaluation study centers on the educational treatment being dispensed. At the very least, one needs to know whether the treatment was carried out. If so, to what extent? Did the treatment get started on time? Were the personnel and materials necessary for the program available from the outset or, as has been the case in a number of externally funded programs, did materials and supplies arrive shortly before the termination of the program? Questions regarding the implementation of the intended program may seem trivial but are, in fact, critical. Often it is simply assumed that an intended program was carried out on schedule and in the way it was intended. This assumption is open to question but, more important, to study. Any responsible evaluation enterprise must determine whether and how an educational program was carried out.

Information about the execution of a program should not only meet the minimal requirement of determining whether a program has been carried out as intended; it should also furnish some descriptive information about the program in operation. Such information can often be used to identify deficiencies in the program as well as possible explanations for success. The collection of information about the program in operation will rely heavily on the regular use of observational procedures and—in some cases—on the use of narrative descriptive material. Who actually gathers such information is a matter that can be decided locally. Evaluation workers, supervisors, or other administrative personnel can share in the performance of this critical function. Maintenance of logs or diaries by teachers in the program can also contribute to meeting informational needs in this area. Even participant–observer instruments, along the lines developed by Pace and Stern (1958), where individuals are asked to report on particular practices and features of an environment, could be useful.

The study of program implementation is not undertaken just to determine how faithfully a program was carried out. Rather, the program that is evaluated is the implemented program. The implemented program can differ markedly from the designed or intended program. Further, there may be very good reasons for such differences. One of the evaluation worker's responsibilities is to be able to describe and compare the intended program, the implemented or actual program and the achieved program. The achieved program refers to learner performance in terms of program objectives. In order to fulfill this task, the evaluation worker will need to know not only the intended program or learning experiences, the achieved program or learner performance in terms of program objectives, but also the implemented or actual program in order to make the necessary comparisons.

### 1.4 Costs

The fourth major class of information is costs. Unfortunately, costs have not received adequate attention in evaluation work. The reason for this is not clear. Perhaps early educational evaluation efforts were directed toward ascertaining the efficacy of competing instructional treatments that had equal price tags. In such cases, cost considerations would not be a major concern. Today, however, the range of available treatments—in the form of units of instruction, courses, programs, curricula, and instructional systems—have widely varying costs. These need to be reckoned so that administrators and educational planners, as well as evaluation workers, can make intelligent judgements about educational treatments. Not only must direct costs be reckoned—for example, the cost of adoption—but indirect costs as well. Costs of inservice training for teachers who are to use a new program, for example, must be determined if a realistic estimate of the cost of the new program is to be obtained. An evaluation specialist, whose training and experience may be in measurement, research methodology, or curriculum development, may not be able to carry out such cost estimations. If one cannot do this, then one needs to find someone who can. An evaluation that makes no reference to costs is rarely of practical value, however interesting it may be academically. The educational administrator usually has a fair idea of what can be accomplished if money were no object. The real problem for the administrator is to make wise decisions when cost is a factor.

## 1.5 Supplemental Information

The fifth class consists of supplemental information about the effects of a program, curriculum, or institution and is composed of three subclasses. The first includes the reactions, opinions, and views of learners, teachers, and others associated with the enterprise being evaluated. These could be administrators, parents, other community members, and even prospective employers. The purpose of gathering such information is to find out how an educational treatment is viewed by various groups. Such information is no substitute for more direct information about what is actually being learned, but it can play a critical role in evaluating the overall worth of a program in a larger institutional context. There have been occasions when programs, instituted by well-intentioned educators, have succeeded fairly well in achieving their objectives, and at a reasonable cost. However, controversy about such programs—inside or outside the institution—have led to their termination. One can cite as examples the installation of programs of sex education in schools in highly conservative communities or the adoption of textbooks that were considered to contain offensive material by a sizable segment of a community.

Supplemental information—in the form of views and reactions of groups connected with an educational venture—can be highly instructive in a number of ways. It can: (a) provide information about how a program is being perceived by various groups; (b) help in the formulation of information campaigns, if there is a serious discontinuity between what is actually taking place in a program and what is perceived to be taking place; and (c) alert evaluation workers and administrators about the need for additional information as to why a particular program is being viewed in a certain way by one or more groups. Such information may also prevent evaluation workers from developing what Scriven (1972) has described as a kind of tunnel vision which sometimes develops from overly restricting evaluation efforts to determining how well program objectives have been achieved.

Information about the views and reactions of various groups connected with an educational enterprise can be gathered fairly easily through the use of questionnaires and interview techniques. The value of gathering such information should neither be underestimated nor over-

estimated. There have been a number of evaluation efforts that have relied solely on the collection of the views and reactions of individuals and groups having some connection to a program. Educational evaluation should not be confused with opinion polling. It is important to find out how well an educational venture is succeeding in terms of what it set out to accomplish. This requires the collection of information about learner performance outlined in the first two classes of information. In addition, supplemental information about how a program is perceived by various groups is important to an overall evaluation of its worth.

The instances cited above, where supplemental information in the form of views and reactions of various groups were rather extreme, do occur. The frequency of such occurrences, however, is low. Generally, reactions to educational programs tend to be on the mild side with a tendency on the part of the public to view new programs in a somewhat favorable light, especially if they have been fairly well thought through and reasonably well-presented. If reactions to educational programs are fairly mild, ranging, for example, from acquiescence to some positive support, little further attention need be accorded such information. However, one is not apt to know in advance what the views and reactions of various groups are likely to be. Accordingly, it is necessary to consciously find them out.

The second subclass of supplemental information involves learner performances not specified in the objectives of the program. Developers of educational programs, courses, and curricula are improving in their ability to specify what should be learned as a result of exposure to instruction. Furthermore, the responsibility for assessing learner performance with regard to specified objectives is now generally accepted. However, it is also reasonable to inquire how well broader goals of education are being served by a particular program. That is, how well is the need which the program was developed to meet being realized? "An ideal evaluation," Cronbach points out (1963 pp. 679–80):

would include measures of all the types of proficiency that might reasonably be desired in the areas in question, not just the selected outcomes to which this curriculum directs substantial attention. If you wish only to know how well a curriculum is achieving its objectives, you fit the test to the curriculum; but if you wish to know how well the curriculum is serving the national interest, you measure all outcomes that might be worth striving for. One of the new mathematics courses may disavow any attempt to teach numerical trigonometry, and indeed, might discard nearly all computational work. It is still perfectly reasonable to ask how well graduates of the course can compute and can solve right triangles. Even if the course developers went so far as to contend that computational skill is no proper objective of secondary instruction, they will encounter educators and laymen who do not share this view. If it can be shown that students who come through the new course are fairly proficient in computation despite the lack of direct teaching, the doubters will be reassured. If not, the evidence makes clear how much is being sacrificed. Similarly, when the biologists offer alternative courses emphasizing microbiology and ecology, it is fair to ask how well the graduate of one course can understand issues treated in the other. Ideal evaluation in mathematics will collect evidence on all the abilities toward which a mathematics course might reasonably aim; likewise in biology, English or any other subject.

Cronbach's view is not universally accepted. Some writers assert that any attempt to test for outcomes not intended by the program developers is imposing inappropriate and unfair criteria on the program. There is always a danger of being unfair. There is also the highly practical problem of deciding what learner–performance information, not specified in the objectives, should be obtained. It would seem that some information along these lines should be gathered. The examples cited by Cronbach above furnish some useful guides about the kinds of additional information program developers should obtain. It is important that supplemental information about learner performance, when obtained, be analyzed and reported separately from information bearing directly on the intended outcomes of a program. Any evaluation effort must not only be done fairly but be seen to be done fairly. The inclusion of information about learners' competencies, not intended as part of an instructional program, must be handled delicately. Separate treatment and reporting of such information is a minimal prerequisite of fairness.

While Cronbach maintains that an ideal evaluation effort would gather evidence about learner performance on all outcomes an educational enterprise might reasonably aim at, in practice the amount of supplemental performance information will, of necessity, be limited. Unless a program is heavily funded and has the requisite staff to develop evidence-gathering measures for the whole range of supplemental performance information desired, it is unrealistic to expect that very much can be done. Some efforts, albeit modest ones, can be made. It would be best to use the bulk of available resources to obtain learner–performance information with regard to intended outcomes and to supplement this with some additional measures. One should not dilute an evaluation effort by trying to measure everything and end up doing a mediocre or even poor job. This is a matter of planning and strategy. One can always expect that the resources available for evaluation will be limited. This is not a tragedy. Failure to use available resources effectively, however, can lead to poor results. It is recommended that the major use of available resources be devoted to obtaining the most relevant information about learner performance. This would entail examining how much has been learned with regard to the intended outcomes; some provision can (and should) be made with regard to other learner–performance outcomes that might result from the kind of program being evaluated.

The third subclass of supplemental information has to do with the side effects of educational programs, courses, and curricula. Admittedly, this is not an easy matter. Just as pharmaceutical researchers have long known that drugs can have effects on patients other than the ones intended, educators are realizing that their undertakings can have side effects too. Sometimes such unintended effects can be beneficial, for example, when a program designed to improve reading skills of learners not only improves reading proficiency but increases self-esteem. Negative side effects may also occur: in a rigorous academic high-school physics course students may learn a great deal of physics but their interest in learning more physics in college may be markedly reduced and, in some cases, extinguished.

While one can cite side effects of educational programs at length, prescriptions about what to look for and how to detect them are hard to give. Evaluation workers must first recognize that side effects can occur in any educational program. They then must strive to be as alert and as sensitive as possible about what is happening to learners as they move through a set of educational experiences. This means attending not only to learner performance in relation to stated objectives, but to any general class of behaviors, including interests and attitudes, that may be developing. This is not an easy task, but if the evaluation workers can maintain a level of receptivity about effects not directly specified by the objectives of a program, there is a fair chance that such behaviors will be discerned when they appear.

Another way of detecting the side effects of educational programs is through the use of follow-up procedures. Following up learners into the next level of education or into their first year of employment can furnish clues. In the example cited above about the rigorous high-school physics course, the critical information about the negative effect of the program on interest in learning more physics came from a follow-up study. (It was found that students who had taken the innovative physics course were taking additional physics courses in college at less than one-half the rate of comparable students who had taken a conventional high-school physics course.) However, it is not likely that formal follow-up studies will yield clear-cut results. Moreover, formal follow-up studies often require more resources than are available at most institutions. Even when such resources are plentiful, it is not usually clear how they should be put to use. The detection of unintended effects is an elusive business. Rather than attempt to conduct formal follow-up studies, it is usually better to use loosely structured procedures. Open-ended questionnaires and relatively unstructured interviews with teachers at the next level in the educational ladder, with employers of graduates as well as with graduates themselves, could furnish clues about side effects of programs that could then be studied more systematically. It is also possible that the first subclass of supplemental information—views and reactions of various groups connected with a program—could provide clues about program side effects. Whatever strategy is used to detect them, it should probably be somewhat loosely structured and informal.

*Bibliography*

Beberman M 1959 *An Emerging Program of Secondary School Mathematics.* Harvard University Press, Cambridge, Massachusetts

Begle E G 1963 The reform of mathematics education in the United States. In: Fehr H (ed.) 1963 *Mathematical Education in the Americas.* Bureau of Publications, Teachers College, Columbia University, New York

Cronbach L J 1963 Course improvement through evaluation. *Teach. Coll. Rec.* 64: 672–83

Eisner E W 1977 On the uses of educational connoisseurship and criticism for evaluating classroom life. *Teach. Coll. Rec.*

78: 345–58

Pace C R, Stern G G 1958 An approach to the measurement of psychological characteristics of college environments. *J. Educ. Psychol.* 49: 269–77

Popham W J 1975 *Educational Evaluation.* Prentice-Hall, Englewood Cliffs, New Jersey

Scriven M 1972 Pros and cons about goal-free evaluation. *Eval. Comment* 3(4): 1–44

Stake R E 1975 Program evaluation, particularly responsive evaluation. Occasional Paper Series 5 The Evaluation Center, Western Michigan University, Kalamazoo, Michigan

Worthen B R, Sanders J R 1973 *Educational Evaluation: Theory and Practice.* Charles A. Jones, Worthington, Ohio

# Naturalistic Evaluation

**D. W. Dorr-Bremme**

Evaluation is a name applied to several different endeavors in the field of education. Here, however, it means but one of these: the act of gathering information and juxtaposing it with some set of criteria to make judgments regarding the strengths and weaknesses, merits or worth of an educational innovation, program, or product. Naturalistic evaluation is any evaluation in this sense in which information is systematically acquired through a naturalistic mode of inquiry. The quintessential example of naturalistic inquiry is anthropological or sociological fieldwork, in which the researcher spends an extended time on site studying a group's culture or social life in naturally occurring circumstances. Thus, naturalistic inquiry can be distinguished from experimental inquiry and other modes of inquiry oriented by psychometric principles. Collectively, the latter are often associated with such terms as quantitative research, scientific research, hard data, variables, hypothesis testing, and statistical. In contrast, naturalistic inquiry—and so naturalistic evaluation—is commonly associated with such phrases as qualitative research, ethnographic research, fieldwork, case study method, soft data, ecological, descriptive, and interpretive (Bogdan and Biklen 1982).

It bears emphasizing that as most often used, the term naturalistic evaluation functions as a generic label. It references only one major aspect of an evaluation: the general approach followed by the evaluator in collecting and analyzing data. The label, then, entails nothing about the particular procedures or criteria employed to assign value or values to the program, innovation, and so on, etc., which is evaluated.

As the distinguishing feature of naturalistic evaluation, the naturalistic mode of inquiry deserves elaboration here. It consists of and is defined by (a) an orientation—a way of thinking about and portraying the activities of human social groups, and (b) an inquiry method—a systematic process for coming to understand human social activities in context.

## 1. The Naturalistic Orientation

The naturalistic orientation flows logically from theoretical concepts and research findings in several disciplines. Chief among these are anthropology and sociology. Increasingly, ethnomethodology (the study of everyday, practical reasoning), linguistics, and sociolinguistics or pragmatics have come to influence the naturalistic perspective. The philosophy known as symbolic interactionism has also influenced the naturalistic viewpoint.

Work from these fields warrants certain premises about the nature of humankind and human social endeavor. These premises, in turn, underlie the naturalistic orientation. They are as follows:

(a) Social groups—even those that exist side by side in a particular community or school; even those with overlapping memberships—can, and in many instances do, generate and sustain different "systems of standards for perceiving, believing, evaluating, and acting" (Goodenough 1971).

(b) Thus, their memberships routinely perceive and interpret phenomena differently and routinely act on the basis of their interpretations, whatever may be ascertainable as "fact" by standards of "scientific" measurement.

(c) A given social group's standards for sensibly and appropriately interpreting phenomena, ascribing meaning and value, and choosing actions can vary with features of the social context or situation—features which themselves are interpreted by members at successive levels of generality, for instance, this moment in this situation in this event in this phase of the program.

(d) The social life of any societal group, whatever its scope, is systematically ordered. Members' ways of conceptualizing and organizing their activities in many domains of social life are interdependent in dynamic, ecological balance, just as are the various life forms in an ecological niche.

(e) Despite the evident complexity of a group's organized social endeavor, the contexts, the standards for interpreting phenomena and selecting actions, and the relationships among societal elements that its members know and experience are accessible to nonmembers. They are apparent in the patterns that recur in time and across time in members' everyday talk and actions. They are clarified by members' accounts of their activities, especially those that they give as they engage in the activity in question.

These premises orient the naturalistic evaluator's (or researcher's) general goals and specific ways of thinking during inquiry. The naturalistic evaluator assumes that it is in terms of their own particular social realities, in terms of their own standards for appropriately making sense of phenomena and determining appropriate actions, that participants come to interpret, to enact, to judge, and so on, the program to be evaluated. From the naturalistic orientation, then, valid description and explication of the program at issue consists, at least initially, of reporting phenomena and how they function in relationship to one another from the perspectives of program participants. Therein lies the naturalistic evaluator's central goal. To achieve it, he or she takes reality and meaning as problematic as inquiry proceeds. This entails continually reflecting on such questions as: what contexts do participants in this setting know and act in terms of? By what features do they identify them? What meanings, values, and relationships do participants routinely ascribe to specific things, forms of behavior, social roles, and individuals? What standards do participants have for selecting actions that are accepted by other participants as appropriate and sensible in context? What does this person mean by what he or she is doing now? From participants' viewpoints, what relationships of function obtain among aspects of their immediate social environment and aspects of the larger worlds which impinge upon it?

In summary, the hallmarks of the naturalistic orientation are (a) a primary focus, during both inquiry and reporting, upon participants' perspectives; (b) a holistic approach, that is, an effort to understand and portray events in context, as they function in the web of interdependent relationships known to participants; and (c) a commitment to using the evaluator himself or herself as the primary instrument of data collection and analysis: a belief that only a human being operating experientially in the program setting can "peel back" and comprehend the layers of context, meaning, and systemic interdependency among phenomena that constitute participants' social realities.

## 2. The Naturalistic Method

The naturalistic inquiry method follows directly from the naturalistic orientation. The naturalistic evaluator begins inquiry with a few, very broad questions. In general, he or she wants to know "What is going on here that seems to be occasioned by, enacted in the name of, and functionally relevant to the program at issue?" Other, only slightly more specific questions, are usually framed in the light of the program's nature, the evaluation's intended purposes, and/or the concerns and interests of various evaluation audiences. Having established these initial questions, the naturalistic evaluator begins a cycle of inquiry steps that recurs for the duration of the effort. These steps consist of (a) gathering data on site, (b) analyzing and reflecting on the data, (c) refining and posing new (usually more specific) questions to guide continuing inquiry, and (d) returning to the site(s) for further data collection. In this cycle, hunches and hypotheses are successively generated, examined in view of the increasing data, and validated, reshaped, or disconfirmed.

Nearly anything the naturalistic evaluator notices or experiences on site can become data. He or she observes and listens to what program participants and relevant others do and say in their everyday lives, attending to when and where they do and say it. Planned interviews and impromptu conversations with participants are also important information sources. Audiotapes of interviews and videotapes of key activities can be made. Often, too, formal and informal documents are read and analyzed.

In narrative field notes, the naturalistic evaluator records what participants say as fully and as literally as possible. He or she also records personal impressions and inferences, carefully keeping these separate from the record of participants' words and deeds. At the end of a day on site, these notes are reviewed and filled in as necessary. Then, they are examined to identify emerging themes and patterns: phrases, actions and action sequences, expressed thoughts and feelings, and so on, that seem to recur in the data and to fit together. The evaluator also looks for apparent contradictions and discrepancies in the field-note record, pinpoints topics on which information seems incomplete, and tries to monitor how his or her preconceptions and biases may be influencing the accumulating record and evolving interpretations of "what is going on."

As the naturalistic evaluator reflects on his or her field notes in these ways, hunches and further questions suggest themselves. These serve to direct the ongoing inquiry when the evaluator returns to the program site(s). And as the evaluator repeats these steps and gathers additional and more detailed information, the evaluator's first, tentative hunches evolve into firmer hypotheses and, with still further inquiry, into findings.

Naturalistic evaluators disagree on whether reports should provide more than description and explication of the program which emphasizes participants' perspectives. Some argue for doing only this, allowing various evaluation audiences to reach their own judgments of value. Others are willing to make evaluative judgments, usually with the caveat that criteria from diverse frames of reference be used for doing so.

## 3. Current Status and Uses

Naturalistic evaluation remains less common than evaluation based on the experimental and psychometric traditions. Nevertheless, it has been conducted in education with increasing frequency since the mid-1970s. Its wider acceptance and use have been stimulated by broadened definitions of evaluation and the emergence of diverse evaluation models (see Guba and Lincoln 1981 pp. 1–22 for a brief history).

Many of the more recent evaluation models have called for more open-ended and flexible inquiry, an emphasis on program activities and processes, orientation to the evaluation audiences' specific information needs, and multiple criteria for assigning value(s) to program components. Naturalistic evaluation is more consonant with these emphases than with those of the more conventional models, in which program outcomes are measured against formally stated program objectives.

More broadly, naturalistic evaluation is a strong approach when the purpose of evaluation is to refine and improve the enactment of a program, to increase the effectiveness of its management, and/or to examine its implementation or adaptation in particular localities. It is also useful when the principal objective is to improve the technical assistance or support services provided by program sponsors to participants in local settings. Frequently, naturalistic evaluation in a few of many program sites is used to prepare for, supplement, or follow up a larger evaluation using survey and test-score measures.

The advantages of naturalistic evaluation for the above purposes are several. The naturalistic evaluator typically provides richly detailed description and holistic explication of program processes and outcomes as they occur amidst the complexity of the "real world." The naturalistic approach is likely to identify program effects and influences on the program that are missed in evaluations oriented by experimental and/or psychometric premises, and by less theoretically informed and systematic "qualitative" methods as well. And since naturalistic evaluation portrays program processes and effects in terms consonant with participants' ways of experiencing reality, it enables program managers and

sponsors to act on the evaluation in ways that take into account and respond to the needs, concerns, and viewpoints of participants in local settings.

While the advantages of naturalistic evaluation are many, it has some practical disadvantages. Naturalistic inquiry requires considerable amounts of time and labor. It tends, therefore, to be costly—a practical disadvantage in most circumstances. In particular, costs tend to restrict the number of settings the naturalistic evaluator can study thoroughly. This becomes a drawback when the number of program settings is great, since it is then difficult for the naturalistic evaluator to provide data that meet the usual standards for generalizability. Furthermore, where evaluation information is required in a short time, the naturalistic approach can be impractical. Some useful impressions can be gleaned quickly by holding the naturalistic orientation in mind and abbreviating the number of inquiry cycles. But to comprehend program activities validly (that is, from participants' perspectives and holistically) is nearly impossible in a brief period. In addition, naturalistic inquiry generates great amounts of narrative data: reducing, analyzing, and reporting it can take from two to three times the period spent in data collection. All this helps to explain why naturalistic evaluation is most often undertaken as an adjunct or supplement in evaluations based principally on statistically manipulable measures. Some exclusively naturalistic evaluations have been done, however, of both national and local programs. And in general, naturalistic evaluation has become an increasingly important alternative in the repertoire of evaluation inquiry.

## Bibliography

Bogdan R C, Biklen S K 1982 *Qualitative Research for Education: An Introduction to Theory and Methods*. Allyn and Bacon, Boston, Massachusetts

Goodenough W H 1971 *Culture, Language, and Society*, Addison-Wesley Modular Publications No. 7. Addison-Wesley, Reading, Massachusetts

Guba E G 1978 *Toward a Methodology of Naturalistic Inquiry in Educational Evaluation*, CSE Monograph Series in Evaluation No. 8. Center for the Study of Evaluation, University of California, Los Angeles, California

Guba E G, Lincoln Y S 1981 *Effective Evaluation: Improving the Usefulness of Evaluation Results through Responsive and Naturalistic Approaches*. Jossey-Bass, San Francisco, California

Spradley J P 1980 *Participant Observation*. Holt, Rinehart and Winston, New York

# Illuminative Evaluation

M. R. Parlett

The basic emphasis of illuminative evaluation applied to education is on investigating and interpreting a variety of educational practices, participants' experiences,

institutional procedures, and management problems, in ways that are recognizable and useful to those for whom the study is made. The research worker contributes to decision making by providing information, comments, and analysis to increase relevant knowledge and understanding. Illuminative evaluation is characterized by a flexible methodology that capitalizes on available resources and opportunities, and draws upon different techniques to fit the total circumstances of each study.

Illuminative evaluation falls within the general definition of a "systems" approach. Thus, it is holistic in outlook; studies tend to be far-ranging, concerned with the entire network of interrelationships rather than focusing on circumscribed programme features and correlations between individual "variables". As in systems thinking generally, illuminative evaluators are concerned with phenomena of organized complexity; they assume that events can usefully be treated as interrelated; they accept the likelihood of multiple causality and see their task as unravelling what is usually a complicated web of causes and effects. The outcome of an illuminative study is some overall model or "map" which attempts to make sense of the system as an organized and coherent totality, in ways which will inform those for whom the study is directed.

The aim is to increase understanding of policy questions related to the educational programme, instructional innovation, school setting, organizational problem, or other "system" studied. The approach is designed to illuminate (or throw light upon) its character and special features as a working system, along with the wider context in which the system operates. The approach is also evaluative in that attention is necessarily paid to qualities, to costs and effects, to desirable and unintended outcomes, and the value (or lack of it) of parts of the system or the whole of it, as perceived by the various constituencies or pertinent subgroups with different investments, perspectives, and allegiances.

## 1. A Coordinated Approach

Illuminative evaluation represents a coordinated research approach—its purposes, working philosophies, strategic methodology, built-in values, and conceptual orientation combine together in a distinctive and necessary way. Each feature contributes to the whole. It needs to be understood as an integrated and "total" approach to investigation—not as simply an espousal of qualitative methodology, ethnographic field work, face-to-face methods of enquiry, and narrative reporting—although these do feature strongly in most studies.

Another way of depicting the approach is in terms of its being responsive, naturalistic, heuristic, and interpretive.

### 1.1 Responsive Features

Illuminative researchers aim to be responsive in several ways. It is a tenet of the approach that studies be of use and interest to the educational practitioners and policy makers who represent the target audiences. If this is to

be more than a pious wish, it means paying special attention to the audiences of each study—their requirements for information, their interests, questions, and needs. It means designing the study in ways that do not affront their common sense, with reports being written lucidly, with minimal resort to jargon, and with attention paid to presentation and brevity. If an illuminative evaluation report is found by policy makers and practitioners to be irrelevant, long-winded, or superficial, the study has failed within its own terms.

The approach requires investigators to be responsive in other ways too. Thus, while all research and evaluation constitutes intervention of some kind in the lives of organizations and persons, the close-up, on-site investigative techniques favoured by illuminative evaluators increase the requirements for researcher sensitivity, the building of trust, and responsibility in the way the study is reported so as to maintain anonymity.

Another way in which the approach is responsive is that studies are kept as brief as possible. Although the orientation derives much from anthropological techniques here is one sharp disjunction from field work as commonly practised by ethnographers. Studies which take years to carry out and to write up are rarely adequate for evaluation purposes. Illuminative evaluation can be adapted to carrying out short, intensive studies when these are called for by special circumstances.

### 1.2 Naturalistic Features

In illuminative studies, educational and other relevant phenomena are examined as they occur "naturally" in real-life institutional settings. No attempt is made to bring them under artificial conditions for purposes of investigation. Moreover, every effort is made to look "beyond the display counter" and to do justice to the observable realities "at the back of the shop". Organizational life is studied in all its natural complexity, with attention paid to the unexpected and the atypical as well as to the routine and obvious.

Overall, the concern is to document the programme or set of issues being studied in an informative and revealing manner, drawing together factual and statistical material, opinions, observations, and historical perspectives, to provide a fuller basis for comprehending and appreciating the special nature of the system studied. The data handled are undoubtedly complex. An attempt is made to do justice to the complexity without being submerged by it in the course of study or passing it on to readers in a way that is confusing or inaccessible.

### 1.3 Heuristic Features

In working practice, the systemic nature of the approach calls for a heuristic design—that is, an evolving strategy of study, continuously updated to accord with the investigators' emerging understandings of the system as a whole, as well as accommodating changes in the system that result from the flux of unfolding events during the course of study. In this regard, the illuminative investigator proceeds like a clinical diagnostician or, perhaps, a historian documenting a particular event: the course of enquiry cannot be charted in advance.

In turn, flexibility of design necessitates having facility with a range of methods—mainly direct observation, interviews, focused group discussions, unobtrusive measures, questionnaires, analysis of background documentary materials and of statistical and other information already collected. Techniques are deployed in various combinations according to the exact nature of the enquiry at different stages, with problems defining methods rather than vice versa. Illuminative evaluations therefore have a custom-built plan of study, rather than one "off the shelf", one which acknowledges the programme's specialized features, the requirements and interests of policy makers, and the constraints, resources, and boundary conditions relating to the particular study.

### 1.4 Interpretive Features

Despite the importance placed upon accurate and full description and reporting, illuminative evaluators believe there is a need to go further. The aim is to provide a distillation of local thinking, to concentrate the wisdom, as it were, dispersed in many different perspectives, and to draw threads together in such a way as to "sharpen discussion, disentangle complexities, isolate the significant from the trivial, and raise the level of sophistication of debate" (Parlett and Hamilton 1972).

In order to focus discussion, heighten awareness, and promote a fresh appreciation of the system studied and the related issues of policy, the investigator goes beyond simple description. Underlying structures and relationships do not declare themselves in obvious ways—they have to be discovered, even created. In this respect, illuminative evaluators align themselves with the functionalist anthropologist Bronislaw Malinowski (1961): "The principles of social organization, of legal constitution, of economics and religion, have to be constructed by the observer out of a multitude of manifestations of varying significance and relevance. It is these invisible realities, only to be discovered by inductive computation, by selection and construction, that are scientifically important in the study of culture."

## 2. History, Context, and Applications

Illuminative evaluation (Hamilton et al. 1977) has been in the forefront of the movement away from evaluation based heavily on preordinate designs, specification of objectives, operationalization of variables, the collection of more or less exclusively numerical data, and the primacy of statistical methods of analysis. While illuminative evaluation needs to be seen in the context of a vigorous critique of the traditional research paradigm

used in evaluation, the chief priority since 1972 has not been on dismantling the previously dominant model but on practising and perfecting an investigative approach located within a different paradigm, which is a genuine, viable, and radical alternative.

Illuminative evaluation originated in work carried out at the Massachusetts Institute of Technology in 1967–1968 and at the University of Edinburgh in the early 1970s. The basic ideas and methods of working were largely discovered through trial and error, in relative ignorance of similar approaches. Discoveries of roots, connections, and overlaps swiftly followed. These helped to solidify and extend the approach which was first fully elaborated and designated as illuminative evaluation by Parlett and Hamilton (1972).

There are family resemblances to a broad variety of naturalistic enquiries in evaluation and to the participant observation-based fieldwork research into schools developed by Smith.

Illuminative evaluation is most often linked with responsive evaluation and shares with this approach concerns to inform decision makers; to represent the complexity and detail of programmes studied; and to use a variety of investigative techniques in order to achieve a portrayal of the system studied.

Illuminative evaluation has been applied in many different forms and contexts (and not only within education). There have been numerous studies in higher education settings, examining undergraduate life and subcultures, student assessment, laboratory instruction in the sciences and engineering, and experiments with new approaches to teaching. One study carried out retrospectively concerned a major innovation in undergraduate physics instruction that had failed (Friedman et al. 1976).

On a larger scale, there has been a national study of mainstreaming or integration of visually impaired children in England and Wales (Jamieson et al. 1977); a study of the cost-effectiveness of an internationally sponsored community development and parent education project in rural Chile (Richards 1984); and a government-funded study of vocational preparation schemes in the United Kingdom. Major studies have also been made of open-plan schooling (Hamilton 1977) and of professional decision making in special education.

While a number of evaluation reports have been published (completely or in extract) most have circulated locally. Few have been confidential or restricted. Most (to the author's knowledge) have been well received. Over 120 persons have been given formal training in the approach by Parlett alone and a growing number of Ph.D. theses in several different countries have been based on the approach.

## 3. Negotiation and Setting Up the Study

In any exercise labelled "evaluation" there are questions regarding policy. Take the following examples: (a) Is this scheme worth trying to replicate elsewhere? (b) What improvements can be made in the running of the organization and the effectiveness of initiatives? (c) Is refunding desirable and on what basis should the effort be judged? (d) What have been the principal benefits attributable to the programme that was funded?

These are the kinds of questions that lead organizations, funding bodies, sponsors, and managers of programmes to consider having an evaluation carried out. Part of a comprehensive study must be to consider the circumstances of its being required. The illuminative evaluator places a premium on discovering: What is really at stake? Do the policy makers want to examine management problems, find a scapegoat, resolve a conflict, cut down a programme to size? And what intentions do sponsors and others have for how the report will be used? To satisfy funding agencies, convince consumers (such as parents), reassure committees, boost the bargaining power of the director? These motives are not disparaged; they are part of the "real world" contexts in which evaluators have to operate.

In illuminative evaluation care and time is taken to surface and wherever possible make explicit the foundations of the study. The evaluator seeks to avoid becoming an unwitting tool of a single power base or pressure group. Illuminative evaluations require a high level of mutual trust if the more delicate (and usually more telling) policy questions are to be opened up to detailed scrutiny. Starting off a study on "the right foot", following extensive negotiation, has been found to be essential and not merely desirable, given the nature and priorities of the approach in action.

Illuminative evaluators treat as a major part of the method how to present the study and win confidence while maintaining its integrity; how to establish working contracts; and how to renegotiate, expanding or contracting the scope of work, if necessary, as the study proceeds.

## 4. Progressive Focusing and Theme Building

In parallel with the initial "negotiation phase" of a study is the "immersion" period: a time of rapid familiarization. Investigators listen and observe, ask numerous questions, read widely, consult a variety of individuals already knowledgeable with the system. Unless a basic familiarity is achieved there is little prospect of subsequent design decisions being adequate or of investigators winning the confidence of programme or organizational members.

Studies then become more selective, with more focused subsidiary investigations being carried out to explore particular themes in depth. Such themes may include problems frequently referred to by teaching assistants; particular sources of pride and felt satisfaction discerned among programme participants; topics avoided or glossed over by administrators; areas of consensus and disagreement among teachers; dis-

crepancies between what is supposed to happen and what in fact happens at the level of day-to-day activities; issues that predominate in off-duty staff talk; and key assumptions about a programme's educational mission that seem to be unquestioned yet central to its operations. These "emerging themes" represent strands of observation and argument which give form and direction to the evolving study. They derive from knowledge gathered in the field as well as from preliminary review of relevant documents, reports of previous studies, and so on, and are "progressively focused" upon in greater detail as the study continues. New themes are added right up to the end of the study. Themes are not cast in permanent fashion but remain "interim" for as long as is compatible with the requirement also to achieve closure and to complete the study. Working themes are likely eventually to become chapter headings and subsections in the report, with the various "points" linked to each theme becoming individual paragraphs.

Perhaps the most distinctive feature of illuminative evaluation is its explicit and conscious concern with progressive focusing and accompanying distillation. In any relatively open-ended study which emphasizes detailed documentation, there is a surfeit of material and numerous possible ways to assemble and summarize it. The illuminative evaluator is like a historian attempting to write an account of a war. So much material is available, so many dimensions of the war-in-context can be covered that a simple commission could easily grow into a life work. The illuminative evaluator has the same obligation as the historian to make judicious selections, devise a manageable structure, and impose intelligent form and meaning to material he or she has gathered.

This form of interpretive work—choosing areas of concentration and key topics and framing the study around these in a series of midway conceptualizations—lies at the centre of illuminative evaluation practice. Progressive focusing on selected themes provides the management criteria for channelling investigative resources and also reduces the likelihood of "data overload" and "not being able to see the wood for the trees". The iterative recycling of emergent themes is also a route to achieving greater clarity, "thickness" of description, and enables the policy relevance of the emerging structure of argument to be selectively tested.

The refinement of themes also provides the procedural vehicle for a critical examination of themes and planning of further enquiries. Asking the questions: "What evidence can be cited?" and "What is the quality of the data being relied upon?" may point to the need for a different form of enquiry or some cross-checking by other methodological means. Such "triangulation" (a term drawn from surveying) refers to key events, processes, practices, outcomes, etc. being examined by different techniques, generating data of various kinds which when considered together give a powerful indication of accuracy and repeatability independently of the mode of enquiry.

## 5. *The Analogy with Map Making*

Illuminative evaluators are like map makers: their job is to represent the system studied and to condense information and analysis. There is continual to and fro movement between the reality to be depicted and the emerging representation of that reality. Like makers of maps, illuminative evaluators have to decide what to include and leave out. In the case of maps, the criteria are governed by the use to which the map will be put (e.g., meteorologists want isobars, political analysts want regional voting patterns) as well as by resource considerations—some information is simply too difficult or expensive to justify collection.

Illuminative evaluators have comparable decisions to reach: Who exactly will read the report, what do they need to know, what will constitute a sufficiently detailed analysis? If the report is long, with many diffuse themes, it is likely to be found irrelevant (like a needlessly cluttered map). On the other hand, a superficial report with little in it (an uninformative map) is equally a waste: it will be easily dismissed or, worse, used to justify simplistic policies. Choosing the appropriate level of detail, scope of enquiry, and apt themes, constitutes the creative work to be done.

The necessary activities of selection and organization are represented by critics of the approach as private, almost artistic processes which cannot be taught and learned as research methods. In practice this is not the case. Most people's "natural" way of mentally ordering everyday experience is to make connections, build some kind of "internal map" of what they are finding out, and to focus on matters of interest and importance to them. In other words, they operate somewhat like the observing and interpreting field investigator. Of course, the ordering of material, the weighing of alternative emerging themes, the self-aware review of inclusion and exclusion criteria, the scrupulous assessment of evidence, and much else that comprises the necessary work of illuminative studies, obviously go far beyond natural ways of knowing and may even contradict them (e.g., by earmarking data that do not fit preconceptions). However, the underlying basis for the necessary interpretive work does not appear to need learning from scratch; instead the capability needs to be revalidated (especially among social scientists taught to distrust their powers of discernment and commonsense ways of knowing), and also made more public and practised with reflexive rigour.

The analogy of map making is helpful in another respect. E. H. Carr, the historian, has written: "To praise a historian for his accuracy is like praising an architect for using well-seasoned timber or properly mixed concrete in his building. It is a necessary condition of his work, but not his essential function." The same goes for illuminative evaluators. A concern frequently expressed before (and only rarely after) an illuminative evaluation study is "How will we know what you say is accurate?" The same question directed at map makers might elicit the reply that once a map is made it can be checked against other sources of information, including the users' experience. Likewise with evaluation reports: those acquainted with the system can normally check most of its observations, challenge its conclusions, and certainly assess its usefulness as an attempt to capture a recognizable reality. This form of quality check is about as demanding as any.

Illuminative evaluation is, in summary, a way of carrying out an investigation into a working system, mapping it for the benefit of interested and responsible readerships. Investigators may serve as conduits—portrayers of individual and collective comment and opinion, summarizing suggestions for changes and system improvements. This "phenomenological mapping" overlays and interlocks with other accounts of the system developed—for example of its history and structure, its purposes and theories of practice, its resources and the use made of them, its stated intentions and the variety of actual consequences. A complete study provides a small atlas of different kinds of programme maps.

A fully successful illuminative evaluation is one which condenses a maximum amount of valid experience and informative commentary about the system studied into a readable report which stimulates talk and brings together key topics, unresolved questions, and practical thinking. Ideally the report is a freely circulating document; it commands respect from different constituencies as a faithful account of their working world; it is "eye-opening" to different groups or interests; and it facilitates substantive discussion and policy formation. Exceedingly hard though not impossible to bring about, such a result certainly is not achievable without utilizing the approach to its full, including careful negotiation; a custom-built design which evolves in the course of study; progressive focusing on to organizing themes; triangulation; the use of multiple enquiry techniques; maintaining the feelings and rights of those participating; attending closely to the ethics of investigation and reporting; writing lucidly for specific audiences; and taking into account the multiple contexts in which the report will represent an intervention.

## Bibliography

Carr E H 1961 *What is History?* Macmillan, London

Friedman C P, Hirschi S, Parlett M R, Taylor E F 1976 The rise and fall of the personalized system of instruction in physics at Massachusetts Institute of Technology. *Am. J. Phys.* 44(3): 204–11

Hamilton D F 1977 *In Search of Structure: Essays from an Open Plan School.* Hodder and Stoughton, London

Hamilton D, Jenkins D, King C, MacDonald B, Parlett M R (eds.) 1977 *Beyond the Numbers Game: A Reader in Educational Evaluation.* Macmillan, London

Jamieson M, Parlett M R, Pocklington K 1977 *Towards Integration: A Study of Blind and Partially Sighted Children in Ordinary School.* NFER Publishing Co., Slough

Malinowski B 1961 *Argonauts of the Western Pacific.* Dutton, New York

Parlett M 1974 The new evaluation. *Trends Educ.* 34: 13–18
Parlett M 1981 Illuminative evaluation. In: Reason P, Rowan J (eds.) 1981 *Human Inquiry: A Sourcebook of New Paradigm Research.* Wiley, Chichester, pp. 219–26
Parlett M, Hamilton D 1972 Evaluation as illumination: A new approach to the study of innovatory programs. Occasional Paper No. 9, University of Edinburgh, Centre for Research in the Educational Sciences. Reprinted in: Glass G V (ed.) 1976 *Evaluation Studies Review Annual*, Vol. 1. Sage, New York
Richards H 1984 *The Evaluation of Cultural Action.* Macmillan, London

# Transactional Evaluation

## R. M. Rippey

Program evaluations and experimental studies of instruction often omit reports of the vicissitudes of change. How did persons involved in new programs contend with discrepant personal needs and aspirations, and institutional demands and sanctions? Transactional evaluation (TE) examines this question.

Classical organizational theory posits a transactional dimension interstitial between the nomothetic (institutional) and the ideographic (personal). New programs and educational experiments strain the academic system and its constituencies. Productive energy is diverted to transactions aimed at reducing the stress. If new roles and demands resemble the old, little energy need be diverted. Unfortunately, personal needs and institutional demands are frequently incongruent. Thus some persons refuse to implement, others are deflected in their purpose, and some experiments unwittingly report on consequences of nonevents.

Although it is useful to know when an innovation fails, it is better to understand why. Programs can fail because they are deficient or because they are badly implemented. Close supervision can force implementation in laboratory settings but rarely in field settings. Thus, effective programs can flounder when disseminated.

Evaluations sometimes overlook the reciprocal character of both the change and the educative process. The changer changes and the teacher learns. One of Ralph Tyler's contributions to curriculum theory was reconceptualizing teaching from a one-way street to a rotary where objectives, instruction, and evaluation interacted. The occasional transformation of this rotary into a cul-de-sac may result from misperceiving the bidirectional character of curriculum reform. Teachers do not apply new educational practices as prescribed any more than students respond uniformly to all stimuli. Resistance of teachers and students against new demands can range from lack of enthusiasm to outright hostility.

## 1. Development of the Concept

Coffey and Golden, in concluding their chapter in the 1957 National Society for the Study of Education (NSSE) yearbook, suggested that the more profound an educational change, the more vigorous the resistance generated. Therefore, changes should begin modestly and experimentally, involving the most enthusiastic as implementors. They further advised careful evaluation. This commonsense approach unfortunately did not answer the question of what to do with the most energetic detractors.

Rippey (1973) asserted that the loyal opposition could serve on an evaluation team as members of the "adversary" squad. The resulting transactional evaluation model differed from its predecessors in four respects: intents, methods, roles, and composition. Its intent was to expand data collection to include social and interpersonal impediments to change. Its methods were conventional except for a special type of questionnaire whose items were not only supplied by evaluation specialists but also solicited from implementors and their critics. The evaluator role was modified to allow for substantial intervention and intimacy. The evaluation team incorporated previously excluded clients and apostates.

Subsequent applications have generally used this model. However, three modifications are: (a) although initially conceived as a means of facilitating change, it has been used to determine the need for change—Harder (1979) used transactional evaluation on a year-long basis in a high-school history class to ascertain student interests and problems; (b) although conceived as formative evaluation, Seidel (1978) used transactional evaluation for "summative evaluation of a *system*" for introducing computer-assisted instruction into the Washington DC public schools; and (c) Schwartz (1977) utilized transactional evaluation not only in evaluating a university-based teacher-training program, but also in working with the evaluation team in formulating the evaluation design.

## 2. Theoretical Issues

Since transactional instruments seek to uncover sources of conflict among pluralistic interest groups, they capitalize on rather than minimize subject–item interactions. Since they intend to discover skewed perceptions, the validity of each item will be in the eye of the beholder. Since they intend to capture the essence of specific programs in unique settings, their generalizability is nil. However, the transactional instrument itself is only part of a proper evaluation and overall validity can be confirmed by analysis of agreement among the multiple sources and methods comprising the comprehensive evaluation.

The objectivity of an intimate and influential evaluator raises questions. However, an evaluator who is remote may fail to capture the essence of a project and may lack access to key information. The evaluator who conceals beneficial informed judgment from a project director, or ignores sensitive political issues may be negligent or naive. On the other hand, can such an evaluator produce an honest account and does such an evaluator interfere with valid findings?

External audits of evaluation reports reveal varied quality independent of intimacy or austerity. Talmage illustrates that dangers to honest accounting may occur subsequent to rather than prior to an evaluation (Rippey 1973). The imperative of replication affects the intimate and the aloof alike.

Data support the modified evaluator role. Cicerelli concludes that National Opinion Research Center community studies of Project Head Start contributed to the resolution of specific social conflicts (Rippey 1973). In a four-year study of college student attitudes toward instruction, Schroder showed that student-contributed transactional evaluation items produced more information than faculty constructed items. Student attitudes appeared to improve as a result of the process. Costs were negligible. Livingston showed increased reading comprehension and speed scores for students assigned to randomly selected reading classes in comparison to equivalent control groups. The experimental groups used frequent transactional analysis assessments of student needs which helped teachers plan instruction.

Transactional evaluation is not restricted to education and has been used by Seidel (1978) in industrial, governmental, and training settings. His data suggest that transactional evaluation is helpful in resolving ambiguity and polarization in collaborative team ventures. However, he believes that it will not be effective in troubled organizations where authority and responsibility have been separated.

Transactional evaluation can lead to more illuminating program evaluations. At the same time, it can increase compliance with and acceptance of experimental treatment and evaluation protocols. Thus it constitutes a useful option for the evaluator's armamentarium.

*Bibliography*

Harder P J 1979 Student comments change curriculum. *Soc. Stud.* 70: 125–28

Rippey R M 1973 *Studies in Transactional Evaluation*. McCutchan, Berkeley, California

Rippey R M 1977 Transactional evaluation and the improvement of instruction. *Educ. Technol.* 17: 7–11

Schwartz H 1977 The use of multiple research methodologies to evaluate an inservice curriculum, Paper presented at the 61st annual meeting of the American Educational Research Association, New York. ERIC Document No. ED 137 335

Seidel R J 1978 Transactional evaluation: Assessing human interactions during program development, Report No. Hum RRO Professional Paper 8–78. ERIC Document No. ED 159 579

Tyler R W 1949 *Basic Principles of Curriculum and Instruction*. University of Chicago Press, Chicago, Illinois

# Intrinsic Evaluation

## M. R. Eraut

The term "intrinsic evaluation" was first introduced by Scriven (1967) to characterize an approach to the evaluation of curriculum proposals and materials which focused on their intrinsic nature rather than their effects. Though he gave little methodological guidance, Scriven argued that all evaluations should include an evaluation of goals and that pure empiricism was impossible. The intrinsic component of an evaluation study should also include a consistency analysis in which divergencies between (a) espoused, (b) implicit, and (c) tested-for goals are disclosed; and a content analysis to appraise the accuracy, coverage, and significance of the content. While an evaluator might himself or herself be responsible for the former, the latter would necessitate consultation with external experts in the subject matter field.

Three possible roles may be played by intrinsic evaluation in the development and evaluation of curriculum materials. Firstly, in formative evaluations independent analysis by an evaluator and/or external experts can begin as soon as draft materials are available. Aims of this early analysis might be to disclose the developers' assumptions about the feasibility, desirability, and utilization of their materials; to relate these assumptions to the standards and values of various external groups; to anticipate issues that might emerge as significant during subsequent field testing; and to collect suggestions for possible improvements. The audience for this intrinsic evaluation would be the development team and its consultative committee; and its purpose both to assist in the formative evaluation and to prevent the developers from early commitment to assumptions that might ultimately prove disadvantageous.

The second role is in the initial stage of a summative evaluation when the audience is the evaluator. In this role the analysis is essentially hypothesis forming and its purpose is to guide subsequent empirical investigation. In addition to providing the basis for any assessment of student performance, an intrinsic evaluation can be combined with knowledge of common school practices to predict likely patterns of use and to anticipate possible incongruencies between intended and observed practice.

Then thirdly, intrinsic evaluation may contribute to the final stage of a summative evaluation by highlighting the major assumptions embedded in the product, evaluating its goals, reporting the findings of content and consistency analyses, and briefing decision makers on the similarities and differences with alternative products. It is only at this stage that the independence of the evaluator is crucial for external credibility.

Other articles in this Encyclopedia describe evaluation activities which rely heavily on intrinsic evaluation. These are rarely performed by people who receive any training for the task; and, while checklists of questions abound, there are few publications which discuss the methodology in any detail. The development of techniques for intrinsic evaluation is still in its infancy, so this article is limited to a review of those approaches which appear to offer the greatest potential.

Content analysis as a systematic technique has been most fully developed in the context of communication research. In essence it involves creating some system for categorizing content, defining a unit of analysis and a set of categorizing rules, and applying them to obtain a profile which depicts the content balance of a communication in terms of the chosen categories. The unit of analysis may be a chapter, a page, a topic, a period of allocated time, or an assignable unit. Several profiles may be used to present a more complete picture, but each needs to have a coherent theoretical base for its characterization. For example, thematic categories indicate the selection and focus of thematic content; categories based on classifications of objectives can indicate levels of thinking demanded of pupils; and other category systems can be devised to show the balance of pupil activities, the difficulty of the language, or the abstraction of the content. While some may be based on existing theories, others may be specifically developed to suit the particular documents being analysed. The most fully developed are probably those relating to the detection of bias against minority groups.

A rather different approach is needed for analysing the structuring and sequencing of content. While Posner and Strike (1976) provide an excellent theoretical framework, there still remain many methodological problems. How, for example, is it possible to assess the validity of the claim by an author or an evaluator that their materials are indeed organized in the way they describe? Can an analyst identify underlying structures without underestimating the richness of good content? Do instructional designers' checklists adequately characterize quality in curriculum materials? As yet there is little systematic advice available but prospective analysts may find useful ideas in several other Encyclopedia articles.

A different style of intrinsic evaluation can be found in writings on curriculum criticism. This notion was introduced by Mann (1969) who argued that the purpose of the critic was to disclose meaning and to relate materials to their social context, making use of their own personal knowledge and stressing their ethical and aesthetic concerns.

Werner (1980) addresses the important issue of validity and suggests three basic validation principles for curriculum criticism: an explicit methodological framework and purpose; public dialogue about the appropriateness of the framework and the validity of the critic's interpretations within it; and evidence that it has contributed to better understanding of the curriculum. All three principles might usefully be applied to intrinsic evaluation in general.

## Bibliography

Mann J S 1969 Curriculum criticism. *Teach. Coll. Rec.* 71: 27–40

Posner G J, Strike K A 1976 A categorization scheme for principles of sequencing content. *Rev. Educ. Res.* 46: 665–90

Sanders J R, Cunningham D J 1973 A structure for formative evaluation in product development. *Rev. Educ. Res.* 43: 217–36

Scriven M 1967 The methodology of curriculum evaluation. In: Tyler R W, Gagné R M, Scriven M (eds.) 1967 *Perspectives of Curriculum Evaluation*. American Educational Research Association Curriculum Evaluation Monographs 1. Rand McNally, Chicago, Illinois

Stake R E 1970 Objectives, priorities and other judgement data. *Rev. Educ. Res.* 40: 181–212

Werner W 1980 Editorial criticism in curricular analysis. *Curric. Inq.* 10: 143–54

# Responsive Evaluation

### R. E. Stake

Responsive evaluation is an approach to the evaluation of educational and other programs. Compared to most other approaches it is oriented more to the activity, the uniqueness, and the social plurality of the program.

The essential feature of the approach is a responsiveness to key issues, especially those held by people at the site. It requires a delay and continuing adaptation of evaluation goal setting and data gathering while the people responsible for the evaluation become acquainted with the program and the evaluation context.

Issues are suggested as conceptual organizers for the evaluation study, rather than hypotheses, objectives, or regression equations. The reason for this is that the term "issues" draws thinking toward the complexity, particularity, and subjective valuing already felt by persons associated with the program. Issue questions such as, "Are the admission criteria appropriate?" "Do these simulation exercises confuse the students about authoritative sources of information" are raised. The evaluator inquires, negotiates, and selects a few issues around which to organize the study.

To become acquainted with a program's issues the evaluator usually observes its activities, interviews those who have some stake in the program, and examines relevant documents. These are not necessarily the data-gathering methods for informing and interpreting the issues, but are needed for the initial planning and progressive focusing of the study. And even later, management of the study as a whole remains flexible whether quantitative or qualitative data are gathered.

## 1. Observations and Judgments

A responsive evaluation study is, of course, directed toward the discovery of merit and shortcoming in the program. It is attentive to the multiple and sometimes contradictory standards held by different groups. Ultimately the evaluators will either make strong summary statements of the program's worth, or they may provide descriptive data and the judgments of others so that report readers can make up their own minds about program worth.

There is a common misunderstanding that responsive evaluation requires naturalistic inquiry or qualitative research. Not so. The evaluators and program staff and evaluation sponsors discuss alternative methods. They negotiate. Knowing more about what different methods can accomplish, and what methods this evaluation "team" can do well, and being the ones to carry them out, the evaluators ultimately determine what the methods will be.

With preliminary emphasis on becoming acquainted with the history and social interactions of the program, it is often decided that the methods of study should be naturalistic or phenomenological. Other times it will become highly quantitative, possibly goal oriented. It depends on the situation. For it to be good responsive evaluation the methods must fit the "here and now," having potential for serving the evaluation needs of the various parties concerned.

It is in fact rather uncommon for a responsive evaluation study to emphasize the testing of students or other indicators of successful attainment of objectives. This is because such instrumentation has so often been found not to be cost effective. Available tests are often not good approximations of the several outcomes intended. And even when possible, developing new tests is very expensive. Test results have too often been disappointing, with educators probably justifiably believing that more was learned than showed up on the tests. With the responsive approach, tests may be used,

but usually are kept in a subordinate role. They are needed when it is clear that they actually can serve to inform about the quality of the program.

People are used more as sociological informants than as subjects here. They are questioned not so much to see how they have changed but to indicate the changes they see.

## 2. Subjectivity and Pluralism

Those who object to the responsive approach often do so on the grounds that too much attention is given to subjective data, for example, the testimony of participants. To obtain a description of what is happening, the evaluation researchers try through triangulation to show the reliability of observations. Part of the description, of course, especially that about the worth of the program, is revealed in how people subjectively perceive what is going on. Placing value on the program is not seen as separate from perceiving it.

The researchers' own perceptions are also recognized as subjective—in choosing what to observe, in observing, and in reporting the observations. One tries in responsive evaluation to make those value commitments more recognizable. Issues are not avoided because they are inextricably subjective. When reporting, care is taken to illuminate the subjectivity of data and interpretations.

Objection to a responsive approach is also expressed in the belief that the program staff, the funding agency, or the research community should specify the key questions. Their questions are worthy of study, but in program evaluation for public use, should never be used exclusively. There is a general expectation that if a program is evaluated, a wide array of important concerns will be considered. Embezzlement, racial discrimination, inconsistency in philosophy, and thwarting of creativity may be unmentioned in the contract, and barely in the evaluation specialist's range of view, but all such shortcomings belong to the evaluation expectation, and the responsive evaluator at least tries not to be blind to them.

Further it is recognized that evaluation studies are administratively prescribed not only to gain understanding and inform decision making but to legitimatize and protect administrative and program operations from criticism, especially during the evaluation period. And still further that evaluation requirements are sometimes made for the purpose of promulgating hoped-for standards.

By seeking out stakeholder issues, the responsive evaluator tries to see that these efforts at extending control over education are not undermining legitimate interests. Responsive evaluation is not intended as an instrument of reform, though reformists might find it useful. It is intended to serve the diverse people most affected personally and educationally by the program at hand—though it is bound to produce some findings they will not like.

## 3. Organizing and Reporting

The feedback from responsive evaluation studies is expected to be in forms and language attractive and comprehensible to the various groups. Thus, even at the expense of inequitable disclosure, different reports may be prepared for different groups. Portrayals and verbatim testimony will be appropriate for some, data banks and regression analyses for others. Obviously a budget will not allow everything, so these different communications need to be considered early in the work.

It is not uncommon for responsive evaluation feedback to occur early and throughout the evaluation period, particularly as a part of refining the list of issues to be pursued. The evaluator may ask, "Is this interesting?" and might, based on the answer, change the priorities of inquiry.

As analyzed by Ernest House (1980) responsive evaluation can be considered "intuitive" or indeed subjective, closer sometimes to literary criticism, Elliot Eisner's connoisseurship, or Michael Scriven's modus operandi evaluation than to the more traditional social science designs. But it differs from them in the most essential feature, that of emphasizing the issues, language, contexts, and standards of stakeholders.

When Stake proposed this "responsive evaluation" approach at an evaluation conference at the Pedagogical Institute in Göteborg, Sweden in 1974, he drew particularly upon the writings of Barry MacDonald, Malcolm Parlett, and David Hamilton, all stressing the necessity of organizing the evaluation of programs around what was happening in classrooms and boardrooms, drawing more attention to what educators were doing and less attention to what students were doing.

It is difficult to tell from an evaluation report whether or not the study itself was "responsive." A final report seldom reveals how issues were negotiated and how audiences were served. Three examples of studies which were clearly intentionally responsive were those of Stake et al. (1978), MacDonald (1975), and Murray et al. (1981).

### Bibliography

Eisner E W 1976 Educational connoisseurship and criticism: Their form and functions in educational evaluation. *J. Aesthetic Educ.* 10: 135–50
House E R 1980 *Evaluating with Validity.* Sage, Beverly Hills, California
MacDonald B 1975 *The Programme at Two: An UNCAL Companion to Two Years On.* Centre for Applied Research in Education, University of East Anglia, Norwich
Murray C A et al. 1981 *The National Evaluation of the Cities in Schools Program,* Final Report. American Institutes for Research, Washington, DC
Parlett M, Hamilton D 1976 Evaluation as illumination: A new approach to the study of innovatory programmes. In: Tawney D H (ed.) 1976 *Curriculum Evaluation Today: Trends and Implications.* Macmillan, London
Scriven M 1974 Evaluation perspectives and procedures. In: Popham W J (ed.) 1974 *Evaluation in Education: Current Applications.* McCutchan, Berkeley, California, p. 7
Stake R E 1980 Program evaluation, particularly responsive evaluation. In: Dockrell W B, Hamilton D (eds.) 1980 *Rethinking Educational Research.* Hodder and Stoughton, London
Stake R E, Easley J, Anastasiou K et al. 1978 *Case Studies in Science Education.* University of Illinois, Urbana, Illinois

# Adversary Evaluation

S. Clyne

Under Anglo–American law, decisions are reached by a jury or judge(s) after hearing opposing testimonies. Disputants or their representatives (lawyers) conduct their own search for evidence. They select, interview, and prepare witnesses to establish points in evidence. Other forms of evidence are introduced by means of witness testimony. Adversary procedures are usually framed by the opening and closing statements of the advocate and adversary lawyer. The testimony of witnesses is elicited by these lawyers in a quasinarrative manner. Testimony aims to attest to the facts of the case and to persuade judge(s) and jury. Extensive swaps of depositions and documents occur between adversaries to enable them to mount effective cross-examinations, which attempt to force witnesses into admissions that will hurt their case and to shake the faith of the judge(s) and jury in the other side's main testimony. In a debate format, evaluators may prepare and argue their cases independently and trust in their skills and expertise to engage in rebuttals.

Within the legal framework, issues are established by reference to definite legal standards and the relevance and admissibility of evidence is strictly determined by the judge(s) in accordance with accepted rules which also protect witnesses from unfair adversarial practices.

Social research paradigms establish what data are to count as facts and how they may be collected and reported. The scientific research model employs experiments or quasi-experiments to measure hypothesized relations between selected variables and by means of statistical techniques reports data in numerical form. Qualitative research models use such techniques as case studies, in-depth interviews, participant observation, and ethnography to allow an "explanation framework" or a "phenomenological understanding" to emerge in the words of the subjects themselves free from pre-existing expectations of researchers.

Decision making in complex social situations depends on comprehensive information about that situation's most salient variables and their interrelationships. Evaluations which combine both quantitative and qualitative data can best meet such needs and a few evaluation models, such as Stufflebeam's decision-making model and Provus's discrepancy model, can accommodate both kinds of data. The adversary approach suggested by Owens (1973) and Wolf (1975) permits such joint use and because of the planned opposition which it espouses, provides what amounts to two independent evaluations.

Adversary evaluation espouses the "fight theory" whereby opposing evaluators strive to win by producing better, that is, more persuasive evidence, and by the use of whatever legal or debating technique or technicalities may yield an advantage. The major advantage claimed for the adversary system is the cross-examination process which is presumed to keep "quantifiers" and "qualifiers" honest. Such a claim is based on the nature of human intelligence as the only research instrument capable of making sense of complex interrelated social variables and of converting them into the language of human testimony which any 12 people of "average ignorance" could be capable of understanding, as a true cross section of the community.

The presentation of at least two viewpoints or evaluations contributes to the elimination of the "yes-man" syndrome which can affect the expert prescribing for a client whose wishes he/she respects. The adversarial instincts of evaluators are presumed sufficient to uncover any hidden assumptions which can infect an opponent's empirical data or logic. The discord and tension inherent in adversarial evaluations, which fail to comply with the demands of Wolf's judicial evaluation model, may simply neutralize biases by balancing them and thus push the positive and negative arguments further apart, thereby anchoring the ends of the decision spectrum and ignoring the middle ground. The behaviour appropriate to adversarial evaluation must always be in doubt in a process or technique which espouses persuasion rather than conviction and which can tolerate data manipulation by omission rather than by commission.

Adversary evaluation depends on crucial human dynamics which are not, and may not be, quantifiable even if detected. The acceptance or rejection of a case can depend on many idiosyncratic factors such as personalities, prejudices, influence, fear, and so on. The weight to be accorded to quantitative versus qualitative data when they are translated into human testimony, which has been rendered palatable for a particular audience, is a matter for conjecture.

The treatment of those issues which are critical to the interests of concerned stakeholders depends on the professional integrity of the adversaries as educational evaluators even when the process itself seeks to rally partisan pressures. The potential of the adversary process to provide information must be sharply distinguished from its potential to produce change, and most importantly the right change. The process encourages the participation of nonprofessionals in education evaluation and conclusions can be reached for reasons other than those which the evidence supports. The limitations which time, personnel, and finances place on the presentation of evidence and analysis of data can seriously affect the quality of the case presentations and the nature of the verdicts passed on them. On the other hand, the opportunity provided for grass-root involvement by concerned constituents, and the popular notion that the adversary process with its extensive cross-examination facilities can afford competence its "day in court", add a popular dimension to decision making which the traditional evaluation methodology does not enjoy. "The touchstones of debate are polemics and persuasion—not truth which is central to the validity of evaluation studies" (Worthen and Owens 1978 p. 341).

The evidence submitted in adversary evaluation depends on the willingness of witnesses to speak in public about matters which they judge to be private or sensitive and can conflict with the public's right to know or the witnesses' right to be protected from public challenges to their credibility. The adversary process enjoys a potential to raise legitimate issues, close enough to the real-world context, and which can be balanced and qualified via cross-examination, so that any charge of propaganda is neutralized. This form of metaevaluation entitles the adversary process to be employed as a fairly useful approach to identify and report on the strengths and weaknesses of some programme or proposed course of action.

Courts judge not issues in general but rather focus on particular cases where the facts are more likely to be determined. The public may lack the sophistication required to distinguish between the appearance of "truth-discovery" and the presentation of varied opinions.

The adversary model affords no directions as to how or what issues should be selected or identified or how cases should be built or presented. Each side can build its own case and pass the other by on matters of major importance. The process makes no demand as to the allocation of time or personnel. It is indifferent as to the number of people engaged in the process or the time or money spent on it. It can only be a value judgment which decides what evidence or which witness to include or exclude, what cross-examination to undertake or forego. The crux of an adversary evaluation is dispute and the jurors or decision makers may in effect choose to ignore—indeed to defy—everything that has been told them. Adversaries can only present their own cases, they may not write the conclusions or calculate the statistical significances.

At least nine adversarial evaluations have occurred to date and a different approach was adopted in each (Worthen and Owens 1978). Each evaluation was conducted by evaluators who sought to impose the procedures of the scientific research method on a technique which synthesizes a number of approaches proper to legal and debating formats. The adversary model or process specifies no methodology to expedite any stage of its implementation and cannot be guaranteed to attend to crucial variables if it is dominated by the need to reach a verdict of success or failure about issues for which standards are notoriously lacking.

The decision audiences can be misled into believing that they have more reliable evidence than they have by the similarity which the process bears to the legal system. Key witnesses and materials cannot be subpoenaed for testimonial purposes and the evaluation may result in the revelation of a greater complexity of issues than was first imagined. The manner in which issues are framed is problematic because no adequate

standards exist in many areas of social science and a simple yes–no mode can obscure many legitimate options, apart from the indictment mentality which it betrays.

## Bibliography

Madaus G F 1982 The clarification hearing: A personal view of the process. *Educ. Res.* AERA 11: 4–11
Owens T R 1973 Educational evaluation by adversary proceeding. In: House E R (ed.) 1973 *School Evaluation: The Politics and Process.* McCutchan, Berkeley, California
Popham W J 1982 Melvin Belli, beware! *Educ. Res.* AERA 11: 5–15
Wolf R L 1975 Trial by jury: A new evaluation method: The process. *Phi Delta Kappan* 57: 185–87
Worthen B R, Owens T R 1978 Adversary evaluation and the school psychologist. *J. Sch. Psychol.* 16(4): 334–45

# Judicial Evaluation

## R. L. Wolf

The judicial evaluation model was conceptualized in the early 1970s as a method which would adopt and adapt procedures from both court proceedings and administrative hearings in the field of law so as to help educational decision makers appreciate the complexity of their programs and base their decisions on a full and complete presentation of available information through the interpretation of two distinct and opposing viewpoints. The politicalization of evaluation, the increased legitimization of subjective forms of evaluation evidence, and the sensitization towards consumer participation in policy formulation suggested that evaluation inquiry could no longer rely exclusively on conventional social science or behavioral research paradigms. The judicial evaluation model was not designed to replicate legal procedures, but rather to use the law to guide more "judicious" evaluation practice. Concepts such as fact finding, human testimony, cross-examination, case preparation, evidentiary rules and procedures, discovery, and structured deliberations were all borrowed from the legal system and modified for evaluation purposes. The intention was to create a process whereby attention could be given to a broad range of educational evidence (both quantitative and qualitative) in a manner that would be educative and instructive to decision makers as well as comprehensible and responsive to the public at large.

The judicial evaluation model was never intended to be a debate between two evaluators with "victory" or persuasion as the desired outcome. It is for this reason that the model has remained separate from adversary evaluation. While the two approaches share a common interest in the legal paradigm, particularly the idea of presenting opposing arguments to a decision-making group, the adversary evaluation approach has ignored

the most compelling aspects of the judicial evaluation model, namely the testimony and cross-examination of witnesses and the structured deliberations of a jury panel. Whereas adversary evaluation is concerned with producing a verdict of success or failure, the judicial evaluation model is aimed at promoting broad program understanding, clarifying the subtle and complex nature of the educational issues in question, and producing recommendations and policy guidelines that lead to institutional growth and/or improved practice.

The judicial evaluation model has been implemented in a wide variety of educational contexts since the early 1970s and a considerable amount of formative evaluation and disciplined research have been applied to it. These inquiry efforts have resulted in an operational framework which defines stages and roles necessary for successful utilization of the judicial evaluation model.

## 1. Implementation Stages

### 1.1 Stage 1—Issue Generation

This stage is the exploratory phase of the inquiry designed to identify as broad a range of issues as possible. A pool of issues emerges out of the content of interviews, through direct observations, and source documents. These preliminary data help to shape the course of inquiry through succeeding stages.

### 1.2 Stage 2—Issue Selection

During this stage the array of issues pooled is reduced to a manageable size for the ultimate public presentation. Issue selection is sensitive to the audience's information needs and involves delineation of the most salient issues.

Extensive analysis of a full range of issues occurs as does a critique of logical inferences relevant to the substantiation of those issues. Because aspects of issues may change over time, frequent analysis for relevance and interpretation is essential.

### 1.3 Stage 3—Preparation of Arguments

This stage involves building cases and preparing final arguments for case presentation. Specific points of contention are developed around each issue so that case presenters may pose distinctively different perspectives. At this juncture, witnesses are selected and reinterviewed relative to their anticipated testimony. Documents and transcripts are analyzed to refine lines of arguments and to develop evidence for the hearings. It is to be noted that arguments are not designed to provoke confrontation. The aim is that each side be given the opportunity to present opposing views thus providing differing perspectives on complex issues.

### 1.4 Stage 4—The Clarification Forum

In this final stage of the inquiry a public presentation of the data is made. The format of the hearings approximates that of a court of law. A panel comprised of policy makers, citizens, and so on, is convened to hear the evidence. Case presenters make their cases through witnesses selected to represent their views relative to a given issue. Direct examination, cross-examination, re-direct examination, and re-cross-examination of all witnesses are employed. And, as in a court of law, opening and closing arguments are presented. Based on the evidence presented, the panel deliberates and makes its recommendations.

## 2. Key Roles

### 2.1 Investigative Teams

Each issue to be "adjudicated" is investigated by two teams directed to explore the different perspectives on a particular issue. The duties of each team include identifying potential witnesses, and conducting in-depth interviews, preparing narrative syntheses for all interviews, and identifying documents, artifacts, and other evidence. Essentially, the teams are responsible for building comprehensive cases and for developing challenges to the case proposed by the other team.

### 2.2 Case Analyst

This person serves as the investigative team supervisor and is responsible for overseeing all activities of a given team. Specifically, the case analyst identifies and screens potential witnesses, conducts in-depth interviews, debriefs team members, and presents interim reports on the procedural and substantive status of interviews and arguments. Analysts continually interact with each other to share information and plan for the clarification forum.

### 2.3 Case Presenter

Case presenters have the responsibility of making the actual arguments at the clarification forum. In the form and style of "attorneys for the prosecution" and "attorneys for the defense," case presenters argue the different positions on any given issue. Arguments are made through the testimony of witnesses and in opening and closing statements. Skillful direct examination and cross-examination of witnesses is critical in this public presentation of the data.

### 2.4 Forum Moderator

The forum moderator enforces the rules of evidence and procedure and directs the scheduled flow of events as the forum proceeds. The moderator also assists the clarification panel to judge the adequacy of the evidence presented and clarifies points of contention. The moderator rules on objections during the course of witness examination and also instructs the panel as to how to weigh evidence and how to structure its deliberations.

### 2.5 Clarification Panel

The clarification panel is composed of persons interested in and perhaps experienced in the particular policy question under consideration, but not necessarily responsible for its formulation and/or implementation. The composition of the panel varies, but it is likely to represent groups such as school personnel, parents, advocacy groups, state and federal educational agencies, and the like. The panel is charged with considering the evidence presented. They are afforded the opportunity to ask questions of the witnesses for purposes of clarification during the course of the public proceedings. Upon completion of their deliberations, the panel presents a written statement of their recommendations. The deliberation period is not public, although a stenographer may record the session to capture the essence of what is being said. However, all statements remain anonymous.

### 2.6 Panel Facilitator

The panel facilitator is a person familiar with the judicial approach who helps the panel meet its responsibilities. The role involves clarifying points of confusion during the deliberation session and helping the panel weigh evidence. In essence, the role is an extension of the forum moderator's function and is provided exclusively for the clarification panel.

Each stage of the judicial evaluation model is governed by both methodological requirements and prescribed rules. Persons assuming responsibility for each major role in the implementation process share input in determining these rules, particularly rules of evidence and rules of procedure. While these rules have remained consistent and stable over different applications of the model they are subject to some modification given the particular use of the model. Originally, the model was envisioned as a summative evaluation tool. However, the judicial evaluation model has since been used for formative evaluation, policy review and analysis, local educational decision making, and national policy formulation. Specific examples of each type of use can be found elsewhere (Wolf 1975, Owens and Hiscox 1977, Wolf 1980).

Through extensive utilization and careful scrutiny the judicial evaluation model's major strengths and weaknesses have been revealed. In essence, the model's major strengths concern its comprehensiveness in design, the breadth, depth, and quality of evidence required, bias control through cross-examination and alternative viewpoint presentations, built-in meta-evaluation mechanisms, responsiveness and relevancy of issues, effective communication to lay publics, and increased potential for evaluation utilization through public clarification and dissemination.

Weaknesses relate to the difficulty in formulating issues in a manner fair to both sides, the selection of an impartial jury, the possible imbalance in the two cases presentations and the differences in oratory skills of the two case presenters, the sometimes lack of specificity revealed through direct and cross-examination procedures, the contrived nature of the hearing due to time restrictions, and the cost and effort involved in case preparation.

Overall, the judicial evaluation model has contributed to the discipline of evaluation by introducing a new way to conceptualize substantive issues and methodological strategies. The model has combined the rigors of intensive field investigation with the public display of a wide range of evaluation evidence. Thus, the model has served as a means of collecting and disseminating information to guide public policy in a manner responsive to educators, decision makers, and citizens alike. Ongoing research about the judicial evaluation model will continue to stimulate new and innovative uses for this unique evaluation approach.

## Bibliography

Owens T R 1973 Educational evaluation by adversary proceeding. In: House E (ed.) 1973 *School Evaluation: The Politics and Process.* McCutchen, Berkeley, California

Owens T R, Hiscox M D 1977 Alternative models for adversary evaluation: Variations on a theme. Paper presented at the Annual Meeting of the American Educational Research Association, New York City, April, 1977. *AERA*, Washington, DC

Popham W J, Carlson D 1977 Deep dark deficits of the adversary evaluation model. *Educ. Res. AERA* 6: 3–6

Thurston P 1978 Revitalizing adversary evaluation: Deep dark deficits or muddled mistaken musings. *Educ. Res. AERA* 7: 3–8

Wolf R L 1973 The application of select legal concepts to educational evaluation. (Doctoral dissertation, University of Illinois) *Dissertation Abstracts International* 1974, 35: 2068A (University Microfilms No. 74–14, 644)

Wolf R L 1975 Trial by jury: A new evaluation method. *Phi Delta Kappan* 57: 185–87

Wolf R L 1979 The use of judicial evaluation methods in the formulation of educational policy. *Educ. Eval. Policy Anal.* 1(3): 19–28

Wolf R L 1980 *Judicial Evaluation: Past, Present, and Future Applications.* Commissioned Monograph, National Institute of Education, Washington, DC

# Delphi Technique

### N. P. Uhl

The Delphi technique, named after the oracle at Delphi in ancient Greece, is a communications process which permits a group to achieve consensus in the solution of a complex problem without face-to-face interaction or confrontation by the individual members of the group. By eliminating face-to-face interaction, this process avoids such problems as the influence of dominant individuals on group decisions, the loss of time and energy on irrelevant or biased discussions, the distortion of individual judgment by group pressure, the inclination to reject novel ideas, and the tendency to defend a previous position. At the same time, it assures independent thought, anonymity, and the assessment without pressure of the ideas of others in the gradual formation of a considered opinion.

In general, the procedure is as follows: (a) participants are chosen and are asked to give anonymous opinions, suggestions, recommendations, or predictions (depending on the topic) to a series of questionnaire items; (b) each participant receives feedback, such as the median response of all participants, and a second round of responding begins in order to ascertain the intensity of agreement or disagreement with the group median response; (c) again feedback is given to the participants in terms of the group median and also the reasons why some participants do not agree with the median response; (d) after reviewing the reasons for the minority opinions, the participants again respond; (e) steps (c) and (d) can be repeated although convergence of opinion usually does not increase greatly after one round of these two steps. A detailed chronological description of how these five steps were employed in an actual study can be found in Uhl's (1971) investigation of institutional goals using the Delphi technique. It is interesting to note that while most studies incorporating the Delphi technique have used questionnaires, a few studies have adopted the technique for computer use which permits participants to respond through separate terminals. Linstone and Turoff (1975), in the most recent compendium of Delphi studies, describe such a study.

The Delphi technique was originally developed by

the Rand Corporation in the 1950s to deal with complex defense problems and since the mid-1960s its use has expanded at a prolific rate. It is being used by business, government, industry, medicine, regional planning, and education in a wide variety of situations including futures forecasting, goal assessment, curriculum planning, establishment of budget priorities, estimates concerning the quality of life, policy formulation, as well as problem identification and formulation of solutions. While the Delphi technique was considered primarily a forecasting tool in its earlier uses, it is currently being utilized more and more as a process to improve communications and generate consensus in the solution to almost any type of complex problem.

The use of the Delphi may be warranted if any or all of the following conditions exist: (a) the resolution of a problem can be facilitated by the collective judgments of one or more groups; (b) those groups providing judgments are not likely to communicate adequately without an intervening process; (c) the solution is more likely to be accepted if more people are involved in its development than would be possible in a face-to-face meeting; (d) frequent group meetings are not practical because of time, distance, etc.; and (e) one or more groups of participants are more dominant than another.

It is surprising that of all the studies performed using the Delphi technique, very few are of a methodological nature. As a result, Delphi has a poor theoretical base and little is known about the variables that affect the process. This lack of a theoretical framework is its main weakness. A systematic research program is needed to determine how and why the method functions.

## Bibliography

Linstone H, Turoff M (eds.) 1975 *The Delphi Method: Techniques and Applications.* Addison-Wesley, Reading, Massachusetts

Uhl N P 1971 *Identifying Institutional Goals: Encouraging Convergence of Opinion Through the Delphi Technique*, Research Monograph No. 2. National Laboratory for Higher Education, Durham, North Carolina

**Part 2**

# Conduct of and Issues in Evaluation Studies

# Part 2

# Conduct of and Issues in Evaluation Studies

---

## Introduction

The second Part of the *Encyclopedia* addresses some of the major issues of concern to evaluators. The four articles in the first section discuss some of the Normative Dimensions of Evaluation Practice, which cut across all of the evaluation approaches reviewed in Part 1. These are followed by a section comprised of ten articles that take up Issues in Test Use and Interpretation. Tests, surveys, and questionnaires are a mainstay of traditional educational evaluation approaches, and can serve as valuable adjuncts even with more naturalistically oriented approaches to evaluation inquiry. Thus, issues pertaining to test use and interpretation should be of practical concern to nearly all evaluators in educational settings. The final section of Part 2 turns to the collection, use, and interpretation of other forms of evaluation data.

The first section, Normative Dimensions of Evaluation Practice, begins with an article discussing the *Role of the Evaluator* as a function of the definition, functions, and object of the evaluation. A goal-based definition of evaluation may entail an evaluator role much like that of a comptroller or auditor, whereas a less judgmental, more descriptive definition of evaluation may cast the evaluator as "public scientist," or educator. The evaluator's role will also vary according to the salience of formative and summative evaluation functions, as well as administrative and "socio-political" functions. (Socio-political functions include motivating desired behavior or drawing attention to a program.) The objects evaluated will also influence the evaluator's role. An evaluator of curricula, for example, will be called on to interact with different groups of stakeholders and to address different kinds of concerns to an evaluator of educational institutions and organizations. In addition to these dimensions, the evaluator's role may refer to his or her status within an organization. Internal evaluators, who must report their findings to their own superiors, may have both opportunities and constraints not shared by external evaluators, who are substantially independent of the entity evaluated.

Regardless of evaluation approach or evaluator role, evaluation may at times involve the collection and interpretation of information that is threatening or unflattering to other persons. The second article in this section, on the *Ethics of Evaluation Studies*, addresses the problem of checking the "natural inclinations" of evaluators that may injure the interests of another person. Several codes of ethics have been written for evaluators, which help to develop and elaborate this basic concern. These address such specific issues as obtaining informed consent from study participants, recognizing the risk of exposing subjects to a loss of self esteem, respect for privacy, and the ethical dimensions of withholding or deferring benefits from one group to better judge their efficacy for another group of recipients. In the evaluation context, a formal, written agreement between the client and the evaluator can provide important protections and safeguards for both parties, and help to avoid later difficulties.

The third article in this section complements the previous, general discussion of codes of ethics with a review of the *Professional Standards for Educational Evaluation*. This document, issued in 1981, includes a total of thirty brief discussions of issues under the rubrics of utility, feasibility, propriety, and accuracy. The article in this section discusses the history of the Standards, including the perceived needs that gave rise to them, and the committee charged with their development then turns to the utility of the Standards, including their value as an exemplar for standards development efforts in different countries.

Considerations of the normative dimensions of evaluation lead naturally to concerns for *Impact of Evaluation Studies*, which is the focus of the fourth article in this section. Impact includes both the planned, purposive application of evaluation information (evaluation use) and other consequences of an evaluation that may be quite unintended. The first category of impacts addressed in this article arise from the application of the information generated by an evaluation. These include not only direct influences on decision making, but also changes in the program or policy evaluated, and changes in attitudes and beliefs. A second category includes impacts of the process of evaluation, such as the diversion of resources from other purposes, and changes in patterns of communication among program participants. The measurement of these and other program impacts is difficult, costly, and unreliable, and while a body of theory on factors explaining evaluation impact has emerged, studies of evaluation impact have not as yet produced a coherent and balanced picture of impacts in general. By considering an organization's patterns of decision making and the perceived information needs of administrators or policy makers, an evaluator may be able to plan and deliver a study that is more likely to be used productively.

The first two articles in the second section, Issues in Test Use and Interpretation, concern norm-referenced and criterion-referenced measurement. These terms refer to two fundamentally different modes of test interpretation. In the area of achievement testing, they have given rise to different methods of content sampling, test development and validation, and reporting. Norm-referencing refers to the interpretation of a test score relative to the distribution of scores for some appropriate reference group, or norming sample. Interpretations in terms of percentiles, quartiles, stanines, normal curve equivalents, grade equivalents, and related statistics are all norm-referenced. Criterion-referencing refers to the interpretation of a test score as indicating directly what an examinee knows or can do. One common form of criterion-referenced interpretation is mastery testing, in which each examinee's score is interpreted in relation to a passing or cutting score, and a pass/fail or master/nonmaster decision is reached. In this section of the *Encyclopedia*, these two interpretive frameworks are discussed and compared, and many of their typical applications are cited. Both norm-referenced and criterion-referenced tests are important tools for the educational evaluator.

Evaluators must not only select tests and interpret testing outcomes, but must also attend to the actual test administration. A variety of issues surrounding this subject are set forth in the next article, *Test Administration*. Test Administration issues are framed in terms of the purposes of testing and the meaning and importance of standardization in particular situations. Among the topics that may be of concern are administration parameters established by the test developer (e.g., time limits), examiner preparation, the physical setting in which the testing is carried out, the emotional climate of the testing, including the state of mind of the examinee, presenting the test (e.g., choosing between group and individual testing, and assuring that examinees understand what they are to do), and finally, a full reporting and appropriate consideration of any unusual features of the administration at the time when tests are scored and interpreted.

A test is designed and used in order to learn about specific areas of knowledge, skills, or dispositions, but performance on the test may also reflect dimensions that it was not intended to measure. The next six articles in this section all deal with such unintended influences on scores, beginning with an article on *Coaching for Tests and Examinations*.

Concern over the effects of coaching appears to be nearly as old as testing itself, but if coaching succeeds in improving the underlying skills a test is intended to measure, then it may have no untoward effect. The potentially unfair advantages conferred by coaching may be minimized by assuring that all examinees are familiar in advance with the instructions, item types, and test format they are to encounter, and that they are as comfortable as possible in the testing situation. Coaching becomes more problematic when it is aimed not at improving the underlying skills to be measured, but at test-wiseness. As the following article, *Test-wiseness* indicates, whether due to coaching or not, test-wiseness may enable some examinees to earn higher scores than their knowledge and skills alone would permit. Test–wiseness concerns arise most frequently in connection with multiple-choice testing. Its effect can be minimized by careful test development and revision, following sound item writing practices. In contrast to the effects of coaching and test-wiseness, *Student Evaluation and Examination Anxiety*, the subject of the following article, can depress the scores of examinees affected. Student evaluation and examination anxiety has been studied in the context of more generalized academic anxiety, and has been related to the assessment method chosen and other factors. Although moderate anxiety may actually facilitate performance, there is clear evidence that excessive anxiety can interfere with performance, sometimes seriously. The article discusses steps that can be taken to minimize the likelihood of such negative effects.

Coaching, test-wiseness, and test-anxiety are each specific sources of unintended variation in test performance. In contrast, test bias and item bias are no more than evidence of unintended systematic variation, usually from an unknown source. Concern over *Test Bias*, the subject of the next article, usually arises in the context of testing for selection of prediction, when it is found that some identified groups, a racial/ethnic minority, for example, appears to be affected adversely by the use of test. In education, contexts where test bias is a concern include admissions testing, special educational placements, competency testing (e.g., for high-school graduation), evaluation of compensatory programs (where test bias may be thought to diminish the measured program effect), and career counseling (where gender bias in interest inventories may perpetuate sex role stereotypes). The detection and analysis of test bias often involves relating test performance to some external indicator of success in the situation for which the test was intended to predict.

Item bias and test bias would appear to be closely related concerns, but the literatures on these two topics are quite distinct. Item bias studies begin with a classification of examinees into groups, and employ various empirical methods to determine whether group differences on some particular items are significantly larger or smaller than would be expected based on the pattern of differences across the remaining items. The article on *Item Bias* surveys a variety of statistical techniques for measuring item bias, then turns to recently developed approaches such as the Mantel–Haenszel statistic and log-linear or logit models. The article concludes with a cautionary note, calling for more attention to the substantive questions of what constitutes item bias, and why particular items are biased. Research directed solely toward the refinement of statistical methods for item bias detection will not illuminate these concerns.

Educational researchers and evaluators have identified a number of additional effects on test scores and other outcome measures which are discussed in the next article, *Unintended Effects in Educational Research*. Educational programs and policies may cause unintended outcomes or side effects. In cases where either intended outcomes or side effects do not become apparent for some time after the treatment occurs, they are termed *after effects* (also called delayed or sleeper effects). In addition, the evaluation itself (as opposed to the implemented program or policy) may engender effects of different kinds. These include reactive effects of measurement, in which the measurement itself affects the behavior measured; the Hawthorne effect and the John Henry effect, in which the groups being tested or the control groups, respectively, exert extra effort; and the Pygmalion effect and the Golem effect, in which positive or negative teacher expectations influence individual learner outcomes.

Decisions about what tests to use in an evaluation must be made in the light of the intended methods of interpretation, practical constraints on test administration conditions, and the relevance and import of threats to validity like coaching, test wiseness, test-taking anxiety, test and item bias, and so forth. Having considered these factors, the evaluator may turn to the final article in this section, on *Guide to Sources and Reviews of Tests*. This article lists nine categories of information to consider in test selection, and then lists major test publishers in the United States, Europe, and elsewhere. Also described are reference works and information retrieval services providing more detailed information on available published tests.

As important as written tests are in evaluation, they by no means exhaust the information sources typically employed. The last section in Part 2 turns from written objective tests to Issues Affecting Sources of Evaluation Evidence. The first article looks at *Handwriting Legibility*, which becomes an issue not only when informants in an evaluation setting respond in writing, but also when observers take written field notes of any kind. This is followed by a consideration of self-report measures—a broad category of approaches used to elicit information about internal processes, about probable behavior in hypothetical situations, and about prior events. The article on *Self-report* reviews the arguments for and against their validity, and describes the sorts of applications in which self-reports are most likely to provide useful data. The final article, *Interviewing*, examines the nature of interviewer skills. Focusing primarily on interviewing technique in clinical situations, the article discusses several alternative theoretical bases for conducting interviews and making use of their findings.

# Normative Dimensions of Evaluation Practice

## Role of the Evaluator

### D. Nevo

The role of an evaluator depends on the way evaluation is being perceived, the purposes it is expected to serve, and the "things" which are the objects of the evaluation. Thus, the role of the evaluator can be understood through a consideration of three aspects: (a) the definition of evaluation, (b) the functions of evaluation, and (c) the objects of evaluation.

### 1. The Definition of Evaluation

Many definitions of evaluation can be found in the literature. They can be summarized here in three major groups. The first group includes the goal-based definitions of evaluation following the definition suggested by Ralph Tyler who defined evaluation as "the process of determining to what extent the educational objectives are actually being realized" (Tyler 1950 p. 69). The second group includes the nonjudgmental descriptive definitions of evaluation. They perceive evaluation as providing information for decision making (e.g., Stufflebeam et al. 1971), or as a systematic examination of educational or social programs (Cronbach et al. 1980). A third group of definitions—the judgmental definitions—point to the judgmental nature of evaluation and define it as the assessment of merit or worth (Scriven 1967, House 1980, Joint Committee 1981) or as a combination of both description and judgment (Guba and Lincoln 1981).

Those various definitions present a very broad view of evaluation which would include assessment, measurement, and testing as parts of evaluation and as terms having a narrower meaning than the term evaluation. Obviously, the various definitions of evaluations imply different perceptions for the nature of the role of the evaluator. The goal-based definitions of evaluation suggest for the role of the evaluator the nature of a controller, a comptroller, or an audit, who direct their efforts to determine the extent that institutional goals are being achieved and approved plans are being carried out. The nonjudgmental descriptive definitions of evaluation suggest an evaluator with the nature of an intelligence officer, a public scientist, or an educator whose roles are to inform their audiences regarding issues and concerns at stake and deepen the audience understanding

of those issues and concerns. The judgmental definitions of evaluation call for an evaluator with the nature of a judge, a referee, or an art critic.

### 2. The Functions of Evaluation

Evaluations are initiated for many purposes and functions, sometimes conflicting ones. Scriven (1967) coined the terms "formative evaluation" and "summative evaluation" referring to two major functions of evaluation. In its formative function, evaluation is used for the improvement and development of an ongoing activity (or program, person, product, etc.). In its summative function, evaluation is used for accountability, certification, or selection.

A third function of evaluation, which has been less often treated by evaluation literature (Cronbach et al. 1980), should also be considered. This is the psychological or sociopolitical function of evaluation. In many cases it is apparent that evaluation is not serving any formative purposes nor is it being used for accountability or other summative purposes. However, it is being used to increase awareness of special activities, motivate desired behavior of evaluees, or promote public relations. Regardless of personal feelings about the use (or misuse) of evaluation for this purpose, it cannot be ignored.

Another somewhat "unpopular" function of evaluation is its use for the exercise of authority. In a formal organization it is the privilege of the superior to evaluate his or her subordinates and not vice versa. In many cases a person in a management position might evaluate someone to demonstrate his or her authority over that person. This may be referred to as the "administrative" function of evaluation.

To summarize, evaluation can serve many functions: (a) the formative function—for improvement, (b) the summative function—for selection, certification, or accountability, (c) the psychological or sociopolitical function—for motivation, to increase awareness, and (d) the administrative function—to exercise authority. An evaluator may be called in to serve any one of those functions and his/her role will be shaped accordingly.

## 3. The Objects of Evaluation

Students and teachers have always been popular objects of evaluation in education. Almost all of the measurement and evaluation literature in education up to the mid-1960s dealt with the evaluation of students' learning. Up to that time it was very difficult to find any substantial guidance regarding the evaluation of other objects such as educational projects, programs, curricular materials, or educational institutions, although data on students' achievements have often been used to make decisions regarding curricula, educational projects, or educational institutions. Various developments in the educational system of the United States (e.g., the Elementary and Secondary Education Act of 1965) led to a significant shift of focus regarding the objects of educational evaluation from students to projects, programs, and instructional materials, which have since then been most common in the writings of the major authors in the evaluation literature in education. Sometimes distinctions were made between the assessment of students and school personnel and the evaluation of educational projects, programs, or curricula. Such distinctions were followed by suggested procedures for the conduct of assessment or evaluation of various objects.

From a review of the contemporary evaluation literature it seems to be evident that almost everything can be an object of evaluation (e.g. Lewy and Nevo 1981) and evaluation should not be limited to the evaluation of students or school personnel. Typical evaluation objects suggested by evaluation literature and evaluation practice in education are as follows: (a) students, (b) school personnel (teachers and administrators), (c) curricula and instructional materials, (d) educational programs and projects, and (e) educational institutions and organizations. Teachers and school psychologists are typical examples of student evaluators. Teachers and school administrators are usually evaluated by their superiors or in some cases by professional evaluators. The evaluation of curricula and instructional materials has become since the early 1960s a prominent specialization among evaluation specialists. Another widely spread specialization among evaluators is program and project evaluation (Stufflebeam et al. 1971, Cronbach et al. 1980, Guba and Lincoln 1981). The evaluation of educational institutions has been demonstrated for a long period by various evaluation practices used for the accreditation of secondary schools, colleges, and universities in the United States.

## 4. Many Roles for the Evaluator

The perception (definition) of evaluation, its functions, and its objects are three independent dimensions which determine the role of the evaluator, although some perceptions of evaluation might be more appropriate than others to serve a certain function of evaluation. For example, the nonjudgmental descriptive approach might be more appropriate for the conduct of formative evaluation rather than the judgmental approach, although both approaches are legitimate for formative as well as for summative evaluation. Considering three types of definitions (goal-based, descriptive, and judgmental), four functions of evaluation (formative, summative, psychological, and administrative), and five kinds of evaluation objects (students, school personnel, curricula, projects, and institutions) will result in a three-dimensional classification of a wide range of up to 60 different roles of an evaluator. He or she may be a goal-based formative evaluator of students, whose role is to determine the extent that students are achieving the educational objectives to help them improve their performance at school. He or she can be a nonjudgmental formative curriculum evaluator assisting a curriculum project to improve its instructional materials, or a nonjudgmental summative evaluator gathering information about several instructional packages to help a school district choose the one most appropriate for its needs. Both of them can be part of a judgmental teacher evaluation team whose function is to motivate teachers by letting them know that their work at school is being evaluated. They can also be a goal-based evaluation team of secondary schools in a developing country hired by the central ministry of education to demonstrate its authority over the local schools. These are only some examples of the wide variety of roles an evaluator has to assume according to his or her perception of evaluation, the function the evaluation is expected to serve, and the object of the evaluation.

According to their roles, evaluators are expected to choose methods of inquiry appropriate for answering particular evaluation questions. However, their work cannot be limited to the technical activities of data collection and analysis. Although there seems to be no agreement among evaluation experts regarding the "best" process to follow when conducting an evaluation, most of them would agree that all evaluations should include a certain amount of interaction between evaluators and their audiences at the outset of the evaluation, to identify evaluation needs, and at its conclusion, to communicate its findings.

The status of evaluators within the administrative structure of the organizations in which they function, defining their authority and responsibility, should also be determined according to their roles. The evaluation literature suggests a distinction between an internal evaluator and an external evaluator. Internal evaluators of a project are usually employed by the project and report directly to its management. Obviously, their objectivity as well as their external credibility might be lower than those of external evaluators who are not employed directly by the evaluated project and who will enjoy a higher degree of independence. At the same time, the internal evaluator is usually less perceived as a threat to the project and has a better chance to develop rapport with its team. To a certain degree both types of evaluators may serve similar functions. The external independent expert can serve not only the summative function of evaluating the project, but also provide invaluable feedback to the project team to improve its ongoing activities. The internal evaluator, who is a member of the project team, can not only serve the formative function of evaluation for the project, but also provide valuable information to demonstrate the merit of the project to funding agencies or other external audiences. However, it seems to be clear that an internal evaluator will be preferred when a formative evaluation is considered, and an external evaluator will be preferred when a summative evaluation is required. A combination of both types for one single object is strongly recommended whenever feasible.

## Bibliography

Cronbach L J, Ambron S R, Dornbusch S M, Hess R D, Hornik R C, Phillips D C, Walker D E, Weiner S S 1980 *Toward Reform of Program Evaluation*. Jossey-Bass, San Francisco, California

Guba E G, Lincoln Y S 1981 *Effective Evaluation*. Jossey-Bass, San Francisco, California

House E R 1980 *Evaluating with Validity*. Sage, Beverly Hills, California

Joint Committee on Standards for Educational Evaluation 1981 *Standards for Evaluations of Educational Programs, Projects and Materials*. McGraw-Hill, New York

Lewy A, Nevo D (eds.) 1981 *Evaluation Roles in Education*. Gordon and Breach, New York

Scriven M 1967 The methodology of evaluation. In: Stake R E (ed.) 1967 *Curriculum Evaluation*. American Educational Research Association (AERA) Monograph Series on Evaluation, No. 1. Rand McNally, Chicago, Illinois

Stufflebeam D L, Foley W J, Gephart W J, Guba E G, Hammond R L, Merriman H O, Provus M M 1971 *Educational Evaluation and Decision-making*. Peacock, Itasca, Illinois

Tyler R W 1950 *Basic Principles of Curriculum and Instruction*. University of Chicago Press, Chicago, Illinois

# Ethics of Evaluation Studies

## E. R. House

Ethics are the rules or standards of right conduct or practice, especially the standards of a profession. What ethical standards have been proposed for the conduct of educational evaluation? What general principles underlie standards? Are these standards and principles sufficient to ensure an ethical practice? These are the questions this article will address. The extent to which evaluation studies actually meet these ethical standards is not addressed here, except by implication.

The ethics of evaluation studies are a subset of ethics or morality in general but, of course, ethics applied to much narrower problems than those of general morality. "In the narrow sense, a morality is a system of a particular sort of constraints on conduct—ones whose central task is to protect the interests of persons other than the agent and which present themselves to an agent as checks on his natural inclinations or spontaneous tendencies to act" (Mackie 1977 p. 106).

Thus the task of an ethics of evaluation is to check the "natural inclinations" of evaluators that may injure the interests of another person, a task made all the more formidable by the fact that these inclinations may be unconscious, built into the very techniques and methods employed by the evaluator. Given the relative power of the evaluator over those evaluated, the ethics of evaluation are critical to the establishment of a responsible evaluation practice.

According to Sieber,

If there were a field of applied ethics for program evaluation, that field would study how to choose morally right actions and maximize the value of one's work in program evaluation. It would examine the kinds of dilemmas that arise in program evaluation; it would establish guidelines for anticipating and resolving certain ethical problems and encompass a subarea of scientific methodology for performing evaluation that satisfies both scientific and ethical requirements; and it would consider ways to promote ethical character in program evaluators (Sieber 1980 p. 52).

There is yet another requirement for an ethics of evaluation: it must be rationally persuasive to evaluators. It seems reasonable to treat evaluators themselves as moral persons. "Thus to respect another as a moral person is to try to understand his aims and interests from his standpoint and try to present him with considerations that enable him to accept the constraints on his conduct" (Rawls 1971 p. 338).

Recently several codes of ethics and standards of practice have been proposed for educational evaluation in particular and for social science research in general. Many of these rules and standards are methodological directives but some are concerned with ethical behavior. For example, in the most elaborate and widely disseminated set of standards, there are four areas of concern—utility, accuracy, feasibility, and propriety. Under propriety the standards are formal obligations, conflict of interest, full and frank disclosure, the public's right to know, rights of human subjects, human interactions, balanced reporting, and fiscal responsibility. These standards relate mostly to privacy, protection of human subjects, and freedom of information. Generally the picture that emerges is that the evaluator should forge a written contract with the sponsor and adhere to that contract. He or she should beware of conflicts of interest in which the evaluator's personal interests are somehow involved. Openness, full disclosure, and release of information are the main ways of dealing with these problems. The limitations on full disclosure are the commonly understood rights of subjects. Ordinarily this means informed consent of the subjects must be obtained. There is also a call for respecting others who are engaged in the evaluation itself, a general admonition to decency.

Anderson and Ball (1978) have compiled a list of ethical responsibilities for the evaluator, as well as a list of ethical obligations for the commissioner of the evaluation. The evaluator is expected to acquaint the sponsor with the evaluator's orientation and values, develop a contract with the sponsor, fulfill the terms of the contract, adhere to privacy and informed consent standards, acquaint the sponsor with unsound program practices, present a balanced report, make the results available to legitimate audiences, allow for other professionals to examine the procedures and data, and publish rejoinders to misinterpretations of the evaluation results. The commissioner of the evaluation has obligations to cooperate in the various tasks of the evaluation. To the degree that they deal with ethics at all, other formal codes of ethics and standards suggest similar ethical principles and sets of problems. Mutual agreement of the evaluator and sponsor is emphasized in most codes.

Ethical issues also emerge from the use of particular techniques in designs, such as the use of control groups. For example, two ethical issues that are of concern in use of control groups are the potential for denying a valuable service to eligible clients who might not be chosen for the beneficial treatment and the equitable allocation of scarce resources to a large group of eligible recipients. Acceptance of the clients as equals is one proposed way of dealing with these problems, and multiple treatment groups is another.

A review of the literature suggests four basic ethical problems: (a) withholding the nature of the evaluation research from participants or involving them without their knowledge; (b) exposing participants to acts which would harm them or diminish their self-esteem; (c) invading the privacy of participants; and (d) withholding benefits from participants. These are all intrusions against the individual's person somehow, or infringements against personal rights.

What principles underlie these ethical concerns? The National Commission for the Protection of Human Subjects of Biomedical and Behavioral Research has identified three underlying principles—beneficence, respect, and justice. Beneficence means avoiding unnecessary harm and maximizing good outcomes. In the opinion of the commission this principle is served by the research or evaluation being valid, by evaluators being competent, by the participants being informed, by the results being disseminated, and by the consequences of the evaluation being weighed with others. The evaluation is supposed to be beneficial.

Respect means respecting the autonomy of others by reducing the power differential between the evaluator and participants, having participants volunteer, inform-

ing participants, and giving participants a choice in matters that affect them. Justice, in the commission's view, means equitable treatment and representation of subgroups within society. Justice is operationally defined by equitable design and measurement, and equitable access to data for reanalysis. These three principles constitute the rationale for ethical human research, including evaluation.

For the most part these ethical codes concentrate upon infringements to personal rights. The codes assume that there are inherent individual rights prior to the conduct of the evaluation, that the participants must be accorded these rights, and that the individual must voluntarily agree to participation. Almost all these codes of ethics require that the evaluator enter into a contractual agreement with the sponsor and adhere to the agreement as a matter of ethics. Not adhering to the agreement would be considered unfair. Those who are not a party to the agreement have certain personal rights, such as the rights to be informed about the study and the right to volunteer.

Fairness suggests that people are obligated to uphold their part of an agreement when they have voluntarily accepted the benefits of an arrangement or taken advantage of its opportunities to further their own interests. People are not to benefit from the efforts of others without doing their fair share.

Not just any agreement is considered binding, however. House and Care (1979) have asserted that a binding agreement must meet certain conditions. For example, a party cannot be coerced into signing the agreement. All parties must be rational, equally informed, and have a say in the agreement itself. Only under certain conditions can the agreement be considered an appropriate basis for the evaluation.

The fundamental ethical notion is that of a contractual ethics, the establishment of an implicit or explicit contract as the basis for conduct. This is consistent and, indeed, entailed by viewing society as a collection of individuals. "The essence of liberalism . . . is the vision of society as made up of independent, autonomous units who co-operate only when the terms of cooperation are such as make it further the ends of the parties" (Barry 1973 p. 166). Voluntary consent of the participants is essential to ethical conduct in this framework, and intrusions upon people without their consent is considered unethical and immoral. Individual autonomy is a primary principle within this conceptual framework, and autonomy is reflected in establishment of agreements, informing participants, and requesting consent. The ethics are essentially personal and contractual.

While these principles capture many of the concerns of those who have codified ethical principles for evaluation, other theorists have held that these notions of ethics are too restricted. Ideology plays an important role in how evaluation studies are conducted. In fact, Sjoberg contends that evaluation studies usually take for granted the structural constraints of the social system. Evaluations are used for effectiveness, efficiency, and accountability within the dominant bureaucratic hierarchies. The categories used by evaluators are those of the status quo, and the social indicators employed are allied to the political power structure. To the degree to which this is true, the formalized ethics of evaluation are limited to concerns which do not threaten the ideological status quo. Many ethical problems are beyond the recognition of evaluators because they are excluded by the prevailing ideology. People are usually not aware of the limits of this ideological consensus until they step outside it.

For example, MacDonald has carried the principle of autonomy a step beyond the prevailing consensus. He has contended that evaluations usually serve the interests and purposes of bureaucratic sponsors or an academic reference group at the expense of those being evaluated. He has proposed that those being evaluated be shown the information collected from them and be given veto power over what is said about them in the evaluation report. Individual autonomy is carried to the extent that "people own the facts of their lives." This is a right not usually accorded to respondents. Within this framework knowledge of social action is the private property of practitioners, and truth is relative to the different interpretive frameworks by which social agents guide their conduct. This position is too extreme for most evaluators but is based upon an extension of an accepted principle. Another unusual ethical position is that evaluators should make themselves more vulnerable to those evaluated, thus redressing the balance of power between the two parties.

Underlying all these various notions of correct behavior in evaluation are contrasting conceptions of justice. The dominant implicit conception of justice is utilitarian, the idea being to maximize satisfaction in society. Any action which maximizes the total or average satisfaction is the right thing to do. Although such a notion seems remote from the practice of evaluation, indicators such as test scores are often taken as surrogate measures of satisfaction and the right thing to do is determine which educational programs maximize these scores. This thinking ultimately leads to a particular kind of evaluation study and technology, even though evaluators may not be fully cognizant of the underlying philosophical assumptions or ethical implications. For example, Schulze and Kneese have shown that the results of a cost–benefit analysis can vary dramatically depending upon which overall ethical system one adopts. They contrast utilitarian, egalitarian, elitist, and libertarian ethical views. As they note, the philosophical underpinnings of current cost–benefit analyses are utilitarian.

Contrasted to utilitarian justice are pluralist conceptions of justice which presume that there are multiple ultimate principles of justice. Such notions often translate into including the perceptions of various interest groups in the evaluation and distinguishing how different groups are served by the program. Pluralist/ intuitionist conceptions of justice hold that there are

several principles of justice and no overriding endpoint or measure of the general welfare. In practical terms, evaluations based on pluralist ideas treat interest groups as several in number and as having distinct interests from one another.

From different perspectives some theorists have argued that the interests of the disadvantaged and the lower classes are ordinarily neglected in an evaluation and that such interests should be represented or even given priority as an ethical matter. Such an obligation edges into the political and is quite different from an admonition to respect the rights of individuals. Current formal codes of ethics for evaluators restrict their content to individual rights within a contractual framework.

An expanded view of the ethics of evaluation would be based upon more principles than that of individual autonomy. Autonomy suggests that no-one should impose his or her will upon others by force or coercion or illegitimate means. No-one should be imposed upon against his or her will. Autonomy is intimately tied to the notion of choice and is manifested in the notion of individual rights and the social contract. Presumably a person's autonomy has not been violated if he or she chooses freely what to do.

However, autonomy alone is not sufficient as a moral basis for evaluation. Each person should have an equal right to advance his or her own interests for satisfaction. The fundamental notion of equality is that all persons should be taken as members of the same reference group and consequently should be treated the same. The satisfaction of each person's interests is worthy of equal consideration in the public determinations of wants. Individual rights are a protection against imposition by others but do not guarantee equal consideration. It is here particularly that social-class differences play a most significant but neglected role in evaluation. Often powerless groups are not entitled to consideration or representation of their interests in evaluation. Too often only the interests of the powerful are represented.

Of course, if each individual and group is allowed to advance its own interests, there are inevitable conflicts, and these conflicts must be settled impartially. An evaluation must be impartial, that is, in its procedures it must be fair to all interests. Sometimes impartiality is confused with objectivity, but it is possible to employ an objective procedure which is reproducible but biased against a particular social group. It is possible to have a test which discriminates in a systematic, reproducible but biased fashion against certain social groups. Impartiality is a moral principle that ensures fair consideration.

Impartiality is especially difficult when the evaluator must face a situation in which there are conflicting values. To what degree should the evaluator become involved with the participants? Eraut has suggested two moral principles in such a situation. First, people have a right to know what an evaluation is doing and why. Second, all those who might be considered as clients have a right to some stake in the evaluation. This position proposes the involvement of participants somewhat beyond the negotiation phase, even to the point of helping with data collection. However, even in such an expanded notion of participant involvement, the evaluator is not expected to side with one group or endorse a particular set of values.

There is one other principle worth considering as a moral basis for evaluation. On the basis of equality, autonomy, and impartiality a person could advance his or her own interests equally, not impose on others, and join others in settling conflicts impartially. Yet what about the losers in such a decision process? The winners have no responsibility for the losers, strictly speaking. Intuitively, a person is disturbed at such a situation. Reciprocity, treating others as you would like to be treated, adds an element of humanity. Reciprocity makes winners at least partially responsible for the losers. Reciprocity is not a primary value of liberalism because it suggests a sense of community which extends beyond the notion of separate individuals who cooperate with each other only to seek their own advantage. One of liberalism's deficiencies is this lack of caring and sense of belonging to a larger community.

Finally, there is the formidable problem of the applications of these principles in the actual conduct of evaluation. Ethical principles are rather abstract notions, and it is not always obvious how such principles should be applied in a given situation. Concrete examples and guidelines are essential if a person is to model his or her behavior on such principles.

Even if a person endorsed all the ethical principles discussed here, their application would not be straightforward. Some of the most intractable ethical problems result from a conflict among principles, the necessity of trading off one against the other, rather than disagreement with the principles themselves. For example, both liberals and conservatives endorse the principles of autonomy and equality but weigh these principles differently in actual situations. The balancing of such principles against one another in concrete situations is the ultimate act of ethical evaluation.

## Bibliography

Anderson S B, Ball S 1978 *The Profession and Practice of Program Evaluation*. Jossey-Bass, San Francisco, California

Barry B 1973 *The Liberal Theory of Justice: A Critical Examination of the Principal Doctrines in 'A Theory of Justice' by John Rawls*. Clarendon Press, Oxford

Evaluation Research Society Standards Committee 1982 Evaluation Research Society standards for program evaluation. *New Directions for Program Evaluation* 15: 7–19

House E R 1980 *Evaluating with Validity*. Sage, Beverly Hills, California

House E R, Care N S 1979 Fair evaluation agreement. *Educ. Theory* 29: 159–69

Joint Committee on Standards for Educational Evaluations 1981 *Standards for Evaluations of Educational Programs, Projects, and Materials*. McGraw-Hill, New York

Mackie S L 1977 *Ethics*. Penguin, London

Rawls J 1971 *A Theory of Justice*. Harvard University Press, Cambridge, Massachusetts

Sieber J E 1980 Being ethical? Professional and personal decisions in program evaluation. *New Directions for Program Evaluation* 7: 51–61

# Professional Standards for Educational Evaluation[1]

## D. L. Stufflebeam

Professional educators, throughout the world, must evaluate their work in order to: (a) obtain direction for improving it; and (b) document their effectiveness. They must evaluate the performance of students, programs, personnel, and institutions. Within various countries, such evaluations have occurred at many levels: classroom, school, school district, state or province, and national system. There have also been international comparisons of the quality of education. The evaluations have varied enormously: in the objects assessed, the questions addressed, the methods used, the audiences served, the funds expended, the values invoked, and, to the point of this article, their quality.

In evaluations, as in any professional endeavor, many things can and often do go wrong: they are subject to bias, misinterpretation, and misapplication; and they may address the wrong questions and/or provide erroneous information. Indeed, there have been strong charges that evaluations, in general, have failed to render worthy services (Guba 1969), and often, findings from individual studies have been disputed (e.g., the Coleman et al. 1966 Equal Opportunity Study). Clearly, evaluation itself is subject to evaluation and quality assurance efforts.

During the past 30 years, there have been substantial efforts in the United States to assure and control the quality of educational evaluation. In addition to creating professional evaluation societies and developing preparation programs and a substantial professional literature, there have been concerted efforts to develop and enforce professional standards for educational evaluation.

1  This article was originally published in the *International Journal of Educational Research*, Vol. 11, No. 1. It appears here with permission from Pergamon Press plc © 1987.

In the mid-1950s, the American Psychological Association joined with the American Educational Research Association and the National Council on Measurements Used in Education to develop standards for educational and psychological tests (APA 1954, AERA/NCMUE 1955); updated versions of the *Test Standards* have been published by APA in 1966, 1974, and 1985, and they have been widely used—in the courts as well as professional settings—to evaluate tests and the uses of test scores. In 1981, the Joint Committee on Standards for Educational Evaluation, whose 17 members were appointed by 12 organizations, issued the *Standards for Evaluations of Educational Programs, Projects, and Materials* (which was originally commissioned to serve as a companion volume to the Test Standards); in 1982, the Evaluation Research Society (Rossi 1982) issued a parallel set of program evaluation standards (intended to deal with program evaluations both outside and inside education). The Joint Committee on Standards for Educational Evaluation has also developed standards for evaluations of educational personnel (which is a companion volume to their program evaluation standards).

The different sets of standards are noteworthy because they provide: (a) operational definitions of student evaluation and program evaluation (soon to include personnel evaluation); (b) evidence about the extent of agreement concerning the meaning and appropriate methods of educational evaluation; (c) general principles for dealing with a variety of evaluation problems; (d) practical guidelines for planning evaluations; (e) widely accepted criteria for judging evaluation plans and reports; (f) conceptual frameworks by which to study evaluation; (g) evidence of progress, in the United States, toward professionalizing evaluation; (h) content for evaluation training; and (i) a basis for synthesizing an overall view of the different types of evaluation.

It is likely that many evaluators, psychologists, and others concerned with the evaluation of education are aware of the Test Standards, but not the Program Evaluation Standards, nor the Personnel Evaluation Standards. The purpose of this article is to inform an international audience—including evaluators, psychologists, and others involved in the evaluation of education—about the *Standards for Evaluations of Educational Programs, Projects, and Materials* (hereafter called the Program Evaluation Standards). While it is hoped this article will provide a useful reference to groups in other countries that may desire standards to guide their evaluation work, the Joint Committee's standards are distinctly American and may not reflect the values, experiences, political realities, and practical constraints in some other countries.

## 1. Introduction to the Program Evaluation Standards

In general, the Joint Committee devised 30 standards that pertain to four attributes of an evaluation: utility, feasibility, propriety, and accuracy. The utility standards reflect a general consensus that emerged in the educational evaluation literature during the late 1960s requiring program evaluations to respond to the information needs of their clients, and not merely to address the interests of the evaluators. The feasibility standards are consistent with the growing realization that evaluation procedures must be cost-effective and workable in real-world, politically charged settings; in a sense, these standards are a countermeasure to the penchant for applying the procedures of laboratory research to real-world settings regardless of the fit. The propriety standards—particularly American—reflect ethical issues, constitutional concerns, and litigation concerning such matters as rights of human subjects, freedom of information, contracting, and conflict of interest. The accuracy standards build on those that have long been accepted for judging the technical merit of information, especially validity, reliability, and objectivity. Overall, then, the Program Evaluation Standards promote evaluations that are useful, feasible, ethical, and technically sound—ones that will contribute significantly to the betterment of education.

### 1.1 Key Definitions

The Program Evaluation Standards reflect certain definitions of key concepts. *Evaluation* means the systematic investigation of the worth or merit of some object. The object of an evaluation is what one is examining (or studying) in an evaluation: a program, a project, instructional materials, personnel qualifications and performance, or student needs and performance. *Standards* are principles commonly accepted for determining the value or the quality of an evaluation.

### 1.2 Development of the Program Evaluation Standards

To ensure that the Program Evaluation Standards would reflect the best current knowledge and practice, the Joint Committee sought contributions from many sources. They collected and reviewed a wide range of literature. They devised a list of possible topics for standards, lists of guidelines and pitfalls thought to be associated with each standard, and illustrative cases showing an application of each standard. They engaged a group of 30 experts independently to expand the topics and write alternative versions for each standard. With the help of consultants, the Committee rated the alternative standards, devised their preferred set, and compiled the first draft of the Program Evaluation Standards. They then had their first draft criticized by a nationwide panel of 50 experts who were nominated by the 12 sponsoring organizations. Based on those critiques, the Committee debated the identified issues and prepared a version which was subjected to national hearings and field tests. The results of this five-year period of development and assessments led, in 1981, to the published version of the Program Evaluation Standards. Presently, that version is being applied and reviewed, and the Joint Committee is collecting feedback for use in preparing the next edition.

### 1.3 Developers of the Program Evaluation Standards

An important feature of the standards-setting process is the breadth of perspectives that have been represented in their development. The 12 organizations that originally sponsored the Joint Committee included the perspectives of the consumers as well as those who conduct program evaluations. The groups represented on the Joint Committee and among the approximately 200 other persons who contributed include, among others, those of statistician and administrator; psychologist and teacher; researcher and counselor; psychometrician and curriculum developer, and evaluator and school board member. There is perhaps no feature about the Joint Committee that is as important as its representative nature, since by definition a standard is a widely shared principle. Just as the breadth of perspectives involved in developing the Program Evaluation Standards enhances their credibility in the United States, the low level of involvement of groups from outside the United States limits the credibility and usefulness of the Program Evaluation Standards in other countries.

### 1.4 Format

The depth to which the Joint Committee developed each standard is apparent in the format common to all of the standards. This format starts with a descriptor, for instance, "Formal Obligation." The descriptor is followed by a statement of the standard, for example "Obligations of the formal parties to an evaluation (what is to be done, how, by whom, when) should be agreed to in writing, so that these parties are obligated to adhere to all conditions of the agreement or formally to renegotiate it," and an overview, that includes a rationale for the standard and definitions of its key terms. Also included, for each standard, are lists of pertinent guidelines, pitfalls, and caveats. The guidelines are procedures that often would prove useful in meeting the standard; the pitfalls are common mistakes to be avoided; and the caveats are warnings about being overzealous in applying the given standards, lest such effort detract from meeting other standards. The presentation of each standard is concluded with an illustration of how it might be applied. The illustration includes a situation in which the standard is violated, and a discussion of corrective actions that would result in better adherence to the standard. Usually, the illustrations are based on real situations, and they encompass a wide range of different types of evaluations. One easy step to extending the applicability of the Program Evaluation Standards to evaluations in fields outside education would be to develop new illustrative cases drawn directly from experiences in evaluating programs outside education. Such a step might also be useful in efforts to adapt the Program Evaluation Standards for use in countries outside the United States.

### 1.5 Content of the Standards

In general, the Utility Standards are intended to guide evaluations so that they will be informative, timely, and influential. These standards require evaluators to acquaint themselves with their audiences, earn their confidence, ascertain the audiences' information needs, gear evaluations to respond to these needs, and report the relevant information clearly and when it is needed. The standards in this category include: audience identification, evaluator credibility, information scope and selection, valuational interpretation, report clarity, report dissemination, report timeliness, and evaluation impact. Overall, the Utility Standards are concerned with whether an evaluation serves the practical information needs of a given audience.

The Feasibility Standards recognize that an evaluation usually must be conducted in a "natural", as opposed to a "laboratory" setting and require that no more materials and personnel time than necessary be consumed. Subjects covered in the Feasibility Standards include: practical procedures, political viability, and cost effectiveness. Overall, the Feasibility Standards call for evaluations to be realistic, prudent, diplomatic, and frugal.

The Propriety Standards reflect the fact that evaluations affect many people in different ways. These standards are aimed at ensuring that the rights of persons affected by an evaluation will be protected. The Propriety Standards cover the following areas: formal obligation, conflict of interest, full and frank disclosure, public's right to know, rights of human subjects, human interactions, balanced reporting, and fiscal responsibility. These standards require that those conducting evaluations learn about and abide by laws concerning such matters as privacy, freedom of information, and protection of human subjects. The standards charge those who conduct evaluations to respect the rights of others and to live up to the highest principles and ideals of their professional reference groups. Taken as a group, the Propriety Standards require that evaluations be conducted legally, ethically, and with due regard for the welfare of those involved in the evaluation, as well as those affected by the results.

Accuracy, the fourth group of standards, includes those standards that determine whether an evaluation has produced sound information. These standards require that the obtained information be technically adequate and that conclusions be linked logically to the data. The subjects developed in this group are object identification, context analysis, defensible information sources, described purposes and procedures, valid measurement, reliable measurement, systematic data control, analysis of quantitative information, analysis of qualitative information, justified conclusions, and objective reporting. The overall rating of an evaluation against the Accuracy Standards gives a good idea of the evaluation's overall truth value. The 30 standards are summarized in Table 1.

**Table 1**
Summary of the standards

(A) **Utility Standards**
The utility standards are intended to ensure that an evaluation will serve the practical information needs of given audiences. These standards are:

(A1) Audience Identification
Audiences involved in or affected by the evaluation should be identified, so that their needs can be addressed.

(A2) Evaluator Credibility
The persons conducting the evaluation should be both trustworthy and competent to perform the evaluation, so that their findings achieve maximum credibility and acceptance.

(A3) Information Scope and Selection
Information collected should be of such scope and selected in such ways as to address pertinent questions about the object of the evaluation and be responsive to the needs and interests of specified audiences.

(A4) Valuation Interpretation
The perspectives, procedures, and rationale used to interpret the findings should be carefully described, so that the bases for value judgments are clear.

(A5) Report Clarity
The evaluation report should describe the object being evaluated and its context, and the purposes, procedures, and findings of the evaluation, so that the audiences will readily understand what was done, why it was done, what information was obtained, what conclusions were drawn, and what recommendations were made.

(A6) Report Dissemination
Evaluation findings should be disseminated to clients and other right-to-know audiences, so that they can assess and use the findings.

(A7) Report Timeliness
Release of reports should be timely, so that audiences can best use the reported information.

(A8) Evaluation Impact
Evaluations should be planned and conducted in ways that encourage follow-through by members of the audiences.

(B) **Feasibility Standards**
The feasibility standards are intended to ensure that an evaluation will be realistic, prudent, diplomatic, and frugal. These standards are:

(B1) Practical Procedures
The evaluation procedures should be practical, so that disruption is kept to a minimum, and that needed information can be obtained.

(B2) Political Viability
The evaluation should be planned and conducted with anticipation of the different positions of various interest groups, so that their cooperation may be obtained, and so that possible attempts by any of these groups to curtail evaluation operations or to bias or misapply the results can be averted or counteracted.

(B3) Cost Effectiveness
The evaluation should produce information of sufficient value to justify the resources expended.

(C) **Propriety Standards**
The propriety standards are intended to ensure that an evaluation will be conducted legally, ethically, and with due regard for the welfare of those involved in the evaluation, as well as those affected by its results. These standards are:

(C1) Formal Obligation
Obligations of the formal parties to an evaluation (what is to be done, how, by whom, when) should be agreed to in writing, so that these parties are obligated to adhere to all conditions of the agreement or formally to renegotiate it.

(C2) Conflict of Interest
Conflict of interest, frequently unavoidable, should be dealt with openly and honestly, so that it does not compromise the evaluation processes and results.

(C3) Full and Frank Disclosure
Oral and written evaluation reports should be open, direct, and honest in their disclosure of pertinent findings, including the limitations of the evaluation.

(C4) Public's Right to Know
The formal parties to an evaluation should respect and assure the public's right to know, within the limits of other related principles and statutes, such as those dealing with public safety and the right to privacy.

*(continued)*

**Table 1**
Summary of the standards *(continued)*

(C5)   Rights of Human Subjects
Evaluations should be designed and conducted so that the rights and welfare of the human subjects are respected and protected.

(C6)   Human Interactions
Evaluators should respect human dignity and worth in their interactions with other persons associated with an evaluation.

(C7)   Balanced Reporting
The evaluation should be complete and fair in its presentation of strengths and weaknesses of the object under investigation, so that strengths can be built upon and problem areas addressed.

(C8)   Fiscal Responsibility
The evaluator's allocation and expenditure of resources should reflect sound accountability procedures and otherwise be prudent and ethically responsible.

(D)   **Accuracy Standards**
The accuracy standards are intended to ensure that an evaluation will reveal and convey technically adequate information about the features of the object being studied that determine its worth or merit. These standards are:

(D1)   Object Identification
The object of the evaluation (program, project, material) should be sufficiently examined, so that the form(s) of the object being considered in the evaluation can be clearly identified.

(D2)   Context Analysis
The context in which the program, project, or material exists should be examined in enough detail, so that its likely influences on the object can be identified.

(D3)   Described Purposes and Procedures
The purposes and procedures of the evaluation should be monitored and described in enough detail, so that they can be identified and assessed.

(D4)   Defensible Information Sources
The sources of information should be described in enough detail, so that the adequacy of the information can be assessed.

(D5)   Valid Measurement
The information-gathering instruments and procedures should be chosen or developed and then implemented in ways that will assure that the interpretation arrived at is valid for the given use.

(D6)   Reliable Measurement
The information-gathering instruments and procedures should be chosen or developed and then implemented in ways that will assure that the information obtained is sufficiently reliable for the intended use.

(D7)   Systematic Data Control
The data collected, processed, and reported in an evaluation should be reviewed and corrected, so that the results of the evaluation will not be flawed.

(D8)   Analysis of Quantitative Information
Quantitative information in an evaluation should be appropriately and systematically analyzed to ensure supportable interpretations.

(D9)   Analysis of Qualitative Information
Qualitative information in an evaluation should be appropriately and systematically analyzed to ensure supportable interpretations.

(D10)   Justified Conclusions
The conclusions reached in an evaluation should be explicitly justified, so that the audiences can assess them.

(D11)   Objective Reporting
The evaluation procedures should provide safeguards to protect the evaluation findings and reports against distortion by the personal feelings and biases of any party to the evaluation.

---

*1.6 Eclectic Orientation*

The Program Evaluation Standards do not exclusively endorse any one approach to evaluation. Instead, the Joint Committee has written standards that encourage the sound use of a variety of evaluation methods. These include surveys, observations, document reviews, jury trials for projects, case studies, advocacy teams to generate and assess competing plans, adversary and advocacy teams to expose the strengths and weaknesses of projects, testing programs, simulation studies, time-series studies, checklists, goal-free evaluations, secondary data analysis, and quasi-experimental design. In essence, evaluators are advised to use whatever methods are best suited for gathering information that is relevant to the questions posed by clients and other audiences, yet sufficient for assessing a program's effectiveness, costs, responses to societal needs, feasibility, and worth. It is desirable to employ multiple methods, qualitative as well as quantitative, and the methods should be feasible to use in the given setting.

## 1.7 Nature of the Evaluations to be Guided by the Program Evaluation Standards

The Joint Committee deliberately chose to limit the Program Evaluation Standards to evaluations of educational programs, projects, and materials. They chose not to deal with evaluations of educational institutions and personnel nor with evaluations outside education. They set these boundaries for reasons of feasibility and political viability of the project.

Given these constraints, the Joint Committee attempted to provide principles that apply to the full range of different types of studies that might legitimately be conducted in the name of evaluation. These include, for example, small-scale, informal studies that a school committee might employ to assist in planning and operating one or more workshops; as another example, they include large-scale, formal studies that might be conducted by a special evaluation team in order to assess and report publicly on the worth and merit of a statewide or national instructional program. Other types of evaluations to which the Program Evaluation Standards apply include pilot studies, needs assessments, process evaluations, outcome studies, cost effectiveness studies, and meta-analyses. In general, the Joint Committee says the Program Evaluation Standards are intended for use with studies that are internal and external, small and large, informal and formal, and for those that are formative (designed to improve a program while it is still being developed) and summative (designed to support conclusions about the worth or merit of an object and to provide recommendations about whether it should be retained, revised, or eliminated).

It would be a mistake to assume that the Program Evaluation Standards are intended for application only to heavily funded and well-staffed evaluations. In fact, the Committee doubts whether any evaluation could simultaneously meet all of the standards. The Committee encouraged evaluators and their clients to consult the Program Evaluation Standards to consider systematically how their investigations can make the best use of available resources in informing and guiding practice.

The Program Evaluation Standards must not be viewed as an academic exercise of use only to well-funded developers but as a code by which to help improve evaluation practice. This message is as applicable to those educators who must evaluate their own work as it is to those who can call on the services of evaluation specialists. For both groups, consideration of the Program Evaluation Standards may sometimes indicate that a proposed evaluation is not worthy of further consideration, or it may help to justify and then to guide and assess the study.

## 1.8 Trade-offs Among the Standards

The preceding discussion points up a particular difficulty in applying the Program Evaluation Standards. Inevitably, efforts to meet certain standards will detract from efforts to meet others, and tradeoff decisions will be required. For example, efforts to produce valid and reliable information and to generate ironclad conclusions may make it difficult to produce needed reports in time to have an impact on crucial program decisions, or the attempt to keep an evaluation within cost limits may conflict with meeting such standards as information scope and selection and report dissemination. Such conflicts will vary across different types and sizes of studies, and within a given study the tradeoffs will probably be different depending on the stage of the study (e.g., deciding whether to evaluate, designing the evaluation, collecting the data, reporting the results, or assessing the results of the study). Evaluators need to recognize and deal as judiciously as they can with such conflicts.

Some general advice for dealing with these tradeoff problems can be offered. At a macro level, the Joint Committee decided to present the four groups of standards in a particular order: Utility, Feasibility, Propriety, and Accuracy. The rationale for this sequence might be stated as "an evaluation not worth doing isn't worth doing well." In deciding whether to evaluate, it is therefore more important to begin with assurances that the findings, if obtained, would be useful, than to start with assurances only that the information would be technically sound. If there is no prospect for utility, then of course there is no need to work out an elegant design that would produce sound information. Given a determination that the findings from a projected study would be useful, then the evaluator and client might next consider whether it is feasible to move ahead. Are sufficient resources available to obtain and report the needed information in time for its use? Can the needed cooperation and political support be mustered? Would the projected information gains, in the judgment of the client, be worth the required investment of time and resources? If such questions cannot be answered affirmatively, then the evaluation planning effort might best be discontinued with no further consideration of the other standards. Otherwise, the evaluator would next consider whether there is any reason that the evaluation could not be carried through within appropriate bounds of propriety. Once it is ascertained that a proposed evaluation could meet conditions of utility, feasibility, and propriety, then the evaluator and client would tend carefully to the accuracy standards. By following the sequence described above, it is believed

**Table 2**
Summarized Functional Table of Contents

| Standards (descriptors) | (1) Decide whether to do a study | (2) Clarify and assess purpose | (3) Ensure political viability | (4) Contract the study | (5) Staff the study | (6) Manage the study | (7) Collect data | (8) Analyze data | (9) Report findings | (10) Apply results |
|---|---|---|---|---|---|---|---|---|---|---|
| A1 Audience identification | X | X | X | X |   | X |   |   | X | X |
| A2 Evaluator credibility | X |   | X | X | X | X | X |   |   | X |
| A3 Information scope and selection |   |   |   | X |   |   | X |   | X |   |
| A4 Valuational interpretation |   | X | X |   |   |   | X | X | X | X |
| A5 Report clarity |   |   |   |   |   |   |   |   | X |   |
| A6 Report dissemination |   |   | X | X |   |   |   |   | X | X |
| A7 Report timeliness |   |   |   | X |   |   |   |   | X |   |
| A8 Evaluation impact | X | X | X |   |   |   |   |   | X | X |
| B1 Practical procedures | X |   | X |   |   | X | X | X |   |   |
| B2 Political viability | X |   | X | X | X |   | X |   |   | X |
| B3 Cost effectiveness | X | X |   |   |   | X |   |   |   |   |
| C1 Formal obligation | X |   | X | X |   | X | X |   |   | X |
| C2 Conflict of interest | X | X | X | X | X | X |   |   |   | X |
| C3 Full and frank disclosure |   |   |   | X |   |   |   |   | X |   |
| C4 Public's right to know |   |   | X | X |   |   | X |   | X | X |
| C5 Rights of human subjects |   |   | X | X |   | X | X |   |   | X |
| C6 Human interactions |   |   | X |   |   | X |   |   |   |   |
| C7 Balanced reporting |   |   |   | X |   |   | X |   | X | X |
| C8 Fiscal responsibility |   |   |   |   |   | X |   |   |   |   |
| D1 Object identification | X | X |   | X |   | X | X | X | X | X |
| D2 Context analysis | X | X |   |   |   |   | X | X | X | X |
| D3 Described purposes and procedures | X | X | X | X |   | X | X |   | X | X |
| D4 Defensible information sources |   |   | X |   |   |   | X |   | X |   |
| D5 Valid measurement |   |   |   |   |   |   | X |   |   |   |
| D6 Reliable measurement |   |   |   |   |   |   | X |   |   |   |
| D7 Systematic data control |   |   |   |   |   | X | X |   |   |   |
| D8 Quantitative analysis |   |   |   |   |   |   |   | X |   |   |
| D9 Qualitative analysis |   |   |   |   |   |   |   | X |   |   |
| D10 Justified conclusions |   |   |   |   |   |   |   | X | X | X |
| D11 Objective reporting |   |   | X |   | X |   |   |   | X |   |

that evaluation resources would be allocated to those studies that are worth doing and that the studies would then proceed on sound bases.

There are also problems with trade-offs among the individual standards. The Committee decided against assigning a priority rating to each standard because the trade-off issues vary from study to study and within a given study at different stages. Instead, the Committee provided a Functional Table of Contents that is summarized in Table 2. This matrix summarizes the Committee's judgments about which standards are most applicable to each of a range of common evaluation tasks. The standards are identified down the side of the matrix. Across the top are 10 tasks that are commonly involved in any evaluation. The checkmarks in the cells denote which standards should be heeded most carefully in addressing a given evaluation task. All of the standards are applicable in all evaluations. However, the Functional Table of Contents allows evaluators to identify quickly those standards that are most relevant to certain tasks in given evaluations.

### 1.9 Attestation

To assist evaluators and their clients to record their decisions about applying given standards and their judgments about the extent to which each one was taken into account, the Committee provided a citation form (see Table 3). This form is to be completed, signed, and appended to evaluation plans and reports. Like an auditor's statement, the signed citation form should assist audiences to assess the merits of given evaluations. Of course, the completed citation form should often be backed up by more extensive documentation, especially with regard to the judgments given about the extent that each standard was taken into account. In the absence of such documentation, the completed citation form can be used as an agenda for discussions between evaluators and their audiences about the adequacy of evaluation plans or reports.

### 1.10 Validity of the Standards

Since the Program Evaluation Standards were published, a considerable amount of information that bears on the validity of the standards has been presented. In general, this evidence supports the position that the Program Evaluation Standards are needed, have been carefully developed, have good credibility in the United States, and have been put to practical use. However, the assessments also point out some limitations and areas for improvement.

Bunda (1982), Impara (1982), Merwin (1982) and Wardrop (1982) examined the congruence between the Program Evaluation Standards and the principles of measurement that are embodied in the Standards for Educational and Psychological Tests (APA 1974). They independently concluded that great consistency exists between these two sets of standards with regard to measurement. Ridings (1980) closely studied standard

setting in the accounting and auditing fields and developed a checklist by which to assess the Joint Committee effort against key checkpoints in the more mature standard-setting programs in accounting and auditing. In general, she concluded that the Joint Committee had adequately dealt with four key issues: rationale, the standard-setting structure, content, and uses. Wildemuth (1981) issued an annotated bibliography with about five sources identified for each standard; these references help to confirm the theoretical validity of the Program Evaluation Standards, and they provide a convenient guide to users for pursuing in-depth study of the involved principles. Linn (1981) reported the results of about 25 field trials that were conducted during the development of the Program Evaluation Standards; these confirmed that the Program Evaluation Standards were useful, but not sufficient guides, in such applications as designing evaluations, assessing evaluation proposals, judging evaluation reports, and training evaluators. Additionally, they provided direction for revising the Program Evaluation Standards prior to publication. Stake (1981) observed that the Joint Committee had made a strong case in favor of evaluation standards, but he urged a careful look at the case against standards. He offered analysis in this vein and questioned whether the evaluation field has matured sufficiently to warrant the development and use of standards.

A number of writers have examined the applicability of the Program Evaluation Standards to specialized situations. Wargo (1981) concluded that the Program Evaluation Standards represent a sound consensus of good evaluation practice, but he called for more specificity regarding large-scale, government-sponsored studies and for more representation from this sector on the Committee. M Linn (1981) concluded that the Program Evaluation Standards contain sound advice for evaluators in out-of-school learning environments, but she observed that they are not suitable for dealing with tradeoffs between standards or settling disputes between and among stakeholders. While the Program Evaluation Standards explicitly are not intended for personnel evaluations, Carey (1980) examined the extent to which they are congruent with state evaluation policies for evaluating teachers; she concluded that only one standard (D11, Objective Reporting) was deemed inappropriate for judging teacher evaluations.

Burkett and Denson (1985) surveyed participants at a conference on evaluation in the health professions to obtain their judgments of the Program Evaluation Standards. While the respondents generally agreed "... that the *Standards* represent a useful framework for designing evaluations and offer substantial potential for application to the evaluation of continuing education (CE) for programs for the health professions," they also issued the following criticisms:

(a) Crucial elements of certain standards lie outside the evaluator's professional area of control.

**Table 3**

Citation form

The *Standards for Evaluations of Educational Programs, Projects, and Materials* guided the development of this (check one):

request for evaluation plan/design/proposal
evaluation plan/design/proposal
evaluation contract
evaluation report
other

To interpret the information provided on this form, the reader needs to refer to the full text of the *Standards* as they appear in Joint Committee on Standards for Educational Evaluation 1981 *Standards for Evaluations of Educational Programs, Projects, and Materials*. McGraw-Hill, New York.

The *Standards* were consulted and used as indicated in the table below (check as appropriate):

| Descriptor | | The Standard was deemed applicable and to an extent feasible and was taken into account | The Standard was deemed applicable but could not be taken into account | The Standard was not deemed applicable | Exception was taken to the Standard |
|---|---|---|---|---|---|
| A1 | Audience identification | | | | |
| A2 | Evaluator credibility | | | | |
| A3 | Information scoop and selection | | | | |
| A4 | Valuational interpretation | | | | |
| A5 | Report clarity | | | | |
| A6 | Report dissemination | | | | |
| A7 | Report timeliness | | | | |
| A8 | Evaluation impact | | | | |
| B1 | Practical procedures | | | | |
| B2 | Political viability | | | | |
| B3 | Cost effectiveness | | | | |
| C1 | Formal obligation | | | | |
| C2 | Conflict of interest | | | | |
| C3 | Full and frank disclosure | | | | |
| C4 | Public's right to know | | | | |
| C5 | Rights of human subjects | | | | |
| C6 | Human interactions | | | | |
| C7 | Balanced reporting | | | | |
| C8 | Fiscal responsibility | | | | |
| D1 | Object identification | | | | |
| D2 | Context analysis | | | | |
| D3 | Described purposes and procedures | | | | |
| D4 | Defensible information sources | | | | |
| D5 | Valid measurements | | | | |
| D6 | Reliable measurements | | | | |
| D7 | Systematic data control | | | | |
| D8 | Analysis of quantitative information | | | | |
| D9 | Analysis of qualitative information | | | | |
| D10 | Justified conclusions | | | | |
| D11 | Objective reporting | | | | |

Name: _____ Date: _____
               (typed)

               (signature)

Position or Title: _____

Agency: _____

Address: _____

Relation to Documents (e.g., author of document, evaluation team leader, external auditor, internal auditor) _____

(b) The Standards assume more flexibility, e.g., in the choice of methods of assessment, than sometimes may exist in institutional settings.

(c) The Standards deal better with external evaluations than with internal, self-evaluations.

(d) The Standards need to be made more useful by ordering them in the same sequence as an evaluation typically unfolds, providing more specific guidelines and examples, and adding bibliographic references.

Marsh et al. (1981) used the Program Evaluation Standards to study the practice of educational evaluation in California and concluded the following: "(a) the standards were perceived as important ideals for the orientation of the process and practice of evaluation; (b) the current practice of evaluation in California was perceived by professional evaluators as being, at most, of average quality; and (c) the practice of low quality evaluation was attributed to a combination of restriction of time, of political and bureaucratic coercions, and of incompetence of the evaluator."

Several evaluators from other countries have examined the Program Evaluation Standards for their applicability outside the United States. Nevo (1982) and Straton (1982), respectively from Israel and Australia, both concluded that while the Program Evaluation Standards embody sound advice, they assume an American situation—regarding level of effort and citizens' rights, for example—that is different from their own national contexts. Rodrigues de Oliveira et al. (1982) published, in Portuguese, a summary and critique of the Program Evaluation Standards in the hope that their contribution would ". . . positively influence the quality of the evaluations conducted in Brazil, help in the training of educational evaluators, and help those who recommend evaluations to improve their value." Lewy (1983 p. 11), from Israel, concluded that the Program Evaluation Standards ". . . provide useful guidelines for evaluators in Israel as well as the USA," but raised questions about the adequacy of their theoretical rationale and criticized their lack of specificity.

Lewy, like Dockrell (1983), saw great possibilities for unhealthy collusion between evaluators and sponsors and disagreed with the position reflected in the Program Evaluation Standards that evaluators should communicate continuously with their clients and report interim findings. Dockrell also observed that evaluation in Scotland and other European countries is much more qualitatively oriented than is evaluation practice in the United States and that the Program Evaluation Standards do not and probably could not provide much guidance for the perceptiveness and originality required of excellent qualitative research. Scheerens and van Seventer (1983) saw in the Program Evaluation Standards a useful contribution to the important need in the Netherlands to upgrade and professionalize evaluation practice; but, to promote utility in their country, they said the standards would need to be translated and

illustrated at the national research policy level, as opposed to their present concentration on the individual evaluation project. Even so, they questioned whether such standards could be enforced in the Netherlands, given the susceptibility of national research policy there to frequently changing political forces and priorities. Marklund (1983) concluded that the Program Evaluation Standards provides a good checklist of prerequisites for a reliable and valid evaluation, but that due to differences in values of program outcomes, such standards do not guarantee that the result of the evaluation will be indisputable. Overall, the main value of the Program Evaluation Standards outside the United States appears to be as a useful reference for stimulating discussion of the need for professionalizing evaluation and the range of issues to be considered.

Six studies were conducted to examine the extent to which the Program Evaluation Standards are congruent with the set of program evaluation standards that was issued by the Evaluation Research Society (Rossi 1982). Cordray (1982), Braskamp and Mayberry (1982), Stufflebeam (1982), McKillip and Garberg (1983), and Stockdill (1984) found that the two sets of standards are largely overlapping.

Overall, the literature on the Program Evaluation Standards indicates considerable support for these standards. They are seen to fill a need; they are judged to contain sound content; they have been shown to be applicable in a wide range of United States settings; they have been applied successfully; they are consistent with the principles in other sets of standards; and they are subject to an appropriate process of review and revision. But by no means are they a panacea. Their utility is limited, especially outside the United States, and several issues have been raised for consideration in subsequent revision cycles.

## 2. Standards for Evaluations of Educational Personnel

An initial decision in developing the Program Evaluation Standards was to exclude the area of personnel evaluation. One reason was that developing a whole new set of standards for program evaluation presented a sufficiently large challenge; another reason was that members of the Committee believed that teachers' organizations would not support development of standards for evaluations of personnel. Also, in 1975 when the Joint Committee was formed, there was little concern for increasing or improving the evaluation of educational personnel.

### 2.1 The Decision to Develop Educational Personnel Evaluation Standards

In 1984, a number of factors led to the Joint Committee's decision to develop standards for evaluations of educational personnel. The Committee had successfully developed the Program Evaluation Standards and felt capable of tackling the personnel evaluation standards issue. They were also convinced that personnel evaluation in education was greatly in need of improvement. Moreover, they saw this need as urgent, because of the great increase in the development of systems for evaluating teachers and because of the great turmoil and litigation that accompanied the expansion of educational personnel evaluation activity. Moreover, they believed that the major teachers' organizations would support the development of professional standards that could be used to expose unsound plans and programs of personnel evaluation.

## 2.2 Expansion of the Joint Committee

In the course of deciding to develop the educational personnel evaluation standards, the Committee also decided to expand its membership to ensure that its members reflected relevant perspectives on evaluations of educational personnel as well as evaluations of educational programs. Additions to the Committee included representatives from the American Association of School Personnel Administrators, the American Federation of Teachers, and the American Association of Secondary School Principals, as well as individual members-at-large with expertise in litigation in personnel evaluation and research on teacher evaluation. New appointments by sponsoring organizations also included the perspectives of industrial/organizational psychology and traditionally underrepresented groups. The 18-member Committee continues to include a balance between the perspectives of educational practitioners and evaluation specialists. The Joint Committee's sponsoring organizations are now the American Association of School Administrators, American Association for School Personnel Administrators, American Educational Research Association, American Evaluation Association, American Federation of Teachers, American Psychological Association, Association for Measurement and Evaluation in Counseling and Development, Association for Supervision and Curriculum Development, Education Commission of the States, National Association of Elementary School Principals, National Association of Secondary School Principals, National Council on Measurement in Education, National Education Association, and National School Boards Association.

## 2.3 The Guiding Rationale

It is appropriate for the Joint Committee to deal with personnel evaluation as well as program evaluation, since both types of evaluation are prevalent in education, and both are vitally important for assuring the quality of educational services. Practically and politically it is usually necessary to conduct these two types of evaluation separately. But logically, they are inseparable.

Practice and literature have lodged responsibility for personnel evaluation with supervisors and admin-

istrators and have created expectations that program evaluators will not evaluate the performance of individuals as such. Program evaluators might provide some technical advice for developing a sound system of personnel evaluation and might even evaluate the personnel evaluation system itself; but they have preferred, and often have insisted on, staying out of the role of directly evaluating individual personnel. To do otherwise would stimulate fear about the power and motives of evaluators, and would undoubtedly generate much resistance on the part of principals and teachers, leading in turn to lack of cooperation in efforts to evaluate programs. Thus, program evaluators typically have avoided any association with personnel evaluation. They have emphasized instead the constructive contributions of program evaluation, and they have promised as much anonymity and confidentiality as they could to teachers and administrators in the programs being evaluated. On the whole, efforts to separate personnel and program evaluation in school districts have remained in vogue.

But a basic problem remains: namely, it is fundamentally impossible to remove personnel evaluation from sound program evaluation. A useful program evaluation must determine whether a program shows a desirable impact on the rightful target population. If the data reveal otherwise, the assessment must discern those aspects of a program that require change to yield the desired results. Inescapably, then, program evaluators must check the adequacy of all relevant instrumental variables, including the personnel. The rights of teachers and administrators must be respected, but evaluators must also protect the rights of students to be taught well and of communities to have their schools effectively administered.

However, personnel evaluation is too important and difficult a task to be left exclusively to the program evaluators. Many personnel evaluations are conducted by supervisors who rarely conduct formal program evaluations. Also, state education departments and school districts are heavily involved, apart from their program evaluation efforts, in evaluating teachers and other educators for certification, selection, placement, promotion, tenure, merit, staff development, and termination.

Undesirably, the literatures and methodologies of program evaluation and personnel evaluation are distinct. The work of the Joint Committee in both areas affords a significant opportunity to bring a concerted effort to bear on synthesizing these fields and coordinating the efforts of program evaluators and personnel evaluators for the betterment of the education service.

## 2.4 The Developmental Process

To achieve its goals for developing standards for personnel evaluations, the Joint Committee employed the approach it found successful in the development of the Program Evaluation Standards. They collected and studied a large amount of information about educational personnel evaluation and developed a tentative set of topics for personnel evaluation standards. A panel of writers, nominated by the 14-sponsoring organizations, wrote multiple versions of each proposed standard. The Joint Committee evaluated the alternative versions and decided which aspects of each standard would be included in the initial review version of the *Educational Personnel Standards* book. The first draft of the book was reviewed and criticized by a national and an international review panel. The Joint Committee used these critiques to develop a semifinal version of the book which was field tested and subjected to hearings conducted throughout the United States. The results of these hearings were used to develop the final version of the book which was published in 1988 and entitled *Educational Personnel Evaluation Standards*. The entire process was monitored and evaluated by a validation panel, whose members represent the perspectives of philosophy, international education, law, personnel psychology, school district administration, educational research, psychometrics, teaching, and the school principalship.

## 2.5 Contents of the Standards

After reviewing a great deal of material on personnel evaluation, the Joint Committee decided that the four basic concerns of utility, feasibility, propriety, and accuracy are as relevant to personnel evaluation as they are to program evaluation. Some of the topics for individual standards are likewise the same, for example valid measurement and reliable measurement. However, there are important differences in the two sets of topics. For example, full and frank disclosure, a program evaluation standard, has not surfaced in the personnel evaluation standards; and service orientation, a key entry in the personnel evaluation standards (requiring that evaluators show concern for the rights of students to be taught well), was not among the Educational Program Evaluation Standards. In general, much work remains to be done before the contents of the first edition of the Educational Personnel Evaluation Standards will be determined.

## 2.6 International Involvements and Implications

The Committee desires to stay in touch with international groups that are involved in evaluations of educational personnel so that it can benefit from the experiences of other countries and share what it learns from this project with interested groups in those countries. Accordingly, an Irish psychologist will serve on the validation panel to add an international perspective, and the Committee will engage an international review panel to evaluate the first draft of the standards. It will also report its progress to international audiences, through a periodic newsletter. However, the Committee realizes that the standards must concentrate on the relevant United States laws and personnel evaluation systems; and it is quite possible that the personnel evaluation standards will not transfer well to other cultures.

## 3. Conclusion

The purpose of this article has been to discuss standards for evaluations of education, including a review of the *Standards for Evaluations of Educational Programs, Projects, and Materials* and coverage of the Joint Committee's decision to develop standards for evaluations of educational personnel. The pervasive message is that all evaluators should strive to make their evaluations useful, feasible, proper, and accurate. However, the Joint Committee has not and undoubtedly will not finalize a set of universal standards, especially as their standards lack direct applicability to evaluation work in other countries. Moreover, professional standards are most useful when developed by the professionals whose work is to be assessed.

Evaluation groups in other countries that might desire to develop their own standards could profit from studying the Joint Committee's work. They have had 10 years experience in organizing a systematic and ongoing process of setting and applying standards for improving evaluation services.

## Bibliography

American Educational Research Association, and National Council on Measurements Used in Education 1955 *Technical Recommendations for Achievement Tests*. National Education Association, Washington, DC

American Educational Research Association, American Psychological Association, and National Council on Measurement in Education 1985 *Standards for Educational and Psychological Testing*. American Psychological Association, Washington, DC

American Psychological Association 1954 *Technical Recommendations for Psychological Tests and Diagnostic Techniques*. American Psychological Association, Washington, DC

American Psychological Association 1966 *Standards for Educational and Psychological Tests and Manuals*. American Psychological Association, Washington, DC

American Psychological Association 1973 *Ethical Principles in the Conduct of Research with Human Participants*. American Psychological Association, Washington, DC

American Psychological Association 1974 *Standards for Educational and Psychological Tests*, rev. edn. American Psychological Association, Washington, DC

Braskamp L A, Mayberry P W 1982 *A Comparison of Two Sets of Standards*. Paper presented at the joint annual meeting of the Evaluation Network and Evaluation Research Society, Baltimore, Maryland

Bunda M 1982 *Concerns and Techniques in Feasibility*. Paper presented at the annual meeting of the National Council on Measurement in Education, New York

Burkett D, Denson T 1985 Another view of the standards. In: Abrahamson S (ed.) 1985 *Evaluation of Continuing Education in the Health Professions*. Kluwer-Nijhoff, Boston, Massachusetts. pp. 53–58

Carey L M 1980 *State-level Teacher Performance Evaluation Policies*. National Council on State and Inservice Education,

Professional Development Occasional Paper No. 1, New York

Coleman J S, Campbell E Q, Hobson C J, et al. 1986 *Equality of Educational Opportunity*. Office of Education, United States Department of Health, Education, and Welfare, Washington, DC

Cordray D 1982 An assessment of the utility of the ERS standards. In: Rossi P H (ed.) 1982 *Standards for Evaluation Practice*. Jossey-Bass, San Francisco, California, pp. 67–81

Division of Industrial-Organizational Psychology, American Psychological Association 1980 *Principles for the Validation and Use of Personnel Selection Procedures*, 2nd edn. American Psychological Association, Division of Industrial-Organizational Psychology, Berkeley, California

Dockrell W B 1983 *Applicability of Standards for Evaluations of Educational Programs, Projects, and Materials*. Presentation at the annual meeting of the American Educational Research Association, Boston, Massachusetts

Guba E G 1969 The failure of educational evaluation. *Educ. Technol.* 9: 29–38

Impara J C 1982 *Measurement and the Utility Standards*. Paper presented at the meeting of the National Council for Measurement in Education, New York

Joint Committee on Standards for Educational Evaluation 1981 *Standards for Evaluations of Educational Programs, Projects, and Materials*. McGraw-Hill, New York

Joint Committee on Educational Evaluation 1988 *Personnel Evaluation Standards: How to Assess Systems for Evaluating Educators*. Sage, Newbury Park, California

Lewy A 1983 *Evaluation Standards: Comments from Israel*. Presentation at the annual meeting of the American Educational Research Association, Boston, Massachusetts, p. 11

Linn M 1981 Standards for evaluating out-of-school learning. *Eval. News* 2: 171–76

Linn R L 1981 A preliminary look at applicability of the educational evaluation standards. *Educ. Eval. Policy Analysis* 3(2): 87–91

McKillip J, Garberg R *A further examination of the overlap between ERS and Joint Committee evaluation standards*. Unpublished manuscript, Southern Illinois University

Marklund S 1983 *Applicability of Standards for Evaluations of Educational Programs, Projects, and Materials in an International Setting*. Presentation at the annual meeting of the American Educational Research Association, Boston, Massachusetts

Marsh D D, Newman W B, Bover W F 1981 *Comparing Ideal and Real. A Study of Evaluation Practice in California using the Joint Committee's Evaluation Standards*. Paper presented to the annual meeting of the American Educational Research Association, Los Angeles, California

Merwin J C 1982 *Measurement and Propriety Standards*. Paper presented at the meeting of the National Council for Measurement in Education, New York

Nevo D 1982 *Applying the Evaluation Standards in a Different Social Context*. Paper presented at the 20th Congress of the International Association of Applied Psychology, Edinburgh, Scotland

Ridings J M 1980 *Standard Setting in Accounting and Auditing. Considerations for Educational Evaluation*. Unpublished dissertation, Western Michigan University

Rodrigues de Oliveira T, Hoffman J M L, Barros R F, Arruda N F C, Santos R R 1981 *Standards for Evaluation of Educational Programs, Projects, and Materials*. Unpublished manuscript, Department of Education of the Federal University of Rio de Janeiro (UFRJ)

Rossi P H (ed.) 1982 *Standards for Evaluation Practice*. Jossey-Bass, San Francisco, California

Scheerens J, van Seventer C W 1983 *Political and Organizational Preconditions for Application of the Standards for Educational Evaluation*. Presentation at the annual meeting of the American Educational Research Association, Boston, Massachusetts

Stake R 1981 Setting standards for educational evaluators. *Eval. News* 2: 148–52

Stockdill S H 1984 *The Appropriateness of the Evaluation Standards for Business Evaluations*. Presentation at the Evaluation Network/Evaluation Research Society Joint meeting, San Francisco, California

Straton R B 1982 *Appropriateness and Potential Impact of Programme Evaluation Standards in Australia*. Paper presented at the 20th International Congress of Applied Psychology, Edinburgh

Stufflebeam D L 1982 *An Examination of the Overlap between ERS and Joint Committee Standards*. Paper presented at the Annual Meeting of the Evaluation Network, Baltimore, Maryland

Wardrop J C 1982 *Measurement and Accuracy Standards*. Paper presented at the meeting of the National Council for Measurement in Education. New York

Wargo M J 1981 The standards: A federal level perspective. *Eval. News* 2(2): 157–62

Wildemuth B M 1981 *A Bibliography to Accompany the Joint Committee's Standards on Educational Evaluation*. Eric Clearinghouse on Tests, Measurement, and Evaluation. Educational Testing Service, Princeton, New Jersey

# Impact of Evaluation Studies

**M. C. Alkin and R. H. Daillak**

Evaluation studies collect, analyze, and report information about programs or policies. Evaluation typically is designed to produce information that will aid decision making. Therefore, beneficial impact, in the form of better decisions about programs or policies, is expected from evaluation.

Evaluation impact may be defined broadly as an evaluation's discernible influence upon the activities or attitudes of individuals or groups. Impacts resulting from information, such as findings or recommendations generated in an evaluation, are the most commonly discussed evaluation impacts. Apart from their informational results, however, the processes of evaluation can also influence activities and attitudes to yield an equally important category of impacts.

Use must be distinguished from impact. The term "evaluation use" is often reserved to mean the purposive application of evaluation information or evaluation processes to achieve desired ends. Some evaluation impacts result from and are the intended ends of evaluation use; other impacts may be quite unintended.

## 1. Impacts of Evaluation Information

Evaluation information can dramatically sway program or policy decisions. More commonly, however, evaluation information is only one of several sources considered by decision makers, and evaluation information's influence on program or policy actions is partial rather than total. Evaluation can, of course, be said to have had influence, hence impact, in cases where it acts as a contributing factor.

Evaluation information can receive serious attention, yet be overruled by other considerations. In such situations, evaluation information will have influenced decision-making activity (to the extent that the information was given a serious hearing), and may even have influenced individual decision makers' choices, yet the program or policy in question may show no overt mark of evaluation influence.

Evaluation information's influence may also be masked, but in a different way, when evaluation results show that a current policy, program, or practice is succeeding. If there is little controversy surrounding a current practice, then positive evaluation results may receive little notice, even though negative findings might have generated great concern. Thus, if evaluation is viewed as corrective feedback, to nudge programs onto a proper course, then impact could be expected to be visible only for programs in difficulty. It would not be possible to conclude that the feedback system, that is, evaluation, had lost its influence simply because of a finding that successful programs had shown no sign of evaluation impact.

Evaluation information's influences upon attitudes or beliefs—sometimes called the conceptual influences of evaluation—are among the most complex impacts. While actions and attitudes may be left unchanged by agreeable evaluation results, beliefs may be strengthened by supportive evaluation results. Partisans in a policy debate, for example, may take great comfort from evaluation data favorable to their position, even if they recognize that the other side will not be swayed by the data. Evaluation's results may be a comfort even in the absence of external debate: a decision maker may welcome information that validates a previous decision.

Significantly, evaluation information can alter attitudes or beliefs without altering actions. For example, evaluation results could persuade school decision makers that preschool programs are worthwhile, without causing them to establish such programs in the schools. "Purely conceptual" impacts of this kind may later result in action.

## 2. Impacts of the Processes of Evaluation

Evaluation processes can have important impacts quite apart from those resulting from evaluation information.

Some of these additional impacts are prosaic (although occasionally overlooked). For example, evaluations consume educational resources. Money is spent directly on evaluation studies, and time is demanded from educators as well as often from students.

Other more subtle impacts include evaluation's influences upon communication within school organizations. The manner and form of the evaluation's conduct have a variety of impacts. Many evaluations focus attention on "goals" and "objectives," thus perhaps altering the terms in which educational work is conceptualized. Some evaluations bring together groups of practitioners to discuss program strategies, encouraging collegiality where there may have been isolationism. Such effects are difficult to prove. Evaluation's effects on some attitudes can be measurable, however. The prospect of evaluation frequently causes staff to become anxious. Prior to evaluative reviews, programs often take steps to comply more fully with regulatory guidelines, and they may attempt to correct deficiencies that would otherwise draw evaluative criticism.

The evaluation process may have political or symbolic impacts as well. Policy making may be deferred until after an ongoing evaluation is completed. The mere fact that a program is evaluated may help to legitimize the program. To the public or to legislators, evaluation may signal program management's cost-consciousness, responsibility, or accountability (Alkin 1975).

## 3. Measuring Evaluation Impact

Measures of evaluation impact are complicated by four principal difficulties: the lack of observability of many impacts, the presence of contributing influences besides evaluation, problems with diffusion of evaluation information, and the manifold nature of impact itself.

Choice, decision making, and attitude formation are mental activities which leave traces that vary in accessibility. When these activities occur in a group context, for example, there may be documentary evidence to indicate the role played by evaluation. Judgments by single individuals, however, are less likely to be well-documented. Indeed, those individual judgments that ratify the status quo (e.g., a manager's decision to continue current activities) may leave virtually no documentary traces. With documentary evidence so often slim, measures of evaluation impact have come to rely heavily upon decision makers' self-reports. In addition, impact is often inferred, or at least suspected, when actions in line with evaluation conclusions occur soon after relevant evaluation information is received by decision makers.

These measurement approaches are quite susceptible to error. The presence of multiple contributing influences upon actions or beliefs make it difficult to infer evaluation's influence in any particular situation. Decision makers' and program participants' assessments may be the best available guide to evaluation's impact, but even these respondents may have difficulty judging evaluation's relative contribution.

As the time span between evaluation and a subsequent impact increases, measurement difficulties multiply. As time elapses, many other potential influences will have had the opportunity to affect events. In addition, evaluation information may diffuse into the general knowledge base underlying the program or policy system, and participants in the system may be affected by evaluation information without ever knowing its source.

Finally, unitary measures of impact are elusive, since it is possible for many different types and degrees of impact to occur, even from the same evaluation. Information and process impacts at levels throughout the educational system must be explored in order to assess fully evaluation's impact.

## 4. Studies of Evaluation Impact

Empirical studies of evaluation impact burgeoned in the 1970s, in large part because it seemed that evaluation was not influencing educational practice in a significant way. Most studies examined information impacts in particular programs, for example, investigating the local school impacts of evaluation information in programs funded through Title I of the United States Elementary and Secondary Education Act (David 1981).

The ensuing research has suggested that evaluation studies have had mixed effects upon education. Most studies have found that uses are made of evaluation information, thus refuting the most pessimistic assertions of earlier observers. However, the impacts of evaluation appear to have been modest. Few dramatic changes in programs or policies can be directly attributed to evaluation. Instead, evaluation information is most often mentioned, when mentioned at all, as one of several convergent factors leading to a decision. For example, program managers may cite positive evaluation results as evidence of program effectiveness. Negative evaluation findings, however, seldom stimulate change directly, but if they persist, and if they are substantiated by other indicators, may lend weight to program or policy reassessments.

A complete and balanced picture of evaluation's impacts upon education is difficult to assemble, however. Because of measurement difficulties, research on impact has relied primarily upon interview surveys and case studies. Consequently, the samples that have been investigated have been relatively small and, to an extent, questionably representative of evaluation studies as a whole. Furthermore, process-related evaluation impacts have received relatively little attention, and little is confidently known about them.

## 5. Factors Explaining Evaluation Impact

Evaluation impact research was stimulated in part by perceptions that evaluation was not having adequate impact. Not surprisingly, therefore, attention was also devoted to explaining why evaluations had greater or lesser impact in specific cases. Explanations for information impacts again garnered the greatest attention. Several themes have emerged from recent studies (Leviton and Hughes 1981, Weiss 1977).

The nature of decision making in organizations appears to have had important implications for evaluation. Formal program or policy decision making—in the sense of a conscious choice at a given point in time between discrete decision alternatives—seems to be less common than was previously thought. More frequently, program or policy activities seem to result from an accretion of actions and small unheralded choices on the part of many different individuals within an organization. The individuals involved may not perceive themselves as being engaged in "decision making," particularly not with regard to macroscopic policies or program directions. They tend to base their actions on quite circumscribed grounds—routines, standard procedures, and immediately relevant considerations—and they may see evaluation's global pronouncements as largely irrelevant to their day-to-day work.

When formal decision making does occur, it is likely to deviate significantly from posited decision-making models. Rather than engaging in an exhaustive search for and assessment of decision options, decision makers are likely to consider a limited number of alternatives and may examine only a small amount of data pertinent to each, focusing on a few particularly critical criteria that a satisfactory choice must fulfill (Simon 1957). Political and bureaucratic needs are often among these critical concerns. Evaluations almost always focus on a different set of concerns, namely, a program or policy's tangible outcomes for a service population. Moreover, evaluations very often seek to avoid the controversy associated with discussions of political and bureaucratic issues. Consequently, evaluation usually provides only part of the data that decision makers desire. When all the critical criteria are taken into account, decision makers may reasonably arrive at judgments that seem at odds with evaluation information.

Evaluation's impact can be moderated by common organizational circumstances. There are also other factors that can affect evaluation information's impact, many of which can be more directly controlled by evaluators, or at least accommodated in constructive ways. These include evaluation's relevance and credibility; the manner in which information is shared between evaluators and users; the information processing styles of administrators; and the degree to which potential information users become actively interested in evaluation (Leviton and Hughes 1981). One unifying point here is that there are important personal and psychological components to information use. Evaluations which attend to these components are more likely to have their findings used.

Evaluation information that is relevant to administrators' or policy makers' self-perceived information needs is more likely to be considered in decision making. The timeliness with which evaluation information is delivered is an aspect of relevance, but research suggests it must be considered in proper perspective: poor timing can preclude the use of evaluation information in particular decisions, but because information's useful life-span can extend for months or years, even tardily delivered information can ultimately have impact.

If information is disbelieved, it is naturally less likely to have impact. Administrators and policy makers appear to judge information's credibility through a variety of means. Evaluation information usually is compared with information from other sources that appear credible; information from first-hand experience or trusted advisors frequently seems to be considered more valid than evaluation information.

Evaluation information is judged in part by judging the messenger, the evaluator: thus, evaluator credibility is important to information credibility and impact (Alkin et al. 1979). Methodological quality has been less convincingly associated with impact, because poor quality is not always detected. In highly politicized situations, however, methods have often come under close scrutiny, and methodological defects have impeded credibility and impact (perhaps appropriately so).

Effective information sharing between evaluators and users appears to facilitate impact in several ways. At the outset of the evaluation, better targeting to the interests and information needs of users can produce more useful information. At the conclusion of the evaluation, careful dissemination of evaluation results, with appropriate follow-up, helps deliver accurate understandable information to those persons who need and can use the information. Also, much has been said about the need to make evaluation presentations in a style that communicates effectively. One way to assure needed effectiveness is to match the preferences and characteristics of information users. Clarity of report language is, of course, critical. Presentations may have to be carefully adapted, since many potential information users are not technically trained in social research procedures. Indeed, managers often prefer regularly held discussions with evaluators, concisely written reports, and qualitative rather than quantitative data.

There is strong evidence that personal commitment and advocacy can affect evaluation information impact. When some administrator or policy maker takes a special interest in evaluation, evaluation is more likely to have impact. An interested user can draw others' attention to evaluation findings and can push for organizational changes suggested by evaluation. It has been suggested that evaluators should seek out and cultivate such potential users (Patton 1978).

## Bibliography

Alkin M C 1975 Evaluation: Who needs it? Who cares? *Stud. Educ. Eval.* 1(3): 201–12

Alkin M C, Daillak R H, White P 1979 *Using Evaluations: Does Evaluation Make a Difference?* Sage, Beverly Hills, California

David J L 1981 Local uses of Title I evaluations. *Educ. Eval. Policy Anal.* 3(1): 27–39

Leviton L C, Hughes E F X 1981 Research on the utilization of evaluations: A review and synthesis. *Eval. Rev.* 5: 525–48

Patton M Q 1978 *Utilization-focused Evaluation.* Sage, Beverly Hills, California

Simon H A 1957 *Administrative Behavior.* Macmillan, New York

Weiss C H 1977 *Using Social Research in Public Policy Making.* Lexington Books, Lexington, Massachusetts

# Issues in Test Use and Interpretation

## Norm-referenced Assessment

### D. Vincent

Educational assessment is said to be norm referenced, or normative, when it compares performance amongst those assessed. "Performance" is used to include a wide variety of cognitive and noncognitive processes which may be assessed for educational purposes. Most characteristic of these are learning outcomes, or achievements, measured by objective tests. However, nonobjective assessment of attainment and performance in the form of response to affective measures are both often entirely amenable to norm-referenced treatment. The following account of the main principles of norm referencing thus applies to these also, although many published accounts of the topic refer primarily to the measurement of achievement in the academic or cognitive sense. The process of comparison takes two forms. First, it may be based simply on the relative performance of individuals within a specified group, for example, candidates in a competitive entrance test for college or university. Secondly, and more generally, norm-referenced assessment involves the estimation of individual or group performance in relation to a level which is in some sense typical or average; the "norm", for a specified population. Thus, the two definitive features of a norm-referenced assessment "instrument"—typically a standardized test—are the capacity to spread out those assessed so that variations in performance can be clearly identified, and the availability of norms of performance, usually estimated population means and associated indices of dispersion. It is this that is meant by the "standardization" of a test.

The more effectively a test discriminates amongst testees of different abilities, the more accurate will be the normative interpretations made subsequently. A number of scaling systems are in use to express individual performance in normative terms. The majority of these express performance relative to the mean of a definitive group, either a population or, more commonly, a "standardization" sample representative of the population. It follows that the more sensitive an instrument is to fine differences of performance in the standardization sample, the more precisely individuals or subgroups can be compared subsequently with the norm.

The history of educational assessment—and of a large

part of mental measurement—has been, effectively, a history of norm-referenced assessment. The expression "norm referenced" became current in the 1960s to contrast this established model of educational assessment with emerging alternatives, particularly criterion-referenced assessment of achievement. A review of the contrasts between criterion- and norm-referenced assessment is given in Mehrens and Lehmann (1969).

Norm-referenced assessment deals with rankings and relative performance amongst individuals. This has a primarily statistical rather than curricular meaning. Norms are thus essentially contingent and neutral indices. They convey little in absolute terms about the quality or content of learning or attainment. The content of a normative attainment test may, of course, be selected to reflect desirable outcomes of learning. However, the norms for a test do not necessarily constitute a desirable standard, only a typical one. Norms describe, they do not prescribe.

In the assessment of skills and achievements a distinction can be made between performance and progress. In practice, education is as much concerned with the latter as the former. Many programmes involving norm-referenced assessment regularly monitor and record progress throughout a school or college career, going beyond once-only appraisals of performance. Published norm-referenced instruments are thus usually designed to take account of progress by provision of equivalent forms of a test, incorporation of appropriate age or grade level adjustments in the scaling system and by adjustments for retesting and, occasionally, time of testing. Such technical refinements eliminate or hold constant influences which may distort evidence of apparent progress or improvement. They provide evidence of progress by default: elimination of extraneous or spurious sources of variation makes it more likely that whatever remains can be attributed to genuine progress. This may provide sufficient precision for many practical applications of norm-referenced assessment. However, it should be noted that the majority of such procedures rely upon data derived from cross-sectional studies. In the case of adjustments for age and grade, linear increases in raw-score levels across age or grade samples are used to infer the extent to which progress can be attributed to developmental, maturational or temporal factors and, thus, to normal progress. Such procedures cannot be as authoritative as direct study of progress through longitudinal monitoring of the same, or equivalent, groups of learners. Strictly speaking, therefore, true norms for progress are rarely available.

## 1. Construction

Two main sets of principles govern the construction of norm-referenced measures: those concerning content and format and those concerning psychometric properties. Matters of content are determined according to the type of process to be assessed. For example, measures of general intellectual ability would be based, ideally, on fully developed theories or models of intelligence. Contrastingly, an attitude scale might develop atheoretically, commencing simply with a pool of statements people have made of their own attitudes to a subject. Most standard texts on achievement tests recommend an initial curriculum analysis be made. This takes the form of a rationale or blueprint which specifies, often as a cross-tabulated grid, processes and content to be assessed. Such an analysis may already exist as a result of systematic specifications of learning objectives at some prior curriculum planning stage. In either case, items are thereafter drafted to accord with the categories of behaviour and content specified. Exact numbers and balance of items will be selected to reflect the relative importance attached to different categories. At this stage it is customary for draft items to be reviewed by subject specialists. This may assist in weeding out poor items and ensuring general content validity of the test. These content planning and review procedures also perform an important consultative function where a large-scale or potentially controversial testing programme is proposed.

Many techniques and formats exist for the presentation of items, but objective formats, particularly multiple choice, are consistently popular, being more economical while no less valid than other methods.

The psychometric characteristics of norm-referenced assessment are fully treated in many textbooks, both introductory and advanced. These show how a sophisticated technology can be brought to bear in evaluating and controlling statistical features of items and tests. However, most judicious authors would accept that technical considerations should not apply to the exclusion of cognate and curricular issues.

The apparent extent of the statistical dimension to normative measurement need not entirely deter teachers who are not test specialists from application of these principles in devising their own tests. For example, use of even simple item analysis procedures would help ensure a school-made test provided the required spread and discrimination amongst testees. In this respect, at least, the teacher-made instrument can approach the efficiency of the published product of the test specialist. Estimations of reliability and error of measurement also

enhance the clarity with which teachers might interpret results on their own tests. However, establishing meaningful norms is a task which, perhaps by definition, lies outside the scope of individual institutions. It is also debatable whether studies exploring underlying dimensions or latent trait structure would be appropriate, although these are of great theoretical interest to the researcher. They are also subject to more academic controversy than routine aspects of item analysis and reliability. Published guides for the nonspecialist in basic principles of normative test construction are certainly available (e.g., Marshall and Hales 1971, Nuttall and Skurnik 1969) although the extent of their actual use has not been widely researched.

## 2. Applications

Norm-referenced assessment is used extensively throughout many education systems in administration and teaching, clinical and guidance work, research, and evaluation. The practical and conceptual basis for applying and interpreting normative measurement in such fields is dealt with in established texts such as Cronbach (1970), and Thorndike and Hagen (1977).

The wisdom of this great reliance upon testing has been questioned (e.g., Broadfoot 1979), particularly where it has been an instrument of administrative policy. Certainly, for national or regional administrators, the potential of norm-referenced measurement to differentiate between students of differing abilities, has proved particularly attractive. Problems of screening and selection can be conveniently tackled by use of instruments with the requisite measuring powers. For example, numerous published tests have been produced to identify children who have difficulty in learning to read English as a first language. These are selected, or devised, to contain a sufficient number of relatively easy items to enable the test to distinguish between poor and average readers and to make fine distinctions and rankings within the former group. Such tests are widely used on an administrative regional scale to identify children who may require specialist remedial instruction. At the other extreme, it is the practice in some countries to employ general ability and scholastic aptitude tests to select candidates for advanced or higher education. Here the emphasis may well be upon above-average difficulty for the relevant population. This will allow the maximum discrimination amongst high performers and thus assist, or indeed determine, the process of selection. Use of norm-referenced instruments for selection and placement in education has aroused criticism in some countries. However, the most telling of these criticisms tend to concern the psychological theories on which such tests are based rather than their psychometric properties. In some countries, concern for accountability in education has brought pressure for greater use of system-wide monitoring and evaluation. This may include a strong component of normative measurement. Indeed the need for comprehensive curriculum coverage and longitudinal continuity in such programmes, has acted as a stimulus for innovations in methods of assessment, notably in the field of item banking.

The social impact of accountability-related assessment programmes can be considerable, particularly where results for individual institutions are published. Here the use of norm-referenced assessment cannot avoid close scrutiny. Even where criticisms of technical adequacy can be answered, a more fundamental question remains. This concerns the capacity of normative measurement to fully express or encapsulate school achievement. In this respect assessment of what is learned (criterion-referenced assessment), as opposed to measurement of normative relationships, is of considerable interest. There are also more radical alternatives, such as those proposed in Burgess and Adams (1980) for assessment in British secondary education.

The purposes served by norm-referenced assessment at national or regional level have close counterparts at the level of school or college administration. Screening, selection, placement, and monitoring of standards are perennial concerns of school administration. There are also some additional purposes, notably the keeping of individual student records, where information from normative assessment may feature as a matter of routine. The extent to which a distinction can be made between the use of norm-referenced assessment as an administrative rather than pedagogic device, depends largely upon local circumstances. Ideally, there would be continuity between the two purposes. In practice, the extent to which the normative assessments made in an institution contribute constructively to the work of individual teachers varies greatly. Much of this is probably determined by the approach and emphasis of national and local policy. Where this has aroused resent-

ment because of its extent, or suspicion over the way results will be used, it may seem ironic to suggest normative measurement has any genuine pedagogic value. Defenders of norm-referenced assessment would, nevertheless, point to intrinsic capacity to clarify and add perspective, if not objectivity, to teachers' judgments of individual and group achievement. Applied at class or group level, it can be illuminative of range and differences in achievement and the effects of changes and innovations in teaching method. It can also dispel conjecture concerning standards of achievement in relation to relevant population norms and elucidate strengths and weaknesses in different skill or subject areas. All this presupposes appropriate training, expertise, and availability of a suitable choice of instruments. In these respects the resources available at school level rarely match those at other levels.

## Bibliography

Broadfoot P 1979 *Assessment, Schools and Society*. Methuen, London

Burgess T, Adams E 1980 *Outcomes of Education*. Macmillan, Basingstoke

Cronbach L J 1970 *Essentials of Psychological Testing*. Harper and Row, New York

Marshall J C, Hales L W 1971 *Classroom Test Construction*. Addison-Wesley, Reading, Massachusetts

Mehrens W A, Lehmann I J 1969 *Standardized Tests in Education*. Holt, Rinehart and Winston, New York

Mehrens W A, Lehmann I J 1975 *Measurement and Evaluation in Education and Psychology*. Holt, Rinehart and Winston, New York

Nuttall D L, Skurnik L S 1969 *Examination and Item Analysis Manual*. National Foundation for Educational Research, Slough

Thorndike R L, Hagen E P 1977 *Measurement and Evaluation in Psychology and Education*, 4th edn. Wiley, New York

# Criterion-referenced Assessment in Evaluation

## R. K. Hambleton

Criterion-referenced tests are constructed to permit the interpretation of examinee test performance in relation to a set of well-defined competencies (Popham 1978). In relation to the competencies, there are three common uses for criterion-referenced test scores: (a) to describe examinee performance, (b) to assign examinees to mastery states (e.g., "masters" and "nonmasters"), and (c) to describe the performance of specified groups of examinees in program evaluation studies. Criterion-referenced tests are presently receiving extensive use in schools, industry, and the military in the United States because they provide information which is valued by test users and different from the information provided by norm-referenced tests. This article will introduce basic criterion-referenced testing concepts, compare these tests to norm-referenced tests, consider some

aspects of criterion-referenced test development, and describe several promising applications.

## 1. Basic Concepts

One of the first articles on the topic of criterion-referenced testing appeared in the *American Psychologist* (Glaser 1963). Over 700 papers on the topic have been published since then, and the scope and direction of educational testing has been changed dramatically. Glaser was interested in assessment methods that would provide necessary information for making a number of individual and programmatic decisions arising in connection with specific objectives or competencies. Norm-referenced tests were seen as limited in terms of providing the desired kinds of information.

At least 57 definitions of criterion-referenced measurement have been offered in the literature. Popham's definition which was introduced earlier in this article is probably the one which is most widely used. Several points about the definition deserve comment. First, terms such as objectives, competencies, and skills are used interchangeably in the field. Second, the competencies measured by a criterion-referenced test must be well-defined. Well-defined competencies make the process of item writing easier and more valid, and improve the quality of test score interpretations. The quality of score interpretations is improved because of the clarity of the content or behavior domains to which test scores are referenced. There is no limit on the breadth and complexity of a domain of content or behaviors defining a competency. The intended purpose of a test will influence the appropriate breadth and complexity of domains. Diagnostic tests are typically organized around narrowly defined competencies. End-of-year assessments will normally be carried out with more broadly defined competencies. Third, when more than one competency is measured in a test it is common to report examinee performance on each competency. Fourth, Popham's criterion-referenced test definition does not include a reference to a cutoff score or standard. It is common to set a minimum standard of performance for each competency measured in a criterion-referenced test and interpret examinee performance in relation to it. But, the use of test scores for describing examinee performance is common (e.g., the best estimate of student A's performance in relation to the domain of content defined by the competency is 70 percent) and standards are not needed for this type of score use. That a standard (or standards) may not be needed with a criterion-referenced test will come as a surprise to persons who have assumed (mistakenly) that the word "criterion" in "criterion-referenced test" refers to a "standard" or "cutoff score." In fact, the word "criterion" was used by Glaser (1963) and Popham and Husek (1969) to refer to a domain of content or behavior to which test scores are referenced.

Three additional points about criterion-referenced tests deserve mention: (a) the number of competencies measured by a criterion-referenced test will (in general) vary from one test to the next, (b) the number of test items measuring each competency and the value of the minimum standard will (in general) vary from one competency to the next, and (c) a common method for making mastery–nonmastery decisions involves the comparison of examinee percent (or proportion-correct) scores on competencies to the corresponding minimum standards. With respect to (c), when an examinee's percent score is equal to or greater than the standard, the examinee is assumed to be a "master" (M), otherwise the examinee is assumed to be a "nonmaster" (NM). There are however more complex decision-making models (for a review, see van der Linden 1980).

It is common to see terms like criterion-referenced tests, domain-referenced tests, and objectives-referenced tests in the psychometric literature. Popham's definition for a criterion-referenced test is similar to one Millman and others proposed for a domain-referenced test. There are no essential differences between the two if Popham's definition for a criterion-referenced test is adopted. The term "domain-referenced test" is a descriptive one and therefore it is less likely to be misunderstood than the term, "criterion-referenced test." One reason for continuing to use the term, "criterion-referenced test," even though it is less descriptive and its definition has become muddled in the psychometric literature, is that there is considerable public support in the United States for "criterion-referenced tests." It would seem to be a waste of valuable time to mount a campaign for a new term.

Objectives-referenced tests consist of items that are matched to objectives. The principal difference between criterion-referenced tests and objectives-referenced tests is that in a criterion-referenced test, items are organized into clusters with each cluster serving (usually) as a representative set of items from a clearly defined content domain measuring an objective, while with an objectives-referenced test, no clear domain of content is specified for an objective, and items are not considered to be representative of any content domain. Therefore, interpretations of examinee performance on objectives-referenced tests should be limited to the particular items on the test.

## 2. Norm-referenced and Criterion-referenced Tests

Proponents of norm-referenced and criterion-referenced tests in the United States waged a battle in the 1970s for supremacy of the achievement testing world. A third group argued that there was only one kind of achievement test from which both criterion-referenced and norm-referenced score interpretations could be made when needed. It is now clear that there was no winner although in the 10-year period the uses of criterion-referenced tests did increase substantially in the United States. Also, there was a reduction in the amount of norm-referenced testing taking place. There was no winner because it is clear that it is meaningful to distinguish between two kinds of achievement tests and both kinds of tests have important roles to play in providing information for test users. Norm-referenced achievement tests are needed to provide reliable and valid normative scores for comparing examinees. Criterion-referenced achievement tests are needed to facilitate the interpretation of examinee performance in relation to well-defined competencies.

Although the differences between norm-referenced tests and criterion-referenced tests are substantial, the two kinds of tests share many features. In fact, it would be a rare individual who could distinguish between them from looking at the test booklets alone. They use the same item formats; test directions are similar; and both kinds of tests can be standardized.

There are a number of important differences, however, between them. The first difference is test purpose. A norm-referenced test is constructed specifically to facilitate comparisons among examinees in the content area measured by the test. It is common to use age-, percentile-, and standard-score norms to accomplish the test's purpose. Since test items are (or can be) referenced to competencies, criterion-referenced score interpretations (or, more correctly, objectives-referenced score interpretations) are possible but are typically limited in value because of the (usually) small number of test items measuring any competency in the test. Criterion-referenced tests, on the other hand, are constructed to assess examinee performance in relation to a set of competencies. Scores may be used (a) to describe examinee performance, (b) to make mastery–nonmastery decisions, and (c) to evaluate program effectiveness. Scores can be used to compare examinees but comparisons may have relatively low reliability if score distributions are homogeneous.

The second difference is in the area of content specificity. It is common for designers of both test types to prepare test blueprints or tables of specifications. It is even possible that norm-referenced test designers will prepare behavioral objectives. But, criterion-referenced test designers must (typically) prepare considerably more detailed content specifications than provided by behavioral objectives to ensure that criterion-referenced test scores can be interpreted in the intended way. This point will be considered further in the next section. Thus, with respect to content specifications, the difference between the two types is in the degree to which test content must be specified.

The third difference is in the area of test development. With norm-referenced tests, item statistics (difficulty and discrimination indices) serve an important role in item selection. In general, items of moderate difficulty (p-values in the range 0.30 to 0.70) and high discriminating power (point biserial correlations over 0.30) are most likely to be selected for a test because they contribute substantially to test score variance. Test reliability and validity will, generally, be higher when test score variance is increased. In contrast, criterion-referenced test items are only deleted from the pools of test items measuring competencies when it is determined that they violate the content specifications or standard principles of item writing, or if the available item statistics reveal serious noncorrectable flaws. Item statistics can be used to construct parallel forms of a criterion-referenced test or to produce a test to discriminate optimally between masters and nonmasters in the region of a minimum standard of performance on the test score scale.

The fourth and final major area of difference between criterion-referenced tests and norm-referenced tests is test score generalizability. Seldom is there interest in making generalizations from norm-referenced achievement test scores. The basis for score interpretations is the performance of some reference group. In contrast, score generalizability is usually of interest with criterion-referenced tests. Seldom is there interest in the performance of examinees on specific sets of test items. When clearly specified competency statements are available and assuming test items are representative of the content domains from which they are drawn, examinee test performance can be generalized to performance in the larger domains of content defining the competencies. It is this type of interpretation which is (usually) of interest to criterion-referenced test users.

## 3. Content Specifications

Behavioral objectives had a highly significant impact on instruction and testing in the 1960s and 1970s. But, while behavioral objectives are relatively easy to write and have contributed substantially to the specification of curricula, they do not usually lead to clearly defined content descriptions defining competencies. Popham (1974) described tests built from behavioral objectives as "cloud-referenced tests." Several suggestions have been made for addressing the deficiency in behavioral objectives and thereby making it possible to construct valid criterion-referenced tests. These suggestions include the use of item transformations, item forms, algorithms, and structural facet theory. Possibly the most versatile and practical of the suggestions was introduced by Popham (1978) and is called domain specifications, item specifications, or expanded objectives. Domain specifications serve four purposes: (a) they provide item writers with content and technical guidelines for preparing test items, (b) they provide content and measurement specialists with a clear description of the content and/or behaviors which are to be covered by each competency so that they can assess whether items are valid measures of the intended competencies, (c) they aid in interpreting examinee competency performance, and (d) they provide users with clear specifications of the breadth and scope of competencies. Some educational measurement specialists have even gone so far as to suggest that the emphasis on content specification has been the most important contribution of criterion-referenced testing to measurement practice (Berk 1980).

Using as a basis the work of Popham (1978), Hambleton (1982) suggested that a domain specification might be divided into four parts:

(a) Description—a short, concise statement of the content and/or behaviors covered by the competency.

(b) Sample directions and test item—an example of the test directions and a model test item to measure the competency.

(c) Content limits—a detailed description of both the content and/or behaviors measured by the competency, as well as the structure and content of the

---

*Description*
The student will identify the tones or emotions expressed in paragraphs.

*Sample directions and test item*
Directions: Read the paragraph below. Then answer the question and circle the letter beside your answer.

Jimmy had been playing and swimming at the beach all day. Now it was time to go home. Jimmy sat down in the back seat of his father's car. He could hardly keep his eyes open.

How did Jimmy feel?

A. Afraid   B. Friendly   C. Tired   D. Kind

*Content limits*
1. Paragraphs will describe situations which are familiar to grade 3 students.
2. Paragraphs should contain between three and six sentences. Readability levels should be at the third grade (using the Dale-Chall formula).
3. Tones or emotions expressed in the passages should be selected from the list below:

| sad | mad | angry | kind |
| tired | scared | friendly | excited |
| happy | lucky | smart | proud |

*Response limits*
1. Answer choices should be one word in length.
2. Four answer choices should be used with each test item.
3. Incorrect answer choices may be selected from the list above.
4. Incorrect answer choices should be tones or emotions which are familiar to students in grade 3 and which are commonly confused with the correct answer.

**Figure 1**
A typical domain specification in the reading area

item pool. (This section should be so clear that items may be divided by reviewers into those items that meet the specifications and those items that do not.) Sometimes clarity is enhanced by also specifying areas which are not included in the content domain description.

(d) Response limits—a description of the kind of incorrect answer choices which must be prepared. The structure and content of the incorrect answers should be stated in as much detail as possible.

An example of a domain specification is shown in Fig. 1. Once properly prepared domain specifications are available, the remaining steps in the test development process can be carried out.

## 4. Criterion-referenced Test Development

It is essential to specify in as clear a form as possible the domain of content or behaviors defining each competency which is to be measured in the test being constructed. The mechanism through which the competencies are identified will vary from one situation to the next. For high-school graduation exams, the process might involve district educational leaders meeting to review school curricula and identifying a relatively small set of important broad competencies (e.g., reading comprehension, mathematics computations). When criterion-referenced tests are needed in an objectives-based instructional program, it is common to define a curriculum in broad areas (and, sometimes into a two-dimensional grid). Then, within the cells of the grid the sets of relevant objectives, often stated in behavioral form, are specified, reviewed, revised, and finalized. With certification exams, it is common to first conduct a "role delineation study" with individuals working in the area to identify the responsibilities, subresponsibilities, and activities which serve to define a role. Next, the knowledge and skills which are needed to carry out the role are identified.

A set of 12 steps for preparing criterion-referenced tests adapted from Hambleton (1982) is suggested in Table 1.

## 5. Applications of Criterion-referenced Tests

Criterion-referenced tests (or domain-referenced tests, mastery tests, competency tests, basic skills tests, or certification exams as they are alternately called) are being used in a large number of settings in the United States to address many problem areas. Criterion-referenced tests are finding substantial use in American schools. Classroom teachers use criterion-referenced test score results to locate students correctly in school programs, to monitor student progress, and to identify student deficiencies. Special education teachers are finding criterion-referenced test scores especially helpful in diagnosing student learning deficiencies and monitoring the progress of their students. Criterion-referenced test results are also being used to evaluate various school programs. While it is less common, criterion-referenced tests are finding some use in higher educational programs as well (e.g., those programs based upon the mastery learning concept). Also, criterion-referenced tests are in common use in military and industrial training programs.

In recent years, it has become common for state departments of education and (sometimes) school districts to define sets of skills (or competencies) which students must achieve in order to be promoted from one grade to the next, or in some states, to receive high-school diplomas. The nature of these criterion-referenced testing programs varies dramatically from one place to another. For example, in some places, students are held responsible for mastering a specified set of skills at each grade level, in other states, skills

**Table 1**
Steps for constructing criterion-referenced tests

| Steps | Comments |
|---|---|
| 1. Preliminary considerations<br><br>(a) Specify test purposes.<br>(b) Specify groups to be measured and (any) special testing requirements (due to examinee age, race, sex, socioeconomic status, handicaps, etc.).<br>(c) Determine the time and money available to produce the test.<br>(d) Identify qualified staff.<br>(e) Specify an initial estimate of test length. | This step is essential to ensure that a test development project is well-organized and important factors which might have an impact on test quality are identified early. |
| 2. Review of competency statements<br><br>(a) Review the descriptions of the competencies to determine their acceptability.<br>(b) Make necessary competency statement revisions to improve their clarity. | Domain specifications are invaluable to item writers when they are well-done. Considerable time and money can be saved later in revising test items if item writers are clear on what it is that is expected of them. |
| 3. Item writing<br><br>(a) Draft a sufficient number of items for pilot-testing.<br>(b) Carry out item editing. | Some training of item writers in the importance and use of domain specifications, and in the principles of item writing is often desirable. |
| 4. Assessment of content validity<br><br>(a) Identify a sufficient pool of judges and measurement specialists.<br>(b) Review the test items to determine their match to the competencies, their representativeness, and their freedom from bias and stereotyping.<br>(c) Review the test items to determine their technical adequacy. | This step is essential. Items are evaluated by reviewers to assess their match to the competencies, their technical quality, and their freedom from bias and stereotyping. |
| 5. Revisions to test items<br><br>(a) Based upon data from 4(b) and 4(c), revise test items (when possible) or delete them.<br>(b) Write additional test items (if needed) and repeat step 4. | Any necessary revisions to test items should be made at this step and when additional test items are needed, they should be written, and step 4 carried out again. |
| 6. Field test administration<br><br>(a) Organize the test items into forms for pilot testing.<br>(b) Administer the test forms to appropriately chosen groups of examinees.<br>(c) Conduct item analyses, and item validity and item bias studies. | The test items are organized into booklets and administered to appropriate numbers of examinees. That number should reflect the importance of the test under construction. Appropriate revisions to test items can be made here. Item statistics are used to identify items which may be in need of revision: (a) items which may be substantially easier or harder than other items measuring the same competencies, (b) items with negative or low positive discriminating power, and (c) items with distractors which were selected by small percentages of examinees. |
| 7. Revisions to test items<br><br>(a) Revise test items when necessary or delete them using the results from 6(c). | Whenever possible, malfunctioning test items should be revised and added to the pools of acceptable test items. When revisions to test items are substantial they should be returned to step 4. |
| 8. Test assembly<br><br>(a) Determine the test length, and the number of forms needed and the number of items per objective.<br>(b) Select test items from the available pool of valid test items.<br>(c) Prepare test directions, practice questions, test booklet layout, scoring keys, answer sheets, etc. | Test booklets are compiled at this step. When parallel-forms are required, and especially if the tests are short, item statistics should be used to ensure matched forms are produced. |

*(continued)*

**Table 1**  (continued)

9. Selection of a standard

   (a) Initiate a process to determine the standard to separate "masters" and "nonmasters."

A standard-setting procedure must be selected and implemented. Care should be taken to document the selection process.

10. Pilot test administration

   (a) Design the administration to collect score reliability and validity information.
   (b) Administer the test form(s) to appropriately chosen groups of examinees.
   (c) Evaluate the test administration procedures, test items, and score reliability and validity.
   (d) Make final revisions based on data from 10(c).

At this step, test directions can be evaluated, scoring keys can be checked, and reliability and validity of scores and decisions can be assessed.

11. Preparation of manuals

   (a) Prepare a test administrator's manual.
   (b) Prepare a technical manual.

For important tests, a test administration manual and a technical manual should be prepared.

12. Additional technical data collection

   (a) Conduct reliability and validity investigations.

No matter how carefully a test is constructed or evaluated, reliability and validity studies should be carried out on an ongoing basis.

---

which must be acquired are specified at selected grade levels, and in still other states, only a set of skills which must be mastered for high-school graduation is specified.

One of the most important applications of criterion-referenced tests is to the areas of professional certification and licensure. It is now common in the United States, for example, for professional organizations to establish entry-level examinations which must be passed by candidates before they are allowed to practice in their chosen professions. In fact, many of these professional organizations have also established recertification exams. A typical examination will measure the competencies which define the professional role and candidate test performance is interpreted in relation to minimum standards which are established. There are now hundreds of professional organizations, including most groups in the medical and allied health fields, which have instituted certification and recertification exams.

*Bibliography*

Berk R A (ed.) 1980 *Criterion-Referenced Measurement: The State of the Art*. Johns Hopkins University Press, Baltimore, Maryland

Glaser R 1963 Instructional technology and the measurement of learning outcomes. *Am. Psychol.* 18: 519–21

Hambleton R K 1982 Advances in criterion referenced testing technology. In: Reynolds C, Gutkin T (eds.) 1982 *Handbook of School Psychology*. Wiley, New York

Hambleton R K, Swaminathan H, Algina J, Coulson D B 1978 Criterion-referenced testing and measurement: A review of technical issues and developments. *Rev. Educ. Res.* 48: 1–47

Popham W J 1974 An approaching peril: Cloud referenced tests. *Phi Delta Kappan* 55: 614–15

Popham W J 1978 *Criterion-Referenced Measurement*. Prentice-Hall, Englewood Cliffs, New Jersey

Popham W J, Husek T R 1969 Implications of criterion-referenced measurement. *J. Educ. Meas.* 6: 1–9

van der Linden W J 1980 Decision models for use with criterion-referenced tests. *Appl. Psychol. Meas.* 4: 469–92

# Test Administration

## P. W. Airasian and S. Terrasi

The primary purpose of testing is to obtain information to help make inferences about an examinee's performance on a behavior domain of interest. Achieving this purpose depends upon good judgment at each of the five steps in the testing process: construction, selection, administration, scoring, and interpretation. This discussion focuses upon standardized test administration, its steps, implementation, and import. While good administration procedures are essential for successful

testing, one must bear in mind that test administration is but one link in the chain of testing practice.

All tests must be administered, although the type of test, the purpose, and the conditions of administration may vary widely. Tests may be administered to a single individual or to a large group. The examinee may be either unaware or acutely aware of being tested. Tests may assess cognitive, affective, or psychomotor aspects of an examinee's performance. To provide focus to this discussion in light of the variegated dimensions of test administration, only standardized test administration will be considered here.

A standardized test is one which is constructed for use in more than one setting. A test is standardized in the sense that the administration procedures, directions, apparatus, and scoring are fixed by the test constructor so that the test may be administered and scored identically by different examiners in different settings to achieve comparable results across all examinees. It is noted that many of the issues to be discussed here also have relevance for the administration of nonstandardized tests.

Test administration is the process of attending and responding to the physical and emotional factors in a testing situation which may have a significant influence on an examinee's performance and therefore on the inferences made on the basis of that performance. Six aspects of test administration will be discussed: (a) administration parameters set by the test developer; (b) examiner preparation; (c) physical setting for testing; (d) emotional setting for testing; (e) presenting the test (individual versus group testing); (f) scoring and reporting. Suggestions for good practice and consequences of poor practice will be discussed for each aspect of the administration process.

## 1. Administration Parameters Set by the Test Developer

A test developer must provide materials and information pertinent to a test's administration. The responsibility of test developers in this regard is delineated in the *Standards for Educational and Psychological Tests* (1974), which includes detailed suggestions for the contents of a manual to aid qualified users to administer, score, and interpret the results of the test. Further, if a test is to be administered appropriately and the results interpreted validly, the test developer must inform the user of the intended audience for and purposes of the test, the construct that the test purports to measure, and the consistency with which it measures that construct.

In addition to other technical information spelled out in the *Standards*, the test developer must provide specific administration guidelines. These should specify the level of expertise required of the examiner, including any special training or certification necessary to administer the test. If the test is intended for a number of uses, the level of expertise required for *each* use should be specified, since different test uses may require different levels of administrative experience and expertise.

The directions for administration should be presented in detail sufficient for the administrative conditions to be duplicated readily across different test settings. Information about the prescribed time limits (if any), oral directions for examinees (often a script is provided to be read to examinees), policy on guessing on test items,

suggestions for the distribution of materials, guidelines for how to deal with examinee questions, and so on all should be described by the test developer.

The developer must provide directions for test taking that are comprehensible to the intended examinees. The validity of the inferences derived from the test is destroyed if examinees fail test items because of poor directions rather than because of lack of knowledge of the content being tested. Sample items help to attain the necessary understanding of the tasks involved in the test, particularly for young or inexperienced test takers. Further, in situations in which the examinees work on the test at their own speeds, printed guides such as "Go on to the next page" or "Stop here" increase the likelihood that examinees will attempt all desired items and stop at the proper place.

The use of separate answer sheets or other manipulative materials should be explained in detail to the examinees. Practice exercises and having the examiner check that examinees understand how and where to record answers is recommended strongly, especially for younger children. While separate answer sheets allow for speedy, convenient scoring, examinees must know how to utilize them correctly before accurate and valid data can be assumed. In general, separate answer sheets are not recommended for children under 6 or 7 years of age.

Finally, the test developer must describe the procedures for scoring responses to the test items. In cases involving objective type items, scoring will not usually present a problem. However, when the responses to items are less structured and require interpretation and judgment in scoring, the developer must establish clear criteria for scoring and must provide evidence of interscorer agreement using those criteria. For some individually administered tests, the examinee's responses determine whether the examiner will stop testing or proceed on to new test items. In such situations, the test is being scored as it is being administered and the necessity of clear scoring instructions and an experienced, certified examiner are apparent. The general issue of concern in test administration and scoring, particularly for less structured types of item formats, is that the testing conditions be sufficiently well-defined that an individual examinee's test score reflects his or her actual performance on the trait of interest, rather than error resulting from faulty administration conditions or inaccurate scoring.

In sum, the test developer is responsible for providing substantial and specific information about the nature, purpose, and audience for the test as well as directions for administering, scoring, and interpreting results. Valid inferences about examinees' performance and fair comparisons among examinees in different test settings are predicated upon standardized conditions of test administration. If time limits, directions, scoring procedures, and the like are allowed to vary widely across administrations of a test, there will be no common or equitable basis on which to compare all test takers. It is for this reason that standardized test administration is so important and that the initial concern with test administration rests with the test developer.

## 2. *Examiner Preparation*

The examiner has responsibilities before, during, and after test administration. This section focuses upon responsibilities prior to actual test administration, although it will be noted that there is overlap among the examiner's responsibilities that occur at different times. Three areas of examiner preparation are discussed: (a) self-preparation of the examiner; (b) preparation of test materials; (c) preparation of examinees.

The examiner must possess the level of expertise required for proper administration, scoring, and interpretation of the test or test results. The level of expertise required may range from the ability to read and follow written directions, as for most group-administered ability and attainment tests, to formal certification from an accrediting agency, as for many individually administered intelligence and projective tests. In general, the procedures for administering most group-administerd tests are relatively simple and straightforward, requiring no special training. Individually administered tests of ability, attainment, or personality require more intensive examiner training and preparation (Brown 1980). The test administrator must possess sufficient knowledge and training to duplicate the conditions under which the test was designed to be given. At the very least, this means that the examiner must have detailed knowledge of the intended administration conditions and procedures *prior to* the time of actual test administration. Most errors in administration are caused by the examiner's failure to prepare sufficiently beforehand.

The examiner is responsible for ensuring that proper quantities and types of materials necessary to administer the test be on hand. Provision for faulty materials should be made by having extras available. Security of the test and test materials prior to test administration must be safeguarded by the examiner. Pretest security is most important when examinee familiarity with the test, test materials, or administrative conditions prior to testing may provide the examinee with an unfair advantage over less familiar peers. Careful attention to counting, collating, distributing, and collecting tests and test materials both before and after test administration can aid greatly in maintaining test security.

Preparation of the examinees is the third facet of the examiner's preadministrative responsibilities. The purposes of such preparation are to inform examinees and often their parents that testing will be carried out, to provide a general description of the types of tasks examinees will be required to perform, and to describe the general purpose for testing. Often, preparation also involves obtaining parental permission for the pupil to sit for the test. In addition to possibly reducing

anxiety on testing day, notification and preparation of examinees represent an effort to adjust for differential test-taking sophistication among examinees. Lack of familiarity with tests tasks and purposes may have detrimental consequences upon less test-sophisticated examinees, reducing their scores, decreasing the validity of comparisons with their more test-sophisticated peers, and affecting decisions made about examinees.

Tutoring, teaching the content of particular tests, and teaching general test-taking strategies are common practices in situations in which performance on a test is an important determiner of an individual's educational or life chances. Studies of the effects of such practices on examinee performance differ in scope, procedure, and results (Cronbach 1970), but in general, gains in test scores from coaching tend to be relatively small. However, the test administrator must realize that a test score is invalidated when a particular experience or training session raises an examinee's score without appreciably affecting the behavior domain that the test samples (Anastasi 1981).

Generally speaking, examinee preparation for test administration will be accomplished by means of booklets or pamphlets provided by the test publisher for distribution to pupils and parents. In situations in which such information is not available, the test administrator may wish to provide information to pupils and parents about the nature, tasks, and purpose of forthcoming testing.

## 3. *Physical Setting for Testing*

Many physical aspects of the test environment must be controlled in order to obtain valid, comparable test results from examinees. An essential part of many test situations is time-keeping. The examiner should use an accurate stopwatch or timing device, preferably with a second indicator. A wall clock visible to all examinees or some other means of posting time information will help examinees in a group testing situation to pace themselves. Time accorded to reading test instructions and directions is not normally included in the time for test taking unless specified by the test author. Comparable test results are not obtained when examinees are given different work periods on a test that calls for a standard time allotment.

The physical comfort of examinees should also be assured as much as is possible during testing. Distractions and physical discomfort can interfere with examinees manifesting their best test performances. A sign indicating "Testing. Please Do Not Disturb" posted on the examination room door can eliminate many unwanted intrusions. Outside noises such as public address systems, telephones, bell schedules, and so on should be suspended during testing whenever possible. Examinees should have adequate work space, comfortable chairs, and level desks or tables on which to work. Adequate lighting, proper ventilation, and a moderate temperature in the testing room are also important.

Many of the guidelines suggested in this section are fairly commonsense notions about the physical comfort of examinees during test taking. It is important to remember that while physical comfort is important in its own right, it is doubly important in the testing situation, since physical discomfort may distract and impair examinees' ability to manifest their best representative test performance.

## 4. *Emotional Setting for Testing*

Testing is a social activity which calls for interaction between examiner and examinees. Consequently, test administrators must be concerned with the emotional setting in which testing transpires. Ideally, the examiner seeks to develop rapport, reduce anxiety, and motivate effort among examinees. While there is no single method or strategy which ensures that these aims will be realized with each examinee, and while the importance of the emotional rapport between examiner and examinee is greater in individual than group testing situations, there are a few general guidelines to follow in order to help attain the proper emotional setting for testing.

In individual or group testing situations, examinee questions should be responded to without disdain, sarcasm, or impatience, no matter how trivial or redundant the questions may appear. Examiners need to be sensitive to the feelings of examinees and to develop techniques for eliciting examinees' best performance. These aims may be difficult to attain in group-administered test situations, since examinees in such situations cannot be singled out from the remainder of the group for special encouragement or explanation. The advantage of increased efficiency in the group testing situation is offset to some extent by the examiner's inability to develop rapport with and to motivate each individual examinee. If possible in group test settings, individual examinee manifestations of poor rapport and motivation such as inattention, restlessness, and giving up should be noted by the examiner for future reference in interpreting scores.

When motivation to do well is excessively high or when the results of the test are perceived to have important consequences for the examinee's educational or life chances, test anxiety may develop and impede the examinee's performance (Sarason 1980). Explaining in a serious but friendly manner the purpose of the test and how results will be used tends to relax anxious examinees and increase the validity of obtained test scores. If the examiner convinces the examinees that the test will be used to help them, the validity of scores increases (Cronbach 1970). Although the examiner may be able to detect test anxiety or other emotional discomfort more easily in an individual than in a group testing situation, it may be difficult to calm and motivate all examinees in either context.

## 5. *Presenting the Test*

Instructions should be read slowly, in a clear voice, and in the exact wording provided by the test developer. Very often, examinees fail to read instructions carefully and thus cannot follow them, despite high interest and motivation to do well on the test. Most standardized test instructions will be complete enough to anticipate the types of questions examinees will ask, but occasionally unanticipated questions may arise. The general guidelines for examiners to follow are (a) to inform examinees *how* to respond to test questions, but not *what* to respond and (b) to answer questions only during the allotted time and only for all examinees simultaneously.

Testing a single examinee presents unique concerns. Usually, the types of decisions resulting from individually administered tests have greater consequences for the examinee than do decisions resulting from group administered tests. This means that the conditions of administration take on heightened importance and the role of the "sensitive" test administrator becomes more crucial. However, since most individually administered tests are characterized by continuous interaction between the examiner and the examinee, the rapport and emotional tone of the testing situation is idiosyncratic and difficult to standardize across all examiners or examinees. It is in the individually administered test situation that the examiner has the most discretion and latitude for structuring the environment and the interaction that takes place. Fortunately, it is individually administered testing which normally requires that examiners have formal certification to administer the test.

Thus, to elicit the examinee's best effort is essential for a test administrator, but the means to do this vary widely in nature and in potential effect upon different examinees. In most circumstances it is recommended that facial expressions, tones of voice, and the like be kept somewhat bland and noncommittal, so as not to provide encouraging or discouraging messages to the examinee and to avoid expectancy effects (Rosenthal 1966). But examinee rapport, interest in the tasks, and motivation may be hard for the examiner to achieve and maintain using the same techniques across different examinees. There has been much discussion, for example, of the effect of the race of the examiner and examinee upon test performance, but there is little hard evidence to support a strong racial effect (Sattler 1982).

Individually administered test items or tasks usually permit a wider variety of examinee responses than do more objective items typically found on group administered tests. So, not only does the examiner have to utilize discretion and sensitive judgment in presenting tasks to individual examinees, but also may often have to exercise the same discretion and judgment in scoring responses.

It is, therefore, not in the least bit platitudinous to talk about the "sensitive" test administrator and the "art" of test administration. Especially for individually administered tests, the humanity, psychological insight, and sensitivity of the examiner will be crucial to good testing practice. Good directions, instructions, and scoring keys set the parameters within which the examiner works, but the "art" of test administration is learning to work effectively within these parameters (Terman and Merrill 1960 pp. 47–48). Both the examiner and the examinee bring to the testing situation a set of attitudes, abilities, biases, and motives. The successful test administrator recognizes this fact and has a variety of strategies to structure the testing situation so as to obtain the best performance from all examinees.

## 6. Scoring and Reporting Issues

Responsible test scoring and reporting include documenting unusual conditions of administration which may have affected an examinee's test results significantly. For example, deviation from the standardized procedures developed by the test author must be considered in reporting and interpreting results. This recommendation has importance for testing special populations, groups on whom the test has not been normed or for whom the standard administration procedures are inappropriate. Modification of procedures is often made to accommodate special needs pupils or pupils from certain racial, ethnic, or language backgrounds. Modifications such as (a) extending time limits; (b) changing the mode of administration (e.g., from oral to visual); (c) translating items into another

language; and (d) using lower than appropriate levels of the test—all may provide more relevant assessment of special groups, but results obtained under altered conditions are not directly comparable to norms obtained under standard conditions. This fact is not meant to imply that such changes in test administration are never warranted; it does however insist that reporting and interpretation of results be done with full disclosure of departures from standard administration conditions.

## Bibliography

American Psychological Association 1974 *Standards for Educational and Psychological Tests*. American Psychological Association, Washington, DC

Anastasi A 1981 Coaching, test sophistication, and developed abilities. *Am. Psychol.* 36: 1086–93

Brown F G 1980 *Guidelines for Test Use: A Commentary on the Standards for Educational and Psychological Tests*. National Council on Measurement in Education, Washington, DC

Cronbach L J 1970 *Essentials of Psychological Testing*, 3rd edn. Harper and Row, New York

Rosenthal R 1966 *Experimenter Effects in Behavioral Research*. Appleton-Century-Crofts, New York

Sarason I G 1980 *Test Anxiety: Theory, Research and Applications*. Erlbaum, Hillsdale, New Jersey

Sattler J M 1982 *Assessment of Children's Intelligence and Special Abilities*, 2nd edn. Allyn and Bacon, Boston, Massachusetts

Terman L M, Merrill M A 1960 *Stanford–Binet Intelligence Scale: Manual for the Third Revision Form L-M*. Houghton Mifflin, Boston, Massachusetts

# Coaching for Tests and Examinations

**W. Haney**

Special preparation for tests and examinations seems to have occurred for as long as such means of assessment have been considered of importance in society. In his brief review of 3,000 years of civil service examinations in China, DuBois (1966) observes that millions of men prepared for the tests, often for decades, though few achieved success. In his book *China's Examination Hell*, Miyazaki (1976) recounts the extent to which special preparation for the Chinese examinations had become institutionalized in the Ming and Ch'ing eras, when the examination system had reached its most complex form:

> Because not very many places in the classics were suitable as subjects for examination questions, similar passages and problems were often repeated. Aware of this, publishers compiled collections of examination answers, and a candidate who relying on these compilations, guessed successfully during the course of his own examination could obtain a good rating without having to work very hard. . . . Reports from perturbed officials caused the government to issue frequent prohibitions of the publication of such collections of model answers, but since it was a profitable business with a steady demand, ways of issuing them sur-

> reptitiously were arranged and time and again, the prohibitions rapidly became mere empty formalities. (Miyazaki 1976 p. 17)

Such concerns foreshadowed worries which have recurred repeatedly over the issue of special preparation and coaching for tests. However, only with the introduction of "new type" objective tests and examinations in the twentieth century has much systematic investigation been brought to bear on worries over test coaching and special preparation. The following paragraphs briefly recount: (a) the history of systematic research on the topic of coaching; and (b) various ways in which coaching may influence test and examination results.

## 1. History of Inquiry

Modern testing can be conveniently dated from the invention of the Binet intelligence scale in 1905. Alfred Binet himself investigated the effects of special preparation on test results. In a 1911 article, for example, he discussed the effects of practice on levels of performance on his intelligence scale. He found that "there was an appreciable progress for all at the time of the second examination" given to 9-year-old pupils roughly 2 weeks after a first examination. Binet mentioned several factors which might have increased pupils' performance including memory (as the same test was used for both the first and second examinations), pupils' becoming accustomed to the testing situation, and instruction and learning. Binet noted too that pupils' gains were greater on some types of tasks than on others.

After the Binet scales were translated into English and Binet-type intelligence tests became common in the United States following the First World War, the effects of coaching became a topic for investigation in this country. Gilmore (1927), for example, investigated "how much a student's score in [Otis group] intelligence tests might be increased as a result of coaching" (p. 119). He concluded among other things that "students can be coached to the point of increasing their standing and score in intelligence tests even in case of the material [used in coaching] being only similar and not identical with that of the basic test" (p. 121).

Other research on coaching has appeared occasionally in the literature, but seems to have garnered special attention only in connection with tests which took on particular social significance. In connection with the British eleven-plus examination, for example, several articles were published in the early 1950s on effects of coaching and practice on group intelligence tests (e.g. Wiseman and Wrigley 1953). These and other inquiries of the time indicated that coaching could raise group intelligence test scores, but left in doubt the magnitude of gains attributable to coaching, the exact definition of coaching, whether effects of coaching persisted over time, whether the effects of coaching derived from increased "test sophistication," decreased text anxiety, or other factors, and what if anything should be done as a result of the finding that coaching increased test scores.

In the United States a similar pattern has been apparent, with coaching and research on coaching appearing mainly in regard to selection and certification instruments having considerable social significance; for example, the Scholastic Aptitude Tests used for college admissions (Whitla 1962, Pike 1978, Messick 1980); the Law School Admissions Test; and the national medical board examination (Scott et al. 1980). The general finding of most of this literature has been that special preparation and coaching can raise test scores, but to what extent, by which means, and with what implications, all have been questions receiving no clear answers.

## 2. Types of Special Preparation and Coaching

Pike (1978) provides a useful elaboration concerning coaching and more general test preparation, and also the various ways in which test scores may be improved as a result. He defined coaching as short-term instruction in test wiseness and in answering questions similar to those appearing on the target examination. Though the exact definition of test coaching has been a topic of some dispute, the essential point of agreement is that special preparation and coaching usually refer to efforts to raise examinees' scores on a particular target examination. Pike's formulation is useful because it indicates that such preparation can influence scores through three quite different means: (a) by altering the underlying skills and abilities which the test is designed to measure (what Pike calls the true score component); (b) by improving examinees' familiarity with the format, conventions, and particular types of tasks encountered in the target test (what Pike calls primary test-specific components); and (c) by improving examinees' levels of confidence and efficiency in test taking ("secondary components influencing test taking").

The influence of special preparation and coaching on test scores via these different paths obviously has different implications for both the validity and social significance of test results. At one extreme coaching might consist of instruction on the exact questions which are later to appear on a test—this possibility has been suggested with respect to the Scott et al. (1980) study of preparation for the medical board examination. Such practices would surely substantially diminish the validity of test results, and the social standing of such preparation is revealed by the fact that it is generally called cheating rather than coaching.

At the other extreme, coaching aimed at developing general skills such as verbal ability or mathematical reasoning becomes virtually synonymous with instruction. As such, questions about coaching begin to merge with long-familiar issues in educational research generally, concerning test validity, transferability of training, and social utility of educational measurement.

## Bibliography

Dersimonian R, Laird N 1983 Evaluating the effect of coaching on SAT scores: A meta-analysis. *Harvard Educ. Rev.* 53: 1–15

DuBois P 1966 Test dominated society: China 1115 BC–1905 AD. In: Anastasi A (ed.) 1966 *Testing Problems in Perspective.* American Council on Education, Washington, DC

French J, Dean R 1959 Effect of coaching on aptitude tests. *Educ. Psychol. Meas.* 19: 319–30

Gilmore M E 1927 Coaching for intelligence tests. *J. Educ. Psychol.* 18: 119–21

Messick S 1980 *The Effectiveness of Coaching for the SAT: Review and Reanalysis of Research from the Fifties to the FTC.* Educational Testing Service, Princeton, New Jersey

Messick S 1981 The controversy over coaching: Issues of effectiveness. *New direct. Test. Meas.* 11: 21–53

Miyazaki I 1976 *China's Examination Hell.* Weatherhill, New York

Pike L W 1978 *Short-term Instruction, Testwiseness, and the Scholastic Aptitude Test: A Literature Review with Research Recommendations.* Educational Testing Service, Princeton

New Jersey
Scott L K, Scott C W, Palmisano P A, Cunningham R D, Cannon N J, Brown S 1980 The effects of commercial coaching for the NBME Part I examination. *J. Med. Educ.* 55: 733–42

Whitla D K 1962 Effect of tutoring on scholastic aptitude test scores. *Pers. Guid. J.* 41: 32–37
Wiseman S, Wrigley J 1953 The comparative effects of coaching and practice on the results of verbal intelligence tests. *Br. J. Psychol.* 44(2): 83–94

# Test-wiseness

**R. E. Sarnacki**

Within an approximately 30-year period, the construct of test-wiseness has risen from a relatively obscure phenomenon to a universally recognized threat to test reliability and validity. Since its formal introduction into the literature (Thorndike 1951), test-wiseness has been operationally defined with subsequent extensive empirical research firmly establishing it as an observable theoretical construct in the domain of cognitive testing (Sarnacki 1979). Test-wiseness is best defined as "a subject's capacity to utilize the characteristics and formats of the test and/or the test-taking situation to receive a high score" (Millman et al. 1965); or similarly, the ability to manifest test-taking skills using the characteristics and formats of a test in order to receive a score commensurate with the criteria being measured.

Test-wiseness has been succinctly described as a "primary test specific component" that may affect observed scores through either (a) the examinee's general test-wiseness skills such as test familiarity, pacing, use of general testing strategies; or (b) his or her specific test-wiseness skills such as recognition of specific item construction flaws (Pike 1978). It should be obvious then that "test-wiseness is logically independent of the examinee's knowledge of the subject matter for which the items are supposedly measures" (Millman et al. 1965). In addition, test-wiseness may be observed through either situationally specific faults of the test, or manifestation of test-wiseness may occur as a persistent trait of individual examinees. Test-wiseness then, may be utilized on any test or test item that allows examinees to substitute test-wiseness for knowledge. Its persistent occurrence in cognitive measuring instruments suggests that test-wiseness may enter into any test score, whether wanted or not.

Although test-wise examinees may use their general test-taking skills on all types of tests, it is safe to say that test-wiseness more readily manifests itself on multiple-choice tests where maximum item-writing skills are required. Indeed, the majority of test-wiseness research has centered around the recognition of secondary item cues that occur in flawed multiple-choice items. For example, one item fault known as "absurd options" allows the test-wise examinee to eliminate one or more of the alternatives because of their logical inconsistencies with the stem.

In Figure 1, option (c) is not logically consistent with the stem since it is not a state, and therefore may be eliminated as a possible answer. A number of similar item faults have been delimited elsewhere (Millman et al. 1965, Sarnacki 1979), and have been subsequently employed extensively in the test-wiseness research. Regardless of which test-wiseness cues are observed, it should be noted that their appearance is independent of the content area being tested, and may occur on either teacher-made or standardized tests.

Since test-wiseness is independent of content area, its contribution to observed scores on any test that does not intentionally measure test-wiseness as the criterion is error variance. This means that test-wiseness may attenuate the test's validity since it typically represents systematic invalid variance that is not related to either the criterion or random error. Similarly, test reliability may be depressed since internal consistency estimates of reliability are deflated by the test-wiseness elements of guessing, clerical errors in responding, and careless omission of responses. More importantly to the individual test taker, individual differences in test-wiseness may exaggerate differences in observed scores, perhaps in the extreme leading to erroneous conclusions concerning levels of content knowledge. In practice, this means that since individuals differ in the amount of test wiseness they possess, students high in test-wiseness skills can profitably employ their talents on any flawed test. On the other hand, low test-wise examinees are penalized for a lack of such abilities, especially when normed against students high in test-wiseness. In addition, Ebel (1972) has pointedly noted that "more error in measurement is likely to originate from students who have too little, rather than too much, skill in taking tests." This problem is compounded daily, due to the ever-increasing use of multiple-choice tests, new multiple-choice item types, and an increasingly heterogeneous pool of prospective test takers.

As a theoretical construct, test-wiseness has received considerable attention in the refinement of its domain

---

The Golden Gate Bridge is located in which state?
a) Texas
b) Florida
c) San Francisco
d) California

*Figure 1*
Flawed multiple-choice item

definition. Researchers have not only experimentally manipulated the elements of the original test-wiseness taxonomy, but also discovered new test-wiseness elements dependent on novel formats of multiple-choice items, or on alternate cognitive strategies employed in answering standard multiple-choice items. Within this process of domain refinement, the test-wiseness construct has been accurately and reliably measured; observed on all types of cognitive test instruments; studied developmentally and cross-sectionally in age groups ranging from preschool children to middle-aged adults; found to be positively correlated with verbal ability; between uncorrelated and moderately positively correlated with intelligence; negatively correlated with text anxiety; and related to culture, but unrelated to sex. Finally, and probably most importantly, test-wiseness skills have been successfully taught to all levels of test-wise subjects through a variety of instructional formats, resulting in increased test performance on test-wise measures, cognitive tests, or both.

Most of the test-wiseness research has been performed in the United States and Canada. However, studies have been enacted in Sweden, demonstrating test-wiseness skills in grade school children and identifying test-wiseness as a source of error variance in cognitive testing (Nilsson 1975). In addition, the educational literature in European countries, which have imported the multiple-choice question, is beginning to focus on the relationships between test-wiseness and faults in item construction.

The large amount of attention that test-wiseness has received in the scientific literature attests to the consensus in recognition of test-wiseness as a source of extraneous variance in test scores. As suggested earlier, this interest has been necessitated in part by the ever increasing use of objective tests, and the development of complex item formats such as the various alternate multiple-choice items used in medical education. In addition, the growing pool of prospective test takers who differ widely in their test-wiseness skills (but are equally vociferous in demanding fair testing practices) has also stimulated researchers to study testing issues such as test-wiseness. This matrix of concern has translated into such practical measures as training in test-construction principles for future test makers, and innumerable programs for instruction in test-wiseness and test-taking skills for future examinees. The concern over test-wiseness skills in various testing environments has caused test-wiseness to become more than an esoteric variable for study by psychometricans only. Test-wiseness has literally achieved a place in the layperson's vernacular, and use of the term no longer carries definitional ambiguity. Consequently, the expanding employment of multiple-choice tests, the persistent nature of test-wiseness, and the demands of test consumers, all suggest that test-wiseness will continue to receive its share of attention.

## Bibliography

Ebel R L 1972 *Essentials of Educational Measurement*, 2nd edn. Prentice Hall, Englewood Cliffs, New Jersey

Millman J, Bishop C H, Ebel R 1965 An analysis of test-wiseness. *J. Educ. Res.* 25(3): 707–26

Nilsson I 1975 The occurrence of test-wiseness and the possibility of inducing it via instruction. *Educ. Rep. UMEÅ* No. 8

Pike L W 1978 *Short-term Instruction, Test-wiseness and the Scholastic Aptitude Test: A Literature Review with Research Recommendations*. Educational Testing Service, Princeton, New Jersey

Sarnacki R E 1979 An examination of test-wiseness in the cognitive test domain. *Rev. Educ. Res.* 49(2): 252–79

Thorndike E L 1951 Reliability. In: Lindquist E F (ed.) 1951 *Educational Measurement*. American Council on Education, Washington, DC

# Student Evaluation and Examination Anxiety

**F. D. Naylor**

Test-taking anxiety may be a specific instance of a more generalized academic anxiety that has chronic effects on performance whether or not the context of performance is test-like in character. On the other hand it may be a response to the particular characteristics of a test situation, in so far as that situation poses unique stresses. How unique the stress might be will depend on the cognitive appraisal of the perceived situation.

The extensive review of test anxiety by Sarason (1980) marked the end of more than a 20-year period of considerable theoretical development and empirical research in the area. Test-taking anxiety is important in education from the point of view of both the educator and the student. In so far as anxiety acts to distort test performance it can be rightly regarded as a source of measurement error that affects both the reliability and validity of tests. When tests are used at crucial decision-making points for students, the associated stress may be sufficient to interfere with performances that might have been anticipated in nonstressful conditions.

## 1. The Conditions for Test-taking Anxiety

The conditions for the arousal of anxiety in the context of testing are similar to those in other contexts: stress, perceived threat, and particularly threats to self-esteem. Spielberger (1966) formulated a theory of anxiety that distinguishes anxiety as a trait (A-Trait) from anxiety as a response or state (A-State). A-Trait refers to individual differences in anxiety proneness, whereas A-State refers to individual differences in the actual response to a particular stressful situation. Measures of both kinds of anxiety tend to be positively correlated. High and low A-Trait are inferred from the reported frequency of anxiety experiences, while differences in A-State, both within and between individuals, are inferred from reports of the intensity of the experience. The trait–state formulation has been most useful in clarifying both the conceptual and experimental understanding of test-taking anxiety.

### 1.1 Test Takers: A-Trait and A-State

The trait–state formulation is not explicit about the origins of A-Trait, though clearly it has both biological and experiential components. It appears to be something more than a residuum of A-State experiences in that it is held to influence the cognitive appraisal that might serve to trigger A-State. However, it is clear that there are substantial individual differences in A-Trait, and these differences are related to A-State responses in test and test-like situations. In general, persons who achieve high scores on measures of A-Trait tend to experience stress in a broader range of situations, and to experience greater intensities of A-State than do low scorers. It would be anticipated, therefore, that persons high on A-Trait would tend to experience greater anxiety (A-State) in test-like situations than those lower in A-Trait. The evidence is consistent with this proposition. Gaudry and Spielberger (1971) have reviewed studies which show that the expected relationship between A-Trait and A-State holds, and that performance decrements are primarily due to the influence of A-State.

There tends to be a negative correlation between measures of A-Trait and intelligence, and this appears to influence the cognitive appraisal of a test-like situation. Gaudry and Spielberger (1971) point out that there are interactions between test anxiety and intelligence in the determination of performance such that at the highest levels of ability, anxiety appears to have a facilitating effect on performance.

### 1.2 Grouping by Ability

Sarnoff et al. (1958) conducted a cross-cultural study of English and American children which led to a great deal more research on the relationship between anxiety and ability grouping or "streaming". Given the British educational practice of streaming by ability in the later years of primary school, and the "eleven-plus" selection examination for secondary education, Sarnoff et al. (1958) predicted that English children would tend to be more test anxious than their American counterparts. The results of the study accorded with the prediction whereas scores on the General Anxiety Scale for Children were comparable in both groups.

Australian studies derived from these findings and reviewed by Gaudry and Spielberger (1971) produced similar results. They showed that mean test-anxiety scores tended to be higher in the lower streams than in the upper streams. The data in all these studies were correlational, and evidence provided by Levy et al. (1969) suggested the possibility that the apparent correlation between streaming practices and test anxiety was really due to the pre-existing negative correlations between test anxiety and ability.

Experimental studies reported by Gaudry and Spielberger (1971) indicated that failure experiences caused the level of reported test anxiety to rise. Even a single failure experience could produce a significant increment in test-anxiety scores, while the reverse is true for a success experience. In a situation where students in all streams are given the same assessments on a particular curriculum, it is inevitable that those in the lower streams will have more profound failure experiences with consequent elevations in test anxiety. As Gaudry and Spielberger (1971) point out, it is the lack of flexibility in the method and content of assessment, not streaming per se, that appears to be the cause of higher test-taking anxiety in the lower streams.

### 1.3 Methods of Assessment

Assessment procedures may vary in a great many respects. Variations occur in the degree of formality–informality of assessment as well as in its form and content. These variations affect the perception of the context of testing and the consequent appraisal of the testing situation.

In general terms, the more important the examination in terms of the consequences that follow from it, the more the high test-anxious student will be disadvantaged because of the reduction in performance it will tend to produce. In these circumstances the way the test is actually presented is very important. The research data here are far from being conclusive but some trends are evident. Emphasis on the importance and difficulty of tests or examinations before their commencement, particularly by prestige figures, increases anxiety and inhibits performance. Instructional effects on test-taking anxiety are well-established experimentally, and they indicate that high-anxious students tend to perform better than low-anxious students when the examination instructions are nonanxiety provoking. The opportunity to comment on difficult or ambiguous items has also been shown to facilitate improvement in the performance of high-anxious students.

The influences of success and failure experiences on levels of A-State in testing situations indicate that arranging test items in order of difficulty mitigates test anxiety, with consequent beneficial effects on performance. Presumably students are able to pay more attention to the qualities of an item when they are not distracted by experiences of anxiety.

In the classroom situation, stress varies according to whether the assessment procedure is progressive or terminal. Progressive assessment occurs in the context of a usual school day without special arrangements. In Australian schools it is based on homework or assignments, or short tests in a regular lesson. Terminal examinations, on the other hand, tend to be conducted under special circumstances. Predominantly they occur in an unfamiliar place such as an examination centre and are conducted with a high level of formality. They are frequently used for purposes of selection and reporting, and can thereby affect future educational and personal opportunities and experiences.

Sarason et al. (1960) hypothesized that the more test-like a situation, the more anxiety interferes with performance. It is a fair inference, therefore, that in the Australian situation, terminal assessment is going to be associated with greater test anxiety than progressive assessment. Accordingly, it can be predicted that the high anxious will tend to perform better in the progressive than in the terminal situation. The evidence confirms this interactive hypothesis and supports the claims of Sarason et al. concerning test-like situations.

## 2. The Effects of Test-taking Anxiety

Although it is tempting to regard test-taking anxiety as a debilitating condition that has inhibitory effects on performance, the preceding outline of some of the conditions for its occurrence does not suggest that such effects are inevitable. That is, the effects tend to follow from interactions of the characteristics of the person and the nature of the testing situation. The evidence indicates that anxiety proneness (A-Trait) is a prime cause of test-taking anxiety in that it influences the cognitive appraisal of the testing situation. If the appraisal is that the situation is threatening, and in particular threatening to self-esteem, an augmented A-State response will occur. The internal stimuli arising from this response will modify the cognitive appraisal of the situation, and the nature of the behaviour towards the test.

Experimental and correlational evidence suggests that test-taking anxiety acts to distract the attention of anxious persons from the veridical appraisal of the testing situation to a preoccupation with their own states. The capacity to cope with the testing situation is thereby impaired. However, there is evidence that this outcome is affected by further interactions. A significant variable here is the difficulty of the test, which is partly determined by the form and content of the test, and the skills, knowledge, and abilities of the testee. Additional variables such as competition might also be important. The interactive effects of these variables sometimes facilitate the performance of highly able anxious students. Presumably their attention to task-relevant aspects of the test situation would be impaired by very high anxiety. Studies of the optimal level of arousal for effective performance, summarized in the Yerkes–Dodson Law which states that the relation between motivation and learning is expressed by an inverted U-shaped curve, indicate that performance is facilitated at a middle level of motivation (anxiety) rather than at high or low levels. A corollary of this is that as tasks increase in difficulty, the optimal motivational level

becomes lower. At a constant anxiety level, therefore, variation in task difficulty between individuals might lead to facilitating or debilitating effects on performance depending on the degree of difficulty involved.

## 3. Conclusions

There is sufficient evidence concerning test-taking anxiety to show overwhelmingly that it interferes with optimal performance. Even where highly able students appear to have their performance facilitated by anxiety, it is not inconsistent to state that their performance would be impaired where the difficulty level of the test was beyond their capacity. The nature of difficulty is not simple and obvious, and both test and personal characteristics contribute to it. Test-taking anxiety is affected by a history of failure whether in the long term or the short term, and in so far as such history creates habits of avoidance and aversion that are part of the definition of A-Trait, the conditions for appraising all test situations as threatening are established. The cumulative effects of such a history are suggested by the increasing magnitude of the negative correlation between anxiety and performance as students progress through grades (Gaudry and Spielberger 1971).

Practical remedial action to counter these effects includes making tests and examinations less "test-like" (Sarason et al. 1960) by reducing needless formalities. Techniques such as the provision of memory supports, grading the difficulty of test items to avoid early failure, progressive rather than terminal assessment, and allowing testees to comment on difficult items have all been used in attempts to minimize the effects of test-taking anxiety with some success. More recently, there have been attempts to raise the levels of self-esteem among poorer performers by the use of cognitive behaviour modification and rational–emotive therapy. The long-term effects of these procedures on the cognitive appraisal of test situations, and the reduction of test-taking anxiety, are not yet clearly established.

## Bibliography

Gaudry E, Spielberger C D 1971 *Anxiety and Educational Achievement*. Wiley Australasia, Sydney

Levy P, Gooch S, Kellmer-Pringle M L 1969 A longitudinal study of the relationship between anxiety and streaming in a progressive and a traditional junior school. *Br. J. Educ. Psychol.* 39: 166–73

Sarason I G (ed.) 1980 *Test Anxiety: Theory, Research and Applications*. Erlbaum, New York

Sarason S B, Davidson K S, Lighthall F F, Waite R R, Ruebush B K 1960 *Anxiety in Elementary School Children*. Wiley, New York

Sarnoff I, Lighthall F F, Waite R R, Davidson K S, Sarason S B 1958 A cross-cultural study of anxiety amongst American and English school children. *J. Educ. Psychol.* 49: 129–36

Spielberger C D 1966 *Anxiety and Behavior*. Academic Press, New York

# Test Bias

## C. K. Tittle

Bias is defined as prejudice or having a particular bent or direction. To say a test is biased is to charge that it is prejudiced or unfair to groups or individuals characterized as different from the majority of test takers. In the United States these groups have included ethnic minorities, women, individuals whose first language is not English, and persons with handicapping conditions. Charges of test bias have been based on examination of individual test items, group differences in average performance, and the use of tests. Test bias has been examined for tests used in the selection of students for admission to institutions of postsecondary education, placement of students in special education classes, certification of minimum competencies or standards of achievement in secondary education, evaluation of educational programs, and career counseling.

Test bias, from a broader, construct-oriented perspective, has been examined in studies of tests used in cross-cultural research and in earlier attempts to develop tests which are culture free or culture fair. Early research in the 1900s on intelligence measures recognized the problems of testing children in different groups, for instance, those whose native language was not English. With the development of group mental tests and the first large-scale use of tests, the Army Alpha in the First World War, these measures came into wider use and to the attention of the public. By the 1920s cross-cultural test results were being used to counter deterministic interpretations of mental test scores. In the 1930s there were studies of the effect of language and culture on test scores. During the 1940s and early 1950s, there were again studies of racial differences in intelligence measures. Havighurst and Davis studied the relation of social class and test performance, and Eells, with others, attempted to develop culture fair mental tests.

No one now would claim that a test can be culture free or culture fair, nor is there consensus on a set of procedures which would establish that a test measures the same construct for groups with different cultural environments. Thus the tensions between professional testing practices and public concerns that arise in court cases and legislation in the United States, such as federal regulations for assessment practices for employment selection and educational placement of the handicapped, have been fruitful. The result has been a series of studies since the early 1970s, studies resulting in renewed attention to the theory underlying tests, the test development process, and a broader view of the validity evidence appropriate for the justification of tests used in educational settings. The issues that have arisen in each test-use setting are described first, followed by a summary of the major methodological approaches in studies used to detect item bias in the

absence of criteria external to the test. This is the usual situation in educational achievement testing. Brief mention is made of experimental and correlational studies which can be used to provide further evidence that tests are measuring the same constructs in different groups.

Detailed reviews of methods and related studies can be found in Berk (1982), Cole (1981), and Jensen (1980).

## 1. Settings for Test Use

The fundamental role of validity in questions of test bias is made clear in describing the settings for test use. Validity of a test, or more accurately, the validity of inferences based on test scores has been established typically through one of three strategies: (a) criterion-related or predictive studies of validity; (b) content analyses for validity; and (c) construct studies of validity. Criterion-related studies examine the accuracy with which a test predicts a criterion, such as the use of a test of developed abilities to predict a criterion of college grades in an admissions setting. Content validity depends upon the definition of a domain of achievement to be sampled, the classification of test items in terms of this domain of reference, and expert judgment that the content of the test samples or represents accurately the achievement domain. An example is the knowledge and application of facts, concepts, and principles in a measure of science achievement. The construct strategy is used to determine how well a score represents a construct, such as achievement motivation, anxiety, or literacy and requires logical and empirical bases in studies testing hypotheses about the relationship of scores on the construct measure to other variables.

The view which suggests that a particular type of validity is appropriate for different types of tests has been challenged by public concerns over the use of tests and the issues raised in studies of test bias. Several authors (most recently Messick 1988) have suggested a more unified view of validity in which it is argued that the role of construct validity is fundamental. The accuracy of an inference that a pupil cannot read based on the results of a single test score labeled as a measure of reading comprehension is dependent on more than expert judgment or classification of the test items in relation to objectives of instruction. The inference that an individual child cannot read assumes that motivation in the testing situation is optimal, that anxiety or unfamiliarity with the testing format does not interfere with performance, that questions can be answered only within the context of the reading passage, that the vocabulary is appropriate, that is, within the child's experience or readily inferred from the context, and so on. Variables such as motivation and anxiety are extraneous to the construct of reading comprehension which the test purports to measure. There are, therefore, questions of an educational and psychological nature that should be examined when group differences in average test performance are observed. One facet of construct validity is to examine alternative explanations for differences in test performance.

Test bias in educational settings has another dimension. If evidence on the accuracy of interpretations is provided and it is satisfactory, there remains the question of the logical and empirical consequences of test use in a particular instance. If in admissions testing, proportionally fewer (in terms of the applicant pool) minority students are selected at elite institutions, what is the social value of this outcome? Similarly, if a career interest inventory used in counseling suggests fewer science and technological occupations to women for exploration than to men, what is the social value of this outcome? Whether one incorporates the social value questions within an expanded conception of validity or considers values as a matter for public policy and hence separate from a technical definition of validity, social values are a part of the study of test bias in educational settings.

## 1.1 Admissions Testing

In the use of tests for admission to postsecondary education an issue has been whether the tests are fair to particular groups of students. Although there have been studies of individual test items for bias, bias in this setting has focused on the use of tests in the selection process. In the selection situation a test is assumed to have predictive validity to the extent that students scoring well on the test also do well on a criterion. When there are differences between test scores, on the average, for groups such as blacks and whites or men and women, the question arises as to whether the group differences are also reflected in criterion differences or whether they represent bias. The criterion is typically limited to college grades and little study has been made of possible criterion bias. Similarly, the majority of studies have compared data for blacks and whites; fewer analyses have examined data for females and males.

In defining bias in the selection setting, initially the relationship of the test (the predictor) to college grades (the criterion) was examined for differential validity: for situations in which the correlations expressing the relationship between the test and criterion were different for minority group and majority (white) groups or between women and men. Within-group regression equations used to estimate criterion scores were also studied. There were several ways in which group differences could occur in the correlations, predictor reliabilities, and differences in slopes, intercepts, or standard errors of estimate. In general, however, the comparison of these statistics for black and white groups of students has shown little evidence of differential validity to date. This is not the case for gender, where

studies do indicate differential prediction, and specifically the underprediction of criterion performance for women (e.g., Gamache and Novick 1985).

There has been a shift from the criterion orientation expressed in the search for differential validities, to a decision orientation found in the study of the use of test results under different models proposed for fairness in selection. Several models or approaches have been proposed as fair procedures for selecting students for an educational institution. In these models a criterion score (grades) and a predictor (test score) are available and a cut score on the test needs to be found for each group such that the definition of fair selection in a particular model is satisfied. As an example, the standard regression approach has been used and a test defined as unfair if use of the common regression line systematically over- or under-predicts criterion scores for members of a particular group. If the regression equations are identical within each group, the use of the common regression line to select students with the highest criterion scores is considered fair. Selection is fair (to individuals) if it is optimal, based on the best prediction available.

An alternative model suggested that if the effect on groups was examined, a smaller proportion of one group than another might be selected with the regression model, even though the potential rates of success (if all applicants were admitted) of individuals in both groups would be similar. A possible decision or policy alternative, then, would be to select from the two groups in proportion to past rates of success for the groups (a constant-ratio model). Other models have been suggested, with variants on the idea of bringing values or utilities for particular outcomes for majority and minority individuals or groups explicitly into consideration. The models of fairness in selection that have been proposed have different outcomes when there are group differences in predictor and/or criterion scores. Decisions about the use of the test scores can place explicit utilities (values) on the possible outcomes for the educational institution and individual or groups of students affected by the decision. Recognition of the social value of different outcomes has also led to the application of statistical decision theory. The general view at present is that the models of fairness in selection will not resolve questions of fairness and bias. Rather, the explicit consideration of values (utilities) placed upon outcomes for the institution, the individual, groups of concern, and the larger social body will further discussions of equity in educational opportunity and outcomes.

Another facet to the fairness discussion has been proposed by Novick (1980), in suggesting a move from defining groups for special consideration on the basis of ethnicity, race, or sex. An alternative is to define disadvantage operationally (e.g., family income). A measure of disadvantage could thus be made for each individual rather than using the group membership as a proxy for the disadvantage for which compensation or equalization is sought. A further refinement of this approach would be to identify the educational and psychological variables for which "disadvantage" is proxy, and link these to educational selection and placement within the university setting. Paradoxically, as the issue of test bias in selection has been clarified into its technical and social components, there is a trend toward less selectivity on the part of many postsecondary institutions in the United States. This trend should reinforce the placement and instructional use of tests, resulting in less reliance on traditional predictors such as aptitude (developed ability) measures.

## 1.2 Special Education Placement

The use of educational and psychological tests in placing students into special classes, as for the mildly retarded, has been the subject of controversy and court litigation. There are two main issues here—overrepresentation of minorities in special education classes and charges of bias in the IQ tests that are often the basis of placements. The assessment process leading to classification and placement typically involves standardized tests, and is most important for the mildly handicapped classifications of learning disability, educable or mild mental retardation, and emotional disturbance/behavior disorders. More severe handicaps occur with lower frequency, standardized tests are less important in classification, and no significant disproportionality by race, social status, or gender exists with the more severe handicaps in the United States.

Questions of test bias have arisen when items on individual measures of intelligence are examined, and when evidence of predictive validity has been used. In two court cases in the United States, *Larry P. versus Riles* and *Parents in Action on Special Education* (PASE) *versus Hannon*, judges reached opposite conclusions on the issue of bias in the test items. In *Larry P.*, the opinion remarks that the cultural bias of the tests was hardly disputed in litigation. In PASE the judge examined test items and found nine items should not be used because of bias.

In relation to validation, which in the employment or admissions settings has meant predicting a criterion, the judge in *Larry P.* defined validity as showing the appropriateness of the test and placement decision to the specific educational needs of the child. Evidence of high correlations between intelligence test scores and school performance in general did not justify placing a child in an environment in which the attempt at academic education would, for all practical purposes, cease (Sherman and Robinson 1981).

Studies of bias or fairness in special-education placement includes issues related to tests and other assessment procedures, among them the question of cultural bias in items (see Sect. 2 for methodology), the potential adverse impact of test use (disproportionate classification of groups into special classes), and studies of effects—evidence that the classification into "treatments" is of educational benefit to children. Special

issues in the testing of linguistic minorities are also relevant (Olmedo 1981), such as language dominance and test translation procedures.

## 1.3 Competency Testing

In the United States minimum competency testing (MCT) programs have been started by local school districts and more than 30 states to assess basic academic skills students are expected to master in order to graduate with a diploma from secondary schools. In many minimum competency testing programs the tests are typically objective in form and measure reading and mathematics, sometimes language and writing skills. A passing score or standard for acceptable levels of student performance is established and the main uses of the test results are to certify students for grade promotion, graduation, or a diploma and to classify or place students in remedial or other special service programs.

Test or item bias issues have been raised in a major court case, *Debra P. versus Turlington*, in the state of Florida (US). The plaintiffs charged that the test was racially biased, that inadequate preparation time had been given, and that use of the test to classify and group students for remediation reinstituted segregation in the public schools. Initially the test was judged not racially biased, although analyses of individual items judged or statistically identified as biased against blacks found differential effects on the pass rate. However, another form of "bias" can be found in lack of opportunity to learn test content. In 1981 the Appeals Court remanded the case for further findings because the state had not made any effort to make certain whether the test covered material actually studied in the classrooms of the state.

In addition to issues of racially biased items, and the match between curriculum, instruction, and minimum competency tests, other questions of bias involve testing special groups, such as those for whom English is a second language, and the handicapped. Can skills included in minimum competency tests be the same for handicapped and nonhandicapped students?.

## 1.4 Evaluating Educational Programs

Issues of test bias in evaluation have been raised primarily in studies of compensatory education programs. The debates over the standardized achievement tests used in evaluation focus on group differences in test scores and individual items which are identified as biased—items that may represent life styles or experiences more typical of middle socioeconomic white groups in United States culture. A second focus is on the interpretation of scores and use of the tests. Criticisms of the interpretation and use of the tests are based on the inference which is sometimes made that students cannot learn what the tests measure. Bias or lack of fairness in this context has included claims that items are set in contexts unfamiliar to urban students and also that tests do not measure the skills being taught in compensatory programs. These issues, as with the issues in minimum competency test programs, require a variety of methods to provide evidence of the fairness or lack of bias in a test.

### 1.5 Career Counseling

Issues of test bias in career counseling have centered on whether career interest inventories are biased against women. Earlier versions of a well-known United States interest inventory had separate forms for men (blue in color) and for women (pink). Fewer occupational scales were developed for women, thus limiting the occupations suggested for consideration by women students. In 1974 the National Institute of Education sponsored the development of *Guidelines for Assessment of Sex Bias and Sex Fairness in Career Interest Inventories.* Several aspects of interest measurement, the inventory itself, technical information and interpretive information, are considered in the *Guidelines.* Sex bias was examined in stereotyping of female and male roles, in the development of new scales, and in providing the same range of occupations for men and women. Gender-neutral language—firefighter, letter carrier, and flight attendant—was recommended. One issue is not readily resolved, the issue of whether the test is sex biased if it results in different distributions of basic interest areas or occupational groups suggested for men and women. This issue, and others that require technical data, as well as the value judgments that are made when particular interest measures are used with women, are discussed in a series of papers edited by Diamond (1975) and Tittle and Zytowski (1978).

What little evidence is available suggests that the validity of interest inventories may be the same for minority and white groups. Because interest measures are frequently used within a program of career guidance in schools, studies of the effects or outcomes of using interest measures have been carried out. Outcome measures can also provide evidence on bias or lack of fairness in the use of interest inventories by using student ratings, the number of occupations considered by females and males, and number of nontraditional occupations considered.

## 2. Item-bias Methodology

The study of test bias in the absence of an external criterion is an active area of research. For the most widely used tests in education—achievement, developed abilities, and basic interest measures—there are no external standards by which judgments of bias or fairness can be made. The statistical methods, which are the main area of research, all make the assumption that the test, over all items, is not biased. The methods rely upon detecting items which are by some definition aberrant from the majority of items in the test.

However, the statistical definition is not the only definition of bias. Critics have examined test content

from several perspectives, making judgments as to whether portrayals of minorities and women are stereotyped or are broadly representative of all the roles—occupational, educational, familial, recreational—that persons in a particular culture can occupy. And, as mentioned earlier, another form of bias detection lies in analyses of the overlap of the opportunity to learn provided by curriculum materials and instruction with the items in standardized tests.

Each of these areas of item-bias detection is examined below. In the development of major standardized tests many test publishers in the United States now conduct judgmental reviews of test material for stereotyping, representativeness and familiarity of content to particular groups, as well as statistical item-bias analyses. The judgments or analyses of overlap among test items, curriculum, and instruction have been examined in research studies but are rarely done routinely and systematically by schools. Together these methods begin to define and document the use of a set of procedures that permit decisions that a test is fair or unbiased for particular groups of students.

### 2.1 Judgmental Reviews

The use of judgmental reviews in the test development process is described by Tittle (in Berk 1982). Test planning, item writing and review, item tryout, selection of final items, and development of norms and scaling are all stages in the test development process where judgments are made that affect perceptions of test bias. Procedures used to judge item bias include review forms and directions to judges that focus on identifying stereotyping of women, minorities, and the handicapped. Judges are asked to identify items that may be more or less familiar to particular groups. Tallies are made of the representativeness of item content and art work in tests for portraying women, men, and minorities in a positive manner (rather than omitting them, as is sometimes the case). Analyses may use categories such as the following for tallies: adult and child characters, female and male, main or secondary character, types of environment, behavior exhibited, and types of consequences of behavior.

Although judges are now being used more consistently in test development, there is little research that answers questions such as, who is an "expert" judge? And, how much agreement exists between judges? Or, should agreement be important? The statistical item-bias approaches described below do not substitute for these judgmental reviews. Also, there is no expectation that judges and statistical procedures will identify the same items as "biased." Both approaches are necessary, although neither may be the final criterion for accepting or rejecting items in a particular measure.

There are more data available on the categories for classification and agreement between judges in the judgments of items, curricula, and opportunity to learn. Although this is a fundamental aspect of examining test validity and establishing the program sensitivity of tests used in evaluation, the types of classification schemes used have varied widely. A series of studies at Michigan State University provide a model for future analyses. A detailed set of categories was developed for analyzing fourth-grade tests of mathematics and curriculum materials. The main dimensions were: mode of presentation, nature of material, and operations. The opportunity to learn judgments are made by using teacher, student or external ratings of the opportunity to learn each item during the instructional process. Little is known about the characteristics of these ratings in terms of reliability and relationship to other variables.

### 2.2 Statistical Methods

Statistical methods of examining items for possible bias are being developed and studied. Research on the results of using different methods has begun, using both computer simulations and empirical data. The item-bias methods have been used when there is no criterion external to the test which can serve as the basis of estimating bias. The methods are intended to be used in the process of test development, to assist in building an unbiased test. Their development was stimulated by findings of group differences in test scores such as those for disadvantaged and advantaged groups.

All methods start by assuming the test as a whole is less biased than the individual items in the test. Thus the test questions designed to measure the same construct are studied together and bias is discovered when an item does not fit the pattern of the majority of items. Bias, as assessed by these methods, is the finding that an item is deviant from others in the test. Thus the definition of item bias is circular—it is possible to detect relative but not constant bias across all items in the test. Recognizing this limitation to the studies, an item can be defined as biased if equally able individuals from different groups do not have the same probability of success on the item.

Although a number of statistical procedures have been proposed, only four general types are mentioned here: (a) transformed item difficulty (TID); (b) item discrimination; (c) item characteristic curve methods; and (d) chi square.

The transformed item difficulty approach has been used since the 1960s. Using Angoff's procedures (see Berk 1982), the item difficulty ($p$) value or proportion getting the item right, is computed for each group. Each $p$ value is transformed to the normal deviate ($z$) that would cut off that proportion of the area under the unit normal curve. The normal deviates may have a second transformation, to a delta value (delta = $4z + 13$). Deltas are plotted, one pair for each item. Items falling away from the principal or major axis of the ellipse are examined for the perpendicular or shortest distance of each point from the line, and the distance is taken as a measure of the degree of item bias. A limitation of the method is that the $p$ values reflect group differences in ability as well as item difficulties.

The item discrimination method uses the difference between point biserial correlations (correlation of the item and the total test score) as a measure of item discrimination. A weakness of this technique is that mean differences in groups will give false indications of biased items. This method does not correlate well with other methods, and it is not frequently used in practice.

Item characteristic curve (latent trait or item response theory) methods are theoretically more satisfying because the characteristics of an item are described in terms of a function with parameters that are invariant over samples. The item characteristic curve describes the probability that a student with a given ability answers a test item correctly in terms of three parameters: the $a$ parameter, the slope of the curve at the inflection point (point at which the slope of the curve changes direction), which reflects item discrimination; the $b$ parameter, the inflection point, which reflects item difficulty; and the $c$ parameter, the lower asymptote, which is the probability of guessing correctly for students of low ability.

For an item to be unbiased, the item characteristic curves must be the same for each group being compared. That is, the item has equal probabilities of success for students of the same ability regardless of group membership. Item characteristic curves may be based on one, two, or three parameters. The one parameter model, called the Rasch model, is a special case of the three parameter model (see *Rasch Measurement Models*). It assumes that there is no guessing on the test (no $c$ parameter) and that all items discriminate equally (no $a$ parameter). Various indices of item bias have been proposed for the three and one parameter models. The three parameter model requires large sample sizes (1,000) and numbers of items (40) for good estimates, as well as a complex computer analysis. The one parameter model has assumptions that are difficult to meet in practice. Both methods essentially require unidimensionality in the item set.

An application of chi square was proposed by Scheuneman. This approach approximates the latent-trait method by establishing categories of ability on the basis of total test score. The correct responses for groups are compared within ability levels. The total score range on the test is usually divided into five categories. Observed and expected proportions are calculated and compared using chi square. A further refinement of this idea is the Mantel–Haenszel procedure. Generally these approaches appear to be useful and practical, if imperfect, approximations to the three-parameter item characteristic curve. Smaller sample sizes are tolerable and large-scale computer facilities are not required.

### 2.3 Experimental Design Studies

Another approach to the study of item bias has been to vary the type of content on which groups might be expected to respond differently. For example, content thought to "favor" black or white students is selected and used in test development. Students of each group are randomly assigned to treatments in which type of item context or content is varied, and scores are compared in an analysis-of-variance design. This approach, although not as extensively applied as the statistical item-bias techniques, has potential for providing an understanding of why items may function differently for groups of students.

### 2.4 Correlational Studies

Correlational methods have also been used both to study the underlying dimensions or constructs in a set of items and to examine the patterns of relationships between a test and other measures. The emphasis is again on whether the dimensions (factors) or patterns of correlations are the same for different groups, using exploratory or confirmatory analyses. These studies fit within the usual view of construct validity.

### 2.5 Structural Equation Modeling and Item Response Theory (IRT)

Of considerable promise is the work of Muthen (1988), which provides an extension of item response theory (IRT) modeling of dichotomous items to include external variables. By including external variables, possible sources of item bias may be examined, that is, the examination of the influence of background and situational or contextual variables on differential item performance of groups of concern. Muthen's work has examined the influence of instructional and attitudinal variables on item performance for different groups, an example of modeling that would be valuable to educational evaluators.

### 3. Summary

Examining a test and test use for bias or fairness to groups and individuals is a many-sided problem and there is no one method which will substantiate the claim that a test is fair. The variety of procedures currently being applied has not resulted in a clear consensus on a single set of procedures. However, research on the relationship between methods as well as their technical adequacy is being conducted. Researchers have argued that there is a conflict between the use of judgments, reviews of test content, and the statistical methods, since there is often little overlap between the items identified as "biased" by these methods. In practice, however, two points can be made. The first is that the judgments and content reviews provide information that

the statistical methods cannot, while the reverse is also true. Second, the published test remains the outcome of a series of decisions made by each test developer, not the result of rote application of any bias procedures. This practice is unlikely to change in the near future.

Studies that may provide additional insight into group differences in test performance are, for example, those examining psychological variables such as test anxiety and responses to changes in item types, formats, and familiarity of context material. Similarly, studies of coaching and test-taking skills may also lead to educational practices that reduce the influence of extraneous variables on test performance. Renewed attention to problems of test bias holds the promise of bringing testing closer to educational practice and to psychological theory.

### Bibliography

Berk R (ed.) 1982 *Handbook of Methods for Detecting Test Bias*. Johns Hopkins University Press, Baltimore, Maryland

Cole N S 1981 Bias in testing. *Am. Psychol.* 36: 1067–77

Diamond E E (ed.) 1975 *Issues of Sex Bias and Sex Fairness in Career Interest Measurement*. National Institute of Education, Washington, DC

Gamache L M, Novick M R 1985 Choice of variables and gender differentiated prediction within selected academic programs. *J. Educ. Meas.*, 22: 53–70

Jensen A R 1980 *Bias in Mental Testing*. Free Press, New York

Messick S 1988 Validity. In: R L Linn (ed.) 1988 *Educational Measurement*, 3rd edn. Macmillan, New York

Muthen B 1988 Some uses of structural equation modeling in validity studies: Extending IRT to external variables. In: Wainer H, Braun H I (eds.) *Test Validity*. Erlbaum, Hillsdale, New Jersey

Novick M R 1980 Policy issues of fairness in testing. In: van der Kamp L J T et al. (eds.) 1980 *Psychometrics for Educational Debates*. Wiley, New York

Olmedo E L 1981 Testing linguistic minorities. *Am. Psychol.* 36: 1078–85

Sherman S W, Robinson N M (eds.) 1981 *Ability testing of Handicapped People: Dilemma for Government, Science, and the Public*. National Academy Press, Washington, DC

Tittle C K, Zytowski D G (eds.) 1978 *Sex-fair Interest Measurement: Research and Implications*. National Institute of Education, Washington, DC

Weiss D J, Davison M L 1981 Test theory and methods. *Annu. Rev. Psychol.* 32: 647–51

Wild C L, Dwyer C A 1980 Sex bias in selection. In: van der Kamp L J T et al. (eds.) 1980 *Psychometrics for Educational Debates*. Wiley, New York

# Item Bias

**R. J. Adams and K. J. Rowe**

Despite an already large and growing literature on the subject of item bias in educational and psychological tests, its seems that no universally accepted definition yet exists. However, in the case of ability tests, Shepard

et al. (1981) are helpful: "an item is biased if two individuals with equal ability but from different groups do not have the same probability of success on an item" (p. 316). The detection of test item bias is an active area of psychometric research that has grown in response to concerns with the possibility of bias in educational and psychological testing for evaluation, selection, and placement purposes. These concerns have primarily grown out of a broader social interest in the equitable treatment of socio-political and ethnic minority groups.

One important distinction which is often made is between bias that is *external* to a test and bias which is *internal* to the test instrument itself. According to Osterlind (1983), "external bias is the degree to which test scores may manifest a correlational relationship with variables independent of the test" (p. 9). External bias issues include the social consequences of test use as well as fairness in tests and procedures for selection. These issues are usually treated under the general heading of "test bias" which focuses interest on the construct and predictive validity of a whole test, rather than on individual test items per se. Alternatively, internal bias is primarily concerned with the psychometric properties of the test items themselves; the focus of interest being the relationship between the construct validity of individual items and that of the total test. In much of the literature, internal bias is known as "item bias".

The major concern of item bias detection procedures involves examinations of whether individual test items behave in a similar manner (i.e. have similar measurement properties) for different subgroups drawn from the same population, without reference to an external criterion. In this context, a test item is said to be biased when there is evidence of interaction between group membership and item performance, when ability or psychological differences between the groups have been controlled.

The identification of item bias is important, even for tests that are mainly dependent on predictive validity (e.g. selection tests), since internal indications of bias make it increasingly likely that the test will also show predictive bias. Hence, techniques for identifying test item bias are useful in test construction, since potentially biased items, in the predictive sense, can be rejected during the initial item-selection process and prior to any attempts to evaluate a test's predictive validity in populations.

The emotive and somewhat perjorative connotations associated with the word "bias", have prompted some psychometricians to adopt the terms "differential item performance" or "differential item functioning" rather than item bias. This alternative nomenclature reflects the aim of item bias detection methods in identifying those items that function differently for different groups of testees. In this article, however, for the sake of consistency with most of the research literature, we use the term "item bias".

## 1. Statistical Techniques for Measuring Item Bias

In recent years there has been a proliferation of statistical techniques for measuring item bias, particularly in tests of educational attainment. Since the large num-

ber of existing techniques and their related literature makes it impossible for them to be fully discussed here, the reader is referred to reviews and handbooks such as Berk (1982) and Osterlind (1983) for more detailed discussions and technical formulations of item bias detection methods, as well as for references to original sources.

Briefly, methods for identifying item bias include: factor analysis, examinations of item discrimination through point-biserial and partial correlations, the examination of item difficulty through various transformations, ANOVA methods, item response theory or latent trait methods, a variety of chi-square approaches, and methods of using log-linear models and the Mantel–Haenszel statistic. From the numerous techniques which have been developed, however, findings from comparative studies suggest that only a few of them are of sufficient value for this use to be encouraged. While, in this article, we focus on methods which have been developed primarily for the detection of item bias in educational and psychological tests of attainment or ability, these methods may also be applied to sets of test items designed to measure any latent trait of interest. First, we outline those methods that provide some indication of bias and are easy to apply, despite their known inadequacies, and then discuss a couple of the more recently proposed, albeit more complex, methods. The application of alternative techniques to the study of a practical problem concerned with sex bias in aptitude testing is found in such studies as Adams (1983).

### 1.1 Quick but Incomplete Methods

A set of methods have been developed which, although incomplete and often misleading, may serve as initial indicators of items that behave differently for separate groups. The first of these requires the calculation of the item difficulties (*p*-values) for each group. The items are then ranked within groups according to the *p*-values, and the rank orders for each group are compared. Any item that notably deviates in its comparative ranking for the groups may be indicative of bias. Nevertheless, like all incomplete methods, the comparison of rank orders can be misleading. For example, if the groups have different ability distributions, the items will not have the same *p*-value ranking unless all of the items have the same discrimination (see Ironson 1983).

A second possibility involves the comparison of the item discrimination indices for each of the groups. These are usually represented as the point-biserial correlations between the item and total test scores. While differences between the point-biserial coefficients for the group can be useful indicators of bias, they are sensitive to differences in the score distributions for each group. Since the point-biserial correlation coefficient is a function of the *p*-value of an item, if the two groups have different ability distributions, a nonbiased item will be more discriminating in the group for which the *p*-value is closest to 0.5.

Factor analysis has also been used for detecting item

bias. If the factor structure of the test is computed separately for each group and then compared, any item which does not produce comparable loadings may be regarded as biased. Factor analysis of biserial correlation matrices has considerable conceptual appeal since it allows for a comparison of underlying constructs in the test for each group. Unfortunately, however, even with tests that are known to contain bias, factor analytic methods often produce the same underlying structure for the groups. Furthermore, it is widely recognized that factor analysis is inappropriate when used with dichotomous data of the type that normally appear in educational and psychological tests of ability. Given these limitations, it may also be considered as an incomplete method for detecting item bias.

Another widely applied method involves the use of ANOVA. If two or more groups, sampled from the same population, are given a common test, the occurrence of a significant Items × Group interaction is used to indicate differential item behaviour, suggesting that the items may not have the same meaning for the different groups in terms of construct validity. Nevertheless, such interpretations are potentially misleading since significant Items × Groups interactions are often observed as a function of either differing ability levels among testees or differences in overall group performance.

Each of these incomplete methods relies on traditional item analyses that produce statistics dependent on the ability distributions obtained from the respondent samples. Consequently, when the distribution of ability in the groups under investigation varies, unpredictable influences on bias indicators invariably occur, thus confounding the identification of item bias.

## 1.2 Transformed Item Difficulty (TID)

The transformed item difficulty (TID) strategy is essentially an extension of the ANOVA approach which seeks to identify the extent to which particular items contribute to the Items × Groups interaction. While the TID approach, like the incomplete methods, is also based on traditional item analyses, its ease of use and strong performance in comparative studies support its utility with small samples and/or short tests.

In the TID method, the $p$-values for each item are calculated separately for each group and are transformed to a scale that is more likely to be interval than the $p$-value scale. The usual method of transformation involves converting the $p$-values to $z$-values, where $z$ is the $(1-p)$th percentile in a normal distribution, and then producing a delta ($\Delta$) scale, where for item $i$ of group $j$,

$$\Delta_{ij} = 4z_{ij} + 13$$

The transformation of $z$ to the $\Delta$ scale is favoured because it removes negative values and adequate precision can be shown using only one decimal place.

When the pairs of $\Delta$ values are shown in a scatter plot, they form an ellipse with major axes given by

$y = bx + a$. $a$ and $b$ are given by Angoff and Ford (1973) as:

$$a = M_x - bM_y$$
$$b = (s_y^2 - s_x^2) \pm [(s_y^2 - s_x^2)^2 + 4r_{xy}^2 s_x^2 s_y^2]^{1/2}/2r_{xy}s_x s_y$$

where $s_x^2$ is the variance of the $\Delta$ values for the group plotted on the horizontal axis, $s_y^2$ is the variance of the delta values plotted on the vertical axis, $M_x$ and $M_y$ are the respective means, and $r_{xy}$ is the correlation between the two sets of $\Delta$'s.

The perpendicular distance between the plotted delta pair for each item $i$, and the major axis is given by:

$$d_i = (bx_i + a - y_i)/(b^2 + 1)^{1/2}$$

where $x_i$ and $y_i$ are the pair of $\Delta$ scores for item $i$. The magnitude of this distance is used to indicate the amount of bias in the item. However, there is some conjecture about the magnitude of the distance that should be used to indicate bias.

In many instances, the TID method is adequate for identifying item bias. It is conceptually simple, easy to compute and provides a visual indication of the amount of bias. Comparative studies of item bias detection techniques have shown that the TID method performs well as an approximation to more sophisticated methods, especially when short tests are being analysed or sample sizes are small. Unfortunately, when using the TID method, like most of the incomplete methods, differences in the group score distributions can unjustifiably make items appear to be biased because of a lack of statistical control over ability differences between the groups. Moreover, the fact the the focus of attention for both the ANOVA and TID approaches is solely on item difficulty gives rise to several problems, not the least of which is that Items × Groups interactions have been shown to occur in any test regardless of item bias.

## 1.3 Chi-Square Methods

In an attempt to avoid these problems, a chi-square goodness-of-fit approach has been used, by examining differences in proportions of groups responding correctly to an item across total test score categories. The score distribution is broken into a number of arbitrary levels and the probabilities of test takers from different groups with the same ability level responding correctly to an item are compared. When the proportions are similar for all groups, an item is said to be unbiased. While the chi-square approach is comparatively simple to compute, it has the disadvantage of being particularly sensitive to within-groups item discriminations, as well as being constrained by the arbitrary selection of ability levels. For a review of chi-square methods, see Marascuilo and Slaughter (1981).

## 1.4 Latent Trait Models

Latent trait theory, sometimes called item response theory (IRT), provides statistical models for describing the relationship of an index of a testee's ability to the probability of a correct response to an item. Under such models, item responses can be described in the form of an item characteristic curve (ICC), which relates the probability of success on an item to a function of the testee's ability position on the latent trait being measured by the test, and the characteristics of the item. For item bias detection, the most frequently used IRT models include the three-parameter logistic model and the Rasch model.

The mathematical form of the three parameter ICC is given by:

$$P_i(\theta) = c_i + (1 - c_i)/[1 + e^{-Da_i(\theta - b_i)}] \; (i = 1, \dots, n)$$

where $P_i(\theta)$ is the probability of a correct response for a testee of ability $\theta$; $a_i$, $b_i$ and $c_i$ are parameters characterizing item $i$, and $D = 1.7$ is a constant scaling factor. Figure 1 shows two possible item characteristic curves. Parameter $b_i$ is a location parameter for the ICC on the underlying continuum and it is generally called the item difficulty. Parameter $a_i$ corresponds to the slope of the ICC at $\theta = b_i$ and is generally regarded as the discrimination index, while $c_i$ gives the lower asymptote for the curve. This parameter is regarded as a pseudo-guessing parameter because it corresponds to the probability of a correct answer for an individual with very low ability.

Thus, under an IRT model, an item would be regarded as unbiased if all individuals having the same underlying ability have an equal probability of getting the item correct, regardless of subgroup membership. In such circumstances there would be no significant differences in group item-characteristic curves.

In the attempt to identify biased items, group ICC's generated by the three-parameter logistic model are compared. This is achieved by first estimating the parameters for items, and placing the obtained values on the same scale. Bias is estimated for an item by observing the differences in ICC's for two groups when $\theta$ is equated (i.e. both groups are placed on the same ability scale), and it is evident that different probabilities of success result for each group. For example, from Fig. 1, it is evident that the probability of a correct response is greater for group A than for group B at all levels of ability, except for group B testees of high $\theta$ values. Moreover, the effects of bias are confounded by both discrimination and difficulty. Since the ICC's for the two groups are demonstrably different, the item does not discriminate equally between the two groups and the presence of bias is thus inferred.

A range of methods has been advocated for accurately examining the differences between the ICC's for different groups. The reader is referred to Shepard et al. (1984), where eight of these methods are briefly described as part of a comparative study of item bias detection methods using the three-parameter logistic model. As a result of their study, they recommend the use of a weighted sum of squares calculated as:

$$SOS_i = \frac{1}{N_A + N_B} \sum_{j=1}^{N_A + N_B} \frac{[\hat{P}_{iA}(\theta_j) - P_{iB}(\theta_j)]^2}{s^2_{\hat{P}_{iA} - \hat{P}_{iB}}}$$

where $\hat{P}_{iA}$ is the estimated probability of an individual with ability $\theta_j$ responding to item $i$, $N_A$ and $N_B$ are the number of individuals in groups A and B respectively, $s^2_{\hat{P}_{iA} - \hat{P}_{iB}}$ is the standard error of the difference in estimated probabilities, and the summation is performed over all values of $\theta_j$ that occur in the analyses.

While the three-parameter logistic model allows items to differ in difficulty, discrimination and guessing, the Rasch model includes only a single parameter for each item, namely, a difficulty parameter. Essentially, the model provides a common measurement scale on which testee ability and item difficulty are simultaneously calibrated. Although derived independently, the Rasch model is functionally equivalent to the three-parameter logistic model with $c_i = 0$ and $Da_i = 1$.

Despite their similarity, the Rasch and three parameter logistic models were developed on very different philosophies. Advocates of the three parameter model claim that its three parameters more closely describe, in psychometric terms, the tests and test data that are most widely used, while Rasch model advocates argue that it is deductively derived from the requirements of valid measurement. If a test or item does not conform to the Rasch model, it is argued that the test or the item must contain some form of bias. This may not be item bias in terms of bias against a minority, but may be indicative of a number of possible threats to valid measurement. For example, Masters (1988) has shown that differences in item discrimination may be due to bias against a minority group.

In comparative studies, however, the three parameter model has generally received more favourable attention for item bias detection. This is mainly due to its feature of more closely describing, in psychometric terms, multiple choice tests as they are currently constructed. In simulation studies it could well be an outcome of the

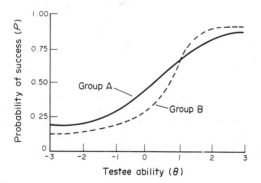

**Figure 1**
Hypothetical equated item characteristic curves for two groups different in discrimination, difficulty and pseudochance. Adapted from Osterlind (1983 p. 64)

fact that most simulated data are generated by the model in the first place.

Among the claimed advantages of IRT or latent trait approaches to item bias detection, perhaps the most important is the "sample-invariant" property of the models' parameters, which implies that differences in ability should not create artifactual instances of bias. This theoretical property of the models means that the item parameters are independent of the distributional characteristics of the sample and are therefore not subject to the distortions described for the incomplete and TID methods. Hence, under any latent trait model, parameters from different samples should be equal. Items whose parameters are notably unequal violate the assumptions of the model, and in consequence are said to be biased because they may be measuring something different for a particular group.

Despite the widespread acceptance of IRT technology, it is subject to some fundamental difficulties. For example, it has been shown in practice that the $a_i$ and $c_i$ parameters of the three parameter model do not exhibit the strong invariance required by the model. Similarly, the ICC's are not entirely independent of the distribution of ability since possibly biased items cannot be excluded from the initial ability estimate. Moreover, the analyses are complex, expensive and require large samples (i.e. preferably $n > 1,000$). Further, IRT models do not only assume that the average item is unbiased, but are incapable of detecting the presence of constant bias across all items.

Of more crucial importance perhaps, is that the applicability of any IRT model in a given testing situation is conditional on the validity of its underlying assumptions. These assumptions, namely, unidimensionality, local independence, and logistic model adequacy, can be debilitatingly stringent, since even the choice of items may be governed a priori by the models, regardless of their substantive educational or psychological appropriateness. In the context of test item selection, Novick (1980) emphasizes that when the particular requirement of a unidimensional latent trait is not satisfied, it is "impossible to differentiate between additional traits which are meaningful in the testing situation and those which are reflective of bias" (p. 132).

## 2. The Future

While item bias detection is among the most active of all areas of psychometric research, much remains to be done before a satisfactory battery of procedures with known properties is available. For example, further work needs to be done in explicating the currently available procedures, developing new procedures and extending item bias technology beyond dichotomously scored tests. In terms of current techniques, the distributional properties of many of the bias detection indices need to be investigated such that the power of the detection methods can be determined.

Future developments will undoubtedly involve the extension of item bias procedures beyond dichotomous items to polychotomous items that result from measurement instruments employing partial credit scoring, graded scoring, or rating scales. Since instruments of this type have widespread application in educational and psychosocial research, the possibility of bias in such instruments is equally important as that for dichotomous tests. A number of latent trait measurement models now exist for the modelling of data of this type and their use in the detection of item bias for data of this type may become an important area of research.

Currently, the most active area of item bias research is concerned with the development of new techniques based on log-linear or logit models, and the Mantel–Haenszel approach to contingency table analysis. These approaches are essentially modifications to chi-square methods and also employ elements of item response theory.

### 2.1 Mantel–Haenszel Statistic

The use of the Mantel–Haenszel statistic (see Holland and Thayer 1986) is a relatively new method for the detection of item bias that is gaining considerable support.

The Mantel–Haenszel approach is a chi-square technique with a number of distinct advantages over its predecessors. To apply the Mantel–Haenszel approach, the two groups being examined are divided into matched subgroups. The simplest method of matching is to use the total test score (research is still required on refining the methods for establishing appropriate groups) and for each matched group a table is calculated, as in Table 1. Using the notation of Holland and Thayer, $T_j$ is the total number of students in the matched set $j$; $n_{R_j}$ is the number from group R, and $A_j$ is the number from group R who got the item correct, and so on. Then, for the item being examined for bias, the $p$-values for each group $P_{R_j}$ and $P_{F_j}$ are calculated. The null hypothesis, $H_0 : P_{R_j} = P_{F_j}$ is then tested. In most chi-square approaches, the $H_0$ is tested against the simple negation of $H_1$ (i.e. $H_1 : P_{R_j} \neq P_{F_j}$) and they are not powerful against any specific violations to $H_0$. In contrast, the Mantel–Haenszel approach reduces the alternatives to $H_0$, to $H_1 : P_{R_j}/Q_{R_j} = \alpha P_{R_j}/Q_{F_j}$ (where $Q = 1-P$). The Mantel–Haenszel statistic for testing the null hypothesis

*Table 1*

Contingency table for the calculation of the Mantel–Haenszel statistic (MH-CHISQ)

| Group | Score on Test Item | | Total |
|-------|------|------|-------|
| | 1 | 0 | |
| R | $A_j$ | $B_j$ | $n_{R_j}$ |
| F | $C_j$ | $D_j$ | $n_{F_j}$ |
| Total | $M_{1_j}$ | $M_{0_j}$ | $T_j$ |

against $H_1$ (after correction for continuity) is given by Holland and Thayer as:

$$\text{MH-CHISQ} = \left[ \left| \sum_j A_j - \sum_j \text{E}(A_j) \right| - \frac{1}{2} \right]^2 \bigg/ \sum_j \text{var}(A_j)$$

where

$$\text{E}(A_j) = n_{\text{R}_j} M_{1_j} / T_j$$

$$\text{var}(A_j) = n_{\text{R}_j} n_{\text{F}_j} M_{1_j} M_{0_j} / T_j^2 (T_j - 1)$$

MH-CHISQ is distributed as chi square with one degree of freedom.

In addition to having greater power than other chi-square methods, the Mantel–Haenszel approach allows the calculation of a measure of the degree of bias in the item. This measure of bias is given through the odds ratio alpha ($\alpha_{\text{MH}}$). The estimate of $\alpha_{\text{MH}}$ is given by:

$$\hat{\alpha}_{\text{MH}} = \left( \sum_j A_j D_j / T_j \right) \bigg/ \left( \sum_j B_j C_j / T_j \right)$$

Holland and Thayer (1986 p. 9) have provided the following interpretation of $\hat{\alpha}_{\text{MH}}$:

> The value of $\hat{\alpha}_{\text{MH}}$ is the average factor by which the odds that a member of R is correct on the studied item exceeds the corresponding odds for a *comparable* member of F. The values of $\hat{\alpha}_{\text{MH}}$ that exceed 1 correspond to items on which the reference group performed better on average than did comparable members of the focal group.

Preliminary studies of the Mantel–Haenszel approach to item bias detection are still in progress and the results are not yet sufficiently clear to make any strong conclusion in respect of its utility. Although its usefulness is yet to be fully determined, early evaluation work indicates that it could be a cheap and effective alternative to the more complex latent trait methods.

### 2.2 Log-linear and Logit Models

Log-linear and logit models are beginning to have an impact on new directions in item research. Recent work by Kelderman (1984), who formulates the Rasch model as a quasi-log-linear model, and van der Flier et al. (1984) who use an iterative logit model, provide the groundwork for future developments in item bias detection technology.

Kelderman provides a method for formulating the Rasch model as a quasi-log-linear model and uses the log linear formulation to test specific violations to the Rasch model's assumptions. Although not directly concerned with item bias, Kelderman shows how various tests of independence on a group × score × item 1 × item 2 ×, . . ., × item $k$ contingency table may be undertaken. Many of these tests can be used to identify specific forms of item bias. While the log-linear Rasch approach requires further development, the theoretical formulations of the approach to date indicate some promise.

Van der Flier et al. also use a contingency table approach where a score × group × item response table is set up for each item. If the score categories are denoted by $i = 1,2, . . ., s$, the groups are denoted by $j = 1,2, . . ., g$ and the item response categories by $k = 1,2$ say, then the expected cell frequency in the table is denoted $F_{ijk}$. The logit is then defined as the natural logarithm of the ratio of the correct and incorrect responses. This is very similar to the formulation of the odds ratio in the Mantel–Haenszel and is also closely related to the basic steps in the formulation of the Rasch model.

The saturated logit model is therefore denoted as:

$$\log(F_{ij_1}/F_{ij_2}) = C + S_i + G_j + (SG)_{ij}$$

with constraints:

$$\sum_i S_i = \sum_j G_j = \sum_i (SG)_{ij} = \sum_j (SG)_{ij} = 0$$

where $C$ is the item difficulty parameter, $S_i$ is the score effect, $G_j$ is the group effect, and $(SG)_{ij}$ is the score by group interaction. This model, by definition, fits the data perfectly.

If the restricted model, $\log (F_{ij_1}/F_{ij_2}) = C + S_i$ fits the data, there is no group effect, so the item is not biased against any group. If the model $\log (F_{ij_1}/F_{ij_2} = C + S_i + G_i$ is required to fit the data, then uniform bias is detected; that is, there is bias against one of the groups which is uniform over score levels. If the saturated model is required to fit the data, then nonuniform bias has been detected; that is, bias that varies over the score levels. Note that it is possible, however, for an item to have bias that changes in direction over ability levels.

In most of the item bias detection procedures, the total test score (or some transformation of it) is used as the criterion against which to judge bias. In other words, the testee's ability is defined by the items being investigated for bias. To avoid this kind of circularity, van der Flier et al. used the logit model iteratively, with biased items being used successively from the calculation of the group score. Iterative methods can be employed with any of the chi-square or item response theory approaches, but they have not been extensively explored. One possible problem with iterative methods is that they are likely to be order-dependent so that the final set of unbiased items may depend on which item is chosen to be deleted first. In many instances, this choice could be somewhat arbitrary. In their comparative study, van der Flier et al. found that the iterative logit method performed favourably when compared to ANOVA and TID methods. Comparisons with IRT approaches have yet to be reported.

### 3. Concluding Comments

Prospects for the further development of item bias detection procedures, the explication of their properties and their relative usefulness, are indeed promising. Nevertheless, there is need for such optimism to be tempered with caution.

In recent years, the issue of bias in educational and psychological tests has received intense public and technical scrutiny, stimulating both public debate and psychometric research. However, despite advances in item bias detection technology, some of which have been reviewed here, it is important to note that apart from statistical criteria, none of the proposed methods for the detection of item bias is able to indicate *why* an item identified as "biased" is biased or *what* constitutes an item being biased. Clearly, in the absence of substantive theoretical criteria, no amount of statistical manipulation of test data can provide the *what* and *why* of "item bias", nor facilitate the drawing of valid inferences about its presence or absence. While psychometric research continues to yield notable improvements in test quality, much of this work cannot be said to have significantly clarified the public controversies, or to have resolved some of the more pressing substantive problems related to the issues of test and item bias. This state of affairs is primarily due to the fact that the efforts directed toward "improvements" have addressed technical rather than the substantive issues of item bias associated with its psychoeducational cognitive correlates.

## Bibliography

Adams R J 1983 *Sex Bias in ASAT*? Australian Council for Educational Research, Hawthorn, Victoria

Angoff W H, Ford S F 1973 Item–race interaction on a test of scholastic aptitude. *J. Educ. Meas.* 10: 95–106

Berk R A (ed.) 1982 *Handbook of Methods for Detecting Test Bias*. Johns Hopkins University Press, Baltimore, Maryland

Holland P W, Thayer D T 1986 Differential item performance and the Mantel–Haenszel procedure. Paper presented at the Annual Meeting of the American Educational Research Association, San Francisco, California

Ironson G H 1983 Using item response theory to measure bias. In: Hambleton R K (ed.) 1983 *Applications of Item Response Theory*. Educational Research Institute of British Columbia, Vancouver, pp. 155–74

Kelderman H 1984 Loglinear Rasch model tests. *Psychometrika*. 49: 223–45

Marascuilo L A, Slaughter R E 1981 Statistical procedures for identifying possible sources of item bias based on $\chi^2$ statistics. *J. Educ. Meas.* 18: 229–48

Masters G N 1988 Item discrimination: When more is worse. *J. Educ. Meas.* 25(1)

Novick M R 1980 Policy issues of fairness in testing. In: van der Kamp J T, Langerak W F, de Gruitjer P N M (eds.) 1980 *Psychometrics for Educational Debates*. Wiley, New York, pp. 123–37

Osterlind S J 1983 *Test Item Bias*. Sage University Paper series on Quantitative Applications in the Social Sciences, Series No. 070-030. Sage Publications, Beverly Hills, California, and London

Shepard L, Camilli G, Averill M 1981 Comparisons of procedures for detecting test-item bias with both external and internal ability criteria. *J. Educ. Stat.* 6: 317–75

Shepard L, Camilli G, Williams D M 1984 Accounting for statistical artifacts on item bias research. *J. Educ. Stat.* 9: 93–128

van der Flier H, Mellenbergh G J, Ader H J, Wijn M 1984 An iterative item bias detection method. *J. Educ. Meas.* 21: 131–45

# Unintended Effects in Educational Research

**S. Ball**

An unintended effect is an outcome that is peripherally related to, and *not* the reason for the implementation of an experimental program or treatment. This article will consider (a) not only side effects, but also other unintended effects that have been observed in research and evaluation; (b) reactive effects; (c) after effects; (d) the Hawthorne effect; (e) the John Henry effect; (f) the Pygmalion effect; and (g) the Golem effect.

## 1. Side Effects

Side effects are usually unintended outcomes, but it is not uncommon for program developers to recognize the possibility of a side effect and plan to have it happen.

An example of an unintended side effect is a foreign-language teaching program that is so heavily structured that the students dislike learning the foreign language. The intended main effect was the learning of the foreign language. The unintended side effect was the development of a distaste for further learning of the language.

Certainly the program developers would not want that to happen. Note, then, that in this instance the unintended side effect was negative. It could have been positive. For example, a children's television show might have as an intended main goal that the viewers learn about children in other countries. An unintended positive side effect might be that viewers take out relevant books from the school library and their reading comprehension and vocabulary are thereby improved.

Intended side effects are hoped-for outcomes that usually are outside the domain of the intended main effects. Thus, if the intended main effecs are achievement and cognitively oriented, then the intended side effects will usually be attitudinally affectively oriented. If the major goal is to improve the students' knowledge and skill in mathematics, the intended side effect might be to enhance the students' self-confidence in and liking of mathematics.

Some side effects may be so important that they outweigh the main intended outcomes. A tragic illustration of this occurred in the drug evaluation field with the tranquilizer, thalidomide. It was found to be effective in its intended role but it was not until it had gone into general use in Europe that it was found to have tragic consequences on the fetuses of pregnant women.

Because side effects can be vitally important in evaluating educational programs, Scriven (1972) proposed a goal-free model of program evaluation. He argued that an evaluator who knows the program goals will be too prone to access only those goal areas ignoring the unintended side effects. With a goal-free evaluation, however, the evaluator according to Scriven is more likely to assess the impact of a program whether intended or not.

Evaluators should be aware that sometimes the intended main effects fail to appear yet positive side effects do occur. For example, innovative educational program A is not superior to traditional program B, but program A does have the positive side effect that students are more motivated to stay on in school. This side effect may itself become the rationale for recommending the substitution of program A for program B.

A difficult question is who decides what side effects to look for. In general, program developers do not want evaluators to search for negative side effects. There should be clarity in the contract or the work order specifying the degree of autonomy given the evaluator in making decisions on what side effects to look for. Ideally this decision should be arrived at only after full consultation among the program developers, funders, clients, staff and evaluators.

## 2. Reactive Effects

Reactive effect is a term used in relation and evaluation when the measurement procedures or research/evaluation design distort the data obtained and the conclusions reached.

Reactive effects in measurement occur when the behavior elicited by measurement procedures is not characteristic of the behavior that would have occurred in the absence of the measurement procedure. For example, suppose a researcher wishes to know the impact of a new teaching technique on student behavior, and suppose further that the measurement procedure involves an observer in a classroom using a behavior checklist as the teacher works with the students. The presence of the observer may cause the students to behave differently in comparison to how they would behave with no observer in the classroom. The observer, in this case, has a reactive effect on the evidence obtained.

Distortions due to reactive effects in measurement may be the result of subjects trying to make a good impression on the data gatherer, of personal interactions between interviewer and interviewee (in this case the sex, race, age, and ethnicity of the interviewer can affect the responses obtained), of response sets (for example

young children tend to answer "yes" to questions posed by authority figures), of initial questions in a test leading to changes in understanding or to a new appreciation by the test taker of what is considered important and so affecting the way the test taker answers the later questions, and of changes in the environment created by the measurer (for example the placing of a videotape machine in a library might affect the way students behave during a library period).

In general, the less obtrusive the measurement procedure, the less reactive it is likely to be. Webb et al. (1966) provide an excellent presentation of unobtrusive measures in their book: *Unobtrusive Measures: Non-reactive Research in the Social Sciences*. A more extensive discussion of response sets, reactive effects, and unobtrusive measures is presented by Anderson et al. (1975).

Reactive effects (distortions) due to research/evaluation design deficiencies may also lead to erroneous conclusions.

## 3. After Effects

An after effect, as the term implies, is an impact that occurs some time after a treatment has been implemented. The term "sleeper effect" has also been used instead of after effect. Sometimes an after effect is noted years after the treatment has ended. Most research and evaluation studies fail to test for the long-delayed after effects because the final posttest occurs too soon after a treatment is ended. If there is a possibility of an after effect occurring, the evaluation design should include both an immediate posttest (at the end of the treatment) and at least one delayed posttest.

An example of after effect is provided by Kersh and Wittrock (1962) in their review of research on teaching techniques. They found that "direct" teaching techniques seemed to show a stronger impact than "discovery learning" techniques when the groups were tested immediately after the respective treatment. However, a delayed posttest (some six weeks after the treatment was over) showed the reverse to be true. The discovery learning group had shown little fade out of results and now performed better than the direct teaching group. Presumably an after effect of discovery learning was motivational, causing the students to continue to rehearse and learn to a degree not matched by the direct teaching group.

A controversial but potentially important example of after effect has been noted in the evaluative research on Head Start, a program for disadvantaged preschoolers. In the first decade of Head Start research it was noted that the program had an initial impact on children but that this impact did not seem to provide a permanent aid. That is, although the impact was observable when the children started regular school at the age of 5 or 6, it seemed to lessen so that there was little or no difference between the erstwhile Head Start participants and their comparable non-Head Start peers by third grade (age 8–9). However, an after effect (sleeper effect) was noted. Children who had been in Head Start seemed to forge ahead of their controls in the middle-school years (grades 6 and 7).

An after effect should not be confused with a side effect. The side effect happens concurrently with the main, intended effects but the after effect, if it occurs, happens at a time after the main and side effects.

## 4. The Hawthorne Effect

The Hawthorne effect is a reactive effect and it refers to the change in behavior that occurs when the subjects in an evaluation or experiment are aware that they are being studied. This awareness is confounded with the independent variable being studied; so any positive impact noted in the research can be causally ascribed either to the independent variable or to the awareness of the subjects.

The Hawthorne effect is well-illustrated by the series of experiments (Pennock 1929) which took place at the United States Western Electric Company factory from 1924 to 1927 at Hawthorne, Illinois. The label "Hawthorne effect" was coined by Pennock to describe the unexpected findings noted by him and his colleagues (Snow 1927). Many independent variables were systematically manipulated (e.g., illumination, rest pauses, pay incentives) and the employees were informed of what was happening. The enigma was that productivity tended to increase irrespective of the experimental manipulation. It became clear that the employees' awareness that they were being studied, itself had a positive impact on their productivity.

A number of researchers have studied the impact of the Hawthorne effect in educational settings (Cook 1962) and some have questioned its strength (Bauernfeind and Olson 1973). Nonetheless there is general agreement among educational researchers that the Hawthorne effect is a potential threat to the validity of educational experiments. Researchers are cautioned to guard against it (Sax 1979).

Consider, for example, a situation where a new kind of textbook is being tested in a random sample of classrooms, while another random sample of control classrooms is also being studied for comparison. If the experimenters had no regard for the Hawthorne effect, the experimental classrooms would receive the new kind of textbook, the teachers and students would be allowed to know they were the mediating variables in a textbook experiment, and observers might even spend time in the experimental, but not the control, classrooms. As a result the teachers and students might work harder; and the positive impact thus seen might then be wrongly ascribed to the new textbook (Trow 1971).

To avoid the contamination by the Hawthorne effect, care should be taken with the teachers and students *not* to emphasize the experiment. The control classrooms should be observed as much as the experimental classrooms, and since the experimental classes are receiving new books, the control classes might at least receive new copies of the old text, a "placebo".

The presence of the Hawthorne effect helps to explain the fads of educational practice. A new idea (e.g., the initial teaching alphabet or i.t.a. approach to reading, or the "open" classroom) is implemented with enthusiasm and with considerable apparent success. Over the following years the fad dies off. It could well be that much of the early success was a manifestation of the Hawthorne effect. As the new treatment becomes routine, the Hawthorne effect and positive impacts accruing therefrom are lost.

The obverse side of the Hawthorne effect is the John Henry effect.

## 5. The John Henry Effect

The John Henry effect is a type of reactive effect in which members of the control group perform better than they typically would perform. The reason why the control group outperform themselves is presumably because they feel competitive about the experimental group thereby creating enhanced enthusiasm to do well. The John Henry effect is to the control group as the Hawthorne effect is to the experimental group.

The term John Henry is taken from a folk hero of the United States, a black railroad worker who was told that the steam drill would replace human labour in laying railroad tracks. By amazing effort he did better than the machine but the exertion eventually killed him.

The John Henry effect was associated with educational research by Saretsky (1972). He pointed out a peculiar phenomenon with respect to the evaluative research that had taken place on performance contracting. Control groups and experimental groups in 18 sites had been studied: the control groups had made much greater than anticipated gains though they were presumably receiving no new or different treatment. It seemed, however, that the teachers of the control classes were definitely trying harder than they would normally have worked.

The John Henry effect (improved control group performance), may lead to the wrong conclusion that the experimental treatment, whatever it may be, is uneffective. Frequently the researcher looks at differences between the mean performance of the experimental group and the control group to see if the experimental treatment is effective. The research should also ensure there is no unusual change in the untreated control group. Perhaps the most appropriate evaluation (research) design to employ when the John Henry effect is thought likely to occur is a time series design in which measures are taken to provide baseline data before the experiment is introduced. Measurement should also occur after the treatment (experiment) is over. If the John Henry effect has occurred, the control group performance should be enhanced during the duration of the experiment and should return to baseline afterwards. If the treatment is effective the experimental group, of course, will also show enhanced performance during the experiment. The comparison might then be made with the experimental group's performance and the baseline or projected baseline performance of the control group, thereby discounting the John Henry effect.

Preferably the John Henry effect should not be allowed to occur. Control groups should not be made to feel threatened or in competition with the treatment group just as the experimental group should not be made to feel special and different.

## 6. The Pygmalion Effect

The Pygmalion effect was given emphasis when Rosenthal and Jacobson (1968) published *Pygmalion in the Classroom*. The term Pygmalion comes from the Greek myth in which life was infused into an inanimate object by the power of positive thinking. In the Rosenthal studies (Rosenthal and Rubin 1978), expectancies of the experimenter (or teacher) lead to improved performance by the subjects (or students). Thus, if a teacher believes a student will do better in the coming year, there is a stronger than chance possibility that this belief will be fulfilled.

## 7. The Golem Effect

Babad et al. (1982) also coined the less used term "Golem effect" after a Jewish myth in which a mechanical creature runs amok and becomes destructive. The Golem effect is a negative expectancy effect (in contrast to the positive expectancy effect called Pygmalion) and it is used to explain in part why students about whom teachers have low expectations often perform more poorly than would be likely given their previous school record.

Because reactive effects can be misleading, it is most important in developing and administering measures and in developing research and evaluation designs to

guard against them. Being aware of their potential mischief is a first step.

## Bibliography

Anderson S B, Ball S, Murphy R T 1975 *Encyclopedia of Educational Evaluation*. Jossey-Bass, San Francisco, California

Babad E Y, Inbar J, Rosenthal R 1982 Pygmalion, Galatea, and the Golem: Investigations of biased and unbiased teachers. *J. Educ. Psychol.* 74: 459–74

Bauernfeind R, Olson C 1973 Is the Hawthorne effect in educational experiments a chimera? *Phi Delta Kappan* 55: 271–73

Cook D L 1962 The Hawthorne effect in educational research. *Phi Delta Kappan* 44: 116–22

Kersh B Y, Wittrock M C 1962 Learning by discovery: An interpretation of recent research. *J. Teach. Educ.* 13: 461–68

Pennock G 1929 Industrial research at Hawthorne: An experimental investigation of rest periods, working conditions and other influences. *Personnel J.* 8: 296–313

Rosenthal R, Jacobson L 1968 *Pygmalion in the Classroom: Teacher Expectation and Pupils' Intellectual Development.* Holt, Rinehart and Winston, New York

Rosenthal R, Rubin D B 1978 Interpersonal expectancy effects: The first 345 studies. *Behav. Brain Sci.* 377–415

Saretsky G 1972 The OEO P.C. experiment and the John Henry effect. *Phi Delta Kappan* 53: 579–81

Sax G 1979 *Foundations of Educational Research*, 2nd edn. Prentice Hall, Englewood Cliffs, New Jersey

Scriven M 1972 Pros and cons about goal-free evaluation. *Eval. Comment* 3(4): 1–4

Snow C E 1927 Research on industrial illumination. *The Tech Engineering News* 8(6): 257–82

Trow M 1971 Methodological problems in the evaluation of innovation. In: Caro F G (ed.) 1971 *Readings in Evaluation Research*, Russell Sage, Rensselaer, New York

Webb E J, Campbell D T, Schwartz R D, Sechrest L 1966 *Unobtrusive Measures: Nonreactive Research in the Social Sciences.* Rand McNally, Chicago, Illinois

Zdep S M, Irvine S H 1970 Reverse Hawthorne effect in educational evaluation. *J. Sch. Psychol.* 8(2): 89–95

# Guide to Sources and Reviews of Tests

C. E. Massad

The primary purpose of this article is to provide information about two sources of published tests: the test publishers and the reviews of tests. In addition, the kind of information important in the test selection process and the information generally available from the two sources above are briefly discussed.

Before referring to sources of information on tests, it is important to have clearly in mind (a) the purpose of testing and the kinds of decisions to be made based on the interpretation of the results (e.g., guidance of individuals, educational program evaluation) and (b) the characteristics of the individuals to be tested (e.g., age, level of educational attainment, language of the

home, language in which educated). Once these things are specified, information about tests can be profitably reviewed and the appropriateness of various tests for the situation can be determined.

Generally, both publishers and reviewers of tests provide information on several characteristics considered to be important in the test selection process. This information should guide each test user in determining the appropriateness of tests for the user's situation. Test descriptions usually include characteristics like (a) population in terms of age or educational level for whom the test was designed; (b) whether the test is to be administered to a group, an individual, or can be used either way; (c) whether there are alternate forms of the test available; (d) whether the test requires machine scoring by the publisher or whether the user can choose to have the test machine or hand scored; (e) how long it takes to administer the test; (f) what materials are available (e.g., re-usable test booklets, administrator's manual, interpretive material, practice material); (g) test reliability information; (h) test validity information; and (i) the types of scores available (for instance, standard scores, percentiles, raw scores, subscores, profiles).

The major test publishers include Addison-Wesley Testing Service (USA); American College Testing Program (USA); American Guidance Service (USA); Australian Council for Educational Research; Bobbs-Merrill Company (USA); Bureau of Educational Research and Service at the University of Iowa (USA); CTB/McGraw-Hill (USA); Centro Editor de Psicologia Aplicada (Brazil); Caribbean Examination Council (Barbados, West Indies); Consulting Psychologists Press (USA); Danish Institute for Educational Research; Educational and Industrial Testing Service (USA); Educational Records Bureau (USA); Educational Testing Service (USA); Follett Publishing Company (USA); Ginn and Company (USA); Institute for Personality and Ability Testing (USA); International Association for the Evaluation of Educational Achievement (Sweden); National Board of Education (Sweden); National Foundation for Educational Research in England and Wales; New Zealand Council for Educational Research; Ontario Institute for Studies in Education (Canada); Oxford–Cambridge School Examinations Board (UK); The Psychological Corporation (USA); Riverside Publishing Company (USA); Science Research Associates (USA); Scottish Council for Research in Education; West African Examination Council (Ghana); Western Psychological Services (USA). Up-to-date addresses for these and other test publishers may be obtained by writing to: Test Collection, Educational Testing Service, Princeton, New Jersey 08540, USA.

In addition, Test Collection makes available on a subscription basis *News on Tests*, a newsletter including new publishers, new references on measurement and evaluation, and references to test reviews. Another regular publication of Test Collection is *Major US Publishers of Standardized Tests*, a pamphlet listing publishers' addresses. A series of annotated test bibliographies has been prepared and is also available from Test Collection on request.

The International Association for Educational Assessment (IAEA), a multinational association of organizations concerned with measurement, can also be contacted for sources of information on tests in various countries.

An information-retrieval system specifically designed to respond to search questions about tests is the Educational Resources Information Center (ERIC) Tests, Measurement, and Evaluation Clearinghouse (ERIC/TM). It contains information on tests and other measurement devices, measurement and evaluation procedures

and techniques, and programs or projects insofar as they relate to evaluation materials, procedures, and techniques. *A Directory of Information on Tests* is available for a nominal fee from ERIC/TM. For information on other ERIC/TM publications and available services, write to: User Service Representative, ERIC/TM, American Institute for Research, 1055 Thomas Jefferson Street NW, Washington, DC 20007, USA.

Of course, the classic source of test information is the Buros *Mental Measurement Yearbook* (MMY), published in eight editions and supplemented by monographs on specific measurement topics. These volumes provide comprehensive information on, and critical reviews of hundreds of, measuring and data collection devices. Two volumes of *Tests in Print* (1961, 1974) serve as master indexes to the first seven editions of the *Mental Measurement Yearbook*. These and the eighth edition (1978) were published by the late Oscar K. Buros under Gryphon Press, Highland Park, New Jersey, USA. New contributions have come from the Buros Institute of Mental Measurements at the University of Nebraska.

Other references published by Buros (Gryphon Press) include: *Reading Tests and Reviews* (1968, 1975), *Personality Tests* (1970, 1975), *Intelligence Tests and Reviews* (1975), *English Tests and Reviews* (1975), *Vocational Tests and Reviews* (1975), *Foreign Language Tests and Reviews* (1975), *Mathematics Tests and Reviews* (1975), *Science Tests and Reviews* (1975), and *Social Studies Tests and Reviews* (1975).

## Bibliography

AERA/APA/NCME Joint Committee 1985 *Standards for Educational and Psychological Testing*. American Psychological Association, Washington, DC

Andrulis R S 1977 *Adult Assessment: A Sourcebook of Tests and Measures of Human Behavior*. Thomas, Springfield, Illinois

Berger B 1969 *An Annotated Bibliography of Measurement for Young Children*. Center for Urban Education, New York

Bonjean C M, Hill R J, McLemore S D 1967 *Sociological Measurement: Inventory of Scales and Indices*. Chandler, San Francisco, California

Borich G D, Madden S K 1976 *Evaluating Classroom Instruction: A Sourcebook of Instruments*. Addison-Wesley, Reading, Massachusetts

Buros O K (ed.) 1974 *Tests in Print II: An Index to Tests, Test Reviews, and Literature on Specific Tests*. Gryphon, Highland Park, New Jersey

Buros O K (ed.) 1978 *Eighth Mental Measurements Yearbook*. Gryphon, Highland Park, New Jersey

Chun K-T, Cobb S, French J R P 1975 *Measures for Psychological Assessment: A Guide to 3,000 Original Sources and Their Applications*. Institute for Social Research, University of Michigan, Ann Arbor, Michigan

Compton C 1980 *A Guide to 65 Tests for Social Education*. Pitman Learning, Belmont, California

Hoepfner R et al. (eds.) 1970 *CSE Elementary School Test Evaluations*. Center for the Study of Evaluation, University of California, Los Angeles, California

Hoepfner R et al. (eds.) 1972 *CSE-RBS Test Evaluations: Test for Higher Order Cognitive, Affective, and Interpersonal Skills*. Center for the Study of Evaluation, University of California, Los Angeles, California

Hoepfner R et al. (eds.) 1974 *CSE Secondary School Test Evaluations*. Center for the Study of Evaluation, University of California, Los Angeles, California

Hoepfner R, Stern C, Nemmedal S G (eds.) 1971 *CSE-ECRC Preschool/Kindergarten Test Evaluations*. Center for the Study of Evaluation, University of California, Los Angeles, California

Massad C E 1977 *Information for Assessment and Evaluation*. Evaluation Improvement program, Educational Testing Service, Princeton, New Jersey

# Issues Affecting Sources of Evaluation Evidence

## Handwriting Legibility

### A. P. Holbrook

The legibility of handwritten letter forms is crucial to the effective communication of written expression. Because legibility has not been precisely defined, its measurement poses problems that are particularly relevant in the area of essay marking.

It is generally acknowledged that legibility consists of letter shape and slant, letter size, the space between letters, their alignment, and, less pertinent in this age of ball-points, thickness of stroke. Other more controversial aspects of legibility, which by their nature make definition difficult, include the aesthetic qualities of a piece of handwriting, the conventionality of letter forms and whether they are acceptable and/or familiar, and the role of syntax and semantics.

The rating scale has been the principal instrument of evaluation. The best known are those of Thorndike in 1910, Ayres in 1912 and 1915, and Freeman in 1912 and revised in 1959 (see Herrick and Erlebacher 1963). These scales are all based on different criteria of legibility. The characteristic handwriting scale is produced for primary and junior secondary levels. It consists of graded samples of handwriting, utilizing a copied or memorized passage that includes all the letters of the Roman alphabet. Not all scales are composite, that is, include both manuscript and cursive styles, nor do they all include left-handed samples. To use a scale a comparison is made between a sample sentence written by a student, and handwritten examples of that same sentence in the scale. If there is a "match", the student's sample is given the value assigned to the appropriate scale sample.

Teachers have been found to judge handwriting more objectively when they use a scale. It has been argued, however, that it is a cumbersome and arbitrary means of assessment, particularly as one scale could not contain the whole universe of style. Also very little is known about the reliability of such scales though in more recent times attempts have been made to redress this deficiency (Phelps et al. 1985). Thus there is a trend towards the development of a simple diagnostic instrument, one that is based on a minimum standard of legibility and where letters are rated as either correct or incorrect. Transparent overlays printed with model letter forms, where deviations from the model can be measured by pupil and teacher alike, are a step in this direction.

Holistic rating systems have also been utilized. They typically involve scoring handwriting samples with a Likert-type scale, though markers may be provided with model letters as a guide. The reliability, validity and utility of the overlay and holistic approaches to rating handwriting were investigated by Graham (1986). Intra-rater and interrater reliability coefficients revealed that the holistic procedures were unreliable, whereas marks assigned by markers using overlays were consistent over time and across markers.

Although there has been very little research into the specific factors that contribute to legibility, it has been shown (see Askov et al. 1970, Peck et al. 1980, Ziviani and Elkins 1984) that there is no significant relationship between legibility and intelligence; females write more legibly and more accurately than males; and legibility deteriorates with speed, and is better among primary students than it is among secondary students and adults. Research into factors influencing essay marks has revealed a significant relationship between handwriting and the grades awarded to essays (Markham 1976). In general, poor legibility results in lower grades, despite the quality of content, though one study found that poor legibility was more likely to influence the marks awarded to essays of poor and average quality (Briggs 1971). In another study, in cases of poor handwriting, markers tended to rely more on their expectations of student performance than on essay content (Chase 1979). Even the clarity of the markers' own handwriting has been found to influence the grades they award (Huck and Bounds 1972). Research in this area, though by no means extensive, does serve to give some idea of the relevance of legibility for educational testing.

## Bibliography

Askov E N, Otto W, Askov W 1970 A decade of research in handwriting: Progress and prospect. *J. Educ. Res.* 64: 100–11

Briggs D 1971 The handwriting handicap. *Where* 58: 170–73

Chase C I 1979 The impact of achievement expectations and

handwriting quality on scoring essay tests. *J. Educ. Meas.* 16: 39–42

Graham S 1986 The reliability, validity and utility of three handwriting measurement procedures. *J. Educ. Res.* 79: 373–80

Herrick V E, Erlebacher A 1963 The evaluation of legibility in handwriting. In: Herrick V E (ed.) 1963 *New Horizons for Research in Handwriting.* University of Wisconsin Press, Madison, Wisconsin, pp. 207–31

Huck S W, Bounds W G 1972 Essay grades: An interaction between graders' handwriting clarity and the neatness of exam papers. *Am. Educ. Res. J.* 9: 279–83

Markham L R 1976 Influences of handwriting quality on teacher evaluation of written work. *Am. Educ. Res. J.* 13: 277–83

Peck M, Askov E N, Fairchild S H 1980 Another decade of research in handwriting: Progress and prospect in the 1970s. *J. Educ. Res.* 73: 283–98

Phelps J, Stempel L, Speck G 1985 The children's handwriting scale: A new diagnostic tool. *J. Educ. Res.* 79: 46–50

Zachrisson B 1965 *Studies in the Legibility of Printed Text.* Almqvist and Wiksell, Stockholm

Ziviani J, Elkins J 1984 An evaluation of handwriting performance. *Educ. Rev.* 36: 249–61

# Self-report

J. W. Newfield

The expression "self-report" is more a general label than a specific term. Self-report refers to the result produced by any measurement technique in which an individual is instructed to serve both as assessor or observer and as the object of the assessment or observation.

One use of self-reports is to investigate internal processes and states such as cognitive processes, motives, or feelings, attitudes, or values. Examples would include asking individuals to report the steps they used in solving a problem, their reasons for participating in a program, or their assessment of self-concept, degree of acceptance of authority, or extent of tolerance. Another application of self-reports is to provide verbal substitutes for behavior samples as when individuals are questioned about the degree of assertiveness they would exhibit in a presented situation. A third application of the use of self-reports is to provide information concerning prior behavior when people are questioned about particular episodes.

Self-reports may be obtained with an open response format, such as a request to "think aloud" or "list aspects of your job which you enjoy." They may also be obtained with a fixed response format. Common forms of fixed response formats are a Likert-type response scale, the Thurstone scale, the Guttman scale, and the semantic differential.

When planning to use self-reports an initial step should be to determine whether the desired information is potentially accessible. There is some division of opinion as to the type of information which can be obtained from self-reports. Some types are generally accepted as unavailable to all individuals. These include knowledge of the process of retrieval from long-term memory and knowledge of recognition and motor-perception processes. Another form of knowledge accepted as non-accessible is knowledge of automatic or highly overlearned processes which occur quickly and do not use short-term memory. Plausible requests could not be made for this type of information. Information accepted as potentially accessible, which has been labeled by Nisbett and Wilson (1977) as a great storehouse of private knowledge, includes personal historical facts, the focus of attention at any given point in time, current sensations and knowledge of emotions, evaluations, and plans (p. 255). Requests for self-reports of this type of information are plausible. Information for which the potential for access is in dispute is knowledge of higher-order cognitive processes. Some (Nisbett and Wilson 1977) claim that individuals may have no direct access to higher-order mental processes. Others (Ericsson and Simon 1980) claim that for conditions which fit theoretical expectations with regard to access there are studies which show sufficient congruence between verbal reports and other behavioral measures to support the view that individuals do have potential access to these processes.

In general the accuracy of self-reports depends upon characteristics of the instruction requesting the information, individual differences in ability to retrieve requested information, and the self-report task attitudes of respondents. Subjects will respond more accurately if the requesting instruction is stated clearly and specifically, and if the requested information is accessible. The instruction must be sufficiently clear and worded at an appropriate level as to be understood by the respondent. In addition, Ericsson and Simon (1980) stress the importance of avoiding the use of probes which are "too general to elicit the information actually sought" (p. 24). Also, the instruction should be of such a nature that the information sought could reasonably be expected to be accessible in memory. The importance of the later characteristic of self-report instructions, especially when probing for processes or reasons for influences on evaluations, choices, or behaviors, is highlighted by the fact that respondents will often answer almost any self-report question. These answers may simply be "implicit, a priori theories about the causal connection between stimulus and response" (Nisbett and Wilson 1977 p. 233), they may be generated by the use of "intermediate processes to infer missing information and to fill out and generalize incomplete memories before responding" (Ericsson and Simon 1980 p. 243), or they may be accurate self-reports. Without careful attention to the characteristics of the requesting instruction these alternatives cannot be evaluated.

With regard to the effects on self-report accuracy related to an individual's ability to retrieve information from long-term memory there are many factors which should be taken into account. Some of these may be influenced by the conditions under which self-report data are gathered. For example, the richness of context clues provided in self-report instructions can facilitate retrieval. Also, the less time lapse there is between events and self-reports related to these events the more retrieval will be facilitated. Other factors related to retrieval which may not be under an investigator's control include the degree of structure in memory and the strength of associations among memory components related to the information being sought.

For some applications, self-reports are more suspect than in other instances since the attitude of the respondent toward the self-report task may lead the respondent to report information inaccurately. This may occur if the nature of the information requested would reflect negatively on the respondent, if the information is deemed too private to report, or if a particular report would generate some desired advantage for the respondent. Through the use of procedures to provide anonymity some of these problems can be reduced, but for some topics and for some uses to which self-report data might be put, obtaining a sufficient degree of accuracy to be of theoretical or practical value is difficult.

For some purposes self-reports may provide the best source of data while in other instances they may provide the most convenient source of data. For these reasons self-reports will continue to play an important role in educational studies. However, it should be emphasized that the validity of self-report measures should be determined empirically in the same fashion as the validity of any other performance measure.

## Bibliography

Ericsson K A, Simon H A 1980 Verbal reports as data. *Psychol. Rev.* 87: 215–51
Hook C M, Rosenshine B V 1979 Accuracy of teacher reports of their classroom behavior. *Rev. Educ. Res.* 49: 1–12
Nisbett R E, Wilson T D 1977 Telling more than we know: Verbal reports on mental processes. *Psychol. Rev.* 84: 231–59

# Interviewing

### R. G. Matarazzo

The interview is ubiquitous in today's society, having an important role in business, government, education, medicine, law, and the social sciences to name several major areas of application. Interviews in different settings vary in their long-range goals, but the immediate purpose ordinarily is similar: encouraging the interviewee to engage in some kind of self-exploration to satisfy a purpose mutual to interviewer and interviewee. Thus interviewers in different settings need to engage in some similar behaviors: defining the goal; deciding what topics need to be covered in order to achieve that goal; establishing a relationship; facilitating a flow of communication from the interviewee; guiding the communication to relevant information; and terminating the interview. The interviewee consumes most of the talking time: ordinarily in excess of 80 percent.

Although the term "interview" dates back at least to the sixteenth century, it achieved special professional meaning through the writings of Freud in the early twentieth century. Freud's psychoanalytic interview came to be primarily a session in which the interviewee engaged in free association while the interviewer listened and gave minimal guidance and interpretation of the meaning or significance of statements. This form of interviewing was found to be wanting even within the professions of psychology and psychiatry. Designed to elicit unconscious impulses and motives, it was an inefficient means both of obtaining additional needed information and of helping the patient to solve problems. In the infancy of the practice of psychotherapy, however, it provided security to the professional who left it primarily for the patient to emit significant material. Providing further security, the doctor–patient interaction was considered so sacrosanct that no outsider should observe or record the interview. This belief hampered research and progress until a psychologist Carl Rogers (1951), first tape-recorded, published, and analyzed therapeutic interviews. In these interviews, also, the interviewer's role in structuring the interaction was minimal while the interviewee expressed his feelings and thoughts, guided only by the interviewer's clarifications and reflections of what had been said.

This "nondirective" interviewing style has also passed from widespread acceptance, because it was not effective and efficient with many types of individuals and problems. It should be noted, however, that some contributions from both nondirective and psychoanalytic interviewing continue to be accepted: for example, Freud's "neurotic defenses" (repression, projection, etc.) and discovery of unconscious cues (slips of speech, forgetting, etc.); and Rogers' analysis of the necessary ingredients in interviewer attitude (such as warmth, genuineness, and positive regard).

Since Rogers' initial breakthrough in unveiling the interview from secrecy, demonstrating that it was amenable to research and need not remain exclusively the domain of one specialty area, the interview has been studied and written about by individuals of diverse backgrounds and purposes. Within psychiatry and the social sciences, interviewing has been studied from the perspective of three major goals; (a) accurate diagnosis, (b) psychotherapy, and (c) research. The diagnostic interview, as previously used, was not a reliable diagnostic instrument across interviewers. In an early study (Ash 1949) in which three psychiatrists participated in one interview and made separate diagnoses, there was only 45 percent agreement for major diagnostic categories and 20 percent for specific subcategories. However, the flaw seemed to lie largely in the definition of diagnostic criteria. It was noted that interviewers often did not agree on the symptoms or behaviors diagnostic of a given psychiatric category. Thus, it was necessary to establish agreed-upon criteria before greater reliability could be achieved. Development of specific criteria was attempted by Feighner et al. (1972), among others, enabling researchers such as Spitzer et al. (1977) to obtain reliability coefficients of approximately 0.80. Similar, operationally defined criteria have recently been adopted officially by the American Psychiatric Association in its latest diagnostic manual (DSM III). For example, schizophrenia residual type, must include: (a) a history of at least one previous schizophrenic episode; (b) no prominent psychotic symptoms at present; and (c) continuing evidence of illness such as blunted or inappropriate affect, social withdrawal, eccentric behavior, illogical thinking or loosening of associations.

With such specific criteria in mind, order is built into the task of verbal inquiry and behavioral observation; interviewers can be trained; and skills can be measured. Standardized interview schedules, conducted by lay individuals, are found to be useful in diagnostic tasks, in research, and in some other situations. Although therapeutic interviewing probably cannot be standardized, Peterson (1968) and others have pointed out that skillful interviewing involves a degree of structure. This consists initially of "scanning" the major interpersonal areas of human functioning (e.g., vocational, social, family, avocational), then covering the apparently significant areas for that individual in more detail.

A number of recent books describe basic interviewing skills for the beginner: how to open the interview, facilitate communication, elicit feelings, deal with specific problems, summarize and close the interview, and so on (Enelow and Swisher 1972, Froelich and Bishop 1977).

Beyond such basic skills, it is difficult to describe exactly what good interviewers do. One important element, however, is attitude. Truax showed that attitude can be a potent determinant of patient outcome, emphasizing the importance of Rogers' aforementioned "ingredients," such as warmth, positive regard, and empathy. Confronting individuals negatively, with their shortcomings and skill deficiencies destroys rapport at the outset, decreases self-exploration by the interviewee, and has a negative effect upon therapeutic outcome (Truax and Carkhuff 1967).

Several professional groups have been concerned with developing effective methods of teaching interviewing skill (Matarazzo 1978). The most effective teaching methods have involved: explicit definition of the behaviors to be learned followed by practice in live interviews; feedback by observers who have carefully rated the behavior in question; videofeedback; and ideally, feedback from the interviewee. A positive supervisor–student relationship has been found to be important, as well as supervisor modeling of empathy, warmth, and respect in that relationship. A program incorporating the above is that described by Ivey, called microcounseling, in which he attempts to teach one interviewing skill at a time (such as "attending" behavior, "accurate reflection," and "summarization of feelings") with immediate feedback, attempts to improve through immediate practice, and more feedback (Ivey and Authier 1978).

In summary, although interviewing takes place in many settings, interviewer skills are basically the same: (a) definition of the goal, (b) facilitation of communication, (c) establishing and maintaining a positive relationship, (d) guiding content, and (e) decision making based upon the interview. Rogers and the nondirective group have placed major emphasis on relationship variables such as warmth, empathy, and positive regard. Facilitation of communication has been a common concern, and is described in most primers on interviewing. The last three skills, however, appear to be the most difficult for interviewers to acquire, and involve a combination of conceptual, experiential, and behavioral learning in a constantly shifting, never duplicated situation. It is in these areas that it remains difficult to define the specific differences between expert and novice interviewers.

## Bibliography

American Psychiatric Association 1982 *Diagnostic and Statistical Manual of Mental Disorders: DSM III*. American Psychiatric Association, Washington, DC

Ash P 1949 The reliability of psychiatric diagnosis. *J. Abnorm. Soc. Psychol.* 44: 272–77

Enelow A J, Swisher S N 1972 *Interviewing and Patient Care*. Oxford University Press, New York

Feighner J P, Robins E, Guze S B, Woodruff R A, Winokur G, Munoz R 1972 Diagnostic criteria for use in psychiatric research. *Arch. Gen. Psychiatry* 26: 57–63

Froehlich R E, Bishop F M 1977 *Clinical Interviewing Skills: A Programmed Manual for Data Gathering, Evaluation and Patient Management*. Mosby, St. Louis, Missouri

Ivey A E, Authier J 1978 *Microcounseling: Innovations in Interviewing, Counseling, Psychotherapy, and Psychoeducation*, 2nd edn. Thomas, Springfield, Illinois

Matarazzo R G 1978 Research on the teaching and learning of psychotherapeutic skills. In: Garfield S L, Bergin A F (eds.) 1978 *Handbook of Psychotherapy and Behavior Change: An Empirical Analysis*, 2nd edn. Wiley, New York, pp. 941–66

Peterson D R 1968 *The Clinical Study of Social Behavior*. Appleton-Century-Crofts, New York

Rogers C R 1951 *Client-centered Therapy: Its Current Practice, Implications, and Theory*. Houghton-Mifflin, Boston, Massachusetts

Rogers C R 1957 The necessary and sufficient conditions of therapeutic personality change. *J. Consult. Psychol.* 21: 95–103

Spitzer R L, Sheehely M, Endicott J 1977 DSM III: Guiding principles. In: Rakoff V M, Stancer H C, Kedward H B (eds.) 1977 *Psychiatric Diagnosis.* Brunner-Mazel, New York

Truax C B, Carkhuff R R 1967 *Toward Effective Counseling and Psychotherapy: Training and Practice.* Aldine, Chicago, Illinois

# Part 3

# Curriculum Evaluation

# Part 3

# Curriculum Evaluation

---

## Introduction

The curriculum is the medium through which instruction is planned and delivered, and curriculum evaluation itself is a major category of educational evaluation. An examination of the curriculum is also likely to be a significant component of evaluations of educational materials, techniques, and practices; educational programs; and educational organizations or institutions. Part 3 is divided into two sections. It begins with a treatment of curriculum Models and Philosophies, and then turns to the Components and Applications of Curriculum Evaluation.

The consideration of evaluation models and philosophies begins with a series of five articles, the first of which takes up the nature of *Alternative Paradigms in Curriculum Inquiry*. This historical review and discussion examines three different conceptions of alternative paradigms: as a classification system to categorize positions on curriculum theory and practice; as alternative perspectives or assumptions about curriculum inquiry; and as conceptions of the dimensions that define curricula and guide curriculum development. The article takes the eclectic, synthetic position that alternative models can coexist productively, and that multiple paradigms can fruitfully inform curriculum inquiry. The second article, *Curriculum Validation*, takes up the question of whether a curriculum realizes its stated intents. The question has both philosophical and empirical aspects, and involves conceptions of validity as well as epistemological and ontological problems. Four procedures are described and discussed for addressing the curriculum validation question: judgement, experimentation, analysis, and consensus. The third article, on *Curriculum Evaluation*, traces the history of this subfield within evaluation, and describes both formative and summative applications. Questions about who should carry out such evaluations, how they should be organized, and what they should encompass are also considered.

Having analyzed the general nature and intents of curriculum evaluation, this section next turns to the subject of *Curriculum Evaluation Models*. In a general article on this subject, two broad categories of models are distinguished: curriculum product evaluations, which focus on products such as course of study, syllabi, textbooks, and so on;

and curriculum program evaluations, which refer to the complex set of interactions between a given instructional program and its setting. Historically, program evaluations began with goal-oriented studies of how successful programs were in attaining their stated objectives. More recently, these have been joined by models that give broader consideration to unintended program effects. Curriculum evaluation models have also evolved in the direction of providing a more detailed description of the curriculum in use, and of showing greater concern for the interest, needs, and perspectives of curriculum users.

The last of the five articles on evaluation in the context of curriculum inquiry, *Curriculum Evaluation Research*, considers curriculum evaluation itself as an object of inquiry, and describes the state of current research on delineation of the questions that curriculum evaluation should address: information gathering; reporting of curriculum evaluation findings; and curriculum evaluation utilization. The conclusion of the article draws attention to the need for further research on curriculum evaluation. Many questions remain to be answered.

The next four articles in Part 3(a) take up the goal-driven, or Tylerian, evaluation models, which focus most strongly on the stated, intended outcomes of a curriculum program. The first of these articles describes the *Eight-year Study*, carried out in the late 1930s. This study involved a dramatic restructuring of 30 high schools, aimed at attaining some goals common to all of the schools, and other goals unique to each of them. The project's evaluation, led by Ralph W. Tyler, was instrumental in founding the modern field of curriculum evaluation. Because goals and objectives are central to the approach of the *Eight-year Study* and subsequent rational–empirical approaches, the next three articles are devoted to educational objectives and to taxonomies of educational objectives, including their evolution over the past two decades. The first of these articles, *Educational Objectives*, clarifies the several meanings of the terms *goal* and *objective* in the literatures of education and evaluation, and discusses the strengths and limitations of specific objectives in curriculum design and evaluation. It further considers the interrelationships among objectives and the contexts in which they are used, some logical ambiguities in the definition and use of objectives, and the political and management implications of objectives-driven instruction. The article concludes with numerous arguments for and against the use of objectives in curriculum development, lesson planning, instructional design, evaluation, and as a means of communicating to students what they are supposed to do. The second article focuses on *Taxonomies of Educational Objectives*. It describes several well-known organizing frameworks for cognitive and for affective learning outcomes, and reviews evidence concerning their reliability and validity. In the cognitive domain, the frameworks reviewed include the Bloom Taxonomy of Educational Objectives, the Guilford Structure of Intellect Model, the Gagné-Merrill Taxonomy, Gerlach and Sullivan's Taxonomy, and De Block's Taxonomy. In the affective domain Krathwohl's taxonomy is reviewed, together with an analysis by De Landsheere that might serve as the basis for an alternative framework. The article concludes with a brief summary of six taxonomies proposed for the psychomotor domain, and some general remarks. The third of these three articles, *A Twenty-year Perspective on Educational Objectives*, provides an historical context, beginning with the programmed instruction movement, and traces the uses of behavioral objectives, as well as the limitations of these uses, up to the present. Criterion-referenced tests are recommended as a method for assessing objective attainment, and guidelines are set forth for the use of educational objectives by evaluators.

As with educational evaluation generally, the field of curriculum evaluation has seen a rapid growth in more naturalistic approaches. These are well-represented by the final articles in the first section. The first of these, *Qualitative Curriculum Evaluation*, presents a general discussion of the subject. Qualitative curriculum evaluation is conceived as a flexible set of approaches aimed at expanding reflective human understanding and promoting moral action within educational settings and their social contexts. It may include empiricism and may employ enumeration, but differs from more scientific or technologically oriented approaches in its concern for the particular, for meaning, and for valuation. The article discusses the nature of qualitative curriculum evaluation, its historical origins, and its relation to the broader realm of naturalistic methodology. The final article in Part 3(a) discusses *Curricular Implications of Educational Connoisseurship and Criticism. Connoisseurship* refers to the private experience and appreciation of the nuances of curriculum and of classroom life. The understandings and insights of the educational connoisseur are made public in the form of criticism, which blends evocative, figurative, or metaphorical language with factual description, to communicate the author's interpretations. The methods of connoisseurship and criticism may be applied not only to ongoing educational programs ("in vivo"), but also to program plans, blueprints, and instructional materials ("in vitro"). The critical process of coming to understand an educational setting as a connoisseur, and the issues of veridicality and generalizability of insights communicated through educational criticism, are manifested in much the same way as for other forms of naturalistic inquiry. These concerns are not to be minimized, but neither can they be avoided altogether by a retreat to positivism or empiricism.

The discussion turns next from models and philosophies to the second section of Part 3, comprising a detailed treatment of some specific Components and Applications of Curriculum Evaluation. The first of these articles, *Curriculum Feasibility Studies*, considers philosophical, pedagogical, political, and economic issues in addressing the worth of a curriculum in a particular situation, and the likelihood of its successful implementation. *Curriculum Tryout*, the subject of the next article, is important for both formative and summative evaluation purposes. Before any curriculum is produced in final form and disseminated, a small scale tryout is recommended with careful monitoring to detect any problems as early as possible. Some of the specific varieties of curriculum tryout are laboratory tryout, pilot tryout, and field tryout. These may be used separately or in sequence as part of the curriculum development process.

The next three articles continue the analysis of specific curriculum components. *Textbooks and Curriculum* considers the manner in which textbooks influence and define curriculum content and organization, distinguishing the role of textbooks in centralized versus decentralized educational systems, and noting recent trends away from content prescriptions and toward outcome-based and process-oriented considerations. The next article considers the analysis of textbooks themselves. For many years, textbook analysis was dominated by the use of readability formulas and, more recently, checklists. Modern approaches attend much more to the rhetorical structure of the text and the clarity with which that structure is marked for the reader. The article on *Textbook Analysis* discusses these trends, and includes a useful list of specific questions that may be used in curriculum evaluation to judge the strengths and weaknesses of texts. Finally, the presentation on *Evaluation of Learning Resources* moves beyond textbook evaluation to consider a variety of instructional media. Evaluation of these materials may serve the ends of selection for purchase or utilization planning, as well as their improvement, modification, or redesign. Instructional resource evaluation procedures for each of these purposes are discussed in the article.

Distance education is a major area of application for curriculum evaluation. *Evaluation in Distance Education* describes the state of knowledge and future evaluation needs with regard to social and educational outcomes of distance education programs, cost considerations, and the organization and management of such programs. Distance education raises some significant and distinctive evaluation concerns, including the likelihood of survival of the program itself, determining whether the program is reaching remote target populations, the adequacy of coverage of the target population, cost effectiveness of distance education versus alternative educational delivery systems, and the interaction of external contextual factors with program organization and operation.

The last three articles in Part 3(b) all deal in a more focused way with varieties of outcome-oriented curriculum evaluation. The first of these, *Error Analysis as a Curriculum Evaluation Method*, entails a careful examination of students' work including homework, school work, tests, and so forth to identify major errors or other evidence of mislearning. This form of outcome analysis is most useful as a formative evaluation tool, and may be employed at several points in the curriculum development process. The second approach, *Impact Analysis of Curriculum*, entails a more holistic consideration of the curriculum's contributions to changes in the school context. These include both immediate and evolutionary changes in teaching practices, administrative and management patterns, and community and parental relationships, as well as learner behaviors. Although no single evaluation may examine all of these impact areas, examples of each have appeared in the curriculum evaluation literature. The last article in Part 3(b) takes up *Long-term Curriculum Evaluation*, which is concerned with the long-term effects of a curriculum. Not only are long-term effects prominent among the explicit intended outcomes of many curricula, but in addition, general outcomes going well beyond the specific content of the curriculum may be among the most important outcomes of any educational program. Examples of long-term curriculum evaluations are described, and the limitations of the approach are discussed briefly. Causal relationships between curricular exposure and later outcomes are difficult to establish for several reasons, including nonrandom assignment and selective sampling, but the retrospective approach offers better control over these factors than do either cross-sectional or longitudinal evaluation research designs.

# Models and Philosophies

## Alternative Paradigms in Curriculum Inquiry

W. H. Schubert and A. L. Schubert

Since the late 1960s the topic of paradigms of inquiry has steadily emerged as a principal issue in curriculum discourse (Schubert 1986). In fact, the educational research community itself has witnessed a surge of interest in clarifying the conceptual assumptions or paradigms that guide inquiry. It can be argued that apart from philosophy of education, which takes as a primary responsibility the clarification of modes of inquiry or epistemological bases, curriculum studies is the subfield of education that provided the earliest in the question of paradigms. Deeply concerned with the nature of inquiry, curriculum scholars in the late 1960s and early 1970s shared with the larger community of scholars in social sciences and humanities an interest in questions that Thomas Kuhn elicited in his landmark book, *The Structure of Scientific Revolutions* (Kuhn 1962). During the next two decades, philosophers began to sketch underlying assumptions and values behind alternative positions on inquiry, noting empirical, analytic, phenomenological, and critical categories (see Bernstein 1976, Bredo and Feinberg 1982). Moreover, concrete approaches to research methodology appeared using pragmatic, phenomenological, and critical orientations under the label "human sciences" (Polkinghorne 1983), a term which has more currency in European circles than American.

The issue of paradigms of inquiry is discussed overtly in the curriculum literature. In 1976 the journal *Curriculum Inquiry* was founded, after beginning under the title *Curriculum Theory Network* in 1968 at the Ontario Institute for Studies in Education, Toronto. Other journals have since emerged to further discourse on matters of curriculum inquiry.

Despite the increasingly widespread interest in the topic of paradigms of curriculum inquiry, the way the term paradigm is used is quite diverse. This diversity is not unique to curriculum, for after Kuhn initiated the discussion in his 1962 classic, Lakatos and Musgrave (1970) identified more than 20 meanings attributed to Kuhn's own treatment of the topic. In curriculum, at least three dominant uses can be found: (a) classification systems; (b) assumptions about inquiry; and (c) dimensions that define curriculum.

## 1. Paradigm as Classification Systems

A number of attempts to categorize existing positions on curriculum theory and practice have emerged since the late 1960s. Each is an attempt to illustrate prevailing differences and contending views, but none is offered with the intent that the categories represent invariant divisions. It must be understood that overlap does exist, often productively, and that differing categories illustrate a richness in diversity rather than contending parties immobilized by a lack of common purpose. Curriculum scholars and practitioners share the common aim of trying to determine that which is worthwhile for learners to know and experience.

Thelen (1960) identified four models for education and sketched a broad portrayal of curriculum elicited by each: (a) personal inquiry, (b) group investigation, (c) reflective action, and (d) skill development. While each of these positions can be used along with the others, it is possible for one to dominate, and the consequences of domination and/or collaboration need to be anticipated carefully in a spirit of action inquiry (Thelen 1960 pp. 208–09).

Eisner (1985) portrays five basic orientations to curriculum, including: (a) development of cognitive processes, which focuses on learning and the intellect; (b) academic rationalism, which emphasizes intellectual attainment through disciplines of knowledge; (c) personal relevance, which involves the centrality of personal meaning derived from teacher–student collaboration in creating curricular experiences; (d) social adaptation and social reconstruction, which focus curriculum on ends that meet social needs; and (e) curriculum as technology, which views curriculum design as a procedural enterprise having the potential to facilitate any substantive purpose.

Pinar (1975) identifies three categories of curriculum developers and theorists: (a) traditionalists, (b) conceptual empiricists, and (c) reconceptualists. Each is illustrated by sets of articles vis-à-vis curriculum, instruction, and evaluation in Giroux et al. (1981). Traditionalists evolved from immersion in school settings where the job had to be done to meet technocratic needs of the system, and thus had difficulty developing new images of what curriculum might be. Conceptual empiricists emerged with post-Sputnik curriculum reform which involved social and behavioral scientists who espoused neopositivist orientations to curriculum inquiry and design. Reconceptualists were born through a configuration of interests in literary sources, post-Marxist political theory, existentialism, phenomenology, and radical psychoanalysis. Curriculum scholars of this category brought matters of personal meaning and social justice to the fore.

Schubert (1986) derived three categories from historical studies of curriculum literature: (a) intellectual traditionalist; (b) social behaviorist, and (c) experientalist. The intellectual traditionalist values the liberal arts, great books, or disciplines and knowledge approach to curriculum. The social behaviorist sees curriculum as a scientifically warranted technique or formula for curriculum design that causes learning of behaviors valued by society. The experientalist values experience that begins with personal interest, moves to pursuit of common human interests, and continuously monitors consequences of such pursuit in terms of the social justice and personal meaning that accrue.

Kliebard (1986) identifies four historical categories: (a) humanists, (b) social effiency advocates, (c) developmentalists, and (d) social meliorists. While social meliorists develop curriculum to make society better, social efficiency experts try to more productively perpetuate status quo bureaucracies. While humanists tie curricular quality to benefit of the intellect through the time-honored liberal arts and sciences, developmentalists argue that intellectual attainment best obtains from curriculum based on study of human growth processes. Earlier, Kliebard (1972) argued that curriculum policy and proposals can be interpreted through three guiding metaphors: travel, production, and growth. Clearly one can see distinctly the travel metaphor in the humanist, the production metaphor in social efficiency, and the growth metaphor in both the developmentalist and the social meliorist.

The above category schemes are illustrative; they are not intended to be all-inclusive, Schiro (1978), for instance, identifies four curricular "ideologies": academic, social efficiency, child-study, and social reconstruction. Orlosky and Smith (1978) offer a four-part classification of curriculum theory styles: humanistic, disciplines of knowledge, technical or analytic, and futuristic, while Huenecke (1982) classifies curriculum theory in three quite different domains: structural, generic, and substantive. As one continues to identify systems it is possible to perceive similarity among them. For instance, McNeil's (1985) use of humanistic, social reconstructionist, technology, and academic subjects bear relationship to the classification language of Eisner, Kliebard, and others. Similarly, one can see many of the above systems reflected by Miller (1983) who introduces a spectrum of seven orientations to curriculum (behavioral, subject/disciplines, social, developmental,

cognitive processes, humanistic, and transpersonal) as well as potential "meta-orientations."

From the foregoing it can be argued that one image of paradigm in curriculum literature pertains to classification systems that attempt to differentiate alternative positions on curriculum theory and practice. Some scholars believe that classification systems impair the complexity of curricular inquiry by oversimplification, and others at the opposite end of the continuum hold that the systems of classification rightly differentiate alternatives within curricular discourse.

## 2. Paradigm as Assumptions about Inquiry

The existence of classification systems directly speaks to substantive positions on curriculum matters, and indirectly implies the need to investigate alternative forms of curriculum inquiry. The issue of forms of inquiry clearly relates to Kuhn's (1962) treatment of paradigm. His analysis addresses revolutionary conceptual changes in natural sciences, for example from geocentric to heliocentric universe, from Newtonian to Einsteinian physics, from pre- to post-Darwinian biology. When any given system dominates, the rules of scientific inquiry are governed by certain presumptions, but as anomalies increase that cannot be explained by the prevailing system, a reconceptualization is required. Thus, a new paradigm is wrought and the system continues.

Habermas (1971) in philosophy, and Bernstein (1976) in social and political theory have elaborated paradigms that pertain to inquiry in the social sciences and to a lesser extent the humanities. The work of Habermas has aided in discussions of paradigmatic reconceptualization of curriculum paradigms. Building upon Habermas (1971), and Bernstein (1976), Schubert (1986) depicts three paradigms of curriculum inquiry: (a) empirical–analytic, (b) hermeneutic, and (c) critical. Each can be interpreted relative to interests served, kinds of organization used to serve those interests, and modes of rationality manifest in each paradigm. It must be noted that considerable variation exists within each paradigm or type of science (inquiry). Moreover, those selected as illustrative of a given paradigm may not perceive themselves as operating within that conceptual orientation to inquiry. This further exemplifies the problematic character of curriculum inquiry.

The empirical–analytic paradigm draws upon research traditions that stem back to E. L. Thorndike, and Willhelm Wundt before him. The interest served is technical, reflecting a positivist vision of science, and the social organization that facilitates empirical–analytic inquiry is that of hierarchies in the work-place. This mode of rationality accepts social reality as it is, values parsimony, assumes knowledge to be objective and value free, seeks to discover empirically testable lawlike propositions, and assumes principles of control and certainty. The canons of replication, validity, and reliability are central to this paradigm. Schwab (1970) argued that the dominance of this paradigm made the curriculum field moribund, preoccupied with easily managed research that finds problems in the minds of researchers rather than in states of affairs, that operates exclusively by inductive and hypothetical–deductive methods of inquiry, that seeks laws of curricular behavior rather than situationally specific insights, and that sees knowledge qua knowledge and publication as the end of inquiry. Schwab called this empirical–analytic orientation "theoretic," drawing upon Aristotelian roots.

The hermeneutic paradigm focuses on interpretation. Literally and historically, hermeneutics refers to the interpretation of religious texts; metaphorically applied to curriculum, the text becomes curriculum, context, practice, and discourse. The interest served by hermeneutic inquiry is practical. Schwab contrasts practical inquiry with theoretic and argues that a move from the theoretic to the practical, quasipractical, and eclectic is the only way to revive curriculum from its moribund state. This would include a problem source for inquiry found in actual states of affairs rather than in conceptualizations of researchers who abstract and combine similarities from situations, disregarding the vast amount of idiosyncrasy left behind. Practical inquiry also values direct and sustained interaction with phenomena under investigation, seeks situationally specific insights, and foresees meaningful and morally defensible decision and action as its end. Such inquiry is clearly in the pragmatic tradition of John Dewey (1938).

The hermeneutic emphasis on serving practical interests through interactive social organization, however, is as relevant to phenomenonology as to pragmatism. At times the two seem to blend in the hermeneutic mode of rationality which sees human beings as active creators of knowledge, emphasizes understanding and communication, views reality as intersubjectively constituted and grounded within a historical and political context, looks for meaning beneath the texture of everyday life, and focuses sensitively on meaning through language.

While Schwab addresses practical and theoretic languages of curriculum discourse, Huebner (1966) calls for languages of a moral and aesthetic character to move beyond the predominantly technical, scientific, and political language of curriculum in use by scholars and practitioners today. Moral language is well-illustrated in work by Macdonald (1977), while aesthetic language is quite evident in work by Eisner (1985).

The journals *Phenomenology and Pedagogy* and *The Journal of Curriculum Theorizing* contain a considerable variety of writing of hermeneutic or interpretive character. The interpretive has found several quite different variations. Willis (1978), for example, provides an array of both concepts and cases of the interpretive study of curriculum evaluation. The debate over quantitative and qualitative inquiry seems to have begun in the evaluation literature and proceeded to embrace the whole of educational research (Smith and

Heshusius 1986). Eisner, in particular, challenges scholars in education to realize the great potential for educational insight and understanding through artistic inquiry and study of the arts.

Critical inquiry in curriculum forms a paradigm of praxis that serves the interest of emancipation and proceeds under the social organization of power. Its mode of rationality assumes the necessity of ideological critique, that is, of interrogating the economic, political, and cultural contexts and assumptions of curriculum as influenced by such factors as gender, class, and race (Apple and Weis 1983).

The works of Apple (1982) and Giroux (1983) have done a great deal to focus attention upon key critical issues. These authors encourage educators to ask such questions as the following, which were outlined in Schubert (1986 p. 315).

(a) How is knowledge reproduced by schools?

(b) What are the sources of knowledge that students acquire in schools?

(c) How do students and teachers resist or contest that which is conveyed through lived experience in schools?

(d) What do students and teachers realize from their school experiences? In other words, what impact does school have on their outlooks?

(e) Whose interests are served by outlooks and skills fostered by schooling?

(f) When served, do these interests move more in the direction of emancipation, equity, and social justice, or do they move in the opposite direction?

(g) How can students be empowered to attain greater liberation, equity, and social justice through schooling?

Encouraging practitioners to engage in critical praxis that attends to such questions is furthered by recent developments in action research. Stenhouse (Rudduck and Hopkins 1985) encouraged this sort of reflection among teachers in England, and Carr and Kemmis (1986), in Australia, built upon Stenhouse's work to develop critical mindedness in practitioners.

## 3. Paradigm as Dimensions that Define Curriculum

Tyler (1949) developed a set of constructs that constitute a paradigm for curriculum work. Moreover, Tyler's guidelines or rationale, as it is called, is the most widely used set of principles in curriculum today. One can hardly find a curriculum guide, a teacher's manual, a lesson or unit plan, or a curriculum and instructional methods book that does not contain Tyler's four main topics: purpose, learning experiences or content, organization, and evaluation. These topics may be used descriptively as categories deemed necessary for analyzing a curriculum, or they may be used prescriptively as the starting point for determining purposes, learning experiences, organization, and evaluation for a given curriculum. Tyler further advocates that it is necessary to "filter" responses to these topics through carefully clarified philosophical and psychological "screens," that is, basic positions or underlying assumptions. Finally, Tyler calls for balance among three knowledge sources for developing purposes: students, subject matter, and society.

Taba and Goodlad have made influential variations on the Tyler rationale. Although Tyler did not intend his four topics (purposes, learning experiences, organization, and evaluation) to be used predominantly as a recipe, they were often followed as a stepwise formula for making curriculum. Taba (1962) expanded the stepwise interpretation into seven phases: (a) diagnosis of needs, (b) formulation of objectives, (c) selection of content, (d) organization of content, (e) selection of learning experiences, (f) organization of learning experiences, and (g) determination of what and how to evaluate. Goodlad (1979) introduced the notion "learning opportunities" to replace Tyler's "learning experiences" as a more tangible category, and set Tyler's categories in a larger content, suggesting that each of these categories can be treated at instructional, institutional, societal, ideological, and individual levels.

The Tyler rationale, in its several incarnations, has received criticism from a number of sources. Walker (1971) provides a conceptual alternative, drawing upon naturalistic study of curriculum decision-making committees. He argues that curriculum committees rarely follow the Tylerian model. Instead, they operate much more politically. They begin with a platform, or set of beliefs, background knowledge, prejudices, hidden agendas, images of what might be, and so on. These all became a formidable part of deliberation or discussion and negotiation, the second phase. The final phase, design, is realized when time constraints mandate that proposed practices be implemented, often regardless of logical closure.

Schwab (1973) argues that a conception of curriculum consistent with practical inquiry invokes four fundamental commonplaces: teachers, learners, subject matter, and milieu or environment (psychosocial, as well as physical and institutional). The curriculum that has impact on the outlook of students is derived from the composite of interactions among the commonplaces.

Berman (1968) offers a set of curricular priorities as alternatives to the conventional subject matter areas. She argues that the curriculum should focus directly on processes such as perceiving, communicating, loving, knowing, decision making, patterning, creating, and valuing. She also suggests that it is possible to integrate these processes with each of the conventional content areas.

Schubert (1986 p. 411) describes curriculum inquiry as increasingly perceived as the process of asking fundamental questions such as: "What is worth knowing and experiencing? What kind of life does such knowing and experiencing assume is good for both individuals and the society? How can worthwhile knowledge and experience be provided by educators? How can we know if it is provided?" To respond fully to such questions requires a sense of perspective (the historical, philosophical, sociological, economic, cultural, psychological, and political contexts of curriculum), paradigm (the empirical–analytic, the practical and hermeneutic, and critical praxis), and possibility (understanding of ways to conceptualize and deal with curriculum problems, ways to provide for the ongoing education of educators, and reflective capabilities to imagine alternative futures, the means to realize them, and the consequences of doing so). To pursue this kind of inquiry requires that all concerned with curriculum, educators and students, address these topics; thus, in many respects one can find that curriculum itself deals with fundamental concerns of curriculum inquiry.

## 4. Conclusion

Three kinds of conceptualizations of paradigm have been described, along with examples of each. Each, of course, has limitations that should be acknowledged, along with potential.

### 4.1 Paradigm as Classification System

Paradigm can be viewed as classification system, that is, as categories of major viewpoints or lines of thinking in the field. To acknowledge prevailing diversity can lead to unwarranted relativism and it can encourage the use of oversimplified lines of demarcation. Moreover, it can give the impression that confusion reigns if the most notable scholars differ extensively. Walker (1980), however, sees this as a sign of robustness, calling it a "rich confusion." To admit uncertainty can be seen as a symbol of maturity that acknowledges a pluralistic universe, rather than immaturity that expresses itself in the false security of clutching to the one idea known well.

### 4.2 Paradigm as Assumptions about Inquiry

Viewing paradigms of curriculum inquiry as assumptions about inquiry has greatest kinship with the treatment of paradigms in the social sciences and humanities. The question has been raised, however, as to whether any of the scholarly alternatives (empirical, analytic, hermeneutic, critical) represent a fundamental departure from one another. Because the result of each is usually rendered available in written form, each can be seen as susceptible to commodification. It is taken from the world of lived experience, and by scholarly rendition in writing ceases to grow as if it remained embedded in action. While scholars must heed such criticism, their world of scholarship is part of lived experience; thus, their analyses and advocacies of paradigms can be seen as clarification of alternative sources of meaning, knowing, valuing, and expressing that which they study.

It remains to be asked whether current attention to paradigms of inquiry is indeed a novel contribution to scholarship or whether it is a renewal of concern that philosophers have long exhibited for fundamental principles in metaphysical, epistemological, axiological, ethical, political, and other realms. For example, is contemporary concern for paradigms of curriculum inquiry significantly different from, say, Phenix's (1964) inquiry into realms of meaning? Nevertheless, today's inquiry into curriculum paradigms enables more persons to question basic assumptions, whether or not the inquiry is of a new variety.

### 4.3 Paradigm as Defining Dimensions

Paradigms viewed as dimensions that define curriculum in turn guide conceptualizations of curriculum development. The disadvantage of this interpretation of paradigm is that one set of categories may be perceived as incompatible with the others. The idea that Tyler's (1949) categories are mutually exclusive from Schwab's (1973) or that either of these is incompatible with those advanced by Walker (1971) may have some validity, but extends little appreciation to an eclectic stance. When exercised reflectively and with careful deliberation, the art of being eclectic (see Schwab 1971) reveals the potential complementarity of sets of dimensions of curriculum heretofore deemed alternative or contradictory.

Finally, any of the three images of paradigm discussed in the article have great potential for enabling a form of internal critique which enriches inquiry in curriculum studies. Simultaneously, if taken as final answers, the idea of paradigms can stultify curriculum inquiry by making categories rigid and causing scholars to take sides. Perhaps the best response to the interest in paradigms is for educators at all levels to take seriously the spirit of questioning exhibited in the literature on paradigms, and to eschew the doctrinaire in exchange for continuous striving to develop through deeper understanding of curricular phenomena.

## Bibliography

Apple M W 1982 *Education and Power*. Routledge and Kegan Paul, Boston, Massachusetts

Apple M W, Weis L 1983 *Ideology and Practice in Schooling*. Temple University Press, Philadelphia, Pennsylvania

Berman L 1968 *New Priorities in the Curriculum*. Merrill, Columbus, Ohio

Bernstein R J 1976 *The Restructuring of Social and Political Thought*. University of Pennsylvania Press, Philadelphia, Pennsylvania

Bredo E, Feinberg W (eds.) 1982 *Knowledge and Values in Social and Educational Research*. Temple University Press, Philadelphia, Pennsylvania

Carr W, Kemmis S 1986 *Becoming Critical: Education, Knowledge and Action Research*. Taylor and Francis, Philadelphia, Pennsylvania

Dewey J 1938 *Logic, the Theory of Inquiry*. Henry Holt, New York

Eisner E W 1985 *The Educational Imagination: On the Design and Evaluation of School Programs*. Macmillan, New York

Giroux H A 1983 *Theory and Resistance in Education: A Pedagogy for the Opposition*. Bergin and Garvey, South Hadley, Massachusetts

Giroux H A, Penna A N, Pinar W F (eds.) 1981 *Curriculum and Instruction: Alternatives in Education*. McCutchan, Berkeley, California

Goodlad J I 1979 *Curriculum Inquiry: The Study of Curriculum Practice*. McGraw-Hill, New York

Habermas J 1971 *Knowledge and Human Interests*. Beacon, Boston, Massachusetts

Huebner D 1966 Curricular language and classroom meanings. In: Macdonald J B, Leeper R R (eds.) 1966 *Language and Meaning*. Association for Supervision and Curriculum Development, Washington, DC, pp. 8–26

Huenecke D 1982 What is curriculum theorizing? What are its implications for practice? *Educ. Leadership* 39: 290–94

Kliebard H M 1972 Metaphorical roots of curriculum design. *Teachers College Record* 72(3): 403–04

Kliebard H M 1986 *The Struggle for the American Curriculum, 1893–1958*. Routledge and Kegan Paul, Boston, Massachusetts

Kuhn T S 1962 *The Structure of Scientific Revolutions*. University of Chicago Press, Chicago, Illinois

Lakatos I, Musgrave A (eds.) 1970 *Criticism and the Growth of Knowledge*. Cambridge University Press, Cambridge

Macdonald J B 1977 Value bases and issues for curriculum. In: Molnar A, Zahorik J A (eds.) 1977 *Curriculum Theory*. Association for Supervision and Curriculum Development, Washington, DC, pp. 10–21

McNeil J D 1985 *Curriculum: A Comprehensive Introduction*. Little, Brown, Boston, Massachusetts

Miller J P 1983 *The Educational Spectrum: Orientations to Curriculum*. Longman, New York

Orlosky D E, Smith B O 1978 *Curriculum Development: Issues and Insights*. Rand McNally, Chicago, Illinois

Phenix P 1964 *Realms of Meaning: A Philosophy of the Curriculum for General Education*. McGraw-Hill, New York

Pinar W F (ed.) 1975 *Curriculum Theorizing: The Reconceptualists*. McCutchan, Berkeley, California

Polkinghorne D 1983 *Methodology for the Human Sciences: Systems of Inquiry*. State University of New York Press, Albany, New York

Rudduck J, Hopkins D (eds.) 1985 *Research as a Basis for Teaching: Readings from the Work of Lawrence Stenhouse*. Heinemann, London

Schiro M 1978 *Curriculum for Better Schools: The Great Ideological Debate*. Educational Technology Publications, Englewood Cliffs, New Jersey

Schubert W H 1986 *Curriculum: Perspective, Paradigm, and Possibility*. Macmillan, New York

Schwab J J 1970 *The Practical: A Language for Curriculum*. National Education Association, Washington, DC

Schwab J J 1971 The practical: Arts of eclectic. *Sch. Rev.* 79: 493–542

Schwab J J 1973 The practical 3: Translation into curriculum. *Sch. Rev.* 81: 501–22

Smith J K, Heshusius L 1986 Closing down the conversation: The end of the quantitative–qualitative debate among educational inquirers. *Educ. Res.* 15(1): 4–12

Taba H 1962 *Curriculum Development: Theory and Practice*. Harcourt, Brace, and World, New York

Thelen H A 1960 *Education and the Human Quest*. Harper and Brothers, New York

Tyler R W 1949 *Basic Principles of Curriculum and Instruction*. University of Chicago Press, Chicago, Illinois

Walker D F 1971 A naturalistic model for curriculum development. *Sch. Rev.* 80(1): 51–65

Walker D F 1980 A barnstorming tour of writing on curriculum.

In: Foshay A W 1980 *Considered Action for Curriculum Improvement*. Association for Supervision and Curriculum Development, Washington, DC, pp. 71–81

Willis G (ed.) 1978 *Qualitative Evaluation: Concepts and Cases in Curriculum Criticism*. McCutchan, Berkeley, California

# Curriculum Validation

## W. H. Schubert

The question of validating the curriculum involves considerations of whether the educational program provides what its stated intent indicates. This relates quite directly to conceptions of validity (construct, context, content, external, internal) as treated in evaluation and research design literatures. While curriculum validation clearly relates to these areas, it extends to even more complex philosophical issues in the question: How can one know a good curriculum?

This question directly invokes epistemological and axiological problems. Epistemological concerns about the character of defensible ways of knowing are raised when one asks how curricular purposes and content can best be determined. Smith et al. (1957) identify four procedures for curriculum developers to use in making such decisions: judgment, experimentation, analysis, and consensus. The consideration of these procedures as alternative methods of decision making in turn invokes basic questions about defensible ways to come to acquire or create knowledge. Thus, the relative merits of such epistemological bases as intuition, experience, utility, authority, tradition, and the scientific method are central to the problem of curriculum validation.

The question of validation procedure is merely technical unless it is coupled with substantive inquiry about the nature of what should be taught. The term "should" is a question of value and thus is rooted in the axiological realm. To what standard of judgment should those who determine curricular purpose and content turn in striving for validation? Smith et al. (1957) also address this question by using a criterial approach. They ask if justification of purposes stems primarily from provision of basic needs, social adequacy, or democratic ideals. The latter serve as criteria for validating educational objectives. Similarly, these authors suggest the following criteria for the selection of curricular content: (a) significance to an organized body of knowledge; (b) longevity of use or the "test of survival"; (c) utility; (d) interest of learners; and (e) contribution to the growth and development of democratic society (p. 131–50).

Smith et al. (1957) emphasize the importance of consistency among objectives. It is central to curriculum validation to insure that objectives are noncontradictory. It is too frequently discovered, upon careful analysis, that objectives within different subject matter areas or at different grade levels contradict one another.

They can even be shown to have counteractive effects upon one another. Recent investigations by Goodlad in the United States have revealed that purposes of state departments of education are often lost or massively distorted by school districts, that are supposed to implement them. Moreover, the character of curriculum changes as it is mediated and interpreted through national and state decision-making hierarchies and through every dimension of local schooling: district administrators, building administrators, supervisors, teachers, and students. As each of the members of the curriculum development and implementation process acts in a capacity that modifies the selection of learning experiences, instructional approaches, patterns of organizing learning environments, and evaluation strategies, the character of the curriculum is altered. Such interdependencies are seldom accentuated as fully as in the selection of instructional materials by schools. Selection of materials that are not consonant with purposes distorts the validity of the entire program. The Educational Products Information Exchange (EPIE) Institute attempts to overcome this problem by providing a consumer service to schools that enables them to explicate the intent, content, instructional strategies, and evaluation procedures implicit in materials; thereby, schools are helped to match characteristics of materials with the needs and interests of teachers, students, the public, and governmental policy. Moreover, EPIE uses a process of learner verification and revision whereby student input is used to test the assertions of publishers about their materials.

While the process of curriculum validation frequently involves the efforts of experts who identify assumptions embedded in the substance and process of determining the curriculum, and while they diligently try to understand the interactive effects among different curricular components, more subtle and complex processes are at work. All individuals who participate in the curriculum process, especially students, act to validate it by judging its merits in relation to their own needs and experiences (Hopkins 1954). A great deal remains to be learned about this activity as it relates to formal conceptions of curriculum validation. While students' perceptions of the curriculum are sometimes used as feedback to curriculum planners, conceptions of active student involvement in curriculum creation are a new frontier for curriculum validation.

*Bibliography*

Educational Products Information Exchange (EPIE) Institute 1979 *Selecting Instructional Materials*. EPIE, Stoney Brook, New York

Hopkins L T 1954 *The Emerging Self in School and Home*. Harper, New York

Smith B O, Stanley W O, Shores J H 1957 *Fundamentals of Curriculum Development*, rev. edn. Harcourt, Brace and World, New York

# Curriculum Evaluation

## J. R. Sanders

Curriculum evaluation refers to the process of studying the merit or worth of some aspect, or the whole, of a curriculum. Depending on the way in which the term curriculum is defined, the focus or objects of curriculum evaluation could include curriculum and/or student needs, curriculum design, instructional processes, materials used in instruction, objectives for student outcomes, student progress through the curriculum, teacher effectiveness, the learning environment, curriculum policy, resource allotment, and the outcomes of instruction.

Theory and practice in curriculum evaluation closely followed the development of educational psychology as a field of study (Clifford 1973) until the 1960s. Exceptions in the United States were the development of the accreditation movement for schools and colleges in the late 1800s and the Eight-year Study directed by Ralph W. Tyler in the 1930s (Smith and Tyler 1942). The accreditation movement led to a process of periodic self-study and reviews by outside teams in educational institutions. The Eight-year Study generated a model for studying the achievement of curriculum objectives that influenced the practice of curriculum evaluation through to present times.

As a field of study, curriculum evaluation underwent a period of rapid development in the United States during the 1960s and 1970s. This expansion of interest in curriculum evaluation and a concurrent development of thought was related to two phenomena of that period. One was the flourishing of curriculum reform, especially in science and mathematics, brought on by post-Sputnik anxiety about the technical preparation of American students. The other influence was a substantial increase of revenues allocated to education by the federal government with concomitant mandates for evaluation. In 1959, the National Defense Education Act, and in 1965 the Elementary and Secondary Education Act, injected millions of dollars into American education for curriculum development, innovation, and reform. The Elementary and Secondary Education Act also carried with it legislative mandates for evaluation of innovations and reforms. Educators soon realized that previous thinking in curriculum evaluation was inadequate to serve the new demands for accountability and curriculum improvement. Curriculum specialists were called on to develop new procedures to meet the changing needs of the times. The need for better methods of curriculum evaluation led to a great expansion of the literature on curriculum evaluation in the 1960s and 1970s.

## 1. The Need for Curriculum Evaluation

Few educators or their constituents would argue that curriculum quality is unimportant in the educational process. Furthermore, few would argue that there is no room for improvement in any curriculum. Curriculum evaluation directly addresses both areas of defensible interest.

Knowing about the quality of curriculum is a concern that extends beyond the local school to the state at large. Education prepares future generations to take their place in society and neither educators nor other members of society can afford to retain substandard educational goals, materials, or instruction. Curriculum evaluation that monitors and reports on the quality of education serves educational policy makers and those who must make decisions that affect the education system at different levels. It contributes to public relations and aids planning. Curriculum evaluation of this type is called summative evaluation (Scriven 1967).

Identifying aspects of a local curriculum which should be improved and then guiding decisions about how to improve them is another role of curriculum evaluation. Professional educators concern themselves with changing curriculum content, teaching methods or experiences, educational facilities, staff selection and development, and objectives for student outcomes as needs of their students and society are identified. This calls for a continual process of local curriculum study and improvement by school personnel. Curriculum evaluation of this type is called formative evaluation (Scriven 1967).

The first role of curriculum evaluation serves the needs of policy makers, administrators, and other members of society for information about the educational system that will help them to make important decisions affecting curriculum. The second role of curriculum evaluation serves the needs of teachers, curriculum specialists, school administrators, and others who are responsible for curriculum development.

## 2. Who Should Evaluate Curricula?

There is no single appropriate person or group who should be assigned the responsibility of curriculum evaluation. Much of the assignment of responsibility depends on the purposes to be served by curriculum evaluation, the availability of professional curriculum evaluators, the credibility of an individual or group to those who are to be served by a curriculum evaluation, consideration of conflict of interest for the curriculum evaluator, and the placement of the curriculum evaluator within or outside the educational system. Circumstances differ from one curriculum evaluation to the next and the decision to assign responsibility and authority for the curriculum evaluation should be responsive to the context of the curriculum evaluation.

If the purpose to be served by a curriculum evaluation is summative (i.e., a report to the public, a basis for determining curriculum policy, or a basis for deciding to discontinue a major part of the curriculum or make major revisions in the curriculum), the curriculum evaluator is best selected from candidates who are independent of, and unaffected by, the object of the evaluation. This is often an individual or group external to the educational system in which the evaluation is being done. If the purpose to be served by a curriculum evaluation is formative (i.e., to guide curriculum development, to identify weaknesses or needs in the curriculum or in students, to monitor curriculum processes so that adjustments can be guided), the curriculum evaluator is best selected from candidates who are close to the object of the evaluation and knowledgeable about the context in which it exists. This is often an individual or group that is internal to the educational system in which the evaluation is being done.

Regardless of purposes to be served, the curriculum evaluator should be knowledgeable and experienced in curriculum evaluation. Payne (1974 pp 9–10) suggested the following areas in which the curriculum evaluator should be competent:

(a) Specifying information needs from program planning for evaluation.

(b) Developing a plan for evaluating a specified curriculum.

(c) Locating, reading, and integrating relevant research, measurement, and evaluation literature.

(d) Specifying evaluation objectives and database requirements in appropriate form(s).

(e) Critically evaluating a given evaluation design or study.

(f) Relating theoretical evaluation models and "real-life" requirements.

(g) Relating input, transaction, and outcome variables.

(h) Demonstrating appropriate interpersonal relationship skills in working with evaluation team and program staff.

(i) Differentiating advantages and disadvantages of cross-sectional and longitudinal studies.

(j) Conducting systems, functions, and task analyses.

(k) Designing an effective measurement–management process.

(l) Compiling a master evaluation system from several systems.

(m) Describing evaluation design and analysis requirements in computer programmer or data processing terms.

(n) Specifying criteria for selection or development of evaluation instruments.

(o) Applying appropriate data-gathering procedures.

(p) Applying appropriate data-analysis procedures.

(q) Making a cost–benefit analysis of a given curriculum.

(r) Using evaluation information to make decisions about curriculum.

(s) Designing a program planning budgeting system.

(t) Administering the activities of an evaluation unit.

(u) Designing a system of data presentation that describes format, responsibility, procedures, recipients, and schedule.

(v) Redesigning and refining evaluation methods when appropriate.

This list may be supplemented by these additional evaluation competencies identified by Sanders (1979):

(a) Describing the object of the evaluation—knowing what is being evaluated, what its limits are, what its important characteristics are, and being able to communicate the essence of the object to others.

(b) Describing the context of the evaluation—knowing what factors surrounding the evaluation are salient in the effect that they have or can have on the object and on the evaluation.

(c) Conceptualizing appropriate purposes for the evaluation—being able to state purposes clearly as a way of giving direction to the evaluation.

(d) Determining value or merit in the object of the evaluation—being able to identify and justify criteria that will be used to prepare judgmental or value statements about the object of the evaluation and then systematically applying those criteria.

(e) Maintaining ethical standards—demonstrating knowledge of proper professional behavior.

A third consideration in selecting a curriculum evaluator is that the individual or group should have credibility to those served by the evaluation. The *Standards for Evaluations of Educational Programs, Projects, and Materials* (Joint Committee 1981) suggest that an evaluator should be trained in curriculum evaluation, have technical competence, be knowledgeable about the object being evaluated, have experience, have integrity, possess public relations skills, and have other characteristics considered necessary by those who will use the evaluation.

A fourth consideration is the absence of conflict of interest on the part of the evaluator. The *Standards for Evaluations of Educational Programs, Projects, and Materials* (Joint Committee 1981) suggest that an individual or group being considered to conduct a curriculum evaluation should not have private interests that would be affected by the evaluation or that would affect the evaluation. Such private interests could include a particular philosophical, theoretical, or political point of view that would affect findings, financial benefit, or loss depending on evaluation results, job security or career development being influenced by evaluation findings, or past history with the people or curriculum being evaluated.

Finally, the placement of the curriculum evaluator within or outside the educational system where evaluation is taking place needs to be considered. The impact that a curriculum evaluation will have depends partially on the level of authority and influence that the curriculum evaluator has with the system. This level of authority or influence is affected by placement within the organizational structure (e.g., a direct line to the chief executive) and affects the level of cooperation and commitment of personnel who will be involved in the evaluation.

## 3. Organization of Curriculum Evaluation

Sanders (1978) indicated that organizing for evaluation can be either internal or external, depending on the considerations presented in the preceding section. Resources, the organizational structure of the educational system, the number of special curriculum projects underway, and requirements for curriculum evaluation by policy or law are factors that affect the decision of how to organize internally for curriculum evaluation. The availability of expertise, legal or contractual requirements, span of control, and the need for independence are factors that affect how to organize externally for curriculum evaluation.

Generally, the organization for internal curriculum evaluation may be carried out either on a centralized organizational basis or on a decentralized organizational basis. The centralized form would require the formation of an evaluation unit or office or evaluation within the system that would serve curriculum evaluation requirements (Stufflebeam et al. 1971). A decentralized form could be:

(a) Individuals within the system. Persons with evaluation and curriculum expertise exist within the system and may be given reduced workloads so that they may take on evaluation responsibilities. Roles such as teacher/evaluator or curriculum specialist/evaluator may be defined and used as a means for incorporating curriculum evaluation into the day-to-day activities of the school system.

(b) Ad hoc groups within the system. Groups with certain configurations of expertise may take on short-term, limited-scope responsibilities for curriculum evaluation.

(c) Existing, permanent groups within the system. Curriculum evaluation may be organized so that it is carried out by departments or grade level personnel or by some other existing organizational form.

(d) New, continuing groups within the system. A new set of units may be created to focus on certain continuing objects of curriculum evaluation (e.g., an office to monitor student progress through a kindergarten to grade 12 curriculum and report on curriculum weaknesses identified through the monitoring system).

The organization for external curriculum evaluation may include:

(a) Individuals outside the system. Persons with evaluation and curriculum expertise who could serve as consultants as needed for curriculum evaluation.

(b) Existing groups or agencies outside the system.

(c) A consortium of educational institutions. Educational systems that have formed a cooperative in order to share expertise to address curriculum evaluation needs of member institutions.

## 4. Limitations of Curriculum Evaluation

Curriculum evaluation often depends on the cooperation of individuals within the learning environment—classroom teachers, school building principals, lecturers, tutors, curriculum coordinators and specialists, curriculum project staff, and others. Without their cooperation in designing and implementing the evaluation, there can be little likelihood of success. Part of this cooperation is in allowing others to view their work; part is in contributing ideas and identifying issues or problems with curriculum that need to be studied; part is in data gathering and the provision of requested information; and part is in reviewing and correcting draft evaluation reports. Curriculum evaluation will be successful to the extent that necessary cooperation is provided.

Curriculum evaluations can be limited by the complexity of measuring or describing certain behaviors or events. For example, classroom processes and instructional experiences have different meanings for different students. It is frequently very difficult to discern or assess how an experience is perceived or assimilated by a particular student and, at best, curriculum evaluators are limited to indicators of student change over long periods of time.

Curriculum evaluators can be limited by time and access to students. The results of curriculum reforms may not show up for years or decades after they are installed. Results of curriculum change may also be a private matter that only student self-reports will reveal and the validity of such data is often suspect.

Curriculum decisions are often based on factors or information that are not part of a curriculum evaluation study and the utility of curriculum evaluation is then questioned. Curriculum evaluators must be aware that they are one part of the decision-making process and that their role in decision making is limited.

Criteria for evaluating curricula or specific aspects of a curriculum depend on rationales and expectations. Rationales and expectations depend on theories. The multiplicity of curriculum theories, expectations, and rationales that exist create problems for the curriculum evaluator. The evaluator needs to select certain criteria on which to base the evaluation (in order to make the evaluation feasible) while at the same time receiving different signals from legitimate recipients of the evaluation's findings. Thus, there is a need to clearly state the limits of any curriculum evaluation.

Curriculum evaluation is a complex but critical undertaking in educational systems. The more that it is integrated into the routine of curriculum operations, the more likely it is that it will affect choices, decisions, and practices. It is a function that is necessary for growth and renewal in the educational branch of any society.

## Bibliography

Bloom B S, Hastings J T, Madaus G F 1971 *Handbook on Formative and Summative Evaluation of Student Learning.* McGraw-Hill, New York

Clifford G 1973 A history of the impact of research on teaching. In: Travers R M W (ed.) 1973 *Second Handbook of Research on Teaching: A Project of the American Educational Research Association.* Rand McNally, Chicago, Illinois

Joint Committee on Standards for Educational Evaluation 1981 *Standards for Evaluations of Educational Programs, Projects, and Materials.* McGraw-Hill, New York

Lewy A (ed.) 1977 *Handbook of Curriculum Evaluation.* UNESCO, Paris

Payne D A 1974 *Curriculum Evaluation: Commentaries on Purpose, Process, Product.* Heath, Lexington, Massachusetts

Sanders J R 1978 School professionals and the evaluation function. *J. Sch. Psychol.* 16: 301–11

Sanders J R 1979 On the technology and art of evaluation. A review of seven evaluation primers. *Eval. News* 12: 11–17

Scriven M 1967 The methodology of evaluation. In: Stake R (ed.) 1967 *AERA Monograph Series on Curriculum Evaluation* No. 1: *Perspectives of Curriculum Evaluation.* Rand McNally, Chicago, Illinois

Smith E R, Tyler R W 1942 *Appraising and Recording Student Progress.* Harper, New York

Stufflebeam D L, Foley W J, Gephart W J, Guba E G, Hammond R L, Merriman H O, Provus M M 1971 *Educational Evaluation and Decision-making.* Peacock, Itasca, Illinois

Worthen B R, Sanders J R 1987 *Educational Evaluation.* Longman, New York

# Curriculum Evaluation Models

### M. C. Alkin

The term "curriculum evaluation" has historically been used to refer to several different but interrelated concepts which have not always been distinguished in the research literature. Some writers have used "curriculum evaluation" to refer to curriculum product evaluation; others have thought of curriculum program evaluation. This article distinguishes between these two activities and discusses the evaluation theories, or points of view, pertaining to each.

## 1. Curriculum Product Evaluation

The first usage of the term "curriculum evaluation" refers to evaluation which focuses on products such as courses of study, syllabi, textbooks, and so on, and makes evaluative judgments about those products.

One type of curriculum product evaluation employs specified external criteria. In this sense, curriculum evaluation is an examination of the adequacy of a curriculum product based on derived characteristics describing appropriateness.

The work of Tyler et al. (1976) offers an example of curriculum product evaluation employing specific criteria. Her evaluation judges characteristics such as: adequacy of the teacher's manual for classroom application and for providing explanation as to the content selection, sequence, and presentation; evidence provided by the developer/publisher as to the effectiveness of the curriculum material; specification of instructional objectives on which the material is based; the appropriateness of the materials given the skills, background knowledge, age, ethnicity, and socioeconomic background of the intended students.

In addition, many subject-matter methodology textbooks discuss evaluation criteria applicable to their specific discipline. For example, McNeil et al. (1980) discuss five general criteria for evaluating the quality of instructional materials used as classroom reading matter: consistency with reading approach; adequacy of objectives; instructional content; instructional methodology; validation. Most textbook publishers also employ evaluative standards in assessing a proposed instructional product, though little has been formally written on this subject by the publishers themselves.

A second type of curriculum product evaluation differs in several respects, primarily in its reliance on field data for judgments of the adequacy of the curriculum product. Curricular products are evaluated in terms of their actual impact on students. In this sense, curriculum product evaluation is an examination, or validation, of the impact of a newly developed product. The evaluation theory for this type is primarily found in the evaluation portions of the literature on curriculum and instructional product development procedures (see, for example, Baker and Alkin 1973, Markle 1969).

Curriculum product evaluation based on field data may be performed both formatively (to shape or modify the curriculum under development) or summatively (to validate the curriculum prior to its release). The type of products included are more limited than for curriculum product evaluation using external criteria. The foci of curriculum product evaluation are typically learning materials such as textbooks or other instructional modules and would not include broader examples of curriculum products such as a comprehensive school program.

## 2. Curriculum Program Evaluation

Another major type of curriculum evaluation theory consists of the evaluation of curriculum programs in operation. The term "curriculum program evaluation" refers to the complex set of interactions between a given instructional program and its setting. Curriculum evaluation activities in this broader context are concerned with looking at how a particular curriculum works within its instructional setting.

The discussion of curriculum program evaluation theory models overlaps substantially with the discussion of program evaluation theory generally. In some respects, this type of evaluation might almost be viewed as program evaluation rather than curriculum evaluation since it is not the curriculum per se that is being looked at but rather the curriculum as part of an operating program in situ. However, the literature on curricula has not tended to make this distinction and has incorporated these models into the curriculum literature. Indeed, a recent book on evaluation published by the Association for Supervision and Curriculum Development (Brandt 1981) included only articles by evaluation theorists who represent program evaluation points of view.

The theories associated with curriculum program evaluation can be further differentiated into several subsets: (a) measurement outcome oriented; (b) research or methodology oriented; (c) values oriented; and (d) decision or user oriented. These approaches have been derived within the context of program evaluation. However, they might be appropriately applicable in various aspects of product evaluation.

### 2.1 Measurement Outcome-oriented Evaluation

One of the earliest models of evaluation, known as the Tylerian evaluation model, has been most associated with the term curriculum evaluation. This model is oriented towards measurement outcomes as a governing basis for the conduct of evaluation, taking as its ultimate purpose the determination of whether a given program (or curriculum) achieved its intended purposes. The following rules and guidelines are meant to delimit and regulate the evaluation activities:

(a) Determine the broad or general goals of the program.

(b) Define goals or objectives in behavioral terms.

(c) Find situations in which achievement of objectives will be shown.

(d) Develop or select appraisal techniques (standardized tests, questionnaires, etc.).

(e) Determine by measuring whether the objectives have been achieved.

For those using this model, then, the important questions ask how the objectives are to be determined, classified, behaviorally defined, and measured. Other important questions include the consideration of short-term and long-term objectives and the use of traditional and nontraditional forms of measurement.

Critics of the Tylerian model point out several areas of concern to evaluators: the Tylerian approach does not take into consideration the unintended effects of curriculum; it does not look at process variables or at an examination of the particular instructional setting (for example, it may turn out that test performance was poor because the student population was atypical or because the program was never implemented properly). Moreover, the Tylerian approach does not take into account learner variables which may be present prior to implementation of curriculum.

### 2.2 Research-oriented and Methodology-oriented Evaluation

Research-oriented or methodology-oriented evaluation represents another program evaluation type. Theorists most strongly associated with the research/methodology orientation are often identified with particular aspects of methodology. For example, Peter Rossi and Scarvia Anderson are associated with experimental research methods in evaluation, while Lou Smith and Egon Guba (in his most recent writings), among others, emphasize the richness that qualitative and descriptive data can contribute to the evaluative process. Other theorists include those whose concern for causal modeling, quasi-experimental procedures, and the like dominate their approach to evaluation.

### 2.3 Values-oriented Evaluation

While most evaluation approaches involve the valuation of acquired data, values-oriented evaluation theorists have values as their primary concern. Within this orientation, there are several positions concerning who should make the value judgments about programs, and how such judgments are best arrived at. Some values-oriented theorists, like Michael Scriven and Elliot Eisner, maintain that the evaluator should be primarily responsible for making value judgments based on his/her own personal background, knowledge, and experience. Robert Stake agrees that the evaluator should be the one to make value judgments, but suggests that he/she should be guided by relevant data collected from appropriate external groups and individuals within the community. Other theorists, such as Robert Wolf, doubt whether a single evaluator can fairly consider and judge the views of all sides; thus he advocates the use of a "judicial" model.

### 2.4 Decision-oriented and User-oriented Evaluation

The final approach to evaluation primarily emphasizes the concerns of decision makers and other users of evaluation information. While decision-oriented and user-oriented theory acknowledges the important roles played by methodological choice and the valuation of data, it nonetheless insists on the precedence within the evaluation process of producing data relevant for decision/user audiences. This approach is reflected in the writings of Daniel Stufflebeam, Malcolm Provus,

and Marvin Alkin. Recent writings by Michael Patton have recognized a dynamic relationship existing between evaluators and users, a relationship in which decision concerns have been replaced by interactions illuminating the more incremental nature of decision-making as it applies to educational programs.

### Bibliography

Baker E, Alkin M C 1973 Formative evaluation of instructional development. *Audio-Vis. Commun. Rev.* 21: 389–418

Brandt R S (ed.) 1981 *Applied Strategies for Curriculum Evaluation.* Association for Supervision and Curriculum Development, Alexandria, Virginia

Cronbach L J et al. 1980 *Towards Reform of Program Evaluation: Aims, Methods and Institutional Arrangements.* Jossey-Bass, San Francisco, California

McNeil J D, Donant L, Alkin M C 1980 *How to Teach Reading Successfully.* Little, Brown, Boston, Massachusetts

Markle S M 1969 *Good Frames and Bad: A Grammar of Frame Writing,* 2nd edn. John Wiley, New York

Tyler L L, Klein M F, et al. 1976 *Evaluating and Choosing Curriculum and Instructional Materials.* Educational Resource Associates, Los Angeles, California

Worthen B R, Sanders J R 1973 *Educational Evaluation: Theory and Practice.* Wadsworth, Belmont, California

# Curriculum Evaluation Research

### J. R. Sanders

There are several ways to organize the research on curriculum evaluation. One might classify studies of curriculum evaluation into empirical and nonempirical groups. One might use the tasks of curriculum evaluation as a categorization scheme, that is, research on (a) delineating, (b) obtaining, (c) providing, and (d) using evaluation information (Stufflebeam et al. 1971, Straton 1977, Stufflebeam and Welch 1986). One might also group research on curriculum evaluation by the various approaches proposed for conducting curriculum evaluation (Van der Klauw and Lubbers 1979, Fraser 1982, Madaus et al. 1983, Worthen and Sanders 1987). There are many other possible organizers for research on curriculum evaluation.

The choice of organizers is somewhat arbitrary, but important, because it creates a certain mindset about what is known about curriculum evaluation and what still needs to be studied. The organization to be used here is in accordance with the tasks of curriculum evaluation. This framework was chosen because it has been used elsewhere, and other useful organizers can be subsumed within it.

The term research is used to include both empirical and nonempirical inquiry aimed at expanding knowledge and understanding of curriculum evaluation. Curriculum evaluation refers to the process of studying the merit or worth of some aspect, or the whole, of a curriculum. Curriculum could include the design of,

needs for, processes of, materials for, objectives of, environment of, policies for, support of, and outcomes of educational experiences (Schubert 1982).

### 1. Research Delineating Curriculum Evaluation

Research on delineating the questions that curriculum evaluation should address has been sparse. Stufflebeam and Welch (1986) identified a few studies aimed at identifying the kinds of questions a curriculum evaluation should address. Worthen and Sanders (1987) identified several checklists that have been developed for evaluating curriculum materials and school curriculum, but few were research based. They also reported research showing that evaluation user involvement in delineating the questions to be answered by evaluation does affect the eventual use of evaluation information. Questions addressed by curriculum evaluation have been found to come from evaluation models, curriculum checklists, research literature, and from clients.

Straton (1977) suggested research that needs to be conducted on the delineation process in curriculum evaluation. Needed research includes studies of alternative methods for identifying evaluation questions and of alternative methods for selecting evaluation questions. It also includes studies of the information that different audiences value in curriculum evaluation.

## 2. Research on Obtaining Information for Curriculum Evaluation

Research on obtaining information for curriculum evaluation has concentrated on techniques to enhance the quality of information being gathered. Research on methods for enhancing the validity and reliability of testing can be found in most testing textbooks. Likewise, references to research on enhancing the quality of surveys, interviews, observations, site visits, and other data collection methods can be found in many research methods textbooks. Straton (1977) and Worthen and Sanders (1987) have provided extensive references to research on information gathering methods used in curriculum evaluation.

Straton (1977) identified research that is needed on information collection processes in curriculum evaluation. This research includes studies of alternative data collection methods (e.g., approach, format, length, administration, sampling procedures) used for different kinds of evaluation questions and with different populations. Criterion variables would include cost and data quality.

## 3. Research on Providing Curriculum Evaluation Information to Various Audiences

The research on providing curriculum evaluation information has grown substantially since 1970. This research is often concerned with methods of providing information so that the chances that it will be used are enhanced, thus linking the providing and using processes in curriculum evaluation.

Worthen and Sanders (1987) reported research indicating that written reports are not always the most effective way to provide information in curriculum evaluation. Studies have found that teachers tend to rely on verbal information and look for it at the time it is needed. Other research on providing information has indicated that the technical quality of a study will affect its use by administrators and policy makers, as will its timeliness, use of nontechnical language, use of illustrations and examples, and focus on practical matters that audiences can do something about. Most guides to curriculum evaluation advise tailoring report format and style to those who will be expected to use the results of curriculum evaluation.

Straton (1977) identified needed research in the area of providing curriculum evaluation information. Needed research includes studies of alternative media for communicating different types of message to different types of audience. Audience studies, looking at difficulty level of communications, timing of delivery of information, and interest in different levels of thoroughness in reporting, are also needed.

## 4. Research on the Use of Curriculum Evaluation

The research on curriculum evaluation use began receiving a considerable amount of attention in 1975. Worthen and Sanders (1987) have provided extensive references to this research.

The findings of research on curriculum evaluation use have indicated that use takes on many forms: some is direct use to make decisions or changes; most is indirect conceptual learning that eventually shapes the thinking of decision makers; and some is proforma use to fulfill some mandated reporting function. Factors found to affect the use of curriculum evaluations have included credibility of the evaluator and the evaluation, the evaluator's commitment to getting the evaluation used, the quality of the evaluation itself, the interest of decision makers in the evaluation, the extent to which the evaluation focused on local needs, the way in which the evaluation findings are presented, and the translation of evaluation results into specific recommendations for action.

Methods for getting curriculum evaluation results used have been found in several field research projects. These methods include staff development through workshops and inservice programs, participation on committees, discussions with parent groups, school board policies governing the use of curriculum evaluations, demonstrations of how using evaluation findings will save money, and the evaluator being available at the right places at the right times.

Studies of the processes of decision making by teachers, principals, and other educational decision makers, the kinds of information they need and use, and methods for making that information available are needed. Studies of methods for integrating curriculum evaluation into curriculum decision making by teachers, administrators, and school board members are also needed.

## 5. Summary of the Research on Curriculum Evaluation

Although research on the process of curriculum evaluation accelerated during the 1970s, there is much that is remaining to be done. There is little known about how curriculum evaluation is conducted in schools of different size or across international boundaries. Stufflebeam and Welch (1986) concluded that overall, research on curriculum evaluation is spotty and inconclusive. It is limited in its usefulness for guiding evaluation practice and for developing an agenda for further research. There is a need for a better research base to help in advancing the theory and practice of curriculum evaluation. Straton (1977) began building the research agenda, and many of the questions he listed are still unanswered. Research on curriculum evaluation remains a priority for those who depend on evaluation to guide curriculum change.

### Bibliography

Fraser B J 1982 *Annotated Bibliography of Curriculum Evaluation Literature*. Israel Curriculum Center, Ministry of Educational Culture, Jerusalem

Madaus G F, Scriven M, Stufflebeam D L 1983 *Evaluation Models: Viewpoints on Educational and Human Services Evaluation.* Kluwer-Nijhoff, Boston, Massachusetts

Schubert W H 1982 Curriculum research. In: Mitzel H E (ed.) 1982 *Encyclopedia of Educational Research*, 5th edn. The Free Press, New York

Straton R G 1977 *Research of the Evaluation Process: Current Status and Future Directions.* The University of Sydney, Sydney

Stufflebeam D L, Foley W J, Gephart W J, Guba E G, Hammond R L, Merriman H O, Provus M M 1971 *Edu-cational Evaluation and Decision Making.* F E Peacock, Itasca, Illinois

Stufflebeam D L, Welch W L 1986 Review of research on program evaluation in United States school districts. *Educ. Admin. Q.* 22: 150–70

Van der Klauw C F, Lubbers M 1979 *Evaluation of Education: A Review.* Department of Educational Research, Erasmus University, Rotterdam

Worthen B R, Sanders J R 1987 *Educational Evaluation: Alternative Approaches and Practical Guidelines.* Longman, New York

# Eight-year Study

## K. Strickland

The concept of the Eight-year Study grew out of the desire of people associated with the Progressive Education Association to attempt a fundamental reconstruction of the American secondary school. Founded in 1919 by a group of parents and teachers associated with experimental schools, the organization had initially concentrated its efforts on implementing changes at the elementary level (Cremin 1961). The decision at the annual meeting in 1930 to focus on the high school in part reflected the increased domination of the group by professional educators, and a growing interest in the active dissemination of progressive ideals. The leaders of the study were also aware of the tremendous growth which had occurred in high-school attendance and they were concerned that the curricula of nearly all American high schools were dominated by college preparatory courses, though only one in every six high-school students actually attended college. The progressives felt that by placing an undue emphasis on preparation for college, schools were failing to provide a significant educational experience for the vast majority of the students whose formal education ended in high school (Aikin 1942).

Members attending the 1930 annual meeting of the Progressive Education Association did not lack ideas for improving secondary education, but they were keenly aware that most high schools were unwilling to risk deviating from the subject-unit requirements dictated for college admission. Although the comprehensive American high school was intended to prepare students both for college and for life, past attempts to change the curriculum had been thwarted by the fear that modification might affect a few students' chances for college admission. In an attempt to alleviate this concern, the progressives directed that a Commission on the Relation of School and College be appointed to examine ways in which school and college work could better be coordinated and to seek an agreement from colleges and universities which would allow high schools the freedom to modify their programs without jeopardizing the possibility of college admission. The 26-member commission composed of school and college officials completed both tasks within two years, delivering a stinging indictment of the American high school in 1931, and reporting the following year that the necessary cooperation of nearly 300 colleges and universities had been secured. Beginning with the class entering college in 1936 and continuing for a period of five years, students from 30 selected high schools would be admitted to college based only on the recommendation of the high-school principal and a carefully compiled record of school life (Aikin 1942).

In the fall of 1933, representatives from the 30 high schools selected to participate in the project met with the Directing Committee to plan the eight years of work ahead. Naming the study from the length of time originally designated for the experiment, the schools examined ways in which each might alter their curriculum, organization, and procedures to better serve the needs of youth. Certain goals were common to all of the schools, including a commitment to help young people understand and appreciate the democratic way of life, and a desire to develop a greater unity and continuity in the curriculum. They wanted to improve the guidance of students and to implement concepts long associated with progressive education: cooperative planning by students and teachers; a curriculum reflecting the present concerns of youth as well as the skills and knowledge demanded by society; active student participation in the learning process; and attention to all aspects of the individual—physical, intellectual, emotional, and spiritual (Cremin 1961). The schools also believed that successful preparation for college did not depend upon the study of certain subjects for a specified length of time, and they recognized that proof of this assumption was vital to the success of the experiment (Aikin 1942).

The 30 public and private high schools chosen to participate in the Eight-year Study varied in size, location, finances, resources, and facilities, as well as in the social, economic, and academic background and ultimate destination of their students. As the experiment progressed, it was also apparent that each school differed in the type of administration and leadership available, and in the commitment of the teachers, parents, and community to change. These factors, as well as the decision to allow each school to proceed independently, led to considerable variation in the amount and type of modification which occurred. The account of the schools' experiences (Giles et al. 1942) reveals that some merely revised their subject matter content, or combined subjects such as biology and chemistry into a single broad field of science. Though all of the schools were characterized by some common developments, such as increased teacher participation in curriculum planning and the use of the community as a resource and topic of study, the less experimental schools adopted these changes within the framework of the subject-discipline design associated with traditional college preparatory work. More significant modifications occurred in those schools which reorganized instruction around the common problems of people in various cultural epochs, and in schools employing a core curriculum focusing on the needs of youth. The latter were designated "experimental schools" by the follow-up staff and appeared to have met the original goals of the Eight-year Study to the fullest extent.

Of the various committees, subcommittees, and consultants available to assist the 30 schools, none were more significant than the evaluation and follow-up staff under the direction of Ralph W. Tyler. The evaluation staff responded to the need of the schools to measure the achievement of objectives such as the inculcation of social attitudes and the development of effective modes of thinking. This cooperative venture not only produced new instruments in value, attitude, and skill areas not previously measured, but also led both teachers and staff to recognize that evaluation must be based upon a clear statement of objectives and should be a continuous and integral part of the curriculum planning process. To the follow-up staff fell the task of determining if the departure from the conventional pattern of college preparation had handicapped students' work in college. Matching 1,475 pairs of graduates from experimental and traditional schools on the basis of age, sex, race, scholastic aptitude scores, home and community background, interests, probable future, and college attended, the staff studied the graduates for a period ranging from one to four years. They concluded that graduates from the 30 schools had performed slightly better academically than matchees in college, and were rated higher in factors such as systematic and objective thinking, intellectual curiosity and drive, resourcefulness, vocational orientation, and concern for world affairs. Significantly, the largest differences in achievement were found among students from the most experimental schools in the Eight-year Study and their traditional matchees (Smith et al. 1942).

The four volumes reporting the work of the Eight-year Study (Aikin 1942, Chamberlin et al. 1942, Giles et al. 1942, Smith et al. 1942) published by the Progressive Education Association were almost immediately overshadowed by the war efforts. In the following decade, the entire progressive education movement was brought under attack, and the positive results of the Eight-year Study failed to have the desired long-term effect on either college entrance requirements or high-school curriculum. Nevertheless, this longitudinal experiment did have a significant impact on American education, for it spawned the field of evaluation, and it emphasized the integral relationship between goal setting, curriculum planning, and the evaluation process. As the United States continues to grapple with the question of how to provide a significant educational experience for all youth within the comprehensive high school, the account of the Eight-year Study may yet provide some insight into this persistent problem of secondary education.

## Bibliography

Aikin W M 1942 *The Story of the Eight Year Study, with Conclusions and Recommendations.* Harper, New York

Chamberlin C, Chamberlin E, Drought N E, Scott W E 1942 *Did They Succeed in College? The Follow-up Study of the Graduates of the Thirty Schools.* Harper, New York

Cremin L A 1961 *The Transformation of the School: Progressivism in American Education.* Random House, New York

Giles H H, McCutchen S P, Zechiel A N 1942 *Exploring the Curriculum: The Work of the Thirty Schools from the Viewpoint of Curriculum Consultants.* Harper, New York

Smith E R, Tyler R W et al. 1942 *Appraising and Evaluating Student Progress.* Harper, New York

# Educational Objectives

## M. R. Eraut

The term "objective" is frequently used by educators and laymen as a synonym for "goal". Sometimes it can be replaced by "aim" or "intention" without appreciable loss of meaning. However, it has also come to acquire a more technical meaning, whose significance is not so readily apparent to those unfamiliar with its use in the education literature. In this more specialized sense, it normally refers to an intended and prespecified outcome of a planned programme of teaching and it is expressed in terms of what it is hoped the student will have learned. The two usages are often distinguished by referring either to general objectives (goals) or to specific objectives (intended learning outcomes).

This more technical use of the term "objectives", with its associated demand for lengthy detailed statements of intended learning outcomes, is criticized by a number of writers on both practical and theoretical grounds. Thus to help the reader understand some of the controversies, as well as the development among some educators of a specialized terminology for communicating objectives, the article begins with a brief historical survey. This introduces different recommendations for the specification of objectives, with special attention to the notion of levels of specification and to various formulations of the concept of behavioural objectives. The ensuing discussion of problems associated with the status of objectives examines structural relationships between objectives, the logic of intentions expressed by an objective, and the political status of statements of objectives. Then finally the uses and usefulness of objectives in curriculum development, in lesson planning, in instructional design, in evaluation, and for communication to pupils are examined.

## 1. Historical Development

The origin of thinking about objectives in a more technical manner is usually attributed to Bobbitt (1918) whose book *The Curriculum* was probably the earliest systematic treatise on curriculum theory. The circumstances were significant. Only five years previously, Bobbitt had been the first to expound principles of educational administration directly based on Taylor's (1912) theory of scientific management. Industrial language suffused the book while Bobbitt readily accepted Spencer's utilitarian approach to knowledge selection. Where Spencer (1860) had merely asserted that "the first step must be to classify, in order of importance, the leading kinds of activity which constitute human life", Bobbitt proposed to use Taylor's time and motion study techniques to make this a reality.

A similar position was advocated by Charters (1924) whose notes for curriculum construction began as follows:

> First, determine the major objectives of education by a study of the life of man in its social setting. Second, analyse these objectives into ideals and activities, and continue the analysis to the level of working units.

Following this advice led Pendleton to list 1,581 objectives for English and Billings to find 888 important generalizations for social studies teachers. Hence the objectives movement was already collapsing under its own weight when its prevailing utilitarian ideology was eclipsed by the progressivism of the 1930s. Its revival by Ralph Tyler, a former student of Charters, was in a different context—that of diagnostic testing and evaluation—and with a different philosophy—one of individual development rather than utilitarian efficiency (Smith and Tyler 1942). Tyler's Eight-year Study was a cooperative venture with a group of progressive schools; one of its main purposes was to formulate educational objectives which involved pupils in thinking for themselves and applying their knowledge rather than merely memorizing it or performing routine exercises. This aspect of the work was further developed by Tyler's former student, Benjamin Bloom, and a group of col-

lege examiners who eventually published two taxonomies of objectives, one for a cognitive domain and one for an affective domain.

Tyler's approach to curriculum development was based on reciprocal interaction between the formulation of objectives and the evaluation of their attainment (Tyler 1949). Evaluation was important for the improvement of educational programmes and proper evaluation required knowledge of what objectives the programmes were aiming to achieve. Thus objectives needed to be formulated with sufficient specificity to guide evaluation and subsequent attempts at course improvement in which the objectives themselves might be altered, both to include new possibilities and to remove that which was no longer considered feasible or of sufficiently high priority. For this purpose Tyler recommended that curriculum planners use behavioural objectives, in which both the content and the intended type of student behaviour are specified, and that course objectives be summarized in a two-dimensional matrix with content categories along one dimension and behavioural categories along the other.

It is sometimes forgotten that Tyler and the taxonomists defined objectives at a relatively general level, and it was Mager's (1962) influential book on preparing objectives for programmed instruction which more fully recaptured the spirit of Bobbitt. Moreover, like Bobbitt before him, Mager derived his position from the behavioural technology approaches of trainers in military and industrial settings.

First Mager (1962) argued that behaviour should be specified only in observable terms and outlawed the use of verbs like "know", "understand", "feel", or "appreciate" that were indicative only of unobservable internal states of mind. Second, he insisted that the standard of performance should be specified in minute detail and with a built-in assumption of mastery or near-mastery, for example 90 percent of the students should get 90 percent of the questions correct on a test covering addition and subtraction of two digit numbers. Then, third, to avoid any ambiguity he asked for the conditions of performance to be clearly identified. Given the emphasis on the nature of the terminal performance itself, objectives which satisfy Mager's criteria are sometimes referred to as performance objectives, though the term behavioural objective is still more usual.

Gagné (1965) was among many psychologists who welcomed Mager's operational definition because it would help to determine the particular type of learning required. Unlike Tyler who was concerned with providing general guidance to teachers and curriculum planners, Mager and Gagné were interested in instructional design, which at that time was seen in terms of the detailed planning of instructional events in accordance with the principles of behaviourist psychology. If the design did not always lead to programmed learning, it was still expected to yield something very like it.

Several authors took up Mager's guidelines on specifying observable behaviours and gave special attention to the action verbs whose incorporation into the statement of an objective was said to meet this requirement. More recently, however, Gagné and Briggs (1974), realizing that operational definitions of performance often conveyed little information about the kind of learning that had taken place, recommended the addition of a "learned capability" component to the specification of an objective. There would seem to be some contradiction between the focus on performance and the abandonment of operationalism implicit in the addition of the learned capability component.

Finally, it should be noted that it is possible for a planning group formulating objectives to pursue each of the four main dimensions noted in this discussion—content, behaviour, conditions, and standards—to varying degrees of specificity, and this issue is further discussed below.

## 2. Levels of Specificity and the Limits of Specification

Krathwohl (1965) has distinguished three levels of specificity and suggests that each is appropriate for a different purpose:

> At the first and most abstract level are the quite broad and general statements most helpful in the development of programs of instruction, for the laying out of types of courses and areas to be covered, and for the general goals towards which several years of education might be aimed or for which an entire unit such as an elementary, junior, or senior high school might strive.
>
> At a second and more concrete level, a behavioural objectives orientation helps to analyse broad goals into more specific ones which are useful as the building blocks for curricular instruction. These behaviourally stated objectives are helpful in specifying the goals of an instructional unit, a course, or a sequence of courses.
>
> Third and finally, there is the level needed to create instructional materials—materials which are the operational embodiment of one particular route (rarely are multiple routes included) to the achievement of a curriculum planned at the second and more abstract level, the level of detailed analysis involved in the programmed instruction movement.

The first level corresponds to what Taba has called a "platform of general objectives" though it may also apply to a specific programme within a school (Taba 1962). The second level corresponds to Tyler's and Taba's version of the term "behavioural objective", and is also the level at which the taxonomies were developed. Davies (1976) calls these "general objectives", a term which Taba reserves for Level 1.

While it is customary to describe levels of specificity in terms of language and purpose, the addition of a quantitative density dimension can also sometimes be helpful. Since objectives are usually formulated in groups or clusters, an index of density can be simply defined as

$$\frac{\text{Number of objectives in list}}{\text{Hours of learning which list is intended to cover}}$$

Thus, when working at Krathwohl's Level 1, a ministry of education lists 8 objectives for primary mathematics over the 5–9 age range, and about 600 hours of learning are involved, so the density is 8/600 or 1/75. Teachers planning a course of 100 hours using a Tyler matrix at Level 2 might well arrive at a list of about 20 objectives that would mean a density of 20/100 or 1/5. Then at Level 3 the objectives for an individual lesson, a self-instructional unit or a chapter in a book are likely to number between about 1 and 10 for a learning period of between 30 minutes and 2 hours, giving a density index that is usually greater than 1.

Another writer to identify three levels of objectives was Scriven (1967), though his perspective was primarily epistemological. His first level, entitled a "conceptual description of educational objectives", gives priority to conceptual structure and to student motivation. Then his second level, "manifestation dimensions of criterial variables", is concerned with the various ways in which a student's conceptual knowledge and understanding and his or her attitudes and nonmental abilities may be manifest or made observable. The third level provides an operational description of an objective in terms of how it is to be assessed. Thus Scriven's second and third levels correspond fairly closely to those of Krathwohl, but the first level has quite a different character, being based on curriculum content rather than general goals.

Both Krathwohl and Scriven state that Level 1 statements of objectives can guide the development of Level 2 objectives and that Level 2 statements can guide Level 3. But this process is much more complicated than simple logical deduction. There is no defensible set of rules or procedures for deriving specific objectives from general objectives because (a) selection decisions are made which involve judgments about appropriateness and priority; and (b) the kind of analysis required goes beyond the existing state of philosophical and psychological knowledge (Hirst 1973).

Gronlund (1970) makes a useful distinction between *minimum essentials* and *developmental objectives*. While minimum essentials can be handled as Level 3 objectives, developmental objectives are so complex that:

(a) Only a sample of representative behaviours can be tested.

(b) Teaching is directed towards the general class of behaviour that the objective represents rather than towards the sample that is specifically tested.

(c) Standards of performance are extremely difficult, if not impossible to define; so it is more meaningful to talk of encouraging and directing each student towards the maximum level of development he or she is capable of achieving.

A more radical distinction is made by Eisner (1969) who argues for separate treatment for instructional and expressive objectives. While instructional objectives can be prespecified and mastered, expressive objectives are concerned with outcomes that cannot and should not be prespecified because some form of original response is being sought. An expressive objective may specify an educational encounter, situation, problem, or task but it cannot predict what will be learned from what is intended to be an idiosyncratic response. While more usually associated with art and literature, the term is equally applicable to essays and projects in which students are encouraged to develop personal perspectives and insights.

## 3. The Status of Objectives

### 3.1 Structural Status

An educational objective cannot be considered in isolation, either from its companion objectives or from objectives which are intended to come before or after it in some planned sequence. It is necessarily embedded in some structure of intentions, whether this is described explicitly in some plan or document or left implicit in the way the curriculum is organized. The list format which is commonly used to communicate sets of objectives is particularly ill-suited to conveying structural information. So quite different assumptions may inform the selection of a set of objectives from those which later guide the grouping and sequencing of those objectives for teaching purposes. There may also be considerable differences between the structure embedded in course materials, the structure in the mind of the teacher, and the structures developing in the mind of each student.

When compilers of objectives do give attention to structural assumptions, they frequently turn to the concept of a learning hierarchy. A group of objectives is said to constitute a learning hierarchy when it can be represented by a structure rather like a family tree, in which the achievement of each objective is dependent on the achievement of all the objectives connected to it on the level below. A hierarchy is usually developed by logical analysis, breaking down an objective into subobjectives until each step constitutes a clearly distinguishable learning task. Both the dependency claims of the hierarchy and the concomitant assumption that the level of analysis is appropriate may need to be empirically verified.

This notion of learning hierarchies, when combined with Carroll's (1963) suggestion that individual differences might be more appropriately attributed to rate of learning than to quality of learning, leads naturally to the type of individualized instruction that is commonly referred to as mastery learning. All knowledge within a mastery learning system is assumed to be essentially hierarchical in nature; instruction is individualized so each student can proceed at his or her own rate; and there is a built-in requirement for every student to master each unit before proceeding to the next. Hence the formulation and sequencing of objectives and the development of assessment instruments to indicate their mastery are an essential part of the strategy (Bloom et al. 1981).

The terms "terminal objective" and "enabling objective" are also associated with sequencing. A terminal objective represents the end of a learning sequence and needs to be justified in its own right; while an enabling objective situated in the middle of a sequence need only be justified in terms of its role in facilitating the achievement of one or more terminal objective(s). The distinction, though useful, is still an oversimplification because many objectives can be justified on both grounds and their description as "terminal" or "enabling" depends mainly on the time-scale adopted: the terminal objective of a lesson becomes an enabling objective in the context of a topic or course; and the terminal objective of a course becomes an enabling objective in the context of a student's subsequent life.

From the student's point of view, what probably matters most is an objective's position on the immediacy–remoteness continuum (Dressel 1976). Many objectives will appear to students both as conceptually remote, because they are far from what seems to be relevant in the community outside school, and as temporally remote because their utility lies far in the future. Perceiving links between their immediate objectives and possible ultimate goals can be crucial for some students' motivation. It has been suggested that objectives being communicated to students should be accompanied by individual rationales or justifications which relate them to more distant and more valued goals.

### 3.2 Logical Status

The logical status of an objective also deserves attention as it greatly affects the part it might play in planning and teaching. First, there is the distinction made by White who noted that the phrase "behavioural objective" can mean one of two things:

(a) objectives which themselves *consist in* pupils behaving in certain ways;

(b) objectives whose attainment is *tested by* observing pupils behaving in certain ways. (White 1971)

To state that no cognitive activity other than the repetition of memorized responses can be behavioural in sense (a) is not to claim that greater clarity cannot be achieved by giving close attention to the formulation of an objective; but it does imply that most educational objectives can be behavioural only in sense (b). Such objectives cannot wholly specify the ways in which they might be assessed, and no form of assessment can provide unambiguous evidence of their achievement. In practice, some forms of assessment are widely accepted as providing adequate evidence of the attainment of certain objectives, some have their adequacy disputed, and some are clearly unsatisfactory. If this were not the case, assessment would not be such a complex and elaborate field of study.

A second problem arises if one questions more carefully the notion of an objective being an intended outcome. In what sense is it intended? Is it expected to happen? Is its achievement specifically planned? Is it always explicit? Much of the writing about objectives seems to imply affirmative answers to all these questions, but observations of practice suggest a more cautious approach. Lists of objectives are often used to express aspirations rather than expectations and course documents often include a mixture of the two. More significantly, perhaps, an objective which is an expectation for one student may be an aspiration for another.

The term "emergent objectives" has been used to refer to objectives which may not even have been formulated in advance, but which, when the opportunity arises, are seen to contribute to important educational aims which tend to get neglected under the pressures of institutional expectations.

## 3.3 Political Status

The status of an objective is also affected by political factors. Who specifies them and with what authority? Who uses them and how strongly do they feel obliged to keep within the specifications? There are a large number of possible situations. For example, influences on objectives from outside school may be of any of the following kinds:

(a) external specification as part of a pattern of curriculum control;

(b) an external requirement for the school to formulate its own objectives, which may or may not be accompanied by a further requirement to have them formally approved;

(c) external specification as part of a system of external examinations;

(d) external specification as part of a package of curriculum materials which the school may choose or be obliged to adopt or adapt;

(e) external comments by district officers, advisers, or inspectors.

Only in the first two uses will objectives necessarily be formally specified. However, evidence from curriculum implementation studies suggests that external specification of objectives alone has relatively little impact unless accompanied by sanctions or by other forms of specification such as textbook approval or external examinations. Congruence between externally specified objectives and classroom practice may be more readily explained by their sharing a common tradition than by hypotheses of cause and effect. Even when objectives have been internally specified, it must remain an empirical question whether they play a significant role in classroom practice. Accounts in the literature would seem to indicate that sometimes they do not.

## 4. Arguments For and Against using Objectives

When discussing the advantages and limitations of planning and working with objectives, it is important to

specify the user, the context, and the type of use envisaged. Five main types of use will be distinguished—curriculum development, lesson planning, instructional design, evaluation, and communication to students. These different uses are often confused in the literature, with arguments for and against one type of use being frequently applied to another. Moreover, it has not been unusual for authors to set up "straw-man" images of their opponents in order to demolish extreme statements while avoiding entanglements with more moderate positions [see, for example, the often quoted papers by Popham (1969) and Macdonald-Ross (1973)].

### 4.1 Using Objectives in Curriculum Development

Attention will be confined here to the use of objectives at Krathwohl's second level, leaving discussion of the use of highly specific objectives for the next section. In doing so, however, it must be remembered that most advocates of instructional objectives at the third level are agreed that prior specification at the second level is essential. But the converse is not true. Objectives may be used in curriculum development without any assumption that more detailed specification by teachers or by instructional designers will necessarily follow.

The principle arguments for using objectives for curriculum development purposes alone would appear to be (a) that they clarify the intentions of the developers and (b) that they focus attention upon the learner as well as the teacher. What the use of objectives cannot do is resolve disputes over what should be taught, though sometimes they may help to map out the issues. Objectives at the second level will never be devoid of ambiguity, and some educators are more skilful than others in using the language of objectives, so the question of whether or not objectives do indeed clarify intentions can only be answered in terms of individual cases.

Many authors have stressed that the clarification of teaching intentions is a difficult exercise involving considerable insight and delicacy of phrasing, and that it is incapable of totally satisfactory resolution. People who prepare curriculum specifications at district, regional, or national level need to understand these problems, if their use of objectives is not to do more harm than good.

At institutional level, however, the context of curriculum specifications is quite different because formal curriculum documents are only a small part of the communication between the teachers concerned. A statement of objectives then has a strongly indexical character in which its meaning is enriched by and partly dependent upon other communications which occurred before, during, and after its preparation. The advantages of using objectives will depend on whether the curriculum developers want to use them or merely feel obliged to use them; on whether they are genuinely seeking agreement as opposed to finding a form of words which maximizes the independence of individual teachers; and on whether intentions are easily communicated by other means, such as a common textbook or examination.

Above the institutional level, the political status of an objective is often critical. While some teachers are used to being told what to teach, others regard the formulation of objectives as the teachers' own responsibility. Normal practice varies greatly between one country and another, but in any country, attempts to alter the balance of power by changing either the locus or the extent of specification of objectives are likely to meet resistance. In practice, however, whether politically welcome or not, objectives may be misunderstood or even ignored by teachers. Even when the process of formulating objectives clarifies the intentions of a curriculum team or committee (and it is not unknown for it to lead to a deliberately vague compromise), the document that results does not necessarily convey those intentions adequately to teachers. This is not an argument against using objectives but rather one against placing too much reliance on them as a form of curriculum communication. The literature on curriculum implementation is replete with examples where misunderstanding or lack of sanctions or infeasibility have prevented externally specified curricula from being implemented as intended.

An important criticism from a theoretical rather than a practical perspective concerns not the use of objectives per se but approaches to curriculum development which assume that statements of objectives are adequate on their own in the first stage of curriculum planning. Several authors (see for example Stenhouse 1970/71), have argued for prime attention to content; others for an early consideration of assessment, which often counteracts the impact of objectives; and yet others for the early specification of certain crucial and often nontraditional learning experiences such as project work, community service, work experience, or artistic performance. Many of these other curriculum elements can be so important for a course that they need discussion prior to any detailed formulation of objectives. Moreover, when curriculum development is viewed as a problem-solving activity with a premium on creative imagination, an early emphasis on objectives may lead only to the reformulation of traditional practice at a time when more radical change is what is really needed (Eraut 1976). Thus, when the emphasis is on curriculum innovation, objectives may not be a starting point but a "late development of the curriculum maker's platform" (Walker 1971).

The argument against using objectives which has probably received the greatest support is that they are only appropriate for some areas of the curriculum. Eisner (1969) has eloquently argued against behavioural objectives in the arts, and their usefulness for describing higher level learning in the humanities (Stenhouse 1970/71) and social sciences (Eraut et al. 1975) has also been questioned. In all these cases it is the individuality and complexity of students' work which is said to limit the applicability of the language of objectives. Two major issues are at stake—the nature of the subject and the autonomy of the learner. Both have been and will long continue to be matters for debate among educators, though many would now agree that objectives are more helpful in some situations than in others. The principal problem lies in recognizing those situations in which the use of objectives is appropriate.

Given the problems of deriving, formulating, and justifying objectives, it is much safer if in the context of the education system as a whole objectives are regarded as means rather than ends. The courses and curricula that are planned constitute the means whereby students have to be guided towards a variety of ends; and the language of objectives provides one means of clarifying intentions during the planning process.

## 4.2 Using Objectives in Lesson Planning

The claim that highly specific objectives at Krathwohl's third level improve the quality of lesson plans and subsequent pupil performance is usually argued by asserting that good lesson planning is logically dependent on knowing what one is seeking to achieve; and that this necessarily entails having learning objectives. Both parts of this assertion have been challenged. To begin with the second—one counterargument is that teachers know what they are doing because they are working in a recognized teaching tradition. Provided that they can relate the content of their lessons to a topic on a syllabus, a chapter in a textbook, or a possible question in an examination, they do not need any separate list of course objectives. Once a tradition is clearly established, objectives become redundant. The use of objectives in such a context is less likely to be one of defining the course than one of inspiring teachers to move their students beyond the level of routine completion of textbook exercises or memorization of content, a purpose for which specifying beyond the second level is clearly inappropriate.

When more informal approaches to teaching are adopted, objectives are less likely to be implicit in textbooks, syllabi, and examinations. But then the first part of the assertion becomes more of an issue. Is good lesson planning logically dependent on knowing what objectives one is seeking to achieve? Sockett (1976) argues that objectives are totally inadequate as a description of a teacher's ends, because a teacher always has other equally important ends, to which his or her actions are directed: being fair to groups, getting students to ask questions, building up weaker children's confidence, developing interpupil discussion, and so on. Though one can argue that these "procedural aims" should be included as general course objectives, they need to be pursued over a long period. Such aims have a justifiably important influence on teaching, but cannot be converted into specific objectives for individual lessons.

Another criticism comes from Jackson (1968) whose interviews with teachers judged as "outstanding" revealed that both their planning and their classroom responding were aimed not directly at the achievement of objectives but at creating productive learning conditions and securing student involvement. Since involvement in learning activities is logically necessary for learning, one might be permitted to modify the original assertion to argue that good lesson planning is dependent on having appropriate activities and strategies to achieve a high degree of student involvement. If that primary goal can be achieved then surely productive learning will follow. Where there is no established tradition, course objectives may be helpful in choosing between possible activities and in alerting a teacher to special opportunities; but it is unreasonable to expect the teacher to sustain a detailed knowledge of how each of 30 or more students is progressing towards each of a dozen or so objectives in every single lesson. Worse still, it might distract the teacher from the primary task of securing involvement in learning.

A further argument against using highly specific objectives in lesson planning is that they overconstrain the teacher. Both Jackson and Sockett characterize good teaching as being strong on opportunism. Atkin (1968) suggests that higher order objectives are best pursued whenever the opportunity arises rather than according to preplanned schedules. For example, when students' questions lead to the discussion of some significant moral problem or issue, the teacher may see the opportunity for pursuing objectives whose introduction might have seemed artificial or nonproductive if the teacher had initiated them. Eisner's expressive objectives also resist very precise planning. In general, support for the use of specific objectives at Krathwohl's third level is now largely confined to situations where the teaching is highly directive and objectives are limited to the lower cognitive levels. Using general course objectives to guide lesson planning is quite a different procedure from allowing lesson planning to be dominated by the detailed specification of behavioural objectives; and there is little conclusive empirical evidence to support either practice. Until there is good evidence of how people who work with objectives plan or teach differently and of how this benefits their students, the use or nonuse of objectives should remain a matter of personal preference.

### 4.3 Using Objectives in Instructional Design

The term "instructional design" commonly refers to the design of teaching and learning materials by a specially designated team, who may or may not include teachers who will be responsible for their implementation. Although some writers on instructional design appear to address ordinary teachers, there is little evidence that their recommendations get used by individual teachers who are not members of a design team.

The claim that using highly specific objectives at Krathwohl's third level improves the quality of instructional design is prominent in the literature. Indeed it is often taken for granted. Yet there is little empirical evidence to support this claim for learning systems other than those based on individualized learning. The detailed specification of objectives is an extremely time-consuming operation, which requires considerable skill if common pitfalls are to be avoided; and it is, perhaps, unlikely to be a good use of scarce personnel when there is an urgent need to create and try out new teaching ideas.

The more restricted claim that highly specific objectives are needed for individualized learning programmes based on mastery learning receives much stronger theoretical and practical backing. The advocates of highly specific objectives adopt a similar theoretical position to advocates of mastery learning; and designers of mastery-learning-based instructional systems consistently use highly specific objectives. It can be argued that designers could proceed directly from second level objectives to criterion tests, but this would ignore the detailed mapping of hierarchies of learning objectives which most designers working in this tradition recommend.

### 4.4 Using Objectives in Evaluation

It is in the context of evaluation that the concept of objectives has been most continuously used and most elaborately evolved. Tyler's primary concern was with evaluation and the taxonomies were also developed for evaluation purposes. Arguments for and against using objectives in evaluation are treated at greater length elsewhere, so the discussion here will be brief.

One of the purposes of an evaluation, sometimes the main purpose, is to examine the realization of intention. To what extent have various people's intentions been realized in practice? People have many kinds of intentions but these usually include at least some that relate to student outcomes. Whether or not they are documented or made explicit, intended student outcomes can often be expressed either as objectives or in terms of performance on some task or in some anticipated situation. Thus an evaluation concerned with the realization of intention will usually need either to collect existing evidence of student performance (folders of work, test papers, etc.) or to devise some means of assessing what students have learned. If some differentiated comment on student performance is required, then this can be achieved by separate reports on each performance task or by using a list of objectives and commenting on the achievement of each. Classification schemes may be used to help set out the range of objectives, either at the data analysis stage or as an aid to constructing assessment instruments where these are deemed necessary.

The convenience of collecting student achievement data in this way and using them for improving the course by what is now called formative evaluation is what led to Tyler's model of curriculum development; and it helps to explain the continuing popularity of that model with many evaluators (Bloom et al. 1981). However, formative evaluation normally requires more than just student performance data. Moreover, as recent disputes about performance contracting (Stake 1973) and careful studies of test performance (Cicourel et al. 1974) have revealed, the kind of cognitive behaviour which leads to a particular performance is not necessarily the same as that which was intended. Students interpret tasks differently and get tested in many different contexts. Even assigning an examination question to a particular level in Bloom's cognitive domain may depend on the assumptions made about the teaching prior to that examination. Thus the usefulness of information about objectives and their achievement is dependent on additional information about transactions and conditions which can assist in their interpretation. Even statements of objectives have to be seen in context because they are not absolute criteria but indications of people's attempts to express their intentions.

In case studies and small-scale evaluations, collecting qualitative contextual evidence to assist with the interpretation of achievement data is a feasible proposition. But the larger the scale of evaluation, the more diverse will be the programme being evaluated, until it becomes extremely difficult to collect sufficient contextual information to provide useful guidance for decision making. A further problem in evaluating large-scale educational programmes is that their objectives are usually negotiated as part of some political compromise, and are therefore ill-suited for bearing the brunt of a programme evaluation based on educational objectives (Cronbach et al. 1980).

Closely related to the use of objectives in evaluation is their use in the monitoring of student achievement and in accountability. In both cases objectives may be used as a guide to test construction or as an aid to data analysis. Their use, however, will not obviate the need for a careful demonstration of the validity of any assessment instruments. It will always need to be argued that an objective is an adequate statement of an intention and that a test item is an adequate indication of the achievement of an objective.

### 4.5 Using Objectives to Communicate to Students

There is much more empirical evidence on this issue than on other uses of objectives, presumably because it lends itself to short simple experiments. Several reviews of this research have been published (Hartley and Davies 1976; Faw and Waller 1976; Lewis 1981). The analysis is complicated by the existence of alternative methods for drawing learners' attention to what is expected of them. Hartley and Davies discuss pretests, overviews, and advance organizers as alternative attention directors; while Faw and Waller also included inserted questions. Most of the evidence reported is based on work with college students, some on work with high-school students and very little with other populations; and it has usually stemmed from situations where students learned from textual material rather than a teacher.

While several studies have shown that providing objectives enhances student achievement, an equal number have reported no significant difference (Lewis 1981). Some of the more favourable results can be "explained" in terms of increased learning time (Faw and Waller 1976). Alternative methods of guidance appear to have a similar impact—sometimes there are positive effects, sometimes there are none, but there are no reports of negative effects. On the whole the evidence for inserted questions seems to be the strongest, especially when applied to long passages of prose. However, the research is beset with methodological difficulties: when, for example, does an introduction become an implicit statement of objectives; and when does a statement of objectives become a form of coaching for a test? The general conclusion of reviewers is that giving a student clearer directions normally enhances his or her learning, but a statement of objectives is only one of several ways of doing it. Such additional guidance may only be necessary when the instruction was not well-designed in the first place.

## Bibliography

Atkin J M 1968 Behavioral objectives in curriculum design: A cautionary note. *Sci. Teach.* 35: 27–30

Bloom B S, Madaus G F, Hastings J T 1981 *Evaluation to Improve Learning.* McGraw-Hill, New York

Bobbitt F 1918 *The Curriculum.* Houghton Mifflin, Boston, Massachusetts

Carroll J B 1963 A model of school learning. *Teach. Coll. Rec.* 64: 723–33

Charters W W 1924 *Curriculum Construction.* Macmillan, New York

Cicourel A V et al. 1974 *Language Use and School Performance.* Academic Press, New York

Cronbach L J et al. 1980 *Toward Reform of Program Evaluations.* Jossey-Bass, San Francisco, California

Davies I K 1976 *Objectives in Curriculum Design.* McGraw-Hill, Maidenhead

Dressel P L 1976 *Handbook of Academic Achievement.* Jossey-Bass, San Francisco, California

Eisner E W 1969 Instructional and expressive educational objectives: Their formulation and use in curriculum. In: Popham W J et al. (eds.) 1969 *Instructional Objectives.* (AERA Curriculum Evaluation Monograph 3.) Rand McNally, Chicago, Illinois

Eraut M R 1976 Some perspectives on curriculum development in teacher education. *Educ. Teach.* 99: 11–21

Eraut M R, MacKenzie N, Papps I 1975 The mythology of educational development: Reflections on a three-year study of economics teaching. *Br. J. Educ. Technol.* 6(3): 20–34

Faw H W, Waller T G 1976 Mathemagenic behaviours and efficiency in learning from prose materials: Review, critique and recommendations. *Rev. Educ. Res.* 46: 691–720

Gagné R M 1965 The analysis of instructional objectives for the design of instructions. In: Glaser R (ed.) 1965 *Teaching Machines and Programmed Learning*, Vol 2: *Data and Directions.* Department of Audio-visual Instruction, National Education Association (NEA), Washington, DC

Gagné R M, Briggs L J 1974 *Principles of Instructional Design.* Holt, Rinehart and Winston, New York

Gronlund N E 1970 *Stating Behavioral Objectives for Classroom Instruction.* Macmillan, New York

Hartley J, Davies I K 1976 Preinstructional strategies: The role of pretests, behavioral objectives, overviews and advance organizers. *Rev. Educ. Res.* 46: 239–65

Hirst P H 1973 Towards a logic of curriculum development. In: Taylor P H, Walton J (eds.) 1973 *The Curriculum: Research Innovation and Change.* Ward Lock Educational, London

Jackson P W 1968 *Life in Classrooms.* Holt, Rinehart and Winston, New York

Krathwohl D 1965 Stating objectives appropriately for program, for curriculum and for instructional materials. *J. Teach. Educ.* 17: 83–92

Lewis J M 1981 Answers to twenty questions on behavioral objectives. *Educ. Technol.* 21: 27–31

Macdonald-Ross M 1973 Behavioural objectives: A critical review. *Instr. Sci.* 2(1): 1–52

Mager R F 1962 *Preparing Instructional Objectives.* Fearon, Palo Alto, California

Popham W J 1969 Objectives and instruction. In: Popham W J et al. (eds.) 1969 *Instructional Objectives.* (AERA Curriculum Evaluation Monograph 3.) Rand McNally, Chicago, Illinois

Scriven M 1967 The methodology of evaluation. In: Tyler R W, Gagné R M, Scriven M (eds.) 1967 *Perspectives of Curriculum Evaluation.* (AERA Curriculum Evaluation Monograph 1.) Rand McNally, Chicago, Illinois

Smith E R, Tyler R W 1942 *Appraising and Recording Student Progress.* Harper, New York

Sockett H 1976 *Designing the Curriculum.* Open Books, London

Spencer H 1860 What knowledge is most worthwhile? In: Spencer H (ed.) 1910 *Education: Intellectual, Moral and Physical.* Appleton, New York

Stake R E 1973 Measuring what learners learn. In: House E R (ed.) 1973 *School Evaluation: The Politics and Process.* McCutchan, Berkeley, California

Stenhouse L 1970/71 Some limitations on the use of objectives in curriculum research and planning. *Paedag. Eur.* 6: 73–83

Taba H 1962 *Curriculum Development: Theory and Practice.* Harcourt, Brace and World, New York

Taylor F W 1912 *Scientific Management.* Harper, New York

Tyler R W 1949 *Basic Principles of Curriculum and Instruction.* University of Chicago Press, Chicago, Illinois

Tyler R W 1964 Some persistent questions on the defining of objectives. In: Lindvall C M (ed.) 1964 *Defining Educational Objectives.* University of Pittsburgh Press, Pittsburgh, Pennsylvania

Walker D F 1971 A naturalistic model for curriculum development. *Sch. Rev.* 80: 51–65

White J P 1971 The concept of curriculum evaluation. *J. Curric. Stud.* 3: 101–12

# Taxonomies of Educational Objectives

## V. De Landsheere

Originally, the term taxonomy (or systematics) was understood as the science of the classification laws of life forms. By extension, the word taxonomy means the science of classification in general and any specific classification respecting its rules, that is, the taxonomy of educational objectives.

A taxonomy related to the social sciences cannot have the rigour or the perfect branching structure of taxonomies in the natural sciences. In education, a taxonomy is a classification constructed according to one or several explicit principles.

The term "taxonomy of educational objectives" is closely associated with the name of B. S. Bloom. This is explained by the extraordinary worldwide impact of the *Taxonomy of Educational Objectives* first edited by Bloom in 1956. This taxonomy was enthusiastically received by teachers, educationists, and test developers because it offered easily understandable guidelines for systematic evaluation covering the whole range of cognitive processes (and not only the lower mental processes, as was too often the case in the past). This taxonomy had also a definite influence on curriculum development and teaching methods for the same reason: it emphasized processes rather than content matter, and helped determine a proper balance between lower and higher cognitive processes.

Bloom's Taxonomy of cognitive objectives was soon followed by taxonomies for the affective and psychomotor domains. Within two decades, several taxonomies were developed by other authors and a great number of philosophical and empirical studies appeared on this topic.

A presentation of the main taxonomies so far published follows.

## 1. The Cognitive Domain

### 1.1 Bloom's Taxonomy

This taxonomy, which has inspired the majority of the other taxonomies, uses four basic principles: (a) the major distinction should reflect the ways teachers state educational objectives (methodological principle); (b) the taxonomy should be consistent with our present understanding of psychological phenomena (psychological principle); (c) the taxonomy should be logically developed and internally consistent (logical principle); and (d) the hierarchy of objectives does not correspond to a hierarchy of values (objective principle).

The taxonomy itself comprises six cognitive levels:

(a) Knowledge: recall or recognition of specific elements in a subject area. The information possessed by the individual consists of specifics (terminology, facts), ways and means of dealing with specifics (conventions, trends, sequences, classifications, categories, criteria, universals), and abstractions in a field (principles, generalizations, theories, and structures).

(b) Comprehension:
- (i) Translation: the known concept or message is put in different words or changed from one kind of symbol to another.
- (ii) Interpretation: a student can go beyond recognizing the separate parts of a communication and see the interrelations among the parts.
- (iii) Extrapolation: the receiver of a communication is expected to go beyond the literal communication itself and make inferences about consequences or perceptibly extend the time dimensions, the sample, or the topic.

(c) Application: use of abstractions in particular and concrete situations. The abstractions may be in the form of general ideas, rules of procedure, or generalized methods. The abstractions may also be technical principles, ideas, and theories which must be remembered and applied.

(d) Analysis: breakdown of a communication into its constituent elements or parts such that the relative hierarchy of ideas is made clear and/or the relations between the ideas expressed are made explicit. One can analyse elements, relationships, organizational principles.

(e) Synthesis: the putting together of elements and parts so as to form a whole. This involves arranging and combining in such a way as to constitute a pattern of structure not clearly there before.

(f) Evaluation: evaluation is defined as the making of judgments about the value of ideas, works, solutions, methods, material, and so on. Judgments can be in terms of internal evidence (logical accuracy and consistency) or external criteria (comparison with standards, rules . . .).

The content validity of the taxonomy is not considered as perfect by any author but, in general, they are satisfied with it: taken as a whole, it allows nearly all the cognitive objectives of education to be classified. Nevertheless, the taxonomical hierarchy is questionable and the category system is heterogeneous. De Corte (1973) has pointed out that the subcategories used are not always based on the same classification principle. He writes: "For knowledge, analysis and synthesis, the subcategories correspond to a difficulty scale of products resulting from cognitive operations. For comprehension, the subdivisions are specifications of operations and not of their products. For evaluation, the subcategories depend on the nature of the criteria chosen to formulate a judgment."

Gagné (1964) has also pointed out that some categories or subcategories only differ in their content and not by formal characteristics which affect their conditions of learning.

According to Cox (De Corte 1973), the agreement on classification among the users of the taxonomy ranges from 0.63 to 0.85. The lack of reliability must come from the vagueness of the concepts for which the authors of the taxonomy propose essential rather than operational definitions.

The taxonomy has been elaborated for evaluation purposes. It has also been very useful in developing blueprints for curriculum development. It helped in identifying and formulating objectives, and, as a consequence, in structuring the material and specifying assessment procedures.

When developing a test for a particular curriculum, the curriculum often only presents a theme (Bacher 1973). No indication is given about which behaviours of the theme are to be tested. The test constructor is left to guess about which behaviours are to be tested. Furthermore, the taxonomy of objectives movement could signal a renaissance of nineteenth-century faculty psychology. Instead of training separate mental faculties such as memory, imagination, etc., one could artificially cultivate memory (knowledge in Bloom), application, analysis, synthesis, judgment, aptitudes.

Several authors are of the opinion that the taxonomy pays too much attention to knowledge, and not enough to higher mental processes.

It is not possible to use the taxonomy without reference to the behavioural background of the individual. There is an obvious difference between the individual who solves a specific problem for the first time and the individual who has met the same problem before. In both cases, however, the answer can be the same.

To test the validity of the hierarchical structure of the taxonomy, Madaus and his associates developed a quantitative causal model (see Fig. 1) to reveal not only the proportion of variance at each level explained directly by the preceding adjacent level, but also any proportion of variance explained indirectly by nonadjacent levels. The statistical techniques used were principal components analysis to identify the role of a factor of general ability $g$, and multiple regression analysis to measure the links between taxonomic levels. Hill (1984) has employed maximum likelihood estimation procedures, using LISREL, to list the hierarchical assumptions of the

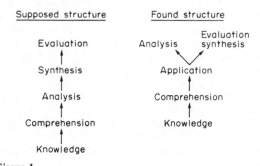

***Figure 1***
Schematic representation of an hypothesized perfect hierarchy and of the hierarchical structure found by Madaus et al. 1973

Bloom taxonomy, and has provided important evidence to support a hierarchical structure between the five higher-order categories.

In a pure hierarchy, there must be a direct link between adjacent levels and only between these two. As one proceeds from the lower to the higher levels in Bloom's taxonomy, the strength of the direct links between adjacent levels decreases and many links between nonadjacent levels appear. Knowledge, comprehension, and application are well-hierarchized. Higher up in the hierarchy, a branching takes place. On one side, analysis is found (even if the *g* factor is taken into account, analysis entertains an indirect link with comprehension). It is what Ebel (1973) calls the stage of content mastery. On the other side, synthesis and evaluation are found; they are differentiated clearly from the rest in that they are highly saturated in the *g* factor. This dependence increases if the material is not well-known to the students, or is very difficult, or if the lower processes have not been sufficiently mastered to contribute significantly to the production of higher level behaviours.

Horn (1972) suggested an algorithm to classify objectives along Bloom's taxonomy. He notes that in lower mental processes, objectives content and problem cannot be separated. For instance, for the objective: "The student will be able to list the parts of a plant", there is no problem. The answer will be possible only if the student has it "ready made" in his or her memory. For higher mental processes, the problem is general, and can be formulated without reference to a specific content.

To quasioperationalize Bloom's taxonomy, Horn takes the level of complexity of the problem posed as a classification criterion. At each level, he considers the formal aspect and the content. Figure 2 presents Horn's algorithm.

Using Horn's algorithm, well-trained judges can reach a high interreliability in their classification of objectives.

Bloom's taxonomy is formulated in an abstract way. To help the users apply the taxonomy properly, Metfessel et al. (1970) suggested a list of verbs and a list of objects which, appropriately combined, give the framework for an operational objective at the different taxonomic levels.

Bloom is aware of the limits of the instrument to whose development he has contributed. What really matters to Bloom is that educators question as often as possible whether they have varied the cognitive level of the tasks, exercises, and examinations they propose, whether they stimulate their students sufficiently, and whether they really help them develop.

### 1.2 Guilford's Structure of Intellect Model

To organize intellectual factors, identified by factor analysis or simply hypothesized, Guilford (1967) designed a structure of intellect (SI) model (see Fig. 3). This model was essentially conceived to serve the heuristic function of generating hypotheses regarding new factors

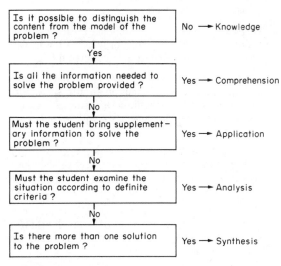

**Figure 2**
Horn's algorithm

of intelligence. The placement of any intellectual factor within this nonhierarchical model is determined by its three unique properties: its operation, its content, and its product.

Content categories are:

(a) Figural: figural information covers visual, auditive, and kinesthesic sense.

(b) Symbolic: signs that can be used to stand for something else.

(c) Semantic: the verbal factor.

(d) Behavioural: behavioural content is defined as information, essentially nonverbal, involved in human interactions, where awareness or attention, perceptions, thoughts, desires, feelings, moods, emotions, intentions, and actions of other persons and of ourselves are important.

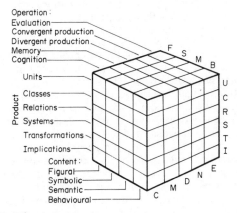

**Figure 3**
Guilford's Structure of Intellect Model

Operation categories are:

(a) Cognition: awareness, immediate discovery or rediscovery, or recognition of information in various forms; comprehension or understanding.

(b) Memory: retention or storage, with some degree of availability, of information in the same form in which it was committed to storage, and in connection with the same cues with which it was learned.

(c) Divergent production: the generation of information from given information where the emphasis is upon variety and quantity of output from the same source; this category is likely to involve transfer.

(d) Convergent production: the area of logical productions or at least the area of compelling inferences. The input information is sufficient to determine a unique answer.

(e) Evaluation: the process of comparing a product of information with known information according to logical criteria, and reaching a decision concerning criterion satisfaction.

Product categories are:

(a) Units: relatively segregated or circumscribed items of information having "thing" character.

(b) Classes: recognized sets of items grouped by virtue of their common properties.

(c) Relations: recognized connections between two items of information based upon variables or upon points of contact that apply to them.

(d) Systems: organized or structured aggregates of items of information, a complex of interrelated or interacting parts.

(e) Transformations: changes of various kinds, of existing or known information in its attributes, meaning, role, or use.

(f) Implications: expectancies, anticipations, and predictions, the fact that one item of information leads naturally to another.

Each cell of Guilford's model represents a factor that is a unique combination of operation, content, and product. For instance, cell 1 (see Fig. 3) represents cognition of figural units.

Can Guilford's model be utilized to formulate or at least to generate objectives? First of all, it can be noted that the three dimensions of the model are hierarchical at least to a certain extent. Furthermore, Guilford has discussed the implications of his model for education. He thinks that it indicates clearly the kinds of exercises that must be applied to develop intellectual abilities. He remarks, in particular, that school, in general, over-emphasizes cognition and the memorization of semantic units. It is important, says Guilford, to apply oneself

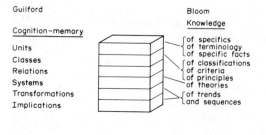

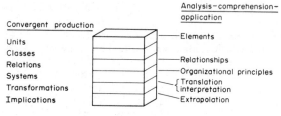

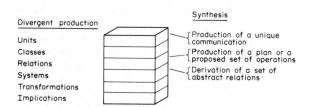

**Figure 4**
Parallelism between Guilford's model and Bloom's cognitive taxonomy

much more to the exercise of the other products: classes, relations, systems, transformations, and implications.

The fact that Guilford compares his model to Bloom's taxonomy and acknowledges important similarities between both of them seems to confirm that Guilford does not exclude the possibility that his model may be used to generate and classify objectives.

Guilford's model can absorb Bloom's whole cognitive taxonomy (see Fig. 4). By its greater precision, the SI model may allow easier operationalization and, more generally, may offer greater taxonomic possibilities.

De Corte (1973) has adapted and transformed Guilford's model. The four dimensions of De Corte's general model of classification are: (a) the subject matter of specific content of a given universe of objectives; (b) the domain of information to which the subject matter belongs (content in Guilford's model); (c) the product: the objectives are classified with respect to the formal aspect of the information they produce (products in Guilford's model); (d) the operation is defined as in Guilford's model.

De Corte focuses on this fourth category and develops Guilford's five operations into a seven category system. Cognition comprises receiving–reproducing operations: (a) perception of information; (b) recall of information; (c) reproduction of information and productive operations; (d) interpretative production of information; (e) convergent production of information; (f) evaluative production of information; (g) divergent production of information.

De Corte's system is of interest in that it develops Guilford's model in such a manner that it becomes a practical tool for the definition of the cognitive objectives of education. It seems to indicate how Bloom and Guilford's contributions could be integrated and be of use to education.

### 1.3 The Gagné–Merrill Taxonomy

Gagné proposes a hierarchy of processes needed to achieve the learning tasks assigned by objectives. Merrill designates the behaviour and psychological condition under which learning can be observed.

With Gagné's learning conditions, the push-down principle constitutes the basis of the Gagné–Merrill taxonomy. In the process of development, a person acquires behaviour at the lower levels before acquiring behaviour at the higher levels. Later, the conscious cognitive demand on the learner increases. Learners have an innate tendency to reduce the cognitive load as much as possible; consequently, a learner will attempt to perform a given response at the lowest possible level. The push-down principle states that a behaviour acquired at one level will be pushed down to a lower level as soon as conditions have changed sufficiently so that the learner is able to respond to the stimulus using lower level behaviour. It is rather surprising that this important principle is often neglected or even ignored in the literature related to the taxonomies of educational objectives.

The Gagné–Merrill taxonomy is an original formulation, integrating the affective, psychomotor, and cognitive domains.

The following is a condensed version of Merrill's presentation:

(a) *Emotional behaviour (signal learning).* In the presence of every stimulus situation, students involuntarily react with physiological changes which they perceive as feelings. The direction (positive or negative) and the relative magnitude of this emotional behaviour can be inferred by observing the students' approach/avoidance responses in unrestrained choice situations.

(b) *Psychomotor behaviour.* A student is able to execute rapidly, without external prompting, a specified neuromuscular reaction in the presence of a specific stimulus situation. The observable behaviour is an overt skeletal–muscular response which occurs in entirety without hesitation. Psychological conditions of importance are the presence of a specific cue and the absence of prompts. Psychomotor behaviour may be further broken down into three constituent behaviours.

First, topographic behaviour (stimulus response) is where a student is able to execute rapidly without external prompting, a single new neuromuscular reaction in the presence of a particular stimulus cue. This can be observed as a muscular movement or combination of movements not previously in the student's repertoire. The important psychological conditions are the presence of a specific cue and the absence of prompts.

Second, chaining behaviour, where a student is able to execute, without external prompting, a coordinated series of reactions which occur in rapid succession in the presence of a particular stimulus cue, is observed as a series of responses, and occurs in the presence of a specified cue and in the absence of prompts.

Third, skilled behaviour is where a student is able to execute sequentially, without external prompting, complex combinations of coordinated psychomotor chains, each initiated in the presence of a particular cue when a large set of such cues are presented. In some skills, cue presentation is externally paced while in other skills cue presentation is self-paced. This is seen as a set of coordinated chains, and occurs when there is a paced or unpaced presentation of a set of cues and an absence of prompts prior to or during the performance.

(c) *Memorization behaviour.* A student immediately reproduces or recognizes, without prompting, a specific symbolic response when presented with a specific stimulus situation. The observable behaviour always involves either reproduction or recognition of a symbolic response, and occurs under psychological conditions similar to those of psychomotor behaviour. Memorization behaviour can be broken into naming behaviour where a student reproduces or recognizes, without prompts, a single symbolic response in the presence of a particular stimulus cue; serial memorization behaviour (verbal association) which occurs in the presence of a particular stimulus cue, so that a student reproduces, without prompting, a series of symbolic responses in a prespecified sequence; and discrete element memorization behaviour (multiple discrimination) where a student reproduces or recognizes, without prompting, a unique symbolic response to each of a set of stimulus cues.

(d) *Complex cognitive behaviour.* The student makes an appropriate response to a previously unencountered instance of some class of stimulus objects, events, or situations. This can further be broken into classification behaviour, analysis behaviour, and problem-solving behaviour.

Classification behaviour (concept learning) is where a student is able to identify correctly the class membership of a previously unencountered object or event, or a previously unencountered representation of some object or event. It occurs when the student must make some kind of class identification, the important psychological conditions being the presentation of unencountered instances or non-instances.

Analysis behaviour (principle learning) is when a student is able to show the relationship between the component concepts of an unencountered situation in which a given principle is specified as relevant. The student must first identify the instances of the several classes involved in the situation and then show the relationship between these classes. The psychological condition of importance is presentation of a situation which the student has not previously analysed or seen analysed.

Problem-solving behaviour is when a student is able to select relevant principles and sequence them into an effective solution strategy when presented with an unencountered problem situation for which the relevant principles are not specified. Creativity and/or divergent thinking occurs when some of the relevant principles are unknown to the student and the strategy developed represents a new higher order principle. It can be observed when the student must synthesize a product which results from analysing several principles in some appropriate sequence and generalize new relationships not previously learned or analysed. The psychological conditions of importance are: an unencountered problem for which the relevant principles are not specified, and which in some cases may require principles not previously analysed by the student or perhaps even by the instructor.

Without any doubt, Gagné–Merrill's taxonomy provides some order in the field of fundamental learning processes. However, it does not claim exhaustivity, and certain categories such as "process learning" and "problem solving" are rather vague.

D'Hainaut (1970) believes that Gagné does not give enough emphasis to the creative processes. Divergent thinking can be categorized under the heading "problem solving", but this category is perhaps too large.

Merrill and Gagné have made two important contributions to the definition of objectives. Their categories are expressed in terms of definite behaviour and the psychological conditions are considered, although these conditions are still to be integrated into an operational definition of objectives.

### 1.4 Gerlach and Sullivan's Taxonomy

Sullivan in association with Gerlach (1967) attempted to replace a description of mental processes in general terms (as in Bloom's taxonomy) by classes of observable learner behaviours which could be used in task description and analysis. Their model is empirical. After listing hundreds of learning behaviours, Sullivan has progressively grouped them into six categories, each headed by a typical verb. The six categories are ordered according to the increasing complexity of behaviours they represent, but the whole does not constitute a rigorous hierarchy and, for that reason, cannot be considered as a true taxonomy.

(a) Identify: the learner indicates membership or non-membership of specified objects or events in a class when the name of the class is given.

(b) Name: the learner supplies the correct verbal label (in speech or writing) for a referent or set of referents when the name of the referent is not given.

(c) Describe: the learner reports the necessary categories of object properties, events, event prop-

erties, and/or relationships relevant to a designated referent.

(d) Construct: the learner produces a product which meets specifications given either in class or in the test item itself.

(e) Order: the learner arranges two or more referents in a specified order.

(f) Demonstrate: the learner performs the behaviours essential to the accomplishment of a designated task according to pre-established or given specifications.

Gerlach and Sullivan consider their "taxonomy" as a check list helping to ensure that no important behaviour is forgotten when planning school activities. This may succeed, as long as "mastery objectives" (i.e., objectives concerning a fully defined behaviour universe) are kept in sight. However, the six categories suggested do not cover creative productions and do not even make a clear place for transfer.

### 1.5 De Block's Taxonomy

De Block (1975) suggests a model of teaching objectives (see Fig. 5). He thinks that teaching pursues objectives in three directions: (a) from partial to more integral learning. Comprehension seems more desirable than rote learning (knowledge); in this perspective, mastery and integration are final objectives; (b) from limited to fundamental learning. Facts gradually become background data; concepts and methods come to the fore; (c) from special to general learning. The objective is thinking in a productive rather than in a reproductive way, taking initiatives, and being able to adapt oneself to a great variety of situations.

The combination of all subcategories yields 72 classes of objectives. De Block's system does not deal sufficiently with the criteria by which it is recognized whether an objective has been achieved or not. However, it can certainly help teachers to reconsider

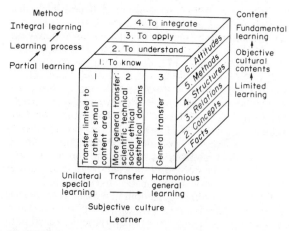

**Figure 5**
De Block's model of instruction

their activities, and to make their students work at higher cognitive or affective levels.

### 1.6 Conclusion to the Cognitive Domain

Not one of these taxonomies can be considered as entirely satisfying. Looking at highly nuanced classifications, only moderate reliability can be hoped for. If the system is reduced to a few operationalized categories, content validity decreases.

The taxonomy of Bloom and his associates has already been used successfully by hundreds of curriculum and test developers throughout the world. Furthermore, it has stimulated fruitful discussion and reflection on the problem of objectives. The several taxonomies that appeared after Bloom are useful to curriculum developers, to test constructors, and to teachers planning their next lesson and preparing mastery tests for their pupils.

## 2. The Affective Domain

According to Bloom, the affective domain includes objectives which describe changes in interest, attitudes, and values, and the development of appreciations and adequate adjustment.

What are the main difficulties in the pursuit of affective objectives? Imprecision of concepts, overlap of the affective and the cognitive domains, cultural bias (Western culture still tends to consider feelings as the most secret part of personality), ignorance about affective learning processes, and poor evaluation instruments.

So far, the only significant taxonomy for the affective domain is the one published by Krathwohl et al. (1964), hence the brevity of this section when compared to the first.

### 2.1 Krathwohl's Taxonomy

The main organizing principles for the cognitive domain were "from simple to complex" and "from concrete to abstract". It soon appeared that these could not be used for the affective domain which dealt with attitudes, interests, values, and so on. After a long search, the authors discovered an ordering principle that was precisely characteristic of affective development: the degree of internalization, that is, the degree of incorporation of the affects within the personality. When the process of internalization is completed, the person feels as if the interests, values, attitudes, etc. were his or her own and lives by them. In Krathwohl's taxonomic terms, the continuum goes from merely being aware that a given phenomenon exists, and giving it a minimum attention, to its becoming one's basic outlook on life. The main organizing principles in Krathwohl's taxonomy are receiving, responding, valuing, organization, and characteristics.

(a) Receiving: "Sensitivity to the existence of certain phenomena and stimuli, that is, the willingness to receive or attend to them." Receiving consists of three subcategories that represent a continuum: (i) awareness; (ii) willingness to receive; and (iii) controlled or selected attention.

(b) Responding: "Behaviour which goes beyond merely attending to the phenomena; it implies active attending, doing something with or about the phenomena, and not merely perceiving them." Subcategories of responding are: (i) acquiescence in responding; (ii) willingness to respond; and (iii) satisfaction in response.

(c) Valuing: "It implies perceiving phenomena as having worth and consequently revealing consistency in behaviour related to these phenomena." The individual is motivated to behave in the line of definite values. Subcategories are: (i) acceptance of a value; (ii) preference for a value; and (iii) commitment.

(d) Organization: "For situations where more than one value is relevant, the necessity arises for (i) the organization of the values into a system; (ii) the determination of the interrelationships among them; and (iii) the establishment of the dominant and pervasive one." Subcategories are: (i) conceptualization of a value and (ii) organization of a value system.

(e) Characteristics by a value or value complex: "The values already have a place in the individual's value hierarchy, are organized into some kind of internally consistent system, have controlled the behaviour of the individual for a sufficient time that he has adapted to behaving in this way." Subcategories are: (i) generalized set and (ii) characterization.

The most striking feature of this taxonomy is its abstract, general character. Krathwohl is aware of the problem. The taxonomy deals with objectives at the curriculum construction level. This means that objectives as defined in the taxonomy are approximately midway between very broad and very general objectives of education and the specific ones which provide guidance for the development of step-by-step learning experiences.

For a short presentation of Krathwohl's taxonomy, G. De Landsheere (1982) tried to find a classification principle that would be easier to formulate in behavioural terms than internalization. He suggested a continuum of activity, or of personal engagement. De Landsheere's frame of reference was developmental psychology. He wrote: "An individual has really reached the adult stage if his behaviour has found its coherence, its logic and stability; he has developed at the same time a sound tolerance to change, contradiction, frustration; he is cognitively and affectively independent; he is, at the same time, able to abide by his engagement and feelings." Education is a long process leading to this ultimate balance.

De Landsheere suggests the following taxonomy:

(a) *The individual responds to external stimulation.*

(i) The individual receives: this is a rather amorphous stage. The individual encounters, for instance, beauty or ugliness without any reaction, like a mirror that would not reflect any image. This behaviour is hard to distinguish from the cognition (in Guilford's sense) that takes place before memorization. Only some manifestation of attention is observable.

(ii) The individual receives and responds to the stimulus: an observable reaction takes place. The individual obeys, manifests pleasure by his or her words or attitudes. At this stage, there is not yet explicit acceptance or rejection that would reflect a deliberate choice.

(iii) The individual receives and reacts by accepting or refusing: now the individual knows what he or she wants or likes, provided things or events are presented.

(b) *The individual takes initiatives.* The individual tries spontaneously to understand, to feel, and then act according to the options available. Here the adult stage is reached. For instance, the individual lives a life in accordance with his or her values, feelings, beliefs, likings, but is also able to change his or her mind if convincing proofs or arguments are offered. This stage is parallel to evaluation in the cognitive domain.

The classification suggested by De Landsheere seems clearer than Krathwohl's taxonomy, but more limited. Objectives can be more easily operationalized, but the criticism of Krathwohl's work also applies here.

## 2.2 Conclusion to the Affective Domain

The situation in the affective domain remains unsatisfactory. Why does it appear that so much work is still to be undertaken in the field? Krathwohl has not succeeded in filling completely the gap in the theoretical framework and the methodology of educational evaluation in the affective domain. A more systematic attack on the problem of affective objectives is required, and, in particular, an inventory of existing studies, experiments, and evaluation instruments in the field should be undertaken. Indubitably, the affective domain will constitute a priority area in the field of educational research in the decades to come.

## 3. The Psychomotor Domain

Why is the psychomotor domain important? First of all, motion is a necessary condition of survival and of independence. Life sometimes depends on physical strength correctly applied, on agility, and on rapidity. Locomotor behaviour is needed to explore the environment and sensory-motor activities are essential for the development of intelligence. Some psychomotor behaviours such as walking and grasping, are also necessary for physical and mental health to be maintained. Dexterity is crucial for the worker, and also in civilizations giving a lot of time to leisure, corporal ability plays a considerable role in artistic and athletic activities.

Numerous taxonomies have been developed for the psychomotor domain. Some of them tend to be comprehensive, in strict parallelism with the taxonomies inspired by Bloom and Krathwohl for the cognitive and affective domains. Others have been developed for specialized fields and have, in many cases, a very technical character. Only six taxonomies which fall in the first category are presented in this article.

Ragsdale, Guilford, Dave, and Kibler's taxonomies are summarized very briefly for they are mainly of historical interest.

### 3.1 Ragsdale's Taxonomy

As early as in 1950, Ragsdale published a classification for "motor types of activities" learned by children. He worked with three categories only: (a) object motor activities (speed, precision): manipulation or acting with direct reference to an object; (b) language motor activities: movement of speech, sight, handwriting; (c) feeling motor activities: movements communicating feelings and attitudes.

These categories are so general that they are of little help in the definition of educational objectives.

### 3.2 Guilford's Taxonomy

Guilford (1958) suggested a simple classification in seven categories that is not hierarchical, and also does not seem of great utility for generating objectives. The seven categories are: power, pressure, speed, static precision, dynamic precision, coordination, and flexibility.

### 3.3 Dave's Taxonomy

Dave's classification (1969), although also rather schematic, can be considered as an embryo of a taxonomy. The categories are: initiation, manipulation, precision, articulation, naturalization (mechanization and internalization). The meaning of the first three categories is clear. Articulation emphasizes the coordination of a series of acts which are performed with appropriate articulation in terms of time, speed, and other relevant variables. As for naturalization, it refers to the highest level of proficiency of an act that has become routine.

### 3.4 Kibler's Classification

Kibler and his associates suggest a classification (1970) more developed than that of previous authors. The main frame of reference is developmental child psychology.

(a) Gross bodily movements: movements of entire limbs in isolation or in conjunction with other parts of the body (movements involving the upper limbs, the lower limbs, two or more bodily units).

(b) Finely coordinated movements: coordinated movements of the extremities, used in conjunction with the eye or ear (hand–finger movements, hand–eye coordination, hand–ear coordination, hand–eye-foot coordination, other combinations of hand–foot–eye–ear movements).

(c) Nonverbal communication behaviours: facial expression, gestures (use of hands and arms to communicate specific messages), bodily movements (total bodily movements whose primary purposes are the communication of a message or series of messages).

(d) Speech behaviours: sound production (ability to produce meaningful sounds), sound–word formation (ability to coordinate sounds in meaningful words and messages), sound projection (ability to project sounds across the air waves at a level adequate for reception and decoding by the listener), sound–gesture coordination (ability to coordinate facial expression, movement, and gestures with verbal messages).

### 3.5 Simpson's Taxonomy (1966)

Simpson's taxonomy can be divided into five main categories.
(a) *Perception.* This is the process of becoming aware of objects, qualities, or relations by way of the sense organs.

(i) Sensory stimulation: impingement of a stimulus upon one or more of the sense organs (auditory, visual, tactile, taste, smell, kinesthesic).

(ii) Cue-selection: deciding to what cues one must respond in order to satisfy the particular requirements of task performance, for example, recognition of operating difficulties with machinery through the sound of the machine in operation.

(iii) Translation: relation of perception of action in performing a motor act. This is the mental process of determining the meaning of the cues received for action, for example, the ability to relate music to dance form.

(b) *Set.* Preparatory adjustment of readiness for a particular kind of action or experience.

(i) Mental set: readiness, in the mental sense, to perform a certain motor act.

(ii) Physical set: readiness in the sense of having made the anatomical adjustments necessary for a motor act to be performed.

(iii) Emotional set: readiness in terms of attitudes favourable to the motor act's taking place.

(c) *Guided response.* Overt behavioural act of an individual under the guidance of the instructor (imitation,

trial and error).

(d) *Mechanism.* Learned response became habitual.

(e) *Complex overt response.* The individual can perform a motor act that is considered complex because of the movement pattern required. A high degree of skill has been attained. The act can be carried out smoothly and efficiently.

(i) Resolution of uncertainty: the act is performed without hesitation.

(ii) Automatic performance: the individual can perform a finely coordinated motor skill with a great deal of ease and muscle control.

Simpson suggests that there is perhaps a sixth major category: adapting and originating. "At this level, the individual might originate new patterns of actions in solving a specific problem."

The weakness of this taxonomy is to be found again in its very abstract and general formulation.

### 3.6 Harrow's Taxonomy

As operationally defined by Harrow (1972), the term "psychomotor" covers any human voluntary observable movement that belongs to the domain of learning. Harrow's taxonomy is the best available for the psychomotor domain, although some of the category descriptives are unsatisfactory:

(a) Reflex movements: segmental, intersegmental, suprasegmental reflexes.

(b) Basic–fundamental movements: locomotor, nonlocomotor, manipulative movements.

(c) Perceptual abilities:
    Kinesthetic discrimination: body awareness (bilaterality, laterality, sidedness, balance), body image, body relationship of surrounding objects in space.
    Visual discrimination: visual acuity, visual tracking, visual memory, figure–ground differentiation, perceptual consistency.
    Auditory discrimination: auditory acuity, tracking, memory.
    Tactile discrimination.
    Coordinated abilities: eye–hand and eye–foot coordination.

(d) Physical abilities: endurance (muscular and cardiovascular endurance), strength, flexibility, agility (change direction, stops and starts, reaction–response time, dexterity).

(e) Skilled movements: simple adaptive skill (beginner, intermediate, advanced, highly skilled), compound adaptive skill (beginner, intermediate, advanced, highly skilled), complex adaptive skill (beginner, intermediate, advanced, highly skilled).

(f) Nondiscursive communication: expressive movement (posture and carriage, gestures, facial expression), interpretative movement (aesthetic movement, creative movement).

In fact, Harrow does not describe her model in relation to a general, unique criterion (i.e. co-ordination), but simply looks for a critical order; mastery at an inferior level is absolutely necessary to achieve the immediate higher level in the hierarchy of movements.

This taxonomy has great qualities. First, it seems complete, not only it its description of the major categories of psychomotor behaviour, but also in terms of the subcategories within the different taxonomic levels. Furthermore, the author defines the different levels clearly. For each subcategory, she proposes a clear definition of the concept and indicates, where necessary, the differences from other authors who have written in this field. She also presents concrete examples.

Harrow's taxonomy seems to be of direct use to teachers in physical education. Level (c) is specially interesting for preschool and for elementary-school teachers. It contains a good example of a battery for testing the perceptive abilities of pupils, diagnosing difficulties, and proposing appropriate remedial exercises. The author underlines the dependence between the cognitive and psychomotor domains at the level of perceptual abilities. Several examples also show the great interrelation between the three domains. However, Harrow's hierarchy is not governed by a specified criterion, such as internalization or coordination. Moreover, the subcategories are not mutually exclusive.

### 3.7 Conclusion to the Psychomotor Domain

It seems that taxonomies in the psychomotor domain have not yet been given the attention they deserve. They should be tried in many varied situations and their relations with the other two domains should be carefully investigated.

### 4. Conclusion

The cognitive domain is the best developed. First, it is by nature favourable to the construction of logical models. Second, schools have traditionally been interested in cognitive learning, especially in the acquisition of factual knowledge which in turn leads to easy evaluation.

Compared with the cognitive domain, the affective domain is less developed. Only since about 1970 has the educational world been trying to change the situation (in the past, affectivity has sometimes been intensively cultivated, but nearly always in terms of indoctrination processes). Affects seem less observable than cognitive activities and in most cases are less susceptible to rigorous measurement.

One would think that the psychomotor domain would present fewer difficulties, but little systematic work has been undertaken. In most Western educational systems,

physical and artistic education is comparatively neglected in the curriculum.

Despite certain weaknesses, the two taxonomies with which Bloom is associated, and Harrow's taxonomy dominate the field. The others should, however, not be neglected, since they supply further clarifications and suggestions.

At present, the taxonomy movement in education is of great value. Even though the instruments are so far imperfect, they stimulate educators to fruitful reflection. Half-way between the great ideological options and the micro-objectives, the taxonomies seem to relate philosophy and educational technology and practice. It is one of their great merits.

### Bibliography

Bacher F 1973 La docimologie. In: Reuchlin M (ed.) 1973 *Traité de psychologie appliquée*. Presses Universitaires de France (PUF), Paris

Bloom B S (ed.) 1956 *Taxonomy of Educational Objectives: The Classification of Educational Goals*, Handbook 1: *Cognitive Domain*. McKay, New York

Dave R H 1969 *Taxonomy of Educational Objectives and Achievement Testing. Developments in Educational Testing*, Vol. 1. University of London Press, London

De Block A 1975 *Taxonomie van Leerdoelen*. Standard Wetenschappelijke Uitgererij, Amsterdam

De Corte E 1973 *Onderwijsdoelstellingen*. Universitaire Pers, Louvain

De Landsheere G 1982 *Introduction à la recherche en éducation*. Thone, Liège; Armand Colin, Paris

De Landsheere V, De Landsheere G 1984 *Définir les objectifs de l'éducation*. Presses Universitaires de France (PUF), Paris

D'Hainaut L 1970 Un modèle pour la détermination et la sélection des objectifs pédagogiques du domaine cognitif. *Enseignement Programmé* 11: 21–38

Ebel R L 1973 Evaluation and educational objectives. *J. Educ. Meas.* 10: 273–79

Gagné R M 1964 The implications of instructional objectives for learning. In: Lindvall C M (ed.) 1964 *Defining Educational Objectives*. University of Pittsburgh Press, Pittsburgh, Pennsylvania

Gerlach V, Sullivan A 1967 *Constructing Statements of Outcomes*. Southwest Regional Laboratory for Educational Research and Development, Inglewood, California

Guilford J P 1958 A system of psychomotor abilities. *Am. J. Psychol.* 71: 164–74

Guilford J P 1967 *The Nature of Human Intelligence*. McKay, New York

Harrow A J 1972 *A Taxonomy of the Psychomotor Domain: A Guide for Developing Behavioral Objectives*. McKay, New York

Hill P W 1984 Testing hierarchy in educational taxonomies: A theoretical and empirical investigation. *Eval. Educ.* 8: 181–278

Horn R 1972 *Lernziele und Schülerleistung: Die Evaluation von den Lernzielen im kognitiven Bereich*, 2nd edn. Beltz, Weinheim

Kibler R J, Barker L L, Miles D T 1970 *Behavioral Objectives and Instruction*. Allyn and Bacon, Boston, Massachusetts

Krathwohl D R, Bloom B S, Masia B B 1964 *Taxonomy of Educational Objectives: The Classification of Educational Goals*, Handbook 2: *Affective Domain*. McKay, New York

Madaus G F, Woods E N, Nuttal R L 1973 A causal model analysis of Bloom's taxonomy. *Am. Educ. Res. J.* 10: 253–62

Merrill M D 1971 Necessary psychological conditions for defining instructional outcomes. In: M D Merrill (ed.) 1971 *Instructional Design: Readings.* Prentice-Hall, Englewood Cliffs, New Jersey

Metfessel N S, Michael W B, Kirsner D A 1970 Instrumentation of Bloom's and Krathwohl's taxonomies for the writing of educational objectives. In: Kibler R J, Barker L L, Miles D J (eds.) 1970 *Behavioural Objectives and Instruction.* Allyn and Bacon, Boston, Massachusetts

Ragsdale C E 1950 How children learn motor types of activities. *Learning and Instruction.* 49th Yearbook of the National Society for the Study of Education, Washington, DC

Simpson E J 1966 *The Classification of Educational Objectives, Psychomotor Domain.* University of Illinois, Urbana, Illinois

# A Twenty-year Perspective on Educational Objectives[1]

## W. J. Popham

Educational evaluation, by most people's reckoning, was spawned as a formal educational speciality in the mid-1960s. In the United States, the emergence of educational evaluation was linked directly to the 1965 enactment by the US Congress of the Elementary and Secondary Education Act (ESEA). Focused on educational improvement, this precedent-setting legislation provided substantial federal financial support to local school districts each year, but only on condition that officials in those districts had evaluated the previous year's federally supported programs. This legislation soon proved effective in motivating US school officials to discover what educational evaluations actually were and, having done so, to carry them out. There were, of course, ample instances wherein school officials reversed the order of those two steps.

During the early years of educational evaluation, considerable attention was given to the role of educational objectives. Indeed, in view of the mid-1960s preoccupation of US educators with educational objectives and educational evaluation, it might reasonably be assumed that they had developed from the same origins. Such, however, was not the case.

## 1. An Alternative Origin

North American educators' attention to educational objectives was not triggered by mid-1960s federal education legislation. A series of developments in the field of instructional psychology, quite separate from such federal initiatives, resulted in the need for heightened attention to statements of instructional intent. It was the activity of instructional psychologists, not educational evaluators, that first focused the attention of US educators on the way in which statements of educational objectives were formulated.

More specifically, in the late 1950s Skinner (1958) captured the attention of numerous educators as he proffered laboratory-derived principles for teaching children. Skinner's notions of carefully sequencing instructional materials in small steps, providing frequent positive reinforcement for learners, and allowing learners to move through such instructional materials at their own pace were, to many educators, both revolutionary and exciting. A key tenet of Skinner's approach involved the tryout and revision of instructional materials until they were demonstrably effective. Because Skinner believed that such "programmed instruction" could be effectively presented to learners via mechanical means (Skinner 1958), the prospect of "teaching machines" both captured the fancy of many lay people and, predictably, aroused the apprehension of many educators.

Central to the strategy embodied in all of the early approaches to programmed instruction, including the small-step scheme espoused by Skinner, was the necessity to explicate, in terms as unambiguous as possible, the objective(s) of an instructional sequence. More precisely, early programmed instruction enthusiasts recognized that if an instructional sequence was to be tried out and revised until successful, it was necessary to have a solid criterion against which to judge the program's success. Hence, programmed instruction specialists universally urged that the effectiveness of instructional programs be judged according to their ability to achieve preset instructional objectives.

Without question, Robert Mager's 1962 primer on how to write instructional objectives served as the single most important force in familiarizing educators with measurable instructional objectives. Consistent with its roots, Mager's introduction to the topic of objectives was originally entitled *Preparing Objectives for Programmed Instruction* (1962). Later, as interest in the book burgeoned, it was retitled more generally as *Preparing Instructional Objectives*. Organized as a branching program, it allowed readers to gain considerable expertise on the topic, in less than an hour's reading. During the mid-1960s copies of Mager's cleverly written booklet found their way into the hands of numerous educators and, even more importantly, influentially placed federal education officials.

When, in the aftermath of the 1965 ESEA enactment,

1  This article was originally published in the *International Journal of Educational Research*, Vol. 11, No. 1. It appears here with permission from Pergamon Press plc © 1987.

federal officials attempted to guide US educators toward defensible ESEA evaluation paradigms, they found an on-the-shelf evaluation approach best articulated by Ralph Tyler (1950). The Tyler strategy hinged on an evaluator determining the extent to which the instructional program being evaluated had promoted learner attainment of prespecified educational objectives. Such an objectives-attainment conception of educational evaluation, while destined to be replaced in future years by a number of alternative paradigms, seemed eminently sensible to many highly placed officials in the US Office of Education. Both implicitly and explicitly, therefore, an objectives-attainment model of educational evaluation was soon being fostered by US federal officials at the precise time that US educators were becoming conversant with the sorts of measurable instructional objectives being argued for by programmed instruction proponents.

In retrospect, it is far from surprising that a Tylerian conception of objectives-based educational evaluation became wedded to a Magerian approach to objectives formulation. That marriage occurred in such a way that many neophyte educational evaluators assumed the only bona fide way to evaluate an educational program was to see if its measurably stated educational objectives had been achieved.

The unthinking adoption of an objectives-attainment approach to educational evaluation led, in many instances, to the advocacy of evaluation models in which positive appraisals of an educational program were rendered if its objectives had been achieved—irrespective of the defensibility of those objectives. Not that Tyler had been oblivious to the quality of educational objectives, for in his writings (Tyler 1950) he stressed the importance of selecting one's educational objectives only after systematic scrutiny of a range of potential objectives.

In his classic 1967 analytic essay on educational evaluation, M Scriven, having witnessed cavalier applications of objectives-attainment evaluations in the numerous national curriculum-development projects then underway, attempted to distinguish between what he viewed as genuine evaluation and mere estimations of goal-achievement (Scriven 1967). In his subsequent observations regarding the role of educational objectives in evaluating educational programs, however, Scriven still came down solidly on the side of measurably stated objectives (Scriven 1971).

As can be seen, then, although educational objectives in the United States trace their lineage more directly from instructional psychology than educational evaluation, such objectives were widely accepted during the early years as an integral component of evaluation methodologies—particularly those based on objectives-attainment.

## 2. The Behavioral Objectives Debate

It was in the late 1960s and early 1970s that instructional objectives per se captured the attention of many educational evaluators. Many evaluators subscribed, at least rhetorically, to the form of measurable objectives set forth in the 1962 Mager booklet. Such instructional objectives had become known as behavioral objectives because, at bottom, they revolved around the post-instruction behavior of learners. Yet, although behavioral objectives were espoused by many (e.g., Glaser 1965, Popham 1965), a number of writers put forth heated criticisms of behaviorally stated objectives (e.g., Arnstine 1964, Eisner 1967).

Proponents of behavioral objectives argued that such objectives embodied a rational approach to evaluation because they enhanced clarity regarding the nature of one's instructional aspirations. Critics countered that because the most important goals of education did not lend themselves readily to a behavioral formulation, the preoccupation with behavioral objectives would lead to instructional reductionism wherein the trivial was sought merely because it was measurable. Disagreements regarding the virtues of behavioral objectives were frequent at professional meetings of that era, some of those disputes finding their way into print (e.g., Popham et al. 1969). Indeed, the arguments against behavioral objectives became so numerous as to be cataloged (Popham et al. 1969).

Although the academic dialogue regarding the virtues of behavioral objectives lingered until the early 1970s, most US educational evaluators who made use of objectives tended to frame those objectives behaviorally. The bulk of professional opinion, whether or not warranted, seemed to support the merits of behaviorally stated objectives. And, because many educational evaluators believed it important to take cognizance of an educational program's instructional goals, behaviorally stated instructional objectives were commonly encountered in evaluation reports, and are to this day.

Perhaps the most serious shortcoming of behavioral objectives, however, was not widely recognized during the first decade of educational evaluation. That shortcoming stems from the common tendency to frame behavioral objectives so that they focus on increasingly smaller and more specific segments of learner post-instruction behavior. The net effect of such hyperspecificity is that the objectives formulator ends up with a plethora of picayune outcomes. Although early critics of behavioral objectives were wary of what they believed to be a tendency toward triviality in such objectives, no critic predicted what turned out to be the most profound problem with small-scope behavioral objectives. Putting it pragmatically, the typical set of narrow-scope behavioral objectives turned out to be so numerous that decision-makers would not attend to evidence of objective-attainment. After all, if decision-makers were quite literally overwhelmed with lengthy lists of behavioral objectives, how could they meaningfully focus on whether such objectives were achieved?

Simply stated, the most important lesson that has

been learned about the use of behaviorally stated objectives for purposes of educational evaluation is that less is most definitely more. Too many objectives benumb the decision-maker's mind. Too many objectives, because decision-makers will not attend to them, are completely dysfunctional.

The discovery, based on experience, that too many behavioral objectives did not result in improved decision-making does not, of course, indicate a need to retreat to an era when educational objectives were fashioned in the form of broad, vacuous generalities. There is a decisively preferable alternative, namely, to coalesce small-scope behaviors under larger, albeit still measurable behavioral rubrics. Thus, instead of focusing on 40 small-scope objectives, evaluators would present decision-makers with only five or six broad-scope, measurable objectives. To illustrate, if an objective describes a "student's ability to solve mathematical word problems requiring two of the four basic operations, that is, addition, subtraction, multiplication, and division," that objective covers a good deal of mathematical territory. A modest number of such broad-scope objectives will typically capture the bulk of a program's important intentions.

## 3. Taxonomies of Educational Objectives

In 1956 Benjamin Bloom and his colleagues brought forth a taxonomy of educational objectives in which they drew distinctions among objectives focusing on cognitive, affective, and psychomotor outcomes (Bloom et al. 1956). In their analysis, Bloom and his coauthors attended chiefly to the cognitive taxonomy, laying out six levels of what they argued were discernibly different types of hierarchically arranged cognitive operations. These cognitive operations, they argued, were needed by learners to satisfy different types of educational objectives. Eight years later, in 1964, David Krathwohl and his coworkers provided us with a second taxonomy focused on five levels of affective-domain objectives (Krathwohl et al. 1964). Although several taxonomies of psychomotor objectives were published shortly thereafter, none attracted the support of the initial two taxonomies dealing with cognitive and affective objectives.

The 1956 *Taxonomy of Educational Objectives: Handbook 1: The Cognitive Domain* initially attracted scant attention. Sales of the book were modest for its first several years of existence. However, at the time that US educators turned their attention to instructional objectives in the early 1960s, they found in their libraries an objectives-analysis scheme of considerable sophistication. Sales of the cognitive taxonomy became substantial and the six levels of the taxonomy, ranging from "knowledge" at the lowest level to "evaluation" at the highest level, became part of the lexicon employed by those who worked with educational objectives. Although the affective taxonomy never achieved the substantial popularity of the cognitive taxonomy, it too

attracted its share of devotees.

Educational evaluators started to use these objectives-classification systems to classify objectives. Much attention was given, for example, to the appropriate allocation of objectives to various taxonomic categories. Some evaluators would classify each of a program's objectives according to its proper taxonomic niche in the hope of bringing greater clarity to the objectives being sought. Several authors even went to the trouble of identifying the action verbs in instructional objectives which would be indicative of particular levels of the taxonomies (e.g., Gronlund 1971, Sanders 1966). Thus, if an objective called for the student to "select from alternatives" this was thought to represent a specific taxonomic level whereas, if the learner were asked to "compose an essay", then a different taxonomic level was reflected. It is saddening to recall how much time educational evaluators and other instructional personnel devoted to teasing out the taxonomic distinctions between different objectives. For, in the main, this activity made no practical difference to anyone.

One problem with the taxonomies is that they focus on covert processes of individuals, processes whose nature must be inferred from observable overt behaviors. For the cognitive taxonomy, to illustrate, teachers could ask students to write an essay in which discrete information is coalesced, and could then infer that the "synthesis" level of the taxonomy had been achieved because the student wrote the requested essay. However, it is quite possible that the student merely parroted an analysis he or she had incidentally overheard a short time earlier. In that instance, memory rather than synthesizing ability would have been displayed and a different level of the cognitive taxonomy been represented. Unless we have a solid understanding of the prior history of the learner, it is difficult, if not impossible, to know whether a given type of learner response represents a higher or lower order process. Answering a challenging multiple-choice test item may represent the "application" level of the taxonomy unless, of course, the correct answer to the question was discussed and practiced during a previous class. There is, obviously, peril in attempting to inferentially tie down the unobservable.

An even more substantial shortcoming with taxonomic analyses of educational objectives is that even were such analyses accurate, the meaningful yield from isolating the taxonomic levels of educational objectives would be questionable. Are educational decision-makers truly advantaged as a consequence of such classification machinations? Is it, in fact, the case that higher-level objectives are more laudable than lower-level objectives? Or, more sensibly, should the defensibility of an educational objective not really be determined on its intrinsic merits rather than its taxonomic pigeon hole?

The taxonomies of educational objectives brought to educational evaluators a helpful heuristic when used as a broad-brush way of viewing a program's educational aspirations. While it is of course useful to recognize, for instance, that there are no affective objectives sought by a program and that its cognitive objectives deal predominantly with rote-recall knowledge, beyond such general appraisals, fine-grained taxonomic analyses yield dividends of debatable utility.

## 4. Measurement and Objectives

There are some educational objectives that require little or nothing in the way of assessment devices to indicate whether they have been accomplished. For instance, if the chief objective of a "make-school-interesting" campaign is to reduce absenteeism, then the verification of that objective's attainment hinges on a clerk's counting absence records. If the nature of the educational objective being considered does not require the use of formal assessment devices such as tests or inventories, then objectives can be employed without much attention to assessment considerations.

Yet, because program objectives in the field of education often focus on improving the status of students' knowledge, attitudes, or skills, determination that most educational objectives have been achieved hinges on the use of some type of formal assessment device. During the past two decades, educational evaluators have learned some important lessons about how to use such assessment devices in order to establish whether educational objectives have been achieved.

For one thing, it is now generally accepted that, for purposes of educational evaluation, criterion-referenced tests are to be strongly preferred over their norm-referenced counterparts. The distinction between traditional norm-referenced tests and the newer criterion-referenced tests had been initially drawn by Robert Glaser (Glaser 1963). Glaser characterized norm-referenced measures as instruments yielding *relative* interpretations such as the percentage of examinees in a normative group whose performance had been exceeded by a given examinee's performance. In contrast, criterion-referenced measures yielded *absolute* interpretations such as whether or not an examinee could master a well-defined set of criterion behaviors. Although the utility of this distinction was generally accepted, precious little attention was given to criterion-referenced testing by educational measurement specialists until the 1970s.

It was during the 1970s, indeed, that increasing numbers of educational evaluators began to recognize a continuing pattern of "no significant differences" whenever norm-referenced achievement tests were employed as indicators of an educational objective's achievement. Evaluators began to recognize that the generality with which norm-referenced test publishers described what those tests measured made it difficult to inform decision-makers of what a program's effects actually were. Of equal seriousness was the tendency of norm-referenced test-makers to delete test items on which students performed well because such items contributed insufficiently to detecting the variance among examinees so crucial for effective norm-referenced interpretations. Such deleted items, however, often tapped the very content being stressed by teachers, hence norm-referenced tests frequently turned out to be remarkably insensitive to detecting the effects of even outstanding instructional programs.

Although almost all educational evaluators recognized that norm-referenced tests were better than nothing, the 1970s were marked by growing dissatisfaction on the part of evaluators with norm-referenced achievement tests. Yet it was soon discovered that not one test that was paraded by its creators as a "criterion-referenced" assessment device was, in fact, a meaningful improvement over its norm-referenced predecessors. Many of the so-called criterion-referenced tests of the 1970s were ineffectual.

The chief dividend of a well-constructed criterion-referenced test, at least from the perspective of educational evaluators, is that it yields an explicit description of what is being measured. This, in time, permits more accurate inferences to be made regarding the meaning of test scores, and because of such heightened clarity, educational evaluators can provide decision-makers with more meaningfully interpretable data.

This clarification dividend, of course, flows only from properly constructed criterion-referenced tests, not merely any test masquerading in criterion-referenced costuming. Educational evaluators, burned too often because of poorly constructed criterion-referenced tests, have learned to be far more suspicious of such tests. Although preferring tests of the criterion-referenced genre, evaluators are now forced to scrutinize such assessment contenders with care. It is impossible to tell whether an educational objective has been achieved if the assessment device used to assess its attainment is tawdry.

The previous discussion was focused on tests used to determine the attainment of educational objectives in the cognitive domain, and also touched on the assessment of affectively oriented educational objectives. The major lesson learned is that there are very few assessment devices at hand suitable for the determination of students' affective status such as, for example, their attitudes toward self, school, or society. There was a fair amount of pro-affect talk by US educators in the 1960s and 1970s, and it was believed by many evaluators that this attention to affect would be followed by the creation of assessment instruments appropriate for tapping affective outcomes of interest. Regrettably, affective instruments suitable for determining whether affectively oriented objectives have been achieved, have yet to be constructed.

Most of the affective measures created by evaluators during the past decade clearly require far more cultivation. Too often an evaluator with modest measurement acumen has attempted to quickly construct an affective inventory (modally, a "modified Likert-type" scale), then introduce it, unimproved, into the evaluation debate. Not surprisingly, such quickly contrived assessment devices usually proved to be of no value. Slapdash affective measures yield information only as good as the effort that went into obtaining it. Evaluators now recognize that there is not a huge array of predefined affective measures to be employed in evaluations, and that the development of acceptable affective assessment instruments is a task more formidable than formerly believed.

This discussion of the relationship between educational objectives and measures leads naturally into a choice-point for evaluators. Should educational evaluators focus on program objectives initially, then move toward measurement, or leap directly toward measurement and dispense with objectives altogether? Although it is true that objectives without assessment often represent only a planner's rhetoric, it is difficult to deny that framing one's intentions clearly can aid in both program design and the subsequent formative and/or summative evaluation of the program. There seems to be virtue, however, in first determining what the range of available assessment options actually is, then framing one's objectives in such a way that those objectives are linked to available instrumentation. To formulate educational objectives while remaining oblivious of assessment possibilities is folly.

## 5. Separable Performance Standards

When Mager (1962) proffered his conception of an acceptable instructional objective, he argued that such an objective would: (a) identify and name the student behavior sought; (b) define any important conditions under which the behavior was to occur; and (c) define a level of acceptable performance. Thus, an example of an acceptable Magerian objective might be something like this:

> The student must be able, in 10 minutes or less, to name correctly the items depicted in 18 of 20 previously unencountered blueprints.

(Note that the student behavior, "to name", is depicted along with two conditions: the necessity to carry out the naming "in 10 minutes or less", plus the fact that the blueprints should be "previously unencountered". In addition, the objective establishes the performance level as "18 of 20" correct.) Twenty years on, however, evaluators have learned that the behavior identified in the objective, and the performance level sought from that behavior, are decisively separable. Indeed, there is substantial virtue in keeping an objective's behavior and performance standards distinct. If evaluators are forced to attach a performance standard to educational objectives in advance of a program's implementation, it is almost always the case that the standard will be arbitrary and indefensible. In most settings it makes far more sense to await the program's impact, then render an experience-informed judgment regarding acceptable levels of performance.

Since the middle of the 1970s we have seen considerable attention directed toward the establishment of defensible performance standards (e.g., Zieky and Livingston 1977). Most of this work has been linked to competency testing programs and the need to establish acceptable performance on competency tests for, say, awarding of high school diplomas. There is no reason why educational evaluators cannot profit from this standard-setting literature and apply it to judgments regarding hoped-for program effectiveness. The isolation of the student behaviors to be sought is, however, a different task to the determination of how well those behaviors must be displayed. Mixing behavioral aspirations and performance standards in educational objectives adds not clarity but confusion.

## 6. Guidelines for Evaluators

In current educational evaluations, the role of educational objectives is typically modest. While early educational evaluators were frequently caught up in the importance of objectives, today's educational evaluators typically focus on evidence of program effects irrespective of whether those effects were ensconced in prespecified objectives. Although objectives are regarded as useful mechanisms for inducing clarity of intent, they are not considered the *sine qua non* of sensible evaluations. For those evaluators who do employ educational objectives in their work, the following guidelines are offered. They have been drawn from the experience-derived observations outlined above regarding the evolution of educational objectives as used by evaluation personnel during the preceding 20-plus years.

(a) *Educational evaluators should formulate or recommend educational objectives so that the degree to which an objective has been achieved can be objectively determined.* Hindsight informed us that the early advocates of behaviorally stated instructional objectives chose the wrong label, namely, behavioral objectives. Not only did that descriptor result in acrimonious repercussions in the 1960s, it still arouses the ire of critics (for example Wesson 1983). However, whether characterized as behavioral, measurable, or performance objectives, an objective that does not permit us to judge reliably when it has been attained is of limited utility to educational evaluators. Elsewhere it has been argued that, for purposes of curricular design, a modest proportion of objectives targeted at the ineffable may be of value (Popham 1972). Yet for educational evaluators who must communicate with decision-makers, the ineffable has its limitations. Thus, if an objective is stated nonbehaviorally, it should be accompanied by an indication of how the attainment of that objective will be established.

(b) *Educational evaluators should eschew numerous narrow-scope educational objectives and, instead, focus* on a manageable number of broad-scope objectives. Educational evaluation is a decision-oriented endeavor. Decision-makers need to have access to information that will increase the wisdom of their decisions. Decision-makers who are inundated with numerous objectives will pay heed to none. Too much information confuses the prospective user of that information. Educational evaluators must encourage program personnel to coalesce narrow-scope objectives under broader rubrics so that decision-makers need contemplate only a comprehensible amount of data. Evaluators who countenance a gaggle of narrow-scope objectives do a disservice to both program personnel and decision-makers. Less is truly more.

(c) *Educational evaluators should employ the Taxonomies of Educational Objectives only as gross heuristics, not fine-grained analytic tools.* When evaluators use the taxonomies to remind themselves and program personnel that there are, in truth, affective, psychomotor, and cognitive objectives—and that most cognitive objectives articulated by today's educators demand only the recall of information—they have discovered the bulk of taxonomic treasure. More detailed use of the taxonomies typically result in analyzing with a microscope objectives fashioned with a sledgehammer.

(d) *If measurement devices are required to ascertain an educational objective's attainment, educational evaluators should employ criterion-referenced rather than norm-referenced measures.* This guideline assumes the existence of properly constructed criterion-referenced tests. Such an assumption requires sufficient sophistication on the part of the evaluator to distinguish between useful and useless criterion-referenced tests. It was also suggested in this analysis that, whenever possible, educational evaluators should encourage program personnel to formulate their objectives so that they are operationally linked to acceptable measuring devices.

(e) *Educational evaluators should keep separate the behavioral focus of educational objectives from the performance levels expected of students.* Above all, educational objectives should bring with them a degree of clarification which elevates the rigor of rational decision-making. Embodiment of standard setting in the objective itself typically adds confusion, not clarity, to statements of instructional intent. Moreover, the premature setting of performance standards often leads to indefensible and arbitrary performance expectations.

## 7. Conclusion

As one looks back over two-plus decades of educational evaluation and the role that educational objectives have played during that period, it is clear that interest in objectives per se has abated. For a while, behavioral objectives were like new toys, and it seemed everyone wanted to play. More than 20 years worth of experience has shown that there are other evaluation games worth

playing. In the late 1980s, test results capture far more of the decision-maker's attention than assertions about how many objectives were or were not achieved. As has been stressed throughout this analysis, statements of instructional intent can accomplish much good. When we clarifiy our educational aspirations in precise form, it is both easier to fashion programs to achieve those aspirations and to mold evaluation endeavors that help us see to what extent our objectives were achieved. Clearly stated educational objectives can help an evaluator if their import is not over-emphasized. Skillfully employed, educational objectives can contribute to more defensible evaluations.

## Bibliography

Arnstine D G 1964 The language and values of programmed instruction: Part 2. *Educ. Forum* 28: 337–46

Bloom B S, Engelhart M D, Furst E J, Hill W H, Krathwohl D R 1956 *Taxonomy of Educational Objectives*, Handbook 1: *The Cognitive Domain*. Longmans, Green, New York

Eisner E W 1967 Educational objectives: Help or hindrance? *Sch. Rev.* 75: 250–66

Glaser R 1963 Instructional technology and the measurement of learning outcomes: Some questions. *Am. Psychol.* 18: 519–21

Glaser R (ed.) 1965 *Teaching Machines and Programmed Learning* Vol. II: *Data and Directions*. Department of Audiovisual Instruction, (National Education Association) NEA, Washington, DC

Gronlund N E 1971 *Measurement and Evaluation in Teaching*, 2nd edn. Macmillan, New York

Krathwohl D R, Bloom B S, Masia B B 1964 *Taxonomy of Educational Objectives: The Classification of Educational Goals*, Handbook 2: *Affective Domain*. David McKay, New York

Mager R F 1962 *Preparing Objectives for Programmed Instruction*. Fearon Press, Palo Alto, California

Popham W J 1965 *The Teacher Empiricist*. Aegeus Press, Los Angeles, California

Popham W J 1972 Must all objectives be behavioral? *Educ. Leadership* 29: 605–08

Popham W J, Eisner E W, Sullivan H J, Tyler L L 1969 *Instructional Objectives*, AERA Monograph Series on Curriculum Evaluation. Rand McNally, Chicago, Illinois

Sanders N M 1966 *Classroom Questions: What Kinds?* Harper and Row, New York

Scriven M 1967 The methodology of evaluation. In: Tyler R W, Gagné R M, Scriven M (eds.) 1967 *Perspectives of Curriculum Evaluation*, AERA Monograph Series on Curriculum Evaluation. Rand McNally, Chicago, Illinois, pp. 39–83

Scriven M 1971 *Evaluation Skills*, AERA Training Tape Series 6B. Audiotape distributed by the American Educational Research Association, Washington, DC

Skinner B F 1958 Teaching machines. *Science* 128: 969–77

Tyler R W 1949 *Basic Principles of Curriculum and Instruction*. University of Chicago Press, Chicago, Illinois

Wesson A J 1983 Behaviourally defined objectives: A critique, Part 1. *Vocat. Aspect of Educ.* 35(91): 51–58

Zieky M J, Livingston S A 1977 *Manual for Setting Standards on the Basic Skill Assessment Tests*. Educational Testing Service, Princeton, New Jersey

# Qualitative Curriculum Evaluation

## G. Willis

Qualitative curriculum evaluation, also known as "educational criticism," cannot be defined by a fixed set of procedures, nor by a specific kind of data. It is not an effort to develop universal, invariant, or even unambiguous knowledge and valuations about educational situations and thus can be contrasted sharply with the typical positivistic pursuits which have dominated Western educational research during much of the twentieth century. Nor should it be confused with forms of research (such as some kinds of ethnography) which deal with qualitative data but from a scientific or technological perspective, thus deriving limited valuations or no valuations at all.

Consistent with, and partially developed in its modern form, from such sources as phenomenology, hermeneutics, and critical theory, qualitative curriculum evaluation aims at expanding reflective human understanding of specific educational situations and promoting moral action within these situations and their social contexts. To do so, qualitative curriculum evaluators immerse themselves in educational situations, not only to discover their tangible characteristics, but also to discern personally their salient but intangible qualities. Each evaluator derives meanings and valuations (including tendencies to action) which he or she shares with others in order to provide new and multiple perspectives on each situation under investigation. However, since neither meanings nor valuations exist apart from context, qualitative evaluators extend their investigations to the personal and social contexts of specific situations. Hence, qualitative curriculum evaluation can be defined as reflective effort to develop the fullest possible range of knowledge (including personal knowledge) about specific educational situations, and to derive meanings and valuations about situations within the fullest possible range of knowledge about their contexts in order to enlarge understanding and to promote moral action. To fulfill these aims, qualitative curriculum evaluation treats curriculum in the fullest possible way, as the experience of the student. In general, it encourages reflection by using naturalistic methodology, proceeding through a case study format, and incorporating four phases of criticism (observation, description, interpretation, and appraisal).

Since qualitative curriculum evaluation includes empiricism and employs enumeration whenever appropriate, it cannot be differentiated from other forms of curriculum evaluation by reference to quantification or lack thereof. Other forms of evaluation consistent with a scientific or technological perspective ordinarily strive for objective, usually hypothetical–deductive knowledge about educational situations by limiting themselves to controlled research designs and statistically derived generalizations about empirical data only. A major contrast between qualitative and scientific or technological studies is, therefore, that the latter are often neither about the fullness of educational situations nor valuations. Their principal concern is precise measurement of specified characteristics of situations. For instance, they may provide evidence about whether certain goals of a program or curriculum have been realized, but may say nothing, in and of themselves, about many other matters, such as whether the goals were worth attempting to realize in the first place. Though the latter kind of study has been used extensively in Western education during the twentieth century, qualitative curriculum evaluation is actually much older. In fact, in rudimentary, undeveloped form it is the means used by virtually all people to derive meanings and valuations in their own lives. Since the mid-1970s it has been developed and refined especially by advocates in the United States and the United Kingdom and has made substantial inroads into the former dominance of self-limited scientific and technologically oriented evaluation studies.

## 1. Origins

For centuries people have made decisions about how to live their lives and what to study in schools. In so far as most of these decisions have been made in naturalistic, informal ways, the origins of qualitative curriculum evaluation are lost in antiquity. However, the curriculum itself can be conceived in several different ways, and it can be evaluated formally in different ways more or less consistent with these conceptions. The curriculum has been commonly conceived throughout history as subject matter or the course of studies. As subject matter it can be evaluated in terms of how accurately it reflects the underlying reality of the universe and how logically it is arranged. This kind of metaphysical and epistemological analysis of subject matter was for centuries the principal means of evaluating the curriculum in Western education. The curriculum can also be conceived as the activities which students undertake in schools, and it can be evaluated in terms of the utilitarian results of these activities. This point of view underlies the scientific or technological orientation to curriculum evaluation. It has developed primarily in the twentieth century, abetted by the testing and measurement movement, and recently has been associated with efforts to improve programs and promote accountability.

A third way of conceiving the curriculum has also developed in the twentieth century. Arising originally from the thought of John Dewey and progressive education, it has recently been shaped by other sources. In this point of view the curriculum is the experience of the individual student. This experience is influenced by the entire environment to which the student is exposed, including the course of studies, and it is comprised of both an external side (the overt activities which the student undertakes) and an internal side (the beliefs, ideas, attitudes, feelings, and the like which the student holds or undergoes). In this view the curriculum can be evaluated by assessing the quality of the student's experience, but this assessment must include all phases of the entire interaction, including the student's autonomous participation.

In this view, evaluation depends on the ability of the evaluator to apprehend the overall situation adequately and fully, to portray it accurately and compellingly, and to make valuations about it wisely. Hence, qualitative curriculum evaluation updates the ancient, informal means of making decisions about schools through personal observations by refining the evaluator's essentially artistic skills of perception and portrayal, and essentially philosophic skills of critical analysis (now extended from subject matter only, to the fullness of educational situations, including contexts and the experiences of individual students). Although there are many examples of qualitative, naturalistic studies of schools extending back to the beginnings of the twentieth century and beyond, the first modern statement to argue that curriculum evaluation is, in fact, educational criticism dealing with the experience of students was probably made by Mann (1968–69). In the 1970s books began to appear taking this same position. Hamilton (1976) pointed out how typically technological–utilitarian evaluations borrow methods developed to measure agricultural production, and with several colleagues (Hamilton et al. 1977) collected a series of essays further extending this critique and developing the modern notion of naturalistic evaluation. Willis (1978) described the art of educational criticism as "qualitative evaluation" and provided a series of essays, many of them written by practising critics, which further defined the theoretical basis for, and offered concrete examples of, educational criticism. However the leading spokesperson for this point of view has been Eisner, who in an influential essay (Eisner 1977) described the skills essential to high quality, formal educational criticism and two years later published the first book (Eisner 1979) to develop a complete rationale for educational criticism. In another influential essay (Eisner 1981) he clearly differentiated artistic and scientific approaches to educational research and evaluation. Such books and articles provide a modern basis for qualitative curriculum evaluation as educational criticism, though many other authors, especially in the 1980s, have added their own statements.

## 2. Procedures and Aims

The methodology of qualitative curriculum evaluation is naturalistic. Naturalistic methodology has been described at length by Guba and Lincoln (1981), who define it in terms of two dimensions. First, the evaluator attempts to encounter the situation as it is. The point is to change the situation as little as possible through the evaluator's presence or by deliberately altering the situation to make it conform to a preordinate research design, which may, in fact, deal with only part of it. Second, the evaluator brings as few preconceptions as possible to the situation. The point is to let meanings and valuations arise as fully as possible out of the situation itself. Naturalistic methodology leaves open a wide variety of ways of encountering the situation fully. The evaluator may or may not attempt to gain an insider's perspective by becoming an organic part of the situation, but in either case the evaluator observes the situation at sufficient length to gain a thorough understanding of it and gleans additional evidence about it from a variety of sources.

Understandings developed naturalistically are usually reported in a case study format. (For a discussion of the case study, see Stake 1978.) Case studies do not attempt to report generalizations abstracted from specific situations. Rather, they attempt to portray the truth about specific situations concretely, vividly, and in context. This is not to say that an evaluator can never suggest any generalizations through a case study nor that an audience cannot infer any generalizations, but it is to say that meanings and valuations conveyed by vivid portrayals of specific situations must be carefully scrutinized for how well they fit the particulars of any other situations.

The phases of criticism present in any thorough evaluation study have been described by McCutcheon (1979). These phases are always interrelated but tend to be more fully developed and carefully balanced in educational criticism than in scientific or technological evaluation studies. The first of these phases, observation, includes whatever means the evaluator uses to gain information and insight. This phase may therefore include not only the direct observations of the evaluator, but also interviewing, the examination of records, the use of unobtrusive measures, and the evaluator's reflective consideration of all evidence. The second phase, description, is how the evaluator chooses to portray the situation. Here the evaluator must choose from among the many things which could be portrayed and the many ways of creating this portrayal. The aim is communicating to the audience of the evaluation significant truths about the situation itself and its larger context. Descriptions are usually written narratives but may include oral, visual, and other forms of communication as well. The third phase, interpretation, is the ascribing of meaning to the situation. (For a detailed discussion of interpretation, see McCutcheon 1981.) Meanings may arise either internally or externally to the situation. Internal meanings arise when participants ask themselves what it means to them personally to live within the situation. External meanings arise when specifics of the situation are compared with ideas, theories, other events, or other situations which provide new ways of viewing or understanding the situation. Both internal and external meanings are ways of attributing significance in context. The fourth phase, appraisal, is the directly evaluative part of educational criticism. Despite the tendency of scientific and technological studies merely to report purportedly objective facts about a situation, there simply is no evaluation until someone derives valuations about it. This means that the critic must comment on the *merit* and *worth* of the overall situation or its parts. Merit deals with value in terms of how well done something is; worth with the value of doing it in the first place. In general, the best studies make clear the basis for the critic's valuations. All four phases are present in any good critical study, which itself can be evaluated in terms of the adequacy of the fit between evidence and situation, the internal consistency of the study's various parts, the significance of its meanings and valuations, and the compellingness of its portrayals.

Since qualitative curriculum evaluation is thus a way of making public the fullest possible range of knowledge about educational situations and their contexts, its general aims of enlarging understanding and promoting moral action are actually one and the same and can best be realized when different insights are openly portrayed and actively tested. Therefore, educational criticism is not limited to formal evaluators; virtually anyone—especially teachers and students—may engage in it, and all honestly held and openly shared meanings and valuations contribute to the realization of these aims (Willis 1981). In this sense qualitative curriculum evaluation is not merely a way of assessing the curriculum,

however conceived, but also a means of increasing the quality of the educative experience of all those who engage in it.

## Bibliography

Eisner E W 1977 On the uses of educational connoisseurship and criticism for evaluating classroom life. *Teach. Coll. Rec.* 78: 345–58
Eisner E W 1979 *The Educational Imagination: On the Design and Evaluation of School Programs*. Macmillan, New York
Eisner E W 1981 On the differences between scientific and artistic approaches to qualitative research. *Educ. Res.* 10 (4): 5–9
Guba E G, Lincoln Y S 1981 *Effective Evaluation: Improving the Usefulness of Evaluation Results Through Responsive and Naturalistic Approaches*. Jossey-Bass, San Francisco, California
Hamilton D 1976 *Curriculum Evaluation*. Open Books, London
Hamilton D, MacDonald B, King C, Jenkins D, Parlett M (eds.) 1977 *Beyond the Numbers Game: A Reader in Educational Evaluation*. Macmillan, Basingstoke
McCutcheon G 1979 Educational criticism: Methods and application. *J. Curr. Theor.* 1 (2): 5–25
McCutcheon G 1981 On the interpretation of classroom observations. *Educ. Res.* 10 (5): 5–10
Mann J S 1968–69 Curriculum criticism. *Curr. Theory Network* 2: 2–14
Stake R E 1978 The case study method in social inquiry. *Educ. Res.* 7 (2): 5–8
Willis G (ed.) 1978 *Qualitative Evaluation: Concepts and Cases in Curriculum Criticism*. McCutchan, Berkeley, California
Willis G 1981 Democratization of curriculum evaluation. *Educ. Leadership* 38 (8): 630–32

# Curricular Implications of Educational Connoisseurship and Criticism

### T. E. Barone

*Educational connoisseurship* and *educational criticism* are terms coined by Eisner (1977) to describe two facets of an arts-based approach to educational inquiry. Connoisseurship refers to a capacity to appreciate subtle and important qualities in educational phenomena. Criticism is the means of disclosing these appreciations, usually in the form of a critical essay.

## 1. Educational Connoisseurship

The connoisseur of fine arts is someone whose perceptive powers have been highly developed through intense experiences with the products of various modes of artistic expression. He or she is able to recognize and appreciate the significant nuances within the art object. Eisner (1985) argues that connoisseurship also extends to more mundane areas of life such as wine-tasting, sports, and other aspects of nature and society. One can develop a level of connoisseurship in educational matters by becoming a sensitive student of curriculum

artifacts and classroom life. This demands, first, attention to curricular and pedagogical phenomena, and secondly, the opportunity to compare the features found in one setting or object with others found elsewhere. This can result in refined powers of discrimination and a set of ideas that allow the critic to place what is seen into an intelligible context.

## 2. Educational Criticism

The perceptual activities of the educational connoisseur are essentially private in nature; educational criticism is the art of publicizing what the connoisseur has appreciated. Usually this disclosure takes the form of a written text, especially an essay.

A critique will often be a blend of two modes of language. The first mode is used when the critic aims to publicize his or her emotional and intellectual responses to the patterns of qualities experienced. This is the metaphorical mode, with language that is artful, suggestive, connotative, evocative, literary. Only figurative language possesses the power to allow a foreign audience direct imaginary access to these experiences, through the rhythms evoked in the structure and form of the writing, by the imagery within the words and phrasing, and so forth.

At other points the critic's narrative requires an explicit, denotative, linear mode of language, one that often takes the form of propositional statements. Factors that determine the quality and manner of the blending of these language modes include the nature of the intended audiences and the talents and proclivities of the critic.

## 3. Structural Dimensions of Educational Criticism

Each of these language modes is also associated with certain structural dimensions of the critique. McCutcheon (1976) has identified three such dimensions: description, interpretation, and assessment. These dimensions are useful for analytical purposes although, in fact, each dimension implies the others to some extent. For example, there is always assessment implicit in description.

Within the descriptive dimension the critic attempts vividly to portray, or render salient, qualities within curriculum artifacts or educational events. The critic's task is thus to re-educate the readers' perceptions enabling them to experience vicariously various aspects of these artifacts or events, and to help them to see aspects that would otherwise be missed. Description is best accomplished using the metaphorical mode of language.

In the interpretative dimension the critic attempts to make sense of the qualities described. Critics have cited the notion of "thick description" as crucial to the role of interpretation in criticism. The critic attempts to explicate the "deep structure" of educational phenomena perceived, construing their significance by viewing them as part of a nexus of social meaning.

Interpretation may involve placing features of an intended curriculum or ongoing program within an historical context or even drawing on a variety of theories from the social sciences for illumination. The interpretative dimension often requires a language that is denotative and discursive, comprised of propositional statements, as does the third dimension, evaluation.

Both the descriptive and interpretative dimensions can be found within science-based modes of qualitative educational inquiry (although usually in forms different from those found in criticism). The evaluative dimension most clearly distinguishes it from those other inquiry modes. Proponents of criticism argue that appraisal is also implicit in the work of social scientists (just as appraisal is implicit in the descriptive and interpretative dimensions of educational criticism). But it is also the task of the educational critic to *explicitly* appraise features of the critical object according to personally held educational criteria. These criteria may

even be spelled out in order to make the perspective of the critic more obvious to the reader, and itself open to criticism. In reading an educational criticism, one should be aware of the voice of the critic speaking about educational phenomena from within a distinct set of educational values. The reader should, therefore, be in a better position to judge the persuasiveness of the critic's appraisal of those curriculum materials or educational practices.

## 4. Two Categories of Educational Criticism

Two distinct categories of educational criticism are identifiable, based on the kinds of educational phenomena treated within each. Biological metaphors have been borrowed to label these categories: the in vitro or "test tube" category of criticism, and the in vivo or "in life" type. Within the former the critic analyzes curricular phenomena such as program blueprints, sets of plans and intentions, curriculum materials of all sorts, or the physical surroundings in a school or classroom, all *apart* from their operation or usage in educational events. These materials are treated in some ways as analogous to pieces of plastic art such as paintings and sculpture, or to literary texts, or to architecture.

Examples of in vitro criticism are few in number. Prominent examples are by Vallance (1977), who applied a set of guidelines distilled from critical descriptions of paintings to a curriculum package called "The Great Plains Experience," and Munby (1979) who reviewed the curriculum "Philosophy for Children." Both critically appraised the materials as a completed work, a static artifact. Both also expressed some discomfort about this approach since program plans and materials usually undergo a process of adaptation, implementation, and modulation by a teacher, and students seldom see the curriculum in the form examined by the critic.

In vivo criticism takes into account that materials exist not in a vacuum but as an integral part of a usually complex educational landscape. In vivo critics thus focus on the curriculum-in-use, or the experienced curriculum: the transactions that occur within the lives of people in schools and classrooms. Unlike paintings, sculptures, or pieces of architecture, the "objects" of concern are events that are played out spatio-temporally, like dances or dramas. Even further, the events analyzed by in vivo critics are "actual" rather than staged. Educational criticism may, therefore, contain features found in social criticism as well as art criticism. Genres of literary nonfiction are potential sources of strategies for effectively criticizing the experienced curriculum (Barone 1980).

Usually the focus of in vivo criticism is an ongoing education program. Individual examples of in vivo critiques include Donmoyer (1980) and Barone (1987). Collections of in vivo critiques are included in Eisner (1985), and issues of *Daedalus* (1981, 1983) devoted to high school and outstanding school arts programs.

Another collection of essays that closely resemble in vivo criticism can be found in Lightfoot (1983), although the author prefers the term "social science portraiture."

## 5. The Critical Process

An educational critic seldom enters the critical process with a preconceived set of hypotheses to be tested, or preformulated questions to be answered, or with a precise set of methodological procedures to be employed. Instead, both the emergent pattern of inquiry and the form and substance of the final product are highly dependent on the unique interactions between the educational perspective of the critic and the phenomena confronted in the particular setting. Nevertheless, several phases have been identified in the process (Barone 1982).

When the educational critic first confronts the critical phenomena there is an initial haziness: the qualities are not yet subordinate to an explicit overall structure or pattern and so appear to be random. In the second phase, relationships between various phenomena begin to be perceived and tentative patterns of qualities discerned. Only in phase 3 does the process climax, as a theme emerges as a mediator for structuring the phenomena that besiege the critic. In phase 4 the thematic structure serves to guide the inquiry and writing tasks, while simultaneously growing in clarity and definition itself. The implications of this controlling idea are "teased out" as it serves to select from among, and reveal relationships between, qualitative phenomena. It also becomes a premise for inferring subthemes. Finally, in phase 5, closure is reached and the critique is judged adequate and complete.

## 6. Issues of Credibility and Generalizability

Opponents to the legitimation of educational criticism as a research genre have objected to the subjective nature of the inquiry approach. Its findings, they submit, are highly suspect due to a lack of rigorous methodological safeguards to insure elimination of personal biases and distortions. Proponents have responded by noting that there are value judgments, and hence subjectivity, involved in all forms of research, including science-based research. These value judgments are more implicit and less obvious, but nevertheless unavoidable, in several phases of science-based research: in the formation of the research question, in the choice of tools to be employed, in the interpretations of information collected (McCutcheon 1976 p. 65). Educational criticism may possess the advantage of avoiding the illusion of objectivity inherent in other inquiry modes.

Proponents of educational criticism view science-based research as undergirded by a false epistemology, one that honors the correspondence theory of truth. In such research the aim is to discover reality apart from

the human mind and to represent this unmediated reality in a statement of findings. Proponents hold that the meaning of phenomena is inevitably construed, and thereby influenced, by previous experience and present perspective. The educational critic may, however, strive to promote a type of intersubjectivity through his or her critique, persuading readers of its credibility and usefulness. Eisner (1985) has cited two processes that are important if an individual critique is to receive this "consensual validation." These are (a) structural corroboration and (b) referential adequacy.

Structural corroboration concerns the coherence of the evidence and arguments presented by the critic. Have general statements and opinions been supported by evidence that builds into a persuasive (i.e., unified and coherent) picture? Have pieces of evidence been effectively assembled to create a structured pattern, a comprehensive entity of information?

Referential adequacy means that new insights attained through educational connoisseurship must be based on empirical phenomena observable by others and conveyed in a critique that adequately refers to those phenomena. Referential adequacy is most appropriately applied to criticisms in which the audience has direct access to the object or situation criticized, allowing them to check the relationship between the critic's subject matter and his or her rendering of it.

Donmoyer (1981) suggested that even a lack of direct access need not present an insurmountable problem for criticism in regard to its credibility. The understanding of a critical text is seen as a means to an end rather than an end in itself. The credibility of a piece of criticism lies in its usefulness for promoting in the reader a "psychological generalization" process that is distinct from the kind of nomothetic generalization found in science-based research. The latter kind of research is concerned with the discovery and/or construction of general abstract theories. Psychological generalization, on the other hand, is concerned with creating anticipatory images in the reader of a criticism. Having confronted these images in a criticism, the reader can then assess their appropriateness for other educational situations to which he or she does have direct access.

## 7. Critics and Audiences

Advocates of educational connoisseurship and criticism see a potential value in its use for a variety of educational constituencies. Beneficiaries might include teachers who desire insightful feedback on their pedagogical methods, administrators and policy makers who make complex decisions on educational matters, parents who would like a fuller picture of the school activities engaged in by their children, and members of the general public who need to be brought closer to the complexities of education than lists of test scores can bring them.

Who, then is the educational connoisseur and critic? Eisner (1985) sees criticism less as a role than as a function. Despite the seemingly elitist connotations of the labels, the connoisseur/critic need not be a member of a "privileged" cadre of evaluators but might be a student, administrator, school board member, or university professor. Peer criticism among teacher colleagues within institutions might lead to more effective pursuance of educational aims. Anyone familiar with schooling is an educational connoisseur to some extent, and can thus aspire to educational criticism. Indeed, Gray (1981) has argued that the term "educational criticism" has clarified and made visible what many practitioners and supervisors have long engaged in under other names. Careful observation, qualitative interpretation and assessment of practice already occur in many educational institutions, although usually in forms less elaborate and polished than those found in published educational criticisms.

## Bibliography

Barone T E 1980 Effectively critiquing the experienced curriculum: Clues from the "new journalism". *Curr. Inq.* 10 (1): 29–53

Barone T E 1982 The Meadowhurst experience: Phases in the process of educational criticism. *J. Curr. Theor.* 4 (1): 156–70

Barone T E 1987 On equality, visibility, and the fine arts program in a black elementary school: An example of educational criticism. *Curr. Inq.* 17 (4): 421–46

*Daedalus* 1981 Vol. 110 (4) (issue devoted to America's schools: Portraits and perspectives)

*Daedalus* 1983 Vol. 112 (3) (issue devoted to the arts and humanities in America's schools)

Donmoyer R B 1980 The evaluator as artist. *J. Curr. Theor* 2 (2): 12–26

Donmoyer R B 1981 Alternative conceptions of generalization and verification for educational research: Toward a rationale for qualitative ideographic inquiry. Doctoral dissertation, Stanford University

Eisner E W 1977 On the uses of educational connoisseurship and criticism for evaluating classroom life. *Teach. Coll. Rec.* 78: 345–58

Eisner E W 1985 *The Educational Imagination: On the Design and Evaluation of School Programs*, 2nd edn. Macmillan, New York

Gray J U 1981 Vintage connoisseurship: A practitioner's view of educational criticism. *Curr. Inq.* 11 (4): 343–58

Lightfoot S L 1983 *The Good High School: Portraits in Character and Culture.* Basic Books, New York

McCutcheon G 1976 The disclosure of classroom life. Doctoral dissertation, Stanford University

Munby H 1979 Philosophy for children: An example of curriculum review and criticism. *Curr. Inq.* 9 (3): 229–49

Vallance E 1977 The landscape of "The Great Plains Experience": An application of curriculum criticism. *Curr. Inq.* 7: 87–105

# Components and Applications of Curriculum Evaluation

## Curriculum Feasibility Studies

### L. A. Sosniak

When presented with a proposed curriculum or a plan for developing a curriculum, at least two broad questions need to be addressed. First, to what extent is the curriculum worthwhile for the educational circumstances in question? Second, how likely is it that the curriculum can be implemented successfully? Attempts to answer these questions constitute feasibility studies of curriculum.

Curriculum feasibility studies are likely to be informal. A decision about feasibility will typically be based on the best judgment of the curriculum specialist or instructional leader in a school or school district. Such a decision is made after careful reading of the materials or proposal and after considerable discussion with staff in the school or district who would be responsible for implementing the curriculum. An extended, highly systematic study of a proposed curriculum is both unlikely and not necessarily desirable. It is unlikely because typically a substantial number of curricular suggestions are put forward each year. If each was subject to systematic evaluation, the cost to a school system would be staggering. Any curricular suggestion judged to be worthy after an informal evaluation can always be pilot tested before being fully implemented in a school or district. Even then, because a pilot situation is seldom—if ever—identical to the circumstances under which the curriculum would be implemented on a large-scale, the "hard data" provided by such an evaluation may cost far more than it is worth. Therefore, a costly, highly systematic feasibility study may also be undesirable. Further, a curriculum is a plan for instruction, and as such is never completely standardizable. The curriculum-in-action will always be moderated by the teachers and students working with the guide. Consequently, effectiveness in one setting is no guarantee of effectiveness in another (Eisner 1985 pp. 196–97).

Although feasibility studies are likely to be informal, they involve a wide variety of specific concerns. These include philosophical, pedagogical, political, and economic issues. Each of these will be considered under a separate heading.

## 1. Philosophical Issues

A curriculum, or an idea for one, may be right for one situation but wrong for others. Determining whether it is right for one's own situation typically begins with an analysis of the fit between the curriculum and the philosophy of one's own school or school system. A test of philosophical fitness can be applied both to the aims or objectives of the curriculum and the means of realizing the curricular intentions. That is, a first consideration might be the extent to which the aims or objectives of the curriculum are consonant with the stated and implicit local educational philosophy. An equally important consideration would be whether the procedures explicit and implicit in the new curriculum are also consistent with the local philosophy for the ways students and teachers should work—individually and together (Peters 1959).

If the philosophy embedded in the curriculum is not consistent with the local educational philosophy, it might be worthwhile to ask whether it is in harmony with the philosophy the school or district is moving toward. If the answer is still no, there may be little reason to look at the curriculum proposal any further. If the philosophy embedded in the curriculum is appropriate, there is one further philosophical question to consider: the question of whether the curriculum proposed constitutes an improvement over the present state of educational affairs. As Schubert (1986 p. 373) reminds us, a curricular change is no guarantee that the change will be for the better.

## 2. Pedagogical Issues

A new curriculum can be analyzed with a view to a variety of pedagogical considerations. Some of these focus specifically on the fit between the curriculum and the students with whom it will be used; others focus on the integrity of the curriculum itself; still others focus on the relationship between the curriculum and the teachers who will be expected to translate it into classroom instruction.

One would probably want to consider, first, whether the educational claims for the curriculum are realistic. Is it likely that the students will be able to learn what the curriculum promises? Do they have the prerequisite knowledge necessary for working through the curriculum? Is it likely that the students will have mastered the most important knowledge and skills of the curriculum even before they begin working through the new course of study? A related, more specific consideration is the degree to which the content and methods of the curriculum are appropriate for the students who will be working through the course of study. On the whole, are they geared to the proper level of difficulty for the students in your school or district? Are they relevant to students' lives?

One can also look at the extent to which the curriculum is coherent within itself. Is the content well-chosen given the aims of the curriculum? Are the explicit and implicit methods of instruction appropriate for both the curricular aims and content? Is the curriculum consistent in its philosophy and methods from beginning to end?

The importance of considering the appropriateness of the curriculum for the teachers who will be using it cannot be overestimated. Recent examinations of curriculum implementation repeatedly show that new curricula often fail to be adopted or to be used as intended because of the difficulties they pose for classroom teachers (Jackson 1983, Tyler 1979). Three considerations seem especially important. First, are the teachers likely to understand and value the aims of the curriculum? Second, are the teachers likely to be knowledgeable about the content and methods of the curriculum? Third, are the methods of instruction for the new curriculum likely to fit well with the teachers' current methods for organizing instruction?

## 3. Political Issues

A curriculum that seems philosophically and pedagogically appropriate for one's situation may prove troublesome nonetheless. When studying the feasibility of implementing a new curriculum, it is important to consider the politics—within the school as well as within the community served by the school—that may interfere with successful implementation of the curriculum. Will both moral and organizational support be available to teachers from high-level administrators within the school or district? Teachers need to be given time, incentive, and payoff for changing their practices and course content (see, for example, Lazerson et al. 1984); they need, especially, the room to flounder and be less-than-successful initially when working with unfamiliar and complex content and methods (Little 1984). Recent analyses of curriculum change indicate further that teachers resist imposed change; the wholehearted support of teachers typically requires involving them meaningfully in the construction or selection of the curriculum (Noddings 1979).

Controversy in the community around a particular curriculum also has proved to be especially troublesome. Two issues seem important to consider in this regard. First, does the curriculum fall within the role of the school as the parents of the school children envisage it? Some new curricula may be seen by the community as usurping the role of the parent in a child's education. Second, does the point of view espoused by the curriculum match the values of the community? If even a small but vocal portion of the community believes that the curriculum espouses a point of view that conflicts with their beliefs or values, the curriculum may be impossible to implement successfully.

## 4. Economic Issues

Although one wouldn't want to make decisions about school curricula solely on the basis of cost, it would be foolhardy and irresponsible to ignore the matter of cost entirely. Changing from one curriculum to another involves a variety of "costs." Some costs are quite obvious while others are "hidden;" some can be measured in dollars and cents while others may not be quantifiable (Wolf 1984 Chap. 7). The price of the new materials required is just a small part of the total investment necessary to implement a new curriculum.

If the new curriculum is to be added to the current school program (rather than replacing a portion of the existing curriculum), one would certainly want to consider student time as a cost. The time students would be required to invest in the new curriculum would have to be subtracted from other portions of the school program. Time is an important variable in any cost estimation even if the new curriculum is intended to replace a portion of the existing school program. It is important to consider the time teachers would have to invest preparing to use a new curriculum (individually and in staff development programs), as well as the time that administrators and other extraclass professional staff would have to devote to implement and maintain the new course of study.

Some curricular proposals may require additional staff. Others may require additional space (for classrooms, offices, or supply rooms) or substantial remodeling of existing space. Still other curriculum proposals may require that a school be kept open longer hours—adding to the cost of heat, light, janitorial services, and so forth.

Finally, all new curriculum proposals are likely to require some new materials. The type of materials—and related costs—can vary considerably. Textbooks which can be used for a period of years will obviously be significantly less expensive than "consumable" materials (e.g., workbooks, science materials) which would have to be replaced each year. Equipment (including movie projectors, microcomputers, and tape recorders) will have to be maintained. Both the nonrecurring and the recurring costs of materials need to be kept in mind.

## 5. Conclusion

Decisions about the feasibility of a proposed curriculum or a plan for developing a curriculum involve multiple considerations. The educational significance and appropriateness of the curriculum for one's particular circumstances are certainly the most important. However, economic and political considerations ought not to be given short-shrift.

## Bibliography

Eisner E W 1985 *The Educational Imagination: On the Design and Evaluation of School Programs*, 2nd edn. Macmillan, New York

Jackson P 1983 The reform of science education: A cautionary tale. *Daedalus* 112: 143–66

Lazerson M, McLaughlin J B, McPherson B 1984 New curriculum, old issues. *Teach. Coll. Rec.* 86 (2): 229–319

Little J W 1984 Seductive images and organizational realities in professional development. *Teach. Coll. Rec.* 86 (1): 84–102

Noddings N 1979 NIE's national curriculum development conference. In: Schaffarzick J, Sykes G (eds.) 1979 *Value Conflicts and Curriculum Issues*. McCutchan, Berkeley, California

Peters R S 1959 *Authority, Responsibility and Education*. George Allen and Unwin, London

Schubert W H 1986 *Curriculum: Perspective, Paradigm, and Possibility*. Macmillan, New York

Tyler R W 1979 Educational improvements best served by curriculum development. In: Schaffarzick J, Sykes G (eds.) 1979 *Value Conflicts and Curriculum Issues*. McCutchan, Berkeley, California

Wolf R M 1984 *Evaluation in Education*, 2nd edn. Praeger, New York

# Curriculum Tryout

**A. Lewy**

The curriculum reform of the 1960s and 1970s brought forward the demand for empirical tryout of instructional materials and curricula prior to their widespread use. The high cost of producing new curricula was one of the factors that motivated sponsors to demand empirical evidence of the quality of new programs. But apart from such demands, one of the basic tenets of the curriculum movement of the 1960s was that only empirical evidence can demonstrate the quality of an educational program. The leaders of the curriculum movement strove to realize Campbell's (1969) vision of the experimental society, where preliminary tryout of social action is adjunct to planning.

## 1. Phases of Curriculum Tryout

The tryout of new curricula is carried out in successive phases with increasing numbers and type diversification of students. Nevertheless, it does not fully cover the entire span of planning activities. Formative evaluation of new curricula already starts at the pretryout stage, when the development team defines the program objectives, selects the contents, and makes decisions about the outline of the course of the study. The tryout of the curriculum can start only at a phase when instructional materials to be used by learners are already available; but it is not necessary to wait until all study materials for a whole course of study become available. The tryout may and should start at a phase when only selected components of the program are available to the learner. Evaluation experts use various terms for denoting the successive stages of program tryout, such as: prototype testing, revision cycles, and product tryout; or laboratory phase, hothouse phase, and utilization phase.

While there may be slight differences among these sets of terms, in practice they delineate three phases parallel to what will be labelled here as: laboratory tryout, pilot tryout, and field tryout.

### 1.1 Laboratory Tryout

Individual components of the program can be tried out on individual students invited to the curriculum laboratory at the very earliest stages of the development activities. The curriculum team itself, together with the evaluator, observes the learner's behavior, takes note of his or her responses to the instructional materials, and, if needed, suggests specific modifications. One of the problems of the laboratory tryout is that certain learning activities must be presented to the learner in a predetermined sequence. In an ordinary school situation lessons are presented to the learner in a day-by-day sequence. During the laboratory tryout phase, a considerable amount of time is often needed to prepare the materials and it may therefore occur that the interval between the tryout of one lesson and that of the subsequent one is much longer than it would be in an actual school setting.

### 1.2 Pilot Tryout

As soon as a fully completed preliminary version of a course is available for learners, it can be tried out in a regular school setting. At this phase the team members themselves usually serve as classroom teachers. The purpose of such a tryout is to examine whether the program can be implemented within the system and to ascertain the conditions (in terms of space, equipment, teacher training, learners' prerequisite knowledge) necessary for ensuring the success of the program, and what modifications, if any, are needed to improve the quality of the program. Harlen (1973) lists a series of issues to be examined at this phase: Do the children enjoy the program? Can they cope with the assignments they are given? Do they participate in the scheduled activities? Are the teachers aware of the unique features of the program? Do they accept or identify themselves with the basic tenets of the program?

### 1.3 Field Tryout

On the basis of the findings of the pilot tryout, a revised version of the program is produced, which is then tried out by school teachers in the regular settings of their classes, and without any direct intervention on the part of the development team. The purpose of this phase is to examine the "exportability" of the program, that is, to ascertain whether it can be used in school without the ongoing support of the development team, as well as to demonstrate the merits of the program to its potential users.

## 2. Procedures and Instrumentation

Curriculum tryout moves from relatively "soft" methodology at the initial phases toward more strictly prescribed design as an advance is made toward the later tryout phases. At the laboratory phase it is necessary to be content with observing a few learners. Nevertheless, studies have shown that even such limited tryouts (with nonrepresentative samples of the target population) may contribute to the improvement of programs (Markele 1967). The major methodological problem at this phase is usually referred to as "distortion filter." The evaluator does more than note what he or she observes; he or she interprets or "filters" what is observed. The ideal tester of instructional materials should be sensitive to subtle manifestations of the pupil's problems. At the pilot phase the utilization of a judgmental sample is recommended. The evaluators, utilizing a variety of instruments, collect information about various aspects of the functioning of the program. They collect information about classroom processes by direct observation supplemented by teachers' remarks at the margins of the textbook pages, by interviews, and by questionnaires. Formal testing plays a relatively minor role at this phase. Evidence of achievement is provided through observing the learners' behavior in the classroom and by "curriculum embedded tests," that is, assignments and homework presented to the learner during the actual teaching–learning process. Only at the field-trial phase does it become feasible to employ random sampling procedures and to compare the outcomes of the program being evaluated with those of alternative programs.

## 3. Utilizing Findings of Curriculum Tryout

Recent research has focused on the question of what use is made of findings obtained from curriculum tryout,

and what factors affect the degree of utilization of such findings. Harlen (1973) reports that data collected through direct observation of classroom processes and through teachers' written comments about flaws detected in the instructional materials are used more frequently as a basis for modifying programs than the results of achievement tests. A survey of evaluation studies conducted in the United States revealed that the credibility of the evaluation results is a crucial factor in determining the degree of their utilization (Boruch and Cordray 1980). This is true mainly with clients who have difficulty in understanding certain technical aspects of the report. In such cases, confidence in the evaluator is very important, and this is one reason why the stability of the evaluator is critical. The interpretability of the information is another critical factor. Printed information is frequently misinterpreted by users and there is a need for oral reporting as well. Absence of regular meetings between evaluators and curriculum developers invites errors in interpretation. Surprisingly enough, lack of timeliness is not mentioned among the obstacles to utilizing results of tryout. This is true mainly with regard to the phases of laboratory tryout and pilot tryout in which the data are based on direct observation, and certain preliminary summaries are produced almost immediately after collection of the data. When these findings are made available for the development teams in the form of oral reports they are put to use long before the written report is completed. Lewy (1977) found that the tryout process provides a moratorium for the development team to reconsider issues which may have been overlooked during the strenuous work of program writings, when they were required to meet strict deadlines. Such considerations are combined with the reported tryout findings, and used for modifying the program. Cronbach (1980) claims that the tryout process creates among the team members an awareness of the importance of certain criteria used for evaluating the program, and in this way affects the quality of their work. The mere existence of tryout may keep certain flaws from occurring. In addition, it contributes to the accumulation of knowledge which teaches team members to avoid certain flaws in the future. Thus the effects of tryout make themselves felt not only with regard to the target program, but also in forthcoming planning activities.

No studies have been conducted either on the direct contribution of program tryout and modification to the outcomes of program utilization or on the payoff of repeated tryouts. Information about these two issues seems to be crucial for future decisions with regard to the planning of curriculum tryouts.

### Bibliography

Boruch R F, Cordray D S (eds.) 1980 *An Appraisal of Educational Program Evaluation: Federal, State and Local Agencies.* Northwestern University, Evanston, Illinois

Campbell D T 1969 Reforms as experiments. *Am. Psychol.* 24: 409–29

Cronbach L 1980 *Toward Reform of Program Evaluation.* Jossey-Bass, San Francisco, California

Harlen W 1973 Science 5-13 Project. In: Schools Council (eds.) 1973 *Evaluation in Curriculum Development: Twelve Case Studies: Papers from the Schools Council's Project Evaluators on Aspects of the Work.* Macmillan, London

Lewy A (ed.) 1977 *Handbook of Curriculum Evaluation.* Longman, New York

Markele S M 1967 Empirical testing of programs. *Sixty-sixth Yearbook of the National Society for the Study of Education, Part II.* University of Chicago Press, Chicago, Illinois

# Textbooks and Curriculum

E. Ballér

From the numerous definitions of the term *curriculum*, this article focuses on two approaches: firstly, the curriculum is viewed as the content of instruction in a subject area within the school system which is selected on the basis of educational considerations and organized into topics and structures according to special principles; secondly, the curriculum is viewed as an overall plan of goals, subjects, timetables, materials, and intended learning outcomes of institutionalized teaching and learning as expressed in official, more-or-less standard, syllabi, usually adopted by educational authorities. The textbook, on the other hand, serving as an educational medium or manual of instruction in a certain subject area, is the product of a "technological process", which specifies and interprets the content of the curriculum and structures it in a way that is suitable for teaching and learning.

The relationship between curriculum and textbook is determined by several factors. It is affected—among other things—by the national traditions, the overall political, cultural, and educational aims of the school system, the curricular policy and the procedures employed for approving the syllabus and authorizing textbooks in a particular country. Thus, even if the content of a particular subject is uniform across countries, the textbooks used for teaching vary considerably.

## 1. Centralized and Decentralized Systems

In exploring this complex issue, a distinction should be made between centralized and decentralized educational systems and their curriculum development practices. The differentiation between centralized and decentralized educational systems emerged in the second half of the nineteenth century, and it usually coincided with the introduction of compulsory education. In some countries the pursuit of cultural homogeneity, which was supposed to be attainable through the acquisition of a common and standardized body of knowledge, resulted in centralistic tendencies. For centuries, especially after the invention of printing, textbooks represented and shaped the school curriculum. Famous authors and eminent educators such as Erasmus (1469–1536), Comenius (1592–1670), Pestalozzi (1746–1827), and Ushinsky (1824–1870) developed school textbooks that profoundly influenced the content of instruction as well as its processes and methods, not only within a single country but even across frontiers (Michel 1973).

When, in a number of countries, centrally produced, mandatory syllabi were introduced, they incorporated this textbook-based and information-loaded knowledge. When this notion of formally legitimized syllabi gained prominence in centralized systems, then curriculum development and textbooks played a secondary role only. Textbooks were evaluated and approved on the basis of their fidelity to the regulations laid down in the official documents, that is, faithfulness to their spirit and sometimes even to their content and structure. This was the major instrument by which centralized administrations could exercise control over teaching–learning processes in the school. This was true not only in most socialist countries, but also in some of the Western types of social systems (Hacker 1983).

Even under such circumstances, however, textbooks have not lost their influence. They have remained the major instructional medium, the most important resource for teaching and learning, the most prominent means for improving pupils' achievement, and indeed they have enjoyed the kudos of official legitimation and support. At the same time they affected the central syllabi, since experience derived from using a particular textbook in the schools has often had an impact upon the centrally initiated curriculum reforms.

In countries with decentralized education systems, the original unity or "symbiosis" between curricula and textbooks prevailed. In the English-speaking world, for example, the improvement and production of instructional materials was regarded as actual curriculum development. Due to the lack of centrally prescribed curricula, schools had a decisive say in selecting textbooks from the range of available choices offered by the publishing companies. In turn, textbook publishing became a commercial enterprise, where profitability and the demand of the market dominated.

## 2. Trends

Since the 1950s, significant changes have influenced the curriculum–textbook relationship in both centralized and decentralized systems. Centralized systems have moved away from merely prescribing curricular content and have begun to emphasize outcome-based and process-oriented management of instruction.

Consequently, central planning assumed the role of an infrastructure, facilitating alternative approaches and instructional innovations which required decision-making at local levels. This, in turn, has had consequences for the selection of the content of instruction and for its organization both in central documents and in textbooks, (Báthory 1986). At the same time, textbooks today constitute only one component of instructional media kits, which comprise a variety of teaching aids.

In decentralized systems of education, on the other hand, one can observe a struggle for controlling the curriculum by prescribing standards and achievement requirements, which in turn influences curriculum and textbook development (Lawton 1983). The effect of widely publicized and successful centrally developed textbooks and curriculum packages has also imposed a certain uniformity on the curricula used by the schools. This tendency has been precipitated by the requirements of external examinations. These trends have resulted in increasing the similarity of curriculum and textbook development and administration in the two main types of educational systems.

## Bibliography

Báthory Z 1986 Decentralization issues in the introduction of new curriculum: The case of Hungary. *Prospects* 16: 33–47

Hacker H (ed.) 1980 *Das Schulbuch. Funktion und Verwendung im Unterricht.* Klinkhardt, Bad Heilbrunn

Hacker H 1983 Kodifizierte Bestimmungsfaktoren Curricularer Lernereignisse: Schulbücher. In: Hameyer U, Fray K, Haft E (eds.) 1983 *Handbuch der Curriculumforschung.* Beltz, Weinheim, pp. 351–60

Lawton D 1983 *Curriculum Studies and Educational Planning.* Hodder and Stoughton, London

Michel G 1973 *Schulbuch und Curriculum. Comenius im 18 Jahrhundert.* Henn, Ratingen, Düsseldorf

*Schulbuchgestaltung in der DDR* 1984. Von einem Autorenkollektiv. Volk und Wissen Volkseigener, Berlin

# Textbook Analysis

**B. B. Armbruster and T. H. Anderson**

Procedures for analyzing textbooks have been dominated by the use of readability formulas (Klare 1982). These formulas yield an index which supposedly makes it possible to match the reading demands of a textbook with the reading capabilities of the reader as determined by reading achievement scores. Two of the more well-known readability formulas, Dale and Chall (1948) and Fry (1977) use measures of word difficulty and sentence complexity to determine the appropriate reading level of the text.

In addition to readability formulas, an array of checklist instruments has been advocated as a potentially helpful way of analyzing textbooks. A sample of these checklists (Ball 1976, Jevitz and Meints 1979, Krause 1976) shows that they direct the textbook analyst to potentially important aspects of the textbook that are not necessarily measured by readability formulas. Checklist items direct the reader to consider such aspects of the textbook as the use of visual aids, cultural and sex biases, teacher's manuals or supplements, the quality of workmanship, the quality of materials, the costs, and the quality of writing. One checklist (Jevitz and Meints 1979) has 72 such items. In addition to the sheer magnitude of items to consider, many of them are stated so vaguely that the analyst may find it difficult to make the judgments required by them.

In this article some theoretical ideas and research findings are presented about how students read, understand, and remember ideas that can contribute to the process of analyzing textbooks. These ideas will enable the textbook analyst to set rational priorities on the potentially large set of criteria (such as those referenced above) and also help clear up the vagueness associated with some of the items.

Current theories suggest that learning from textbooks is a function of characteristics of the text itself and cognitive strategies used by the reader during reading.

## 1. The Text

One factor affecting learning from text is structure. Structure refers to the way ideas are connected together in logical organizational patterns. A few basic rhetorical structures appear to reflect fundamental patterns of human thought: (a) simple listing—a listing of items or ideas where the order of presentation of the item is not significant; (b) conclusion/evidence—a special case of simple listing, consisting of a proposition and a list of reasons serving as evidence for that fact; (c) comparison/contrast—a description of similarities and differences between two or more things; (d) temporal sequence—a sequential relationship between items or events considered in terms of the passage of time; (e) cause–effect—an interaction between at least two ideas or events, one considered a cause or reason and the other an effect or result; and (f) problem–solution—similar to the cause–effect pattern in that two factors interact, one citing a problem and the other a solution to that problem. These basic structures can be subsumed in higher order structures that underlie particular text genres (e.g., narratives, newspaper articles) and content areas (e.g., biology, history) (Anderson and Armbruster 1984).

The structure of text can be conveyed in many ways: (a) words denoting relationships (because, before, for example, in comparison); (b) explicit statements of the structure; (c) previews or introductory statements, including titles; and (d) summary statements. Information in the text that points out aspects of structure has been called "signaling" (Meyer 1975). Research has shown that better organized text, and text that makes the organization clear to the reader (for example, through the use of signaling), increases the likelihood of the reader's understanding, remembering, and applying information learned from the text (Meyer 1979).

Another characteristic of text that influences learning outcomes is local coherence, also called cohesion by linguists (Halliday and Hasan 1976). Local coherence is achieved by several kinds of simple linguistic links or ties that connect ideas together within and between sentences. Among the most common links are various forms of reference (e.g., pronoun, anaphora, etc.) and conjunctions or connectives (e.g., and, or, but, because, however). Research has established the importance of cohesive ties in understanding and remembering text. For example, repeated references that help to carry meaning across sentence boundaries can decrease reading time and increase recall of text as an integrated unit (deVilliers 1974, Haviland and Clark 1974, Kintsch et al. 1975, Manelis and Yekovich 1976, Miller and Kintsch 1980). Also, children prefer to read, read faster, and have better memory for sentences connected by explicit conjunctions, particularly causal connectives, than sentences in which the conjunction is left to be inferred (Katz and Brent 1968, Marshall and Glock 1978–79, Pearson 1974–75).

Characteristics of the content itself also affect learning from reading. Kintsch and his colleagues have shown that one of these characteristics—idea density—contributes to reading difficulty. For example, Kintsch and Keenan (1973) kept text length constant while varying the number of propositions (ideas) in text. They found that reading time was more a function of the number of propositions than the number of words. Kintsch et al. (1975) showed that reading times were longer and recall less for texts with many different word concepts than for texts with fewer word concepts. In other words, it is easier for readers to process and retain in memory a proposition built from old, familiar elements than to process propositions which introduce new concepts into the text. In sum, the denser the text (the greater the number of new ideas per unit of text), the longer it takes to read and the less the likelihood of remembering it.

Another aspect of content that affects learning outcomes is the proportion of important to unimportant information, or main ideas to details. In a series of experiments by Reder and Anderson (1980), college students who read summaries one-fifth the length of original texts were better able to recognize important facts and learn new, related material than students who read the full version. Reder and Anderson (1980) conclude that text that helps students focus attention and avoid having to time-share between main points and details is an effective way to aid learning.

Another finding from research is that learning and memory are improved when people are given infor-

mation clarifying the significance of facts that might otherwise seem arbitrary, particularly causal elaborations that establish a causal relationship between ideas (Bransford and Johnson 1973, Bransford et al. 1980). For example, in research on narratives, provision of information about the character's goal and events leading up to the goal has a significant effect on comprehension and memory (Kintsch and van Dijk 1978, Rumelhart 1977, Thorndyke 1977). Presumably, knowledge of the goal and the events leading up to the goal helps readers understand the significance of the character's actions and the consequences of those actions.

In sum, various features of the text itself—structure, local coherence, content—influence learning from reading. Characteristics of the reader, however, probably play an even more crucial role in learning from textbooks. Of particular importance are the cognitive strategies used during reading.

## 2. Cognitive Strategies

Cognitive strategies are what the students use to get the information from the text page into their heads. These information-processing strategies include not only the initial focusing of attention and the subsequent encoding of the information attended to but also an "executive level" aspect of these processes called metacognition. Metacognition refers to both the awareness and control that readers have over their own thinking and learning (Baker and Brown 1983). Research has demonstrated that several cognitive strategies (including the metacognition component) are associated with learning from text. Some of these strategies are discussed below. (For additional strategies of effective learners, see Baker and Brown 1983).

One beneficial strategy in learning from text is selective attention to, and processing of, the most important information in text as defined by the criterion task (that is, what students must do to demonstrate that learning has occurred; for example, answer questions at the end of the chapter or take a test). Numerous studies have shown a clear relationship between learning outcomes and readers' knowledge of or expectations about criterion tasks. For example, one line of research has examined the effect on learning of questions inserted periodically in the text. These studies have shown that questions inserted in the text have a striking focusing effect on studying behaviors and learning outcomes. Students tend to spend more time studying the text that is relevant to the types of inserted questions they receive and they tend to perform better on posttest items testing the type of information tapped by the inserted questions they receive (Reynolds et al. 1979). The inserted questions establish expectations about the criterion task, which then guides cognitive processing.

A second strategy associated with effective learning from text is selective attention to, and processing of, the most important information in text as defined by the author's structure. Mature readers, at least, are able to detect the most important information from text and remember it. The ability to do this seems to develop gradually; immature or less competent readers are less likely to identify and process important information than more mature readers (Brown and Smiley 1977, 1978, Meyer et al. 1980). However, an encouraging line of research indicates that less mature students can be taught to identify and use text structure to facilitate learning. For example, Bartlett (1978) taught ninth graders (14-year-olds) to identify and use four common expository text structures as an aid to learning. Likewise, Dansereau (1983) has successfully trained college students to identify and use the inherent structure of text as an aid to learning.

Another strategy that can help students learn from text is to make use of their own prior knowledge to interpret and remember new information. Research has confirmed that what readers know already greatly influences what they learn and remember from text (Anderson et al. 1977, Spilich et al. 1979). One must not only have the relevant knowledge but also activate it at the appropriate time. In other words, readers must be able to "call up" appropriate prior knowledge when it is needed to understand new information. Research indicates that children often fail to spontaneously activate relevant prior knowledge when it could help them in learning from text, but that they can be trained to do so (Bransford et al. 1980, Bransford 1984).

Another important cognitive strategy is to encode information in such a way that it can be remembered. Research shows that some kinds of studying strategies or learning activities are particularly helpful. Studying strategies that involve the identification and manipulation of the author's structure (structuring strategies) appear to be especially helpful in learning, given that students know how to use the strategy. For example, students taught to outline can use outlining as a learning aid (Barton 1930), and students instructed in semantic mapping techniques (diagrammatic representations of text structure) can improve their memory for text (Armbruster and Anderson 1980, Dansereau 1983). Another studying technique that appears to promote processing is causal elaboration. Bransford and his colleagues (Bransford 1979, Bransford et al. 1980) have shown that people remember ideas better if they can establish a meaningful causal relationship between them. That is, in causal elaboration, readers use prior knowledge (information from the text or from their heads) to construct a significant connection between ideas that might otherwise seem unrelated. For example, readers might use prior knowledge of the function of an object to help them understand and remember the object's structure.

Selectively attending to and processing "important" information, engaging prior knowledge, and using high pay-off studying techniques are some of the cognitive strategies that research has shown to facilitate learning from text. Research has also shown that instruction in strategies can have a positive effect on learning outcomes. Research has already been mentioned in which instruction in identifying the author's structure and in using studying strategies has resulted in improved learning. Research has not only shown that instruction can be effective but has also suggested how teachers can best help students learn to learn from reading. The major practical implication from the research is that students should be taught to use cognitive strategies with awareness. That is, students should be informed about why, when, where, and how they should use particular strategies (Brown et al. 1981).

## 3. Implications for Practice

A prime reason for analyzing textbooks is to enable educators to make wise decisions when selecting textbooks for classroom use. As mentioned in the introduction, two techniques are rather widely used in analysis-for-selection. One is the use of readability formulas to index the general language complexity of the textbook prose. The other is checklist instruments which direct the analyst to various aspects of textbooks that are not indexed by the readability formulas. Both of these techniques can be helpful in deciding which textbooks are generally appropriate for classroom use.

In addition to these techniques, some questions are proposed that respond to the interpretation of what recent research on reading has to suggest about textbook evaluation. Answering these questions should add important information to the textbook selection decision. The first series of questions relate to the text:

(a) Does the textbook make a systematic effort to help the reader connect new ideas with ideas already learned? Does the author include well-written introductions, summaries to chapters, and questions that encourage students to use relevant prior knowledge?

(b) Are the texts coherent at a global level? Are they well-structured and is that structure readily apparent to the reader as evidenced by chapter titles, headings, outlines, introductions, conclusions, and topic sentences?

(c) Are the texts coherent at a local level? Do pronouns have clear referents and are the relationships between ideas explicit or obvious?

(d) Do the texts work toward some important purpose at an appropriate rate by introducing new, main ideas when they are needed? Are the intervening ideas between main ones the type that extend, elaborate, and make explicit the relationship between the main ones, or do the intervening ones simply introduce irrelevant detail?

The following questions concern student exercises.

(a) Do the student exercises at the end of chapters and in workbooks help students learn to locate and process important information from the text? If the students were to learn well the answers to questions at the end of the chapters, would they have an important body of knowledge to help them read and understand the next chapter, or next year's textbook?

(b) Do the student exercises at the end of chapters and in workbooks help students learn a variety of studying techniques? Are the when's, where's, how's, and why's of the studying techniques explained?

The final questions concern the teacher's materials.

(a) Do the teacher's manuals which accompany some textbooks explain to teachers the when's, where's, how's, and why's to teach students about some of the difficult studying aspects, such as text structure and what-to-do-when-something-is-not-well-understood?

(b) Do the teacher's manuals which accompany some textbooks explain to teachers the when's, where's, how's and why's students should be taught to become aware of and monitor their own cognitive processes while studying?

## Bibliography

Anderson R C, Reynolds R E, Schallert D L, Goetz E T 1977 Frameworks for comprehending discourse. *Am. Educ. Res. J.* 14: 367–82

Anderson T H, Armbruster B B 1984 Content area textbooks. In: Anderson R C, Osborn J, Tierney R J (eds.) 1984 *Learning to Read in American Schools: Basal Readers and Content Texts.* Erlbaum, Hillsdale, New Jersey

Armbruster B B, Anderson T H 1980 *The Effect of Mapping on the Free Recall of Expository Text.* (Tech. Rep. No. 160). Center for the Study of Reading, University of Illinois, Urbana, Illinois

Baker L, Brown A L 1983 Cognitive monitoring in reading. In: Flood J (ed.) 1983 *Understanding Reading Comprehension.* International Reading Association, Newark, Delaware

Ball H G 1976 Standards for material selection. *J. Read.* 20: 208–11

Bartlett B J 1978 Top-level structure as an organizational strategy for recall of classroom text. Unpublished doctoral dissertation, Arizona State University

Barton W A 1930 *Outlining as a Study Procedure.* Teachers College, Columbia University, New York

Bransford J D 1979 *Human Cognition: Learning, Understanding, and Remembering.* Wadsworth Belmont, California

Bransford J D 1984 Schema activation and schema acquisition: Comments on Richard C. Anderson's remarks. In: Anderson R C, Osborn J, Tierney R J (eds.) 1984 *Learning to Read in American Schools: Basal Readers and Content Texts.* Erlbaum, Hillsdale, New Jersey

Bransford J D, Johnson M K 1973 Considerations of some problems of comprehension. In: Chase W (ed.) 1973 *Visual Information Processing.* 8th Symposium on Cognition, Carnegie-Mellon University, 1972. Academic Press, New York

Bransford J D, Stein B S, Shelton T S, Owings R 1980 Cognition and adaptation: The importance of learning to learn. In: Harvey J L (ed.) 1980 *Cognition, Social Behavior, and the Environment.* Erlbaum, Hillsdale, New Jersey

Brown A L, Smiley S S 1977 Rating the importance of structural units of prose passages: A problem of metacognitive development. *Child Dev.* 48: 1–8

Brown A L, Smiley S S 1978 The development of strategies for studying texts. *Child Dev.* 49: 1076–88

Brown A L, Campione J C, Day J D 1981 Learning to learn: On training students to learn from texts. *Educ. Res. AERA.* 10: 14–21

Dale E, Chall J S 1948 A formula for predicting readability. *Educ. Res. Bull.* 27: 11–20, 37–54

Dansereau D F 1983 Learning strategy research. In: Segal J, Chipman S, Glaser R (eds.) 1983 *Thinking and Learning Skills: Relating Instruction to Basic Research*, Vol. 1. Erlbaum, Hillsdale, New Jersey

de Villiers P A 1974 Imagery and theme in recall of connected discourse. *J. Exp. Psychol.* 103: 263–68

Fry E B 1977 Fry's readability graph: Clarification, validity, and extension to level 17. *J. Read.* 21: 242–52

Halliday M A K, Hasan R 1976 *Cohesion in English.* Longman, London

Haviland S E, Clark H H 1974 What's new? Acquiring new information as a process in comprehension. *J. Verb. Learn. Verb. Behav.* 13: 512–21

Jevitz L, Meints D W 1979 Be a better book buyer: Guidelines for textbook evaluation. *J. Read.* 22: 734–38

Katz E, Brent S 1968 Understanding connections. *J. Verb. Learn. Verb. Behav.* 1: 501–09

Kintsch W, Keenan J M 1973 Reading rate as a function of the number of propositions in the base structure of sentences. *Cognit. Psychol.* 5: 257–74

Kintsch W, van Dijk T 1978 Toward a model of text comprehension and production. *Psychol. Rev.* 85: 363–94

Kintsch W, Kozminsky E, Streby W J, McKoon G, Keenan J M 1975 Comprehension and recall of text as a function of content variables. *J. Verb. Learn. Verb. Behav.* 14: 196–214

Klare G R 1982 Readability. In: Pearson P D (ed.) 1982 *Handbook of Reading Research.* Longman, New York

Krause K C 1976 Do's and don'ts in evaluating textbooks. *J. Read.* 20: 212–14

Manelis L, Yekovich F R 1976 Repetitions of propositional arguments in sentences. *J. Verb. Learn. Verb. Behav.* 15: 301–12

Marshall N, Glock M D 1978–79 Comprehension of connected discourse: A study into the relationship between the structure of text and information recalled. *Read. Res. Q.* 16: 10–56

Meyer B J F 1975 *The Organization of Prose and its Effects on Memory.* North Holland, Amsterdam

Meyer B J F 1979 Organizational patterns in prose and their use in reading. In: Kamil M L, Moe A J (eds.) 1979 *Reading Research: Studies and Applications.* 28th Yearbook of the National Reading Conference

Meyer B J F, Brandt D M, Bluth G J 1980 Use of top-level structure in text: Key for reading comprehension of ninth-grade students. *Read. Res. Q.* 16: 72–103

Miller J R, Kintsch W 1980 Readability and recall of short prose passages: A theoretical analysis. *J. Exp. Psychol: Human Learning and Memory* 6: 335–54

Pearson P D 1974–75 The effects of grammatical complexity on children's comprehension, recall, and conception of certain semantic relations. *Read. Res. Q.* 10: 155–92

Reder L M, Anderson J R 1980 A comparison of texts and their summaries: Memorial consequences. *J. Verb. Learn. Verb. Behav.* 19: 121–34

Rumelhart D E 1977 Understanding and summarizing brief stories. In: LaBerge D, Samuels J (eds.) 1977 *Basic Processes in Reading: Perception and Comprehension.* Erlbaum, Hillsdale, New Jersey

Spilich G J, Vesonder G T, Chiesi H L, Voss J F 1979 Text processing of domain-related information for individuals with high and low domain knowledge. *J. Verb. Learn. Verb. Behav.* 18: 275–90

Thorndyke P W 1977 Cognitive structures in comprehension and memory of narrative discourse. *Cognit. Psychol.* 9: 77–110

# Evaluation of Learning Resources

**M. R. Eraut**

For this article, a learning resource will be defined as an identifiable physical object which carries information that can be used to promote learning. This includes printed, audio, and pictorial materials, and will also be taken to include computer programs and television programmes, since these can be stored and evaluated as distinct entities. It excludes physical objects such as scientific apparatus, communication equipment like a telephone, human resources, and resource-rich locations such as a museum or learning centre.

Learning resources range in significance from a complete curriculum package, through sets of booklets, to a single audiotape, film, slide, or worksheet. Hence, it is important to stress that the evaluation effort should be commensurate with the significance of the learning resource. If the resource is to be used for a long time or with a large number of students, then more than a token evaluation is called for. But if it is intended for only a few students for part of a lesson, the application of sophisticated evaluation techniques is clearly inappropriate. Since this article seeks to avoid the obvious and trivial, it will be mainly concerned with resources of sufficient significance to merit giving considerable attention to their evaluation. However, some of the methods discussed may also be useful for short quick evaluations of materials of lesser consequence.

Four main approaches to the evaluation of learning resources are reported in the literature.

(a) Evaluation by a panel or committee, whose inspection or viewing of the resource is followed by a discussion of its merits and weaknesses.

(b) Canvassing the opinions of users or potential users with a simple questionnaire, but without advice on techniques of resource evaluation. A simple popularity contest, with the proviso that certain types of criticism, for example, bias, will be seen as particularly important.

(c) Intrinsic evaluation, in which the learning resource is subjected to prolonged study in depth by reviewers and their reports are used as a basis for further discussion.

(d) Field testing in which the resource is tried out in one or more classrooms to assess its impact and its effects.

These four approaches may be combined in several ways. For example, in Japan, the textbook approval procedure involves intrinsic evaluations by specially appointed reviewers being passed on to a committee for discussion and recommendation; and in some districts of the United States, teacher members of a selection committee may briefly field test resources in their own classrooms. This article is mainly concerned with intrinsic evaluation and field testing, because these approaches are considered essential for improving the quality of learning resource evaluation.

First, however, let us distinguish the three main purposes which evaluation of learning resources may serve: (a) selection or purchase; (b) utilization planning; and (c) improvement, modification, or redesign. When a resource has been developed by a teacher for use in his or her own classroom, these purposes will overlap. Otherwise they are likely to be distinct. For each purpose is normally associated with a different context and with a different group of evaluators.

## 1. Evaluation for Selection or Purchase

Purchasing decisions for textbooks are made at national, provincial, district, or even school level. Such decisions may involve free choice by individual schools (as in the United Kingdom); central prescription at national (Kenya) or provincial level (Pakistan); or restricted choice from a list approved by a higher level of government (national in Japan, provincial in Canada and the Federal Republic of Germany). Above school level, decisions about approval or adoption are usually made by a system of committees with clearly specified procedures, and this is often extended to include supplementary materials as well. Supplementary materials, however, are likely to be approved rather than specified; and their purchase will be severely limited by cost in all but the wealthiest countries.

Large numbers of purchasing decisions are also made by the staff of libraries and resource centres. Their job is to develop and maintain collections of learning resources from which teachers or students may borrow. They are spared the burden of having to make a single absolute choice, but instead have to constantly consider the range and diversity of their collection as a whole and the needs of many potential users. New purchases have to take into account the resources that have already been assembled.

Finally, there is an important distinction between resources that are used in a single school or classroom, such as books and simple audiovisual materials, and resources that are too expensive to be allocated to a single site. Purchasing, production, and distribution systems for films, television, or computer-based learning are usually made by specialized agencies at the district or regional level. But it may still be left for the school to decide what use it makes of them. This pattern may well extend to other types of resource if electronic modes of distribution become more widely adopted.

The process of selection for purchase is usefully divided into four stages, though only the more elaborate evaluations will use all four.

Firstly, there is a descriptive analysis of the resource, which can vary in intensity from a cursory inspection by a potential user to a thorough intrinsic evaluation. Its purpose is (a) to discuss the main features of the learning resource, its structure, and its principal qualities; (b) to disclose the educational and pedagogic assumptions which explicitly or implicitly underpin its design; (c) to note any subsidiary features of special significance, for example, obscurities, inaccuracies, minor bias, creative treatment of a topic, and so on.

Secondly, there is a field testing of the resource in classrooms to ascertain its impact on pupils in various contexts and conditions.

Thirdly, there is evaluation by assembling arguments for and against choosing the resource. Each argument will need to be constructed by combining evidence from the descriptive analysis and the field testing with evaluative criteria derived from user opinion, consultation with interested parties, policy documents, or the education literature. Some of these arguments will be unproblematic, in the sense that all decision makers agree that a certain passage is inaccurate or that a certain characteristic is an asset. Other arguments will be contested because the same feature may be regarded positively by some people and negatively by others, according to their views about the curriculum and pedagogy of the area concerned. Eraut (1982) argues strongly that this kind of divergency should be mapped rather than hidden or removed.

Finally, decision making, the final stage, involves deliberation of the evidence, discussion, and eventually choice. Various approaches to purchasing and selection decisions are discussed in the methodology section below.

While there is now a growing body of prescriptive literature suggesting how selection and purchasing decisions ought to be made, there is very little research describing how such decisions are made. When systematic appraisal is used, it is usually only the procedures which are reported, not which factors were critical in determining the decision or which people's views prevailed. However, such systematic appraisal is itself still relatively rare. More often, appraisal amounts to little more than a cursory inspection; and it is perhaps unsurprising that so little attempt has been made to develop the necessary expertise.

## 2. Evaluation for Utilization Planning

The utilization of a learning resource can be planned at two levels, that of course design and that of lesson planning. When there is a detailed and elaborate teachers' manual, it could be argued that lesson planning is unnecessary: only preparation is needed. But such slavish adherence to a manual is unusual; and, though such manuals may appear to provide a complete specification of teaching, this is often illusory because utilization problems may not surface until the teacher is in front of the class. Indeed, many authors have argued that it is impossible to specify teaching in that degree of detail (Harris 1982).

Frequently, complete specification of teaching is not even attempted. The course design team recommends learning resources or sections of such resources for particular topics, but does not attempt to discuss how they might be used. Or there may be a general syllabus and a prescribed textbook without any course design. The teachers are left to plan the detailed lesson-by-lesson use of learning resources on their own; and for this purpose they need either to evaluate the resource themselves or to read an existing evaluation that conveys the right kind of information.

The approach to utilization planning can vary considerably, according to differences in the assumptions of teacher and designer and the degree to which each is prepared to accommodate the other. Figure 1 shows six possible outcomes, recognizing that discussions of curriculum implementation which assume a single teaching style or a single type of "correct" implementation can oversimplify. Even a fairly inflexible teacher will have more than one lesson-type in the repertoire though none may be very suitable for some kinds of resource. Similarly, resource designers may suggest several patterns of use, though some may deviate so far from common practice that even flexible teachers reject them

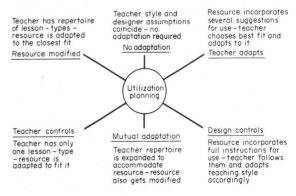

*Figure 1*

Outcomes of utilization planning

as impractical. In theory, there is an important distinction between utilization planning which attempts to fit resources to existing practices, often without studying them sufficiently to even become aware of other possibilities; and utilization planning which attempts to maximize the potential of the resource by considering several patterns of use and choosing that which seems to offer the most benefit to pupils. In practice, research on educational innovation suggests that the former is common and the latter unusual. Only when long-term classroom-based inservice education is provided is there a reasonable chance of teachers expanding their repertoire to include novel patterns of teaching; and then it is mutual adaptation rather than simple teacher adaptation which has the best chance of long-term survival.

In practice, evaluation by teachers is likely to merge with utilization planning, with early evaluation being influenced, possibly even terminated, by early utilization ideas and later evaluation being largely determined by the experience of use. Nevertheless it is useful to consider a three-stage model of evaluation for utilization planning even though the stages will normally overlap.

(a) Inspection and analysis of the resource.

(b) Generation of ideas for different patterns of use and possible modifications.

(c) Selection of the most appropriate idea, followed by detailed lesson planning.

A constructive use of the model would be to train teachers to approach learning resource evaluation in this kind of way, and to encourage the circulation among teachers of resource evaluation documents which incorporate the first two stages.

On the whole, good utilization of learning resources is not promoted by evaluations that either ignore the diversity of usage which most resources receive or regard such diversity only in terms of a mismatch between designer aspirations and teacher practice. However, empirical evaluations which gather data about the impact of a learning resource in a manner that takes into account variations in patterns and contexts of use, are an important contribution to the continuing professional development of teachers and the improvement of their resource utilization practice.

## 3. Evaluation for Improvement

Evaluation for improvement, modification, or redesign is perhaps the most advanced form of learning resource evaluation. Two traditions have contributed to our knowledge. "Developmental testing" was the term originally used by designers of programmed learning sequences, whose commitment to improving learning resources by cycles of testing and revision evolved during the 1960s. "Formative evaluation" was the term introduced by Scriven (1967) to describe the role of course improvement in curriculum evaluation.

Markle (1967), writing within the instructional technology tradition, describes three stages in the empirical testing of a learning resource: (a) developmental testing, during which early drafts or even short excerpts are tried out with several groups of students and immediate revisions are made; (b) validation testing, in which a later draft is tested with larger numbers of students under the designer's general supervisions; and (c) utilization testing, when designer supervision is abandoned, variation in pattern of use is studied, and longer term evidence of impact is collected.

Sanders and Cunningham (1974), writing within the curriculum evaluation tradition, identify and define four types of formative evaluation activity as follows:

(a) *Predevelopmental activities*—formative evaluation work that occurs before formal product development has started. Formative evaluation tasks related to the evaluation of needs, tasks, or other planning acitivies fall into this category.

(b) *Evaluation of objectives activities*—formative evaluation work directed at judging objectives in product development. The emphasis of work in this category is on the provision of reliable information about the worth of goal statements produced by the product developer.

(c) *Formative interim evaluation activities*—formative work dealing with the appraisal of early product development efforts.

(d) *Formative product evaluation activities*—formative evaluation work that focuses on the appraisal of a finished draft of the proposed product.

To this they added three main sources of information to obtain a two-dimensional matrix with 12 cells. These sources are:

(a) *Internal Information*—information that could be generated by inspecting the entity itself. Included in this category is descriptive information about and critical appraisals of the entity.

(b) *External Information*—information concerning the effects of an entity on the behaviours of relevant groups. Student achievement after using a product or parental attitudes toward the objectives of a product are examples of information placed in this category.

(c) *Contextual Information*—information concerning the conditions under which an entity is expected to function. Classroom environment, pupil characteristics, and time of year are three examples of information that fall into this category.

## 4. Intrinsic Evaluation Methodology

Techniques for the descriptive analysis stage of intrinsic evaluation are discussed in other articles: content analysis in, comprehensibility in, and outcomes analysis in.

This section focuses, therefore, on the evaluation and decision-making stages. First, however, it should be stressed that using checklists to collect reviewer opinions on resource characteristics is no substitute for a proper analysis. The methods by which reviewers arrive at their opinions cannot remain undiscussed and unexamined if our knowledge of learning resources and their potential is to progress. Such checklists can serve a useful reminder role to reviewers but cannot substitute for evidence and argument. Moreover, they are usually too vague for questions to have a common meaning for all reviewers, and there is a tendency for them to build in assumptions from theories that are by no means universally accepted.

Two distinctive approaches to the evaluation and decision-making stages have been developed by the Educational Products Information Exchange in New York (EPIE 1974) and an Anglo–German research team based at the University of Sussex (Eraut et al. 1975). Both have been used in a number of countries, and have published sample analyses to illustrate their approaches. The Sussex report also reviews work undertaken in the Federal Republic of Germany, Sweden, and North America.

Central to the EPIE approach is the attempt to find the best fit between materials—as revealed by an instructional design analysis—and context—as revealed either by a needs analysis or by an analysis of an existing curriculum for which the materials are being considered. The various design features are grouped under four main headings: goals and objectives, scope and sequence of content, teaching–learning methods, and approaches to student evaluation. Then a direct comparison is made under each of these headings between alternative sets of materials and some preexisting programme or set of criteria. Additional information about teacher and student characteristics and community concerns may also be brought into the decision-making arena.

The Sussex scheme also begins by examining the curriculum strategy underpinning the design of the resource, and uses four similar constructs to describe it. Objectives and outcomes, subject matter, teaching–learning and communication methods, and assessment patterns. But then it proceeds to explore different ways of using the resource and possible modifications. By expecting diversity rather than a single uniform pattern of use, it seeks to ascertain the potential of the resource under different implementation conditions and in different user contexts. External congruence is then handled through considering implications for implementation in different schools, with special attention to pupil, teacher, school, and community characteristics.

The approach to evaluation which follows is deliberately divergent and pluralistic. Before the decision-making stage is reached, it is argued that the strengths and weaknesses of the materials should be appraised from a range of different value positions. Otherwise important educational issues will be ignored and less

powerful groups will feel that the process was biased against them from the start. Focusing is achieved by devoting attention in turn to aims, curriculum strategy, and quality of materials; and each is considered in terms of different patterns of use and implementation factors.

The other main difference between the EPIE and Sussex approaches is that EPIE either provides or recommends the development of checklists and rating scales for most sections of the analysis, while Sussex prefers a more open approach. The reasons are twofold. The EPIE analyses are much shorter than those produced by Sussex, and they appear to envisage selection from a large number of alternatives. They also expect learning resources to be based on coherent theoretical positions, which can easily be detected and discussed. Sussex sees theory more in terms of "ideal types" which influence but do not determine many crucial aspects of the design strategy. Materials evolve out of curriculum traditions and can usefully be criticized from several theoretical viewpoints without being completely identified with any. Alternative options are generated from considerations of practice in other schools or districts; and evaluation criteria can be derived from (a) critical differences between these options, (b) suggestions in the guide to the scheme, (c) the views of users, evaluators, and other interested parties, and (d) the education literature, especially that specific to the subject and age-group concerned. Trying to tidy up the decision-making process too much is dangerously reductionist, and useful analyses have to be fairly long.

## 5. Field-testing Methodology

Large-scale field testing of learning resources makes use of standard research techniques such as observations, interviews, and questionnaires, each of which is discussed in a separate article; and, in general, models derived from curriculum evaluation will be applicable. Small-scale field testing presents rather different problems, and these are discussed below. Two types of small-scale field testing are particularly important—student tryout in the early stages of resource development, and quick evaluations of small resources like films and audiotapes.

Small-scale developmental testing involves the designer or an associate trying out a prototype version of a learning resource with a relatively small number of students, either individually or in small groups. The purpose is to get quick feedback of sufficient quality (a) to improve the designer's understanding of student problems and perspectives, and (b) to suggest possible modifications. The students should be carefully chosen but are unlikely to be representative of the intended user population which will usually be more varied. With resources of short duration, it is sometimes possible for the designer to make small modifications on the spot or to give an alternative explanation which can subsequently be incorporated into a revised version of the resource. With larger resources it may still be possible for the designer to try out sections and modify or develop ideas at an early stage, before too much time and effort is committed to a particular approach.

Piloting of complex resources is discussed in considerable detail by Nathensen and Henderson (1980), with special attention to Open University courses. Their discussion of the use of in-text feedback questions for concurrent data collection, in addition to the usual posttests and interviews, is particularly helpful. They suggest collecting six types of try-out data and provide a checklist of questions under each of these headings: student performance, clarity of materials, level of materials, student actions (choice of routes, take-up of options, reaction to self-assessment, etc.), student attitudes, and student use of time.

Another agency using a qualitative, small-scale, interactive approach to field testing is the Media Center for Children in New York (Gaffney 1981). In this case the resource is in its published form, so the purpose is not to guide revision but to guide selection and utilization. There is a strong emphasis on children's rather than adult's responses to media; and priority is accorded to the affective rather than the cognitive. Their scheme for film evaluation comprises four sections. Section 1 notes children's behaviour during screening. Section 2 records children's responses in discussion to questions about the film, how it affected them, what they thought it was about, things they might change in it, and so on. Section 3 asks the teacher/evaluator to summarize the experience and interpret the children's response, and to answer questions about the film's appropriateness for various groups of children and different modes of utilization. Section 4 summarizes the overall impact of the film and the evaluation process. This approach could be adapted to other kinds of learning resource which generate emotional involvement or arouse children's curiosity, and makes an interesting contrast to the more usual custom whereby the teacher, evaluator, or designer asks all the questions.

This section has deliberately focused on small-scale qualitative approaches to complement the techniques discussed in much greater length elsewhere. It is also useful to be reminded that accounts of children's interaction with learning resources convey information that cannot be adequately summarized by other methods. Such information is vital for resource improvement, and probably equally important for utilization planning.

## Bibliography

Educational Products Information Exchange (EPIE) 1974 *Selecting and Evaluating Beginning Reading Materials*. EPIE Report Nos. 62–63, New York

Eraut M R 1982 Handling value issues. In: House E R, Mathison S, Pearsol J A, Preskill H (eds.) 1982 *Evaluation Studies Review Annual*, Vol. 7. Sage, Beverly Hills, California, pp. 271–86

Eraut M R, Goad L, Smith G 1975 *The Analysis of Curriculum Materials*. Educational Area Occasional Paper 2. University of Sussex, Brighton

Gaffney M 1981 What's going on? Evaluating children's media. In: Brown J W, Brown S N (eds.) 1981 *Educational Media Yearbook 1981*. Libraries Unlimited, Littleton, Colorado

Harris I B 1982 Communication for guiding teachers: The impact of different conceptions of teaching and educational practice. Paper presented at the Annual American Educational Research Association Meeting, AERA, Washington, DC. ERIC Document No. ED 217 040

Markle S M 1967 Empirical testing of programs. In: Lange P C (ed.) 1967 *Programmed Instruction*. 66th National Society for the Study of Education Yearbook Part 2. University of Chicago Press, Chicago, Illinois

Nathensen M B, Henderson E S 1980 *Using Student Feedback to Improve Learning Materials*. Croom Helm, London

Sanders J R, Cunningham D J 1974 Formative evaluation: Selecting techniques and procedures. In: Borich G D (ed.) 1974 *Evaluating Educational Programs and Products*. Educational Technology, Englewood Cliffs, New Jersey

Scriven M 1967 The methodology of evaluation? In: Tyler R W, Gagné R M, Scriven M (eds.) 1967 *Perspectives of Curriculum Evaluation*. American Educational Research Association, Curriculum Evaluation Monographs 1. Rand McNally, Chicago, Illinois

# Evaluation in Distance Education[1]

E. G. McAnany, J. B. Oliveira, F. Orivel, and J. Stone

"Distance education, simply and somewhat broadly defined, is 'education which either does not imply the physical presence of the teacher appointed to dispense it in the place where it is received, or in which the teacher is present only on occasions or for selected tasks.' This French Government definition of the term *télé-enseignement* (Loi 71.556 du 12 juillet 1971) contains two basic elements: the physical separation of teacher and learner and the changed role of the teacher, who may meet students only for 'selected tasks' such as counselling, giving tutorials or seminars, or solving study problems.

Distance education methods can be successfully used for catering to groups who, for geographical, economic, or social reasons, are unable or unwilling to make use of traditional (e.g., classroom-based) provision. In so doing, they can liberate the student from constraints of space, time, and age." (Kaye 1985, Vol. 3, p. 1432)

---

1   This article was originally published in *Evaluation in Education: An International Review Series*, Vol. 6, No. 3. It appears here with permission from Pergamon Press plc © 1982.

Evaluation in distance education (DE) raises significant and distinctive issues and questions. The costs, institutional and management structures, and outcomes for these alternative educational approaches are conceived differently from different disciplinary perspectives. For the economists, cost measures and their integration into planning and management are of concern. For the educational evaluator most DE projects have had few outcome measures that would allow useful comparisons with traditional systems or even useful formative evidence that might help better internal functioning. For planners and managers, very little evidence of a rigorous nature is available to delineate better ways to structure and operate the variety of DE projects. This article suggests some directions evaluation of DE might take, from these different perspectives. The degree of need in each area is partly reflected in the relative lengths of the respective sections: economists are clearest (and briefest) on what needs to be done, organizational evaluators have the most yet to do, and social and educational outcomes researchers are in between.

## 1. Social/Educational Outcomes and Future Needs

The article poses a series of questions about outcomes that include aspects of the consideration on cost and organization to be treated later. However, answers to these questions can be a guide toward what still needs to be learned about DE. The questions are divided according to a basic set of evaluation questions that Suchman (1967) asked a number of years ago, and still seemed to be a good way of summarizing studies of social interventions. These are questions of effort, effect, adequacy, efficiency, and process and may be defined as follows: Effort—what treatment or intervention is devised and how and to whom it is delivered? Effect—what impact does the treatment have on the target audience? Adequacy—does the intervention offer a substantial reduction in the problem? Efficiency—are there any alternatives that offer the same solution for a cheaper cost? Process—how does the intervention operate and how does this, as well as certain contextual factors, affect outcomes? A number of specific questions about DE projects may be summarized as follows:

(a) Effort
   Can DE survive? What factors count most heavily in project survival?
   Can DE reach the right target audiences with the right inputs?

(b) Effect
   Can DE teach basic cognitive skills; literacy and numeracy to adults; technical skills (agriculture, technology, building trades, personal economic planning, etc.); and family practice skills (health, nutrition, family planning)?

Can DE motivate participants? Can it teach discipline and basic self-instructional skills? Can it create affective/attitude changes?
   Can DE change behavior patterns and create changes in status, income, or general family welfare?

(c) Adequacy
   Can DE reach enough of a given population at need to affect the problem significantly (socially, not statistically speaking)? Can DE grow to meet greater demand?

(d) Efficiency
   Is DE the best alternative to achieve the given objectives at the least cost, or are there other feasible ways of doing the same things more efficiently?

(e) Process
   What factors in DE's organization and operation most affect the outcomes and what external, contextual factors affect outcomes and to what degree? How can these factors be mitigated or incorporated to improve DE outcomes?

It is clear that the answers to these questions are not all available at present, nor are all of the implications of the questions themselves well defined. The task of future planners and evaluators of DE in social and educational outcomes may best be concentrated in the following areas: Effort—reaching the right people and project survival; effect—motivation and study skills; adequacy—flexibility and growth; and process—contextual factors.

### 1.1 Survivability

The evaluation literature speaks of evaluability of projects but not of the survival chances of those same projects. The rate of survival of DE projects has often been discussed, but no satisfactory explanation has been provided. Some blame large technology, others lack of teacher acceptance, others poor planning, and still others lack of changing pedagogical philosophies. The fact that DE projects have gone out of business at what, to traditional educators, seems an alarming rate calls for more serious study into the conditions which affect the very basic social outcome assumed by all evaluators namely, that the project should survive in order to deliver its services and have an impact.

A number of authors have made reference to specific projects (Schramm et al. 1981, Escotet 1980a) but no one to date has tried to go beyond specific cases and look for more generalized conditions that may explain the fact that projects often fail to survive. It may be that contextual factors peculiar to a single project can explain the failure but when a series of cases are analyzed perhaps a pattern of conditions may emerge that could provide planners and project directors with some guidelines for future work. Thus, it is too superficial a judgment to say that television failed in Samoa, Niger, Colombia, and the Ivory Coast simply because it was television. On the other hand, neither is teacher acceptance an adequate explanation in all cases though it clearly looms large in Samoa and perhaps the Ivory Coast. In any case, conclusions about various conditions that threaten drastic outcomes like failure of the project need, at the very least, to be cataloged and placed at the disposal of planners of DE. Paying adequate attention to teacher response to an intrusive medium like television might have prevented some actions in Samoa, but a number of other factors, cultural, and political, contributed to failure not only in Samoa but in other DE projects as well.

The future task is one of case study summaries and a taxonomy of conditions that planners have some control over in prospect. This could insure that projects survive long enough to have expected impacts on participants.

## 1.2 Target Audiences

Problems that have arisen in the equity arena would suggest that DE does not always automatically reach the intended audience. The use of a monitoring evaluation approach would provide a better idea for project managers as to whether this objective is being attained, but two other aspects are important in the planning and outcome evaluation stages.

In planning DE projects, the identification of the target in a more complete sense is usually difficult and often not accomplished. The equity question is most relevant here. Those persons who self-select to participate in a DE undertaking may not be those in greatest need, nor even the target audience originally planned for. The consequences can be either a widening of social class divisions if too many better-off people participate or lack of an adequate number of participants because of a variety of obstacles for the poorer members of society. There are no built-in guarantees as to how DE can overcome the structural constraints of given audiences, but better knowledge about the target audience, its needs, interests, and limitations would help enhance impact in the long term (see Contreras and de Dios 1982 for more on rural audiences and the need for better information about them).

At the outcome stage, at least in longer-term measures, one DE area almost totally neglected is adequate follow-up or tracer studies of students to find out what they do with their distance education once they are finished with the course. In most cases, there is little information as to whether students go on to regular schools, get better jobs, improve their lives, or return to their previous situation. Such studies are complex and costly to perform, yet many evaluation questions about outcome remain unanswered unless the movement of students can be followed up after they finish their studies. To take but one example, the Telesecundaria in Mexico (Mayo et al. 1975) asked whether one social outcome of the success of the project might not be to encourage the best young people to leave the rural area. Again, although much is known about the learning of students in the prestigious British Open

University and cost comparisons are more than adequate, no one has really investigated the social and economic impact of an Open University degree.

## 1.3 Motivation

Practically all researchers in DE agree that motivation is critical to success, yet there are no extant studies that tackle the problem of measurement or observation head on. The advantage of understanding the motivational structure of a given audience better is two-fold: in a planning sense, a more adequate provision of content, organization, and structure would build upon the level of participant interest and help overcome obstacles to achieving a certificate or acquiring a given skill; at the outcome end, a better understanding of the variety of motivations in different participants might also help explain a variety of learning outcomes. It has been argued that DE often taps into a rural audience without previous opportunity and takes advantage of those highly motivated and the more gifted among this audience who first participate. Evaluations of such projects in the early stages of their histories will give too positive a picture of outcomes because of the selection involved (see Carnoy and Levin 1975). Unfortunately, at this point, little is known about selection and motivation in DE to know whether this is a valid criticism or not. What is called for is not only a better focus on motivation but also some kind of adequate measurement of this variable. At the very least, planners need to do better needs analysis to ascertain what the audience perceives its needs are and what seems to motivate them to undertake an often difficult chore of study.

## 1.4 Study Skills

The assumption that motivation is enough to make a student successful in a school setting has long been dismissed by educators. Distance education also calls for more than goodwill from students. All DE projects place a greater responsibility on students for their learning and study skills which are a necessary prerequisite for success. Kaye and Rumble (1981) point out the importance of these skills for success in the British Open University and indicate that this institution provides noncredit modules for this purpose to beginning students. They fail to provide any evaluation evidence about how well students master these modules, or to what extent their levels of proficiency in these skills correlate with later success.

The British Open University is, however, almost an exception in its care in teaching students how to learn in a DE context; many projects assume that instruction is self-evident and that mastery can be achieved with proper motivation. Among the possible explanations of the relatively high dropout rate in some projects (Escotet 1980a cites 90 percent in the Venezuela Open University) is the inadequate provision, printed or interpersonal, of support for students who may be incapable of organizing themselves properly. No matter how self-instructional materials may be, some study skills need to be taught before students can take advantage of the materials.

An evaluation of how different DE projects deal with this problem with different audiences (literacy, primary, junior secondary, etc.) would provide planners at least with the basis for appropriate responses under a variety of circumstances.

## 1.5 Flexibility and Growth

From an outcome perspective, organizational rigidity may be related to two important phenomena, survivability (see above), and growth to respond to the true dimensions of a problem. There has been a long tradition in the sociology of education concerning the study of the effects of bureaucracy in large school systems, but little more than passing reference has been made to the problems in nontraditional settings. The case studies in survivability mentioned above might find one important ingredient of survival or extinction in the rigidity and bureaucratic mentality developed in some DE projects. This rigidity would take special forms if it were tied to large, expensive and/or complicated technology.

Even if rigidity did not destroy the organization, it may easily make it slow to adapt to new challenges or goals, or simply to dynamic growth. The Telesecundaria project in Mexico is an example of an organization that was able, under pressure from student demand to grow. Without this flexibility and potential for growth, DE projects will reach a plateau and remain there. A major criticism of DE and other nontraditional solutions to social problems is that pilot projects so often remain just that and do not grow as predicted to national levels. An example of this is the SACI (Satélite Avançado para Communicações Interdisciplinares) case in Brazil (McAnany and Oliveira 1980).

A review of DE cases for survivability may be added to by a similar review of cases where the projects have remained at a limited stage and have not grown to meet the demand that they were designed for. No serious analysis has been done in this area, and yet conditions for change and growth in DE organizations should provide valuable information for planners.

## 1.6 Context Evaluations

What is called for in this area is greater attention in the evaluations of DE to factors external to the DE institution itself. The Asociacion Latinoamericana de Educacion Radiofonica (ALER) study (1982) of 26 Latin American radio schools emphasized the factors in the operating environment that most affected their success. Two are worth mentioning as examples. The relationship of the radio school, a private entity, with the central government is critical because the government grants the license to operate. If the radio school is seen as too political in dealing with its large constituency of the rural poor, it may be closed down. Thus relations with the government centrally concern the director of the radio school, but the rural audiences are also sensitive about whose side the radio school is on. Again, if the radio school wishes to have some of the DE courses accepted for credit, it needs good relations with the government ministry of education.

There are a series of other context factors that enter into a final assessment of outcome that goes beyond the measurement of cognitive skills most central to educational outcome. Social outcomes are an important added element in the adult programs and these are open to even more influence by constraints in the environment. Planners and managers would benefit from both a taxonomy of contextual variables most likely to affect outcomes, and better methods for observing if not always measuring such factors.

## 2. Cost Considerations and Future Needs

Cost evaluation findings have shown that originally distance education was not principally supposed to reduce costs, but to give access to education to people excluded from the formal system. The cost reduction effect of DE was actually an accident, however, this is no longer the case. Budgetary constraints in most countries, especially in the field of education, make decision-makers anxious to promote cost-effective projects, if possible without sacrificing social and equity concerns.

The clear advantage of DE is potentially to satisfy both these objectives, and one can expect further developments as a consequence. The main obstacle is now a shift in priorities. During the last two decades, the rates of expansion of higher education, and to a lesser extent, of secondary education, have been regularly above those of primary education in a majority of developing countries. In those countries where the objective of universal access to primary education has not yet been achieved, the development of primary education is both a serious equity and a cost-effectiveness issue. It should be noted, however, that DE is less likely to be cost-effective at this level of education because younger pupils generally cannot study on their own.

Numeracy and literacy projects using a DE approach are aimed at adults or adolescents in many countries, but there are relatively few evaluations of such projects, especially cost-effective evaluations. The ambitious program of functional literacy for adults sponsored by UNESCO in the late 1960s and early 1970s did not prove to be cost-effective. However, other mass literacy campaigns, promoted in countries where, very often, decisive political changes have taken place, seem to be more cost-efficient in spite of the absence of adequate evaluation studies (for example, Cuba, The People's Republic of China and, more recently, Nicaragua). Recent projects in West Africa try to provide some kind of literacy to young rural adults by using local languages and agriculturally oriented programs. There again, the cost-effectiveness ratio seems rather doubtful, but more evaluation is clearly needed to assess this assumption.

Generally speaking, in the field of literacy, DE is more

difficult to implement, either because the audience is too young (the case of 6–12 year olds), or because illiterate adults need more assistance than literate ones. Any innovative project in this field should be carefully evaluated from a cost-effectiveness point of view.

The introduction of individual electronic hardware in education is likely to change the concept of distance teaching. It will be more and more home-study oriented, and didactic material will be produced by private firms, bypassing educational institutions. In the near future, however, there is still little prospect for such use in the poorest developing countries. This is less true in middle income countries, such as the South Asian belt, or in Brazil or Mexico. There again, carefully designed evaluation should be carried out in pioneering countries, developed countries included, to monitor the development of educational technology in this area.

The last field of future research in the field of educational technology in the context of developing countries is linked with the general question of limited public resources allocated to education. This constraint will be more and more a structural change, which means that new private resources will have to be raised to finance educational services. It is easier to introduce private financial participation for new and innovative projects than in the framework of previously free traditional teaching services. Our assumption is that future educational innovation will be more concerned with the economic question of optimal use of scarce resources, and the question of the selection of the most cost-effective educational inputs. This concern will open the scope of the issue, in the sense that questions like choice of teaching languages, pupil/teacher ratio, teachers' qualification, textbooks and printed material, health and nutritional status of pupils, design and progression of curricula, and the like, will be included as determinant variables in the study of cost-effectiveness of educational services. In this context, DE will only be one possible way of increasing the productivity of educational services, along with any other alternatives which tend to increase the effectiveness of the system more rapidly than its costs.

## 3. Organization/Management and Future Needs

Much is known in the field of administrative theory to guide managerial practices in general. Administrative, as well as evaluative research, has as much potential as any other field of applied social research to influence decision making within organizations. However, the utilization of knowledge encounters several limitations, not only because of the inadequate training of managers, but most often because of the complexities of the political, interpersonal and interorganizational forces closely involved in the life of social groups.

In the following section, three concrete problems of planning and management in DE projects are focused upon. First, there are the problems managers face in organizing staff, particularly the interface of pro-fessionals and semiprofessionals, the handling of outside consultants, and the balance between knowledge and power segments of projects. Second, there is the problem of managing students who remain at a distance, with special attention to their motivation. Third, there are problems of managing three key functional areas in DE: media production; planning and implementation; and evaluation.

### 3.1 Management of Staff

Distance Education organizations deal with the complex problem of managing professionals, semiprofessionals, artists, researchers, consultants, and evaluators. Much is known about the organizational behavior and the managerial consequences of dealing separately with these groups, and there is a considerable body of research on most of these topics (Mintzberg 1979, Clark 1980, Etzioni 1969, and Benveniste 1977). However, by the nature of their work DE institutions have to deal with all these people in interaction. In many projects, the issue of professionalism alone can make the difference between success and failure.

There are two situations in which semiprofessionals interact in most DE projects. First, as staff and participants in the curriculum development and production teams at headquarters and second, as facilitators, monitors, or managers of learning at reception centers. Semiprofessionals exist because they are still not professionals, because they are not seen as professionals by people who consider themselves professionals (producers, scholars, content specialists), or because they do not behave professionally, given individual or institutional constraints (e.g. monitors, paraprofessional teachers or tutors in charge of predetermined activities in the learning centers).

The main source of mistakes for managing in such situations lies in the establishment of inadequate teaming structures and in the misplacement of control. Professionals tend to avoid control other than self-regulation; semiprofessionals like to be treated as professionals, or behave like bureaucrats in the face of bureaucratic and rigid controls; artists have difficulty working within explicit constraints, and avoid situations in which their creativity has to be defined more operationally; consultants and evaluators dislike being limited by any kind of institutional constraint.

"Polyvalent" teachers or monitors (that is, teaching personnel who have responsibility for all subjects rather than specializing in one subject) seem to be common in DE projects which utilize the mass media. Examples of this are the Mexican Telesecundaria which uses as coordinators certified primary school teachers in secondary levels and the Educational Television (ETV) project in Maranhão, Brazil which used learning orientators. The hope is that the generalist approach may reduce costs and not have a prejudicial effect on quality, given the fact that much of the instruction comes through the media. The impact on costs and learning outcomes of using generalist rather than specialized teaching personnel in such projects has been documented only rarely (see Mayo et al. 1975), while preliminary results from a study conducted in the early 1980s in Maranhão indicate that the monitors do not like their polyvalent role and would prefer to teach only subjects which they know well.

Since materials development is most often the key component in DE, structuring this activity into teams requires more than just effective managerial techniques and tactics of conflict resolution. It implies knowledge (research and evaluation-based, or otherwise acquired) and skills to simultaneously deal with structurally divergent perspectives. The issue is further complicated to the extent that the technology adopted tends to become more rigid or is conceived in such a way that frequent interaction is required. Trade-offs will have to be made between preinvestment in team building versus conflict management later on. Potential sources of complication lie in two specific issues: the establishment of standards, and the institutional affiliation of members.

A few studies (Kaye and Rumble 1981, Oliveira and Walker 1982, Gallagher 1978) have asked the question of how standards for materials' production teams are set, and who sets them. When producers are strongest, formats become the guide; when content specialists, such as university professors are involved, they tend not to pay much attention to pedagogical and other technical requirements; when educationalists and educational technologists take the leadership, other groups have to accommodate this new and (for most of them) unusual situation. Sequential attention to problems have been attempted in a few cases (the approach of the Children's Television Workshop in New York, for example), and team building and collaboration are reported (though neither studied nor compared) in many projects. Everyman's University in Israel is an interesting example of such problems occurring in a context in which the issue of the establishment of standards also arises. Well-established scientific, and in some cases, professional disciplines have very clear notions of standards, competence, excellence, and so on. Such scientific background is lacking in most educational technology groups, which seldom come to duly appreciate and follow the processes of scientific and technological hard-headed thinking. Standards for practice and work excellence are derived from technical models (systems approach models and the like) and, in a few rare cases, from an aesthetic perspective. Moreover, such differing perspectives are seldom shared by group members. When dealing with underprivileged students and other clientele who are not on the higher end of the intellectually gifted scale, competence, success, and effective education might mean quite a different thing. Everyman's case points to a clear institutional option and its consequences: legitimacy for the project was linked to the acquisition of a strong reputation for quality of their general studies courses. As a result outside specialists were consulted for each set of materials produced, while inside only a part-time

evaluator worked to produce reports, not taken very seriously. For Everyman's University professional legitimacy and standards came from outside.

Understanding the interplay of such inside and outside groups, coming to an acceptable definition of standards, patterns, and concepts of what the system is about, adapting the interorganizational structure to fit within the technology-imposed structure or the dominant-group perspectives requires not only a dynamic view of the process of organizing large-scale operations, but also a more profound analysis relating structures to outcomes. Both fine-grained case analysis and comparative evaluations are needed (Mayo and Hornik 1981), but have until now rarely been undertaken.

Kaye and Rumble (1981), and Oliveira and Walker (1982) introduce discussions of the interaction of the academic style of management and the technological imperatives of distance education organizations. Rumble points to the difference between institutions and organizations. Universities are value-creating institutions, that is, adherence to and acceptance of common beliefs about academic freedom, standards of excellence, individual responsibility and performance, departmental independence, and such things require a loose coupling between intrainstitutional units, and very weak administrative interference from above and from outside. Distance education projects, on the other hand, are more similar to industrial organizations, with deadlines, cost control requirements, sophisticated logistical arrangements, and they also have to deal with numbers of contracts and subcontracts, requiring complex interinstitutional relations. When both organizational constraints and institutional values meet, there is potential for trouble. Distance Education projects associated in some way with university education require carefully designed organizational structures to accommodate the different values about how to achieve basic objectives. Difficulties arise because perspectives on what the objectives should be and how they should be met can be opposed. Oliveira and Walker (1982) illustrate the problem with DE projects, as does Mody (1979) for the SITE project in India. This evidence reinforces the conclusion that the future questions of team integration and interinstitutional management will need to be on the planning agenda for new DE projects.

From a practical/evaluation perspective, the main focus should concentrate on highlighting the costs and benefits of differential structuring. Benefits should be more related to prevalent concepts of economic efficiency and effectiveness. They should also deal with issues of organizational learning (how different arrangements contribute to better integration of the group-members' skills; how formative and summative evaluation feeds back into various subgroups of the team, what the impact is on ongoing practices, and so on). On the cost side, not only traditional economic measures should be used (mostly comparing alternative ways of producing materials) but also such things as human costs, levels of conflict, inhibition versus promotion of creativity, and so on. Comparing outputs of differently structured groups could be highly instructive and provide insights into the nature of teaming and its effects on outputs. Schramm's (1972) advice for standards should serve as a guide—materials for learning should be clear, and simple, and effective!

International consultants present an important issue in DE management and evaluation since many of these projects in developing countries still depend upon foreign aid for both beginning and continuing efforts. Tendler (1975) has already illuminated at the macro level much about the logic and dynamics of foreign aid: money exists, international staff of lending institutions have their careers tied to spending money, sometimes without regard to how it is spent, and solutions and problems can be reasonably manipulated to fit each other. Many developing countries continue to expect that their DE projects will be funded externally and this means that the problems of outside consultants will continue as well.

As mentioned above, consultants are the main vehicle for transferring technology, standards, and values as well as agendas. It is not an accident that most of the literature and evaluation on DE is written by people located outside the country in which the project is developed. Such evidence, to a great extent, explains the avoidance of evaluations of managerial and administrative practices. Besides being foreigners, and generally coming from developed countries, outsiders and experts typically find themselves in an unbalanced (dominant) relationship with the recipient of the "know-how."

One of the major consequences of such asymmetry is due to lack of appreciation of contextual variables (Mayo and Hornik 1981, Lenglet and McAnany 1977, McAnany 1980) and the introduction of standards, patterns and models which complicate the appropriateness of the technology to the project. Consultants, consciously or not, impose priorities, define problems, set standards, and determine work structures and hierarchies which do not always fit with the environments of project implementation. For example, they may require planning technologies with a high level of rationality not found even in their own countries, thus creating a false sense of inferiority and incompetence among project people and hindering rather than helping performance. This issue has never appeared in the DE literature, even though it is a recurrent theme in the field of technology transfer studies (Hancock 1982).

As evaluators, consultants set standards for practice and for interpretation of reality. Standards define what is good and what is bad, what works and what does not work. Economic rationalities alien to highly turbulent and extremely poor countries (or projects) may prevent evaluators from appreciating the "miracle" of making a local project operate and survive, in spite of irregular cash flow and all sorts of environmental pressures. Using outside ethical and moral positions, or strict functionalist perspectives, a consultant may be unable

to adequately evaluate and understand the roles of bureaucracy, red tape, corruption, and other "irrationalities" as instrumental, or even essential to overall effectiveness.

Few studies deal with such important issues in case histories, nor are there serious options for alternative technologies other than those defined by foreign aid. Lateral transfer of experiences from other developing countries with similar problems which might be better able to interact are precluded by the nature of international and often bilateral aid. Training by foreign consultants and institutions helps to lead project personnel in the adoption of certain planning, production, managerial, and hardware selection procedures. Few of these aspects of transfer of technology have been studied in the evaluation literature in general and hardly at all in the transfer of educational technology.

### 3.2 Management of Students at a Distance

The Accion Popular Cultural (ACPO), the radio school DE institution in Colombia, was one of the first institutions to introduce the idea of learning centers for distance students (Morgan et al. 1980). Radio forums and campaigns (McAnany 1973) have often utilized monitors and intermediate regional structures in order to mediate the relation between messages and audiences. Agricultural extension programs have widely utilized such mechanisms, in a variety of ways. Mayo and Hornik (1981) question the meaning of participative planning, implying that alternative consulting structures have been used to integrate students and audiences with production mechanisms.

There are few studies showing different results according to organizational structure. Comparisons generally include home study, compulsory learning centers, optional learning centers, and differences in the functions of learning centers (teaching, tutoring, motivating, socializing, and so on). Educational outputs cannot be seen as the only effectiveness measure, given other supporting needs for the final success of any educational effort. For instance, very little is known and published outside the British Open University about what happens to the self-learner during and after a distance learning course. In fact interaction amongst DE students is undesirable because it creates student mobilization and unrest. As such DE projects could be seen as a mechanism of social control, and not simply as an educational alternative. Since groups promote personal and social support for teachers scattered in rural villages, group meetings may be important to enhance the students' chances of finishing training courses, and to improve their actual practices. Using television or radio as a pacesetter may be much more important than the actual contents delivered by such media. These examples illustrate nontrivial questions with managerial implications, and every one of them requires adequate organizational formats or structures.

What is lacking, in general, is more, and better evaluations and research studies of the management of motivation, particularly for adults. Structural constraints (available space at home, competing demands for the television or radio set, and a supportive environment in the family, among others) have not been adequately studied, nor have the organizational consequences of such constraints. A few studies report changes of organizational arrangements based on formative evaluation and ongoing information coming from site visits and other sources. On the other hand, the production of materials also requires correction on the basis of information such as to what extent the structure of materials and the structure of the groups could be changed so that evaluation data would show that DE programs reinforce producers or scholars to a much greater extent than they reinforce students or project participants. The problem of who sets up the criteria is not a simple matter, and appropriate organizational channels can maximize the participation of certain groups in the definition of these standards.

Another empty area in which there is certainly scattered knowledge and vast experience from field personnel, is the help that projects can give students in terms of managing their own study habits and conditions. These projects are learning activities carried out by individual students in their homes which supplement the instruction provided through the distance education media. Projects become another form of instructional activity used to organize students' time. Correspondence teaching, particularly individualized correspondence teaching, for example, could be an interesting source for comparative research with other forms of organizing student learning.

A less studied area is the impact on students of semiprofessionals, monitors, tutors and other less-than-regular full-time teachers. The question here is not only in terms of learning gains and socialization, but in the transmission of professional role models. The impact of intermediate or surrogate figures in relation to students' expectations, specialists versus generalist tutors, expected and actual competence and credibility, and limited opportunity for repetition of concepts (one of the greatest advantages of regular schools), constitute interesting topics with profound implications in terms of the organization of intermediate "personalized" media in DE. A related issue yet to be explored is the question of the relative power, influence, and role of such intermediaries in the instructional process. A final topic is the career dynamics of semiprofessionals, their role expectations, and the long-term chances of using them to work under limited conditions of professional autonomy as monitors or tutors.

### 3.3 Management of Media

Distance education projects described in the literature review (that is, large-scale programs, almost always under government sponsorship, intended to deliver instruction via distance education) present a large variation of combinations of media and institutional arrangements for the production of multimedia within DE. Though print is the main medium in most DE projects, even the limited use of other media present challenging managerial and organizational problems.

Decisions to use media are seldom "rational," in the perspective of the economist or the system's planner. Very few studies deal with the problem, but most of them suggest that, in principle, some decision to use one (or more) specific media was taken. Blue ribbon commissions, influential reports, outside money flowing in search of projects, merchants with attractive new technologies, a group of people trained at one given institution, a minister who was impressed with the marvellous promise of a given technology seen abroad (generally in the United States, Europe, or Japan, seldom in less glamorous countries), a media-based organization in search of objectives—these are typical "reasons" to start a project or to adopt a given medium as the central focus of a new project. Sometimes problems meet solutions in more or less predictable ways. Availability of equipment or trained people also play a role in the decision process. Consultants, nationals or foreign, are not an irrelevant source of such decisions, and correlations must be found between a consultant's (and an organization's, for that matter) background and the kinds of recommendations presented to decision makers. The choice of alternative advice (and media) can have tremendous impact on future costs, given the heavy load of sunk costs associated with some technologies, and the difficulties, technical and human, in retraining and reallocating media specialists. Questions like minimizing costs, given a fixed decision on the use of a medium could be studied in connection with more conventional cost studies. Such an approach presents a potentially new contribution to organizational studies. Here, again, the manager and other project staff have problems of how to deal with experts and expertise. Some media and some technologies, once adopted, result in dependence on the superior knowledge of a given group, so that a decision to adopt certain media and technologies will affect subsequent decisions, power, resource allocation, and group structuring. For example, changing to color television, dropping individual or collective tutoring, contracting, leasing, buying, or developing broadcasting facilities may impose further organizational constraints. Studies performed at the British Open University explicitly deal with such problems, and additional insights can still be obtained from more detailed analysis of such arrangements.

Technology, particularly broadcasting and other sophisticated technologies like computers for elaborate monitoring and evaluation presents once again the problem of interorganizational relations. Issues of technological dominance, transfer of institutional doctrines, values and standard operating procedures from one organization to another, technology transfer between a technologically and a nontechnologically oriented organization and the imbalances such relations create, as well as issues of collaboration and competition are but a few of the themes already studied in the general literature of organization and management. All of these studies may be applied and extended in DE organizations. Case studies and anecdotal information available in DE, as well as the experience acquired by managers and consultants, constitute a solid base for evaluating management of DE media systems.

Another issue related to media management concerns innovation and innovative institutional behavior. Unless a technological innovation or medium is very cheap—seldom the case in DE—the use of an established medium or instructional model makes it harder to adopt radical departures with it, even when there are strong economic incentives for doing so. Few if any studies illustrate the transition of an innovative use of a medium or model from a pilot project to full implementation. To the extent that an organization is heavily committed to a specific medium in DE (for example, radio, television, correspondence) and not to the solution of educational problems, it is more difficult for it to behave innovatively with regard to the innovation after a short time. The medium itself becomes the institution's power base and that of its members, and this will not be risked with radical change. Adoption of technological innovations in DE often precludes organizational adaptability.

Finally, media management in DE demands better trained people than many other educational enterprises which use simpler technologies. The relationship between bureaucratic structure and technological need requires clarification from further studies. Adapted structures, as seen above, tend to lose adaptability. Educational technology is often a poorly understood concept that creates undesirable analogies with industrial enterprises. Education cannot satisfactorily deal with the unidimensional value embedded in the original industrial applications of technology (efficiency, effectiveness, savings, profit, and so on are examples of the ambiguity of terms applied to DE). Even fairly specific prescriptions for instructional design as proposed by Gagné and Briggs (1974) or, for example, media selection procedures advanced by a number of authors, are not easy to put into practice when dealing with real-world teams composed of communicators, media specialists, educators, and subject matter experts.

Training and socialization of the teams (or alternatively, their separation into highly segmented units with sequential monitoring of the activities by outside management) constitute crucial steps in the structuring of DE organizations (Bates 1981) since they are the best ways of future performance control. In the present situation, adherence to organization (team-built) values, in place of, or in addition to professionally-held values is the best guarantee against destructive conflicts. In many instances, the survival, change and adaptability of projects in DE institutions lie much less in the ability and competence of managers and staff than in context variables. In a few cases, as suggested by both the oral and written histories of projects, the ability to manage the environment and influence the decisions of outside institutions is more crucial than internal management skills. One may, for instance, consider the survival of the Telesecundaria in Mexico and the disappearance of such projects as Tele-Niger, or the fading of the Ivory Coast or Samoa projects, from the perspective of external management skills. The research agenda should include better historical studies of these cases and a better understanding of how socialization and training of managers may have influenced their ultimate institutional outcomes.

### 3.4 Management of Planning and Implementation

The literature on organization and management analyzes planning and routine operations to a much greater extent than it deals with implementation. This is true of administrative literature which, like research in education and communications, emphasizes planning and evaluation but neglects the critical area of implementation. Moreover, the formative evaluation dealing with this stage seldom leads to publication in journals. Often such research raises delicate issues of management that the public is not supposed to know of.

Most researchers and evaluators recognize that political realities limit the role of planning and policy recommendations in DE projects (Mayo and Hornik 1981, Kaye and Rumble 1981, Bates 1981). Nonetheless, the rational bias concerning planning and decision making influences so much thinking in this area that most studies contain implicit assumptions that the project depends heavily on intentional action and rationally guided intervention. Rumble's otherwise excellent analysis of the dilemmas involved in trying to interface DE projects with higher education institutions proposes a rational planning-implementation model, and, while recognizing the strong forces of institutional and political factors, includes them as some kind of inevitable evil that has to be dealt with somehow. Lenglet and McAnany's (1977) analysis of the relations between evaluation and decision making in DE assumes that the real world comes first, and that evaluation is but one component of a broad spectrum of information sources. Mayo and Hornik (1981) recognize the double role of the evaluator as an expert *and* as a political actor.

Whilst planning is essential, plans do vary widely in their usefulness. Plans are necessary for a variety of reasons, most of them unrelated to project management—they justify resources, keep people busy, have a catalytic effect when they deal with consensual objectives stated in very broad terms, and sometimes they help implementation. Like memories, plans can be good or bad, depending on the directions a project has taken. Plans that are useful as guides for implementation and management depend to a large extent on their level of detail and the degree of their certainty. That is why microplanning and subunit planning become useful instruments for action, and long-term plans need constant reviewing. The problem in many instances is that planning about predictable and controllable phenomena as well as about trivial ones is important, but not crucial. Dealing with uncertainty, conflicting views, political forces, institutional inertia, standard operating procedures, professional and semiprofessional demands, abrupt budget cuts, constantly changing laws and regulations, unstable cabinets, underpaid staff, and difficulties in correcting previously established technologies and procedures are but a few examples of realities that require data and guidance from organizational and administrative research and evaluation that go beyond planning. Routine drives out planning, and the wisdom embedded within traditional ways of doing things paradoxically contains the seeds for inertia as well as for innovation.

Much analysis is needed on the functions, real and symbolic, of plans, and the strategies to maximize them. Plans, like reorganizations, may help institutions to define superordinate goals which may automatically define organizational objectives, set up conflicts, outline strategies and legitimize the organization. How this works and how it can work better in DE projects has yet to be clarified.

Very few studies comment on the issue of institutional identity or the definition of the business of an institution. The case of Everyman's University is one example: it emphasizes that its business is to compete for quality, while using DE for a specific clientele. The definition of *business*, in many DE cases (Kaye and Rumble 1981), points to a critical issue, namely that many projects become associated with low-quality, low-standard activities, particularly due to the choice of clientele or market niches. The dynamics of such "underdog" organizations must be better known if they are going to be redesigned to become successful or at least to survive.

Leadership and the institutionalization of charisma is also another topic lightly touched upon in the literature, but nowhere carefully spelled out. Many projects are said to be the direct result of influential leaders—Beneke (El Salvador), Mendonca (SACI-Brazil), Block [AID (Agency for International Development) satellites], and Sarabai [SITE (Satellite Instructional Television Experiment)-India]. The interaction between obviously needed leadership and the contextual forces that made both leaders and projects possible is much less studied and understood. Moreover, the transition between the original charismatic leadership style and the institutionalization of the project's values, routines, and procedures is even less understood. How could a project not die or barely survive after the great leader is gone? What invisible leaders (arrangements, structures, organizational and economic pressures, and so on) explain the success of some DE organizations? Understanding such factors is a necessary first step in acting upon them. General organizational literature has made some advance in this matter of leadership and

institutionalization, which may be useful to guide future and more applied evaluation efforts in DE.

### 3.5 Management of Evaluation

Evaluation, like planning, can guide management in the process. There is nothing intrinsic to evaluation activities, however, that make them more likely than other organizational events to influence managerial practices.

Much has been written about the relationship between evaluation and decision-making, and the DE community has witnessed more than one international meeting dealing at length with the matter. However, the matter is complicated by the fact that formative evaluations seem limited to making marginal changes and summative evaluations remain unused on book shelves, while there is very little evidence that either greatly affect decisions in the real world of DE project operation.

A first question about evaluation may be to what extent the actual and symbolic values of evaluations can be useful to the variety of clients (and decision-makers), but particularly to the dominant coalition. The previous discussion on consultants and experts suggests that managers who have a certain degree of freedom in hiring evaluators can expect some significant effects on both evaluation outcomes and the impact of the findings. Managers can and will hire evaluators who will produce the kind of findings most supportive of project goals.

Another area of managerial discretion (including the level of internal evaluation and the definition of control mechanisms within the project) is the decision as to who defines issues to be evaluated. There are a series of nontechnical issues that are decided by management. These include timing of reports, setting up direct reporting channels, asking for further research and qualification of findings, stamping as "confidential" certain information, sending selected information to the "right" people, and relying on effective (or ineffective) computer feedback systems. Important as these are, little of this is reported in the DE evaluation literature. Evaluation is most often discussed as a technical matter and is commonly assigned a formal-rational function in decision making. Such treatment assumes a set of conditions seldom found in the real world of decision-makers. There are, however, some indications of progress. Mayo and Hornik (1981) recognize the political nature of evaluation decisions and the political use of evaluation tools, but there remain practical reasons for viewing the formal mechanisms of evaluation as separate from the ongoing managerial decision-making process. Until this is done, it will be difficult to understand how to maximize the chances for utilization of research and evaluation in managerial activity.

Oral information and the use of verbal reports as a key source of influence of evaluations are also underestimated, even in the extensive case-study literature. Given the recognized importance of this channel in the political science, sociological, and administrative literatures, it seems useful to further investigate report formats and variables affecting the maximization of advantages for the various parties (evaluators and project managers or decision-makers, and eventually the clientele).

Evaluation and research on organizational variables can also illuminate important aspects related to the design of controlling mechanisms and interunit relationships. Rumble (Kaye and Rumble 1981) points to the case of higher education in DE institutions, in which loosely coupled units are the only organizational format apt to accommodate the institutional values of academic professionals. Small units, rather than the overall organization are very useful as places to understand major workings of organizations.

A less studied theme is the definition of success and reputation gained from evaluations. In the world of DE, many projects became famous or successful at birth: good plans, good intentions, and the right people backing the project were enough to promote interest and give the impression that projects like the ones in Samoa, El Salvador, the Ivory Coast, India (SITE), and others were a success well before a sound evaluation was undertaken. International agencies and good communications strategies contributed to the dissemination of such ideas. Poorly funded projects and evaluations performed by people not connected to the mainstream have seldom, if ever, been known and used as models or paradigms.

The indirect influence of such models operates in the sense of introducing external criteria to the manager's agenda under an umbrella of credibility and objectivity. Such influences come in the definition of the problems to be attacked, the solutions to be adopted, the issues to be evaluated, the standards and criteria of performance (which determine the types of equipment, technologies, and the like to be used), the types and profiles of consultants to be hired, and so on. Variables such as environmental factors are commonly ignored or misperceived. Most importantly, the symbolic and ritual effects of evaluation are not adequately managed, since evaluation tends to follow its own logic in such contexts.

All in all, the literature reviewed is extremely provocative in terms of suggesting items for a research agenda, but rather limited in the analysis of such items, generally naive in the description and appreciation of organizational and managerial components, and fairly confident about the potential role of all kinds of evaluation as a factor influencing decision making.

A research agenda in such an applied field as DE will necessarily be derived from a compromise between available knowledge from relevant social science fields, some change in the profile of project evaluators and researchers in the field of DE, as well as a selection of priorities to be negotiated between the principal actors and potential sponsors of such a socially relevant and potentially useful undertaking.

## Bibliography

Arena E, Jamison D, Oliveira J B, Orivel F 1977 *Economic Analysis of Educational Television in Maranhão, Brazil.* UNESCO, Paris

Bates A W 1981 *The Planning and Management of Audiovisual Media in Distance Learning Institutions.* International Institute of Educational Planning, UNESCO, Paris

Benveniste G 1977 *The Politics of Expertise*, 2nd edn. Boyd and Fraser, San Francisco, California

Carnoy M, Levin H M 1975 Evaluation of educational media: Some issues. *Instr. Sci.* 4: 385–406

Clark B R 1980 *Academic Culture.* Yale Higher Education Research Group, Working Paper 42, Yale University, New Haven, Connecticut

Contreras E, Dios R de 1982 *Analisis de los Sistemas de Educacion Radiofonica.* Asociacion Latinoamericana de Educacion Radiofonica (ALER), Quito

Escotet M 1978 Factores adversos para el desarrollo de una universidad abierta en America Latina. *Revista de Tecnologia Educativa* 4(1): 66–83

Escotet M 1980a *Tendencias de la Educacion Superior a Distancia.* Editorial Universidad Estatal a Distancia, San Jose, Costa Rica

Escotet M 1980b Adverse factors in the development of an open university in Latin America. *Programmed Learning and Educational Technology* 17(4): 262–70

Etzioni A 1969 *The Semi-Professions and their Organization.* The Free Press, New York

Gagné R, Briggs L 1974 *Principles of Instructional Design.* Holt Rinehart, and Winston, New York

Gallagher M 1978 Good television and good teaching: Some tensions in educational practice. *Educational Broadcasting International* 11: 203–06

Hancock A (ed.) 1982 *The Transfer of Teaching Technology in Education and Communications.* UNESCO/International Institute of Educational Planning (IIEP), Paris

Kaye A, Rumble N (eds.) 1981 *Distance Teaching for Higher and Adult Education.* Croom Helm and the Open University Press, London

Kaye A R 1985 Distance education. In: Husén T, Postlethwaite T N 1985 *The International Encyclopedia of Education*, Vol. 3. Pergamon Press, Oxford, pp. 1432–38

Lenglet F, McAnany E G 1977 *Rural Adult Education and the Role of Mass Media: A Comparative Analysis of Four Projects.* Institute for Communication Research, Stanford University, Stanford, California

Mayo J K, McAnany E G, Klees S J 1975 The Mexican Telesecundaria: A cost-effectiveness analysis. *Instr. Sci.* 4: 193–236

Mayo J K, Hornik R C 1981 *Evaluation and Research in the Planning, Development, and Support of Media-based Education.* International Institute for Educational Planning, (IIEP) Paris

McAnany E G 1973 *Radio's Role in Development: Five Strategies of Use.* Clearinghouse on Development Communication, Bulletin No. 4. Washington, DC

McAnany E G 1980 Understanding "success" in communication technology: A review of some Third World projects. In: *The Economics of New Educational Media*, Vol. 2. UNESCO, Paris pp. 48–60

McAnany E G, Oliveira J B 1980 *The SACI/EXERN Project in Brazil: An Analytical Case Study.* Reports and Papers on Mass Communication No. 89. UNESCO, Paris

Mintzberg H 1979 *The Structuring of Organizations.* Prentice-Hall, Englewood Cliffs, New Jersey

Mody B 1979 Programming for SITE. *Journal of Communication* 29(4): 90–98

Morgan R, Muhlman L, Mansor P 1980 *Evaluacion de Sistemas de Communicacion Educativa*. Accion Popular Cultural, Bogota

Oliveira J B, Walker R 1982 Studies of the development of teaching and transfer of educational technology in Brazilian universities. In: Hancock A (ed.) 1982 *The Transfer of Teaching Technology in Education and Communications*. UNESCO International Institute of Educational Planning (IIEP), Paris

Schramm W (ed.) 1972 *Quality in Instructional Television*. University of Hawaii Press, Honolulu, Hawaii

Schramm W, Nelson L M, Betham M T 1981 *Bold Experiment: The Story of Educational Television in American Samoa*. Stanford University Press, Stanford, California

Suchman E A 1968 *Evaluative Research*. Russell Sage, New York

Tendler J 1975 *Inside Foreign Aid*. Johns Hopkins University Press, Baltimore, Maryland

# Error Analysis as a Curriculum Evaluation Method

T. N. Postlethwaite

Error analysis consists of analysing students' work—homework, school work, tests—to identify the major errors they are making, or to identify mislearning which is occurring. Error analysis is usually undertaken at two or three points in the curriculum development cycle. The first point is at the small-scale tryout stage of new curriculum materials. The second point is at the larger-scale tryout stage; however, this stage is only undertaken in a few countries. The third point is at the quality-control stage when a probability sample of children is tested after the curriculum has been fully implemented in all schools.

The error analysis undertaken at the first point is more comprehensive than at the second and third points. The error analysis conducted for all three points consists of two analyses.

The first is to discover where an objective is being achieved by only a "few" students. "Few" must be operationally defined by the curriculum team. It is often defined as fewer than 40 percent of students.

At the small-scale tryout stage where perhaps only six classrooms are being used, the pattern of percentage correct for the first three items (one item measuring one objective) could be as shown in Table 1. It can be seen that the objective measured by Item 1 is well-achieved, by Item 2 is poorly achieved, and by Item 3 is well-achieved in some classes and poorly achieved in other classes.

What is "going wrong" with Item 2? At this point, the evaluator turns to the item analysis. This is also the analysis which is used for the larger-scale tryout and quality-control stages. For all students the analysis may be as presented in Table 2 for a multiple-choice item with five possible responses.

Response C is considered to be the right answer or best answer. Responses A, B, D, and E are wrong answers but have been constructed such that they are errors which the students are likely to make. These responses are usually based on teachers' experience. Only 22.2 percent of the students obtained the correct answer. However, Response B was answered by 51.2 percent of all students and the discrimination index, which is typically a point biserial correlation, is positive. This indicates that the better students on the test as a whole are opting for Response B. Assuming that the item is a good item, then an error in learning has been discovered.

The next question is why or how has this error arisen? At the larger-scale tryout and quality-control points all that can be done is to examine the curriculum materials and hope that it is possible to identify what might be the cause. At the small-scale tryout stage the evaluators

*Table 1*
Percentage of correct responses in a sample of six schools

|  | Schools | | | | | |
|  | A | B | C | D | E | F | Average |
|---|---|---|---|---|---|---|---|
| Item 1 | 90 | 80 | 85 | 87 | 93 | 78 | 85.50 |
| Item 2 | 20 | 30 | 27 | 19 | 15 | 22 | 22.16 |
| Item 3 | 90 | 80 | 15 | 20 | 50 | 90 | 57.50 |

*Table 2*
Item analysis for Item 2

|  |  | Responses | | | | |
|  | Omit | A | B | $C^a$ | D | E |
|---|---|---|---|---|---|---|
| Item 2: |  |  |  |  |  |  |
| Percentage of students selecting | 0.6 | 8.0 | 52.2 | 22.2 | 7.6 | 9.4 |
| Discrimination | −0.04 | −0.09 | 0.26 | 0.12 | −0.12 | −0.14 |

a The correct response

have usually collected other information of a qualitative nature from the teachers and students about problems they have had with the curriculum text or with the teaching–learning strategy used. By referring to the qualitative data it is usually possible to identify the cause. The two most frequent causes are that the level of language used is too difficult for the students or that the sequencing is inappropriate. The curriculum team is then in a position to revise the materials and/or the accompanying teacher guide.

The examples given above have used tests with multiple-choice format. However, it is also possible to use students' homework or classwork for such an analysis. There are certain types of achievement for which multiple-choice tests are inappropriate (Thorndike and Hagen 1969). The basic technique is to go through the set homework or school work of the group or sample of students in question and make a frequency count of the "errors" occurring. This yields information about the most frequent errors and again it is usually possible to identify "causes" in the small-scale tryout but not in the larger-scale tryout and quality-control stages.

Three other ways in which error analysis is used are worthy of brief mention. The first is the construction of distractors in multiple-choice items such that the wrong answer chosen by the student indicates to the teacher the likely error. Take for example the item

$(-17) + (-14) =$ A. $-31$

B. $+31$

C. $-3$

D. $+3$

If a student answers B, the most likely error is that the student is confusing $(-) + (-)$ with $(-) \times (-)$. The second use links errors to the way in which teachers explain rules and principles. For example, it was found that some children in a particular target population were calculating $3 + (-7)$ as 10 and $(-6) + (-15)$ as 9. A small study then discovered that these errors were being made only in classes where teachers were attempting to teach the concept and operation of negation numbers using a number line—for example a line with unit intervals along it from $-30$ passing through zero to $+30$.

A third way (Lundgren 1976) in which error analysis is used is in the drawing of profiles of achievement of individual students as compared with what objectives they are meant to learn. Objectives are classified by theme and behaviour (in the taxonomic sense). Hence, there may be one category which involves the calculation of simple multiplication. If 12 items are involved in the testing of the objective, the profile indicates how many of the items are correctly answered. This, in turn, indicates to the teacher where remedial work is needed with an individual student.

## Bibliography

Johnstone A H 1981 Diagnostic testing in science. In: Lewy A, Nevo D (eds.) 1981 *Evaluation Roles in Education*. Gordon and Breach, New York

Klahr D (ed.) 1976 *Cognition and Instruction*. Erlbaum, Hillsdale, New Jersey

Lewy A (ed.) 1977 *Handbook of Curriculum Evaluation*. UNESCO, Paris

Lundgren U 1976 *Model Analysis of Pedagogical Processes*. Stockholm Institute of Education, CWK, Gleerup

Postlethwaite T N, Nasoetion N 1979 Planning the content of teacher upgrading programs: An approach in Indonesia. *Stud. Educ. Eval.* 5: 95–99

Thorndike R L, Hagen E 1969 *Measurement and Evaluation in Psychology and Education*. Wiley, New York

# Impact Analysis of Curriculum

M. C. Alkin

Curriculum impact analysis is the study of changes in the total society influenced by implementing curricula. A new curriculum might itself lead to dramatic changes in the school context. More typically, however, curriculum changes combine with other factors (community values, changes in resource availability, demographics, etc.) to have an impact. Furthermore, it should be noted that the impact of a new curriculum is not always immediate—often, the effects are not felt for some time. In this section, curriculum impact refers to instances when curricula contribute to changes in the school context.

What are the areas of impact? Curricula are designed to have impact on students' subject matter mastery; thus, investigations of curricula typically focus on how closely learners reach prescribed objectives. Looking only at learner behavior changes, however, ignores other important factors. Several researchers have urged that changes in teaching practices, administrative and management patterns, community and parental relationships with the school, and learner social behavior be studied also. Curricula must be judged in terms of the various impacts (intentional and unintentional, long range and short range) which they have on all elements of the school system.

## 1. Teaching Practices

Various curricula demand that certain types of relationships be established between teacher and student. The consultative role demanded by heuristic learning, for example, requires the development of new communication patterns from a teacher who is accustomed to lecturing. Similarly, a "back-to-basics" curriculum may require that much more structured roles be developed by teachers who have used an open education curriculum. Curricula which mandate a team teaching approach require instructors to form new kinds of relationships with fellow teachers and to be more sensitive in the ways they interact with parents and community members.

Some curricula demand a change in the way a subject matter is presented. Curricular approaches which require such techniques as individualization, discovery learning, or the extensive use of audiovisual materials have a direct effect on teaching practices. Teachers who are accustomed to other instructional modes may have to change their practices to accommodate such curricular changes. Schramm (1977), for example, has noted the changes in teaching practices caused by the introduction of nationally sponsored multimedia curricula in several developing countries.

But teachers do not always completely adopt the instructional mode prescribed for a given curriculum. Teachers may modify a curricular approach or continue to use methods which differ from those specified. Thus, examinations of the impact of curricula must examine the methods that teachers actually use, not just those that they were supposed to have used.

Teachers also make use of practices developed in one curriculum when teaching other courses. As an example, a particular program may use individualized instruction. If a teacher chooses to individualize courses which are not using that program, or if the teacher vigorously rejects individualization in all other contexts, the curriculum has had an impact on teaching practices.

The impact of a curriculum on teacher morale will affect the curriculum's impact on student learning. Gordon et al. (1979), for example, found that teachers using Project Follow Through curricula were led to pursue further professional career development activities. This would indicate a positive impact on attitude. Other curricula may create negative teacher attitudes.

## 2. Administrative and Management Patterns

Administrative patterns are influenced by curricular decisions in numerous ways. To fully understand schools, analysts must consider curricula's impact on this educational subsystem.

The introduction of new curricula may cause unrest, lack of understanding, and sometimes misunderstanding among teachers, parents, and the community. Administrators must develop effective communication channels to ameliorate communication problems. The changes must be explained to faculty and their support gained. Parent and community groups must be reassured (Mann 1977).

Curricula have impact on administrative resource allocation decisions. The adoption of a laboratory approach in the science curriculum, for example, can have a tremendous impact on the school budget. Finding both the space and the money to implement a new curriculum can require shifting resources formerly allocated to other areas. Administrators might find themselves facing entrenched groups not ready to accept resource reductions.

Curricula also impact on school staffing decisions. A school which stresses an academic curriculum needs different kinds of teachers than a school which places importance on a vocationally oriented curriculum. The introduction of a curriculum which calls for individualization may require that the administrator hire additional paraprofessional staff. A new curriculum may be usable by the existing staff, but the staff may need inservice training to successfully implement it.

The impact of curricular change on roles and role relationships has been recognized by several researchers. Fullan and Pomfret (1977), for example, assert that this is the main problem in curriculum implementation. In a curriculum which calls for team teaching, assignment to teams must take into account the relationships among team members. New curricula can also result in administrative role changes. An open education curriculum calls for a consultative role; a traditional academic curriculum, on the other hand, demands a much more formalized role.

Existing curricula have impact on administrative behavior as well. The organization of curricula affect the way in which administrators receive and maintain their power and leadership roles (Goodlad et al. 1979). Some curricula are organized so that the administrator can establish a leadership position through acknowledgement as the most experienced subject matter expert. In other instances, it is unrealistic to expect that an administrator should have a high degree of knowledge about all of the specialized fields which are included. Thus, the administrator must use different tactics to establish a leadership role.

## 3. Community and Parental Relationships

A curriculum's impact on parents and the wider community is often overlooked. Curricula which deal with topics that typically provoke a reaction in parents such as sex education, evolution and creation, and political systems could cause disruption in parental and community support for the schools. Schools must assess the impact of such curricula on the community in order to successfully implement them. Unfortunately, it is sometimes impossible to predict community reaction.

Recently, multicultural curricula have been introduced in several countries both to challenge the "melting pot" philosophy and to improve school–community relations. Stahl (1979) found that use of a curriculum which recognizes the contributions and culture of Oriental Jews in addition to those of European Jews has resulted in better relations between parents and teachers in the schools.

Gordon et al. (1979) present one illuminating example of the many kinds of impacts which curricula can have on parents and communities. They discovered that Project Follow Through curriculum projects had a consistent impact on both the home–school partnership and the career development of parents and community aides. Parents used the desirable teaching behaviors which they had learned through the curricula with younger children not yet involved in the projects. The rate of parental volunteerism increased significantly as a result of the programs, and parents became actively involved in the political processes of their communities. A further impact of the curricula was to increase parental motivation to continue their own education.

## 4. Learner Behavior

Curricula also impact on learner behavior—the way students think, learn, and approach life. Examples of these process outcomes (as opposed to cognitive outcomes) include student attitudes toward school, their expectations, self-images, and preparation for adult life. A number of writers have addressed this issue, but examples of a few recent studies will illustrate the point.

Stallings (1975) provides an informative view of this aspect of learner behavior in her evaluative studies of Project Follow Through. Since a variety of curricula were used, Stallings was able to compare the effects of various curricula on learner process behavior. She discovered that independence, cooperation, and non-verbal problem-solving ability were highest in classrooms where the curriculum called for self-selected activities, individualization, use of audiovisual materials, and a wide variety of activities. Classes using this type of curriculum also had significantly lower rates of absenteeism. She found that curricula which stressed work with textbooks and workbooks produced high learner task persistence. In classes which utilized a behaviorist curriculum, students tended to feel responsible for their own failures but not for their successes; they attributed their success to the teacher or the materials.

Kerkhoff (1977) investigated the effect of English and American curricula on shaping the educational expectations of boys. His hypothesis that the English curriculum would produce more realistic expectations earlier in adolescents was generally supported, but British boys overestimated the importance of ability. He found overall that the older American boys had the most realistic expectations of all.

Ballard et al. (1977) looked at the curriculum impact of a peer tutoring program on educable mentally retarded students. They were interested in discovering if working in a peer tutoring environment would improve the social acceptance of the retarded students and found that the social acceptance of those retarded students who had been in the tutoring curriculum was significantly improved over that of those retarded students who had not been involved. On a related note, Stahl's (1979) findings suggested that the inclusion of a multicultural curriculum results in a more positive self-image of Oriental Jewish students.

Macdonald (1975) theorized that schools develop and transmit social patterns to learners. He suggests that most school curricula require learners to play a passive role. He maintains that the impact of this learned role has serious long-range implications since he believes that this role is not what will be expected of students in their adult lives. He speculates that one short-range impact is the development of boredom and a lack of seriousness in students; a long-range implication is a dysfunctional attitude toward later careers. Finally, Macdonald suggests that the curriculum of modern schools produces students who work for social rewards rather than personal satisfaction.

## 5. Summary

Curriculum impact analysis views the school as a social system made up of learners, teachers, administrators, parents, and the wider community. While recognizing that curricula are designed to increase student subject matter learning, consideration of impact must focus on issues beyond changes in learner cognitive knowledge. Analysis of the impact of curricula must assess a curriculum's effects on teaching practices, administrative and management patterns, parent and community relationships with the school, and learner behavior in areas other than subject matter knowledge.

## Bibliography

Anderson R E 1979 The deterioration of the college-educated labor market: Implications for secondary schools. *Teach. Coll. Rec.* 79(2): 274–78

Ballard M, Corman L, Gottlieb J, Kaufman M J 1977 Improving the social status of mainstreamed retarded children. *J. Educ. Psychol.* 69: 605–11

Fullan M, Pomfret A 1977 Research on curriculum and instruction implementation. *Rev. Educ. Res.* 47: 335–97

Goodlad J L, Sirotnik K S, Overman B C 1979 An overview of "A Study of Schooling." *Phi Delta Kappan* 61: 174–78

Gordon J I, Olmsted P, Rubin R, True J 1979 How has Follow Through promoted parent involvement? *Young Child.* 34: 49–53

Hanson E 1979 *Educational Administration and Organizational Behavior.* Allyn and Bacon, Boston, Massachusetts

Kerkhoff A 1977 The realism of educational ambitions in England and the United States. *Am. Sociol. Rev.* 42: 563–71

Macdonald J B 1975 The quality of everyday life in school. In: Macdonald J B, Zaret E (eds.) 1975 *Schools in Search of Meaning.* Association for Supervision and Curriculum Development, Washington, DC

Mann D 1977 The politics of changing schools. *National Association of Secondary School Principals (NASSP) Bull.* 61: 57–66

Schramm W 1977 *Big Media, Little Media: Tools and Technologies for Instruction*. Sage, Beverly Hills, California
Stahl A 1979 Adapting the curriculum to the needs of a multiethnic society: The case of Israel. *Curric. Inq.* 9: 361–71

Stallings J 1975 Implications and child effects of teaching practices in Follow Through classrooms. *Monographs of the Society for Research in Child Development* 163: 40 (7–8)

# Long-term Curriculum Evaluation

## P. Tamir

Retrospective curriculum evaluation is a process by which the merits of a particular instructional program are determined on the basis of its long-term effects. The rationale and goals of many curricular innovations include long-term effects. For example, Bruner (1960) suggests that "massive general transfer may be achieved by appropriate learning, even to the degree that learning properly under optimum conditions leads one to learn how to learn" (p. 6). Cronbach (1963) is even more explicit and asserts that "outcomes of instruction are multidimensional . . . hence the outcomes observed should include general outcomes ranging far beyond the content of the curriculum itself—attitudes, career choices, general understandings and intellectual powers, and aptitude for further learning in the field" (pp. 675, 683). Thus, one major justification of retrospective curriculum evaluation is its potential for evaluating long-term effects.

The second justification is even more compelling; it suggests that *only* long-term evaluation can adequately assess certain merits of a given program. This suggestion is based on Ausubel's theory of meaningful learning, which asserts that the best and, perhaps, the only way to find out whether learning has been meaningful is by looking at the impact of the learning on subsequent achievement. Although details may be forgotten, the cumulative effects of having learned them remains on the cognitive structure of the learner. On the other hand, Ausubel seriously questions the validity of results obtained in an immediate final examination for assessing the worth of a curriculum, since "motivated students can learn for examination purposes large quantities of overly sophisticated and poorly presented material that they do not really understand" (Ausubel 1968 p. 578).

## 1. Examples of Retrospective Evaluation

The following examples are illustrative cases of retrospective evaluation.

In 1966 Ausubel evaluated the Biological Science Curriculum Study (BSCS) approach by content analysis of its three versions which were designated as Blue, Yellow, and Green. He wrote:

The Blue Version presents biological material of college level difficulty and sophistication to students who had not had the necessary background in chemistry, physics, and elementary biology for learning them meaningfully. . . . It is so impossibly sophisticated for its intended audience as to be intrinsically unlearnable on a long-term basis. . . . It is

not only unnecessary and inappropriate for the beginning course, but also hinders learning and generates unfavorable attitudes toward the subject.

If biochemical content is included, it is probably better to provide a minimal background in chemistry and to consider biochemical topics at a somewhat lower level of sophistication (Yellow Version), than to provide almost no background in chemistry and to consider biochemical topics at a very high level of sophistication (Blue Version).

Only the Green Version has a unifying theme . . . is reasonably well organized and integrated and makes an original contribution to and introduces a new (i.e., ecological) approach in the teaching of high school biology. (Ausubel 1966 pp. 176, 177, 180–81, 183)

When the results of achievement tests administered immediately at the end of the course were compared it was found that Blue Version students outscored Green and Yellow Version students (The Psychological Corporation 1967). Yet, when the long-term effects of the three versions were compared by evaluating students in their first year biology course at the university several differences were observed. Some of them are the following.

(a) BSCS students, compared with traditional students, were less likely to fail or drop out of introductory biology.

(b) Among the BSCS versions, "Blue" students showed the highest rates of failure and attrition, but "Yellow" students rarely failed or dropped out.

(c) Green Version students, compared with all other students, demonstrated the highest rate of retention with respect to ecology.

(d) Yellow Version students had the most positive, and Blue Version students the least positive attitudes toward biology.

(e) In their performance in tests that required critical thinking and an understanding of science, BSCS graduates tended to rely on higher cognitive abilities more than did non-BSCS graduates.

It may be seen that the results of the retrospective evaluation confirmed many of Ausubel's predictions, especially in relation to the inadequacy of the Blue Version for most 10th-grade students and the meaningful learning offered by the Green Version. On the other hand, in spite of Ausubel's assertions, Yellow Version students have demonstrated significant and consistent superiority in various aspects of achievement and attitudes (Tamir 1970).

Another example of retrospective evaluation is the evaluation of the chemistry program known as CHEM Study. It was found that:

> CHEM Study students have a distinct advantage in selective courses.
>
> The improved completion record of CHEM Study students in college chemistry courses suggests that they are more persistent, hence more interested in chemistry, due to their background. This record indicates that it is just as advantageous for the marginal students to have had CHEM Study as it is for the best. (CHEM Study 1967)

A study of first-year university students' perceptions of their high-school biology (Tamir et al. 1980) revealed, among other things, firstly, that students valued most highly the help of prior biological knowledge for the understanding and retention of new material presented in lectures, and secondly that students who specialized in high-school biology, as well as those who studied the Israeli BSCS adaptation, had considerable advantage over others in understanding the lectures and in their work in the laboratory.

## 2. The Nature and Limitations of Retrospective Evaluation

As already explained, the essence of retrospective curriculum evaluation is the long-term transfer paradigm which assumes the existence of relationships between early and subsequent levels of education. These relationships can be identified in two ways: (a) evaluation of actual students' behaviors at an advanced stage in reference to their learning experiences at earlier stages; and (b) examination of students' perceptions of the contribution of an earlier program (e.g., high school) to their subsequent studies (e.g., university).

Retrospective studies have certain limitations. One limitation of retrospective evaluation is the lack of control of events that have occurred in the interval between the two stages (e.g., high school and university). Another is that the samples are, by necessity, selective, since they include only those students who have moved from the lower to the higher level (e.g., from high school to the university).

Two alternative strategies have been traditionally used to study long-term effects: cross-sectional and longitudinal. Both strategies have severe limitations. Thus in longitudinal studies the same students are supposed to be followed for several years and their behaviors are measured at different points of time. However, not only is it difficult and costly to locate the subjects, but it is often impossible to maintain the original sample, hence attrition becomes a major handicap. Cross-sectional studies are free of this handicap, but suffer from the fact that different students represent different stages of growth, and one can never be sure of the magnitude of the effects of individual differences. The strategy suggested here, namely retrospective evaluation, overcomes the limitations mentioned above, since it deals with the same sample and there is practically no attrition.

## 3. Conclusion

Retrospective curriculum evaluation is built on sound theoretical grounds and its value has been demonstrated by several empirical examples. It may serve three major purposes: (a) the evaluation of long-term effects; (b) the evaluation of the meaningfulness of learning within the framework of a particular curriculum; (c) the long-term views and perceptions of students who are the major clientele of any given curriculum.

## Bibliography

Ausubel D P 1966 Evaluation of the BSCS approach to high school biology. *Am. Biol. Teach.* 28: 176–86

Ausubel D P 1968 *Educational Psychology: A Cognitive View*. Holt, Rinehart and Winston, New York

Bruner J S 1960 *The Process of Education*. Vintage, New York

CHEM Study 1967 A study of CHEM study students after reaching college. *CHEM Stud. Newsletter* 7: 1

Cronbach L J 1963 Course improvement through evaluation. *Teach. Coll. Rec.* 64: 673–83

Tamir P 1970 Long-term evaluation of BSCS. *Am. Biol. Teach.* 32: 354–58

Tamir P, Amir R 1981 Retrospective curriculum evaluation: An approach to the evaluation of long-term effects. *Curric. Inq.* 11: 259–78

Tamir P, Amir R, Nussinvoitz R 1980 High school preparation for college biology in Israel. *Higher Educ.* 9: 399–408

The Psychological Corporation 1967 *A Report of Biology Science Curriculum Study Evaluation Program 1964–1965*. The Psychological Corporation, New York

# Part 4

# Measurement Theory

# Part 4

# Measurement Theory

---

## Introduction

Part 4 presents a body of theory critical for measurement in evaluation. Although the models of classical test theory and item response theory (IRT) were developed for the most part with objective paper-and-pencil tests in mind, they apply more broadly to any data collection procedure where the ultimate aim is to arrive at quantitative scores for each of the entities measured. Concepts like reliability and validity apply even more broadly, to qualitative as well as quantitative data. The title of this Part, Measurement Theory, should by no means suggest that the material presented is not of direct practical value. Familiarity with this Part should give all evaluators, whether quantitative or naturalistic in their orientation, a better understanding of the data collection approaches they use. It should especially help to acquaint evaluators with the powerful statistical models and procedures now available for designing, scoring, and interpreting quantitative instruments in both the cognitive and affective domains.

Part 4 begins with a section on General Principles, Models, and Theories, including validity and reliability, classical test theory and its extensions, and IRT models. It then turns to the section on more Specialized Measurement Models and Methods, including rating scales and achievement tests, techniques for test construction and validation, models for measuring attitudes, values, and personality constructs, and some specialized topics in the measurement of achievement.

The first section opens with an article which provides a broad historical overview of *Measurement in Educational Research*, beginning with the origins of psychological measurement as a field of inquiry in the late nineteenth century. The discussion then turns to axiomatic systems for measurement, especially conjoint measurement and the Rasch model. The remainder of the article surveys some strong true-score models, alternative parameterizations of ability, criterion-referenced measurement, attitude measurement, and multivariate measurement approaches, including factor analysis.

The second article extends this general discussion, turning to *Future Developments in Educational Measurement* and commenting on likely and desirable advancements in the light of recent trends. Four areas are highlighted: the construction of variables and the investigation of generalizability and construct validity; IRT models, especially methods of estimation and extensions to multidimensional models; ability theory, including new models for human abilities, incorporation of speed of processing into such models, and improved tests that are more nearly unidimensional; and lastly, the measurement and analysis of learning and educational achievement, including improved representations of students' evolving knowledge structures, and improved methods of achievement test construction.

The body of theories that undergird modern measurement are not exclusively mathematical and statistical. There are also theories to guide the examination of the meaning or appropriateness of a given measurement operation in a given situation. A measure is valid to the extent that it does what it is intended to do. Validity implies that score-based inferences are warranted, and that a measure purported to indicate some concept (or construct) largely reflects the dimension it is intended to measure, and not some other. A variety of different kinds of evidence might be brought to bear on a test's validity. These are generally organized under the rubrics of content validity, criterion-related validity, and construct validity. The article on *Validity* defines and illustrates these categories of validatory evidence, and also describes the relation of new, structural equation models to the investigation of validity.

One of the earliest and best developed areas of classical test theory concerns the reliability, or replicability, of measurements. A test is reliable to the extent that test performance accurately represents performance on the broader universe of measurement operations which the test is intended to represent. The third article, *Reliability*, presents the classical reliability model and describes some of its major implications. It then turns to the reformulation of that model using variance components, which permits a much more general, multifaceted treatment of measurement error. Designs for estimating reliability are considered, and in a brief concluding section, consideration is given to the reliability of domain-referenced or mastery tests, where the intent is to estimate an individual's domain score or mastery status, rather than to rank order examinees consistently.

One application of the concept of test reliability is in accounting for the effects of measurement error on correlations. The brief article on *Attenuation* provides simple formulas for adjusting correlations to obtain estimates of the strength of underlying relationships, in effect removing the influence of measurement error on the observed correlation.

Within classical test theory, the observed score is analyzed into just two components, true score and error, and different possible sources of error are generally not distinguished. In an important extension to this classical model, generalizability theory allows not only for multiple sources of error, but also for multiple definitions of the true score. The machinery of generalizability theory permits rigorous statements about the universe of admissible observations about which a given observation is intended to generalize. For each facet across which generalizations are to be made, there may be a nonzero variance component which contributes to the measurement error. The article on *Generalizability Theory* extends and elaborates the treatment of reliability in the preceding articles. It introduces the basic concepts and terminology of this important topic, and illustrates several of the most widely used measurement designs.

The article on *True-score Models* sets forth some of the relationships among classical test theory models, IRT models, and other less well-known strong true-score models. This overview serves as a bridge to a set of three articles on *Item Response Theory*, *Latent Trait Measurement Models*, and *Rasch Measurement Models*. Item response theory and latent trait models, which include the class of Rasch measurement models, all describe the functioning of single test items. Each model expresses the probability distribution of possible responses by one examinee to one item, as a function of parameters characterizing the item and the examinee. The properties of the test as a whole are then derived from the properties of the items. In contrast, the models of classical test theory are generally specified at the level of the test as a whole. Several advantages flow from the specification of IRT models at the item level. Once the parameters for a set of items are estimated (a process known as *item calibration*), scores on tests constructed from different subsets of these items can easily be converted to a common scale. This greatly simplifies test equating, and makes possible adaptive testing methods in which efficiency is improved by giving different items to more versus less able examinees. Once items are calibrated, it is also possible to determine how much information they will yield when administered to examinees at different levels of ability. This feature of IRT models provides a firm statistical basis for scientific test design. The article on *Item Response Theory* reviews the fundamentals of these important models, and describes a number of applications. The article on *Latent Trait Measurement Models* contrasts some specific variants within the area of IRT models, and offers support for use of the Rasch models as one of several alternatives. Finally, the article on *Rasch Measurement Models* describes this important class of models more fully, and provides further applications.

The second section of Part 4 turns from this general treatment of topics in measurement theory to a more focused consideration of models and methods for specific purposes and specific types of data. It begins with two articles providing a theoretical treatment of analysis and scaling for rating scales and for achievement tests. Rating scales generally force examinees to choose one of a series of ordered response categories for each of a number of items designed to reflect the same underlying dimension. Thus, rating scale analysis involves the treatment of ordered polytomous responses. Achievement tests are usually forced choice instruments for which responses are scored correct or incorrect. Therefore, scaling of achievement tests involves the treatment of dichotomous responses. The article on *Rating Scale Analysis* covers the uses and scoring of such scales, the Thurstone and Rasch measurement models, and a number of specific issues that may arise in the development and use of rating scales. The article on *Scaling Achievement Test Scores* offers an extensive treatment of types of scales, the assumptions implicit in the use of number-correct scores, classical and item response theoretic (IRT) approaches to scoring, and commonly used derived scores, including linear and area conversions as well as age and grade conversions. The article goes on to consider alternative models and methods of test equating, which is the process of mapping two or more tests onto a common scale, and then turns to moderation procedures, which generalize equating methods to the case where different tests may not be strongly correlated, or may not even measure the same areas of knowledge. Finally, the use of item banking to define a generalized measurement scale is described.

The next two articles discuss specific methods useful for test construction and validation. Each combines a theoretical exposition with useful, practical advice. *Item Analysis*, discussed in the first of these articles, describes methods for the statistical analysis of items during test development. The statistics generally computed describe an item's difficulty and its accuracy in discriminating different levels of ability, referred to as *discrimination*. For criterion-referenced tests, somewhat different statistics are often used than for norm-referenced tests. A number of useful statistics and formulas are presented, including methods for predicting test statistics from the item statistics computed. *Validation of Individual Test Response Patterns*, discussed in the second of these articles, refers to the systematic study of patterns of responses across items in order to detect possible disturbances of the measurement process. Item response theory models are quite helpful for this purpose, because they provide an explicit model for the probability of each obtained item response as a function of examinee ability. Thirteen specific sources of disturbance are listed, and the major item response validation methods are described.

The next five articles each describe specific models for measuring attitudes, values, or personality constructs. In contrast to the more general mathematical models presented earlier, these approaches each specify the design and format of the measurement instrument, as well as the method for calculating scale scores from the responses obtained. The first of these articles, on *Thurstone Scales*, presents the law of comparative judgment, the idea of subjective values, the method of equal appearing intervals, and other fundamental ideas contributed by Thurstone. *Guttman Scales* and the related method of scalogram analysis, both described in the second of these five articles, provide an alternative approach to the measurement of attitudes. The Likert scale is among the most widely used scale formats, and one of the most flexible. The article describing *Likert Scales* presents a step-by-step outline of how to construct them. The next scale type considered, *Semantic Differential Measurement*, was designed as a tool for measuring the meaning of different concepts, but has also been widely used as an attitude measurement technique. Respondents rate concepts on scales anchored by a number of bipolar adjective pairs. Several alternative scaling methods have been devised for deriving scores from the resulting data. The last of the five articles in this group describes the *Repertory Grid Technique* developed in connection with Kelly's personal construct theory. The article presents the rationale for the technique, defines terms, explains procedures, and gives applications.

The most common procedure in achievement testing is to ask examinees to select or produce the correct answer to each question, and then calculate the number of questions answered correctly. The final three articles in Part 4 each discuss alternative procedures that may offer significant improvements over the standard approach in special situations. The first of these articles discusses *Diagnostic Assessment Procedures* that may be used in regular classroom settings to increase the information yield of tests. These generally entail a more fine-grained analysis of test performance, or the use of tests designed to measure narrow learning objectives rather than broad achievement constructs. Some of these approaches also incorporate specific information about the structure of the subject-matter domain. For example, they may consider the implications of response patterns over sets of arithmetic problems designed so that distinct misconceptions will yield discernable error patterns. *Confidence Marking*, the subject of the next article, refers to alternative marking systems in which, for example, students may not only select a response, but also report their degree of confidence in the response selected. The result may be a more challenging and more informative assessment for the student. The final article in this group concerns *Correction for Guessing*. These are scoring formulas that distinguish between incorrect and omitted responses, in effect imposing a penalty for incorrect responses. Guessing corrections are often used in conjunction with instructions to examinees designed to discourage random guessing, with the aims of increasing overall accuracy of measurement and eliminating any relative advantage for those students more prone to guess than others. In addition to the traditional formulas, the article discusses guessing corrections from an IRT perspective.

# General Principles, Models, and Theories

## Measurement in Educational Research

### J. A. Keats

In describing the application of measurement principles to educational research, it is impossible to separate the contributions which have come from the disciplines of education, psychology, sociology, physical sciences, and mathematical statistics. There is little to be gained from making such separations but certain approaches tend to be known by the name of their principal protagonist and this reference tends to imply that a particular person's discipline is the one making the contribution. No such implication is intended in the present account when techniques are referred to by their customary name.

Measurement in education has been practiced for more than a millenium in China and for centuries elsewhere. However it was not until the beginning of the twentieth century that research workers studying educational problems became self-conscious about measurement methods. This situation also existed in the physical sciences where Campbell's (1917) account of physical measurement was the first to be widely recognized and adopted. It was not until educational measurement methods had developed considerably that it was possible to compare them with physical measurement and this was done by a committee of the British Association for the Advancement of Science in 1938 (Ferguson et al. 1940).

In the first four decades of the twentieth century two quite different educational measurement techniques were developed for quantifying individual differences. The first of these was developed by Binet in the context of an educational problem associated with compulsory education. Binet not only constructed an instrument for deciding whether or not a child could benefit from formal education as it was in those days, but also established the criteria of item difficulty and discriminating power which are still currently used for the selection of items, tasks, and so on to be used in educational and psychological tests.

While Binet was constructing a psychological instrument to solve an educational problem, others, such as Sir Francis Galton and Spearman (1904), were developing and applying statistical methods suitable for the study of individual differences. Binet's criteria of difficulty and discriminating power which he defined graphically were soon converted to statistical indices which in the case of discriminating power was sometimes associated with a test of statistical significance. However, Binet's developmental measure, the mental age, was severely criticized by those with a more statistical approach as being ambiguous in definition and lacking generality (Thurstone 1926). Thurstone recommended measures based on the standard score at particular age levels.

It has only recently been pointed out (Keats 1982a) that the differences between the approaches of Binet and Thurstone were not only those of the convenience of one measure as opposed to another but went much deeper. Both approaches implied that cognitive growth could be described by a single number. However Binet's approach implied that individual differences at any age level could be accounted for by differences in rate of growth whereas Thurstone's approach implied that individual differences at all ages arose from differences in the value approached at intellectual maturity, but that rate of approach to the ultimate level is the same in percentage terms. According to Thurstone's implicit assumption everyone reaches a given fraction, for example one-half of his or her ultimate level at a particular age level. In the case of physical height this assumption is very nearly correct. With Binet's assumption, all human beings are approaching the same ultimate level but at quite different rates. Both Binet's and Thurstone's implicit assumptions have been shown to be seriously in error (Keats 1982a).

While these arguments were proceeding, a third criterion for selecting items, that of item homogeneity, was being ignored. Spearman (1904) had established conditions which would lead to the conclusion that the relationships between a given set of measures could be accounted for by a single variable or factor. Spearman used these techniques to try to establish a single general ability underlying all tests of cognitive performance (the techniques are known as factor analysis). While Spearman's thesis was proved incorrect empirically, his methods could have been used to establish criteria for concluding that a given set of cognitive tasks or items all measured the same underlying variable, that is were homogeneous. This condition for educational and psychological measurement was not stressed until the

237

middle of this century. Thus the three criteria for incorporating cognitive tasks into a single instrument with a single score are difficulty, discriminating power, and homogeneity.

## 1. The Relationship Between Educational Measurement and Physical Measurement

The conditions for physical measurement stated by Campbell (Campbell 1917) involved two basic operations each requiring a condition to be satisfied. The first of these is an operation of ordering whereby two objects can be compared with respect to (say) weight and a decision made as to which is heavier. In this case the condition to be met is that of transitivity so that if object A is judged heavier than object B and object B heavier than object C then object A *must* be judged heavier than object C. Failure to meet this condition could be due to unreliability in the comparing instrument or to a confusion in the dimensionality on which the objects are being compared.

Given that the ordering condition can be met with consistency, a second operation, that of combining must be possible, that is, two or more objects can be combined with respect to the dimension being measured in such a way that the combination can be compared on that dimension with any other object or combination of objects. With a consistent ordering operation and a combining operation it is possible to associate a number with any object by combining standard units and subunits. The combining or additivity condition is that the number associated with object A plus that associated with object B must equal the number associated with the combination of A and B. If the additivity condition holds for all pairs of objects then the set of numbers associated with these operations and objects is unique apart from a multiplying constant to convert, for example pounds to kilograms.

With the development of educational measurement using objective testing methods, rating scales, attitude scales, and soon, the question of the extent to which these methods can be made to satisfy Campbell's conditions naturally arose. A Committee of the British Association for the Advancement of Science (BAAS) in 1938 examined this question in the context of psychological applications of these techniques and concluded that they did not do so completely (Ferguson et al. 1940). The ordering operation and condition could be met by a number of methods with allowance for unreliability of comparisons but a suitable combining operation could not be identified and so the additivity condition could not be checked.

Following the BAAS report, Gulliksen (1946) has pointed out that in the case of the method of paired comparisons a combining of differences operation was in fact defined and additivity of differences could be checked. This observation led naturally to the definition of interval scales, that is, scales for which differences between objects could be measured but for which no

zero point could be defined from the data obtained by the method of measurement used. Stevens (1951) proposed a fourfold classification of measurement methods:

(a) Nominal scales which are really unordered classifications of objects.

(b) Ordinal scales which have an operation of ordering which exhibits transitivity.

(c) Interval scales which have ordering and combining operations for *differences* and these meet the consistency conditions of transitivity and additivity.

(d) Ratio scales which satisfy Campbell's criteria for fundamental measurement of individual objects.

Stevens' classification has been widely adopted in the literature reporting educational and psychological research since the early 1950s. However his conclusion that certain types of statistical procedures are applicable or inapplicable to one or more types of scale has caused considerable controversy. This conclusion has not been substantiated in terms of the assumptions underlying the various statistical techniques and so should not be taken seriously.

## 2. Conjoint Measurement

The general lack of a combining operation in educational and psychological research was finally overcome by research workers in Denmark and the United States, apparently independently, developing conjoint measurement at approximately the same time. Technical accounts of this theory are contained in Luce and Tukey (1964) and Ross (1964). The latter account is marred by a general "theorem" which is not only incorrectly proved but is in fact untrue. Rasch (1960) working at the Danish Institute for Educational Research published what amounts to an application of conjoint measurement to the preparation of objective tests and analysis of data obtained from their application. His method has been developed and widely applied in recent years.

The simple account given here follows Coombs et al. (1970) using objective testing as an example. The measurement method is based on a matrix or table in which rows correspond to groups of subjects who have each attempted all of the items which define the columns. The entries in the cells of the table, for example $P_{gi}$, are the proportions of subjects in group $g$ who give the correct response to item $i$. Table 1 displays such a table. If the letters $a$, $b$, $c$ denote the measures corresponding to any three of the groups of subjects and $p$, $q$, and $r$ to the measures corresponding to any three of the items then it must be possible to define three functions, $\phi$, $f$, and $h$ such that:

(a) $\phi(a, p) = f(a) + h(p)$, that is, the function $\phi$ is decomposable into two additive components which separately are functions of $a$ and $p$.

**Table 1**

Proportions of subjects in groups giving the "correct" responses to items

| | | Items | | | | | | |
|---|---|---|---|---|---|---|---|---|
| | | 1 | 2 | 3 ... | $i$ ... | $j$ ... | $N$ | |
| Groups of subjects | 1 | $P_{11}$ | $P_{12}$ | $P_{13}$ ... | $P_{1i}$ ... | $P_{1j}$ ... | $P_{1N}$ | |
| | 2 | $P_{21}$ | $P_{22}$ | $P_{22}$ ... | $P_{2i}$ ... | $P_{2j}$ ... | $P_{2N}$ | |
| | | ⋮ | ⋮ | ⋮ | ⋮ | ⋮ | ⋮ | |
| | $g$ | $P_{g1}$ | $P_{g2}$ | $P_{g2}$ ... | $P_{gi}$ ... | $P_{gj}$ ... | $P_{gN}$ | |
| | | ⋮ | ⋮ | ⋮ | ⋮ | ⋮ | ⋮ | |
| | $n$ | $P_{n1}$ | $P_{n2}$ | $P_{n3}$ ... | $P_{ni}$ ... | $P_{nj}$ ... | $P_{nN}$ | |

(b) $\phi\,(a, p) \geqslant \phi\,(b, q)$ if and only if $P_{ap} \geqslant P_{bq}$.

The following axioms are sufficient for the existence of functions satisfying the above conditions:

(a) The cancellation axiom: if $P_{ap} \geqslant P_{bq}$ and $P_{br} \geqslant P_{cq}$ then $P_{ar} \geqslant P_{cp}$.

(b) The solvability axiom: if $P_{ap} \geqslant t \geqslant P_{ap''}$ for some real $t$ then there exists a $p$ such that $P_{ap} = t$ and the corresponding condition for the individual differences subscripts.

All measures of the type $a$, $b$, $c$ and $p$, $q$, $r$ satisfy the conditions for an interval scale which may under certain circumstances be transformed to a ratio scale.

Rasch (1960) proposed a transformation of the proportions obtained in tables such as those in Table 1. He observed that if

$$\frac{P_{gi}}{1 - P_{gi}} = \frac{A_g}{D_i} \tag{1}$$

where $A_g$ is now used to denote the ability of group $g$ and $D_i$ the difficulty of item $i$ then:

$$\text{Logit}\,(P_{gi}) = \log \frac{P_{gi}}{1 - P_{gi}} = \log A_g - \log D_i \tag{2}$$

which meets the order preserving and additivity conditions. The values of $\log A_g$ satisfy interval-scale conditions and the values of $A_g$ thus satisfy ratio-scale conditions. Similarly the values of $D_i$ satisfy the conditions for a ratio scale. Rasch presents examples of test data which satisfy the conditions of this model and some which do not. Other workers have made empirical investigations of the applicability of the model to tests which were not constructed in accordance with the model and often report satisfactory fits of the data by the model.

Many years before Rasch's publication, Lord (1952) had developed the theory of the normal ogive latent ability model. The methods of estimating ability values for the normal model are very complex and certainly require computer assistance. It is thus not surprising that latent ability models and measures were not used in educational and psychological research until after Rasch's logit model had appeared with its much greater simplicity.

From the time that advances in electronic computers made the normal ogive model a viable alternative to the logit model (sometimes called the "one parameter logistic model", a title which is somewhat misleading) there has been considerable discussion as to which model should be used. Before summarizing the points made in this controversy it is as well to remember that the advantages of using latent ability measures are not questioned. The most efficient way of obtaining estimates of these measures however, is the subject of considerable current debate.

One of the reasons for the greater simplicity of the Rasch logit model lies in the fact that the model assumes that although the test items have different difficulties, they all have the same discriminating power. This restriction places an added restraint on selecting items for a test: they must not only have significant discriminating power but also, at least approximately *equal* discriminating power. The advantage claimed for such instruments is that the simple, number correct score is a sufficient statistic for estimating ability. There are other consequential advantages related to chaining or equating tests.

The disadvantages of the logit model are argued in terms of the fact that, given (say) 200 trial items, a test of 80 items chosen with tight restriction on discriminating power will in general have lower reliability than one, also of 80 items, in which the highly discriminating as well as the moderately discriminating items are included. However, to utilize this greater reliability for the estimation of latent ability, it would not be possible to use the simple, number correct score as the basis of estimation. Some kind of weighted score would be required. These matters are demonstrated by Birnbaum (1968).

Birnbaum suggested what is usually taken to be the inclusion of an item discrimination parameter in the logit model but what is really a different model—the two- (or more correctly three-) parameter logistic model. In terms of the logit model, Birnbaum's model would be

$$\frac{P_{gi}}{1 - P_{gi}} = \left(\frac{A_g}{D_i}\right)^{C_i} \tag{3}$$

where $C_i$ is the index of discriminating power of the item. In terms of dimensional analysis this equation is unbalanced unless $C_i$ is dimensionless for all items which it is not. Thus the Rasch form is the only logit model which is dimensionally balanced.

However, Birnbaum and others write the alternative model by transforming $A_g$ and $D_i$ into $a_g$ and $d_i$ where $A_g = e^{a_g}$ and $D_i = e^{d_i}$, from which

$$\frac{P_{gi}}{1 - P_{gi}} = \frac{e^{c_i a_g}}{e^{c_i d_i}} \text{ or logit } (P_{gi}) = c_i(a_g - d_i) \tag{4}$$

or

$$P_{gi} = \frac{e^{c_i a_g}}{e^{c_i a_g} + e^{c_i d_i}} \text{ or } \frac{e^{c_i(a_g - d_i)}}{e^{c_i(a_g - d_i)} + 1} \tag{5}$$

This logistic model is dimensionally balanced if $C^i$ is taken to be of dimensionality (ability)$^{-1}$ which is defensible. Similar definitions are used in the normal ogive model (Lord 1952). The sacrifices made for this additional parameter are firstly that the number correct score is no longer a sufficient statistic for the estimate of ability and the ability estimates obtained are not on a ratio scale. However, the additional care needed to construct tests to meet the conjoint measurement conditions in the way Rasch suggests is worthwhile. The further application of latent ability measures to the measurement of cognitive growth will be discussed later.

### 3. Frequency Distributions of Educational and Psychological Measurements

A further problem associated with measurement of individual differences relates to the frequency distribution of scores on objective tests obtained from administration to large random samples. This problem has practical significance because of the use of percentile ranks and normalized percentile scores as derived scores. Keats (1951) was the first to suggest on general theoretical grounds that the negative hypergeometric distribution should give a reasonable representation of score distributions. Because of computational problems he followed Karl Pearson (1930) in using the Beta function to estimate the theoretical frequencies. Keats demonstrated that this method gave good representations of most frequency distributions found in practice and was useful not only in providing stable estimates of percentile points but also in revealing bias in samples.

At approximately the same time Mollenkopf (1949) showed that the error variance of an objective test was greatest for the middle range of scores and least for extreme scores. Keats (1957) showed that a binomial error distribution accounted for this phenomenon and Lord (1965) gave a general account of the binomial error model. Keats and Lord (1962) showed that the binomial error model together with linear regression of true score on raw score leads to a derivation of the negative hypergeometric distribution. This finding stimulated considerable further research into representations of data obtained from objective tests. Lord (1965) looked into possible additional forms of the distribution of true scores while Keats examined some

of the effects of nonlinear regressions of true scores on raw scores. Many of these results and some additional ones were brought together in Lord and Novick (1968).

The practical usefulness of theoretically based frequency distributions in defining percentile values on objective tests for carefully defined populations has seldom been applied in practice despite the obvious advantages in standardizing and equating tests. More recently Huynh (1976) has confirmed the robustness of the negative hypergeometric distribution and suggests its use when criterion-referenced as opposed to normatively based tests are being developed (see below).

### 4. Parameters of Persons

Gulliksen (1950) based his theory of mental tests essentially on the notion that a raw score on the test could be thought of as consisting of a true score and an error score which were additive and uncorrelated. He showed that much of the existing test theory could be derived in these terms. There were, however, problems of strict definition and of estimation which were not developed. Lord and Novick (1968) attempted to solve these problems by means of axioms they claim to be not inconsistent with conjoint measurement. However Lumsden (1976) severely criticized true score theory on the grounds that any set of axioms which had been proposed for the definition of true score was unlikely to be satisfied in any domain so far explored.

Rasch (1960) also implicitly criticized true score theory when he complained that as a student he was always being assessed on an arbitrarily difficult set of tasks and relative to an undefined population. He argued strongly for ability measures which did not have these relativities associated with them but were "person parameters" in an absolute sense. Criticism of a similar kind was being expressed by Bayley (1955) who pointed out that it was impossible to develop a quantitative theory of cognitive development unless such an absolute measure could be developed. She did not seem to accept the notion that latent trait measures of the Rasch type could meet these requirements. Subsequently two extensive longitudinal studies, those reported by McCall et al. (1973) and by Hindley and Owen (1979), have been carried out without using such measures.

More recently Lumsden (1978) has proposed that, in addition to a level parameter of the latent trait kind, one could also distinguish between subjects in terms of the extent to which their performance varies with the difficulty of the task. Some subjects obtain most of their score on what are usually called "easy" items and fail on "difficult" items whereas others perform almost as well on the difficult items as they do on the easy ones. This concept is the person's equivalent of the concept of discriminating power of an item, that is, the extent to which a low-scoring subject gives the right answer much less often on more difficult items than less difficult items. Attempts to establish this as a reliable and valid dimension for persons have not so far been very successful. A possibly related measure of a subject's tendency to guess (Miles 1973) has also not been developed to a stage where it can be regarded as an established dimension.

Keats (1982a) criticized the term "person parameter" which has been commonly used following Rasch (1960) on the grounds that in the cognitive area subjects continue to develop up to an age of approximately 20 years. Thus an estimate of this parameter at age 10 years will be consistently different from one at 15 years. Such a variable quantity hardly deserves to be called a parameter. He proposed a more basic parameter which determines the greatest level the subject will approach with age and raised the question as to whether this was the basic person parameter or whether a rate of development parameter might be required as well as, or even instead of, a greatest level parameter.

By assuming that cognitive development could be represented in terms of a latent ability being projectively related to time, Keats (1982a) showed that Binet's mental-age measure was only a consistent measure if all subjects were approaching the same adult value at quite different rates. The deviation measure advocated by Thurstone (1926) and Wechsler (1939) among others is, on this assumption, stable only if the rate of development is approximately the same for each subject but the adult value approached varies from person to person. Using longitudinal data reported by Skodak and Skeels (1949), Keats was able to show that both a rate parameter and an adult level parameter seemed to be important. In a subsequent paper Keats (1982b) considered mechanisms which could be thought of as underlying cognitive development and thus gave these parameters a theoretical significance independent of their mensurational significance.

Even though current evidence suggests that in the quantification of general ability an independent rate and asymptote parameter are required to represent development, this must not be taken to mean that purely rate of development models are not applicable in educational research. If one considers minimal skills in reading and number work which almost all can master, it is still significant to measure how quickly they are mastered by subjects of different ability and in different settings. There is much more research to be done investigating personal parameters in these areas.

## 5. *Criterion-referenced Testing*

This form of educational measurement arose in part as a reaction to normative testing which relates a person's performance to that of a particular norming group, for example an age group or a grade group. The objective of this form of testing is to relate the person's performance to some kind of standard or level of mastery but the problem arises of attempting to define such a standard in terms of a test performance. This problem exists whether or not the score on the test has been converted to some kind of derived score such as a standard score or even to an estimate of some underlying latent trait.

Various ways of solving the basic problem of setting a mastery level in terms of a test score have been suggested. These range from the exercising of a value judgment by curriculum experts through decision theory approaches which assume knowledge of a true mastery score to utilizing the ratio of the two costs of misclassification, that is false positives and false negatives and alternatively the use of an independent criterion such as degree of success in a referral task. Huynh (1976) suggests that mastery classification should imply a high probability of success in training to which only persons classed as masters at the lower level are admitted. He explores the statistical implications of this approach in terms of the beta–binomial model (Keats and Lord 1962) with constant losses and pass–fail referral performance.

There are very few areas of knowledge for which content criteria can be specified precisely. One could consider mechanical arithmetic as one such and require a criterion of (say) 90 percent accuracy in adding and/or multiplying two digit numbers by two digit numbers. However such criterion referencing ignores the fact that some combinations are more likely to produce errors than others and also the fact that some students make systematic errors due to inappropriate strategies. Thus the problems of developing criterion-referenced instruments touch on the very core of the educational process. Until more of the theoretical problems of education are solved the possibility of developing useful criterion-referenced instruments seems to be unattainable.

In this context the development of computer-administered tests is proceeding rapidly. The further goal of adapting items to the level of performance of the student is also being approached in some areas. It should also be possible to develop programmes to explore the patterns of errors made by a particular student to determine deficient strategies that can be corrected. The interaction between measurement and diagnosis and treatment of weaknesses in performance must be studied in detail before criterion referencing can be successful and the wide use of computers should facilitate this work.

## 6. *Measurement of Attitudes*

Attitude measurement began as a result of Thurstone's development of scale values for stimuli on dimensions for which there is no corresponding physical measure. Using the method of paired comparisons Thurstone and Chave (1929) showed that it was possible to find scale values for statements reflecting positive and negative attitudes and that subjects could be measured in terms of the scale values for statements they agreed with. Shortly after Thurstone's contribution, Likert (1932) suggested that the methods which had been developed for constructing objective tests of cognitive abilities could be applied to the construction and use of scales for measuring attitudes. Later still, Guttman (1947) proposed criteria that could be used to select statements which formed a scale.

A valuable collection of scales for the quantification of attitudes has been provided by Shaw and Wright (1967). Their publication corresponds in many ways to the *Mental Measurements Yearbooks* published by Buros (1978) in the field of psychological testing but is more immediately useful because the scales are presented in full along with the evaluative material. As a means of organizing their material, Shaw and Wright classify scales according to the quantified attitudes. The classes of attitudes that are distinguished are attitudes towards social practices, social issues and problems, international issues, abstract concepts, political and religious issues, ethnic and national groups, "significant others", and social institutions. A revised edition of this volume is urgently needed.

The three methods, Thurstone's, Likert's, and Guttman's, use different models as the basis of their quantification methods and all have some current use. Allport and Vernon (1931), among others, have used essentially ranking methods to obtain measures which are then interpreted as if they corresponded to Likert's scales. This confusion of models by Allport and Vernon is quite unscientific as it can lead to unjustified interpretations of data and the neglect of other possible interpretations. Models for ordinal data are relatively recent.

The Likert method of constructing and applying attitude scales is by far the most common as it resembles most nearly the objective test approach. The major difference arises from the fact that whereas items in cognitive tests are usually scored as either +1 (correct) or zero (incorrect), the Likert items often have alternatives of the kind "strongly agree, agree, undecided, disagree, strongly disagree" which are scored 2, 1, 0, −1, and −2 respectively. However the inclusion of the alternative "undecided" has been shown to lead to anomalous results and so should not be used.

There was little practical or theoretical development of this method from the 1930s until quite recently. Andrich (1978) applied the Rasch approach to model building to the analysis of attitudinal data collected by either the Likert or the Thurstone method. In particular he indicated ways in which data could be collected and analysed to test the assumptions of these two methods. Andrich also quotes some results from empirical studies which tend to support the use of integral values allocated to the possible categories in the Likert method.

The Thurstone method depends on the possibility of reliably scaling statements in terms of the attitude level of persons who would endorse the statement. He suggested the method of paired comparisons as a way of determining these scale values but because of the experimental time required by this method he developed other, quicker procedures. Thurstone emphasized that the scale values obtained by one of these methods should be independent (up to a linear transformation) of the attitudes of the judges scaling the statements. This condition has rarely been checked in practice and is similar to the requirement of the Rasch model that the estimates of the difficulties of items should be independent of the abilities of the subjects used to obtain them.

Given that sufficient numbers of appropriately scaled statements are available, a subject's attitude can be measured by averaging the scale values of those items he or she endorses. Again, the second requirement for the Rasch model should apply in that the measurement obtained for a subject should not depend on the particular set of statements with which the subject is presented. This condition is harder to check because Thurstone scales currently available tend to have a relatively small number of items so that any sampling of these statements would tend to give unreliable as well as coarse measures.

Guttman scales can best be thought of as Likert scales with items of infinite discriminability. If the Likert scale items meet the requirements of the Rasch model then the Guttman scale property that a person's score indicates precisely which items he or she endorsed is weakened to the extent that, for each score, the probability of its being obtained with each of the possible patterns can be calculated. If the items in the scale have a wide range of item parameter values and high discrimination there will be a most probable pattern for each score. In the rarely obtained case of a perfect Guttman scale these most probable patterns will, of course, have a probability of unity.

The unifying effect of applying the Rasch model to methods of measuring attitudes should be clear from the above discussion. Only with the restrictions of this model is it possible to justify giving a unique interpretation to the usual raw score whether from an ability test, an attainment test, or an attitude scale. If more general models which allow for variation in the discriminating power of items are used then the value of the measure differs from one pattern of responding to another. Even for an instrument of only 20 items, there are at least one million patterns of responding but only 21 possible raw scores. Thus the data reduction possibilities obtained by using the Rasch model are enormous.

## 7. Multivariate Approaches to Measurement in Education

Spearman (1904) proposed that measures of cognitive achievement, including sensory judgments could be accounted for by an underlying single factor or general ability. Much of the data he used came from school achievement measures and the balance from the psychophysical laboratory. This approach was developed and explored for almost 30 years before Thurstone (1931) proposed multivariate factor analysis.

Both methods were directed towards the problem of representing human cognitive performance in terms of a relatively small number of cognitive factors. The technical problems of factor analysis have been actively investigated for more than 50 years and although they cannot be said to have been solved many least squares and maximum likelihood methods are now available for exploring and testing data. Most, if not all, are available in the form of computer programs. However, there is still debate as to which method is the most appropriate in a given situation and the various methods do not produce the same results.

On the substantive side many attempts have been made to define the significant factors by means of which individual differences in cognitive behaviour can be represented. Thurstone proposed a set of primary mental abilities and provided research instruments to measure these. More recently groups working with French (Ekstrom et al. 1976) have after a great deal of empirical research proposed 23 cognitive ability factors and provided at least three tests measuring each of these. The tests are referred to as cognitive factor reference tests and are intended for use in identifying factors rather than for direct use in assessment or selection situations.

The predominant tendency today is to use a large number of group factors rather than to retain Spearman's concept of a general factor and supplement this with well-established group factors. However this practice tends to obscure the one most pervasive and substantiated result from cognitive achievement studies, namely that measures of cognitive performance with quite different content are almost always positively related. It is probably true to assert that if the general plus group factor approach were adopted the number of cognitive factors to be referenced would be reduced from 23 to perhaps as few as 15 uncorrelated measures.

In the case of personality or temperament factors the group led by French (Dermen et al. 1978) have had a much more difficult task as there is far less agreement about which factors have been clearly and reliably defined. The manual of reference tests for temperament factors reflects this uncertainty by the fact that only 18 of the 28 factors listed could be confirmed by the group, the remainder, however, have often been reported in the literature. A further problem with temperament scales is that they are far more susceptible to the effects of response styles than are cognitive tests.

While the French group has provided a valuable service to educational research by investigating both cognitive and personality factors in this almost exhaustive fashion, it should be noted that almost all of their work has been carried out on adults. There is still the task of determining to what extent they also apply to children of primary and secondary schools. For at least some factors this question has some urgency for educators who wish to obtain a concise way of recording children's cognitive performance.

Factor analytic methods can also be regarded as ways of accounting for patterns or structures in correlations between variables by postulating more fundamental variables underlying the manifest observations. Two other ways of accounting for such patterns in correlation are also of concern when considering measurement in educational research. The first concerns the special patterns that arise in developmental studies when measures are administered on several different occasions to the same group of subjects. The second seeks to interpret patterns in terms of causal relationships and is called path analysis.

Anderson (1940) was the first to propose an explanation for the particular pattern of correlations obtained in developmental studies when performance on a particular measure, at a given age level, is correlated with performance on the same measure at other age levels. When all such correlations are tabulated the table obtained usually exhibits a distinctive pattern sometimes called a simplex pattern (Anderson 1940). Anderson demonstrated that such a pattern could be generated by means of cumulations of random numbers. Thus the first measure would be a random number and the second measure would consist of the first measure plus a second random number and so on. In due course there would be considerable overlap between one measure in the series and the next and so high correlation. Thus development could be thought of as random cumulations of the products of experience without any individual differences parameters.

This possible explanation of development was repeated by many writers without any great amplification until Drösler (1978) demonstrated, using time series methods, that it was possible to distinguish graphically between simplex patterns which could have arisen in this fashion and those which could not. From published data Drösler showed that educational achievement tests provided correlation patterns which were *not* inconsistent with Anderson's proposed explanation over most of the compulsory education period. However, general ability or aptitude tests reject the Anderson proposal for age levels above approximately 5 years. This finding has been confirmed for other sets of published data. Thus educational measures can be classified into those that do and those that do not conform to the random cumulation model. Factor analysis is not an appropriate method in the case of developmental data.

A second situation in which the factor analytic model is not an appropriate one for analysing tables of correlations between measures obtained in educational research, is one in which relationships are asymmetric in that A can influence B but B cannot influence A. An example would be where a social class measure is related to school achievement. It is most unlikely that a child's school achievement could affect his or her parents' social class whereas social class could influence school achievement. A method which accounts for patterns of correlations under these circumstances is path analysis and both least squares and maximum likelihood programmes are available for estimating the weightings of causal paths. With present knowledge of causal paths in education it is probably desirable to use the least squares method which makes fewer assumptions and so is much more influenced by the data than maximum likelihood methods.

A related form of studying correlations between educational measures is the method of Herbst (1970) which he termed cyclic network analysis. In that publication Herbst illustrates application of this method using measures of pupil's work effort, boredom, and anxiety in relation to work expected by the teacher as perceived by the pupil. However, as Herbst notes, path analysis applied at the group level will often yield different results from those obtained by cyclic network analysis at the group or individual level.

## Bibliography

Allport G W, Vernon P E 1931 *A Study of Values: A Scale for Measuring the Dominant Interests in Personality: Manual of Directions*. Houghton Mifflin, Boston, Massachusetts

Anderson J E 1940 *The Prediction of Terminal Intelligence from Infant and Pre-school Tests*. Thirty-ninth Yearbook, National Society for the Study of Education. American Educational Research Association, Chicago, Illinois, pp. 385–403

Andrich D 1978 A rating formulation for ordered response categories. *Psychometrika* 43: 561–73

Bayley N 1955 On the growth of intelligence. *Am. Psychol.* 10: 805–18

Birnbaum A 1968 Some latent trait models and their use in inferring an examinee's ability. In: Lord F M, Novick M R (eds.) 1968 *Statistical Theories of Mental Test Scores*. Addison Wesley, Reading, Massachusetts, pp. 395–479

Buros O K (ed.) 1978 *The Eighth Mental Measurements Yearbook*. Gryphon Press, Highland Park, New Jersey

Campbell N R 1917 *Foundation of Science: The Philosophy of Theory and Experiment*. Dover Publications, New York

Coombs C H, Dawes R M, Tversky A 1970 *Mathematical Psychology: An Elementary Introduction*. Prentice-Hall, Englewood Cliffs, New Jersey

Dermen D, French J W, Harman H H 1978 *Guide to Factor Referenced Temperament Scales 1978*. Educational Testing Service, Princeton, New Jersey

Drösler J 1978 Extending the temporal range of psychometric prediction by optimal linear filtering of mental test scores. *Psychometrika* 43: 533–49

Ekstrom R B, French J W, Harman H H 1976 *Manual for Kit of Factor-referenced Cognitive Tests, 1976*. Educational Testing Service, Princeton, New Jersey

Ferguson A, Meyers C S, Bartlett R J 1940 Quantitative estimation of sensory events. Final report. *Advancement of Science* 2: 331–49

Gulliksen H 1946 Paired comparisons and the logic of measurement. *Psychol. Rev.* 53: 199–213

Gulliksen H 1950 *Theory of Mental Tests*. Wiley, New York

Guttman L 1947 The Cornell technique for scale and intensity analysis. *Educ. Psychol. Meas.* 7: 247–79

Herbst P G 1970 *Behavioural Worlds: The Study of Single Cases*. Tavistock, London

Hindley C B, Owen C F 1979 An analysis of individual patterns of DQ and IQ curves from 6 months to 17 years. *Br. J. Psychol.* 70: 273–93

Humphreys L G 1960 Investigations of the simplex. *Psychometrika* 25: 313–23

Huynh H 1976 Statistical consideration of mastery scores. *Psychometrika* 41: 65–78

Keats J A 1951 *A Statistical Theory of Objective Test Scores*. Australian Council for Educational Research, Hawthorn, Victoria

Keats J A 1957 Estimation of error variances of test scores. *Psychometrika* 22: 29–41

Keats J A 1982a Comparing latent trait with classical measurement models in the practice of educational and psychological measurement. In: Spearritt D S (ed.) 1982 *The Improvement of Measurement in Education and Psychology: Contributions of Latent Trait Theories*. Australian Council for Educational Research, Hawthorn, Victoria, pp. 61–72

Keats J A 1982b Ability measures and theories of cognitive development. In: Messick S (ed.) 1982 *Festschrift for F. M. Lord*. Educational Testing Service, Princeton, New Jersey

Keats J A, Lord F M 1962 A theoretical distribution of mental test scores. *Psychometrika* 27: 59–72

Likert R 1932 A technique for the measurement of attitudes. *Arch. Psychol.* 140

Lord F M 1952 A theory of test scores. *Psychometric Monogr.* 7

Lord F M 1965 A strong true-score theory, with applications. *Psychometrika* 30: 239–70

Lord F M, Novick M R 1968 *Statistical Theories of Mental Test Scores*. Addison-Wesley, Reading, Massachusetts

Luce R D, Tukey J W 1964 Simultaneous conjoint measurement: A new type of fundamental measurement. *J. Math. Psychol.* 1: 1–27

Lumsden J 1976 Test theory. *Ann. Rev. Psychol.* 27: 251–80

Lumsden J 1978 Tests are perfectly reliable. *Br. J. Math. Stat. Psychol.* 31: 19–26

McCall R B, Appelbaum M I, Hogarty P S 1973 Developmental changes in mental performance. *Monogr. Soc. Res. Child Dev.* 38 (3, Serial No. 150)

Miles J 1973 Eliminating the guessing factor in the multiple choice test. *Educ. Psychol. Meas.* 33: 637–51

Mollenkopf W G 1949 Variation of the standard error of measurement. *Psychometrika* 14: 189–230

Pearson K (ed.) 1930 *Tables for Statisticians and Biometricians*, 3rd edn. Cambridge University Press, Cambridge

Rasch G 1960 *Probabilistic Models for some Intelligence and Attainment Tests*. Danish Institute for Educational Research, Copenhagen

Ross S 1964 *Logical Foundations of Psychological Measurement: A Study in the Philosophy of Science*. Munksgaard, Copenhagen

Shaw M E, Wright J M 1967 *Scales for the Measurement of Attitudes*. McGraw-Hill, New York

Skodak M, Skeels H M 1949 A final follow-up study of one hundred adopted children. *J. Genet. Psychol.* 75: 85–125

Spearman C 1904 "General intelligence," objectively determined and measured. *Am. J. Psychol.* 15: 201–93

Stevens S S (ed.) 1951 *Handbook of Experimental Psychology*. Wiley, New York

Thorndike, R L (ed.) 1971 *Educational Measurement*, 2nd edn. American Council on Education, Washington, DC

Thurstone L L 1926 The mental age concept. *Psychol. Rev.* 33: 268–78

Thurstone L L 1931 Multiple.factor analysis. *Psychol. Rev.* 38: 406–27

Thurstone L L, Chave E J 1929 *The Measurement of Attitude: A Psycho-physical Method and Some Experiments with a Scale for Measuring Attitude toward the Church*. University of Chicago Press, Chicago, Illinois

Wechsler D 1939 *The Measurement of Adult Intelligence*. Williams and Williams, Baltimore, Maryland

# Future Developments in Educational Measurement

## J. B. Carroll

It would be presumptuous to try to predict the precise way in which the field of educational measurement will evolve over the next few decades. This article attempts only to comment on likely developments, and to indicate what developments might be most desirable, in view of advances that have occurred in the last decade.

Educational measurement is concerned basically with the devising and construction of variables that may be useful in education—in educational research and/or in practical actions such as selection and guidance of students and the diagnosis and appraisal of student learning. The scientific aspects of educational measurement pertain to assessing the characteristics of those variables in respect to their accuracy and faithfulness to the intentions of their creators or, in somewhat more technical terms, in respect to their reliability and validity. Examples of variables are scores of psychological and educational tests; ratings of behavior, performance, or learning by teachers or observers; measures of socioeconomic status or home background; and quantitative evaluations of schools or social settings. Over the years, educational measurement science has progressed toward ever more precise ways of establishing and assessing such variables. The trend has been toward better linking variables with appropriate statistical, mathematical, and psychological theories to support them. The future will probably see further strengthening of these linkages.

Educational measurement comprises a number of relatively separate and, in some cases, highly specialized fields. This article will survey these fields chiefly from the standpoint of their possible future development. It will not go into much detail or cite many references, since details and references are covered in separate articles in this volume.

## 1. Constructing Variables

A broad distinction can be made between variables that arise from single observations or judgments and variables that arise from some kind of compositing of multiple observations or judgments that are not necessarily equivalent. Examples of the former are ratings, such as teacher's grades or observers' ratings of learning ability, and measurements of single attributes like height and weight. Examples of the latter are test scores that are a weighted sum of scores assigned to single items or tasks that compose a test, the single items being not necessarily equivalent in difficulty, reliability, or validity. Note, however, that *after* a variable of the second type has been established through appropriate techniques, it becomes a variable of the first kind, amenable to study by various techniques of classical test theory. The distinction is made in order to contrast applications

of classical test theory with applications of item response theory.

Many aspects of classical test theory will continue to pertain to the former type of measurement. Concepts of reliability and validity, true and error scores, and parallelism of equivalent measure will continue to be applicable to these types of variables. It would be a mistake to abandon the fundamental principles and techniques of classical test theory, because they are the only principles and techniques that are applicable to variables that arise from single observations or judgments. Note that a single variable can be of this kind, even though it can be matched by other variables of the same kind. For example, even though the measurement of height comes from a single observation, one could be concerned with the reliability of such measurements by obtaining similar measures on multiple occasions and performing appropriate statistical procedures on them.

In this realm, one can foresee the further development and application of generalizability theory, concerned with the degree to which measurement errors can be identified as attributable to different sources (Brennan 1983). For example, the reliability of teachers' ratings of essays can be studied as a function of teacher, student, essay, subject matter, etc. A difficulty is that multi-faceted studies of this type tend to become large and unwieldy if conducted according to presently available procedures. Whether it would be possible to overcome these difficulties is unclear, but it would in any case be desirable to conduct generalizability studies on many types of variables.

Issues concerning reliability and construct validity can now easily be addressed with linear structural relationships analysis (LISREL) modeling applied to multitrait–multimethod data, in order to determine the relative variances due to traits and to particular methods of measuring those traits (Marsh and Hocevar 1983, Schmitt and Stults 1986). This procedure should be applied to a wide variety of educationally important variables.

## 2. Item Response Theory

Undoubtedly the most striking development of the past several decades in educational measurement has been the establishment and elaboration of what has become known as "item response theory" (IRT), closely related to latent trait measurement models. It is important to notice that these theories and models apply to variables of the second kind noted above, that is, to variables that arise from multiple measurements that are not necessarily equivalent. In the usual case, these measurements are responses to a series of test items or tasks that are not necessarily equivalent in difficulty or validity in measuring the presumed underlying trait or traits. The basic idea of these theories and models is that from a set of observed responses to a set of items it is possible to derive measures or estimates of the underlying trait or traits that have superior measurement and interpretive properties as compared to, say, an unweighted sum of the item scores. Item response theory is essentially a theory of the relation between item response and an underlying trait. Usually, the underlying trait is assumed to be an "ability" of some kind, that is a property of the person such that there is a systematic relation between the ability levels of different individuals and their probabilities of "passing" or correctly responding to different items.

Actually, such a theory was assumed from the earliest days of the history of educational measurement (Carroll 1987). In the 1930s and 1940s, it was generally assumed that the relation between ability and item response could be well-described by a normal ogive model; the implications of this model were not fully followed up in detail because of the apparent intractability of the mathematics required by this model. Present-day item response theory has been developed mainly on the basis of a more mathematically tractable model, namely the logistic function, which gives results closely similar to those from the normal ogive model. IRT admits several alternative models based on the logistic function, differing mainly in the number of parameters that are required to describe the function. In frequent use are the one-parameter "Rasch" model, that specifies only the position of an item on a difficulty scale, and the three-parameter model that specifies position, slope, and "guessing" parameters for each item.

Item response theory can be successfully applied only for what has been called "serious testing," that is, to multi-item tests and examinations that are intended to be, or have been, applied to hundreds or even many thousands of examinees. For example, Educational Testing Service has used IRT in an interesting way to develop a so-called Reading Proficiency Scale on the basis of matrix-sampled test responses from thousands of persons tested at various ages in a national assessment of reading comprehension ability (National Assessment of Educational Progress/Educational Testing Service 1985). Educational Testing Service, like many other testing organizations, regularly uses IRT in compositing and equating various types of aptitude and achievement examinations. Undoubtedly the future will see many more uses of IRT for these purposes.

A further motive for the development and use of IRT has been the need and possibility of so-called "adaptive testing", also called "tailored testing", that is, testing that is conducted in such a way that items or tasks administered at any point in the testing can depend upon the individual's responses to previous items. Adaptive testing is nothing new in educational measurement; a simple form of it occurs in the administration of individual tests like the Stanford–Binet, where the particular tasks administered to the individual depend upon the examiner's initial impression of the subject's ability and upon the individual's success in passing progressively more difficult items. IRT makes it possible, however, to select items for presentation that, in the light of the individual's total pattern of responses up to any given point, will maximize the reliability of the score and at the same time minimize the number of items that have to be presented to arrive at a sufficiently reliable score. Such use of IRT normally requires extensive computations throughout the testing, but with the increasing availability of computer terminals and personal microcomputers, it is certain that adaptive testing will make its way into many testing situations. For example, the United States armed forces are presently making serious studies of the possibilities of using computerized adaptive testing in a wide variety of selection and training functions (Green et al. 1984).

Nevertheless, there are many difficult and worrisome aspects of IRT and related theories. The state of the art has not reached anything like a completely satisfactory condition, although there is now a tremendous amount of activity and research. The chief difficulty centers in problems of estimating item and ability parameters. Classical maximum likelihood procedures require large data sets and extensive computations, with results that are sometimes unreliable or even meaningless. Various other procedures and algorithms are being investigated; Bock (1985) proposes that Bayesian estimation procedures are likely to give the best results. A related difficulty concerns the choice of IRT models. Generally, the more parameters in the model (e.g., three as opposed to two or even just one), the more difficult the problems of estimation and computation become. A particular problem has to do with models that assume a "guessing" parameter, i.e., a parameter that specifies the probability of correct response from an individual with (theoretically) infinitely low ability, who can often make a correct response by "guessing." It seems that this parameter is critically necessary for analyzing sets of multiple-choice items such as are very often employed in tests. There is a further problem connected with this, incidentally, namely that some item response curves show "valleys" or "troughs," there being some individuals who are likely to respond less correctly than they would by chance, since they are unduly attracted to incorrect alternatives. Researchers are now working on models to take care of this problem (Thissen 1986). It would seem important to do this because multiple-choice distractors are often written with the deliberate purpose of misleading persons of low ability.

There is a set of further problems with IRT that urgently call for solutions. Simple item response theory assumes that there is a single dimension of "ability" that underlies performance on a test. This assumption may be reasonable enough in the case of certain kinds of tests, for example, tests of verbal ability, reading comprehension ability, or spatial ability. (One application of IRT is to determine which items best measure the single underlying ability, and to eliminate the items that measure it poorly or not at all, thus reducing the dimensionality of the test.) Unidimensionality may not be a reasonable assumption in the case of certain types of achievement tests, where in a sense each item may measure a separate ability—an ability unique or specific to itself. IRT procedures tend not to work well in such cases. There is a need for alternative procedures to deal with these cases, or at least a need for procedures to indicate when all is not well.

Dimensionality is a multifaceted problem. It has long been known that factor-analytic procedures, often employed to investigate dimensionality, are at best problematic when they are applied to binary or dichotomous data. Test items scored either 0 or 1 depending on correctness of response are perfect examples of such data, and cause difficulties in factor analysis, particularly if there is a chance guessing factor, as is usually the case with multiple-choice items, or if there are many "omit" responses. Recent developments, under the heading of what is called "full-information factor analysis" (Muraki and Engelhard 1985), appear to have surmounted many of these difficulties, but further exploration and testing of these procedures in a variety of situations should command a high priority.

Another aspect of dimensionality is this: in using the common factor model with binary data, one has to assume that each item score is a function of one or more dimensions of ability; regression weights or factor loadings would indicate the extent to which each ability affects item response, for every individual. But this model ignores at least two possibilities: (a) that the weights are different for different individuals, depending upon their strategies of item solution, and (b) that the ways in which abilities affect item response cannot be described by a linear model. (The first of these possibilities, of course, represents a limitation of factor analysis even when applied to nonbinary variables.) For example, it could be that in order to be successful in passing an item, an examinee would have to be above a certain critical point on each of two or more abilities. Solutions to these difficulties are much to be sought; possibly, they will arise from current work on multicomponent latent trait models (Fischer 1983, Embretson 1985a). This work also has implications that will be discussed later when we look at substantive issues about how ability and content are relevant to test construction.

Problems of dimensionality also arise in connection with the equating of tests, either horizontally or vertically. It has been shown that test equating can be inaccurate when the unidimensional assumptions of normal item response theory are violated (Holland and Rubin 1982). This problem becomes exacerbated if attempts are made to equate achievement tests that do not have an underlying ability of the usual kind. Under these conditions it may be desirable to investigate the applicability of more classical methods of test equating.

Despite all the problems mentioned, item response theory makes possible highly sophisticated analyses of test data in the case of large data sets, that is, where the number of examinees is at least 200, and preferably many more, and where the number of items is within the range of usual test lengths. The standard version of LOGIST, a program distributed by Educational Testing Service, permits use of $N = 15,000$ examinees and $n = 400$ items, but this test length would probably be only rarely encountered and would entail excessive computational costs. Use of LOGIST frequently runs into problems that are due to violations of assumptions. Researchers will probably continue to explore the problems of this and other computing algorithms.

Full use of item response theory with classroom tests is generally impractical, but certain principles and simplifications may be applicable (Harnisch 1983, Izard and White 1982, Yen 1984). Conventional item analysis procedures are certainly in order and incorporate some of the principal notions of item response theory.

There has been interest in the concept of "appropriateness," that is, the extent to which an individual's pattern of responses is consistent with the general pattern found in a large sample of examinees (Drasgow and Levine 1986, Trabin and Weiss 1983). An extreme case of an "inappropriate" pattern would be one where an individual fails easy items but passes difficult items. One purpose of appropriateness measurement would be to identify examinees who misunderstand directions, cheat, or otherwise fail to respond to the test on the basis of ability alone. An excessive number of inappropriate patterns might also reveal an underlying multidimensionality of the test. There is a need for investigations of these possibilities.

Closely related to this is the concept of the person characteristic curve, obtained by plotting probabilities of passing, or individuals, or for groups of individuals with closely similar abilities, as a function of item difficulties. If the test is essentially unidimensional, person characteristic curves will form a family of generally parallel curves and will be useful in interpreting patterns of ability. Carroll (1985) has proposed that this technique is useful in defining abilities as a function of item or task difficulty; his work needs to be extended over a wide range of abilities. The concept of the person characteristic curve can easily be applied to classroom tests with small $N$ and relatively small numbers of items.

## 3. Ability Theory

We now consider a number of substantive issues with which educational measurement has been, and will continue to be, concerned.

One dominant issue has been the nature, variety, and organization of human abilities and their potential relevance to students' educational progress. The last decade has seen the introduction of a surprising variety of new theories and theoretical standpoints.

As summaries or reconceptualizations of more or less

traditional views, mainly based on factor-analytic work, we can mention: Humphreys' (1985) discussion of general intelligence (*g*); Jensen's (1984) defense of *g* against a "specificity doctrine" according to which intelligence is broken down into many separate abilities; Horn's (1985) reformulation of the Cattell hierarchical model of intelligence; Gustafsson's (1984) validation of a hierarchical model through confirmatory factor analysis; Royce and Powell's (1983) new structural model of intellectual abilities; Jäger's (1984) "Berlin model of intelligence"—an interesting reformulation based in part on Guilford's "Structure-of-Intellect model"; and Snow et al.'s (1984) presentation of a radex model of abilities. There are basic similarities in all these viewpoints, along with differences that will have to be resolved by further consideration and empirical research. Snow and Lohman (1984) have presented a promising theory of the relevance of aptitude to learning and instruction.

In the category of new theories of intelligence we can mention: Sternberg's (1985a) "triarchic" theory of intelligence that features a theory of information-processing components of intellectual activity; and Gardner's (1983) theory of "multiple intelligences," proposing that intellectual abilities can be classified as linguistic, musical, logical–mathematical, spatial, bodily–kinesthetic, and personal relations. At the same time, these and other writers propose that more attention be devoted to the measurement of "social" intelligence (Frederiksen et al. 1984, Sternberg and Smith 1985), and "practical intelligence" (Sperber et al. 1985, Wagner and Sternberg 1985). How all these proposals can be actualized and interrelated could be a major concern of future research in the nature and variety of cognitive abilities.

Much of the impetus for these new research directions has come out of recent developments in cognitive psychology. Carroll (1976) pointed out that most psychometric tests of abilities can be viewed as cognitive tasks. Much of the research in the past decade has centered on detailed examinations of cognitive abilities in terms of their information-processing components. Examples of such studies can be found in several volumes edited by Sternberg (1982a, 1982b, 1984, 1985b) and by Dillon (1985) and Dillon and Schmeck (1983). The essential idea behind this work is that cognitive tasks can often be subdivided into components, each of which may represent a distinct ability or personal characteristic; further, that the difficulties, response-time latencies, and other measurable aspects of performance on these tasks can be related to particular features of the stimuli and of the response requirements of the tasks. By studying these relations, it is possible to attain better understanding of the nature of abilities and to find foundations for them in theories of cognitive psychology. Thus far, this idea has been implemented on only a small number of abilities—certain kinds of verbal, reasoning, and spatial abilities, and the available studies raise numerous questions still to be answered. There is a need to extend this type of investigation to still other abilities.

Recent studies have reopened the question of whether there is some kind of intrinsic relation between general intelligence and mental processing speed as measured by reaction time (Barrett et al. 1986, Jensen 1985, Vernon and Jensen 1984). This research has been highly controversial, with alternative interpretations and counterclaims proposed by Longstreth (1984) and Smith and Stanley (1983), among others. Further, British research cited by Eysenck and Barrett (1985) suggests that general intelligence is related to physiological measures as obtained by the average evoked potential and the electroencephalogram. There is a further need to confirm these findings and to resolve the differences of interpretation that have arisen.

Some of these developments have an interesting relation to what Embretson (1985b p. 3) calls "test design": "specifying the aspects of individual differences that a test measures by constructing and/or selecting items according to their substantive properties." The collection of papers edited by Embretson presents useful examples of test design studies that could be emulated in future research, as well as appropriate mathematical techniques for implementing such studies.

Given the present state of the art, it should be possible to develop a scientific theory of cognitive abilities that would consistently identify and describe all the major and minor cognitive abilities and provide unquestioned methods of measuring them and stating how they enter into different types of cognitive behavior, learning, and performance. More large, well-designed factorial studies are needed to specify the status of various factors or latent traits of ability in the hierarchy of abilities.

Throughout the history of factor analysis, there has been the tantalizing hope that it would eventually be possible to construct so-called "pure factor" tests of abilities. In general, this hope has proved elusive, but that may have been because the theory and technology used were not adequate. Theories of cognitive abilities and the technology of test construction are now adequate to justify mounting a new program of constructing tests of separate cognitive abilities, with alternate forms appropriate for different age ranges, that would be demonstrably unidimensional. One important aspect of such a program would be the careful control of level of mastery and speed effects.

Sternberg (1986) provides a good summary of some current trends and activities in intelligence testing.

## 4. Measurement and Analysis of Learning and Educational Achievement

Cognitive psychology has had a considerable influence on the measurement and analysis of learning and educational achievements or more generally, on what has been called instructional psychology. Discussions of this point can be found in volumes edited by Plake (1984) and Ronning et al. (1987). As in the case of abilities, viewpoints from cognitive psychology stress the importance of analyzing tasks—in this case, learning tasks—in terms of the types of perceptions, understanding, declarative and procedural knowledge, and response capabilities that the student must possess or acquire in order to achieve learning success. In the past, constructors of achievement tests have tried to apprehend these matters on an intuitive basis and incorporate them in these tests. Insights from cognitive psychology may enable test constructors to approach these problems more systematically (Resnick 1983).

Recent studies of the learning of reading comprehension, science, and mathematics confirm the idea, long held by many teachers, that students' errors come about not so much from carelessness or lack of memory but because they have constructed incorrect rules or algorithms for solving the problems presented. This fact has given rise to measurement procedures designed to diagnose student's "bugs" or incorrect rules (Tatsuoka and Tatsuoka 1983). On the other hand, Resnick (1984) has argued that detailed diagnosis of incorrect rules is less important than trying to understand the incorrect mental representations that lead students to make errors. Resnick's work was in the area of elementary mathematics teaching. In any event, achievement tests must be better oriented to assist teachers in diagnosing incorrect mental representations and erroneous procedural rules, and one can expect further refinements and applications along these lines.

A pronounced trend of the last two decades has been increased recognition of a distinction between *norm-referenced* and *criterion-referenced* tests, with an effort to construct better tests of the latter kind (Berk 1984). It is not often realized, however, that in many cases, one and the same test can be treated either as a norm-referenced or a criterion-referenced test, depending upon how scores are interpreted. Many tests originally constructed as norm-referenced tests could readily be criterion referenced by analyzing, in concrete terms, the levels of performance or achievement that their scores indicate. A recent example of this process has been the criterion referencing of the Reading Proficiency Scale developed by NAEP/ETS (1985) by specifying types of reading performances characteristic of five discrete score levels. This criterion-referencing information helps in interpreting the normative information that is also provided.

Writing items for achievement tests has always been regarded as almost an arcane art possessed by very few people. Recently, however, there have been renewed attempts to reduce this art to a system accessible to ordinary mortals (Roid and Haladyna 1982), and it is proposed that computers can be programmed to construct items and tests (Bejar 1985). Computer generation of items may indeed be possible in some limited domains, and this possibility deserves to be further explored. However, it is likely that most domains of educational achievement will continue to require item construction by the creative effort of subject-matter experts in collaboration with experts in testing.

In the meantime, teachers and test constructors will continue to be aided by the increasing availability of large banks of items at appropriate locations throughout the world (Millman and Arter 1984). Items in such banks can be indexed not only in terms of subject matter but also in terms of their item difficulty and discrimination parameters derived from item response theory. It will continue to be the case, despite possible claims to the contrary, that these item parameters must be evaluated in terms of the kinds of samples from which they are derived. It is not yet clear whether ways of circumventing this difficulty can be devised.

The use of computers in testing has already been mentioned in several connections. There will also be increasing use of computers in instruction, offering the possibility of what Baker (1984) has called "nonintrusive testing", that is, testing that occurs automatically in the course of instruction. Special attention should be given to the problem of separating level of mastery and speed dimensions of ability and/or achievement; acquisition of data by computers should facilitate this work because the computer can separately record speed and accuracy aspects of performance.

## 5. *Some Final Remarks*

Educational measurement should not be concerned only with the construction of variables; it must also participate in the investigation of causal and associative relations among variables. For example, there needs to be further concern with models of cognitive growth over the life-span and in a variety of mental functions (Bock 1983, Keats 1983). The structural modeling of important educational variables such as home background, cognitive ability, personality, motivation, type of instruction, during of learning, and education achievement is a topic that should continue to receive devoted and sophisticated attention.

Educational measurement will undoubtedly continue to become more professionalized and specialized. The construction and publication of measurements used in education will be held to increasingly high standards (AERA, APA, and NCME 1985, Levy and Goldstein 1984, Mitchell 1985). It is difficult indeed to keep abreast of the many books, monographs, and journals that are now being published in this field in many countries. Volumes such as the present one, however, may enable educational measurement specialists to take the long view and retain a modicum of sanity amidst the profusion.

## Bibliography

American Educational Research Association (AERA), American Psychological Association (APA), National Council on Measurement in Education (NCME) 1985 *Standards for Educational and Psychological Testing*. American Psychological Association, Washington, DC

Baker F B 1984 Technology and testing: State of the art and trends for the future. *J. Educ. Meas.* 21: 399–406

Barrett P, Eysenck H J, Lucking S 1986 Reaction time and intelligence: A replicated study. *Intelligence* 10: 9–40

Bejar I I 1985 Speculations on the future of test design. In: Embretson S E (ed.) 1985 *Test Design: Developments in Psychology and Psychometrics.* Academic Press, Orlando, Florida pp. 279–94

Berk R A (ed.) 1984 *A Guide to Criterion-Referenced Test Construction.* Johns Hopkins University Press, Baltimore, Maryland

Bock R D 1983 The mental growth curve reexamined. In: Weiss D J (ed.) 1983 *New Horizons in Testing: Latent Trait Test Theory and Computerized Adaptive Testing.* Academic Press, New York, pp. 205–19

Bock R D 1985 Contributions of empirical Bayes and marginal maximum likelihood methods to the measurement of individual differences. In: Roskam E E (ed.) 1985 *Measurement and Personality Assessment.* North Holland, Amsterdam, pp. 75–99

Brennan R L 1983 *Elements of Generalizability Theory.* American College Testing Program, Iowa City, Iowa

Carroll J B 1976 Psychometric tests as cognitive tasks: A new "Structure of Intellect." In: Resnick L (ed.) 1976 *The Nature of Intelligence.* Erlbaum, Hillsdale, New Jersey, pp. 27–56

Carroll J B 1985 Defining abilities through the person characteristic function. In: Roskam E E (ed.) 1985 *Measurement and Personality Assessment.* North Holland, Amsterdam, pp. 121–31

Carroll J B 1987 Measurement and educational psychology: Beginnings and repercussions. In: Glover J, Ronning R R (eds.) 1987 *Historical Foundations of Educational Psychology.* Plenum, New York

Dillon R F (ed.) 1985 *Individual Differences in Cognition,* Vol. 2. Academic Press, Orlando, Florida

Dillon R F, Schmeck R R (eds.) 1983 *Individual Differences in Cognition,* Vol. 1. Academic Press, New York

Drasgow F, Levine M V 1986 Optimal detection of certain forms of inappropriate test scores. *Appl. Psychol. Meas.* 10: 59–67

Embretson S 1985a Component latent trait models for test design. In: Weiss D J (ed.) 1985 *Proceedings of the 1982 Item Response Theory and Computerized Adaptive Testing Conference,* Department of Psychology, University of Minnesota, Minneapolis, Minnesota, pp. 295–316

Embretson S E (ed.) 1985b *Test Design: Developments in Psychology and Psychometrics.* Academic Press, Orlando, Florida

Eysenck H J, Barrett P 1985 Psychophysiology and the measurement of intelligence. In: Reynolds C R, Willson V L (eds.) 1985 *Methodological and Statistical Advances in the Study of Individual Differences.* Plenum, New York, pp. 1–49

Fischer G H 1983 Logistic latent trait models with linear constraints. *Psychometrika* 48: 3–26

Frederiksen N, Carlson S, Ward W 1984 The place of social intelligence in a taxonomy of cognitive abilities. *Intelligence* 8: 315–37

Gardner H 1983 *Frames of Mind: The Theory of Multiple Intelligences.* Basic Books, New York

Green B F, Bock R D, Humphreys L G, Linn R L, Reckase M D 1984 Technical guidelines for assessing computerized adaptive tests. *J. Educ. Meas.* 21: 347–60

Gustafsson J-E 1984 A unifying model for the structure of intellectual abilities. *Intelligence* 8: 179–203

Harnisch D L 1983 Item response patterns: Applications for educational practice. *J. Educ. Meas.* 20: 191–206

Holland R W, Rubin D B (eds.) 1982 *Test Equating.* Academic Press, New York

Horn J L 1985 Remodeling old models of intelligence. In: Wolman B B (ed.) 1985 *Handbook of Intelligence: Theories, Measurements, and Applications.* Wiley, New York, pp. 267–300

Humphreys L G 1985 General intelligence: An integration of factor, test, and simplex theory. In: Wolman B B (ed.) 1985 *Handbook of Intelligence: Theories, Measurements, and Applications.* Wiley, New York, pp. 201–24

Izard J F, White J D 1982 The use of latent trait models in the development and analysis of classroom tests. In: Spearritt D (ed.) *The Improvement of Measurement in Education and Psychology: Contributions of Latent Trait Theories.* Australian Council for Educational Research, Hawthorn, Victoria, pp. 161–88

Jäger A O 1984 Intelligenzstrukturforschung: Konkurrierende Modelle, neue Entwicklungen, Perspektiven. *Psychol. Rundsch.* 35: 21–35

Jensen A R 1984 Test validity: g versus the specificity doctrine. *J. Soc. Biol. Struct.* 7: 93–118

Jensen A R 1985 Methodological and statistical techniques for the chronometric study of mental abilities. In: Reynolds C R, Willson V L (eds.) 1985 *Methodological and Statistical Advances in the Study of Individual Differences.* Plenum, New York, pp. 51–116

Keats J A 1983 Ability measures and theories of cognitive development. In: Wainer, H, Messick S (eds.) 1983 *Principals of Modern Psychological Measurement: A Festschrift for Frederick M. Lord.* Erlbaum, Hillsdale, New Jersey, pp. 81–101

Levy P, Goldstein H (eds.) 1984 *Tests in Education: A Book of Critical Reviews.* Academic Press, London

Longstreth L E 1984 Jensen's reaction-time investigations of intelligence: A critique. *Intelligence* 8: 139–60

Marsh H W, Hocevar D 1983 Confirmatory factor analysis of multitrait multimethod matrices. *J. Educ. Meas.* 20: 231–48

Millman J, Arter J A 1984 Issues in item banking. *J. Educ. Meas.* 21: 315–30

Mitchell J V Jr. (ed.) 1985 *The Ninth Mental Measurements Yearbook,* 2 vols. Buros Institute of Mental Measurements, University of Nebraska, Lincoln, Nebraska

Muraki E, Engelhard G Jr. 1985 Full-information item factor analysis: Application of EAP scores. *Appl. Psychol. Meas.* 9: 417–30

National Assessment of Educational Progress/Educational Testing Services (NAEP/ETS) 1985 *The Reading Report Card: Progress Toward Excellence in Our Schools; Trends in Reading over Four National Assessments. 1971–1984.* Educational Testing Service, Princeton, New Jersey

Plake B S (ed.) 1984 *Social and Technical Issues in Testing: Implications for Test Construction and Usage.* Erlbaum, Hillsdale, New Jersey

Resnick L B 1983 Toward a cognitive theory of instruction. In: Paris S G, Olson G M, Stevenson H W (eds.) 1983 *Learning and Motivation in the Classroom.* Erlbaum, Hillsdale, New Jersey, pp. 5–38

Resnick L B 1984 Beyond error analysis: The role of understanding in elementary school arithmetic. In: Cheek H N (ed.) 1984 *Diagnostic and Prescriptive Mathematics: Issues, Ideas, and Insights.* Research Council for Diagnositic and Prescriptive Mathematics, Kent, Ohio, pp. 2–14

Roid G H, Haladyna T M 1982 *A Technology for Test-Item Writing.* Academic Press, New York

Ronning R R, Glover J, Conoley J C, Witt J C (eds.) 1987 *The Influence of Cognitive Psychology in Testing*. Erlbaum, Hillsdale, New Jersey

Royce J R, Powell A 1983 *Theory of Personality and Individual Differences: Factors, Systems, and Processes*. Prentice-Hall, Englewood Cliffs, New Jersey

Schmitt N, Stults D M 1986 Methodology review: Analysis of multitrait-multimethod matrices. *Appl. Psychol. Meas.* 10: 1–22

Smith G A, Stanley G 1983 Clocking *g*: Relating intelligence and measures of timed performance. *Intelligence* 7: 353–68

Snow R E, Kyllonen P C, Marshalek B 1984 The topography of ability and learning correlations. In: Sternberg R J (ed.) 1984 *Advances in the Psychology of Human Intelligence*, Vol. 2. Erlbaum, Hillsdale, New Jersey pp. 47–103

Snow R E, Lohman D F 1984 Toward a theory of cognitive aptitude for learning from instruction. *J. Educ. Psychol.* 76: 347–76

Sperber W, Wörpel S, Jäger A O, Pfister R 1985 *Praktische Intelligenz: Untersuchungsbericht und erste Ergebnisse*. Freie Universität, Berlin

Sternberg R J (ed.) 1982a *Advances in the Psychology of Human Intelligence*, Vol. 1. Erlbaum, Hillsdale, New Jersey

Sternberg R J (ed.) 1982b *Handbook of Intelligence*. Cambridge University Press, Cambridge

Sternberg R J (ed.) 1984 *Advances in the Psychology of Human Intelligence*, Vol. 2. Erlbaum, Hillsdale, New Jersey

Sternberg R J 1985a *Beyond IQ: A Triarchic Theory of Human Intelligence*. Cambridge University Press, Cambridge

Sternberg R J (ed.) 1985b *Human Abilities: An Information-Processing Approach*. Freeman, New York

Sternberg R J 1986 The future of intelligence testing. *Educ. Meas. Iss. Prac.* 5(3): 19–22

Sternberg R J, Smith C 1985 Social intelligence and decoding skills in nonverbal communication. *Soc. Cognit.* 3: 168–92

Tatsuoka K K, Tatsuoka M M 1983 Spotting erroneous rules of operation by the individual consistency index. *J. Educ. Meas.* 20: 221–30

Thissen D 1986 The formulation and representation of item response models for multidimensional ability tests with guessing. Paper presented at the meeting of the Psychometric Society, Toronto, Canada.

Trabin T E, Weiss D J 1983 The person response curve: Fit of individuals to item response theory models. In: Weiss D J (ed.) 1983 *New Horizons in Testing: Latent Trait Test Theory and Computerized Adaptive Testing*. Academic Press, New York, pp. 83–108

Vernon P A, Jensen A R 1984 Individual and group differences in intelligence and speed of information processing. *Pers. Indiv. Diff.* 5: 411–23

Wagner R K, Sternberg R J 1985 Practical intelligence in real-world pursuits: The role of tacit knowledge. *J. Pers. Soc. Psychol.* 49: 436–58

Yen W M 1984 Obtaining maximum likelihood trait estimates from number-correct scores for the three-parameter logistic model. *J. Educ. Meas.* 21: 93–111

# Validity

## R. A. Zeller

That valid measurement is essential to successful scientific activity is widely accepted among science methodologists, theoreticians, researchers, and philosophers. Nonetheless, this importance has not led, until quite recently, to a systematic, focused approach to the problem of evaluating the validity of particular measurement procedures. Indeed, the reaction of most scientists to the question of validity has been one of the recitation of abstract ritualistic dogma of validity's importance, rather than a serious investigation of the place of validity in scientific research. In this discussion, validity will be defined and contrasted with its companion concept in the measurement process, reliability. Then the types of validity will be described and the procedures used to evaluate each type of validity will be developed and illustrated.

## 1. The Definition of Validity

A measure is valid if it does what it is intended to do. Alternatively stated, an indicator of some abstract concept is valid to the extent that it measures what it purports to measure. In science, indicators "purport" to measure concepts. To the extent that the indicators provide accurate empirical representations of their respective concepts, theoretical statements about the relationships among concepts based upon an analysis of their respective indicators can proceed in an orderly fashion. However, when indicators do not represent their respective concepts (i.e., when indicators are invalid), scientific statements about the relationships among concepts become distorted.

There is virtual agreement on the importance of valid measurement to the success of scientific endeavors. For example, Hauser (1969 pp. 127–29) stated: "I should like to venture the judgment that it is inadequate measurement, more than inadequate concept or hypothesis, that has plagued social researchers and prevented fuller explanations of the variances with which they are confounded." In a similar vein, Greer (1969 p. 160) stated:

> The link between observation and formulation is one of the most difficult and crucial of the scientific enterprises. It is the process of interpreting our theory or, as some say, of "operationalizing our concepts." Our creations in the world of possibility must be fitted in the world of probability; in Kant's epigram, "Concepts without percepts are empty." It is also the process of relating our observations to theory; to finish the epigram, "Percepts without concepts are blind."

But why, when it is so crucial to the success of scientific endeavors, does valid measurement receive ritualistic recitations instead of serious investigation? There are two important interrelated answers to this question. First, theoretical considerations (and hence, considerations of validity) were excluded from an early, important definition of "measurement." Second, as shall be seen, it is immensely difficult to provide compelling evidence of the validity of measurements. Each of these impediments to a vigorous and rigorous investigation of validity will be discussed.

## 1.1 An Inadequate Definition of Measurement

Stevens (1951 p. 22) defined measurement as ". . . the assignment of numbers to objects or events according to rules." While this definition takes into account the empirical activities associated with the measurement process, it ignores the theoretical ones. For example, suppose that a researcher wanted to measure the concept "self-esteem." According to Stevens, the researcher would have accomplished that task by constructing a set of rules for the assignment of a number to each individual. Presumably, that number would empirically represent that individual's level of self-esteem. One possible "rule for assigning numbers of objects" is: father's weight (in pounds) divided by mother's height (in inches). Thus, if a respondent's father weighed 200 pounds and mother was 50 inches tall, the number "4" (i.e., 200/50) would be assigned to that respondent. If the father weighed 120 pounds while the mother was 60 inches tall, the number "2" (120/60) would be assigned.

However, as is obvious from this example father's weight and mother's height do not give a valid representation of an individual's self-esteem. The problem is that this "rule" fully satisfies Stevens' definition of measurement. Any definition of measurement that considers only the world of sense experience and omits consideration of abstract theoretical concepts is an inadequate definition of measurement. Widespread use of Stevens' exclusively empirical definition of measurement may have impeded efforts to come to grips with the problem of validity in social research.

While Stevens allegedly defined "measurement," he actually provided the context for assessing reliability. Reliability focuses on the extent to which a measurement procedure consistently yields the same result on repeated observations. Alternatively stated, reliability is the degree of repeatability or consistency of empirical measurements. In scientific discourse, when indicators are unreliable, scientific statements about the relationships among the variables become obscured. Thus, an appropriate epigram concerning reliability and validity is: unreliability obscures; invalidity distorts.

Stevens' definition of measurement establishes the context for reliability because it lays the empirical groundwork but does not lay the theoretical groundwork for the measurement process. Correspondingly, reliability focuses upon the empirical aspects, but ignores the theoretical aspects, of the measurement process. Validity, on the other hand, focuses on the theoretical aspects of the measurement process and seeks to interweave these concerns with the empirical ones. In this sense, it is much easier to assess reliability than it is to assess validity, for the assessment of

reliability requires no more than manipulation of empirical observations while the assessment of validity requires the manipulation of both empirical observations and theoretical concepts simultaneously.

## 1.2 An Adequate Definition of Measurement

In this regard, Blalock (1968 p. 12) has observed that ". . . theorists often use concepts that are formulated at rather high levels of abstraction. These are quite different from the variables that are the stock-in-trade of empirical sociologists." In this tradition, measurement can be defined as the process of linking abstract concepts to empirical indicants. To illustrate the measurement process, the situation where a researcher wants to measure the concept "self-esteem" can again be used. According to Blalock, the research must engage in a variety of tasks to provide a valid empirical measure of this concept. These tasks include: (a) defining the concept "self-esteem"; (b) selecting indicants that will provide empirical representations of the concept "self-esteem"; (c) obtaining empirical information for those indicants; and (d) evaluating the degree to which those indicants did, in fact, provide a valid representation of the concept "self-esteem." These four tasks will briefly be carried out in the attempt to establish the validity of a measure of self-esteem.

(a) *Defining the concept "self-esteem."* Rosenberg (1979 p. 54) defines self-esteem as a positive or negative orientation towards oneself. An individual of low self-esteem ". . . lacks respect for himself, considers himself unworthy, inadequate, or otherwise seriously deficient as a person." On the other hand, a person of high self-esteem considers himself or herself to be a person of worth. High self-esteem carries no connotations of ". . . feelings of superiority, arrogance, conceit, contempt for others, [or] overweening pride." This, then constitutes a widely used theoretical definition of the concept "self-esteem."

(b) *Selecting measures of self-esteem.* Having defined "self-esteem" theoretically, Rosenberg then constructed indicants that he thought would measure the concept (Rosenberg 1979 p. 291). The indicants are statements about oneself; subjects respond to these indicants by expressing strong agreement, agreement, disagreement, or strong disagreement. Some indicants are written with a positive description of self; examples include: "On the whole, I am satisfied with myself," and "I feel that I'm a person of worth, at least on an equal plane with others." Other indicants are written with a negative description of self; examples include: "I feel I do not have much to be proud of," and "I wish I could have more respect for myself." Rosenberg constructed 10 such indicants; five were positive statements while the other five were negative statements.

(c) *Obtaining empirical information for indicants.* Rosenberg then obtained empirical information for these indicants by asking adolescents to respond to each indicant in terms of the response categories.

(d) *Evaluating the validity of the indicants*. Having completed the first three steps in the measurement process, it is then possible to examine the validity of the indicants as empirical representations of the concept. The question being asked at this stage in the research process is: "To what degree do the indicants represent the concept 'self-esteem' empirically?" The answer to this question is a major challenge in scientific discourse. There are a variety of approaches to this problem. Section 2 describes these different types of validity.

## 2. Types of Validity

Validity refers to the extent to which an empirical indicant measures what it purports to measure. Such activity does not go on inside a vacuum. Instead, it occurs within the context of a measurement situation, as described above. Thus, it is not the indicant itself that is being validated, but rather, it is the purpose for which the indicant is being used that is submitted to validation procedures. In Cronbach's words (1971 p. 447): "One validates, not a test, but an *interpretation of data arising from a specified procedure*."

There are a variety of approaches that social researchers have taken in order to establish the validity of their measures. These different approaches to the assessment of validity will now be considered; for each, their different meanings, uses, and limitations will be described and illustrated.

### 2.1 Content Validity

Fundamentally, content validity focuses upon the extent to which the content of an indicant corresponds to the content of the theoretical concept it is designed to measure. For example, the self-esteem indicants focused upon the same content as the conceptual definition of self-esteem. Thus, Rosenberg's self-esteem measure could be judged as a content valid measure of the concept "self-esteem" because the content of the indicants corresponded to the content of the concept.

Establishing content validity, therefore, involves specifying the domain of content for the concept and constructing and selecting indicants that represent that domain of content. Neither of these tasks can be done unequivocally. Self-esteem can again be used as an example. One question concerns the theoretical development of the concept. Does Rosenberg's definition include all relevant aspects of the concept? Does his definition exclude any relevant aspects of the concept? Neither of these questions can be answered with certainty because of the fundamental openness of meaning that is characteristic of concepts. As Kaplan (1964 p. 63) asserts: "As the theory is used—for scientific as well as practical purposes—its meaning is progressively more fixed; but some degree of openness always remains." Thus, in content validation, "acceptance of the universe of content as defining the variable to be measured is

essential" (Cronbach and Meehl 1955 p. 282). Obtaining this acceptance has proved to be exceedingly difficult for many of the concepts in the social and behavioral sciences.

The second question concerns the construction and/or selection of indicants designed to represent a domain of content. Do Rosenberg's indicants include all relevant aspects of his definition of self-esteem? Do his indicants exclude any relevant aspects of this definition? Neither of these questions can be answered with certainty either, because of the fundamental nature of indicants. Specifically, empirical indicants are designed to be as specific, as exact, and as bounded as the conceptual definitions and the research settings will allow. Hence, indicants never duplicate nor fully exhaust the meaning of the respective concept. While Rosenberg chose to represent the concept "self-esteem" by 10 indicants, he could have used 100 or 1,000. Even if he had done this, he would not have established the content validity beyond doubt. This is so because there is no agreed-upon criteria for evaluating whether content validity has or has not been established. Thus, while it is important to make a reasonable effort to establish the content validity of a set of indicants, these two liabilities prevent content validation from being sufficient for establishing the validity of indicants as measures of their respective concepts.

### 2.2 Criterion-related Validity

Criterion-related validity focuses upon the correlation between an indicant and some criterion variable of interest. Within this context, the criterion-related validity of college board exam scores is established by the degree to which they are correlated with performance in college. Frequently, the criterion-related validity of coaching effectiveness is established by the won–lost record of the team. Thus, criterion-related validity is the degree of correspondence between the indicant and the criterion. If this correlation is high, the indicant is considered to be criterion-related valid *for that criterion*.

There are two types of criterion-related validity: concurrent validity and predictive validity. Concurrent validity describes a criterion-related validity situation where the criterion variable exists in the present. For example, a researcher might wish to establish the awareness of students about their performance in school during the past year. In this situation, each student could be asked the question: "What was your grade point average last year?" This response could then be concurrent criterion validated by correlating it with the grade point average obtained from the school's record office.

Predictive validity describes a criterion-related validity situation where the criterion variable will not exist until a later point in time. For example, a researcher might wish to have students anticipate their performance in school during the next year. In this situation, each student could be asked the question: "What do you think your grade point average will be next year?" This response could then be predictive criterion validated by correlating it with the grade point average obtained from the school's records office after the elapse of a year's time.

Most tests used to screen applicants for various occupational and educational opportunities are, by nature, concerned with predictive validity. In each case, the purpose of the test is to differentiate between those who will be successful in the position in the future and those who will not. Ordinarily, one cannot fully establish the predictive validity of such an instrument. This is because the instrument is actually used to choose who will and who will not be allowed into the respective positions. For example, suppose that a university entrance examination is administered to 2,400 applicants to a particular university. The university then establishes a minimum score for admission. The university then wishes to discover whether the entrance examination is effective in predicting who will and who will not succeed in the program. It embarks upon "an evaluation research project" to assess the predictive validity of the entrance examination. The following is a discussion of the practical and conceptual difficulties that such a research team would face.

In order to explore this situation, some reasonable assumptions should be made about the nature of the situation faced by "the research team." First, there is a positive and relatively strong correlation between score on the entrance examination and performance in the program. Second, the university can only admit half of the applicants. Third, the university uses performance on the entrance examination as the criterion for admission. Fourth, only those students who exhibit a certain level of performance or better "succeed" at the program. Figure 1 provides a scatterplot of the behavior that would occur if these assumptions were, in fact, the case. In Fig. 1, the horizontal axis represents score on the entrance examination, where 1 represents the lowest score and 6 represents the highest. The vertical axis

represents performance in the program, where 1 represents the lowest performance and 6 represents the highest. In this contrived situation, there are 100 observations at each of the 24 locations designated by the letters, A, B, C, and D; these represent the 2,400 applicants to the program. An examination of this scatterplot reveals that it is consistent with the assumption that there is a positive and relatively strong correlation between score on the entrance examination and performance in the program. This product moment correlation coefficient is 0.64; thus, 41 percent of the variance in performance in the program is associated with entrance examination score. By social science standards, this is a relatively strong association.

Recall, however, that the university can only admit half of the applicants to the program, and that it uses the entrance examination scores as the criterion for admission. Since half of the applicants have entrance examination scores of 4 or higher, these individuals are admitted to the program; applicants whose entrance examination scores are 3 or less are not admitted. Thus, only those applicants designated in Fig. 1 by the letters A and C are admitted into the program; applicants designated by the letters B and D are not admitted. Moreover, the university requires a minimum level of performance of 4 in order for that individual to "succeed" in the program; those whose program performance is 3 or less fail in the program. Hence, A's are admitted and succeed in the program; B's are not admitted to the program, but they would have succeeded if they had been admitted; C's are admitted to but fail in the program; and D's are not admitted to the program, and would have failed in the program if they had been admitted.

The university thus admits the A's and the C's; it rejects the admission requests of the B's and the D's. The A's and the C's participate in the program; the A's succeed in the program; the C's fail. At the end of this time, the evaluation research team is commissioned to investigate the effectiveness of the entrance examination in predicting success in the program. This research team compiles the data on entrance examination scores and performance in program ratings. They then calculate the product moment correlation between these two variables. However, they discover that they only have information on both variables for the 1,200 A's and C's who were admitted into the program; they have no information on "performance in program" for those B's and D's who were not admitted. Hence, instead of the 0.64 correlation that was conjectured from Fig. 1, their observed correlation is a mere 0.32; thus, from their observations, only 10 percent of the variance in performance in the program is associated with entrance examination score. By social science standards, and much to the delight of critics of the entrance exam, this is a relatively weak association. Hence, critics charge, the entrance examination provides little useful information about the potential for success in the

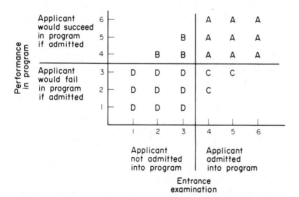

*Figure 1*
Relationship between entrance examination and performance in program

program, and the entrance examination should therefore be scrapped forthwith.

A more sober look at the research situation, however, reveals that the critics were guilty of making an *ad hominem* argument; they were appealing to prejudices about entrance tests rather than to the believability of the evidence. A reexamination of Fig. 1 shows that 75 percent of those admitted to the program succeeded at it, while only 25 percent of those who were not admitted would have succeeded if they had been admitted. Any admissions officer will testify to the fact that an admissions criterion that has a 75 percent predictive success rate (above the 50 percent success rate if applicants were admitted randomly) is a valuable tool in deciding which applicants are most likely to succeed in the program.

This example illustrates one fundamental difficulty in the use of predictive validity in social research. This difficulty is that when a predictor is used to choose which subset of applicants from a larger pool of applicants will be provided an opportunity to succeed in a program, later attempts to assess the effectiveness of that indicator are inextricably intertwined with the operation of that predictor as an admissions criterion. The result is that the predictor may appear to be only marginally correlated with success in the program when it may well be strongly correlated with success in that program.

A second fundamental difficulty in the use of criterion-related validity in social research settings is that there simply do not exist appropriate criterion variables for many of the concepts that social researchers wish to investigate. For example, no appropriate criterion variable is known for a measure of self-esteem. That is, there is no group in society that has a clear and undeniably high (or low) self-esteem such that this group could be used as a criterion variable to validate a measure of self-esteem. Moreover, the more abstract the concept, the more difficult it is to establish the viability of appropriate criterion variables for use in criterion-related validity analysis. Thus, while criterion-related validity would appear to be an attractive method for establishing the degree to which a measure represents what it purports to measure, its value is primarily by and large an illusion, for it is extremely difficult to satisfy the theoretical demands of validity in its empiricist character.

## 2.3 Construct Validity

Construct validity focuses on the assessment of whether a particular measure relates to other measures consistent with theoretically derived hypotheses concerning the relationships among the concepts. As Cronbach and Meehl (1955 p. 290) observe: "Construct validation takes place when an investigator believes his instrument reflects a particular construct, to which are attached certain meanings. The proposed interpretation generates specific testable hypotheses, which are a means of confirming or disconfirming the claim." Thus, of

necessity, construct validity is assessed within a given theoretical context.

Establishing construct validity, therefore, involves the following steps:

(a) construction of a theory by defining concepts and anticipating relationships among them;

(b) selecting indicants that represent each concept contained within the theory;

(c) establishing the dimensional nature of these indicants;

(d) constructing scales for each of the respective sets of indicants;

(e) calculating the correlations among these scales; and

(f) comparing these empirical correlations with the theoretically anticipated relationships among the concepts.

The problems and opportunities inherent in the assessment of construct validity (and hence, each of the above steps) can be illustrated by again examining the concept of self-esteem.

Step 1 involves construction of a theory by defining concepts and anticipating relationships among them. Consistent with Rosenberg (1979), the theory will assert the theoretical relationships among (A) social background factors, (B) self-esteem, and (C) social and political knowledge, attitudes and behavior as follows:

$$
\begin{array}{ccccc}
\text{A} & + & \text{B} & + & \text{C} \\
\text{Social} & \rightarrow & \text{Self-esteem} & \rightarrow & \text{Social and} \\
\text{background} & & & & \text{political knowledge,} \\
& & & & \text{attitudes, and behavior}
\end{array}
$$

In words, social background factors cause self-esteem which, in turn, causes social and political knowledge, attitudes, and behavior. The plus signs ($+$) in the above theoretical digraph represent the anticipation that the relationship between the cause and the effect will be positive. Thus, the theoretical digraph suggests that a more positive social background will cause a more positive self-esteem and that a more positive self-esteem will cause greater social and political knowledge and more positive social and political attitudes and behaviors.

Step 2 involves selection of indicants that represent each concept contained within the theory. For the purpose of this example, the following are the indicants selected to represent each concept:

(A) Social background is represented by:

+ $a_1$ is years of father's formal education
+ $a_2$ is years of mother's formal education
+ $a_3$ is father's occupational prestige

(B) Self-esteem is represented by the following 10 Likert attitude indicants:

+ $b_1$ is "I feel that I have a number of good qualities"
− $b_2$ is "I wish I could have more respect for myself"
+ $b_3$ is "I feel that I'm a person of worth, at least on an equal plane with others"

- $b_4$ is "I feel I do not have much to be proud of"
+ $b_5$ is "I take a positive attitude toward myself"
- $b_6$ is "I certainly feel useless at times"
- $b_7$ is "All in all, I'm inclined to feel that I am a failure"
+ $b_8$ is "I am able to do things as well as most other people"
- $b_9$ is "At times I think I am no good at all"
+ $b_{10}$ is "On the whole, I am satisfied with myself" (Rosenberg 1979 p. 291)

(C) Social and political knowledge, attitudes, and behavior is represented by:

+ $c_1$ is understanding of democratic principles
+ $c_2$ is knowledge of government services
+ $c_3$ is knowledge of political authorities
- $c_4$ is political cynicism
+ $c_5$ is political efficacy
+ $c_6$ is participation in community activities
+ $c_7$ is participation in school activities

The positive (+) and negative (−) signs to the left represent whether the specific indicant is a positive or negative measure of its respective concept. For instance, agreement with the statement $b_6$, "I certainly feel useless at times" indicates less self-esteem than disagreement with that statement. Moreover, there are many ways to measure each of these concepts other than those illustrated. For example, social background could have been measured by marital status of parents, degree of parental disagreement, disciplinary consistency, disciplinary extremes, and so on; such measurement would be consistent with much theory in child development.

The theoretical model can now be reformulated to include the anticipated measurement properties and using the symbolic representations as presented in Fig. 2. Again, the arrows represent a causal linkage from the cause to the effect. Also, the algebraic sign represents the nature of the relationship. Moreover, the arrows between capital letters represent a causal relationship among the concepts. The arrows from the capital letters to the lower case letters represent the causal effect of the concept on its respective indicant. These arrows, called "epistemic correlations," are the major structural building blocks on which the assessment of validity proceeds. Thus, the indicants have been selected and have been represented within the theoretical model.

*Table 1*
Factor analysis of self-esteem indicants[a]

| Items | Extracted | | | Rotated | | |
|---|---|---|---|---|---|---|
| | I | II | $h^2$ | I | II | $h^2$ |
| 1 | 0.590 | 0.109 | 0.360 | 0.493 | 0.339 | 0.360 |
| 2 | 0.328 | −0.176 | 0.138 | 0.109 | 0.356 | 0.138 |
| 3 | 0.581 | 0.314 | 0.436 | 0.633 | 0.187 | 0.436 |
| 4 | 0.600 | −0.085 | 0.367 | 0.365 | 0.483 | 0.367 |
| 5 | 0.669 | 0.198 | 0.487 | 0.614 | 0.332 | 0.487 |
| 6 | 0.577 | −0.346 | 0.453 | 0.165 | 0.653 | 0.453 |
| 7 | 0.731 | −0.202 | 0.575 | 0.376 | 0.659 | 0.575 |
| 8 | 0.549 | 0.387 | 0.451 | 0.662 | 0.113 | 0.451 |
| 9 | 0.640 | −0.359 | 0.539 | 0.200 | 0.706 | 0.539 |
| 10 | 0.480 | 0.196 | 0.269 | 0.478 | 0.200 | 0.269 |

a Items 2, 4, 6, 7, and 9 have been reflected such that higher scores indicate higher self-esteem

Step 3 involves establishing the dimensional nature of the indicants designed to measure their respective concepts. The illustration of step 3 will focus on the indicants of self-esteem, as an attempt is being made to establish the construct validity of the concept, self-esteem. Similar analyses can and should be carried out for measures of all concepts within the theory. The data to be used in this analysis come from a study of 340 high-school students (Carmines 1978). Each respondent was asked to respond to each of the 20 indicants illustrated in step 2. A principal components factor analysis of the 10 self-esteem indicants was performed and is presented in Table 1. For an excellent, extensive discussion of the use of factor analysis in this context, see Marradi (1981).

An examination of Table 1 reveals two possible interpretations for the indicants of self-esteem. One interpretation is represented by the extracted factor loadings on the left; the other is represented by the rotated factor loadings on the right. The two possible interpretations will be discussed in turn.

The extracted factor loadings in Table 1 reveal one factor of great strength and a second factor of moderate strength. Since the negative indicants were reflected such that higher scores indicate higher self-esteem, a reasonable interpretation is that the first factor represents the concept "self-esteem" empirically; within this context, factor I will be called the "self-esteem" factor. That is, the higher a respondent's answer to each

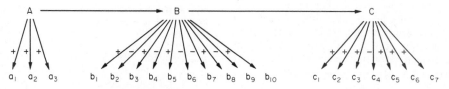

*Figure 2*
Theoretical measurement model

item, the higher his or her self-esteem is inferred to be. The second factor has positive factor loadings for the positively phrased indicants and has negative factor loadings for the negatively phrased indicants. A reasonable interpretation of factor II is that it represents a method artifact known as "response set," the general tendency to respond to interview or questionnaire items in a particular manner, irrespective of their content. In this context, response set would occur if the respondent would agree (or disagree) with all 10 indicants. The theoretical inference to be made from this extractional scheme is that the conceptualization of self-esteem was correct. Specifically, there is only one conceptual dimension of self-esteem that operates in the theoretical arrangement of things; thus, only one such concept is included in the theoretical model. This assertion has been made repeatedly by Rosenberg (1979). This analysis also identifies the method artifact "response set" as reliably but invalidly influencing the indicants.

An alternative interpretation of the factor analysis would occur by examining the rotated factor loadings in Table 1. This set of factor loadings reveals two distinct factors. Factor I is defined by strong loadings for items 1, 3, 5, 8, and 10; factor II is defined by strong loadings for items 2, 4, 6, 7, and 9. The common content that defines the former set of items is that each is a positive statement of self-esteem; the common content that defines the latter set of items is that each is a negative statement of self-esteem. Hence, in this interpretation, factor I is named "positive self-esteem" while factor II is named "negative self-esteem." The theoretical inference to be made from this rotational scheme is that the conceptualization of self-esteem was erroneous. Specifically, two different conceptual dimensions of self-esteem, one positive and the other negative, operate in the theoretical arrangement of things and, thus, should be included in the theoretical model.

Since these two interpretations are contradictory, both cannot apply to the situation. More precisely, factor analysis cannot resolve this issue, because both interpretational structures are consistent with accepted factor analytic practice. Moreover, the most common "default" interpretation, the rotated factor structure, will be the erroneous interpretation, as will be shown. However, a construct validational approach to the problem can provide evidence consistent with one interpretation and inconsistent with the other. This evidence focuses on the relationship of the self-esteem indicants to the indicants of the other concepts contained within the theoretical model. In this case, self-esteem is theoretically anticipated to be related both to social background factors and the social and political knowledge, attitudes, and behavior. If the positive and negative self-esteem factors measure different theoretical components of the self-image, they should relate differentially to indicants of these theoretically relevant concepts. If, on the other hand, the factors measure

a single dimension of self-esteem with the bifactorial structure being due to a method artifact, the two factors should relate similarly to these theoretically relevant variables. Thus, the dimensional nature on these indicants cannot be unequivocally established until the remaining steps in the process of establishing construct validity take place. This process will now be looked at.

Step 4 involves the construction of scales for each of the respective sets of indicants. Because the interpretational contradiction described above is unresolved, new scales must be created in such a way so as to resolve the contradiction. Thus, one scale will be created out of the positive self-esteem indicants (1, 3, 5, 8, and 10) and a second scale out of the negative self-esteem indicants (2, 4, 6, 7, and 9). These will be called the "positive self-esteem" and the "negative self-esteem" scales respectively. The scales were created by the simple expedient of summing the scores of each respondent on each scale.

Step 5 involves the calculation of correlations among the scales. Step 6 involves the comparison of these empirical correlations with the theoretically anticipated relationships among the concepts. While the theoretical anticipations of the nature of the relationship were presented in Fig. 2, the appropriate empirical correlations for the construct validity analysis are presented in Table 2. Specifically, the correlations of the "positive self-esteem" and the "negative self-esteem" scales with the social background indicants and with the social and political knowledge, attitudes, and behavior indicants are presented. Most of these correlations are statistically significant (at the 0.05 level) with the anticipated algebraic sign. Thus, the positive and negative self-esteem scales appear to capture an important dimension of adolescent self-esteem. Moreover, the two scales appear to measure the same, rather than different, dimensions of self-esteem, for their correlation with these theoretically relevant indicants are almost identical to one another in terms of direction strength, and consistency. Indeed, the average difference between correlations across all 10 indicants is approximately 0.03, with the highest difference being 0.05. None of these differences is statistically significant (at even the 0.25 level), and there is no compelling theoretical interpretation of such differences.

Thus, a construct validity analysis supports the theoretical unidimensionality of self-esteem as asserted by Rosenberg (1979) rather than theoretical bidimensionality. The two-factor (rotated) solution, thus, offers only spurious evidence for the dual theoretical dimensionality of self-esteem. The more appropriate interpretation is that the bifactorial structure of the indicants is a function of a single theoretical dimension of self-esteem that is contaminated by a method artifact response set.

This example graphically illustrates a key point that this article has attempted to make: that in spite of the usefulness of factor analysis, it does not always lead to

**Table 2**
Correlations between positive and negative self-esteem scales and indicants of theoretically relevant concepts

| Comparison indicant | Positive self-esteem scale | Negative self-esteem scale | Difference between correlations | N |
|---|---|---|---|---|
| *Socioeconomic background factor* | | | | |
| Father's education | 0.17[b] | 0.15[b] | 0.02 | 198 |
| Mother's education | 0.11[a] | 0.08 | 0.03 | 208 |
| Father's occupation | 0.12[a] | 0.08 | 0.04 | 198 |
| *Social and political knowledge, attitudes, and behavior* | | | | |
| Understanding of democratic principles | 0.16[b] | 0.13[b] | 0.03 | 334 |
| Knowledge of government services | 0.12[a] | 0.10[a] | 0.02 | 333 |
| Knowledge of political authorities | 0.14[b] | 0.09[a] | 0.05 | 331 |
| Political cynicism | −0.09[a] | −0.13[b] | 0.04 | 331 |
| Political efficacy | 0.18[c] | 0.22[c] | −0.04 | 334 |
| Participation in community activities | 0.05 | 0.02 | 0.03 | 228 |
| Participation in school activities | 0.14[b] | 0.11[a] | 0.03 | 338 |

a $p < 0.05$   b $p < 0.01$   c $p < 0.001$

unambiguous inferences about the theoretical dimensionality of concepts. Therefore, factor analysis cannot be used as the sole criterion for establishing the adequacy of the concept–indicant linkage. On the contrary, naive and simplistic interpretation of factor structures (such as the automatic use of the default varimax rotation) can be misleading in terms of the theoretical nature of the empirical indicants. It has been shown how response set can artificially produce an inference of two underlying dimensions when in fact there is only one. Any method artifact that can systematically alter the correlations among the indicants may produce this kind of faulty inference.

From the above discussion, it should be clear that the process of construct validation is, by necessity, theory laden. Indeed, strictly speaking, it is impossible to "validate" a measure of a concept unless there exists a theoretical network that surrounds the concept. Without such a network, it is impossible to generate theoretical predictions, which, in turn, lead directly to empirical tests involving measures of the concept. This should not lead to the erroneous conclusion that only formal fully developed theories are relevant to construct validation. On the contrary, Cronbach and Meehl (1955 p. 284) note: "The logic of construct validation is involved whether the construct is highly systematized or loose, used in ramified theory or a few simple propositions, used in absolute propositions or probability statements." What is required is only that one be able to

state several theoretically derived hypotheses involving the particular concept.

In the self-esteem example described above, the construct validity evidence was positive. That is, the self-esteem scale correlated as theoretically anticipated with the indicants of the theoretically relevant concepts. Moreover, it is possible to have relatively strong confidence in this construct validation because positive construct validational evidence was found for multiple measures of more than one theoretically relevant concept. For a more complete discussion of the procedures for handling external associations with sets of indicants, see Curtis and Jackson (1962), and Sullivan and Feldman (1979).

But what would the appropriate inference have been if the construct validity evidence had been negative? That is, what should a researcher conclude if the empirically observed relationships are inconsistent with those that were theoretically anticipated? Four different interpretations are possible (Cronbach and Meehl 1955 p. 295). One possible interpretation is that the indicant of the concept lacks construct validity; that is, that the indicants do not measure the concept that they purport to measure. Unfortunately, negative construct validity evidence is also consistent with three other interpretations:

(a) the theoretical arrangement of the concepts was incorrect; and/or

(b) the procedures for deriving empirical hypotheses from the theory were incorrect; and/or

(c) the indicants of the other concepts in the theory lack construct validity.

There is no foolproof procedure for determining which of these interpretations of negative evidence is correct in any given instance. Bits of evidence can be accrued from additional data analysis that suggests one or more of these interpretations. However, it is important to acknowledge that the process of construct validation is more analogous to a detective searching for clues than it is analogous to an accountant proving out a balance. A researcher does not establish validity once and for all; instead, a researcher obtains bits of information that are consistent or inconsistent with a construct validity interpretation. The more systematic the pattern of such bits of information that are consistent with construct validity, the more confidence one has in that interpretation.

## 3. Conclusion

In this article, validity has been considered. An indicator is valid to the degree that it empirically represents the concept it purports to measure. As such, valid measurement becomes the *sine qua non* of science. There are several strategies for establishing valid measurement including content, criterion-related, and construct validity. It has been argued that construct validity is most appropriate for most questions in social research. Construct validity not only has generalized applicability for assessing validity of social science measures, but it can also be used to differentiate between theoretically relevant and theoretically meaningless empirical factors. This is a crucially important contribution to measurement, because reliability assessment in general and factor analysis in particular are insensitive to this problem. Heise (1974 p. 12) comments: "The meaningfulness of a factor does not depend on the statistical characteristics of its indicators but on their theoretical content, and in ordinary analytic procedures these considerations are not entered as constraints on the numerical analysis." Thus, however useful factor analysis may be for assessing the reliability of a measure, it is not directly relevant to assessing its validity. Viewed from this perspective, efforts to assess validity within a strictly factor-analytic approach—as with Heise and Bohrnstedt's (1970) validity coefficient and with Jöreskog's (1973) linear structural equation system—have the important limitation that they *assume* what a researcher wants to test in validity assessment— whether the set of items measure what they are intended to measure. Thus, ". . . there should be no question that an internal index of validity is not a complete substitute for an external check on the validity of a composite scale" (Smith 1974 p. 177). Specifically, it is believed that analysis of a set of indicants designed to

measure a concept can never be an adequate substitute for a theoretically oriented assessment of a measure's validity.

Moreover, the key question underlying validity— inferring the dimensional nature of the posited theoretical concepts—is not a question that lends itself to a solely statistical solution. On the contrary, in order to properly decide which of the empirical factors represents the respective concept, it is necessary to go beyond the statistical criteria used in factor analysis to the more explicit theoretically relevant criteria used in construct validation. Only in this way can the social researcher ensure that his or her measures are valid.

## Bibliography

Blalock H M 1968 The measurement problem. In: Blalock H M, Blalock A B (eds.) 1968 *Methodology in Social Research*. McGraw-Hill, New York, pp. 5–27

Carmines E G 1978 Psychological origins of adolescent political attitudes. *Am. Pol. Q.* 6: 167–86

Carmines E G, Zeller R A 1979 *Reliability and Validity Assessment*. Sage, Beverly Hills, California

Cronbach L J 1971 Test validation. In: Thorndike R L (ed.) 1971 *Educational Measurement*, 2nd edn. American Council on Education, Washington, DC, pp. 443–507

Cronbach L J, Meehl P E 1955 Construct validity in psychological tests. *Psychol. Bull.* 52: 281–302

Curtis R F, Jackson E F 1962 Multiple indicators in survey research. *Am. J. Sociol.* 68: 195–204

Greer S 1969 *The Logic of Social Inquiry*. Aldine, Chicago, Illinois

Hauser P 1969 Comments on Coleman's paper. In: Bierstedt R (ed.) 1969 *A Design for Sociology: Scope, Objectives, and Methods*. American Academy of Political and Social Science, Philadelphia, Pennsylvania, pp. 122–36

Heise D R 1974 Some issues in sociological measurement. In: Costner H L (ed.) 1974 *Sociological Methodology 1973– 1974*. Jossey-Bass, San Francisco, California

Heise D R, Bohrnstedt G W 1970 Validity, invalidity, and reliability. In: Borgatta E F, Bohrnstedt G W (eds.) 1970 *Sociological Methodology 1970*. Jossey-Bass, San Francisco, California

Jöreskog K G 1973 A general method for estimating a linear structural equation system. In: Goldberger A S, Duncan O D (eds.) 1973 *Structural Equation Models in the Social Sciences*. Seminar Press, New York, pp. 85–132

Kaplan A 1964 *The Conduct of Inquiry: Methodology for Behavioral Science*. Chandler, San Francisco

Marradi A 1981 Factor analysis as an aid in the formation and refinement of empirically useful concepts. In: Jackson D J, Borgatta E F (eds.) 1981 *Factor Analysis and Measurement in Sociological Research: A Multi-dimensional Perspective*. Sage, Beverly Hills, California, pp. 11–49

Rosenberg M 1979 *Conceiving the Self*. Basic Books, New York

Smith K W 1974 Forming composite scales and estimating their validity through factor analysis. *Social Forces* 53: 168–80

Stevens S S 1951 Mathematics, measurement and psychophysics. In: Stevens S S (ed.) 1951 *Handbook of Experimental Psychology*. Wiley, New York, pp. 1–49

Sullivan J A, Feldman S 1979 *Multiple Indicators: An Introduction*. Sage, Beverly Hills, California

# Reliability[1]

## R. L. Thorndike

Any test presents a set of tasks that sample from some universe of responses by the examinee. The universe corresponds, it is hoped, to the latent attribute in which one is interested. In evaluating a test two broad questions are encountered that are different but overlapping. A first question is how accurately the test sample represents the broader universe of responses from which it is drawn; a second is how faithfully that universe corresponds to the latent attribute in which one is interested. The first relates to what is commonly called the "reliability" of the test, the second to its "validity". Collectively, they have been spoken of by Cronbach et al. (1972) as the generalizability of the test score—the range of inferences that can be made from it.

There are typically three sides to the issue of reliability: the basic rationale, the procedures for data collection, and the statistical procedures for data analysis. These facets interact, in that certain empirical data sets are appropriate for certain conceptions of the universe to which inference is desired, and the possible types of statistical analysis depend on the data at hand. Ideally, one would feel that the rational analysis of the universe to which generalization was desired should be primary and that data collection and statistical treatment should flow from this analysis. Realistically, however, practical considerations may limit the data that it is possible to collect, and these limitations may set boundaries on the universe to which inferences can logically be made and on the statistical analyses that can be carried out.

This article starts with a consideration of "classical" reliability theory. This is the true-score-and-error model of a test score that was presented by Spearman in 1904 and that provided the accepted theoretical model for discussions of reliability for the next 50 years. There follows an analysis of the multifacet model of reliability presented by Lindquist (1953) and elaborated by Cronbach and his associates (1972). Then the discussion returns to the practical issues involved in data collection and analysis. Finally, the meaning of reliability in the context of domain mastery or criterion-referenced testing is briefly considered.

## 1. The Classical Reliability Model

The classical reliability model views a test score as having two additive components, the "true" score and a random "error". The error is defined as unrelated to the true score and as unrelated to the error that would occur in another measurement of the same attribute.

The true score is defined as the value that the average of repeated measurements with the identical measure approaches as the number of measurements is increased without limit. The term "identical" implies that it is possible to measure an individual repeatedly without changing that individual—a condition that obviously cannot be achieved in the real world. Though the model is in this respect, and some others, an oversimplification and not a representation of reality, development of the model brings out a number of relationships that are instructive and useful in the design and construction of tests and in the evaluation of test scores.

### 1.1 Basic Assumptions and Resulting Relationships

The basic assumptions of the model are as follows:

(a) The obtained score is the sum of true score plus error; that is, $X_{\text{obt}} = X_{\text{true}} + X_{\text{error}}$. The subscripts $o$, $t$, and $e$ will be used for observed score, true score, and error, respectively. The subscript $x$ is used for the variance ($s_x^2$) of $x_o$.

(b) Over the population, error is independent of true score; that is, $r_{te} = 0$.

(c) In pairs of measures, the error in one measure is independent of the error in the other; that is, $r_{ee'} = 0$.

Given these assumptions, it can be concluded that, as the number of persons or the number of measurements increases, the mean error approaches 0 as a limit. That is, $\bar{X}_e \cong 0$ when the number of measures increases without limit. This follows from the definition of errors as *random* deviations from the true score that are equally likely to be positive or negative. Any consistent direction to "error" would be indistinguishable from, and hence assimilated as part of, the operational "true" score.

It follows that, in the limit, the mean of observed scores is equal to the mean of true scores; that is:

$$\bar{X}_o \cong \bar{X}_t \tag{1}$$

This relationship holds both for repeated measures of an individual and for the mean of a group. That is, as the number of observations increases, the observed mean approaches the mean of true scores and is an unbiased estimate of the true-score mean.

It is shown next that the variance of observed scores equals the true-score variance plus the error variance. Most of the development from here on will work with

---

1 This article is an edited version of material by R L Thorndike which first appeared in *Applied Psychometrics* (1982), Chap. 6 pp. 143–83. It appears here by permission of Houghton Mifflin, Boston, Massachusetts © 1982.

scores that are expressed as deviations from the mean; that is, $x = X - \bar{X}$.

$$s_x^2 = \frac{1}{N} \sum (x_t + x_e)^2$$

$$= \frac{1}{N} \sum (x_t^2 + x_e^2 + 2x_t x_e)$$

$$= \frac{1}{N} \sum x_t^2 + \frac{1}{N} \sum x_e^2 + \frac{2}{N} \sum x_t x_e$$

$$= s_t^2 + s_e^2 + 2s_t s_e r_{te}$$

But, by definition, $r_{te} = 0$, so

$$s_x^2 = s_t^2 + s_e^2 \tag{2}$$

It can also be shown that the correlation between two equivalent test forms is equal to the true-score variance divided by the observed variance; that is:

$$r_{xx'} = \frac{s_t^2}{s_x^2} \tag{3}$$

Thus the alternate-forms reliability of a test equals true-score variance divided by observed variance. From this it follows that $s_t^2 = s_x^2 r_{xx'}$ and $s_t = s_x \sqrt{[r_{xx'}]}$. The standard deviation of true scores can be estimated by multiplying the observed standard deviation by the square root of the reliability coefficient.

Returning to Eqn. (2) and transposing, gives $s_e^2 = s_x^2 - s_t^2$. But it has been seen that $s_t^2 = s_x^2 r_{xx'}$, therefore $s_e^2 = s_x^2 - s_x^2 r_{xx'}$, or:

$$s_e = s_x \sqrt{1 - r_{xx'}} \tag{4}$$

Thus the standard error of measurement is estimated from the observed standard deviation and the alternate-forms reliability coefficient.

Next the correlation between observed score and true score, and the correlation between observed score and measurement error can be derived. Remembering that $x_o = x_t + x_e$,

$$r_{x_o x_t} = \frac{\frac{1}{N} \sum (x_t + x_e) x_t}{s_x s_t}$$

$$= \frac{\frac{1}{N} \sum x_t^2 + \frac{1}{N} \sum x_t x_e}{s_x s_t}$$

But the second term in the numerator approaches zero because of the independence of true score and error. Hence

$$r_{x_o x_t} = \frac{s_t^2}{s_x s_t} = \frac{s_t}{s_x} \tag{5}$$

Referring to Eqn. (3), it was found that $r_{xx'} = s_t^2 / s_x^2$ so $r_{x_o x_t} = \sqrt{[r_{xx'}]}$. The correlation of an observed measure with the underlying true score is equal to the square root of the alternate-forms reliability coefficient.

Turning to observed score and error,

$$r_{x_o x_e} = \frac{\frac{1}{N} \sum (x_t + x_e) x_e}{s_x s_e}$$

$$= \frac{\frac{1}{N} \sum x_t x_e + \frac{1}{N} \sum x_e^2}{s_x s_e}$$

Once again referring to the independence of true score and error, it can be seen that the first term of the numerator approaches 0, and

$$r_{x_o x_e} = \frac{s_e^2}{s_x s_e} = \frac{s_e}{s_x}$$

But it can be seen from Eqn. (4) that $s_e / s_x = \sqrt{[1 - r_{xx'}]}$ and therefore $r_{x_o x_e} = \sqrt{[1 - r_{xx'}]}$. This correlation of observed score with error is a specific example of the more general expression $\sqrt{[1 - r_{xy'}]}$ which has been called the coefficient of alienation when predicting $y$ from $x$.

### 1.2 Effects of Increasing or Decreasing Test Length

The discussion turns now to the effects of increasing (or decreasing) the length of a test, considering en route the general expressions for the correlations of sums (and differences; a difference is, algebraically speaking, still a sum).

The equation for the mean of the unweighted sum of two or more variables is simply:

$$\text{Mean}_{(X_1 + X_2 + \cdots + X_k)} = \bar{X}_1 + \bar{X}_2 + \cdots + \bar{X}_k$$

Illustrating with the case of two variables, gives

$$\bar{X}_{(1+2)} = \frac{1}{N} \sum (X_1 + X_2)$$

$$= \frac{1}{N} \sum X_1 + \frac{1}{N} \sum X_2$$

$$= \bar{X}_1 + \bar{X}_2$$

If $X_1$ and $X_2$ are equivalent forms of the same test, each will have the same mean, because in each case the observed mean will equal the true-score mean, and one can write:

$$\text{Mean}_{2X} = 2(\text{Mean } X)$$

When the length of a test is doubled by adding equivalent items, the mean can be expected to double. More generally:

$$\text{Mean}_{kX} = k(\text{Mean } X)$$

If the variables are combined with different weights, we then get

$$\text{Mean}_{\text{wtd sum}} = \sum W_i \bar{X}_i \tag{6}$$

261

Turning now to the variance of a sum, gives:

$$s^2_{(x_1 + x_2)} = \frac{1}{N} \sum (x_1 + x_2)^2$$

$$= \frac{1}{N} \sum x_1^2 + \frac{1}{N} \sum x_2^2 + \frac{2}{N} \sum x_1 x_2$$

$$= s_1^2 + s_2^2 + 2 s_1 s_2 r_{12}$$

Coming back to the situation of dealing with equivalent forms of the same test, the effect of doubling the length of the test will be investigated. One then has:

$$s^2_{(x+x')} = s_x^2 + s_{x'}^2 + 2 r_{xx'} s_x s_{x'}$$

But because the test forms are equivalent, and so have the same standard deviation, this can be expressed as:

$$s^2_{(2x)} = 2 s_x^2 + 2 r_{xx'} s_x^2$$

$$= s_x^2 (2 + 2 r_{xx'})$$

and

$$s_{2x} = s_x \sqrt{2 + 2 r_{xx'}} \qquad (7)$$

In general terms, when the length of a test is increased by a factor of $k$, the variance can be expected to increase by a factor of $k + k(k-1)r_{xx'}$, in which case $s_{kx} = s_x \sqrt{[k + k(k-1)r_{xx'}]}$. The rate at which the standard deviation increases as the length is increased depends on the correlation between unit-length tests. At one limit, as the correlation approaches 0.00, the increase is proportional to $\sqrt{[k]}$. At the other, as the correlation approaches 1.00, the increase is proportional to $k$.

Though covariance and correlation between tests has been applied here, average interitem covariance or correlation could also be applied. The relationships developed between unit-length tests and longer tests also apply at the limit where the unit is a single item, and the $k$-length test is a test composed of $k$ items.

What happens to the variance of true scores and to the variance of errors when the length of the test is doubled? Using Eqn. (7) and remembering that the correlation of true scores on alternate forms is 1.00, it can be seen that:

$$s^2_{(2t)} = 2 s_t^2 + 2 r_{tt} s_t^2 = 4 s_t^2$$

$$s_{(2t)} = 2 s_t$$

For the variance of errors, remembering that the correlation of errors on alternate forms is by definition 0, one has:

$$s^2_{(2e)} = 2 s_e^2 + 2 r_{ee} s_e^2 = 2 s_e^2$$

$$s_{(2e)} = s_e \sqrt{2}$$

In the general case of increasing test length by a factor $k$,

$$s^2_{kt} = k^2 s_t^2, \qquad s_{kt} = k s_t$$

and

$$s^2_{ke} = k s_e^2, \qquad s_{ke} = s_e \sqrt{k}$$

Thus it can be seen that true-score variance increases as the square of test length, whereas error variance increases only as a linear function of test length. This relationship accounts for the progressively greater reliability of a test as its length is increased.

A variety of interesting relationships can be derived when the sum of variables $x_1 + x_2 + \cdots + x_m$ is correlated with the sum of variables $y_1 + y_2 + \cdots + y_n$. Consider first the case in which there is the same number of elements in each sum and in which all of both the $x$'s and the $y$'s represent equivalent forms of the same test. Then, if the tests are in fact equivalent, all the covariances will be equal, except for sampling fluctuations, and the same will be true of all the variances. It can be shown that:

$$r_{(1 \text{ to } m)(1 \text{ to } m)} = \frac{m \bar{r}_{ii'}}{1 + (m-1)\bar{r}_{ii'}} \qquad (8)$$

This is the general form of the Spearman–Brown Prophecy Formula to estimate the reliability of a test the length of which has been increased by a factor of $m$. When $m = 2$, then

$$r_{2x} = \frac{2 r_{xx'}}{1 + r_{xx'}} \qquad (9)$$

This is the specific form for a double length test. It is most frequently encountered in adjusting a split-half reliability coefficient obtained by correlating score on odd-numbered items with score on even-numbered items to give the reliability of the complete test.

When all the $x$'s are to be considered equivalent forms of one test and all the $y$'s equivalent forms of another test, the correlation when one or both of the two tests are lengthened can be estimated. If both are lengthened, it can be shown that:

$$r_{(x_1 + \cdots + x_m)(y_1 + \cdots + y_n)}$$

$$= \frac{\bar{r}_{xy}}{\sqrt{\frac{1}{m} + \left(\frac{m-1}{m}\right)\bar{r}_{xx'}} \sqrt{\frac{1}{n} + \left(\frac{n-1}{n}\right)\bar{r}_{yy'}}} \qquad (10)$$

For proofs of these relationships see Thorndike (1982).

This equation makes it possible to estimate what the effect would be on the correlation between any two variables, say a predictor test and some type of criterion measure, if more (or less) data were gathered for either or both. Suppose, for example, it had been found that the correlation between two forms of an aptitude test was 0.80, the correlation between two independently obtained supervisory ratings was 0.60, and the correlation of a single test with a single rating was 0.25. One might ask what the correlation would be between a test twice as long and the average of 5 ratings. As an estimate it would be found that:

$$r_{2x \cdot 5y} = \frac{0.25}{\sqrt{\frac{1}{2} + \frac{1}{2}(0.80)}\sqrt{\frac{1}{5} + \frac{4}{5}(0.60)}}$$

$$= \frac{0.25}{\sqrt{(0.90)(0.68)}} = \frac{0.25}{0.78}$$

$$= 0.32$$

If one of the tests, say $x$, remains of unit length while the length of the other is changed, then:

$$r_{x(y_1 + \cdots + y_n)} = \frac{\bar{r}_{xy}}{\sqrt{\frac{1}{n} + \frac{n-1}{n}r_{yy'}}}$$

If the length of $y$ is now increased without limit, giving in effect the correlation between $x$ and $y_t$, the true score on $y$, then:

$$r_{xy_\infty} = r_{xy_t} = \frac{r_{xy}}{\sqrt{r_{yy'}}}$$

Furthermore, if the length of both tests is allowed to increase without limit then:

$$r_{x_\infty y_\infty} = r_{x_t y_t} = \frac{r_{xy}}{\sqrt{(r_{xx'})(r_{yy'})}} \quad (11)$$

This is the general form of the correction for attenuation. It provides an estimate of the correlation between true scores on $x$ and $y$, or measures that are of such a length that measurement errors are negligible. Taking the values from our previous illustration would give:

$$r_{x_t y_t} = \frac{0.25}{\sqrt{(0.80)(0.60)}} = \frac{0.25}{0.693} = 0.36$$

## 1.3 Problems in Defining True Score and Error

True score and error, of course, are not observables. Behavior samples are observed, and from these observations inferences about the constructs of "true score" and "error" are made. And the inferences that can legitimately be made depend on the nature of the samples of behavior that are observed.

The key point is that a universe has a dimension of *content* as well as one of trials or occasions and/or one of judges or appraisers, and variable performance arises in part from the extent of variation in the specific content in terms of which the universe is assessed. Content may be defined quite narrowly, as when all the words in a vocabulary test are drawn from a single area of knowledge such as biology, or broadly to cover the whole of a field. The universe may be defined solely in terms of content, or it may also be limited in terms of format—as when the measure of vocabulary consists only of words out of context presented in pairs, with the examinee to judge whether the members are synonyms or autonyms. As the definition of the universe is broadened, any single task or narrow sampling of tasks becomes less adequate to represent that universe. Thus any estimate of reliability for a testing procedure appropriately refers to its precision as estimating some *particular* universe score, and it will depend as much on the definition of the universe as on the instrument.

## 2. Reliability Estimates and Variance Components

### 2.1 Error Variance

The classical definition of reliability was framed in terms of true score and error variance and took the form:

$$r_{xx'} = \frac{\sigma_t^2}{\sigma_t^2 + \sigma_e^2}$$

What is included under the heading "error variance" depends on how the universe that the test score is presumed to represent is defined, with certain sources of variance being treated as error under one definition of the universe and as true score under another definition. In theory, at least, an ideal set of data and an ideal analysis would be those that made it possible to estimate the magnitude of each possible component of variance, so that estimates could be made of the reliability of an instrument as representing universes defined in various ways, and so that the effectiveness of various alternative strategies for increasing the reliability of generalization to a particular universe score could be compared.

If the different facets that are likely to be sources of variation in the resulting score have been identified, the theoretically ideal data-gathering and data-analysis design for getting information about the sources of error in an instrument or procedure would seem to be that of a completely crossed multidimensional analysis of variance.

A two-dimensional illustration is shown in Fig. 1. Suppose that each of $N$ examinees has written answers to $m$ test questions. Each answer has been evaluated by the same single reader. One then has an $N \times m$ data

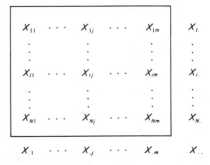

**Figure 1**
Two-dimensional matrix representing $N$ examinees answering $m$ questions.

matrix that can be represented by the entries in the box. The border entries represent summations, where a subscript of a dot ($\cdot$) indicates summation over that facet. In this matrix, each row represents a person and $X_{i.}$ is the sum over questions for person $i$, whereas each column represents a question and $X_{.j}$ represents the sum over all persons for question $j$. The usual computations for analysis of variance (see, for example, Winer 1971) are:

$$\text{Total sum of squares} = \sum_1 \sum_1 (X_{ij})^2 - (X_{..})^2/mN$$

$$\text{Persons sum of squares} = \frac{1}{m} \sum_1^N (X_{i.})^2 - (X_{..})^2/mN$$

$$\text{Questions sum of squares} = \frac{1}{N} \sum_1^m (X_{.j})^2 - (X_{..})^2/mN$$

Residual sum of squares =

$$\text{(Total SS} - \text{persons SS} - \text{questions SS)} \quad (12)$$

and then

$$\text{Persons mean square} = \frac{(\text{persons sum of squares})}{(N-1)}$$

$$\text{Questions mean square} = \frac{(\text{questions sum of squares})}{(m-1)}$$

$$\text{Residual mean square} = \frac{(\text{residual sum of squares})}{[(N-1)(m-1)]}$$

$$(13)$$

A numerical illustration is shown in Table 1, in which each of a group of six examinees responded to the same set of four questions. All were evaluated by one exam reader.

The precision of the scores that result from a test composed of a set of $m$ questions can now be investigated. Note that the only facet of the domain that can be studied is that of questions rated by a single rater. There is no evidence on the variability that would be introduced if the examinees were tested on different occasions or if the questions were rated by different judges. To obtain evidence on these facets, they would have to be systematically introduced into the data-gathering and data-analysis design.

In this context, the usual situation is that all examinees respond to the same questions. When that is the case, "questions" becomes a fixed condition, does not vary, and consequently introduces no variance. Then the only source of error variance is the residual term: the inter-action between persons and questions—that is, the fact that each examinee does better on some questions and worse on others than would be expected in light of that person's average performance and the difficulty of a given question for all examinees. The *observed* variance among persons includes both "true" between-persons variance and error, so we must subtract the error, to

*Table 1*
A numerical illustration of six examinees responding to a set of four questions

| Examinees | Questions 1 | 2 | 3 | 4 | Sum |
|---|---|---|---|---|---|
| 1 | 9 | 6 | 6 | 2 | 23 |
| 2 | 9 | 5 | 4 | 0 | 18 |
| 3 | 8 | 9 | 5 | 8 | 30 |
| 4 | 7 | 6 | 5 | 4 | 22 |
| 5 | 7 | 3 | 2 | 3 | 15 |
| 6 | 10 | 8 | 7 | 7 | 32 |
| Sum | 50 | 37 | 29 | 24 | 140 |

$$\Sigma(X_{ij})^2 = 972 \qquad \Sigma(x_{i.})^2 = 3{,}486$$
$$\Sigma(X_{.j})^2 = 5{,}286 \qquad (X_{..})^2 = 19{,}600$$

Total SS = $972 - 19{,}600/24 = 155.3$
Examinees SS = $3{,}486/4 - 19{,}600/24 = 54.8$
Questions SS = $5{,}286/6 - 19{,}600/24 = 64.3$
Residual SS = $155.3 - 54.8 - 64.3 = 36.2$
Examinees MS = $54.8/5 = 10.96$
Questions MS = $64.3/3 = 21.43$
Residual MS = $36.2/(3 \times 5) = 2.41$

get an estimate of $\sigma_t^2$. Thus, $\sigma_t^2 = $ examinees MS $-$ residual MS, and hence:

$$\text{Reliability} = \frac{\text{examinees MS} - \text{residual MS}}{\text{examinees MS}} \quad (14)$$

In the illustrative example presented in Table 1, this becomes:

$$\text{Reliability} = \frac{10.96 - 2.41}{10.96} = 0.78$$

and the standard error of measurement is $\sqrt{2.41} = 1.55$.

The foregoing estimate applies to the total score, in this example the score based on four questions. It is also possible to estimate the average error variance and the average reliability of a single element, in this illustration the response to a single question. The relationships are as follows:

$$\sigma_E^2 = \frac{\text{residual MS}}{m}$$

$$\text{Reliability} = \frac{\text{examinees MS} - \text{residual MS}}{\text{examinees MS} + (m-1) \text{ residual MS}}$$

$$(15)$$

For the illustrative example being considered, the values come out:

$$\sigma_E^2 = \frac{2.41}{4} = 0.60$$

$$\text{Reliability} = \frac{10.96 - 2.41}{10.96 + 3(2.41)} = 0.47$$

and the standard error of measurement equals $\sqrt{[0.60]} = 0.77$. Naturally, a score based on just a single question provides a much less accurate estimate of the universe score than one based on the pooling of a number of questions.

It is possible, of course, that questions are not uniform across examinees, and that it is not known which, from a pool of possible questions, a given examinee is going to encounter. If that is so, and the questions vary from examinee to examinee, "questions" variance becomes part of error and must be so treated. There are then only two distinguishable components, examinees and residual, in which case:

$$\text{Total SS} = \sum \sum (X_{ij})^2 - (X_{..})^2/mN$$

$$\text{Persons SS} = \frac{1}{m} \sum (X_{i.})^2 - (X_{..})^2/mN$$

$$\text{Residual SS} = \text{total SS} - \text{persons SS}$$

$$\text{Persons MS} = \frac{\text{persons SS}}{N-1}$$

$$\text{Residual MS} = \frac{\text{residual SS}}{N(m-1)}$$

Applying these relationships to the illustrative example considered here, gives

$$\text{Examinees SS} = 54.8$$

$$\text{Residual SS} = 100.5$$

$$\text{Examinees MS} = \frac{54.8}{5} = 10.96$$

$$\text{Residual MS} = \frac{100.5}{18} = 5.58$$

$$\text{Reliability of total score} = \frac{10.96 - 5.58}{10.96} = 0.49$$

$$\text{Reliability of single item} = \frac{10.96 - 5.58}{10.96 + 3(5.58)} = 0.19$$

The reduction in reliability is quite dramatic in this example—and rightly so, because the questions obviously differed widely in their mean score for this group of examinees.

The approach to reliability through analysis of the facets of variance can be quite instructive, as the example shows. It indicates in this case that a great deal of precision will be lost if different examinees are given different questions. However, for this conclusion to be dependable, it is important that the sample of questions be representative of the universe of admissible questions. Of course, if the estimate of examinee variance is to be meaningful, it is also important that the sample of examinees be representative of the population of examinees to which one wants to generalize. However, research workers in general and test makers in particular are used to worrying about their sample of persons. The point is that if estimates are to be made about the size

of effects from varying any other facet of the situation, *equal attention must be devoted to sampling from the other facet*. It may be desirable to have as large a sample from the facet of questions, or of raters, or of observation periods, as from the facet of persons.

## 2.2 The General Multifacet Model

In the illustration considered so far only one facet of the domain was varied—the facet represented by questions. Table 2 illustrates a two-facet problem. Suppose that each of the questions had also been read by a second reader and that this reader had assigned scores as shown on the right below. (The scores assigned by the first reader are repeated on the left.)

The actual scores on single questions are enclosed in the two boxes. The sums over questions and over questions and readers are shown on the right. The sums over examinees and over examinees and readers are shown at the foot of the table.

The raw material is now available for a three-way analysis of variance allowing the possibility of obtaining estimates of seven distinct components of variance. If the facet that is represented by raters is designated $k$, the sums are as follows:

$$\sum_i \sum_j \sum_k (X_{ijk})^2 = 2{,}214 \quad \text{squares of single observations}$$

$$\sum_j \sum_k (X_{.jk})^2 = 12{,}014 \quad \text{squares of sums over persons}$$

$$\sum_i \sum_k (X_{i.k})^2 = 8{,}026 \quad \text{squares of sums over questions}$$

$$\sum_i \sum_j (X_{ij.})^2 = 4{,}258 \quad \text{squares of sums over readers}$$

$$\sum_j (X_{.j.})^2 = 23{,}522 \quad \text{squares of sums over both persons and readers}$$

$$\sum_k (X_{..k})^2 = 45{,}200 \quad \text{squares of sums over both persons and questions}$$

$$\sum_i (X_{i..})^2 = 15{,}878 \quad \text{squares of sums over both questions and readers}$$

$$(X_{...})^2 = 90{,}000 \quad \text{square of grand sum}$$

*Table 2*
A two-facet problem representing six examinees responding to a set of four questions evaluated by two readers

| | First reader | | | | Second reader | | | | Sum | | |
|---|---|---|---|---|---|---|---|---|---|---|---|
| Question | 1 | 2 | 3 | 4 | 1 | 2 | 3 | 4 | | | |
| Examinee | | | | | | | | | First reader | Second reader | Both readers |
| 1 | 9 | 6 | 6 | 2 | 8 | 2 | 8 | 1 | 23 | 19 | 42 |
| 2 | 9 | 5 | 4 | 0 | 7 | 5 | 9 | 5 | 18 | 26 | 44 |
| 3 | 8 | 9 | 5 | 8 | 10 | 6 | 9 | 10 | 30 | 35 | 65 |
| 4 | 7 | 6 | 5 | 4 | 9 | 8 | 9 | 4 | 22 | 30 | 52 |
| 5 | 7 | 3 | 2 | 3 | 7 | 4 | 5 | 1 | 15 | 17 | 32 |
| 6 | 10 | 8 | 7 | 7 | 7 | 7 | 10 | 9 | 32 | 33 | 65 |
| Sum | 50 | 37 | 29 | 24 | 48 | 32 | 50 | 30 | 140 | 160 | 300 |
| Item sum for both readers | 98 | 69 | 79 | 54 | | | | | | | |

From these sums, the sum of squares associated with each component can be derived.

$$\text{Total sum of squares} = 2{,}214 - \frac{90{,}000}{48} = 339.0$$

$$\text{Persons sum of squares} = \frac{15{,}878}{8} - \frac{90{,}000}{48} = 109.8$$

$$\text{Questions sum of squares} = \frac{23{,}522}{12} - \frac{90{,}000}{48} = 85.2$$

$$\text{Readers sum of squares} = \frac{45{,}200}{24} - \frac{90{,}000}{48} = 8.3$$

$$P \times Q = \frac{4{,}258}{2} - \frac{90{,}000}{48} - 109.8 - 85.2 = 59.0$$

$$P \times R = \frac{8{,}026}{4} - \frac{90{,}000}{48} - 109.8 - 8.3 = 13.4$$

$$Q \times R = \frac{12{,}014}{6} - \frac{90{,}000}{48} - 85.2 - 8.3 = 33.8$$

$$P \times Q \times R = 339.0 - (109.8 + 85.2 + 8.3 + 59.0 + 13.4 + 33.8) = 29.5$$

The mean squares for each of the seven components can now be derived by dividing by the number of degrees of freedom, as shown in Table 3.

It is now possible to estimate the seven variance components. To do this, it must be noted that each mean square at a given level already includes, within itself, variance represented in the higher levels of interaction. That is, the persons-by-questions mean square includes a contribution from persons $\times$ questions $\times$ readers, and the persons mean square includes contributions from persons $\times$ questions and from persons $\times$ readers. It must also be noted that the mean squares represent the values that attach to a sum of several observations. For example, the mean square for persons is a sum over four questions each read by two readers. If the variance component for a single observation is wanted, the given value must be divided by the number of observations on which it is based.

Taking these two points into account gives the fol-lowing set of equations from which the variance com-ponents can be determined:

$$\sigma_{pqr}^2 = \text{MS}_{pqr}$$

$$\sigma_{pq}^2 = \frac{1}{n_r}(\text{MS}_{pq} - \text{MS}_{pqr})$$

$$\sigma_{pr}^2 = \frac{1}{n_q}(\text{MS}_{pr} - \text{MS}_{pqr})$$

$$\sigma_{qr}^2 = \frac{1}{n_p}(\text{MS}_{qr} - \text{MS}_{pqr})$$

$$\sigma_{p}^2 = \frac{1}{n_q n_r}(\text{MS}_{p} - \text{MS}_{pq} - \text{MS}_{pr} + \text{MS}_{pqr})$$

$$\sigma_{q}^2 = \frac{1}{n_p n_r}(\text{MS}_{q} - \text{MS}_{pq} - \text{MS}_{qr} + \text{MS}_{pqr})$$

$$\sigma_{r}^2 = \frac{1}{n_p n_q}(\text{MS}_{r} - \text{MS}_{pr} - \text{MS}_{qr} + \text{MS}_{pqr}) \quad (16)$$

In this problem the values become:

$$\sigma_{pqr}^2 = 1.97$$

$$\sigma_{pq}^2 = \tfrac{1}{2}(3.93 - 1.97) = 0.98$$

$$\sigma_{pr}^2 = \tfrac{1}{4}(2.68 - 1.97) = 0.18$$

$$\sigma_{qr}^2 = \tfrac{1}{6}(11.27 - 1.97) = 1.55$$

$$\sigma_{p}^2 = \tfrac{1}{8}(21.96 - 3.93 - 2.68 + 1.97) = 2.16$$

$$\sigma_{q}^2 = \tfrac{1}{12}(28.40 - 3.93 - 11.27 + 1.97) = 1.26$$

$$\sigma_{r}^2 = \tfrac{1}{24}(8.30 - 2.68 - 11.27 + 1.97) < 0$$

The values for the seven components of variance pro-vide estimates of how important the various facets will be in producing variation in the estimates of a given examinee's ability. These values are worth examining with some care.

First, note that the estimate for readers is less than zero. Of course, variation less than zero is meaningless. What this value points out is that it is, after all, *estimates* that are being dealt with. These estimates may in some cases fall above the universe value and in some cases below. Furthermore, the estimates are often (and cer-tainly in our data) based on a small number of degrees of freedom and are correspondingly unstable. There were only two readers. It happened that these two were

**Table 3**
Data matrix of mean squares

| Source | Sum of squares | Degrees of freedom | Mean square |
|---|---|---|---|
| Persons | 109.8 | 5 | 21.96 |
| Questions | 85.2 | 3 | 28.40 |
| Readers | 8.3 | 1 | 8.30 |
| $P \times Q$ | 59.0 | 15 | 3.93 |
| $P \times R$ | 13.4 | 5 | 2.68 |
| $Q \times R$ | 33.8 | 3 | 11.27 |
| $P \times Q \times R$ | 29.5 | 15 | 1.97 |

similar in the overall severity of their grading standards (though they differed rather markedly in their severity on *specific* questions), and when account was taken of the interactions of readers with questions and with examinees, the residual contribution of readers per se appeared to be nil.

The result on readers points out the need, in studies of the importance of different variance components, to sample adequately from each of the facets—in this case examinees, questions, and readers. Practical realities often make it difficult to get as large or as well-designed a sample from such facets as test tasks, evaluators, and occasions as the sample of examinees, but the need is as great in the one case as in the other.

Returning to the list of variance components, it should be noted with satisfaction that the largest single component is that for persons (or examinees). This is the component that represents "true score" or "universe score" and is of primary interest in this assessment. The next largest component is that designated $\sigma_{pqr}^2$. This should more accurately be labeled $\sigma_{pqr}^2 + \sigma_{\varepsilon}^2$, because it incorporates both the second-order interaction of person × question × reader and the random "error" in its purest form. With only one observation in each $p \times q \times r$ cell of Table 3, it is impossible to separate these two elements. In most instances it will happen that at the highest level of interaction there *will* be only a single observation, so that "error" and this highest interaction will be confounded.

The next three components, in order of size, are question-by-reader interaction (1.55), questions (1.26), and person-by-question interaction (0.98). All these involve the sampling of questions, and collectively they indicate that the particular set of questions included in the test is a very potent determiner of the score that a given examinee will achieve. From the viewpoint of a strategy for accurate measurement, the size of these components indicates that it will be important (a) for all examinees to answer the same questions and (b) for the number of questions to be large.

The importance of the different variance components can be seen more clearly if the "coefficient of reproducibility," (the ratio of expected true score or universe variance to expected observed variance) is calculated. Universe variance for score, that is, the sum of observations on $n_q$ questions, each rated by $n_r$ readers, is given by:

$$\sigma_{true}^2 = (n_q n_r)^2 \sigma_p^2$$

where $\sigma_p^2$ is the estimate of the *persons* variance component. This follows from the formula given in Sect. 1.2, because to add questions and readers is in effect to increase the length of the behavior sample. The expected observed variance is given by:

$$\sigma_{obs}^2 - (n_q n_r)(n_q n_r \sigma_p^2 + n_p \sigma_r^2 + n_r \sigma_q^2 + n_q \sigma_{pr}^2$$
$$+ n_r \sigma_{pq}^2 + \sigma_{qr}^2 + \sigma_{pqr}^2) \quad (17)$$

With appropriate divisions in both numerator and denominator, the coefficient of generalizability becomes:

$$\frac{\sigma_{true}^2}{\sigma_{obs}^2} = \frac{\sigma_p^2}{\sigma_p^2 + \dfrac{\sigma_q^2}{n_q} + \dfrac{\sigma_r^2}{n_r} + \dfrac{\sigma_{pq}^2}{n_q} + \dfrac{\sigma_{pr}^2}{n_r} + \dfrac{\sigma_{qr}^2}{n_q n_r} + \dfrac{\sigma_{pqr}^2}{n_q n_r}} \quad (18)$$

Using the data derived from Table 3, this gives:

$$\frac{\sigma_{true}^2}{\sigma_{obs}^2} = \frac{2.16}{2.16 + \dfrac{1.26}{4} + \dfrac{0}{2} + \dfrac{0.98}{4} + \dfrac{0.18}{2} + \dfrac{1.55}{8} + \dfrac{1.97}{8}}$$

$$r_{xx'} = \frac{2.16}{3.25} = 0.66$$

This coefficient is an estimate of the correlation that would be obtained between two sets of scores for a group of examinees, when each examinee is tested with a random set of four questions chosen independently for that examinee and rated by a random two readers also chosen independently for each examinee.

Looking only at the denominator, the source of most of the "error variance" becomes evident. Thus:

$$\sigma_{obs}^2 = 2.16 + (0.32 + 0 + 0.24 + 0.09 + 0.19 + 0.25)$$
$$\qquad\quad p \qquad q \quad r \quad pq \quad\ pr \quad\ qr \quad pqr$$

It can be seen that the largest components of the error variance, in order of size, are questions (0.32); the interaction of persons, questions, and readers (0.25); and the interaction of persons and questions (0.24). The strategy for reducing all these would be to increase the number of questions. This would increase the divisors in the largest terms of the denominator of Eqn. (18)—and hence would reduce those largest terms and increase the precision of the resulting score. If the number of questions were doubled, this would give

$$\sigma_{obs}^2 = 2.16 + (0.16 + 0 + 0.12 + 0.09 + 0.10 + 0.12)$$
$$= 2.75$$
$$r_{xx'} = \frac{2.16}{2.75} = 0.79$$

By contrast, if the number of readers were doubled without any change in the number of questions, this would give:

$$\sigma_{obs}^2 = 2.16 + (0.32 + 0 + 0.24 + 0.04 + 0.10 + 0.12)$$
$$= 2.98$$
$$r_{xx'} = \frac{2.16}{2.98} = 0.72$$

and the gain in precision would be a good deal less.

## 2.3 Nonrandom Questions and Readers

Up to this point, it has been assumed that both the questions facet and the readers facet have been sampled at random, such that a given examinee could have any four questions drawn from the universe of admissible questions rated by any two readers drawn from the universe of admissible readers. It is a good deal more common for the set of questions (and possibly the readers) to be the same for all examinees. If the set of questions will be uniform for all examinees, the variance component associated with questions $(\sigma_q^2)$ disappears, which gives:

$$\sigma_{\text{obs}}^2 = 2.16 + (0.24 + 0.09 + 0.19 + 0.25) = 2.93$$

$$r_{xx'} = \frac{2.16}{2.93} = 0.74$$

Naturally enough, an estimate of a person's standing in the group is appreciably more precise when it is known that all members of the group will take the same test. If it is *also* known that the readers will be the same for all examinees, two other variance components ($\sigma_r^2$ and $\sigma_{qr}^2$) drop out of the observed variance, leaving:

$$\sigma_{\text{obs}}^2 = \sigma_p^2 + \frac{\sigma_{pq}^2}{n_q} + \frac{\sigma_{pr}^2}{n_r} + \frac{\sigma_{pqr}^2}{n_q n_r}. \tag{19}$$

For the data given this becomes:

$$\sigma_{\text{obs}}^2 = 2.16 + (0.24 + 0.09 + 0.25) = 2.74$$

$$r_{xx'} = \frac{2.16}{2.74} = 0.79$$

Thus, in the illustrative example considered here, keeping the questions and readers uniform for all examinees raises the true-score variance, as a percentage of the total, from 66 to 79.

It is also possible that one may be interested only in a *specific* set of test questions, considering these to be the universe to which it is wished to generalize. The questions facet then becomes a *fixed* facet, rather than one that is sampled randomly from some larger universe. Considering a certain facet to be fixed has two effects: (a) the interaction between persons and that fixed facet, $\sigma_{pq}^2$ in the illustration under consideration, is treated as a component of true score rather than error; (b) the component associated with that fixed facet $(\sigma_q^2)$ disappears. Thus

$$\sigma_{\text{true}}^2 = \sigma_p^2 + \frac{\sigma_{pq}^2}{n_q}$$

$$\sigma_{\text{obs}}^2 = \left(\sigma_p^2 + \frac{\sigma_{pq}^2}{n_q}\right) + \left(\frac{\sigma_r^2}{n_r} + \frac{\sigma_{pr}^2}{n_r} + \frac{\sigma_{qr}^2}{n_q n_r} + \frac{\sigma_{pqr}^2}{n_q n_r}\right)$$

$$\sigma_{\text{true}}^2 = 2.16 + 0.24 = 2.40$$

$$\sigma_{\text{obs}}^2 = 2.40 + (0 + 0.09 + 0.19 + 0.25) = 2.93$$

$$r_{xx'} = 0.82$$

If there were interest in generalizing only to this set of

questions as appraised by these specific readers, this could be shown by:

$$\sigma_{\text{true}}^2 = 2.16 + 0.24 + 0.09 = 2.49$$

$$\sigma_{\text{obs}}^2 = 2.49 + 0.25 = 2.74$$

$$r_{xx'} = 0.91$$

*2.4 Confounding of Variance Components*

In all of these analyses, the situation has been one in which the design for *collection* of the original data was completely "crossed"—that is, every examinee answered every question and every response was evaluated by every rater. Collection of the original data in this format has very real advantages in that it allows for the generation of estimates (though somewhat fragile ones because of small *n*'s for some of the facets) of *all* the variance components. However, it may not always be possible to gather such data. Thus the readers might vary from one examinee to another and it might not be known which reader had read a particular examinee's paper. It might only be known that two from a sizable universe of readers had read a given paper. In this case, the reader is said to be "nested within persons". When it is not known which readers have read a given examinee's paper, certain of the variance components become confounded and cannot be separated from one another. Specifically, reader variance $(\sigma_r^2)$ cannot be separated from the interaction between reader and examinee $(\sigma_{pr}^2)$, because information for a particular pair of readers can be identified only within the data for a single examinee. Similarly, $\sigma_{qr}^2$ and $\sigma_{pqr}^2$ cannot be separated. Thus the only identifiable variance components are $\sigma_p^2$, $\sigma_q^2$, $\sigma_{pq}^2$, $(\sigma_r^2, \sigma_{pr}^2)$, and $(\sigma_{qr}^2, \sigma_{pqr}^2)$. Table 4 shows how the data for our illustrative problem are analyzed.

It should be noted that both the sum of squares and the number of degrees of freedom collapse for the two components that are confounded and cannot be separated.

The analysis of variance components also reduces to just the five that can be isolated. Thus:

$$\sigma_{qr,pqr}^2 = \text{MS}(Q \times R, P \times Q \times R)$$

$$\sigma_{pq}^2 = \frac{1}{n_r}[\text{MS}(P \times Q) - \text{MS}(Q \times R, P \times Q \times R)]$$

$$\sigma_{r,pr}^2 = \frac{1}{n_q}[\text{MS}(R, P \times R) - \text{MS}(Q \times R, P \times Q \times R)]$$

$$\sigma_q^2 = \frac{1}{n_p n_r}[\text{MS}(Q) - \text{MS}(P \times Q)]$$

$$\sigma_p^2 = \frac{1}{n_q n_r}[\text{MS}(P) - \text{MS}(P \times Q) - \text{MS}(R, P \times R)$$

$$+ \text{MS}(Q \times R, P \times Q \times R)] \tag{20}$$

**Table 4**
Analysis of confounded variance components

| Component | Sum of squares | Number of degrees of freedom | Mean square |
|---|---|---|---|
| $P$ | 109.8 | 5 | 21.96 |
| $Q$ | 85.2 | 3 | 28.40 |
| $(R, P \times R)$ | 8.3 + 13.4 | 6 | 3.62 |
| $P \times Q$ | 59.0 | 15 | 3.93 |
| $(Q \times R, P \times Q \times R)$ | 33.8 + 29.5 | 18 | 3.52 |

For the data of the example shown in Table 4, this becomes:

$$\sigma^2_{qr,pqr} = 3.52$$

$$\sigma^2_{pq} = \tfrac{1}{2}(3.93 - 3.52) = 0.20$$

$$\sigma^2_{r,qr} = \tfrac{1}{4}(3.62 - 3.52) = 0.02$$

$$\sigma^2_q = \tfrac{1}{12}(28.40 - 3.93) = 2.04$$

$$\sigma^2_p = \tfrac{1}{8}(21.96 - 3.93 - 3.62 + 3.52) = 2.24$$

The analyses of true score and observed variances parallel the development previously given, except that the confounding prevents the testing of some of the models. Thus, for generalization to a situation in which each examinee is tested with a random set of four questions drawn from the universe of admissible questions:

$$\sigma^2_{\text{true}} = 2.24$$

$$\sigma^2_{\text{obs}} = 2.24 + \left(\frac{2.04}{4} + \frac{0.02}{2} + \frac{0.20}{4} + \frac{3.52}{8}\right)$$

$$= 2.24 + (0.51 + 0.01 + 0.05 + 0.44) = 3.25$$

$$r_{xx'} = \frac{2.24}{3.25} = 0.69$$

If it were known that all examinees would have the same questions, then:

$$\sigma^2_{\text{obs}} = 2.24 + (0.01 + 0.05 + 0.44) = 2.74$$

$$r_{xx'} = \frac{2.24}{2.74} = 0.82$$

If, however, there were interest only in generalizing to

a universe of scores on these specific questions, then the following could be derived:

$$\sigma^2_{\text{true}} = 2.24 + 0.05 = 2.29$$

$$r_{xx'} = \frac{2.29}{2.74} = 0.84$$

The effects of uniform readers or a universe of only specified readers cannot be analyzed because the required variance components involving readers are confounded.

It is even conceivable that both questions and readers could be confounded with persons (though it is unlikely that data would be gathered in this form). This would occur if all that was known was that, in the original analysis of the test, each examinee had taken *some* form of a test composed of four questions and that each person's paper had been read by *some* pair of readers. Confounding then becomes complete, and all that can be isolated are between-persons and within-persons components of variance, as shown in Table 5.

$$\sigma^2_p = \frac{1}{m_q n_r} [\text{MS}(p) - \text{MS}(\text{within})]$$

$$= \tfrac{1}{8}(16.50) = 2.06$$

$$\sigma^2_{\text{obs}} = 2.06 + \frac{5.46}{8} = 2.06 + 0.68 = 2.74$$

$$r_{xx'} = \frac{2.06}{2.74} = 0.74$$

The estimate is that, for a randomly chosen four-question test by two randomly chosen readers, 74% of the variance is true-score or universe variance of persons and the other 26% is contributed by the composite of all

**Table 5**
Analysis of completely confounded variance components

| Component | Sum of squares | Number of degrees of freedom | Mean square |
|---|---|---|---|
| $p$ | 109.8 | 5 | 21.96 |
| Within $p$ | 229.2 | 42 | 5.46 |

other components. No further analysis of the situation is possible. This value may be compared with the 66% found in Sect. 2.2, which results from the variance components of the completely crossed data. That the agreement is not better than this must be attributed to the small number of degrees of freedom underlying several of the specific variance components.

This two-facet illustration of the variance-components approach to analysis of reliability and the precision of measurement has been discussed in some detail, because it serves to exhibit both the logic and the empirical possibilities of the method. The same type of approach is possible with three or more varied facets, but the number of variance components approximately doubles each time a facet is added. In such multifacet studies, obtaining the full set of completely crossed data becomes quite an undertaking. Furthermore, obtaining samples of adequate size and of suitable randomness for each facet can present serious practical difficulties.

The variance-components model is one into which practically all the conventional procedures for gathering data on reliability can be fitted, and understanding any procedure is enhanced by seeing how it handles the several components of variance. The simplest procedure is to test each examinee with two forms of a test, giving everyone form *A* followed by form *B*—either immediately or at some later date. It has then been the usual procedure to compute the correlation between form *A* and form *B*. This is a single-facet problem, but the facet is a compound one that could be designated test-form-confounded-with-order. Thus there are three variance components: (a) persons, (b) test-form-and-order, and (c) the interaction of components (a) and (b). Component (b) shows up as a difference between mean scores on the two forms and does not influence the correlation, because product–moment correlations are based on deviations from the respective group means. Thus,

$$r_{AB} = \frac{\sigma^2_{\text{persons}}}{\sigma^2_{\text{persons}} + [\sigma^2_{(\text{persons} \times \text{forms})}/2]}$$

(This is divided by 2 because the persons-by-forms components are based on two forms.)

Coefficient alpha ($\alpha$) (Cronbach 1951) and its special case, Kuder–Richardson Formula 20, are also single-facet approaches in which analysis is carried out at the item level. Thus, in the case under consideration there is: (a) a between-persons variance component, (b) a between-items component, and (c) an interaction-of-persons-with-items component. Once again, items are thought of as a fixed effect. The results from this analysis can be shown to be algebraically equivalent to coefficient alpha, computed by the equation:

$$\alpha = \frac{n}{n-1} \left( 1 - \frac{\sum\limits_{i=1}^{m} s_i^2}{s_x^2} \right) \tag{21}$$

where $s_i^2$ is the variance of item $i$ and $s_x^2$ is the variance of test $x$.

If a test is appreciably speeded and there are a number of students who do not have time to attempt a number of items then coefficient alpha tends to become meaningless. Furthermore, in the persons-by-items data matrix, there are a number of empty cells. In effect one assigns a value of zero to each of these empty cells, but it is done in the absence of data. The series of zeros for a given examinee produces a kind of spurious consistency in his or her scores on the later items and consequently inflates to some degree the estimate of the reliability coefficient.

## 3. Reliability with Conventional Data-collection Strategies

Carrying out a systematic analysis of variance components is the most instructive way to obtain a complete understanding of the sources of error in a measurement procedure. However, collecting the data for such a complete analysis is rarely practical and perhaps not really necessary. The circumstances of life usually *do* make it possible (a) to give two presumably equivalent forms of a test and study the correlation between the resulting two sets of scores, (b) to give the same test form on two separate occasions and study the correlation between the results from the two testings, or (c) to give a single test form consisting of several sections or a number of items and study the consistency of performance over the sections or items. Much of the evidence on test reliability stems from one or another of these procedures.

The foregoing procedures permit the allocation to error of only certain components of variance. Consequently each provides a somewhat different and a somewhat limited definition of the universe being sampled by the test. However, each offers some information about the generalizability from a testing procedure.

### 3.1 Reliability Estimated from Equivalent Forms

If two equivalent forms of a test are administered (forms that are measures of the same latent attribute and that can both be expected to measure it with the same precision), the correlation between them serves as an estimate of the reliability coefficient. That is, it can be shown that, if the foregoing conditions hold,

$$r_{12} = \frac{\sigma^2_{\text{true}}}{\sigma^2_{\text{observed}}} = \frac{\sigma^2_{\text{true}}}{\sigma^2_{\text{true}} + \sigma^2_{\text{error}}}$$

The value obtained for this coefficient is critically dependent on the heterogeneity of the group to which the two forms are administered—that is, on the size of $\sigma^2_{\text{true}}$. For this reason, an estimate of the error variance or of its square root, called the standard error of measurement, is often a more serviceable statistic. It is a good deal less sensitive to the range of talent in the sample on which the reliability estimate is based. This standard error of measurement is given by $\sigma_{\text{meas}} = \sigma_{\text{obs}}\sqrt{[1 - r_{xx'}]}$.

So far the error variance has been treated as though it kept the same value at all levels of the latent attribute. Of course, this is not necessarily the case. A test often measures more accurately within certain limits on the latent attribute than it does at other points; the location of higher accuracy depends on the way in which the items that compose the final test were chosen. The standard error of measurement, estimated from the correlation between two forms of a test, is a kind of pooled overall estimate of precision, an estimate that is often better replaced by estimates at each of a number of different score levels. A procedure for obtaining those estimates is provided by Thorndike (1982).

## 3.2 Reliability Estimated from Retesting

As indicated above, an alternative data-gathering strategy is to use one specific measure of a latent attribute and to repeat the identical measure after an interval. This is a reasonable strategy if (a) all test exercises are so similar in content or function that any one sample of exercises is equivalent to any other and (b) the exercises are so numerous and/or nondescript that, at the second testing, there will be little or no memory of the responses given on the initial testing. Specific memory will, of course, become less and less of a problem as the interval between the two testings is lengthened. However, as the time interval is lengthened, the variation from one testing to the other reflects in increasing proportion the impact of intervening experiences or of differential rates of growth. The variation then becomes, in increasing proportion, an indicator of instability of the underlying attribute over a time span, rather than of lack of precision in the measuring instrument.

The standard error of measurement at each score level can appropriately be obtained from retesting with the identical test. It now provides information about the consistency with which persons at different ability levels respond to the test tasks. The difference in mean score between the first and second testing constitutes a variance component reflecting some mixture of practice effect and growth between the two testings. The two are not separable, but the relative importance of each can be inferred at least crudely from the length of the interval between testings.

## 3.3 Reliability Estimated from Internal Consistency

The third data-collecting strategy relies on the internal analysis of a single test administration. This has very great practical advantages, because (a) it requires development of only a single form of the test and (b) cooperation of examinees is required for only a single period of testing. These practical advantages have led test makers and research workers to use procedures of internal analysis frequently, in spite of their fairly severe theoretical limitations. One limitation is, of course, that all testing is done within a single brief period, so that no evidence can be obtained on diurnal variability—changes in individual performance from one occasion to the next. Another limitation is that the estimates of reliability become more and more inflated as the test is speeded. This issue will be discussed further after the basic procedures have been set forth.

The early procedure for extracting reliability estimates from a single administration of a test form was to divide the test items into equivalent fractions, usually two equivalent halves, and obtain two separate scores—one for each fraction. The correlations between the sets of scores were then obtained and were corrected by the Spearman–Brown Prophecy Formula to give an estimate of the reliability coefficient for the full-length test. As indicated in Sect. 1.2, when the test is divided into halves, the correction formula becomes:

$$r_{11} = \frac{2r_{1/2\ 1/2}}{1 + r_{1/2\ 1/2}}$$

When items are numerous and arranged either by subarea or in order of gradually increasing difficulty (or by increasing difficulty within subareas), putting alternate items into alternate test forms has often seemed a sound strategy for achieving equivalence: hence the odd–even correlations often reported. An investigator or test maker must decide in each case whether this or some other procedure is the most reasonable way to define equivalent halves for the instrument she or he is studying.

In recent years, those extracting reliability estimates from a single test administration have tended increasingly to base the estimates on analysis of variance approaches, in which single items constitute the units on which the analysis is based. The analysis is built on the assumption that all items are measures of the same underlying attribute—that is, that the test is homogeneous in content. For this reason, when a test is composed of two or more diverse subtests, it is usually necessary to apply the analysis to each subtest separately and then to use a formula for the correlation of sums to estimate the reliability of the total. Analysis of variance procedures do not depend on any particular choice in subdividing the items, and they approximate an average of all the possible correlations that might have been obtained by different ways of assigning items to alternate forms. When the assumption of homogeneity of function measured is justified, this would appear to be the most objective way to determine consistency across the items of the test.

The most general form of the analysis of item variance is provided by Cronbach's coefficient alpha (Cronbach 1951), the formula for which is:

$$\alpha = \frac{n}{n - 1}\left(1 - \frac{\sum s_i^2}{s_t^2}\right) \tag{22}$$

where $n$ is the number of items in the test, $s_i^2$ is the variance of item $i$, and $s_t^2$ is the variance of the total test. This expression is quite general in its application. It will handle test exercises in which score can take a range of values, as in essay tests or in inventories that provide multiple levels of response. It can even be applied when the "items" are themselves groups of test exercises.

When all the items are scored either 0 or 1, coefficient alpha reduces to the form reported earlier by Kuder and Richardson (1937) and known as Kuder–Richardson Formula 20. It is:

$$\text{Reliability} = \frac{n}{n-1}\left(1 - \frac{\sum p_i q_i}{s_t^2}\right) \qquad (23)$$

A lower-bounds estimate of this value, which is exact if all items are of the same difficulty, is provided by Kuder–Richardson Formula 21, which takes the form:

$$\text{Reliability} = \frac{n}{n-1}\left(1 - \frac{\sum n\bar{p}\bar{q}}{s_t^2}\right)$$

where $\bar{p}$ is the mean percent of correct responses, and $\bar{q}$ the mean percent of incorrect responses. K.R. 21 can also be expressed as:

$$\text{Reliability} = \frac{n}{n-1}\left\{1 - \frac{\bar{X} - [(\bar{X})^2/n]}{s_t^2}\right\} \qquad (24)$$

This formula provides a convenient way to get a quick, conservative estimate of coefficient alpha, because it requires information only on the mean, standard deviation, and number of items in the test. It differs from the full formula by the amount $ns_p^2/s_t^2$ where $s_p^2$ is the variance of the item difficulty indices, $p$. For a test of 50 or more items, this element is likely to be no greater than 0.02 or 0.03. For example, if the items have a range of $p$-values from 0.30 to 0.90 with a standard deviation of 0.10, and the test's standard deviation is 6 points (a realistic figure), for a 50-item test, this gives:

$$\frac{50(0.10)^2}{6^2} = \frac{0.50}{36} = 0.014$$

Thus, with tests of a length commonly encountered in practice, Eqn. (24) provides a very serviceable approximation.

It was indicated earlier that coefficient alpha in its standard form is applicable only to homogeneous tests in which all items are designed to measure the same common latent attribute. When test items are not designed to be measures of a single homogeneous attribute, a test may often be divided into subtests each of which is designed to be homogeneous in what it measures. Then Eqns. (22), (23), or (24) can be applied to each subtest separately to estimate the reliability (in the internal-consistency sense) of the subtest.

## 4. Reliability of Domain Mastery or Criterion-referenced Tests

In discussing reliability up to this point, the main concern has been the precision with which an individual can be located on the scale of a latent attribute through the administration of a test. Within limits, this conception can still be applied to a domain mastery test. The adaptation that may be required is to think of the attribute as having a limited range, because the tasks that fall within a precisely defined domain may have a limited range of difficulty. Within that range, correlations may be attenuated because of the presence of substantial numbers of perfect (or zero) scores. Such scores indicate individuals who fall at the boundaries of the difficulty range of the domain and who are in a sense not fully measured. The presence of such scores acts to attenuate correlation coefficients. The location of these extreme cases on a continuous scale representing the domain is in a sense indeterminate, so it is difficult to estimate a meaningful standard error of measurement for them.

Within the domain mastery model, interest usually focuses on some one level of performance—often 80% or 90% of correct answers—that has been defined as constituting "mastery" of the domain. When this is the case, the critical issue so far as reproducibility of results is concerned would appear to be whether another sample from the domain would lead to the same decision (mastery or nonmastery, as the case may be) for each individual.

The most direct approach to answering the question of consistency in the critical decision is to obtain two test scores for each individual by administering two equivalent test forms—equivalent in that each sampled by the same rules from the defined domain. The two could be given concurrently or with a lapse of time, depending on the nature of the universe to which one wished to generalize. From the test results, one could produce a $2 \times 2$ table such as the one shown in Table 6. Table 6 would present the basic data on consistency, but finding a statistic that adequately evaluates the test is not easy. The simple percentage of cases with consistent decisions depends on the range and level of talent in the group. In the extreme case, if one is dealing with a group for whom the domain is completely new and untaught (no one approaches mastery), we will get an appearance of a very accurate test, because all cases

*Table 6*
Results of mastery domain tests

| | | Form A | |
| --- | --- | --- | --- |
| | | Nonmastery | Mastery |
| Form B | Nonmastery | | |
| | Mastery | | |

will fall in the upper left-hand cell. Of course, consistency of performance could also appear if the test were extremely easy for all members of the group. Furthermore, if the group were extremely varied in competence (including a number for whom the test was very hard, a number of others for whom it was very easy, and very few who were just about at the threshold of mastery), high consistency of placement would be the rule. In all of these cases, consistency in placement reflects properties of the groups tested rather than excellence of the test. Furthermore, in the intermediate range of excellence of examinees, both percentage of agreement and the point correlation represented in the phi-coefficient are sensitive to the proportional split between the two groups.

If the two forms of the test have been equated for difficulty and if it is reasonable to assume that, within the domain as defined, competence shows a normal distribution, then one can postulate a normal bivariate distribution of competence underlying the score distribution on the tests, and one can appropriately calculate a tetrachoric correlation for the fourfold table. This should be relatively independent of the average *level* of ability in the group tested, though it would be sensitive to the variability in the ability being studied and would be higher for a group that is more heterogeneous in ability. However, the tetrachoric correlation coefficient will not be sensitive to differences in the proportion achieving the criterion score level on form *A* and form *B*. If these differences appear to be due to something in the forms themselves, rather than to the sequence of testing, the tetrachoric correlation will yield an overestimate of the test's reliability.

Various measures that have been proposed for use with criterion-referenced tests depend in some way on the average of squared deviations of test scores from the established "mastery" level, developed as formulas analogous to those for error variance. However, these formulas are substantially (perhaps even primarily) dependent on level of competence within the group of examinees, and they reveal little about the properties of the test as a testing instrument. They seem to be heading in an unproductive direction.

If one is dissatisfied with the conventional reliability coefficient when a test is being used for mastery decisions, perhaps the best alternative is the standard error of measurement for scores within a range of a few percentage points above and below the critical percentage that is defined as "mastery". This is one index that does *not* depend to any substantial degree on the range or level of talent within the group, but solely on consistency of performance from trial to trial. Though this statistic might be difficult to interpret in terms of proportion of cases receiving the same decision on two testings (that *does* depend on the nature of the group), the standard error would permit comparison of one test with another.

The procedures for calculating a standard error of measurement are described in Thorndike (1982), and these procedures can be applied in the present case. The form that the results might take can be illustrated for a triad of tests (unfortunately not designed to be mastery tests) for which standard errors by score level happen to be available. Consider the Cognitive Ability Tests at Level A. Standard errors of measurement based on a sample of 500 and expressed as percentage of items got right were as follows for examinees with an *average* score of from approximately 70% to 90% of correct answers:

(a) verbal test, 3.96%;

(b) quantitative test, 3.99%;

(c) non-verbal test, 3.15%.

Within the limits of the data, these results would be interpreted as showing that the verbal test and the quantitative test are quite comparable in the precision with which a judgment can be made that a person has achieved "mastery" of their domain, but that the non-verbal test permits this decision to be made with appreciably greater precision.

## Bibliography

Cronbach L J 1951 Coefficient alpha and the internal structure of tests. *Psychometrika* 16: 297–324
Cronbach L J, Gleser G, Nanda H, Rajaratnam N 1972 *The Dependability of Behavioral Measurements*. Wiley, New York
Kuder G F, Richardson M W 1937 The theory of estimation of test reliability. *Psychometrika* 2: 151–60
Lindquist E F 1953 *Design and Analysis of Experiments in Psychology and Education*. Houghton Mifflin, Boston, Massachusetts
Thorndike R L 1982 *Applied Psychometrics*. Houghton Mifflin, Boston, Massachusetts
Winer B J 1971 *Statistical Principles in Experimental Design*, 2nd edn. McGraw-Hill, New York

# Attenuation

## R. M. Wolf

Attenuation refers to the reduction in the relationship between variables that is due to imprecision or unreliability in the measurement process. Suppose an investigator was interested in determining the relationship between two theoretical variables, say, ability and achievement. The investigator would develop or select two scales to measure them. He or she would then administer the two scales to a group of individuals. If the relationship between these variables is linear, then the correlation coefficient ($r$) indicates the strength of relationship between the scales. However, these scales contain measurement error, that is, they are not perfectly reliable. Thus, the correlation between the scales is less than the correlation between the two theoretical variables. This reduction in the correlation due to error in the measuring process is called attenuation.

If it can be assumed that the true scores on the scales can be considered to represent the theoretical variables of interest, then there are formulas available to estimate the true correlation between the theoretical variables. These formulas are intended to correct for the attenuation in the correlation due to unreliability. The most common formula for correction for attenuation is:

$$r_{1\infty2\infty} = \frac{r_{12}}{\sqrt{r_{11}r_{22}}} d$$

where $r_{1\infty2\infty}$ is the correlation between the theoretical true scores; $r_{12}$ is the correlation between the scale scores; and $r_{11}$ and $r_{22}$ are the reliabilities of the two scales.

Thus, if the correlation between an ability test and an achievement test was found to be 0.73 and the reliability coefficients of the two tests were 0.89 and 0.85, the following is true:

$$r_{1\infty2\infty} = \frac{0.73}{\sqrt{(0.89)(0.85)}} = 0.84$$

In thinking of the two theoretical variables, it would be appropriate to think of the correlation as 0.84 even though the tests correlate was only 0.73.

A second formula for correction for attenuation allows the correlation between the observed score on one measurement and the true score on a second measurement to be estimated in terms of the correlation between the observed scores on the two measurements and the reliability of the second measurement. This formula is:

$$r_{12\infty} = \frac{r_{12}}{\sqrt{r_{22}}}$$

The terms are as defined above. In this second formula, however, the unreliability of only one of the scales is considered in contrast to the first formula where the effects of unreliability in both scales are considered.

Correction for attenuation is considered important in theoretical studies where it is desired to estimate the relationships between theoretical variables.

## Bibliography

Lord F M, Novick M R 1968 *Statistical Theories of Mental Test Scores*. Addison-Wesley, Reading, Massachusetts
Nunnally J C 1967 *Psychometric Theory*. McGraw-Hill, New York

# Generalizability Theory

## L. Allal

Generalizability theory provides a conceptual framework for estimating the reliability of behavioral measurements obtained by a wide range of procedures—tests, rating scales, observation forms, attitude scales—used in educational research and decision making. The statistical techniques of generalizability analysis can be applied to virtually any set of data collected by means of a factorial design which includes persons (or other objects of measurement) as well as one or several factors formed by the random sampling of conditions of measurement (for instance, items, examiners, moments of test administration).

Historically, within the context of classical test theory, a variety of procedures were developed for estimating different aspects of reliability: calculation of test–retest correlations to estimate the stability of measurements over different testing occasions; correlation of scores obtained from parallel forms of a test to estimate the equivalence of measurements based on different sets of items; application of various formulas to estimate the internal consistency, or homogeneity, of a pool of test items. Generalizability theory offers a comprehensive set of concepts and estimation procedures for treating any one or, simultaneously, all of these aspects of reliability. It is applicable, moreover, to designs which include other sources of fixed or random sampling variations than those typically considered by the classical procedures. In conducting a generalizability analysis, the effects of multiple sources of potential error can be assessed. It is then possible to determine the improvements of design that are needed to reduce error and increase precision of measurement.

This article will present the basic concepts of generalizability theory, as developed by Cronbach et al. (1972). Several of the more recent extensions of the model will be briefly discussed. An example will be used to illustrate the types of analyses that can be carried out using generalizability theory. Finally, several areas of application of the theory will be indicated.

## 1. Basic Concepts

Behavioral measurements used in educational research and decision making are almost always based on procedures involving one or more sources of potential error due to fluctuations in the conditions of measurement. In generalizability theory, the design of a measurement procedure implies the specification of the admissible variations that can occur along one or several facets, for instance, items, occasions, correctors, observers. The universe of admissible observations is defined by all possible combinations of the conditions corresponding to the levels of the facets. Any given observed score is thus a sample from the universe of scores that would exist if measurements were obtained under all admissible conditions. The classical concept of "true" score is replaced in generalizability theory by the concept of universe score, which Cronbach and co-workers (1972 p. 15) define as follows:

> The ideal datum on which to base the decision would be something like the person's mean score over all acceptable observations, which we shall call his "universe score." The investigator uses the observed score or some function of it as if it were the universe score. That is, he generalizes from sample to universe. *The question of "reliability" thus resolves into a question of accuracy of generalization, or generalizability.*

In conducting a generalizability study, it is necessary to include all relevant facets of the universe of admissible observations in the design used for data collection. The design must include at least one facet formed by the random sampling of measurement conditions. It may include, however, any number of other facets constituted by random or fixed modes of sampling. For example, if data are collected by a design in which persons are crossed with a random sample of items, the facet "items" could be nested within the levels of a fixed facet such as "instructional objectives," or it could be crossed with levels of a random facet such as "occasions." It would also be possible to construct a design in which items are nested within objectives and crossed with occasions.

Once the data have been collected, the standard procedures of analysis of variance are applied to determine the mean square for each source of variation present in the design. By successively inserting the numerical values of the observed mean squares into the equations for the expected mean squares, estimates are obtained for the variance components corresponding to all sources of variation. The choice of the analysis of variance estimation model (that is, use of the random effects model or the appropriate mixed effects model) is determined by the mode of sampling (random, finite random, fixed) of the levels of the facets.

For a simple design in which persons are crossed with items, variance components can be estimated by the random effects model for three sources of variation: persons ($\hat{\sigma}_p^2$), items ($\hat{\sigma}_i^2$), and error ($\hat{\sigma}_{pi,e}^2$). For a more complex design in which items are nested in fixed objectives, the appropriate mixed effects model would be used to estimate the variance components for five sources of variation: persons ($P$), items ($I:O$), objects

($O$) and the interactions $P \times (I:O)$ and $P \times O$. If items were crossed with the facet occasions, variance components could be estimated by the random effects model for seven sources of variation: persons ($P$), items ($I$), occasions ($O$) and the interactions $P \times I$, $P \times O$, $I \times O$, $P \times I \times O$.

Once the variance components have been estimated, the principles of generalizability theory are used to determine the allocation of the components for the estimation of three major parameters. After a general definition of each parameter, the formula will be given for the estimate corresponding to the $p \times i$ design in which the objects of measurement are persons crossed with a random sample of items.

(a) *Universe-score variance.* This parameter, symbolized by $\sigma^2(\mu)$, is defined as the variance of the expected values of the scores belonging to the universe of admissible observations. It reflects the systematic variations due to differences among the objects of measurement. For the $p \times i$ design described above, it is estimated by the variance component estimate due to persons: $\hat{\sigma}_p^2$.

(b) *Relative error variance.* Observed scores are frequently interpreted by comparing the relative positions of the objects of measurement within the score distribution. In this case, the sources of error are limited to the interactions of the objects of measurement with the facet(s) formed by random sampling of the conditions of measurement. The relative error variance, symbolized by $\sigma^2(\delta)$, is estimated by the sum of the weighted variance component estimates corresponding to the sources of relative error. Each component is weighted inversely to the number of times its effect is sampled when calculating the average score of one of the objects of measurement. For the $p \times i$ design, the estimate of relative error variance is based on a single variance component estimate: $\hat{\sigma}^2(\delta) = 1/n_i \hat{\sigma}_{pi,e}^2$, where $n_i$ is the number of levels of the facet items.

(c) *Absolute error variance.* For some situations, particularly in the areas of criterion-referenced and domain-referenced measurement, the observed scores are used as estimates of universe scores. In crossed designs, if decisions are based on the absolute rather than the relative values of the observed scores, additional sources of error must be considered. The absolute error variance, symbolized by $\sigma^2(\Delta)$, includes the components of relative error plus the components that are due specifically to the facet(s) formed by random sampling of the conditions of measurement. Thus, for the $p \times i$ design, the estimate of absolute error variance is based on two variance component estimates: $\hat{\sigma}^2(\Delta) = 1/n_i \hat{\sigma}_{pi,e}^2 + 1/n_i \hat{\sigma}_i^2$.

The precision of measurement provided by a given design is assessed by a generalizability coefficient, defined as the ratio of the universe-score variance to the expected observed-score variance. For the case of relative comparisons of observed scores, the expected observed-score variance is composed of the universe-score variance plus the relative error variance. The corresponding generalizability coefficient for the $p \times i$ design would be estimated as follows:

$$\frac{\hat{\sigma}_p^2}{\hat{\sigma}_p^2 + \hat{\sigma}^2(\delta)}$$

In crossed designs, if decisions are based on the absolute rather than the relative values of the observed scores, the estimate of absolute error variance, $\hat{\sigma}^2(\Delta)$, would be used in place of $\hat{\sigma}^2(\delta)$, and the corresponding coefficient estimated as follows:

$$\frac{\hat{\sigma}_p^2}{\hat{\sigma}_p^2 + \hat{\sigma}^2(\Delta)}$$

The interpretation of these coefficients is analogous to that of classical reliability coefficients. Values approaching 1.0 indicate that the scores of the persons can be differentiated with a high degree of accuracy while generalizing over random variations in the sampling of items.

Cronbach and co-workers (1972) distinguish two stages in the application of generalizability theory. The first is the generalizability (G) study carried out by the developer of the measurement procedure. Its aim is to provide future users of the procedure with the information they will need to assess the adequacy of the design, or of various modified versions of the design, with respect to the purposes of their investigations. A generalizability study is therefore designed to furnish estimates of the variance components for all sources of variation of potential interest to future users. It may also provide estimates of generalizability parameters for one or more versions of the basic design.

On the basis of this information, a variety of decision (D) studies may then be conducted by the persons planning to use the procedure. In carrying out a decision study, various modifications of the initial generalizability-study design may be considered. Certain modifications may be required because of practical constraints affecting the application of the procedure. For example, due to limitations on the availability of training supervisors, the number of observations of each trainee may be reduced in the decision-study design as compared to the frequency of observation in the generalizability study. Other design modifications may be considered in order to improve the precision of measurement. The most obvious example is the reduction of measurement error by increasing the sample of the levels of the random facets which, as shown in the generalizability study, make the largest contributions to the error variance. For example, in the case of the $p \times i$ design, an increase of the number of items ($n_i$) would lead to a decrease of the estimates of both relative and absolute error, as defined by the formulas presented above. Once an appropriate decision-study design has been defined, the corresponding generalizability parameters can be estimated using the data already collected in the generalizability study.

## 2. Extensions of Generalizability Theory

An article by Shavelson and Webb (1981) offers a detailed review of the contributions to generalizability theory since the 1972 publication by Cronbach and co-workers. Two areas of development will be mentioned here.

The first is the work by a number of researchers on problems associated with the underlying statistical models used in generalizability analysis. A paper by Brennan et al. (1980) deals with several important aspects of the estimation and interpretation of variance components for balanced and unbalanced designs used in generalizability studies. Their paper offers useful clarifications with respect to the definition and estimation of generalizability parameters based on variance components estimated by mixed models. It also points out the limitations of many existing statistical approaches and computer programs as far as their application in the context of a generalizability study is concerned. Continued work in this area is needed since unbalanced designs and designs involving fixed facets are relatively frequent in the field of educational measurement.

The work on underlying statistical models also includes efforts to develop multivariate extensions of the basic univariate procedures for generalizability analysis. In addition to the proposals of Cronbach et al. (1972) for the generalizability analysis of profiles of scores, some work has been carried out on multivariate methods for estimating the components of variance and covariance associated with composite scores defined by canonical coefficients or other weighting schemes. Much of the work in this area involves issues of statistical estimation that are far broader than the specific concerns of generalizability theory.

A second area of development is based on the principle of symmetry, which as proposed by Cardinet et al. (1981 p. 184), affirms "that each factor of a design can be selected as an object of study, and generalizability theory operations defined for one factor can be transposed in the study of other factors." This principle has led Cardinet and his colleagues to develop a framework for generalizability analysis that is applicable to a very wide range of situations in educational measurement. The procedures proposed in this framework can be used not only in the classical situations focused on the measurement of individual differences, but also in a variety of other situations where the objects of measurement are factors other than persons. In addition, these procedures can be applied to designs in which the objects of measurement (whether persons or other factors) are defined by the crossing and/or nesting of the levels of several fixed or random factors. Generalizability theory is thus extended to the analysis of the sources of error and of bias that occur when multifaceted measurement procedures are applied to multifaceted populations.

A further advantage of the proposed framework is its

usefulness in situations where data are collected in order to carry out comparisons along each of several facets which are of interest to educational decision makers. In multipurpose educational surveys, for example, school administrators may wish to compare achievement levels of classes or of school districts, whereas curriculum developers may be interested in comparisons of achievement levels for different items or sets of items. To deal with these multiple measurement aims, Cardinet and co-workers (1981) propose a clear separation between the initial phases of analysis based on analysis of variance (that is, computation of mean squares and estimation of variance components) and the subsequent phases of analysis based on the principles of generalizability theory. This separation implies that variance components are estimated without reference to any particular aim of measurement. Subsequently, several alternative measurement designs can be defined by distinguishing, in each case, two types of facets: the facets of differentiation (corresponding to the objects of measurement) and the facets of instrumentation (corresponding to the conditions or instruments of measurement). It is then possible to determine the allocation of the variance component estimates for the estimation of the variance of differentiation (universe-score variance) and the error variances associated with each design. In the final phase of the framework, various modifications of the initial design are considered in order to optimize the measurements needed for different decision-making or research purposes.

## 3. An Illustration of Generalizability Analysis

In this illustration, the principles of generalizability analysis will be applied to a relatively complex design that typifies several aspects of data collection in the field of education measurement. In many instances, rather than simple random sampling of persons from a homogeneous population, persons are randomly sampled within levels of one or more fixed stratification variables. The data collection design thus entails the nesting of the facet persons within other facets. For example, pupils may be nested within facets such as age, sex, grade, instructional treatment, or in the case of a study of teaching behavior, teachers may be nested within facets such as type of training, years of experience, sector of employment. In a similar manner, measurement procedures (tests, rating scales, and so on) are often constructed by the generation of randomly equivalent items nested within levels of one of more fixed classification variables (for example, objectives, content chapters, tasks) corresponding to the dimensions of a predetermined table of specifications. In addition, designs often include one or more sources of random sampling fluctuations due to facets such as examiners (observers, correctors) or occasions (moments of observation or of test administration).

To illustrate the application of generalizability theory for designs of this type, the following example will be used: A 30-item multiple-choice test has been administered on two occasions to a sample of 100 eighth grade pupils, 50 boys and 50 girls. The test has been constructed to measure pupil achievement with respect to three instructional objectives, and is composed of 10 items per objective.

The data collection design for this example is formed by five facets. The random facet pupils ($P$) is nested within the fixed facet sex ($S$). Items ($I$) constitute a second random facet nested within the fixed facet objectives ($O$). The facets $P:S$ and $S$ are crossed with the facets $I:O$ and $O$. In addition, the random facet moments of testing ($M$) is crossed with the other four facets.

For this design, variance components can be estimated for 17 sources of variation, the five sources corresponding to the main effects of the facets ($S$, $P:S$, $I:O$, $O$, $M$), and the 12 sources corresponding to the interactions among facets: $S \times O$, $S \times (I:O)$, $S \times M$, $(P:S) \times O$, $(P:S) \times (I:O)$, $(P:S) \times M$, $O \times M$, $(I:O) \times M$, $S \times O \times M$, $S \times (I:O) \times M$, $(P:S) \times O \times M$, $(P:S) \times (I:O) \times M$. Since two facets of the design, $S$ and $O$, are fixed, the variance components would be estimated using the appropriate mixed model of analysis of variance.

Once the variance components have been estimated, several directions of generalizability analysis could be considered, depending on the aim of measurement. For illustrative purposes, two contrasting cases will be described using the terminology proposed by Cardinet and co-workers (1981). The description of each case will be limited to the definition of the measurement design and the corresponding allocation of the variance component estimates for the estimation of the generalizability parameters.

The first, and more conventional, case is the use of the test scores to compare pupil achievement levels in the context of school certification or placement decisions. In this situation, the aim of measurement is to differentiate pupils while generalizing over testing moments and over items based on a fixed set of objectives (see Table 1). If decisions pertain to individual pupil scores regardless of sex, the measurement design is defined by two facets of differentiation ($P:S$ and $S$) and three facets of instrumentation ($I:O$, $O$, and $M$).

The estimation of the differentiation (that is, universe-score) variance is based on the variance component estimates for the two facets of differentiation, $P:S$ and $S$. The relative error variance is estimated on the basis of the variance component estimates due to the interactions of the differentiation facets with the random instrumentation facets. For this design, the sources of relative error correspond to the following interactions: $(P:S) \times (I:O)$, $(P:S) \times (I:O) \times M$, $(P:S) \times M$, $S \times (I:O)$, $S \times (I:O) \times M$, $S \times M$. The estimate of absolute error variance includes the above interaction components plus the variance component estimates due to the effects of the random instrumentation facets and

**Table 1**

Allocation of the variance component estimates for the estimation of generalizability parameters associated with two contrasting aims of measurement

| Generalizability parameters | Aim of measurement | |
|---|---|---|
| | Differentiation of pupils | Differentiation of objectives |
| Differentiation variance | $P:S$<br>$S$ | $O$ |
| Relative error variance | $(P:S) \times (I:O)$<br>$(P:S) \times (I:O) \times M$<br>$(P:S) \times M$<br>$S \times (S:O)$<br>$S \times (I:O) \times M$<br>$S \times M$ | $I:O$<br>$(P:S) \times (I:O)$<br>$(P:S) \times (I:O) \times M$<br>$(I:O) \times M$<br>$O \times (P:S)$<br>$O \times (P:S) \times M$<br>$O \times M$ |
| Absolute error variance | Components of relative error plus:<br>$I:O$<br>$M$<br>$(I:O) \times M$ | Components of relative error plus:<br>$P:S$<br>$M$<br>$(P:S) \times M$ |

the interactions among these facets: in this case, $I:O$, $M$, and $(I:O) \times M$.

The second case to be considered is the comparison of the achievement levels attained for different instructional objectives, as might be required in the context of curriculum evaluation or in a survey monitoring educational outcomes of the school system. In this case, the aim of measurement is to differentiate objectives, while generalizing over random variations in items, moments, and pupils nested within sex. The measurement design therefore includes a single differentiation facet ($O$) and four instrumentation facets ($I:O$, $M$, $P:S$, $S$).

The corresponding allocation of the variance component estimates differs in several respects from that of the previous design (see Table 1). The estimation of the differentiation variance is based on the variance component estimate for the facet $O$. The estimate of the relative error variance includes the estimated variance component for the random facet $I:O$, and the components for the interactions of $O$ and $I:O$ with the remaining random instrumentation facets $P:S$ and $M$, that is, a total of seven components, as shown in Table 1. The absolute error variance is estimated on the basis of the above components plus the components due to the random instrumentation facets and their interactions: $P:S$, $M$, and $(P:S) \times M$.

In examining the indications in Table 1, it can be seen that the allocation of the variance components is quite different depending on the aim of measurement. Only two sources of relative error, $(P:S) \times (I:O)$ and $(P:S) \times (I:O) \times M$, and one additional source of absolute error, $M$, remain the same in the two cases under consideration. It should be noted, moreover, that further differences would arise in computing the esti-

mates of the generalizability parameters for these designs. Adjustments of certain components would be required in each case due to the presence of fixed differentiation facets (compare with Brennan et al. 1980), and different coefficients would be used for the weighting of the components entering into the formulas for the estimated error variances.

## 4. Areas of Application

In addition to the application of generalizability theory in the classical area of norm-referenced test construction for the measurement of individual differences, a number of other areas of application have been developed over recent years. In the brief description that follows, several selected references are given for four areas. Further indications can be found in the review article by Shavelson and Webb (1981).

### 4.1 Criterion-referenced and Domain-referenced Measurement

For some of the specific problems of criterion-referenced mastery testing, such as the fixing of the criterion score so as to minimize false positive and false negative decision errors, Bayesian methods are likely to provide the most adequate approach. However, when dealing with the broader aspects of domain-referenced interpretation of test scores, several basic concepts of generalizability theory can be applied to estimate levels of competency within a multifaceted domain and the error associated with absolute decisions. Brennan and Kane (1977) have developed an "index of dependability" for domain-referenced testing in which observed scores are used to estimate the positions of universe scores with respect to a specified criterion.

### 4.2 Surveys of Educational Attainments

The flexibility of generalizability theory, as enlarged by the principle of symmetry, is particularly useful for dealing with multiple problems of reliability in large-scale surveys involving multifaceted measurement procedures applied to multifaceted populations. An example of multidirectional generalizability analysis based on data from a survey of mathematics achievement is briefly described in Cardinet et al. (1981). An article by Tourneur and Cardinet (1981) provides a more detailed presentation of the analyses carried out for a complex design involving content domains crossed with pupils, nested in age and class, and with test forms in which item series and classes are nested.

### 4.3 Observational Studies

Generalizability theory provides an appropriate framework for dealing with the multiple aspects of reliability (time and event sampling, interobserver agreement) that must be considered in designing observation procedures for the measurement of student or teacher behaviors. Proposals for the design and analysis of generalizability and decision studies based on observational data are provided by Mitchell (1979). At present, however, solutions have not been found for problems arising from the degree of correlations that may exist among observations collected within various time spans (class period, day, week, etc.).

### 4.4 Ratings of Occupational Skills and Instruction

Both univariate and multivariate generalizability procedures were applied in a study by Webb and Shavelson (1981) of ratings of educational skills required for different types of occupations. This study considered multiple facets of error (occasions × centers × raters nested in centers) associated with the ratings of three skills (reasoning, mathematics, language) needed in various jobs (jobs being the objects of measurement). An example of generalizability analysis applied to student ratings of instruction can be found in Gillmore et al. (1978).

### Bibliography

Brennan R L, Kane M T 1977 An index of dependability for mastery tests. *J. Educ. Meas.* 14: 277–89

Brennan R L, Jarjoura D, Deaton E L 1980 Some issues concerning the estimation and interpretation of variance components in generalizability theory. *ACT Technical Bulletin* No. 36. American College Testing Program, Iowa City, Iowa

Cardinet J, Tourneur Y, Allal L 1981 Extension of generalizability theory and its applications in educational measurement. *J. Educ. Meas.* 18: 183–204

Cronbach L J, Gleser G C, Nanda H, Rajaratnam N 1972 *The Dependability of Behavioral Measurements: Theory of Generalizability for Scores and Profiles.* Wiley, New York

Gillmore G M, Kane M T, Naccarato R W 1978 The generalizability of student ratings of instruction: Estimation of the teacher and the course components. *J. Educ. Meas.* 15: 1–15

Mitchell S K 1979 Interobserver agreement, reliability and generalizability of data collected in observational studies. *Psychol. Bull.* 86: 376–90

Shavelson R J, Webb N M 1981 Generalizability theory: 1973–1980. *Br. J. Math. Stat. Psychol.* 34: 133–66

Tourneur Y, Cardinet J 1981 L'étude de la généralisabilité d'un survey. *Educ. et recherche* 3(1): 33–50

Webb N M, Shavelson R J 1981 Multivariant generalizability of general education development ratings. *J. Educ. Meas.* 18: 13–22

# True-score Models

**R. R. Wilcox**

Suppose $N$ examinees take an $n$-item test. A frequent goal in mental test theory is making inferences about the examinees, or items, that go beyond the observed test scores. For example, the items on a test might represent some larger item domain, and the goal might be to estimate the proportion of items an examinee would get correct if he/she answers every item in the item pool. Another goal might be to determine how well an examinee would perform if he/she were to take the same $n$ items at another point in time. There are many related problems as well. For example, if examinees either pass or fail a test, how can observed scores be used to characterize how well a test is performing? How many items should be used on a test?

True-score models are essentially probability models that yield solutions to the problems described above. The term "true score" refers to some unknown parameter that represents an examinee's ability level. However, there are several notions of true score which represent different conceptualizations of ability. The true score used in a particular situation will depend on the goals of the test constructor, the related measurement problems, and the assumptions that are reasonable in a given situation. Thus, it is important to have a precise description of the different true scores, and to understand how they relate to one another. The remaining sections outline these differences.

### 1. Classical Test Theory

Consider a single examinee responding to a specific item that is scored either right or wrong. Suppose the item is repeatedly administered to the same examinee, and that the examinee's responses are independent of one another. If a 1 indicates a correct response, and a 0 an incorrect response, then an examinee's responses can be represented by a sequence of 1's and 0's. The distribution of the 1's and 0's is called a propensity distribution. The examinee's expected score, $\mu$, where the expectation is taken with respect to the propensity distribution, is the examinee's true score. That is, $\mu$ is the average value of the 1's and 0's over the independent and repeated responses to an item.

In this particular situation, the examinee's true score is just the probability of a correct response, where the probability $\mu$ is defined in terms of the repeated, independent, and identically distributed trials. However, this notion of true score is easily extended to any measuring instrument. In particular, let $x$ be an examinee's score on some test. Then the examinee's true score is defined to be $E(x)$, that is, the expected value of $x$, where the expectation is taken with respect to the propensity distribution of $x$.

In order to make inferences about $\mu$, classical test theory makes some additional assumptions about the observed scores of examinees. Measurement journals are replete with articles on characterizing tests under these assumptions, and the work continues. Here the important point is the interpretation of $\mu$. For a summary of the basic ideas in classical test theory, see Lord and Novick (1968).

## 2. Latent Trait Models

A class of true-score models that grew out of classical test theory are known as latent trait models. These models consist of a mathematical equation that proposes how an examinee's "ability" level combines with certain item characteristics to yield the probability that an examinee will produce the correct response. An appealing feature of these models is that once an examinee's ability level has been estimated, it is possible to determine the probability of a correct response to an item the examinee has never taken, assuming that certain item parameters have already been determined.

Let $p_i(\theta)$ be the probability that a specific examinee with ability $\theta$, $-\infty < \theta < \infty$, answers the $i$th item correctly on an $n$-item test. Several mathematical forms for $p_i(\theta)$ have been proposed (Lord 1980).

For present purposes, the important point is how these probabilities are interpreted. It might seem that the term "probability" is a precise description of $p_i(\theta)$, and in a certain sense it is; however, probabilities are frequently interpreted in terms of some process. In classical test theory, the process is repeatedly administering the same item to the same examinee which leads to the true score $\mu$. A similar interpretation is sometimes given to $p_i(\theta)$. That is, $p_i(\theta)$ is the examinee's expected score (assuming dichotomously scored items) where the expectation is taken with respect to a propensity distribution. However, Lord (1980 Chap. 15) objects to this interpretation, and suggests that one of two alternative interpretations be used instead. The first imagines a pool of items that have the same item parameters. For a randomly sampled item, $p_i(\theta)$ is the probability of a correct response from an examinee having ability level $\theta$. The second interpretation is that $p_i(\theta)$ is the probability of a correct answer from a randomly sampled examinee who has ability level $\theta$.

## 3. Item Sampling Models

A third class of true-score models is known as item sampling models. Again consider a single examinee responding to an $n$-item test. This time items are viewed as being randomly sampled from some item domain. In some cases the item domain exists de facto, and tests do indeed consist of randomly sampled items. In other situations, sampling items from an item domain is just a convenient conceptualization.

The binomial error model is the most commonly used item sampling model. This means that if $\xi$ is the proportion of items an examinee would get correct if he/she were to respond to every item in the item pool, the probability of getting $y$ correct on an $n$-item test is:

$$f(y \mid \xi) = \begin{bmatrix} n \\ y \end{bmatrix} \xi^y (1 - \xi)^{n-y}$$

Note that $\xi$ is different from $\mu$, $\theta$, and $p_i(\theta)$; $\xi$ does not, for example, involve a propensity distribution—examinees are assumed to respond only once to an item in the definition of $\xi$. Also, latent trait models are usually assumed to be unidimensional (e.g., Lord 1980) while item sampling models do not require this assumption. This is not necessarily a criticism of latent trait models since it has been argued that tests should be homogeneous in some sense. A disadvantage of the binomial model is that it implies that all the items on a test have the same level of difficulty when every examinee takes the same items. However, this problem can be avoided (Lord and Novick 1968 Chap. 23), and it appears that it is not a serious problem in practice (Wilcox 1981).

It might be surmised that Lord's first interpretation of $p_i(\theta)$ is the same as $\xi$, and this conclusion might be reinforced by observing that when latent trait models are assumed, the probability of $y$ correct responses to an $n$-item test reduces to a binomial probability function in certain special cases (Lord and Novick 1968 p. 385). The quantities $p_i(\theta)$ and $\xi$ are related, but they are not necessarily the same. To see this, note that under a latent trait model each item in a domain of items has some set of item parameters $a$, $b$, and $c$; and the value of these parameters will presumably vary over the items. If $g(a,b,c)$ is the joint probability function of $a$, $b$, and $c$ for the item domain, then the probability of a correct response to a randomly sampled item is:

$$\xi = \int \int \int p(\theta, a, b, c) g(a, b, c) da \, db \, dc$$

Of course, if Lord's second interpretation is used, $\xi$ and $p(\theta, a, b, c)$ again represent different quantities.

## 4. Latent State Models

A fourth class of true-score models assumes examinees responding to an item belong to one of finitely many states. The most common situation is a two-state model where examinees are assumed to either know or not know the correct response. Other models include the possibility of having misinformation. That is, an examinee eliminates the correct response on a multiple-choice item in the belief that it is indeed incorrect. The problem is that an examinee's response might not reflect his/her true state. If, for example, an examinee does not know the answer to a multiple-choice item, he/she might choose the correct response by chance.

Numerous latent structure models have been proposed for measuring and correcting errors at the item level such as guessing. As a simple illustration, one of these models is described on the next page.

Suppose randomly sampled examinees respond to an answer-until-correct test. That is, examinees choose an alternative on a multiple-choice test item, and they are told immediately whether they are correct. This can be accomplished by having examinees erase a shield on an especially designed answer sheet. If the symbol underneath the shield reveals that the examinee is incorrect, he/she chooses another alternative. This process continues until the correct response is identified.

Among the population of examinees, let $p_i$ be the proportion of examinees who would choose the correct response on the $i$th attempt of a particular item. Let $\zeta$ be the proportion of examinees who would know, and suppose $\zeta_i$ is the proportion who can eliminate $i$ distractors ($i = 1, \ldots, t - 2$) where $t$ is the number of alternatives. The idea is that some examinees might be able to eliminate certain responses from consideration via partial information without knowing the correct response. If after eliminating as many distractors as possible, a testee chooses at random from among those that remain, then:

$$\zeta = p_1 - p_2$$

(Wilcox 1982). Thus, if among $N$ examinees, $y_1$ is the number who get an item right on the first try, and if $y_2$

get it correct on the second try, the estimate of $\zeta$, the proportion of examinees who know the correct response, is just $\zeta = (y_1 - y_2)/N$. A similar model can be used to estimate the proportion of skills among a domain if skills that an examinee has acquired, and a modification of the model can be used to measure misinformation. Many other measurement problems can be solved including an exact test for random guessing, and an empirical method of determining how many distractors are needed on multiple-choice items. For results on related models, see Macready and Dayton (1980) and the references therein.

## Bibliography

Lord F M 1980 *Applications of Item Response Theory to Practical Testing Problems*. Erlbaum, Hillsdale, New Jersey

Lord F M, Novick M R 1968 *Statistical Theories of Mental Test Scores*. Addison-Wesley, Reading, Massachusetts

Macready G B, Dayton C M 1980 The nature and use of state mastery models. *Appl. Psychol. Meas.* 4: 493–516

Wilcox R R 1981 A review of the beta-binomial model and its extensions. *J. Educ. Stat.* 6: 3–32

Wilcox R R 1982 Some empirical and theoretical results on an answer-until-correct scoring procedure. *Br. J. Math. Stat. Psychol.* 35: 57–70

# Item Response Theory

## F. M. Lord and M. L. Stocking

Item response theory (IRT) models the relationship between a person's level on the trait being measured by a test and the person's response to a test item or question (Lord 1980). Because trait levels are inherently unobservable, item response theory falls into the general class of latent trait models.

In contrast to classical test theory, item response theory makes strong assumptions about a person's behavior when responding to items. Many advantages accrue from these strong assumptions: (a) it is possible to characterize or describe an item, independently of any sample of people who might respond to the item; (b) it is possible to characterize a person independently of any sample of items administered to the person; (c) it is possible to predict properties of a test in advance of test administration.

Item response theory has some disadvantages. It is currently not possible to completely check the accuracy with which the assumptions are met by the data. For data that appear to meet the assumptions, however, it is reassuring that predictions made from item response theory can often be independently verified. Applications of item response theory are generally more expensive than similar applications of classical test theory, and many applications of item response theory require the use of a computer.

## 1. Basic Concepts of Item Response Theory

### 1.1 Assumptions

Most item response theory models assume that only a single latent trait underlies performance on an item. This is often a reasonable assumption: most tests are constructed to measure a single trait, for example, verbal ability. Models that incorporate more than one latent trait are currently beyond the state of the art.

All of item response theory assumes that it is possible to describe mathematically the relationship between a person's trait level and performance on an item. This mathematical description is called an item response function, an item characteristic curve, or a trace line.

### 1.2 Item Response Functions

For dichotomously scored items (items that are scored right or wrong), the item response function (IRF) states mathematically the probability of a correct response for a given level of trait. This conditional probability is a function of the item characteristics or parameters. Usually, the mathematical function chosen to represent this conditional probability is from the logistic ogive family or the normal ogive family of functions. There is family or the normal ogive family of functions. There is little difference between the two. More practical work has been done using the logistic family, because of its mathematical simplicity.

If $u_i$ stands for a response to item $i$ (0 for incorrect and 1 for correct) and $\theta$ stands for the trait being measured, then the logistic item response function is:

$$P(u_i = 1|\theta) = c_i + (1 - c_i)/(1 + e^{-1.702a_i(\theta - b_i)}) \quad (1)$$

The normal ogive item response function is:

$$P(u_i = 1|\theta) = c_i + (1 - c_i)\Phi[a_i(\theta - b_i)] \quad (2)$$

where $\Phi[\ ]$ is the normal cumulative distribution function. In these equations $a_i$, $b_i$, and $c_i$, are parameters that describe characteristics of item $i$. Figure 1 displays a typical item response function and the meaning of the three item parameters. The pseudo-guessing parameter $c_i$ is the probability that an examinee with very low $\theta$ will respond correctly to the item. The item discrimination parameter $a_i$ is related to the steepness of the curve at the point of inflection. The item difficulty $b_i$ is the $\theta$-level at the point of inflection.

Not all items require three parameters to characterize them adequately. Some work has been done with two-parameter models ($c_i = 0$). A great deal of work has been done with one-parameter models in which the items vary only in difficulty ($a_i$ = constant, $c_i = 0$). If this latter model is logistic, it is called the Rasch model. Note that the three-parameter model in Eqn. (1) and Eqn. (2) subsumes models with fewer parameters.

Item response models have also been developed for items with more complex scoring procedures. Consider a multiple-choice item for which it is informative to know which incorrect option was selected by a person. Item response theory applicable to this type of scoring has been developed by Bock (1972) and Samejima (1969).

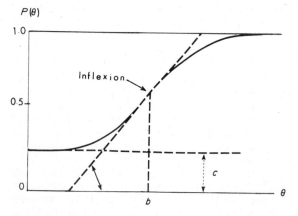

$P(\theta)$

### 1.3 Information Functions

Information functions (Birnbaum 1968) are used to describe the measurement effectiveness of a test or an item at each level of the trait being measured. In contrast, classical test theory usually provides only one measure of effectiveness, which is applied to all people regardless of their $\theta$.

The test information function for a particular scoring method has two equivalent definitions, both of which are useful. By the first definition, the information function for test score $y$, $I(\theta, y)$, is inversely proportional to the square of the length of the asymptotic confidence interval for estimating trait $\theta$ from score $y$. A high level of information at a particular $\theta$ means that this $\theta$ can be more precisely estimated from score $y$ than a $\theta$ for which the level of information is relatively low.

The second definition states that the information function for test score $y$ is the square of the ratio of (the slope of the regression of $y$ on $\theta$) to (the standard error of measurement of $y$ for fixed $\theta$). In this context, $I(\theta, y)$ can be viewed as a signal-to-noise ratio. The signal is the change in mean $y$ due to a change in $\theta$. The noise is measured by the standard error of measurement of $y$ for fixed $\theta$.

An item information function $I(\theta, u_i)$ is defined as $I(\theta, u_i) \equiv [P_i'(\theta)]^2/[P_i(\theta)Q_i(\theta)]$, where $p_i(\theta) \equiv P(u_i = 1|\theta)$ is the item response function, $Q_i(\theta) = 1 - P_i(\theta)$; and $P_i'(\theta)$ is the derivative of the item response function with respect to $\theta$. The test information function $I(\theta)$ is defined as the maximum information available from a test, regardless of the scoring method. The test information function is the simple sum of the item information functions: $I(\theta) = \Sigma_{i=1}^n I(\theta, u_i)$, where $n$ is the number of items in the test. For conventional tests $I(\theta)$ is typically a bell-shaped curve. Each item contributes to $I(\theta)$ independently of all other items in the test. In classical item and test analysis, the contribution of each item to test reliability and test validity depends upon what other items are in the test.

Information functions are useful when the metric established for measuring $\theta$ is not subject to challenge. However, slight changes in this metric can drastically alter the shape of an information function and therefore the conclusions drawn.

### 1.4 Relative Efficiency Functions

Suppose there are two tests, $x$ and $y$, both measuring the same trait $\theta$. The relative efficiency (R.E.) function of test $y$ versus test $x$, R.E. $(y, x)$, is the ratio of their information functions at corresponding values of $\theta$: R.E. $(y, x) = I(\theta, y)/I(\theta, x)$ (Birnbaum 1968). Most practical applications of item response theory will rely on relative efficiency functions since, unlike information functions, relative efficiency is invariant under any monotonic transformation of the metric used to measure $\theta$.

If R.E. $(y, x) > 1$ for a particular $\theta$, then test $y$ gives more information than test $x$ at that $\theta$. Relative efficiency functions are useful tools for redesigning existing tests and for investigating novel tests, without actually administering them.

## 2. Illustrative Applications

The first steps in any application of item response theory to practical problems are to choose a model for the item response function and to obtain estimates of item parameters and $\theta$'s. The process of obtaining these estimates (frequently referred to as calibration) is generally accomplished by one of the many available computer programs (see Wingersky 1983). The following sections describe some applications.

### 2.1 Test Construction

Tests with prespecified measurement properties can be constructed from a pool of calibrated items. The first step is to specify a target information function for the new test. The shape of this target indicates the $\theta$ levels at which the test should provide the most precise measurement. Next select items for the new test that will fill in areas under the target that might be difficult to fill, for example, areas where relatively few items are available. Compute the test information function for this part test. Then add items that contribute information in areas that are far from meeting the target. Continue to choose items, always comparing the information function of the part test to the target, until a satisfactory approximation to the target has been reached.

### 2.2 Redesigning an Existing Test

Relative efficiency functions provide a convenient way of investigating various design changes in a test and comparing them with the original test. Figure 2 illustrates this.

The curves in Fig. 2 are relative efficiency functions for three different tests designed from an original 50-item test. Curve 1 is a test containing only the 25 harder items. This half-length test is less efficient for all test scores. The loss of efficiency is small, however, for high scores. Curve 2 is a test containing only the 25 easier items. This half-length test is less efficient at high scores but is actually more efficient than the full-length test at low scores. This is true because guessing on hard items by low-scoring people destroys information. Better measurement is obtained for these people by discarding the harder items. Curve 3 is a 50-item test with all $b_i$ changed to a middle value. This "peaked" test measures very much better for the middle range of scores.

### 2.3 Equating

Equating is a measurement topic of interest to test publishers who produce many different forms of a test but wish to report scores on a single scale. The process of finding corresponding scores on different forms of a test is called equating. In general, observed scores on two different forms of a test cannot be equated except under conditions that make the equating unnecessary (Lord 1980). However, true scores can be equated under a wide variety of conditions, and item response theory facilitates true-score equating.

Suppose there are two tests, $x$ and $y$, both measuring the same trait. The items in both tests are calibrated on the same scale. A person's (number-right) true score $T_x$ on test $x$ is a transformation of the person's $\theta$: $T_x = \sum_{i=1}^{n} P_i(\theta)$, where $P_i(\theta)$ is the item response function for item $i$ evaluated at $\theta$, and $n$ is the number of items in test $x$. Similarly, the true score on test $y$ is $T_y = \sum_{i=1}^{m} P_i(\theta)$, where the sum is taken over the $m$ items in test $y$. These two expressions imply that for any particular $\theta$, a true score on test $x$ and a corresponding true score on test $y$ can be computed. These two true scores are equated because they represent the same trait level on two different measuring scales.

In practice, estimated item parameters are substituted into the two expressions and equated pairs of true scores are computed for arbitrary values of $\theta$. Even though only observed scores are known, the process continues as if the true-score equating holds for observed scores as well.

### 2.4 Item Bias

Items in a test that measures a single trait must measure the same trait in all subgroups of the population to which the test is administered. Items that fail to do so are biased for or against a particular subgroup. Since item response functions in theory do not depend upon the group used for item calibration, item response theory provides a natural method for detecting item bias.

Suppose a test is administered to two different groups and the item response functions are estimated separately for each group. If, for a particular item, the item response function for one group is uniformly higher than for the other group, then a person in the first group has a higher probability of a correct response for the same $\theta$. This item is clearly biased in favor of the first group. Typical instances of item bias are not this clear.

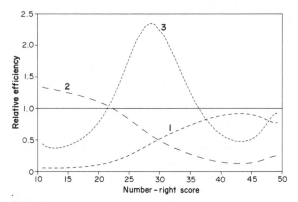

*Figure 2*
Relative efficiency functions of three modified tests

Usually item response functions will cross, rather than lie all above or all below each other. This means that the item is differentially biased at different $\theta$ levels.

### 2.5 Mastery Testing

Mastery tests are designed to determine if a person has reached a specified level of achievement, in which case the person is a "master." Item response theory can be used to construct optimal mastery tests.

Suppose there is a pool of calibrated items, and subject matter experts have defined the mastery level. The test construction specialist then selects items from the pool that have the highest item information functions at that level. The test constructed in this way will measure most precisely at the mastery level, thus minimizing errors in classifying people. In addition, item response theory can aid in the determination of the optimal item difficulty, item weights, and cutting score, also the necessary test length. Various test designs may be compared in relative efficiency.

### 2.6 Tailored Testing

Conventional tests are usually designed to measure best near the middle of the $\theta$ range for some group. A tailored test is one in which every person is administered items that measure that person's $\theta$ best. The general testing algorithm is as follows: (a) obtain an estimate of a person's $\theta$; (b) from a pool of calibrated items, select an item that measures best at that $\theta$; (c) administer and score the item, revise the estimated $\theta$; (d) if the estimate is precise enough, stop, otherwise, return to step (b). Many tailored testing designs are possible, most of which require a computer for item administration.

Information functions for tailored tests are generally higher than for conventional tests over a broad range of $\theta$. Much work has been recently done in this field, investigating and implementing various designs (McBride 1979).

Item response theory is essential for many aspects of tailored testing. For example, conventional scoring does not apply, since every person may take a different test. In contrast, item response theory provides estimates of $\theta$ that are independent of the particular items administered. With item response theory, many different designs can be examined and evaluated using relative efficiency functions.

### Bibliography

Birnbaum A 1968 Some latent trait models and their use in inferring an examinee's ability. In: Lord F M, Novick M R (eds.) 1968 *Statistical Theories of Mental Test Scores.* Addison-Wesley, New York

Bock R D 1972 Estimating item parameters and latent ability when responses are scored in two or more nominal categories. *Psychometrika* 37: 29–51

Hambleton R K, Swaminathan H, Cook L L, Eignor D R, Gifford J A 1978 Developments in latent trait theory: Models, technical issues, and applications. *Rev. Educ. Res.* 48: 467–510

Lord F M 1980 *Applications of Item Response Theory to Practical Testing Problems.* Erlbaum, Hillsdale, New Jersey

McBride J R 1979 Adaptive mental testing: The state of the art, TR No. 423. United States Army Research Institute for the Behavioral and Social Sciences, Alexandria, Virginia

Samejima F 1969 Estimation of ability using a response pattern of graded scores. *Psychometr. Monogr.* No. 17, Psychometric Society

Wingersky M S 1983 LOGIST: A program for computing maximum likelihood procedures for logistic test models. In: Hambleton R K (ed.) 1983 *Applications of Item Response Theory.* Educational Research Institute of British Columbia, Vancouver, British Columbia

# Latent Trait Measurement Models

## G. Douglas

The theory and practice of educational and psychological measurement, whereby society's educational intentions are evaluated through achievements, abilities, aptitudes, and attitudes, has for most of the twentieth century been founded on a model which views the score, $X$, that a person receives on a test, as the sum of two unobservable components, $\tau$ and $\varepsilon$, which form the relationship $X = \tau + \varepsilon$, where $X$ is the total observed score, $\tau$ is the "true score", and $\varepsilon$ is the "error score". This true-score model produces units for both the estimated true score and the estimated standard deviation of error scores (the standard error of measurement, $SE_{meas}$), which are necessarily on the same scale as are the units for the observed score $X$. This means that for tests composed of items scored 0 for incorrect and 1 for correct, $\tau$ is bounded by 0 and $L$ where $L$ is the maximum possible score on the test. The random part of this model, which allows conventional statistical confidence statements, is embodied in the assumption that

$$\varepsilon \sim NID[0, \sigma_\varepsilon^2]$$

that is, errors are normally and independently distributed with expectation 0 and variance $\sigma_\varepsilon^2$, where $\sigma_\varepsilon$ and $SE_{meas}$ are alternative notations for the precision of measurement.

An understanding of the basics of a latent trait approach to measurement can be gained by identifying those aspects and axioms of true-score theory which have been too restrictive, unsubstantiated, or of inadequate scope for the measurement required in many educational and psychological circumstances. In view of its inadequacies, it may appear puzzling that true-score theory was ever useful; however, the differences between true-score and latent trait approaches, when translated into practice, are more ones of enhanced understanding of the latter approach rather than of theoretical conflict between the two.

The core of the problem in the true-score model is that the units of $X$ (and of $\tau$), do not lie on an interval scale. The increase in ability arising from one more item correct on test A is not necessarily the same as that from one more item correct on test B (even when A and B are designed to measure the same ability and have the same number of items). The very use of the word "ability" presupposes the existence of an underlying scale (a latent trait), with some equal-interval units. The symbol $\theta$ will be used for this ability. Whether the latent variable $\theta$ has an equal-interval scale is axiomatic and can never be proved "correct" or "incorrect". However since equal intervals and the corresponding linearity are crucial in most, if not all other types of measurement, there is some precedent for demanding these concepts in mental measurement. It is also axiomatic that $\theta$ is continuous, admitting of all possible values within its range. Hence there is a sense in which $\tau$, the true score, and $\theta$, the latent trait measure, represent the same ability but on different scales with $0 < \tau < L$ and $-\infty < \theta < \infty$.

A plot of one against the other is necessarily monotonic and nonlinear and demonstrates the nonintervality of the true scores. This point and others are illustrated in Fig. 1.

In order to make a meaningful comparison in which the number of items, $L$, does not play a role, the true score $\tau$ has been converted to a relative true score, $\zeta$, where $\zeta = \tau/L$ and $0 < \zeta < 1$.

In Fig. 1, relative true score $\zeta$ is plotted against latent trait value $\theta$ for tests A and B of the same trait. For test A of 20 items, 19 points may be plotted, of which 14 are shown on the figure. For test B of 10 items, 9 points may be plotted and all 9 are shown on Fig. 1. The incompatibility of the $\zeta$-scores is demonstrated by two observations:

(a) the latent trait value corresponding to a $\zeta$ of 0.6 depends directly on which test is used—this dispar-

ity is a function of the differing difficulty levels of the items within the two tests. Since a lower $\theta$ value is obtained for a $\zeta$ of 0.6 on test B, it would be argued that test B is "harder" than test A;

(b) a given increment in $\zeta$ for test A (changing from a $\zeta$ of 0.5 to a $\zeta$ of 0.6, for example), results in a change in trait $\theta_A$ which is not of the same magnitude as the corresponding change in trait $\theta_B$.

Associated with both true-score and latent trait models are certain item characteristics, such as difficulty, discrimination, and intercorrelations. A limiting factor in the applicability of true scores has been the sample dependence of the indices used to describe these characteristics. The proportion of persons in a calibrating sample who get an item incorrect (item difficulty) changes when a shift is made from a sample whose mean ability is low to one whose mean ability is high. Item indices which remain "invariant" from one sample to another have been viewed as the desideratum of any well-formulated psychometric theory since the earliest writings of Thurstone. The discovery of these invariant indices has eluded many psychometricians along the way, although the call for their use has been frequent.

On the other hand, few calls have been heard for person ability indices (raw score, true scores, etc.), which are "invariant" from one test to another (see Fig. 1); the usual way to handle this problem has been through "test equating" via parallel forms. A methodology in which unrestricted selection of different numbers of precalibrated, valid, and relevant items from a pool can lead to ability measures freed from the characteristics of the particular items, has been even more elusive.

Any limitations which arise from using true scores instead of ability measures carry over to the concept of measurement error. Without the concept of a latent ability, it is not possible to give expression to the fact that, other things being equal, a person with a score of 48 out of 50 is not measured with the same precision as is one whose score is 25 out of 50. The standard error of true-score measurement is in the metric of the raw scores and actually decreases as $\zeta$ tends to the extremes of 0 and 1. But, as can be seen from Fig. 1 again, it is just at these extreme scores where one increment in $\zeta$ produces a large $\theta$-increment, that there is most uncertainty about the actual location of $\theta$. This paradox is resolved if the errors of measurement are expressed in the metric of $\theta$. When $\theta$ tends to its extremes, the error variance increases. The score of 48 out of 50 transforms to a $\theta$ estimate with a larger error of measurement than that arising from the transformation of the score of 25. This sensible arrangement of measurement error follows automatically if $\theta$ is estimated by powerful statistical procedures (maximum likelihood) in which formulas for standard errors follow directly from the theory. A useful theory of mental measurement must address the question of precision of ability indices with respect to the problems outlined above.

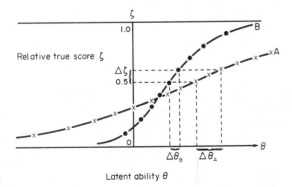

**Figure 1**
Latent ability versus relative true score for two tests A and B

Perhaps the most fundamentally important aspect which serves to illustrate the restrictive nature of the traditional methodology revolves around what latent trait theorists call "fit of data to the model". If items are ordered according to increasing difficulty from easy to hard and simultaneously order people from least able to most able and arrange the observed data matrix accordingly, the observed patterns in the data may be compared with expected patterns, the expectations being governed by the choice of latent trait model.

Figure 2 shows a hypothetical data matrix of three persons' responses to five items, and conveys the essence of fit. Persons are ordered by their raw scores and items by the count of the number of persons who had each item correct, although some latent trait models would use different criteria for ordering.

In Fig. 2, the items and persons are still ordered according to the previous criteria; however, there are no inversions to the "triangular" pattern which the model dictates. This particular set of patterns is known as a "Guttman scale". Its defining characteristic is that knowledge of a person's raw score tells everything about the person's behaviour on every item or, in other words all it is necessary to know about the person's ability. Some years prior to the development of probabilistic latent trait models, Guttman presented this deterministic scale and the associated concept of reproducibility. Guttman postulated an underlying unidimensional latent trait, but the nonprobabilistic nature of his model prevented a satisfactory analysis of fit. Only in the context of probabilities of response patterns does a truly sensible concept of fit emerge. The degree to which modelled patterns depart from those of real data, and the implications of ignoring varying amounts of departure, is of fundamental importance to latent trait theory. This is because the predictions from, and utility of, any model are of value only to the extent that the data conform in some specified way with that model.

The contrasts between true scores and latent traits lead into a more formal definition; a latent trait is a psychological dimension (construct) whose existence is postulated to account for replicable variation in observations of behaviour in certain well-articulated situations. There is no question of physical existence for psychological traits; the value of any "trait" lies wholly in its utility as a tool for understanding experience

through behaviour. Since a trait is an abstraction, it may be manipulated, restricted, varied, and otherwise transformed according to whatever purpose is to be served.

Latent trait models are probabilistic models which describe the probability relationship between observations (and their summaries), and unknown parameters (representing the trait). The probabilistic aspect insures that the mathematical form of the model provides just the probability and not the certainty of occurrence of prescribed events. These models contain three sets of elements: an enumeration of the possible events (the "sample space"), an identification of the latent parameter(s) deemed necessary to account for systematic item "behaviour", and an identification of the latent parameter(s) deemed necessary to account for systematic person behaviour. In the discussion which follows, some limits are placed on these elements to keep to fundamentals:

(a) There are only three sets of elements (some models have more).

(b) The sample space consists of the numbers 0 and 1 (multiple-choice items need not be stipulated for this sample space to be operative). Some models have other sample spaces.

(c) There is only one parameter $\theta$ to account for person behaviour.

(d) The mathematical form of the model is a monotonically increasing function of $\theta$, that is, the probability of success on an item increases with increasing $\theta$. This orderliness requirement has particular appeal for the practice of measurement.

The use of the term "systematic" to describe behaviour of either persons or items is deliberate. There is a need for assurance that the parameters identified as necessary, relate to characteristics which are persistent, replicable, and invariant within a well-defined frame of reference. The existence is not denied of other characteristics which might influence responses (since there must surely be an infinity of them), but there can be no legitimate reason to parameterize them unless they display the above characteristics. This point is crucial to understanding the difference among competing latent trait models.

Since knowledge of traits can only arise from responses to items, it has been customary to formulate the mathematical equations in terms of "item characteristic curves" (ICCs), that is, in terms of the probability of success on an item as a function of $\theta$. One such formulation is plotted in Fig. 3. $P_i(\theta)$ is the notation used to convey the fact that the item characteristic curve is for item $i$ (and that its shape, location along the abscissa, and other characteristics depend on item parameters), and that $\theta$ is an independent variable.

Some psychometricians use the label "item response theory" (IRT) for this formulation. Others find this alternative detracts from understanding persons' behav-

| | | Items | | | | |
| --- | --- | --- | --- | --- | --- | --- |
| | Easy | | | | Hard | |
| Low ability | 1 | 2 | 3 | 4 | 5 | Person score |
| 1 | 1 | 1 | 0 | 0 | 0 | 2 |
| Persons 2 | 1 | 0 | 1 | 1 | 0 | 3 |
| 3 | 1 | 1 | 1 | 0 | 1 | 4 |
| High ability | | | | | | |
| Item count | 3 | 2 | 2 | 1 | 1 | |

*Figure 2*
Guttman pattern of response

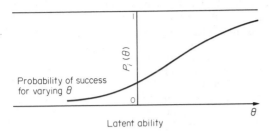

**Figure 3**
Item characteristic curve—item *i* and varying $\theta$

iour through traits. This latter group writes the probability statement connecting observed data and latent parameters as $P(\lambda_{vi})$, where $\lambda_{vi}$ is a suitable function of item and person parameters, and the identification of $\theta$ as a type of "independent variable" is little more than a convenience for plotting curves like Fig. 3. With this latter orientation it makes equal sense to describe the "person characteristic curve" (PCC) in Fig. 4.

Figure 4 describes the probability of success for person *v* according to encounters with items whose latent characteristic (for example, difficulty level), is increasing. Upon justification of a particular shape for the item characteristic curve (or person characteristic curve), $\theta$ may be related monotonically to the probability of success.

The identification of $\theta$ and $\delta$ with a line running from $-\infty$ to $+\infty$ is an important aid in understanding latent trait theory since it relates items to people directly in the same metric. Furthermore, since the models are probabilistic, it is sensible to show $P_i(\theta)$ [or $P(\lambda_{vi})$], reaching its limits asymptotically. The shape of the curve depends on the choice of mathematical function; this choice is governed, in turn, by the number, nature, and arithmetic arrangement of item and person parameters and these are ultimately governed by the philosophy of what it means to make useful psychological measures of people.

A selection of the best-known models is now described. The "normal ogive" model, used by Thurstone from psychophysics, is now mainly of historical interest since other forms of the probability distribution pose less problems for parameter estimation and yet still

retain the essential characteristics of a measurement model.

Birnbaum (1968) borrowed ideas from bioassay to justify his logistic model of mental measurement:

$$P_i(\theta) = p(x_i = 1; \theta, \alpha_i, \delta_i)$$

$$= \frac{\exp[\alpha_i(\theta - \delta_i)]}{1 + \exp[\alpha_i(\theta - \delta_i)]}$$

The alternative notation for $P_i(\theta)$ has been chosen to emphasize that, from one point of view, all latent trait measurement models are genuine probability distributions relying on discrete random variables and one or more parameters. According to the logistic model, the probability of success on an item is governed by the logistic distribution in which:

(a) $\alpha_i(\theta - \delta_i)$ is the "logit";

(b) $\delta_i$ is an item parameter called the item difficulty;

(c) $\alpha_i$ is an item parameter called the item discrimination; and

(d) $\theta$ is the (latent) independent variable of ability.

The arbitrary inclusion of additional parameters beyond one for person and one for item leads, however, to an irreconcilable disparity between assumed sophistication and the actual practice of measurement. On the other hand, this model (and its extension to one with three item parameters) is in use, particularly in the United States, so some further comments are pertinent.

One claim to the validity of these models is that the item characteristic curve has a shape which closely parallels those shapes which arise when unrestricted and unedited real data are plotted. These empirical plots are usually of raw score (on the abscissa) versus proportion of correct answers (on the ordinate). Although the abscissa has finite bounds, it is argued that a suitable transformation of this scale to an ability scale would produce curves like the logistic. Therefore, for example, if curves actually do differ in slope, this is taken as evidence of the necessity for the inclusion of the item discrimination parameter, and hence $\alpha_i$ has to be modelled. In this sense there are no a priori grounds for this model—"it must be justified on the basis of the results obtained, not on a priori grounds" (Lord 1980 p. 14).

There are at least four problems with this approach to modelling data (apart from the serious practical ones of parameter estimation with real and realistic data sets). In the first instance, the intersection of the item characteristic curves leads to a counterintuitive and complex description of the concepts of "easiness of an item" and "ability of a person". That is, the simplicity of equating "easiness" directly with chances of success (the easier the item, the greater the chance of success), and the corresponding simplicity of equating "ability of the person" directly with number of items correct is lost. This loss of simplicity is a result of the absence of sufficient statistics for the parameters.

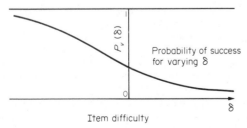

**Figure 4**
Person characteristic curve—persons *v* and varying $\delta$

Secondly, if the sole criterion for model choice is a closer and closer fit to observed data, then there is theoretically no limit to the number and nature of item and person parameters (already four item parameters have been proposed by some writers). Complexities of this nature do not occur in physical science measurements and they do retard the development of social science measurement since the clear interpretation of data in the presence of many parameters is a difficult exercise.

The third point relates to practice. The unrealistic nature of models with more than one parameter per person and/or per item, is well-appreciated by those working daily with tests and measurements. Even though classroom teachers, for example, may not acquire a full knowledge of latent trait theory, the underlying principles of the simplest and recommended model have been known and adopted for many decades. Working with this model, for example, the analysis of person response patterns (across a set of items) is made conceptually and operationally very simple whereas with the two- and three-parameter models the exercise is exceedingly complex and unlikely to gain acceptance.

Fourthly, it is unclear how to carry out successfully a number of central measurement tasks with two- and three-parameter models: equating, linking, test design, and person measurement are some examples of exercises which present little difficulty under the one-parameter model. For those whose job it is to make measurements, evaluate them and report results, one dominant criterion for the adoption of new procedures is: does it make an appreciable difference? It is suggested that the answer to this, from the point of view of latent trait theory in general, is positive, but that the additional benefit from the complexities of two- and three-parameter models is not forthcoming.

Latent trait models which go under the name of "Rasch" models were derived by the Danish mathematician, Georg Rasch, and have been promoted in the United States by B. D. Wright in Chicago and in Europe by G. Fischer in Vienna, and by their respective colleagues. For binary-scored data, the Rasch model has the form:

$$p(X_{vi} = 1; \theta_v, \delta_i) = \frac{\exp(\theta_v - \delta_i)}{1 + \exp(\theta_v - \delta_i)}$$

At first impression it would appear that this model may be made equivalent to Birnbaum's by setting all discriminations equal to the value 1.0. However, despite the algebraic identity between them, it should be noted that two fundamental differences exist between the Rasch model and the equal-discrimination version of the Birnbaum model. In the first case, Rasch arrived at the shape of his item characteristic curve by an a priori argument about what he believed to be the essential nature of measurement and hence the class of models which must follow from his measurement axioms of invariance. Secondly, the double subscripting of the

random variable $X_{vi}$, and the consequent subscripting of $\theta$ gives a status to $\theta_v$ equivalent to that of $\delta_i$. This means that attention may be focused on an individual person $v$ to the same extent and in the same way that attention is paid to an individual item $i$. Thus realistic study of individual differences arises in which person $v$ may be studied in his or her own right, and not just as a representative number of the population of persons. In other words, both $\theta_v$ and $\delta_i$ are seen as "fixed" effects rather than "random and fixed" effects. This makes possible the extension of this model to other facets (person and items represent two facets), since all that is required is a suitable subscripting of $X$ and the inclusion of extra parameters, provided the logit combines all parameters additively.

Thus a Rasch model for measuring written composition, in which the decision concerning the numerical value to attach to a given response is possibly made by different graders for different person's essays, might require the random variable $X_{vig}$ with the logit $\theta_v - \delta_i - \gamma_g$ where the parameter $\gamma_g$ is identified as "grader harshness". The inclusion of extra facets, and the extension to other polychotomous scoring systems, takes place within the framework of a single, undimensional latent trait.

Historically, the different orientations to latent trait theory exposed here arise from an uncritical adaptation from a similar theory in biological assay. The fundamental difference between the bioassay models and the psychometric models is that the former operate with known values of the independent variable (for example, drug dosage), whereas $\theta$ remains an unknown parameter and must always be estimated in the psychometric models.

In a discussion of the theory of latent traits not much attention need be paid to peripheral aspects such as estimation; however, since this topic and "tests of fit" really have no counterpart in true-score theory, some comment is warranted. When psychometricians advance from the linearity of the true-score model and its simplistic distributional assumptions to the nonlinearity of logistic distributions with explicit parameters, they are able to take advantage of a range of powerful parameter estimation techniques. In particular, the method of maximum likelihood has been well-developed and used by statisticians working with a wide variety of probability models. A considerable literature has evolved around estimation in latent trait models and someone wishing to make use of latent trait theory would be advised to consult this literature.

Somewhat later on the scene, but proposed with equal enthusiasm, have been the various tests of fit. Most of these have been associated with the Rasch model and encompass "person" fit as well as the more conventional "item" fit. The relationship between fit of data to the Rasch model and such topics as unidimensionality, local independence, and varying discriminations occupy a large part of the recent literature on Rasch models. It is sufficient here to point out that the use of a formal probability model and all its contingent framework of estimation and fit strategies, has given to modern psychometrics a status that is not only of theoretical soundness but one which permits ready adoption to the practical realm of educational and psychological measurement.

## Bibliography

Andrich D 1973 Latent trait psychometric theory in the measurement and evaluation of essay writing ability. Doctoral dissertation, University of Chicago

Birnbaum A 1968 Some latent trait models and their use in inferring an examinee's ability. In: Lord F M, Novick M R (eds.) 1968 *Statistical Theories of Mental Test Scores.* Addison-Wesley, Reading, Massachusetts

Fischer G H 1973 The linear logistic test model as an instrument in educational research. *Acta Psychol.* 37: 359–74

Guttman L 1954 The principle components of scalable attitudes. In: Lazarsfeld P F (ed.) 1954 *Mathematical Thinking in the Social Sciences.* Free Press, Glencoe, Illinois

Lord F M 1980 *Applications of Item Response Theory to Practical Testing Problems.* Erlbaum, Hillsdale, New Jersey

Rasch G 1980 *Probabilistic Models for Some Intelligence and Attainment Tests.* University of Chicago Press, Chicago, Illinois

Thurstone L L 1929 Theory of attitude measurement. *Psychol. Rev.* 36: 222–41

Wright B D 1971 Solving measurement problems with the Rasch model. *J. Educ. Meas.* 14: 97–116

Wright B D, Stone M H 1979 *Best Test Design.* MESA Press, Chicago, Illinois

# Rasch Measurement Models

**B. D. Wright**

The "Rasch measurement" models developed by Danish mathematician Georg Rasch between 1951 and 1959 and explained in his 1960 book, *Probabilistic Models for Some Intelligence and Attainment Tests*, are the most important advance in psychometrics since Thurstone's 1927 *Law of Comparative Judgment*. Objective measurement depends on measuring instruments which function independently of the objects measured. This requires a response model for calibrating their functioning which can separate the effects of instrument and object. Rasch was the first psychometrician to realize the necessity and sufficiency for objectivity of logistic response models with no interaction terms. The methods introduced in his book go far beyond measurement in education or psychology. They exemplify the principles of measurement on which all scientific objectivity is based.

Rasch models are practical realizations of "fundamental measurement." When data can be selected and organized to fit a Rasch model, the cancellation axiom of additive conjoint measurement is satisfied, a perfect Guttman order of response probabilities and hence of item and person parameters is established, and items are calibrated and persons measured on a common interval scale.

The nuclear element from which all Rasch models are built is

$$P(x; \beta, \delta) = \exp(\beta - \delta)/[1 + \exp(\beta - \delta)] \quad (1)$$

with raw-score statistics $r$ for person parameter $\beta$, and $s$ for item parameter $\delta$. The linear relation between $\beta$ and $\delta$ in the exponent enables $P(x; \delta | r)$ to be non-informative concerning $\beta$, and $P(x; \beta | s)$ to be non-informative concerning $\delta$. It follows that $r$ is sufficient for $x$ concerning $\beta$ and ancillary concerning $\delta$, while $s$ is sufficient for $x$ concerning $\delta$ and ancillary concerning $\beta$. Margining to $r$ and $s$ estimates $\beta$ and $\delta$ sufficiently while conditioning on $s$ and $r$ enables their inferential separation.

## 1. Rasch Models

The Poisson and item analysis models introduced in Rasch's 1960 book belong to the family of measurement models described by him in his 1961 article "On general laws and the meaning of measurement in psychology." Four models from this family have come into use.

The general unidimensional Rasch model can be written

$$P[k; \beta, \delta, (k), (\phi)] = \exp[\phi_x(\beta - \delta) - k_x]/\gamma \quad (2)$$

where the available response categories are labeled 0, 1, 2, . . . , $m$, a response in the $x$th category by a person to an item is denoted by $x$, the parameters $\beta$ and $\delta$ are the metric positions of the person and the item on their common variable, $(k)$ is a vector of $m + 1$ response category parameters, $(\phi)$ is a vector of $m + 1$ nonparametric category coefficients and

$$\gamma = \sum_{j=0}^{m} \exp[\phi_j(\beta - \delta) - K_j] \quad (3)$$

is the sum of all possible numerators.

### 1.1 Rating Scale Model

When $m$ is finite and the $m + 1$ response categories are ordered, two simplifications occur. Andersen (1977) shows that the nonparametric category coefficients $(\phi)$ must be equidistant and may as well be successive integers. Andrich (1978) shows that the category parameters $(k_j, j = 0, m)$ can be interpreted in terms of thresholds $(\tau_j, j = 1, m)$ that govern the transitions across adjacent categories. With these interpretations

$$\phi_x = x = 0, 1, 2, \ldots, m \qquad (4)$$

$$k_0 = 0 \qquad (5)$$

$$k_x = \sum_{j=1}^{x} \tau_j \qquad (6)$$

$$\gamma = 1 + \sum_{k=1}^{m} \exp[x(\beta - \delta) - \sum_{j=1}^{k} \tau_j] \qquad (7)$$

and Rasch's general unidimensional model becomes the rating scale model studied by Andrich (1978) and Wright and Masters (1982)

$$P[x; \beta, \delta, (\tau)] = \exp[x(\beta - \delta) - \sum_{j=1}^{x} \tau_j]/\gamma \qquad (8)$$

### 1.2 Poisson Model

When the response process allows $x$ to take any positive integer so that $m = \infty$, and individual contributions to $x$ occur independently, then $k_x = \log(x!)$, $\gamma = \exp[\exp(\beta - \delta)]$ and the rating scale model becomes the Poisson model Rasch used for the analysis of oral misreadings and reading speeds

$$P[x; \beta, \delta] = \exp[x(\beta - \delta)]/x! \exp[\exp(\beta - \delta)] \qquad (9)$$

### 1.3 Partial Credit Model

When the thresholds $\tau_j$ are individualized to the item difficulties $\delta$ to form $\delta_j = \delta + \tau_j$ so that each item has its own set of internal step difficulties and $\delta_0 = 0$, the model becomes:

$$P[x; \beta, (\delta_j)] = \exp \sum_{j=0}^{x} (\beta - \delta_j) \bigg/ \sum_{k=0}^{m} \exp \sum_{j=0}^{k} (\beta - \delta_j) \qquad (10)$$

which is useful for the analysis of graded performance and partial credit data (Wright and Masters 1982).

### 1.4 Item Analysis Model

When there are only two alternatives so that $m = 1$, the model becomes

$$P(x; \beta, \delta) = \exp[x(\beta - \delta)]/[1 + \exp(\beta - \delta)] \qquad (11)$$

which is the simple logistic "Rasch Model" so widely used for the sample-free calibration of educational test items and the test-free measurement of individual attainment (Wright and Stone 1979).

These four models, and a fifth for finite numbers of independent trials, can be expressed in the partial credit form as in Eqn. (10) by specifying

$$\delta_j = \delta_j \ldots\ldots\ldots\ldots\text{partial credit}$$
$$\delta_j = \delta \ldots\ldots\ldots\ldots\text{item analysis}$$
$$\delta_j = \delta + \tau_j \ldots\ldots\ldots\ldots\text{rating scale}$$
$$\delta_j = \delta + \log(j) \ldots\ldots\ldots\text{Poisson counts}$$
$$\delta_j = \delta + \log(j) - \log(m + 1 - j) \ldots\ldots\text{binomial trials}$$

## 2. Methods of Estimation

Measurement models require methods for estimating their parameters. The LOG method Rasch used for item calibration in 1953 is easy to follow and brings out the necessity of additivity in the construction of a measuring system.

Rasch also describes a pairwise calibration in which the ability parameters of persons scoring one on two-item tests cancel when estimating the difficulty difference between the two items. This leads to a PAIR method of item calibration in which items are tabulated against one another in all possible pairs and the responses of persons attempting each pair but succeeding on only one item provide the item calibrations.

The PAIR method can also be used for person measurement because the difficulty parameters of items attempted by both of a pair of persons but succeeded on by only one of them cancel when estimating the ability difference between the two persons. In this case the persons are tabulated against one another in all possible pairs and responses to items attempted by each pair of persons, but succeeded on by only one of them, provide the person measures. This method is useful when one has too few persons to establish a useful item calibration and is sufficiently satisfied that the items work together to define a useful variable to get along without verifying this by trying to calibrate them.

Log uses ability estimates when the ability parameters could have been removed by conditioning. PAIR does not use information based on item relationships more complex than pairwise comparisons. To improve on this, Rasch outlines a conditional method of estimation, FCON, in which all person parameters are explicitly removed by conditioning and all data are used for item calibration. Simulations done in 1965 and 1974 (Wright and Douglas 1977a), however, show that tests exceeding 30 or 40 items can encounter round-off errors which spoil FCON estimates. This provoked the development of an unconditional counterpart UCON (Wright and Panchapakesan 1969). In FCON, the person parameters are replaced by a term indexed to items as well as person scores, and calculated from symmetric functions of item estimates. In UCON this term is indexed to person scores only and its variation over items averaged out.

Rasch (1960 p. 182) shows why UCON works. The symmetric functions $\sigma_{ri}$ in FCON can be written $\beta_{ri} = \log(\sigma_{r-1,i}/\sigma_{ri})$ so that the conditional probability of a person with score $r$ succeeding on item $i$ becomes

$$\exp(\beta_{ri} - \delta_i)/[1 + \exp(\beta_{ri} - \delta_i)] \qquad (12)$$

The item parameter $\beta_{ri}$, which replaces person parameter $\beta_r$ is calculated from the set of item difficulties with $\delta_i$ removed. But removing the current estimates $d_i$ one at a time has little effect on the matrix of estimates $(b_{ri})$. As a result person parameter conditioning is well-approximated by reducing each vector of $(b_{ri})$ to $b_r$ so that the working probability of a person with score $r$

succeeding on item $i$ becomes

$$\exp(b_r - d_i)/[1 + \exp(b_r - d_i)] \tag{13}$$

Wright and Douglas (1977b) show that the average effect of using $b_r$, the estimated ability of any person with score $r$, instead of calculating the symmetric functions of the item difficulty estimates, can be removed by multiplying centered UCON item difficulties by $(L - 1)/L$, where $L$ is the number of items.

If items and persons are more or less normally distributed, an even simpler method of estimation, PROX, can be used (Wright and Douglas 1977a; Wright and Stone 1979 pp. 30–45). The PROX equation for estimating item difficulty $d$ from item score $s$ in a sample of $N$ persons normally distributed in ability with mean $M$ and standard deviation $S$ is

$$d = M + [1 + (S/1.7)^2]^{1/2} \log[(N - s)/s] \tag{14}$$

The divisor 1.7 scales the standard deviation of item difficulty from logits to probits. When persons and items are symmetrically distributed around one mode and targeted on one another, PROX produces item estimates equivalent to those of UCON or FCON.

Once an item bank is calibrated, a person can be measured with any suitable selection of items. An especially reasonable choice is a sequence of items evenly spaced over the region where the person is thought to be. This motivates an interest in how to estimate measures from tests of evenly spaced items.

The UFORM method for estimating person ability $b$ from relative score $f = r/L$ on a uniform test of $L$ items with average difficulty $H$ and difficulty range $W$ is

$$b = H + (f - 0.5)W + \log(A/B) \tag{15}$$

where

$$A = 1 - \exp(-fW),$$

and

$$B = 1 - \exp[-(1 - f)W].$$

This makes the transformation of test scores into measures simple. The ability measure implied by $f = r/L$, a proportion correct on a particular uniform test, is determined by adding $H$, the average difficulty of the test items and the easily tabled increment based on $f$ and $W$ given above. A standard error for this measure can be calculated by looking up an error coefficient in a corresponding table and dividing it by the square root of $L$ (Wright and Stone 1979 pp. 143–151).

## 3. The Analysis of Fit

Before estimates are used as calibrations and measurements, it is necessary to verify that the data from which they came are suitable for measuring. The requirements for measuring are specified by the model. If the data cannot be managed by the model, then they cannot be used to calibrate items or measure persons.

To evaluate the fit between data and model, the validity of item response patterns must be examined during item calibration, and the validity of person response patterns examined during measurement.

The fit analysis Rasch (1960 pp. 88–105) applies to his LOG method of estimating parameters for the item analysis model is simple and elegant. Its graphical form brings out the essential part additivity plays in the construction of measures. A useful alternative for the item analysis model is to compare each response of each person to each item with its estimated expectation $p = \exp(b - d)/[1 + \exp(b - d)]$ in which $b$ and $d$ are the current estimates of person ability and item difficulty. When this comparison is summarized over persons for an item, it indicates the overall validity of that item. When it is summarized over items for a person, it indicates the overall validity of that person's responses (Wright and Stone 1979 pp. 66–80). More detailed and more sensitive analyses of fit can be implemented by partitioning these comparisons into relevant classes of items and/or persons and analyzing the variance structure of these partitions.

If the observed response $x = 0$ or $1$ has an expectation $E$ estimated by

$$Ex \simeq \exp(b - d)/[1 + \exp(b - d)] = p \tag{16}$$

in which $b$ and $d$ are used exactly as they come from the estimation procedure [*before* unbiasing by $(L - 1)/L$ in the case of UCON] and a variance estimated by

$$Vx \simeq p(1 - p) = w \tag{17}$$

then the BIAS statistic

$$g = \Sigma(x - p)/(wL)^{1/2} \tag{18}$$

and the NOISE statistics

$$v_1 = \Sigma[(x - p)^2/w]/L$$
$$v_2 = \Sigma(x - p)^2/\Sigma w \tag{19}$$

with expectations

$$Eg = 0$$
$$Ev = 1 \tag{20}$$

and variances

$$Vg = 1$$
$$Vv_1 = \Sigma[(1/w) - 4]/L^2 \tag{21}$$
$$Vv_2 = (\Sigma w - 4\Sigma w^2)/(\Sigma w)^2$$

test the fit of responses ($x$) to their corresponding expectations ($p$). The average restriction in the mean squares caused by replacing the unknown probabilities by estimates based on $N$ persons taking $L$ items can be corrected by multiplying $v$ by $[NL/(N - 1)(L - 1)]$. The development and use of fit statistics for the other models are discussed and illustrated in detail by Wright and Masters (1982 pp. 90–117).

## 4. Applications of Rasch Measurement

### 4.1 Item Banking

When a family of test items are constructed so they calibrate along a single dimension, and when they are used so they retain these calibrations over a useful realm of application, then a scientific tool of great simplicity and far-reaching potential becomes available. The resulting "bank" of calibrated items defines the variable in exquisite detail. Its item contents serve the composition of an infinite variety of pre-equated tests: short or long, easy or hard, wide in scope or sharp in focus. Neither the difficulty nor shape of these tests need have any effect on their equating. All possible scores on all possible tests are automatically equated in the measures they imply through the common calibrations of their bank items. Whatever the test, its measures are expressed on the common variable defined by the bank. Furthermore the validity of these calibrations and of each measure made with bank items can be verified at every step.

### 4.2 Test Design

The positioning of items along the dimension they define makes test design easy. Tests can be targeted on any region along the variable represented by calibrated items. The items chosen for a particular test can be spread over the target region in whatever way is most informative. The best designs are obtained by bunching items at decision points to maximize decision information and by spreading them evenly over targets to maximize target information.

### 4.3 Tailored Testing

The basic recipe for turning $f = r/L$, the proportion of correct answers on a test of average item difficulty $H$, into $b$, its corresponding measure in logits, is:

$$b = H + \log[f/(1 - f)] \tag{22}$$

A simple formula for optimal sequential testing follows. If each succeeding item is chosen on the basis of prior performance, the logit difficulty of the best next item can be estimated from $h$, the average logit difficulty of preceding items, and $f$, the proportion of these items answered correctly,

$$d = h + \log[f/(1 - f)] \tag{23}$$

The final measure equals the last difficulty chosen. Response validity can be checked by periodic administrations of off-target items for which the expected response is all but certain. Should invalidity emerge it can be used to revise or terminate the session.

### 4.4 Self-tailoring

Persons can also make their own choice of item difficulty as they go along. The items in their test can be arranged to increase in difficulty. People may choose their own

starting point. If they feel strong, they may work ahead into harder items until they reach their limit. If they feel weak, they may stay with easy items. Capitalization on opportunity can be controlled by scoring persons on all items contained in the item segment their easiest and hardest item selections embrace, whether they attempt them all or not.

### 4.5 Response Validation

The analysis of fit enables the validity of each response to be examined. This is an important step in estimating a measure from test performance. The items used will vary in their positions along the variable. This will happen when items are spread to cover the target. It will also be forced by limitations in item resources. As the simplicity and necessity of verifying response pattern validity are appreciated, items for measuring will be selected which spread out enough to facilitate the evaluation of the response patterns they stimulate.

When items vary in their difficulty, persons are expected to do better on easier items than on harder ones. Because the response model is explicit in this regard, this expectation can be formulated into an analysis of fit for any response pattern. This enables the validity of each and every test performance to be examined before any measures estimated from it are reported.

### 4.6 Item Bias

The analysis of response pattern fit allows each person's item responses to be diagnosed in detail. If any theory is possessed that classifies items by response format, page layout, booklet location, item text, topic, or approach, then it is possible to calculate how much each person's responses are disturbed by these categories.

When a disturbance is found, it is possible to estimate the extent to which the unusual category is biased for each person. There is no other objective basis for the analysis of item or test bias. Bias estimated from groups can never satisfy the right of each individual to be fairly treated regardless of membership.

### 4.7 Individual Diagnosis

More important is the identification of each test taker's strengths and weaknesses and the use of this diagnosis to find what he or she needs next. Most test takers are associated with programs dedicated to improving them. The justification for testing is the intention to use tests to help test takers. For this, an item content diagnosis of each test taker's response pattern is essential. Since the response residuals from the measurement model manifest all the diagnostic information the test contains, their analysis is also all that can be done statistically.

## 5. Connections with Traditional Test Statistics

The person and item statistics of a Rasch analysis do not correspond directly to the indices of item difficulty, test reliability, and test validity of traditional test theory. Nevertheless, Rasch item difficulties and person abilities are closely related to traditional *p*-values and test scores, and the Rasch model provides valuable insight into traditional concerns for test reliability and validity.

### 5.1. Item p-values

The traditional approach to item difficulties uses a "*p*-value" or "proportion of persons attempting the item who are successful". These *p*-values have two shortcomings. First, they are dependent upon the abilities of the persons who took the test: the more able the persons, the higher the proportion of persons succeeding on each item. This makes it awkward to compare the difficulties of items taken by different groups of persons. Second, because they are bounded by zero and one, *p*-values cannot form an interval or linear scale: equal differences in *p*-values cannot represent equal differences in item difficulties.

Rasch item difficulty estimates are freed from both of these shortcomings. The way in which this is done can be illustrated for the particular case in which person abilities are assumed to be normally distributed. In this case, sample-free item difficulties can be approximated from item *p*-values using the formula

$$D = M + Y[\log(1 - p)/p)]$$

where $Y = (1 + S^2/2.89)^{1/2}$, $D$ is the Rasch item difficulty, $M$ is the mean ability for the sample of persons, $S$ is the standard deviation of these abilities, and $p$ is the traditional item *p*-value. The values of $D$, $M$ and $S$ are in logits on the linear scale shared by item calibrations and person measures and the factor $2.89 = 1.7^2$ rescales the normal distribution to follow the logistic.

This formula removes the two shortcomings of *p*-values. First, the *p*-values are transformed onto a linear scale by the logit function $\log[(1 - p)/p]$. Second, this transformed *p*-value is rescaled so that the influence of the sample standard deviation $S$ and sample mean $M$ are removed. If the person abilities are more or less normally distributed, the resulting item calibration $D$ is sample free. This means that the difficulties of items can be compared even though they might come from quite different samples of persons.

### 5.2. Test scores

A Rasch ability estimate is reported for each person taking a test, provided that the test is not so easy that the person answers all items correctly or so difficult that they are able to answer none. The traditional approach to reporting a person's ability is to count the number of correct answers made and to report either this raw test score or some norm-based transformation of it. But like *p*-values, these raw scores have two shortcomings. First, they are dependent upon the difficulties of the items in the test. If the items are easy, raw scores will be high. This makes it awkward to compare the abilities of persons taking tests of different

difficulty. The second disadvantage is that, because they are bounded by zero and the maximum possible score, raw scores are also not on an interval scale. The result is that a difference of one score point does not represent the same difference in ability from one end of the score range to the other.

Rasch ability estimates are freed of these disadvantages. Under the assumption that items are normally distributed, ability estimates can be approximated from raw scores with the formula:

$$B = H + X\{\log[r/(L - r)]\}$$

where $X = (1 + W^2/2.89)^{1/2}$, $B$ is the person's ability measure, $H$ is the mean difficulty of the test items, $W$ is the standard deviation of these item difficulties, all in logits, $r$ is the person's raw score, and $L$ is the number of items in the test. Once again, the disadvantages of the raw scores are removed in two steps: First by transforming the scores onto an interval scale using the transformation $\log[r/(L - r)]$ and second by removing the influence of the mean and standard deviation of the test item difficulties. If the item difficulties are more or less normally distributed, then the resulting person measures are test free. This means that they can be compared even though pesons take quite different sets of items. The general formula which can be used for any distribution of item difficulties is slightly more complicated. For details, see Wright and Stone (1979).

### 5.3 Reliability

The reliability of a test is intended to specify the accuracy with which the test measures the variable it is designed to measure. The traditional formulation of test reliability can be derived from a "true score" model which assumes that the observed test score of each person can be resolved into two components: an unknowable true score and a random error. The reliability of a test is defined as the proportion of a sample's observed score variance $SD^2$, which is due to the sample's true-score variance $ST^2$

$$R = ST^2/SD^2 = 1 - (SE^2/SD^2)$$

where $SD^2 = ST^2 + SE^2$, and $SE^2$ is the error variance of the test, averaged over that sample.

The size of this traditional reliability coefficient, however, depends not only upon the test-error variance $SE^2$ which describes how precisely the test measures (i.e., for a given $ST^2$, the greater the precision of measurement, the smaller $SE^2$, and so, the larger $R$), but also on the sample true-score variance $ST^2$ which describes the ability dispersion of the sample (i.e., for a given $SE^2$, the greater the sample true-score variance $ST^2$, the larger $R$). Rather than combining $ST^2$ and $SE^2$ into one compound statistic which is easily mistaken for a sample-free index of how accurately a test measures, it is more useful to distinguish between these two components of variance in the traditional reliability expression and to examine $ST^2$ and $SE^2$ separately.

The observed sample variance $SD^2$ can be calculated directly from the observed measures, but the test error variance $SE^2$ must be derived from a model describing how each score occurs. The traditional approach to estimating this error variance is to estimate the reliability first. This is done in various ways, for example, by calculating the correlation between repeated measurements under similar conditions, or by correlating split halves, or by combining item point biserials. An average error variance for the test with this particular sample is then estimated from $SD^2(1 - R')$ where $R'$ is the estimate of $R$.

The magnitude of the estimated reliability $R'$, however, also depends upon a third factor, namely the extent to which the items in the test actually work together to define one variable. The traditional estimate of $R$ can be expressed as a function of an observed sample variance $SD^2$ and an "actual" test-error variance $SA^2$:

$$R' = 1 - (SA^2/SD^2)$$

This actual error variance has two parts. The modeled test error variance $SE^2$ is its theoretical basis. But it is also influenced by the extent to which the items actually fit together, and are thus internally consistent. When item inconsistency is estimated by a fit mean square $V$ for the test as a whole, then the actual error variance is

$$SA^2 = V.SE^2$$

so that the estimated reliability becomes

$$R' = 1 - (V.SE^2)/SD^2$$

The Rasch analysis resolves these complications by dealing separately with each of the three components $V$, $SE$ and $SD$ which are submerged in the traditional test reliability coefficient.

First, the model provides a direct estimate of the modeled error variance $SE^2$. This modeled error indicates how precisely each person's ability can be estimated when the test items are internally consistent. Unlike the traditional reliability coefficient, this estimate is not influenced by any sample variance or fit and is not sample specific. It is a sample-free test characteristic which estimates how precisely any person's ability can be estimated from their particular score, regardless of any sample to which they may belong. Also unlike the traditional reliability coefficient, this estimate is not an average for the entire test, but is particular to whatever test score is actually obtained.

Under a Rasch analysis, the term "reliable" is best reserved for this single score-specific, sample-free aspect of traditional reliability. Rather than referring to the reliability of a whole test with respect to some sample, the term is used to describe the precision of each person's measure. Analogously, the estimate of the standard error for each item makes it possible to refer to the "reliability" of each item's calibration.

Once values for the test measurement error $SE^2$ of each person observed are available, an estimate of the true-sample variance $ST^2$ can be obtained:

$$ST^2 = SD^2 - MSE$$

where $MSE$ is the sample mean of the individual error variances:

$$MSE = \left( \sum_{n=1}^{N} SE^2 \right) \Big/ N$$

The third factor influencing estimates of traditional test reliability namely the internal consistency among items, is treated as the "internal validity" of the instrument.

### 5.4 Validity

In traditional test theory, a distinction is made between internal and external validity. The usual statistics employed to assess the internal validity of a test are the item point biserials and their accumulation into the test reliability estimate. Since the magnitude of this item statistic depends on the ability distribution of the sample, in particular, on the relationship between the item $p$-value and the sample ability spread, it has the disadvantage of being sample dependent. When an explicit measurement model is used, the internal validity of a test can be analyzed in terms of the statistical fit of each item to the model in a way that is independent of the sample ability distribution. A mean-square test of fit can be used to estimate the extent to which the data on each item are consistent with the latent variable implied by the collection of items in the test. The evaluation of this fit is a check on internal validity. If the fit statistic of an item is acceptable, then the item is "valid".

The pattern of each person's performances can be analyzed in the same way and, if the fit statistic for a person's performance is acceptable, then that person's test performances are interpreted as a "valid" basis for inferring a measure of that person's ability. To the extent that person's test performances do not approximate the model (e.g., if the person tends to get easy items wrong and hard items right), the validity of that person's ability estimate is in doubt.

### 6. Conclusion

Rasch has devised a truly new approach to psychometric problems . . . . He makes use of none of the classical psychometrics, but rather applies algebra anew to a probabilistic model. The probability that a person will answer an item correctly is assumed to be the product of an ability parameter pertaining only to the person and a difficulty parameter pertaining only to the item . . . the ability assigned to an individual is independent of that of other members of the group and of the particular items with which he is tested; similarly for the item difficulty . . . . Thus Rasch must be credited with an outstanding contribution to one of the two central psychometric problems, the achievement of nonarbitrary measures. Rasch is concerned with a different and more rigorous kind of generalization than Cronbach,

Rajaratnam, and Gleser. When his model fits, the results are independent of the sample of persons and of the particular items within some broad limits. Within these limits, generality is, one might say, complete. (Loevinger 1965 p. 151)

## Bibliography

Andersen E B 1977 Sufficient statistics and latent trait models. *Psychometrika* 42: 69–81

Andrich D 1978 A rating formulation for ordered response categories. *Psychometrika* 43: 561–73

Loevinger J 1965 Person and population as psychometric concepts. *Psychol. Rev.* 72: 143–55

Rasch G 1960 *Probabilistic Models for Some Intelligence and Attainment Tests*. Danmarks Paedogogiske Institut, Copenhagen. (Reprinted 1980 University of Chicago Press, Chicago)

Rasch G 1961 On general laws and meaning of measurement in psychology. *Proceedings of the Fourth Berkeley Symposium on Mathematical Statistics and Probability*, pp. 312–33

Rasch G 1977 On specific objectivity: An attempt at formalizing the request for generality and validity of scientific statements. *Danish Yearbook of Philosophy* 14: 58–94

Wright B D, Douglas G A 1977a Best procedures for sample-free item analysis. *Appl. Psychol. Meas.* 1: 281–95

Wright B D, Douglas G A 1977b Conditional versus unconditional procedures for sample-free item analysis. *Educ. Psychol. Meas.* 37: 47–60

Wright B D, Masters G N 1982 *Rating Scale Analysis*. MESA Press, Chicago, Illinois

Wright B D, Panchapakesan N 1969 A procedure for sample-free item analysis. *Educ. Psychol. Meas.* 29: 23–48

Wright B D, Stone M H 1979 *Best Test Design*. MESA Press, Chicago, Illinois

# Specialized Measurement Models and Methods

## Rating Scale Analysis

### D. Andrich and G. N. Masters

Rating scales are used to help identify the degrees of a property, or in modern terms trait, an object or person may have when no instrument for measuring the trait directly is available. One common example of rating scales in education is in attitude questionnaires where responses to statements on an issue are expressed using alternatives like: strongly disagree; disagree; neutral or undecided; agree; and strongly agree. Another is in performance ratings where judges classify performances on tasks in categories like: poor; fair; good; excellent. The former, with a neutral category, are said to be bipolar scales, while the latter are said to be unipolar.

Many variants on the above formats for rating scales have been suggested. In some cases, the only cues given are descriptions of the two extreme categories, with the remaining categories simply being cut-off points on a line segment. In others, such as in judgment of essay-writing ability, examples of specimens at each level are provided. In each case the trait rated needs to be made as clear as possible with the examples or cues clarifying the way it is operationalized.

Because direct measurements of variables in the social sciences are difficult, rating scales are extremely common. Dawes (1972) points out that some 60 percent of studies have rated variables as the only form of dependent variable.

## 1. Contingency Table Contexts

In many contexts individuals who belong to well-defined classes or populations may be asked to rate their opinions with respect to some issue. For example, educators identified and involved with different aspects of education may be asked to provide an opinion on, for example, public examinations or minimum competency testing. Table 1 shows the kind of format in which responses may be collected and presented. A topic such as public examinations may prompt more than one statement being considered. Then results are often reported statement by statement and inferences are drawn regarding the level of support enjoyed by each issue.

## 2. Individual Classification Contexts

Often more refined classifications than those provided by contingency tables are required. First, the performance of each person rated, or providing an opinion, may need to be considered individually rather than as a member of some population. Secondly, it may be necessary to obtain more precise information about that person than that which can be obtained from one statement or rating. Therefore, either more than one statement on a related topic is presented, or more than

*Table 1*
Format for ratings in contingency tables

| Please respond to the following statement in one of the categories provided: There should be publicly defined standards which all students should pass before leaving high school | | | | | |
|---|---|---|---|---|---|
| Response score | | Strongly disagree (0) | Disagree (1) | Agree (2) | Strongly agree (3) | Total number |
| Teaching level | Elementary | $f_{10}$[a] | $f_{11}$ | $f_{12}$ | $f_{13}$ | $N_1$ |
| | Secondary | $f_{20}$ | $f_{21}$ | $f_{22}$ | $f_{23}$ | $N_2$ |
| | Tertiary | $f_{30}$ | $f_{31}$ | $f_{32}$ | $f_{33}$ | $N_3$ |

a $f$ denotes frequency

**Table 2**
Format for ratings of individuals

| Person (ratee) | Rating score $x$ | Statements of tasks | | | | | | | | |
|---|---|---|---|---|---|---|---|---|---|---|
| | | *1* | | *2* | $\ldots$ | *i* | $\ldots$ | *I* | |
| | | 0  1  2 | | 0  1  2 | | 0  1  2 | | 0  1  2 | |
| 1 | | $x_{11}$ | | $x_{12}$ | $\ldots$ | $x_{1i}$ | $\ldots$ | $x_{1I}$ | |
| 2 | | $x_{21}$ | | $x_{22}$ | $\ldots$ | $x_{2i}$ | $\ldots$ | $x_{2I}$ | |
| 3 | | $x_{31}$ | | $x_{32}$ | $\ldots$ | $x_{3i}$ | $\ldots$ | $x_{3I}$ | |
| $\vdots$ | | $\vdots$ | | $\vdots$ | | $\vdots$ | | $\vdots$ | |
| $n$ | | $x_{n1}$ | | $x_{n2}$ | $\ldots$ | $x_{ni}$ | $\ldots$ | $x_{nI}$ | |
| $\vdots$ | | $\vdots$ | | $\vdots$ | | $\vdots$ | | $\vdots$ | |
| $N$ | | $x_{N1}$ | | $x_{N2}$ | $\ldots$ | $x_{Ni}$ | $\ldots$ | $x_{NI}$ | |

one task is required to conduct the rating, or sometimes both. In situations with two or more statements or two or more tasks, the information is collapsed into a single value for each person. Table 2 shows the kind of format in which the responses may be collected and presented.

With respect to the case where many statements or tasks are provided, whether in opinion, attitude, performance, or achievement ratings, the statements or tasks have the same role as they do in Thurstone scales to which dichotomous responses rather than ratings are required. That is, they serve to define a continuum, and the ratings can be seen as extensions and refinements to dichotomous responses such as disagree or agree, and correct or incorrect. Viewed from this perspective, the increase in the number of categories beyond two helps increase the precision. The greater the number of categories, and to the degree that the categories can be used meaningfully, the greater the precision.

Unlike performance ratings, where a rater rates a performance explicitly, the rater in attitude testing is the person whose attitude is to be assessed. Attitude questionnaires requiring such ratings are said to be of the Likert style following the work by Likert (1932) on attitude measurement.

## 3. Scoring the Response Categories

Whether in contingency table or individual testing contexts, the issue which has received a great deal of attention is the scoring of the ordered response categories. The most elementary approach follows closely the measurement analogy.

With a formalized measuring instrument, any object can be placed between the two cut-off points or thresholds on a continuum mapped onto a real line. On a typical measuring instrument the thresholds are represented by line segments of equal width which cut the real line at equal intervals. The measure then is the number of thresholds which the object is seen to pass

and this measure may be refined by having smaller intervals between thresholds and by having thresholds represented by finer lines. Often, measurement errors are considered sufficiently small relative to the variation of the measured property that they may be ignored and the measures are then treated as continuous variables.

By analogy, in the rating scale the thresholds are placed so that they indicate equal spacing, and the raters are supposed to place their response between two thresholds. Elementary quantification and analysis extends this measurement analogy. Thus the successive categories are scored with successive integers, and the resultant numbers are again treated as continuous variables. The integers may start with either 0 or 1. For convenience here, they will be taken to commence with 0 and to have a maximum of $m$, where there are $m$ thresholds and therefore $m + 1$ categories.

In the contingency table context, the relative status of each group $g$ is calculated then simply by

$$r_g = \sum_{x=0}^{m} x f_{gx}$$

while in the assessment of individuals on statements or tasks $i$, $i = 1, \ldots, k$, the status of each individual $n$ is calculated simply by

$$r_n = \sum_i x_{ni}$$

That is, the integer ratings are simply summed.

Standard analyses based on these summary statistics, and following the true score model of traditional test theory, have been developed. Guilford (1954 Chap. 11) provides a comprehensive discussion on the construction of rating scales and on the analyses using the above scoring.

However, the assumption of equality of intervals, on which the integer scoring is supposed to be based, has often been questioned. This has led to more formal representations of the rating process.

## 4. Mathematical Response Models

In the analysis of ratings which is more sophisticated, two qualifications to the elementary analogy of the measuring instrument are made. First, the error in classification is recognized explicitly by formulating a continuous random variable $d$ for a response process when a rater makes a rating according to $d = \mu + \varepsilon$ where $\mu$ is the true location or true value of the rating, and $\varepsilon$ is the error with mean 0 and variance $\sigma^2$. This simple additive equation may be subscripted in different ways depending on the context. Thus with contingency tables and ratings on a single statement or task, it may take the form $d_g = \mu_g + \varepsilon$ for every person in group $g$. In the rating of a person $n$ on more than one statement or task $i$, it may take the form $d_{ni} = \mu_{ni} + \varepsilon_i$ in which case the error variance $\sigma_i^2$ depends only on the statement or task. The true value $\mu_{ni}$ of the rating may then be taken to depend on both the location value $\beta_n$ of person $n$ and the location value $\delta_i$ of task $i$. This value is then usually resolved according to $\mu_{ni} = \beta_n - \delta_i$. In performance rating, $\beta_n$ is an ability of person $n$ and $\delta_i$ is the difficulty of task $i$, while in attitude ratings the formulation may be identical, with $\beta_n$ representing the attitude of person $n$ and $\delta_i$ the affective value of statement $i$.

Whatever the context, the rating is then supposedly determined by the interval in which the value of the random variable $d$ falls. This formulation leads to the second qualification to the measurement analogy: instead of distances between thresholds simply being presumed to be equal, they are estimated.

### 4.1 The Traditional Threshold Model

The traditional model, which has its origins in the work of Thurstone (1927), assumes either a normal or a logistic distribution for the random response process. After a simple linear scaling, the two are indistinguishable numerically. Therefore, the latter is usually preferred because it is more tractable. Then the probability of a response above each threshold is the area beyond the threshold in the cumulative normal or the cumulative logistic, whichever is used. Figure 1 shows the process formalized for the logistic distribution, in which the probability $p_x^*$ of a response *above* threshold $\tau_{x'}x = 1, m$, is given by:

$$p_x^* = \frac{1}{\gamma} \exp[(\mu - \tau_x)/\sigma] \qquad (1)$$

$$= \frac{1}{\gamma} \exp[\alpha(\mu - \tau_x)]$$

where (a) $\alpha = 1/\sigma$ is termed the discrimination and (b) $\gamma = 1 + \exp[\alpha(\mu - \tau_x)]$ which ensures that $p_x^*$ and its complement, the probability of a response below threshold $x$, sum to 1. The probability $p_x$ of a response in category $x, x = 0, 1, 2, \ldots, m$ is then given simply by the difference between successive cumulative

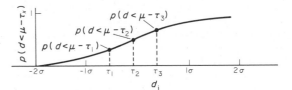

*Figure 1*
Probability that $d$ is less than $\mu - \tau_x$ for each $\tau_x$ in the traditional threshold model

probabilities as $p_x = p_x^* - p_{x+1}^*$ with $p_0 = 1$ and $p_{m+1} = 0$. It is worthwhile noting that the ratio of $p_x^*$ and $1 - p_x^*$ gives:

$$\frac{p_x^*}{1 - p_x^*} = \exp[\alpha(\mu - \tau_x)]$$

of which the natural logarithm

$$\ln\left(\frac{p_x^*}{1 - p_x^*}\right) = \alpha(\mu - \tau_x)$$

is called the logit.

Just as $\mu$ may be qualified depending on the context, so may the threshold values $\tau_x$. For example, in the contingency table context, the exponent of Eqn. (1) may take the form $\alpha_g(\mu_g - \tau_x)$ or the same discrimination may be retained for all groups, giving simply $(\mu_g - \tau_x)$, where the discrimination is absorbed into the location parameters. Alternatively, not only may the discrimination be different from group to group, but so may the threshold values. The exponent would appear then as $\alpha_g(\mu_g - \tau_{xg})$.

In the case for the assessment of individual $n$ and across more than one task or statement $i$, $\mu$ again is resolved according to $\mu_{ni} = \beta_n - \delta_i$. Then if each task or statement is assumed to have the same discrimination and equal thresholds, the exponent in Eqn. (1) may take the form $(\beta_n - \delta_i - \tau_x)$. If each task or statement has a different discrimination and different threshold values, this exponent may be written as $\alpha_i(\beta_n - \delta_i - \tau_{xi})$.

The estimation of the parameters may be carried out in various ways. In the early work, and in the case where ratings are associated with a group or population, the proportions of responses in the respective categories were taken as a direct estimate $\hat{p}_x$ of the corresponding probabilities $p_x$. Then the estimates of $\mu - \tau_x$ were given simply by either the corresponding standard normal deviate, or the logit given by $\ln(\hat{p}_x^*/(1 - \hat{p}_x^*))$ for each group. More recent techniques usually involve so-called maximum likelihood estimation (MLE) procedures. This requires identifying the values of the parameters of the chosen model which maximize the probability of obtaining the data observed.

It is interesting to note that Likert originally investigated the possibility of deriving weights for categories in the manner described above. Thus he considered that as far as the calculation of weights was concerned, the persons to be assessed for attitude belonged to some general population. Then with his emphasis on the subsequent assessment of individuals, he used as his criterion for the quality of the weightings the correlation between scores obtained by summing simply the integers and by summing the empirically derived weights. These correlations were generally almost the maximum. As a result, and for the obvious reason of simplicity, Likert and the majority of users of rating scales since then have used the simple integer scoring followed by simple summing. That is, in their statistical work, they have continued with the measurement analogy.

While the simple characterization or measurement of individuals is often the main criterion, understanding and controlling the rating mechanism is also important for researchers. Therefore, researchers have continued to show concern about the assumption of equal intervals on the rating scales. The traditional threshold model and its mathematical formulation described above is one attempt to accommodate these concerns, for which Bock (1975 Chap. 8) provides the mathematics for contingency tables and Samejima (1969) for the assessment of individuals.

## 4.2 The Rasch Rating Model

A more recent formulation of a mathematical model for ratings (Andrich 1978) accommodates not only the features of a random response process and the estimation of thresholds but also the simple integer scoring of the successive categories and the simple summing among tasks or statements. If $p_x$ is again the probability that a rating, governed by a true value $\mu$, is in category $x$, the model takes the form:

$$p_x = \frac{1}{\gamma} \exp\left(x\mu - \sum_{k=1}^{x} \tau_k\right) \qquad (2)$$

where

$$\gamma = \sum_{k=0}^{m} \exp\left(k\mu - \sum_{j=1}^{k} \tau_j\right)$$

is a normalizing factor ensuring that

$$\sum_{x=0}^{m} p_x = 1$$

and where $\tau_x$, $x = 1, 2, \ldots, m$ are again $m$ thresholds on the continuum. This model has been called the Rasch rating model because it has all the distinguishing properties of the Rasch model for dichotomously scored responses. Figure 2 shows the response probability curves for three ordered categories. As with Eqn. (1), the exponent of Eqn. (2) can be modified to suit the particular data collection format. Thus for contingency tables, the exponent may take the form

$$\left(x\mu_g - \sum_{k=1}^{x} \tau_k\right).$$

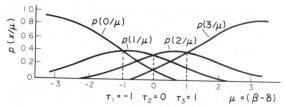

**Figure 2**
Probability of response $x$ for a value of $\mu$ in the Rasch rating model

Alternatively, if the thresholds are considered differently spaced from group to group, it may be modified to

$$\left(x\mu_g - \sum_{k=1}^{x} \tau_{kg}\right)$$

It is important to note an essential similarity and three essential differences between Eqn. (1) and Eqn. (2). The similarity is that they both take the logistic form. One difference, however, is how the logistic response process is formalized. As has been seen, in Eqn. (1) there is one process across *all* thresholds and the logit is identified by forming the ratio of the cumulative probabilities on either side of each threshold. In Eqn. (2) there is a process at *each* threshold and the logit is identified by forming the ratio of probabilities of adjacent categories, that is, by $p_{x+1}/p_x$ giving

$$(p_x/p_{x-1}) = \exp(\mu - \tau_x)$$

from which:

$$\ln(p_x/p_{x-1}) = \mu - \tau_x$$

The second difference is that the exponent in Eqn. (2) has parameters which are additive. That is, there is no general discrimination $\alpha$ as in the exponent of Eqn. (1). The third difference is that even though the same term "threshold" is used in both models, because they are defined differently, they have different values.

In the case where the ratings pertain to members of a population or group, the proportion of responses in each category can be used to estimate the probability $p_x$. The simple logistic transform given above can be used to estimate the parameters in the exponent. This technique, however, is not elegant or efficient when some categories have small response frequencies. Therefore, the maximum likelihood estimation approach to estimation is again usually preferred.

When the maximum likelihood estimation is used, it becomes evident that the sufficient statistic for the estimate of $\mu_g$ is $r_g = \Sigma_x x f_{gx}$ and that the sufficient statistic for the estimate of $\tau_x$ is $t_x = \Sigma_x f_{gx}$. Further, the solution equations for $\mu_g$ and $\tau_x$ respectively are

$$r_g = \frac{1}{\gamma} N_g \sum_x \exp\left(x\hat{\mu}_g - \sum_{k=1}^{x} \hat{t}_k\right) \quad g = 1, G$$

$$t_x = \frac{1}{\gamma} \sum_g \exp\left(x\hat{\mu}_g - \sum_{k=1}^{x} \hat{t}_k\right) \quad x = 1, m$$

These equations with the imposed constraints $\Sigma_g \hat{\mu}_g = 0$ and $\Sigma_x \hat{t}_x = 0$ must be solved iteratively because they are implicit, and not explicit, equations in the parameters.

The existence of sufficient statistics is particularly important because it indicates that these statistics contain all the information about the parameters which is available in the responses. But it is equally important that these statistics, containing all the information, are the simple sums of the integers. That is, the statistic $r_g$ is exactly the one used in the elementary measurement analogy. The probabilistic model [Eqn. (2)] and its form serves to rescale the constrained qualitative responses onto an additive or linear scale, and in the process also scales the thresholds. The simple total score $r_g$ is then not seen as the sum of equally spaced thresholds as in the full measurement analogy, but as a count of the number of thresholds which have been passed. The actual weighting of the thresholds, obtained as estimates, is taken account of separately. Andrich (1979) discusses the application of the rating model to contingency table contexts.

In the case of assessment of individuals, the location $\mu$ in the exponent of Eqn. (2) is again modified to include a person parameter $\beta_n$ and a difficulty or affective value parameter $\delta_i$ so that $\mu_{ni} = \beta_n - \delta_i$ giving the exponent

$$(\beta_n - \delta_i) - \sum_{k=1}^{x} \tau_k$$

In this case, the sufficient statistic for the person parameter $\beta_n$ is $r_n = \Sigma_i x_{ni}$, for the task or statement parameter $\delta_i$ it is $s_i = \Sigma_n x_{ni}$ and for the threshold parameter $\tau_x$ it is $t_x = \Sigma_n\Sigma_i I_{nix}$ where $I_{nix} = 1$ if the response is in category $x$, and 0 otherwise. That is, $t_x$ is simply the total number of responses in category $x$ across all tasks or statements and across all persons. The solution equations for $\beta_i$, $\delta_i$, and $\tau_x$ respectively, are given by

$$r_n = \frac{1}{\gamma} \sum_i \exp\left[x(\hat{\beta}_n - \hat{\delta}_i) - \sum_{k=1}^{x} \hat{t}_k\right] \quad n = 1, N$$

$$s_i = \frac{1}{\gamma} \sum_n \exp\left[x(\hat{\beta}_n - \hat{\delta}_i) - \sum_{k=1}^{x} \hat{t}_k\right] \quad i = 1, I$$

and

$$t_x = \frac{1}{\gamma} \sum_n \sum_i \exp\left[x(\hat{\beta}_n - \hat{\delta}_i) - \sum_{k=1}^{x} \hat{t}_k\right] \quad x = 1, m$$

with the constraints $\Sigma_i \delta_i = 0$ and $\Sigma_k \hat{t}_k = 0$.

Again, the statistic $r_n$ for estimating the person parameter is identical to that used in the elementary measurement analogy and shown by Likert to be satisfactory for the measurement of persons. In fact, because $\beta_n$ and $r_n$ are monotonically related, their correlation is nearly perfect. The transformation of $r_n$ to $\beta_n$ again maps or transforms the qualitative responses onto a linear scale.

If it is assumed that the threshold spacings, whatever they are, are not equal across tasks or statements, then the exponent of Eqn. (2) may be qualified further to: $x\beta_n - \Sigma_{k=1}^{x} \tau_{ki}$. Masters (1982), Wright and Masters (1982), and Masters and Wright (1984) provide comprehensive treatment of the Rasch model for rating and the various qualifications in the exponent of Eqn. (2). Masters (1988) provides an overview of extensions of the rating model including the Rasch Model for Partial Credit Scoring. In all these models, the total score $r_n = \Sigma_i x_{ni}$ continues to be the sufficient statistic in relation to the person parameter $\beta_n$, thus indicating the appropriateness of scoring successive categories with successive integers while taking account of variations in spacing between the thresholds.

## 5. Connecting Ratings to Measurements

Because the Rasch rating model does not require that the distances between thresholds are equal, the integer score on each rating is not itself a measure. However, the parameter estimates are on a linear scale and are measures up to an interval level. With respect to a conformable set of statements or tasks, the only difference between usual measures and those estimated through the Rasch model for ratings is one of degree. The precision can be increased by increasing the number of tasks or statements. Thus the Rasch rating model formally completes the measurement analogy.

A related aspect of the Rasch rating model is that it formalizes the popular and simple, yet theoretically weak, Likert approach to the attitude measurement of individuals. Likert had originally proposed his approach to circumvent the time-consuming requirement of scaling statements required by the approaches of Thurstone. The formalization permits the Likert approach to subscribe to all the rigorous requirements of Thurstone for scales including the scaling of tasks or statements. In particular, and with respect to a conformable set of tasks or statements, any subset will lead to the same measure of a person. Similarly, the scale values of the statements and thresholds will be invariant across the abilities or attitudes of the persons measured. The linearity and this form of invariance are key aspects of Thurstone Scales. Andrich (1982) presents a full discussion of the way the Rasch rating model unifies the Thurstone and Likert approaches to scaling and measurement.

## 6. Quality Control

It should be appreciated that these invariance properties hold in observed responses only if they conform with the Thurstone or Rasch models. Thus, the Rating Model will connect ratings to measurements only if these ratings conform to the model, and whether or not they do so conform is an empirical question.

There are two related advantages with the above explicit measurement model to which the ratings may be expected to conform. The obvious one is that the measures, not simply ratings, are available. The second, and equally important, is that in the very process of attempting to obtain formal measurements, a greater understanding of the variable or trait in question should follow. A close examination of response patterns which do not conform to the rating model may be as informative in understanding the variable as when they do conform, and the Rasch rating model permits a refined analysis which detects lack of conformity in various ways. These issues are discussed in detail in Wright and Masters (1982).

### 6.1 The Response Pattern

One important and necessary feature for measurement, which can be checked, is whether the response pattern is internally consistent. According to the rating model, every person is expected to score higher on an easier question in achievement testing, or a smaller affective value in attitude measurement. If the ratings do not conform satisfactorily to this pattern, then a single measure to represent the responses cannot be justified.

### 6.2 The "Halo" Effect

There can be many sources of inconsistency, as in all measurement data. When judges rate performances, a judge may gain an overall impression which affects all ratings of the performance, even if these ratings are supposed to reflect different criteria. This is called the "halo" effect. The ratings in this case are "too consistent" as a result of the artificial dependence among them.

### 6.3 Rater Leniency

In performance ratings, some raters may be more lenient or more harsh than others. If more than one rater rates with respect to a single task, then the Rating Model accounts for this effect. In particular, when $\delta$ is made to characterize the rater, it represents rater harshness. Alternatively, if more than one rater and more than one task is involved, then the exponent in Eqn. (2) may be further modified to include the rater effect. For example, it may take the form $x(\beta_n - \delta_i - \eta_j) - \Sigma_{k=1} \tau_k$ where $\eta_j$ is the harshness of rater $j$. Other qualifications are also possible.

### 6.4 Response Sets

Another possible systematic source of inconsistency occurs when different individuals use the categories differently. For example, some raters may use the extreme categories, while others may use the central categories, relatively too often. Both types of response patterns, reflecting what are known as response sets, can threaten valid measurement.

### 6.5 Number of Categories and the Neutral Category

In constructing rating response formats which will minimize the above problems, two further issues need to be considered. Firstly, the number of categories should be large enough to take advantage of the judge's capacity to discriminate, but not greater. Guilford (1954 Chap. 11) gives empirical evidence to guide the choice of the number of categories. Usually four or five are used for unipolar scales and five to nine for bipolar scales.

Secondly, in bipolar scales, the "neutral" or "undecided" category has been the subject of much study. It seems not to attract responses consistent with those found on either side of it, it being a "catch all" category in which people who do not understand the question, as well as people who are genuinely undecided, or neutral, respond. It seems best to construct statements which would attract few responses in this category, and then to exclude the category when the statements are used to obtain measures.

## Bibliography

Andrich D 1978 A rating formulation for ordered response categories. *Psychometrika* 43: 561–73

Andrich D 1979 A model for contingency tables having an ordered response classification. *Biometrics* 35: 403–15

Andrich D 1982 Using latent trait measurement models to analyse attitudinal data: A synthesis of viewpoints. In: Spearritt D (ed.) 1982 *The Improvement of Measurement in Education and Psychology*. Australian Council for Educational Research, Hawthorn, Victoria

Bock R D 1975 *Multivariate Statistical Methods in Behavioral Research*. McGraw-Hill, New York

Dawes R M 1972 *Fundamentals of Attitude Measurement*. Wiley, New York

Guilford J P 1954 *Psychometric Methods*, 2nd edn. McGraw-Hill, New York

Likert R 1932 A technique for the measurement of attitudes. *Arch Psychol*. No. 140

Masters G N 1982 A Rasch model for partial credit scoring. *Psychometrika* 47: 149–74

Masters G N 1988 Measurement models for ordered response categories. In: Langeheine R, Rost J (eds.) 1988 *Latent Trait and Latent Class Models*. Plenum, New York

Masters G N, Wright B D 1984 The essential process in a family of measurement models. *Psychometrika* 49: 529–44

Samejima F 1969 Estimation of latent ability using a response pattern of graded scores. *Psychometric Monogr*. Supplement 13(4)

Thurstone L L 1927 Psychological Analysis. *Am. J. Psychol*. 38: 368–89

Wright B D, Masters G N 1982 *Rating Scale Analysis*. MESA Press, Chicago, Illinois

# Scaling Achievement Test Scores

## J. P. Keeves

This article is concerned with the scaling procedures that are employed in the field of education, not only to make the scores on achievement tests more readily interpretable in a variety of practical situations but also, and more importantly, to strengthen the scores resulting from the assessment of educational achievement so that more effective and meaningful analyses can be carried out on the data, and more valid conclusions can be obtained. The article considers the types of scales used in the assessment of performance on achievement tests, the classes of scaling models used, the alternative approaches to scaling available for the obtaining of achievement test scores, the scaling procedures used for converting achievement test scores to measures on specific scales, the equating of different test forms, and the moderation of scores obtained using different scales. There is growing recognition that latent trait procedures will in the future perform an important function in scaling, equating, and moderation and that there is a need for research in this field of educational measurement. Consideration is limited to the scaling of achievement test data. Other aspects of scaling are examined in other articles (see *Scaling Methods*).

## 1. Preliminary Steps to Scaling Students' Responses

Prior to undertaking scaling it is necessary to carry out one or more of the necessary preliminary steps of (a) classifying, (b) ordering, and (c) measuring. These processes are defined as follows:

(a) Classifying is the process of assigning students' responses to qualitatively different classes or categories.

(b) Ordering is the process of ranking students' responses to qualitatively different classes or categories.

(c) Measuring is the process of estimating the location of the students' responses (or ordered categories) on an underlying trait. Locations are expressed in terms of some unit that retains a consistent meaning across all locations.

### 1.1 Types of Scales

The assessment of students' responses involves the assigning of numbers to the individual students for their responses according to some defined rule. The rule specifies a quantitative aspect of a response with respect to the categories of an attribute, and thus defines the scale which is used for obtaining the associated measures. In this operation, four types of data exist. The four types of data involve four properties which the data may or may not possess. These properties are:

(a) identity: the responses that are classified together into one category are identical in nature;

(b) transitivity or order: the responses may be ranked in order from least to greatest or greatest to least;

(c) metric: the responses can be quantitatively distinguished from each other in terms of a fixed or constant sized unit of measurement;

(d) functional zero: the underlying scale of measurement has a known functional zero point and the measurements made are related to this functional zero point.

The types of scales and related data arise from these four properties.

(a) *Categorical or nominal data.* These possess identity only. For example, students may be classed into categories according to whether they answered a multiple-choice test item correctly or incorrectly, indicated that they guessed the answer, or omitted the item. These four types of response are essentially categorical in nature. Neverthelesss, the presence of a response could be scored +1 and the absence of a response scored 0, and a very crude scale could be formed. More elaborate procedures have been developed for the scaling of such data.

(b) *Ordinal scales and data.* These possess both identity and transitivity properties. For example, students' essays may be classified into one of five ordered classes in which placement in a higher class is associated with superior performance than that required for those essays placed in a lower class. Much of the data collected in educational research studies is essentially ordinal in nature, and a wide range of procedures has been developed in order to scale these data.

(c) *Interval scales and data.* These possess the properties of identity, transitivity, and metric. In the measurement of educational achievement, for example, in assessing the number of correct responses to a sample of 50 items on a test of a limited domain of knowledge such as knowledge of the basic number facts, an interval scale is frequently assumed. However, achievement measured in this way does not involve the use of a truly interval scale. Latent trait measurement procedures seek ways of converting such data into measures on a scale that approximates more closely to an interval scale. These measurement procedures are discussed more extensively below.

(d) *Ratio scales and data.* These possess all four properties of identity, transitivity, metric, and a functional zero. For example, a student may take 5 minutes 25 seconds to solve a specified problem. Here time is measured on a ratio scale. The functional zero is that time at which the student commenced work on the problem.

Togerson (1958) has drawn attention to a fifth type of scale, namely an ordinal scale with a natural origin, rather than a functional zero. Such scales include bipolar attitude scales, where the uncertain category provides a natural origin. A simple ordinal scale of achievement associated with number of books read during a semester would have a natural origin that also had the characteristics of a functional zero.

In order to investigate relationships between variables in educational research, it is desirable to obtain measures on a scale which permits the data to hold as many of the four properties as possible. By employing an interval scale instead of an ordinal scale to make observations in the investigation of an educational problem, it is possible to add and subtract measures, and by using a ratio scale instead of an interval scale multiplication and division may also be applied to the measures. Thus the strength of such scales and the data they provide may range from strong ratio scales and the associated measures to relatively weak ordinal scales and measures.

In the analysis of data different statistical procedures have been developed for data possessing different properties, and since the power of these analytical techniques increases with the strength of the scales employed, considerable effort is directed towards increasing the strength of the scales used in educational research and practice. These attempts to improve the strength of the scales, and the data they yield, must be seen to be different from the efforts made to increase the accuracy of the data by more careful measurement or by more effective sampling. Scaling as a procedure in educational measurement is directed towards upgrading the data by the use of operations that will change the properties of the data with respect to transitivity and metric. For example, the rankings of essay markers are subject to error as a consequence of both within-judge errors (which arise when a judge fails to discriminate consistently) and between-judge errors (when judges differ in the rankings they assign). These rankings form at least an ordinal scale. Through the multiple marking of the essays by two or more judges, and through the use of an average ranking, the strength of the scale can be increased. Similarly, the percentage of passes achieved by a class group on an examination scored 1 and failures on the examination scored 0, are at least quasi-interval data and the strength of the scale concerned with the proportion passing can be increased through the use of the logit transformation (Snedecor and Cochran 1967) prior to analysis. The use of logits transforms the data to a normal distribution that has many properties that facilitate the analysis of the data.

## 2. Achievement Test Scores and Scales

The strategies employed in the measurement of educational achievement are, in general, based upon samples of student behaviours that are responses to requests for the student to perform clearly identified tasks. Commonly, achievement tests employ multiple-choice test items which are questions with alternative answers provided, from which the student must choose the most appropriate answer. This answer must be indicated by a pencil mark on a printed paper booklet or separate paper answer sheet. Tightly specified instructions are provided by the examiner. If the student is well-motivated to perform in this test situation, and if the student has understood correctly the examiner's instructions, it is assumed that the pencil and paper record will provide an accurate measure of the student's level of achievement on the field of tasks under survey. Other types of behaviour can be assessed in a similar way by, for example, constructing a response, writing an extended answer, pressing an identified key on a keyboard of a computer terminal, or by an observer observing behaviour and making a record of the type of behaviour observed. For the simplest types of test items, and using the simplest scoring procedure, a student is assigned a score of $+1$ for each response that is classed as correct, and 0 for each response that is classed as incorrect. Because of the complex structures associated with the organization of knowledge in the mind of each student, the responses made on one question are not completely independent of answers to other questions. However, it is generally assumed that each question answered, and each score $+1$ or 0, has provided an independent sample of student behaviour.

### 2.1 Sources of Error

It is also assumed that the number of correct responses made by a student has a rough one-to-one relation to the amount of knowledge possessed by the student in the area under investigation or to the student's ability to perform the skill being measured. Likewise, it is assumed that there is a strong one-to-one relation between the response made by the student and the score assigned in the scoring process. However, each response made by the student or each score assigned has a component of error associated with it, which arises from several sources.

(a) The response made by a student may exhibit random fluctuations associated with factors such as carelessness that are not related to the extent of knowledge held by the student.

(b) Since it is rarely possible to require students to respond to a complete population of tasks associated with an area of knowledge or performance it is necessary, in general, to sample behaviour by requiring a limited number of tasks to be answered. Consequently, there are errors associated with the sampling of tasks from the total population of such tasks.

(c) Although it is common to develop procedures that are standardized and objective, errors can occur in the scoring process. It is assumed that such errors are the result of random fluctuations in the scoring process and are not related to the extent of knowledge held by the student.

(d) There is a further source of error associated with the appropriateness of the rule involved in defining the scale which is used in the measurement process for the type of performance being assessed. If the errors associated with this source are systematic they can be detected and adjustments made. However, commonly such errors are not systematic and, like the other three types of error, can be considered to be random fluctuations which have arisen in the measurement process. The existence of such errors is common in all types of measurement.

## 2.2 Scaling Methods

The problems confronting research workers engaged in educational measurement are those of constructing a scale that has the properties of transitivity, metric, and if possible a functional zero, as well as the property of identity, so that the separate scores on individual items or tasks can be used to indicate extent of achievement on a defined scale. The functions of theory and practice in educational measurement are to upgrade the procedures involved in the measurement process, so that the measures obtained possess as fully as possible these four properties. The use of an appropriate scaling procedure is an important step in the measurement process, and much of the work of scaling involves transforming data that are essentially ordinal in nature to interval data with metric properties.

There are three broad classes of scaling models that can be employed with educational achievement tests. First, there are those scaling models that are concerned with attributes of the stimulus tasks to which the student is asked to respond. Second, there are those scaling models that are concerned with the attributes of the responder in relation to a defined population of responders. In these models there is dependence on differences between individuals in their attributes or characteristics and in their observed behaviour in order to establish an appropriate scale. However, since it is rarely possible to administer a test to a complete population of students, it is necessary to employ an appropriate sample of students and, as a consequence, errors of sampling are introduced into the measurement process in order to establish the scale of measurement. Third, there are those scaling models in which both the stimulus tasks and the responders are assigned scale values. In these scaling models the purpose of the scale is to assign scale values to both the stimulus tasks and to the responders. This third model assumes specifically that there is an underlying latent trait of performance that is common to both individuals and tasks and that the items or tasks employed assess performance of the individuals with respect to that latent trait.

## 2.3 Approaches to Measurement

There are also two broad approaches to measurement in education and psychology that are employed to con-

vert the scores on individual tasks to measures on a defined scale. In the first approach to measurement it is assumed that extent of knowledge or level of performance in the area under investigation is in some sense cumulative along a linear dimension. In addition, it is assumed that there is an identity relationship, with allowance made for the types of errors considered above, between the amount of knowledge that each individual possesses, or the level of performance of each individual, and the algebraic sum of the scores assigned for individual items. These assumptions have led to two separate theories of measurement—classical test theory and random sampling theory. The difference between these two theories lies in the emphasis placed in the latter on the random sampling of items or tasks from a specified population of tasks. These models are essentially deterministic models. Using these theories of measurement the scales developed are at best quasi-interval scales.

Nevertheless, there are significant problems with this class of theories, particularly within classical test theory. Suppose that an 80-item test has been developed comprising multiple-choice items, with four distractors, which are arranged in order of difficulty from the easiest to the hardest items. Suppose one student answers correctly the first 40 items and a random one-quarter of the remainder. With a simple scoring procedure, in which each item answered correctly is scored +1, each item answered incorrectly is scored 0, and the scores on individual items are added together, this student would obtain a total score of 50. Then suppose a second student answers correctly the 40 odd-numbered items, and a random one-quarter of the even-numbered items. Under the same scoring procedure this student would also obtain a total score of 50. These two students exhibit extreme and perhaps artificially different patterns of response. However, there are likely to be significant differences in the levels of achievement of the two students, because the latter student was able to answer correctly more hard items, even though missing many easy items, while the former student obtained the same score largely by getting more easy items right. In general, this approach to measurement takes no cognizance of attributes of the responders to the test items. It considers only the characteristics of the items. However, some work has been undertaken to investigate the problem typified by the patterns of responses of the two students (Harnisch and Linn 1981).

In order to overcome this problem between the two different types of attribute involved in the calculation of scores, namely, the characteristics of the responders and the characteristics of the stimulus tasks, it is necessary to assume the existence of an underlying latent trait that is common both to all responders as well as to all the stimulus tasks or test items which are used. Both stimulus tasks and individual responders are located at levels along a scale defined by the latent trait. The level of performance of an individual responder on this latent trait scale is that level at which the responder would answer correctly with a specified degree of probability a stimulus task located at that level. Commonly, a probability of 0.50 is employed. Thus it might be expected that an individual responder would answer correctly more than 50 percent of the tasks below this level and answer incorrectly more than 50 percent of the tasks above this level. In a similar manner the location of a stimulus task or test item on this scale is identified in terms of the probability that a specified proportion, commonly 50 percent of responders located at that level, would answer correctly the item associated with the task. Whereas the first approaches to measurement described above were deterministic in nature with a regard to the location of items or individuals on a scale, this second approach to measurement, namely latent trait theory, is essentially probabilistic in nature.

In latent trait measurement the stimulus task or achievement test item must be designed in such a way that responders depend on the latent attribute which the examiner is seeking to measure in order to answer it correctly. Consequently, for an item to be acceptable, the probability of a responder answering correctly the item must increase regularly as the level of standing of the responder on the latent trait increases. In Fig. 1 the probability $P_g(\theta)$, of a responder with ability $\theta$ scoring 1 on an item $g$ is plotted against $\theta$. This relationship between probability of success and the latent trait is known as the item characteristic curve.

In general, an item characteristic curve can be described by three parameters:

(a) $a_g$, the steepness of the curve, or the discrimination index;

(b) $b_g$, the difficulty of the item;

(c) $c_g$, chance level of success on the item.

Two mathematical models are available for theoretical work on test items and the tests that are produced using the latent trait approach. The first uses the normal curve function of the form:

$$P_g(\theta) = \int (b_g - \theta)\theta(t)\,dt$$

where the symbols in the formula are defined above.

The second model is the logistic function of the form:

$$P_g(\theta) = C_g + \frac{1 - C_g}{1 + e^{-Da_g(\theta - b_g)}}$$

where the symbols have been defined above, and $D$ is a constant of scale, according to the units in which $\theta$ is recorded, so that the scale units for the logistic function are equivalent to those for the normal curve function.

These two functions, the logistic function and the normal curve function yield very similar results. The advantage of one over the other lies largely in the mathematics of subsequent analytical and computational work in which the functions are employed.

Independently of the development and use of these two functions in educational measurement Rasch proposed the use of the logistic function, in a form in which the parameter $a_g$ for the slope of the item characteristic curve is considered uniform across all items, and the chance level of success $c_g$, is considered to be zero.

We may wish to calculate an expected score on a set of items which are located at different levels on the latent trait continuum and so to plot a test characteristic curve between test scores and scores on the latent attribute. The expected number of correct responses for a given value of $\theta$ can be found by obtaining the probability of success on each item separately ($P_g\theta$) and then summing the $P$ values over items to give the expected score. Using the logistic function form we obtain

$$E(x\mid\theta) = \sum_{g=1}^{n} P_g(\theta) = \sum_{g=1}^{n} C_g + \frac{1 - C_g}{1 + e^{-Da_g(\theta - b_g)}}$$

A typical test characteristic curve for an 80-item multiple choice test with four alternatives is shown in Fig. 2.

The test characteristic curve shows the correspondence between expected scores of responders and the scale defined on the latent attribute. It is clear that equal increments in raw scores do not correspond with equal increments in $\theta$ across the range of the latent attribute scale. Thus the scaling procedure has provided an equal interval scale which has considerable advantages in ana-

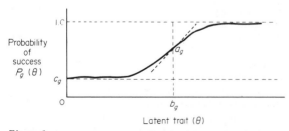

*Figure 1*
Item characteristic curve

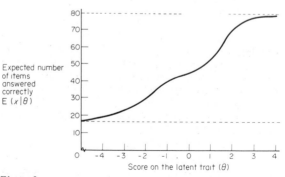

*Figure 2*
Test characteristic curve

lytical work. However, it should be noted that while the raw score scale appears to have a functional zero, the existence of this zero point is artificial insofar as guessing on items with four alternatives is likely to take place. Consequently the lowest score with a very high level of probability for a correct response commonly lies between 0 and 20. Moreover, it will be noted that the latent attribute scale clearly does not have a functional zero, and as a consequence this scale is not a ratio scale but an interval scale.

## 3. Scaling

Thorndike (1982) has identified four types of procedures that are used for converting achievement test scores to measures on specific scales. They can employ one or other of the three scaling models, namely, attributes of the stimulus task, attributes of the responder, or the latent trait model in which both stimulus tasks and responders are considered. The converted score values are assumed to have the properties of an interval scale, although the raw data are clearly not interval data. However, the extent to which an interval scale is achieved varies considerably. In addition, in the conversion of scores to a new scale consideration is customarily given to the meaning that can be attached to the scale values employed, and care is often taken to avoid conversion scales that have similar values to the percentile scales and the IQ scales.

### 3.1 Linear Score Conversions

Linear score conversions, in general, simply transform the raw score scale to a more convenient scale. It is assumed that the raw score distribution obtained by adding together scores on individual items indicates, in at least an adequate way, the distribution of the attribute assessed by the set of items. As a consequence no attempt is made to change the shape of the distribution of raw scores. The linear conversion formula is

$$Z(x) = X_s = S_s \frac{(X_r - \bar{X}_r)}{S_r} + \bar{X}_s$$

where $X$ refers to score values, $\bar{X}$ refers to score mean values, $S$ refers to standard deviations, $r$ refers to the raw score values, and $s$ refers to the standard score values.

Scores which have been converted in this way to a standard score scale are generally referred to as standard scores. Commonly occurring scales are $50 - 10$ scores ($\bar{X} = 50$, $S = 10$); $Z$ scores ($\bar{X} = 0$, $S = 1$); College Board scores ($\bar{X} = 500$, $S = 100$).

Figure 3 shows an example of a raw score frequency distribution expressed as $Z$ scores in standard deviation units.

### 3.2 Area Conversions

Area conversions are, in general, employed when the shape of the raw score distribution is considered inap-

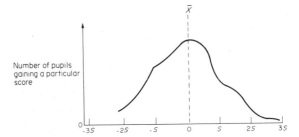

**Figure 3**
Example of raw score frequency distribution expressed in standard deviation units

propriate. It must be assumed that the distribution of the attribute in the population under survey can be characterized by a known frequency distribution, or that the statistical and analytical procedures being employed in the examination of the data require a particular type of distribution. Under these circumstances it is appropriate to convert the raw scores to a scale with the defined distribution. In this scale conversion, equal areas associated with the cumulative frequency distributions of the raw scores and the scores which are associated with a defined scale are equated.

In situations where it is desired to obtain a maximum spread of scores, the *rectangular distribution* is defined to be the underlying score distribution. Such a spread of scores arises in practice where all items are at the 50 percent difficulty level. However, where maximum spread is required and the items do not have a common difficulty level of 50 percent, the rectangular distribution is employed. This conversion is readily applied in the case of percentile ranks to yield centile scores, and decile ranks to yield decile scores.

In situations where multivariate analyses are carried out, the statistical tests are based on the multivariate *normal distribution*. There are also cases where the analytical procedures being used assume the multivariate normal distribution. For example, in linear structural relations analysis (LISREL), the shape of the distribution of the criterion measures must be known, and commonly a normal distribution is selected. While it is unlikely that proof can be obtained to support the assumption of a normal distribution, several sources of evidence recommend the choice of this distribution in practice. First where raw scores are added together and averaged, the central limit theorem indicates that averaged scores tend quite rapidly to a normal distribution. Second, where in nature an attribute is generated by many small, independent causes, a normal distribution of that attribute in a population might be expected. This assumption requires that a large probability sample has been drawn from the population, so that the score distribution in the sample will approximate to that occurring in the population. Third, where a test is comprised of a large number of independent items scored +1 and 0, the negative hypergeometric

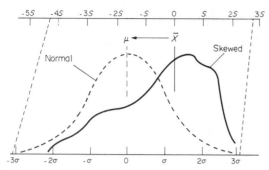

**Figure 4**
Skewed, transformed to normal distribution

**Table 1**
Details of stanine scale

| Stanine | Z score range | Centile score range | Population percentage in stanine |
|---|---|---|---|
| 9 | +1.75 and over | 96–99 | 4 |
| 8 | +1.25 to +1.75 | 89–95 | 7 |
| 7 | +0.75 to +1.25 | 77–88 | 12 |
| 6 | +0.25 to +0.75 | 60–76 | 17 |
| 5 | −0.25 to +0.25 | 41–59 | 20 |
| 4 | −0.75 to −0.25 | 24–40 | 17 |
| 3 | −1.25 to −0.75 | 12–23 | 12 |
| 2 | −1.75 to −1.25 | 5–11 | 7 |
| 1 | −1.75 and below | 1–4 | 4 |

distribution provides the theoretical underlying score distribution, but with a large number of items this can be approximated to by the normal distribution.

Conversion of raw scores to a normal distribution is undertaken by means of the probit transformation (Fisher and Yates 1963). With this score conversion procedure the cumulative frequency distribution of the raw scores is calculated and scores associated with that distribution are converted to normal standard scores in order to correspond with equal areas under the normal curve whose equation is given by

$$P(X) = \int_{-\infty}^{\infty} \frac{1}{\sqrt{2\pi}} \exp\left(\frac{-x^2}{2}\right) dx$$

Commonly occurring scales are normal standard scores ($\bar{X} = 0$, $S = 1$), and IQ deviation scores ($\bar{X} = 100$, $S = 15$).

Figure 4 illustrates the conversion of a skewed raw score distribution to a normal standard score distribution. It should be noted that the phrases "normalized, standard" scores or "normal standardized" scores have not been used. "Standardized" score is a term that has generally been reserved for other somewhat arbitrary conversion systems, while the term "standard" score is reserved for Z scores, and closely related scales. Likewise, to a mathematician "normalizing" involves producing scores each equal to Z with the sum of squares (instead of the standard deviation) set at N or unity; a procedure that does not involve the normal distribution.

A commonly used scale is the stanine scale, which also involves an equal area conversion procedure. In Table 1, details of the stanine scale and its relation to the Z score range and the centile range, together with the proportion of the population in each stanine score category, are recorded.

A similar scale is the sten scale that has a mean value of 5.5 and 10 score categories. Figure 5 shows the normal distribution score equivalents for the Z scale, the IQ deviation scale, centiles, stens, and stanines.

### 3.3 Age and Grade Conversions

Age and grade scaling involves the making of the assumption that a year of growth in the attribute being

measured represents an equal unit whether there is concern for years of schooling as provided by the grade index or years of natural development as provided by the age index. The two aspects are necessarily related, but there seems little basis for the supposition that for individuals, development or schooling occur uniformly; although for populations, individual fluctuations will probably average out. Nevertheless, both age and grade norms are widely employed as indexes of growth and learning with respect to such attributes as intelligence, verbal ability, reading, vocabulary, numerical ability, arithmetic achievement, and spatial ability (Lindquist 1951).

Since the construction of age and grade scales is dependent on attributes of the students who responded to the tests in the particular areas of educational achievement, it is essential that high quality representative samples from the specified age and grade populations should be drawn in order to establish standards of performance at the age and grade levels under investigation. While in general the evidence obtained by those engaged in norming studies to develop appropriate scales indicates that marked fluctuations do not

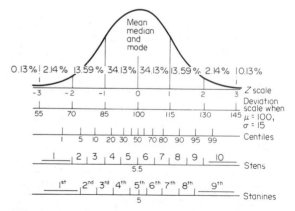

**Figure 5**
Some normal distribution scale equivalents

occur, and that sampling irregularities can be smoothed by the careful drawing of norming curves, the errors associated with the construction of such scales have commonly been underestimated. Particular problems arise through sampling errors associated with non-response bias and the clustering of students in schools, to the extent that the effective numbers of students in samples are commonly many times smaller than the numbers of students who were tested. Further problems arise for both age and grade norming from the fact that reading and arithmetic performance is dependent on the time of the school year at which testing was undertaken. However, the procedures of interpolation assume that growth in the attribute being measured occurs uniformly across a school grade or a year of life.

Thorndike (1982 p. 109) has summarized the basic steps involved in constructing age and grade scales:

(a) Obtain large and representative probability samples of students from the target populations, so that stable estimates with known errors of sampling can be calculated.

(b) Administer the tests to the samples at appropriate age and grade levels.

(c) Determine the average raw score for each age or grade grouping. Where possible with age samples subdivide each year sample into three-month subgroups. These scores are then assigned to the specific age and grade values.

(d) Interpolate between successive age and grade levels to determine an age and grade equivalent for each raw score on the tests.

(e) Extrapolate beyond the lowest and highest age and grade levels at which testing occurred in order to locate scale values at the tails of the raw score distribution.

(f) Construct a table showing age and grade equivalents for each raw score value.

Interpolation and extrapolation can be carried out graphically where straight lines do not appear appropriate. However, where straight lines can be drawn, numerical estimates can be readily calculated. Sometimes theoretical score distributions such as the negative hypergeometric distribution or the normal distribution are employed, with these distributions being fitted to the data. With the increased availability of computers some attempts have been made to fit empirical curves to age and grade data in order to improve the accuracy with which the age and grade norms are estimated. For a more detailed account of norming procedures Angoff (1971) should be consulted.

Since the early 1970s there has been some criticism of the use of tests that have been normed by procedures of age and grade conversion, or standardized, as the scaling process is commonly called. However, normed tests continue to be extensively used in such countries as the United States and the United Kingdom.

## 3.4 Latent Trait Scaling

Latent trait scaling is a technique that is being used increasingly for the scaling of ability and achievement tests in both educational and psychological research and practice. Different methods of latent trait scaling have been developed using variations of the statistical model involving the logistic function given above. The simplest and most widely used model is the one parameter or Rasch model which employs the location parameter only. Use is also being made of a variation of the three-parameter model, which employs the difficulty parameter and the guessing parameter, but because of problems in obtaining convergence in the estimates of the three parameters, the third parameter—the discrimination parameter—is sometimes set at a fixed value for all items. The two-parameter model which involves the difficulty and the discrimination parameters does not appear to have been widely used in practical applications. In addition, variations of the general logistic function have been developed for use with attitude scales and rating scales and for use with polychotomous responses where partial credit is given for a less than complete answer. In the paragraphs that follow only the use of the Rasch model for scaling will be extensively discussed.

The use of a latent trait approach requires the assumption of a clearly defined underlying trait associated with a specific dimension of knowledge or skill, together with the assumption that individual respondents can be located at specific positions along the defined continuum. This approach does not demand a hypothetical universe of items from which random samples of items can be drawn, although it could work within such a situation. However, it does postulate that the response of a student to a given item is a function of the responder's position on the continuum associated with the latent trait, together with random error. For a set of items, the error terms associated with each item in the set must be uncorrelated with each other and with the latent trait. This assumption is referred to as one of local independence of the items and implies a unidimensional trait. If the items have been chosen in such a way that they are related to a highly specific educational achievement objective or with a specific ability, experience has established that the statistical procedures employed work well. Nonetheless, as Bejar has pointed out:

> ... unidimensionality does not imply that performance on the items is due to a single psychological process. In fact, a variety of psychological processes are involved in the act of responding to a set of items. However, as long as they function in unison—that is, the performance on each item is affected by the same processes and in the same form—unidimensionality will hold. As a violation of this principle, consider an achievement test, some of the items in which call for numerical computation, whereas the rest of the items call for the recall of factual material. If within the populations being tested with this instrument there is variability with respect to numerical ability, then the performance

on the test as a whole will depend on that ability and achievement. (Bejar 1983 p. 31)

In the illustration of the Rasch model on the following pages a primary-school mathematics test associated in the main with numerical computation has been chosen as an appropriate application of the use of these procedures. All questions are constructed response items and not multiple-choice items, so that a guessing parameter is not required in the model. Furthermore, the items in the test do not have widely discrepant discrimination indexes, so that the discrimination parameter need not be included in the model.

The Rasch model uses the logistic function to relate the position of the items on the scale associated with the latent attribute to the probability of success on the item. According to this model, when the difficulty of an item and the ability level of the group of students just match, 50 percent of the students will get the item right and 50 percent will get it wrong, or the odds are even, or one to one.

The odds of getting an item right can be stated as:

$$\frac{P_i}{N - P_i}$$

where $N$ is the total number of students in the group and $P_i$ is the number of persons in the group getting the item right.

Using the logistic function, with the natural logarithm this ratio can be restated as follows:

$$b - d_i = \log\left(\frac{P_i}{N - P_i}\right)$$

where $b$ is the ability or achievement level of the group, and $d_i$ is difficulty parameter of item $i$ when

$$b = d_i, \quad \log\left(\frac{P_i}{N - P_i}\right) = 0 \quad \text{and} \quad \frac{P_i}{N - P_i} = 1$$

so that the proportion of correct responses $P_i$ is 0.50. In Table 2 the proportion of correct responses corresponding to integral scale values of $b - d_i$ are recorded.

The nature of the relationship specified for an item, with respect to the scale associated with the latent attribute, is assumed to remain unchanged with changes

**Table 2**
Proportion of correct responses for integral scale values

| $b - d_i$ | percentage correct |
|-----------|--------------------|
| +3.0 | 95 |
| +2.0 | 88 |
| +1.0 | 73 |
| 0.0 | 50 |
| −1.0 | 27 |
| −2.0 | 12 |
| −3.0 | 5 |

in mean level of performance and the spread in performance of the group of responders. Thus the analysis is considered to be largely sample-free. A systematic investigation of sampling errors associated with different sample sizes and different sample types by Farish (1984), has shown that small sampling errors can be expected. The effects of sampling will be greatest where the students responding have been subjected to different curricula, and where there is not a perfect fit of the data with the latent attribute. Thus the analyses will only be sample-free where perfect fit occurs, and the items are in agreement with the specified relationship (Douglas 1982).

Once a reference point for locating the scale of the latent attribute has been chosen, the zero point for the scale determined by analysis for a set of items and persons can be referred to this reference point. Likewise, an appropriate spread of scores can be chosen and can be related to the scale units found from the analysis of the data. Thus while the zero point and spread of scores remains arbitrary, it is possible to define an appropriate and meaningful scale. A variety of procedures are available for the analysis of the data in order to estimate the scale values and with large sample sizes, where there is concern for maximum precision, the use of a maximum likelihood procedure would seem to be the most satisfactory. Wright and Stone (1979) should be consulted for a more detailed account of appropriate procedures.

In Fig. 6, a kid-map for a student is presented in the form of a mathematics report to students, parents, and teachers. A scale has been defined with a mean score of 250 and a scale unit of 20 score points. It is evident from the figure that both the students and the items can be located on the same scale through the use of the Rasch scaling procedure. The student whose performance is recorded in Fig. 6 has a mean score of 280 on this scale with a relatively small error as indicated by the upper and lower boundaries of the box in the kid-map. An error in responding to the item $(5 \times 18 = ?)$ is unexpected since the difficulty of the item is marginally below the expected level of performance on the scale. However, the remaining items that have not been mastered are above the expected performance level. The kid-map provides not only information on level of achievement and reports the type of test items that have and have not been mastered but it also provides information of a diagnostic nature for teachers. It is possible that the incorrect response to the item $(5 \times 18 = ?)$ was the result of a careless error. However it is also possible that the skill of carrying in multiplication had not been mastered. It would seem appropriate for a teacher to select multiplication items at the level between 270 and 290. These items should then be used to diagnose further the problems experienced by the student in calculating answers to items which were appropriate to the expected level of performance and were equivalent in difficulty to the item that the student might have been expected to answer

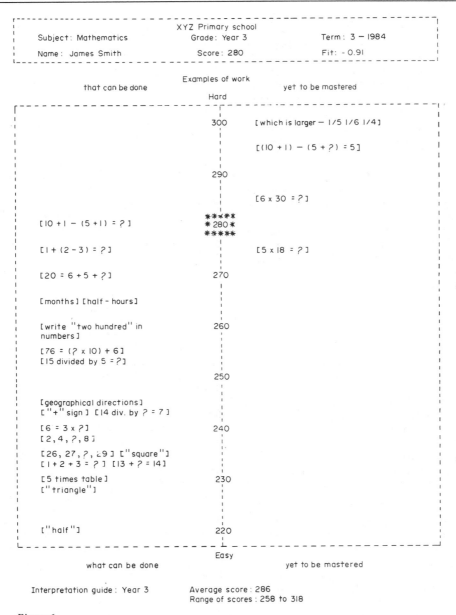

**Figure 6**
Kid-map

correctly but had not mastered. Maps of student performance, class group performance, and levels of difficulty of individual items provide information of both a mastery and diagnostic nature by combining student performance and item difficulty on a single scale.

A scale developed by latent trait scaling procedures can be likened to a ladder of achievement. The student is able to climb this achievement ladder, and at an appropriate rung a diagnostic test can be used to identify accurately particular weaknesses in the student's performance, as well as to identify curricular areas where

the student is ready for further instruction. The principles of student assessment which have been discussed with respect to the performance of an individual student can be extended to yield evidence on the performance of class groups, and thus to provide information on which a teacher could base classroom instruction.

## 4. Equating Test Forms

Where test items are sampled at random from a universe of test items, or where test items are constructed to specification or to match existing items, it is possible to generate what are known as parallel forms of a test. Such parallel forms of a test do not, in general, have identical mean values or standard deviations. However, it is assumed that the parallel forms of a test are strongly correlated, and that the associated correlation coefficient does not differ significantly from 1.0. Under these circumstances it is possible to equate the parallel forms of a test so that equivalence can be maintained. Further problems are encountered in measuring achievement outcomes in longitudinal studies in so far as it is clearly inappropriate to use the identical test instruments at different age levels, and it is commonly necessary to make changes to the test items between occasions. Nonetheless, it is possible to construct tests that have common items across adjacent age or grade levels, and that have common items at the same level between occasions. The equating of tests using common items between age or grade levels is referred to as vertical equating, while the equating of tests administered at the same level between occasions is referred to as horizontal equating. In theory the same procedure could be used for vertical equating as for horizontal equating. Nevertheless, it must be recognized that in practice, because of ceiling and floor effects in vertical equating, and because of substantial curriculum change effects in horizontal equating, significant problems may be encountered in maintaining a high level of equivalence between the tests employed in longitudinal studies.

Three general procedures are available for use to bring achievement test scores to a common scale. These procedures correspond in kind to those described above in the discussion of scaling, namely linear score conversion, equal area score conversion, and latent trait scaling. The further approach referred to above—of age and grade conversion—involved setting up a scale that had an external frame of reference, and the equating of parallel forms of tests would become redundant if each parallel form had been scaled by conversion to an age or grade scale. It is of course possible to equate parallel forms before carrying out the conversion of one of the forms to an age or grade scale. However, it should be noted that age and grade scales are rarely constructed with sufficient accuracy to permit their use in longitudinal research studies.

The article will only consider the general issues associated with the equating of tests. A general introduction is provided by Angoff (1971) and by Thorndike (1982). A comprehensive technical discussion of the problems of test equating is given in the volume edited by Holland and Rubin (1982).

### 4.1 Linear Equating

The procedure of linear equating is appropriately used whenever the shapes of the two raw score distributions being equated are the same, or when it can be assumed that both the test items and the persons tested represent appropriate samples for the measurement of an attribute that has a specified distribution with respect to both test items and persons. The scores are converted to standard scores, commonly to a mean of zero and a standard deviation of one, and the line of equivalence is used to equate one set of scores with the other (see Angoff 1971 p. 569). This procedure was used in the First IEA Science Study to bring scores on the science tests, which were administered across countries and across three age levels, to a common scale. The data available on common items were used to establish two lines of equivalence for the 10-year-old to the 14-year-old age levels, and for the 14-year-old to the terminal secondary-school levels respectively, by pooling data to obtain three grand mean values and the corresponding grand standard deviations. National mean values were set along these lines of equivalence through the use of all items in the tests at each age level (see Comber and Keeves 1973).

### 4.2 Equal Area or Equipercentile Equating

In this procedure it is similarly assumed that both the test items and the persons tested represent appropriate samples for the measurement of a specific attribute. In the use of this procedure cumulative frequency distributions are calculated, the scores are obtained at equal percentile points for each test, and a line of equivalence is plotted (see Angoff 1971 p. 571). This method of equating allows for differences in the shapes of the score distributions. As a consequence there is a more accurate location of equivalent scores in the tails of the tests, which is of some consequence if one or both of the score distributions are highly skewed. This procedure may prove to be more accurate and effective in vertical equating, but experience suggests that with large samples the procedure has few advantages in horizontal equating where the tests measure an attribute that is normally distributed in the population under survey. The equipercentile equating technique has been used in the equating of College Board Achievement Test Scores over time in the United States. However, linear equating was used in the equating of Scholastic Aptitude Test Scores until 1981; since 1982, latent trait procedures have been used (Donlon 1984).

### 4.3 Latent Trait Equating

It is also possible to employ models based on the assumption of an unobservable, but underlying, latent trait which exhibits a relationship that can be represented by a logistic function. Morgan (1982) has illustrated the use of Rasch scaling procedures with the Australian Scholastic Aptitude Test. In addition, Cowell (1982) has employed the three-parameter model with a language test (TOEFL). Goldstein (1980) has challenged the use of latent trait procedures in the development of a scale for horizontal equating which involves a common scale of measurement over time, particularly for educational achievement, because of the alleged problems of finding sensible interpretations of any results from such models for other than narrowly defined psychological attributes. Nevertheless, experience is being gained in the use of latent trait procedures for the equating of achievement tests in educational research, which seems to indicate that the procedures are both robust and meaningful.

Sontag (1984) has provided evidence to support the use of the one-parameter model for the logistic function in the vertical scaling of the data collected in the IEA Six Subject Study across the 10-year-old, the 14-year-old, and terminal secondary-school levels in the areas of science, reading comprehension, and word knowledge. The one-parameter model was found to yield more stable results than the two- and three-parameter models. Sontag concluded that:

> These results may be due to several factors. The first is the overfitting of the model to the data. In a cross-comparison design, a complicated model can overfit to a specific sample. Thus the analysis may be unique to a given group and not reproducible because of the idiosyncrasies specific to that group. The second factor is that a model with few parameters will be most consistent due to small variance alone. Lastly, this particular data set might not fit the item response theory models. On several occasions the three parameter model was unable to converge due to misfits of the items. (Sontag 1984)

Beaton (1987) has reported that the National Assessment of Educational Progress (NAEP) used latent trait scaling procedures for the vertical equating of tests across the 9-year-old, 13-year-old, and 17-year-old age levels in the development of a combined reading scale. Instead of identifying the reading scale employed in a particular NAEP testing programme as the standard for past and future assessments, the research workers, who were engaged in the task of scaling the reading tests, advanced the idea of a hypothetical reading proficiency test with idealized properties. The key properties of this hypothetical test were:

(a) it contained 500 items, so that scores ranged from 0 to 500,

(b) all item characteristic curves were logistic in shape,

(c) correct answers to items could not be achieved by guessing,

(d) an average level of discrimination was assumed to apply to all items,

(e) item difficulties were evenly distributed along the $\theta$ scale of difficulty from $-4.99$ to $4.99$,

(f) the function used to transform scores from the $\theta$ scale to the reading proficiency scale was linear and of the form $RP_s = 250.5 + 50\ (\theta)$, where $RP_s$ was the score for subjects on the reading proficiency scale. This reading proficiency scale then had a mean over all age groups of 250.5 and a standard deviation of 50.

This scale is a latent trait scale and is not norm-referenced. In order to give meaning to this scale, it was decided to anchor scale points and identify items that discriminated between each pair of adjacent points.

For the NAEP reading scale a decision was made to anchor the following points: 150, 200, 250, 300, and 350, since these points spanned the range in which most students scored. The results were presented on a Reading Report Card and the five levels of proficiency were described as rudimentary (150), basic (200), intermediate (250), adept (300), and advanced (350). Two sample items were provided to indicate the standards achieved with a probability of a correct response of 0.8 on the chosen items by the students located at those score levels with which the items were associated. Expressed in other words, 80 percent of the students performing at each of the specified score levels could be expected to answer correctly the items associated with each level. The findings of the four NAEP reading surveys conducted so far have shown that practically no 13-year-old students and a small proportion of the 17-year-old students could read at the advanced level. Less than 20 percent of the 13-year-olds and about 40 percent of the 17-year-olds could read at or above the adept level. Over 60 percent of the 13-year-olds and 80 percent of the 17-year-olds could read at the intermediate level, and practically all students of both ages could read at the rudimentary and basic levels. While the anchoring process was not a necessary consequence of the use of latent trait theory, this theory was used to establish the scale, equate the tests at the 9-year-old, 13-year-old, and 17-year-old levels, and identify the scale points at which anchoring would occur (Beaton 1987). This work has made highly significant advances towards the development of a meaningful and valid scale of reading achievement that could endure over a substantial period of time.

### 4.4 Models of Data Collection

Angoff (1971) and Thorndike (1982) have identified three basic data collection models from which equating could be carried out that (a) would be free from bias, and (b) would, for a given cost of both effort and money, be as accurate as possible. These three methods are: (a) equivalent random samples of students, (b) double cross-tested samples of students, and (c) anchor or core test procedures.

(a) *Equivalent random samples.* In this procedure the total sample of students is divided into the required number of random balanced subsamples and a different form of a test is administered to each subsample of students. While this procedure has the advantage that the students are only required to take one form of the test, it is a necessary requirement that the different parallel forms of the test should be rotated in an appropriate way and randomly distributed within each primary sampling unit, for example, each classroom. Equating can be undertaken using either linear or equipercentile procedures. However, this strategy is a relatively inefficient one since the standard errors of equating under this model are large.

(b) *Double cross-tested samples.* In this model all students are required to take two forms of the tests which are being equated, but the total sample of students must be divided into two matched subsamples, and the order in which each subsample takes the forms should be crossed. This approach yields markedly increased precision in the standard errors of equating. In general, this model is four times as precise as the equivalent random sample model, but precision is obtained at a cost of twice the total time of testing. It should be noted, moreover, that 16 times as many students would need to be tested in the equivalent random sample model to achieve the same level of precision as would be obtained for the double cross-tested sample model. There is, however, the problem of reduced motivation during the second testing in this second model, and the need to make an appropriate adjustment for practice to the results of both groups.

(c) *Core test procedures.* In the third model, all students in the total sample take a common core test, or anchor test, as well as one or more of the parallel forms. The core test may be conceived of as a separate relatively short test or as a common set of test items. In either case the core test should be given at similar locations in the testing programme so that any effects of practice or fatigue apply equally to the different test forms. The capacity for the core test to provide a bridge with the different forms of the test depends on its correlation with each of the parallel forms being equated. In addition, the core test should have adequate reliability so that its correlations with the tests being equated are not markedly reduced. The advantage of this procedure is that it is not essential for the different forms of the test to be administered at the same time.

If linear equating of two or more different forms is being carried out, then a mean value on each test must be estimated for the total group, by using the data from the bridging test. This estimate is calculated as the sum of a subgroup's score on one form of the test together with the regression of the score of that test on the bridging test. In a similar way the standard deviations for the total group on that form can be estimated. Once these estimated values have been calculated for the different forms they can be used in the standard equation for linear scaling, since the mean and standard deviation for each form have been estimated for the total group of students. With only moderate correlations between the core test and the different forms there is a substantial loss in precision for this third model compared to the second model but a considerable advance on the precision provided by the equivalent random sample model.

Equipercentile scaling can also be carried out when a core test has been employed to bridge two or more different forms. Details of these procedures are given in Thorndike (1982). Rock et al. (1985) have used a modified three-parameter latent trait model to score and equate with core test procedures two tests in mathematics each comprising 25 items, of which 12 items were identical and 6 had minor editorial and format changes. The two forms of this mathematics test were administered to large samples in 1972 and 1980 respectively in a study of factors associated with decline in test scores of high school seniors between the two occasions.

## 5. Moderation

Moderation is a procedure that was first employed at Oxford University to compare and equate levels of performance in the examinations conducted within the colleges of the university. The statistical procedures that have been developed to serve the purposes of equating levels of achievement on different examination papers have also come to be known as "moderation". The main advantage of using these procedures in examining is that they provide greater scope for flexibility of syllabus and teaching methods, and greater opportunities for matching the examinations with individual and local needs. Thus teachers are less restricted by an examination conducted internally or within a school or group of schools and externally moderated than by any other methods of examining. The function of moderation in this situation is to establish and maintain comparable standards between different examinations in the same subject area that are conducted on different syllabuses or in different settings. A further use of moderation occurs when a total score must be calculated from examination marks in different subject areas. The procedures employed for the equating of marks in different subject areas is sometimes referred to as "standardization". However, this term should not be confused with the calculation of standard scores, a procedure that has been discussed above.

Howard (alias used by Sir Cyril Burt) (1958) identified the key requirements of moderation procedures. They are that candidates should not be disadvantaged by the marking patterns of examiners nor by the candidatures with whom they compete. In practice these requirements demand that the same mark on different examinations should imply the same level of performance relative to a common population. Moderation, in its different forms, of the scores awarded within schools either by examinations or by the systematic assessment of student class work, is required on four counts. First, there are differences between subjects in the quality of the candidatures they attract. Second, there are differences between schools in the characteristics of the students who attend them. Third, there are differences between markers, both between and within schools, in the mean level of scores awarded, the spread of scores, and the shapes of the distributions of scores that they give to students. Fourth, there are differences between the courses of instruction that the students have studied and as a consequence in the assessment procedures employed. Moderation procedures are needed to provide effectively for these differences in a way that satisfies equitably the key requirements advanced by Burt.

It is necessary to recognize that in situations where moderation is applied, for example, between two sets of scores, the correlations between those scores may differ significantly from 1.0. If the correlation did not differ from 1.0 then equating procedures could be employed. As a consequence distinctions can be drawn between the procedures of rescaling, equating, and moderation, although the three procedures have much in common. In rescaling, the mean values may be changed; the spread of scores changed; and the shape of the score distributions may or may not be changed; but the relative location of the component scores do not change with respect to one another. A conversion or transformation procedure is applied to achieve the rescaling of scores. In equating, two or more tests essentially similar in kind that correlate strongly are brought to a common scale. A special case of test equating is where the same essay examination is marked by two or more markers and the scores assigned by the different markers are brought to a common scale. This is sometimes erroneously referred to as moderation. However, in true moderation it is not assumed that the examinations or tests are identical in kind, since they do not correlate perfectly, and an external scale of reference is required to bring the scores to a common scale. Thus moderation has some features in common with the procedure of scaling. However, where scaling involves the conversion of only one set of scores, moderation commonly involves the bringing of two or more disparate sets of scores to a single scale which must be defined.

As with scaling, there are three broad classes of procedures that can be employed in the moderation of examinations. First, there are procedures for moderation that involve attributes of a common stimulus task to which the groups of students are required to respond. Second, there are those procedures used for moderation that are concerned with the attributes of the groups of students with respect to a larger population of students. Third, there are moderation procedures that are concerned with both common stimulus tasks and the attributes of students. This third set of moderation procedures involve essentially predictive methods, and a prediction equation is developed for separate groups of students whose performance is measured on a set of tasks to provide a criterion measure. The statistical procedures that are employed in moderation also draw upon the different theories of educational measurement, and the different types of scaling procedures, namely, linear, equal area, or latent trait procedures as discussed above.

The different procedures described below are employed in the different circumstances that arise in the conduct of examinations, particularly those associated with entry into higher education.

## 5.1 Use of a Moderator Test

In its simplest form this type of moderation procedure involves the moderation of scores on the $i$th achievement test $Y_i$ using a moderator test $X$. Cooney (1975) has considered in some detail the issues associated with the procedures of moderation. If two assumptions are

made, namely, (a) the joint distribution of the moderator test and the achievement test scores is bivariate normal, and the marginal distributions are normal, and (b) the moderator test has a significant correlation $r$ with the achievement test, then the following linear equation can be employed in the process of moderation.

$$T_{ij} = Y_{i.} + \frac{rS_{yi}}{S_x}(X_j - X.) \tag{1}$$

where $T_{ij}$ is the moderated score for student $j$ on achievement test $i$, $Y_{i.}$ is the mean score on the achievement test $i$, $X_j$ is the score of student $j$ on the moderator test, $X.$ is the mean score on the moderator test, $S_{y_i}$ is the standard deviation of the achievement measure $Y_i$, and $S_x$ is the standard deviation on the moderator test $X$.

An extension of this procedure is employed in the United States for the scaling of College Board subject examination scores using the two moderator tests of verbal scholastic aptitude (SAT$_V$) and mathematical scholastic aptitude (SAT$_M$). In formulating the linear equation for moderation, the partial regression coefficients for predicting achievement using SAT$_V$ and holding SAT$_M$ constant, and using SAT$_M$, holding SAT$_V$ constant, are used. The major problem is that performances in different subject areas do not correlate equally with the Scholastic Aptitude Tests. The greater the correlations between the achievement test scores and the moderator variables the greater the values of the adjustments made in moderation (Donlon 1984). Equipercentile scaling could also be used if the evidence suggested that the assumption of a bivariate normal distribution did not hold and either the achievement test scores or the moderator test score departed markedly from a normal distribution. These approaches to moderation have been rejected in Australia because the scores obtained in different subject examinations do not correlate equally with scores on the moderator variables available.

## 5.2 Use of Characteristics of Candidatures

Two approaches have been developed to use characteristics of the candidatures in the process of moderation of examinations at the terminal secondary-school level.

The first approach uses achievement characteristics. The most obvious achievement characteristic that is available for adjusting the level of performance of a student group to allow for differences in the quality of the candidatures is the performance of the students on the other subjects that they sat on the same occasion. This procedure involves the calculation of an aggregate score on a specific number of other subjects which were taken by the students. For each subject group these aggregate scores can be averaged for the group, and the mean score and standard deviation for the group on a particular examination can be rescaled using these values of the mean and standard deviations of the averaged aggregate scores for the group. This is a simple linear rescaling operation. This operation can be expressed symbolically as follows:

$$T_{ij} = \sum_{i=1}^{m} \sum_{j=1}^{n_i} \frac{X_{ij}}{mn_i} + \frac{(Y_{ij} - Y_i)}{S_{y_i}} S_x \qquad (2)$$

where the symbols are similar to those in Eqn. (1), except that $X_{ij}$ is the score for student $j$ on achievement test $i$, and where there are $n_i$ students in each subject group, and a maximum of $m$ subjects are used in the aggregate. $S_x$ is the standard deviation of the averaged aggregated achievement test scores.

The moderated score $T_{ij}$ replaces $X_{ij}$ for each subject in turn and the process can be repeated iteratively until the values of $T_{ij}$ converge. With a large number of students taking each subject and with considerable overlap in the candidatures between subjects this iterative procedure gives stable estimates. However, because of the high intercorrelations between certain achievement test scores, those groups of students taking subjects that correlate highly, such as the mathematics and sciences subjects, have a greater spread of scores ($S_x$) than are estimated for those groups of students taking subjects that do not correlate highly with each other (Keeves and Parkyn 1979). As a consequence this procedure may be seen to be biased in favour of certain student groups.

An alternative procedure using aptitude characteristics employs the characteristics of a student group given by the average performance of the group on a scholastic aptitude test. In this procedure the quality of the candidature is assessed by the average level of scholastic aptitude of the group of students. This operation is expressed symbolically by:

$$T_{ijk} = X_i + \frac{(Y_{ijk} - Y_{i..})}{S_{y_i}} S_{x_i} \qquad (3)$$

where the symbols employed correspond to those in Eqns. (1) and (2) above except for the addition of terms to include consideration of $k$ schools (Keeves et al. 1977).

Superficially this procedure is similar to that associated with the use of a moderator test, and the similarity arises from the fact that for all examination subjects the correlation between the subject and the moderator variable is set at unity, to account for the differences in the magnitudes of the correlations which were seen to pose particular problems for that method. In a similar way this procedure overcomes some of the problems which arise from the differences in the intercorrelations between subjects when achievement characteristics of student groups are used. In practice this procedure described above establishes a scholastic aptitude test scale on which the qualities of the candidatures of the different school and subject groups are measured. The performances of the groups as groups are moderated using measured ability on this scale. The shortcomings of this approach are that it gives little recognition to the quality of instruction in a school and it depends heavily

on the meaningfulness and consistency of the scholastic aptitude test that is used as the basis for the scaling of the student groups. Where student groups differ significantly in their performance on this reference test, for example where male and female students and ethnic groups differ in their performance on this test, problems become obvious, whereas similar problems while present in the other procedures described above, are not so obvious. Some research has been undertaken into these problems (Adams 1984, Masters and Beswick 1986).

## 5.3 Prediction Methods

Prediction methods of moderation that incorporate both the characteristics of the achievement-based examinations and those of student groups are available for use in moderation. Their use is implied when external moderators from a higher level of education undertake moderation programmes to compare both scripts and the quality of the candidatures who come from different institutions and with different academic backgrounds. These judgmental approaches to moderation suffer from the high level of subjectivity of the decisions required (Goldstein 1986). In addition, difficulties are encountered in showing publicly that the methods employed are fair and just, as is necessary when large numbers of candidates from different social backgrounds are involved.

Research studies that examine the predictive powers of different selection procedures are not uncommon and the investigations by Parkyn (1959), Choppin and Orr (1976), and Donlon (1984) are important studies. However, examples where these principles and the findings of predictive studies have been applied to the process of moderation have not been found. The development of a profile of information might be proposed for use in such situations. The components of the profile would be combined into a prediction equation using weights that sought to optimize student success at a later stage in education. The weights could be calculated as regression weights obtained from prior predictive studies. This approach would merely formalize and quantify what has previously been carried out by moderators using their judgments based on experience.

## 5.4 Item Banking

Choppin (1985) has discussed the concept of an item bank and the ideas presented below are drawn largely from that source. An item bank is a collection of test items organized, classified, and catalogued in order to facilitate the construction of a variety of achievement and other types of test. The item bank can be seen as a replacement for tests that have been converted to a specific scale, such as the age and grade scales described above. The key characteristic that changes a pool of test items from one in which random sampling can occur into a potential item bank is a comprehensive procedure for deriving the properties (reliability, precision, difficulty, etc.) of the tests constructed in this way using the statistical properties of the items with which the tests are built. Inasmuch as item banks are not mere collections of test items, but are organized and scaled in order to provide a basis for generalized measurement, they must rely on some underlying theory or model of the test-taking process. An approach to the construction of an item bank which is steadily increasing in influence stems from a proposal by Choppin (1968) to use latent trait theory, and specifically the Rasch model, for this purpose. A good example of the use of this approach is to be found in Cornish and Wines (1977).

The availability of large banks of items would permit their employment as a source of tests which were scaled in advance of use. An examiner in a school or school district in a particular curriculum area would be able to select either at random, or to a specified plan, a set of items that would form a test from the bank of items in that curriculum area. Since the characteristics of the items were already known, the characteristics of the test formed from the set of items would also be known with respect to an underlying scale. Consequently, the performance of individual students and school or classroom groups could be mapped within a specified curriculum area. However, the major advantage of the latent trait scaling of the items in a bank is the possibility of comparing scores on different tests administered at different points in time. Nevertheless, this leads to a new problem, namely, the changing validity of an item bank as changes in the school curriculum occur. It is too early to say whether regular updating and rescaling of the items in an item bank can successfully maintain its validity over substantial periods of time. Even if this problem cannot be completely solved, the item bank should provide a sound basis for quantitative description of curriculum change that is more powerful than has previously been available.

It will be seen from this brief discussion of item banks and their use that they involve the application of latent trait measurement procedures to develop a generalized scale associated with the field of knowledge represented by the items in the bank. Any test which employs a set of items drawn from the bank is automatically equated to other tests that can be drawn from the bank. The benefits of setting up such a bank of test items are that the bank can be used to moderate student performance between schools in the field of knowledge associated with the bank. The performance of students in a particular school can be compared with the performance of students in any other school, provided that it can be assumed that the differences in curricula between the two schools are not so great as to invalidate the scaling of items in the bank and their use. A more flexible approach to the use of item banks has been explored by Palmer (1980) who sought not to compare performance between schools directly, but to use the information obtained from the administration of tests based on items drawn from a bank to establish levels of performance and tolerance limits outside of which measured per-

formance would not be expected to occur. This approach applied the ideas of quality control to school performance.

## 6. Conclusion

With a growing emphasis on standards of achievement in school at the same time as there is movement towards universal secondary education and the completion of 12 years of schooling by each age cohort, it seems likely that increased attention will be given to the moderation of examinations and achievement tests at the terminal secondary-school level. The advantage of the use of moderation procedures is that it will allow teachers to have greater flexibility in the design and development of appropriate curricula for particular groups of students. Moderation procedures will permit the standards of achievement of different groups to be compared. Moreover, it seems probable that latent trait procedures that have the capability to scale accurately sets of achievement test items, provided the items assess performance on a clearly specified trait, will be used increasingly in the future. Furthermore, there is a need for research and developmental work in the field of item banking, which involves the application of latent trait theory to a range of practical problems.

## Bibliography

Adams R J 1984 *Sex Bias in ASAT?* Australian Council for Educational Research (ACER), Hawthorn, Victoria

Angoff W H 1971 Scales, norms and equivalent scores. In: Thorndike R L (ed.) 1971 *Educational Measurement*, 2nd edn. American Council on Education, Washington, DC

Beaton A E 1987 Implementing the new design: The NAEP 1983–84 technical report. National Assessment of Educational Progress/Educational Testing Service, Princeton, New Jersey

Bejar I I 1983 *Achievement Testing: Recent Advances*, Sage University Paper Series on Quantitative Applications in the Social Sciences Series No. 07–036. Sage Publications, Beverly Hills, California

Choppin B H 1968 Item bank using sample-free calibration. *Nature* 219:870–72

Choppin B H 1985 Item bank. In: Husén T, Postlethwaite T N (eds.) 1985 *The International Encyclopedia of Education.* Pergamon, Oxford, pp. 2742–45

Choppin B H, Orr L 1976 *Aptitude Testing at Eighteen Plus.* National Foundation for Educational Research (NFER), Slough

Comber L C, Keeves J P 1973 *Science Education in Nineteen Countries.* Almqvist and Wiksell, Stockholm

Cooney G H 1975 Standardization procedures involving moderator variables. *Aust. J. Educ.* 19(1): 50–63

Cornish H G, Wines R 1977 *ACER Mathematics Profile Series.* Australian Council for Educational Research (ACER), Hawthorn, Victoria

Cowell W R 1982 Item-response-theory pre-equating in the TOEFL testing program. In: Holland P W, Rubin D B (eds.) 1982 *Test Equating.* Academic Press, New York

Donlon T F (ed.) 1984 *The College Board Technical Handbook for the Scholastic Aptitude Test and Achievement Tests.* College Entrance Examination Board, New York

Douglas G A 1982 Conditional inference on a generic Rasch model. In: Spearritt D (ed.) 1982 *The Improvement of Measurement in Education and Psychology.* Australian Council for Educational Research (ACER), Hawthorn, Victoria

Farish S J 1984 *Investigating Item Stability.* Australian Council for Educational Research (ACER), Hawthorn, Victoria

Fisher R A, Yates A 1963 *Statistical Tables for Biological, Agricultural, and Medical Research*, 6th edn. Oliver and Boyd, Edinburgh

Goldstein H 1980 Dimensionality bias independence and measurement scale problems in latent trait test score models. *Br. J. Math. Stat. Psychol.* 33: 234–46

Goldstein H 1986 Models for equating test scores and for studying the comparability of public examinations. In: Nuttall D L (ed.) 1986 *Assessing Educational Achievement.* Falmer Press, London

Harnisch D L, Linn R L 1981 Analysis of item response patterns: Questionable test data and dissimilar curriculum practices. *J. Educ. Meas.* 18(3): 133–46

Holland P W, Rubin D B (eds.) 1982 *Test Equating.* Academic Press, New York

Howard M 1958 The conversion of scores to a uniform scale. *Br. J. Stat. Psychol.* 11(2): 199–207

Keeves J P, McBryde B, Bennett L A 1977 The validity of alternative methods of scaling school assessments at the HSC level for the colleges and high schools of the Australian Capital Territory. In: Australian Association for Research in Education (AARE) 1977 *Curriculum Evaluation: Conference Papers.* AARE, Canberra

Keeves J P, Parkyn G W 1980 *The Higher School Certificate Examination in New South Wales.* New South Wales Board of Senior School Studies, Sydney

Lindquist E F (ed.) 1951 *Educational Measurement.* American Council on Education, Washington, DC

Masters G N, Beswich D G 1986 *The Construction of Tertiary Entrance Scores: Principles and Issues.* Centre for the Study of Higher Education, University of Melbourne, Melbourne

Morgan G N 1982 The use of the latent trait measurement model in equating of scholastic aptitude tests. In: Spearritt D (ed.) 1982 *The Improvement of Measurement in Education and Psychology.* Australian Council for Educational Research (ACER), Hawthorn, Victoria

Palmer D G 1980 Item banking. *Educ. Technol.* 1(3): 17–24

Parkyn G W 1959 *Success and Failure at the University.* New Zealand Council for Educational Research (NZCER), Wellington

Rock D A, Ekstrom R B, Goertz M E, Hilton T L, Pollack J 1985 *Factors Associated with Decline in Test Scores of High School Seniors, 1972 to 1980.* Center for Statistics, US Department of Education, Washington, DC

Snedecor G W, Cochran W G 1967 *Statistical Methods*, 6th edn. Iowa State University Press, Ames, Iowa

Sontag L M 1984 Vertical equating methods: A comparative study of their efficacy. Ph.D. thesis, Teachers College, Columbia University, New York

Thorndike R L 1982 *Applied Psychometrics.* Houghton Mifflin, Boston, Massachusetts

Togerson W S 1958 *Theory and Methods of Scaling.* Wiley, New York

Wright B D, Stone M H 1979 *Best Test Design.* Mesa Press, Chicago, Illinois

# Item Analysis

## R. Wood

The case for preferring item analysis procedures based on item characteristic curve theory (ICC) is made elsewhere. Here it is sufficient to observe that for a good deal of practical work in test construction, direct use of the basic sample statistics on which ICC theory builds, and of the original item response data themselves, can take the user a long way. Paradoxically, perhaps, these conventional or classical item analysis procedures gain more value as the connections with modern methods are better understood. A transformation of item difficulty like $\Delta$, and a coefficient like the biserial correlation, no longer seem ad hoc when it is realized how they fit into ICC theory (Thorndike 1982). And, of course, an appreciation of the limitations of the classical statistics must act as a curb on any tendency to overinterpret results. It might be added that the virtue of placing ICC theory in the hands of neophyte users is not at all obvious. An apprenticeship with the classical methods, even if a short one, seems obligatory.

## 1. Item Difficulty

For any item, the raw response data consist of frequency counts of the numbers of individuals choosing each option, together with the number not answering the item at all, known as the "omits". From this information, it is immediately possible to calculate the proportion or percentage of individuals choosing the right answer. This statistic is known as the item difficulty or facility, depending on which nomenclature is preferred. Facility is perhaps the more felicitous term, since the greater the percentage correct, the easier the item.

Item difficulty or facility—usually termed $p$—suffers, like all percentages, from the drawback that the scale implied cannot be regarded as calibrated in equal intervals. The difference (in intensity of difficulty) between items with facilities of 0.40 and 0.50 is not the same as, rather it is somewhat smaller than, the difference between items with facilities of 0.10 and 0.20. This elasticity in the scale makes for misjudgments in comparing facilities and rules out simple statistical manipulations of $p$, except for summation which results in an estimate of the total test mean (see Sect. 5.1).

A solution to this problem which, incidentally, gives a direct measure of item difficulty, is to transform $p$ to an ostensibly equal interval scale according to the following rationale (Henrysson 1971). A very common assumption made in test theory is that the ability to answer a particular item varies from very low ability to very high ability in a population of subjects. It is

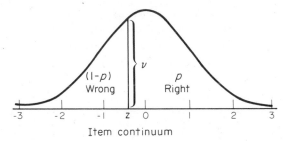

**Figure 1**
Normal distribution of subjects on the item continuum

Other transformations of $z$ are possible; this one merely happens to have been used over the years by the Educational Testing Service. An alternative would be $50 + 10z$, which gives difficulty measures with a mean of 50.

It is not imperative that $p$ be transformed. It can be left as it is providing its limitations are observed. Note that $\Delta$ does not have, as $p$ has, a direct relationship with a test statistic like the mean, but this is easily remedied by transforming the total score so that it has the same mean and standard deviation as $\Delta$. The same applies to other transformations.

assumed that the subjects are distributed on this item continuum according to the normal distribution as illustrated in Fig. 1.

The item continuum is a hypothetical construct specific to each item, that is, a scale measuring the ability to solve the item in question. In practice, however, it is dichotomized into only the two categories, right and wrong, in proportions $p$ and $1 - p$. This is illustrated in Fig. 1. The value $z$ expresses this point of categorization in standard score form. A table of normal probability curve values is used to find $z$ corresponding to $p$ and gives the level of ability (as measured in standard scores $z$ on the item continuum) necessary to answer the item correctly.

For the item analysed in Table 1, the item proportion is $p = 0.46$. From a normal curve table it is found that the standard score that divides this distribution in proportions 0.54 and 0.46 is $z = 0.10$ (entering with area equal to 0.04). This is the difficulty index of the item. Because $z$ can run from $-3$ to $+3$, there is merit in transforming it to a scale of all positive values. The standard score $z$ with mean equal to 0 and standard deviation equal to 1 can be transformed into scores $\Delta$ with mean equal to 13 and standard deviation equal to 4 by the linear transformation equation $\Delta = 13 + 4z$. $\Delta$ will in practice take values from about 6 to 20, a high value indicating a difficult item. In the example, with $z$ equal to 0.1, $\Delta$ equals 13.4. This indicates that the item is of a little more than average difficulty.

## 2. Item Discrimination

A discrimination index is meant to communicate the power of an item in separating the more from the less capable on some latent attribute. Operationally, the usual procedure is to compute a correlation, either biserial or point biserial, between success and failure on the item and score on a measure that is considered to represent the latent attribute. This is typically and conveniently the total score on the test to which the item belongs, but other measures will do. The idea is that the higher the correlation between candidates' scores on an item and their scores on the test, the more effective the item is in separating them. Naturally, this relationship is a relative one; when included in one test, an item could have a higher item–test correlation than when included in another, yet produce poorer discrimination. Those who are uncomfortable with an internal criterion because the reasoning behind the choice seems to be circular, are advised to seek an external criterion.

Choice of correlation lies between two forms, although there are some outsiders which will be considered briefly. The point biserial correlation is a special case of the general Pearson product–moment correlation, where one of the variables (test score) is regarded as continuous and the other (item score) can take one or other of two discrete values, typically 1 for correct and 0 for incorrect. The biserial correlation is based on the assumption that both variables are continuous but

**Table 1**
Example of the analysis of one item

| Score | Options | | | | | | Item |
|---|---|---|---|---|---|---|---|
| | A | B | C | D | E | O | reached |
| | 146 | 13 | 54 | 22 | 82 | 2 | 319 |
| | 0.46 | 0.04 | 0.17 | 0.07 | 0.26 | 0.01 | 1.00 |
| 0–18 | 9 | 6 | 18 | 7 | 21 | 2 | 63 |
| 18–22 | 16 | 5 | 16 | 8 | 19 | 0 | 64 |
| 22–29 | 30 | 1 | 7 | 7 | 19 | 0 | 64 |
| 29–35 | 42 | 1 | 8 | 0 | 13 | 0 | 64 |
| 35–47 | 49 | 0 | 5 | 0 | 10 | 0 | 64 |
| Mean criterion | 30.79 | 18.77 | 22.02 | 19.18 | 23.45 | 12.50 | 26.02 |

that one has been divided at some point into two groups, those who pass the item and those who fail it. The passers are thought to differ from the failers only in having more of whatever the item measures—that is, as having enough to get over the threshold and get the item right (Thorndike 1982 p. 71). The two variables are each assumed to follow a normal Gaussian distribution in the population of persons from whom the sample is drawn. That assumption was already made for the dichotomized scale (item continuum) when $p$ was transformed to $z$ and $\Delta$. Note that the biserial is *not* a form of product–moment correlation; rather it should be thought of as a measure of association.

## 2.1 Point Biserial Correlation

The standard form for the sample point biserial correlation is

$$r_{pbis} = \frac{M_R - M_W}{S_T} [p(1 - p)]^{\frac{1}{2}} \tag{1}$$

but it may be more convenient to use the equivalent form

$$r_{pbis} = \frac{M_R - M_T}{S_T} \left(\frac{p}{1 - p}\right)^{\frac{1}{2}} \tag{2}$$

where

$M_R$ = mean score on continuous variable for those getting item right
$M_W$ = mean score on continuous variable for those getting item wrong
$M_T$ = mean score on the continuous variable for the whole sample
$S_T$ = standard deviation of scores on the continuous variable for the whole sample
$p$ = percentage getting the item right or item facility. $(1 - p)$ is often written as $q$.

Evidently $r_{pbis}$ serves as a measure of separation through the action of the term

$$\frac{M_R - M_T}{S_T}$$

It is also a function of item facility and the effect of this will be looked at presently.

To calculate $r_{pbis}$ for the item in Table 1, the values of $M_R$ and $M_T$ can be found in the row directly underneath the body of the table labelled, "mean criterion", where "criterion" means test score. These mean test scores provide useful supplementary information. Thus, the mean score on the test obtained by those choosing A, the correct answer, was 30.79. This is $M_R$. Similarly, the 13 candidates choosing B scored an average of 18.77 on the test, which made them the lowest scoring of the four distractor groups. The mean score on the test for the entire group, $M_T$, is given at the right end of the "mean criterion" row, and is 26.02. The value of the

standard deviation, $S_T$, which is not given in the table, was 8.96. The calculation for $r_{pbis}$ is therefore

$$\frac{30.79 - 26.02}{8.96} \cdot \left(\frac{0.46}{0.54}\right)^{\frac{1}{2}}$$

which turns out to be 0.49.

The question immediately arises, "Is a value of 0.49 good, bad, or indifferent?" This is a fair question to ask of any correlation taking this value. If it were an ordinary product moment correlation, one might interpret the value within the limits −1 to +1 but with the point biserial that will not work because it has a curtailed range. If the distribution of scores in the total group is normal, the point biserial can never go beyond ±0.8 (Thorndike 1982). Furthermore the range of possible values depends on the percentages of passers and failers, contracting as the split becomes more uneven. The maximum values of $r_{pbis}$ for $p = 0.10$ and $p = 0.25$ when the total score distribution is normal are 0.58 and 0.73 respectively, (0.80 when $p = 0.50$). In these circumstances a value of 0.49 signifies quite powerful discrimination.

## 2.2 Biserial Correlation

The formula for calculating the sample biserial correlation coefficient resembles that for the point biserial quite closely, being

$$r_{bis} = \frac{M_R - M_T}{S_T} \cdot \frac{p}{y} \tag{3}$$

where the terms are as before, except for $y$, which stands for the ordinate or elevation of the normal curve at the point where it cuts off a proportion $p$ of the area under the curve (see Fig. 1). $y$ enters into the formula because of the assumption about the normally distributed underlying variable. It will usually be found in the same statistical tables as $z$.

In theory, the biserial can take any value between −1 and +1. Negative values usually indicate that the wrong answer has been keyed. Values greater than 0.75 are rare, although, in exceptional circumstances, the biserial can exceed 1, usually due to some peculiarity in the test score or criterion distribution. For the item in Table 1, the biserial estimate was 0.62, about which it is possible to say the same as about the point biserial value, that it signifies quite powerful discrimination.

## 2.3 Biserial and Point Biserial Correlations Compared

The point biserial $r$ is always lower than the biserial $r$ as can be seen from the relationship

$$r_{pbis} = r_{bis} \cdot \frac{y}{[p(1 - p)]^{\frac{1}{2}}} \tag{4}$$

It follows from this formula that $r_{pbis} = 0.82 r_{bis}$ when $p = 0.50$ and that $r_{pbis}$ shrinks with respect to $r_{bis}$ the further $p$ gets from 0.50, although the effect is only dramatic when $p$ becomes very high or very low. While it is always a simple matter to convert from one coefficient or index to the other, their respective strengths and weaknesses need to be understood. Where the point biserial *r* is used, there are considered to be only two distinct positions on the item continuum, right or wrong. But passers would seem to differ from failers more in degree than in kind, which makes the assumption of continuity underlying the biserial correlation more plausible, although the requirement that it should take a particular distributional form (normal) is harder to believe.

It has been seen that the point biserial is confounded by item difficulty. This is not necessarily a bad thing; in fact, it may be argued that the point biserial value is rather more informative about the item's contribution to the functioning of the test, because very easy or very difficult items make relatively few differentiations between more and less capable examinees. Even so there is no hiding the fact that the point biserial is effectively a combined index of difficulty and discrimination. Those who believe that the two concepts should not be muddled up in a single index (Thorndike 1982) will incline towards the biserial. Because it is less influenced by item difficulty, it has been thought that the biserial might prove to be invariant, or at least reasonably stable, from one examinee group to another. This is necessarily a matter for empirical investigation (Lord and Novick 1968) and the results are still not available. For what it is worth, personal experience indicates that even with ostensibly parallel groups of candidates, biserial estimates for the same item can "bounce" around beyond what would be expected from a "guestimated" margin of error, guestimated because no really good estimate of precision is available for this statistic—a mark against it.

The biserial plays a part in item characteristic curve theory (in the equation for estimating the steepness parameter of the curve); the point biserial does not. Against that, and importantly, the point biserial fits directly into the algebra of multivariate analysis (Thorndike 1982). When it comes to estimating test parameters from item parameters (see below) it is the point biserial which is needed. For the sort of bread and butter item analysis with which this article is concerned, this is an important plus. Indeed, it may be stated quite generally that any item statistic which does not bear a definite (preferably a clear and simple) relationship to some interesting total test score parameter (Lord and Novick 1968) is of limited value for practical test construction purposes.

Evidently both biserial and point biserial have shortcomings, serious enough to rule either out if the objections were to be pressed. The practical user will find that as long as a markedly nonnormal distribution of ability is not anticipated, substantially the same items will be selected or rejected, whichever index is used to evaluate discrimination. It is when item selection is linked to the engineering of test score distributions with desirable properties, as it ought to be for conventional

group testing situations grounded in more or less norm-referenced contexts, that the point biserial has the edge. Otherwise the best advice is to fasten on to one or other statistic, learn about its behaviour (for available information about sampling error is not impressive), and stick with it. Switching from one to the other, or trying to interpret both simultaneously, is likely to be futile.

### 2.4 Other Discrimination Indices

Of all the discrimination indices which have been proposed, the simplest is undoubtedly $D$, or net $D$, as it is sometimes called. If, for any item, $P_h$ is the proportion of correct answers achieved by the 27 percent highest scorers, and $P_l$ is the corresponding figure for the 27 percent lowest scorers, then $D = P_h - P_l$. It may seem odd that just as good results can be obtained by discarding middle scores of the score distribution as by using the whole distribution, but providing the ability being measured is normally distributed, and that is a big proviso, this is the case. Incidentally, it has been shown that the correct percentage is more like 21 percent, but, even so, 27 percent, or more conveniently 25 percent, cannot be far from optimal.

It is important to remember that the $D$ statistic was invented to fill a need at the time for a shortcut manual method of estimating the discriminating power of an item. For those who want or need to carry out an item analysis by hand—and it is still a good way of getting the "feel" of item performance—it can be said that $D$ agrees quite closely with biserial correlation estimates, even when the underlying distribution is non-normal. Like the point biserial and even the biserial, the $D$ index is dependent on item facility. In particular, it decreases sharply as the facility approaches 0 or 1, when it must be interpreted with caution but then, as already noted, the test constructor will probably not be interested in these items anyway. (Thorndike 1982 provides tables for calculating $D$.)

Those who prefer a discrimination index which is independent of item difficulty might be interested in the rank biserial correlation coefficient (Henrysson 1971). However, there are problems with this index when frequent ties among test scores occur, and it is, therefore, not recommended for large groups ($n > 50$). Many other discrimination indices have been proposed. A recent Monte Carlo study of 10 such indices (Beuchert and Mendoza 1979) concluded that selection of an index should be based solely on ease of computation or the need for statistical tests of significance. Such advice ignores the need for linkage with test parameters and should be viewed circumspectly, but it may be regarded as a judgment on the utility of "fringe" indices.

### 2.5 Correcting Estimates for Spuriousness

It is argued (Henrysson 1971 p. 150) that the point biserial between item score and total test score is spuriously high because the item score enters in both variables. It is further argued that the obvious correction, removing the item score from the test score and correlating with the sum of the remaining $n - 1$ items, is misconceived because the criterion changes each time a new item is analysed, and the construct validities for each dimension may shift subtly. To overcome this objection it has been argued that what is required is the correlation of each item with the common factor (the latent attribute measured by the whole set of items), freeing it of any specific variance of the item in question (Thorndike 1982).

The amount of correction for spuriousness is in inverse proportion to $n$, the number of items entering into the total score with which the item is correlated. When $n$ is large—say 40 to 50—the correlation is too small to be of any practical significance. Furthermore, the correction will rarely alter noticeably the relative size of the correlations themselves. Thus decisions about which items to include in the final form of a test are not often likely to be changed as a result of applying the correction (Thorndike 1982). It is said that if a computer program is used routinely for item analysis, there is good reason to include the correction formula in the program but that is debatable.

## 3. Fractile Tables

Whatever item statistics are concocted, being of a summary nature they are bound to be less informative than we would like. Evidently an infinite number of items can have different response patterns, yet possess the same discrimination index, or the same difficulty. The message is that it is a mistake to rely too heavily on item statistics; in particular they cannot describe how persons of different levels of achievement or ability respond to specific items. By defining fractiles of the distribution of test scores, and classifying item responses according to membership of these fractiles, the user can observe the behaviour of items across the ability range and also keep an eye open for malfunctioning distractors, something which will not be revealed by plots (see below). It is a matter of doing informally what item characteristic curve theory does more formally, although usually only for the correct response.

Items may

(a) fail to differentiate between persons in the lower, and sometimes the middle fractile bands;

(b) be useful over lower fractiles but give little or no information about persons in the higher fractiles;

(c) discriminate in a way which fluctuates wildly over fractiles.

By way of illustration, consider Table 1. The item generating data belonged to a 50-item chemistry test taken by 319 candidates. The correct (starred) answer was option A, chosen by 146 candidates, which, as the number underneath indicates, was 0.46 of the entry. The facility of this item was, therefore, 0.46, and the difficulty ($\Delta$) 13.42. As already noted, the point biserial

correlation was 0.49. Of the distractors, E was most popular (endorsed by 82 candidates, or 0.26 of the entry), followed by C, D, and B. Only two candidates omitted the item.

The five ability bands—and five is a good number to use, although three would do—have been constructed so as to contain equal numbers of candidates, or as nearly equal as possible, which means that, unless the distribution of scores is rectangular, the score intervals will always be unequal. However, there is no reason why the bands should not be defined in terms of equal score intervals or according to some assumption about the underlying distribution scores. If, for instance, a person wanted to believe that the underlying score distribution was normal, the bands could be constructed so as to have greatest numbers in the middle bands and smallest in the outer bands. The problem then is that, given small numbers, any untoward behaviour in the tails of the distribution would be amplified or distorted. Also, interpretation of the table would be more prone to error because of the varying numbers in the bands.

Turning to the body of the table, a pattern will be evident. Whereas under the correct answer A the count increases as the ability level rises, under the distractors (excepting D, where the trend is unclear), the gradient runs in the opposite direction. This is just as it should be if we want the item to discriminate in terms of total test score. The pattern we should *not* want to see would be one where the counts under A were equal to those under another distractor or, worse, where the count in each cell of the table was the same. As it is, the distribution of answers tells us quite a lot. Relatively speaking, options B and C were much more popular in the bottom ability band than in the rest, and in the bottom band the correct answer was barely more popular than B and D, which were almost totally rejected by the top two bands. Taken as a whole, the table underlines the observation that wrong answers are seldom, if ever, distributed equally across the distractors, either viewing the candidates as a whole, or in bands. Nor is there any evidence of blind guessing, the sign of which would be an inflated number in the top left hand cell of the table—the one containing a "9"—causing the gradient to flatten out at the bottom, or even go in the other direction. (The writer takes the view that most guessing is informed and that the best instructions are those which exhort examinees to answer as many questions as possible; see Wood 1977.)

The question arises as to whether there is some percentage below which a distractor score should not fall if it is to be regarded as "working" satisfactorily. There is not, if only because the percentage of wrong responses to be shared among the distractors depends on the percentage correct. That said, anything of the order of 5 percent or less should be looked at askance. Such distractors are clearly wrong to nearly everybody and a search should be made for more plausible wrong answers.

It will be seen that "omits" have been treated as

incorrect responses in computing a difficulty index. This is a strictly pragmatic decision. Theoretical work has properly sought to treat omits as a conceptually distinct category of response and there is still much to be learned about omitting behaviour. It should be obvious that displaying response data in fractile table form enables the user to keep an eye on omit levels and on who is omitting (via the mean criterion score).

## 4. Generalized Item Statistics

It is always desirable to inspect fractile tables, but it may still be asked whether there is any way of summarizing all response patterns simultaneously. The appropriate statistics would be generalizations of the point biserial and biserial coefficients, and these have, in fact, been developed. To calculate the point multiserial, each response option, including the right answer, is treated as a separate nominal category, as if each represented a character such as eye colour. With the polyserial, on the other hand, being a generalization of the biserial, it is necessary that the distractors can be ordered or graded in terms of degree of "wrongness" or "rightness", so that the assumption of an underlying normally distributed trait can be better met. It is doubtful whether items often lend themselves to this kind of ordering, at least not on a large scale. The polyserial coefficient will generally find a more suitable application when the polychotomized variable is something like an examination grade or a rating, where there is a natural order of measurement. The point multiserial is the more suitable statistic, but it is rather cumbersome to calculate (although not once it is programmed). Whether it is any more informative than the ordinary point biserial is another matter. The feeling is that these generalized statistics are not of much value in regular item analysis. The user would be just as well off with point biserial estimates calculated for each distractor, and some item analysis programmes do provide this information.

## 5. Estimating Test Parameters from Item Statistics

There are three aspects to this. Firstly, there are the algebraic relationships between test parameters and item statistics; secondly, there is the utilization of these relationships in the choice of items to produce (hopefully) desired test score distributions; and thirdly there is the practical business of selecting items to meet the test specification.

### 5.1 Estimating the Mean, Standard Deviation, Average Intercorrelation, and Reliability

As with any comparable estimation procedure, it is necessary, or certainly preferable, for the sample on which the estimates are based to have the same characteristics as the population with which the final test will be used.

The relationship between item difficulties and mean test score is very simple. If $\bar{x}$ is the mean test score and $p_i$ is the difficulty of item $i$, then for an $n$ item test

$$\bar{x}_T = \sum_{i=1}^{n} p_i \tag{5}$$

This relationship can be checked out easily by drawing up a person-by-item response matrix composed of entries of 0 or 1, and summing the item and person scores in the borders.

The standard deviation of test scores is estimated by the expression

$$s_T = \sum_{i=1}^{n} (p_i q_i)^{\frac{1}{2}} \cdot r_{it} \tag{6}$$

where $q_i = (1 - p_i)$ and $r_{it}$ is the point biserial correlation of item $i$ with the total test. There are certain grounds for believing that estimates of discrimination gained from tryouts will be lower than in the test proper, for example, poorer quality criteria, and more casual responses from examinees and this should be allowed for when using Eqn. (6).

Once a trustworthy estimate of the standard deviation is to hand, an estimate of the internal consistency of the test in the form of Kuder–Richardson 20 can be obtained using the following formula

$$r_{TT} = \frac{n}{n-1} \left( 1 - \frac{\sum_{i=1}^{n} p_i q_i}{S_T^2} \right) \tag{7}$$

Item intercorrelation is not a statistic that pertains to any one item and in that sense fails to satisfy the Lord and Novick test of a useful item parameter. However, in other respects, it (or rather the average item intercorrelation) is a most useful statistic, especially when it comes to engineering or forecasting the shape of test distributions. The relationships between item intercorrelations, item–test correlations, and test reliability are shown in Eqn. (7). It can be seen that reliability depends entirely on item intercorrelations.

$$r_{TT} = \frac{\bar{r}_{ij}}{\bar{r}_{it}^2} = \frac{n\bar{r}_{ij}}{1 + (n-1)\bar{r}_{ij}} = \frac{n\bar{r}_{it}^2 - 1}{(n-1)\bar{r}_{it}^2}$$

$$\text{or} \quad \frac{n}{n-1} \left( 1 - \frac{1}{n\bar{r}_{it}^2} \right) \tag{8}$$

where $\bar{r}_{ij}$ is the average item intercorrelation. (Silverstein 1980 shows how these statistics can be related through mean squares if item analysis is treated as an ANOVA problem, as it can be.)

The last expression is handy for back-of-the-envelope calculations where the test constructor has a good idea of what the average point biserial is likely to be. Likewise, if a "guestimate" of the average item difficulty, $\bar{p}$, is available, the mean score can be estimated as $n\bar{p}$, and the standard deviation as $n(\bar{p}\bar{q}r_{it})^{\frac{1}{2}}$. Note that because $n(\bar{p}\bar{q})^{\frac{1}{2}}$ is always greater than $\Sigma(pq)^{\frac{1}{2}}$, the foregoing expression tends to overestimate slightly the standard deviation that will result (Thorndike 1982).

## 5.2 Engineering Test Score Distributions

The influence of item difficulty and discrimination on the properties of the total test is a rather complicated matter, especially if multiple-choice items are involved (Henrysson 1971). A full account of the subject is still awaited, and those who have studied it in the past have not always agreed on the effects of various selection strategies. It used to be said that there was no consensus concerning the best method of obtaining a rectangular score distribution (Scott 1972), but authorities now seem to be agreeing that what is wanted are intercorrelations of 0.33 and difficulties of 0.50. (Stanley 1971 shows that it must be necessary but not sufficient to have this degree of item intercorrelation if a person wishes to obtain a rectangular distribution from 50 percent difficulty items.) Above the item intercorrelation of 0.33, the total scores tend to become more frequent at the extremes and less frequent in the middle, until for the perfect intercorrelation situation only the extreme two scores have any frequencies. Test constructors prevent this by varying the item difficulty from easy to difficult, rather than setting it at approximately 0.50 for each item, so that even with high intercorrelations, thinning out in the middle does not occur (Stanley 1971). In fact, few if any achievement tests have average item intercorrelations approaching 0.33; they are more often of the order of 0.10 to 0.20, and even 0.20 would be high. Thus the test constructor who wishes to discriminate maximally among candidates is always liable to be frustrated. The optimum strategy in these circumstances of item heterogeneity is to choose items in the difficulty range 0.60 ($\Delta = 12$) to 0.40 ($\Delta = 14$), the departure from the theoretically desirable figure of 0.50 being necessary to ring the changes on content (Henrysson 1971). In other words, one acts as if rectangular distributions were realizable.

Experience indicates that many people think intuitively that item difficulties should be widely distributed. The argument goes something like this. If all items are of the same difficulty, they can only measure efficiently those whose ability level corresponds to the difficulty level. Only if items are distributed across the difficulty range so that everyone has something they can tackle, can everyone be measured reasonably efficiently. This argument is impeccable—as far as it goes. The fact is that neither item selection policy will give the best results, the first because it neglects the most and least able candidates, and the second because, unless the test is to be grotesquely long, there are too few items at each point of the difficulty/ability range to provide effective measurement. The equal difficulty strategy is simply the better of two poor alternatives for large candidate populations. If candidates at the extremities are to be measured efficiently, what is needed are tests tailored to their abilities. Therein lies the motivation for developing individualized testing procedures.

Naturally, there are specialized measurement needs which require special treatment; an example would be a severe selection situation where, say, only 5 percent of candidates are to be selected. In these circumstances, items should all be of a difficulty level commensurate with the cut-off point and discriminations (and therefore intercorrelations) should be as high as possible.

## 5.3 Selecting Items in Practice

When selecting items in practice, a handy way of displaying the available items in terms of their statistical characteristics is to plot values of facility or difficulty against values of the discrimination index, whatever that is. It is conventional to plot difficulty along the horizontal axis and discrimination up the vertical axis, with the position of items being signified by the item number, and also, perhaps, by some coding, like a box or a circle or a colour, to indicate different item types or content areas. On top of the plot can be superimposed horizontal and vertical lines indicating the region within which "acceptable" items are to be found depending on the specifications (Wood 1977). A similar effect is obtained by using the Shewart control chart.

## 6. Item Analysis For Criterion-referenced Tests

The writer counts himself among those who wish to deemphasize the distinction between norm-referenced and criterion-referenced testing but when it comes to item analysis there are undeniable differences.

Item analysis has always been a source of ambivalence among advocates of criterion-referenced testing. Doctrine requires belief in perfect congruence between objectives, item generators, and items, so that items which function less than satisfactorily are not supposed to occur. Experience, however, indicates that there will always be subjective and uncertain elements in the formulation of objectives and therefore in the production of items, suggesting that there is room for some kind of item analysis.

This empirical view is generally accepted nowadays but in the beginning, ambivalence led to some gratuitous inversions. It was argued that items with facilities as near as possible to 100 percent should be favoured above all others, when a moment's thought would have shown that such items can provide no evidence on the effectiveness of instruction, or on progress towards mastery. What was wanted, it was said, were items with nonsignificant item-test correlations; items that discriminate positively usually indicate a need for revision. This, of course, was simply to misuse norm-referenced item statistics. If the idea is to find items which are sensitive to changes within individuals, then it is necessary to test items out on groups before and after they have received instruction. Items showing little or no difference, indicating insensitivity to learning, would then be discarded. The best items, in this view, are those which have $p$ values approaching 0 prior to instruction, and $p$ values approaching 1 subsequent to instruction.

Various refinements of the simple difference measure have been proposed. There is no point mentioning them all here because no two writers seem to be able to agree on the superiority of any one statistic. Besides, there now seems good reason to view them all with suspicion (van der Linden 1981). Noting that all the item analysis statistics (or validity coefficients, as he calls them) are based on the same idea of instructional sensitivity, require pretest–posttest administration, and entail gain scoring, van der Linden acknowledges that such features are welcomed in many papers as being typically criterion-referenced but argues that these coefficients have many disadvantages and serious interpretation problems. When the validity of instruction is not established, low pretest–posttest differences may be due to poor instruction rather than to weak items. Two items with the same difference between pretest and posttest $p$ values may cover different intervals of the mastery continuum with different degrees of discrimination. Complicating everything are the threats to internal validity—history, maturational effects, scaling effects—which are inherent in all quasi-experimentation, of which criterion-referenced item validation is clearly an instance. The pretest–posttest method mixes up two sources of information—the characteristics of the item and the differences between the pretest and posttest mastery distributions—and blames the former for the peculiarities of the latter. By doing so, it is not surprising to find that it weeds out items of high quality (van der Linden 1981). A latent trait analysis, with prominence given to the "information function"—which does not mix up the two sources of information—is recommended. The critique is persuasive and those who wish to persist with simple difference measures will have to deal with it.

## 7. Choosing Items to Discriminate Between Groups

Not only may items be chosen to discriminate between and within individuals, but also between groups of individuals. The principal importance of such a measure lies in the evaluation of teaching programmes or instructional success. Suppose a number of classes within a school have been taught the same material, and it is desired to set all class members a test to find out which class has learnt the most. The items which differentiate within classes will not necessarily register differences between classes (Lewy 1973). This is what would be

expected, given that the basic units of observation—the individual score and the class average—are so different. For item selection to differentiate between classes, the appropriate discrimination index is the intraclass correlation. Using indices like the biserial will most likely result in tests which are not sensitive to differences between class performance. (Critics of the American studies which claimed that school makes little or no difference to achievement, make much of this point.)

It will be evident that there are other possibilities once the distinction between unit of observation and unit of analysis is observed. Interest may lie in maximizing discrimination among students within particular classes or, more generally, in differentiating between individuals within their respective subgroups rather than among all of them (Lewy 1973). The current lively interest in the unit of analysis problem is bound to touch item analysis. Personal experience with intraclass correlation on item response data from achievement tests has been that the highest values occur with items on topics that are either new to the syllabus or are controversial. If, as seems likely, these topics are taken up by only some teachers, the effect will be to create a possibly spurious impression of greater between-school variability than really exists.

## Bibliography

Beuchert A K, Mendoza J L 1979 A Monte Carlo comparison of 10 item discrimination indices. *J. Educ. Meas.* 16: 109–17

Henrysson S 1971 Gathering, analyzing and using data on test items. In: Thorndike R L (ed.) 1971 *Educational Measurement.* American Council on Education, Washington, DC

Lewy A 1973 Discrimination among individuals vs. discrimination among groups. *J. Educ. Meas.* 10: 19–24

Lord F M, Novick M R 1968 *Statistical Theories of Mental Test Scores.* Addison-Wesley, New York

Scott W A 1972 The distribution of test scores. *Educ. Psychol. Meas.* 32: 725–35

Silverstein A B 1980 Item intercorrelations, item-test correlations and test reliability. *Educ. Psych. Meas.* 40: 353–55

Stanley J C 1971 Reliability. In: Thorndike R L (ed.) 1971 *Educational Measurement.* American Council on Education, Washington, DC

Thorndike R L 1982 *Applied Psychometrics.* Houghton Mifflin, Boston, Massachusetts

van der Linden W J 1981 A latent trait look at pretest–posttest validation of criterion-referenced test items. *Rev. Educ. Res.* 51: 379–402

Wood R 1977 Multiple choice: A state of the art report. *Eval. Educ.* 1: 191–280

# Validation of Individual Test Response Patterns

### R. M. Smith

Aberrant response patterns have long been considered as a source of potential error in the measurement process. Thurstone was keenly aware of the need to eliminate population considerations from the measurement

of people. In his attempts to build absolute scales he screened out individuals whose response patterns were erratic.

Mosier (1940), Glaser (1949), and Lumsden (1978)

used Thurstone's work on equal appearing intervals and the law of comparative judgment to develop various methods of identifying aberrant response patterns. The techniques developed by these authors require that consistency of responses, either correct or incorrect, must be a characteristic of responses to items that lie considerably above or below a person's ability. It is not a feature of responses to items targeted on an individual's ability.

The relationship between the consistency of responses and the difference between a person's ability and an item's difficulty can be modeled by the probabilistic function that underlies latent trait theory. Using the probabilities of a correct response derived from these models, Wright and Stone (1979) and Levine and Rubin (1979) have developed a variety of measures of the validity of the response pattern. These measures are based on the departure of the observed response pattern from the modeled probabilities.

Another approach to validating response patterns is based on Guttman scaling (see *Guttman Scales*). Several indices have been developed to measure the departure of the individual's response pattern from the predicted pattern (Tatsuoka and Linn 1981). These indices assume that a person's responses to a test are perfect when they form a Guttman scale. A person whose response pattern to items ordered from easy to hard is 11110000 is said to fit the model perfectly. A person whose response pattern to items is 00001111 is an example of the worst possible case of misfit. These indices have two disadvantages. They must be calculated for the entire test, since it is impossible to test the fit of a single response or a subset of responses to the predicted pattern. In addition, the indices are dependent on the sample that took the test. The validity of a person's responses is therefore dependent on the people with whom that person is compared.

## 1. Specific Threats to the Measurement Process

In order to evaluate the various procedures for validating individual response patterns it is necessary to understand the possible range of individual measurement disturbances. Measurement disturbances are those things which interfere with the measurement process. These disturbances are problematic since they often result in a systematic over- or under-estimation of the person's true ability. Measurement disturbances can be classified into two basic types: disturbances that are characteristics of the testee and independent of the items, and disturbances that can be thought of as an interaction between the person and the item. There do not appear to be any measurement disturbances that are properties of the item and independent of the item.

The first general class of measurement disturbances are problems that are considered characteristics of the person being tested. These include, but are not necessarily limited to the problems listed below.

(a) *Startup/test anxiety.* Unexpected incorrect responses at the beginning of the test which will result in an underestimate of the person's ability.

(b) *Plodding/excessive cautiousness.* Unexpected omitted responses at the end of the test. If scored as incorrect the person's ability will be underestimated.

(c) *Copying from another person.* This will result in groups of unexpected results throughout the test unless the entire test is copied. Usually this will result in an overestimation of the person's ability.

(d) *Illness.* If the onset of the illness occurs during the test and impairs the person's ability to perform, the person's ability will be underestimated.

(e) *External distractions.* External distractions, for example mowing the lawn outside the window, can cause a person to perform below their ability on a subsection of the test. This will result in an underestimation of the person's ability.

(f) *Guessing to complete test/random guessing.* This behavior will result in both unexpected correct and incorrect responses. Generally it will result in an overestimate of the person's ability.

(g) *Lack of interest/boredom.* General lack of interest in the entire test or sections of the test will often result in unexpected incorrect responses, resulting in an underestimate of the person's ability.

(h) *Fatigue.* Long tests can often introduce a fatigue factor which causes unexpected incorrect responses late in the test resulting in an underestimate of the person's ability.

The second class of measurement disturbances, presented below, involves the interaction between a property of an item and a characteristic of a person:

(a) *Guessing when the correct answer is not known.* This usually occurs on items that are very difficult for the person and results in an overestimate of the person's ability.

(b) *Sloppiness/excessive carelessness.* This usually occurs on items that are very easy for the person and results in an underestimate of the person's ability.

(c) *Item content/person interaction.* This usually occurs when one of the skills or topics included on the test is overlearned or underlearned. This may result in an over- or under-estimate of the person's ability.

(d) *Item type/person interaction.* This usually occurs when one of the item formats differentially favors a person. It may result in an over- or under-estimate of the person's ability.

(e) *Item bias/person interaction.* This usually occurs when a subset of items differentially favors an ethnic group, age group, sex, curriculum, or cognitive style. This may result in an over- or under-estimate of the person's ability.

This type of disturbance is difficult to detect because it involves an interaction and thus can affect individuals to different degrees depending on the individual's susceptibility to the particular property of the item. Some people will guess on every item that is too difficult for them while some people will never guess on an item. The detection of this type of disturbance requires the identification of sets of items that exhibit such tendencies before it is possible to test the effect of the interaction on a person's ability estimate.

## 2. Item Group Formation

There are three methods of forming the item sets necessary to test for the interaction between the properties of the item and the characteristics of the person. The choice of the particular method depends on how easy the property or characteristic is to detect. People with differential familiarity with a particular item content, item format, or cognitive level are difficult to identify prior to testing. However, the classification of items into subsets based on observable characteristics can often be accomplished by expert judges.

In the case of differential familiarity based on some readily observable characteristic of the person (sex, race, age, or curriculum), it is usually easier to group people by these characteristics than it is for expert judges to identify items that will be differentially familiar to these subpopulations. Items can be calibrated separately for each identifiable subpopulation, and the item difficulties from each calibration compared.

In cases where the measurement disturbance (guessing or sloppiness) involves both a property of an item and a characteristic of a person that are both difficult to observe, it is possible to detect the tendency of the item to evoke this type of behavior by analyzing the item characteristic curves. The item characteristic curves (ICC) for normality, guessing, and sloppiness are shown in Fig. 1. Item characteristic curves that depart from the expected form can be detected by graphical analysis or by the systematic analysis of the residuals in the tails of the item characteristic curve.

## 3. Possible Methods of Correcting for Disturbances

There are at least four basic responses to the question of what to do about measurement disturbances. The

most popular one is to ignore the problem. Any time a test score is based on the number correct or some standardization based on the total raw score and no attempt is made to validate the individual response pattern, a decision has been made to ignore all possible sources of measurement disturbance. In terms of the group this may be an acceptable decision since most measurement disturbances can be thought of as random variables. Therefore, the overall effect on the group mean may be zero. In terms of the individual however this may be the worst possible decision since an individual may be helped or hurt by factors unrelated to what is being measured.

A second possible solution is to assume that every person is affected to the same degree by the measurement disturbance. Two examples of this type of solution are guessing corrections and total score corrections based on the number of "biased" items in the test. Techniques for removing disturbances based on this assumption continue to be popular despite evidence suggesting that all individuals are not equally affected by guessing or the presence of biased items.

A third possible solution is to use some method of robust estimation to moderate the effect of the unexpected responses in any response pattern (Wainer and Wright 1980). These procedures are based on the capacity to calculate the probability of a correct response for any item/person interaction within the framework of latent trait theory. These procedures make no assumptions about the presence or absence of measurement disturbances, nor do they attempt to classify the cause of the disturbances, but rather, check each response pattern for unexpected responses and make an appropriate statistical correction. One advantage of these corrections is that they are applied at the individual, rather than group, level. Persons without unexpected responses will not have their overall ability estimate changed by these procedures.

A fourth solution is to use all the information available about the items and the persons in a systematic analysis of each person's response pattern. This analysis seeks to identify the cause and magnitude of the measurement disturbance and is referred to as person analysis. The procedure employs a variety of comparisons between expected and observed scores to detect the measurement disturbances (Wright and Stone 1979).

Once such disturbances have been detected there are four possible decisions that can be made: (a) rather than report a single overall ability, report several separate abilities, for example, one for addition and one for multiplication; (b) modify the response string and re-estimate the person's ability, for example, eliminate the 10 unreached items at the end of a person's response pattern; (c) decide that there is not enough information in the response pattern to report any score, that is, retest the individual; or (d) decide that the error introduced into the estimation procedure by the measurement disturbance is small enough so that the impact to

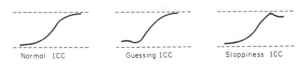

**Figure 1**
Typical item characteristic curves

the person's total ability estimate is marginal. This decision can be based on a comparison with the standard error of measurement associated with each ability estimate.

## 4. Person Analysis with the Rasch Model

Person analysis with the Rasch model is based on the analysis of individual item/person residuals. The residual is the difference between the observed response and the expected response:

$$R = O - E \tag{1}$$

where $O$ = the observed item score $(1, O)$, and $E$ = the expected score. The expected score is the probability of a correct response, which under the Rasch model is

$$P = \frac{\exp(\beta - \delta)}{1 + \exp(\beta - \delta)} \tag{2}$$

where $\beta$ = the ability of the person, and $\delta$ = the difficulty of the item.

One method of detecting measurement disturbances is to order the items from easy to hard and plot the residuals $(R)$ for every item/person interaction (see Fig. 2).

In the typical example the person answered the easy items correctly, the hard items incorrectly, and about half of the medium difficulty items correctly. There are no unexpected residuals in the response pattern. Thus there is no reason to believe that the person's overall ability estimate is not an accurate reflection of his or her true ability. In the guessing case there are several observations that can be made. This person missed two relatively easy items and answered two difficult items correctly. Thus there are four surprising responses in this response pattern. There are enough unexpected responses to signal that the person's ability estimate may not be accurate.

Residual plots have two drawbacks. A single plot summarizes only part of the available information. To adequately analyze a person's response string it may be necessary to make as many as five plots per person. For a large number of examinees reviewing all of the plots

may be tedious. In addition the task of differentiating between a plot marginally acceptable and those which show signs of moderate measurement disturbances is difficult. It is possible to overcome these two drawbacks by summarizing the information contained in the residuals by collecting it into a series of fit statistics. These are known as person fit statistics.

There are three basic methods of summarizing the information contained in the residuals. The unweighted total fit statistic squares the raw residual, standardizes it, and sums it over all the item/person interactions. The unweighted total is

$$UT = \sum_{i=1}^{L} \frac{(O_i - E_i)^2}{E_i(1 - E_i)} \tag{3}$$

The unweighted between fit statistic is a direct test of the item-freed measurement property of the Rasch model. If the data fit the model the overall ability estimate should accurately predict the person's score on any subset of items. By comparing the person's predicted score $(\Sigma E)$ with the observed score $(\Sigma O)$ on any subset of items it is possible to test the fit of the data to the model. The unweighted between fit statistic is

$$UB = \left[\frac{1}{(J - 1)}\right] \sum_{1}^{J} \frac{(\sum_{i \in J} O_i - \sum_{i \in J} E_i)^2}{\sum_{i \in J} [E_i(1 - E_i)]} \tag{4}$$

where $J$ is the number of subsets. Both the total and the between fit statistic are based on the overall ability estimate. To test the fit of the response to the subset of which that item is a member it is possible to estimate the person's ability on that subset alone and create an unweighted within-set fit statistic for each subset. This fit statistic is

$$UW = \sum_{i=1}^{L_J} \frac{(O_i - E_i)^2}{[E_i(1 - E_i)]} \tag{5}$$

where $E$ is based on the subset ability estimate. These summary statistics can be converted into standard statistics symmetry about the mean by using a cube root transformation.

Each fit statistic plays a different role in the process of detecting measurement disturbances. The total fit statistic which provides a single overall test of fit is better at detecting guessing, sloppiness, and other types of random measurement disturbances.

The between fit statistic is better at detecting more systematic forms of measurement disturbances, for example, startup, plodding, guessing to complete, and all disturbances resulting from item/person interactions. This test of fit requires the a priori development of nonoverlapping subsets of items for each test, grouping the items on the basis of item difficulty, position on the test, item type, specific forms of bias, etc. It is possible to perform any number of between tests on each response pattern.

The within fit statistic is not very useful in detecting new instances of measurement disturbance. Its greatest

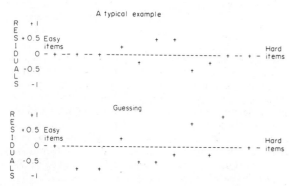

**Figure 2**
Residual plots

utility is in helping to distinguish between possible causes of measurement disturbance detected by the other two fit statistics. It is possible to compute a within fit statistic for each subgroup used in the between fit analysis.

The use of these three statistics to systematically examine response patterns and to select cases with unexpectedly large fit statistics for individual analysis, can greatly reduce the time necessary to validate the individual response patterns. Given existing programs, it is possible to perform this type of analysis for as little as US$10 per person—a small price to pay to assure that the individual abilities being reported are in fact accurate estimates of the person's true ability.

## Bibliography

Glaser R 1949 A methodological analysis of the inconsistency of responses to test items. *Educ. Psychol. Meas.* 9: 727–37

Levine M V, Rubin D B 1979 Measuring appropriateness of multiple choice test scores. *J. Educ. Stat.* 4: 269–90

Lumsden J 1978 Tests are perfectly reliable. *Br. J. Math. Stat. Psychol.* 31: 19–26

Mosier C I 1940 Psychophysics and mental test theory: Fundamental postulates and elementary theorems. *Psychol. Rev.* 47: 355–66

Rasch G 1980 *Probabilistic Models for Some Intelligence and Attainment Tests.* University of Chicago Press, Chicago, Illinois

Tatsuoka K K, Linn R L 1981 Indices for detecting unusual item response patterns in personnel testing. *Computerised Adaptive Testing and Measurement.* Research Report 81–5. University of Illinois, Urbana, Illinois

Wainer H, Wright B D 1980 Robust estimation of ability in the Rasch model. *Psychometrika* 45: 373–91

Wright B D, Stone M 1979 *Best Test Design.* Mesa Press, Chicago, Illinois

# Thurstone Scales

## D. Andrich

Thurstone's extensive work on the construction of scales for understanding and measuring educational, psychological, and sociological variables, shows great care in formalizing the fundamentals of measurement. Such care, exemplified in the following remarks which preceded an analysis of opinion data, reflect a concern in the very foundations of scientific enquiry.

> We shall avoid mere correlational procedures since it is possible to do better than merely to correlate the attributes. When a problem is so involved that no rational formulation is available, then some quantification is still possible by the coefficients of correlation of contingency and the like. But such statistical procedures constitute an acknowledgement of failure to rationalize the problem and to establish the functions that underlie the data. We want to measure the separation between the two opinions on the attitude continuum and we want to test the validity of the assumed continuum by means of its internal consistency. (Thurstone 1959 p. 267)

For Thurstone, the rationalizing principle was that of linearity, which means that if the value of object *A* is greater than that of object *B* by an amount $a_1$, and if the value of object *B* is greater than that of object *C* by an amount of $a_2$, then the value of object *A* should be greater than that of object *C* by an amount close to the sum $a_1 + a_2$.

Many of Thurstone's papers on scaling, written in the 1920s and 1930s as the one from which the above quote has been drawn, are republished in Thurstone (1959).

## 1. Unidimensionality

Preceding the formalization of linearity is the notion of a single continuum or unidimensionality. Unidimensionality is a relative concept and is constructed either to understand complex phenomena or to facilitate decision making. Attitudes of people are clear examples of complex phenomena; yet Thurstone argued convincingly that there was a sense to placing them on a single continuum.

> When we discuss opinions, about prohibition for example, we quickly find that these opinions are multidimensional, that they cannot all be represented in a linear continuum. The various opinions cannot be completely described merely as "more" or "less". They scatter in many dimensions, but the very idea of measurement implies a linear continuum of some sort, such as length, price, volume, weight, age. When the idea of measurement is applied to scholastic achievement, for example, it is necessary to force the qualitative variations into a scholastic linear scale of some kind.
>
> And so it is also with attitudes. We do not hesitate to compare them by the "more or less" type of judgment. We say about a man, for example, that he is more in favour of prohibition than some other, and the judgment conveys its meaning very well with the implications of a linear scale along which people or opinions might be allocated. (Thurstone 1959 pp. 218–19)

## 2. Defining a Continuum

Whatever the property, or in modern terminology, trait, for which a scale is to be constructed, it is necessary to operationalize and formalize the continuum. In the case of mental tests, such as intelligence, aptitude, or achievement, this is done by formalizing the notion of the difficulty of a question, and by spacing the questions on the continuum according to their relative difficulties.

We shall, therefore, locate these test questions on the scale as landmarks of different levels of intellectual growth. (Thurstone 1925 p. 434)

The continuum identifying a particular attitude, and termed by Thurstone generally as the "affective continuum" (Thurstone 1959 p. 292), is characterized in the same way. Statements such as "I feel the church services give me inspiration and help to live up to my best during the following week", and "I think the church seeks to impose a lot of worn-out dogmas and medieval superstitions" (Thurstone 1959 p. 267), are scaled so that they have affective values which locate them on the particular continuum.

## 3. Statistical Formulations

Thurstone's mathematical–statistical formulations for his scales arise from the psychophysical methods and models of Fechner and Weber in which the basic data collection design is that of pair comparisons. In such a design, each of a group of persons compares objects with respect to some physical property, such as weight or brightness, and declares which of the pair has more of the property. Thurstone contributed to the logic of psychophysics, and in the process, liberated the construction of scales for subjective values from the need of any physical continuum.

### 3.1 The Law of Comparative Judgment

The basis for this liberation was Thurstone's law of comparative judgment (Thurstone 1959 p. 39), which may be summarized as follows:

(a) When person $n$ reacts to object $i$, the person perceives a value $d_{ni}$ of the property in question. This value is assumed to be a continuous random variable defined by

$$d_{ni} = \alpha_i + \varepsilon_{ni} \qquad (1)$$

where $\alpha_i$ is the subjective scale value of object $i$ and is constant with respect to all persons in a specified population, and $\varepsilon_{ni}$ is the error component associated with person $n$. Over the population of persons, $d_{ni}$ is defined to be normally distributed with mean $\alpha_i$ and variance $\sigma_i^2$.

(b) When person $n$ compares two objects $i$ and $j$ then the person judges that object $i$ has more of the property if the difference $d_{ni} - d_{nj} > 0$. In the population, this difference:

$$d_{ij} = d_{ni} - d_{nj} = (\alpha_i - \alpha_j) + (\varepsilon_i - \varepsilon_j) \qquad (2)$$

is a continuous random variable normally distributed with mean value $\alpha_{ij} = \alpha_i - \alpha_j$ and variance

$$\sigma_{ij}^2 = \sigma_i^2 + \sigma_j^2 - 2\rho_{ij}\sigma_i\sigma_j.$$

This difference process for a fixed $\alpha_{ij}$, is shown in Fig. 1 in which the shaded region represents the prob-

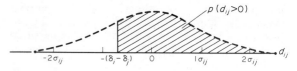

**Figure 1**
Probability that $d_{ij} > 0$ for fixed $(\delta_i - \delta_j)$ in a pair comparison design

ability that $d_{ij} > 0$.

In empirical data, the proportion of persons who judge that object $i$ has more of the property than object $j$ is an estimate of this probability. The associated estimate of $\alpha_i - \alpha_j$ then is the corresponding normal deviate. The step of transforming a proportion, taken as an estimate of a probability in a normal distribution, was, in fact, the key step in Thurstone's linearization of his scales.

The expression for $\sigma_{ij}^2$ was further modified by Thurstone (1959 p. 39) into special cases. One special case is to assume that the correlation $\rho_{ij}$ is zero. A further specialization is to let $\sigma_i^2 = \sigma_j^2 = \sigma^2$. This produces Thurstone's Case V of the law of comparative judgment, and is the easiest case to apply. Torgerson (1958) and Bock and Jones (1968) elaborate on the law of comparative judgment and develop more advanced techniques for estimating the scale values. Edwards (1957) provides an excellent elementary treatment.

### 3.2 Attitude Testing—Subjective Values

Thurstone stressed that comparisons need not be constrained to physical objects:

> One of the main requirements of a truly subjective metric is that it shall be entirely independent of all physical measurement. In freeing ourselves completely from physical measurement, we are also free to experiment with aesthetic objects and with many other types of stimuli to which there does not correspond any known physical measurement. (Thurstone 1959 pp. 182–83)

For constructing attitude scales, statements reflecting different intensities of attitude may be scaled through the pair comparison design.

### 3.3 Mental Testing

Thurstone applied the principles of the law of comparative judgment to mental testing by a simple redefinition of one of the variables. Effectively, the ability of each person replaced the value of one of the two entities which were compared. Thus, the ability of a person was compared with the difficulty of a question.

A common classification of persons taken by Thurstone was an age group. Then the proportion of any age group which succeeded on any question was transformed to a normal deviate and used as a basis for scaling. This principle is described in detail in Thurstone (1925).

### 3.4 The Absolute Zero of Scales

Armed with the law of comparative judgment, and its various modifications which gave him scales with equal intervals, Thurstone pushed rational measurement even further. He sought to find natural origins for scales both in the measurement of intelligence (Thurstone 1928) and in the measurement of subjective values.

With respect to the former, Thurstone established that, when measured on an interval scale, the variance of intelligence at any age group was proportional to the mean of the age group. Accordingly, he extrapolated the relationship to the age level at which the variance was zero, and concluded that this was a reasonable estimate of the natural origin of intelligence scales.

With respect to the natural origin of subjective values, the principle used was to first scale single objects using the pair comparison design, and then to scale objects in combinations. The values of the objects were relative to a natural origin when the sum of the values of two single objects was the same as the value assigned to the objects as a combination.

This work on a rational origin has not had much impact on psychometric research, but it is exemplary methodologically, and may yet prove to be important, particularly in understanding intellectual growth and development.

### 3.5 The Methods of Equal Appearing Intervals and Successive Intervals

Two disadvantages of the pair comparison design are that it is time consuming and taxing on judges. As a result of these disadvantages, the much simpler method of rank ordering was adapted to the law of comparative judgment (Thurstone 1959) and models for incomplete pair comparison designs have been developed (Bock and Jones 1968).

Another adaptation of the law of comparative judgment was with respect to the design of *equal appearing intervals* and its extension to the method of successive intervals. This design was specifically considered in relation to the construction of an attitude scale as an instrument for measuring attitudes of persons. After creating a list of some 100 statements, based on a literature search of the topic in question and opinions of experts, the statements are placed by 200 or 300 judges into 11 intervals. These intervals are to be considered equally spaced in intensity on the affective continuum.

Scale values for the statements are then computed on the assumption that the equal appearing intervals actually operate as if they were equal. For the method of successive intervals, the data collection design is essentially the same, but instead of assuming that equality of intervals prevails, estimates of scale values of intervals are calculated.

The model for computing the scale values is a direct extension of the model in Fig. 1. As in the derivation of the law of comparative judgment, it is assumed that a continuous random variable $d_i$ is induced when the person encounters and reacts to a statement. Then if there are $m$ boundaries or thresholds between the $m + 1$ successive intervals on the affective continuum designated by $\tau_1, \tau_2, \ldots, \tau_k, \ldots, \tau_m$, the response corresponds to the interval in which the value of the random variable falls.

The estimate of the appropriate model probabilities is again given by a proportion; this time by the proportion of persons who classify the statement to be in or below a given category. By transforming these probability estimates to corresponding normal deviates, the scale values of both the statements and the category boundaries can be estimated.

The approach and modelling associated with the method of successive intervals has been used as a basis for the analysis of qualitative data in which three or more categories have some order, and the mathematical statistical and computing techniques have been advanced considerably (Bock 1975). A contrasting approach to dealing with ordered categories is presented in Andrich (1978).

## 4. Checks on the Scales

Once a set of statements or questions has been placed on a continuum, various checks or controls on the scales must be made. Because Thurstone was concerned that measurement be scientifically defensible, he stressed that the scales must be checked for validity, and that it must be possible for the data not to accord with the theory underlying the scale construction. The first check is that the ordering and spacing of the questions or statements is consistent with an informal appreciation of the continuum. If the observed ordering or spacing violates this informal understanding, then a closer examination of the scale construction should follow. Perhaps only some questions or statements need to be eliminated. Alternatively, it may be that the effects of dimensions other than the one intended have played too great a role. Finally, it may be that the scale construction is sound, and that a new understanding about the continuum, not appreciated before the construction of the scale, has been revealed.

### 4.1 Statistical Tests

More formal statistical checks are also usually applied. Many of these checks take advantage of the feature that the estimates of the scale values of questions are a summary of the data. From this summary, and the particular mathematical model, an attempt is then made to "recover" the observed details of the data, usually the relevant proportions. To the degree that the detail is recovered, to that degree the scale is confirmed to be internally consistent. Such statistical checks on the model are generally called tests of fit: they test the fit between the data and the model.

Finally, it is possible to test directly the degree to which the differences among scale values of questions, taken in threes, satisfy the requirement of additivity mentioned in Sect. 1. It should be appreciated that no test of fit is necessary and sufficient for the models, and the results of the different tests of fit are not mutually exclusive. Bock and Jones (1968) elaborate on the statistical tests of fit.

### 4.2 Principles of Invariance

Another fundamental requirement which can be applied in checking the validity of a scale is that of invariance of scale values of statements across populations of persons who may have different attitudes.

> If the scale is to be regarded as valid, the scale values of the statements should not be affected by the opinions of the people who help to construct it. This may turn out to be a severe test in practice, but the scaling method must stand such a test before it can be accepted as being more than a description of the people who construct the scale. (Thurstone 1959 p. 228)

To the degree that the invariance is demonstrated across different groups of persons, including those with known differences on the trait under investigation, to that degree the scale is applicable across those groups. The scale is deliberately constructed both to capture the trait in questions and to exhibit the desired properties of a measuring instrument.

### 4.3 Person Measurement

Thurstone also appreciated the complementary requirement that a person's measure should not depend on the actual questions used in a scale. In the context of constructing a mental test, among the requirements he listed is the following:

> It should be possible to omit several test questions at different levels of the scale without affecting the individual score. (Thurstone 1926 p. 446)

Interestingly, however, Thurstone never seemed to formalize a person parameter in his mathematical statistical models. And despite the specifications of invariance, both in the scaling of questions or statements and in the measurement of persons, he seemed to be constrained by considering persons always to be sampled from some specified population. Possibly it was this constraint which prevented his formalizing a person parameter in his models.

The procedure for attitude measurement of individuals, though based on a set of scaled statements and though eminently plausible, is essentially ad hoc. A person responds to an attitude scale, which consists of statements approximately equally spaced on the continuum, by either agreeing or disagreeing with each statement. Then the person's measure of attitude is taken as the median of the scale values of the statements endorsed.

It seems that a further reason why Thurstone did not formalize the person parameter in attitude scales was that he dealt with only one of the two types of scales, and in particular, the one in which it is more difficult to formalize a person parameter. The type of scale with which he dealt implies that a person would tend to endorse the statements in a given range on the scale which represented his or her attitude, and would tend not to endorse statements more extreme in either direction. The other type of scale, subsequently elaborated by Guttman (1950), implies that if a person endorses a statement of a particular scale value, then the person will tend to endorse all statements with smaller scale values and tend not to endorse all statements with greater scale values.

> In a small 1929 monograph I described two types of attitude scales. . . . These were called the *maximum probability type* and the *increasing probability type*. All our work was with the first type. Recently, there has been interest in the second type of scaling, which lends itself to certain types of attitude problems. The scaling of attitude statements can be accomplished directly from the records of acceptance and rejection for a group of subjects without the sorting procedure that we used, but, as far as I know, such a scaling procedure has not yet been developed. (Thurstone 1959 p. 214)

The model which (a) is a probabilistic version of the Guttman-type scale; (b) permits measurement of persons and the scaling of statements from the direct endorsement or otherwise of the persons; and (c) which also captures all the properties of linearity articulated by Thurstone, is the simple logistic model known as the Rasch model (Rasch 1960, 1980). The scales produced are those of the increasing probability type.

### Bibliography

Andrich D 1978 A rating formulation for ordered response categories. *Psychometrika* 43: 561–73

Bock R D 1975 *Multivariate Statistical Methods in Behavioral Research*. McGraw-Hill, New York

Bock R D, Jones L V 1968 *The Measurement and Prediction of Judgment and Choice*. Holden-Day, San Francisco, California

Edwards A L 1957 *Techniques of Attitude Scale Construction*. Appleton-Century-Crofts, New York

Guttman L 1950 The problem of attitude and opinion measurement. In: Stouffer A et al. (eds.) 1950 *Measurement and Prediction*. Wiley, New York

Rasch G 1960 *Probabilistic Models for Some Intelligence and Attainment Tests*. University of Chicago Press, Chicago, Illinois, repr. 1980

Thurstone L L 1925 A method of scaling psychological and educational tests. *J. Educ. Psychol.* 16: 433–51

Thurstone L L 1926 The scoring of individual performance. *J. Educ. Psychol.* 17: 446–57

Thurstone L L 1928 The absolute zero in intelligence measurement. *Psychol. Rev.* 35: 175–97

Thurstone L L 1959 *The Measurement of Values*. University of Chicago Press, Chicago, Illinois

Torgerson W S 1958 *Theory and Methods of Scaling*. Wiley, New York

# Guttman Scales

## L. W. Anderson

Guttman scales (Guttman 1944) contain a set of statements which all relate to a person's attitude toward a single object (e.g., attitude toward school). Guttman scales possess two characteristics. First, the statements included on such scales represent increasingly positive feelings with respect to the attitude object. This characteristic differentiates Guttman scales from Likert scales. Second, the endorsement of any statement implies the endorsement of each less positive statement. Scales possessing this second characteristic can be referred to as cumulative scales (Anderson 1981). This latter characteristic differentiates Guttman scales from Thurstone scales.

When a Guttman scale is administered the respondents are directed to indicate whether they agree with (endorse) or disagree with (do not endorse) each statement. Each respondent's score is simply the number of statements endorsed. Because of the cumulative nature of Guttman scales this total score provides information about the particular statements that were and were not endorsed. If, for example, a person received a score of five on an eight-statement Guttman scale, he or she would have most likely agreed with the five least positive statements on the scale. Furthermore, he or she would have most likely disagreed with the three most positive statements.

The reasonableness of inferring the pattern of responses from the total score depends on whether a scale is, in fact, a Guttman scale. Unlike Thurstone and Likert scales, judges are not used to examine the appropriateness of the statements to be included on Guttman scales. Rather, the determination that a scale is a Guttman scale is made solely on the basis of two empirical criteria: the coefficient of reproducibility and the coefficient of scalability. In order to compute these two coefficients the tentative Guttman scale must be administered to a fairly large sample of the population for whom the scale is intended. The responses are submitted to a Guttman scale analysis, typically performed by a standard computer program.

The Guttman scale analysis begins with an examination of the number of inappropriate response patterns. Based on the two characteristics of Guttman scales mentioned earlier, certain response patterns are appropriate while others are inappropriate. Consider, for example, a scale in which five statements are ordered from least positive to most positive. Suppose that responses of agree are designated by the number "1" and responses of disagree are designated by the number "0." A response pattern of 1 1 1 0 0 is appropriate since the three least positive statements were endorsed while the two most positive statements were not endorsed. On the other hand, a response pattern such as 1 1 0 1 0

is inappropriate since the fourth most positive statement was endorsed while the third most positive statement (that is, a less positive statement) was not. As a rule, any response pattern in which a "1" appears to the right of a "0" is an inappropriate response pattern. Furthermore, for each inappropriate response pattern an error is counted every time a "1" appears to the right of a "0." In the example above one error is present in the inappropriate response pattern.

The total number of errors is computed by summing across all of the response patterns of the sample of respondents. The total number of responses is found by multiplying the number of statements appearing on the scale by the number of respondents in the sample. The percent of errors is calculated by dividing the total number of errors by the total number of responses. Finally, this percent of errors is subtracted from 100 percent to yield what Guttman refers to as the coefficient of reproducibility (CR). Guttman suggests that this coefficient should be larger than 90 (that is, the percent of errors does not exceed 10 percent) if the scale is to be considered a Guttman scale.

That the coefficient of reproducibility is greater than 90 is a necessary but not sufficient condition for a Guttman scale. A second empirical criterion must be met if a scale is a Guttman scale. This second criterion is based on Guttman's coefficient of scalability (CS). According to Anderson (1981), "Guttman believed that it was impossible to interpret the magnitude of the coefficient of reproducibility without some knowledge of the minimum value that this coefficient can assume. He also was aware that the minimum value of the coefficient of reproducibility (which he called the minimum marginal reproducibility, or MMR) would be computed for the scale" (p. 256). In common terms, the minimum marginal reproducibility index represents a chance score. That is, the minimum marginal reproducibility index is the percent of appropriate response patterns that would occur "by chance" given the number of respondents receiving the various total scores and the number of respondents endorsing each statement.

Several computations are needed to produce the coefficient of scalability from the index of minimum marginal reproducibility. The first involves the subtraction of the minimum marginal reproducibility from the coefficient of reproducibility. This computation yields what Guttman referred to as the percent improvement (PI), the difference between the actual and minimal coefficient of reproducibility. The second computation involves the subtraction of the minimum marginal reproducibility from 100 percent. This computation yields the possible percent improvement (PPI), the difference between the maximal and minimal coefficient of reproducibility.

The third computation requires dividing percent improvement by possible percent improvement and results in the coefficient of scalability. This coefficient, then, represents the extent to which the coefficient of reproducibility is substantially beyond that which could be expected by chance. Guttman suggested that the coefficient of scalability should exceed 60.

These dual criteria of 90 and 60 are used to determine a Guttman scale. If both criteria are met, then a Guttman scale has been developed. If not, then a Guttman scale is not present. As can be seen, then, a scale either is or is not a Guttman scale; there is no room for close approximations. Proctor (1970) expressed some concern about this dichotomous nature of Guttman scales. As a consequence, he developed a probabilistic formulation of the Guttman scale model. Interested readers are referred to the Proctor formulation for additional information. Sato (1975) has also extended the model in order to analyze and evaluate achievement tests.

Guttman scales are difficult to construct. Statements may appear to be cumulative in nature, but the results of the Guttman scale analysis may fail to support this appearance. If either the coefficient of reproducibility or the coefficient of scalability is too low, the assumptions underlying Guttman scales are not met. If this is the case several alternatives are possible. First, modifications in statements can be made based on the evidence obtained from the initial administration of the scale. These modifications may result in legitimate Gutt-man scales. Second, the Proctor reformulation can be used to transform Guttman's original deterministic model into a probabilistic model. Such a transformation may be especially beneficial for scales closely approximating Guttman scales.

Despite the difficulty in developing Guttman scales, such scales do have several advantages over Thurstone and Likert scales. First, as has been mentioned, it is possible to determine the entire pattern of responses to the statements from a single total score. Thus, more specific information about the nature of the respondent's attitude is possible. Second, the cumulative nature of Guttman scales makes it feasible to assess change in attitude. An increase of one point on the total score means that the respondent has moved up the attitude continuum by one statement. Change then becomes additive.

In summary, then, Guttman scales are difficult to construct but extremely useful as measures of attitude. In general, the benefits of achieving a Guttman scale far outweigh the difficulties in achieving one.

## Bibliography

Anderson L W 1981 *Assessing Affective Characteristics in the Schools*. Allyn and Bacon, Boston, Massachusetts

Guttman L 1944 A basis for scaling qualitative data. *Am. Sociol. Rev.* 9: 139–50

Proctor C H 1970 A probabilistic formulation and statistical analysis of Guttman scaling. *Psychometrika* 35: 73–78

Sato T 1975 *The Construction and Interpretation of S–P Tables*. Meiji Tosho, Tokyo (in Japanese)

# Likert Scales

## L. W. Anderson

Likert scales (Likert 1932) consist of a series of statements all of which are related to a person's attitude toward a single object (for instance, attitude toward teachers). Two types of statements appear on Likert scales. The first type includes statements whose endorsement indicates a positive or favorable attitude toward the object of interest (to be called "favorable statements"). The statement "I like the teachers in this school" is an example of a favorable statement. The second type includes statements whose endorsement indicates a negative or unfavorable attitude toward the object (to be called "unfavorable statements"). The statement "Most teachers make life in school miserable" is an example of an unfavorable statement. An approximately equal number of favorable and unfavorable statements typically are included on a Likert scale.

People to whom a Lickert scale is administered are directed to indicate the extent to which they endorse each statement. Typical response options are strongly agree, agree, not sure, disagree, and strongly disagree. A numerical value is assigned to each response option. For a favorable statement five points can be assigned to a "strongly agree" response, four points to an "agree" response, and so on. For an unfavorable statement the scoring is reversed (that is, five points are assigned to a "strongly disagree" response). After a numerical value has been assigned to each response made by a particular individual, the numerical values are summed to produce a total score. For this reason, Likert scales are sometimes referred to as summated scales.

According to Anderson (1981), satisfactory Likert scales can be developed if a series of eight steps are followed by the designer. These steps are described below:

(a) Statements must be written that are favorable or unfavorable with respect to the attitude object.

(b) Judges are called in to examine the statements that have been written. The judges should be selected from the population for whom the scale is designed. They are asked to examine each statement and classify it either as favorable, unfavorable, or neither.

(c) Any statement not classified as favorable or unfavorable by the vast majority of the judges is eliminated.

(d) The remaining statements are placed on a piece of paper in a random order. Appropriate directions and response options are added. The directions typically indicate that the respondents should indicate how they feel about each statement by marking SA if they strongly agree, A if they agree, NS if they are not sure of their feelings, and SD if they strongly disagree. The directions also may indicate the purpose of the scale and suggest that there are no right or wrong answers. At this point an initial version of a Likert scale has been prepared.

(e) The initial version of the Likert scale is administered to a sample of the population for whom the scale is intended. In order to gather meaningful, reliable data on statements individually and collectively, a sample that is several times larger than the number of statements should be used.

(f) The correlation between the responses made to each statement and the total scale scores is computed.

(g) Each statement whose correlation with the total score is not statistically significant is eliminated. The fact that each statement must be correlated with the total scale score if it is to be included on the final form of the scale is referred to as Likert's Criterion of Internal Consistency.

(h) The final form of the scale is prepared.

Following these eight steps will produce a traditional Likert scale.

Over the years various modifications have been made by developers and users of Likert scales. These modifications fall into one of two categories: (a) modification of the response options, and (b) modification of the statement format.

Original Likert scales contained five response options ranging from strongly agree to strongly disagree as indicated earlier. Two-, three-, four-, six-, and seven-response options have been used on subsequent scales. The use of an even number of response options reflects the concern on the part of scale designers that respondents might use the "not sure" response option to avoid making a real choice. With an even number of response options the respondents are "forced" to choose between favorable and unfavorable responses to the attitude object.

The use of a larger number of response options reflects the attempt to increase the internal consistency

of the scale by increasing the number of total response opportunities given to the respondents. Increasing the number of response options on a Likert scale is similar in this regard to increasing the number of items in dichotomously scored cognitive tests. The use of a smaller number of response options, on the other hand, reflects the attempt to make the scale more appropriate for younger or less well-educated respondents. These types of respondents typically are able to make fewer reliable differentiations. Fewer response options require fewer differentiations.

In addition to modifications in the number of response options, alterations have been made in the statement format. Incomplete statements rather than complete statements have been used. When incomplete statements have been used, appropriate modifications in the response options also have been made. The following illustrates these modifications.

When school is cancelled because of bad weather, I am:

(a) very happy

(b) happy

(c) sad

(d) very sad

In this example, an unfavorable incomplete statement has been written. The response options suggest different degrees of attitude, as do the more traditional response options. At the same time, however, these response options are more appropriate given the nature of the incomplete statement.

The advantages of Likert scales include ease of construction (relative to Guttman and Thurstone scales); adaptability to a wide variety of attitude objects, situations, and settings; and ability to assess both directions and intensity of attitude. The major disadvantage is that different response patterns can produce the same total score. Likert scales therefore are not as sensitive to assessing change as are Guttman and Thurstone scales.

In summary, then, Likert scales consist of statements possessing two characteristics. First, the statements represent either favorable or unfavorable attitudes as determined by judges. Second, the responses to each statement are significantly correlated with the sum total of responses to the entire set of statements. Statements not possessing these characteristics are eliminated from the final form of the scale. For this reason designers of Likert scales are encouraged to write more statements than will ultimately be needed.

## Bibliography

Anderson L W 1981 *Assessing Affective Characteristics in the Schools*. Allyn and Bacon, Boston, Massachusetts
Edwards A L 1957 *Techniques of Attitude Scale Construction*. Appleton-Century-Crofts, New York
Likert R 1932 A technique for the measurement of attitudes. *Arch. Psychol.* No. 140 (whole issue)

# Semantic Differential Measurement

## J. L. Phillips

The semantic differential is a method for measuring aspects of the meaning of various concepts. In addition, it is widely used as an attitude measurement technique. It was developed to tap connotative meaning by Charles Osgood and his associates at the University of Illinois during the 1950s. Used in its original form and in various transformations, it is attractive for its simplicity and its versatility, but is not without controversy.

## 1. Description

The semantic differential consists of a set of seven-point bipolar scales and a set of concepts. Each concept (a word, short phrase, picture, etc.) is rated on each scale (for instance, good–bad, loud–quiet, old–young). A typical format presents a concept at the top of a printed page with the set of scales below, but there are variations. Single concept–scale pairs are often isolated. Subjects are instructed to mark towards the extremes of each scale if a concept is closely related to one of the bipolar adjectives and toward the middle if a concept is only slightly related. The midpoint of the scale means that the concept is neutral on the scale, ambivalent on the scale, or the scale is irrelevant to the concept.

## 2. Results and Applications

The simplicity of the format provides an unusual economy in data collection. For example, a semantic differential instrument consisting of 30 concepts and 12 scales administered to 50 subjects generates, in an hour, $30 \times 12 \times 50 = 18,000$ data points. While such economy has value, it creates a need for data reduction. An advantage of the semantic differential is that data reduction techniques are available. It has been shown that when concepts are sampled representatively, data subjected to factor analysis will allow a partition of scales into three categories or factors. These factors are evaluation (E), potency (P), and activity (A). These factors accounted for over 47 percent of the variance in the original (Thesaurus) study and 58 percent or more in a recent study (Mann et al. 1979). This EPA structure is robust and replicable. Reduction of semantic differential data into evaluative, potency, and activity scores is empirically warranted.

Evidence for robustness has been summarized by Osgood et al. (1975). These writers have claimed that EPA is independent of specific scales, age, sex, political orientation, and pathology of subject, as well as specific concepts. They have reported evidence for this trifactorial pattern across 21 different language communities. Invariance has been shown by Mann et al.

(1979) over procedural and analytic variations. A study by Chapman et al. (1980) identified EPA using evoked brain potentials.

The semantic differential has been adapted for many uses. Recently, articles using the semantic differential to measure attitudes have been approximately four times as frequent as those directed to semantic concerns. It has been applied to such domains as sports, health, familial issues, industrial/organizational considerations, and to ecological concepts. The semantic differential has been geographically widespread. From 1977 through 1981, articles about the semantic differential have appeared in at least eight countries. By a conservative estimate, approximately 15 articles about the semantic differential appear each year.

In most applications, the concepts were determined by the objectives of the study. They were not selected through any sampling process or else were sampled from the limited domain of interest. This presents no problem for the semantic differential methodology. Assuming an appropriate selection of scales, these concepts can be scaled on each of the three factors. Investigators often report using "semantic differential-type" scales, by which they mean bipolar scales chosen to be appropriate to the concepts to be rated. The investigator should be aware that using such ad hoc scales may preclude the scaling of concepts using EPA. If such scale values are desired, then semantic differential scales with known relationships to EPA should be used. Frequently, however, the study may have objectives for which the EPA-structure is neither of practical nor theoretical significance. Adaptations (for instance, Alexander and Husek 1962, Franks and Marolla 1976, Guttentag and Bray 1976, and Hurwitz et al. 1975) have proven useful despite this lack of correspondence.

## 3. Criticisms of the Semantic Differential

In most applications the procedures associated with the semantic differential can be used as if they were theoretically neutral. Indeed, measures of evaluation, potency, and activity can be treated as stable descriptions of the concepts. While criticisms of the semantic differential have detracted from this utility (for instance, does the semantic differential have equal scale intervals?) there is no convincing evidence that such defects have any practical significance, nor is there evidence that alternatives to the semantic differential do not have similar problems.

Nevertheless, the semantic differential has received criticism. Of the articles about this technique, nearly one-third have addressed methodological or theoretical criticisms. Criticisms may be classified into three major categories. One group has directed itself to a set of scaling assumptions fundamental to the semantic differential methodology. Criticisms concerning the bipolarity of semantic differential scales and the integrity of the midpoint fall into this category. A second group deals with the interpretation of semantic differential data in terms of EPA. These criticisms include concept–scale interaction, and concept domain differences. A third group relates to the choice of the analytic model used to transform semantic differential data into the EPA structure. While this third group is important, its discussion is beyond the present scope. Readers should refer to such sources as Maguire (1973) or Murakami (1977).

### 3.1 Criticisms of Scaling Assumptions

Previously it was noted that the midpoint had the meanings of neutrality, ambivalence, and irrelevance. The semantic differential has been criticized for this confound (Forthman 1973). Mann et al. (1979) found that variations in the meaning of the midpoint have only a minimal effect on the data, but did recommend separating out the irrelevance meaning.

Efforts to deal with the midpoint issue have focused on scale irrelevance as the point of contention. The fact, however, that the midpoint can stand for ambivalence points up a conceptual difficulty. If a concept is simultaneously "good" and "bad" for example, and if this holds for many concepts, then "good" and "bad" would not represent the polar opposition required. This view of concepts as imbued with both properties suggests something other than the perfect negative correlation assumed by semantic differential scales.

Concepts can be constructed for which a scale would lack bipolarity in some phenomenological sense. The bipolar scale "hot–cold" seems other than bipolar when applied to concepts like "frozen enchilada" or "laid-back nymphomaniac." Green and Goldfried (1965) showed that unipolar variations of semantic differential scales did not manifest perfect negative correlations over a range of ordinary concepts. The correlation between the polar anchors varied across concepts. Such lack of bipolarity is damaging to the semantic differential and challenges the well-established EPA structure. It would not be expected, however, that unipolar scales exhibit perfect negative correlations. Given that neither of the unipolar scales have perfect reliability, their actual correlation would be constrained by their reliabilities. Mann et al. (1979) corrected unipolar scale correlations for unreliability and found that the median correlation, over 15 scales, was approximately $-0.97$. While this correlation is not perfect, it suggests that concerns about bipolarity have been exaggerated.

### 3.2 Criticisms of the EPA Structure

Despite the ubiquity of the EPA structure, not all data will generate EPA. Data that fail to reflect EPA can be obtained easily. If a list of things valued by some group are used as concepts to be rated by that group, the EPA structure will not emerge because there will be no evaluative factor. This is so because all concepts will be rated positively on all evaluative scales. A set of data based upon arbitrarily chosen concepts may thus not yield the EPA structure and this failure does not discredit the generality of EPA.

Despite this, many studies have "failed to find" EPA and have claimed that some alternative to EPA is the appropriate structure for their domain of interest. Because EPA has been proposed, not for a specific domain of concepts, but for the universe of concepts, it is not clear how this issue of universality versus domain specificity is to be resolved. While it may be the case that certain domains may have unique scale organizations, the demonstration of a divergent factor structure does not tarnish the universalistic claim of EPA. The issue is more complicated. From the standpoint of the semantic differential, the universal domain is nothing less than those concepts uniformly distributed through a "semantic space" defined by the dimensions of E, P, and A. A sample of concepts that reflect this uniformity is likely to display the EPA structure. A sample that does not may show a different organization, but such a sample would be rejected as nonrepresentative by the prior logic. If this issue is resolvable at all, then the focus of resolution would be on the methods of random sampling from some hypothetical "universal domain of concepts."

Of promise in this regard is empirical work dealing with an issue raised originally by Osgood et al. This is the issue of concept–scale interaction. Concept–scale interaction occurs whenever "the meanings of scales and their relation to other scales vary considerably with the concept being judged." For example, the scales good–bad, beautiful–ugly, valuable–worthless, and wise–foolish are evaluative in nature, and positively evaluated concepts are highly rated on all. Such a positively evaluated concept is "puppies." Indeed, "puppies" is seen as good, beautiful, and valuable, but also as foolish. In the context of "puppies," "foolish" most likely functions as a positive attribute, roughly synonymous with "cute."

Osgood et al. noted a high degree of such concept–scale interaction but also observed that this interaction does not obscure the EPA structure. Mann et al. (1979) showed that concept–scale interaction accounted for 10–15 percent of the variance, under typical conditions of administration, and that it did not alter the factor structure.

What has not been widely appreciated is that concept–scale interaction may be evidence for concept domain differences. If semantic differential scales have a different meaning for one set of concepts than for another, a research strategy would be to treat them as separate groups. The argument for EPA would be the demonstration of this structure for each group of concepts, rather than the demonstration of EPA for the total sample.

## Bibliography

Alexander S, Husek T R 1962 The anxiety differential: Initial steps in the development of a measure of situational anxiety. *Educ. Psychol. Meas.* 22: 325–48

Chapman R M, McCrary J W, Chapman J A, Martin J K 1980 Behavioral and neutral analyses of connotative meaning: Word classes and rating scales. *Brain Lang.* 11: 319–39

Forthman J H 1973 The effects of a zero interval on semantic differential rotated factor loadings. *J. Psychol.* 84: 23–32

Franks D D, Marolla J 1976 Efficacious action and social approval as interacting dimensions of self-esteem: A tentative formulation through construct validation. *Sociometry* 39: 324–41

Green R F, Goldfried M R 1965 On the bipolarity of semantic space. *Psychol. Monogr.* 79 (6)

Guttentag M, Bray H 1976 *Undoing Sex Stereotypes: Research and Resources for Educators.* McGraw-Hill, New York

Hurwitz D, Wiggins N, Jones L 1975 A semantic differential for facial attribution: The face differential. *Bull. Psychol. Soc.* 6: 370–72

Maguire T O 1973 Semantic differential methodology for the structuring of attitudes. *Am. Educ. Res. J.* 10: 295–306

Mann I T, Phillips J L, Thompson E G 1979 An examination of methodological issues relevant to the use and interpretation of the semantic differential. *Appl. Psychol. Meas.* 3: 213–29

Murakami Y 1977 On stratum factor structure: Containing the critics and theorizing of semantic differential method. *Psychologia* 20: 98–106

Osgood C E, May W H, Miron M S 1975 *Cross Cultural Universals of Affective Meaning.* University of Illinois Press, Urbana, Illinois

Osgood C E, Suci G J, Tannenbaum P H 1971 *The Measurement of Meaning.* University of Illinois Press, Chicago, Illinois

# Repertory Grid Technique

## R. J. Alban-Metcalfe

Repertory grid (repgrid) technique was devised by George Kelly within the context of his "personal construct theory", but has come to be used as a technique in its own right. In essence, it is an approach designed to carry out effectively the everyday process of trying to find out how people view the world from their own perspectives. For this reason, in its simpler forms, repertory grid technique has been compared to a well-structured interview. It can, however, be modified in a wide variety of ways, and can be augmented by sophisticated statistical and other mathematical procedures.

In repertory grid technique, the term element is used to denote the persons (including self), things, and events that together constitute an individual's environment. The term construct denotes the dimensions or reference axes used by the individual to discriminate between elements. According to Kelly, each person characteristically builds up an internal representation of the world in terms of a finite number of constructs. Constructs are conceived of as being bipolar, for example, "nice to know, versus not nice to know", "interesting, versus boring". Each person's constructs, which are based on the unique way that he or she perceives the world, are themselves unique, though individuals living in the same culture tend to have similar constructs. Unique also is the way that constructs are interrelated to form that person's construct system. Repertory grid technique can be used specifically to determine (a) which constructs an individual uses, (b) how those constructs are used, and (c) the interrelationships between the constructs.

The commonest ways of eliciting constructs are verbal, for example, by an interviewer asking people to indicate what similarities and what differences they see between specified groups of elements, though nonverbal approaches have also been developed. It is important to recognize, however, that a construct is a dimension; it is not a verbal label. Thus, different individuals are likely to have subtly (or in some cases fundamentally) different constructs to which the same verbal label is attached. As an example, the verbal label "funny, versus not funny" may be used to indicate two very different constructs used by a pupil and a teacher. Conversely, though, in the vast majority of instances, people from the same culture use mutually agreed verbal labels to indicate similar constructs. The particular constructs that given individuals use can be determined directly by asking them to verbalize discriminations they make between elements with which they are familiar. How they used these constructs, and the meaning of the constructs, can be inferred by asking the individuals to apply the same constructs to other elements, or exploring the implications of each discrimination. The interrelationships between constructs, and more information about their meaning, can be inferred either by eliciting a series of constructs that the individual sees as being causally related (i.e., laddering), or by recourse to mathematical techniques.

In eliciting constructs from individuals, a number of procedures can be adopted. Of these, the simplest involves presenting the person with combinations of three elements at a time (triads), with the name of each element written on a separate card, and asking for some important way in which two of the elements are similar to each other, and different from the third. The way in which two of the elements are similar is referred as the emergent pole of the construct. The other pole can either be the way in which the third element was different, or be the logical opposite of the emergent pole. As an alternative, the elements can all be presented at the same time, written in a row across the top of a piece of paper marked out into squares, and the

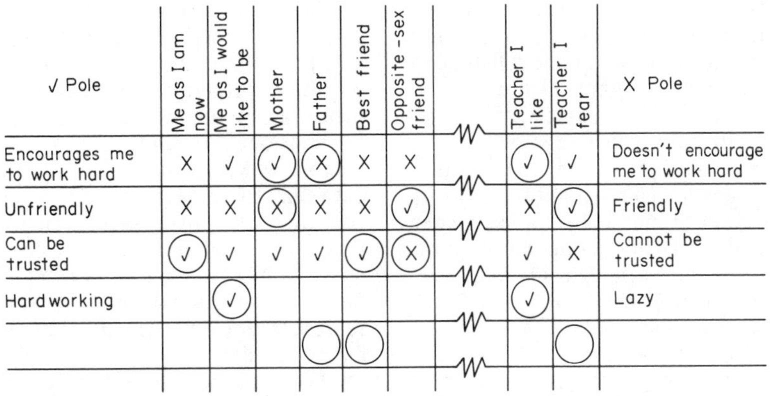

| √ Pole | Me as I am now | Me as I would like to be | Mother | Father | Best friend | Opposite-sex friend | | Teacher I like | Teacher I fear | X Pole |
|---|---|---|---|---|---|---|---|---|---|---|
| Encourages me to work hard | X | √ | (√) | (X) | X | X | | (√) | √ | Doesn't encourage me to work hard |
| Unfriendly | X | X | (X) | X | X | (√) | | X | (√) | Friendly |
| Can be trusted | (√) | √ | √ | √ | (√) | (X) | | √ | X | Cannot be trusted |
| Hard working | | (√) | | | | | | (√) | | Lazy |
| | | | | (○) | (○) | | | (○) | | |

**Figure 1**

A partially completed repertory grid. Constructs elicited with reference to the triads of elements indicated by the circles

constructs elicited by the interviewer directing attention to specified triads (or dyads) (see Fig. 1). After a specified number of constructs has been elicited, and written in columns at each side of the sheet of paper, the person can be asked to construe each of the elements in relation to each of the constructs. Indication of which pole applies to each element can be made either by dichotomous or rated responses, or by rank ordering the elements. A third approach to eliciting constructs is through "free" description, oral or written. "Self-characterization" grids, for example, can be devised by extracting bipolar constructs from individuals' descriptions of themselves. Such descriptions are usually given in the third person, as if they were descriptions of the principal character in a play or film.

Two major developments of the repertory grid have been laddering and pyramid construction. In the first of these, a construct is chosen by the interviewer, and the person asked which pole applies to a given element, say, for example, the element "me as I am now", and why. For example, a teacher might say that the construct pole "like to work in a large school, versus don't like to work in a large school" best describes "me as I am now". In response to a series of "Why?" questions, the sequence of constructs elicited might be—"like to have lots of other teachers around me" (versus the opposite), "like to have other adults to talk to" (versus the opposite), "like to have my mind stimulated by intelligent conversation" (versus the opposite), and "keeps me sane" (versus the opposite). Note (a) that the constructs elicited are related logically to one another (at least from the individual's point of view), and (b) that the sequence of constructs can be thought of as being arranged in an hierarchical manner. Thus, "like to work in a large school" is a relatively subordinate construct, whereas "like to have my mind stimulated by intelligent conversation" is relatively superordinate. Note also, that the teacher could not be expected to give a reasoned answer to the question "Why do you want to remain

sane?" "Keeping sane" is a core construct, that is, a construct that is essential to that person's very being as a person.

The elicitation process just described is known as laddering up a construct system. The opposite process of laddering down can be achieved by asking questions of the type, "How do you know that construct pole X applies to element A?", or "What evidence is there that X is true of element A?" In this way, subordinate constructs can be elicited.

In pyramid construction, individuals are asked, first of all, to think of some other element, say, a teacher or a pupil, with whom they feel most relaxed, and to specify an attribute which is characteristic of that element. Secondly, the request is made to state the kind of element (in this case a person) that would represent the opposite of the selected attribute. Having elicited two poles of a construct, the interviewer inquires what kind of a person the first element is. The third stage involves laddering down each of the opposite poles of the construct, so identifying a "pyramid" of relationships between constructs.

Two principles should govern the choice of elements in the repertory grid technique: (a) the relevance of the elements to the part of the construct system to be investigated, and (b) the representativeness of the chosen elements. Thus, if intimate personal relationships are the focus of interest, then the elements should include persons who correspond to role titles such as, "me as I am now" (and perhaps also "me as I would like to be", "me as my best friend/mother/wife sees me", and so on), members of close family and friends, and "significant" others, such as teachers, and older friends and acquaintances who are loved, admired, or feared. Similarly, if the focus of interest is relationships at school or work, or school subjects, hobbies and interests, careers, or clothes, then representative elements from these areas should be chosen. Relevance of elements selected is important because constructs have only limited ranges of convenience, or appropriateness: thus, the construct "printed, versus not printed" is relevant to construing books and syllabi, and also dresses and skirts, but it cannot be used meaningfully in relation to people, school subjects, or careers. Further, it is likely that a complete range of relevant constructs will be elicited only if the elements constitute a fully representative sample. The number of elements used commonly varies from around 10 to 25. The greater the number of elements, the more likelihood of representativeness being achieved, though in some circumstances, the subject matter may mean that fewer elements are available, or the nature of the sample (e.g., less able pupils) may mean that fewer are desirable.

Just as with elements, the greater the number of relevant constructs that are elicited, the greater their likelihood of being representative. Again, optimal numbers range from around 10 to 25, though most people appear to use fewer than 20 different constructs in relation to people, and some use as few as one or two. Constructs can be classified in a number of ways, such as into physical, for example, "tall" (versus the opposite), situational, for example, "is a pupil from this school" (versus the opposite), behavioural, for example, "writes quickly" (versus the opposite), and psychological, for example, "is likely to do badly under exam pressure", (versus the opposite); or into vague, for example, "is OK" (versus the opposite), and excessively precise, for example, "is a medical student" (versus the opposite).

Repertory grid data can be analysed in a wide variety of ways, and manipulated using a wide range of procedures. Thus, the interviewer may simply be concerned to note which constructs a given individual uses, and in the case of laddering or pyramid construction, also to infer relationships between constructs. Alternatively, elicited constructs can be used in idiographic or nomothetic instruments, relevant to a particular individual or group of individuals, or to particular elements. In some forms, repertory grid data can be subjected to statistical or other mathematical procedures, or used as the basis for devising interactive computer programs.

Mathematical analyses of repertory grids have been used to calculate a number of "structural" indices concerned with relationships between elements and constructs. Notable among these are cognitive complexity, cognitive differentiation, and articulation, which are measures of tendency to construe elements in multidimensional ways; identification and assimilative projection, which are concerned with perceived similarity between self and others; and constellatoriness and the coefficient of convergence, which measure similarities in the use of constructs. Mathematical techniques commonly applied to repertory grid data include cluster and factor analysis, and on the bases of these, diagrammatic representations of element and construct relationships have been devised.

The applications of repertory grid technique fall into two principal groups, "static" and "dynamic". In both groups, repertory grids can either be idiographic, in which case the individual's own constructs (or a mixture of own and provided constructs) are used, or nomothetic, in which case, for purposes of comparison, provided constructs are used commonly (though not exclusively). Examples of the "static" use of repgrid data are determination of a student's (or teacher's) perceptions of, say, self, family, and peers, or perceptions of self in relation to career opportunities in vocational guidance. "Dynamic" use of the repertory grid can involve completion of a comparable grid on two or more occasions, in order to give a measure of the extent to which an individual's construct system changes over time. This can be useful, for example, in studying the development of self-awareness, or friendship development. Alternatively, repertory grid data can form the basis of interactive computer programs, for example, in decision-making exercises.

## Bibliography

Fransella F, Bannister D 1977 *A Manual for Repertory Grid Technique*. Academic Press, London
Pope M L, Keen T R 1981 *Personal Construct Psychology and Education*. Academic Press, London
Shaw M L G (ed.) 1981 *Recent Advances in Personal Construct Technology*. Academic Press, London

# Diagnostic Assessment Procedures

## G. Delandshere

A diagnostic assessment procedure is a means by which an individual profile is examined and compared against certain norms or criteria. Diagnostic assessment focuses on individuals whereas diagnostic evaluation is centered on schooling processes such as the curriculum, program, administration, and so on. In both cases the task is to determine the strengths and weaknesses of the individual or process under study. Testing is used for diagnostic assessment of student learning problems and focuses on the construction and utilization of tests as well as their interpretation. Mastery tests can also be used for diagnostic purposes since they describe the teaching/learning process and student performance. Finally, a distinction must be made between diagnostic procedures used for assessing specific learning disabilities and those used in the regular classroom for assessing learning difficulties. Only the latter will be discussed here.

Different explanatory mechanisms, or analogies, have been used in this field but their adequacy can be questioned. When the term "diagnosis" is used, it is often assumed that a medical model is implied. A set of objectives is to be reached; the student's actual performance is then measured and any pattern of discrepancies is examined and analyzed to find a "remedial treatment" or "prescription." Another analogy found in the literature is based on computer technology and refers to "procedural bugs" or "student bugs" when describing difficulties in learning. Not all researchers and educators accept the value of these analogies because most learning problems involve teaching problems as well. Hence, diagnosis should not focus on the student alone. There is nothing "pathologically" wrong with a student who has learning problems, as there is in the case of a diseased patient, but rather an incompatibility exists between a particular teaching method and the student's learning activity or cognitive style. These issues are important and need to be kept in mind when considering the uses of diagnostic testing and diagnostic evaluation in the classroom.

## 1. Diagnostic Assessment

Diagnostic assessment differs from summative types of assessment, such as minimum competency tests or final or certification examinations. The difference between summative, formative, and diagnostic assessment lies in the type of question each of them is addressing. Summative assessment is concerned with a final product whereas formative assessment provides a description of student progress. Diagnostic assessment draws a profile of student achievement, considering (a) the discrepancies between expected and actual achievement, (b) the cause for such discrepancies, and (c) appropriate "remedial treatment." This last type of assessment requires the definition of clear learning objectives and assessment techniques. A global approach to diagnostic assessment relies on teacher observations, analysis of student work, results obtained on achievement tests, and is not concerned with the construction of specific diagnostic instruments. From this perspective, diagnosis of student learning difficulties cannot be made through the examination of a single specific skill. Rather, student achievement on a broad range of objectives should be documented. Only after examining the entire student profile will it be possible to evaluate the possible causes of learning problems and make an accurate diagnosis. This "case study" approach is not intended to be used for each student in a classroom but only for those who experience persistent learning difficulties. Such a thorough examination is time consuming, and most students do not require this kind of assessment.

Effective diagnostic assessment relies on the right kind of data being collected and their correct interpretation. The danger exists that a diagnostician might define a limited set of learning-problem categories, label students according to these categories, and subsequently only prescribe familiar or readily available treatments. At each level of this process the validity of the diagnosis and the "treatment" is in question. Continuous evaluation of "prescribed treatments" is necessary. In addition, empirical data are needed to test the efficacy of the model as a whole (Thomas 1981).

## 2. Diagnostic Testing

If diagnostic testing is defined as providing feedback to teachers and students regarding their strengths and weaknesses, almost any test would be diagnostic. In effect, a score on any standardized test gives some indication of the student's performance and also informs the teacher as to how successful he or she was in teaching the material. But the total score does not give any real information concerning specific areas of difficulty or their causes. Examination of the individual items would tell us which answers are correct and which are wrong. However, most available tests have not been constructed for diagnostic purposes; they have too few items per objective and the analysis of the wrong answers cannot lead to a diagnosis of learning problems. Diagnostic testing is seen as one component of the ongoing teaching/learning process. In order to use tests for diagnosis, they should be specifically designed for that purpose.

Guidelines for constructing "good" multiple-choice tests for diagnostic purposes are needed. As with any other test, a clear definition of learning objectives is required; but each test addresses a very specific skill (e.g., addition, subtraction, etc.) and the items are designed to test a particular subskill from various perspectives. Each item provides information to the student and the teacher since each distractor has a precise meaning in terms of learning difficulties and possible remedial strategies. Here the emphasis is on the significance of each particular answer and the response patterns in general. The total score has no real importance or meaning, and guessing is not usually a concern in diagnostic testing since evidence that a student guesses does not provide the specific information needed for diagnosis and remediation.

A consensus does not exist concerning the use of distractors as sources of information for diagnosis. The three main approaches to this issue can be described as follows. One view maintains that the choice of a given distractor has a specific meaning in terms of learning difficulties (Baker and Herman 1983). Working from open-ended questions, Tatsuoka and Tatsuoka (1983) analyze the responses to discover which rules are followed in finding the answers. And finally, in adaptive or sequential testing, the only information taken into consideration is whether or not the answer is correct. The last approach does not analyze or ascribe any meaning to the answers given by students.

In adaptive or sequential testing, the items are selected on the basis of the student's responses to previous items. More specifically, a correct response leads to a more difficult item, whereas an incorrect response leads to an easier one. Item selection does not depend on which distractor was chosen but in whether or not the answer was correct. This type of testing is usually administered by a computer which records the answers and selects the items. The pool of items used in one sequence is pretested for unidimensionality, and item difficulty is the basis for their selection. Finally, hypotheses about learning difficulties are formulated on the basis of the response pattern.

One problem with sequential or adaptive testing is that decisions are often made based upon the answer to a single item. However, certain diagnostic characteristics have been attributed to these tests. As they are currently designed, their main advantage is in improving the precision of measurement since each individual receives a different set of items corresponding to his or her level of performance. In order to effectively use adaptive testing for diagnostic purposes the number of items on which diagnostic decisions are made would need to be increased. Also, since adaptive testing has the flexibility to readily adjust to the subject's performance level, potential exists for its use in diagnostic assessment.

A final research perspective found in the literature attempts to explain why errors are made by identifying the "misconceptions" or "bugs" that produce them. The first task is to construct a "procedural network" for each skill under study by breaking down problems into the requisite subskills. What are the correct and incorrect procedures that can be followed in attempting to perform a task? Breaking the skill down into subskills is crucial because, in order to be efficient, a diagnostic model "must contain all of the knowledge that can possibly be misunderstood by the student or else some student misconceptions will be beyond the diagnostic capabilities of the system" (Brown and Burton 1978). Secondly, a set of items must be generated that provides opportunities for students to demonstrate all the identified subskills. Student answers are then examined to reveal those subskills which have not yet been answered. Based on these student "misconceptions" a second set of problems is administered to confirm the initial hypothesis. The information gained from this testing should suggest possible remedial strategies.

This approach has been implemented through the use of the "Buggy system" (Brown and Burton 1978), a computerized game used mostly for teacher training. The computer plays the role of the student, while the teacher has to recognize the source of student error (or bugs) and be able to replicate them. Hence, teachers become more sensitive to the causes of student learning problems. It seems evident that by following this model, single "bugs" can be easily diagnosed. However, when a student has "multiple bugs" or when different "bugs" interact, the diagnosis becomes more problematic. Also, if subskills or possible misconceptions have been omitted from the "procedural network" some of the response patterns may be interpreted as random error.

This research perspective is primarily concerned with developing a model to account for hundreds of "bugs" that can occur when skills being studied become more complex. A probabilistic model seems to be more appropriate for detecting aberrant response patterns when several hundred "bugs" are possible. Brown and Burton's model showed that it was possible to give the correct answer even when using "erroneous rules." Tatsuoka and Tatsuoka (1983) refined that aspect of the model by introducing the Individual Consistency Index (ICI). A low total score and a high Individual Consistency Index indicate that the student is using the wrong rules to solve the problems. This index can be used as a signal to point out students who need remediation and more refined diagnoses. Also, using item response theory, they demonstrate that when the possibility exists to respond correctly by using the wrong rule, the data set obtained reveals multidimensionality. In other words, the test measures different dimensions depending on whether the student masters the skill or not. This finding has definite implications not only for diagnostic testing but for testing in general and points out the importance of checking for construct validity.

All "bugs" do not affect the learning process in the same way but a typology of "bugs" or misconceptions still has to be developed. Furthermore, teaching strategies to remediate these diagnosed learning problems are not always available. Before making any concluding comments, the testing techniques of mastery learning will be briefly examined to demonstrate how they may also be classified as diagnostic instruments.

## 3. The Mastery Learning Approach

This model uses testing in a way that is not always considered "diagnostic," but in fact does serve this function. It involves the use of "formative" or "mastery" tests at frequent intervals to test student performance on each item as compared to a "mastery standard." Examination of these answer patterns provides information on the level of learning and indicates whether a student needs more practice or another teaching method. Some theorists in the area of mastery learning contend that the construction of formative tests is based on a theory of learning. An underlying theory is useful in designing the test in such a way as to identify not only the learning problems but also the cause of the problems.

The difference between mastery and diagnostic testing is not always obvious. Since the term "diagnostic" is used in so many different ways, confusion regarding the application of this term persists. For example, the model of diagnostic assessment developed by the Scottish Council for Research in Education (Black and Dockrell 1980) differs little from a mastery learning model. The former model uses criterion-referenced tests constructed according to a taxonomy of objectives. These objectives, or intended outcomes, are directly linked to the curriculum. While the model is designed to assess mastery it does not necessarily provide information for detecting potential sources of learning difficulties. Therefore, although this has been labeled a diagnostic model, it does not contain many of the diagnostic features of some of the models presented here.

Formative or mastery tests have some of the same objectives as diagnostic tests. One difference may be with the way they are constructed. As indicated above, mastery tests seem to correspond to a theory of learning whereas most diagnostic instruments are constructed to test hypothesized erroneous rules that students follow in solving problems. Mastery tests are attached to a teaching method; they are used to assess student learning and provide students and teachers with feedback regarding skill mastery. This method may not be sufficient for all students, and more refined instruments with better interpretation techniques may be needed to diagnose skill mastery for some students. These are not necessarily included in mastery learning programs. Generally, the type of information sought determines the appropriate kind of test to be used. If the teacher wants to know who has mastered a particular skill and who has not, almost any testing instrument will suffice. However, if partial knowledge is considered important and if it is believed that knowing in detail what kind of error the student makes helps adjust teaching methods, then multiple testing and more refined instruments are necessary.

## 4. Conclusion

As has been seen, diagnostic assessment can be conducted in a variety of ways, ranging from global evaluation to more refined diagnosis of very specific skills. The particular demands of each situation will determine which type of assessment is most appropriate. Other factors such as time and cost effectiveness will influence the decision as well. For example, some learning difficulties are a function of developmental lag, therefore intensive diagnosis would be unnecessary and unproductive.

Diagnosis of temporary learning problems can also lead to persistent "labeling" that endures even after the learning problem has disappeared. Research has shown that teachers' expectation can influence their attitudes and behavior toward students.

A final point concerns the assumptions upon which diagnostic testing rests. The first is that learning can be "decomposed" into a set of discrete subunits or subskills. The second is that items can be generated to measure accurately and validly these subskills. All the diagnostic testing models described above are predicated on these assumptions. The practical or educational value of these models, therefore, depends on the validity of these assumptions, which in many areas of education remains to be established.

### Bibliography

Baker E L, Herman J 1983. Task structure design: Beyond linkage. *J. Educ. Meas.* 20: 149–64
Black H D, Dockrell W B 1980 *Diagnostic Assessment in Secondary Schools: A Teacher's Handbook*. Scottish Council for Research in Education, Edinburgh
Brown J S, Burton R R 1978 Diagnostic models for procedural bugs in basic mathematics skills. *Cognit. Sci.* 2: 155–92
Tatsuoka K K, Tatsuoka M M 1983. Spotting erroneous rules of operation by the individual consistency index. *J. Educ. Meas.* 20: 221–30
Thomas R M 1981 A model of diagnostic evaluation. In: Lewy A, Nevo D (eds.) 1981 *Evaluation Roles in Education*. Gordon and Breach, London

# Confidence Marking

### D. A. Leclercq

According to Ebel (1965), "the term confidence weighting refers to a special mode of responding to test . . . items, and a special mode of scoring those responses . . . . The examinee is asked to indicate not only what he believes to be the correct answer to a question, but also how certain he is of the correctness of his answer. When his answers are scored he receives more credit for a correct answer given confidently than for one given diffidently. But the penalty for an incorrect answer given confidently is heavy enough to discourage unwarranted pretense of confidence."

This article considers how the credits and penalties are assessed.

## 1. The Underlying Models

The choice of a level of confidence (from amongst those available) must be considered in the perspective of decision theory. Technical problems such as validity, reliability, and acuity of confidence answers must be based on a sound model of mental activity, on carefully written instructions, and on the selection of appropriate tariffs. The tariffs are the points attributed: for a correct response ($T_c$), for an incorrect one ($T_i$), or for an omission ($T_o$). A set of three tariffs ($T_c$, $T_i$, and $T_o$) is called a $t$-scale. The best known $t$-scale is the $St$-scale (simple $t$-scale) where $T_c = +1$, $T_i = 0$, and $T_o = 0$. The expected score on a given question (ESQ) is computed according to the following formula:

$$\text{ESQ} = (p \cdot T_c) + (q \cdot T_i) + (r \cdot T_o)$$

where $p$ = probability of a correct answer, $q$ = probability of an incorrect answer, and $r$ = probability of an omission.

### 1.1 Classical Models and Corrections for Guessing

In the usual "correction for guessing" scoring formula, $T_i$ is equal to $-(1/k-1)$. This tariff characterizes the *Gt*-scale (where *G* stands for Guessing), contrived in such a way that ESQ = 0 when the probability for a successful guess is $1/k$, and is based on the model "Students who do not know the correct answer choose randomly among the *k* alternatives." Procedures such as eliminating the incorrect alternatives instead of choosing the correct one (Coombs et al. 1956) are based on a second model of test taking behavior: "Students who do not know the correct answer first eliminate the alternatives they know to be wrong. Then they choose randomly amongst those that remain." This gives rise to a generalized *Gt*-scale that allows for the existence of partial knowledge.

It is well-known that the *Gt*-scale is unfair. In some cases, it undercorrects and in others it overcorrects. Other statistical "corrections for guessing" have been proposed (Chernoff 1962), but in spite of their sophistication, these approaches are not sound for two reasons. First, the percentage of students that have chosen a given alternative (i.e., the alternative's popularity) is not a good index of the (subjective) individual attractiveness of the alternative. Second, item difficulty must be combined with students' ability to explain the probability of a correct answer (a basic assumption of the Rasch model).

### 1.2 Subjective Probabilities

The apparent difficulty of a question is a subjective experience since it depends upon the student's own ability that varies from individual to individual. The way to cope with this is to take into account the personal attractiveness of the alternatives (i.e., the individual's subjective estimate of the probability that each alternative is correct). Accordingly, the tariffs depend on the subjective probability *and* on the correctness of the response. This suggests a matrix of tariffs. In educational tariff matrices the $T_c$ values are positive, the $T_i$ values are negative, and the $T_o$ value is equal to zero.

This third model is distinguishable from the earlier ones because it does not refer to the dichotomy "when the student knows . . . when the student does not know." This model supposes a continuity of cognitive states, from perfect knowledge to null knowledge. Between these two extremes exist many intermediate states of knowledge, of partial information.

Model 3 states that when a student is faced with the various alternatives, he or she attributes to each of them a probability of being the correct one. If a student is requested to give only one answer, he or she will choose the alternative with the greatest probability.

More and more researchers and teachers share De Finetti's opinion (1965): "Partial information exists; to detect it is interesting, necessary and feasible. Instruction in using these methods . . . has, moreover, a high educational value. Such methods, including the way of *scoring*, and not only the response systems, must be

appropriately chosen by the experimenter and clearly explained to the subjects who must understand the nature of the game they are playing. If this is done, questions about guessing disappear."

### 2. The Instructions

In order to obtain "admissible measures of subjective probability" (Shuford et al. 1966), that is, valid and reliable measures, instructions must be carefully designed. It is not sufficient to ask the students to emphasize those answers of which they are confident, or to ask them to choose among the degrees of an ordinal scale (such as "1 = not sure, 2 = fairly sure, 3 = very sure," etc.). Such definitions are vague and will be interpreted in different ways by different students, although despite these shortcomings, they have been frequently used in combination with various tariff matrices.

It is better to express the level of confidence in probabilistic terms. A student can hardly distinguish 0.3 from 0.35, so it would appear useless to request answers of such an acuity. For this reason, a few areas are delimited on the probability scale, so that the student has to choose a zone of probabilities and not pinpoint a single probability. Table 1 gives one set of instructions as used in Belgium (Leclercq 1982), with a nondecision tariffs matrix (*A*) and a relevant tariffs matrix (*B*).

### 3. Psychometric Considerations

The score on a test computed with a *Ct*-scale (Confidence *t*-scale) is a payoff, a reinforcement, but not a measure. It is an arbitrary weighted mixture of two different measures: the measure of the student's knowledge in the content area and the measure of the student's ability in self-estimation. Various indices of this last ability have been suggested (Lichtenstein et al. 1977, Leclercq 1982): indices of individual coherence, realism, calibration efficiency, acuity, and stability in the use of confidence degrees.

De Finetti (1965) stresses that "It is only subjective probability that can give an objective meaning to every response and scoring method."

Nevertheless, more valid or more reliable information about a student's ability in a given domain can be

*Table 1*
Tariff matrices for model 3

| If you attribute to your answer a chance of success from | then choose confidence degree number | Tariffs *A* | | Tariffs *B* | |
|---|---|---|---|---|---|
| | | $T_c$ | $T_i$ | $T_c$ | $T_i$ |
| 0 to 25% | 0 | 0 | 0 | 0 | 0 |
| 25 to 50% | 1 | +1 | −1 | +3 | −1 |
| 50 to 75% | 2 | +2 | −2 | +4 | −2 |
| 75 to 100% | 3 | +3 | −3 | +5 | −5 |

obtained from his or her confidence responses only if he or she is a good estimator of his or her own capacity and if he or she tells the truth.

Tariff matrices are computed according to a decision theory in order to encourage students to express their convictions honestly and without faking.

## 4. Implementation Considerations

Students usually use poor strategies (e.g., follow optimistic or pessimistic rules) instead of simply telling the truth. They need to experience the consequences of their choices (i.e., the tariffs must be applied to them) in two or three tests before they will fully appreciate that the matrix is "fair" for the honest student.

The whole scoring system is more challenging to the student. The best performance must not only be correct, but moreover be strongly backed by confidence. The procedure should include a "correct-for- severity" coefficient to adjust the final *C* scores to the usual ones (as computed with the *St*-scale).

## 5. Educational Importance

Sound estimates of the chances of success in an undertaking are of importance for physicians, nurses, and surgeons in a hospital, for teachers in a school, for workers in a factory, and for drivers on the road. If someone is confident of his or her correctness, but is wrong half of the time, he or she is a perpetual source of annoyance and danger to himself or herself and to others. It is thus important that adults are able to estimate realistically the chances of success of any project they undertake.

## 6. Research Interest

In many cases, overt behavior is more related to the individual's beliefs than to objective measures of knowledge.

Research on subjective probabilities in education raises theoretical and methodological problems similar to those that arose in psychology when psychophysics developed. Strict definitions had to be found for "stimulus" and for "response." In the same way, concepts like "knowledge," "doubt," "uncertainty," "confidence," "information," begin to acquire a new operational meaning in the framework of subjective probability.

Subjective probability enables people to assess partial knowledge with valid, reliable, sensitive, and convenient methods and techniques. Specific principles must be respected, and clear distinctions must be made between measures, payoffs, and degrees. When this is done, promising perspectives appear concerning the study of information processing by humans, a central concern for educators.

## Bibliography

Chernoff H 1962 The scoring of multiple choice questionnaires. *Ann. Math. Stat.* 33: 375–93

Coombs C H, Milholland J E, Warner F B 1956 The assessment of partial knowledge. *Educ. Psychol. Meas.* 16: 13–37

De Finetti B 1965 Methods for discriminating levels of partial knowledge concerning a test item. *Br. J. Math. Stat. Psychol.* 18: 87–123

Ebel R L 1965 Confidence-weighting and test reliability. *J. Educ. Meas.* 2: 49–57

Leclercq D A 1982 Confidence marking: Its use in testing. *Eval. Educ.* 6(3)

Lichtenstein S, Fischhoff B, Phillips L 1977 Calibration of probabilities: The state of the art. In: Jungermann A H, De Zeeuw G (eds.) 1977 *Decisionmaking and Change in Human Affairs.* Proc. of 5th Research Conf. on Subjective Probability, Utility, and Decision Making, Darmstadt, 1–4 Sept, 1975. Reidel, Dordrecht

Shuford E H, Albert A, Massengill H E 1966 Admissible probability measurement procedures. *Psychometrika* 31: 125–45

# Correction for Guessing

## B. H. Choppin

Guessing on tests includes both the apparently random selection of an answer to a question without consideration of the alternatives, and the selection of an answer on criteria unrelated to the trait being assessed (e.g., the strategy of "always choosing option C"). It is a problem on mental tests to the extent that it can affect total scores in a way not directly related to the trait being assessed. This means that in practice it is important only for multiple-choice tests. Three separate effects give rise for concern:

(a) Guessing introduces an apparently random factor into test scores which lowers reliability and validity.

(b) Lucky guesses inflate the score of the candidate leading to the possible overestimation of his or her level of achievement.

(c) This inflation of scores gives an unfair advantage to candidates who guess frequently as opposed to those who do not.

## 1. The Standard Correction

Since multiple-choice tests came into widespread use in the 1920s, there has been a steady stream of research studies aimed at finding ways to ameliorate the effects of guessing. Many of the early papers were based on a simple model that said if a candidate knew the correct answer to a question he or she would choose it; if not, he or she would omit the item or would select at random from among all the alternatives presented. This permits an estimate of the number of items on which guesses have been made;

$$G = \frac{m}{(m-1)} W$$

where $W$ is the number of incorrect alternatives selected and $m$ is the number of alternative choices per question. Assuming that $1/m$ of the guessed responses are correct, this suggests that the subtraction of $W/(m-1)$ from the raw score $R$ would remove the inflation caused by guessing. This, the so-called "standard correction" for guessing, has come into widespread use. (It should be noted that the same principle can be applied to items rather than to persons in order to estimate the number of testees who can really solve an item.)

The standard correction has been criticized ever since it was first introduced. Its assumptions are too simple to be credible. In general students who do not know the right answer may still know enough to be able to eliminate one or more of the distractors so that, when they come to guess, their probability of success would be greater than $1/m$. This would suggest a higher proportion of correct guesses so that, in general, the standard guessing correction would be too small. However, a number of empirical studies (e.g., Brownless and Keats 1958) have shown that even the standard formula leads to too many negative corrected scores (i.e., the correction is too large). Other research, using score reliability and validity as criteria, confirms this result (Diamond and Evans 1973, Choppin 1974). Optimal gains in reliability and validity were achieved with corrections only one-third to one-half as large as those produced by the standard formula. Other important studies based on the "standard correction" were reported by Ziller (1957) and Traub et al. (1969).

## 2. Other Models and Formulas

Chernoff (1962) proposed that different weights should be accorded to items depending on how much guessing was estimated to have occurred *on that item*. Thus more credit would be earned for a correct answer on an item where there were few incorrect responses, than on one in which the responses were evenly distributed across all the alternatives. This model treats guessing as a phenomenon associated with particular items rather than particular people, and does not enjoy empirical support.

Coombs et al. (1956) suggested that students be directed to cross out each alternative answer that could be definitely identified as incorrect. The special scoring formula they proposed is claimed to minimize the effects of guessing by overconfident testees. De Finetti (1965)

tackles guessing by asking students to assign probabilities of correctness to all the different alternatives on each question.

Wainer and Wright (1980) treat the regular one/zero persons-by-items response matrix that occurs with conventional response and scoring modes. They propose a jackknife technique applied to scaled estimates of ability, and report that, for simulated data at least, the method appears to work very well.

## 3. Latent Trait Theories

Latent trait theories represent a different approach to the problem of guessing on multiple-choice tests. They attempt to examine guessing by plotting relative rates of success on the item for examinees of different abilities to produce item characteristic curves (ICCs). The simplest of the latent trait models in common use, the Rasch model, assumes that no random guessing is taking place. Indeed, Rasch pointed out that the presence of guessed correct responses in a data set violated the requirements for objective measurement.

However, the three-parameter latent trait model developed by Lord includes an item parameter representing the asymptotic probability of success on an item for a person of very low ability. A weakness of this approach is that it regards "guessing" as a property of a particular item rather than a behavior exhibited by a particular person on a specific occasion. The parameter, usually represented by $c_i$ (and misleadingly described as the guessing parameter), is estimated from considering the pattern of responses for *all* the people who attempted the item under consideration rather than modeling guessing behavior for any individual and it actually describes the shape of the item characteristic curve for the group as a whole. Item response theory does offer a way of estimating ability on a multiple-choice test that allows for the possibility of guessing—by giving less credit than normal for correct responses to difficult questions—but some uncertainties about the validity of this approach remain.

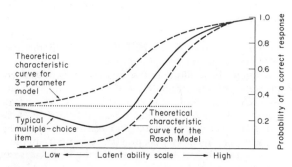

*Figure 1*
Empirically established characteristic curve for a typical multiple-choice item compared to curves for two latent trait theories

Several research studies (e.g., Choppin 1982) have demonstrated that item characteristic curves for mult-iple-choice items intended to measure achievement have a shape similar to the solid curve shown in Fig. 1, so that neither the Rasch model nor item response theory can be expected to provide a satisfactory account of test-taking behavior for students of low ability. The trough in the item characteristic curve appears to result from students with fairly low achievement levels tending to act on the basis of misinformation so as to sys-tematically choose one or the other of the distractors in the item, and hence to choose the correct res-ponse much less often than chance would suggest. The location and depth of the trough varies considerably from item to item. This is an area where more research is needed.

## 4. The Avoidance of the Guessing Problem

In multiple-choice testing situations where the existence of guessing poses a serious problem to the interpretation of the results, several alternative strategies to minimize the effects are available. The major alternatives are discussed below with the most effective being con-sidered first and the least effective last.

### 4.1 Choose Item Formats that Minimize the Problems Associated with Guessing

Although students lacking needed information to solve a problem directly may frequently guess on open-ended items, the chances of success in most cases are too small for the behavior to spoil the measurement. The problem becomes serious when the student has to select the correct response from only a limited number of alterna-tives (only two in the extreme case of "true/false" tests). One way to handle the problem is, therefore, to avoid the multiple-choice format altogether, and to use item formats which require constructed responses. Alterna-tively, if multiple-choice items have a relatively large number of distractors (say five or more), and they are reasonably plausible so that the typical low-achieving student will not be able to rule out many of them, then the success rate on guessing is likely to be quite low and the problem will not be serious.

### 4.2 Prepare Appropriate Instructions to the Test-taking Student

Here two quite different strategies may be followed depending on whether the test is intended for ranking the students (norm referenced), or for measuring as accurately as possible what each student knows (cri-terion referenced). In the first case, a guessing problem arises if some students are more inclined than others to guess, rather than to omit an item when they do not know enough to be able to solve it directly. In this case, the appropriate instruction to the students is to tell them to guess if they are not sure of the answer, and *not to omit any items* at all. In the second case, the problem

arises from correctly guessed responses by individual students which could lead to inappropriate deductions about the student's level of achievement. In these cir-cumstances the opposite type of instruction is appro-priate. The students should be told *not to guess*, and to omit items to which they do not know the correct answer. It may be appropriate to warn of a heavy penalty being imposed for incorrect responses. Unfor-tunately, experience shows that both sets of instructions are of only limited effectiveness. In practice some stu-dents still omit items even though they were told to attempt all of them, and other students still guess when they are not sure even though they are warned of the penalties.

### 4.3 Use a Latent Trait Model to Adjust for Guessing Behavior

If it is not possible to arrange the test session so as to minimize the guessing problem by one of the methods outlined above, then it is suggested that a latent trait model be employed to analyze the results. Where aggre-gated results for a group of individuals are of interest, the three-parameter model may be appropriate.

Alternatively, if individual estimates of achievement are the goal, then the procedure for editing the obser-vation matrix and applying the Rasch model proposed by Choppin (1982) is suggested.

### 4.4 Use the Standard Correction for Guessing

Although there is little reason for believing that this procedure is fair to all students, or that it improves the psychometric quality of the measures, this procedure is simple to apply and appears to be a small step in the appropriate direction. Where large variations in the frequency of guessing between testees exist, then the standard correction can remove a substantial proportion of the bias in the ranking of raw scores.

## Bibliography

Brownless V T, Keats J A 1958 A retest method of studying partial knowledge and other factors influencing item response. *Psychometrika* 23: 67–73

Chernoff H 1962 The scoring of multiple choice questionnaires. *Ann. Math. Stat.* 33: 375–93

Choppin B H 1974 *The Correction for Guessing in Objective Tests* (IEA Monograph Series No. 4). International Associ-ation for the Evaluation of Educational Achievement (IEA), Stockholm

Choppin B H 1982 *A Two-parameter Latent Trait Model* (CSE Technical Report). Center for the Study of Evaluation, UCLA, Los Angeles, California

Coombs C H, Milholland J E, Womer F B 1956 The assessment of partial knowledge. *Educ. Psychol. Meas.* 16: 13–37

De Finetti B 1965 Methods for discriminating levels of partial knowledge concerning a test item. *Br. J. Math. Stat. Psychol.* 18: 87–123

Diamond J, Evans W 1973 The correction for guessing. *Rev. Educ. Res.* 43: 181–91

Traub R E, Hambleton R K, Singh B 1969 Effects of promised reward and threatened penalty on performance on a multiple choice vocabulary test. *Educ. Psychol. Meas.* 29: 847–61

Wainer H, Wright B D 1980 Robust estimation of ability in the Rasch model. *Psychometrika* 45: 373–91

Ziller R C 1957 A measure of the gambling response-set in objective tests. *Psychometrika* 22: 289–92

# Part 5

# Measurement Applications

# Part 5

# Measurement Applications

---

## Introduction

This Part of the *Encyclopedia* examines the major roles that measurement plays in evaluation research, and prepares the evaluator to design and use sound instrumentation for different applications in evaluation. The first section addresses the Creation, Scoring, and Interpretation of Tests for different purposes. The second section then takes up the actual uses of tests for selection and for description.

Part 5(a) begins with three articles on general principles of item and test development, and the first of these concerns *Item Writing Techniques*. The creation of test exercises is still more art than science, but a number of procedures have been developed for generating items according to more or less objective (algorithmic) procedures, intended to improve the replicability and interpretability of tests. This article provides useful guidelines for traditional item writing techniques, reviews computer-based test authoring systems, and also describes more objective, algorithmic approachs to item and test construction. In the following article, attention turns from item writing to *Item Bank*. An item bank, perhaps better called an item library, is a test construction resource offering advantages of economy, flexibility, consistency, and security in test construction and use. Item banks can be helpful in defining item domains and permitting "domain referencing" of tests created by systematic item sampling. Illustrative applications are presented, from both Europe and the United States. The last of the three articles on general item and test development principles takes up the practical problem of *Readability and Reading Levels*. These terms are defined, and readability formulas are discussed. These formulas can be a useful adjunct to common sense in striving to ensure that items and test instructions are comprehensible to the intended test takers.

Having covered the general principles of item development, the section proceeds to examine the creation of measuring instruments for some of the special purposes that often arise in evaluation studies, beginning with an article on *Domain-referenced Tests*. Domain-referencing is a form of criterion-referenced test interpretation that assumes the test content is representative of a content domain. A score on the test can then be used to characterize performance across the entire domain, sometimes referred to as a domain score estimate. Among the approaches that have been developed for domain specification and test construction are objective item generation methods, creation of highly detailed test and item specifications (e.g., amplified objectives), and enumeration of specific literary works or content topics from which test content may be selected. A small body of statistical theory has also evolved to address issues such as domain-referenced test length and the precision of domain score estimates. A second article on specialized testing purposes addresses *Culture-fair Assessment*. Although complete culture fairness may be impossible to attain in practice, it remains a useful ideal to strive for. To the extent that cultural biases cannot be eliminated by careful test design, rules for scoring and for interpreting test scores may be adjusted to reduce inequities among groups. A third article on specialized testing purposes examines the subject of *Attitudes and their Measurement*. Terms like emotion, consistency, target, direction, and intensity may be used to distinguish attitudes from other affective characteristics (e.g., self-esteem or value). Different types of scales developed for measuring attitudes are reviewed, and a helpful set of item writing guidelines is developed. The interpretation of attitude measurements and future directions in this important area are also discussed. The last of the four articles on specialized testing purposes is devoted to *Questionnaires*. Questionnaires of different kinds and for different purposes are described, and advice is offered about questionnaire focus, questions of a personal nature, questionnaire length, and other matters. A step-by-step approach to questionnaire development is then presented, beginning with the identification of variables to be studied and proceeding through question development, small tryout, pilot decisions about questionnaire layout, field testing of a draft instrument, and the creation of a final instrument.

The section proceeds from creating tests for different purposes to scoring and interpretation, beginning with three articles which discuss scaling methods in general. The article *Scaling Methods* surveys a variety of useful models and methods, with practical guidelines for the construction of rating scales as well as a survey of mathematical models for scaling. Many of these methods apply to data types obtained by specific procedures, for example, dominance data, profile data, proximity data, or conjoint data, and so methods of instrument design and data collection must be considered in conjunction with alternative scaling methods.

The *Partial Credit Model* is one of the family of Rasch models, which applies to ordered polytomous item responses. This scaling model makes stronger assumptions about the data than most, but where the model applies, all of the advantages of Rasch models for scale definition and estimation are gained. The article which examines this model begins with an illustration, then turns to the algebra of the model, special cases in its application, and its relation to other models in the Rasch family. Finally, applications of the model in the definition of variables, item banking, and computer adaptive testing are described.

The group of three articles on scaling methods concludes with a practical treatment of *Test Norms*, primarily for achievement test data. The importance of a clear population definition and careful sampling is emphasized to assure the accuracy of norm-referenced interpretations. Discussion then turns to various derived scores and scales including both linear conversions and those employing area conversions to normalize the shape of the score distribution. A concluding section provides detailed guidance in using norm tables to arrive at interpretations of individual test performance and to provide confidence bands for such interpretations.

*Automated Scoring Systems* may be of substantial value in large-scale evaluation studies. In this article, specialized scoring equipment ranging from high-capacity optical scanners through desk top scanners and card readers is described. The use of microcomputers for test scoring is also described, and automated scoring is discussed in the context of broader educational activities. The final article in this section examines *Computer Scoring of Essays*. To date, this area of computer application is seriously limited by the difficulties of converting handwritten text to machine readable form, and by the difficulty of natural language processing. Nonetheless, as word processing becomes more widely used, and as methods for computer-based text analysis improve, computerized essay scoring may become more useful.

The second section of Part 5 examines the issues involved in Using Tests in Evaluation Contexts. A series of five articles address uses of tests for selection and prediction, and an additional six articles discuss the use of tests for description. Selection and prediction per se do not figure prominently in evaluation research, but comprehensive evaluations of special educational programs and of educational institutions will often entail an examination of selection mechanisms for those programs or institutions. Adequate descriptions of the populations served are indispensable in establishing reasonable expectations for the levels of outcomes a program should achieve and for finding appropriate control groups in evaluation research designs. Tests and decision rules used in selecting participants, clients, or matriculants serve to define such populations. The selection and prediction articles begin with a treatment of *Selection Mechanisms for Entry to Secondary Education*. After considering the problem of defining "secondary" education in different national contexts, the article discusses the need for selection; the types of tests, interviews, and other mechanisms employed; and the organization and political ramifications of these mechanisms. Formal selection mechanisms at the secondary-school level are most important in less developed parts of the world, where the demand for secondary schooling still exceeds the national capacity to provide it. *Selection Mechanisms for Entry to Higher Education*, the subject of the next article, are important for industrialized as well as developing nations. A typology of possible selection mechanisms includes enrollment without further selection, lotteries, use of secondary school records, interviews, standardized tests, entrance examinations, and access based on work experience. These approaches are illustrated by descriptions of the systems used in a number of nations around the world. The third article in this group considers the *Prediction of Success in Higher Education*, using school records, achievement tests, interviews, and other criteria. Research on this prediction problem has been hampered by the difficulty of defining and quantifying academic success, and by the restriction of range implicit in studying only those who have been admitted. The fourth article on selection and prediction examines *Credentialing* for different professions, and the fifth article considers the use of *Interviews for Selection*, especially selection into higher education.

Description of program and schooling outcomes is basic to most educational evaluation studies, and so the last six articles of Part 5(b) are devoted to this area of testing applications. *Educational Profiles*, the subject of the first article in this group, are a narrative-based method of recording educational outcomes, popular in the United Kingdom and in Australia. Although the rationale for prose descriptions of student strengths, weaknesses, and attainments is compelling, there are difficulties with the implementation and use of educational profiling. These documents tend not to be standardized, and reliability is difficult to establish. More objective alternatives are described in the next article, on *School Records and Reports*. Records are for internal use, and reports are for communication with external audiences. It follows that records are more easily changed and updated, and that somewhat different information is appropriate for each type of document. The article describes in some detail typical contents and formats for each type of document.

Environmental measures are distinctive in that the object of measurement is the climate or environment of the home or classroom. The article on *Environmental Measures* distinguishes two approaches to such measurement, involving either an environmental press approach or an interpretive mode of investigation. The histories of these two approaches are reviewed, and methods are described for assessing participants' perceptions of home and classroom settings using standardized instruments. Interpretive, ethnographic, or case study approaches offer an alternative approach to environmental measurement. Such methods have yielded significant insights, but the reader is cautioned against brief, "hit-and-run" forays in the name of naturalistic inquiry. An important direction for future research will be the integration of environmental press and interpretive approaches.

Applications of measurement for the description of educational programs are illustrated in the article on *"Title I" Evaluation Programs*. The history of "Title I" program evaluations is described, and three evaluation designs are described in detail. The logic, assumptions, strengths, and weaknesses of the "norm-referenced," "comparison group," and "regression" designs are discussed in turn.

The last two articles on descriptive uses of tests move beyond the level of the program to the problem of characterizing educational systems. The first of these is concerned with *Monitoring National Standards*. It discusses the purposes of such monitoring, the varieties of cognitive and affective outcomes that may be evaluated, and the design of monitoring systems. It then describes achievement monitoring in the United States and in the United Kingdom in some detail. The final article of Part 5 describes the *National Assessment of Educational Progress: Retrospect and Prospect*, one of the oldest national assessment programs. It reviews the original design and rationale for the assessment, then describes the evolution of NAEP in response to new information needs, as well as a policy context more favourable to interstate comparisons. The article concludes with a description of possible future directions for national assessment, and new technologies becoming available.

# Creation, Scoring, and Interpretation of Tests

## Item Writing Techniques

J. L. Herman

Item writing techniques provide rules and prescriptions for constructing sound test items, items that measure what they are intended to measure. Until relatively recently, these rules have incorporated the conventional wisdom of test writers and have provided only general guidance on how to devise test items that do not clue or unnecessarily confuse an examinee's response. Since the 1960s, however, in tandem with the growth of criterion-referenced testing, item writing techniques increasingly have focused attention on the nature and structure of test content and ways to define and operationalize what is being measured. The match between the intended content of a test and that of test items is no longer left to the implicit understanding of the item writer; rather, newer item writing technologies provide explicit, specific rules to help insure that test items measure particular domains of knowledge, skills, and/or abilities. This article provides an overview to a range of current item writing techniques. It is limited to techniques for measuring academic achievement and focuses principally on selected response or "objective" measures.

## 1. Conventional Guidelines

Conventional item construction guidelines help inhibit the inclusion of extraneous factors in test items that confound an examinee's response. They concentrate on factors such as linguistic, semantic, and grammatical features that may enable an unknowing examinee to give a correct response or that may prevent a knowing examinee from responding correctly. Typical rules for multiple-choice items, short answer and completion items, and true–false response items are given in Fig. 1 (Gronlund 1971, Conoley and O'Neil 1979).

## 2. Techniques for Constructing Replicable Test Items

While general guidelines of the sort listed in Fig. 1 are useful for constructing sound test items, they represent necessary but not sufficient criteria. Left open is the issue of how to construct items that capture and validly reflect intended test content. A number of approaches

to this problem have evolved over the years; these approaches differ in the degree of specificity, amount of discretion left in the hands of the item writer, and replicability of the items generated.

Content–process matrices represent the loosely structured end of the continuum, where item writers are accorded a great deal of discretion in devising individual items. Derived from a curriculum general scheme described by the work of Tyler and Bloom et al., broad subject domains are partitioned into two dimensions of content and process. Content includes the key concepts of the subject field and process the levels of reasoning specified by Bloom's taxonomy. Subject area experts write items they consider appropriate for each cell of the matrix, guided only by the simple content–process designation.

Criterion-referenced approaches, exemplified first by objectives-based techniques and later by domain referencing, provide more direction for item writers' efforts. Objectives specify observable stimulus and response conditions that describe the nature of the task that is expected of the learner and conditions under which the task is to be performed. The objective becomes the target of assessment, and test items are generated to match the conditions specified, for example, "Given a short story, the student will select, from among four given alternatives, the main idea."

The probability that items produced by two writers will be parallel is higher for objectives-based approaches than for content–process schemes; however significant discretion and areas of item writer variability still exist. For example, different writers may vary in their definitions of "short story," in the extent to which main ideas are stated or implied, in the amount of supporting detail, and so on.

More fine-grained specifications of the intended test content have been developed to control this variability and to more precisely define the domain of behavior to be assessed—descriptions that serve to prescribe test item development. The goal of these more elaborate specifications is to define a pool of items that represents an important universe of knowledge or skill domain—such that student performance on one set of items drawn from the domain would generalize to a second set of

---

*Typical rules for multiple-choice items:*

1. The stem of the item should be meaningful by itself and should present a clear problem.
2. The stem should be free from irrelevant material.
3. The stem should include as much of the item as possible except where an inclusion would clue. Repetitive phrases should be included in the stem rather than being restated in each alternative.
4. All alternatives should be grammatically consistent with the item stem and of similar length, so as not to provide a clue to the answer.
5. An item should include only one correct or clearly best answer.
6. Items used to measure understanding should contain some novelty and not merely repeat verbatim materials or problems presented in instruction.
7. All distractors should be plausible and related to the body of knowledge and learning experiences measured.
8. Verbal associations between the stem and correct answer or stereotyped phrases should be avoided.
9. The correct answer should appear in each of the alternative positions with approximately equal frequency and in random order.
10. Special alternatives such as "none," "all of the above" should be used sparingly.
11. Avoid items that contain inclusive terms (e.g., "never," "always," "all") in the wrong answer.
12. Negatively stated item stems should be used sparingly.
13. Avoid alternatives that are opposite in meaning or that are paraphrases of each other.
14. Avoid items which ask for opinions.
15. Avoid items that contain irrelevant sources of difficulty, such as vocabulary, or sentence structure.
16. Avoid interlocking items, items whose answers clue responses to subsequent items.
17. Don't use multiple choice items where other item formats are more appropriate.

*Typical rules for short answer and completion items:*

1. A direct question is generally better than an incomplete statement.
2. Word the item so that the required answer is both brief and unambiguous.
3. Where an answer is to be expressed in numerical units, indicate the type of units wanted.
4. Blanks for answers should be equal in length. Scoring is facilitated if the blanks are provided in a column to the right of the question.
5. Where completion items are used, do not leave many blanks.
6. For completion items, leave blank only those things that are important to remember.
7. In composing items, don't take statements verbatim from students' textbook or instruction.

*Typical rules for true–false or alternative response items:*

1. Avoid broad general statements for true–false items.
2. Avoid trivial statements.
3. Avoid negative statements and especially double negatives.
4. Avoid long complex sentences.
5. Avoid including two ideas in a single statement unless cause–effect relationships are being measured.
6. Include opinion statements only if they are attributed to particular sources.
7. True statements and false statements should be approximately the same length.
8. The number of true statements and of false statements should be approximately equal.
9. Avoid taking statements verbatim from students' text or instruction.

**Figure 1**
General guidelines for item writing

items and to the entire defined domain. In its most highly prescribed form, domain specifications provide an exhaustive set of rules for generating a set of related test items. For example, item forms developed by Hively et al. (1973) include:

(a) general description of what the item form is about;

(b) item form shell, which provides a sample item as it would be administered to examinees and the common unvarying elements of each item generated;

(c) stimulus and response characteristics, which describe the theoretical characteristics of the item generation scheme and the dimensions which are varied to comprise the replacement sets;

(d) replacement schemes and replacement sets, which detail the exact mechanics of generating item pools for the given domain;

(e) scoring specifications, which describe the properties to be used to distinguish between a correct and an incorrect response (see Fig. 2).

Similarly, Osburn has described item forms which (a) generate items with a fixed syntactical structure; (b) contain one or more variable elements; (c) define a class of item sentences by specifying the replacement sets for the variable elements. Facet design, originated by Guttman, likewise specifies a universe of content in terms of a mapping sentence that contains variable facets—the latter operates like replacement sets in Hively's item forms.

The most highly specific item forms and mapping sentence approaches permit computerized test item writing. Using author languages such as COURSE-WRITER, PLANIT, and TUTOR, a series of computer commands define the wording of an item form and the way the variable elements are chosen or computed.

Producing a number satisfying a given order relation to specified numbers(s) (spoken form).

**General description**

The child is asked to say the name of a number that bears a specified order relation ("greater than" or "less than") to a given number or numbers in the range 0 through 20. Given numbers are presented in spoken form and response is spoken.

**Stimulus and response characteristics**

Constant for All Cells

The presentation is completely spoken; a spoken response is required.

Distinguishing Among Cells

Three scripts are used asking respectively for a number greater than a given number, for a number less than a given number, and for a number greater than one given number and less than another

Within the third script, three conditions are allowed: (1) first given numeral greater than second with required number possibly an integer; (2) first given numeral greater than second with required number necessarily not an integer; and (3) first given numeral less than second so that the solution to the problem is the empty set.

Varying Within Cells.

Within each cell, the given numbers are integers from the range 0 through 20 chosen so that the correct response (when it is not the empty set) can be a real number from the range 0 through 20.

**Cell matrix**

| Script (a) | "greater than $b_1$" | "less than $b_1$" | "greater than $b_1$" but less than $b_2$ | | |
|---|---|---|---|---|---|
| Numerals (b) | $0 \leq b_1 \leq 19$ | $1 \leq b_1 \leq 20$ | $0 \leq b_1 \leq 18$ $b_1 + 2 \leq b_2 \leq 20$ | $0 \leq b_1 \leq 19$ $b_2 = b_1 + 1$ | $1 \leq b_1 \leq 20$ $0 \leq b_2 < b_1$ |
| | (1) | (2) | (3) | (4) | (5) |

**Item form shell**

| Materials None | |
|---|---|
| Directions to examiner | Script |
| Read script to child. Write down child's exact words. | Tell me a number that is |

**Replacement scheme**

(a) Script
  Cell 1: "less than $b_1$," "greater than $b_1$,"
  Cells 3,4,5: "greater than $b_1$ but less than $b_2$,"

(b) Numerals within Script
  Cell 1: **Choose** $b_1$ from R.S. 9.1
  Cell 2: **Choose** $b_1$ from R.S. 9.2
  Cell 3: Choose two numbers from R.S. 9.3
  Cell 3: Choose two numbers from R.S. 9.3
    Let $b_1$ = smaller number; $b_2$ = larger number
    Reject if $b_2 - b_1 \leq 1$
  Cell 4: Choose $b_1$ from R.S. 9.3
    Let $b_2 = b_1 + 1$
  Cell 5: Choose two numbers from R.S. 9.3
    Let $b_1$ = larger number; $b_2$ = smaller number
    Reject if $b_1 = b_2$

**Replacement sets**

  R.S. 9.1: Whole numbers 0,1,2,...,19.
  R.S. 9.2: Whole numbers 1,2,3,...,20.
  R.S. 9.3: Whole numbers 0,1,2,...,20.

**Scoring specifications**

  Cell 1: Any real number X where $X > b_1$
  Cell 2: Any real number X where $X < b_1$
  Cell 3: Any real number X where $b_1 < X < b_2$
  Cell 4: Any real number X where $b_1 < X < b_2$
  Cell 5: Any response equivalent to saying that there are no numbers which can fulfill the conditions.

*Figure 2*
Sample item form

The applicability of highly specific item forms has been questioned for content areas which are not highly structured; their cost feasibility and widespread practical utility are also a concern. Popham and Baker have both suggested a compromise strategy to optimize descriptive rigor and feasibility. Derived from Hively's work, their approach features an expanded objective which delimits the nature of the intended content and response and provides explicit rules for generating test items. First known as amplified objectives and in their more recent refinement, domain specifications, these statements detail (a) a general description of the knowledge, skill, or attitude being measured; (b) content limits, which describe the range of eligible content for constructing the item stem; (c) response limits, which describe the nature of the correct response, including specific criteria for judging the adequacy of a constructed response, or rules for generating distractors for multiple-choice items; and (d) sample items and directions for administration. Figure 3 provides a sample domain specification.

## 3. Item Writing Algorithms

Domain specifications provide rules for generating test items, and the source of such rules has received modest attention. Hively has indicated the curriculum as a source, and has described inductive and deductive approaches to generating item generation rules and schemes. Others have attempted to describe rules for item generation which are applicable across curricula

and content areas, for instance, assessing prose learning and comprehension and concept learning.

### 3.1 Linguistic-based Approaches to Item Writing

Bormuth was among the first to stress the need for an item writing technology, and pioneered linguistic-based approaches to assess prose learning and assure a logical connection between test items and instructional materials. Bormuth proposed a detailed set of rules for transforming segments of prose instruction into test items, using his "wh-transformation." He described transformations for two types of items: those derived from a single sentence, and those derived from the relationship between sentences. For example, a sentence is selected from the instructional materials, a substantive word is deleted and replaced with the appropriate *wh* word (*who, what, when, where,* etc.), and the item is constructed by transforming the sentence into a question.

Anderson emphasized the use of paraphrasing in constructing such test items. He pointed out that verbatim questions do not require comprehension, but merely recall. To assess whether an examinee has comprehended the original information, it must be paraphrased and then transformed. He outlined two requirements for paraphrased statements: (a) they have no substantive words in common; (b) they are equivalent in meaning. In addition to assessing comprehension of prose materials, Anderson also outlined a method for testing concepts and principles by substituting particular terms for superordinate ones and

| | |
|---|---|
| *Grade level:* | Grade 3 |
| *Subject:* | Reading comprehension |
| *Domain description:* | Students will select from among written alternatives the stated main idea of a given short paragraph. |
| *Content limits:* | 1. For each item, student will be presented with a 4–5 sentence expository paragraph. Each paragraph will have a stated main idea and 3–4 supporting statements. |
| | 2. The main idea will be stated in either the first or the last sentence of the paragraph. The main idea will associate the subject of the paragraph (person, object, action) with a general statement of action, or general descriptive statement. For example, "Smoking is dangerous to your health," "Kenny worked hard to become a doctor," "There are many kinds of seals." |
| | 3. Supporting statements will give details, examples, or evidence supporting the main idea. |
| | 4. Paragraphs will be written at no higher than a third grade reading level. |
| *Response limits:* | 1. Students will select an answer from among four written alternatives. Each alternative will be a complete sentence. |
| | 2. The correct answer will consist of a paraphrase of the stated main idea. Paraphrased sentences may be accomplished by employing synonyms and/or by changing the word order. |
| | 3. Distractors will be constructed from the following: |

(a) One distractor will be a paraphrase of one supporting statement given in the paragraph (e.g., alternative "a" in the sample item).

(b) One or two distractors will be generalizations that can be drawn from two of the supporting statements, but do not include the entire main idea (e.g., alternative "d" in the sample item).

(c) One distractor may be a statement about the subject of the paragraph that is more general than the main idea (e.g., alternative "b" in the sample item).

| | |
|---|---|
| *Format:* | Each question will be multiple choice with four possible responses. |
| *Directions:* | Read each paragraph. Circle the letter that tells the main idea. |
| *Sample item:* | Indians had many kinds of homes. Plains Indians lived in teepees which were made from skins. The Hopi Indians used bushes to make round houses, called hogans. The Mohawks made longhouses out of wood. Some Northeast Indians built smaller wooden cabins. |

What is the main idea of this story?
   a. Some Indians used skins to make houses.
   b. There were different Indian tribes.
   c. Indians built different types of houses.
   d. Indian houses were made of wood.

*Figure 3*
Sample domain specifications

replacing with synonyms all remaining substantive words, a process further operationalized by Conoley and O'Neil.

Bormuth's transformational approaches were further refined by Finn who used case grammar to develop an 82-step algorithm for selecting sentences and for transforming them into questions. Finn's procedures were subsequently streamlined into three major steps:

(a) Analyzing the text and selecting the sentences, including procedures for screening tests and selecting the most instructionally relevant and significant sentences, for writing summary sentences, and for using word frequency analyses to identify keywords.

(b) Transformation of sentences into questions, by clarifying referents and simplifying the selected sentences, replacing the keyword noun, and rewriting the sentences and a question.

(c) Construction of distractors, from learner-free responses, from a fixed list of keywords, or from other similar function words in the instructional passage.

### 3.2 Concept Learning Approaches to Item Writing

Tiemann and Markle's research on concept learning provides guidance on how to circumscribe and define valid domains for teaching and assessment. A concept represents a class of objects, events, ideas, or relations which vary among themselves, but are nonetheless classified as the same. For example, the concept "dog" includes dobermans, spaniels, poodles, mutts; "democracy" subsumes parliamentary and congressional varieties; "reinforcer" includes endless specific instances. Concept testing basically involves assessing generalization to *new* examples and discrimination of nonexamples of a particular concept.

Systematic analyses of the critical and variable attributes of a concept are central to both teaching and testing. Critical attributes are those which are common to all members of the class, while variable attributes are those which may differ among members; these attributes define and differentiate the concept domain. For example, all dogs have four legs and a tail, but vary in size, color, length of hair, and so on. Examples and nonexamples of the concept, embodying the presence and/or absence of these various attributes, are constructed for teaching, and new, previously unencountered examples of both types are used to test students' understanding. Novel examples are essential—otherwise simple recall rather than higher levels of thinking are being assessed. Further, examples and nonexamples representing systematic variation of critical and variable attributes can heighten the diagnostic value of resultant test items.

### 3.3 Other Approaches to Higher Levels of Learning

Williams and Haladyna's typology is also concerned with constructing higher level test items and provides rules for matching syntactical forms with objectives at various cognitive levels. They define a three-dimensional matrix for classifying objectives and test items: content (including facts, concepts, and principles); task (including reiteration, summarization, illustration, prediction, evaluation, application); and response mode (selected and constructed). Generic objectives for each cell describe the type of situation to which the examinee must respond, the nature of the information or stimulus presented, and the type of response required, for instance, "name," "identify," "define." After selecting the content and task to be tested, the item writer can then use the matrix to determine how to construct an appropriate test item. The Instructional Quality Inventory, developed for use in United States military training, relies on a similar content by task matrix and is particularly concerned with objective/test consistency and adequacy.

### 4. Summary and Conclusions

In summary, a range of item writing strategies has been advanced since the 1970s. These strategies have been aimed predominantly at defining a universe or domain of knowledge to be tested and at assuring a match between test items and significant instructional content; they seek to maximize instructional and content validity.

Unfortunately, however, there appears to be conflict between features which maximize such validity and those which affect feasibility. For example, the approaches which offer the greatest descriptive rigor are least likely to be implemented by teachers because of time, cost, and technical sophistication requirements. These more elaborate approaches may be more feasible for large-scale national, state, and province assessments, and for creating item banks which are maximally useful for instructional planning and certification—situations where greater resources are available, and resultant items are intended for widespread use.

Item writing is but one step in the test development process. Sound procedures must be used at all steps to assure test validity.

### Bibliography

Anderson R C 1972 How to construct achievement tests to assess comprehension. *Rev. Educ. Res.* 42: 145–70
Bormuth J R 1970 *On the Theory of Achievement Test Items.* University of Chicago Press, Chicago, Illinois
Conoley J, O'Neil H F 1979 A primer for developing tests items. In: O'Neil H F (ed.) 1979 *Procedures for Instructional Systems Development.* Academic Press, New York
Finn P J 1975 A question-writing algorithm. *J. Read. Behav.* 4: 341–67
Gronlund N E 1971 *Measurement and Evaluation in Teaching,* 2nd edn. Macmillan, New York
Hively W, Maxwell G, Rabehl G, Sension D, Lundin S 1973 *Domain-referenced Curriculum Evaluation: A Technical Handbook and a Case Study from the Minnemast Project,* CSE Monograph Series in Evaluation No. 1. Center for the Study of Evaluation, University of California, Los Angeles, California
Millman J 1980 Computer-based item generation. In: Berk R (ed.) 1980 *Criterion-referenced Measurement.* Johns Hopkins University Press, Baltimore, Maryland
Roid G, Haladyna T (eds.) 1980 The emergence of an item writing technology. *Rev. Educ. Res.* 50: 293–314
Roid G, Haladyna T 1982 *A Technology for Test–item Writing.* Academic Press, New York
Tiemann P W, Markle S M 1978 *Analyzing Instructional Content: A Guide to Instruction and Evaluation.* Stipes, Champaign, Illinois
Williams R G, Haladyna T 1982 Logical operations for generating intended questions (LOGIQ): A typology for higher level test items. In: Roid G, Haladyna T (eds.) 1982

# Item Bank

B. H. Choppin

An item bank is a collection of test items, organized, classified, and cataloged, like the books in a library, in order to facilitate the construction of a variety of achievement and other types of mental test. (The term "question bank" is used synonymously with item bank in the British literature.) Unstructured collections of items (some of which have been available for several decades) are generally referred to as item pools. It is the recent development of classification and calibration procedures for individual items that makes possible the construction of tests with particular pre-specified characteristics that distinguishes the item bank from an item pool. The term item bank came into use following a research project of the 1960s (Wood and Skurnik 1969). Unfortunately the implied analogy to a financial bank, and its associated concepts of credit and debit, have caused some confusion. It is perhaps better to think of an item bank strictly as an item library from which items can be withdrawn in order to compose tests.

## 1. Problems of a Standardized Test

An item bank can be seen as a replacement for a single standardized test, or for a whole network of such tests. The development of item banks derives in some part from the growing dissatisfaction with standardized testing. Standardized tests need to be given under standard conditions (the original meaning of standardized test) in order that the score on the test be interpretable. This is often inconvenient as the length of the test, and the time it requires, may not exactly fit the circumstances of the application. Further, even when all or part of a test does not exactly match the objectives of the tester, he or she has no real choice other than to use the test in its entirety or not at all. Any variations in the test invalidate the norms, which are the only mechanism for interpreting the scores. This is especially important with achievement tests, where the instrument's validity for a particular use may depend upon the extent to which it matches the particular curriculum and instructional treatment. Custom-designed tests for specific applications get around this, but at the expense of abandoning norms. Tests without norms may be used to make comparisons as long as all the people to be compared were measured by the same test. Sometimes this condition is satisfied, but there are many circumstances in which references to scores on another test or some external level of performance is needed. Test norms, themselves, present other problems. The individuals that are to be measured are rarely typical members of any particular group for which norms are available, so the use of norms to interpret a test score involves introducing an unknown degree of uncertainty or error into the measurement process.

## 2. Advantages of Item Banks

Item banks have been developed to improve testing practice in a number of ways. These may be conveniently classified under four headings: economy, flexibility, consistency, and security. These will be considered in turn.

### 2.1 Economy

Each year, and in each main subject area of the school curriculum, tens of thousands of new test items are written. The composition of these new items has exercised the ingenuity of some of the finest teachers and examiners in almost every country in the world. Most of the test items they have created are used once, and once only, and then discarded. Many of the items are not worthy of preservation, but each year a substantial number of original, stimulating items of high quality are lost. A major advantage of item banking is that it thrives on the repeated use of items. Careful screening ensures that only high-quality items are included in the item bank, but once an item has been so included it is likely to remain on the "active" list for a number of years, and may be sensibly employed in a variety of different tests. Furthermore, the initial trial of the items, and the storing in the bank of appropriate statistical data about their functioning, provide the necessary information from which to develop an adequate statistical description of any test constructed from a subset of these items without a further trial stage. This applies both to the psychometric characteristics of reliability, validity, and so on, and to the calibration of scores on the test, and results in a considerable saving of work and expense.

### 2.2 Flexibility

As has already been suggested, an important advantage of an item bank is that it offers the facility for tailoring tests to specific applications. New tests may be built from materials stored in the bank with relatively few constraints. They may be long or short; covering a wide range of ability or concentrating on items at a particular level; providing comprehensive coverage of the curriculum or focusing on a narrowly defined area, and so on. In each case, the classificatory and statistical information cataloged for each item permits a realistic assessment of the test's reliability and validity, a calibration of scores of the test onto a fixed scale, and a guide to the interpretation of those scores in terms of performance on particular tasks. Individual items can be removed from, or added to, a test with predictable effects on the test's characteristics. Item banks may even be used to generate fully adaptive tests in which each item presented to the student is chosen from the collection in the bank on the basis of the student's performance on the items preceding it.

### 2.3 Consistency

The complete calibration of items leads to the cross-calibration of all tests derived from them, and gives the measurement system a degree of coherence and consistency unobtainable from networks of standardized tests. From an item bank it is relatively straightforward to construct parallel tests by varying some parameters, particularly the difficulty level of the test (e.g., to make an easier version for less advanced students). In this case, since both sets of raw scores are still translated onto a common scale, it is possible to compare the performance of individuals taking different tests.

### 2.4 Security

Traditional achievement tests and examinations all depend upon a certain degree of surprise. The candidate may well know in general what to expect in an examination paper, but if the details of the questions are known beforehand then the examination will not function as intended. Candidates will attempt to memorize the answers to the questions they will meet, rather than working on increasing their understanding of the full range of subject matter. The items included in the test represent only a sample of the full domain of achievement being assessed, and for the test to be valid, each candidate's response to the included items should be in some sense representative of his or her potential responses to all the items from the domain (including those that are not a part of the test).

Sometimes this need for surprise, and the consequent requirement for test security, is a serious problem; sometimes not. In general it depends on how much hangs on the test result. In educational systems with limited resources, and hence very strong competition for places in the secondary or tertiary levels of education, the importance of an examination's result to an individual may be very great indeed. In such countries, it is not unknown for pirated versions of the national school-leaving examination or university entrance test to be circulated furtively before the date of the examination itself.

Item banking systems seek to overcome the security problem in two ways. First, the size of the bank means that it is impracticable for the individual student to attempt to memorize the answers to all questions without first mastering the content matter. With large banks of, say, 2,000 or more items, it may even be advantageous to publish the complete collection of a limited scale. This would further discourage the idea that anybody who comes into possession, authorized or unauthorized, of some or all of the item collection, has secured some sort of special advantage. Security may also be increased by preparing, as a routine matter, several alternative forms of tests and examinations for all those applications where leakage of test content might pose serious problems. Having available four or five alternative forms of the examination, with no one knowing until the final moments which form is to be administered to a particular individual, will itself do much to enhance the integrity of the examination system. The possibility of substituting a different examination form from the one originally planned, either as a result of suspected leakage, or because analysis of the first set of results reveals strong evidence of malpractice, allows recovery from a potentially scandalous situation. Three thousand years ago the discovery of malpractice in the civil service examinations of Imperial China led to the execution of the chief examiners. Item banks can contribute to lessen the insurance premiums paid by their modern counterparts.

## 3. Measurement Models

The psychometric key that turns an item pool into a potential item bank is a comprehensive procedure for deriving the properties of tests (reliability, precision, difficulty, etc.) from the statistical properties of the items from which they are built. Inasmuch as item banks are not mere collections of test items, but are rather organized, scaled, and calibrated to provide a basis for generalized measurement, they must rely on some underlying theory or model of the test-taking process.

One such model, deriving from the statistical technique of generalizability, concentrates on the estimation of an individual's domain score; that is the proportion of some defined domain of test items that the candidate has mastered. Shoemaker (1975) proposed a comprehensive framework for achieving testing based on this approach. At about the same time, a number of American researchers, interested primarily in the definition of item domains, devised several systems for the computer generation of test questions according to specified item forms that could be used to create item banks (Byrne 1975). Since this date, the domain-referenced approach to item banking appears to have lost much of its impetus. The underlying model which treated items as completely interchangeable, has proved to be of strictly limited utility when applied to educational problems.

The other approach to establishing item banks, which is steadily increasing its influence in the testing world, stems from a proposal by Choppin (1968) to use latent trait theory, and specifically the Rasch model, for item calibration.

One of the early objectives of the change in emphasis from norm-referenced to criterion-referenced measurement was to establish criteria of performance in terms of tasks appropriate to life in the real world, rather than the classroom. However, with the exception of a few skills (typing and swimming, for example) this has not been found to be possible. Instead, criterion referencing has usually meant the relating of performance on one set of test items to the complete dimension of achievement as described by other items. Far from treating items as interchangeable, latent trait theory scales them according to difficulty, and spreads them out in a complete map of the curriculum area. Measurement of the student via the item bank then means locating him or her somewhere on the achievement map. Good examples of this approach are to be found in Cornish and Wines (1977) and Connolly et al. (1971).

## 4. Applications

Both the examples cited above are small-scale item banks designed for use by a teacher with a single student. Other banks designed for the generation of group tests have been published commercially or made available to teachers through official channels. These are more concerned with establishing group levels of performance than mapping individual achievement, and the curriculum analysis underlying them may not be as detailed, though some classification of the items in curricular terms is usually considered essential.

In the United States, whose public school system exhibits local autonomy and explicit concerns with both curriculum specification and standards of performance, the main interest in item banks has been in supporting test programs at a district or state-wide level for monitoring overall standards *and* assessing individual students. For example, all students in the Los Angeles County School District are tested with materials drawn from a central bank, and the information collected is analyzed for the individual student, and aggregated by classroom and school to provide detailed diagnostic feedback. Similarly, the Evaluation Department of the City of Portland Public Schools in Oregon uses extensive item banks to assess its students at several grade levels each year (Doherty 1976).

Two other roles of item banking deserve consideration. Both involve large-scale testing programs spread over a number of years. The first is that of supporting a national examinations system where, apart from its contributions to economy and security, the item bank can facilitate the maintenance of standards from one year to the next. Such systems are being developed in a number of countries including Hong Kong, India, and Indonesia. The other application is in research projects for the longitudinal monitoring of achievement standards such as the Assessment of Performance Unit in the United Kingdom (Choppin 1978, 1981). Here the major advantage of latent trait scaling, the possibility of comparing scores on different tests administered at different points in time, itself leads to a new problem— the changing validity of an item bank as changes in the school curriculum occur. It is too early to say whether regular updating and recalibration of the bank can successfully maintain its validity over the substantial periods of time envisaged by the designers of the monitoring exercise. Even if this problem cannot be completely solved, the item bank will provide a sound basis for quantitative description of curricular change more powerful than any we have had before.

## Bibliography

Byrne C J 1975 *Computerised Question Banking Systems*. Open University, Milton Keynes
Choppin B H 1968 Item bank using sample–free calibration. *Nature* 219: 870–72
Choppin B H 1978 *Item Banking and the Monitoring of Achievement*. National Foundation for Educational Research, Slough
Choppin B H 1981 Is education getting better? *Br. Educ. Res. J.* 7: 3–16
Connolly A J, Nachtman W, Pritchett E M 1971 *Key Math Diagnostic Arithmetic Test*. American Guidance Service, Circle Pines, Minnesota
Cornish G, Wines R 1977 *ACER Mathematics Profile Series*. Australian Council for Educational Research, Hawthorn, Victoria
Doherty V 1976 Developments in goal based assessment in the Portland Public School. ERIC Document No. ED 126 566
Shoemaker D M 1975 Toward a framework for achievement testing. *Rev. Educ. Res.* 45: 127–47
Wood R, Skurnik L S 1969 *Item Banking: A Method for Producing School-Based Examinations and Nationally Comparable Grades*. National Foundation for Educational Research, Slough

# Readability and Reading Levels

## A. Davison

The term readability is generally used to refer to the assessment of the difficulty that a reader of a certain level of skill may have in reading a piece of connected written discourse, or text. These assessments are important in rank ordering different texts by difficulty, and in matching readers' abilities to the difficulty of the material they must read. While the term sometimes refers to factors which motivate readers to read, such as content and mode of presentation, for the most part what is meant by readable is comprehensible. The difficulty of a text is generally measured in terms of how well readers are able to understand it, that is, able to give correct answers to questions about the texts.

The most commonly used method of measuring readability in the last 50 years has been the application of one or more readability formulas. These formulas, or formula-like procedures, measure average values for certain features of the text in question, such as the familiarity or abstractness of the vocabulary used, or the length and consequent complexity of the sentences. The average values of these factors for samples of 100 words each are multiplied by various coefficients, and the final result of the calculation is either a grade-level score or a score corresponding to a range of grade levels. The readability score represents a prediction that a certain percentage of readers with reading skills of a certain grade level (or higher) will be able to read and comprehend the text. That is, readability scores have a fairly high correlation, between 0.5 and 0.7 or 0.8, with other measures of comprehension.

These predictions hold for certain kinds of texts and readers. The original rationale for readability formulas was to insure that school materials would be of an appropriate level for the students who were supposed to use them, and also to give teachers a less subjective measure than intuition, and a less cumbersome method than scanning an entire text, for assessing difficulty and rank-ordering texts. But even though they represent predictions, and not guarantees, readability formulas have been widely used for judging texts of all kinds, including texts using figurative language, or texts expressing difficult concepts and employing a technical vocabulary. The use of formulas has been extended to many kinds of readers, including adults with low reading skills, but without taking into consideration the specific purposes which a reader might have in reading, the background knowledge which the reader brings to the text, level of motivation, and so on. These are factors which may vary between readers, and so may make a big difference in how well the reader comprehends the text. Finally, readability formulas are so widely used and influential in the choice of educational materials that it is inevitable that they would come to shape the kind of writing used in graded materials. Since vocabulary and sentence enter into the calculation of readability scores, there is inescapable pressure on writers to use familiar and standard vocabulary and to keep sentences short and simple.

Certainly, the prediction which readability formulas make is that a text will be easier to read if the vocabulary is simplified and if the sentences are shortened. But this prediction is false, of course. If readability scores are correlated with measures of comprehension, they do not measure the factors which directly cause difficulty of reading. They measure only certain factors which may reflect difficulty, for some text types, readers, and situations, at least. Formulas are not in themselves a characterization of reading comprehension and all the factors which enter into the processing and interpretation of language in connected discourse. As more is understood about reading, language processing, and learning, in general, the more questions arise as to whether readability formulas are valid and adequate as measures of reading difficulty.

The history of readability formulas goes back to the 1920s, though the kind of formula still in use today did not come into general circulation until the 1930s, when measures of sentence length were combined with measures of vocabulary. Before that, the early formulas made use of lists such as Thorndike's (1921) list of frequent words in English. Some formulas compared the percentage of words of Germanic origin, likely to be familiar and frequent, with words of Latin and Greek origin, which generally are more technical and abstract in meaning. The same factors were also measured by comparing monosyllabic with polysyllabic words, or number of concrete references versus abstract references. To these measures was added the measure of sentence length, in number of words or syllables, in 100-word samples taken from various parts of the text being evaluated. The formulas in use today all include averages of sentence length, as well as various measures of vocabulary complexity, such as number of syllables per 100 words, percentage of words on a list of frequent words, and so on.

The earlier formulas were validated against a standard set of graded reading passages and comprehension questions, the McCall–Crabbs passages (1925, revised 1950), and some more recent formulas were revised in accordance with the passages (Klare 1963). A new procedure for validating the scores obtained with readability formulas was the cloze procedure introduced by Taylor (1953). This procedure involves the deletion of every nth word—every 5th word for example—in a portion of the text in question. Readers are asked to supply the missing word, and the percentage of exactly correct responses is used to calculate the reading level of the text. This procedure is based on the assumption that the reader must be able to understand a text in its truncated form in order to reconstruct the missing words. Hence the text must contain a certain amount

of redundancy—at least for a skilled reader. The procedure is somewhat more sensitive than formulas to texts which are conceptually difficult even though the sentences may not be long or the vocabulary technical.

Most formulas, by their nature, give equal weight to one factor at all grade levels, so that the interaction of vocabulary and sentence length follows a "straight line." The best-known formula which does not follow this pattern is the Fry formula (1968), which weights vocabulary and sentence length differently at higher and lower grade levels. For this reason the "formula" has to be represented in a graph format, rather than as a multiple regression equation like other formulas. For Fry, vocabulary contributes more to difficulty at higher grade levels than sentence length, and the reverse is true at lower grade levels, where sentence length is the greater obstacle to comprehension. The distinction made here is at least a suggestion of a definition of what might cause reading difficulty, and an attempt to match features of a formula to the stages which children go through in acquiring language, and in learning to interpret written text with the same grammatical principles, vocabulary, and real-world knowledge which they use for spoken discourse. Research on these questions is still going on; for instance, it is fairly clear that some parts of language, especially sentence structures, are difficult and are learned later by preschool children and young school-age children in the process of first language learning. But it is not known whether these are the same complex structures which contribute to reading difficulty; and if they are, whether they are complex for the same reason that young preliterate children have trouble with them.

The originators of the earlier formulas seemed to be interested in measuring factors which cause difficulty of comprehension, as well as sentence length and vocabulary. Many of the formulas of the 1930s included additional factors, such as the percentage of pronouns in the 100-word samples, the number of prepositional phrases, or definite articles, finite verbs, compound and complex sentences, affixes within words, abstract references, and Latinate vocabulary. Most of these factors were abandoned in later formulas. More recently, there have been attempts to measure reading difficulty, particularly syntactic complexity, without simplistic averages. Some procedures for determining sentence complexity are based on the results of systematic studies of language acquisition in young children, and experiments in language processing in children and adults. Dawkins (1975) gives a taxonomy of difficult constructions, while Botel and Granowsky (1972) use a similar taxonomy to assign weightings to parts of a sentence, so that its total complexity can be calculated if it is made up of many parts. Its overall complexity could then be compared with another sentence of the same length or similar structure. Von Glasersfeld (1971) incorporates a model of language processing, Yngve's Depth Hypothesis, which predicts greater difficulty the more deeply embedded a structure is, and the more material that needs to be held "in storage" before the whole structure can be processed. Von Glasersfeld also incorporates semantic links between sentences that would facilitate processing.

Interest persists in the question of defining exactly what it is that causes difficulty of processing, either absolutely or relatively speaking. The question is all the more difficult in the light of the findings of Bormuth (1966). The results of a cloze procedure, with children in grades four to eight (ages 9–13) as subjects and excerpts from school materials as texts, were matched with other factors in the texts. These factors included depth of embedding, syntactic complexity measured in various ways, as well as the factors mentioned in connection with early formulas. These factors turned out to be intercorrelated in various ways, but the most highly correlated values were the results of the cloze tests and the scores obtained by applying readability formulas.

From the statistical point of view, the correlation of readability formulas with comprehension tests or cloze tests is quite high—0.5 to 0.7 or 0.8. Yet no formula gives a perfect prediction in all cases, as their partisans freely admit. They may predict success for 50 percent of readers with fair accuracy, if used for the texts and readers for which they were intended. But if it is necessary that the prediction be more accurate, or if the difficulty of the text needs to be lowered, the readability formulas give no useful help at all. This is particularly true for adults. It has been shown that the instructions which a judge gives the jury on points of law can be made more comprehensible in certain ways, but not only by shortening sentences and simplifying complex and technical vocabulary—the implied message of readability formulas. Different formulas often give different scores to the same text [this article, however, is "college" by the Fry formula, 13th–15th grade by Dale–Chall, and 43 (difficult) on the Flesch Scale]. But even given some amount of variation, the formulas fail to make accurate predictions of difficulty for technical materials read by adults.

For younger readers, the use of readability formulas raises questions about the choice of presenting meaning in a series of short sentences, with inferred connections, or in complex and long sentences, with an explicit connective. It has been shown that fourth and fifth grade (age 9–11) students prefer, and understand more successfully, a causal relation presented in a complex sentence with an explicit connective, "because." This result runs contrary to the predictions of formulas. While the proponents of readability formulas have never claimed that formulas measure the only factors which reflect ease or difficulty, it has become more and more clear that many factors enter into success in comprehension, and what is an important factor in some situations may not be important in another. For example, poor text organization and lack of connection between the parts can make comprehension more difficult, but the negative effect may be less if the reader has a rich store of background knowledge of the subject of the text. Without adequate background knowledge, or definition of the topic of the passage, even a well-organized and coherent text may be difficult. The roles of background information and text organization are particularly important in comprehension. But these factors are not well-suited for measurement by formula-like measures. They are assumed beforehand, as formulas are intended to be applied to otherwise well-formed and coherent texts. Factors which may vary from one situation to another are not reflected in the absolute values which formulas give.

Researchers are still investigating how people, particularly younger children, understand connected written discourse. Many factors are involved and the relations between the factors are subtle and difficult to measure. Readability formulas are capable of being used to reflect some of the factors which sometimes contribute to difficulty. Because of their simplicity, they have an obvious utility and attraction, which may distract attention from other important features of texts. As formulas are not models of reading processing, they do not represent strong hypotheses which can be used to accumulate new knowledge about readability, and to relate factors which enter into success in comprehension with other experimental or observational results in learning theory, cognition in general, or language ability. Much remains to be discovered in these areas. If formulas are used to measure readability, they should be used with caution, in accordance with the limitations imposed by their originators. They should not be used to revise or simplify texts; and they should not be used to the exclusion of judgments about other factors, such as the background and motivation of potential readers, and the organization and coherence of the texts being measured.

## Bibliography

Bormuth J 1966 Readability: A new approach. *Read. Res. Q.* 1: 79–132

Botel M, Granowsky A 1972 A new formula for measuring syntactic complexity: A directional effort. *Elem. Engl.* 49: 513–16

Dawkins J 1975 *Syntax and Readability.* International Reading Association, Newark, Delaware

Fry E 1968 A readability formula that saves time. *J. Read.* 11: 513–16

Klare G R 1963 *The Measurement of Readability.* Iowa State University Press, Ames, Iowa

Klare G R 1974 Assessing readability. *Read. Res. Q.* 10: 62–102

McCall W, Crabbs L 1925, 1950, 1961 *Standard Test Lessons in Reading.* Bureau of Publications, Teachers College, Columbia University, New York

Taylor W 1953 Cloze procedure: A new tool for measuring readability. *Journalism Q.* 30: 415–31

Thorndike E 1921 *The Teacher's Word Book.* Teachers College, Columbia University, New York

von Glasersfeld E 1971 The problem of syntactic complexity in reading and readability. *J. Read. Behav.* 3: 1–14

# Domain-referenced Tests

### E. L. Baker

A domain-referenced test attempts to provide clear specifications about the nature of the tested performance in order to clarify what is being measured and to provide a basis for assessing the representativeness of the items with regard to the competency in question.

Domain-referenced testing is a special case of criterion-referenced testing. Criterion-referenced testing focuses upon assessing the respondent's performance with respect to a well-defined level or body of knowledge. When the test designer wishes to describe well the content and skills sampled by the test, the use of domain-referenced testing is suggested. The domain that is referred to in this context does not correspond to the term domain as used by Bloom et al. (1956) in describing broad areas of competency in their well-known taxonomies of objectives. Rather, domain refers to the specifically circumscribed universe from which performance is sampled and to which performance is expected to generalize. Thus, in domain-referenced testing, part of the problem is devising or describing the parameters of the domain and another is devising a rule of algorithm to permit sampling.

## 1. Specifications for Domains

All tests have certain specifications, describing the broad range of content and skills to be assessed. Domain-referenced tests present specifications that attempt to reduce successively the uncertainty first of the test item writer in creating comparable items, that is, items which represent the same universe of skills and content, and second, of the test user who is attempting to understand what a test score means. Because criterion-referenced testing emphasizes measuring what or how much the learner knows, the first problem is to describe that general area. Various writers have attacked this problem using their own special language. More generally, however, the problem consists of describing what content the respondent will be faced with under what conditions, in what form the response is expected, and what criteria will be used to judge the adequacy of performance. Because of the history of criterion-referenced testing in general and domain-referenced testing in particular, a common starting point is in the description of the objectives of the instructional program that the tests purport to measure. The point of entry derives from objectives because the entire movement of criterion-referenced tests and domain-referenced tests grew out of a preoccupation with assessing instruction (Glasera 1963). A common way for educators to think about domains is in terms of clarifying the objectives that they want to assess, [e.g., the "amplified objectives" of Popham (1981)].

At a practical level, it is necessary to assure that items used to assess a particular area conform in some

regularized way to specifications. Although at the outset of this movement, in the late 1960s in the United States, much emphasis was given to the behavior that was to be elicited by the test, further effort pointed to the major problem of clarifying the content in the objective. The content limits of the domain are its most critical feature. How may content be circumscribed? One approach, taken by Hively et al (1973) depends upon the use of an item shell into which specific content may be inserted according to an algorithm, for example, $a + b =$ -----, where $a$ equals any two-digit number and $b$ equals any three-digit number. Given such a shell, and the rule "any," comparable items may be developed and an estimate may be made of the performance in respect to the entire universe of two-digit and three-digit sums. Because of the relative simplicity of using an algebraic form for a mathematical task, it is not surprising that the earliest efforts in domain-referenced testing came from mathematics and science problems that involved quantity (Hively et al. 1973). Naturally, the problem of content becomes unwieldly as a move is made from content that has a clear structure to content with arbitrary arrangements. For that reason, domain-referenced tests are easier to prepare in those fields where either there exists a complete list of content itself (e.g., English consonants), rather a vast set of information, or creative works that differ in more ways than they are similar, for example, French novels. Nonetheless, domain-referenced testing has developed some approaches to describing and limiting content for testing. One procedure involves describing features of the content thought to be critical to an assessment of competency. For example, in the assessment of reading comprehension, children may need to be presented with both fiction and nonfiction as stimuli, but because the cognitive processes for understanding may differ, such content domains might be separated and further specified in a domain-referenced test. Therefore, the content limits might specify not only the genre, (fiction or nonfiction,) but also the length of passage, the complexity of the writing, and the novelty of the information. Clearly such limits exclude certain passages from consideration, but permit enormous variation in those selected, raising the question of what is comparable content. Another approach to the problem of content limits in fields such as social studies or literature has been to enumerate the concepts or works to which students will be expected to generalize, for example, mercantilism, capitalism, economic socialism, or *The Duinio Elegies* by Rilke and *Four Quartets* by Eliot. In this approach, there is no attempt to equate the concepts or pieces to which the student is supposed to respond. Instead, the list is simply to assure that the test items (and, as well, the preceding instruction) take the enumerated content explicitly to heart.

Thus, content established by enumeration communicates content on a practical and concrete level rather than an abstract, rule level. Another type of enumeration occurs when all of a particular set of information represents the universe. The rule is simply "go to" a reference or resource and use it as a base for content. For example, to be able to read aloud any passage from the *London Times*. An effective universe of discourse has been circumscribed and clearly what is fair game for testing is any sort of article or advertising in the periodical named. Operationally, such a limit communicates a good deal to test writer, teacher, and perhaps to the learner (should the specifications be made available to students).

Another example is to refer to a particular text, for example, any anthropological concept from Beals and Hoijer, *Introduction to Anthropology*. The table of contents provides the functional content limits. However, the topics included in the book itself may be arbitrary and reflect the biases of the authors rather than some more generally applicable structure of the field. So in the same way that specifying particular concepts such as mercantilism is arbitrary, so is the reference to a particular work a weakened form of domain-referenced testing. Whereas the student may demonstrate competency with respect to the defined limits, the validity of those limits still needs demonstration.

A second feature of content limits relates to the determination of the adequacy of the students' responses. For constructed responses, the typical approach is to provide scoring criteria, and training regimens for their application. Thus, in the domain of expository writing, scoring criteria include (a) mechanical, (e.g., grammatical) errors, (b) topic-related criteria (e.g., correct information), and (c) stylistic criteria (e.g., support provided for assertions). When the explication of criteria is too complex, some examples of domain-referenced testing have used excellent, average, and poor samples of student effort to assist the scorer in classifying responses. To the extent such criteria can be identified into components, the domain-referenced test takes on more utility as a diagnostic or placement tool, for on the basis of poor performance on specific criteria, instruction can be developed or revised. The source of these performance criteria may be at best arbitrary, for example, no more than three spelling errors, thereby opening the test developer to the charge of casual curriculum design. It is probably best to include as criteria those features of performance that are expected to be subtasks of the major goal, for example, the inclusion of a thesis statement in an expository essay, or else those known to be prerequisites to a next course or unit in the same instructional sequence (e.g., past tense of Spanish verbs).

When the student is asked to make a selection from a set of options rather than to produce a response, the criteria of adequate performance are used as the basis for constructing the response options. For instance, if a student is to set the proper modifier for a given sentence,

it may be critical that the test provide options that are modifiers but which differ according to semantic (does it make good sense?), and syntactic (adjective or adverb) features. Perhaps the greatest contribution of domain-referenced tests will be to regularize the manner in which response options are generated so that a right answer means some mastery over a comparable set of options, and a wrong answer has direct diagnostic value.

The next major feature of domain-referenced test specifications is the description specifically of the item format, the directions, and the conditions under which the response is observed. Although more properly the focus of the item writing article, format decisions have strong implications for assessing the validity of the domains.

## 2. Problems in Domain-referenced Testing

A number of theoretical and practical problems remain in domain-referenced test generation and validation. One problem relates to the relative broadness and narrowness of the domain and whether it is practical to use specific domains in the large-scale assessment of a performance developed under a variety of conditions. Some efforts have been made to use domain-referenced testing in regional assessments and evaluations in the United States, but as yet no specific analysis of this problem has been undertaken. In addition, questions have been raised about the sampling rules, including the number of items necessary to get reasonable estimates of a domain. This problem has a tautological component since number of items, or test length, depends upon the cut score used, which may very well be a function of the quality of instruction. A third major question involves the addition of components explicitly addressed to the linguistic features of the test rather than to its content or response features. Of interest is the extent to which variation can be attributed to language rather than to more traditional characteristics of tests and instruction.

A fourth issue involves the match between items and the domain specifications to which they presumably relate. Present procedures are particularly weak, in that simple on–off judgments are usually made about a match. Clearly, the level of detail of the specifications will interact with the quality of judgment, for with very broad specifications almost any item will fit. However, some application of set theory appears promising.

## Bibliography

Baker E L 1974 Beyond objectives: Domain referenced achievement. In: Hively W (ed.) 1974 *Domain Referenced Testing*. Educational Technology Publications, Englewood Cliffs, New Jersey

Bloom B S (ed.) 1956 *Taxonomy of Educational Objectives:*

*The Classification of Educational Goals.* Handbook 1: *Cognitive Domain.* McKay, New York

Glaser R 1963 Instructional technology and the measurement of learning outcomes: Some questions. *Am. Psychol.* 18: 515–21

Hively W, Maxwell G, Rabehl G, Sension D, Lundin S 1973 *Domain Referenced Curriculum Evaluation,* CSE Monograph Series No. 1. Center for the Study of Evaluation, University of California at Los Angeles, Los Angeles, California

Popham W J 1981 *Modern Educational Measurement.* Prentice Hall, New Jersey

# Culture-fair Assessment

## S. Hegarty

Most tests and other forms of assessment rely on content which is specific to a given culture or reflect the values of a particular societal group. A form of assessment devised for use within one context cannot then be validly used to assess people from a different culture or value system. Culture-fair tests seek to address this problem by providing a means whereby people of diverse backgrounds can be assessed fairly and not suffer disadvantage on account of their backgrounds.

## 1. Defining Culture Fairness

The purpose of assessment is to obtain information on individuals' functioning or ability. This commonly entails discriminating between them. Thus, job selection procedures choose one candidate from a group and reject the others, IQ scores assign individuals a number on a scale and imply a rank ordering between them, and so on. In each case the discrimination must relate to the purposes in view. In job selection, IQ score may not be a primary criterion since other qualities such as specific knowledge or the ability to relate to colleagues may be more important.

In general terms, an assessment procedure will be fair if it discriminates on relevant grounds and avoids discriminating on irrelevant ones, relevance in each case being decided by reference to the purposes in hand. It will be culture fair if these grounds encompass a comprehensive range of cultural factors. Both negative and positive aspects are important. The negative side of culture-fair assessment is the requirement that gross cultural factors such as place of birth or ethnic group membership be ignored as sources of differentiation. This is on the assumption that such factors will generally be irrelevant to the action and decisions to be taken on the basis of the assessment. The positive, and more problematic, aspect is the need to take account of relevant differences deriving from the cultural background. If a particular group of children has had diminished learning opportunities or been socialized to regard school in a negative way, this will be relevant to any future learning they engage in and must be taken account of in educational programmes for them. It must likewise be allowed for in the assessment procedures that lead to placement in such programmes.

## 2. Psychometric Models of Culture Fairness in Assessment

The notion of culture fairness has proved difficult to translate into operational terms. A number of psychometric models have been produced to specify what culture-fair selection means and what it entails in practice. These incorporate the different notions people have of culture-fair selection. Petersen and Novick (1976) give a comprehensive overview.

Three models will be described briefly here. First, the regression model or Cleary's model (Cleary 1968) sees test fairness in terms of efficient prediction. If a test is being used to choose between different applicants, it must select the one with the highest predicted performance. When a test is being developed it is necessary to settle on some relevant aspects of performance that can serve as criteria and demonstrate that the new test predicts well to them. One criterion for a test of academic aptitude would be performance on a subsequent examination. If the test is satisfactory in this respect one can assume that high scorers on it would also do well on the examination and that low scorers would do badly.

When there are clearcut groups with different average levels of performance on the criteria such as whites and blacks in the United States the predictions must be carried out separately. This may appear to be just a technical point but it is of great practical significance. The prediction is done by means of regression analysis. Unless separate regression equations are used for different subpopulations, a high-scoring subgroup will in general be discriminated against by underprediction. In the present example American whites would be placed at a disadvantage.

A constant ratio model has been proposed by Thorndike (1971). This focuses on the proportion of applicants selected from different subgroups and in particular on any discrepancy between their respective mean performances on the test and on criteria. If for example two groups are such that the discrepancy between their test means is greater than the discrepancy between their criterion means, the group with lower test scores will be discriminated against by the regression model. Use of a common cut-off score will mean that a smaller proportion of individuals likely to succeed (as measured by criterion performance) will be selected from this group than from the high-scoring group. In general it will be necessary to have different cut-off scores for the different groups. These will be related to the fraction of the groups which reach a specified level of criterion performance. If the specified criterion score is such that 40 percent of group A and 10 percent of group B attain it, then the cut-off scores must be set so that individuals will be chosen from the two groups in the ratio 4:1.

Another model known as the conditional probability model is due to Cole (1973). This focuses on those applicants who would succeed if selected and gives all such an equal chance of being selected, regardless of group membership. This is done by again having different selection cut-off points for the different groups, these points being chosen so that the conditional probability of selection given success will be the same for each group. It can be noted that this model requires lower cut-off scores for "minority" groups than the Thorndike Model.

These various models differ from each other because of the notions of fairness they incorporate. The regression model, for example, sees fairness in terms of efficient prediction. This avoids discriminating on irrelevant grounds but it takes little account of the positive aspects of culture fairness. Efficient prediction does not require one to take account of factors which may be depressing present performance. In fact, it may be hampered by seeking to do so; if the reasons why present performance is low are not diagnosed, present performance may well be a good predictor of future performance (since unidentified problems are unlikely to be solved). If, however, an assessment procedure seeks to identify possible limitations on present performance levels and take account of them, that would be recognized as a fairer procedure.

The constant ratio model sees fairness in terms of the selection of comparable numbers from different subgroups. This does not ignore potentially relevant differences in the same way, but the effort to be culture fair is relatively crude. The model is usually applied to ethnic groups: if the proportion of white people to black people in the population at large is 70:30 then a fair assessment procedure will produce seven white people for every three black people. This is fairness of a sort, but it does assume that being white or black is a crucial variable. In practice there are many variables which are more relevant to the outcome of an assessment than ethnic group membership.

## 3. Achieving Culture Fairness

In practice, culture fairness in assessment can only be achieved by taking account of the context in which the assessment is carried out. The objectives of the assessment must be identified clearly and related to the discrimination capacities of whatever assessment procedure is in use. Many different procedures can be used in this way as long as the relationship between objectives and discrimination capacities is clearly analysed.

A more direct way of achieving culture fairness is to construct tests with culture fairness specifically in mind. Learning ability tests are one major way of doing this; Hegarty (1988) and Gredler (1988) have reviewed recent efforts to construct tests of learning ability. Other culture-reduced tests are reviewed by Jensen (1980). They include group tests such as Raven's Progressive Matrices and individual tests like the Leiter International Performance Scale. While these tests embody many different approaches many of them are psychometrically underdeveloped.

### Bibliography

Cleary T 1968 Test bias: Prediction of grades of Negro and white students in integrated colleges. *J. Educ. Meas.* 5: 115–24
Cole N 1973 Bias in selection. *J. Educ. Meas.* 10: 237–55
Gredler G 1988 Assessment of learning ability: A current appraisal. In: Gupta R, Coxhead P 1988 *Cultural Diversity and Learning Efficiency: Recent Developments in Assessment.* Macmillan, London
Gupta R, Coxhead P 1988 *Cultural Diversity and Learning Efficiency: Recent Developments in Assessment.* Macmillan, London
Hegarty S 1988 Learning ability and psychometric practice. In: Gupta R, Coxhead P 1988 *Cultural Diversity and Learning Efficiency: Recent Developments in Assessment.* Macmillan, London
Hegarty S, Lucas D 1979 *Able to Learn? The Pursuit of Culture-fair Assessment.* National Foundation for Educational Research, Slough
Jensen A R 1980 *Bias in Mental Testing.* Methuen, London
Petersen N, Novick M 1976 An evaluation of some models for culture-fair selection. *J. Educ. Meas.* 13: 3–30
Thorndike R L 1971 Concepts of culture-fairness. *J. Educ. Meas.* 8: 63–70

# Attitudes and their Measurement

## L. W. Anderson

Allport referred to attitude as "the most distinctive and indispensable concept in contemporary American social psychology." Thurstone boldly asserted that "attitude can be measured." In view of these two quotes it is no surprise that attitude has become an important concept within the field of education. At the same time, however, attitude has been a misunderstood concept. In the introduction to their book Fishbein and Ajzen

(1975) suggest that attitude is "characterized by an embarrassing degree of ambiguity and confusion." The purpose of this article is to clarify the meaning of attitude and to suggest ways in which attitude can be measured.

## 1. Definitions of Attitude

Attitude has been defined in many different ways over the years. Allport (1935) cites some 16 definitions of attitude that were formulated prior to the preparation of his manuscript. He attempted to glean from the various definitions the common elements or what he referred to as the essential features of attitude. He arrived at three such features: (a) preparation or readiness for favorable or unfavorable responses, (b) which is organized through experience, and (c) which is activated in the presence of all objects and situations with which the attitude is related.

Fishbein and Ajzen (1975) also identify three essential features of attitude. "Attitude is learned, . . . it predisposes action, and such actions are consistently favorable or unfavorable toward the object." The similarity of the essential features is striking. Over a period of some 40 years, then, a certain degree of agreement as to the nature of attitude has been achieved.

In an effort to understand attitude in relationship to other elements of the affective domain, Anderson (1981) began by delineating the essential features of affective characteristics in general. He identified five such characteristics: (a) emotion, (b) consistency, (c) target, (d) direction, and (e) intensity. Each of these features will be described briefly below and their relationship with attitude will be described where appropriate.

(a) *Emotion*. Affective characteristics involve primarily the feelings and emotions of persons. Affective characteristics typically are contrasted with cognitive characteristics (which primarily involve knowing and thinking) and psychomotor characteristics (which primarily involve acting and behaving). Since an attitude is an affective characteristic it also involves a person's feelings and emotions. Quite likely, then, the preparedness or readiness mentioned by Allport is emotional (in contrast with intellectual or behavioral preparedness or readiness). In fact, Chave had defined attitude as a complex of feelings, desires, fears, convictions, prejudices, or other tendencies that have given a set or readiness to act to a person because of varied experiences. In Chave's definition feelings are directly mentioned; desires, fears, convictions, and prejudices are quite clearly emotions.

(b) *Consistency*. Consistency differentiates affective characteristics from affective reactions induced by particular situations or settings. A reasonable degree of consistency of responses is necessary before it can be inferred that a person possesses a particular affective characteristic. If a great deal of inconsistency of responses is noted, it may be suggested that the person does not possess the particular affective characteristic

being sought. Rather the responses are determined more by factors external to the person than factors internal to the person (i.e., characteristics of the person). Both Allport, and Fishbein and Ajzen cite consistency as an essential feature of attitudes. While Fishbein and Ajzen explicitly mention consistency ("such actions are consistently favorable or unfavorable"), Allport implies consistency in his third essential feature. If preparedness or readiness is activated in the presence of all related objects and situations, consistency of activation is clearly implied.

(c) *Target*. As is indicated in Allport's third essential feature and in the above discussion, affective characteristics are related to particular objects, situations, ideas, and experiences. These objects, situations, ideas, and experiences can be subsumed under the general label "target." All emotions and feelings, including attitude, are directed toward (or away from) some target. While Allport identifies these targets as objects and situations, Fishbein and Ajzen limit the targets to objects.

(d) *Direction*. Given a target, affective characteristics prepare people to approach or avoid it. Hence, direction (or in Allport's terms "directedness") is an essential feature of affective characteristics. Direction is concerned with the positive or negative orientation of the emotions or feelings toward the target. Differences in orientation are typically expressed in terms of bipolar adjectives which indicate the opposite directions. Both Allport, and Fishbein and Ajzen suggest the appropriate bipolar adjectives for attitude are favorable and unfavorable.

(e) *Intensity*. Intensity refers to the degree or strength of the emotions or feelings. Intensity is an essential feature of affective characteristics; some people experience more intense emotions than other people. Similarly, some emotions are more intense than other emotions. "Hate," for example, is a more intense emotion than "dislike." Intensity per se is not addressed in the definitions of Allport, or Fishbein and Ajzen. It seems likely, however, that intensity is related to the level of preparedness (Allport) and the extent to which attitude predisposes action (Fishbein and Ajzen).

As has been mentioned, Anderson (1981) identified his five essential features so that attitude could be differentiated from other affective characteristics. Interestingly enough, the first two features (emotion and consistency) do not permit such differentiation. Rather, all affective characteristics possess these two features. Likewise, that attitude is learned (Fishbein and Ajzen) or organized through experience (Allport) does not allow the differentiation of attitude from other affective characteristics.

The differentiation of attitude from other affective characteristics is possible only if the last three essential characteristics identified by Anderson are considered: target, direction, and intensity. Anderson was able to differentiate some of the more common affective characteristics discussed in the field of education from attitude on the basis of these three essential features.

As has been indicated above, the most common target of attitude is an object; frequently a social object. In contrast, the most common target of interest is an activity. That is, people develop interest in doing things. The most common target of value is an idea or abstraction. Rokeach refers to a value as a standard. Unlike the targets of attitude which are fairly concrete, the targets of values are largely abstract. Consider the "study of values" for example. This instrument was designed to measure six value types: aesthetic, economic, political, religious, social, and theoretical. As can be seen, these types are clearly abstract in nature.

The measurement of preferences requires the specification of two or more targets since preferences involve a choice to be made between or among alternatives. On the *Kuder Preference Record*, *Vocational*, for example, students are presented with three alternative activities. The targets of the preferences measured by the KPR-V correspond with 10 vocational areas, including outdoor, mechanical, artistic, and literary.

Self-esteem is an affective characteristic gaining in popularity in the field of education. Quite clearly, the target of self-esteem is the persons themselves. Often more specific aspects of self-esteem are examined. One such component is termed academic self-esteem. Here the target is the persons as students in academic settings.

As can be seen, then, attitude differs from other affective characteristics in terms of target. While targets of other related affective characteristics include activities, abstractions, and perceptions of self, the targets of attitude are most likely fairly concrete, social objects.

Attitude also can be differentiated from other affective characteristics in terms of direction. As has been noted the directional indicators of attitude are favorable and unfavorable. Other affective characteristics are associated with other directional indicators. For interest these indicators are disinterested and interested. Several directional indicators are appropriate for defining value depending on the definition being used: undesirable and desirable, unimportant and important, and unacceptable and acceptable.

The directional indicators for preference are in fact the targets themselves. That is, the directions indicated by preferences are toward one target and, by definition, away from another target. For self-esteem the directional indicators for self-esteem are negative and positive, or worthless and worthy.

Finally, attitude can be differentiated from other affective characteristics in terms of intensity. From the definition of attitude it can be inferred that attitude is an emotion of moderate intensity. An attitude is more or less a reactive emotion. That is, when an object is encountered by an individual, attitude is activated. Several affective characteristics are more intense than attitude.

Interest is a more intense emotion. According to Getzels an interest "*impels* an individual to *seek out* particular objects, activities, understandings, skills, or goals for attention or acquisition" (emphasis added). In contrast with attitude, then, interest is a proactive emotion. Interest impels a person to action; either covert action (attention) or overt action (acquisition).

Similarly, value is a more intense emotion than attitude. Each of the definitions referred to earlier include words and phrases that indicate quite clearly the high intensity nature of value. Getzels suggests that a value influences the selection of behavior. Rokeach defines a value as a standard that guides and determines action, attitudes toward objects and situations, ideology, presentations of self to others, evaluations, judgments, justifications, comparisons of self with others, and attempts to influence others. That a value "guides and determines" suggests that it is a highly intense emotion. Tyler indicates that the educational significance of value stems from its role in "directing . . . interests, attitudes, and satisfactions." The inclusion of the verb "directing" again suggests a fairly high intensity level.

Self-esteem also tends to be a more intense emotion than attitude largely because the target of the emotion is the self. Virtually all emotions related to the self tend to be of high intensity. Finally, preference tends to be a fairly low intensity emotion. A preference demands a choice between or among targets. Since the choice is "forced" on the individual, a great deal of emotion may not accompany the choice. If, of course, the targets are all related to a great deal of interest or value, the intensity level may rise greatly. This increase in intensity, however, is associated more with interest and value than with preference per se.

In summary, then, attitude can be considered a moderately intense emotion that prepares or predisposes an individual to respond consistently in a favorable or unfavorable manner when confronted with a particular object. This definition contains all five of the essential features of affective characteristics identified by Anderson (1981). In addition, this definition is consistent with the composite definitions offered by Allport (1935) and Fishbein and Ajzen (1975). Furthermore, this definition permits the differentiation of attitude from other related affective characteristics such as interest, value, preference, and self-esteem. Such a differentiation is based primarily on (a) the nature of the targets toward which the emotion is directed, (b) the directionality of the emotion, and (c) the intensity of the emotion. As can be seen, then, attitude is a fairly specific affective characteristic. It has unique features and should not be equated with the general concept, affect. Unfortunately one of Thurstone's later definitions virtually equates attitude with affect. Failure to consider the unique features of attitude, and failure to differentiate attitude from other related, yet distinct affective characteristics have led in part to the embarrassing degree of ambiguity and confusion identified by Fishbein and Ajzen.

## 2. Measurement of Attitude

Attempts to measure attitude fall into one of three categories. All such attempts require the making of inferences about attitude from some observable indicator. The categories can be formed on the basis of the type of indicator on which the inference is made. The first category contains those methods that enable inferences to be made based on individuals' responses to a series of sentences or adjectives. Methods falling into this category are called scaling techniques and the instruments developed are called scales.

The second category contains those methods that permit inferences to be made from individuals' overt behaviors. These methods require the gathering of observational data and the establishment of sufficiently strong attitude–behavior relationships. The third category includes those methods that allow inferences to be made based on individuals' physiological responses. Each of these methods will be discussed in one of the following sections.

### 2.1 Inferences made from Responses to a Set of Statements or Adjectives

The most prevalent means of measuring attitudes is providing individuals with a list of sentences or adjectives and asking them to respond to each sentence or adjective in accordance with their true feelings. As has been mentioned previously these lists are called scales. The most frequently used scales are Thurstone scales, Likert scales, Guttman scales, and semantic differential scales. Although other scaling techniques have been developed since 1952, these four types of scales continue to enjoy the greatest popularity.

Several key differences exist among the four aforementioned types of scales. Semantic differential scales can be differentiated from the other three types in terms of format. A semantic differential scale consists of a set of bipolar, evaluative adjectives (e.g., good–bad, nice–awful, relaxed–tense). Thurstone, Likert, and Guttman scales contain sentences, not adjectives.

Differences among Thurstone, Likert, and Guttman scales can be seen by viewing attitude as existing along an underlying continuum. Such a view is consistent with the definition of attitude presented in an earlier section. The target is indicated above the continuum. The midpoint of the continuum indicates change in direction. The distance from the midpoint in either direction indicates intensity.

The placement of the sentences along the continuum differentiates Likert scales from Thurstone and Guttman scales. Sentences included on Likert scales are written only at (or near) the two ends of the continuum. In fact, sentences that may be interpreted as representing points around the midpoint are excluded from Likert scales by judges. In contrast, sentences included on Thurstone and Guttman scales are written to represent points all along the continuum.

The extent to which the scale is cumulative distinguishes Guttman scales from Thurstone scales. Guttman scales are cumulative. That is, a positive response to a sentence positioned somewhere along the continuum implies a positive response to all statements to the left of that statement on the continuum. Thurstone scales are noncumulative. While sentences are written to reflect feelings at approximately equal intervals along the continuum, there is no assumption that the responses are cumulative. Rather the assumption is that positive responses should cluster around a particular point on the continuum. Sentences to the left of that cluster represent overly negative feelings given the attitude of the individual being measured. Similarly, sentences to the right represent overly positive feelings given the attitude.

In summary, three features distinguish the four most frequently used types of attitude scales. These features and the relevant differentiations are presented in Table 1.

Once the type of scale has been identified, it is then necessary to either select adjectives or write statements. Two sources are available for the selection of adjectives for inclusion on a semantic differential scale. The first source is Osgood, Suci, and Tannebaum (1957). This volume contains lists of bipolar adjectives that have been examined empirically as part of the field testing of the semantic differential technique. The second source is Allport and Odbert (1936). This manuscript contains a list of 17,953 adjectives that seem appropriate for use

*Table 1*
Features differentiating Thurstone, Likert, Guttman, and semantic differential scales

| Feature | Type of scale | | | |
|---|---|---|---|---|
| | Thurstone | Guttman | Likert | Semantic differential |
| Format | Sentence | Sentence | Sentence | Adjective |
| Position on continuum | Points along | Points along | Endpoints only | |
| Nature of continuum | Noncumulative | Cumulative | | |

in designing attitude scales. Either these adjectives can be combined to form bipolar adjectives for use on semantic differential scales, or they can form the basis for generating appropriate sentences for use on Thurstone, Likert, or Guttman scales.

Edwards (1957 pp. 13–14) has identified 14 "informal criteria" for writing statements for inclusion on attitude scales. These 14 criteria are as follows:

(a) Avoid statements that refer to the past rather than the present.

(b) Avoid statements that are factual or capable of being interpreted as factual.

(c) Avoid statements that may be interpreted in more than one way.

(d) Avoid statements that are irrelevant to the psychological object under consideration.

(e) Avoid statements that are likely to be endorsed by almost everyone or almost no one.

(f) Select statements that are believed to cover the entire range of the affective scale of interest.

(g) Keep the language of the statements simple, clear, and direct.

(h) Statements should be short, rarely exceeding 20 words.

(i) Each statement should contain only one complete thought.

(j) Statements containing universals such as *all*, *always*, *none*, and *never* often introduce ambiguity and should be avoided.

(k) Words such as *only, just, merely*, and others of a similar nature should be used with care and moderation in writing statements.

(l) Whenever possible, statements should be in the form of simple sentences rather than in the form of compound or complex sentences.

(m) Avoid the use of words that may not be understood by those who are to be given the scale.

(n) Avoid the use of double negatives.

Fiske (1971) has proposed what may be termed a more formal approach to the generation of attitude statements appropriate for inclusion on affective scales. Kifer (1977) has operationalized the approach as a series of steps to be followed. The first step involves the identification of the specific affective characteristic and appropriate target (e.g., attitude toward school). The second step involves the delineation on the kinds of actions or opinions that would be exhibited or expressed by people possessing a positive attitude toward school. Such people may (a) discuss school matters with parents and friends, (b) participate in school-related activities and functions, (c) volunteer to talk to incoming students about the school, (d) enjoy the vast majority of their classes, (e) volunteer to participate in school-improvement projects, and (f) enjoy friendships with a large number of students in their class(es).

The third step requires the identification of facets and elements of attitude toward school. Kifer suggests two general facets. The first is the behavior to be exhibited or the opinion to be expressed if a positive attitude is to be inferred. The second facet is the settings or situations in which the behavior is likely to be exhibited or the opinion is meant to be elicited. The elements of each facet are identified by examining and categorizing the actions and opinions resulting from the second step of the approach. Continuing with the attitude toward school example, the following elements of the two facets may be identified. The elements of the situation facet may be, for example: (a) at home; (b) outside of school; (c) in school; (d) in the classroom; (e) after school. The elements of the behavior/opinion facet may be, for example: (a) enjoys friends, classes; (b) participates in activities; (c) volunteers services; (d) discusses school.

The fourth step involves the formation of sentences by selecting one element from the situation facet and one element from the behavior/opinion facet. These elements are then combined into a grammatically correct sentence. For example, "*After school*, I frequently *participate in* extracurricular *activities*." Or, "I *enjoy the friends* I've made *in school*." Quite clearly, Edwards' (1957) "informal criteria" could serve a useful editing function at this point in the process.

One final topic must be addressed prior to moving on to the next category of instruments. That topic is the technical adequacy (i.e., objectivity, reliability, and validity) of the data gathered by means of attitude scales.

The nature of Thurstone, Likert, Guttman, and semantic differential scales ensures a high degree of objectivity. All responses can be scored with the aid of a scoring key or template. Computer scoring of responses is also possible.

Two types of reliability estimates are appropriate for attitude scales: internal consistency and stability. Internal consistency estimates for well-developed attitude scales containing as few as 10 items can approach 0.80 (Anderson 1981). For well-designed scales of 20 items the internal consistency estimates can approach 0.90. Thus attitude scales of sufficient internal consistency can be developed.

Estimates of the stability of attitudes have been computed less frequently than estimates of internal consistency. One possible reason is the issue of interpretation of such estimates. Quite clearly, the degree of stability of attitude scores should approximate the degree of stability of attitude as a construct. Put simply, before stability estimates are interpreted, it is necessary to know the degree of stability expected from the construct over the time period between administrations of the attitude scale.

The little available evidence that does exist suggests that reasonable stability can be expected over periods as long as four to five weeks. Stability coefficients over this time period can approach 0.90 with the majority falling between 0.85 and 0.90 (Anderson 1981).

Two of the scaling techniques have reliability estimates included in the technique itself. The Guttman technique requires the computation of two coefficients: the coefficient of reproducibility and the coefficient of scalability. Combined, these two coefficients estimate the degree to which a cumulative scale is present. As such, these coefficients provide information about the internal consistency of the responses.

In the Thurstone technique reliability can be computed separately for each person. In fact, traditional indicators of internal consistency (e.g., split-half, alpha) do not provide accurate internal consistency estimates. Each sentence on a Thurstone scale is associated with a scale value ranging from 1 to 11. The extent to which a person is responding consistently can be estimated by examining the range of scale values associated with the sentences endorsed by the person. The larger the range of scale values, the more inconsistent the responses.

The major problems of attitude scales lie in the area of validity. Several threats to validity are commonly cited. The most common threat is social desirability. Socially desirable responses are those that are inconsistent with the true feelings of the person; rather the responses are consistent with what the person believes to be expected or acceptable responses. A second common threat is acquiescence. Acquiescence refers to the tendency for persons to agree with sentences when they are unsure or ambivalent. Despite these problems validity of attitude scales can be enhanced by using appropriate hypotheses in order to empirically test the construct validity of the scales.

## 2.2 Inferences made from Overt Behaviors

Sechrest (1969) argues that inferences about attitude should be made based on people's behavior. Part of Sechrest's advocacy of this position stems from the concerns for validity of attitude scales mentioned in the previous section. In order to enhance the validity of the inferences made from behavior Sechrest suggests that the observations of the behavior be naturalistic. He defines naturalistic measures as those that "(a) do not require the cooperation of the subject, (b) do not permit the subject's awareness that he is being measured or treated in any special way, and (c) do not change the phenomenon being measured" (p. 152). Sechrest questions the almost total reliance on attitude scales for the measurement of attitudes and recommends that such observations of behavior be used to supplement these traditional measures.

To what extent can attitudes be inferred from overt behaviors? This is an interesting question in view of the extremely low correlation between attitude scale scores and behavioral indicators that have continuously been reported in the literature. Wicker (1969) summarizes his review of relevant studies as follows:

Taken as a whole, these studies suggest that it is considerably more likely that attitudes will be unrelated or only slightly related to overt behaviors than that attitudes will be closely related to actions. Product–moment correlation coefficients relating the two kinds of responses are rarely above .30, and often are near zero. Only rarely can as much as 10% of the variance in overt behavioral measures be accounted for by attitudinal data. (p. 65)

Much of the lack of relationship can be attributed to the use of single behavioral indicators in the research. That is, typically the presence or absence of a single behavior is correlated with the scores on an attitude scale. Examples of such behaviors include whether a person signed a petition for fair employment and whether a person cheated on a self-graded examination. Given the unreliability of single-item measures, in general, the lack of relationship cited above should come as no surprise. Thus while the inclusion of behavioral data may have the potential of increasing the validity of the inferences made about attitude, more reliable measures of behavior must be made if this potential is to be realized. Reliability of such measures can be enhanced in several ways. It can be increased by identifying a variety of behaviors that can reasonably be associated with a given attitude. Reliability also can be enhanced by increasing the number of observations of such behaviors. Both of these ways of increasing reliability are similar to increasing internal consistency of tests by increasing the number of items.

As can be seen, increasing the reliability of the observation of behaviors is necessary before sound inferences about attitude can be made from overt behavior. Some such attempts have been made in a related area, namely, the measurement of self-esteem of students (Coopersmith 1967). Both of these attempts involve the preparation of a checklist of behaviors. The checklist includes a variety of behaviors believed to be related to the self-esteem of students. Once the checklist has been prepared it is to be completed by the student's teacher. The assumption is that teachers will base their responses to the checklist items on multiple observations of, and experiences with, the students. The reported reliabilities of these measures are quite reasonable (e.g., internal consistency estimates from 0.70 to 0.80).

## 2.3 Inferences made from Physiological Responses

Many of Sechrest's (1969) concerns could be alleviated if an appropriate physiological measure of attitude could be found. To date a number of such measures have been proposed; the galvanic skin response (GSR), pupillary dilation and constriction, respiration, and heart rate are among them. While such measures do detect arousal (i.e., intensity), the information they provide is not specific enough for the measure of attitude. Specifically, the direction and target of the arousal remains unknown and probably unknowable. As Fishbein and Ajzen (1975) conclude in their discussion of physiological measures, "it would definitely be desirable to have a non-verbal measure of attitude not under the subject's control, but it appears unlikely that any known physiological reaction will serve this purpose" (p. 94).

## 3. Interpretation of Attitude Measures

Even with sufficiently objective, reliable, and valid measures of attitude, problems of interpretation will likely remain. Norm-referenced interpretations, common to cognitive measures, are of limited utility when interpreting data obtained from attitude measures. That one fifth-grade student has a more positive attitude towards mathematics than 99 percent of all fifth-grade students provides very limited information. Anderson (1981) discusses two other approaches to interpretation that will likely result in improved interpretation.

The first approach is to identify groups of people who are known or suspected to possess varying degrees of attitude toward the target. Each group is described in terms of the relevant characteristics that define group membership (e.g., highly motivated, eager learners). The mean scores for each group are computed. As a check on the validity of the data the differences among the group means can be subjected to a statistical test such as the analysis of variance. If the mean scores of the groups do in fact differ in the expected direction, then a person's score can be interpreted by describing the characteristics of the group whose mean score is most similar to the person's score.

Anderson's (1981) second approach involves an understanding of the underlying attitude continuum. As has been mentioned the attitude continuum contains a point at which the direction changes from negative to positive. For interpretive purposes this point may be referred to as a neutral point. For Thurstone scales the neutral point corresponds with statements having a scale value of six. For Likert and semantic differential scales the neutral point can be computed by multiplying the value assigned to the middle response option for each statement or adjective by the total number of statements or adjectives. For Guttman scales the neutral point must be estimated by considering the position of the statements on the attitude continuum.

Based on the estimate of the internal consistency of the measure, the standard error of measure for the score corresponding to the neutral point can be computed. Two standard errors of measure can be added to and subtracted from the neutral point score. Scores falling within the band of scores formed by the neutral point plus or minus two standard errors of measure are interpreted as indicating a neutral attitude toward the target. Scores to the right and left of this band are interpreted as indicating a positive or negative attitude respectively.

Anderson suggests that the use of both approaches (combined with the norm-referenced approach as needed) will provide a more complete interpretation of the data.

## 4. The Future of Attitudes and their Measurement

If the future of attitudes is to be bright, several conditions must exist. First, the importance of attitudes in relation to school learning must be realized. In certain conditions, attitudes are important as entry characteristics, as outcomes, and as consequences (i.e., unplanned outcomes).

Second, the precision with which people talk and write about attitude must be increased. Vagueness in the meaning attached to attitude serves no useful purpose. Third, attitude measures of sufficient technical quality must be developed and used. Such measures are necessary if the nature of attitude in the field of education is to be better understood.

### Bibliography

Allport G W 1935 Attitudes. In: Murchison C A (ed.) 1935 *Handbook of Social Psychology*. Russell and Russell, New York, pp. 798–844

Allport G W, Odbert H 1936 Trait names: A psycho-lexical study. *Psychol. Monogr.* 211

Anderson L W 1981 *Assessing Affective Characteristics in the Schools*. Allyn and Bacon, Boston, Massachusetts

Coopersmith S 1967 *The Antecedents of Self-esteem*. Freeman, San Francisco, California

Edwards A L 1957 *Techniques of Attitude Scale Construction*. Appleton-Century-Crofts, New York

Fishbein M, Ajzen I 1975 *Belief, Attitude, Intention, and Behavior: An Introduction to Theory and Research*. Addison-Wesley, Reading, Massachusetts

Fiske D W 1971 *Measuring the Concepts of Personality*. Aldine, Chicago, Illinois

Kifer E 1977 An approach to the construction of affective evaluation instruments. *J. Youth Adolescence* 6: 205–14

Osgood C E, Suci G, Tannenbaum P 1957 *The Measurement of Meaning*. University of Illinois Press, Urbana, Illinois

Sechrest L 1969 Nonreactive assessment of attitudes. In: Willems E P, Raush H L (eds.) 1969 *Naturalistic Viewpoints in Psychological Research*. Holt, Rinehart and Winston, New York

Wicker A W 1969 Attitudes vs. actions: The relationship of verbal and overt behavioral responses to attitude objects. *J. Soc. Issues* 25: 41–78

# Questionnaires

R. M. Wolf

A questionnaire is a self-report instrument used for gathering information about variables of interest to an investigator. It consists of a number of questions or items on paper that a respondent reads and answers.

The questions or items can be structured or unstructured. That is, the categories of response may be specified or left unspecified. A structured item such as sex would have the two categories, male and female, and the respondent is asked to check the one that describes him/her. An unstructured item, on the other hand, may ask the respondent to describe how he/she spent his/her last vacation.

A questionnaire, as a self-report instrument, is based on three assumptions. These are:

(a) the respondent can read and understand the questions or items;

(b) the respondent possesses the information to answer the questions or items; and

(c) the respondent is willing to answer the questions or items honestly.

These assumptions may or may not be warranted for a particular questionnaire in a particular study. Accordingly, the assumptions often have to be tested through adequate developmental work before a questionnaire can be used with confidence. Such developmental work often includes interviewing, piloting, and pretesting.

The variables of interest for which information is sought in a questionnaire can be quite varied. They can include factual questions about the respondent such as age, sex, and occupation, attitudes, opinions, interests, beliefs, aspirations, expectations, past, present, and planned activities in particular areas, memberships in various groups, and perceptions of various things. The list of what can be included in a questionnaire is almost without limit. What is included in a questionnaire will obviously be limited by the interests of an investigator, what can reasonably be asked in a questionnaire, and time constraints.

An investigator should limit the questions or items in a questionnaire to variables of primary interest. Each question or item should be explicitly or implicitly related to a particular research question or hypothesis. Even when investigators so restrict themselves, they often find it difficult to fully investigate all variables of interest without making the questionnaire so long as to substantially reduce the likelihood that respondents will answer it. Consequently, even when investigators restrict themselves to variables of interest, decisions will still need to be made about what can and should be included in a particular questionnaire.

The second constraint on what will be included in a questionnaire involves the sensitivity or delicacy of the content of particular questions or items. Matters of a personal nature such as sexual behavior and attitudes are a case in point. Many individuals do not wish to reveal their attitudes and behavior in an area that they consider to be a matter of privacy. Respondents may simply refuse to answer such questions, give what they believe to be socially desirable responses or, perhaps even worse, consign the questionnaire to the nearest wastebasket.

It is clear that asking highly personal questions can produce problems in a questionnaire. It is less obvious that apparently straightfoward and objective questions can also create problems for a respondent. For example, a question regarding the amount of schooling may pose a problem for a respondent. If the residents of a community have, by and large, earned a university degree, an individual with only a high-school diploma may feel threatened by a question regarding the amount of schooling. Similarly, divorced people may feel reluctant to report their true marital status if they view divorce as containing some social stigma. Sensitivity on the part of the individual developing a questionnaire is needed along with considerable developmental work if such problems are to be fully identified and provisions made to deal with them.

The third constraint as to what will be included in a questionnaire is time. Respondents cannot be expected to spend a great deal of time answering a questionnaire. Experience with adults suggests that 30 minutes is the upper limit that can be expected in the way of answering time when questionnaires are administered in a group setting. When questionnaires are mailed to respondents, about 15 minutes appears to be the limit of respondent time. Questionnaires that are administered to students would need to be shorter and require less time. There are two issues involved here. The first is respondent fatigue. Simply stated, answering questionnaire items requires effort. After a while, respondents will tire and this can lead to careless or inaccurate responses. How much questionnaire material can be presented to a respondent is an issue to be addressed in development work. The second issue is more serious. It is the issue of respondent cooperation. A lengthy, time-consuming questionnaire may cause a respondent to cease to cooperate after a period of answering questions. At best one will receive an incomplete questionnaire and, at worst, the questionnaire will not be returned. Again, careful developmental work is needed to establish how much questionnaire material can be presented to a particular target group.

A well-made questionnaire is highly deceptive. It appears to be well-organized, the questions are clear, response options are well-drawn and exhaustive, and there is a natural ordering or flow to the questions that keeps the respondent moving towards completion of the questionnaire. These desirable attributes and the deceptive simplicity of a well-made questionnaire do not spring naturally out of the process of questionnaire construction but are the result of a great deal of painstaking developmental work. The remainder of this article will describe the steps that are needed to achieve such a result along with some attention to the problems that arise and decisions that are required at each step.

The first step in developing a questionnaire is the identification of variables to be studied. Such identification will depend on the nature of the research problem to be studied and the specific hypotheses and questions to be investigated. Theory and previous research will be a major guide in this area as well as conversations with knowledgeable individuals. It is also at this initial stage that the population of interest that will be studied needs to be identified.

Once the list of relevant variables has been identified, it is necessary to decide how data will be collected. A questionnaire is only one means of data gathering. Interviews, tests, and observational procedures are some of the other ways in which information can be gathered. A decision about an appropriate method of data collection will depend on: (a) the nature of the variables to be studied, (b) the nature of the target population that is to be studied, and (c) the amount of resources available for the investigation. Kinsey, for example, decided that the nature of the variables he wished to study, that is, sexual behaviors, were of such a delicate nature that only a carefully structured and sensitively conducted interview could elicit the information he needed. Other examples can be cited. The point is that the use of a questionnaire as a method of data gathering is neither automatic nor obvious.

Assuming that a decision has been made to use a questionnaire to gather data as a result of a conscious, deliberate process, it is then necessary to translate the variables into questions that can elicit the desired information. At this early stage it is generally recommended that the questions or items be unstructured. That is, no attempt be made to provide a set of response categories for the items. The items should then be organized into an order that appears reasonable to the investigator for tryout in an interview format. The investigator and one or two co-workers would then try out the questions in an interview with a few, for example, four or five, respondents from the population that will be studied. The aim of such an exercise is to obtain some information on the comprehensibility of the questions and whether they appear to elicit the desired information. Such an exercise is important in helping to provide a reality base for further development work and to furnish some feedback on how the questions and items are being received and interpreted as well as some idea as to the range of responses.

On the basis of such small tryout work it should be possible to revise the initial set of questions so that both their clarity and the likelihood of eliciting the desired information are increased. While it is expected that the wording of the initial questions will be modified and that additional questions may have to be added, it is possible that other questions will be eliminated. In the case of the tryout of several alternative ways of asking a particular question, it should be possible to decide which of the alternatives is most suitable. Also, it may be found that particular questions fail to elicit the information that is needed with regard to a variable of interest and, consequently, may need to be eliminated.

While considerable revision can and will take place on the basis of an initial tryout in an interview format, it is premature to structure the items by providing a set of response categories for each item. The information to structure items at this point in the developmental

work is too limited. What is recommended rather is that the items and questions be organized into a pilot questionnaire that is reproduced for administration to a group of respondents from the target population. Such a pilot questionnaire would require some introductory statement informing the respondent of the nature of the study being undertaken, why the requested information will be important, a request for cooperation, and a pledge of anonymity and confidentiality in the treatment and use of information supplied by the respondent. This last requirement is the easiest to honor since the information supplied by the respondent will be used solely for further developmental work. Not having the respondent supply his or her name at this stage will usually enhance cooperation. Whether respondents do or do not supply their names in the main collection of data is an issue that will be addressed later.

At the pilot stage there are still likely to be many more questions than will be included in a final questionnaire. This is to be expected since many decisions about the selection of a final set of questions or items will require additional information. Since the tryout questionnaire is apt to contain considerably more questions than a final questionnaire and since questions will be asked in an unstructured or open-ended form, the amount of time that would be required to complete the questionnaire might be considerable. If this is so, the questionnaire could be fractionated into two, three, or, even more parts for the tryout. This would reduce the amount of time required for answering since the respondent would be answering only a fraction of the questions. Since the object of the tryout is to find out how individual items or, at most, groups of items are being answered, such fractionation is not only permissible but probably even desirable. Generally, when fractionating a questionnaire one tries to develop several forms of about equal length or, more important, of equal answering time. In administering the tryout questionnaire(s), one seeks to have roughly equivalent groups take each of the several forms. The desired number of respondents for each form should be at least 30 with a goal of about 50 people who are fully representative of the target population.

The results of the tryout will yield a wealth of information. Since this is the first set of results of the questions and items administered in written form, it will be interesting to determine whether the questions provided the desired type of response data or whether further work on the wording of questions is needed. Examination of the response data will also provide a basis for structuring many of the questions or items. For example, if one question asks respondents to indicate the number of books in their home, it will be possible to produce a frequency distribution of the number of books in the home, and, on the basis of that frequency distribution, produce a set of categories that will encompass the distribution and have sufficient variability for later analysis. Other variables that yield quantitative responses can be handled similarly. For qualitative variables, the data should permit the identification of a number of response categories and a frequency count for each category. In this way, it should be possible to structure or "close" many of the items. This will considerably facilitate later coding and analysis in the main study.

It may not be possible to structure all the items in a questionnaire although this remains a goal. For example, items about occupation, either the respondent's or his or her father's and mother's, may require unstructured items in order to obtain sufficient descriptive material to permit classification into an occupational categorization scheme. In such a case, a closed-ended item will not suffice. In addition, unstructured questionnaire items can be a source of rich and spontaneous response material that can enhance the interpretation of results. On the other hand, unstructured items place an additional burden on the respondent that can result in a reduction of the level of cooperation. Consequently, an investigator needs to achieve a delicate balance between the number of structured versus unstructured items. Information from the next phase of developmental work, pretesting, should furnish some guidance on the appropriate balance between the two types of items.

The results of the questionnaire in tryout form should enable an investigator to produce a penultimate version of the questionnaire. This version should consist largely of items in a structured form. However, since one cannot be sure that the response categories for all structured items are exhaustive, it is common practice to provide an extra category labeled "Other (please specify)" for many items and to allow ample space for the respondent to supply the needed information.

There are a number of other considerations that are necessary at this stage of the developmental work. A short statement of the purpose of the questionnaire needs to be placed at the beginning of the questionnaire along with the specific directions for answering. The material from the tryout version, with appropriate modification, should be used. It is also customary to begin the body of the questionnaire with an item asking the respondent to note the time he or she started to answer the questionnaire, requesting that the questionnaire be answered in a single sitting and, at the end of the questionnaire, requesting that the ending time be noted. In this way, it will be possible to estimate the time required to complete the questionnaire. This is important for two reasons. First, it will enable an investigator to decide whether to further shorten the questionnaire or not. Second, it will furnish a basis for scheduling the administration of the final questionnaire. The last task in the assembly of the questionnaire for pretesting is to affix a short statement at the end of the questionnaire instructing the respondent how to return the questionnaire to the investigator and to thank the respondent for his or her cooperation. Instructions regarding the return of the questionnaire are critical if the questionnaire is to be mailed.

One variable that is critical at this stage of development is the layout of the questionnaire. A good deal of work is required to produce a draft of the questionnaire in which the items are presented in a format that is attractive and will assist the respondent to complete the instrument. Consideration needs to be given to the size of type, sequencing of items, provision of adequate space to answer unstructured items, and other details of presentation. Unfortunately, there are few detailed guides for such work. Experimentation with different layouts and review by a few people from the population on whom the questionnaire will eventually be used are often undertaken for guidance on such matters. It is not necessary that the questionnaire actually be administered at this time, merely that it be reviewed on the basis of layout.

One area in which there has been research and where there is a fair degree of agreement is with regard to classificatory items such as sex, age, race, and the like. It is generally recommended that such items be placed at the end of a questionnaire and be preceded by a short introductory statement that such items are supplementary and will be used for classificatory purposes. The reason for this recommendation is that if the questionnaire began with such items and the stated purpose of the questionnaire was to survey, say, television viewing, a respondent might be put off by the apparent irrelevance of the items and, consequently, not answer the questionnaire. It is better to begin with items that are clearly related to the stated purpose of the questionnaire.

The draft questionnaire, reproduced in bulk, should be administered to a sample of individuals from the target population. A sample size of 50 to 100 respondents should be sufficient. Postadministration analysis should focus on producing frequency distributions of responses for each variable. Additional "closing-up" of items should take place, if warranted. The investigator will also need to pay attention to items in which the rate of nonresponse, or of "don't know" responses, exceeds 5 percent of the respondent sample. Such high rates are usually indicative of ambiguities that are still inherent in items or inadequacies in the response categories. Such problems will need to be dealt with in one way or another. If the variable that the item is measuring is central to the study, further developmental work might be needed. Finally, an analysis of the data on time to complete the questionnaire will have to be made to determine whether the questionnaire will have to be shortened or not. Even if the time data indicate that the time needed to answer the questionnaire is reasonable, a suggested time limit needs to be established for purposes of administration. It is generally recommended that a time limit be set at the time corresponding to the 90th percentile in the distribution of time data. This will ensure that virtually everyone will have sufficient time to answer the questionnaire.

At this point, a final questionnaire should be ready

for use in a study. It should be attractive and present no problems for a respondent. If so, it is the fruit of a long and often painstaking process of development. The questionnaire should consist largely of structured items in which the respondent can easily find and check an appropriate response category. The number of items in which the respondent has to supply an answer in his or her own words should be small. The full questionnaire should require certainly less than 30 minutes to complete and, preferably, less than 15 or 20. It should also be possible to develop a codebook for easy post administration coding and analysis.

The above presentation is intended to describe the process of questionnaire development. It is by no means exhaustive. Further information about each step can be found in the references. Particular attention will also need to be given to question wording so that subtle or not so subtle cues are not supplied, that suggest responding in a particular way. For example, consider the following questions:

(a)  Do you approve of school prayer?

(b)  You *do* approve of school prayer, don't you?

(c)  Don't you disapprove of school prayer?

(d)  You don't approve of school prayer, do you?

While the above four questions appear to be asking the same question, they are not. Questions (c) and (d) are highly suggestive and question (b) is rather suggestive. It should not be surprising that if each question was given to an independent random sample from the same population, results would differ. The point is that sen-

sitivity and care are required in question wording if unbiased results are to be obtained.

A final note should be made about the use of questionnaires with students, especially those aged 12 and lower. It is obvious that great care needs to be taken in the development and use of questionnaires with children. Subtleties of language and complexity of wording must be avoided at all costs. Vocabulary must be at the simplest level. In addition, certain kinds of questions need to be avoided. Questions that deal with past experiences or actions as well as future intentions should not be asked since children's memories are apt to be faulty on past matters and future intentions are usually unclear. Thus, an investigator who is soliciting information from children is best advised to restrict questions to the present. Within the domain of the present, however, it is possible to inquire about actions and present circumstances as well as attitudes, opinions, and beliefs.

## Bibliography

Berdie D R, Anderson J F 1974 *Questionnaires: Design and Use.* Scarecrow, Metuchen, New Jersey
Jacobs T O 1974 *Developing Questionnaire Items: How to Do It Well.* Human Resources Research Organization, Alexandria, Virginia
Labaw P J 1980 *Advanced Questionnaire Design.* Abt, Cambridge, Massachusetts
Oppenheim A N 1966 *Questionnaire Design and Attitude Measurement.* Basic Books, New York
Payne S L 1951 *The Art of Asking Questions.* Princeton University Press, Princeton, New Jersey

# Scaling Methods

### P. Dunn-Rankin

Since the early 1960s relative measurement (scaling) in the social sciences has surged forward on the crest of the enumerative speed and accuracy available from modern computers. In education, where almost all measures are value based and relative to a specific population, the sophisticated measurement of attitudes and perceptions about education in general and learning in particular are just now beginning to emerge. Subkoviak (1975) has described possible ways in which multidimensional scaling methods may have relevance in educational use and Dunn-Rankin (1983) has indicated how both unidimensional and multidimensional methods are utilized in educational research.

Kruskal and Wish (1978) provide a good introduction to multidimensional scaling and Napier in Shepard et al. (1972) provides an effective presentation of the use of nonmetric techniques in the analysis of summated ratings.

Cliff (1973) and Carroll and Arabie (1980) provide extensive reviews related to the development of scaling algorithms since the early 1960s. The educational

researcher should be aware of the extensive number and diversity of such methods and should become familiar with the source programs (the software) to carry on analyses in the affective domain. This article is not exhaustive but attempts to outline several of the most useful methods of scaling as they relate to the field of education. For specific methods and computer programs the reader should consult the references provided. Today all scaling methods are made tractable by the use of high-speed computers.

## 1. Psychological Objects

Psychological objects can be tangible, such as chairs and postcards, but they can also be almost anything which is perceived by the senses and which results in some cognitive affect. Psychological objects can be colors, words, tones, and sentences as well as houses, gold stars, and movie stars. Psychological objects are most often sentences or statements, such as "There will always be wars" or "I hate war." With young children the objects are often pictures. In marketing analysis, psychological objects are the products of industry: cars, soap, televisions, and toothpaste.

Rensis Likert's suggestion that statements (psychological objects) should be chosen so that people with different points of view will respond to each statement differently is still valuable. He suggests that statements may vary widely in emphasis although their content remains similar. Thus the statements: "I would recommend this course to a friend," and "This is the worst course I have ever taken" should evoke different responses but remain generally evaluative in nature or dimensionality. Specifically social scientists should use statements that:

(a) refer to the present rather than the past;

(b) have only one interpretation;

(c) are related to the continuum under consideration;

(d) will have varied endorsement;

(e) cover the range;

(f) are clear and direct;

(g) are short (rarely over 20 words);

(h) contain a complete thought;

(i) are nonuniversal;

(j) are positive; and

(k) contain simple words.

Scaling is concerned with classes of objects about which people can manifest some attitude. Usually the experimenter wishes to know the relationship among the objects; that is, how far apart they are and in what relative directions the objects may lie. Generally, the familiar Euclidean space provides a framework within which numbers can be assigned to objects in a relative but meaningful way.

This use of Euclidean space in one dimension is demonstrated by the scaling of lower case letters of the English alphabet. Letters are the psychological objects placed on a linear scale in terms of their similarity to specific target letters (Dunn-Rankin 1978). Note that when the letter $a$ is used as a target the other letters are scaled in their perceived similarity to $a$ as follows:

In this scale the letter $l$ is seen as least similar to the target letter $a$ while $o$, $e$, and $c$ are judged much closer to $a$.

Distances are not a necessary requisite for a scale. A set of objects could be selected for which order is the scale. If, for example, the following mathematics problems were presented to a group of school children they would be well-ordered in difficulty:

(a) $2 + 2 =$

(b) $24 - 16 =$

(c) $375.5 \div 4 =$

(d) $4!/2!(4 - 2)! =$

(e) $d(3x^2 + 4)/dx =$

Each succeeding problem is more difficult than the one before it. The questions or psychological objects constitute a scale based on difficulty and the numbers (the ranks) have been assigned in a meaningful way. If a 1 is scored for each correct answer and 0 for an incorrect answer, the pattern of ones and zeros over the five questions will indicate where the student is on this mathematics difficulty scale. Thus a person who has the pattern 11110 is farther along on the scale than the student who scored responses of 11000.

## 2. Judgments or Choices

The measurement objectives of a particular study or experiment must be decided prior to commencement. If a psychological scale is to be constructed then the responses to the objects should initially be judgments of similarity. Subjective preference between objects is used when a description of the data from a sample is desired instead of a scale, or when it is felt that the sample is an accurate representation of some population, or both. Thus the two main kinds of responses that subjects can make are (a) judgments and (b) choices (preferences).

Figure 1 presents a diagrammatic outline for attitudinal measurement. First the psychological objects are chosen. The selection is dictated by the interests of the experimenter. Once the objects have been obtained or formulated they are presented in a task. If the task requires judgments, unidimensional or multidimensional methods are used to scale the objects. From this analysis a subset of the objects may be chosen and the objects formulated into a psychological scaling instrument. These instruments can then be presented to the target group(s) and their responses scored. Should judgments of similarity between tangible objects, such as letters, odors, sounds, and so on be obtained in several dimensions, the distance between the objects can be used in future studies as specific measures of similarity. Should preferences instead of judgments be obtained, a descriptive analysis occurs directly. Such analyses can generate or test hypotheses.

## 3. Tasks Used in Assessing Subjective Perception

Psychological objects can be any object about which subjects have some perception or attitude. A taxonomy of tasks for assessing people's judgments or choices about psychological objects is provided in Table 1. See Dunn-Rankin (1983) for a fuller description of tasks.

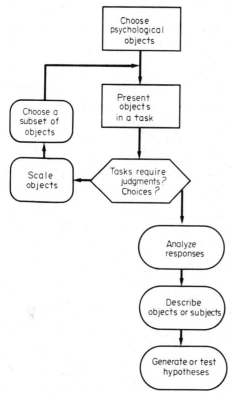

**Figure 1**
Diagrammatic representation of attitudinal measurement

## 4. Data Types and Associated Procedures

The data that are collected after the presentation of different kinds of tasks can be identified as consisting of four major forms. (See Shepard et al. 1972 for a more complete discussion.) These forms of data are dominance, profile, proximity, and conjoint.

**Table 1**
Taxonomy of tasks for assessing people's judgments or choices about psychological objects

| Types of tasks | Examples |
| --- | --- |
| Placing or grouping | Clustering: "Put the similar ones together." |
| Naming or categorizing | Opinion polls: "Do you agree or disagree?" |
| Ordering | Judging a contest: "Who is the best?" |
| Quantifying | Fixing a price: "I say it's worth $20." |
| Combinations | Ordered categories: <br> *onions* <br> × <br> Good — — — — Bad |

### 4.1 Dominance Data

One subject, object, or group is chosen, preferred, or judged over another, that is it dominates. The data may be directly ranked. Pairs may be formed and indirectly ranked by judgment or preference for one object of each pair. Pairs of pairs may be formed and indirectly ranked.

### 4.2 Profile Data

Subjects respond to or are evaluated by a set of variables or stimuli. Objects or variables may also be scored. The variables can be quantitative, binary, or qualitative. Ordered categories fit this data type. By interrelating the columns or rows of this basic data matrix (subjects by variables) a proximity data set can be formed between objects or subjects.

### 4.3 Proximity Data

The data are some form of similarity, confusion, association, correlation, or distance measures between pairs of objects or subjects. The data can be drawn from profile information or by methods of direct appraisal and assessment.

### 4.4 Conjoint Data

The position of a point in a matrix is represented by its value in two or more simple dimensions. Thus a point could represent a person with regard to health, sociability, and intelligence at the same time.

## 5. Measures of Proximity

Proximities are numbers which tell how similar or different objects are. A great number of proximity measures are available that relate to the tasks and types of data that can be collected. These can be categorized as measures of (a) correlation, (b) distance, (c) direct estimates of similarity, and (d) association. In order to analyze a set of objects by clustering or multidimensional scaling, some measure of similarity or dissimilarity between all the pairs of the objects is needed.

Some specific representative measures of proximity are: Pearson's $r$; Kendall's tau; Gamma; scalar product; direct estimation; association (percent overlap); and Gower's similarity measure.

## 6. Unidimensional Scaling Methods

Four major unidimensional methods are presented. Despite recent advances in multidimensional scaling, unidimensional methods have value because of their simplicity and versatility, and because they are amenable to hand-calculated solutions. It is theoretically just as advantageous to create three separate unidimensional scales as it is to derive three dimensions from one multidimensional analysis. In fact, one methodology can serve as a check on the other. (Judgments rather than preferences are more frequently used in unidimensional methods.)

Each of four methods presented offers something unique to scaling analysis. With rank scaling it is simplicity and tests of significance. In comparative judgment it is meeting normality assumptions about attitude. Scalogram analysis provides an "order" definition of scaling. In ordinal categories, profile data is handled instead of paired data. Popular "Likert" scaling is a form of ordered-category scaling.

## 6.1 Rank Scaling

(a) *Scale values proportional to rank sums.* The variance stable rank method of scaling (Dunn-Rankin 1983) is an adaptation of a two-way analysis of variance by ranks. In other words it is a nonparametric subject by treatment analysis in which the treatments are the psychological objects which are scaled. The basic assumption of the method is that the scale values are proportional to the sum of the ranks assigned by the judges to each of the objects. In this method the maximum and minimum possible rank totals, for a given number of judges and objects, act as a convenient and interpretive frame of reference within which the objects are scaled. A linear transformation of these two extreme rank totals into 100 and zero respectively defines the limits of the scale.

(b) *Variance stable rank sums.* The psychological objects can be ranked directly or the ranks can be determined from the votes given to the objects when they are arranged in all possible pairs and a choice made of the most preferred of each pair. A group of second grade children were asked what they most preferred as a reward after a job was well-done; an A grade, a score of 100, a gold star (GS), or the word excellent (Ex). For these children the objects were formed in all ($K(K-1)/n$) possible pairs. The circled objects in Fig. 2 indicate the preferred choice in each pairing for subject 1. The figure also shows the preference values for subject 1.

### Reward pairings

(Circled object was preferred in each pairing)

### Sum of the choices

| Ex | GS | A | 100 |
|----|----|----|-----|
| 0 | 1 | 2 | 3 |

*Figure 2*
Subject 1's preference for the objects is shown and the rank values obtained by counting the choices for each object

These values are found by summing the votes for each different object. In this case three choices or votes were made for a 100, two votes for an A, 1 vote for the gold star, and no preference for the word Excellent. The 3, 2, 1, and 0 rank values are the reverse of the rank order of the objects but are utilized in this position so that the value associated with most preferred object has the largest magnitude.

Table 2 shows the rank values obtained for 24 subjects over the same objects. After obtaining the rank totals ($R_k$), the scale values (SV) are obtained by dividing each rank total by the maximum rank possible and multiplying by 100. These values and a unidimensional graph are presented in Fig. 3.

The scale scores obtained by this simplified rank method can be utilized in traditional ways and are strikingly isomorphic with values obtained under Thurstone's Case V model.

## 6.2 Comparative Judgment

L. L. Thurstone provided a rationale for ordering objects on a psychological continuum. Psychological objects are stimuli for which some reaction takes place within the sensory system of the individual. The objects could be a beautiful girl, a telephone's ring, sand paper, sugar water, or nitrous oxide. They could also include visual statements, such as, "stop," "I hate school," "patriot", and so on.

(a) *Reactions are normally distributed.* Thurstone postulated for any psychological object, (i) reactions to such stimuli were subjective and (ii) judgment or preference for an object may vary from one instance to another. Thurstone suggested that, while a person may have more or less favorable reactions to a particular psychological object, there was a most frequent reaction to any object or stimulus. The most frequent reaction is called the modal reaction. The mode can be based on repeated reactions of a single individual or the frequency of the reactions of many subjects.

Thurstone assumed that reactions to various stimuli were normally distributed. Because the normal curve is bell shaped and symmetrical the most frequent reaction (the mode) occupies the same scale position as the mean. Thus the mean can represent the scale value for the particular psychological object.

Scale values can only be acquired, however, within a relative frame. Thus it is necessary to have at least two objects so that a comparison can be made. In this case Thurstone assumed that the reactions to each object would be normally distributed and additionally that the variance of the reactions around each mean would be the same for both objects. Figure 4 illustrates this case.

*Figure 3*
Graph of reward preference scale values

**Table 2**
Calculation of scale values (SV) from sum of the rank values

| Subjects | Min | Ex | GS | A | 100 | Max |
|---|---|---|---|---|---|---|
| 1 | 0 | 0 | 1 | 2 | 3 | 3 |
| 2 | 0 | 0 | 1 | 3 | 2 | 3 |
| 3 | 0 | 0 | 1 | 2 | 3 | 3 |
| 4 | 0 | 1 | 1 | 1 | 3 | 3 |
| 5 | 0 | 3 | 2 | 0 | 1 | 3 |
| 6 | 0 | 0 | 1 | 2 | 3 | 3 |
| 7 | 0 | 1 | 0 | 3 | 2 | 3 |
| 8 | 0 | 0 | 3 | 2 | 1 | 3 |
| 9 | 0 | 0 | 1 | 3 | 2 | 3 |
| 10 | 0 | 2 | 0 | 2 | 2 | 3 |
| 11 | 0 | 1 | 0 | 2 | 3 | 3 |
| 12 | 0 | 1 | 0 | 3 | 2 | 3 |
| 13 | 0 | 0 | 1 | 3 | 2 | 3 |
| 14 | 0 | 3 | 2 | 0 | 1 | 3 |
| 15 | 0 | 1 | 0 | 2 | 3 | 3 |
| 16 | 0 | 0 | 1 | 3 | 2 | 3 |
| 17 | 0 | 3 | 0 | 2 | 1 | 3 |
| 18 | 0 | 0 | 1 | 2 | 3 | 3 |
| 19 | 0 | 0 | 3 | 2 | 1 | 3 |
| 20 | 0 | 0 | 3 | 1 | 2 | 3 |
| 21 | 0 | 2 | 0 | 2 | 2 | 3 |
| 22 | 0 | 0 | 1 | 3 | 2 | 3 |
| 23 | 0 | 0 | 1 | 2 | 3 | 3 |
| 24 | 0 | 0 | 1 | 2 | 3 | 3 |
| Sums ($R_k$) | 0 | 18 | 25 | 49 | 52 | 72 [$N(K-1)$] |
| SV ($100\ R_k/R_{max}$) | 0 | 25 | 34.7 | 68.1 | 72.2 | 100 |

Suppose $i$ and $j$ are two psychological objects which are to be judged on a continuum of positive affect toward school. Suppose $i$ is "I hate school," and $j$ is "Sometimes school is dull." A group of subjects might be asked to judge which statement is more favorable toward school attendance. If 80 percent of the subjects choose $j$ as more favorable than $i$ and therefore 20 percent choose $i$ as more favorable than $j$, it might be argued that the average reaction to $j$ should be higher on a scale than the average reaction to $i$, or $\bar{s}_j > \bar{s}_i$. The separation between $\bar{s}_j$ and $\bar{s}_i$ is a function of the number of times $j$ is rated over $i$. Using paired comparisons the votes can be counted and proportions of preference obtained. If, with 50 subjects, $j$ (sometimes school is dull) is chosen 40 times over $i$ (I hate school) then the proportion is 40/50 or 0.80.

**Figure 4**
Theoretical distribution of responses about two different psychological objects

The proportions in this method, however, can be expressed as normal deviates, that is, ($z$) standard scores can be obtained for proportions. In this case the normal deviate $(z_{ij}) = 0.84$ (for $p = 0.80$). The scale separation between two reactions can be made in terms of this normal deviate, that is $z_{ij} = \bar{s}_j - \bar{s}_i$. Diagrammatically it can be said that somewhere on the continuum of "attitude toward school attendance" $j$ and $i$ are separated by a distance of 0.84 as shown in Fig. 5.

(b) *Thurstone's Case V.* Thurstone's procedure for finding scale separations starts with the votes derived from some paired comparison schedule of objects. The votes can be accumulated in a square array by placing a 1 in each row and column intersection in which the column object is judged or preferred over the row object.

One matrix can accumulate a large number of different subjects' responses to the objects.

Initially the column sums of the frequency matrix are found and if the sums are not in order the rows and columns of the matrix are rearranged so that the column sums are ordered from smallest to largest. Under the variances table or simplified rank method the sum of the votes could be used directly as scale scores. But, under Thurstone's rationale, the individual frequencies are first converted to proportions.

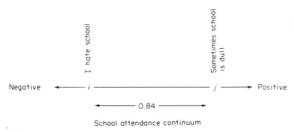

**Figure 5**
"Attitude toward school attendance" continuum

A proportion of 0.50 is placed on the diagonal of this matrix under the assumption that any object judged against itself would receive a random number of votes. The expectation is that 50 percent of the time the subject would choose the column object and 50 percent of the time the row object. Next the proportions are converted to normal deviates by reference to the normal distribution. Finally the differences between column stimuli are found. If the data are complete, the differences between the column sums of the normal deviates are equal to the sums of the column differences.

Knowing the differences between the objects, scale values can be assigned to each by accumulating the differences or distances between them. Should proportions greater than 0.98 occur in the data they are reduced to 0.98. This is similarly true for proportions less than 0.02 which are made equal to 0.02. The reason for this restriction is that normal deviations for extreme proportions usually result in an extreme distortion of the scale values. If data are missing, the entries are left blank and no column differences are found for the blank entries. Averages of column differences are then found by dividing by an $n$ reduced by the number of incomplete entries. The Case V method requires assumptions of equal dispersion of reactions and uncorrelatedness between judgments of different objects. If these assumptions cannot be met, some other method or case may have to be used. The Case V is the simplest of the various cases that Thurstone explored.

### 6.3 Ordered Categories

When the number of objects becomes increasingly large, greater than 20, for example, the number of pairs necessary for rank or paired-comparison methods becomes unwieldy (for 20 objects it would equal $20(19)/2 = 190$ pairs). While some experimenters have asked subjects to compare 50 (1,225 pairs) and 70 (3,660 pairs) items, such studies are atypical and usually involve single items in the comparison rather than statements.

The most popular unidimensional method of attitude measurement involves ordered categories. In this method the judges are asked to place items in a fixed number of categories usually 2, 3, 4, 5, 7, 9, or 11. A typical example of this format is given in Table 3.

In this case a unidimensional scale of attitude toward reading is proposed for these eight statements. Judges

are asked to indicate the degree of positive affect toward reading for each statement by marking appropriately. It is clear that the format can accommodate a great many statements since it calls for only one action per statement by each judge. It is the accumulation of the responses of a number of judges that provides the data for creating the scale.

The scaling method of successive intervals is an attempt to accommodate more items than other unidimensional techniques and in addition to estimate the distance or interval between the ordered categories.

When a number of judges have marked the items, a distribution of judgments for each item is created. In this method the average of the normal deviates assigned to the cumulative proportions of responses in each category represents the scale score of the item but only after each deviate is subtracted from the category boundary. As in the Case V model, variances around scale values are assumed to be equal.

The boundaries of the intervals are located under the assumption that the judgments for each item are distributed normally. In order to analyze the items under the cumulative normal distribution, the categories are numbered from least to most favorable and the cumulative frequency distributions are found.

These frequencies are converted to cumulative probabilities. Any probabilities greater than 0.98 or less than 0.02 are rejected and the cumulative proportions are converted into normal deviates by referring to areas of normal distributions.

The differences between the categories for each item are found and the average of the differences is equal to the boundary between the two columns. For missing entries no differences are found and the average is found for those items for which a difference is available.

Initial item selection for ordered category scaling can be aided by the guidelines prescribed. "Foldback" analysis should be carefully avoided in which a selection of discriminating items is used to predict differences in the sample from which the items were originally selected.

The steps used in creating an ordered category scale are as follows:

(a) Decide on the number of dimensions. (If more than one use multidimensional methods.)

(b) Collect objects. (Make pilot instrument.)

(c) Make a semantic description and exclude semantic outliers.

(d) Present instrument to judges, obtain their judgments.

(e) Find item statistics [mean (proportion passing), SD, $r$ with total test score].

(f) Analyses using successive intervals.

(g) Revise scales.

In the finished scale the category continuum is

**Table 3**
Example of ordered category rating scale

| | | Positive 7 | 6 | 5 | 4 | 3 | 2 | Negative 1 |
|---|---|---|---|---|---|---|---|---|
| 1 | I try reading anything I can get my hands on. | — | — | — | — | — | — | — |
| 3 | When I become interested in something I read a book about it. | — | — | — | — | — | — | — |
| 2 | I read when there is nothing else to do. | — | — | — | — | — | — | — |
| 7 | I don't read unless I have to. | — | — | — | — | — | — | — |
| 4 | I have never read an entire book. | — | — | — | — | — | — | — |
| 5 | I seldom read anything. | — | — | — | — | — | — | — |
| 6 | I almost always have something I can read. | — | — | — | — | — | — | — |
| 8 | I only read things that are easy. | — | — | — | — | — | — | — |

changed to one of agreement–disagreement instead of judgment.

If an ordered category instrument contained a large number of items and many are eliminated, it may be expected that the instrument contains more than one unidimensional scale. If this is the case the multidimensional methods of clustering, factor analysis, or multidimensional scaling methodologies may be used.

### 6.4 Summated Ratings

Likert argues that (a) the intervals between categories are generally equal, (b) preference categories should be established immediately, and (c) the judgment phase of creating a scale should be replaced by item analysis techniques. These three arguments mean that in Likert scaling a person's reaction to or preference about all the psychological objects replaces the direction and intensity of specifically rated objects, that is a respondent's judgments. Surprisingly, both successive intervals and Likert scaling, when carefully applied, yield similar results. Since Likert scaling is easier it is more popular.

The methodology of Likert scaling is as follows: the objects are chosen by the experimenter and unit values are assigned to each ordered category; for example, the integers 1 through 5. After subjects respond by checking or marking one of the categories for each item, an $N \times K$ (subject by item) matrix of information is generated. Each subject's categorical value is provided in the body of the table.

Next, item analyses are performed on the data. The mean (item difficulty) and standard deviation of each item are calculated and the Pearson's $r$ correlation of each item with the total score on all items is found. This correlation acts as a discrimination index for each item. That is, if the item correlates highly with the total score it is internally consistent and should be retained. Finally, a split-half reliability is found or Cronbach's alpha reliability coefficient. Items are eliminated on the basis of poor internal consistency, very high or low endorsement, or lack of variability.

### 6.5 Guttman Scaling

Louis Guttman described a unidimensional scale as one in which the subject's responses to the objects would place individuals in perfect order. Ideally persons who answer several questions favorably all have higher ability than persons who answer the same questions unfavorably. Arithmetic questions make good examples of this type of scale.

Suppose elementary-school children are given the following addition problems:

| (a) 2 | (b) 12 | (c) 28 | (d) 86 | (e) 228 |
|---|---|---|---|---|
| +3 | +15 | +24 | +88 | +894 |

It is probable that if subject A responds correctly to item (e) that he or she would also respond correctly to items (a), (b), (c), and (d). If subject B can answer item (b) and not item (c), it is probable that he or she can answer item (a) correctly but would be unable to answer items (d) and (e). By scoring 1 for each correct answer and 0 otherwise a profile of responses can be obtained. If the arithmetic questions form a perfect scale then the sum of the correct responses to the five items can be used to reveal a person's scale type in terms of a series of ones and zeros. In this example:

| | Items 1 2 3 4 5 | | Sum |
|---|---|---|---|
| Subject A has scale type | 1 1 1 1 1 | = | 5 |
| While Subject B has scale type | 1 1 0 0 0 | = | 2 |

Given a perfect scale the single summed score reveals the scale type. Thus a single digit can be used to recreate all of the responses of a subject to a set of items that constitute a perfect scale.

With five questions, and scoring the item as correct or incorrect there are only six possible scale types. These are:

| | Scale type | | | | | Score |
|---|---|---|---|---|---|---|
| 1 | 1 | 1 | 1 | 1 | 1 | 5 |
| 2 | 1 | 1 | 1 | 1 | 0 | 4 |
| 3 | 1 | 1 | 1 | 0 | 0 | 3 |
| 4 | 1 | 1 | 0 | 0 | 0 | 2 |
| 5 | 1 | 0 | 0 | 0 | 0 | 1 |
| 6 | 0 | 0 | 0 | 0 | 0 | 0 |

While there exist 32 possible arrangements of five ones and zeros, only six of these form scale types. In general the number of scale types for dichotomously scored data is $(K + 1)$ where $K$ is the number of objects. While the perfect Guttman scale is unlikely to be found in practice, approximations to it can be obtained by a careful choice of items and careful analysis of a set of pilot subjects' responses to a larger number of items than are to be used in the final scale.

## 7. Multidimensional Scaling Methods

The technique of factor analysis, traditionally developed and utilized with tests of ability and achievement, has also been applied extensively to the reduction of matrices of proximities. Restrictive assumptions of linearity between variables and homogeneity of variance as well as the multiplicity of factors generated, however, allow the simpler assumptions underlying multidimensional scaling to be utilized in a different and generally more parsimonious description of a data matrix. Preference mapping and individual differences scaling are extensions of factor and multidimensional scaling analyses which provide insights into how individuals differ with regard to the same psychological objects.

### 7.1 Factor Analysis

Factor analysis attempts to simplify a large body of data by identifying or discovering categories of variables. These categories are called structures, dimensions, or more commonly factors. It is, statistically, an analysis of the interdependence between variables and can be used to (a) describe, (b) fulfill hypotheses, or (c) discover new relationships.

Factor analysis starts with a correlation matrix $(R)$ derived from a set of responses of $N$ subjects to $K$ variables or stimuli. (A matrix is a rectangular or square arrangement of data.) All the columns of the raw data matrix are intercorrelated by pairs to produce the square matrix of correlations. The standard or $Z$ score representing the raw score is equal to the raw score minus the mean divided by the standard deviation or

$$Z_i = \frac{X_i - \bar{X}}{S} \tag{1}$$

Pearson's correlation is defined as the average cross-product of the standardized scores:

$$r_{ij} = \frac{\Sigma Z_i Z_j}{N} \tag{2}$$

Each entry of the correlation matrix $(R)$ is a measure of the relationship between two stimuli as perceived by the subjects. Because science is constantly trying to simplify a complex array of data, it is one purpose of factor analysis to present the information contained in a correlation matrix in more concise terms, that is, a smaller matrix called a factor matrix.

Once the factor matrix [for example, $(F)$] has been determined, its elements can be plotted and analyzed spatially as shown in Fig. 6.

If it was known, for example, that tests C and D were tests of arithmetic and A, B, and E were tests of reading, then psychological meaning could probably be attached to this two-dimensional representation. As has been suggested, what is meant by factors is nothing more than the dimensions of the space required to contain a certain set of correlations. It is therefore the central problem in factor analysis to find a dimensional (factor) matrix which is the simplest and most meaningful explanation of a larger matrix of correlations.

Multidimensional scaling is the name for a number of methods which attempt to spatially represent the proximities between a set of stimuli. The methods can determine metric Euclidian distances between objects with only ordinal assumptions about the data. The method is applicable to a wide number of measures of similarity or dissimilarity and unlike factor analysis can be used on data derived from a small number of subjects and with few assumptions about the data. Its primary purpose is a parsimonious spatial representation of the objects.

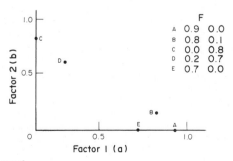

*Figure 6*
Plot of variables of the factor matrix

### 7.2 *Shepard and Kruskal's Nonmetric Monotonic*

Multidimensional scaling proceeds as follows:

(a) There is a given set of *n* objects.

(b) For every two objects (*i* and *j*) some measure or function of proximity $f(\int_{ij})$ is obtained. (These measures may be correlations, similarities, associations, distances, etc.) If similarities are obtained $(\int_{ij})$, they are usually converted to theoretical distances $(\hat{d}_{ij})$ by subtracting from a constant.

(c) A number of dimensions (*t*) are selected which may fit the data. The *n* objects are then placed (randomly or selectively) in the dimensional space.

(d) Multidimensional scaling (MDS) searches for a replotting of the *n* objects so that physical distances $(\hat{d}_{ij})$ between pairs of objects in the plot are related to their measures of proximity $f(\int_{ij}) = (\hat{d}_{ij})$. The relation is such that if the distance between two objects is large the expectation is that their original similarity measure will be small, that is, distances and similarity measures are related inversely but monotonically (in regular order). If, for example, the similarity between the words "war" and "peace" is estimated to be small then the two words should be a relatively "large" distance apart, farther apart than the words "lady" and "mother," for example. If *d* is a measure of distance then its relation to similarity (*s*) can be stated as $d_{ij} < d_{kl}$ when $s_{ij} > s_{kl}$, that is, the distance is greater when the similarity is smaller or specifically: $d_{\text{lady–mother}} < d_{\text{war–peace}}$ when $s_{\text{lady–mother}} > s_{\text{war–peace}}$.

The process of arriving at the best spatial configuration to represent the original similarities has been presented most effectively by Kruskal (1964). In this method a resolution of the spatial configuration is made by steps (iterations). At each step the objects are moved from their initial placement in the dimensional space and the physical distances between all pairs of objects are calculated. The distances $(d_{ij})$ between pairs of objects in the new placement are ordered and then compared with the original proximities $(\hat{d}_{ij})$ between the same pairs of objects, which have also been ordered. If the relationship is increasingly monotonic, that is, if the order of the new distances is similar to the order of the original distances, the objects continue to move in the same direction at the next step. If the relationship is not monotonic, changes in direction and step length are made. It is clear that a measure of monotonicity is primary in nonmetric scaling. This measure is provided by ordering the proximity measures $(\hat{d}_{ij})$ on the *x* axis and measuring horizontal deviations of the newly obtained distances in the plot $(d_{ij})$ from the original distances $(\hat{d}_{ij})$. The deviations are squared so they can be summed. The object is to make the sum of the squared deviations as small as possible. That is, to make

$$\sum_{i<j} (d_{ij} - \hat{d}_{ij})^2 \qquad (3)$$

a minimum.

Kruskal averages the raw stress sum of squares by dividing by $\Sigma d_{ij}^2$. He then gets the formula back into the original linear units by taking the square root. He calls this index stress (*S*):

$$\left( S = \frac{\Sigma(d_{ij} - \hat{d}_{ij})^2}{\Sigma d_{ij}^2} \right)^{1/2} \qquad (4)$$

In general, minimum stress means better fit.

Stress is a numerical value which denotes the degree of departure of the observed or calculated similarity from the true or judged similarity among objects taken two at a time. More precisely, stress is analogous to the standard error of estimate in bivariate regression. Note that in linear regression, the best line location is fitted to points while in Kruskal's nonmetric the points are best arranged to fit a line. Stress is a normalized sum of squared deviations about a monotonic line fit to the scatter plot of corresponding distances and proximity values. Because of normalization, stress can be expressed as a proportion or a percentage, and the smaller the stress, the better (Subkoviak 1975).

Distances can be calculated in *n* dimensions and three or four dimensions may make better fits to the data than one or two dimensions. One way to determine the dimensional space is to plot the stress values for each dimensional solution against the evenly spaced number of dimensions and test the configuration using Cattell's scree test. Since the spatial configuration in multidimensional scaling is arbitrary with regard to the coordinate axes around which they have been assigned, rotation of these axes is often used to make the spatial representation more clearly recognizable.

### 8. *Preference Mapping*

For almost any entity, grape jelly, University of Florida, Enrico Valdes, and so on, a directional identification can be made. That is, given two or more psychological objects the subject (amost automatically) prefers one of the elements of the set.

Individual differences in preference are of interest to the behavioral scientist because the interaction between attitude and treatment has not been fully explored. Different people may react differently to the same stimulus. Some people prefer spinach, others dislike it. Some children prefer teacher approval as a reward; others prefer freedom, competitive success, peer approval, or consumable rewards. Children vary in their preferences for reinforcers.

The methods previously discussed have looked at psychological objects from the view of the average subject. A unidimensional scale may be thought of as a single axis or vector that represents this average. When all subjects' responses are consistently similar such scaling is reasonable. A multidimensional mapping of objects (like a unidimensional scale) is also represented as the average subject's judgment or preference between the pairs of objects. It is important, however, to look at the specific individual's preference.

### 8.1 Inclusion of the Ideal Point

A simple way to measure individual preference is to include an "ideal" stimulus among the authentic stimuli and obtain similarity estimates among all the $n + 1$ pairs of stimuli. If, for example, the "ideal professor" is included among the names of the graduate faculty and similarity estimates between faculty members are obtained from each graduate student in a department, it is assumed that those professors scaled closest to their ideal are most preferred. The scaling is done using multidimensional methods for each subject.

Configuration of stimuli obtained in this manner, however, are not always meaningful or stable since they are based on the responses of a single subject. It is also questionable whether similarities between the "ideal" and other stimuli are interpretable as preferences. Nevertheless preference mapping in this manner can yield important results and is thus included.

### 8.2 Carroll's Multidimensional Vector Model

The vector model of preference mapping is analogous to scoring a subject's preference on a unidimensional scale in multidimensional space. The process usually starts with a two- or three-dimensional configuration of objects whose interpoint distances have been derived from judgments of their similarity and then the subject's preference mapping is included on that configuration. The results from a multidimensional scaling by an appropriate sample are often used as a starting point.

Suppose, for example, the similarity between four desserts (chocolate cake, chocolate ice cream, pound cake, and vanilla ice cream) was judged by a panel of householders and the resulting configuration from multidimensional scaling was as shown in Fig. 7.

It is easy to label the dimensions as (a) chocolate versus nonchocolate and (b) cake versus ice cream. Next, suppose two children were asked to rank order

**Table 4**
Rank order preference for four desserts judged by two children

| | Preference scale values | | | |
|---|---|---|---|---|
| | Chocolate cake ■ | Chocolate ice cream ● | Pound cake □ | Vanilla ice cream ○ |
| Child | | | | |
| A | 1 | 2 | 3 | 4 |
| B | 3 | 1 | 4 | 2 |

their preference for the four desserts and these results were as shown in Table 4.

Surprisingly, the direction and scale scores for each subject can be estimated by the constraints imposed by the initial configuration on the subjects' rank order of preference. In Fig. 8 the two vectors are taken as scales upon which the desserts have been projected. In order to accommodate the rank order in each subject's preference the vectors can only be drawn as shown in Fig. 8.

Notice that the closest (perpendicular) projection of the stimuli on each vector preserves each subject's preference values (rank order). The direction of the vectors is of particular interest since it reveals individual differences in preference with regard to these desserts. A large number of different vectors may be accommodated in a two-dimensional space. When there are several objects and their configuration has been well-defined (as by the householders in this case), the direction of each subject's preference vector is uniquely determined. The case in which the object configuration is determined in advance of the preference mapping has been called external analysis.

## 9. Individual Differences Scaling

The recent development of methodologies which relate differences between individuals to the dimensional aspects of the objects promises to have wide application

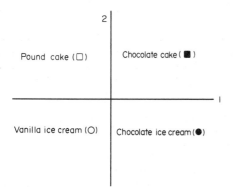

**Figure 7**
Householder panel configuration of four desserts

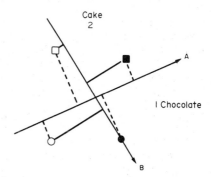

**Figure 8**
Subject vectors drawn to accommodate configuration and rank order of preference

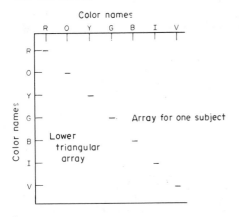

**Figure 9**
Lower triangle matrix for data on subject response to "color names"

in the behavioral sciences. In factor analysis and multidimensional scaling a description of the objects was the primary purpose. In those methods, an average measure of similarity between pairs of objects is used as the primary data. The subject's individual emphasis is lost in the average.

In order to measure individual differences, similarity or preference information between the objects must be obtained for each subject. Each subject responds to the same set of stimuli, for example, "color names" paired in all possible ways. Estimates of the similarity between colors represented by the names are obtained from each subject. Each subject has therefore a matrix of similarity representing all pairs of stimuli. The data can be displayed in a redundant square array or in a lower (or upper) triangular matrix as shown in Fig. 9.

The most useful and popular representation of individual differences is a model of a weighted Euclidean space elucidated by Carroll and Chang (1970). Their procedure is called INDSCAL for *In*dividual *D*ifferences *Scal*ing. This model assumes that different subjects perceive stimuli on common sets of dimensions. The

authors assume that some dimensions may be more important for one individual than another. It seems clear that a color-blind individual might weight the red–green dimension differently than subjects with normal vision. The importance of a dimension for an individual, however, can be zero. (A weight of zero can occur for an individual who fails to use a dimension in making decisions of similarity, for example.)

Individual differences scaling is similar to factor analysis since it seeks to represent a large body of information in a more parsimonious way. The analysis seeks a small-dimensional solution for the objects and an individual weighting for each subject of these few ($t$) dimensions.

Once a solution (a set of weights or loadings for each object and subject) is determined, calculated distances ($d_{ij}$) between the objects are compared with the original or theoretical distances ($\hat{d}_{ij}$) between the objects provided by the proximity data. Pearson's $r$ is used as a criterion in the comparison.

## Bibliography

Carroll J D, Arabie P 1980 Multidimensional scaling. *Annu. Rev. Psychol.* 31: 607–49
Carroll J D, Chang J J 1970 Analysis of individual differences in multi-dimensional scaling via an n-way generalization of "Eckart-Young" decomposition. *Psychometrika* 35: 283–319
Cliff N 1973 Scaling. *Annu. Rev. Psychol.* 24: 473–506
Dunn-Rankin P 1978 The visual characteristics of words. *Sci. Am.* 238(1): 122–30
Dunn-Rankin P 1983 *Scaling Methods*. Erlbaum, Hillsdale, New Jersey
Kruskal J B 1964 Multidimensional scaling by optimizing goodness of fit to a nonmetric hypothesis. *Psychometrika* 29: 1–27
Kruskal J B, Wish M 1978 *Multidimensional Scaling*. Sage, Beverly Hills, California
Shepard R N, Romney A K, Nerlove S B (eds.) 1972 *Multidimensional Scaling: Theory and Applications in the Behavioral Sciences*, Vol. 1: *Theory*. Seminar, New York
Subkoviak M J 1975 The use of multidimensional scaling in educational research. *Rev. Educ. Res.* 45: 387–423

# Partial Credit Model

## G. N. Masters

The partial credit model is an extension of the Rasch model for dichotomously scored test data to outcomes recorded in more than two ordered response categories. One approach to the analysis of polychotomously scored data is to group the ordered response categories and to carry out multiple dichotomous analyses. A preferable approach is to implement a model for ordered response categories directly. The partial credit model is a general polychotomous item response model belonging to the Rasch family of measurement models.

## 1. An Illustration of Use of the Model

There are many situations in educational research in which students' attempts at a task can be categorized into several ordered levels of outcome. The use of multiple outcome categories is common practice when scoring performances on complex tasks like essay writing and problem solving. But even in situations in which it is usual to score students' performances dichotomously (right/wrong), it is often possible to identify among students' "incorrect" answers varying degrees of partial understanding, and so to define more than two levels of outcome on an item. This can be illustrated with the following item from a test of basic mathematics: "A calculator shows the figure 25.634817. Express this correct to two decimal places". Students give a variety of answers to this item, but by far the most common are 25.63, 25.64, 2563.4817, and .25634817.

The usual dichotomous scoring of this item would give full credit for the first of these answers and no credit for any other. However, the second answer, 25.64, shows partial understanding: students who give this answer understand that correcting a number to two decimal places involves reducing to two the number of digits after the decimal point. These students appear to believe that because the original number is greater than 25.63 it must be rounded *up* to 25.64. The last two answers indicate no understanding of rounding and result from moving the decimal point two places (as in multiplication and division by 100). The most that can be said for these two answers is that they show some understanding of "two decimal places". This is more than can be said for the other answers that students give to this item (e.g. 25.634.817).

The answers given to this mathematics item by a group of 570 ninth-grade students are summarized in Fig. 1. Students' answers have been grouped to form four ordered outcome categories: (a) 25.63, (b) 25.64, (c) either 2563.4817 or .25634817, (d) some other answer. The 570 students have been divided into 10 equal-sized groups on the basis of their total mathematics test scores. Students with the lowest test scores are at the bottom of Fig. 1, and those with the highest

test scores are at the top. Figure 1 shows the proportion of students in each test score group in each of the four outcomes categories.

Among the lowest-scoring group of students (at the bottom of Fig. 1), only about 20 percent of students gave the correct answer, 25.63, to this item. The most common answer given by this group was either 2563.4817 or .25634817. More than 60 percent of incorrect answers given by this low-scoring group were of this type. Among the highest-scoring group (at the top of Fig. 1), about 80 percent of students gave the correct answer. Ninety percent of high-scoring students who gave incorrect answers to this item gave the answer 25.64.

Figure 1 shows that the types of errors made on this item change with increasing mathematics test score. Very few of the incorrect answers given by students with low test scores show any understanding of rounding. In fact, about 20 percent of low-scoring students give "other" answers like 25.634.817, suggesting that these students may not even understand "two decimal places." In contrast, the incorrect answers given by high-scoring students display some understanding of rounding but reveal confusion about when to round up or down. In an instructional setting, it would be inappropriate to treat every student giving an "incorrect" answer to this mathematics item in the same way. The type of instruction in rounding decimal numbers required by most low-scoring students in Fig. 1 is likely to be very different from the instruction required by most high-scoring students.

The partial credit model is a statistical model for the analysis of test and questionnaire items for which two or more ordered levels of outcome are defined. Its purpose is to model changes in the distribution of students' answers over the available outcome categories with increasing competence. For the mathematics item described above, the four outcome regions as modelled by the partial credit model are shown in Fig. 2. The four regions of this map correspond to the four regions in Fig. 1. The difference is that these regions no longer show the observed proportions of students in each category, but show *modelled* proportions. The basic shapes of the smooth curves in Fig. 2 are fixed by the algebra of the partial credit model. The locations of these curves were estimated from the answers this group of 570 students gave to this item.

When students' answers to an item approximate the partial credit model (i.e. Fig. 1 resembles Fig. 2), that item can be used to help estimate students' locations on the path of developing competence that runs up the left edge of these figures. It is in this sense that the partial credit model is a "measurement" model: it provides a probabilistic connection between the categories of observed outcome on an item and locations on a latent path of developing competence. This probabilistic connection provides a basis for constructing measures of competence from students' performances on a set of items with multiple outcome categories.

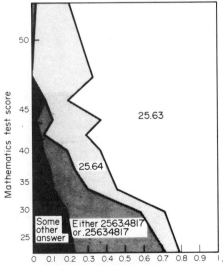

*Figure 1*
Observed outcome map

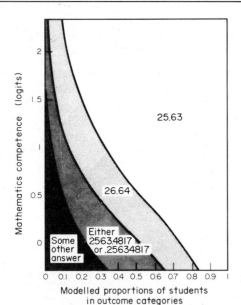

**Figure 2**
Modelled outcome map

## 2. The Algebra of the Model

In common with all latent trait models, the partial credit model represents each student's level of competence or achievement as a location on a *continuum* of increasing competence. In Figs. 1 and 2, this continuum runs up the left edge of the figure. The location $\beta_n$ of student $n$ on this continuum is estimated from that student's answers to a set of appropriate items. Answers to each item are classified into a set of ordered outcome categories labelled $0, 1, 2, \ldots, m_i$ for that item. Under the partial credit model, the probability of student $n$'s answer being in outcome category $x$ of item $i$ is given by

$$
P_{nix} = \begin{cases} \dfrac{1}{1 + \displaystyle\sum_{k=1}^{m_i} \exp \displaystyle\sum_{j=1}^{k} (\beta_n - \delta_{ij})} & \text{for } x = 0 \\[2em] \dfrac{\exp \displaystyle\sum_{j=1}^{x} (\beta_n - \delta_{ij})}{1 + \displaystyle\sum_{k=1}^{m_i} \exp \displaystyle\sum_{j=1}^{k} (\beta_n - \delta_{ij})} & \text{for } x = 1, 2, \ldots, m_i \end{cases} \tag{1}
$$

where the parameters $\delta_{i1}, \delta_{i2}, \ldots, \delta_{im_i}$ are a set of parameters associated with item $i$ which jointly locate the model probability curves for that item (see Fig. 2). There are $m_i$ item parameters for an item with $m_i + 1$ outcome categories.

For the mathematics item described above, four outcome categories were defined, meaning that $4 - 1 = 3$

parameters $\delta_{i1}$, $\delta_{i2}$, and $\delta_{i3}$ were estimated for this item. These three estimates and the algebra of the model provide the modelled outcome regions in Fig. 2. At any estimated level of competence $\beta_n$, the partial credit model provides the widths $P_{ni0}$, $P_{ni1}$, $P_{ni2}$ and $P_{ni3}$ of the four outcome regions at that level. These widths can be interpreted either as the estimated probabilities of a student at that level of competence responding in outcome categories 0, 1, 2, and 3, or as the expected proportions of students at that level of competence responding in these four categories. For values of $\beta_n$ near the bottom of Fig. 2, $P_{ni0}$ and $P_{ni1}$ are larger than $P_{ni2}$ and $P_{ni3}$. For values of $\beta_n$ near the top of Fig. 2, $P_{ni3}$ is large, and all other probabilities are small. A more complete discussion of the algebra of the partial credit model is provided by Masters (1980, 1982), Wright and Masters (1982), and Masters and Wright (1984).

## 3. Ordered Outcome Categories

The partial credit model could be applied to any set of test or questionnaire data collected for the purposes of measuring students' abilities, achievements or attitudes provided that responses to each test or questionnaire item are scored in two or more ordered categories. There are many different ways in which a set of ordered outcome categories might be defined for a task. Some of these are considered below.

### 3.1 Levels of Partial Understanding

The four outcome categories defined for the mathematics item above were the product of a careful study of all answers given by students to this item. This approach to developing a set of outcome categories is described in some detail by Dahlgren (1984). For some tasks, the types of misconceptions and errors that are likely to occur will be well understood, making it possible to construct a set of outcome categories before the task is given to a group of students. For most tasks, however, the construction of a set of categories which capture levels of partial understanding will probably require a close study of students' responses. These might then be grouped according to the levels of understanding that they reflect: "Starting with a comparatively large number of categories the researcher will gradually refine these, arriving at a smaller set of categories that may finally be difficult or impossible to collapse further" (Dahlgren 1984 p. 26). Dahlgren describes this approach to constructing a set of outcome categories as the partitioning of the "outcome space" associated with a task. The final set of categories is then used in future applications of the task.

### 3.2 Multistep Problems

For complex problems which require the completion of a number of steps, it is usual to identify several intermediate stages in the solution of each problem and to award partial credit on the basis of the number of steps a student completes. This scoring procedure is common in subject areas like mathematics and the physical sciences where students must first identify the problem type, select an appropriate solution strategy, and then apply this strategy which may itself involve a number of steps. By awarding credit for the steps a student has successfully completed, a set of ordered outcome categories can be defined for each multistep problem.

### 3.3 Rating Scales

Another common method for recording performances on an item is to rate students' attempts at the item on a scale (e.g., 1 to 5). This ordering procedure is popular for recording performances on tasks like building a model, assembling a piece of apparatus, carrying out a procedure, and writing an essay. To ensure a degree of comparability across raters and over time, the criteria to be applied in rating performances on a task might be made explicit and accompanied by samples of student attempts at that task to illustrate the available score points.

Rating scales are also common methods of measuring attitudes and personalities. In these contexts, respondents are usually provided with a fixed set of response alternatives like "never", "sometimes", "often", "always", or "strongly disagree", "disagree", "agree", "strongly agree" to be used with all items on the questionnaire. Questionnaires of this form can be analyzed with the partial credit model. However, the fact that the response alternatives are defined in the same way for all items introduces the possibility of simplifying the partial credit model by assuming that, in questionnaires of this type, the pattern of modelled outcome regions (Fig. 2) will be the same for all items on the questionnaire and that the only difference between items will be a difference in location on the measurement variable (e.g. difficulty of endorsement). This assumption yields the rating scale model.

### 3.4 Question Clusters

Occasionally, test and questionnaire items come in clusters with all items in a cluster relating to the same piece of introductory text. Each item in a cluster could be treated as an independent item to be scored "right" or "wrong". However, if items of this type are to be treated as independent dichotomously scored items, then the assumption of local independence must be made. Each student's response to any one item must be assumed to be uninfluenced by his or her responses to the other items in that cluster. In most dichotomously scored tests, this is a reasonable assumption. But in an item cluster, items have a shared dependence on a common stem and so are less likely to be locally independent. In this context, it is often more appropriate to treat a cluster as a single "item" on which students' scores are counts of the questions in that cluster answered correctly

and take values between 0 and $m_i$ (where $m_i$ is the number of questions in the cluster). In this way, $m_i + 1$ ordered levels of outcome are defined for each cluster (Andrich 1982, Masters and Evans 1986).

### 3.5 Interactive Items

Finally, ordered outcome categories can be constructed from students' performances on computer-administered items which provide feedback to students during a test. The feedback given during a test may simply inform students of their success or failure on an item and offer a second attempt if the item is failed. Failure on a second attempt might be followed by a third or fourth attempt and credit awarded on the basis of the number of attempts required to provide the correct answer. This procedure usually is referred to as "answer-until-correct" scoring. Alternatively, students failing on their first attempt at an item might be given a "hint" and offered an opportunity to try again (Trismen 1981). Failure after a hint might be followed by further assistance and each student's score based on the number of hints required to arrive at the correct answer. This format not only defines several ordered levels of outcome for each item but also, through the careful construction of hints, might be used to trace students' misunderstandings to their source.

## 4. Related Models

The partial credit model is a latent trait (or item response) model and, in particular, is a member of the Rasch family of latent trait models. The relationship of the partial credit model to a number of other members of this family (e.g. Poisson counts model, binomial trials model) is described by Masters and Wright (1984). Several of these related models are described briefly here.

### 4.1 Dichotomous Rasch Model

The dichotomous model is designed for the analysis of test items for which only *two* levels of outcome are defined ($x = 0$ and $x = 1$). The dichotomous model is obtained by setting $m_i = 1$ in Eqn. (1). This provides the model probabilities.

$$P_{nix} = \begin{cases} \dfrac{1}{1 + \exp(\beta_n - \delta_{i1})} & \text{for } x = 0 \\[2mm] \dfrac{\exp(\beta_n - \delta_{i1})}{1 + \exp(\beta_n - \delta_{i1})} & \text{for } x = 1 \end{cases} \tag{2}$$

The resulting outcome map (compare with Fig. 2) contains only two regions (fail and pass) and the single parameter estimate $\delta_{i1}$ locates the modelled boundary between these two regions. This model is the best known of the item response models and is widely used for the analysis of educational tests.

## 4.2 Rating Scale Model

The rating scale model can be used to analyze questionnaires in which a fixed set of response alternatives like "strongly disagree", "disagree", "agree", "strongly agree" is used with every item on the questionnaire. The rating scale model is obtaining by resolving the general item parameter $\delta_{ij}$ in Eqn. (1) into two components: one for item $i$, and one associated with the transition between response alternatives $j = 1$ and $j$:

$$\delta_{ij} = \delta_i + \tau_j$$

The rating scale model is obtained by substituting $(\delta_i + \tau_j)$ for $\delta_{ij}$ in Eqn. (1):

$$P_{nix} = \begin{cases} \dfrac{1}{1 + \sum\limits_{k=1}^{m} \exp \sum\limits_{j=1}^{k} (\beta_n - \delta_i - \tau_j)} \\ \text{for } x = 0 \\[2em] \dfrac{\exp \sum\limits_{j=1}^{x} (\beta_n - \delta_i - \tau_j)}{1 + \sum\limits_{k=1}^{m} \exp \sum\limits_{j=1}^{k} (\beta_n - \delta_i - \tau_j)} \\ \text{for } x = 1, 2, \ldots, m \end{cases} \quad (3)$$

When this model is applied, a single location $\delta_i$ is estimated for each item and $m$ parameters $\tau_1, \tau_2, \ldots, \tau_m$ are estimated for the $m + 1$ response alternatives provided with the questionnaire.

## 4.3 Other Constraints

Other cases of the partial credit model can be generated by imposing constraints on the values of the item parameters $\delta_{i1}, \delta_{i2}, \ldots, \delta_{im_i}$ for each item. One simple constraint is to restrict these parameters to a *uniform* spacing such that $(\delta_{i2} - \delta_{i1}) = (\delta_{i3} - \delta_{i2}) = \ldots = (\delta_{im} - \delta_{im-1}) = \sigma_i$. Under this constraint (Andrich 1982), only the mean item parameter $\delta_i$ and the uniform spacing $\sigma_i$ are estimated for each item $i$. If there is a reason to expect that the outcome categories for every item on a test will be uniformly spaced, and the data conform to this expectation, this case of the partial credit model offers a more parsimonious representation than the full-rank model in that it requires the estimation of fewer parameters. This constrained version of the model also may be useful with small data sets which provide insufficient data to reliably estimate all parameters for an item.

Further cases of the partial credit model have been proposed by introducing other constraints on the item parameter [e.g. steadily increasing or steadily decreasing differences $(\delta_{i2} - \delta_{i1}) < (\delta_{i3} - \delta_{i2}) < \ldots < (\delta_{im} - \delta_{im-1})$]. In general, constraints such as these are only likely to be of value if they have a basis in theory (i.e. if they follow from the way in which the ordered categories have been defined).

## 5. Applications

Estimation algorithms for the partial credit model are described by Masters (1982) and Wright and Masters (1982). Computer programs to implement these algorithms have been developed by Wright et al. (1981), and Andrich (1982). Since the development of these programs, the partial credit model has been applied to a variety of measurement problems. Some of these are summarized briefly here.

### 5.1 Variable Definition

Figures 1 and 2 illustrate how, by classifying "incorrect" answers to an item into a number of ordered levels of understanding or completion, it is possible to build a more detailed picture of how competence in a subject area develops. This is an important general application of the partial credit model. The probabilistic connection between categories of observed outcome on an item and the latent continuum that these items are constructed to measure, enables each level of competence on the measurement variable to be interpreted in terms of the types of misconceptions or processing errors that are likely to be found among students at that level. Students with estimated locations near the top of Fig. 2, for example, are likely to have very different misunderstandings from students with estimated locations near the bottom of this figure.

Adams et al. (1987) have used this method to build a detailed picture of a path of developing competence in second language learning. The items in their instrument were questions posed to second language learners in face-to-face interviews. Each learner's response to each question was rated using a set of ordered outcome categories specific to that question.

The Education Department of Western Australia has taken a similar approach to analyzing students' performances on written expression tasks. They have identified a number of aspects of writing competence and have developed a set of rating points for each of these aspects of writing. Each set of ordered rating points is illustrated using samples of student writing. In this way, a number of "ladders" of developing competence corresponding to different aspects of writing ability have been constructed and calibrated. These are used as a framework for scoring students' performances on writing tasks and provide a detailed picture of the development of writing competence.

### 5.2 Item Banking

Calibrated item banks usually are limited to dichotomously-scored test items. This is a serious limitation if the bank is to be used as part of a programme of educational assessment. A large proportion of what is taught in schools is not adequately assessed with items that can be scored either right or wrong. If an item bank is to be useful as an assessment resource, it must be capable of incorporating calibrated tasks like essay writing, problem solving, and model building.

The partial credit model provides a basis for the calibration of a range of tasks which cannot adequately be scored dichotomously. If these tasks are to be calibrated and included in an item bank, then it will usually be necessary to provide explicit guides to the scoring of individual tasks, possibly with samples of student responses to illustrate the score points to be used with each task. Some experimental work on the construction of banks of non-dichotomously scored items is described by Masters (1984) and Masters and Evans (1986).

### 5.3 Computer Adaptive Testing

The availability of a bank of calibrated items introduces the possibility of selecting items to suit an individual's current level of competence. If items are administered by computer, then the items to be presented to a student can be selected automatically during the course of a test. After each item is answered, the student's level of competence is reestimated and the bank is searched for the most appropriate remaining item. (This is the item that provides most information at the student's current estimate.)

Computer adaptive testing can be generalized to items which use systems of partial credit scoring, thereby enabling the construction of tailored tests based on more complex outcome spaces than right and wrong answers. The simplest adaptive testing algorithm for the partial credit model uses the statistical "information" $I_{ni}$ available from bank item $i$ at competence level $\beta_n$. This can be calculated as

$$I_{ni} = \sum_{k=1}^{m_i} (k^2 P_{nik}) - \left( \sum_{k=1}^{m_i} P_{nik} \right)^2 \qquad (4)$$

where $P_{nik}$ $(k = 1,2, \ldots, m_i)$ is the model probability of person $n$ with an estimated level of competence $\beta_n$ giving an answer in outcome category $k$ of item $i$. The value of this information might be calculated for each item in a bank, given student $n$'s current estimate, and the item with the largest value of $I_{ni}$ chosen as the next item to be administered to person $n$.

Important foundational work on the extension of computer adaptive testing procedures to items which use systems of partial credit scoring has been done by Koch and Dodd (1985, 1986) and Dodd and Koch (1985, 1986). They describe a number of potential applications of this methodology, including the possibility of constructing computer adaptive questionnaires in which items designed to measure attitudes or opinions might be calibrated and selected to maximize the information available from a questionnaire. Another very promising application of this method is the construction of computer adaptive tests in which feedback is provided and multiple attempts are permitted at individual computer-administered test items.

### Bibliography

Adams R J, Griffin P E, Martin L 1987 A latent trait method for measuring a dimension in second language proficiency. *Lang. Test.* 4: 9–27

Andrich D 1982 An extension of the Rasch model for ratings providing both location and dispersion parameters. *Psychometrika* 47: 105–13

Dahlgren L O 1984 Outcomes of learning. In: Marton F, Hounsell D, Entwistle N (eds.) 1984 *The Experience of Learning*. Scottish Academic Press, Edinburgh

Dodd B G, Koch W R 1985 Item and scale information functions for the partial credit model. Paper presented at the annual meeting of the American Educational Research Association, Chicago, Illinois

Dodd B G, Koch W R 1986 Relative efficiency analyses for the partial credit model. Paper presented at the annual meeting of the American Educational Research Association, San Francisco, California

Koch W R, Dodd B G 1985 Computerized adaptive attitude measurement. Paper presented at the annual meeting of the American Educational Research Association, Chicago, Illinois

Koch W R, Dodd B G 1986 Operational characteristics of adaptive testing procedures using partial credit scoring. Paper presented at the annual meeting of the American Educational Research Association, San Francisco, California

Masters G N 1980 A Rasch model for rating scales. Doctoral dissertation, University of Chicago, Illinois

Masters G N 1982 A Rasch model for partial credit scoring. *Psychometrika* 47: 149–74

Masters G N 1984 Constructing an item bank using partial credit scoring. *J. Educ. Meas.* 21: 19–37

Masters G N, Evans J 1986 Banking non-dichotomously scored items. *Appl. Psychol. Meas.* 10: 355–67

Masters G N, Wright B D 1984 The essential process in a family of measurement models. *Psychometrika* 49: 529–44

Trismen D M 1981 The development and administration of a set of mathematics items with hints. ETS-RB-81-5, Educational Testing Service, Princeton, New Jersey

Wright B D, Masters G N 1982 *Rating Scale Analysis*. MESA Press, Chicago, Illinois

Wright B D, Masters G N, Ludlow L H 1981 CREDIT: A Rasch program for ordered response categories. MESA Psychometrics Laboratory, University of Chicago, Illinois

# Test Norms

## R. Sumner

Norms are essentially social data describing features or behaviour shared by groups of individuals. Test norms can only be understood in terms of defined populations producing specific distributions of scores. Large population norms are established by testing samples which ought to be fully representative of their parent populations. Usually, the raw score distribution provided by a sample is transformed into a rescaled normal distribution. These normalized standard scores are useful for comparing group or individual performance with any normative group which is appropriate. Test manuals should give details of the sampling design and the samples achieved for each population for which norms are provided. Users should beware of norms based on inadequate samples.

A norm typifies a pattern which is peculiar to a specified group of individuals. These may form natural groupings, such as all of the children attending a neighbourhood school, or may be otherwise defined, for example, all students in a school district taught by bilingual teachers. Certain groups may be identified readily; such as every pupil in an educational system with ages between 5 years 0 months and 7 years 0 months; or all students in a nation applying for university places. Other groups are not as sharply defined or their members clearly identified; for example, pupils with immigrant parents (in a multiethnic community); or adults with low attainments in literacy.

When a well-defined group is available for study it is possible to assess behaviour quite reliably. If the membership of a group is open to doubt, the norms ascribed to that group may well be misleading. Compared with other kinds of behaviour, such as "amount of alcohol consumed in a year", test results can be quantified with some precision. Even so, the attribute measured by a test performance must be inferred. Hence, assessment validity must always be borne in mind when any results are interpreted.

## 1. Populations

Individuals may belong to a very large number of groups, for example, all males in the world; children of statutory school age, students of agriculture, and so on. In principle, all of the people in such groups can be counted. In practice it is often unnecessary to enumerate all members of a population, and in many cases it would be impossible to find every individual. Some populations may be quite small; for example the sixth year students in a school district; all motor mechanics attending night school classes at a technical college.

Testing small populations may be feasible and economic but large populations are best approached through sampling. When adequate samples are tested the costs and administrative effort can be kept to the minimum necessary to give a fairly accurate picture of performance. Bearing in mind that norms typify a population, any sample chosen to show how the population behaves must be genuinely representative of it.

When no other information about a population is available, other than its basic description, bias in sampling may be guarded against by selecting sample members at random. Thus, every member of the population would be numbered and statistical tables of random numbers (or a computer-generated string of random numbers) used to choose sample members. In education, such a procedure might be cumbersome.

But, because children are not systematically strong or weak, bright or dull, and so on, at different times, date of birth can be used to choose pupils for a sample. For instance, testing children born on the 10th, 20th, and 30th of each month will yield results for about a 10 percent sample.

Whilst random sampling might be the best that can be done, bias may still occur; for example, there could be a preponderance of hearing impaired children—purely by chance. To avoid such events, when sub-populations can be identified, certain "strata" may be designated and individuals chosen randomly within each stratum up to a certain quota. For example, if 60 percent of a school population attempts a school leaving examination overall sample quotas would specify a 6 to 4 ratio of examinees to nonexaminees.

Again, it may not be practicable to choose a sample by considering every individual in the population. As pupils are already grouped in schools and classes, these "clusters" may be taken as the sampling points. A rule to avoid obtaining a biased selection of pupils will have to be promulgated; otherwise teachers tend to choose their most able classes. For instance, in selecting a sample of one third of a population, schools with six classes could choose the two whose teachers have names beginning with a letter nearest in the alphabet to K (or any other letter).

It is evident that a great deal of care is required to ensure that samples do represent their parent populations without undue bias. On occasions test authors show little awareness of this crucial aspect of obtaining norms. Common sense indicates that it is better to choose randomly, say, 100 pupils singly from 100 randomly selected schools than to test 100 pupils from a single (randomly chosen) school. Because involving 100 schools would be inconvenient, a good compromise should be sought; for example, testing 20 representative pupils in each of five randomly selected schools.

When population strata or "clusters" form part of the sampling design, strata sample numbers should match the between-strata proportions in the whole population otherwise certain subpopulations will carry undue weight, and vice versa. Also within clusters the members tend to be alike, hence the influence of clustering needs to be examined (Kish 1965).

The deficiencies of choosing so called "opportunity samples" to provide norms are now apparent; for example, obtaining test results from 20 schools willing to cooperate because they are known to the test author or traditionally work closely with his/her institution. Despite the justification which may accompany such norms, for example, that the social class composition of the sample resembled the national class distribution, such norms are to be regarded with suspicion.

Indeed, populations can only be represented correctly by samples which are (a) properly designed and (b) adequately achieved. Consequently, unduly high abstention rates or uneven response within strata would induce bias.

A sampling design to obtain pupils' test results might comprise several stages, for example stage 1, the random sampling of a proportion of school districts, within strata, such as inner-city, suburban, and country districts. Stage 2, the random sampling of schools in the chosen districts, within strata, such as secular or religious affiliation. Stage 3, selecting at random a proportion of teaching groups at each school. Such a "cluster sampling" design should provide an equivalent probability of every pupil being selected as a representative of a specific population.

*1.1 Subpopulations*

These are defined for a variety of reasons, principally that test score distributions for certain groups differ significantly from the overall population distribution. It may be sensible to obtain samples to represent (a) the two sexes; (b) geographical regions; (c) year groups or age-bands; (d) ethnic groups; (e) pupils with handicapping conditions; (f) socioeconomic disadvantage; (g) (in some educational systems) instructional grades; (h) (for counselling) successful trainees or competent practitioners, and (i) (for guidance/remedial education) low performance groups or maladjusted children. In some countries legislation may preclude the publishing of norms for some subpopulations, for example, for males/females.

## 2. Scores

Individual test performance is measured initially by the total raw score, that is, the number of correct responses credited to the person taking the test. A sample of persons will usually produce a range of raw scores. Occasionally, as in simple proficiency tests, only a small minority of a sample will yield low scores. For example, a test of 20 single digit addition sums (e.g. $6 + 7 = ?$) might show that 85 percent of the sample score either 19 or 20; the remaining 15 percent would score 18 or less. In such a case, the average score would be relatively high (say 19.3) and the score distribution heavily skewed. The sample percentage obtaining each raw score (i.e. the different $X$ values) would provide the score distribution. Here, the norm would be the average raw score obtained by the sample as a whole; the norms would be the percentage obtaining each score.

Tests which are neither very difficult (for a certain population) nor easy, with a range of questions from relatively easy to hard, and which effectively spread the students measured along a dimension representing the attribute tested, will produce a fairly well-balanced distribution of raw scores. As with any frequency distribution (i.e. the percentage of sample awarded each possible score), a mean (i.e. average) and standard deviation (index of dispersion or spread) can be calculated. Thus, the score distribution can be described minimally by two statistics, that is, the sample's test mean and standard deviation (often denoted by $\bar{X}$ and

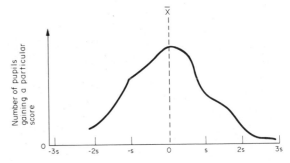

**Figure 1**
Example of raw score frequency distribution expressed in standard deviation units

$s$, respectively). A distribution of scores might be graphed as shown in Fig. 1.

In Fig. 1, the mean raw score on the standard deviation scale is equated to zero; $s$ is defined as the square root of the summed raw individual score minus mean values divided by the number in the sample. Thus $s$ is

$$\sqrt{\frac{\Sigma(X - \bar{X})^2}{N}}$$

when $X$ is each individual's score. $\Sigma$ is "the sum of", and $N$ is the number of individuals in the sample.

In the example given above, the $s$ units would compute to a particular raw score value; for example, one $s$ might equal 6.3 units of raw score. If $\bar{X}$ had worked out at 31.6 (for a 100 item test), a pupil scoring 57 would have a standard deviation unit score of $(57 - 31.6) \div 6.3$; that is, $25.4 \div 6.3 = 3.0300$. Clearly, a score lower than $\bar{X}$ would have a negative sign. (Using $s$ as the scale unit produces what are termed $Z$ scores.)

Two types of transformation have become accepted. One changes $Z$ units into scales with a readily recognized mean; thus $\bar{X}$ can be given a value of, say, 50 or 100. Similarly, $Z$ can be allocated any convenient value, for example, 10, 15, 16, 20, or 24.

The other transformation changes the obtained sample distribution into a "normal" distribution. This is symmetrical about its mean and has a percentage of candidates allocated to each standard deviation unit or part unit (Guilford 1965 describes the procedure in some detail). Normalizing distorts the raw score units so that different segments of the standardized scale are equivalent to unequal numbers of raw score units. Figure 2 illustrates the change from skewed to normal distribution.

It is obvious that raw score scale units below $\bar{X}$ are compressed, those above are stretched out. The standard deviation units for the normalized scale are called sigma (symbolized as $\sigma$) units and the mean is shown by mu (symbolized as $\mu$). (The conventions or notions are not entirely standard; those given have followed Haber and Runyan 1973.)

## 3. Standardized Score Norms

When raw scores have been normalized, the percentage of candidates below or at a given point in the distribution is known. For example, if $\sigma$ is set at 15, and $\mu$ at 100, then approximately 84 percent of a population would score below or at 115. There would only be about 2·5 percent at or below $-2\sigma$, that is, a scale point of 70.

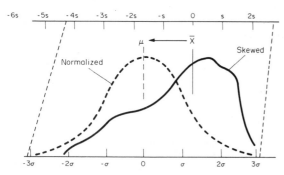

**Figure 2**
Skewed transformed to normal distribution

A testee's performance is expressed in relation to a population; for example, someone with a standardized score of 93 (when $\mu = 100$ and $\sigma = 20$) would be at a point $\frac{7}{20}$ of $\sigma$ below the mean (i.e., $Z = \frac{7}{20} = 0.35$). Values in tables show that approximately 24 percent of the population would score less or the same; hence this person would be said to be at the 24th centile. Note how the raw score distribution obtained from a sample now represents population norms.

Because centiles are regarded by some test authors as having a spurious accuracy, broader divisions of the centile scale are adopted. One system is known as "stens" (i.e., "standard tens"), another as "stanines" (i.e., "standard nines"). The 50 percent centile

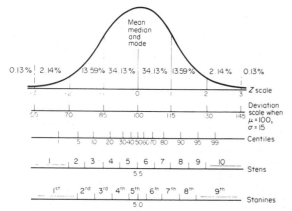

**Figure 3**
Some normal distribution scale equivalents

**Table 1**
Details of stanine scale

| Stanine | Z range | Centile range | Population % in stanine |
|---|---|---|---|
| 9 | +1.75 and over | 96–99 | 4 |
| 8 | +1.25 to +1.75 | 89–95 | 7 |
| 7 | +0.75 to +1.25 | 77–88 | 12 |
| 6 | +0.25 to +0.75 | 60–76 | 17 |
| 5 | −0.25 to +0.25 | 41–59 | 20 |
| 4 | −0.75 to −0.25 | 24–40 · | 17 |
| 3 | −1.25 to −0.75 | 12–23 | 12 |
| 2 | −1.75 to −1.25 | 5–11 | 7 |
| 1 | −1.75 and below | 1–4 | 4 |

corresponds to a sten value of 5.5 and a stanine value of 5.0 (see Fig. 3).

The units on both sten and stanine scales each span one half of a $Z$ unit. Details for the more commonly used scale, stanines, are shown in Table 1.

## 4. Norm Tables and their Interpretation

Norms should show how scores on a test are distributed across a given population. The transformation to a normal distribution is carried out, basically, to enhance the interpretation of an individual's score. For example, intelligence tests such as the WISC-R (Wechsler 1974) or the BAS (Elliott 1979) assess individuals of different ages for, say, vocabulary. Vocabulary has been shown to mature as people grow older, so norms are produced for separate age bands.

A pupil tested on three occasions with scores (on a scale with $\mu = 100$, $\sigma = 15$) of 97 at age 3 years 6 months, 104 at age 8 years 5 months and 101 at age 11 years 10 months would be close to the 43rd, 62nd, and 54th percentiles, respectively. These appear, at first sight, to be quite large fluctuations in performance. In fact, all scores fall in the 5th or 6th stanine. With two standard errors of score (at the 95 percent level of confidence) highly reliable tests would require a band of about $\pm 7$ points. The two extreme scores of 97 and 104 are marginally more likely to differ significantly; hence, it would be misleading to interpret the scores as showing relatively accelerated maturation, followed by relative decline. It would be reasonable to say that the pupil had at least kept pace with his or her peers.

This illustration also shows that, with the confidence bands set at two standard errors, a person's stanine or sten score would have a standard error of $\pm 1$ stanine or sten. For tests with reliability coefficients about 0.9, or less, the error band would be correspondingly bigger.

Clearly, whatever a person scores on a test is the starting point for interpretation. A certain raw score may place the testee high in one population and low in another. For example, on a mechanical ability test of

70 items a raw score of 35 would locate a grade 8 pupil (aged about 13 in United States' school system) at the 25th centile for boys and the 45th for girls. For grade 12 students (aged 17), the same raw score (i.e. 35) would qualify only for the 10th and 30th centiles, respectively. For the same test in a developing nation— in which testing was only recently introduced—a score of 35 was near the 80th centile for male 10th grade students (aged 15) and above the 90th centile for their female counterparts.

Norm-referenced testing has been subject to an increasing amount of criticism since the early 1960s. In an attainment test a centile or stanine level does not indicate what a pupil can do properly. Thus, someone with a sound knowledge of basic mathematics might only rank low in a centile list, and consequently be regarded as almost totally ignorant. Similarly, the practice of defining "remedial" pupils as those scoring at or below, say, 80 (with scale $\mu = 100$, $\sigma = 15$) would identify approximately the lowest 10 percent of the norming population. In a school district with an overall mean of, say, 106, there might only be a group of about 4 percent of the cohort with scores at or under 80. But choosing only individuals in this low score range could be damaging to the children whose capabilities had not been measured particularly accurately, that is, those within the standard error band around the score of 80. Furthermore, 80 may not provide a sound criterion of handicap and a norm-referenced test might do little to illuminate how a pupil was disadvantaged or to what extent.

This drawback is especially apparent when scores are expressed as "grade norms" or "age norms". In these the score distributions for grade or age sample are inspected to find the median (the middle ranked) person's score. A child of 8 may be found to obtain a score typical of $10\frac{1}{2}$-year-old pupils; that is, his or her reading age would be $10\frac{1}{2}$. The concept of age equivalence is somewhat dubious owing to the assumptions involved in the interpretations; for example, in what sense is a $12\frac{1}{2}$-year-old pupil with reading age $10\frac{1}{2}$ similar as a reader to the 8-year-old with the same reading age.

For these and other technical reasons, age and grade equivalents have tended to be dropped.

Standardized scores are particularly useful when different measures are compared, as in a test battery. They are also helpful when comparing groups, for example, when examining whether, in general, the intake to a secondary school is somewhat more or less able than previous intakes. Such information could affect school policy regarding the curriculum, amount of remedial education provided, the formation of teaching groups, and the deployment of staff and other resources. Averaged results for groups of students or pupils can be compared more confidently with published norms (as group statistics have lower standard errors) and interpretations concerning a group accepted more readily.

Test users are advised to apply normed results to individuals critically and carefully, with due importance given to other kinds of evidence, if possible. For example, several pupils low down the centile scale on a reading test produced intelligible and interesting single-page essays for a research project, to the great surprise of their teacher.

A final point is that norms should be reasonably up to date. For attainment tests, when changes in curricula can radically affect the nature of performance through the school population, renorming a test every five to ten years may be advisable. In such an event, a revised test and fresh norms would be a better alternative. Abilities tests may not be as susceptible to curriculum effects though cultural changes (for example, high unemployment) may have fundamental consequences for human attributes and test-taking behaviour.

## Bibliography

Elliott C 1979 *British Ability Scales*. NFER–Nelson, Windsor
Guilford J P 1965 *Fundamental Statistics in Psychology and Education*, 4th edn. McGraw-Hill, New York
Haber A, Runyan R P 1973 *General Statistics*, 2nd edn. Addison-Wesley, Reading, Massachusetts
Kish L 1965 *Survey Sampling*. Wiley, New York
Wechsler D 1974 *Manual for the Wechsler Intelligence Scale Children—Revised*. Psychological Corporation, New York

# Automated Scoring Systems

## F. B. Baker

In the early 1950s it was recognized that the existing techniques for scoring and analyzing test results were not able to meet the needs of large-scale educational testing programs. As a result a number of efforts were initiated to employ advances in electronics to automate the scoring of multiple-choice examinations. The first of these modern automated scoring systems was due to E. F. Lindquist at the University of Iowa (USA). It was followed shortly by the SCRIBE machine built for the Educational Testing Service. Because of the use of

photo transistors to detect the marks on the answer sheets, the equipment has become known as an optical mark reader (OMR). These early systems were able to process several thousand answer sheets per hour and represented a significant advance in the state-of-the-art in test processing. Since then a wide variety of automated test scoring equipment has been developed and used to provide nationwide, regional, local, and classroom testing with accurate, economical test scoring services.

The basic automated test scoring system consists of three major components: the OMR equipment (generically referred to as the scanner); a digital computer with its attendant mass storage, keyboard, and video display terminals; and a computer-driven printer for producing reports. The answer sheets are processed by the scanner and the examinee's item response information and test score(s) are transmitted to the computer. In many systems, these data are then stored on a mass storage medium such as a disc. When all of the answer sheets for a group of examinees have been scanned and meet quality control standards, the computer uses the data to compute the summary statistics of the test and perform an item analysis for the test. Finally the computer-driven printer is used to produce a report for each student, a summary report of the test results for the group, and present the results of the item analysis (Baker 1971). The basic system logic underlies all but the "stand alone" test scoring devices which do not communicate with a computer.

## 1. Optical Mark Reading Equipment

Optical mark reading equipment is available with a wide range of capabilities and the present section provides a brief description of the major classes of equipment. The classes vary primarily on the basis of the number of answer sheets scanned per hour and secondarily on the relationship of the OMR to a separate digital computer.

### 1.1 High Capacity

Optical mark reading equipment in this class can process upwards of 6,000 $8\frac{1}{2} \times 11$ inch answer sheets per hour while scanning both sides of the answer sheet. Although the several thousand marking positions are predetermined by the design of the OMR, the test constructor has considerable flexibility in how these positions are employed. Consequently a wide variety of answer sheet layouts exist for a given scanner. Modern high capacity OMR have internal microprocessors, read only memory (ROM) as well as random access memory (RAM) that is employed to perform sophisticated quality control checks on the scanning process.

As each mark on the answer sheet is detected it is converted to a numerical representation corresponding to the amount of light reflected from or passing through the page. This value can be compared with predetermined standards to evaluate whether the mark is acceptable or not. A running total of the number of improper marks can be maintained and when this total exceeds a threshold, the answer sheet is flagged as being in error. The microprocessor can also compare test scores against upper–lower bounds and identify potentially erroneous scores. In some equipment, the answer sheets that fail these procedures are shunted to a separate output hopper to facilitate subsequent inspection. The high capacity scanners operate in an "online" mode with a minicomputer that is dedicated to the scoring

system. This configuration allows editing of the data via a video display terminal, statistical analysis of the results for previous groups, and report generation to be performed simultaneously with the scanning process. In fact, this class of OMR equipment is not designed to "stand alone" but must be part of a test scoring system. The NCS-Sentry 80 and the Westinghouse W-201 are examples of such high capacity automated scoring systems.

### 1.2 Medium Capacity

The medium capacity OMR has the ability to process about 1,000 $8\frac{1}{2} \times 11$ inch answer sheets per hour and is usually designed to operate either as a "stand alone" machine or as a computer input device. In both modes the examinees' item responses are scored and the test score(s) printed on the answer sheet. In addition, a mark is often printed along the edge of the sheet identifying a wrong answer, thus providing a crude item analysis. In the input terminal mode, the item response data are transmitted to a separate computer, often via a direct link. This communication can also take place in the asynchronous EIA RS-232 format and the data can be transmitted over telephone lines to a remote computer.

Once received by the computer, the editing, data processing, and analysis procedures are much the same as those for a high capacity OMR. The printed output such as student reports, test reports, and item analyses would be identical. Optical mark readers of this class use sheet-compile techniques where the first sheet scanned contains the answer key and an embedded microprocessor uses the key to set up its internal test scoring routines. The NCS-7001 is representative of an OMR in this class.

### 1.3 Desk Top Scanners

The desk top scanner is a recent development in OMR equipment and due to its comparatively low cost is used widely in elementary schools, high schools, colleges, and universities. The typical desk top scanner is no larger than an office typewriter, often weighs less than 30 pounds, and the answer sheets are hand fed, one at a time, by the user of the scanner. There are desk top scanners that strictly "stand alone," those that can serve as input devices to a computer, and those that can function in both modes. Like the medium capacity OMR, the desk top scanner that produces test scores uses the sheet-compile approach to enter the answer key. This class of OMR equipment lacks the sophisticated internal quality control checks on the detected marks that are typical of the medium and high capacity scanners. As a result initial quality control procedures such as checking for multiple marks, poor erasures, stray marks, and smudges must be performed manually before the sheets are scanned. However, small batches of answer sheets are the rule here so that such procedures do not constitute a burden to the user of this type of OMR equipment. The "stand alone" equipment provides a means of printing the test score on the answer sheet as well as identifying wrong answers. Some of these display the test score and class average on a small read-out panel (SCANTRON 2002, Kajaani EVALMATIC). Presumably this information could then be copied by hand onto a report sheet. A large percentage of the available desk top scanners are equipped to act as a computer input device via an RS-232 or similar interface. In this configuration, the desk top scanner fulfills the same role as higher capacity scanners in an automated scoring system. However, the desk top scanners use a much more limited array of marking positions than do higher capacity machines. The answer sheets usually employ only a half page marking array of, say, 64 rows of 12 positions each and often less than this. As a result, answer forms can be printed on 4 inch wide paper strips that can have lengths from 6 to 22 inch. Because the forms are hand fed the processing rate is modest. Using a SCANTRON 5098 as an input terminal to a DEC PDP-11/70 the author obtained an average time of 6.6 seconds per sheet for a rate of about 500 sheets per hour. Thus the raw scanner speeds are somewhat higher. In a "stand alone" mode, the Kajaani EVALMATIC has a processing time of 1.5 seconds for a sheet having 60 items each with five alternatives.

When used as a computer input device, the desk top scanner can meet a variety of classroom needs for test scoring. Because of the computer, the results produced for such classroom testing can be identical to those yielded by the high capacity automated testing programs. However, classroom teachers may not always be interested in the full range of outputs so less complete results may often serve their immediate needs.

## 1.4 Card Readers

A wide variety of equipment exists that is designed to use mark sense Hollerith cards as input to a computer. In recent years the practice has been to produce small desk top units that can serve as computer terminals via an RS-232 or similar interface. Although this equipment has been primarily designed for low volume industrial data collection purposes, it can also be used as a means of entering examinees' item response choices into a computer. In this type of equipment, optical mark sensing or electrical current sensing are used to detect pencil marks on the card. While the standard Hollerith card has 12 rows and 80 columns of marking positions which can be sensed by some readers, most card readers use a much less dense marking array such as $10 \times 40$. In contrast to the desk top scanners which are hand fed, most card readers have an input stack hopper with automatic card feed mechanisms. As a result processing rates of up to 300 cards per minute can be achieved. The Chatsworth 4000 is a representative card reader.

As a test scoring device the card readers are not as attractive as the desk top scanner. In addition to not functioning as a "stand alone" device, they usually require the answer form to be printed on punched card stock which can be expensive.

## 2. Use of Microcomputers in Automated Scoring Systems

One of the major developments of the late 1970s and early 1980s has been the "personal" microcomputer. Although reasonably priced, these microprocessor-based machines are versatile and quite powerful computers. Since test scoring, test analysis, and item analysis involve only modest data processing requirements, the microcomputers are capable of serving as the computer in an automated scoring system. This is particularly true when a desk top scanner or a card reader is used. The first such system reported (Baker et al. 1978) was based upon an early microcomputer constructed from a hobby kit and a SCANTRON-5098 OMR. The manufacturers of desk top scanners have recognized the market potential of the desk top scanner–personal computer combination and some provide the computer software needed to input item response data from the scanner. SCANTRON provides software for using with their desk top scanner in combination with the TANDY TRS-80 Model II computer. Similar software is available for the Chatsworth MR-500 card reader and the Apple II computer. The remaining software for scoring the test, computing the test statistics, and performing the item analysis must then be written for each machine. Given the answer sheet image in memory, the remaining software is very easy to develop in a language such as BASIC, PASCAL, or FORTRAN. Using the first sheet scanned as the answer sheet it is a simple process to score the test and record which items the examinee answered correctly and incorrectly. Once the test score is obtained, its sum and sum of squares can be calculated and the score added to a vector for the sum of scores for those who answered each item correctly. All of this can be done on a sheet by sheet basis. Once the last sheet is processed the summary statistics of the test and its items can be calculated and appropriate reports printed. The nice feature of this process is that there is no real need to store the item response data on mass storage as all the calculation can be done "on-the-fly" thus minimizing data storage requirements.

The Nippon Electric Corporation has developed a microcomputer-based test scoring system that has a unique component. The system includes a mark sense card reader, a microcomputer (NEC-$\mu$PD-8080A), and I/O typewriter unit, and an S–P keyboard unit. This latter unit has 50 keys arranged in two rows on a panel. The user sets the keys to a 1 for correct, 0 for incorrect item response and this vector is transmitted to the computer. This makes it possible to enter the data needed for a student-problem analysis that uses a data array similar to that of Guttman's scalogram analysis. Sato et al. (1981) provide a description of the SPEEDY system and its usage.

### 3. Automated Scoring Systems as a Component of Larger Educational Activity

In recent years considerable interest has been shown in the ability to develop pools of items and store them in the mass storage devices of a computer (Lippey 1974). Given such an item bank, tests can be constructed either completely automatically or interactively by a test designer using a video display terminal. The resultant test is then administered to the examinees and the answer sheets processed by an automated scoring system employing the same computer. Thus, the feedback loop is closed as the item and test statistics produced become part of the descriptive data for the items in the item bank. This information can then be used the next time a test is to be constructed. Brenner (1980) provides an example of such an integrated item banking and test scoring system.

Individualized schemes of instruction rely heavily upon tests to collect achievement data in a classroom setting which is then used to decide upon a student's sequence of instructional activities. Because such instructional approaches are not feasible without computer support, a field known as computer-managed instruction (CMI) has arisen. Desk top scanners in the classroom transmit test data to a computer which performs a diagnosis based upon the test results and generates an instructional prescription for each examinee. The computer also generates reports for teachers to use in directing the student activities (Baker 1978). Because the classroom has a desk top scanner to input item response data and a typewriter-type terminal to print the computer-generated reports, the teacher is freed from the low-level clerical tasks associated with managing individualized instruction. In addition, considerable flexibility is provided as the testing can be done whenever a student reaches the appropriate point in his or her educational activities rather than at a fixed time for the whole classroom or a group of students.

In the United Kingdom, the Open University makes extensive use of OMR equipment to process tests mailed in by individual students. Other student work is graded by instructors who use mark sense forms to score work as well as select computer-generated comments. These forms are then scanned and the student reports with appropriate comments are generated via the computer's printer and mailed to the student. Variations on this approach are used by correspondence schools in several countries.

### 4. State of the Art

Since the early 1970s the high capacity OMR equipment, computers, and associated peripheral devices have reflected the advancements achieved in electronic technology. As a result these systems are more compact, embody more sophisticated quality control techniques, and provide economical support for testing programs.

However, the major new development has been the desk top scanner. The "stand alone" versions enable tests to be scored in the classroom for immediate use. The desk top scanners that can serve as computer input devices either directly or via telephone links are making comprehensive test and item analysis data readily available in situations out of the context of standard testing programs. As a result, automated test scoring is becoming an integral part of many innovative educational schemes such as CMI.

Although the electronic technology used in automated test scoring systems is up to date, the same cannot be said for the measurement theory they implement. Most of the text and item analyses performed are based upon classical test theory rather than modern latent trait/item response theory such as presented by Lord (1980). However, in Europe there is considerable interest in using modern test theory and in the Rasch model in particular. Hopefully, the discrepancy between theory and practice will narrow in the future (see *Latent Trait Measurement Models*; *Item Response Theory*; *Rasch Measurement Models*).

A major hindrance to greater use of automated scoring systems is the cost of answer sheets. Because the answer sheets must be printed with the marking positions in precise locations, and nonreflective ink and high quality paper must be used (especially when the transmitted light approach is used, Baker 1971), the answer sheets are expensive. In 1981, the prices ranged from about 6 cents (US) per sheet in small lots (<10,000 sheets) to 2 cents (US) in large lots (>100,000 sheets). While these costs are easily borne by large-scale once-a-year testing programs, they loom quite large in high frequency classroom testing such as under CMI. Hopefully a means will be found to reduce these sheet costs in the future.

Due to the low cost of microprocessors and their associated components as well as to their increasing power, greater reliance will be placed upon this technology. Two trends will probably develop in the near future. First, certain types of desk top scanners will be designed specifically to operate as a component in a microcomputer-based automated test scoring system, and a better balance of task allocation between the two components achieved. This will result in lower cost scanners that will have improved mark sensing abilities and greater internal quality control procedures. Some additional quality control and the actual test scoring and analysis will be performed in the microcomputer. Second, greater capability will be incorporated into the "stand alone" scanner so that it becomes a self-contained automated test scoring system. Such a system would consist of the desk top scanner with its onboard microcomputer and a small, inexpensive printer to produce the student reports, summary statistics of the test, and the item analysis results. While the internal microprocessor could be programmed by the user, it will be more likely that read only memory and random access memory devices will contain a general purpose test processing program. The current sheet-compile technique could then be used to tailor the general purpose program to the specific answer-sheet format being used and to select the particular reports to be printed, the result being a portable automated test scoring system that could be taken wherever it is desirable to do testing. Such a system could be shared within a school, used to collect research data, and would be an extremely useful set of equipment. It is clear that such exploitation of advances in technology will result in automated scoring systems that will offer a wide range in services at an increasingly attractive per examinee cost.

## Bibliography

Baker F B 1971 Automation of test scoring, reporting and analysis. In: Thorndike R L (ed.) 1971 *Educational Measurement*. Council on Education, Washington, DC

Baker F B 1978 *Computer Managed Instruction: Theory and Practice*. Educational Technology Publications, Englewood Cliffs, New Jersey

Baker F B, Ratankesdaten P, McIsaac D N 1978 A microcomputer based test scoring system. *Educ. Technol.* 18(2): 31–39

Brenner L P 1980–81 On-line item banking in health sciences education. *J. Educ. Technol. Sys.* 9: 213–27

Lippey G (ed.) 1974 *Computer-assisted Test Construction*. Educational Technology Publications, Englewood Cliffs, New Jersey, p. 244

Lord F M 1980 *Applications of Item Response Theory to Practical Testing Problems*. Erlbaum, Hillsdale, New Jersey

Sato T, Takaya M, Kurata M, Mirimoto Y, Chimura H 1981 An instructional data analysis machine with a micro-processor: SPEEDY. *NEC Res. Dev.* 61: 55–63

# Computer Scoring of Essays

**E. B. Page**

The computer analysis of essays written by students has been explored in several major research studies. The outcomes have consistently showed that computers can match the power and accuracy of expert human teachers in evaluating essays, once essays are presented in a form readable by machine. It may be predicted therefore that, when certain problems are solved, there may be a revolution in essay testing similar to that which has transformed objective testing following the development of multiple-choice testing, scoring, and analysis programs. Here will be considered the advantages of machine essay analysis; research work on stylistic grading; research work on content essay tests; problems of essay input; and the prospects for practical implementation.

## 1. Advantages of Machine Essay Analysis

Secondary-school teachers have long recognized an unfairness among disciplines in the responsibility for reading and marking student papers. Among the most privileged and least burdened are apt to be teachers of art, industrial and vocational courses, or mathematics. Among the most encumbered are teachers of classes requiring much written work, especially teachers of writing and usage, whose responsibilities for grading may be considered endless. But it is the students, in all grades, who are the most deprived by the current situation. Though they should have daily writing practice, they are fortunate, in the United States and other nations, to have an essay assignment several times in a month, and such assignments are apt to be returned to them without intensive analysis or encouragement.

As computer costs drop spectacularly, it becomes possible to hope that much essay analysis and comment may be automated, so that students' progress may be facilitated from fumbling solecism to apt and effective expression. As the science and technology of essay analysis become more powerful, it is possible to forecast daily writing stints being handed in on assigned topics, and returned the next school day with comments appropriate to the individual and the class goals. And this may be projected not only in writing classes but in others depending on written responses to test items or homework questions.

## 2. Essay Analysis for Style

Though computer scoring of essays has many contacts with other disciplines, the earliest major direct efforts have been those at the University of Connecticut (USA), where a framework was first established and tested with remarkable success. Beginning in 1964, researchers used multivariate statistics to simulate the stylistic evaluations of high-school essays made by expert English teachers. The general research design was as follows:

(a) Samples of essays by students were judged independently by four (and later eight) expert English teachers. Their numerical ratings were pooled to form the criterion for any machine program of evaluation, since it is clear that a "good" essay is one thought to be good by qualified readers.

(b) Hypotheses were generated by the researchers, together with any colleagues, about variables which the computer might read, which might be correlated with these human judgments. It was recognized that these computer variables may be only approximations of the intrinsic qualities evaluated by the teachers. Thus the computer variables were termed "proxes," and the human judgments "trins."

(c) Computer routines were written to measure these proxes in the essays, and to record the scores.

(d) Essays were prepared for computer input, if they were not already entered at a terminal. For research purposes, the handwritten essays were key punched, letter by letter, on computer cards, and then entered on magnetic tape.

(e) The essays were passed through the computer under control of the program from step (c) above. The prose string was broken into words and punctuations, which were then measured in various ways, looked up in various lists, and checked for their relationship with other words. For each essay, this analysis produced 30 or more measures, including such variables as: title present (yes or no), length of essay in words, mean length of words, proportion of misspellings found, how many kinds of parts of speech or sentence, and all identified punctuations, proportion of subject–verb openings, and so on. These were necessarily "proxes," not "trins."

(f) Taking the human judgments from step (a) as the goal, these computer variables were used in a multiple regression program to predict the expert rating. Automatically, good predictors were weighted heavily, and poor predictors were virtually ignored by the program.

Using very conservative, cross-validated ratings, such a program produced marks which were not distinguishable from those of the human experts. For both the human and the machine judge, the average intercorrelation among judges was about 0.50. Not only this, but the researchers extended the stylistic grading to the most important major essay traits: ideas, organization, style, mechanics—and even creativity, which had been predicted by many scholars to be outside the computer's power. Again, the results were surprising. With a sample of 256 essays and 8 independent human ratings on each trait for each essay, the program did as well with creativity as with mechanics, but this was not true of the human-group reliability (Page 1968).

## 3. Essay Scoring for Content

A major extension of this strategy occurred in research on grading the content of high-school essays in different subject matter areas. Beginning in 1969, Connecticut researchers selected a random sample of public secondary-school teachers in four broad areas: science, social studies, literature, and foreign language. Each of those who volunteered and who gave appropriate tests was asked to provide at least two essay items answered by their students, together with a copy of the question asked; the grade given each essay; a teacher key for each question; and a "model student essay"—that response which the teacher felt was the best written in the class. The design of the research was three-dimensional, with $4 \times 3 \times 4$ levels: four subject matter fields, by three grade levels (7–8, 9–10, 11–12), by four teachers in each. There were then 48 teachers, with two essay items studied for each teacher. The results, therefore, were widely generalizable across secondary-school classes.

Additional subject matter teachers were recruited, four in each major division, and these provided independent ratings of each essay, with generally good agreement among judges, ranging from about 0.48 for English to about 0.68 for foreign language. Again, the pooled ratings served as the criterion for computer scoring, with a multiple regression method used to select the best computer variables. Beside the stylistic variables already proved, special vocabulary was identified in the teacher key and the model student essay, and these words were used, together with their synonyms. A number of strategies were explored for counting any such key words or phrases within a student response.

The results of such methods, once again, were surprisingly sound. The techniques worked well for all four of the major subject matter fields, with the following predictions of the expert judgments: for science, 0.73; social studies, 0.70; English, 0.63; and foreign languages, 0.74. These are, once again, at the performance level of the individual experts themselves (Ajay et al. 1973).

## 4. The Input Problem

Given these striking early successes, it may seem surprising that more research and applications have not yet resulted from them. The principal problem, in today's educational structure, is in producing the student essays in machine-readable form. As computation drops rapidly in price, and small electronic devices become more commonplace, it may be hoped that terminals or other noiseless individual machines are produced which can record essays (perhaps on small magnetic cards), which may then be printed out, commented on, evaluated, and returned to students. Where papers are routinely typed, as for some college assignments, computer programs may be expected to read the typed pages with precision (at this writing, available systems still fall short, and are quite expensive, but this will predictably change). It would be a mistake to hope for an early reading of handwriting: this would depend on great leaps in basic understanding of linguistics and psychology which cannot be accurately predicted.

## 5. Practical Prospects

Where the measurement of knowledge or intelligence is the goal, the essay test is basically handicapped by the inefficiency of asking so few items in a given span of time. For this reason, it will not fully replace the multiple-choice exam, even when its technology is more developed. Yet for the measurement of writing skills, the essay has much face validity; and for instruction in writing, the essay assignment is indispensable. Furthermore, in many courses other than a student's own language, the essay item requires recall and mastery of an area, and in itself practices these accomplishments. Yet many students today can go for months without writing any essay.

One may expect the practical installation of computer essay analysis to occur both at the national level, and at the school. At the national level, it may be expected that computer analysis will replace the "holistic" ratings sometimes used in large programs, and in some nations' screening examinations. For such programs, the secretarial copying of essays would be a minor part of current testing fees, and could be installed very soon. Other uses may be expected to become practicable for university and able secondary students, as computers learn better to read typescript. But many of the most important uses will be instructional, and must depend on the student's entering the essay directly in machine-readable form. This depends on the wide availability of small, quiet, and inexpensive keyboards which produce magnetic records as well as visible copy.

When such implementation does appear, some of the same large advantages (for correction, guidance, and evaluation) which have accompanied the advent of the multiple-choice test may be expected.

## Bibliography

Ajay H B, Tillett P I, Page E B 1973 *Analysis of Essays by Computer (AEC-II)*. Final Report for United States Department of Health, Education and Welfare. University of Connecticut, Storrs, Connecticut

Minsky M L (ed.) 1968 *Semantic Information Processing*. Massachusetts Institute of Technology, Cambridge, Massachusetts

Page E B 1968 The use of the computer in analyzing student essays. *Int. Rev. Educ.* 14: 210–25

# Using Tests in Evaluation Contexts

## Selection Mechanisms for Entry to Secondary Education

E. A. Yoloye

The term secondary education has different meanings in different countries. Conventionally, three levels of education are commonly recognized, namely (a) primary, (b) secondary, and (c) tertiary. Occasionally they are also referred to as first level, second level, and third level.

In recent years the term "basic education" came into vogue to designate the minimum level of education that any child should have. In general it was felt that primary education of six years' duration as was common in many countries of the world was inadequate.

Many developed countries of the world had implicitly expressed the same view by imposing minimum ages for the termination of compulsory schooling for their youth. Such ages range from 14 to 16 years old. Assuming that children usually start primary schooling at the age of 6, such a compulsory minimum school leaving age would imply that children should have a minimum of eight to ten years of schooling.

Consequently, in a number of developed countries, what is defined as primary education lasts eight or more years (for example in Canada, the United States, and New Zealand). A number of countries divide secondary education into junior and senior. The duration of each part varies from two to four years. Many African countries are adopting this pattern by having six years of primary schooling, two or three years of junior secondary, and two or three years of senior secondary. Zambia recently decided to group the three years of junior secondary with the six years of primary to form nine years of "basic education". Nevertheless, many countries, both developed and developing, still keep the term primary education for the first six years, and secondary education for what comes immediately after. Examples are England, Wales, Netherlands, Belgium, Singapore, Nigeria, and most anglophone African countries. Italy is unique in having only five years of primary schooling.

There are several categories of schools within secondary education. The two most common types are the "comprehensive" secondary schools and the grammar schools. In African countries there are also several teacher-training institutions that correspond to second level education although they are not called secondary schools.

In England, Wales, Ireland, Belgium, and Thailand, comprehensive secondary schools run side-by-side with grammar schools and children go into either straight from primary schools. Australia and New Zealand have only comprehensive secondary schools. Canada runs four years of comprehensive high school (grades 9–12) followed by one year in grade 13 for the more academically able. Most African countries that have adopted the junior secondary and senior secondary format, try to implement a comprehensive curriculum in the junior secondary while making the senior secondary more academically oriented. Finland operates a similar system with grades 7–9 (ages 13–15) being comprehensive while the *gymnasium* follows for another three years (grades 10–12).

### 1. The Need for Selection

Selection for secondary school places is usually necessitated by two factors:

(a) A shortage of secondary-school places as is the case in African and most other developing countries.

(b) The desire to give more able students an academically oriented education as is the case in England and Wales.

In Africa, delegates of 39 African States and five European States (the Colonial powers) met in Addis Ababa in May 1961 under the auspices of UNESCO and the Economic Commission for Africa (ECA) to discuss education in Africa. Among other things, the conference—usually referred to as the Addis Ababa Conference—set targets for secondary-school enrolment as percentages of first-level enrolment (UNESCO 1961).

In 1976, a similar conference in Lagos took stock of the progress in the first 12 years. Table 1 gives the relevant figures.

These figures indicate the dimension of the problem of shortage of secondary-school places in Africa. Data from the World Bank Education Sector policy paper (1980) indicate that the position for 1977 is considerably better. Nevertheless over 50 percent of the 33 countries

*Table 1*
Second-level enrolment in African countries as percentages of
first level[a]

| Year | Target % | Observed % |
|------|----------|------------|
| 1960 | —        | 5.7        |
| 1965 | 10.4     | 9.1        |
| 1970 | 15.0     | 12.8       |
| 1972 | 16.4     | 13.2       |

a Source: UNESCO 1975

cited have enrolments lower than 30 percent, and over
75 percent of the countries have enrolment lower than
50 percent.

Given this situation, it becomes imperative that mechanisms should be devised for selecting candidates for
places in secondary schools.

In many developing countries, selection into secondary schools is carried out for reasons similar to those
in Africa.

## 2. Mechanisms of Selection

In general, comprehensive schools are nonselective.
Exceptions are found in the Netherlands and Thailand.
Nevertheless, certain criteria usually guide decisions as
to what school a child attends. In many cases children
are allocated by ministries of education or similar education authorities into neighbourhood schools. In some
cases, for example, in Belgium, parents have a free
choice as to which schools to send their children to.

Where selection is necessary as in the situations discussed in the preceding section, the usual mechanism is
an examination. What differs from country to country
is the content of such an examination.

### 2.1 Kinds of Selection Tests

Four kinds of tests have been employed in selecting
candidates for secondary schools. These are:

(a) achievement tests;

(b) intelligence tests;

(c) aptitude tests;

(d) oral tests or interviews.

Some countries use achievement tests only, for
example Ireland, Singapore, and Thailand (for secondary-grammar schools). Many others use a combination of two or more kinds of tests. England and
Wales for example used a combination of achievement
and intelligence tests for the well-known 11+ examination. (In 1983, a few local education authorities still
used this exam.) The Netherlands use a combination of
achievement, intelligence, and aptitude tests for selection to secondary-grammar schools. In many African
countries, a combination of achievement tests, aptitude

tests, and interviews are used. Italy uses a combination
of achievement tests and oral tests.

(a) *Achievement tests*. These are usually based on the
content of what the child is expected to have learnt in
primary schools. Such achievements tests are, however,
often heavily weighted with language and mathematics.
Sometimes a general paper is also set to cover other
areas of school learning. In Nigeria many schools also
set what was called a "general knowledge" paper which
tested knowledge of current affairs.

(b) *Intelligence tests*. These are used extensively in
England and Wales. They are not based on school
syllabi although performance in them is influenced to
some extent by school achievement. In principle, intelligence tests attempt to assess reasoning ability in various intellectual areas, for example verbal reasoning,
numerical reasoning, nonverbal reasoning, and so on.
Scores in intelligence tests may be given as intelligence
quotients (IQ), as grade equivalents, or as age equivalents.

(c) *Aptitude tests*. These are similar to intelligence
tests in that they focus strongly on reasoning. However,
test items try to identify also the kind of skills required
for various kinds of activities. Thus, for example, Scholastic Aptitude Tests (SAT) focus on verbal and numerical
reasoning. Commercial aptitude on the other hand, in
addition, seeks to assess finger dexterity and ability
to code data. The Test Development and Research
Office of the West African Examinations Council
(WEAC) has a battery of aptitude tests known as
1-D tests. Combinations of different tests in the
battery form particular aptitude tests. Aptitude test
scores are usually recorded as stanines, or grade equivalents.

(d) *Interviews*. These aim at assessing personality
characteristics in addition to academic achievement.
In the area of academic achievement, interviews are
particularly suitable for assessing the candidates' speech
and facility in using the relevant language of instruction
in secondary schools.

More importantly, interviews provide opportunities
to assess such personality variables as politeness, grooming, temperament, and physical fitness. In a number of
African countries, where most secondary schools have
hostel facilities, efforts are also made to assess the
adjustment of candidates by making them live together
for a few days and observing how they interact with
each other. Typically, the interview technique is
employed only after written tests have been administered and shortlists have been prepared on the basis
of performance on the written tests.

## 3. Agencies of Secondary-school Selection

There are various degrees of centralization or decentralization in the procedures for secondary-school selection. At the most decentralized level, individual schools
take the responsibility of organizing their own selections. In effect, the principal or headteacher of the

secondary school invites applications from primary-school leavers, and thereafter proceeds to organize the selection tests, and so on. This procedure is wasteful in time, money, and human resources because the same child often applies for admission and is admitted to several schools. Consequently, principals are never sure of what pupils will come to their schools until the beginning of the academic year. Then begin a series of supplementary admission exercises.

In centralized systems, the ministry of education or a central examination body organizes the selection. Such a central examination body may be a national or subregional examination board. In West Africa for example, the West African Examinations Council (WAEC) conducts common entrance examinations in the five countries of Nigeria, Ghana, Liberia, Sierra Leone, and Gambia.

In some of the African countries, for example Gambia and Sierra Leone, the Common Entrance examination is also the certification for completion of primary-school education. This procedure tends to heighten anxiety among the pupils because a child who fails to gain admission to a secondary school is then deemed to have failed primary education.

Many countries use a combination of the centralized and the decentralized systems. Shortlisting is done through a common entrance examination but the final selection is done by individual schools.

## 4. Political Factors in Selection to Secondary Schools

One of the major concerns in developing countries is the equalization of opportunities for education. Historical factors sometimes create imbalances in access to education. In Nigeria for example, Western education came into the country through the coastal areas of the south. The hinterland was therefore slower in profiting from Western education. Secondly, Western education was brought predominantly by Christian missionaries. In the northern part of the country, Islam had made inroads via the Sahara. The religious difference further contributed to the imbalance. With the coming of independence, the pressure to eliminate such imbalance has been very high. One of the measures that has been taken in this regard is to introduce a quota system for the admissions process into secondary schools. The system operates mainly in federal secondary schools. In this system, each of the 19 states has a specified number of places reserved for its candidates. Thus for the so-called educationally disadvantaged areas, lower levels of achievement in the selection examinations are usually accepted for the candidates.

A different kind of political influence appears when particular political parties enunciate policies which affect selection. For example the Unity Party of Nigeria (UPN) governments in five of the states (Lagos, Ogun, Ondo, Oyo, and Bendel) in Nigeria have introduced 100 percent transition from primary to secondary schools thus eliminating the need for selection examinations.

## 5. Studies in Secondary-school Selection

Early studies in England, Wales, and Australia focused on two main issues namely:

(a) The predictive validity of the selection procedures.

(b) The effects of coaching and practice on test performance.

Examples of such studies are Jorgensen (1935) and Watts et al. (1952).

A number of more recent studies in West Africa also deal with the predictive validity of common entrance examinations (e.g. Skurnik and Safo 1971).

In West Africa, the great concern for equalization of opportunities has given three other foci for study, namely:

(a) the relative performance of urban and rural children in the common entrance examination (e.g. Soriyan and Awuwoloye 1979);

(b) relative performance of different states in Nigeria (e.g. Soriyan 1975);

(c) relative performance of children from public schools and private schools in Ghana (e.g. Agbenyega 1972).

The Agbenyega study is interesting in that it led to a policy decision by the Ministry of Education. The study came out with the expected result that candidates from private schools performed better than those from public schools. It was hypothesized that this was because these private schools concentrated more on common entrance-related subjects while public schools operated a broader curriculum. The Ministry of Education therefore insisted on social studies being included as a subject in the common entrance examination. After the implementation of this policy, the study was repeated and this time the rural/urban factor was investigated as well. Results showed that:

(a) the private schools still performed better than the public ones in all papers including the newly added social studies paper;

(b) rural children performed better than urban children in the social studies paper.

No further policy decision was taken on the matter.

## 6. Conclusion

Although most countries of the world had at some stage in their history needed to select children into secondary schools, such selection today is more important in Third World countries where secondary-school places are severely limited. In these countries, in addition to academic factors, political factors also play important roles in determining selection mechanisms.

## Bibliography

Agbenyega C O 1972 *Performance Analysis of Candidates in Public and Private Schools on the Ghana Common Entrance Examination 1972.* Test Development and Research Office (TEDRO) Research Report R P99. West African Examinations Council (WAEC), Accra

Jorgensen C 1935 Intelligence tests and entrance examinations as instruments for selecting and grading students. *Three Studies in the Prediction of Scholastic Success.* Australian Council for Educational Research (ACER), Hawthorn, Victoria

Skurnik L S, Safo E 1971 *The Validity of the Ghana Common Entrance Examinations: A Summary of Current Findings.* TEDRO Research Report. West African Examinations Council (WAEC), Accra

Soriyan M A 1975 *Performance of Candidates State by State in the 1973 Nigeria National Common Entrance Examination*

*to Secondary Schools.* TEDRO Research Report RP75/10. West African Examinations Council (WAEC), Lagos

Soriyan M A, Awuwoloye E O 1979 *Rural–Urban Effects on the Nigeria National Common Entrance Examination to Secondary Schools.* TEDRO Research Report RP 79/2. West African Examinations Council (WAEC), Lagos

UNESCO 1961 *Conference of African States on the Development of Education in Africa Addis Ababa 15–25 May 1961. Final Report.* UNESCO, Paris

UNESCO 1975 Regional educational targets and achievement in Africa, 1965–1972. ED-76/MINEDAF/REF/2, Paris

Watts A F, Pidgeon D A, Yates A 1952 *Secondary School Entrance Examinations: A Study of Some of the Factors Influencing Scores in Objective Tests with Particular Reference to Coaching and Practice.* 2nd interim report on the allocation of primary school leavers to courses of secondary education. Newnes, London

World Bank 1980 *Education Sector Policy Paper.* World Bank, Washington, DC

Yates A, Pidgeon D A 1957 *Admission to Grammar Schools.* 3rd interim report of the allocation of primary school leavers to courses of secondary education. Newnes, London

# Selection Mechanisms for Entry to Higher Education

## W. Mitter

Up until the eighteenth century, no selection mechanisms for entry to higher education existed since general upper-secondary education and higher education were closely interrelated, with many institutional and curricular links. The most frequent variant was the existence of "preparatory courses" which were the responsibility of the university and whose primary purpose was to provide a classical liberal arts education. Beginning at the end of the eighteenth century in Europe and continuing throughout the nineteenth century the two levels of education separated. This separation process, which is now a world-wide phenomenon, has resulted in a diversity of transition structures. The individual structures reflect national or regional traditions and are determined both by external political, economic, and sociocultural pressures, and by conventions and ideas inherent in the educational system as such. Considering the latter impact, it must be kept in mind that the selection procedures which educational systems use are essential elements of their institutional control.

## 1. Historical Determinants

Taken as a whole, the historical determinants of the transition structures form a framework which consists of several factors which will be illustrated below. In view of their manifestation in national or regional educational systems, one has, above all, to remember that the framework is characterized by a high degree of complexity and by various forms of interaction between the individual factors.

### 1.1 Place of Preparatory Courses

The function of the former preparatory courses has been assigned either to the higher or to the upper-secondary levels. The outcome of this differentiation has been valid until today. The most striking model of the first type is represented by the American liberal arts college which offers a general educational curriculum, the contents of which appear in the curricula of upper-secondary schools in Europe. Higher education in the United States—and, to give another example, in Japan—usually starts with a broad general base comprising arts, sciences, and social sciences. It is gradually completed by courses qualifying the students for specialized academic careers. Traditional European universities, on the other hand, offer specialized studies from the beginning. The placement of the "preparatory courses" is closely determined by the modal age of the students, as can be derived from comparative age schemes.

### 1.2 Diversification of the System

Higher education has expanded considerably since a variety of profession-oriented educational institutions have grown up around traditional universities, devoted predominantly to the technological and commercial fields. Having their origins in secondary-level training establishments, these now upgraded institutions (e.g., polytechnics, *Instituts Universitaires de Technologie*, and *Technische Hochschulen*) have increased the amount and variety of professional training available at the higher education level. Formerly professional training at this level had been restricted to the university faculties of medicine, jurisprudence, and theology. Education as a profession-oriented discipline has attained higher education status relatively late in the form of independent teachers colleges or of university faculties, schools, or departments.

### 1.3 Access to Higher Education

International higher education has been characterized from the beginning by the contrast between (a) restricted admission procedures under the responsibility of the university, as has been developed in the Anglo–Saxon countries, and (b) various forms of "open access", with little direct admissions control by the university. In the regulations valid on the European continent during the past two centuries, "open access" has never meant, of course, uncontrolled admission. On the contrary, more or less rigid school-leaving examinations, be they *Abitur* or *baccalauréat*, held at the end of upper-secondary-school attendance, were designed as articulate selection mechanisms, either under the auspices of the university (e.g., in France) or under the direct control and supervision of the school authorities responsible for general secondary education (e.g., in Germany and the other countries of Central Europe). After the October Revolution, the Soviet universities were opened for all persons over the age of 16 years without any formal selection. This radical experiment, rooted in the revolutionary concept of a totally open educational system, lasted however, only until 1923. It was superseded by the tightly organized admission system which has been in operation up to the present. Combining elements of the Anglo–Saxon and the French variants, it consists of a school-leaving examination in addition to an entrance examination which is given by the university or an equivalent higher educational institution.

### 1.4 Selection During the Courses of Study

Selection for higher education in some countries (e.g., France) is closely linked to selection mechanisms operating thoughout a student's course of study at university. By providing assessment at regular intervals in the form of standardized tests or conventional inquiries, the importance of entry procedures is reduced in comparison to educational systems which do not provide, or at least set a minor value upon, any selection mechanisms during the study courses as has been the case in the traditional German faculties of arts.

### 1.5 Mass Education and its Consequences

The last factor in the framework of historical determinants is embodied in the concept of "mass education" which has, to a greater or lesser degree, affected higher education all over the world, having changed many former elitist universities with comparatively small numbers of students into big and complex establishments. This trend has not only altered the character of subject matter and teaching methods within the university, but has also affected the selection mechanisms for entry to higher education to a remarkable extent. The effect has not only been quantitative but also qualitative because the expansion has predominantly strengthened the profession-oriented task of higher education and thus weakened the concept of "purposeless" studies which had formerly determined the curricula in the arts faculties. While at the beginning of the 1970s there seemed to be no end in sight with regard to the expansion of higher education, the following period of disenchantment has resulted in curtailments of budgets and in reductions of admission quotas, particularly in Western countries. Although the effects of this recent trend must not be overlooked, it is doubtful whether it has stopped the expansion as such. This is shown by the numbers of young people continuing on to higher education as derived from absolute number of enrolments.

## 2. Typology of Selection Mechanisms

The following overview presents eight models of selection mechanisms which demonstrate how access to a university or an equivalent higher educational institute can be achieved. The basic criterion common to all of them is that of formal graduation from a general education upper-secondary school or an equivalent institution, except in the case of the last model. In the context of this article no detailed attention is given to the question of how secondary-school graduation is arranged in individual educational systems. Generally speaking, a distinction can be drawn between the traditional form of organizing a terminal examination at a given point (usually in written and oral form) and the replacement of this practice by summarizing the attainments of the whole of the upper-secondary stage or at least the uppermost grade. The replacement of an examination to assess achievement at a given point with tasks to be done at home, in which examinees can prove their capacity for elementary inquiry, also points to a departure from the traditional formal school-leaving examination. While in a few countries, such as Sweden and the United States, examinations at a given point have been totally abandoned, many countries have developed mixed examination systems combining formal terminal procedures (in written and oral form) with the continuous assessment of attainments. Another criterion of distinction worth noting is the agency which lays down the requirements and is responsible for the assessment procedure as regards content and method: either ministries of education as is the case in most European countries, or public examination boards, the most prominent example being the General Certificate of Education (GCE) in the United Kingdom. Finally, the status of the examiners plays a differentiating role. Comparison can be made between the appointment of university or secondary-school teachers as external examiners (e.g., the United Kingdom, France, and Italy) and the commissioning of the examinees' own subject teachers with this task (e.g., Federal Republic of Germany, East European countries, and the Soviet Union). The relevance of this overview seems to be justifiable in so far as it reveals, on the one hand, the dichotomy of objective and subjective components of secondary-school graduation and, on the other, a world-wide trend characterized by the departure from rigid terminal examinations at a given point to various forms of continuous assessment—at least in the function of completing the examinations—and, therefore, a broadening of the assessment base as a whole.

## 2.1 Enrolment without Further Selection

In this enrolment model the secondary-school-leaving certificate entitles its holder to formal enrolment in higher education without having to overcome any further barriers. The traditional certificates used on the European continent, such as the French *baccalauréat*, the German *Abitur* or the Italian *esame di maturità* (in their original forms), which enable open access to any university or faculty, are examples of this model. It must be contrasted to the following ones in which the secondary-school-leaving certificate is only recognized in its function as the "first threshold" in the admission process.

## 2.2 Lottery

The lottery model has in common with the following two models the basic fact that the holder of the secondary-school-leaving certificate has to (a) submit a formal application for entry to higher education and (b) fulfil the requirements of one of the selection mechanisms marking the "second threshold". In the lottery model selection is effected by way of unweighted or weighted lotteries, the latter being used as part of the admission procedures in the Netherlands and the Federal Republic of Germany.

## 2.3 Weighted Examination of School Marks

The applicants' school-leaving certificates are subjected in this model to special examination by an admission board set up by either the individual university or a centralized agency. Selection is dependent upon the quality of the school marks. The individual selection procedure can be based either on the average mark of the certificate taken as a whole, or with total or partial emphasis given to those subjects which are directly or indirectly related to the university disciplines the applicant wishes to study (e.g., mathematics and sciences for medical studies). This model is the purest embodiment of the concept of *numerus clausus* (*numerus fixus*) which has become a current and controversial issue in all educational systems which use this method as a means of selection.

## 2.4 Consideration of School Records

The admission board, after examining and usually weighting the school marks, often bases its final decision on additional documentary testimony, such as letters of reference, which are provided by school records or other sources. Unlike school marks which provide only subject-bound assessment, such letters, usually written by the headteacher of the upper-secondary school the applicant has attended, afford an insight into the applicants' affective and social qualities. A special variant of this model applied in socialist countries includes reports on their social activities (in youth organizations or harvest work brigades, production campaigns, etc.). This kind of "subjective" scrutiny is rooted in the assumption that the degree of importance attached to individual or social characteristics should be at least equivalent to the anonymity inherent in the "objective" components of selection procedures.

## 2.5 Interviews

Similar justification is given for the model in which the examination of the school-leaving certificate is completed by interviewing the applicants. The use of interviews as an additional, though limited, selection method, is seen to be most beneficial in borderline cases where school marks and tests need to be supplemented. For these cases interviews are considered useful provided certain requirements are met, such as clarity of assessment criteria and standardization of interview conditions.

## 2.6 Standardized Tests

The use of scholastic aptitude tests and achievement tests has spread widely since the 1960s. Although they are not used exclusively anywhere, they are regarded as a way of increasing the validity of predictions of success in higher education. The results obtained vary, and are evaluated differently, according to the historical and social background of the country's educational system, and in particular the position occupied by the secondary school-leaving certificate. The usefulness of the tests also varies from one field of study to another. Generally, however, such admission tests are thought to be useful provided they are tried under realistic conditions of operation and under careful scientific control. Difficulties in meeting these prerequisites are the reason why personality tests (to measure, for example, attitudes and character) are generally regarded as unsuitable for selection purposes. Responsibility for the production and application of standardized tests generally rests with special boards, such as the College Entrance Examination Board (CEEB) and the American College Testing Program (ACT) in the United States, or the Institute of Test Development and Research of the German National Scholarship Foundation in the Federal Republic of Germany.

## 2.7 Conventional Entrance Examinations

According to this model the "second threshold" is represented by more or less conventional types of written and oral examinations. Very often this means that two examinations have to be passed within a short period, first the school-leaving examination and then the entrance examination at the higher educational institution. In comparison to the lottery model, entrance examinations are usually focused on subjects which are related to the desired study lines, but often include general education requirements too, such as knowledge of a foreign language. The "duplication" resulting from this procedure has raised much criticism and has resulted in various schemes designed to combine all or part of the two examinations.

### 2.8 Access Based on Work Experience

In opposition to all the models outlined above, there has developed an increasing interest in ways to open up access to higher education to people who have not passed a formal secondary-school-leaving examination. As a compensatory criterion, work experience has been proposed. Although its use as an admission criterion is commonly linked with the requirement for some formal professional qualification and even a general education certificate of minor degree (compared to the "classical" terminal award), this alternative model relates, in some ways, to the previous "open access" practice which determined the entry to higher education before upper-secondary schools were established as a separate preparatory stage.

To summarize this typological outline, there is a fundamental duality with regard to the role the applicants play in the selection mechanism. In the models discussed in Sects. 2.2 to 2.4 they are restricted to passivity, since they cannot influence the procedures after having submitted their terminal secondary awards and their formal applications. The models of Sects. 2.5 to Sect. 2.7 in contrast are characterized by the applicants' opportunities to "intervene" and revise the outcomes of their school achievements—with the risk of succeeding or failing. The first and last models represent the extremes of this model structure, whereby the latter shows some affinity to those models discussed in Sects. 2.5 to 2.7 so far as the individual work experience is usually examined by the admission board on the basis of certain records or certificates.

## 3. Case Examples

There is little compatibility between the models discussed above and the structures and mechanisms actually found in educational systems around the world, as each country's system is affected by the sociocultural, economic, and political circumstances peculiar to that country. Various combinations of the models exist, each assigning differing degrees of importance to the various factors. The following overview is considered as an exemplary presentation of most characteristic cases.

### 3.1 United States

Higher education admissions criteria are as diversified as the institutions to which the students apply. During the past few decades many institutions have adopted a policy of open admissions in order to give students the opportunity to prove their ability in the college classroom. Traditional requirements for state universities are sometimes established by a state law, but in spite of these variations there are standard procedures to which most college and university admissions officers adhere. Applicants are expected to have a high-school diploma or an equivalent certification before enrolling at a higher institution. However, most high-school students apply to colleges and universities during the final (senior) year of secondary school, submitting applications to several institutions. The factors which most often govern a student's acceptance by a college or university are secondary-school marks, successful completion of specified secondary-school courses (such as advanced placement programmes), scores on specific nationally administered achievement and scholastic aptitude tests, recommendations of high-school teachers, and interviews with college admissions officers.

### 3.2 Japan

Students become entitled to university admission by completing high school or by demonstrating an equivalent level of intellectual attainment. Anyone who believes that he or she will become qualified prior to the beginning of the academic year can apply to one first-division national university, one second-division national university, and as many public and private institutions as desired. Concern for the inefficiency of the examination system used in secondary education and for the stress experienced by many youths has prompted the recent experiments with new criteria for university admissions (including a unified entrance examination).

### 3.3 Soviet Union and Eastern European Countries

In the Soviet Union and most socialist countries in Eastern Europe the secondary-school-leaving certificate merely entitles a person to apply for admission to higher education; to be accepted an applicant is required to pass more or less conventional types of written and oral examinations. Several universities (particularly in the Soviet Union and Poland) have incorporated experimental tests into the examinations as well.

The definitive selection is based upon a competitive system closely related to the annual entry quotas which are set by the state and computed from economic planning data. Work experience, military service, and excellent scholastic achievements in the desired study subjects all enter into the scores and thus improve the applicant's chances. The interrelationship between the university entrance examination and the secondary-school graduation has become a subject of separate study, especially in Hungary. Different methods of combining the school-leaving examination with the entrance examination have been developed on an experimental line in some subjects (comprising, to date, mathematics, physics, and biology).

## 3.4 United Kingdom

The universities are autonomous bodies fixing their admission conditions individually, and without state control; they may confirm or amend them from one year to another or, at least in theory, change them altogether. Polytechnics, which are the responsibility of the local education authorities, have similar conditions. The basic admission requirement is three General Certificate of Education (GCE A level) passes. The marks given individually for each subject reflect the fact that upper-secondary education tries to meet individual interests and abilities. In addition to a personal reference from the headteacher, scholastic aptitude tests and personal interviews may also play a role. The only factor which this "free market system" has in common with the otherwise so divergent systems of state control in socialist countries, is the value placed on the examinations taken at the end of secondary school which entitle a school leaver to apply for admission.

## 3.5 France

The centralized structure of education has retained its traditional focus on the *baccalauréat* (introduced in 1808 by Napoleon) as qualification for university entrance. The system does not provide for any further threshold to university entrance, especially since the content and methods of the *baccalauréat* depend on the university standards. Generally speaking, the holders of the *baccalauréat* may enrol at any university, irrespective of the type of *baccalauréat* they have acquired (*baccalauréat général* with six subtypes; *baccalauréat de technicien* with 11 subtypes). The individual types (or subtypes) only have recommending character with regard to admission to a particular area of study. As a matter of fact, however, the deans of medical and science faculties can refuse those who don't have a *baccalauréat* type C (science oriented) which is considered to be the most selective. In any case, the risk of success or failure is one which students must take upon themselves. Selection takes place during a course of study and because of this the system of higher education has managed to maintain its traditional machinery of selection. The selection process occurring during the first year in medicine serves as a striking example of the rigidity of this process. The elitist *grandes écoles* with their rigid selection mechanism (two- to three-year preparatory courses and entrance examinations) have a special position outside the general regulations.

## 3.6 Sweden

The Swedish education system which is in the process of changing from a centralized system to a decentralized one, has been based on the idea of broadening admission to higher education from the qualitative as well as quantitative aspect. The new admission regulations in force since 1977 differ according to categories of applicants. On the one hand the regulations offer students with school-leaving certificates access to higher education. These certificates are obtained after two to three years' attendance at upper-secondary schools and are achieved on the basis of continuous assessment only, since the previous terminal examination (*studentexamen*) was abolished. On the other hand the new admission criteria include academic aptitude tests for adults who have work experience but do not hold the upper secondary-school-leaving certificate. Thus the admission regulations contain elements of the French model (open admission for secondary-school leavers) as well as the British model (special admission procedures), and the model of socialist Eastern Europe (quota restrictions for categories of applicants in cases where demand exceeds available places).

## 3.7 The Netherlands

For several years selection in the Netherlands has been based on the type of previous school education (ending in a terminal examination). In some subject areas, emphasis is given to marks in those subjects which correspond to the intended course of study (*numerus clausus*). Selection is particularly rigid for those seeking entry to faculties of medicine. As the system of education traditionally permitted holders of a secondary-school-leaving certificate to enter any university, the introduction of *numerus clausus* drastically changes the relationship between secondary and higher education. While in the 1970s a weighted lottery system had been used as a "second threshold", this mechanism had been limited to one-third of the applicants; for another third admission tests have been introduced.

## 3.8 Federal Republic of Germany

Like the Netherlands, the Federal Republic of Germany has also been concerned with the problem of departing from the previous "open access" policy (based on the leaving certificate of upper-secondary schools) and implementing a second threshold in the process of admission (though limited to certain study areas where the demand exceeds the capacities). Since *numerus clausus* (merely depending on the weighting of school marks) has been criticized, an experiment has been introduced into the selection of students of medicine (ongoing since 1980). This experimental procedure gives applicants the opportunity to participate in scholastic aptitude testing. This participation is totally voluntary, and the outcome can only be used to improve the chances in those cases where the test results are better than the corresponding school marks.

## 4. Open Issues

Conclusions to be drawn from a comparative overview point, first of all, to the fact that secondary-school marks, whether resulting from continuous assessment or terminal examinations, are considered as the most reliable predictor of success at university in most cases. In certain disciplines and fields of study where the number of applicants exceeds the number of places available, school marks alone do not constitute a sufficient basis for selection. It must not be forgotten that factors such as marking standards often vary and contribute to distorting the validity of marks. Hence additional procedures must be employed to select applicants—be it in the form of conventional examinations or by the use of scholastic aptitude and achievement tests. Interviews may in some cases perform a useful function especially where comparable school marks and test results call for an additional process that permits an applicant to exert a direct influence. Experience made with interviewing applicants with work experience but not holding a secondary-school-leaving certificate leading to university deserves special attention.

In those countries which have been compelled to replace the former "open access" policy (based on upper-secondary schooling) by some form of second threshold, the new methods for selection are unpopular and many people would prefer to return to the alternative of open admission for secondary-school-leaving certificate holders, as is still practised in Austria, Belgium, Italy, Switzerland, and Latin America. However, retaining the open access involves the danger of overcrowded universities, as is the case in Italy and Latin American countries. It also has to be kept in mind that optimal solutions of solving the selection issue must include a system of counselling to help students choose a particular career or course of study. In this context scholastic aptitude tests and even personality tests may be of importance.

Finally, fundamental attention has to be paid to the dichotomy inherent in the selection system as such. On the one hand the aim of selection procedures is to assess the applicants' intellectual (and manual, as is true of technological and medical studies) capacities predicting success at university. So far the discussion of selection mechanisms and the implementation of corresponding experiments have focused almost entirely on this goal. On the other hand, there remains the open question of how to develop predictors for abilities needed in the professional areas students want to enter on the basis of their university qualifications. Prediction in this field, though being far more difficult than in the admission sector, may gain increasing importance in a period which is characterized by overproduction of the academic work force. In this context, work experience (in various forms) as a prerequisite for certain courses of study (e.g., for medicine) has aroused considerable interest beyond its being regarded as an exceptional selection mechanism.

## Bibliography

Choppin B H, Orr L 1975 *Aptitude Testing at Eighteen Plus*. National Foundation for Educational Research, Slough

Furth D 1978 Selection and equity: An international viewpoint. *Comp. Educ. Rev.* 22: 259–77

Hearnden A 1973 *Paths to University: Preparation, Assessment, Selection*. Schools Council Research Studies. Macmillan, Basingstoke

Husén T 1976 Problems of securing equal access to higher education: The dilemma between equality and excellence. *Higher Educ.* 5: 407–22

Mitter W 1979a *Secondary School Graduation: University Entrance Qualification in Socialist Countries: A Comparative Study*. Pergamon, Oxford

Mitter W (ed.) 1979b *The Use of Tests and Interviews for Admission to Higher Education: A European Symposium*. National Foundation for Educational Research, Slough

# Prediction of Success in Higher Education

## B. H. Choppin

In most parts of the world the provision of places in universities and colleges is insufficient to meet the demand from the young people who aspire to higher education. For this reason, some selection procedure is essential. Even in those countries where the provision of postsecondary places is extensive, such as the United States, there is still competition to obtain admittance to the most prestigious colleges (e.g., Harvard) or faculties (e.g., medicine) so that here too selection procedures are necessary.

A number of European countries (e.g., Austria, Belgium, France, Italy) have established the principle that successful completion of secondary education entitles a young person to admission to the tertiary stage, but this does not entirely avoid selection problems since many more students wish to become doctors and lawyers, for example, than the society can readily absorb. Only in France (and then excepting the *Grandes Ecoles*) does the qualified student retain the right to enroll anywhere within the university system, and there the selection takes place during, rather than before, the course, with large numbers of students failing in their first year.

It has been argued that if selection among qualified candidates is necessary, it must be random if it is to be fair. In the Netherlands, for example, all students successfully completing secondary school may enter a lottery for a place in a specific university department.

However, most countries eschew strict egalitarianism for a more basic economic consideration. The failure of a student in higher education represents a waste of valuable national resources and specialist facilities, and is to be avoided if possible. As a result, the selection of students is explicitly directed towards identifying those who will successfully complete their program of study to the benefit of themselves and of society. Since reducing the wastage (or dropout) rate has a direct economic impact on the institution and on society at large, the question of developing selection mechanisms that would maximize prediction of scholastic or academic success has received wide attention and has been the subject of much research. Comprehensive summaries can be found in Lavin (1965) which covers the situation in the United States and Mitter (1979) which concentrates on research in Europe.

## 1. Alternative Selection Criteria

### 1.1 School-based Assessment: Grades

Almost all school systems keep detailed records of student progress and many formalize this by grading the student's performance in each subject studied on an annual basis, or more frequently. Cumulative summaries of these grades ("grade point average" or GPA in the United States) are frequently used as evidence on which to base the admission of a student to a university program. In most cases the GPAs are used directly, but in some they are first used to rank the student within his/her age group in the school concerned, and then these ranks are reported. This type of school-based measure is usually reliable since it is based on performance spread over several thousand hours of school study in a wide variety of subjects. However, its relevance to the prediction of academic success at the tertiary level where the educational environment may be quite different has been questioned. Moreover, schools have varying standards and an average grade of B in one school will not, in general, indicate the same level of achievement as an average grade of B in another. Although rank in class is an attempt to overcome this problem, it makes no allowance for the fact that the distribution of intellectual talent among schools may be very uneven.

### 1.2 Achievement Measures: Tests and Examinations

In many countries these are preferred to the school-based measures described above since they assess students from different schools on a common scale. There are two main variations. In the first (exemplified by the General Certificate of Education in the United Kingdom), examinations are set by the ministry of education or independent examination boards, and candidates from all schools in the country are entered. In the second pattern, as used for example in the Soviet Union, entrance examinations are set in appropriate subjects by each university. Only those students who applied to a particular faculty at that university will take the examination. In both cases, the examinations are aimed at measuring the achievement of the specified secondary-school curriculum or syllabus. Although overcoming some disadvantages of school-based assessment, these examinations have been criticized because of the extent to which preparation for them may distort the whole educational process in the upper-secondary school. Also, since they are single occasion events, they are less reliable indicators of students' overall levels of performance.

### 1.3 Aptitude Tests

These are tests specifically designed to predict success in higher education. Although bearing some similarity to tests of general intelligence, they tend to assume familiarity with the content of the regular secondary-school curriculum, and to set problems involving abstract reasoning and symbol manipulation, skills considered necessary for success at the college level. The best-known instrument of this type is the Scholastic Aptitude Test (SAT) developed by the College Entrance Examinations Board in the United States and first used in 1926. This test is currently administered to well over one million students each year, and yields two scores, mathematical and verbal aptitude, which have differential predictive validity for different fields of study. A number of other countries have experimented with, or are still investigating, similar types of test. These tests are relatively inexpensive to administer and do not take much of a student's time. The major criticism leveled against them is that in many circumstances they do not appear to predict future success very well.

### 1.4 Interviews

In many countries the interview is one of several instruments of selection and/or counseling used by universities with potential students. In some cases it is used primarily for candidates whose examination performance is borderline, while in others it is a critical part of the selection process and is required of every candidate.

Interviews are widely thought to be unreliable as predictive instruments, and are open to abuse. Even when they are conducted with great care and scrupulous regard to fairness, the public in general, and unsuccessful candidates in particular, may still be skeptical about the honesty of the procedure. On the other hand, many university staff feel that the opportunity to explore candidates' interests and orientation in some depth is the only satisfactory way of identifying those who will make best use of what the university has to offer.

### 1.5 Other Criteria

The utility of a number of other forms of evidence for predicting future success has been explored in research studies. These include personality rating scales completed by the secondary-school authorities, intelligence tests and personality measures (e.g., neuroticism and extraversion) completed by the student, and data about the educational standards of parents and siblings. Although these have shed some light on which factors affect success in university study, none have been considered suitable components of regular selection procedures.

In some countries, particularly in Eastern Europe, job performance on work undertaken after leaving high school is evaluated as part of the selection process, but evidence of predictive validity is not available.

## 2. Predictive Validity

Several methodological problems surround the evaluation of alternative selection measures. The first concerns the choice of a criterion variable which the selector variables are supposed to predict. There has been debate about whether it is better to try to predict successful completion of a university program on a pass/ fail basis, or to concentrate on a measure of the extent of the success achieved (for example, course grades or marks in an examination). In general, researchers in the United States have used college grade point average as the criterion, whereas European investigators have used successful completion of the program of study and/ or the class of degree awarded. This may account for some of the discrepancy in results since it is generally believed that college grade point averages are substantially more reliable than end-of-program "final" examinations.

A second problem surrounds the choice of a statistical index to measure the strength of the predictive relationship. Almost all researchers have used some form of correlation index despite misgivings about its appropriateness.

A third problem is in some ways more fundamental. The typical research study attempts to predict final results only for those students who were admitted to a university course (i.e., those who had obtained fairly high scores on the instruments used for selection). Investigation of the full range of student applicants would require the admission to the university of one or more cohorts for which the usual selection mechanisms were suspended. Apart from lowering the apparent predictive strength of the selection variables, this restriction of range leaves open the question of whether such predictive studies have any relevance at all for the group of candidates whose applications are rejected.

Despite these reservations, there have been a great many investigations particularly with regard to the predictive validity of the SAT. The results of many studies carried out by individual colleges in the United States give simple correlations of SAT with college grades in the range of 0.2 to 0.4, but when the SAT is used in conjunction with a school-based assessment measure, multiple correlations of 0.5 are usually obtained (Angoff 1971). Bloom and Peters (1961) showed that a procedure in which SAT scores were used to adjust for different standards, both in the high school from which the students were coming and the colleges to which they

were applying, could raise the multiple correlation up to about 0.7. A number of other research studies, using many diverse predictors, appear to suggest that the upper limit for predicting college grades from measures obtained prior to the commencement of the course is a multiple correlation of about 0.7. This implies that about half of the total variance in college grades can be accounted for by events which occur during the course and which were not predictable beforehand (Choppin and Orr 1976). Many colleges in the United States have used data on past student performance to set up regression equations which, for that college, predict optimally in terms of aptitude and achievement scores, and these equations are used to guide student admission procedures.

The experimental use of scholastic aptitude tests outside North America has yielded much lower correlations, usually of the order of 0.1 (Rechter 1970, Powell 1973, Choppin and Orr 1976). They have also revealed that aptitude tests are more effective in predicting success in some areas of specialization than in others. In general, the results for courses in mathematics, engineering, and the natural sciences give higher correlations, while predictions of performance in the humanities and the social sciences give lower correlations.

The use of interviews as a selection technique has not been studied as comprehensively as has the use of tests. Educational researchers in general have not shown much respect for the interview, and Lavin (1965), in his detailed literature review of prediction studies, does not discuss the interview as a selection technique at all. Albrow (1967), summarizing a number of British studies, concluded that interviews had virtually no predictive value, despite the high regard in which many European academics still hold the technique.

Most of the research studies cited above have compared the predictive power of a variety of selection instruments used separately or in combination. Mitter (1979) observed that the consensus that emerges from this research is that achievement measures (grade point average or external examinations) are the best predictors of future success. Aptitude tests are the next most effective predictors, almost as good as achievement measures in the United States, but much less effective elsewhere. Intelligence tests, personality data, and interviews emerge as even less effective predictors in those studies that have used them.

A small United Kingdom study (Orr 1974) suggested that those young people who took a break between school and university to work for a year or more were subsequently more successful as undergraduates. In view of this and the importance attached to work experience in the selection policies of Sweden, the Soviet Union, and elsewhere, this topic appears worthy of more detailed investigation. In general, however, the research data currently available supports the continuance of the use of achievement tests and examinations as the most effective predictors of success at the university.

## Bibliography

Albrow M C 1967 Ritual and reason in the selection of students. *Universities Q.* 21: 141–51

Angoff W H (ed.) 1971 *The College Board Admissions Testing Program.* College Entrance Examinations Board, New York

Bloom B S, Peters F R 1961 *Academic Prediction Scales.* Free Press, New York

Choppin B H, Orr L 1976 *Aptitude Testing at Eighteen-plus.* National Foundation for Educational Research, Slough

Lavin D E 1965 *The Prediction of Academic Performance: A Theoretical Analysis and Review of Research.* Russell Sage Foundation, New York

Mitter W (ed.) 1979 *The Use of Tests and Interviews for Admission to Higher Education: A European Symposium.* National Foundation for Educational Research, Slough

Orr L 1974 *A Year Between School and University.* National Foundation for Educational Research, Slough

Powell J L 1973 *Selection for University in Scotland.* A first report on the Assessment for Higher Education Project. University of London Press, London

Rechter B 1970 *Admission to Tertiary Studies: An Account of an Experimental Test Battery and a Proposal for its Use.* Australian Council for Educational Research, Melbourne

Stanley J C 1971 Predicting college success of the educationally disadvantaged. *Science* 171: 640–47

# Credentialing

## D. L. McArthur

Credentialing is a process, sometimes voluntary but frequently carrying the weight of law, through which an individual is approved by a recognized authority to engage in sanctioned professional practices and in some cases to use specific words to properly describe their services. In certain professional fields, primarily those related to physical or mental health, the subject of credentialing has been hotly debated. The various commentators address two major questions: is there any agreement about what constitutes appropriate credentials within a given professional field; and is there any evidence that those who possess such credentials perform better in their work than those who do not.

Credentials were first invented in the nineteenth century, with an explicit intent of providing the public with a statement of competence about a practitioner. Some professions began to build legal procedures for credentialing immediately. For example, teacher certification was first implemented before 1900 in the United States. Its primary goal at that time was to assure the public that the individual had rudimentary skills in the three R's (reading, writing, and arithmetic); as educational opportunities increased and the number of teachers multiplied, the corresponding need for more certification was addressed by approving programs rather than individuals. Physician certification, in contrast, was being extensively revised early in this century with deliberate emphasis on demonstrable individual abilities. Other professions were slower to acquire licensing regulations; in the United States credentialing of psychologists did not appear until 1945, but has now blossomed into multiple tracks of certification and licensure, with more legal regulations than in any other country.

Two professions, interpreting for the deaf and psychotherapy, provide a study in contrasts. The former demonstrates a highly consistent single-track credentialing process, with explicit performance characteristics mandated by one authority at each step. The latter demonstrates a highly diversified process by which persons with any one of a variety of degrees may pass through one or another of several overlapping certifications administered by several separate authorities. The Registry of Interpreters for the Deaf administers a multistage credentialing program at the national level, which involves a hierarchically constituted program of professional sanction. The Comprehensive Skills Certificate is awarded to an individual who successfully undergoes a multiple-part examination with a panel of five members. The exam involves an interview, which to a large extent focuses on ethical issues, and at least three demonstrations of the interpreter's skill. Each skill area constitutes a recognized speciality within interpretation for the deaf, including (a) the interpretation of English to American Sign Language and the reverse, (b) the transliteration of spoken English to manually coded English, and (c) the voicing of English from sign. Interestingly, successful performances in (b) and (c) earn a special certificate in transliteration alone, and in (a) and (c) a special certificate in interpreting alone. Beyond this comprehensive credential is a certificate at the master's degree level, and in addition to the comprehensive credential is a skills certificate which sanctions the individual in the use of interpreting in court. Under study at present is another speciality certification, this in the use of interpreting in mental health. An obvious reason for the success of this registry is its direct evaluation of performance at the individual level, not the least because such performance, when satisfactory, can be appraised objectively. More subtle explanations for its viability rest with the relative singleness of purpose, lack of competition for the service with persons from other disciplines, and unambiguous, ongoing impact on a moment-by-moment basis with clients. Following the passage of national legislation governing equal access to educational opportunities, an upsurge of pride and political strength on the part of the deaf community, and increased recognition of their unique needs by the hearing public, the trend has been to increase, wherever possible, the number of qualified interpreters.

The profession of psychotherapy presents an entirely different set of circumstances. More than 150 laws govern the actions of persons who choose to practice psychotherapy in the United States. Each state has enacted licensing regulations, many of which differ in significant ways from state to state. During the past several years, a number have entertained "sunsetting" legislation, a political economizing through reductions in government workforce and elimination of agencies; by this means large numbers of regulations in force can be totally or partially rescinded. In many cases the state psychological association memberships on the whole opposed such efforts. However, sunsetting legislation actually was instigated by the association in at least one state, following flagrant abuses by the statutory licensing board of its powers to grant exceptions to certification prerequisites.

Considerable argument exists regarding the number of routes of access to certification in psychotherapy, since more than three dozen educational programs at the undergraduate or graduate level attempt to train persons in one or more aspects of the profession, broadly defined. The American Psychological Association has played a strong advocacy role first for the drafting of appropriate enabling legislation for certification, and later for strengthening and clarifying existing systems of regulation at the state level. The American Psychiatric Association was in opposition to these efforts for many years, claiming that the practice of therapy was either the sole province of those with medical training, or that such practice must be carried out only under the direct supervision of a physician. Meanwhile, training programs developed in related areas using titles like counseling psychology, pastoral counseling, mental health technician, alcoholism and drug counseling, marriage and family counseling, recreational therapy, guidance counseling, school counseling, and psychoanalysis. There continue to be moderate overlaps as well with the fields of medicine, rehabilitation, nursing, and psychometry, to name a few. Each of these titles is defined and overseen by different professional organizations. Distinctions blur between aspects of the separate professions as they relate to the delivery of direct services in psychotherapy. Many statutes mention psychotherapy only in the vaguest of terms, and to some degree the present condition of certification in psychotherapy has been defined instead by legal processes.

Without stretching the point, a single individual could reasonably step through five separate jurisdictions for certification as a psychotherapist. The least restrictive is the position of "psychological assistant," a title reserved for persons registered with the state working under the direct supervision of someone appropriately certified. In many states the title is available to those with bachelor's degrees. With a master's degree and supervised experience, another credential given by many states is that of marriage and family counselor. A third credential is that of psychologist, intended to certify (generally) doctoral level practitioners who possess appropriate training and internship experience and pass a written exam. Recent collaboration among the various states has resulted in the adoption of a nationwide examination, which covers material in a variety of topics relevant to all phases of psychology. A subsequent oral exam is generally intended to touch more specifically on the training and career intentions of the applicant. A fourth certification is by the American Board of Professional Psychology, and a fifth is by various psychoanalytic institutes. The American Board of Professional Psychology exam consists of direct observation by a team of examiners of the applicant in a session with a client, a critical review of a transcript or related work sample, and additional questions about psychological ethics and theory. It is interesting that only these last two certifications involve direct observation of the applicant at work.

Durlak (1979) reported that in 42 separate studies which compared credentialed psychologists to nonprofessionals, all but two pointed to a lack of advantage in performance of the former over the latter. Hogan (1979), in a massive study of regulations governing the work of psychotherapists, draws a distinction between "friendly" and "unfriendly" licensing laws. The first are the result of actions initiated by the organization most directly related to the profession, while the second are usually the outgrowth of vociferous territorial battles between opposing organizations. Additionally, there are certificates which imply no more than minimum competency or the absence of reasons to withhold certification, while others imply maximal competency and achievement in the particular field. He concludes that licensing legislation has been

> . . . a significant factor in (a) unnecessarily restricting the supply of practitioners; (b) decreasing their geographic mobility; (c) inflating the cost of services; (d) making it difficult for paraprofessionals to perform effectively; (e) stifling innovation in the education and training of practitioners and in the organization and utilization of services; and (f) discriminating against minorities, women, and the poor. In addition, licensing laws, as currently conceived, tend to promote unnecessary and harmful consumer dependence, since their implicit philosophy is that the public is incapable of making use of information to decide on practitioner competence. (Vol. 1, p. 239)

Hogan goes on to state that the introduction of licensing laws in specific reference to psychotherapy has not made any significant impact on the quality of psychotherapy services. Single cases requiring disciplinary action by the state licensing authority have been known to drain all of the authority's available funds, thus immobilizing effective monitoring.

At present a substantial amount of activity is underway in terms of the credentialing and licensing of health and health-related occupations, and there are a handful of studies each year which examine the relationship between training, credential obtained, and subsequent performance in occupations such as nursing. In employment unrelated to health, the number of research efforts has been painfully small. In reference to the field of education, for example, Pottinger (1976) pointed out that virtually no research work had been conducted, not least because of the extraordinary difficulty of assessing all the variables relevant to the role of teacher. A recent study of nonprofessional and clerical workers conducted in India (Parmaji 1979) found job efficiency to rise with level of credentials, but job satisfaction to decline. Many of the remaining efforts are broad-based speculations about agenda for future improvements in professional education (Kinney 1964); however, more recent authors give the problem of individual credentials far less importance than curricular development and accreditation of programs (Nyre and Reilly 1979).

## Bibliography

Dore R 1976 *The Diploma Disease: Education, Qualification and Development.* Allen and Unwin, London

Durlak J A 1979 Comparative effectiveness of paraprofessional and professional helpers. *Psychol. Bull.* 79: 80–92

Hogan D B 1979 *The Regulation of Psychotherapists, 1: A Study in the Philosophy and Practice of Professional Regulation.* Ballinger, Cambridge, Massachusetts

Kinney L B 1964 *Certification in Education.* Prentice-Hall, Englewood Cliffs, New Jersey

National Commission for Health Certifying Agencies 1979 *Perspectives on Health Occupational Credentialing.* United States Department of Health and Human Services, Washington, DC

Nyre G F, Reilly K C 1979 *Professional Education in the Eighties: Challenges and Responses.* AAHE-ERIC/Higher Education Research Report No. 8. Washington, DC

Parmaji S 1979 *Education and Jobs.* Leeladevi, Delhi

Pottinger P 1976 Techniques and criteria for designing and selecting instruments for assessing teachers. In: Levitov B (ed.) 1976 *Licensing and Credentialing in Education: The Law and the State Interest.* Study Commission on Undergraduate Education and the Education of Teachers, Washington, DC

Washburn G 1980 The relationship of achievement test scores and state board performance in a diploma nursing program. ERIC Document No. ED 203 752

# Interviews for Selection

## G. Trost

The selection interview may be defined as a conversation with the purpose of providing information about an applicant which enables the interviewer to decide upon the applicant's admission to a given institution, educational programme, or occupation. In personnel selection around the world, the interview has certainly been used more frequently than any other instrument of assessment. The present review is focused on the issue of interviewing applicants for institutions of higher education. In this context, the typical aims, contents, and types of selection interviews are described, research results on their psychometric qualities in terms of reliability and validity are summarized, and recommendations are given concerning the most efficient use of this instrument.

## 1. Use of Interviews for Admission to Higher Education

In many industrialized countries, the interview has its place as an instrument of selection for admission to institutions of higher education. In the more selective universities of the United States, the final decision upon the admission of graduate students is based on interviews with faculty members or alumni. Virtually all American medical schools use interviews for the selection of their students. Usually the interview is not the only assessment device in the selection procedure but goes with an evaluation of the applicants' academic records and results in aptitude or achievement tests. In the United Kingdom most of the applicants for university studies go through an interview. In the German Democratic Republic every applicant has to pass an interview with a commission of three faculty members. Interviews are part of the admission procedures in certain universities of Australia, Canada, Ireland, Japan, and Spain. In France and in the Soviet Union the entrance interview has the character of an oral examination. In the Federal Republic of Germany the interview has great importance with regard to selection for scholarships, though in the early 1980s it was not used as an instrument of selection for admission to higher education.

Interviews vary in type, duration, in the extent to which they are structured, and in the kind of evaluation of their outcome. The most frequently used types of interviews are (a) the individual interview in which one interviewer meets one applicant at a time; (b) the board interview where several interviewers meet one candidate at the same time; (c) the group interview conducted by one interviewer with several applicants at a time. The duration of selection interviews in higher education usually ranges from 15 minutes to one hour; the average duration appears to be 30 minutes.

In terms of their structure, the interviews can be categorized as completely structureless, free-flowing conversations; as "semistructured" interviews following a guideline which makes sure that all important topics are covered; and as highly structured interviews with preformulated questions. The possibilities for evaluating the result of an interview vary from a simple pass–fail rating to scaled or verbalized overall judgments or judgments about specific traits of the applicants.

## 2. Content and Aims of Interviews

Typically, the interviewers' questions tap the following areas: biographical background, experience with school and learning, extracurricular interests and activities, career plans, and motives for these plans. However, by asking these questions, the interviewers aim at finding out far more about the applicants, for instance, about their mental abilities, flexibility of mind, maturity of judgment, oral communication skills, ability to cope with problems, self-confidence and self-appraisal ability, skills in social interaction, attitudes to academic and professional work, task commitment, and ethical values in general. For many of the attributes mentioned, it is highly questionable whether, in a selection situation, they can be detected at all because they can be easily faked. But even if it is assumed that some of these traits can reasonably be assessed by an interview, it is necessary to consider whether they cannot be examined in a more reliable, valid, and efficient way by aptitude tests, biographical and interest questionnaires, or even leaderless group discussions.

Assessment, though, is not the only purpose of the selection interview. It is also used as "public-relations device" (Ulrich and Trumbo 1965 p. 114) intended to pay the applicants personal attention by going into their individual situation and to tell them informally about the institution's particular characteristics. Clearly, this can best be done in the face-to-face confrontation.

## 3. Reliability and Validity of the Interview

The interview as a selection device has to be evaluated primarily in the light of those criteria which have traditionally been used to judge the quality of any instrument for educational assessment or prediction. These are the criteria of reliability and validity. In addition, there are some non-scientific criteria such as the relation of costs and benefits and the acceptance of the instrument by the candidates and the public which must be taken into account.

The reliability of the interview, that is, its accuracy and consistency as an assessment device, can be defined and measured in two ways: as the stability of the interviewers' ratings when reinterviewing the same candidates (intrarater reliability), and as the agreement of the judgments of two or more interviewers independently evaluating the same candidates (interrater reliability).

Very little effort has been invested in determining the intrarater reliability so that there is no sound basis for an appraisal of this aspect. However, a fair amount of research has been carried out to inquire into interrater reliability. Prevailing evidence indicates that the reliability of the selection interview in terms of the correspondence of ratings given by several interviewers on the same applicant is at best moderate and certainly lower than what is usually required of instruments for assessment and prediction.

In the relevant literature hints can be found as to the reasons for the very limited reliability. The outcome of an interview seems to depend upon:

(a) individual characteristics of the interviewer, such as his or her leniency or severity, verbal and nonverbal behaviour, attitudes, values, and interests, as well as the extent of training and experience in interviewing;

(b) irrelevant traits on the part of the interviewee, such as outward appearance;

(c) peculiarities of the particular interview situation, such as the "rapport" between candidate and interviewer, the course and outcome of preceding interviews (contrast effects), the amount and quality of the interviewer's information on the candidate before the interview, and the sequence in which the interviewer obtains information about the candidate during the interview.

Selection interviews tend to be more reliable (and probably more valid) if the interviews are structured; if the criteria for the ratings are precisely stipulated; if the judgments are made by means of a set of defined categories or scales; if the interviewers are carefully selected and trained; if more than a single interviewer is involved; and if each interviewer meets a reasonably large sample of applicants. However, by its very nature, the interview will never reach the same reliability as a standardized test—if it is not to be merely a preformulated question-and-answer game that can be easily replaced by a questionnaire.

The validity of the selection interview, defined as the relation of the interview result with subsequent performance in higher education or as the interview's "predictive power", is controversial. Research results differ widely—not surprisingly in view of the variety of aims, contents, and techniques of the interviews used in the respective studies. In most cases it is not clear whether the rating was based solely on the observations made during the interview or whether the interviewer's knowledge of the candidate's previously earned marks and test scores was taken into account as well.

The majority of the findings suggest that the selection interview is of little predictive value; if it is added to other selection instruments, the gain in predictive power is small. It is true that, in following up only those applicants who have been admitted as a result of their high scores in the selection programme, the validity of the selection device is generally underestimated because the (presumably poor) academic achievement of those who performed poorly in the predictor cannot be observed. But even then school marks and test scores consistently prove to be better predictors than interview ratings.

## 4. Conclusions

Nothing that can be measured by a good test should be left to the interview. Yet there are relevant traits, especially in the domain of interpersonal skills, which can better be judged in a face-to-face situation than by paper-and-pencil techniques. Consequently, the interview ratings should be based only on those observations which can directly be made during the interview. Moreover, the interview is the appropriate instrument if the institution selecting the applicants sets value on giving the procedure a personal touch and on facilitating two-way communication. But even then, because of the interview's limited validity and high costs, it should be reserved for those candidates who already have been preselected by other measures.

The interview should be structured. A questionnaire providing all factual information on the applicant can serve as a guideline and enable the interviewer to inquire into the "why" and "how" as well as to check for inconsistencies. The interview ratings should be made using fixed criteria and in a structured form. Used in this way, the interview may certainly not assess "the whole person", but it may serve as a useful complement to other, more anonymous selection instruments.

## Bibliography

Mayfield E C 1964 The selection interview: A re-evaluation of published research. *Pers. Psychol.* 17: 239–60

Moffatt G W 1969 The selection interview: A review. *Pers. Pract. Bull.* 25: 15–23

Triebe J K 1976 *Das Interview im Kontext der Eignungsdiagnostik: Eine Problemanalyse aufgrund der neueren Literatur.* Huber, Bern

Trost G 1979 Research in the Federal Republic of Germany with regard to interviews for admission to higher education. In: Mitter W (ed.) 1979 *The Use of Tests and Interviews for Admission to Higher Education.* National Foundation for Educational Research, Slough

Ulrich L, Trumbo D 1965 The selection interview since 1949. *Psychol. Bull.* 63: 100–16

Wagner R 1949 The employment interview: A critical summary. *Pers. Psychol.* 2: 17–46

Walden T 1979 The graduate admission interview: Benefits and costs. *Coll. Univ.* 55: 50–59

Wright O R 1969 Summary of research on the selection interview since 1964. *Pers. Psychol.* 22: 391–413

# Educational Profiles

**L. Kant and L. Orr**

Profiles are a means of recording the outcomes of education in the form of a comprehensive statement referring to the range of a pupil's educational experience, competencies, and interests. In the United Kingdom, the subject of profile reporting has generated considerable educational and political interest and aroused widespread debate. Although profile schemes are used in some states of the United States, in Australia, and within some European countries as a result of European Economic Community (EEC) educational initiative, this article pays particular attention to profile developments within England and Wales. These countries share a devolved educational structure, a public examination system, and in both there are a number of profile schemes in operation.

Interest in extending such local initiatives into a standardized national profile system has been expressed by British politicians and educationists. In the early 1980s it appeared probable that a common profile scheme would be introduced into Northern Ireland secondary schools and that such a move would be likely to have implications for schools in England and Wales. In Scotland, where the education system is subject to greater central direction than in England and Wales, experiments with pupil profiles have had a chequered history.

In 1973, the Headteachers Association of Scotland decided "to consider the manner and range of assessments in secondary schools that might result in a form of report or certificate applicable to all pupils completing S4"—the final year of compulsory education in Scotland (SCRE 1977). The resulting report scheme records teacher assessments of the skills of listening, speaking, reading, writing, visual understanding and expression, use of number, physical coordination and manual dexterity, and personal qualities, enterprise, and perseverance. Assessment is on a four-point scale and each point represents approximately 25 percent of the year group within a school. There is also a section for "other observations" which includes details of "school activities, other awards, and comments on positive personal qualities". This scheme has been much discussed but even in Scotland was not widely adopted in the original form; many schools which participated in the pilot scheme have since dropped out. This was partly because the operation proved very time consuming and partly because of the difficulties of recording in cross-curricular areas in an education system where subject-based teaching is the rule. In the early 1980s, probably only half a dozen Scottish schools remained actively involved in profile reporting.

## 1. Aspects of Educational Practice in England and Wales

In England and Wales, profile initiatives have tended to occur as a result of teacher dissatisfaction with current systems of providing information about school leavers. In order to comment on these it will be helpful to describe relevant features of the English and Welsh educational systems. Education is compulsory up to 16 years of age. In the public sector, secondary education—from the age of 11 years—is provided in a range of educational institutions, according to the policies of a particular local education authority of which there are 104 in England and Wales. The majority of schools are comprehensive—catering for the full ability range—but some 10 percent of schools still select according to ability. A majority of pupils leave school at the age of 16 though some of these continue with their education at colleges through full-time or part-time study.

The documentary evidence most 16-year-olds have to show as a result of five years of secondary education is a public examination certificate and five years of school reports intended mainly for parents. School leavers also have the opportunity to ask their school for a testimonial or reference. The information provided by these documents is regarded by some as insufficient for placement in employment or further education. The results of public examinations are not available at the time when most job placements are made and school reports are not intended to be used in this way, being provided primarily for parents and pupils. School testimonials and references tend to be the prerogative of a few senior teachers who may not be familiar with the achievement of a particular pupil and they may be compiled without sufficient reference to detailed records. Some employers who have found that examination results and testimonials or references do not give them all the information that they need have created proformas which schools are asked to complete. This can prove onerous for school staff when several different forms need to be filled in for one pupil.

In any case, examination grades provide only a limited picture of a particular student's academic ability. Some employers have suggested that they would prefer to have guarantees of pupils' competence in basic skills and information on those personal attributes they see pertinent to employment, such as perseverance, initiative, and the ability to relate to other people. Examination results do not provide such information and the ad hoc nature of references and testimonials is unlikely to produce any consistency in terms of content or judgment across the pupil range.

## 2. The Rationale for Profiles

Profile reports are seen by some people as a means of solving most of these educational concerns. It is argued that they may be a means of offsetting many of the constraints imposed on schools by the public examination system; this method of accreditation offers a means of directing attention towards those areas such as social learning which the examination system fails to foster. The opportunity for more extensive recording of intellectual and cognitive qualities can also be enlarged. In the school inspectors' secondary survey (Department of Education and Science 1979) it was stated that "schools should promote valuable personal and intellectual qualities such as curiosity, the ability to express views orally, the capacity to work as a member of a team and to work independently". It may be claimed

that examination study and many individual examination syllabi do not preclude such worthy objectives. Nevertheless few teachers believe the public examination system fosters such developments and the grading schemes do not allow for detailed recording or certification. Even in subjects where a discrete body of practical skills and abilities is defined, such as craft subjects, sciences, and languages, these distinct components are not isolated for the purpose of grading and certification. In practice, schools which operate profile schemes have introduced them to supplement the examinations system; examination entries and results are frequently recorded in addition to a spectrum of other information and thus public examinations can be viewed in the context of the pupils' wider achievements.

Pupils whose achievements tend to be ignored or go unnoticed at present, are likely to be more motivated by an educational process and system of recording which allows their individual strengths to be recognized. This group traditionally contains pupils who are disenchanted and disaffected by the schooling process; these pupils form the bulk of early school leavers and the school inspectors' secondary survey suggests that schools in general have failed to provide these pupils with a suitable curriculum which they perceive as relevant to their anticipated needs. They leave school without accreditation and not unreasonably feel this diminishes their achievements both in their eyes and those of potential employers.

Schools are anxious to facilitate their leaving pupils' placement in suitable employment. Records of pupils' qualities, abilities, and achievements, especially in those areas which employers appear to esteem such as personal and social skills, competence in basic skills and practical areas, offer a basis for preliminary introductions and interviews. Employers, particularly those who are based in the school locale and who are likely to recruit on a small-scale but regular basis, have indicated that such information offers greater likelihood of satisfactory recruitment than examination results which are viewed with a mixture of bewilderment and derision. The inability of the examination system to offer any guarantee of competence in a particular area is apparently its major drawback. There is little doubt that the increasingly stringent employment market has been a powerful inducement for schools to expend considerable attention on mechanisms through which pupils' employability is enhanced. Conversely employers argue that it behoves them to select the most deserving candidates. Profile reports appear to meet both these criteria.

## 3. Profile Schemes in Operation

The variety of rationales for profiles combined with a lack of consensus over terminology and content coverage suggests that there is not likely to be agreement over what constitutes a profile report. In practice, profiles go under a variety of pseudonyms which range from "personal achievement record" and "record of personal experience" to "school leaving certificate" and "open testimonial". Because of this diversity of interpretation it may be helpful to describe two differing schemes.

### 3.1 Record of Personal Achievement (RPA), Record of Personal Experience (RPE)

The RPE is an offshoot of RPA and both schemes have sufficient in common to be described together. Pupils record in their own file their individual curriculum vitae of the last two years of compulsory schooling. The intention is that through this recording they will develop personally and also reveal qualities, attitudes, and values through describing their school and leisure pursuits. All the records are pupil compiled and the entries decided by the pupil; the schemes are seen as procedures rather than courses and formal assessment plays no part in the process. In theory, the scheme is open to all pupils; in practice it is employed mainly for nonexamination candidates. It was anticipated that the record would provide a useful instrument for mediation between prospective employer and employee. However, an evaluation of RPA suggested that employers gave it scant consideration. It also pointed out that few employers were agreed about the qualities they deemed necessary in their employees. The evaluator suggests that such a record is unlikely to be valued as a qualification unless there is some reconciliation of pupils' aspirations with society's needs. The scheme "had not fulfilled its potential as a leaving qualification for the majority of pupils involved" (Swales 1979).

### 3.2 Evesham School: Personal Achievement Record (PAR)

The idea of pupil recording and self-evaluation has been incorporated into other profile reports. Evesham School's scheme, which has been seminal, includes a section on personal interests and out-of school activities which the pupil compiles. The Evesham record entries also include details of courses followed, results of attainment tests and examinations, and a comprehensive breakdown of a number of specific skills and competencies which are grouped under the headings of language skills, mathematics skills, practical and social skills. Validation and recording of competence in the requisite item is precipitated by pupil request to a relevant teacher; the teacher's role is to authenticate. Pupil participation in the scheme is optional and pupils have responsibility for their own profile. Few pupils opt out. The items included imply a mastery assessment model although there is some evidence that normative judgments may be applied in practice. The skills included are an eclectic selection and within an area—for example language—are not related in any hierarchical order. Employers were consulted in the course of the scheme's development and have contributed to the printing costs. The influence of the Evesham model can be detected in many other schemes.

The general expectation of profiles appears to rest on a model which includes some final assessment with a structured reporting format and some consistent school approach to recording. There is probably less agreement on whether the final report is exclusively the responsibility of the pupil and whether the profile report should be available to all pupils in the full ability range. However, the first three criteria if applied rigorously would rule out the RPA and RPE schemes and many open testimonials. Such a definition identified approximately 40 profile report schemes in England and Wales in a recent survey (Balogh 1982).

## 4. Concerns over Profile Reports

### 4.1 Purpose

A major problem is a lack of consensus on the purpose of such a record. Many schools perceive the value of a diagnostic instrument: a record which can offer useful feedback to the student and teacher, allowing the identification of strengths and weaknesses, and providing an opportunity for explicit guidance and an appropriate shift in teaching and learning strategies. Employers and institutions which receive students may recognize and support the value of these objectives. They also see a need for a document which provides a final valid assessment of a pupil's abilities, skills, and competencies which is also comparable and reliable. This suggests a summative document which would present a snapshot of achievement at 16+ and would require summative judgments in the academic, personal, and social domains. Such approaches are not likely to prove compatible within the same document and each offers a range of advantages and disadvantages depending on viewpoint and need. Disadvantages are likely to dominate if one document attempts to carry out both functions. If the purpose of profile reports is to supplement public examination results, more detailed information on those aspects of a pupil's performance which are not readily measured by traditional examining methods would need to be included. Basic literacy and numeracy skills, practical skills such as using a telephone or ability to type, cross-curricular skills such as listening and talking, personal and social qualities such as punctuality, perseverance, interests, and out-of-school activities are candidates for inclusion.

### 4.2 Interaction with Curriculum

A profile report which fails to reflect the taught curriculum or an individual child's learning experience may prove a punitive rather than stimulating instrument; the opportunity may not be provided for pupils to demonstrate their capacity in particular areas. It is possible that the introduction of profile reports would encourage schools to discuss their curricula so that these inconsistencies would not arise but this has so far not been evident. Additionally, there are areas of the school curriculum where attempts to reconcile specification of teaching objectives with assessment objectives are particularly difficult; where conceptual understanding or complex abilities such as reasoning, interpretation, abstraction, and synthesis are involved it is not only difficult to state clearcut objectives but also to specify in advance what level of performances would enable the validation to be met. This suggests that the curriculum objectives would either have to be set at a fairly low level which many teachers might feel would undermine the schools' broader educational objectives, or if set at a higher level could pose considerable assessment problems. Certainly the specification of a range of basic skills in, say, numeracy and literacy could be accomplished, but the end result may be viewed as narrow and rigid and reflecting a functionalist approach to education.

### 4.3 Pupil Alienation

Profile reports could prove punitive for low achievers or pupils with behaviour problems. There are cases of pupils who dislike school and so truant or behave badly but who become exemplary employees. The profile target group is contentious in a wider sense. Most schools have designed their profile systems with the nonacademic in mind and job placement rather than educational development is seen as a priority. Occasionally schools make their scheme voluntary and it is interesting to note that at one school where pupils can opt out of the scheme, those who have done so comprise the most academically able and the least able. This suggests that the former perceive the scheme as irrelevant to their particular needs (which they see as 16+ examination success to be followed by academic study). The latter view the scheme as a mechanism by which the school continues to categorize and homogenize its pupils.

### 4.4 Ethics

The ethics of making judgments about a pupil's character or qualities is a frequently expressed concern. It is accepted that teachers are frequently put into positions where they are expected to make judgments about a pupil's character or personal skills; these judgments are generally the staple of references, testimonials, and school reports and teachers have rarely been chary of committing such conclusions to paper. However, it is argued that a move towards profile reports would result in the present arbitrary system being superseded by a formalized system carrying with it the associated cachet of objectivity.

### 4.5 Time: Teachers

A further problem is the time needed to complete profile reports, especially if they are introduced to all pupils. Not all teachers appear to be happy to perform the clerical tasks associated with producing a profile report.

### 4.6 Time: Employers

Although some employers and the Confederation of British Industry (CBI) have welcomed profile devel-

opments, there has been no real evaluation of their use by employers. There may well be some contradiction in what employers say they prefer and what they do in practice. Other studies suggest employers favour information in an accessible and condensed format. A comprehensive profile system may fail to be sufficiently brief to encourage an employer to read, digest, and act upon it. Employers faced with wide-scale selection might prefer to make use of a system which takes on board a preliminary sifting: ironically, the public examination system with its emphasis on ranking does this. It would take a dedicated employer to wade through the contents of a profile scheme which lists a pupil's educational outcomes and positive achievements in order to match the employment needs with an individual profile record.

## 5. Assessment Methods

It is not always easy to assess language skills such as "can read and understand an article in a popular newspaper", but it is even more difficult to reach a decision on the social and personal qualities which appear in many profile reports and which employers are anxious to have included. Schools use a number of different methods of assessment in their profile reports: some have adopted a norm-referenced five-point scale or a four-point scale linked to criteria. Many lay claim to a criterion-referenced system; schools which have adopted an "Evesham" model state that they are employing mastery-based assessment.

### 5.1 Normative Judgments

Much of the opprobrium levelled at normative assessment derives from the association of norm referencing (with its intent to discriminate between candidates) and the concepts of failure and success usually linked with this discrimination. It is argued that criterion referencing enables candidates to show what they can do—though the concept of pass/fail is itself an integral aspect of such a technique. It is held that users would prefer to have a clear statement of what applicants have achieved in examinations than to know that they have obtained, for example, a Certificate of Secondary Education (CSE) grade 4, with its normative definition with which they are unlikely to be familiar.

### 5.2 Criterion Referencing

A positive statement of a pupil's ability in a particular subject area would appear to be desirable. For example, for English a statement such as "this pupil has shown himself/herself capable of handling simple written sentence structures, is able to read at a literal level material such as a contemporary novel and a popular newspaper, can follow straightforward verbal and written instructions, can write a simple narrative in the first person, and can express himself/herself orally in direct language" would be helpful to the pupils and say more about their capacity in English than an examination grade.

Agreement on competence in meeting these criteria may not prove too difficult. However, if the ability to read, understand, and interpret a modern novel becomes a criterion, at what point is that competence reached? This suggests that the assessment is likely to be normative—that is, influenced by an apprehension of what most pupils can do.

### 5.3 Teacher Judgments

Teacher assessment seems particularly inappropriate for personal and social qualities such as "helpfulness", and "reliability", let alone "relationships with others" or "cleanliness" and "health". These qualities hardly lend themselves to a definition of absolute criteria. The questions underlining the desirability of including such qualities are only matched by questions regarding the feasibility of assessing such qualities. Who assesses and how consistency is maintained are also important. Many employers seem happy for teachers to assess affective qualities but no training exists. Ingenkamp (1977) says,

> We have a disquieting situation in which teachers make their judgements like amateurs in the field of those objectives (the social non-cognitive) which are often regarded as the most important and are subject to all those prejudices, stereo-types, distortions, etc., to which all people are exposed when they have only their common sense to rely on.

A fairly commonly offered remedy to this problem is to ask a number of staff to make the judgment on the pupil and then aggregate their opinions. This might result in a degree of consistency within a school but it seems unlikely that the resulting profiles would bear much resemblance to the pupil.

### 5.4 Testing

Evidence from a number of schools which operate a profile scheme suggests that an increasing number of tests are employed in order to relate the students' performance, particularly in numeracy and literacy, to an explicit profile criterion. However, testing on a large scale may in practice prove as much a constraint on the curriculum as the examinations that profiles are designed to replace.

### 5.5 Comparability

The question of comparability, which is a constant in the public examination arena, would be a major concern if profiles were introduced on a national scale. At present, profile reports have no national currency; their present take-up is at a local level and most schools have indicated their belief that this individual and localized character is their particular strength. A movement towards a national public scheme—particularly one in which profiles are viewed as an alternative to public examinations—would raise all the problems of comparability, reliability, and standards with which the English and Welsh examination system is consumed in addition to the ethical and other concerns raised above.

### Bibliography

Balogh J 1982 *Profile Reports for School Leavers*. Schools Council Programme 5 Pamphlet. Longman, London

Burgess T, Adams B 1980 *Outcomes of Education*. Macmillan, London

Department of Education and Science 1979 *Aspects of Secondary Education in England: A Survey by HM Inspectors of Schools*. Her Majesty's Stationery Office, London

Duffy M N 1980 A logbook of personal achievement. *Education 5*: 119–20

Goacher B 1983 *Recording Achievement at 16+*. Schools Council Programme 5 pamphlet. Longman, London

Ingenkamp K 1977 *Educational Assessment*. National Foundation for Educational Research, Slough

Raven J C 1979 *Education, Values and Society: The Objectives of Education and the Nature and Development of Competence*. Lewis, London

Scottish Council for Research in Education (SCRE) 1977 *Pupils in Profile: Making the Most of Teachers' Knowledge of Pupils*. Hodder and Stoughton, London

Stansbury D 1975 *Record of Personal Experience, Qualities and Qualifications: Handbook*. RPE Publications, South Brent, Devon

Stanton G 1982 Profiling and profile reporting. *Coombe Lodge Reports* 14(13)

Swales T 1979 *Record of Personal Achievement: An Independent Evaluation of the Swindon RPA Scheme*. Pamphlet 16. Schools Council, London

# School Records and Reports

**B. J. Goacher**

School records and reports constitute almost universally the formal documented endpoints of the assessment of an individual in school. Together they form the major visible aspect of the whole assessment process. A school record can be defined as a collection of information about an individual which may be used as evidence to arrive at decisions concerning that individual. As such the record may be updated in response to changes in circumstances, performance, or behaviour. A school report essentially contains judgments about an individual although the evidence upon which these judgments have been based may be included. Once completed, the report is not open to alteration. Thus, although both documents carry information it is of a different order and it is intended for a different audience.

Access to school records has frequently been limited to fellow professionals although summaries of content were made available to, for example, doctors, psychologists, and employers. This position has changed in the United States, Canada, and most European countries where parental rights to access to such records have been the subject of legislation. Parents form the main audience for school reports. Specialist leaver reports or profiles for employers have been developed in a number of industrialized countries.

In practice records and reports are by no means as mutually exclusive as would at first appear and there is a considerable confusion about their content and purpose on the part of both teachers and members of the general public.

## 1. School Records

The prime intention in production of a school record is administrative, to provide information for use within the educational system. The information is available to help solve individual problems, that is, to be used as a diagnostic tool within the school, and to help solve institutional problems such as the selection of appropriate courses or schools, and the preparation of reports and testimonials.

A common document for this purpose is therefore often provided at either national or at regional administrative level although such records are frequently supplemented by individual schools. Many are produced in the form of a folder to facilitate the inclusion of additional material such as copies of school reports, letters from parents, and specimens of work.

School records may contain information of two essentially different kinds, cumulative information and informal or anecdotal information and both normally appear on most records.

The cumulative record consists of evidence which may be classified under a number of headings. Typically these include:

(a) basic identification data, for example, name, sex, address, and date of birth;

(b) health, for example general health, recorded illness, physical handicap, the results of auditory and visual testing;

(c) family background, for example parents, parental occupation and attitude to school, siblings, religion;

(d) educational background, for example schools attended, outline curricula, test, examination, and other achievement ratings, ratings of general ability, standardized test scores, special aptitudes and school achievements;

(e) personal and social development, for example attitudes to teachers and peers, personality traits, and any psychological test scores;

(f) vocational information is usually added to the record over the last years of compulsory schooling.

The anecdotal record consists of descriptions and frequently, in practice, of interpretations of classroom and school incidents involving the individual.

The boundary between the cumulative and the anecdotal aspects is often blurred since certain areas of the cumulative record may become dominated by subjective opinion rather than objective fact. Information in areas such as parental involvement in school, home background, and personal and social development is particularly open to value-laden and judgmental recording. Descriptions of events and particularly the interpretation of events is inevitably subject to all the pressures of partial recall and value positions, and even where these can be minimized semantic difficulties can lead to misunderstanding and to prejudicial outcomes.

Because records seek to "capture" the whole individual they necessarily resort to a summative approach in order to reduce the quantity of information which they contain. Such an approach carries with it the risk of subsuming within single grades or scores wide individual differences of performance, sometimes adding incompatible data, sometimes hiding important individual variation. A further problem has been that, as with many routine activities, errors may be built into the record at any stage and inaccurate information be subsequently transferred.

Two trends have exacerbated these inherent problems, the increasing value placed upon personal and social development in many industralized societies and the development of computerized information storage and recall systems in those same societies. While an increasing emphasis upon individual personality and social performance can be defended on psychosocial and educational grounds it has led to a proliferation of personality trait rating scales which appear to offer objective assessments of behaviour which few professional psychologists would feel able to substantiate. An example would be the grading of an individual over a number of behavioural dimensions such as cooperativeness or sociability using an A–E five-point scale. The introduction of computers has made possible the transfer of such school-gathered information to a centrally stored lifelong cumulative record.

The present use made of school records is extremely variable. In the United States, for example, the record is the fundamental focus of the whole individual guidance system both within and between institutions. Extensive use gives rise to clearly articulated statements of the uses of school records such as can be found in the New York State (1962) Manual on Pupil Records. This contains 33 uses for records grouped into five main categories. Decentralized systems such as that found in England and Wales, although often providing common documentation at the regional administrative level, give rise to infrequent use of the record within school, in some schools access to records is even limited to specific staff within the institution, and minimal use to aid selection or transfer (Goacher and Reid 1983). Even where considerable research and development is undertaken to bring about a uniform approach to school records many teachers may remain unclear of their purpose and make minimal use of them (Humphreys and Elwood 1976).

School records have been the subject of much public debate since the early 1970s culminating in various national movements towards providing a more open record system. This has now been achieved and is the subject of legislation in most technological societies. The position regarding school records in the United Kingdom remains an ambiguous one since the confidentiality of school records is upheld while the prevailing European Economic Community regulations provide for an open access to school records for parents and students over the age of 18. Debate continues concerning the individual right to privacy in the face of computer storage and retrieval systems although this has also been the subject of legislation notably in the United States.

A number of principles can be identified which offer guidelines for the completion and use of the school record. These include:

(a) the record should have a unity and not be a random collection of material;

(b) it should be easy to understand and include guidance for its use;

(c) it should be easy to complete and update;

(d) it should contain factual, useful information and be free of speculation;

(e) it should be accessible and open to inspection while providing individual privacy;

(f) those completing the record should be offered training in the skills of observing, assessing, and recording.

## 2. School Reports

Despite considerable changes in pedagogy and a widespread reevaluation of the role of parents in the educational process, the school report remains the most commonly used method of communication between school and home. Although reports frequently provide only information concerned with the school performance of an individual they are sometimes the only point of home–school contact.

Such widespread usage does little to assist in the identification of a clear and unambiguous definition since there are wide variations in the frequency, the content, the format, and the underlying intention of school reports. For example, while in many cases the report is primarily concerned with individual school performance, it may contain other information such as the skills and knowledge contained within the curriculum, the school structure, and classroom process. Reporting may also be conducted through a face-to-face interview. While such a discussion is commonly used to supplement a written report it is occasionally the only reporting technique in use.

Even within the confines of written reports there are a number of alternative approaches in common use. Almost all written reports include graded information most commonly in the form of achievement grades within different areas of the curriculum. A five-point scale (A–E, 1–5) is most commonly used. While some written reports consist of little else (grade cards) in others this approach is supplemented with a descriptive account. In a few cases the report specifically excludes grades (e.g. the standardized report in use in Italy).

Attempting to provide an overview of reporting practice is made still more difficult by the presence of national and regional standard forms of reporting.

While a number of countries and regions do produce a standardized report, often varying this with the age of the pupil, it cannot be assumed that such an approach leads to a uniformity of practice within the schools. Nationally approved report forms appear to be as commonly rejected as they are accepted in some countries (e.g. Denmark and Scotland), while in others they are used almost exclusively (e.g. Italy and Luxembourg). Regionally initiated documents appear to be more regularly adopted by schools (e.g. the Federal Republic of Germany and France) than those introduced nationally. In a few cases, notably in the Federal Republic of Germany, standardized reports also carry out a certification function and are used to assist in selection much as school records are used in other contexts (Macbeth 1982).

A range of reporting functions have been identified extending from the presentation of a formal account, much in the same way that a statement might be issued by a bank, through attempts to change (pupil) behaviour, to reports which carry the intention to involve pupils, parents, and teachers in a collaborative effort (Goacher and Reid 1983).

The formal account often results in documents which are bureaucratic in presentation. It can rely upon unexplained grades or symbols and be abrupt and unhelpful. Such reports can be seen as a way of evading accountability. Reports seeking to change behaviour offer more easily understandable information and provide guidance and advice but continue to affirm the role of teacher as expert. Where participation is the fundamental intention reports encourage two-way communication and seek to involve pupils and parents. Some include an element of student self-assessment while more offer parents a right of reply.

The format of written reports often reflects these underlying purposes and those most commonly in use include:

(a) The grade card—traditionally used for routine reporting in the United States the grade card is elsewhere more commonly used to provide brief interim reports. The document seldom contains space for comment and usually consists of a series of boxes for achievement grades.

(b) The criterion-referenced or profile report based upon criteria derived from the curriculum. Both knowledge and skills may be listed and achievement may be recorded by tick boxes or conventional grades. Additional comment is added in some cases.

(c) The single-sheet report—the balance between graded information and descriptive comment is often a very fine one. Some single-sheet reports allow sufficient space for a single word of comment.

(d) The cumulative report—this usually consists of a series of single-sheet reports bound into a book and used over several years. Occasionally criterion-referenced reports may be used for repeated measures in the same way but over a single year.

(e) The slip report—teachers each complete a separate slip of paper which may or may not include graded information. The slips are then stapled together to form a small booklet. Such an approach avoids the possibility of teachers being influenced by each others' judgments.

(f) Two-way diaries—while these may include marks and grades from teachers the major emphasis is upon written information and this is added to the report by parents as well as teachers. This approach is most fully developed in the *Carnet de liaison* used in secondary technical schools in Luxembourg.

The use of computers to assist in the production of school reports has been developed in a number of countries, notably the United States and the Federal Republic of Germany, but its use has frequently been restricted to the production of grades and marks. A system of selecting comments from a computerized comment bank is currently in use in Wales and the report is produced in the form of a computer printout.

The relative merits of comment and grades and the value to be placed upon grades and marks as methods of recording progress have been the subject of much educational debate. The National Educational Association (1970) study of reporting in the United States included an all-out attack upon the use of grades, questioning their validity, reliability, and usefulness for reporting. Little evidence is available to document pupil or parent reactions to school reports. In a study of English and Welsh school reports (Goacher and Reid 1983) it was found that parents and pupils welcomed written comments, particularly those from classroom teachers. While grades were acceptable, ipsative grades where the pupil is assessed in respect of previous performance, were preferred to normative grades, where comparisons were made with other pupils. Both pupils and their parents wanted the report to offer more guidance in the selection of appropriate courses and suitable careers.

The timing and frequency of reports show considerable variation. In many countries there has been a decrease in the number of reports issued annually, although an end-of-year (end-of-course) summative report is still commonly issued. Such a report can have little effect on student performance and its utility to parents is questionable.

At present school reporting practice offers examples of problems at all points in the educational system. At national and regional level the difficulties are largely those of continuity, coordination, and standardization. Within the school the problems are frequently presented as organizational although aspects such as the skill levels of teachers, notably in areas such as descriptive writing, interviewing technique and assessment are of more crucial importance. For teachers the issues are those of acquiring the necessary skills and the workload involved in reporting. Parental problems are those concerned with comprehending and gaining sufficient confidence to approach an often complex institution. The timing of reports remains a major problem for pupils, and they too sometimes have difficulty in understanding the true meaning of the report they receive. To be effective the school report should:

(a) facilitate the conveying of information about individual progress, attitudes, and behaviour;

(b) review past performance, predict future potential, and offer guidance; provide sufficient background information and explanation to allow understanding;

(c) ensure that, where used, grades are fair, intelligible, and useful; lead to an exchange of views between the school and the home and encourage the formation of a partnership between parent, pupil, and teacher.

It may well be that no single approach to reporting can accomplish these ideals and the reporting processes necessary for their achievement have yet to be developed.

## Bibliography

Butler H E, Moran K D, Vanderpool F A 1972 *Legal Aspects of Student Records*. National Organization on Legal Problems of Education, Topeka, Kansas

Clift P, Weiner G, Wilson E 1981 *Record Keeping in Primary Schools*. Schools Council, London

Goacher B J, Reid M I 1983 *Reporting Achievement in the Secondary School*. NFER/Nelson, Slough

Henrysson S, Wedman I 1977 *The Necessity and Uses of Tests and Marks* (in Swedish). University of Umeå, Stockholm

Humphreys E H, Elwood B C 1976 *Effectiveness of the Revised Ontario School Record System*. Institute for Studies in Education, Toronto, Ontario

Macbeth A M 1982 *The Child Between: A Report on School Family Relationships in the Countries of the European Community*. European Economic Community, Brussels

National Educational Association of the United States 1970 *Marking and Reporting Pupil Progress*. National Educational Association Research Division, Washington, DC

New York State Education Department 1962 *Manual on Pupil Records*. New York State Education Department, Albany, New York

# Environmental Measures

## K. Marjoribanks

Families and classrooms are two of the most significant learning environments that influence students' school outcomes. In this article, methods that have been used in educational research to measure those two environments are examined. The methods have been classified as involving either an environmental press approach or an interpretative mode of investigation.

## 1. Environmental Press Approach

Perhaps the most influential theoretical framework for generating environmental press measures has been Murray's theory of personality. Murray (1938 p. 16) suggests that if the behaviour of individuals is to be understood then it is necessary to devise a method of analysis that "will lead to satisfactory dynamical formulations of external environments". He proposes that an environment should be defined by the kinds of benefits or harms that it provides. If the environment has a potentially harmful effect then Murray claims that individuals attempt to prevent the harmful occurrence by avoiding the context or by defending themselves against it. In contrast, if the environment has a potentially beneficial effect, then it is assumed that individuals will attempt to interact with it.

The directional tendency implied in Murray's framework is designated as the press of the environment. Each press is defined as having a qualitative aspect which is the kind of effect that the environment has or might have upon an individual. Each press also has a quantitative element, which is assessed by the variation in power that an environment has for either harming or benefiting different individuals or the same individual at different times. In his framework, Murray (1938, p. 122) distinguishes between the *alpha press* "which is the press that actually exists, as far as scientific discovery can determine it", and an environment's *beta press* "which is the subject's own interpretation of the phenomena that is perceived". Studies that have used measures to assess the press of family and classroom environments are considered in the following section.

### 1.1 The Press of Family Environments

It was not until Bloom (1964) and a number of his doctoral students examined the environmental correlates of children's affective and cognitive characteristics, that a school of research emerged to assess the alpha press of family environments. Bloom defined the environment as the conditions, forces, and external stimuli that impinge on individuals. It is proposed that these forces, which may be physical or social as well as intellectual, provide a network which surrounds, engulfs, and plays on the individual. As Bloom (1964 p. 187) suggests, "such a view of the environment

reduces it for analytical purposes to those aspects of the environment which are related to a particular characteristic or set of characteristics". That is, the total context surrounding an individual may be defined as being composed of a number of subenvironments. If the development of a particular characteristic is to be understood, then it becomes necessary to identify that subenvironment of press variables which potentially is related to the characteristic.

In the initial subenvironment studies, Dave (1963) and Wolf (1964) examined relations between the family environment and measures of academic achievement and intelligence, respectively. Dave defined six press variables as constituting the family learning environment and they were labelled as achievement press, language models, academic guidance, activeness of the family, intellectuality in the home, and work habits in the family. These variables were defined further by process characteristics such as parental aspirations for their children, the quality of parents' language use and the use of television and other media. A semistructured home interview schedule was designed to assess the variables and their associated process characteristics. Scores on the total environment measure were related to approximately 50 percent of the variance in arithmetic problem solving, reading, and the word knowledge performance of 11-year-olds. Wolf proposed that the intellectual environment of the home could be defined by three press variables that were categorized as press for achievement motivation, press for language development, and provisions for general learning. When combined into a predictor set, the measures were associated with nearly 49 percent of the variation in children's intelligence test scores.

In a penetrating study of the press of family environments, Keeves (1972) collected data on Australian children when they were in the final year of elementary school and in their first year of secondary school. Family contexts were assessed by three dimensions that were categorized as structural, attitudinal, and process. The structural dimension included variables such as sibsize, birth order, parents' occupation, education and income, parents' ages and linguistic background. In the attitude dimension there were measures of parents' attitudes towards their child's present education, their ambitions for the child's future education and occupation, and the parents' hopes and aspirations for themselves. Educational practices in the family such as the use of books and library facilities, provision of help with formal schoolwork, and arrangements made for undertaking home assignments were used to gauge the process dimension. The three dimensions had moderate to strong associations with mathematics and science achievement and low to modest concurrent validities with the children's attitudes to mathematics and science.

In a further example of the environmental press approach, Marjoribanks (1986) investigated the impact of family environments and individual characteristics at 11 years of age on the aspirations of 16-year-olds, in different social status groups. A typology devised by Merton (1968, 1976) was used to construct a family environment measure. The typology suggests that individual behaviour can be related to the goals that are set for individuals and to the means that are used to achieve those goals. In the environment measure, parents' goals for their children were assessed by questions such as: "How much education would you like your child to receive if at all possible?" and "What kind of job would you really like your child to have?" Procedures adopted by parents to support their aspirations were assessed by scales that measured parent–child learning interactions and the family press for independence. In the interaction scale there were items of the form: "When your child was small, how often did you read to her or him?" and "How often would you help your child now with reading?" Press for independence was measured by items in which parents indicated the age at which they would allow their child to undertake certain activities. Also included in the scale were statements similar to those used by Strodtbeck (1961) to measure independence of the family, such as: "Even when children get married their main loyalty still belongs to their family", and "When the time comes for children to take jobs, they should try and stay near their parents even if it means giving up good opportunities". Scores on the items for each dimension were factor analysed to generate factor scales that had reliability estimates greater than 0.75.

In the follow-up survey, a structured questionnaire consisting of 5-point items was used to gather information about the adolescents' perceptions of their parents' educational and occupational aspirations for them, the encouragement they had received from their parents in relation to schooling, and their parents' general interest in their education. From the responses, two scales were constructed and they were labelled as adolescents' perceptions of father support and mother support for learning. The findings from the investigation indicated that in different social status groups, adolescents' aspirations are influenced strongly by the interaction between ability, attitudes to school, and the situational variables of parents' early aspirations for their children and the adolescents' later perceptions of their parents' support.

These illustrative studies indicate that by defining family learning environments by proximal social-psychological dimensions, it is possible to measure potentially alterable variables that make significant unique contributions to variations in students' school outcomes. Bloom (1980 p. 16) claims that:

> If we are convinced that a good education is necessary for all who live in modern society, then we must search for the alterable variables which can make a difference in the learning of children . . . Our basic research task is to understand further how much alterable variables can be altered and their consequent effect on students, teachers and learning.

What is required now in educational research are investigations that define the alpha press with even more elegance and then relate those press variables to a more complex set of affective and cognitive characteristics. McCall (1983 p. 408) suggests, for example, that most of the family variables which have been investigated are "characteristics that distinguish the general environment of one family from another, and they might be expected to influence all children within a family to approximately the same extent. As a result they are called 'between-family environmental factors'".

He goes on to suggest, however, that while between-family environmental factors are influential, they are not the only kind of environmental circumstances and that within-family factors should be investigated. Such factors are those not typically shared by siblings and thus they tend to make them different from one another. The variables might include sibling interactions, birth order and spacing, differential treatment of siblings by parents, illness and separation, cohort differences, and nonfamily effects specific to individual children. McCall (1983 p. 408) also suggests that

> One might add to this list, environmental events that impinge on all family members (e.g., relocation, divorce, neighbors, death of relatives) but they have different effects on individual members because of differences in their ages, personalities, genetic dispositions, and other factors.

It is proposed further that nonshared within-family influences may be of two types. First, there are those factors that exert a continuing influence over one child versus another. There may be, for example, differential patterns of consistent parental support for siblings in a family. Second, there are discontinuous nonshared within-family environmental factors such as moving into a new neighbourhood or the death of a sibling or another family member. As McCall (1983 p. 414) observes, to study such within-family factors we must "abandon our arm's length approach and get closer to our subjects and their families and friends".

In part, getting closer to families may be achieved by combining alpha and beta family measures in studies. There are now many investigations that have included students' perceptions of significant others in analyses of outcome measures. Increasingly, the studies have used adaptations of what has become labelled as the Wisconsin model of status attainment (e.g. Carpenter and Hayden 1985, Davis 1985, Natriello and McDill 1986). In the model, students' perceptions of parent, teacher, and peer group influences are typically included as mediating variables between social background measures and the students' aspirations and eventual educational and occupational attainment. Unfortunately, in much of the research, family influences are assessed by limited measures. Typically, parent effects are gauged by single items that require respondents to answer questions such as "How much encouragement have you received from your parents to stay at school, or to go on to university?"

In a review of such investigations, Campbell (1983 p. 53) claims that "there is a need to go into the sources of family effects more deeply". He proposes, for example, that "if one could show, by whatever means, that family background affects the aspiration formation process in terms of timing, clarity and focus, and the ways in which that occurs, he or she would make a significant contribution" (Campbell 1983 p. 60; also see Alwin and Thornton 1984, Jencks et al. 1983, Schulenberg et al. 1984 for other criticisms of measurement in analyses using students' perceptions of family influences). In a later section of this article, studies that have used ethnographic approaches to examine family learning environments are reviewed.

### 1.2 The Press of School Environments

In a comprehensive review, Fraser (1986) provides an assessment of 20 years of research that has used perceptual measures to gauge the press of classroom and school learning environments. He suggests that classroom environment measures have typically been used:

> to assess student perceptions of what a classroom is actually like. But especially in more recent studies, classroom environment instruments have been used to assess (a) student perceptions of preferred environment, (b) teacher perceptions of actual environment, and (c) teacher perceptions of preferred environment. (Fraser 1986 p. 21)

In contrast to methods which rely on observers, the perceptual approach defines classroom environments by the shared perceptions of students and sometimes by teachers' perceptions. The schedules are often referred to as high inference measures, as opposed to low inference techniques that assess specific explicit phenomena such as the number of questions asked by students in a certain section of a lesson. It is suggested that perceptual measures of classroom and school environments have the advantages that they:

> are more economical than classroom observation techniques which involve the expense of trained outside observers . . . they are based on students' experiences over many lessons, while observational data usually are restricted to a very small number of lessons . . . they involve the pooled judgments of all students in a class, whereas observation techniques typically involve only a single observer . . . students' perceptions, because they are determinants of student behaviour more so than the real situation, can be more important than observed behaviours . . . perceptual measures of classroom environment typically have been found to account for considerably more variance in student learning outcomes than have directly observed variables. (Fraser 1986 p. 3)

Four of the most commonly used perceptual measures of classrooms are the Learning Environment Inventory (LEI) (Fraser et al. 1982), the Classroom Environment Scale (CES) (Moos 1979), the Individualized Classroom Environment Scale (ICEQ) (Fraser 1986), and the My Class Inventory (MCI) (Fraser et al. 1982).

The Learning Environment Inventory, for example, consists of 15 scales that are labelled as cohesiveness, diversity, formality, speed, environment, friction, goal direction, favouritism, cliqueness, satisfaction, disorganization, difficulty, apathy, democraticness, and competitiveness. Each scale is assessed by seven Likert-type items. Typical items are "All students know each other very well" (cohesiveness), "Certain students in this class are responsible for petty quarrels" (friction), "Students do not have to hurry to finish their work" (speed), and "The class is well organized and efficient" (disorganization). The MCI is a simplification of the LEI, designed for children between 8 and 12 years of age. It differs, however, from the LEI in a number of ways. First, to minimize fatigue among younger children it contains only five of the original LEI scales (cohesiveness, friction, satisfaction, difficulty, and competitiveness). Also, item wording has been simplified and the LEI's 4-point response format has been reduced to a Yes–No answer choice.

The Classroom Environment Scale assesses three general categories that are labelled as the relationship dimension, the personal development dimension, and the system maintenance and system change dimension. In the latest version of the schedule there are nine scales, each with 10 items using True–False responses. It has been designed to measure the actual (or real) classroom environment and the preferred (or ideal) environment. Fraser suggests, however, that:

> despite the wide application and proven usefulness of the LEI and CES, these instruments exclude some of the aspects of classroom environment which are particularly relevant in classroom settings commonly referred to as individualized, open or inquiry-based. Consequently, the ICEQ was developed to measure those dimensions which differentiate conventional classrooms from individualized ones involving either open or inquiry-based approaches. (Fraser 1986 p. 27)

In the ICEQ there are 50 items that are assessed by 5-point scales. It has four separate forms which assess, respectively, student perceptions of actual environment, student perceptions of preferred environment, teacher perceptions of actual environment, and teacher perceptions of preferred environment.

From an analysis of research findings from studies that have used such perceptual measures, Walberg (1985 p. 754) concludes that:

> student perceptions of the social environment of learning accounted for a median of 30 percent (range = 13 percent to 46 percent; all significant) of the variance in cognitive, affective, and behavioral postcourse measures beyond that accounted for by parallel precourse measures. Efforts at generalizing these results suggest consistency across different school subjects and different languages and cultures (also see Haertel et al. 1981 for a meta-analysis of classroom perception studies).

Many educators will argue that classrooms and schools need to be examined with a greater sensitivity than can be generated from perception schedules.

Researchers using such perceptual scales, however, generally suggest that the measures provide a portrayal of learning environments that may be enhanced by adopting other investigative methodologies. In the following section of the article, interpretative models of investigating classrooms are examined.

## 2. Interpretative Models of Investigation

Increasingly, in family and classroom environment research, concepts and methodologies are being adopted from a number of theoretical orientations such as social phenomenology, cognitive sociology, ethnomethodology, symbolic interactionism, dramaturgical sociology, and ethnogenic theories of human behaviour. Although there are significant conceptual differences in the orientations, Bernstein (1977) suggests that they share common features such as an opposition to structural functionalism, a view of individuals as creators of meanings, a focus on the assumptions underlying social order together with the treatment of social categories as themselves problematic, a distrust of quantification and the use of objective categories, and a focus on the transmission and acquisition of interpretative procedures.

In learning environment research these interpretative perspectives have emphasized the need to investigate the processes by which individual members of families and classrooms define and manage their everyday lives. Studies typically adopt variations of ethnographic methods to obtain accounts of why students perform certain acts and what social meanings they give to the actions of themselves and of others. Taft suggests that one of the main advantages of the ethnographic approach is that:

> . . . in the course of becoming involved in the group, the investigator becomes acculturated to it. This means that he or she develops personal knowledge about the rules of the group and begins to perceive the same meanings in events as do the members of the group. The investigator learns what behaviour is expected when, where, and in response to what situations. (Taft 1985 p. 1731)

Fensham et al. (1986), for example, used case study techniques to investigate alienation in three high schools. In relation to family–school influences it is suggested of one of the schools, that:

> Another aspect of home background was that (as always) the staff as a whole lacked knowledge of what went on in the homes in general, and the lives of individual pupils in particular. This is the inevitable result of teaching being a middle-class profession, but is accentuated by teachers living outside the area in which they teach. This lack of knowledge makes it difficult for teachers either to relate school knowledge to their pupils' out-of-school experience, or to understand pupils' problems, academic and social. (Tripp 1986 p. 141)

In another investigation using case study techniques, Hatton (1985) examined the relations between parental control and teaching practices within an elementary school that was in an established and prestigious suburb of an Australian city. From interviews with teachers, Hatton concludes that their autonomy was limited by the power of parents.

Although such interpretative studies have provided fresh insights into students' learning contexts, Rist (1980) has been critical of much ethnographic research. He claims that:

> Ethnography is becoming a mantle to legitimate much work that is shoddy, poorly conducted, and ill-conceived. And when such work is questioned, the response is to turn to the terminology for defence. The logic of the method becomes inverted. Rather than make the uncommon and unknown comprehensible, the defence becomes one of privatizing what ought to have been open to scrutiny. (Rist 1980 p. 8)

Rist is extremely critical of "qualitative researchers" who adopt "hit-and-run" forays rather than spending considerable time in schools or families. He proposes that:

> Just as educational research has accrued some heavy costs from an overreliance on quantitative methods when they were inappropriate and unable to answer the questions at hand, so also qualitative research faces growing costs. The more the reliance on the method as an end in itself, the less it is a meaningful research tool. (Rist 1980 p. 9)

Hammersley (1985) suggests that although the interpretative approach has provided a sensitive awareness of some previously underestimated problems in educational research, its orientation has been primarily descriptive. Karabel and Halsey (1977) express a further concern of interpretative studies of learning environments. They suggest, for example, that while:

> stress on the fact that relations in educational institutions are humanly constructed products is a welcome antidote to the deterministic and reifying tendencies of some of the "old" sociology of education . . . emphasis on "man the creator" often fails to take adequate account of the social constraints on human actors in every day life. There is, to be sure, a considerable latitude available to those engaged in struggles over the "definition of the situation", but the question of whose definition will ultimately prevail is preeminently one of power. Battles between students and teachers as to who will define the situation, for example, clearly illustrate this point . . . there is, without doubt, an important element of creativity in student–teacher interaction; but there are also limits to the extent to which "definitions of the situation" may be negotiated. (Karabel and Halsey 1977 p. 58)

They propose further that "if empirical work is confined to observation of classroom interaction, it may miss the process by which political and economic power sets sharp bounds to what is negotiable" (Karabel and Halsey 1977 p. 58).

Similar conceptual concerns are expressed by Scott-Jones (1984) who observes, for example, that the contexts in which parents and children live are important in understanding the family's influence on children's school outcomes. It is suggested that the family is an important context but that it is embedded in other contexts. She claims that there is a need to study "children who develop normally or excel under conditions such as low-income status. The family may be able to cope with adverse conditions in a manner that prevents the expected effects on the child". (Scott-Jones 1984 p. 262)

This would mean that for a more refined analysis of families and schools, ethnographic studies of families and schools need to be complemented by measures of the social constraints that surround parents and their children.

## 3. Some Future Research Orientations

If learning environment research is to advance significantly then measures adopted in the environmental press approach and the interpretative model of analysis need perhaps to be brought together. Studies are required that analyse with greater discrimination the interactions within families and classrooms, and the relations of those interactions to the position of students' learning contexts in different social settings. As well as examining between-context variation, more attention needs to be directed at differences that operate within families and classrooms. By using such a combination of alpha press measures and ethnographic environment studies we may generate a more complete understanding of the relations between students' learning contexts and their outcomes, and hopefully develop a more appropriate social theory of children's learning outcomes.

## Bibliography

Alwin D F, Thornton A 1984 Family origins and the schooling process: Early versus late influences of parental characteristics. *Am. Sociol. Rev.* 49: 784–802

Bernstein B B 1977 *Class, Codes, and Control*, 2nd edn. Towards a Theory of Educational Transmissions, Vol. 3. Routledge and Kegan Paul, London

Bloom B S 1964 *Stability and Change in Human Characteristics.* Wiley, New York

Bloom B S 1980 The new directions in educational research: Alterable variables. In: Sloane K D, O'Brien M L (eds.) 1980 *The State of Research on Selected Alterable Variables in Education.* Department of Education, University of Chicago, Chicago, Illinois

Campbell R T 1983 Status attainment research: End of the beginning or beginning of the end? *Sociol. Educ.* 59: 47–62

Carpenter P G, Hayden M 1985 Academic achievement among Australian youth. *Aust. J. Educ.* 29: 199–220

Dave R 1963 The identification and measurement of home environmental process variables related to educational achievement. Unpublished doctoral dissertation. University of Chicago, Chicago, Illinois

Davis R A 1985 Social structure, belief, attitude, intention and behaviour: A partial test of Liska's revisions. *Soc. Psychol. Q.* 48: 89–93

Fensham P, Power C, Tripp D, Kemmis S 1986 *Alienation from Schooling.* Routledge and Kegan Paul, London

Fraser B J 1986 *Classroom Environment.* Croom Helm, London

Fraser B J, Anderson G J, Walberg H J 1982 *Assessment of*

*Learning Environments: Manual for Learning Environment Inventory (LEI) and My Class Inventory (MCI), (third version).* Western Australian Institute of Technology, Perth, Western Australia

Haertel G D, Walberg H J, Haertel E H 1981 Sociopsychological environments and learning: A quantitative synthesis. *Br. Educ. Res. J.* 7: 27–36

Hammersley M 1985 From ethnography to theory: A programme and paradigm in the sociology of education. *Sociology* 19: 244–59

Hatton E J 1985 Equality, class and power: A case study. *Br. J. Sociol. Educ.* 6: 255–72

Jencks C, Crouse J, Mueser P 1983 The Wisconsin model of status attainment: A national replication with improved measures of ability and aspiration. *Sociol. Educ.* 56: 3–19

Karabel J, Halsey A H (eds.) 1977 *Power and Ideology in Education.* Oxford University Press, New York

Keeves J P 1972 *Educational Environment and Student Achievement.* Australian Council for Educational Research, Hawthorn, Victoria

Marjoribanks K 1986 A longitudinal study of adolescents' aspirations as assessed by Seginer's model. *Merrill–Palmer Q.* 32: 211–30

McCall R B 1983 Environmental effects on intelligence: The forgotten realm of discontinuous nonshared within-family factors. *Child Dev.* 54: 408–15

Merton R K 1968 *Social Theory and Social Structure.* Free Press, New York

Merton R K 1976 *Sociological Ambivalence and Other Essays.* Free Press, New York

Moos R H 1979 *Evaluating Educational Environments.* Jossey-Bass, San Francisco, California

Murray H 1938 *Explorations in Personality.* Oxford University Press, Oxford

Natriello G, McDill E L 1986 Performance standards, student effort on homework, and academic achievement. *Sociol. Educ.* 59: 18–31

Rist R C 1980 Blitzkrieg ethnography: On the transformation of a method into a movement. *Educ. Res.* 9(2): 8–10

Schulenberg J E, Vondracek F W, Crouter A C 1984 The influence of the family on vocational development. *J. Marriage Fam.* 46: 129–43

Scott-Jones D 1984 Family influences on cognitive development and school achievement. In: Gordon E W (ed.) 1984 *Review of Research in Education.* American Educational Research Association, Washington, DC, pp. 259–304

Strodtbeck F L 1961 Family integration, values and achievement. In: Halsey A H, Floud J, Anderson C A (eds.) 1961 *Education, Economy and Society.* Free Press, New York, pp. 315–47

Taft R 1985 Ethnographic research methods. In: Husén T, Postlethwaite T N (eds.) 1985 *The International Encyclopedia of Education* Vol. 3. Pergamon, Oxford, pp. 1729–33

Tripp D H 1986 Greenfield: A case study of schooling, alienation and employment. In: Fensham P, Power C, Tripp D, Kemmis S (1986) *Alienation from Schooling.* Routledge and Kegan Paul, London, p. 141

Walberg H J 1985 Classroom psychological environment. In: Husén T, Postlethwaite T N (eds.) 1985 *The International Encyclopedia of Education* Vol. 2. Pergamon, Oxford, pp. 750–55

Wolf R M 1964 The identification and measurement of home environmental process variables that are related to intelligence. Unpublished doctoral dissertation, University of Chicago, Chicago, Illinois

# "Title I" Evaluation Programs

## G. D. Borich

In 1965 the United States Congress passed the Elementary and Secondary Education Act (ESEA). The primary objective of this legislation was to equalize educational opportunities across the nation's elementary and secondary schools. To bring about this equalization a number of funding programs (called Titles) were implemented, including what is known as the Title I program. Title I was designed specifically to assist economically disadvantaged elementary and secondary schools in improving the quality of their instructional methods, materials, personnel, and activities.

Title I has developed from a five million dollar program beginning in 1965 to a three billion dollar program in 1981. Currently, Title I programs operate in approximately 17,000 school districts nationwide in each of the 50 states.

To obtain Title I funds, local school districts apply directly to their respective state education agency. Based on an auditable percentage of low-income children in their district, the state education agency determines a school or school district's eligibility. Once funds have been approved, school districts distribute funds to eligible schools within their district on the basis of educational need.

In 1971 the United States Congress added a provision to the Elementary and Secondary Education Act requiring that evaluations be conducted for each project funded. Guidelines in the form of models for the evaluation of Title I programs are conveyed to prospective grantees in an ESEA manual published by the United States Department of Education. To further aid local school districts in the evaluation of their programs and in reporting the results to the federal government, 10 Title I technical assistance centers serving three or more states each have been established across the country. These centers advise local schools in the selection of tests to be given to students to determine educational need and assist in implementing one of the following models deemed appropriate for evaluating the effectiveness of local projects.

The Title I evaluation system currently comprises three evaluation models: a norm-referenced model, a comparison group model, and a regression model. These models comprise statistical procedures designed to yield a measure of children's achievement who have received Title I services compared to an estimate of what their performance would have been in the absence of Title I services. The models are intended for use with specifically designed projects or programs at the elementary- and secondary-school level in reading, language arts, and mathematics. Individual schools or school districts choose the model most appropriate to their own circumstances.

With each of these models, a specially prepared normal curve equivalent (NCE) scale is used for interpreting and reporting results. This is an equal interval scale that matches the percentile ranks of the normal curve at the 1st, 50th, and 99th percentile. The normal curve equivalent scale was developed to foster aggregation and standardization in reporting Title I evaluation results across sites and to give individual school districts freedom in choosing achievement tests used to evaluate the effectiveness of their programs. A brief description of each of the three Title I evaluation models follows.

## 1. Model A: The Norm-referenced Model

Model A requires the administration of a national norm-referenced achievement test (or a test that has been equated with a nationally normed test) at pretest and posttest times. In this model, pretest and posttest raw scores are converted to normal curve equivalents using the appropriate norm tables. The mean pretest normal curve equivalent represents the "no-project" expectation or the expected performance of Title I children had they not been given Title I services. The difference between the pretest and posttest means, expressed in normal curve equivalents, is taken as the achievement gain attributable to the provision of Title I services.

The no-project expectation is derived under the assumption that students will maintain their status with respect to the norm group from pretest to posttest. It is assumed that students who score at a certain percentile on the pretest would also score at that percentile on the posttest if no Title I services had been provided. Conversely, if students participate in the Title I project and if the project was successful in raising the achievement levels of project children, the project students would receive a higher percentile rank on the posttest than was attained on the pretest. The assumption that students receiving project services will remain at the same percentile rank does not suggest, however, that they would obtain the same raw scores on the posttest that had been achieved on the pretest. Due to extracurricular activities, normal maturation processes, and other school-related experiences, even students not receiving Title I services would be expected to answer more questions correctly on the posttest than were answered correctly on the pretest. However, the relative achievement of both project and nonproject students with respect to national norms, as expressed by their percentile ranks and normal curve equivalents, would remain the same from pretest to posttest. This relative ranking is achieved through the translation of pretest and posttest raw scores to expanded standard scores (normalized equivalents of raw scores provided by the test publisher) and then to normal curve equivalents. Hence, the mean pretest normal curve equivalent corresponds to the same percentile rank and equivalent raw score as that which would be expected for non-Title I students at the time of the posttest.

In order to make valid comparisons between the performance of Title I students and the performance of students in the norming sample using this model, it is important that:

(a) Title I students be tested close to the time when the students in the norming sample were tested;

(b) students in the Title I project have the same characteristics as those students in the norming sample who received the same test scores;

(c) test level match the functional level of the students and test items reflect the instructional content;

(d) pretest scores used in the computation of the normal curve equivalents gain not be used for selecting children for Title I services, unless adjusted for the regression toward the mean effect; and

(e) if a norm-referenced test is used, the same form be chosen as that given to the norming sample.

(a) *Strength*. When a comparison group is not available or when the composition of such a group suggests that it may not come from the same population as the project group, the norm-referenced model provides a plausible estimate of the no-project expectation.

(b) *Weakness*. The validity of the model rests on the assumption that in the absence of special services the achievement gain of a particular subgroup is the same relative to the norm group over the pre-to-posttest interval. When the Title I group does not possess the same characteristics with respect to achievement as does the norm group, this assumption is not tenable and the model should not be used.

## 2. Model B: The Comparison Group Model

Model B represents a more extensive effort in time and cost than Model A, but provides a more rigorous test of the effectiveness of Title I services. This increase in rigor derives essentially from the assumption that local students who are drawn from the same schools as the Title I students provide the most accurate no-project expectation.

Model B requires the identification of students not only who will form the Title I group, but also who will serve as a no-project comparison similar in composition to the project group. With this model, either normed or nonnormed tests are given to the project and comparison groups at pretest and posttest times. As is the case with each of the Title I evaluation models, non-normed test results must ultimately be referenced to national norms. The difference in mean posttest performance between the comparison and project group, expressed in normal curve equivalents, is taken as the

achievement gain attributable to the provision of Title I services.

With this model it is essential that the comparison group include students whose characteristics are similar to the Title I group. This criterion assumes that the two groups are similar in terms of age, sex, intelligence, race, ethnicity, socioeconomic status, pretest achievement level, and any other characteristics that may create differences in project achievement.

To avoid differential regression effects across project and nonproject groups, it is recommended that students in the project and comparison groups be pretested after they are selected, or failing this, that the same proportion of students be selected from the comparison classrooms to form the comparison group as was selected from the Title I classrooms to form the project group.

To determine if posttest scores need to be adjusted based on differences in the mean pretest scores of comparison and project students, the difference between mean pretest scores for project and nonproject groups are expressed in normal curve equivalents and compared. If the difference in normal curve equivalents is greater than one, it is recommended that posttest scores be adjusted for initial group differences. Adjustment methods are described in Tallmadge et al. (1981).

(a) *Strength*. This model provides a method for adjusting observed posttest scores for random differences that may have occurred on the pretest, thus eliminating the confounding effect of the pretest on posttest scores. Additional features of this model are that it permits the use of different tests for pretest and posttest and testing times need not coincide with norming dates.

(b) *Weakness*. The model assumes that Title I and comparison students are random samples from a single population and that any difference in pretest performance is only the result of sampling error and random error of measurement.

## 3. Model C: The Regression Model

Model C, the regression model, represents the least rigorous and most complex of the three Title I models.

Model C consists of dividing a preexisting group into a program and a comparison group based on their pretest scores. Those below a given score are placed in the project group (Title I), and those above the cutoff score are placed in the comparison group. In the case of Model C the no-project expectation is determined by regressing the comparison group's pretest scores onto their posttest scores. The resulting regression line is then extended downward and onto the area occupied by the pretest-on-posttest regression for Title I students. This extended regression line constitutes the no-project expectation. This procedure allows an estimate of how well Title I students, all of whom scored below the cutoff, would have scored on the posttest had they not participated in the project. The difference between the no-project expectation and the project group's actual mean posttest scores, converted to normal curve equivalents, constitutes the achievement gain attributable to the provision of Title I services. In order for this model to provide interpretable results, it is recommended only when there are greater than 30 students in each group and the correlation between pretest and posttest for the comparison group is 0.4 or greater.

(a) *Strength.* This model makes use of an available comparison group that may be more comparable to the project group than the group used to establish national norms.

(b) *Weakness.* The model makes the assumption that group regressions will be linear over the entire range of the pretest. When lowest scoring students make the largest gains this assumption is not tenable and the model should not be used.

## Bibliography

Echeternacht G (ed.) 1980 *New Directions for Testing and Measurement: Measurement Aspects of Title I Evaluations.* Jossey-Bass, San Francisco, California

Tallmadge G K, Wood C T 1980 *Comparability of Gains from the Three Models in the Title I Evaluation System.* RMC Research Corporation, Mountain View, California

Tallmadge G K, Wood C T, Gamel N N 1981 *ESEA Title I Evaluation and Reporting System: User's Guide.* RMC Research Corporation, Mountain View, California (Available from the US Department of Education, Office of Program Evaluation, Washington, DC)

# Monitoring National Standards

## I. D. Livingstone

A dictionary definition of "standard" is: "the degree of excellence required for particular purposes; the measure of what is adequate; a socially or practically desired level of performance". In the educational context, then, standards should be regarded as objectives to be attained, or expectations of desirable attitudes or levels of performance. There is, however, a popular use of the word "standard" to denote an actual level of performance, often the mean score of a group of pupils on a standardized test. In the interests of precision of language this should more properly be termed a "norm", since it represents the "normal" or average level of performance on the test measure. But since average performance levels tend to be internalized in the minds of the public over a period of time and come to be regarded as typical, norms tend to be confused with standards.

Thus the monitoring of national standards is generally seen as a process of checking at intervals on levels of educational achievement or performance, and will be so interpreted in this article. However, there is a good argument to keep "norms" and "standards" conceptually separate, and an attempt to do this will be made in what follows.

## 1. Why Monitor?

Numerous reasons have been advanced by proponents of national assessment as to why the monitoring task should be carried out. Some of the reasons carry different weight in different societies in different stages of development, but characteristic of most attempts to monitor standards is some desire to find how the education system is "performing", so that remedial action can be taken where performance differs from expectation.

Particularly important in less developed countries are such issues as the following:

(a) There is an expressed need to produce baseline information on levels of achievement, against which the effectiveness of various national development plans can be measured at some time in the future.

(b) There is a desire to update and upgrade school curricula, and this requires objective data on achievement, so that curriculum developers, advisers, and teachers can plan for improvements in the quality and relevance of the education offered to students.

(c) The pressure for equalization of opportunity becomes apparent in education systems which are expanding rapidly and moving from a form of "elitist" education towards something approaching the "universal" systems exemplified by developed countries. Central educational authorities wish to know the range of achievement levels which exist in different regions of the country, the size of urban–rural and ethnic differentials in performance, and the way these are related to the allocation of resources, both human and financial.

(d) Comprehensive information is needed on the effects on achievement of introducing new language policies throughout a whole school system. An example of this would be the cycle of national assessments set in train in Indonesia in the mid-1970s, which, as one of its objectives, sought to determine the impact on achievement of the introduction of Bahasa Indonesia as the national language of instruction, from the third year of primary schooling.

In developed countries, however, other reasons for introducing monitoring procedures may be paramount:

(a) Particularly where administration of the education system is decentralized, education authorities from time to time must face strong calls for accountability from those who support the system through their taxes. These cries typically become more strident in times of national economic constraint. In order to allay public anxieties and convince the taxpayers that students are receiving the best possible education, some form of national assessment is frequently called for. Such enquiries are characteristically triggered by complaints from employers and the general public about alleged declines in standards in the basic subjects, particularly reading, spelling, writing, and mathematics. As education continues to claim a proportionately larger share of national budgets in many developed countries, along with health and social welfare, some form of national monitoring of standards, preferably by an independent body, is seen to be legitimate and necessary.

(b) In many developed countries the need for accountability in the basic subjects has been fulfilled, in part, by means of external examinations in the secondary schools backed up by regular inspection of teachers' work by ministry of education officers at different levels. Both these forms of accountability are in the process of change in many countries. Various types of internal assessment have been introduced for the purpose of certification, and the role of inspectors has become largely an advisory one in response to the increasing professionalism of teachers. This often brings a call from the public for more objective ways of measuring the output of school systems.

(c) In periods of rapid curriculum reform, such as have occurred in many countries since the early 1960s, teachers engaged in the development of new approaches to learning (sometimes within new patterns of school organization, for example, mixed-ability grouping), are asking for more adequate evidence to support and give direction to the changes being made. Traditional knowledge-based objectives as represented by current external examination systems have not been found adequate to cater for the much broader range of objectives of many new courses. Wider forms of assessment are being called for, often on a national basis, since large-scale curriculum reform tends to be centralized. On the other hand, teachers are cautious about forms of assessment imposed from the outside, appreciating the freedom to teach without the restriction of externally prescribed examination syllabi. They are likely to be alert to any form of monitoring of standards which is too closely tied to specific syllabus content.

(d) Providing for the educationally disadvantaged, especially disadvantaged immigrants, is another reason that has been advanced in favour of national assessment, in some developed countries. If significant differences in achievement, particularly the incidence of so-called underachievement, can be shown to be related to the circumstances in which children learn, it may be possible to take remedial action by redirecting resources within national ministries or local education authorities.

(e) Secondary benefits have been claimed from the extensive test development exercises necessary to carry through a national assessment programme. Well-trialled "question banks" in various subject fields can be made accessible to local authorities and schools, and sound models for assessment become publicized. An inservice training function in assessment for teachers has also been suggested as a by-product of the use of teachers to carry out some parts of national assessment programmes.

## 2. *What is Being Monitored?*

To date, most national assessment programmes have concentrated on analyzing achievement outcomes, using the scores of students on various standardized tests, either norm- or criterion-referenced, as the main dependent measures. This process has characteristically begun from a detailed content analysis of the curriculum, which has then led to the development of tests made up of items fitting a predetermined grid, following a prescribed weighting of skills beginning with simple recall of information, and moving through to the higher intellectual skills of application and analysis. The scores on individual items are regularly used to allow for the comparison of levels of performance over time, and subtest scores can be similarly compared in particular skill areas, provided they have not been rendered invalid by changes in syllabus over the period between assessments.

Although generalized attitudes towards schooling and towards particular subjects have been measured in a number of studies, in particular by the very extensive series carried out by the International Association for the Evaluation of Educational Achievement (IEA) since the 1960s, it would be true to say that monitoring in the affective domain is not as well-developed as monitoring in the cognitive domain. This is in spite of the fact that strictly cognitive objectives in official syllabi are often in the minority, and affective ones (such as developing an attitude of enquiry, or an awareness of the importance of a subject in daily life) are commonly emphasized by curriculum developers.

Studies along the typical IEA model have attempted to penetrate beyond simple outcome measures, and evaluate the influence of underlying variables, seeking to answer such questions as: What are the causes of variations in performance? How much learning can be attributed to schooling? Which curricula and methods improve performance? Large-scale assessment surveys on this model, however, demand highly sophisticated methodology (such as path analysis) to be fruitful; at this point, research moves beyond simple monitoring, and well-controlled experimental studies involving classroom process variables are necessary if unambiguous answers are to be obtained.

Another significant new thrust is the emphasis on the monitoring of curriculum programmes, with the very helpful distinction being made between the intended curriculum (as prescribed by the educational authorities), the translated or implemented curriculum (as taught by the teachers) and the achieved curriculum (as indicated by the performance of the students on tests or other outcome measures).

## 3. The Monitoring Process

Paper-and-pencil tests have generally been the main measuring techniques used to monitor national standards, along with supporting questionnaires to gather background information, and in some cases, a measure of attitudes and opinions. There is some debate as to whether measurements in the affective domain can be made reliably by these methods, but certainly they allow for highly reliable assessments of performance in the basic skill areas. The major concern in most monitoring programmes has centred around whether it is possible to measure generalized achievement without dictating specific content. Most assessment programmes have had to grapple with the problem of avoiding tests which are "syllabus bound", covering a broad range of objectives which reflect the goals of the education system and society but at the same time not defining the particular body of information with which each student is expected to be familiar.

The use of multiple-matrix sampling, in which each student is only required to attempt a fraction of the total number of items needed to cover the curriculum, is a relatively new development which can minimize testing time and also allow a much broader and more reliable monitoring of performance. Under this approach, different students may take different combinations of items (and so individual scores and comparisons are meaningless), but it is still possible to establish local and national norms, which are the objectives of the assessment.

It should, of course, not be forgotten that large, centralized examination systems, which continue to operate at various levels in most secondary-school systems, themselves constitute a form of national assessment, although they are not usually geared to assessing changes in performance over time because the questions are not standardized. In spite of elaborate techniques for moderating the standards which examiners use in marking and scaling pupil scores, it is difficult to monitor small changes which may and do occur from year to year under such a system. External examinations do, however, allow for comparisons to be made between different regions of a country, and amongst different subgroups of the population, and as such are a useful monitoring device.

The use of structured, subjective assessments by observers, teachers, and pupils has been mooted by the

Assessment of Performance Unit (APU) in the United Kingdom, as a component in their monitoring programmes. Generally, in the past, such methods have been regarded as too unreliable and expensive to implement on a national basis. Certainly the use of interviews has the potential for allowing more valid assessments to be made in noncognitive areas. But informal, unstructured inspections by officials from education authorities, although commonly used as a means of quality control in schools, leave much to be desired as a sound monitoring technique where educational standards are concerned.

## 4. Some Examples of Monitoring

A number of different models for monitoring national standards have been tried out, but basically the process can be illustrated by the flow chart in Fig. 1. The method, at least on paper, is relatively straightforward. Committees of teachers, curriculum advisors, employers, and so on, draw up lists of skills, understandings, and attitudes which in their view constitute the minimal level of performance for effective participation in adult society and employment. This list provides the brief for the test developers, who devise the test and other instruments necessary to show how many children exceed the stated criteria, and how many fall short. In theory, the results from this monitoring

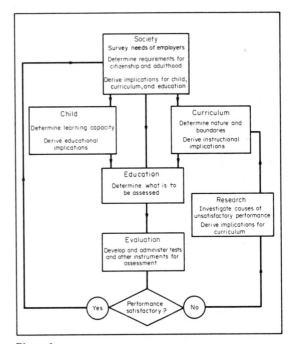

*Figure 1*

National assessment: A flow chart

a First published in Reid (1978)

exercise are then fed back into the system, so that remedial action can be taken, where necessary, on the basis of well-controlled, empirical research. It is unlikely that this ideal is often attained so neatly in practice, but the theory appears to be sound.

Perhaps the best-known example of such a monitoring programme is the National Assessment of Educational Progress (NAEP) set in motion in the United States in 1964. The first testing was carried out in 1969. In brief, the NAEP approach has followed these lines:

(a) Committees of educators and laypersons were set up to identify educational objectives worth assessing in 10 subject areas: reading, writing, literature, mathematics, science, social sciences, music, art, citizenship, and career and occupational development.

(b) Test "exercises" were devised by specialist item writers, to assess the extent to which these goals were achieved in national cross-section samples of students. These exercises tested knowledge, skills, and other outcomes considered important. The exercises were designed to cover a wide range of content and levels of difficulty, and were not confined to paper-and-pencil tests. They included, for example, a measure of skill in playing a musical instrument.

(c) Each year the tests in two or three subjects have been distributed to a representative national sample of students at three age levels (9, 13, and 17 years) and initially, to a sample of young adults. The first national assessment carried out in 1969 involved three subject areas: writing, science, and citizenship.

(d) Approximately 30,000 students are tested annually at each age level, but each exercise (or item) is attempted by only 2,000 students. This method of sampling has been deliberately used to maintain the anonymity of pupils and schools, and to keep the time demands on pupils to a minimum.

(e) The results on half the items are reported to the public; the remainder are kept confidential until follow-up studies are conducted, usually after about four to five years, the initial assessment thus providing a "benchmark" against which subsequent change can be assessed.

(f) Initially, the results were reported in percentage form, item by item, for the national sample, for four geographic regions of the United States, for four kinds of community settings, and two socio-economic levels. Subsequently, the sampling strategy has been modified to provide at least one primary sampling unit within each state to allow "statewide" information to be made available.

(g) Public reaction to the results is sought by asking panels of laypersons, educators, and administrators to analyse and interpret their meaning.

The NAEP is a novel and expensive venture, with an annual budget of more than US$4 million. It has pioneered new approaches to sampling, data collection, and reporting of results, and identified several areas of perceived weakness and strength in the American curriculum, and changes in performance over time, findings which could not be readily obtained with confidence in any other manner.

Another more recent example of an attempt to monitor national standards is reflected in the setting up of the Assessment of Performance Unit (APU) in the United Kingdom in 1974. Interestingly enough, this was less a response to a demand for monitoring standards of literacy and numeracy among school pupils, than a response to problems of providing for the educationally disadvantaged, especially disadvantaged immigrants. The terms of reference made it clear, however, that the APU should concern itself with the performance of children in schools generally, and not only those children failing to reach acceptable minimum standards. Particular features of the APU approach are summarized below:

(a) Under the control of a coordinating committee, working groups were established in six broad curriculum areas: linguistic, mathematical, scientific, personal and social, aesthetic, and physical. It was argued that the diversity of permissible subject combinations, particularly at the secondary-school level, necessitated such a broadly based, cross-curricular model. Rigid subject boundaries were not seen to be appropriate.

(b) Each working group has been allowed to devise its own methods of assessment, and the intention is that these will go far beyond paper-and-pencil tests to include interviews, observational techniques, and assessments of practical work.

(c) Initially, it is intended to assess the performance of representative, national samples of 11-, 13-, and 15-year-olds; a sample size of about 12,000 at each level has been planned. The first subject area to be tested was mathematics, in 1978, followed in 1979 and 1980 by English language and science. The three remaining areas have yet to be explored.

(d) An innovation in the methodology of the assessment has been the use of Rasch item scaling methods, in an attempt to allow levels of performance to be compared from year to year even though the tests contained different items. The validity of this approach has, however, come under criticism on statistical grounds, and is still being debated.

(e) It is planned to publish separate reports for each aspect of the curriculum monitored and each age group, tabulated by sex of pupil, school size and type, location (metropolitan or nonmetropolitan area), and region. The possibility of analysing the results against selected indices of social disadvantage was also advanced, but apparently this was found impracticable and not proceeded with.

Although the NAEP and APU are perhaps the most widely known national assessment programmes, other countries have monitored national standards in less spectacular, and probably less expensive, ways. A number of countries carry out surveys of achievement in individual subjects, perhaps in relation to the norming of standardized tests of achievement; the periodic renorming exercises provide a limited form of monitoring of performance. In some countries (such as Australia and New Zealand), these tests have been developed primarily to assist teachers to tailor the level and pace of their instruction to their particular groups of pupils; in others (such as Sweden) they are administered on a voluntary basis to allow local school districts to establish uniformity in grading standards for the award of national certificates. In both cases, some limited monitoring of standards is possible although this is not the main reason for the testing, and curricular objectives tend to be rather narrow. The minimal competency testing programmes in some states of the United States could also be said to perform a "standard-setting" function.

Probably the most ambitious and complex programme of national assessment ever set in motion has been the series of studies undertaken by the International Association for the Evaluation of Educational Achievement (IEA). This collaborative network of research centres began with an international study of achievement in mathematics in 1964, and followed it with a combined study in six subject areas: science, reading comprehension, literature, French as a foreign language, English as a foreign language, and civic education (1973–1976). A second study of mathematics was commenced in 1976, including a longitudinal component concentrating on classroom processes as well as the usual cross-sectional survey designed to provide a general picture of mathematics achievement in participating countries across the world. Other IEA projects, including a second science study and a study in written composition, are currently in progress.

Although the demands of international comparability for the test instruments have undoubtedly limited their usefulness as a valid measure of curriculum objectives in any particular country, the results from IEA surveys have been widely publicized by the education authorities in participating countries, and have been used, formally or informally, as a means of monitoring educational performance in particular subjects of the curriculum.

A number of less developed countries have participated in the IEA studies, and others (such as Chile and Indonesia) have mounted their own national assessments on the IEA model. That in Indonesia is particularly ambitious, and has now moved into a second cycle to monitor changes in achievement associated with a series of five-year national development plans implemented by the Ministry of Education and Culture.

The World Bank has also been active in sponsoring national assessment surveys, particularly in the less developed countries of Africa and South America.

## 5. *Some Constraints and Problems*

Not all countries are persuaded of the value of large-scale national assessment programmes. Some of the concerns which have been expressed are as follows.

(a) *Resources*. National assessment programmes take a long time to plan, set in motion, and bring to completion with some form of published outcome, often as long as five years in any one subject area. They are also expensive. The NAEP programmes were reported to have cost over US$55 million by 1979, and involved over 800,000 students in assessment exercises.

(b) *Coverage*. In spite of advances in methodology, such as the use of multiple-matrix sampling and a reduced reliance upon traditional multiple-choice objective tests, national monitoring programmes have been criticized for concentrating on the assessment of a few, more easily measured basic skills of literacy and numeracy, and failing to take into account other, less easily measured but equally important objectives (creative writing skills or noncognitive objectives, for example). In decentralized school systems, too, the possibility exists that nationally selected items may not be relevant to the local curriculum or experience of children being tested (inner-city children, or racial minorities for example), and this may reduce the validity of the findings.

(c) *Usefulness*. The results of national assessment programmes are generally aimed at educational policy makers, to assist them to make wise decisions. While there are some examples where this has occurred (such as a major curriculum change in Hungary following the results of the IEA reading comprehension study, and considerable political activity in Italy in the 1970s when regional disparities were highlighted by IEA reports), it is probably true to say that much less use is made of the results from national assessment programmes in curriculum development, resource allocation, or setting priorities for school reform, than their advocates would wish. Whether the benefits justify the costs is an issue which is still being debated vigorously in many countries, and how to disseminate the findings to a broad public in a way which prevents misinterpretation is a matter currently under widespread scrutiny.

(d) *Causes*. Another argument suggests that simply monitoring standards from year to year is of limited value unless some effort is also made to identify the underlying reasons for the changes which have been observed. This demands in addition a careful programme of experimental, classroom research, so that the information can be made available to help teachers improve their teaching. Advocates of this view claim that the same amount of money spent on "action research" programmes in the classroom may prove to be a more fruitful way of improving standards of teaching and learning. Properly controlled educational intervention may be more cost-effective in the long run.

## Bibliography

Great Britain, Department of Education and Science 1978 Assessing the performance of pupils. *DES Report on Education*, No. 93. Department of Education and Science, London

Marklund S 1980 *From Assessment of Individual Students to Evaluation of School Systems*. Stockholm University, Stockholm

Moegiadi, Mangindaan C, Elley W B 1979 Evaluation of achievement in the Indonesian education system. *Eval. Educ.* 2(4): 281–355

Postlethwaite T N (ed.) 1974 What do children know? International studies on educational achievement. *Comp. Educ. Rev.* 18(2): 155–333

Reid N 1978 *Standards, Basics and National Assessment* (Set), No. 1, Item 13. New Zealand Council for Educational Research, Wellington

Sumner R (ed.) 1977 *Monitoring National Standards of Attainment in Schools*. National Foundation for Educational Research, Slough

United States, Comptroller General 1976 *Report to Congress. The National Assessment of Educational Progress: Its Results Need to be Made More Useful*. National Center for Education Statistics, Department of Health, Education and Welfare, Washington, DC

Womer F B, Martin W H 1979 The national assessment of educational progress. *Stud. Educ. Eval.* 5(1): 27–37

World Bank 1974–81 Numerous assessment studies by Education Department Staff/Consultants. World Bank, Washington, DC (largely mimeo)

# National Assessment of Educational Progress: Retrospect and Prospect[1]

## H. J. Walberg

In 1867 Congress passed legislation to create the United States Office of Education whose task was to collect statistics with a view toward improving education in the United States. Today it is increasingly apparent that accurate, comprehensive data are necessary for raising educational productivity and helping to increase the quality of national life.

The National Assessment of Educational Progress (NAEP) is a major informational vehicle for accomplishing these purposes. Sometimes called the Nation's Report Card, the NAEP was created in 1969 to obtain dependable data on the status and trends of achievement in a uniform, scientific manner (see Tyler 1985). The NAEP remains the only regularly conducted national survey in the United States of achievement at the elementary, middle-, and high-school levels (young adults have also been sampled). Unlike the longitudinal projects High School and Beyond and the National Educational Longitudinal Survey of 1988 (NELS-88) that follow the same students longitudinally over time, the NAEP is a periodic series of cross-sectional surveys of successive groups of students of the same age.

The subject areas assessed most often include reading, writing, mathematics, science, and social studies, although citizenship, computers, literature, art, music, and career development are also assessed. By 1988, the NAEP had tested about 1.3 million young Americans, making it one of the largest social surveys ever conducted and the most expensive, comprehensive, and long-standing educational survey in the United States, and perhaps the world.

The NAEP is designed with advice from teachers, subject matter experts, and citizens with a variety of points of view and representing various constituencies. By a process of consensus, they suggest the design objectives for the subject areas and specify general goals that students should achieve by the three ages usually tested: 9, 13, and 17, and now Grades 3, 7, and 11. After review and revision, these specifications are turned over to item writers, who develop questions and other exercises appropriate to the objectives.

The items are reviewed for appropriateness and possible bias, then field tested, revised, and administered to stratified, multistage probability samples. The resulting data are analyzed in various ways and then disseminated. The general purpose of NAEP is to provide information that will help educators, legislators, and others to improve education. This article discusses the evolution of the NAEP and several future prospects for accomplishing its long-term general purpose.

## 1. A Retrospective on the NAEP

At the 1967 meetings of the American Educational Research Association (AERA), arguments were presented about whether or not the United States should have a national assessment and, if so, about how it should be designed. At the outset, some educational reformers spoke actively and eloquently for the assessment to measure progress in improving education. However, several professional education associations and state authorities resisted the idea because they feared

1 This article has been adapted from an article, "National Assessment for Improving Education: Retrospect and Prospect" by H J Walberg which was originally published in the International Journal of Educational Research, Vol. 12, No. 7. It appears here with permission from Pergamon Press plc © 1988.

that schools and states would be identified. A concession was made that only broad regions and subgroups of students would be compared, and the emphasis would be on changes over time. In the 1980s the situation is very different as a large number of governors, legislators, and interested citizens want to study specific comparisons of states and to evaluate ongoing educational reforms.

In the 1970s, the NAEP began to extend its scholarly usefulness significantly when the National Science Foundation explored together with several scholars the idea of using NAEP science data for secondary analyses or studies going beyond trend analyses. The University of Illinois at Chicago was awarded a grant with subcontracts to two other universities and to the Education Commission of the States that conducted NAEP at the time. The project converted the massive NAEP data files to a uniform format with control statements for the Statistical Package for the Social Sciences that would make it easier for secondary or non-NAEP investigators to analyze the data. The project also produced sample analyses, and trained a group of other secondary users from about 20 universities and research agencies.

This grant resulted in a number of publications and an active special interest group of secondary analysts of NAEP data within the American Educational Research Association. NAEP analysts fall into three classes: subject matter specialists, who determine how students perform on individual items and clusters as related to curriculum policy; psychometrists interested in item response patterns; and researchers who try to determine what home, school, and other conditions appear optimal for educational achievement so as to suggest possible changes in educational policies and practices. The NAEP contractors themselves have reported item results and scores by region and types of students, and have recently begun some causal analyses to suggest policies.

The NAEP has extended its utility considerably by enabling secondary users to purchase data tapes at low cost and to analyze the immense bank of data that has accumulated. At little extra cost and human time, many opinion and background items on home, class, school characteristics, and conditions are now given to students, teachers, and principals.

Such items need not be given to entire samples but only random fractions of students taking the achievement tests. They can show how educational conditions and practices, as well as test scores, are changing over time. Analyses of items focusing on public opinion are in the tradition of the General Social Survey conducted by the National Opinion Research Center at the University of Chicago. *Core items* are used in every survey to measure trends in opinion or conditions of enduring importance. *Piggy-back* items may be added temporarily for one or more surveys to detect important short-term trends, or those of interest to particular analysts or project sponsors. In these ways, the NAEP has become an even greater national asset by providing additional valuable information efficiently, since the cost of adding items is small relative to the fixed costs of administration, sampling, data collection, computer processing, and archiving.

## 2. Causal Inference

The opinion and background items of the NAEP also allow a degree of causal inference. They may, for example, allow the inference that leisure-time reading and homework enhance achievement, other things being equal, since students who engage in these activities achieve better results than students who do not. Of course, causal directionality is uncertain since, for example, motivation may cause leisure reading, homework, and achievement, and achievement itself may cause the other things, even though attempts are made to control all the variables in regression and other analyses.

NAEP is, of course, a periodic survey of cohorts rather than longitudinal study that follows the same students over time. Longitudinal studies are better designed to detect variations in learning and other personal characteristics during and after schooling which are attributable to educational practices and conditions. Experimental studies of smaller groups of students randomly assigned to conditions and control groups may even be stronger indicators of their effects.

Neither longitudinal studies nor experiments are infallible. Some members of longitudinal studies refuse to participate or can no longer be located; and they may differ considerably from the original sample. Despite efforts to statistically control the alternative causal variables, analyses of longitudinal data may suggest spurious effects that cannot be completely ruled out, no matter how much sociologists may hope to rule them out. Experiments that psychologists prefer yield stronger causal confidence since groups differ only in random assignment and the conditions are closely observed, but they may be criticized as studies of how people act under contrived conditions rather than in the real world.

For purposes of causal inference, NAEP can partly compensate for the weaknesses of longitudinal surveys and experiments since it comes closest to estimating policies and conditions in the nation rather than those encountered by samples remaining from longitudinal surveys and the small, idiosyncratic samples generally obtained in the usual small-scale, single-site experiments. Some effects such as student motivation, the amount of instruction, its quality, homework, and the curriculum of the home seem powerful enough to be detectable in longitudinal, cross-sectional, and experimental studies (Walberg 1986). Thus, each of these approaches has something to contribute, not only in assessment but in suggesting improvements in practice.

## 3. State, International, and Other Comparisons

The original intentions of the NAEP were to accumulate data that could be compared with future data to measure progress and to compare broad regions of the country and subclasses of students such as boys and girls, and members of various ethnic and social groups. These may be worthwhile comparisons but they do not provide answers to all the important questions that might be gleaned from an upgraded NAEP. Of course, the public wants to know how the nation is progressing in achievement; but there is even more interest in how it compares with the status and progress of other countries. Policy makers in education want to know why achievement has changed and how to raise it. International cooperation on such matters is mutually beneficial since the variations among countries are generally larger than within any particular country and this makes causal effects more detectable.

Even so, the United States, like Australia, Canada, and the Federal Republic of Germany, has no centralized ministry of education; it could be said that the United States has 50 or more ministries, one for each state. If state policies led to increased science achievement in the state of Vermont and decreased it in New Hampshire, the differences and causes could not be detected if the results were averaged by regions or by the whole nation. Some state governments are paying a greater share of the costs of education than previously, and they have initiated different reforms, with more radical choice plans on line. Some state governments want to know how schools compare within their states as well as how their state averages compare with those of other states. The states can learn from one another's experience, and so can the nation as a whole.

The new demand for results and their measurement, of course, began with *A Nation at Risk*, the report of the federally-appointed National Commission for Excellence in Education (1983) and the several dozen other reform reports that followed it. The National Commission pointed out the poor performance of United States students by international standards and the potential contributions of education to national prosperity and welfare. As a result of the reform reports, considerably more money was spent on education and many reforms were made; but it does not seem clear that education is yet as efficient as it should be, and that funds are wisely spent.

Data released on science achievement in March 1988 by the International Association for the Evaluation of Educational Achievement (IEA) and the National Science Foundation again showed comparatively poor United States achievements and rankings near the bottom of affluent countries and rivaled by several developing countries.

Even more pointedly, the National Governors' Association (NGA 1986) issued the bluntly titled *A Time for Results* which calls for higher achievement and deeper and wider reforms in United States schools. Some recommendations in their report on achievement comparisons, school-site management, parental involvement, governance, diversity, magnet schools,

and choice of attendance were not widely considered a decade ago, but are now being enacted in many districts and states. In *Results in Education* (1987) the NGA called for indicators that reflect state educational goals, measure higher-level skills demanded by society, and meet the information needs of educators, policy makers, and the public. In addition, the Council of Chief State School Officers voted to compile state indicators including achievement.

At one time, failure rates on the Selective Service Examinations for the military draft were available by state. The state failure rates ranged widely from less than 1 percent in Minnesota to about 35 percent in one Southern state, and they were related to various educational conditions (Walberg and Rasher 1979). In recent years, wall charts have been issued by the US Department of Education showing average student performance on the Scholastic Achievement Test, the American College Test, and other educational indicators for each of the 50 states. Since these tests have been taken by selective, nonrandom, and varying fractions of age groups within states and across time, they are less desirable as indicators than NAEP scores. However, widespread publicity and comments about state and international achievement show the enormous public and professional interest in comparisons.

The prospect of better state comparisons, as well as school and international comparisons, comes at the right time. NAEP can help fulfill this important national interest as suggested in the National Academy of Education report (1987), however, it may also accomplish several less obvious purposes in the long term.

## 4. NAEP by Tailored Testing

Even NAEP-based calibration, however, would necessarily change this century's convention of giving each child within a class or grade the same test which is similar to old-fashioned "batch processing" in industry. A far more efficient and time-saving approach is *tailored testing* (Carroll 1982) which flexibly adapts test items to students over great ranges of ability, and might be developed by NAEP, or developed with and anchored to NAEP scales.

For several decades, it has been possible both in principle and in practice to program computers to assign the most discriminating items to each student, based upon her, or his prior responses during the testing session. In fact, the idea goes back to the origins of mental testing. Alfred Binet administered intelligence test items of a given difficulty to children depending on how well they did on the first few items tried (Carroll 1982). As few as 10 such tailored items can yield scores as reliable as many more batched items suited to the average student. Alternatively, an hour or two of tailored items might yield accurate individual assessments, not in one subject but in all the major subjects of the standard curriculum. Alternately, at the same time, such items could provide highly detailed assessments of skills in a single discipline, for example, word choice, grammar, spelling, and punctuation in written composition. From such results, tailored instruction can be suggested. Educators could avoid teaching what students already know and what they are yet incapable of learning until they meet prerequisite skills.

The increased efficiency in time use and the computer's capacity to record large amounts of information make it feasible to monitor individual student progress more frequently, accurately, and comprehensively. With a thorough, continuing assessment of what each student needs to learn, it should become equally feasible to provide computer-adapted or tailored instruction. Such instruction is by no means a panacea, but it is among those educational methods that provide moderately superior achievement; and it has the further advantage of saving students' study time (Walberg 1986). It can be expected that computer costs will continue to fall, while software increases in sophistication and interest.

## 5. *NAEP by Modem*

NAEP itself could, in a decade or two, be carried out by computer hookups and this possibility seems worth exploration. In principle, it would be feasible to conduct sample surveys of districts, schools, and students directly by computers. Students, for example, could rapidly complete tailored tests and questionnaires by terminal and modem. In compensation, students and schools could receive an instant report on the results. At present, schools receive no feedback from NAEP, except perhaps a newspaper report a year later if they chance to come across it. The further advantage of a national hookup is the speed at which surveys and tests can be completed. The time-consuming steps of printing tests and questionnaires, mailing, scanning and screening data, and the like could be bypassed. Even analyses could be automated, and produced at electronic speed.

Just as national polls of 1,500 respondents provide reasonably accurate estimates of public opinion in the nation, direct sampling by telephone controlled by computer would make NAEP fast and cheap. Quarterly or even monthly survey reports on important output measures could be made routine as they are in commerce and industry. Local, state or national assessments of special topics might be commissioned and completed in less than a month. The rapid educational reforms occurring in the states cannot be monitored if the information is obsolete before it is processed.

## 6. *Conclusion*

The late 1980s seem a time for great opportunity in educational reform and research in education. Agriculture, engineering, and medicine made great strides in improving human welfare as doubts arose about traditional, natural, and mystical practices; as the widened measurement of results intensified; as experimental findings were synthesized; and as their theoretical and practical implications were coordinated and vigorously implemented and evaluated.

Education is no less open to humanistic and scientific inquiry and no lower in priority since half the workers in modern nations are in knowledge industries, and the value of investments in people is now more apparent than ever (Walberg 1983). Although it is possible to find fault with federal statistics on education, the last decade or two has been a period of quiet but significant accomplishments; and larger amounts of valuable data are being accumulated and put to good use by policy makers.

The NAEP has become a national asset. It can serve as a sturdy benchmark for accomplishments and failures at reform; and policy makers need to know about both.

## *Bibliography*

Carroll J B 1982 The measurement of intelligence. In: Steinberg R J (ed.) 1982 *Handbook of Human Intelligence*. Cambridge University Press, Cambridge, Massachusetts, pp. 29–120.

*Indicators of Education Status and Trends* 1985. US Department of Education, Washington, DC

National Academy of Education 1987 *The Nation's Report Card: Improving the Assessment of Student Achievement. Report of the Study Group*. National Academy of Education, Washington, DC

National Governors' Association 1986 *Time for Results*. NGA, Washington, DC

National Governors' Association 1987 *Results in Education*. NGA, Washington, DC

National Commission on Excellence in Education 1983 *A Nation at Risk*. US Dept. of Education, US Government Printing Office, Washington, DC

Tyler R W 1985 National assessment of educational progress (NAEP). In: Husén T, Postlethwaite T N (eds.) 1985 *The International Encyclopedia of Education*, Vol. 6. Pergamon, Oxford, pp. 3478–80

Walberg H J 1983 Scientific literacy and economic productivity in international perspective. *Daedalus* 112(2): 1–28

Walberg H J 1986 Synthesis of research on teaching. In: Wittrock M C (ed.) 1986 *Handbook of Research on Teaching*, 3rd edn. Macmillan, New York

Walberg H J, Rasher S P 1979 Achievement in the 50 states. In: Walberg H J (ed.) 1979 *Educational Environments and Effects*. McCutchen, Berkeley, California, pp. 353–68

**Part 6**

# Types of Tests and Examinations

# Part 6

# Types of Tests and Examinations

## Introduction

Three parts of the *Encyclopedia* are devoted to testing and measurement. Whilst Part 4 is concerned with theoretical models, and Part 5 with applications, Part 6 is devoted to more practical concerns. It is divided into four sections, comprising Test Security, Timing, and Administration Conditions; Testing Formats Used in Evaluation; Testing in Educational Settings; and Testing Domains of Knowledge, Ability, and Interest.

The opening articles of Part 6(a) examine *Computer-managed Testing* and *Adaptive Testing*. As these two articles attest, computers are playing an increasing role in the preparation, administration, and scoring of tests. They are used to maintain item pools, prepare test materials, administer tests, and to process and score the test results. Adaptive testing is a specialized administration procedure in which different sets of test questions may be administered to different examinees, depending on their patterns of responses. The adaptive testing approach is used to improve efficiency, permitting accurate assessment of more distinct abilities within the same period of time.

The next article, *Closed Tests and Security*, briefly reviews procedures used by testing companies to ensure the security of their test materials. These include keeping materials under lock and key, serial numbering of proof copies and tests, and restricting access to demonstrably qualified individuals, for example, members of relevant professional organizations.

Two more articles on test administration conditions complete the first section of Part 6. The first of these, on *Individual and Group Testing*, highlights the increased flexibility possible with individual testing, versus the usually lower cost, greater objectivity, and better norming of published group-administered instruments. The article concludes with recommendations for individual testing with exceptionally poor readers or emotionally disturbed children. The second article on administration conditions takes up the well-known distinction between *Power and Speed Tests*. These terms are defined, and threats to the validity of speed tests are described. The implications of computerized test administration for the speed–power distinction are also discussed briefly.

The second section of Part 6 is concerned with specific Testing Formats Used in Evaluation. Different types of examinations have distinctive strengths and weaknesses, and the choice of measurement methods for a particular evaluation problem represents a trade-off among them. Thirteen significant considerations that enter into such decisions are presented in Table 1, which illustrates these concerns by rating them as strengths or weaknesses for essay, short-answer, and objective test items. For example, all three of these examination types can be used to measure ability to solve novel problems, but it is easier to construct essay or objective test questions for this purpose than short-answer or completion items. For measuring ability to organize, integrate, or synthesize information, essay tests are probably best, although short-answer or completion items may also be used. Objective items, which typically require the examinee to choose among a small number of prespecified alternatives or to match terms in one list with terms of another, would probably be quite unsuitable for this purpose. The additional examination types discussed in Part 6 could be rated in the same way, on these and the remaining dimensions. Depending on the specifics of a given test and testing application, precise ratings might differ, of course, as would the amount of weight given each factor in reaching a decision, but the factors are generally applicable.

Part 6(b) consists of a series of nine distinct testing formats that may be used in

**Table 1**
Considerations in the Selection of Measurement Approaches[a]

| Factor | Essay | Short Answer or Completion | Objective |
|---|---|---|---|
| Can measure ability to solve novel problems | ++ | + | ++ |
| Can measure ability to organize, integrate, or synthesize | ++ | + | -- |
| Can measure originality or innovative approaches to problems | ++ | + | -- |
| Can isolate specific abilities in subject area from general skills of writing, spelling, and language usage | -- | - | ++ |
| Has potential value for diagnosis | -- | + | ++ |
| Can sample adequately the objectives of instruction | -- | - | ++ |
| Can sample adequately the content of instruction | -- | - | ++ |
| Is free from opportunities for guessing answer | ++ | ++ | -- |
| Gives consistent scores from scorer to scorer | -- | - | ++ |
| Is accurate in differentiating levels of competency among examinees | -- | - | ++ |
| Can be scored by unskilled clerk or machine | -- | - | ++ |
| Can be scored quickly | -- | - | ++ |
| Takes little time for writing items | + | + | - |

a Adapted from Thorndike R L, Hagen E 1969, *Measurement and Evaluation in Psychology and Education*, 3rd edn. John Wiley and Sons, New York. Reproduced by permission of John Wiley and Sons Inc. © 1969. All Rights Reserved.

evaluation. The first four of these are paper-and-pencil testing formats that may be helpful in assessing typical cognitive and affective learning outcomes; the fifth article takes up oral examinations; the sixth offers a general treatment of nonverbal tests; and the last three turn to learning outcomes that may be quite important, but are most likely to be manifest in out-of-school settings.

The paper-and-pencil formats for testing typical learning outcomes begin with a discussion of *Cloze Tests*. These tests are exceptionally easy to prepare and to score objectively. A passage is selected from the text to be tested, and in this passage a number of words are deleted and replaced with standard-length blanks. Words may be deleted at random, but more typically every fifth word is removed. Examinees must attempt to fill in the missing words, and are scored according to their success. The development, use, and interpretation of these tests is described, including guidelines for using cloze scores to judge the readability of texts for a given group of learners.

The next format described, *Cognitive Preference Tests*, was designed for use in evaluation to assess students' interest in course content, and their propensity to work with it intellectually. Cognitive preference tests employ a forced-choice format, and yield scores for different modes of knowledge utilization. The format and method appear promising, but further validation is called for.

Third to be discussed is the very broad category of *Objective Tests*, used to measure intelligence, aptitude, and achievement. The article points out that strictly speaking, objectivity is a property of the scoring method, not the test format. It takes up areas of application, item formats amenable to objective scoring, the advantages and disadvantages of objective tests, and cautions that considerable care in construction is required if these tests are to realize their full potential.

In the next article, *Sentence Completion Tests* are described. These have been used not only for the measurement of educational achievement, but also in personality research. They are not considered an objective testing format, and they can be both difficult and costly to score. Their principle advantage in educational evaluation may be a more accurate measurement of retention than is typical with forced-choice objective tests.

The article on *Oral Examinations* reviews the history and research literature on this form of test, and then turns to modern applications. Because they are more costly to administer and score than written tests, oral examinations are used primarily to measure skills that cannot be tested otherwise; primarily oral language skills themselves, especially in foreign language instruction. Eight different approaches are described, including reading aloud, conversation on a prepared subject, question and answer, and story narration, among others.

*Nonverbal Tests*, the subject of the sixth article in the series on testing formats, offer a method of testing general intellectual ability that does not depend on verbal fluency and may therefore reflect linguistic and cultural factors to a lesser extent than verbal tests. Nonverbal tests are quite diverse, including both performance tests and paper-and-pencil tests of general reasoning ability. They may be group or individually administered, and may focus on a single ability dimension or a mixture of abilities.

The last three testing formats discussed may be useful for examining the application of knowledge and skills in practical problem solving, as well as the transfer of school learning to out-of-school settings. These include *Performance Tests, Practical Examinations,* and *Written Simulation in the Assessment of Problem Solving*. Performance tests are a general category of nonverbal tests that require responses in terms of actual tasks or behaviors. The article in which they are discussed reviews their history and general features, and refers briefly to their use in science education. The discussion of practical examinations focuses much more extensively on the assessment of laboratory skills in science courses, especially those using inquiry-oriented curricula. They may be defined as tasks which require some manipulation or apparatus or some action on materials, and which involved direct experiences of the examinee with the materials or events at hand. A taxonomy of laboratory learning outcomes is presented, and several types of practical examinations are described and illustrated. Written simulations may provide a more feasible approach to the testing of knowledge application. A realistic written simulation of some complex performance or problem is developed, such that information is revealed or choices are presented contingent on the earlier responses of the examinee. Patient–management problems in medicine are among the best developed examples.

The third section of Part 6 addresses tests tailored to specific educational settings, beginning with a general discussion of *Achievement Tests*. The article on achievement testing first distinguishes between standardized tests and classroom tests, according to the purposes for which they are used, the audiences they serve, and their levels of specificity. Design considerations are presented for each type of test, together with their respective strengths and weaknesses. Each variety of test has a role to play, but difficulties arise when they are misused. The most common misuse cited is excessive reliance on externally mandated tests to guide detailed instructional planning at the classroom level.

Following this general discussion of achievement tests, several more specific categories of tests are described. The first of these are *Placement Tests*, used to determine appropriate starting points in learning sequences, and to capitalize on aptitude–treatment interactions by assigning students to alternative instructional treatments. The second is *Criterion-referenced Tests*, which include both domain-referenced and mastery tests. The article discusses item domains and domain specification, item construction and analysis, and such practical matters as test length, the creation of parallel forms, and methods of standard setting. It concludes with discussions of criterion-referenced testing applications, reliability, and validity. Following *Criterion-referenced Tests*, the next article turns to *Standardized Tests*. Several senses of standardization are discussed, including standardized testing conditions, norm-referenced and domain-referenced standardized tests, and comparison to specific performance standards, as in mastery testing. The use of item response theory to develop absolute measurement scales offers yet another example. Different methods may be optimum for different purposes, but the evaluator's choice may be constrained by the substantial investment of resources required to accomplish any large-scale development of standards.

*Minimum Competency Tests, External Examinations*, and *Differential Test Batteries and Omnibus Tests* are the focus of the last three articles in the series on tests for specific educational settings. The first of these distinguishes minimum competency tests from more general tests of educational progress in terms of their purpose, difficulty, and content sampling. Standards, criteria, and policy implications are discussed. The article on *External Examinations* briefly surveys the history, development and distribution, uses, and content of external examinations, leading to an operational definition of such tests as "norm-referenced, terminal written tests designed for those in full-time education" (p.503). Future directions for the development of external examinations are also described. The article on *Differential Test Batteries and Omnibus Tests* discusses the structure and uses of such instruments, and the reporting of score profiles. Caution is urged in the interpretation of score profiles and differences, due to the well-known problem of low reliabilities for difference scores.

Part 6 closes with a series of articles on Testing Domains of Knowledge, Ability, and

Interest. Five articles on testing language and literacy deal with *Reading Comprehension Assessment, Assessing Communication Skills, Essay Examinations, Vocabulary Measures,* and *Foreign Language Performance Tests.* Together, these articles address the definition of linguistic abilities, formats used in their assessment, test design and content, scoring, interpretation, and reporting. Problems of bias and invalidity may arise because of the difficulty of separating language comprehension from prior knowledge, and high reliability may be difficult to attain in writing examinations, because of the small number of independent writing samples that can be obtained from an examinee in a reasonable amount of time. The training of examiners to administer tests of oral and aural proficiency may pose a significant challenge in foreign language testing.

The next five articles deal with the testing of cognitive abilities, beginning with a general discussion of *Models of Intelligence.* In this article, the historical development of intelligence models is reviewed, focusing in part on the long-standing controversy between conceptions of general mental ability as a unitary construct versus a composite of several correlated abilities. Major models proposed by British and American researchers are briefly reviewed, concluding with recent studies that have used structural equation models to reach a synthesis of competing positions. Implications for measurement are derived next, including recommendations that multiple tests rather than a single, homogeneous test be used to measure general ability, and that even when a single, narrower ability is to be measured, it may be necessary to use several different tests so that general ability can be partialled out of performance on more specific measures. The next article takes up the question of *Cognitive Style.* This refers to abilities that may indicate students' preferred modes of learning, as in aptitude–treatment–interaction research. The cognitive style constructs discussed include field independence versus field dependence, reflectivity versus impulsivity, convergence versus divergence, and others. *Verbal Reasoning Tests, Learning Ability Tests,* and *Culture-free Tests* are discussed in the final three articles on cognitive abilities.

The last two articles of Part 6(d) examine the testing of *Vocational Aptitude* and *Vocational Interest Measures.* These measures are generally designed to reflect the aptitude and skill requirements of specific occupational groupings, and show little connection to psychological theories. They may be used in educational settings to select students for shop and business classes, for admission to post-secondary vocational training, or simply as an impetus to vocational exploration and career planning. Vocational tests are often organized into batteries measuring multiple aptitudes, and scaled to predict success in a number of different occupational types. Vocational interest measures also tend to be largely atheoretical in their design and construction. Items are selected and keys are developed following empirical-statistical procedures, on the assumption that examinees may wish to consider occupations whose practitioners express interests and personality characteristics similar to their own. The use of interest batteries in vocational counseling is described, as are computer-based interpretation and guidance systems. The important issue of sex bias in vocational testing and counseling is also discussed.

# Test Security, Timing, and Administration Conditions

## Computer-managed Testing

**D. A. Leclercq**

As their capacities and speed increase and their costs decrease (on average by about 20 percent each year), computers are coming to play an increasingly significant role in the preparation, administration, and scoring of tests. In the past, a clear distinction has been drawn between computer-assisted instruction (CAI) and computer-assisted testing on the one hand, and computer-managed instruction (CMI) and computer-managed testing on the other. In the first group, the computer's role was only to help the teacher who remained the primary decision maker. In the second group, the computer software was extended to provide a self-contained instructional and/or testing experience for the student. However, a range of new applications combines features from both approaches so that the demarcation between them is becoming increasingly blurred.

## 1. Item Pools

Item pools can themselves be stored as computer files. Classification of the items based on taxonomies or catalogues of instructional objectives, on the "universe" of possible questions (Hively et al. 1968), and/or on psychometric and technical characteristics (such as item difficulty, format, etc.) can be conveniently organized by a computer. The computer is helpful in managing and updating such pools and can retrieve items appropriately for test instruction purposes.

Ways in which the computer can use an item bank for test construction to serve specialized purposes have been described by a number of writers. These special topics include "multiple matrix sampling" (Shoemaker 1973), "quasi-parallel tests with defined characteristics" (Choppin 1978, Wright and Stone 1979), and "individualized tailored testing" (Wood 1969, Leclercq 1980).

## 2. Preparation of Test Materials

Advances in computer-controlled printing techniques, specifically including laser printers, make it possible for items which include complex drawings or pictures to be reproduced inexpensively on paper from computer files.

Using the computer to print test forms is of special interest to the examiner who wants to scramble the order of questions in a test, or the order of alternative responses in multiple-choice questions. The resulting variations of an original test constitute an effective way to minimize cheating by students, and the computer is adept at unscrambling what it has previously scrambled. The computer can also provide another kind of quasiparallel test in which the phrasing of the questions is fixed but the numerical values included are generated at random.

## 3. Test Administration

An individually administered interactive criterion-referenced test can be conveniently administered by a computer. A decision algorithm applied repeatedly during the testing sequence determines the sequence of questions to be asked, and perhaps the point at which testing may be discontinued (Weiss 1982). In interactive testing situations, the computer can be programmed to control a variety of peripheral devices so that test items can be displayed on a cathode ray tube (a television or monitor), on slides, or via sound recordings, and so on. The videodisc has excited considerable interest as a storage medium for test material since it can handle still and motion pictures, sound, and digital information, and has a very large capacity.

## 4. Data Processing and Test Scoring

Even when the testing is not individualized and adaptive, computers are regularly used to process test data. Various techniques are used to facilitate the introduction of student test responses directly into the computer system without the need for a keypunching stage. These include optical mark-sense sheets, bar-code reading, and direct optical character recognition. In these areas, educational testers are benefiting considerably from technology originally developed for other purposes.

A major advantage of the computer scoring of test protocols is the possibility of computing numerous and complex scores and indices and of providing detailed and individualized feedback. For instance, students can receive comments on each category of questions or on each individual question including recommendations for subsequent learning activities. Teachers can receive individual results detailing, for instance, which students have mastered which objective (Cooley and Glaser 1969). Some special modes of test response, such as intervals or fractiles (Hardy 1981) imply sophisticated scoring formulas for which the computer is the only convenient solution.

## 5. Integrated Packages of Computer-managed Instruction and Testing

Computer-managed testing is often integrated into systems of computer-managed instruction. Many formal activities in the classroom can be managed by a computer, for example in the "Individually Prescribed Instruction" system (Glaser 1977) where each student follows at his or her own pace a curriculum according to the mastery learning approach. The computer assesses students' achievement after each learning sequence and prescribes the next learning activity in which each student is to engage.

## Bibliography

Choppin B H 1978 *Item Banking and the Monitoring of Achievement.* (Research in Progress Series No. 1.) National Foundation for Educational Research, Slough

Cooley W W, Glaser R 1969 The computer and individualized instruction. *Science* 166: 574–82

Glaser R 1977 *Adaptive Education: Individual Diversity and Learning.* Holt, Rinehart and Winston, New York

Hardy J L 1981 Computer-based feedbacks to improve estimation ability. In: Lewis R, Tagg E D (eds.) 1981 *Computers in Education: Proc. of the IFIP TC-3 3rd World Conf. on Computers in Education, Lausanne, Switzerland, July 27–31, 1981.* North-Holland, New York

Hively W, Patterson H, Page S 1968 Defined system of arithmetic tests. *J. Educ. Meas.* 5: 4

Leclercq D A 1980 Computerised tailored testing: Structured and calibrated item banks for summative and formative evaluation. *J. Eur. Educ.* 15: 251–60

Shoemaker D M 1973 *Principles and Procedures of Multiple Matrix Sampling.* Ballinger, Cambridge, Massachusetts

Weiss D J 1982 Improving measurement quality and efficiency with adaptive testing. *Appl. Psychol. Meas.* 6: 4

Wood R 1969 The efficacy of tailored testing. *Educ. Res.* 11: 219–22

Wright B D, Stone M H 1979 *Best Test Design.* MESA Press, Chicago, Illinois

# Adaptive Testing

**D. J. Weiss**

An adaptive test is one in which different sets of test questions (items) are administered to different individuals depending on each individual's status on the trait being measured. Adaptive tests contrast with conventional tests in which all examinees are administered the same fixed set of items (e.g., a typical paper-and-pencil test). Adaptive testing has also been referred to as tailored, response-contingent, programmed, computerized, automated, individualized, branched, and sequential testing.

In an adaptive test, one or more items are administered to an examinee and scored correct or incorrect. Based on the responses of the examinee, additional items are selected from an item bank (pool) with items of known difficulties and discriminations. The items selected for administration to the examinee during the process of testing are selected to be those in the item bank which are most appropriate for measuring that individual, primarily in terms of their difficulties. In this way, the items are adapted to the characteristics of the examinee during the process of testing. The items administered to each individual are those that are neither too easy nor too difficult for the individual.

Some adaptive tests are designed for individual administration by a trained psychometrist. Others are amenable to paper-and-pencil administration. Still others require that test items be administered by an interactive computer. The latter approach takes full advantage of the capabilities of adaptive testing. While most adaptive tests have been developed for measuring ability or achievement variables, the technology of adaptive testing can be fruitfully applied to the measurement of homogeneous personality and attitudinal variables.

Adaptive tests have demonstrated substantial advantages over conventional tests. A major advantage is that of efficiency. Adaptive tests yield measurements of comparable or superior quality to those of conventional tests with considerably fewer items administered to each individual. These increases in testing efficiency are reflected in savings in test administration time, making it possible to measure two or more traits using adaptive tests in the same amount of time that would be required to measure a single trait using conventional tests. Along with the increases in measurement efficiency, adaptive tests provide improved measurement characteristics in terms of greater precision of the measurements for all or most trait levels, which translate into higher degrees of reliability and potentially higher levels of validity. Even with a set of items that constitute a conventional test, computer-administered adaptive tests can improve measurement efficiency with no loss in the psychometric characteristics of the measurements. Adaptive testing can also result in efficient and more accurate mastery classifications, and provides an efficient and practical approach to the measurement of individual change.

## 1. The Test Constructor's Bandwidth–Fidelity Dilemma

Given the requirement of administering a fixed set of items to a group of examinees, a test constructor can construct a "peaked" conventional test or a "rectangular" conventional test, with possible variations in between these two extremes. The peaked conventional test has all of its items concentrated at one level of difficulty. It will measure very well for individuals whose trait levels are at or near that level of difficulty, but as the trait levels of individuals deviate from the point at which the test is peaked, the precision of the measurements obtained by the conventional test decreases very rapidly since items peaked at an average level of difficulty will be too difficult for individuals with lower trait levels or too easy for individuals with higher trait levels. A rectangular conventional test includes several very easy items which will be appropriate for individuals with very low trait levels, several moderate difficulty items which will be appropriate for individuals at moderate trait levels, and several items at each of a number of levels of higher difficulty which will be appropriate for individuals with higher trait levels. However, only a few of the items in each test will be appropriate for individuals at any trait level. As a consequence, while a rectangular conventional test will provide measurements of relatively equal precision at most trait levels, the overall magnitude of precision of these measurements will be relatively low.

Thus the constructor of a conventional test is caught in a "bandwidth–fidelity" dilemma: a peaked conventional test provides measurements of high fidelity (precision) at the point at which it is peaked, but it has little bandwidth, that is it has little capability of differentiating examinees at other trait levels. By contrast, a rectangular conventional test has good bandwidth—it is capable of differentiating trait levels all along the trait continuum; but it has low overall fidelity—the differentiations it can make are of relatively low precision.

Since a test peaked in difficulty at an individual's trait level provides the best measurements for that individual, adaptive testing solves the bandwidth–fidelity dilemma by selecting from an item bank for each individual a test designed of items which are appropriate in difficulty level for each examinee. The result of a good adaptive testing procedure is a set of items selected for each examinee which have 0.5 probability of a correct response (assuming no guessing) for that individual. This test is the test that is designed to differentiate each individual's trait levels from contiguous trait levels with maximum precision.

## 2. Principles of Adaptive Testing

### 2.1 Adaptive Tests Using Prestructured Item Banks

The general principles of adaptive testing were first applied by Alfred Binet in the Binet intelligence test, developed in France in the early 1900s and later made available as the Stanford–Binet Intelligence Test in the English-speaking countries. In the language of adaptive testing, Binet's intelligence test, which used an item pool prestructured by age (difficulty) levels, is a mechanical branching strategy using a fixed branching rule, a variable entry point, and a variable termination criterion. The entry point for Binet's adaptive test is the level at which the individual is assumed to be functioning. Items are administered and scored immediately.

If all items are answered correctly at a given age (difficulty) level, items at a higher level are administered until an age level is identified at which all items are answered incorrectly (ceiling level). If all items are answered incorrectly at a given age level, items at lower age levels are administered until an age level is identified at which the individual answers all items correctly (basal level). The termination criterion is to stop testing when both a ceiling level and a basal level have been identified. In between the ceiling and basal levels, the examinee will have answered some items correctly and some items incorrectly, providing a set of items approximately adapted to the individual's ability level. The variable termination criterion usually results in different numbers of items administered to different individuals.

Other adaptive tests developed beginning in the late 1950s used paper-and-pencil administration but did not use variable entry and variable termination (Weiss 1974). The two-stage adaptive test (Lord 1980) has minimal adaptive capability. All examinees take a short test, called a routing test, which is typically a test of average difficulty. Based on their scores on the routing test, examinees are branched to a second stage "measurement" test which is roughly adapted to their trait level. The pyramidal adaptive test consists of a set of items prestructured by difficulty into a structure resembling a pyramid. At the top of the pyramid is an item of average difficulty which is the first item administered to an examinee. At the next stage of the test are two items whose difficulties are slightly above and below the difficulty of the first item. At subsequent stages, each item leads to two additional items—a slightly more difficult item, or a slightly easier item. The slightly more difficult item is administered following a correct response to any item, and the slightly easier item is administered following an incorrect response to an item.

The flexilevel test (Lord 1980) consists of a series of items with one item at each of a number of equally spaced difficulties varying from very easy to very difficult items. Individuals begin the test with the item of average difficulty; a correct response leads to the next more difficult item not previously administered, and an incorrect response leads to the next less difficult item not previously administered. A person with a high level on the trait will receive the highest difficulty items, and an individual with a low trait level will receive the 50 percent of the lower difficulty items, while examinees in between will receive a subset of items that span their trait level.

The stratified adaptive (stradaptive) test, like the Binet test, operates from an item bank stratified into item subsets of different difficulty levels (Weiss 1979). Testing can begin at any difficulty level, and a new item is selected after each item is administered. A correct response to an item leads to the most discriminating unadministered item in the next higher level of difficulty. An incorrect response leads to the most discriminating unadministered item at the next lower level of difficulty. Similar to the Binet test, testing continues until a "ceiling" stratum has been identified—a level of difficulty at which the individual answers none of the items correctly (or in the case of multiple-choice items, answers at or below the chance level). The fixed-branching strategies are useful if adaptive tests are to be administered by paper and pencil or by simple testing machines.

## 2.2 Adaptive Testing Using Item Response Theory and Unstructured Item Banks

The full power of adaptive testing is made available through variable-branching strategies based on item response theory (latent trait test theory or item characteristic curve theory), and using computerized item administration. The item response theory item information curve, which combines information on an item's difficulty, discrimination, and "guessing" parameters, describes how precisely an item measures at various points along the continuum or how well an item differentiates between contiguous trait levels. In addition, item response theory-based methods of scoring tests permit estimation of individuals' trait levels based on their responses to one or more items and provide an error of measurement associated with the trait level estimate (Lord 1980).

The maximum information adaptive testing strategy selects items which provide maximum levels of item information at an individual's currently estimated trait level. An item is administered, an estimate made of the individual's trait level based on the responses to one item (using Bayesian estimation procedures) or two or more items (using maximum likelihood estimation procedures). The new trait level estimate is then used to select the next item to be administered to that examinee. This process—selecting the item that provides maximum information at the current estimated level of the trait and reestimating trait level—is repeated until a termination criterion is reached. Adaptive tests of this type can be terminated when the current trait level estimate has a given standard error of measurement (or its reciprocal, precision of information) derived from maximum likelihood scoring, or using Bayesian scoring a given Bayesian posterior variance of the trait level estimate (squared standard error of estimate).

A Bayesian-based variation of the maximum information item selection procedure (Owen 1975) uses Bayes's theorem to select the one item from all the unadministered items that will minimize the Bayesian posterior variance of the trait level estimate after it is answered. The trait level is then reestimated using Bayesian estimation procedures, and the item pool is again searched to identify the single item as yet unadministered that minimizes the posterior variance. The procedure is repeated until some predetermined level of the Bayesian posterior variance is reached. This procedure permits more explicit use of prior information to determine starting points than does the maximum information item selection procedure. However, the use of prior information introduces biases into the scoring procedure which reduce levels of measurement precision for individuals whose trait levels are not near the prior estimate, at least in relatively short adaptive tests.

## 3. Applications of Adaptive Testing

### 3.1 Adaptive Testing to Improve Measurement Efficiency and Measurement Precision

These tests, comprising most of the adaptive testing literature, are those that are designed to solve the tester's bandwidth–fidelity dilemma. Adaptive tests of this type approximate "equiprecise" measurement at all trait levels, that is, measurements that measure all trait levels equally well. The successful implementation of adaptive tests for this purpose requires: (a) an adequate item bank, (b) an efficient item selection routine and scoring method, and (c) an appropriate termination criterion.

In order to have enough good items at all possible trait levels so that each individual will be administered a test peaked at his or her trait level, there must be a reasonably large number of items spanning a wide range of difficulties. Good results have been achieved with item banks ranging from 100 to 200 items, with banks of 116 to 150 items providing excellent results. Regardless of the size of the item bank, however, there must be a relatively equal number of items throughout the range of item difficulties. The adaptive testing item bank designed for equiprecise and efficient measurement will function best with items of high discrimination. The higher the discriminations, assuming an adequate distribution of difficulties, the more efficient will be the adaptive test.

Different adaptive testing strategies have differential efficiency. The most efficient strategy in terms of providing equiprecise measurement is the maximum information strategy combined with maximum likelihood scoring. Second is the Bayesian strategy with Bayesian scoring, although its efficiency tends to decrease for trait level estimates that are discrepant from the prior estimate, at least for relatively short adaptive tests. The stradaptive strategy also yields relatively equiprecise measurement.

Equiprecise measurement is best achieved by using a variable termination criterion. In this way, testing can continue until a specified degree of measurement precision is reached for each examinee. If the item pool permits, this will guarantee equiprecise measurement across all trait levels.

Research on adaptive tests designed to improve both measurement efficiency and measurement precision supports the theoretical expectations (Weiss 1982, 1983). Adaptive tests can solve the bandwidth–fidelity dilemma, resulting in tests of high precision and equal levels of precision across all trait levels measured. Adaptive tests also generally show higher reliabilities at very short test lengths, with reliabilities equal to those of peaked conventional tests with two or more times the number of items. In addition, adaptive tests have shown equal or higher validities with substantially fewer items, in comparison to conventional tests.

## 3.2 Adaptive Testing to Improve Efficiency of Measurement

While adaptive tests can be designed to improve both measurement efficiency and provide equiprecise measurement by using an appropriately designed item bank, adaptive testing can also be used to improve test efficiency with the kinds of item pools typically found in conventional tests (Weiss 1979). In this case, the objective is to select from a fixed subset of items (which might comprise a conventional test) only those items that are necessary to measure a given individual. Adaptive tests of this type can result in substantially shorter tests, and therefore more efficient tests, without any loss in the measurement characteristics of the test. Test length reductions may range up to 80 percent of the items in a conventional test, with typical reductions of about 50 percent.

To improve measurement efficiency with a fixed and relatively small item bank (e.g., 20 or 30 items), adaptive tests can use a maximum information item selection strategy. As indicated, this strategy selects at each stage in the adaptive test the single item providing most information at the individual's current estimated trait level. Testing continues until there are no items left in the bank that provide more than some predetermined minimum amount of information. If the minimum information cut-off value is very low (e.g., 0.01 or 0.05), the adaptive test administered will have captured from all of the items available all potential psychometric information in the item subset. Any remaining items will be items that provide no capability of differentiating between contiguous trait levels at the individual's final trait level estimate.

When more than one trait is to be measured (e.g., in the case of a multiple aptitude battery) this intra-subtest adaptive testing procedure can be combined with information on the intercorrelations of the subtests, in order to further improve testing efficiency. Based on the known intercorrelations of the subtests in some reference group, predictions of probable trait levels on subsequent subtests can be made from the trait level estimates for tests already completed and the known regression of the current test on previous tests. These starting points can then be used for the administration of subsequent adaptive tests within each subtest. Ability estimates at the end of each subtest then are combined in later regression equations to predict starting points for other subtests in the battery. When combined with intrasubtest adaptive item selection, additional savings in items administered will be realized, depending upon the values of the intercorrelations among the subtests.

## 3.3 Adaptive Testing for Classification and Mastery Decisions

All of the adaptive testing strategies described thus far have been concerned with measuring trait level status on an assumed continuous underlying variable. Frequently, however, the problem in testing is one of classification, that is determining whether an individual is below or above a specified cut-off value. This problem is characteristic of the use of tests in personnel selection, where it is desired to know whether an individual possesses the minimum qualifications for a job, or in mastery (criterion-referenced) testing where the objective is to determine whether an individual has mastered at a sufficient level the material in a course of instruction. The classification problem can also be a polychotomous one, for instance, whether an individual is above some minimum cut-off value and below some maximum cut-off value, or a multicategory mastery decision analogous to the grade classification of assigning grades A, B, or C.

Adaptive testing can be used to improve measurement efficiency for making dichotomous or polychotomous classification decisions by selecting only those items from a fixed small item bank that are necessary for any particular individual in order to make the desired classifications. In this context, adaptive testing can be contrasted with sequential classification procedures. In a sequential classification procedure, a fixed sequence of items is determined a priori for everyone to be classified. Items are administered one at a time, and a classification decision is attempted after each item has been administered. If a classification can be made within predetermined error rates, the item administration procedure is terminated. Otherwise, item administration continues until a classification can be made for each individual, or until all of the items available have been administered.

Adaptive classification procedures do not require a fixed item sequence for all individuals. Although both the adaptive and sequential procedures may use a fixed item bank, the adaptive procedure selects at each stage of the testing process the item from the entire available item bank that provides the most capability of differentiating the individual from the predetermined cut-off criterion level. As a consequence, different individuals may be administered different sequences of items. Similar to the sequential procedure, however, the adaptive procedure would administer tests of different lengths to different individuals, terminating the classification process when an appropriate decision or classification can be made.

An adaptive classification or mastery testing procedure based on item response theory first converts the cut-off value(s) to the item response theory trait metric by the test characteristic curve. Items are then selected by a maximum information procedure and scored by a Bayesian scoring procedure. The first item to be selected, and the Bayesian prior distribution used, assumes that the individual is at the cut-off value. This serves to draw all trait level estimates toward the cut-off value, permitting maximum discrimination around the cut-off level. After an item is administered, a Bayesian trait level estimate and its confidence interval (based on its standard error) are computed. If the confidence interval includes the cut-off value, no decision is made as to whether the individual is reliably above or below the cut-off value, and testing continues. Once the confidence interval no longer includes the trait level, a classification decision is made depending upon whether the individual's trait level is above or below the cut-off level.

An advantage of this procedure is that, assuming an adequate item bank, the confidence level of the decision will be at the same minimum level for all individuals tested. This leads to the capability of controlling decision accuracy for each individual and for the group as a whole.

This adaptive testing approach has resulted in better classifications (i.e., more accurate classifications) with fewer items than a "best conventional test," which is one designed with all items peaked at the cut-off level. The adaptive testing strategy also performed better than a sequential test, particularly when the items used were realistic multiple-choice items which differed in their item response theory item parameters (Weiss 1982).

### 3.4 Other Potential Applications

Adaptive testing also has potential for the measurement of individual change. In the adaptive testing approach to the measurement of individual change, each individual can be measured to a prespecified degree of precision at a given point in time. Later, when it is desired to determine whether change has occurred, testing can begin at the trait level associated with the upper limit of the error of measurement of the individual's trait level estimate at the first testing. Testing can proceed by administering and scoring items one at a time, and determining the measurement error associated with each new trait level estimate. Termination of the test at a second point in time can result when the new trait level estimate lies significantly outside of the trait level estimate observed at the first point in time, or when an indication of no change can be confidently made. This procedure can continue at subsequent testings utilizing the same item pool (since all the items will be on the same metric), but ensuring that no items previously administered will be administered. This approach can also incorporate mastery classifications, terminating testing when change has occurred and/or when a specified level of mastery has been reached.

### Bibliography

Lord F M 1980 *Applications of Item Response Theory to Practical Testing Problems*. Erlbaum, Hillsdale, New Jersey

Owen R J 1975 A Bayesian sequential procedure for quantal response in the context of adaptive mental testing. *J. Am. Stat. Ass.* 70: 351–56

Weiss D J 1974 *Strategies of Adaptive Ability Measurement*. Research Report 74–5, University of Minnesota, Department of Psychology, Psychometric Methods Program, Minneapolis, Minnesota

Weiss D J 1979 Computerized adaptive achievement testing. In: O'Neil H F (ed.) 1979 *Procedures for Instructional Systems Development*. Academic Press, New York

Weiss D J 1982 Improving measurement quality and efficiency with adaptive testing. *Appl. Psychol. Meas.* 6(4): 473–93

# Closed Tests and Security

## R. Sumner

Educational and psychological tests vary greatly in their complexity and basis in theory. Test results also serve a wide variety of purposes. According to complexity and/or purpose certain tests are restricted to particular users or types of qualified user.

For example, when an education authority wishes to use test results to choose which pupils may be offered a special type of provision (such as admission to a college course or selective school) any tests given to the students must be tightly controlled. Hence, the tests will be printed at a printer with secure premises and good security precautions, such as locked storerooms, numbered proof copies passed only to trusted readers, and good accounting procedures for the copies printed including the serial numbering of every test. Similarly, quantities of tests would be delivered only in sealed packages with test numbers recorded; test administrators would have instructions about accounting for copies, locking tests away when not required, and ensuring that no copies are taken. These measures would be continued through the dispatch of tests returned to the authority, their processing for scoring, and final destruction or storage pending appeals or other enquiries.

Tests restricted in this manner are sometimes called closed tests. On occasions, such tests can be issued to licensed test centres which, for tests such as spoken second language, may be required to have special equipment as well as trained administrators.

Besides the obvious reason of preventing unfair knowledge of items and answers being gained by some candidates before attempting a test, having a test "closed" is helpful in having standard administration procedures properly observed for all candidates.

Another form of control is operated by certain test publishers with the tacit encouragement in some countries of professional bodies (of psychologists in particular). Accordingly, certain types of test (e.g., personality, occupational-guidance batteries, projective techniques, motivation questionnaires, individual intelligence tests) are supplied only to appropriately qualified users, such as psychologists, teachers, or training personnel in industry, with supplementary qualifications in educational measurement or test administration. These will have completed a recognized course, either as part of professional training or as a specific additional qualification. The publishers concerned take the trouble to ensure that tests are supplied only to individuals whose record confirms adequate qualification. Some

classes of user, such as teachers, may not be required to supply details of qualifications, but their orders must be made on official stationery; teachers attempting to obtain tests in a private capacity would not be supplied.

The tests available from publishers to various types of qualified user may be referred to as "open" tests. But responsibility for the ethical use of a test, its custody, and keeping test results secure rests with the user.

The foregoing remarks apply to conventionally produced and distributed tests, i.e., ones that are printed and purchased from publishers who recognize certain ethical standards. Increasingly, microcomputer discs which incorporate instructions, scoring routines, and questions are being marketed through software firms. These firms may regard their products as available to any purchaser. As a consequence, the use of the results from a test or a series of tests are not always confined to specialists, and test takers might have access in order to practice extensively. It is clear that this degree of "openness" requires vigilance when test results from computer administration are considered for decision-making purposes.

# Individual and Group Testing

## R. M. Wolf

Group and individual testing refers to the manner in which tests are administered. Group tests are designed to be administered to a number of examinees at once while individual tests require that an examiner administer a test to one individual at a time.

The basic differences in the manner of test administration have a number of consequences for test administration, the role of the examiner, test interpretation and use, and test design. At the most obvious level, group tests that can be administered to a large number of examinees simultaneously are highly efficient with regard to the use of examiner time. In addition, the role of the examiner is kept to a minimum in group testing. In contrast, individual tests invariably require highly trained examiners who present test material, usually orally, in a face-to-face situation. In the individual testing situation, the examiner is able to develop rapport with the examinee and to take into account the influence of temporary conditions in the testing situation such as illness, fatigue, distraction, and frustration on the part of the examinee and adjust the testing situation accordingly.

Test interpretation and test use are both affected by whether a test is group or individually administered. Generally, group tests provide better established norms than individually administered tests. Because of the relative ease of administration, it is customary to test very large, representative samples in the standardiza-

tion process of group tests. In the most recently standardized tests it is not uncommon to test as many as 100,000 examinees in contrast to the 2,000 to 4,000 examinees typically accumulated in standardizing the most carefully developed individual tests. In contrast, a trained examiner can take note of a number of aspects of an examinee's performance during the administration of an individual test and take this into account when interpreting an individual's test performance.

The manner of test administration also has consequences for test development and presentation. Individual tests allow for a variety of item formats including open-ended items, each with separate time limits, while group tests rely on printed presentation of test material, usually in multiple-choice format and with a single longer time limit. Such lack of flexibility in group tests has been the subject of some criticism (Hoffman 1962). On the other hand, the inclusion of a number of short subtests in an individual test can be the source of timing errors on the part of less experienced or less careful examiners. Finally, the scoring of group tests is virtually completely objective and can be carried out by clerks or machines while the scoring of responses to individual tests often requires careful judgment on the part of trained examiners.

Studies in which group and individual tests measuring the same attribute have been administered to the same group of examinees show reasonably consistent results on the whole. More detailed analyses, however, suggest that poor readers are apt to suffer from a group-administered ability test in contrast to an individually administered ability test. Also, emotionally disturbed children are apt to perform better on individual than on group-ability tests (Willis 1970). This may well be due to the more flexible nature of the individually administered test that can be adjusted to the examinee's behavior in the testing situation.

## Bibliography

Anastasi A 1982 *Psychological Testing,* 5th edn. Macmillan, New York
Hoffman B 1962 *The Tyranny of Testing.* Crowell-Collier, New York
Thorndike R L, Hagen E P 1977 *Measurement and Evaluation in Psychology and Education,* 4th edn. Wiley, New York
Willis J 1970 Group versus individual intelligence tests in one sample of emotionally disturbed children. *Psychol. Rep.* 27: 819–22

# Power and Speed Tests

## R. Sumner

Some educational or psychological tests are administered for completion within a fixed time limit. For other tests candidates may be allowed as much time as they wish. A simple, though outdated, view of these procedures is to regard the untimed tests as ones which measure "the power" of an attribute, whilst the timed tests measure "speed of performance". In fact the relation between quality of task performance and rate of completion is likely to be highly complex.

Many tests are given within relatively generous time limits designed to allow the majority of candidates to attempt most of the questions. Such tests are often composed of items which are sequenced according to difficulty, that is, data from trial administrations of drafts are used to rank order items from the highest percentage of correct responses to the lowest. Accordingly, during the trials candidates signify progress at successive time intervals by changing from pen to pencil or recording elapsed time in the margin. With the final test versions, the less able or the sophisticated testees may abandon their attempt to complete the test well before the time limit expires. In contrast, the highly motivated or able testees may answer every question comfortably within the time allowed. In this context another concept of "power" is now evident, that is, task complexity or level (of cognitive demand) compounded with rate of working.

Ideally, speed of test performance ought not to be confounded by other personal attributes such as reading comprehension, physiological response time, strategies for scanning an information display, or temperamental factors associated with competition and motivation. In the event complete independence is hardly possible. To reduce or control for concomitant effects it is usual to arrange for practice at the type of response required by the test tasks with liberal time allowance before asking for responses at optimal speed.

Complicated tasks presented as power tests would be impossible to rehearse without enhancing subsequent performance, though some tests of "learning ability" measure performance based upon task rehearsals. In certain tests (notably the WISC-R Performance Scales) bonus points are added for rapid item completion with the clear intention of including both level and speed in a single measure.

The distinction between speed and power tests might well disappear with the more widespread use of computer-based testing. In this context it is possible to incorporate a model of information processing in the test structure. The speed of task completion can be recorded accurately and the complexity of cognitive process and task components can be varied systematically. For some purposes assessment might focus on a person's speed within time limits as compared with time taken to respond without time constraints. Assessments such as these may be highly relevant for examining, say, decision taking whilst handling information presented via multimedia channels. Testing in conventional educational settings will more probably be concerned with questions about the nature of children's learning, of which speed is only one aspect. Test users need to view time allowances critically, particularly when tests established in one cultural context are used in another.

# Testing Formats Used in Evaluation

## Cloze Tests

### C. G. Robinson

Cloze was introduced in 1953 by Wilson Taylor as an objective means of assessing the readability of a text. Words are deleted at random and subjects are invited to replace them. The degree of success is used as an indication of the ease of that passage for that reader and, taken over a number of readers, an indication of readability is achieved. A great deal of research has since established the method as a valid and reliable instrument for assessing both readability and reading ability.

### 1. Introductory Work

Taylor's original idea of the "cloze unit" (Taylor 1953) was derived from the Gestalt phenomenon of "closure" which refers to the tendency of the mind to complete an unfinished pattern. Taylor extended this to the completion of a written (or spoken) idea. Faced with an incomplete thought, a reader would complete it so as to make sense of what the original writer was trying to convey. Taylor argued that, given a text from which words had been deleted at random, the greater number of words a subject could replace, the greater the concordance of their thoughts and therefore the easier the passage for that reader.

In a series of small-scale experiments Taylor showed that a cloze test of more than 16 deletions successfully ranked passages in the same order as did the Flesch and Dale-Chall formulas, and that with rather more deletions successful discrimination among subjects could be achieved. Further, Taylor demonstrated that the formulas were frequently oversensitive to such superficial aspects of language as sentence or word length. Cloze tests were used on passages from the works of Gertrude Stein, James Joyce, and Erskine Caldwell, whose styles tended to produce results from the formulas that over- or under-rated their true difficulties as judged by experts. In Taylor's experiment the cloze tests ranked the passages in the same order as did the experts.

### 2. The Method

The fundamental principle is that the deletions should be random. It is this that clearly distinguishes cloze from sentence completion tasks where the words are examined by the test constructor to determine which word should be removed. Thus the efficiency of the test depends upon the ability of the constructor. In cloze the words are not evaluated and it is not therefore subject to the bias of the test constructor. Also, "if *enough* words are struck out at random, the blanks will come to represent proportionally all kinds of words to the extent that they occur" (Taylor 1953 p. 419). Tests normally have 50 blanks, allowing for swift conversion to a percentage.

Various authors have discussed the necessary frequency of deletions and it is generally agreed that one in five is the most efficient for adult readers but that for children a deletion rate of more than 10 percent causes unnecessary frustration. Taylor found no particular advantage in using random numbers to specify the blanks and most researchers have followed the practice of deleting every *n*th word starting at a randomly selected word.

A word is defined by the white spaces with which the author has separated it from other words, contractions such as *can't* or *don't* counting as single words. The hyphen is treated as white space if the parts are free forms as in *self-conscious* but *re-activate* would be regarded as a single word.

There has been some discussion as to whether it is necessary for each blank to be the same length, or whether the blanks can vary according to the length of the word. If it is not necessary, then photocopies may be used, giving the reader a great deal of nonverbal information from the original such as pictures, diagrams, and of course word length. In readability studies it may result in a fairer assessment than using a retyped passage where such clues are removed, but normal practice maintains equal sized blanks particularly where passages are to be contrasted.

In Taylor's early work he awarded half points for synonyms of the word originally used by the author. He regarded as suspect the subjectivity involved in marking them and, as there is a correlation of 0.95 with the results of verbatim cloze, where only exact replacements are accepted, little benefit accrues from accepting them.

## 3. Development

Two names stand out in the development of the procedure—Bormuth and Rankin. John Bormuth refined Taylor's original methods in a number of articles in the 1960s and established the reliability of the method for assessing readability and reading ability. Bormuth (1969) investigated the relationship between cloze test results and those obtained in oral reading and multiple-choice comprehension questions in a study which set out to challenge the findings of Weaver and Kingston (1963) who claimed that the major factor in cloze tests was a "cloze" factor which was not found in other types of reading tests. In Bormuth's results one factor had an eigenvalue greater than one and he had "little difficulty in applying the name 'reading comprehension ability' to that factor" (Bormuth 1969 p. 364). He suggested that the different results found in the earlier work might have been caused by the truncated sample used.

Rankin developed cloze in his doctoral thesis (Rankin 1957) in which he introduced a distinction between two types: structural and lexical cloze. Structural cloze is the every $n$th deletion system that had been used by Taylor and Bormuth, so-called because the majority of the words deleted are those indicating relationships between words. Lexical cloze deleted every $n$th noun or main verb (and sometimes adjectives), the words that carried the substantive meaning. Structural words form a finite closed class and any native speaker can be expected to know most of them whereas it would be impossible for any single person to know every noun or verb that exists. It follows therefore that it is likely to be easier to replace structural words than lexical and that replacing correctly a lexical item shows a greater concordance with the original writer. Rankin found that structural cloze had high correlations with other reading ability tests and with intelligence but lexical cloze was a better test of the "substantive content" of the passage. Many researchers have since used Rankin's distinctions effectively but it is important not to generalize findings from one deletion system to another.

Most of the research into the use of cloze has been carried out in the English-speaking world and upon English texts but, since 1972, the method has been developed in other languages, particularly French.

The major hurdle to be overcome in transposing a test construction method from one environment to another lies in ensuring that the principles are maintained in such a way that the results in the new environment may be taken to be compatible with those in the old.

Early attempts to use cloze in French followed the strict definition of a word as being separated from other words by white spaces. Under this system, for example, *l'homme, n'est, jusqu'à* are treated as only three words. It is obvious that in the normal course of events far more "words" containing such elisions are to be found in the romance languages than in English and a deletion

system based upon such a definition is likely to be inherently more difficult to restore.

Such was found to be the case and the work of G. Henry in Liège introduced the convention of treating elided forms separately so that *l'homme* is judged to be two words—*l'* and *homme*. The resulting system though treating the text somewhat differently to the English is obviously compatible.

Studies have also been carried out in which cloze has been used on texts in other languages but there has been insufficient work for any established method to be obvious. In constructing cloze passages in languages without a strong tradition it would be wise to consider the effects of such things as the definition of the word before assuming that the English method is suitable.

## 4. Cloze and Entropy

In information theory, entropy is the uncertainty or "lack of organization" in a passage. In a connected passage, the choice of word at any point is restricted by its context. If there is total certainty as to the word used, entropy is zero; total uncertainty means 100 percent entropy. This has a remarkable similarity to verbatim cloze. If the author's word is totally predictable, the cloze score will be 100 percent and entropy zero; if the subjects give totally random answers the cloze score will be zero and entropy 100 percent. But if all the subjects give the same answer then the entropy score will be zero but if that answer is not the same as the author's original, then the cloze score will also be zero. In this case Taylor (1954) suggests that there has been total "misdirection". Intermediate cases are catered for by the formula: Cloze score percent + Entropy percent + Misdirection percent = 100 percent, and it is frequently the misdirection score that characterizes an idiosyncratic style.

McLeod and Anderson (1970) defined a new measure based upon the reduction in uncertainty contributed by each subject and using a group of fluent native speakers as a referent sample to determine the "initial uncertainty". The method is mathematically tedious and necessitates the use of a computer in most cases but their findings, which showed a high correlation between their uncertainty reduction index scores and raw cloze scores, may be used as a further validation of the raw-score method now traditional with cloze tests.

## 5. Comment

It has been suggested that "the cloze procedure enlists the subject in a hierarchical process which goes beyond the ordinary demands of reading" (Weaver 1965).

It is certainly true that it is an exercise which tests much more than traditional "reading comprehension". There is at least a twofold process involved—selecting the appropriate class of word and then choosing the correct one from that class. The necessity for an awareness of style marks cloze as a great improvement upon traditional tests of reading ability.

There is one major area of concern in the use of cloze. Cloze scores of 44 percent and 57 percent are regarded as comparable with traditional comprehension scores of 75 percent and 90 percent respectively and therefore may be taken as indications of instructional or independent reading levels. However a score of 57 percent will appear very low to an independent reader who expects to achieve 90 percent on a test of reading. There will be words that will be almost completely unpredictable even to fluent native speakers—this is a feature of the creativity of language but there must be a doubt as to their value in the test. In readability studies it is necessary to have direct comparability between the methods used to mutilate the different texts for comparison, and the pure every-*n*th system must be used. In testing reading ability, words of near 100 percent entropy are of negligible psychometric value. There can be little doubt that dropping such words from the test will not only raise raw scores to more intuitively acceptable levels but is also likely to lead to increased motivation and an improvement in the reliability of the instrument.

## Bibliography

Bormuth J R 1969 Factor validity of cloze tests as measures of reading comprehension ability. *Read. Res. Q.* 4 (3): 358–65
De Landsheere G 1972 *Le Test de closure mesure de la lisibilite 'et de la compréhension.* Nathan, Paris
Fram R D 1972 A review of the literature related to the cloze procedure (M.Ed. thesis, Boston University, Boston, Massachusetts) ERIC Document No. ED 075 785
Henry G 1974 *Comment mesurer la lisibilite.'* Labor, Brussels
McLeod J, Anderson J 1970 An approach to the assessment of reading ability through information transmission. *J. Read. Behav.* 2(2): 116–43
Rankin E J 1957 An evaluation of the cloze procedure as a technique for measuring reading comprehension (Doctoral thesis, University of Michigan, Ann Arbor, Michigan)
Taylor W L 1953 Cloze procedure: A new tool for measuring readability. *Journalism Q.* 30: 415–33
Taylor W L 1954 Application of 'cloze' and entropy measures to the study of contextual constraint in samples of continuous prose (Doctoral thesis, University of Illinois, Urbana, Illinois)
Weaver W W 1965 Theoretical aspects of the cloze procedure. In: Thurston E L, Hafner L E (eds.) 1965 *The Philosophical and Sociological Bases of Reading.* 14th Yearbook of the National Reading Conference, Milwaukee, Wisconsin
Weaver W W, Kingston A J 1963 A factor analysis of the Cloze procedure and other measures of reading and language ability. *J. Commun.* 13: 252–61

# Cognitive Preference Tests

## E. Jungwirth

Cognitive preference tests (CPTs) have been in use mainly in science education as instruments in comparative curriculum evaluation (where the results are meant to represent the dependent variable), but also for purposes of comparing different types of schools, school systems, and student populations. Heath (1964), the first to use a cognitive preference test—to compare the Physical Sciences Study Committee (PSSC) with "traditional" physics—pointed out that "the interest is not in whether students can identify correct or incorrect information, but rather what they are likely to do with information intellectually". His four modes of "attending to scientific information" have been used by cognitive preference test researchers ever since with slight modifications. They are: (a) recall (*R*), that is a preference for scientific information for its own sake, without consideration of its implications, applications, or limitations; (b) principles (*P*), a preference for scientific information because it exemplifies or explains some fundamental principle or relationship; (c) questioning (*Q*), critical questioning of scientific information as regards its completeness, general validity, or limitations; and (d) application (*A*), a preference for scientific information in view of its usefulness and applicability in a general, social, or scientific context. A sample item is given as follows:

The process of photosynthesis is influenced by environmental conditions.

(a) The rate of photosynthesis at 20°C is 10 times higher than at 10°C. (*R*)

(b) By growing plants in greenhouses one can increase the rate of photosynthesis and thus speed up development and increase yields. (*A*)

(c) Is there an optimal temperature for photosynthesis? (*Q*)

(d) The influence of environmental conditions on photosynthesis is an example of the "Law of Limiting Factors". (*P*)

Cognitive preference test results have generally been taken to portray what the pupil "typically does do" in contradistinction to what he or she "can do", or as evidence of constructive-mode behaviour as contrasted with analytical-mode behaviour. There are two possible ways of responding to cognitive preference tests— either by ranking or by rating of the *RPQA* statements. The first method produces intrapersonal (ipsative) data, a fact which makes interpersonal and interpopulation comparisons difficult both on logical and methodological grounds, but which has nevertheless been the prevalent method in cognitive preference test research so far. The second method produces normative data, which are amenable to usual statistical treatments, but this method has rarely been used.

The most frequently recurring findings in cognitive preference test research, when studying *RPQA*-mode intercorrelations, are two bipolar scales; the *R–Q* scale, termed "scientific curiosity scale" and the *P–A* scale, termed "utility scale". It has been stipulated that the first "provides a measure of the commitment to the learning of science, for instance a high negative ($Q$ minus $R$) score would suggest an intrinsic satisfaction with knowledge already gained . . .. The quality of "ambition to learn more" would be lacking in such a student". Similarly, the continuum of the *A–P* scale identifies the student's orientation towards "practical" versus "pure" science. The interpretations of the *R–Q* scale have been disputed (Jungwirth 1980). Another often-repeated finding is the usually positive, but slight, correlation of $Q$ with $IQ$ and/or academic achievement. Similarly a negative correlation was found with $R$. This has often been taken as a corroboration of the cognitive preference test constructs, but is also prone to alternative interpretations. For comprehensive reviews of cognitive preference test research and problems see Tamir (1975), Brown (1975), and Jungwirth (1979, 1980).

The main problems with cognitive preference test research are those of validity: the *RPQA*-constructs have not been proven to be either unequivocal or mutually exclusive. Introspective reports by respondents (from ninth grade to university levels) have revealed that item content and specificity have a great and possibly overriding effect on expressed preferences, that is, there is no certainty about the nature of the crucial stimulus triggering subjects' responses. The built-in negative correlation of the ipsative (ranking) procedure has been regarded as a confounding factor in interpreting cognitive preference test results. The intra-individuality of the ipsative cognitive preference test scores gives no intimation of the absolute degree of cognitive preferences since they are expressed relatively to each other, and ties are not permitted. Absolute degrees can be diagnosed only by the normative (rating) method, but that method begs the question whether what is rated actually represents a genuine cognitive preference or a general response set, since normative cognitive preference-mode intercorrelations are usually found to be significantly positive. Attempts to demonstrate construct validation by convergence of data across test formats and/or instruments have not been very convincing, in spite of the demonstrated convergence of data across disciplines and/or subject matter. The question has remained open as to whether Heath's original demand, that is, that students show what they are "likely to do" can actually be satisfied by using a multiple-choice format. Recent attempts to correlate multiple-choice cognitive preference test data with open-ended (associative) responses have been singularly unsuccessful. No studies involving predictive validations have so far been undertaken. There has been no proof that cognitive preference data as obtained hitherto can indeed be taken as a substitute principle which takes one behaviour as an index of another, that is, as representing a cognitive style. Some authors have actually used the term "cognitive-preference style" when referring to cognitive preference test findings.

Since the cognitive preference test modes are, obviously, embedded in a content medium, and particular cognitive preference test statements are more or less discernible within such a medium, it has been hypothesized that certain personality factors are essential for the disembedding of these modes from their medium or contextual content matrix. Attempts to correlate cognitive preference with, for instance, field (in-)dependence have, however, produced only nonsignificant results so far.

Predictive studies in cognitive preference test research have been few. Contrary to expectations, students in agricultural or nursing schools were found to be no more *A*-inclined than their peers in nonvocational institutions.

Opinions as to the actual usability of cognitive preference tests in curriculum evaluation, or in determining instructional strategies, differ widely. In this author's view many of the conclusions to be found in the literature should be held in abeyance at least until some of the more basic questions of internal and external validity of cognitive preference tests are settled satisfactorily.

## Bibliography

Brown S A 1975 Cognitive preferences in science: Their nature and analysis. *Stud. Sci. Educ.* 2: 43–65

Heath R W 1964 Curriculum, cognition and educational measurement. *Educ. Psychol. Meas.* 24: 239–53

Jungwirth E 1979 Cognitive-preference testing in the natural sciences: Some question marks. *Eur. J. Sci. Educ.* 1: 417–25

Jungwirth E 1980 Alternative interpretations of findings in cognitive preference research in science education. *Sci. Educ.* 64: 85–94

Tamir P 1975 The relationship among cognitive preference, school environment, teachers' curricular bias, curriculum and subject matter. *Am. Educ. Res. J.* 12: 235–64

# Objective Tests

## B. H. Choppin

Objective methods of observation are those in which any observer who follows the prescribed rules will assign the same values or categories to the events being observed as would another observer. Similarly, an objective test is one for which the rules for scoring it are so specific and comprehensive that anyone who marks a test script in accordance with these rules will arrive at the same test score. Most objective tests used in education are composed of a sequence of individual "objective" test items (sometimes called structured-response items) in which the testees must choose their answers from a specified list of alternatives rather than by creating them for themselves. It is important to remember, however, that the definition relates to the method of scoring the test and not to the format of its constituent items as such. Not all objective tests require the student to select from a presented list. Items which require the student to write down a phrase, a word, or a number, and in the scoring of which there are clear and unequivocal rules for deciding whether the response is right or wrong, also qualify as "objective."

Objective tests stand in clear contrast to essay examinations and other forms of open-ended tests in which few constraints are put on the testee. Such tests are characterized by the very great variation in the responses that are produced even among students of similar ability or attainment, and their scoring requires the examiner to weigh a variety of evidence, a task which calls for substantial amounts of personal judgment. As a result, different examiners usually arrive at different scores for the same essay, and hence this type of assessment is not regarded as objective.

Objective tests may also be distinguished from short-answer (or restricted-response) tests in which, although the testee must produce his or her own answers, the constraints imposed by the formulation of the question are such as to make the scoring more objective. For example, students might be asked to draw a diagram of a terrestrial telescope paying particular attention to the characteristics and positioning of the lenses. The scoring instructions might dictate that the student's response be accepted as correct if and only if the objective lens has a longer focal length than the eye-piece. Tests of this last type are sometimes referred to as semiobjective tests.

## 1. Areas of Application

Objective tests are widely used to measure intelligence, aptitude, and achievement (or attainment). Almost all tests of aptitude and intelligence are of the objective type because of the uses to which such measures are put. Raw scores of intelligence or aptitude have little meaning in themselves, and need to be translated to well-established scales before they can be used. In consequence, reliability of the scores is a major consideration and using objective test formats is one way to maximize this.

However, the appropriateness of objective tests for the measurement of achievement is much more controversial. Essay tests are still preferred to objective tests for most educational purposes in many countries. Where the teacher scores the tests for a single class, objectivity as such is less important, and the advantages of getting the students to express themselves fully and openly tend to outweigh the demands for a reliable score. For example, although the typical American high-school teacher will use objective tests (self-developed) for routine assessment of students on a weekly or monthly basis, the teacher in England or Wales will almost always prefer to use nonobjective tests for this purpose. The system of public examinations in England and Wales, which certify levels of attainment for secondary-school leavers, are largely nonobjective despite the need for reliability (given the importance of the results to the future careers of individual students). However, it should be noted that the proportion of objective test material in these examinations has been increasing in recent years.

## 2. Item Formats

Most objective test items appear in one of four alternative formats. These will be considered in turn below, and examples of each type appear in Fig. 1.

### 2.1 Supply Items

Unlike the other types in which the student is selecting from a list of alternative responses presented to him or her, the supply type of item requires a student to construct a response. However, the question is so structured as to limit the scope of the student's response so that (ideally) there will be one, and only one, acceptable answer. Demanding that the student construct rather than recognize the response avoids some of the common criticisms of objective tests described below. However, it does give up some of the convenience (such as automated scoring) that selection-type items offer. The format's most frequent area of application is in mathematics on questions which call for a specific quantitative answer. However, Fig. 1 demonstrates that it can be used effectively in other areas.

Specification of the acceptable answers is an essential part of the item construction process, but there is always the danger that certain students will invent unforeseen answers that could arguably be accepted as correct. For example, on item 1(b) in Fig. 1 the student might respond "$N_2$." It is advisable with supply items

1. *Supply-type items*

   (a) A new school building has 12 classrooms. The school ordered 30 desks for each classroom. Only 280 desks were delivered. How many more are needed?

   ———————
   (Scoring key: 80)

   (b) The gas which is most abundant in the atmosphere is:

   ———————
   (Scoring key: Nitrogen)

   (c) Through which country does the canal that links the Mediterranean Sea to the Red Sea pass?

   ———————
   (Scoring key: Egypt or UAR)

   (d) A solid element X forms two oxides which contain respectively 71.1% and 62.3% of X. Calculate the equivalent weight of X in each oxide. The specific heat of X is 0.084. Given that the product of the atomic weight and specific heat of a solid element is approximately 6.4, write down the formulae for the two oxides of X.

   ——————— and ———————
   (Scoring key: $XO_2$ and $XO_3$)

2. *True/false items*

   (e) The capital city of Sweden is Stockholm ........................................... True : False

   (f) The rate of juvenile delinquency is usually higher in the older parts of a city ........... True : False

   (g) The oceans are deepest at the center and shallowest near the edges .................. True : False

   (h) Light rays always travel in straight lines ........................................ True : False

3. *Multiple-choice items*

   (i) The amount of heat required to raise the temperature of one gram of a substance by one degree (°C) is called:
   (i) its thermal conductivity
   (ii) its specific heat
   (iii) its thermal capacity
   (iv) its thermal expansion

   (j) John brought the skull of an animal to school. His teacher said she did not know what the animal was but she was sure that it was one that preyed on other animals for its food. Which clue, do you think, led her to this conclusion?
   (i) The eye sockets faced sideways
   (ii) The skull was much longer than it was wide
   (iii) There was a projecting ridge along the top of the skull
   (iv) Four of the teeth were long and pointed
   (v) The jaws could work sideways as well as up and down

4. *Matching item format*

   For each piece of apparatus listed below, identify the scientist who invented it, and enter the appropriate code letter on the answer sheet.

   | | *Apparatus* | | *Inventor* |
   |---|---|---|---|
   | (l) | X-ray spectrometer | (i) | Angstrom |
   | (m) | Reflection grating | (ii) | Bragg |
   | (n) | Interferometer | (iii) | Helmholtz |
   | (o) | Ophthalmoscope | (iv) | Michelson |
   | | | (v) | Newton |
   | | | (vi) | Rowland |
   | | | (vii) | Thomson |

**Figure 1**
Examples of objective test items

to compile a comprehensive list of answers that give appropriate evidence of achievement before scoring begins. Note that the criterion is not grammatical correctness nor even truth. The answer "invisible" to question 1(b) makes the statement true, but does not demonstrate that the student has achieved the objective being tested.

## 2.2 The True/False Item Format

The true/false item presents a declarative statement and requires the examinee to indicate whether he or she judges it to be true or false. (Some generally similar items have other dichotomous response options such as yes/no or appropriate/inappropriate.) Although such items are easy to construct, this is not a format to be generally recommended. Tests composed of true/false items tend to be rather unreliable, and are particularly susceptible to contamination by guessing. Ebel (1970) argues that this is not serious and that true/false tests may be very efficient, but few other writers support this view. True/false items can be quite effective for assessing factual knowledge (especially if great precision is not required), but are usually inappropriate for testing more complex skills.

## 2.3 Multiple-choice Item Format

The multiple-choice item is by far the most frequently used in educational achievement testing. The number of alternative answers offered varies but is usually four or five. As a rule only one of the alternatives is correct, the others (the distractors) being constructed so as to provide plausible examples of common errors. If the distractors are carefully written a wrong-answer analysis can yield valuable diagnostic information about the types of error being made by students. Many variations of the basic format have been developed (Wood 1977) mainly to increase the amount of information elicited by an item or to improve its applicability to the testing of higher mental processes.

The chief difficulty in constructing good multiple-choice questions is to find appropriate distractors. To be effective they must be plausible at least to a substantial minority of students, yet they must be clear and unambiguously wrong in the judgment of experts. Distractors should not give inadvertent clues which permit test-wise students to eliminate them irrespective of their ability to correctly solve the question. The multiple-choice questions given in Fig. 1 may be regarded as exemplars of the type.

Although they too may effectively be used to assess specific knowledge, multiple-choice items are readily adaptable to measure more complex skills involving reasoning and analysis. It has been found to be relatively straightforward to construct an achievement test, all of whose items are in the multiple-choice format which assesses student performance on a wide range of objectives involving different skill levels.

## 2.4 Matching Items

The fourth widely used item format to be considered is the matching exercise. This is a logical extension of the multiple-choice item in which the same list of alternative responses is used for several items in sequence. An example of this format is included in Fig. 1.

The most obvious advantage of the matching item format is one of economy. More responses are obtained from the student for the same amount of reading. The format can be effectively employed to test knowledge of specific facts, but is generally unsuitable for more complex objectives. However, it has been suggested (Thorndike and Hagen 1969) that a variation of the format, the classification task, can be used to appraise comprehension and application type objectives.

## 3. Disadvantages of Objective Tests

Many critics of the multiple-choice format have pointed out that it required students only to recognize the correct answer rather than to recall and/or construct it for themselves. It is suggested that recognition is a fundamentally lower form of behavior, and that many students who are able to recognize the correct answers on a test are unable to apply what they have learned in practice. In general, the research evidence does not support this. Students who are good recallers of knowledge are also good recognizers. Several studies (e.g., Godshalk et al. 1966, Choppin and Purves 1969) which compared objective tests with free-response essays written by the same students showed that the objective tests predicted overall performance on the essay about as well as the limited reliability of the essay scoring would permit.

Associated with this criticism is the complaint that objective tests place an undue emphasis on reading rather than writing skills, so that the latter tend to become devalued. Wood (1977) comments that although this may have some validity in the United States, elsewhere (in the United Kingdom for example) traditional testing practices have paid entirely too much regard to the ability of the testees to express themselves in writing.

A third form of criticism is that the multiple-choice test item typically presents the student with three or four times as many false answers as correct ones. As a rule the distractors are written so as to be quite plausible, and thus the opportunities for the student to "learn" incorrect information during the test session are substantial. Thorndike and Hagen (1969) note that little research had been done on this point.

Two other disadvantages of objective tests deserve mention. The first is that it is in general much easier to write objective test questions to test comparatively low-level skills (e.g., factual knowledge) rather than the more complex skills of analysis and synthesis. As a result, many existing objective tests are over-loaded with items focusing on pieces of specific knowledge. Objective test items (particularly in the multiple-choice format) can be constructed to assess higher mental processes, but in general this is rather more difficult to do, and too often professional test constructors have not paid sufficient attention to this problem.

The other criticism is that objective tests encourage guessing behavior. Although a minority of critics (e.g., Hoffmann 1962) appear to regard guessing itself as an immoral activity on a par with betting on horses or using illegal drugs, most feel it is an appropriate behavior for the student, in a restricted choice situation, who lacks sufficient information to solve the test item directly. The problem arises from the number of correct guesses that occur. They can lead to an overestimate of an individual student's level of achievement, and tend to lower the measurement reliability for a whole group. Various countermeasures have been proposed (see *Correction for Guessing*.

## 4. Advantages of Objective Tests

Against these real or imagined disadvantages, there are clearly a number of benefits ensuing from the use of objective tests of achievement. The first is that by focusing the attention of the student, it is possible to gather information rapidly on particular parts of his or her learning—a feature especially important in diagnostic work and in formative evaluation. This focusing of individual items allows the test maker to control the scope of what is being assessed by the complete test, so that items may be sampled from across a very broad domain or from only a very narrow part of it. In contrast, responses on an essay-type examination are less subject to control by the examiner, and it is often difficult to persuade all students to provide evidence about their mastery of particular skills.

Minute by minute, an objective test is probably the most efficient basis for obtaining information about an individual's learning. Because of its structure, the instrument is relatively easy to score, is reliable, and its data are amenable to a wide range of statistical analyses. Automated scoring procedures have played a major part in making the multiple-choice item format so popular. These have ranged from a simple template (which when placed over a test or answer sheet allows the scorer to quickly observe how many correct responses have been selected), to computer-controlled electronic scanning machines which can "read" the pattern of pencil marks made on an answer sheet very rapidly. The use of such methods whether on a large or small scale substantially reduces the time and cost of achievement testing. However, it should be noted that some of the time saved in scoring

may be used up by the additional time required for test preparation. Constructing clear, unam-biguous, and valid objective test items is not an easy task.

Since each objective test item is usually short, many of them can be included in a single test, and this con-tributes to the higher reliability that is usually achiev-ed. The items can be spread more evenly over the topics to be covered, so that a more representative sampling of performance is obtained. Another way of stating this is to note that the score from a well-made objective test is likely to be more accurate than that from a comparable essay test. Two separate ob-jective tests, based on the same content area, will rank an individual at more nearly the same place in his or her group, than would two free-response measures.

## 5. Summary

Objective tests have been found to be efficient and effective instruments for obtaining measures of learn-ing as well as of general mental ability and aptitude. They yield scores that are more dependable than those from comparable open-ended tests, and their quality can be readily assessed through statistical item analysis.

Nevertheless, their full advantages are only realized when considerable care is exercised in their con-struction. Writers of objective items for achievement tests have an unfortunate tendency to concentrate on factual, and often trivial, information, and to produce tests which seem to distort the full range of educational goals. It is possible, however, to create objective test items which assess abilities to comprehend, interpret, and apply knowledge, to analyze and to synthesize ideas. The extra effort needed to write such items is justified when valid and reliable measures of achieve-ment are desired.

## Bibliography

Choppin B H, Purves A C 1969 Comparison of open-ended and multiple-choice items dealing with literary under-standing. *Res. Teach. Eng.* 3: 15–24
Ebel R L 1970 The case for true–false test items. *Sch. Rev.* 78: 373–89
Ebel R L 1979 *Essentials of Educational Measurement*, 3rd edn. Prentice-Hall, Englewood Cliffs, New Jersey
Godshalk F I, Swineford F, Coffman W E 1966 *The Measure-ment of Writing Ability*. College Entrance Examinations Board, New York
Hoffmann B 1962 *The Tyranny of Testing*. Collier Macmillan, New York
Roid G H, Haladyna T M 1982 *A Technology for Test-item Writing*. Academic Press, New York
Thorndike R L, Hagen E 1969 *Measurement and Evaluation in Psychology and Education*, 3rd edn. Wiley, New York
Wood R 1977 Multiple-choice: A state of the art report. *Eval. Educ.* 1: 191–280

# Sentence Completion Tests

## M. C-L. Yeh

In a sentence completion test each item consists of a string of words which form an incomplete sentence. The subject is asked to provide words to complete the sentence, and the response is scored according to what words are supplied. Some examples of items from sentence completion tests are presented in Fig. 1.

Sentence completion tests have been used projectively in the investigation of personality. For example, Loevinger and Wessler (1970) based their whole methodology for measuring ego development on the sentence completion procedure. Many psychologists and psychiatrists have found sentence completion tests to be valuable in uncovering information about a subject's needs, perceptions, attitudes, and style.

In education, sentence completion tests have been used primarily in the assessment of achievement. Here, in contrast to the projective uses mentioned above, answers are scored according to whether or not they are correct. Because they require the student to construct and supply a response, and generally there will be a very large number of different responses that would all be considered correct, they are not considered to be objective tests. In consequence they can be costly and difficult to score, and the scoring may be a source of unreliability. However, careful attention to drawing up detailed and specific rules for scoring can yield high interscorer correlations and test reliabilities comparable with those for multiple-choice tests.

It is difficult, but not impossible, to devise test items in a sentence completion format to measure achievement on instructional objectives other than at the "knowledge" level. The exception to this is the use of this type of item to test comprehension. For example, a picture or a short prose passage may be presented, and the student asked to complete statements on the basis of information contained in the stimulus.

---

*Example items from a personality measure:*
(a) Women are fortunate because ..................
(b) The worst thing about me is.....................
(c) Being with my parents ...........................

*Example items from tests of achievement:*
(d) An example of a fossil fuel is ...................
(e) An element that is found in proteins but not in fats is ..............................................
(f) A hot liquid in a vacuum flask slowly loses its heat by ...............................................
(g) Some drivers prefer their driving mirrors to be . . . rather than plain because ..............

---

*Figure 1*
Examples of sentence-completion test items

However, the vast majority of applications and almost all the relevant research have been concerned with the sentence completion format's capacity for testing knowledge.

It is generally held that sentence completion tests measure the ability to recall required information, while "choice" tests (true–false, multiple choice, or matching) measure only the ability to recognize the required information when it is encountered. This would appear to account for the lower scores consistently found on sentence completion tests when compared to their equivalent multiple-choice forms (Darley and Murdock 1971, Follman et al. 1974). Several empirical studies have found evidence to support the treating of recall and recognition as two distinct mental processes (Boyd 1971, Kumar et al. 1979). Of course this would imply that sentence completion tests are not equivalent (or parallel) to multiple-choice tests even when the content area being assessed is the same because the skill being measured is different. Nevertheless, many test constructors have found it convenient to employ both sentence completion and multiple-choice formats.

Most educational practitioners appear to believe that recall is a more relevant and important ability than recognition. For this reason, the sentence completion test is preferred on theoretical grounds. It is also clear that many practitioners are bothered by the extent to which guessing can influence scores on multiple-choice tests. While this is rarely a significant problem with supply-type items, the convenience of scoring procedures for objective tests combined with their generally good psychometric properties, mean that, in many parts of the world, the use of objective tests is increasing. However, many constructors of objective tests use sentence completion items, or items in a similar supply format, at an early stage of test development in order to generate plausible distractors for the final multiple-choice form of the items. It has been claimed (Mason 1979) that supply-type items are most appropriate in formative evaluation activities where the richness of the information obtained by testing is more important than the accuracy of ranking or selecting students. This argument can readily be extended to cover most routine classroom testing by the teacher.

A further aspect which deserves consideration is that tests and testing are themselves part of the learning experience of students. A number of empirical studies (e.g., Duchastel 1981) have suggested that sentence completion tests tend to enhance the retention of the tested material better than do multiple-choice tests. However, Gay (1980) concludes that this effect is only perceptible when the follow-up stage of the evaluation itself uses sentence completion tests rather than multiple-choice-type instruments. Whether or not this result invalidates the claimed educational advantage for sentence completion tests depends on one's appreciation of the relative values of recall and recognition.

## Bibliography

Boyd R N 1971 Influence of test form on assessment. *Aust. J. Educ.* 15: 161–70

Darley C F, Murdock B B Jr 1971 Effects of prior free recall testing on final recall and recognition. *J. Exp. Psychol.* 91: 66–73

Duchastel P C 1981 Retention of prose following testing with different types of tests. *Contemp. Educ. Psychol.* 6: 217–26

Follman J, Hall B, Wiley R, Hartman J 1974 Relationship between objective test formats. *Educ. Rev.* 26: 150–51

Gay L R 1980 The comparative effects of multiple-choice versus short-answer tests on retention. *J. Educ. Meas.* 17: 45–50

Kumar V K, Rabinsky L, Pandey T N 1979 Test mode, test instructions and retention. *Contemp. Educ. Psychol.* 4: 211–18

Loevinger J, Wessler R 1970 *Measuring Ego Development.* Jossey-Bass, San Francisco, California

Mason G P 1979 Test purpose and item type. *Can. J. Educ.* 4: 9–13

# Oral Examinations

**G. M. Forrest**

Educational historians believe that the first written examinations were held in China in the second century BC. These were organized by the Chinese Imperial Service and were designed so that the selection of successful applicants could be done in as fair a way as possible. Written examinations did not reach the West for many centuries because, as one theory has it, cheap writing materials were not readily available.

In medieval Europe the "disputation" was the means whereby university bachelor degree students were examined: a candidate was required to expound upon and to debate points of logic and of theology in front of teachers and fellow students. (The origins of the name of the Cambridge University tripos examination date from these times—the tripos was the three-legged stool on which the candidate sat.) In the sixteenth century the Jesuits introduced written examinations into their schools, success in which was required before progress was possible to the next year of study. The nineteenth century saw the introduction of formal written examinations in universities, schools, and other educational institutions which have spread rapidly to all parts of the world.

Many universities still require students, particularly those aspiring to higher degrees, to be examined orally when their written work (in the form of a thesis or dissertation) is the focus of attention. The student is likely to be asked to explain what has been written, to expand certain sections of it orally perhaps, but most likely to justify the methodologies used and the conclusions reached. The overall result for the degree is based not only on the submitted written work but also on the performance of the student in this *viva voce* examination. In some universities, students being examined for their doctorates may be examined "in public", in that university staff and fellow students may exercise a right to be nonparticipating observers: the modern equivalent to the medieval disputation.

Oral examinations feature most frequently in school examinations when foreign languages are being examined. Although there is currently a tendency for exam-inations in the mother tongue to involve an oral component, an oral examination has formed a part of examinations in the United Kingdom since the formalization of public examinations in 1918. Both in Europe and in the United States there were movements in the nineteenth century to make the teaching of languages more realistic by using the spoken word along the lines suggested by Francke (1884) in Germany and by Ticknor (1832) in the United States. Once public external examinations became established, it was normal to include an oral component but because of the administrative difficulties, that component has always tended to be a small element only.

## 1. Research on Oral Examinations

By far the most comprehensive set of complementary investigations on examinations were those carried out in a number of European countries in the 1930s under the auspices of the Carnegie Corporation, the Carnegie Foundation, and the International Institute of Teachers College, Columbia University. In England and Wales a wide range of examinations were investigated, and although most attention has since been paid to the findings on school certificate examinations, one investigation involved a *viva voce* (interview) examination (Hartog and Rhodes 1936). The aim of this study was to "test the degree of consistency" (p. 168) between groups of examiners. Each group of examiners interviewed independently the same candidates. In order to provide motivation for the candidates, a prize of £100 was offered. So that the candidates were "approximately of the same age" and had "received the same kind of training" (p. 168), applicants were limited to those aged between 21 and 23 and who were university or college students. University or college authorities were required to countersign applications and to certify that applicants could be considered as suitable for appointment to the junior grade of the administrative class of the civil service. Of the applicants, 16 were each interviewed by two groups of examiners all experienced in interviewing. After each applicant had been interviewed each examiner recorded the mark (out of 300) which was thought to be appropriate before any discussion took place. Following that discussion, a mark was agreed by the group of examiners; after the last interview had taken place the examiners reviewed their markings so as to ensure that the final marks "translated correctly their impressions of the relative abilities of the candidates" (p. 172).

The results showed that in both groups of examiners there was very close agreement among the examiners on the marks of some candidates whereas little agreement was found with other candidates. The final orders of merit based on the agreed marks of the two groups of examiners were, however, very different, the correlation coefficient not being statistically different from zero. The candidate ranked first by one group of examiners was ranked 13th by the other group while the top candidate in this group was ranked 11th by the former group of examiners. The prize was awarded to the candidate ranked second by one group and equal fourth by the other. The report suggests that it "is probable that the different questions asked of the candidates affect the marks finally awarded" (p. 173) and concluded that "the actual evidence produced seems to have been so different that we might almost have supposed different candidates to have been examined" (p. 173). In a note by one of the authors, based on his impartial observations of the groups of examiners, the opinion was expressed that although both groups of examiners "were equally skilful in cross-examining . . . it was largely a matter of chance whether they struck on a topic in which a candidate felt so strongly that he was able to display his individuality" (p. 176).

As Heywood (1977) points out, such research as has followed the work of Hartog and Rhodes in the 1930s merely supports their misgivings about oral examinations.

## 2. Measurement of Oral Skills

In general terms, oral examinations are usually used to measure skills which cannot be measured by written means. Oral skills in the modern languages tend to overlap with aural skills since the ability to converse with another person presupposes the ability to understand what that person is saying. Nevertheless, oral skills can usefully be specified in two areas: the ability to answer questions (using certain specified language structures) and the ability to ask questions so as to obtain particular information. In making assessments, an examiner is likely to distinguish between and award separate marks for fluency, pronunciation and intonation, the use of vocabulary and idioms, as well as the command of the structures in the foreign language. A variety of techniques is used in the oral examinations organized by external examining authorities. Some require the examiner to conduct the examination on an individual basis; sometimes it is necessary to involve the teacher in making the assessments in which case steps have to be taken to ensure the impartiality of the assessments. The usual techniques are as follows.

(a) Reading aloud: although it is possible to assess a candidate's ability to read aloud in a reliable or consistent way, for practical purposes this special skill is of doubtful value.

(b) Prepared questions: the advantage for the candidate is that what is to be asked is known but candidates can be trained to respond and the weaker candidates may not even understand fully the answers they give.

(c) Conversation on a prepared topic: this technique has the same disadvantage as prepared questions have but it can nevertheless be more demanding. Discrimination among candidates can be improved if they are allowed to develop and express their own ideas spontaneously.

(d) General conversation: if the conversation is conducted properly (and this requires considerable skill on the part of the interviewer), the conversation can be pitched at a level suitable for the candidate.

(e) General questions: this is a useful technique for testing specific language structures, vocabulary, and so on provided that the construction of the questions is carefully carried out.

(f) Questions on pictures: the pictures provide different stimuli so that it is possible to control, to some extent, the language produced. A careful sequence of pictures can ensure that the candidate starts at a simple level. All candidates respond to the same set of pictures.

(g) The narration of a story based on a sequence of pictures: the suitability of the stimulus is a crucial factor and the test is a demanding one since the candidate, after studying the pictures for a set time, is required to tell the story given in the pictures. The main advantage is that all candidates are given the same task, thereby making the standardization of the marking less difficult.

(h) Role playing: although there is, to some extent, an artificial element, role playing is a useful teaching technique. In an examination, it is used to test language in a realistic way since candidates are placed in a specific situation in order to obtain certain information. The candidate, for instance, is told (in the mother tongue) that he/she is at a particular railway station and that a ticket for a certain destination is to be purchased; the times of departure and arrival of the train are to be discovered. The instructions may also be presented in written form. To make the situation as realistic as possible the examiner would, in this example, play the role of the railway official.

Not all these techniques would of course be used

in the same examination, but several might well feature in the oral component of an external school examination.

It is sometimes suggested that a written question paper should be replaced by an oral examination for those candidates who have difficulty in expressing themselves in writing. Where the overall result is determined by the aggregation of examination component marks (the great majority of university, college, and school examinations are based on this practice) difficulties can arise since the candidates examined orally will achieve higher marks than they could have been expected to achieve with a written paper. It is not logical therefore to compare such candidates in terms of their aggregated marks with those candidates whose aggregated marks include the written examination.

Developments in the form of graded tests in foreign languages overcome the difficulties associated with the current practice of aggregating marks by dividing the examination performance in the language into four elements: listening, speaking, reading, and writing. Proficiency in each element is recognized at two or more levels. Candidates for the highest grade will have achieved at the top level in each element but a candidate not capable of writing in the foreign language can still be rewarded for successful performances in listening and speaking. Such a form of examination is likely to encourage the teaching of foreign languages thereby enabling candidates, who at present are dissuaded by the emphasis in examinations on the written element, to show their skills in the practical aspects of the language. Inevitably, the use of graded tests will lead to a greater use of oral examinations.

## Bibliography

Franke F 1890 *Die praktische Spracherlernung, auf Grund der Psychologie und der Physiologie der Sprache*, Reisland, Leipzig

Hartog P, Rhodes E C 1936 *The Marks of Examiners: Being a Comparison of Marks Allotted to Examination Scripts by Independent Examiners and Boards of Examiners, Together with a Section on a Viva Voce Examination.* International Institute Examinations Enquiry. Macmillan, London

Heywood J 1977 *Assessment in Higher Education.* Wiley, London

Ticknor G 1832 *The Best Methods of Teaching the Living Languages: Lectures.* Harvard University Press, Cambridge, Massachusetts

# Nonverbal Tests

## C. D. Elliott

Nonverbal tests, as their name implies, are tests which do not require the person taking the test to solve verbal problems or to give verbal responses (oral or written) to any questions in the test. Such tests have been widely used from the earliest days of the development of psychological and educational tests. A number of items in the Binet Intelligence Scale, the first individually administered intelligence test to be developed, were nonverbal. Similarly, as far as group tests are concerned, the earliest example of a nonverbal test was the Army Beta in the United States, developed during the First World War for testing the general intellectual ability of illiterate soldiers. Since those days there has been a continued development of nonverbal tests, which are generally used in an effort to assess general ability or intelligence independently of the cultural effects associated with language. As will be seen later in this article, although nonverbal tests can be performed by people who have not developed language adequately, such as those who are deaf or language disordered, or those who are from different ethnic backgrounds or who have come from deprived environments, the possession of good language skills is undoubtedly an aid in the solution of most nonverbal problems. It is, therefore, dubious whether any test could be considered to be a "pure" nonverbal test. Nonverbal test items are usually found in so-called "culture fair" tests and in so-called "learning ability" tests. Although nonverbal tests are mostly used for the measurement of general intellectual ability, nonverbal objective procedures have been developed (Cattell and Warburton 1967) for the assessment of personality and temperament. Such procedures might involve, for example, the use of the Galvanic Skin Response (GSR) or performance measures such as those obtained from radar-type vigilance tasks. Yet another type of nonverbal test would be certain tests devised for purposes of vocational selection and guidance, such as manual-dexterity tests. The scope of this article, however, will be restricted to nonverbal tests used for the assessment of general intellectual ability.

Nonverbal tests may be contrasted with verbal tests in terms of their instructions to the testee, their test materials, and the responses required from the testee. Whereas verbal tests always use either oral or written instructions to the testee about the nature of the task, nonverbal tests never provide written instructions, but often provide oral instructions. In a few cases they do not even provide oral instructions but rely instead on completely nonverbal instructions in the form of mime and gesture, such as in the Leiter International Performance Scale, and in the Hiskey-Nebraska Test of Learning Aptitude. In verbal tests, the test problems are always verbal, being presented either orally or in writing and involving the use and understanding of verbal concepts. On the other hand, the very nature of nonverbal tests precludes the use of language in the test items themselves. Hence the items are generally in a visual form. Yet again, the responses required of testees from verbal tests are generally oral or written, whereas in nonverbal tests such responses are eliminated: the testee is usually required to construct something with his or her hands, or to do drawings or simply indicate (with a pencil or by pointing) which of a number of alternative responses is the correct one.

Nonverbal tests may be individually administered or group administered. Individually administered tests are often given by psychologists, but may be given also in certain circumstances by other professional workers, to clients in one-to-one settings. Their major advantage is that they enable the tester to observe the testee's reactions very carefully and thus to ensure as far as possible that the testee understands the nature of the task and is cooperating and performing at an optimal level. Such considerations are particularly important for nonverbal tests, since they are often used in an effort to make the test procedures fairer for individuals who may be disadvantaged when presented with verbal tasks. Such individually administered procedures are, however, very expensive in terms of labour, and consequently many group-administered procedures have been developed in which testees are tested in groups, with the tester giving them general instructions about the completion of the test. Such group-administered nonverbal tests are very popular both for testing school children and for testing job applicants, situations in which it is often necessary to test large numbers of individuals. Group administrations do have their disadvantages, however: it is sometimes difficult to ensure that all testees fully understand the nature of the task and that all of them are working hard while completing the test.

The aims of nonverbal ability tests are in general to obtain as "pure" a measure of reasoning ability as possible, reducing the contaminating effects of language and previous educational experience to a minimum. This is not to say, of course, that it is even possible to conceive of any mental test that could possibly be performed without the individual having learned anything in the past or having developed reasoning processes as a result of past experience. The aim is, however, to reduce specific knowledge and specific past experience to a minimum.

Nonverbal tests have certain disadvantages. The tester may have problems in interpreting low scores. Are they the result of low ability or of poor motivation or failure to understand instructions? These problems are less pronounced in the case of individually administered nonverbal tests, although a considerable premium is placed upon the skill of the tester in developing rapport with the testee and in using a close observation of the testee's behaviour whilst taking the test, in order to inform the interpretation of the score obtained by the testee. Another disadvantage of nonverbal tests is that, because they are designed to measure abilities with the contaminating effects of language and previous direct experience kept to a minimum, inevitably they tend to correlate less well than verbal tests with most performance criteria that testers are interested in, such as scholastic achievement and job success. School teachers often have considerable difficulty in interpreting the practical importance of a high nonverbal ability score in a child who is doing badly in school work. Because of the lower correlation of nonverbal ability scores with school success, a higher proportion of discrepancies between nonverbal scores and achievement test scores are found than are found between verbal test scores and achievement. As with the interpretation of many test results, test users often have difficulty in drawing practical conclusions and recommendations from obtained test scores, and this is a particular problem in the case of nonverbal tests whose correlation with performance criteria may be relatively low.

There are, however, a number of advantages in the use of nonverbal tests. Often, because of the emphasis which is placed on language and past experience in communication and dealings with other people, an evaluation of a person who has an unusual or a deprived background in terms of language and cultural experience may be unduly influenced. The scores of such persons on a nonverbal test may help them to be seen in a different light and to realize that they are capable of reasoning and handling information at a relatively high level even though their verbal performance may appear to be limited. It is difficult to conceive of a situation in which such information could be obtained more economically and effectively than through the use of nonverbal tests. In cases where large numbers of individuals need to be tested, the process of test administration and scoring can be speeded even more through the use of computer-automated scoring systems. The cautions expressed above about the interpretation of such test scores still hold, however, even though a computer printout may appear on first sight to be the ultimate in scientific precision.

In terms of their item content, nonverbal tests can be cross-classified in two distinct ways. Firstly is the question of whether the test is individually or group administered. Secondly is whether the test contains items measuring a homogeneous, single dimension, or whether the test is constructed according to what Cronbach (1970) calls the "hodge-podge" principle, whereby a whole range of different types of problem are included in the test. A good example of the homogeneous test is that of matrices. Such items are generally reckoned to provide a pure measure of nonverbal reasoning. An example of a matrix item is shown in Fig. 1. In such items the testee is required to perceive the relationships in the design of the matrix either horizontally or vertically, and to produce an appropriate solution in the blank square. The item illustrated is taken from the

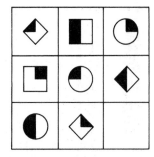

**Figure 1**
Example of matrix item

Matrices Scale of the British Ability Scales (Elliott 1983). A multiple-choice version which is very popular is Raven's Progressive Matrices, first published in 1938. In this version, which can be either group or individually administered, the testee chooses the correct solution from one of six alternatives. In these homogeneous matrices tests, all the items are of the same matrix type. They vary, of course, in terms of the complexity of the problems in the test: such tests commonly have an enormous range of difficulty. The individually administered versions are usually given with no time limit, the final score representing the ability of the testee to solve the items with no time constraints.

Group-administered tests are often of a more heterogeneous type and usually impose time limits. The items illustrated in Fig. 2 are taken from Cattell's culture-fair intelligence tests (Cattell and Cattell 1973). Such item types are, however, found in many nonverbal tests developed in many countries of the world. Such items require a broader range of reasoning skills and

some degree of flexibility in being able to switch from one problem to another. Characteristically, testees are given some initial practice in the different types of items which they will encounter in the test. Typically, since such tests are usually timed, the final score provides a measure of the testee's ability to solve such problems quickly as well as accurately.

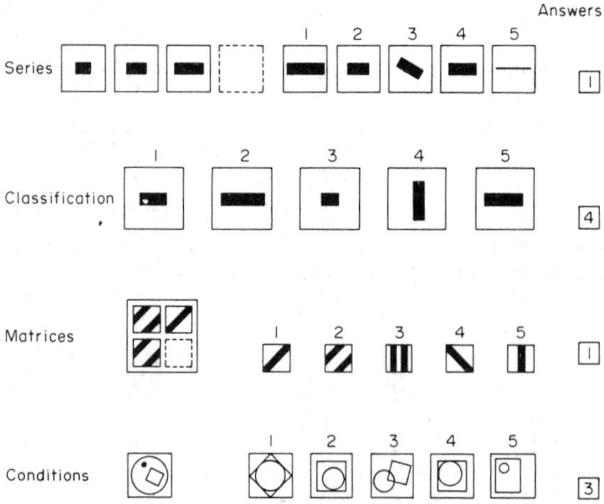

Finally, it should be stressed that nonverbal tests, while being of a distinctly different character and serving a different purpose to verbal tests, are often substantially correlated with verbal tests. This should not be seen as surprising, since the performances of persons on all cognitive tasks are usually positively related. As stated earlier, while nonverbal tests attempt to reduce the effects of language and cultural experience to a minimum, it is not possible to eliminate them. Persons who have a high level of verbal–conceptual development are likely to do well in all analytic tasks whether these are verbal or nonverbal, because they are able to use their verbal abilities to label, structure, and solve even so-called nonverbal problems. Consequently, persons who have had little opportunity to develop language may be relatively handicapped even on nonverbal tests. Such groups as deaf people typically tend to score lower on nonverbal tests, presumably because they have not had the opportunity to develop the higher order language concepts which would be of help to them in solving nonverbal problems. It is virtually impossible to devise nonverbal problems which are not susceptible to verbal mediation.

To summarize, nonverbal ability tests provide a quick and efficient means of measuring higher order reasoning functions with the effects of language and cultural experience being much reduced in comparison with verbal tests. In consequence, they are of use in providing us with insights into the reasoning abilities of children and adults whose educational or other verbal performances are relatively low. Such tests are used in educational and occupational testing programmes in order to make such testing fairer to culturally disadvantaged or minority groups. As with all educational and psychological tests, considerable care needs to be taken in interpreting results obtained from nonverbal tests.

**Figure 2**
Example of matrices test to be administered to groups

## Bibliography

Anastasi A 1982 *Psychological Testing*, 5th edn. Macmillan, New York

Cattell R B, Cattell A K S 1973 *Culture Fair Intelligence Test*. Institute for Personality and Ability Testing, Champaign, Illinois

Cattell R B, Warburton F W 1967 *Objective Personality and Motivation Tests*. University of Illinois Press, Urbana, Illinois

Cronbach L J 1970 *Essentials of Psychological Testing*, 3rd edn. Harper and Row, New York

Elliott C D 1983 *The British Ability Scales. Manual 1: Introduction and Rationale*. National Foundation for Educational Research, Nelson, Slough

# Performance Tests

## S. Kojima

In fields such as psychology and education, the term "performance test" is used to refer to a nonverbal test which requires responses in terms of actual tasks or behaviors, rather than a test which requires verbal responses. However, the full range of tasks and behaviors which can be categorized as performance tests has yet to be explored, and an exact definition agreed.

Adkins (1947) defined performance tests to mean a test that is used only to evaluate the manipulation of instruments, physical movements, manual dexterity, and so on. Her definition would exclude a pencil-and-paper test even if it was used for the observation of behavior. On the other hand, on intelligence scales such as the Wechsler Intelligence Scale for Children (WISC), such items as a maze which require the subject to trace a figure with a pencil are categorized as performance tests.

The term performance test describes the form of the test rather than its use. Such tests have been developed and used for various purposes. In this sense it is different from the terms "intelligence test" and "personality test" which describe tests created for a particular purpose without any specifications about their form.

## 1. Historical Development of the Performance Test

It is said that the origin of the performance test can be traced back to E. Sequin's experiment. In 1846 he devised a form-board (a task requiring the setting of variously shaped plates into appropriate slots) for testing feebleminded people. In 1915 Goddard developed it into a test, and since then various versions have been developed. The Pinter–Patterson Performance Scale (1917) and the Arthur Performance Scale (1933, 1943) are examples of standardized performance tests.

In this sense, the idea of a performance test has been gradually incorporated into the concept of an intelligence test and has come into wide use as in the Wechsler Performance Scales.

Wechsler developed various tests for different age groups; among them the Wechsler Intelligence Scale for Children (WISC—1949), the Wechsler Adult Intelligence Scale (WAIS—1955), the Wechsler Preschool and Primary Scale of Intelligence (WPPSI—1967) are well-known. The WAIS, for instance, includes the following kinds of subtests:

(a) Verbal tests—information; comprehension; arithmetic; similarities; digit span; vocabulary.

(b) Performance tests—digit symbol; picture completion; block design; picture arrangement; object assembly.

Here the term "performance test" is used to refer to nonverbal forms of test which require subjects to respond to pictures or figures shown to them, and it does not necessarily include the use of physical instruments.

The driving test required for getting a driving license, and a test which involves giving a sample to a subject and asking him or her to make the same thing (i.e., copy it) can be considered to be performance tests. They are tests on which success or failure is judged in accordance with the established performance criteria. Such types of tests have been used in various fields of industry for a long time although usually without standardization of the judgment criteria.

The General Aptitude Test Battery (GATB) is a widely known aptitude test designed to measure general aptitude toward occupations. GATB was developed by the United States Department of Labor over a period of about 10 years until general release in 1946. It consists of 15 subtests which are designed to measure 10 aptitudes including intelligence, and this includes a kind of "performance test" which measures manual dexterity and speed of movement.

In recent years, the professional literature includes a number of articles relating to performance tests in such fields as vocational education, military training, medicine and nursing, and automobile engineering. Most of these deal with tests concerning special techniques or skills required in their respective fields. With the recent development of electronic technology, simulations using computers are now available for a wide range of training purposes, and they can also be considered to be a kind of formative performance test.

## 2. General Features of Performance Tests

Performance tests emphasize responses in terms of actual behaviors, and thus they measure different aspects of achievement than do pencil-and-paper tests used for assessing intellectual ability. However, they also have several disadvantages.

In the first place, it often takes considerable time to administer such a test. Further, it gives tasks to an individual subject, and unlike pencil-and-paper tests, it is often difficult to administer a performance test at the same time to a group of people. One of the ways to overcome such a difficulty may be to divide performance test items into short subtests and to administer them simultaneously to a group of subjects but on a rotation basis.

Secondly, they may be more expensive than a pencil-and-paper test if they require the use of various costly instruments and expendable supplies. One way of overcoming this disadvantage may be to explore the possibility of using films and/or slides instead of actual objects, and of using simulations for measurement.

It is also rather difficult to set an objective criterion for judgment. Even if only the results of the tasks or behaviors are evaluated, the criteria adopted by the evaluators may differ from one to another. This point directly affects the validity and reliability of the test. If too much emphasis is given to the practical aspect of behaviors and tasks, the validity and reliability of the test may suffer in contrast to a pencil-and-paper test which measures similar intellectual content.

## 3. Utilization of Performance Tests in Science Education

Mager (1962) proposed that educational objectives be described by a precise statement indicating the performance expected of the learner in terms of specific behavior. In science education, behavioral objectives have been emphasized in the evaluation of learning, as experiments and observations occupy a major part of science instruction. As a consequence, a form of performance test is frequently used. The analytical results show that the practical examination seems to measure different aspects of ability than other paper-and-pencil tests.

### Bibliography

Adkins D C 1947 *Construction and Analysis of Achievement Tests: The Development of Written and Performance Tests of Achievement for Predicting Job Performance of Public Personnel.* United States Civil Service Commission, United States Government Printing Office, Washington, DC

Karmel L J 1970 *Measurement and Evaluation in the Schools.* Collier–Macmillan, Don Mills, Ontario

Kojima S 1974 IEA science study in Japan with special reference to the practical test. *Comp. Educ. Rev.* 18: 262–67

Mager R F 1962 *Preparing Instructional Objectives.* Fearon, Palo Alto, California (Japanese translation 1968 Sangyo Kodo Kenkyujo)

Nedelsky L 1965 *Science Teaching and Testing.* Harcourt, Brace and World, Chicago, Illinois

# Practical Examinations

## P. Tamir

With the advent of the inquiry-oriented science curricula which stress the processes of science and emphasize the development of higher cognitive skills, the laboratory has acquired a central role, not just as a means for demonstration and confirmation, but rather as the core of the science learning process. What is so special about laboratory experiences? Olson asserts that through learning experiences two types of information are acquired: the first, reflecting the features of the objects and events more or less invariant across different experiences, may be called "knowledge." The second, reflecting the features of the experience across different objects and events, may be called "skills." Gilbert Ryle's famous distinction between propositional knowledge (knowing that) and procedural knowledge (knowing how) corresponds to the distinction between "knowledge" and "skill." Olson has further observed that our schools are reasonably successful in serving the goals pertaining to the acquisition of knowledge but they serve poorly the educational goals pertaining to the development of skills, mainly because instruction relies heavily on symbolically coded information (speech, print, pictures, films), which happens to be a convenient and efficient way for transmitting bodies of knowledge to large groups of students. The science laboratory is certainly an exception in this regard. The most important role that the laboratory can play is to provide opportunities for direct experiences, which are so rare in our schools, and which may be conducive to the development of motor as well as intellectual skills. At the same time these experiences also help in the acquisition of knowledge as well as in the development of attitudes. Hence, assessment of outcomes of laboratory instruction needs to include all three domains, namely cognitive, psychomotor, and affective.

## 1. Assessment of Science Laboratory Outcomes

No learning experience can be classified exclusively in any one of the three domains. This article, however, will deal primarily with practical examinations which focus on the cognitive and psychomotor domains, and specifically affective outcomes such as curiosity, perseverance, interest, and enjoyment will not be discussed. Although practical examinations can be used to assess such affective outcomes, so far they have not been used for this purpose. There is evidence, however, which indicates that many students enjoy practical tests and prefer them over regular paper and pencil tests. Table 1 presents a laboratory outcomes inventory.

Unlike the objectives presented by Klopfer (1971) in his table of specifications, the outcomes in Table 1 have been arranged in a sequence which will fit that of a laboratory investigation. The list does not imply, however, that each outcome is to be represented in each examination; rather it is intended to serve as reminder and check list for a comprehensive assessment of laboratory outcomes. The following approaches have been used to assess laboratory outcomes:

(a) Continuous assessment by the science teacher based on systematic observations and records.

(b) Evaluation of laboratory reports made by students on the basis of their laboratory experiences.

*Table 1*
Laboratory outcomes inventory

1. Planning and design
   1.1 Formulates a question or defines a problem to be investigated
   1.2 Predicts experimental results
   1.3 Formulates hypothesis to be tested in this investigation
   1.4 Designs observation or measurement procedure
   1.5 Designs experiment
       1.5.1 Identifies dependent variable
       1.5.2 Identifies independent variable
       1.5.3 Designs control
       1.5.4 Fits the experimental design to the tested hypothesis
       1.5.5 Provides a complete design (including replication, for example)
   1.6 Prepares the necessary apparatus

2. Performance
   2.1 Carries out observations and measurements
       2.1.1 Carries out qualitative observations
       2.1.2 Carries out quantitative observations/measurements
   2.2 Manipulates apparatus; develops techniques
   2.3 Records results; describes observations
   2.4 Performs numeric calculations
   2.5 Explains or makes a decision about experimental technique
   2.6 Works according to own design
   2.7 Overcomes obstacles and difficulties by himself
   2.8 Cooperates with others when required
   2.9 Maintains orderly laboratory and observes safety procedures

3. Analysis and interpretation
   3.1 Transforms results to standard forms
       3.1.1 Arranges data in tables or in diagrams
       3.1.2 Graphs data
   3.2 Determines relationships, interprets data, draws conclusions
       3.2.1 Determines qualitative relationships
       3.2.2 Determines quantitative relationships
   3.3 Determines accuracy of experimental data
   3.4 Defines or discusses limitations and/or assumptions that underlie the experiment
   3.5 Formulates or proposes a generalization or model
   3.6 Explains research findings and relationships
   3.7 Formulates new questions or defines problem based upon results of investigation

4. Application
   4.1 Predicts, based upon results of this investigation
   4.2 Formulates hypothesis based on results of this investigation
   4.3 Applies experimental technique to new problem or variable
   4.4 Suggests ideas and ways to continue this investigation

(c) Individual student projects based on practical skills.
(d) Paper and pencil test items pertaining to laboratory experiences and laboratory-related issues.
(e) Practical examinations.

Items (a), (b), and (c) represent important evaluation strategies; yet, as long as tests are used to complement the teacher's continuous informal and formal evaluation, as well as for the purpose of research and curriculum evaluation, there is no reason to treat practical examinations differently. The general tendency in the United States and elsewhere has been to test for most of the objectives listed in Table 1 by paper and pencil tests. In the few cases where practical tests were used, they tended to focus on performance categories, mainly on categories 2.2 and 2.3. In the United Kingdom there has been a long tradition of practical work followed by practical examinations. Even there the general tendency has been to test for processes included in Table 1 under categories 1.0, 3.0, and 4.0 in paper and pencil tests and restrict the practical examinations to some of the subcategories of category 2.0.

Most recently the Assessment of Performance Unit (APU) in the United Kingdom identified the following six process skills to be included in their assessment scheme: using symbolic representations (graphs, chemical symbols, formulas, diagrams); using apparatus and measuring instruments; observation; interpretation and application; design of investigations; performing investigations. Only three of the six processes, namely manipulation of apparatus, making observations, and performing investigations, were assessed by the actual performance of students while the other three were tested by paper and pencil tests.

## 2. The Justification of Practical Examinations

Five arguments are offered as justification for carrying out practical examinations: (a) Grobman (1970), summarizing the state of the art in the United States writes:

> There has been little testing which requires actual performance in real situation, or in a simulated situation approaching reality . . . to determine not whether the students can verbalize a correct response but whether he can perform an operation, e.g., a laboratory experiment or an analysis of a complex problem. . . . This is an area where testing is difficult and expensive, yet since in the long run, primary aims of projects generally involve doing something rather than writing about something, this is an area which should not be neglected.

(b) Tamir (1975) suggests that "important relationships exist between instruction and assessment." The relative importance assigned to different assessment procedures determines how the student learns and what efforts he invests in different learning tasks. (c) In addition "assessment procedures may have profound effects on instruction." For example the use of open-ended laboratory examinations as part of the matriculation examination in high-school biology in Israel has dramatically changed the laboratory instruction, which has become significantly more prominent and much more inquiry oriented. (d) Kelly and Lister (1969) suggest that "the need for some measurement of pupils' performance in practical work is based on the desirability of reflecting the important role of practical work in courses they take." (e) Lastly and most importantly: "practical work involves abilities, both manual and intellectual, which are in some measure distinct from those used in non-practical work" (Kelly and Lister 1969). This last argument needs elaboration.

## 3. The Practical Mode

While discussing inquiry abilities or skills (such as "the ability to discern a problem" or "the ability to interpret data") Schwab identifies two facets to each of these abilities. On the one hand there is the ability to actually construct a problem or to actually phrase in one's own words the interpretation. This facet was designated as the constructive mode. On the other hand, there is the ability to follow, understand, and judge the soundness of these scientific operations when they are reported in summary of research. This facet was designated as the analytic mode. Tamir argues that the expression of these abilities in the context of actual practical work constitutes yet another facet which he designated as the practical mode. Tamir (1975) provides empirical evidence collected from a number of studies all over the world, including the study by the International Association for the Evaluation of Educational Achievement in *Evaluation of Science Education in Nineteen Countries* (Comber and Keeves 1973) which support the distinctness of the practical mode. Three kinds of items were administered within the framework of the international study mentioned above: paper and pencil items dealing with theoretical material, paper and pencil items dealing with practical laboratory material, and laboratory practical performance items. High correlations ($r = 0.75$) were obtained between the first two types while the correlations between the practical performance scores and the two other types were similar and rather low ($r = 0.24$ to $0.45$). The international study concludes: "these figures indicate that the laboratory practical tests are measuring some attributes quite distinct from those measured by the written examination and that these attributes are only probed to a limited extent by pencil and paper-type 'practical items.'" Following trials of different test items the Assessment of Performance Unit (1978) concludes: "Trials . . . revealed how important it is to go to the trouble of assessing the actual performance of investigations. . . . Pupils were frequently found to be able to produce a reasonable plan on paper, but were quite unable to do in practice anything of what was planned. . . . It is not just manipulative skill which makes the difference between theory and practice in problem solving, but the interaction of ideas with events as they take place."

## 4. Types of Practical Examinations

Based on the arguments and evidence presented above, practical examinations can be defined as tasks which require some manipulation of apparatus or some action on materials and which involve direct experiences of the examinee with the materials or events at hand. Practical examinations may be administered individually or to groups.

### 4.1 Individually Administered Examination

This involves a student who performs the required tasks and an examiner who observes and/or guides the performance and assigns marks. Three different procedures will be described.

In the first, the examiner observes the performance and assigns marks following a prepared checklist. Usually he or she neither asks questions nor gives directions, but rather allows the examinee to follow written directions and hence assessment is confined to the observed behaviors. Figure 1 presents an example based on Tyler's microscope checklist (Tyler 1942).

The second kind of individually administered practical examination is essentially an interview quite similar to that developed by Piaget. Piaget did not limit himself to asking children the same set of questions. Rather, after beginning an interview with a standard question or two, he felt free to create spontaneous additional queries designed to probe the thought process that produced the child's initial answer. This approach was used, for example, by Nussbaum (1979) in assessing the understanding of the concept "Earth" by children. Using a globe, a small figure of a person that could be attached to the globe, a styrofoam ball with a long

---

The teacher's goal is to see whether the student is able to operate a microscope so that a specimen present in a culture is located.

(a) Does the student wipe the slide with lens paper? Yes No
(b) Does the student place one drop or two of culture on slide? Yes No
(c) Does the student wipe cover glass properly? Yes No
(d) Does the student adjust cover glass adequately? Yes No
(e) Does the student wipe off surplus fluid? Yes No
(f) Does the student place slide on stage adequately? Yes No
(g) Does the student look through eye piece and hold closed one eye? Yes No
(h) Does the student turn to objective of lowest power? Yes No
(i) Does the student adjust light and concave mirror? Yes No
(j) Does the student adjust diaphragm? Yes No
(k) Does the student use properly coarse adjustment? Yes No
(l) Does the student break cover glass? Yes No
(m) Does the student locate specimen? Yes No

*Figure 1*
A checklist example for an individually administered examination

Ruth (11 years old) told in detail how astronauts go on a space voyage and how they see from their space ship that the Earth is round. Only after probing with the aid of the concrete props was it found that she had believed that we live on a flat Earth. The round Earth is up in the sky and when astronauts go high enough they can photograph it and thus see that the Earth is round.

*Figure 2*
Example of assessment by interview

straight hole in it to demonstrate holes in three dimensions, and a set of drawings, he was able to identify a number of alternative notions of Earth held by different children. These alternatives then become categories to be used in the assessment of other students' understanding of Earth. An example of what can be deduced from one interview is given in Fig. 2.

The Assessment of Performance Unit (1978) has employed a combination strategy in their category designated as "performing investigations." They wrote: "The problems lie in finding a way to take advantage of the richness of information the answers provide and to interpret the performance as correctly as possible. In some cases it is possible to assess the performance by observation using a checklist or sets of categories; in a few cases, the pupils' writing gives a fair account of what they have done; in other cases, it may be necessary to use a combination of these two kinds of information plus additional data from interviewing pupils when they have finished."

The third kind is an oral examination based on concrete phenomena or materials. Examples are identification of parts in a prepared dissection or the kind of oral included in the matriculation of high-school biology students in Israel who carry out an ecological project for several months and then bring a selection of organisms that they had studied to serve as objects for their oral examination (see Fig. 3).

Individually administered performance examinations are quite common in vocational and professional sub-

On the table lie a few pine tree branches with flowers and cones of different ages. The examinee is asked to suggest as many ways as he can to determine the age of a particular branch. He has to examine the branch to identify and point at the clues that may be used such as the stage of development of the ovulate cones, the bare patches created by the falling of the staminate flowers—one patch per year—and the pattern of new growth. During the discussion the student talks and demonstrates and reveals his general familiarity with the structures and their functions.

Although the examination started with one specific question, it continued in accordance with the student's responses and the questions they led the examiner to ask.

*Figure 3*
Example of a structured oral examination

jects such as typing, driving, medicine, and agriculture. Here, however, we confine ourselves to practical examinations in science.

### 4.2 Group Administered Practical Examinations

While the one (examinee) to-one (examiner) practical examinations described above have their place as an important research tool and as a means of evaluation under special circumstances in schools, they are too expensive to become a routine assessment procedure in most schools, in which group-administered examinations are usually to be preferred. Unlike the one-to-one examination where assessment is based on direct observation and oral probing, group examinations are based on written responses. Three types of group-administered practical examinations are described below, all of which have been used in the matriculation examinations in Israel as well as in high schools and universities in the United Kingdom. They have been used in other countries such as Japan, Hungary, and the United States to some extent, but many countries have avoided them because of the difficulties involved in their design, administration, and scoring, as well as the low reliabilities which are often associated with their results. In the United Kingdom and in Israel great care is taken to ensure that the tests in use are valid and reliable.

The first type of group-administered examination to be described involves the use of a dichotomous key to identify the name of an unrecognized object such as a rock or an organism. Tamir describes this type of examination as follows: "The ability to identify an unknown plant with aid of a key is considered an important skill in biology. While developing this skill some corollary objectives may be achieved, such as developing observational skills, getting acquainted with principles of taxonomy, getting to meet and observe plants, experiencing the diversity of type, and the unity of patterns: one of the major themes of biology." Figure 4 outlines the procedures.

The second type of examination which is used often in the United Kingdom and in college science courses elsewhere is often designated as a "circus" or "stations." Each table in the laboratory room constitutes a station. Each station provides equipment, materials, and instructions for a particular task. The student gets between 5 and 25 minutes to perform depending on the nature of the task. It is essential that the tasks require more or less the same length of time so that students can be conveniently moved from one station to another. For example in the framework of the lower level of matriculation examination in biology in Israel examinees are required to perform three tasks, each lasting 25 minutes. One examiner can control six sets of three students each, a total of 18 students. Examinees perform such tasks which ask for written reports so that marking is, by and large, based on the written report. In certain tasks, the examiner is asked to make occasional checks. For example in a task which requires the use of a

A group of students, usually no more than 30, is seated one student per desk. A key, magnifying glass, needles, razor blade, pencil and paper, and a plant bearing flowers, fruit, and roots are provided. On some occasions students are asked to make a full description of the plant referring to the unique characteristics of roots, stem, arrangement of leaves, shape of leaves and their edges, arrangement of flowers, structure of flower, type of fruit. Following this description they proceed to the actual process of identification. In order to save time it was decided in Israel to skip the advance description and to proceed directly to the identification with the aid of the key. However, in order to keep track of the sequence used by the examinee and his ability to identify correctly the different features of the organism, the student is required to record the numbers of items which he followed as well as the descriptions in the text which fit the organism under examination. A detailed scoring key is used according to which the student loses a preagreed number of marks for each mistake. Half of the marks are assigned to correct identification of the family, genus and species, while the other 50 percent are assigned to the correct recording of sequence and features. The examination lasts 30 to 45 minutes and interrater reliability averages 85 percent of agreement.

*Figure 4*
A practical examination for group administration of the type used in Israel

microscope the student is instructed to call the examiner when he or she has completed mounting a slide for observation. The examiner checks the preparation, lighting, and adjustment and assigns a mark which will constitute part of the overall mark of this particular task. Figure 5 gives an example of a station task for 13-year-old students taken from the Assessment of Performance Unit.

A third type of examination was developed within the framework of the Israeli matriculation examination and is used each year with 3,500 twelfth-grade students (see Fig. 6). It was designated as inquiry-oriented practical examination; its test problems have been selected and designed with the following considerations in mind (Tamir 1974):

(a) They should pose some real and intrinsically valuable problems before the students.

(b) It should be possible to perform the task and conclude the investigation within a reasonable time limit (i.e., two hours).

(c) The problems should be novel to the examinee, but the level of difficulty and the required skills should be compatible with the objectives of and experience provided by the curriculum.

(d) Since every student will be able to perform just one full investigation, several different problems must be used simultaneously to ensure independent work within a group setting. However, for the sake of comparability the different tests should be con-

vergent on a number of skills with specific weights given to each skill (for example: manipulation—10 points; self-reliance—10; observation—10; experimental design—25; communication and reporting—15; reasoning—30). It will also be necessary to control for differences in the levels of difficulty as well as for the heterogeneity of variance by employing appropriate statistical procedures.

(e) The student performing a complete investigation may encounter certain difficulties at various steps of his work. It is inconceivable that he should fail the whole examination just because, for instance, he made some incorrect observations. Therefore a procedure is needed for prompting—or providing certain leads during the examinations without damaging the standards of assessment.

(f) Since the tests are based on open-ended problems, measures of divergence are needed, but accepted limits of this divergence must still be set.

(g) When tests of this kind are used as external examinations, special logistic problems are to be solved. For example, while certain materials can be prepared by the schools some materials and organisms must be brought by the examiners in order to prevent the examinees from obtaining clues regarding

---

*Materials:* Three dropping bottles labelled P (distilled water), Q (acetone in water), R (citric acid in water). Dry cobalt chloride paper in dessicator; blue litmus paper; six clean test tubes; safety spectacles.

*To the student:* You are given three clear liquids labelled P, Q and R, one of which is just water on its own. Follow the instruction below to find out which is just water.

(a) When cobalt chloride paper is put in a liquid which contains water it changes color from blue to pale pink.

(b) When blue litmus paper is put in a liquid which is acid it changes color from blue to red.

1. Test each liquid, one after the other using a clean test tube and fresh piece of the indicator paper each time, first by the cobalt chloride paper and then by the blue litmus paper. Record your results in the table below.

2. Smell each liquid and tick in the table below which of the liquids has a smell.

| Test | Liquid P | Liquid Q | Liquid R |
|------|----------|----------|----------|
| Cobalt chloride paper | | | |
| Litmus paper | | | |
| Smell | | | |

3. Which liquid is just water? Give your reasons.

*Figure 5*
An example of a practical examination used in the United Kingdom

*Materials:* a toad, beakers, thermometer, crushed ice, bunsen burner, table salt, a watch or a stopper.

*To the Student: Part A:*

Observe the toad on your table and design an investigation of the toad, using some or all of the materials on your table. The investigation should involve quantitative measurements the results of which can be reported by making a graph. It should be completed in about 90 minutes.

1. What is the problem you are going to investigate?
2. What hypothesis do you intend to test?
3. Design an experiment to test your hypothesis
   (a) What is the dependent variable? How will you measure it?
   (b) What is the independent variable? How will you change it?
   (c) Describe your procedure in detail.

Hand Part A to the examiner and obtain Part B

*To the student: Part B:*

Even though your design may be appropriate, please follow the instructions below which will enable you to test the effects of different temperatures in the toad's activity.

4. The activity of the toad will be measured by counting the throat movements. What is the assumption behind this measuring procedure?
5. Place the toad in the 400 ml beaker in about 4 cm of water. Cover the beaker and insert a thermometer through the cover. Practice counting the throat movements during 30 seconds. If the movements are too fast, put the beaker with the toad into a larger beaker containing crushed ice to lower the temperature. Record your results.
6. Measure the activity of the toad at 20°C, 10°C, 5°C. Repeat each count three times. Record your results.
7. What do you think will happen to the toad if you lower the temperature to −5°C? Explain.
8. Perform the observation of the toad at −5°C. Describe your procedure step by step. (Don't be afraid. The toad will *not* die.)
9. Record the results at −5°C. Take out the small beaker with the toad and put it on the table.
10. Summarize the results in a table.
11. Draw a graph presenting the results.
12. What happened to the toad when it returned to room temperature?
13. How would you explain the toad's behavior at different temperatures? Is this behavior of value in the toad's adaptation to the external environment? Explain.
14. Would you expect a similar behavior with a mouse? Explain.

***Figure 6***

An example of an inquiry-oriented practice examination

(a) *Drawing a graph*

| | |
|---|---|
| Adequate and perfect drawing | 5 |
| No or inadequate title | 4 |
| Inadequate scaling and relating of x and y axes | 3 |
| Inadequate connection between points of the graph | 2 |
| Combination of at least two of the above | 1 |

(b) *Recording of variables*

| | |
|---|---|
| Dependent variable on y and independent on x axis | 6 |
| Independent variable on y and dependent on x axis | 5 |
| Inappropriate recording of variable names and units | 4 |
| No recording of the variable names and units | 3 |
| Confusing the variables on the axes | 2 |
| Combination of at least two of the above | 1 |

***Figure 7***

An example of a Practical Tests Assessment Inventory for making graphs

In order to standardize the assessment of students' responses a Practical Tests Assessment Inventory (PTAI) was developed and empirically validated. It contains 21 categories beginning with problem formulation and concluding with application of knowledge discovered in the investigation. Figure 7 presents an example from the Practical Tests Assessment Inventory illustrating possible skill areas, student behavior, and their respective point values.

To sum up, the practical mode has a significant role to play in schools, and hence should not be overlooked either in instruction or in assessment. It is possible to do this today better than in the past since there now exist the knowledge and the tools to make valid, reliable, useful, and challenging practical examinations in science.

## Bibliography

Assessment of Performance Unit 1978 *Science Progress Report 1977–78.* Elizabeth House, London

Comber L C, Keeves J P 1973 *Science Education in Nineteen Countries: An Empirical Study.* Wiley, New York

Doran R L 1980 *Basic Measurement and Evaluation of Science Instruction.* National Science Teachers Association, Washington, DC

Grobman H 1970 *Developmental Curriculum Projects: Decision Points and Processes.* Peacock, Itasca, Illinois

Kelly P F, Lister R E 1969 Assessing practical ability in Nuffield A level biology. In: Eggleston J F, Kerr J F (eds.) 1969 *Studies in Assessment.* English Universities Press, London

Klopfer L E 1971 Evaluation of learning in science. In: Bloom B S, Hastings J T, Madaus G F (eds.) 1971 *Handbook of Formative and Summative Evaluation of Student Learning.* McGraw-Hill, New York

Lunetta V N, Tamir P 1979 Matching lab activities with teaching goals. *Sci. Teach.* 46: 494–502

Nussbaum J 1979 Israeli children's conceptions of Earth as a cosmic body: A cross age study. *Sci. Educ.* 63: 83–93

Tamir P 1974 An inquiry oriented laboratory examination. *J. Educ. Meas.* 11: 25–33

Tamir P 1975 Nurturing the practical mode in schools. *Sch. Rev.* 83: 499–506

Tyler R W 1942 A test of skill in using a microscope. *Educ. Res. Bull.* 9: 493–96

the tasks to be assigned during the examination. Also, careful preparation is needed for test administration as well as for assessment in order to provide standardized criteria. Moreover, since novelty is an important feature, new problems must be designed each year.

# Written Simulation in the Assessment of Problem Solving

## C. H. McGuire

Simulation is commonplace in the instruction and assessment of airplane pilots, astronauts, and even entire armies ("war games"), where the associated costs and hazards make training and testing in the "real world" either unacceptable or plainly unfeasible. With the advent of computers, analogous simulation techniques began to be employed more generally in formal educational settings. Recent technical developments (Morantz et al. 1981) have now made it possible to simulate complex problems in inexpensive paper-and-pencil format, that is economically feasible to utilize in the teaching and assessment of sophisticated decision-making and general problem-solving skills.

## 1. Requisites of a Valid Simulation of the Decision Process

Any exercise that purports to simulate the decision-making process must have the following characteristics. First, it must be initiated in a realistic way, as the problem would be posed in reality, not by a predigested summary of its salient features. Second, it must require a series of sequential, interdependent decisions representing the various stages actually demanded in defining, analyzing, and resolving a similar real-life situation. Third, the examinee must be able to make decisions and to obtain information in realistic form about the results of each decision, as a basis for subsequent action. Fourth, once these data are obtained, it must be impossible to retract a decision that is revealed to be ineffectual or harmful. Fifth, the simulation must be constructed so as to allow each person to approach the problem in any way he or she wishes, and to pursue that approach throughout. Hence, provision must be made for alternate paths through the exercise and for variation in the feedback appropriate to the approach each individual selects. Sixth, the problem should evolve and the situation change in response to the specific actions each individual takes. Finally, these changes in conditions must differ, according to the unique configuration of prior decisions each individual has made (McGuire et al. 1976).

## 2. Description of a Written Simulation of a Patient Problem

While the nature of the decision process is to some extent unique to each field, or even to each specific problem within a field, simulations of medical problem solving may be taken as exemplars of a much larger universe. Two variants of problems meeting the above criteria are now being widely used for instruction, self-assessment, certification, and licensure of students and practitioners in virtually all the health professions in the United States (McGuire 1980). The sequential management problem (SMP) which employs free responses followed by corrective feedback at each stage of data gathering and management, is well-adapted to small group, classroom testing (Berner et al. 1974). The patient management problem (PMP), which is fully objective, is more difficult to construct but also more amenable to large-group testing (McGuire et al. 1976). Both are useful for individual and group instruction.

In its most sophisticated form, a PMP is introduced by a very brief description of the patient's presenting complaint, together with any information that the health professional would ordinarily have immediately available on seeing the patient (see Fig. 1—problem statement). The examinee must then decide how to approach the patient, that is, what, if any, further data gathering seems indicated. Each decision is recorded by erasing the opaque overlay or rubbing a chemical marker over the relevant area of a specially treated answer sheet to reveal an instruction directing the respondent to the appropriate next section of the test booklet. Each data gathering and management section contains a long list of possible inquiries or interventions (see Fig. 1—test booklet). On selecting one or more of these options and recording that decision, the examinee receives a realistic report of the patient's response (see Fig. 1—answer sheet). On the basis of these new data, the examinee must decide upon the next step. In this fashion a problem may be carried through many stages, at each of which further decisions must be made based on the specific responses of the patient evoked by an individual's earlier decisions.

Each PMP contains many sections (stages) some of which are not necessarily relevant to the optimal management of the patient. The various stages and the responses to each specific decision are meticulously designed to simulate an actual clinical situation: for example, in response to an order for a laboratory test, X-ray, electrocardiogram, or blood smear, persons are given the actual laboratory report or referred to a high-quality photographic reproduction of the X-ray, tracing, or blood smear; in response to medication orders, changes in the patient's clinical condition are reported. No interpretation of these data is offered and none is explicitly demanded of the examinee. Each is merely given the data requested and is required to act on them as does the physician in the conventional clinical setting. The complications which must be managed differ from person to person depending (as they do in the office or clinic) on the unique combination of specific interventions each has selected at earlier stages. If at any stage individuals take inadequate or inappropriate measures they may be instructed that the problem is terminated because the patient has suffered a relapse, has been sent to another hospital, has been referred to a consultant, or has died.

## 3. Use of Written Simulation

Written simulations of the type described above were first employed in formal testing of United States medical students in the early 1960s (Charvat et al. 1968) and were quickly extended to examination of physicians applying for licensure or specialty board certification, and to older practitioners who needed or wanted some method of assessing themselves and identifying their own strengths and weaknesses. Meanwhile, both students and practitioners who had experienced written simulations as an examination technique made it abundantly clear that the method had very significant implications for the development of instructional materials.

In response to this demand, numerous books of clinical simulations have been developed which are appropriate both for individual, independent study and small-group discussion and problem solving (McGuire et al. 1977, 1978). These instructional simulations differ from the assessment simulations only with respect to the nature of the feedback furnished to the user (McGuire et al. 1976). Instructional simulations are always accompanied by some discussion of optimal approaches to, and management of, the problem; often this discussion is extended to include a detailed rationale for each recommended decision, or even a debate between experts regarding alternative approaches. In contrast, simulations used for testing purposes contain only the kind of immediate feedback that life itself provides. Subsequently, each examinee may be given a set of scores that represents the percentage of optimal data gathering and management decisions represented by

---

**Problem statement**

Thirty minutes after a light luncheon, a 50-year-old woman executive develops severe abdominal pain, during a board of directors meeting. The chairman of the board calls you and asks you to see her as soon as possible. At your request he agrees to arrange for her immediate transfer to a nearby hospital.

When you arrive there 30 minutes later, you find the patient lying on a cart in the Emergency Room. She appears to be in severe pain and begs you for relief.

| Test booklet | Answer sheet |
|---|---|
| You would now (choose only one) : | |
| 1. Obtain further history | 1. |
| 2. Perform a physical examination | 2. |
| 3. Hospitalize patient for further evaluation and therapy | 3. Turn to Section F |
| 4. Hospitalize patient for immediate surgery | 4. |
| 5. Hospitalize patient for urgent surgery after preoperative preparation | 5. |
| 6. Hopsitalize patient for conservative management without further evaluation | 6. |
| 7. Request a consultation | 7. |
| **Section F** | |
| You would now order (select as many as you consider indicated) | 208. 11 g percent |
| | 209. 15 mg/100ml |
| | 210. 31 meq/l |
| 208. Hemoglobin determination | 211. Specific gravitiy 1.022; 2 + glucose; negative acetone; a few epithelial cells |
| 209. Blood urea nitrogen | |
| 210. $CO_2$ combining power | |
| 211. Urinalysis | |
| 212. Chest x-ray | 212. See x-ray number 72 |
| 213. Electrocardiogram | 213. See tracing number 72 |
| 214. Blood smear | 214. See color plate 47 |
| etc. | etc. |

Note that when the student receives the answer sheet it appears to be completely blank; only the item numbers are visible. As the student records each decision the material to the right of the item number irrevocably appears.

**Figure 1**
Excerpt from a patient management problem (adapted from McGuire et al. 1977 and reprinted with permission)

the unique configuration of his or her decisions; this score report may or may not be accompanied by a diagnostic profile describing the nature of the errors—omission or commission—that were made at each stage of the decision process and/or in each problem area (McGuire et al. 1976).

Interest in simulation for both instruction and assessment has spread rapidly from the various medical specialities to virtually all other health professions. The methodology has now been extended to a variety of subject matter fields outside the health professions and to all levels of education, from secondary school through higher education to continuing education (McGuire 1976).

## 4. The Advantages and Limitations of Written Simulation

Simulation imitates, it does not duplicate, life; this is both its greatest strength and, in the minds of some, greatest weakness. Clearly, there are some aspects of reality that cannot at the present time be economically simulated, if they can be simulated at all. Furthermore, it is important to recognize that, even within the realm of the possible, simulation is not necessarily the most appropriate method for enhancing or for measuring all aspects of performance. Factual information is more economically conveyed and more directly measured by conventional techniques of teaching and testing. Personal and professional habits and skills are more firmly entrenched by repeated reinforcement, in diverse settings, over a long time span; they are most reliably assayed under similar conditions. Between these two extremes, simulation provides the following important advantages.

### 4.1 Perceived Relevance

Learning materials, diagnostic tests, and summative examinations composed of simulations appear more relevant to students of all ages than do typical textbooks and conventional examinations.

### 4.2 Preselection and Standardization of Tasks

This perceived relevance can be achieved without being dependent on the accidents of nature or the flow of real problems available at the time and place of instruction or assessment. Indeed, if for either instructional or assessment purposes it is necessary to sample problems that evolve over many years or in which the full effects of an intervention are long delayed, it is possible to

compress a lifetime—individual, corporate, or societal—into a half-hour simulation exercise. Simulation also permits the teacher or examiner to predetermine and to standardize both the task which individuals are to perform and the criteria for judging performance, to focus on the elements of primary concern, and to eliminate irrelevant complexities that would complicate instruction and contaminate assessment. Finally, it is possible to instruct students and to sample their performance on a much broader and more representative group of problems than is possible in a real-life situation.

### 4.3 Ultimate Responsibility and Enhancement of Learning

One of the most important advantages of simulation is that even inexperienced neophytes may be given full responsibility for dealing with the most critical of problems and may be allowed to pursue a frankly appalling course of action without subjecting anyone to inconvenience or danger. Such responsibility combined with the prompt, specific, and unequivocal feedback provided in well-designed simulations makes them a powerful tool for enhancing learning and for motivating students to direct their attention toward developing those cognitive skills most educators claim to prize.

## Bibliography

Berner E S, Hamilton L A Jr, Best W R 1974 A new approach to evaluating problem-solving in medical students. *J. Med. Educ.* 49: 666–72

Charvat J, McGuire C H, Parsons V 1968 *A Review of the Nature and Uses of Examinations in Medical Education.* Public Health Papers No. 36. World Health Organization, Geneva (English, French, Spanish, Russian)

McGuire C H 1980 Assessment of problem-solving skills. *Med. Teach.* 2: 74–79, 118–22

McGuire C H, Nerenberg R, Forman P M (eds.) 1978 *A Spectrum of Clinical Simulations in Basic Medicine.* World Health Organization, Geneva

McGuire C H, Solomon L M, Bashook P G 1976 *Construction and Use of Written Simulations.* Psychological Corporation of Harcourt Brace Jovanovich, New York

McGuire C H, Solomon L M, Forman P M (eds.) 1977 *Clinical Simulations: Selected Problems in Patient Management*, 2nd edn. Appleton–Century–Crofts, New York (English, Japanese)

Morantz D, Clarke W D, Stevens A L 1981 BLAT Occasional Article No. 1: An invisible ink process for use as an educational tool. *Information* [from the British Life Assurance Trust (BLAT) Center for Health and Medical Education] 3: 61–63

# Testing in Educational Settings

## Achievement Tests

### E. H. Haertel

Achievement tests are assessment devices used to measure pupils' attainment of the intended cognitive outcomes of schooling. The term most often refers to individually administered paper and pencil examinations, which may include objective questions, problems or problem sets, essay questions, or a mixture of these forms, as well as other formats. These written tests certainly cannot measure attainment of all of the goals that schools espouse, but the learning outcomes they are designed to measure are among the most important that schools strive to attain.

### 1. Categories of Achievement Tests

It is useful to divide achievement tests into the two broad categories of *classroom tests* and *standardized tests*. Classroom tests are those given by individual teachers, for purposes of grading, instructional planning, or occasionally to evaluate their own instruction. They may include tests provided by publishers to accompany instructional materials (curriculum-embedded tests) as well as tests created by teachers themselves. Standardized tests are those given under the auspices of some authority outside the classroom, including local or regional educational administrations. Although results may be reported to pupils, teachers, and parents as a record of progress and a tool for planning, one major purpose of these tests is usually to monitor the performance of the educational system at the classroom, school, or some higher level of aggregation. Standardized achievement tests are generally given less frequently than classroom tests, and cover a broader range of curriculum content. In comparison to classroom tests, they present a more synoptic, less fine-grained view of student learning.

The distinction between standardized tests and classroom tests roughly parallels that sometimes made between norm-referenced and criterion-referenced tests, although the terms *norm-referenced* and *criterion-referenced* are better used for modes of test interpretation than for tests themselves. Interpretations of standardized tests are primarily norm referenced. Performance is reported in terms of percentiles, stanines, grade equivalents, or other scales that indicate a child's standing relative to some appropriate comparison group, although criterion-referenced interpretations of the absolute level of performance on homogeneous subsets of items may also be reported for diagnostic use.

Interpretations of standardized tests at the school or district level also tend to be norm-referenced, and special norms may be created for comparing schools on the basis of their achievement score means. These will be different from norms for scores at the individual level; there is no simple relationship between the percentile rank of a school and the percentile ranks of its students. It is also common for schools or systems to be evaluated or compared using some summary of student-level derived scores. For example, the proportion of a school's students scoring in the lowest quartile, the proportion below grade level, or the proportion at least one year below grade level may be reported. Comparisons of schools or larger units are sometimes based on the average grade equivalents or the average percentile ranks of students, although measurement specialists generally discourage the averaging of these derived scores.

Interpretations of classroom tests are most often used to infer each individual child's progress or mastery of the content of the curriculum, and tend to be criterion-referenced. Performance is most likely to be reported as a proportion of items correct, although rankings or other norm-referenced scales may be used when course grades are assigned. The marking of classroom tests may include written diagnostic or evaluative comments by the teacher and, under some instructional approaches, children may even be given an opportunity to correct their errors and retake the same or an equivalent test.

### 2. Standardized Achievement Tests

There is substantial diversity among standardized achievement tests. They include specialized instruments to provide a profile of attainments or to aid in diagnosing learning difficulties in specific content areas; test batteries designed for general use with school children; college placement tests; and instruments used in regional, national, or international testing programs. In this section, achievement batteries and regional or national assessment instruments are considered in turn. Information about more specialized tests for specific content areas may be found in other articles.

### 2.1 Standardized Achievement Test Batteries

The achievement batteries used by many school districts in the United States offer one prototype of standardized achievement tests. These may include subtests measuring reading comprehension, listening skills, spelling, word analysis, punctuation, or vocabulary; arithmetic computation, arithmetic concepts, or problem solving; science, social studies, reference skills, or other areas. They are designed to inform teachers, parents, and children about the standing and progress of individual children relative to their age or grade cohorts beyond the local classroom or school, and to inform administrators at the school and higher levels about the relative standing of classrooms, schools, or school systems.

Achievement batteries offer several advantages over separate tests in different content areas. It is efficient and economical to purchase test materials and scoring services from a single source, and test content is likely to be better coordinated than would be possible with tests from different sources, providing coverage of most central curriculum topics, while avoiding needless redundancy from one subtest to another. Equally important, most batteries provide two or more tests forms at a range of age or grade levels, and offer score reports at the child, classroom, and building levels that can profile achievement across grades and content areas using norms based on common comparison groups. This provides the continuity necessary to track academic progress over time, and facilitates building-level or district-level comparisons of schooling outcomes across grade levels. It also facilitates "out-of-level" testing, whereby exceptionally advanced or retarded pupils are given tests at higher or lower than their more typical peers. Achievement batteries are also designed for efficient administration, following common testing procedures for different subtests, and often combining several subtests in one sitting.

Major achievement test publishers offer sophisticated scoring services, which users can purchase along with test materials. These may include the development and reporting of local norms based on district-wide performance, and an impressive variety of computer-generated score reports. A variety of derived scores may be ordered, presented through tables and graphs in attractive formats tailored for use by parents, teachers, principals, and district administrators. Teacher reports may include classroom-level summaries of performance by item or item clusters, so that instruction can be targeted on specific skills needing improvement. Some publishers even provide tables keying particular item clusters to specific pages in widely used textbooks.

The major disadvantage of achievement batteries is their imperfect articulation with the curricula of particular classrooms, schools, or districts. The costs of developing, norming, and publishing a test battery require that it be developed for as large a market as possible, but the United States includes 50 states comprising over 15,000 public school districts, each exercising a degree of independent control over the school curriculum. Consequently, the content of standardized tests tends to be limited to core topics covered in most major textbook series and common to the curricula of most states and districts. Not only is coverage limited to typical curriculum topics, but perhaps more important, it is largely limited to those forms of learning that can be demonstrated by responding to multiple-choice test items. Objective items offer enormous efficiencies relative to formats requiring children to produce a response, and have excellent psychometric properties. It is difficult to demonstrate statistically that the information gained using production rather than selection items justifies the increased cost of processing and scoring tests employing alternative formats (Linn 1986). Fortunately, there has been a trend in recent years toward the inclusion of different kinds of test items in large-scale assessments, especially brief writing samples (Quellmalz 1984). The program of national assessment in the United Kingdom shows that a variety of free response and even individualized testing approaches can be incorporated into large-scale assessments, and in the United States, the National Assessment of Educational Progress (NAEP) also includes some free response exercises.

The imperfect linkage of achievement tests to school curricula can become problematical when these tests exercise undue influence on the curriculum, or when they are used as outcome measures in educational research and evaluation. In an effort to exercise control over schooling processes, administrators may turn to tests as tools of educational policy. School-level test results may be published to bring community pressure to bear on low-performing schools, or teachers may be evaluated on the basis of their students' test score gains. These kinds of policy or accountability uses of standardized tests will create strong incentives to raise scores. Teachers and school principals will study test results to determine which items children tend to miss, and will target instruction to the corresponding skills. Children may indeed learn more of what is tested, but knowledge and skills that do not appear on the test may be crowded out of the curriculum. Over time, instructional activities may come to resemble testing activities more and more. Class discussion, extended writing, and other activities that bear little resemblance to objective testing will occur less frequently, and there will be an increase in the use of worksheets, short-answer questions, and other activities more likely to transfer to test-taking skill (Haertel and Calfee 1983).

Achievement tests provide widely accepted, efficient, objective measurements of important learning outcomes and, for that reason, the intended outcomes of educational curricula or programs are sometimes defined in terms of achievement test score gains. This leads in turn to the use of standardized tests as outcome measures in curriculum evaluation studies, often with disappointing results (Walker and Schaffarzick 1974). Not only is test–curriculum match likely to be imperfect, but traditional methods of test construction and broad content coverage tend to yield tests that measure the cumulative effects of many years of schooling, rather than the focused effects of immediately antecedent instruction (Snow 1980). In addition, overreliance on standardized achievement tests as outcome measures in evaluations is likely to encourage the kinds of curricular distortions described above.

## 2.2 Large-scale Assessments

Regional or national assessment instruments are standardized tests of a distinctly different kind than achievement batteries. Assessment programs typically involve thousands of examinees, and are designed primarily to provide aggregate-level data on outcomes at the school level or above. Such instruments may be designed following a matrix sampling approach, in which different items are given to (randomly equivalent) subsamples of respondents. In the National Assessment of Educational Progress, for example, used to track achievement in the United States, roughly 100 exercises for use at a given grade level may be organized into about 20 blocks, and each examinee is exposed to only two or three of these blocks according to a complex design (Messick et al. 1983). This permits the inclusion of many more items than any single examinee would have time to answer, and so permits better sampling of content than would be possible if all examinees were exposed to all items.

If the skill of two individuals is to be compared, the most accurate approach is to give them the same task on which to demonstrate that skill. If the tasks set for them differ, then comparison becomes more difficult. The purposes of a large-scale assessment are more complex, however, and matrix sampling designs in which different examinees respond to different items offer some important advantages. Regional comparisons may be carried out on a large number of learning objectives, with the intention, implicit or explicit, of generalizing beyond the particular items used to larger universes of items and to applications of the measured skills in situations other than test taking. When items as well as persons are conceived as samples from larger populations, it becomes clear that item sampling may limit precision at least as much as person sampling. Moreover, the useful life of an item is finite. Practice effects may become a problem with repeated use of an item, and the particular content of an item (for example, the topic of a reading passage) may become less relevant after a number of years. A mechanism is needed for gradual replacement of items, without jeopardizing the continuity of long-term trends over time. Statistical methods have been developed in conjunction with matrix sampling designs to address these problems (Bock et al. 1982). The use of a large number of items

and the inclusion of only a small portion of these in each test booklet also help to keep assessment tests secure, and make it less likely that testing results will be compromised by direct instruction on the answers to specific items.

Of course, complex, matrix-sampled assessment designs have disadvantages as well as advantages. The results may be more difficult to communicate clearly to policy makers and the public, and matrix-sampled data are difficult to use for secondary analysis. Moreover, scores for individual examinees can only be obtained using item response theoretic (IRT) models, such as the Rasch model or related models with additional parameters.

Individual students and teachers are unlikely to have as large a stake in the results of large-scale assessments as in testing programs built around standardized achievement batteries. Nonetheless, if rewards or sanctions are attached to performance on large-scale assessments, these tests may also press the curriculum in the direction of greater attention to tested knowledge and skills, and may encourage instructional activities that resemble test tasks. In the United States, some states have conferred monetary awards or other forms of recognition on schools showing exceptional assessment performance or year-to-year improvement, in an explicit effort to use the test to influence curriculum and instruction. Others have enacted strong sanctions which may be triggered when schools or school districts turn in test scores below minimum standards, including the direct intervention of the state in the administration of local school districts with exceptionally poor test performance. These approaches have generated heated debate, and have both their adherents and detractors (Airasian 1988, Anderson and Pipho 1984).

It must be pointed out that large-scale assessment programs may have salutary as well as deleterious effects on curriculum and instruction. In the United Kingdom, a program of national assessment of student performance was initiated in 1975, which includes tests of oral skills, writing, and arithmetic problem solving in which children give free responses rather than selecting among predefined alternatives. There is some evidence that these tests have encouraged teachers to focus more broadly on oral as well as written modes of communication, and to try harder to assure the transfer of arithmetic skill to practical situations (Burstall 1986).

## 3. Classroom Tests

Classroom tests include both curriculum-embedded tests and teacher-constructed tests. Curriculum-embedded tests are the quizzes, unit tests, and other examinations published in textbooks, or in workbooks and other ancillaries; and teacher-constructed tests are those created by teachers themselves, typically for use in their own classrooms or schools. Classroom tests of both kinds are of uneven quality, and curriculum-embedded tests are by no means necessarily superior to those constructed by teachers.

These curriculum-embedded and teacher-constructed tests differ from standardized tests in several ways, but especially in the audiences and purposes they serve, and in their close articulation with instructional content. They rarely approach the psychometric rigor of published standardized tests, but are far more salient and important to students and teachers. Classroom tests are designed and used according to the particular curricular and instructional intents of curriculum developers and teachers. They most often cover content just presented, but may also be used to evaluate pupils' prior knowledge of forthcoming topics, or to measure retention of material covered somewhat earlier. Because they are typically given to groups of pupils no larger than a class and are generally hand scored, classroom tests may readily incorporate production item formats, calling for pupils to generate responses rather than selecting among prespecified alternatives (Stiggins and Bridgeford 1985).

Classroom achievement tests may serve as a major vehicle of communication between students and teachers. They can inform students of teachers' standards and expectations, and can direct students' attention to areas of weakness in their own performance. They can inform teachers about the relative progress of different students, and about the overall effectiveness of the instruction provided. In addition to communicating teacher standards and student achievement, a major purpose of classroom testing is to inform and justify the assignment of marks and grades. Classroom tests and quizzes may also serve as motivational devices. Students may be willing to work harder for high marks, and the threat of a quiz may help to assure that they come to class prepared.

It is rare that norms of any kind are developed for either curriculum-embedded or teacher-created classroom tests, although some individual teachers might maintain records of classroom performance on a given test or even on particular test items from year to year. Performance on classroom tests is often reported as a percentage correct, which may sometimes be interpreted loosely as the proportion of course content a student has mastered. Such interpretations were encouraged by the widespread use of "behavioral objectives" in the 1960s, which were supposed to include an explicitly stated mastery criterion (Mager 1962). Given the range of factors that can influence item difficulties, such interpretations are clearly suspect, and the excesses of behavioral objectives are now generally recognized. The current practice of expressing classroom test performance as a percentage correct may not be strictly defensible, but appears harmless (Haertel 1987).

Classroom tests may have powerful effects on curriculum and instruction. For this reason, and also because they are largely criterion-referenced, it is important in evaluating, selecting, or creating these instruments to consider both the content covered and the range of processes or operations elicited. Examples of such cognitive process categories are the six categories of educational objectives set forth by Bloom et al. (1956), including knowledge, comprehension, application, analysis, synthesis, and evaluation. A traditional method for organizing content and process information is through a test blueprint, or content-by-process grid. This is a two-dimensional table in which rows might correspond to different cognitive processes or operations, and columns represent different units or other content elements in the curriculum. A target number of test items is entered in each cell of the grid, indicating the relative emphasis different content–process combinations are to receive in the final instrument. The grid may also be used in analyzing an existing instrument, by having several judges determine the cell represented by each item (Bloom et al. 1971).

Over the years, content-by-process grids have probably led to better test construction by teachers, by encouraging systematic planning for content balance, and by directing teachers' attention to the ways in which students were required to work with the material covered to arrive at their test responses. In the absence of such consideration, content balance may be uneven, unimportant details may be tested rather than major ideas, and the forms of cognition engaged may be lower-level thought processes like rote recall or routine application of learned procedures, rather than more complex and significant forms of reasoning.

At the same time, content-by-process grids have significant limitations as models for test development or analysis. Such classification schemes encourage the identification of different item formats with different cognitive processes, when in fact the processes elicited by an item depend critically on its relationship to antecedent instruction. The same item may test complex reasoning in one context, and routine application of learned algorithms in another. An item asking for an analysis of a poem or the historical significance of an Act of Parliament likewise may test different things depending on the antecedent instruction. It may be useful in designing classroom tests of higher level thinking to reserve some content just for assessment purposes, assuring opportunities to assess transfer or application of analytical or problem-solving skills using material that has not been directly taught.

## 4. Conclusions

Achievement tests encompass a great variety of different forms of instruments, serving different needs of different audiences. As one surveys these instruments from the classroom level through school, district, regional, and national levels, it is noticeable that their character changes substantially. At higher levels of aggregation, testing occurs at less frequent intervals, content coverage broadens, linkage to the curriculum becomes weaker, and interpretation tends more toward norm referencing than criterion referencing. A major division along this continuum separates classroom tests, which are under the control of individual teachers, from standardized tests, which are mandated by authorities beyond the classroom. As the size of testing programs increases, efficiency in scoring, data processing, and reporting becomes more important, and so standardized achievement tests are often limited to objective, multiple-choice items, although there are some important exceptions. Classroom tests typically employ a greater variety of item formats.

The many varieties of achievement tests can be of significant value when properly used but can cause mischief when used improperly (Airasian 1988). Deleterious outcomes are especially likely when substantial rewards or sanctions are attached to test performance. When tests are used as tools of educational policy, high scores on the tests may become ends in themselves, rather than indicators of other, valued learning outcomes. Such testing can indeed influence curriculum and instruction, but these influences may not always be what the policy makers intend.

## Bibliography

Airasian P W 1988 Measurement driven instruction: A closer look. *Educ. Meas. Issues Practice* 7(4): 6–11
Anderson B, Pipho C 1984 State-mandated testing and the fate of local control. *Phi Delta Kappan* 66: 209–12
Bloom B S, Engelhart M D, Furst E J, Hill W H, Krathwohl D R 1956 *Taxonomy of Educational Objectives*, Handbook I: *Cognitive Domain*. David McKay, New York
Bloom B S, Hastings J T, Madaus G F 1971 *Handbook on Formative and Summative Evaluation of Student Learning.* McGraw-Hill, New York
Bock R D, Mislevy R, Woodson C 1982 The next stage in educational assessment. *Educational Researcher* (AERA) 11(3): 4–11, 16
Burstall C 1986 Innovative forms of assessment: A United Kingdom perspective. *Educ. Meas. Issues Practice* 5(1): 17–22
Haertel E 1987 Scores and scales for school achievement. *Stud. Educ. Eval.* 13: 61–71
Haertel E, Calfee R 1983 School achievement: Thinking about what to test. *J. Educ. Meas.* 20: 119–32
Linn R L 1986 Barriers to new test designs. In: *The Redesign of Testing for the 21st Century: Proceedings of the 1985 ETS Invitational Conference.* Educational Testing Service, Princeton, New Jersey, pp. 69–79
Mager R F 1962 *Preparing Instructional Objectives.* Fearon, Palo Alto, California
Messick S, Beaton A, Lord F 1983 *National Assessment of Educational Progress Reconsidered: A New Design for a New Era.* Educational Testing Service, National Assessment of Educational Progress, Report No. 83–1, Princeton, New Jersey
Quellmalz E S 1984 Toward successful large-scale writing assessment. Where are we now and where do we go from here? *Educ. Meas. Issues Practice* 3(1): 29–32
Snow R E 1980 Aptitude and achievement. In: Schrader W B (ed.) 1980 *Measuring Achievement: Progress over a Decade. New Directions for Testing and Measurement.* Jossey-Bass, San Francisco, California pp. 39–59
Stiggins R J, Bridgeford N J 1985 The ecology of classroom assessment. *J. Educ. Meas.* 22: 271–86
Walker D F, Schaffarzick J 1974 Comparing curricula. *Rev. Educ. Res.* 44: 83–111

# Placement Tests

### R. M. Wolf

Placement tests are used to decide which of two or more alternative treatments will carry each individual further toward a common goal. Suppose there are two ways of teaching a particular school subject, one that emphasizes "discovery" and logical relationships, and one that emphasizes relatively rote learning. Suppose, further, there is reason to believe that students with certain characteristics can learn the subject better by one method and that students with other characteristics by the other method. The goal for both groups of students is the same, namely, mastery of the particular school subject. Placement research seeks to develop tests that will distinguish between those who will progress better by one method and those who will progress better by another method so that each student can be placed in an instructional group in which he or she is likely to learn best. The treatments are different but the desired outcomes are the same.

Figure 1 sets forth a situation in which a test functions effectively for placement. Students who score low on the placement test achieve higher performance in the subject under Treatment II, while students who score

high on the placement test achieve higher performance when taught by Treatment I. Conversely, students who score low on the placement test do poorly under Treat-

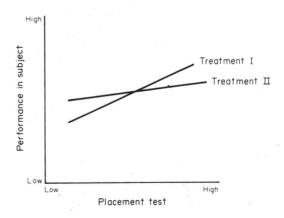

*Figure 1*
Effective functioning of a placement test

ment I while students who score high on the placement test do poorly under Treatment II.

The model of placement research described here also appears in the educational and psychological literature under the headings "aptitude–treatment interaction" or "trait–treatment interaction." An extended discussion of the model and of research on it is provided by Cronbach and Snow (1977). The literature is fairly voluminous but often contradictory and inconclusive. The past history of successes when tests are used for placement decisions has not been impressive. It is not clear whether this is due to inadequacies in the tests or an inability to develop effective alternate treatments.

## Bibliography

Cronbach L J, Snow R E 1977 *Aptitudes and Instructional Methods*. Irvington, New York

Thorndike R L, Hagen E P 1977 *Measurement and Evaluation in Psychology and Education*, 4th edn. Wiley, New York

# Criterion-referenced Tests

### R. A. Berk

A criterion-referenced test is deliberately constructed to assess an individual's performance level with respect to a well-defined domain of behaviors. The principal concern in its development is obtaining rigorous and precise domain specifications to maximize the interpretability of an individual's domain score. This emphasis on the domain has prompted some measurement experts to refer to the test as domain-referenced (see *Domain-referenced Tests*). Such a distinction is meaningful inasmuch as another type of criterion-referenced test has also emerged in practice. This alternative conceptualization, derived from mastery learning theory and popularized by many of the recent technical articles on item statistics and reliability, is represented by the mastery test. It is used to classify students as masters and nonmasters of an objective in order to expedite individualized instruction. Empirical item analysis procedures are recommended to determine whether the items are instructionally sensitive or discriminate between instructed and uninstructed groups. Methods for setting performance standards for mastery, the estimation of classification errors, and the determination of mastery–nonmastery decision consistency are particularly important elements in its development.

To date there have been four books (Berk 1980c, Berk 1984, Brown 1980, Popham 1978) and one issue of a journal (*Appl. Psychol. Meas.* 1980 Vol. 4 No. 4) devoted exclusively to the topic of criterion-referenced tests. They describe the procedures for test construction, score use, and interpretation. Very often the technical characteristics are compared to those of norm-referenced tests. For purposes of clarification, the specific differences between norm-referenced tests and the two types of criterion-referenced tests defined above are summarized in Table 1. A brief explanation of the characteristics of mastery and domain-referenced tests is given next.

## 1. Domain Specification

The mastery test is built on a set of instructional and behavioral objectives. While the objectives-based definition is relatively less precise and "ambiguous" compared to the strategies used to construct a domain-referenced test, it is extremely practicable. In addition, it is possible to improve upon this definition by using amplified objectives, instructional objectives exchange (IOX) test specifications, or mapping sentences.

The primary emphasis in the development of a domain-referenced test is at this first stage. The "unambiguous" definition of a behavioral domain and the generation of an item domain from that definition have been recommended to provide the most useful interpretation of an individual's domain score. These goals are difficult to achieve even with the technologies currently available (Roid and Haladyna 1981). Among the various domain specification strategies, only item transformations, item forms, and algorithms come close to attaining unambiguous definitions via sophisticated rule structures (Berk 1980a).

## 2. Item Construction

The objectives-based strategies associated with the mastery test necessitate a heavy reliance upon traditional item construction rules. The use of mapping sentences (facet theory) in conjunction with objectives holds considerable promise for refining this process so that it is more systematic and mechanical.

The domain-referenced approach requires detailed, explicit rules for generating the test items. The unambiguous specification strategies noted previously provide objective, computer-based technologies for producing item domains.

## 3. Item Domain

Until recently, the distinction between infinite and finite item domains was rarely considered in the test development process. The technological advances since the early 1970s in the specification of behavioral domains, however, have made it possible to actually generate "all possible items" in a domain. The level of precision in the specifications necessary to produce a finite domain

*Table 1*
Technical characteristics of norm-referenced tests and criterion-referenced tests

| Characteristic | Norm referenced | Criterion referenced | |
| --- | --- | --- | --- |
| | | Mastery | Domain referenced |
| Domain specification | Content outline<br>Table of specifications | Instructional and<br>behavioral objectives | Possible strategies:<br>(a) Amplified objectives<br>(b) IOX test specifications<br>(c) Mapping sentences<br>(d) Item transformations<br>(e) Item forms<br>(f) Algorithms |
| Item construction | M–C, T–F, matching<br>Short answer<br>Essay | Traditional rules used to<br>produce traditional<br>formats | Generation rules used to<br>produce traditional formats |
| Item domain | Infinite (or finite) | Infinite (or finite) | Infinite or finite |
| Test length | Based on reliability | Based on decision validity<br>and decision reliability | Based on estimate of<br>domain score |
| Item analysis | Difficulty<br>Discrimination<br>(item-total score $r$)<br>Choice response<br>analysis to revise faulty<br>items | Item-objective congruence<br>Difficulty (mastery group)<br>Difficulty (nonmastery<br>group)<br>Discrimination (between<br>mastery and nonmastery<br>group performance)<br>Choice response analysis to<br>revise faulty items | |
| Item selection | Nonrandom | Nonrandom | Random |
| Parallel forms<br>assumption | Classically parallel | Classically parallel | Randomly parallel |
| Standard setting | Optional | Judgmental or<br>judgmental–empirical<br>method (state or<br>continuum model) | Optional |
| Validity | Content<br>Criterion related<br>Construct | Content<br>Criterion related<br>Construct (Decision) | Content<br>Construct |
| Reliability | Possible approaches:<br>(a) Parallel forms<br>(b) Test–retest<br>(c) Internal<br>consistency | Possible approaches:<br>(a) Threshold loss<br>estimate of $p_o$ or $\kappa$<br>(b) Squared-error loss<br>estimate of $k^2(X, T_X)$ | Possible approaches:<br>(a) Squared-error loss<br>estimate of $\phi(\lambda)$ or $\phi$<br>(b) Point estimate of<br>domain score (individual<br>specific or group specific<br>standard error of<br>measurement) |

is quite unlike that of the objectives-based schemes. There are at least two advantages to the exact specification and enumeration of the items in a domain: (a) the items that comprise one test form or alternate forms can be drawn from the domain using a random or stratified sampling plan, and (b) the characteristics of the domain can be identified and, consequently, can be incorporated into the sampling design (for example, stratification by difficulty level), and other stages of test construction and score analysis (for example, parallel forms assumption, selection of an appropriate reliability index).

The objectives employed to define the content domain for a mastery test may suggest either a finite or an infinite domain. Typically, such a distinction is theoretical except in the case of very specific behavioral objectives; for example, the student will be able to multiply all combinations of single digit numbers. The items written to be included on a given test are usually not sampled from any domain. Rather, those items viewed collectively are assumed to constitute a sample from the domain of "all possible items" that could have been written from the objectives. Since the distinction between item domains makes little practical difference in the context of mastery test construction, the concept of "all possible items" is often associated with the assumption of an infinite item domain.

## 4. Test Length

The problem of determining how many items should be written for each objective on a mastery test has been approached from both practical and statistical perspectives. The former considers a multiplicity of factors, including importance and type of decision making, importance and emphases assigned to objectives, number of objectives, and practical constraints; the latter deals with the relationship between number of items and decision validity and decision reliability indices.

For the domain-referenced test, the analogous test length issue is translated into how many items should be sampled from the domain. It has been studied from the same perspectives. The statistical methods, however, have focused on the relationship between number of items and the reliability of the domain score estimate.

## 5. Item Analysis

An item analysis is desirable for mastery test items due to the intended uses of the test scores for mastery–nonmastery decisions and to the traditional, relatively subjective procedures employed in writing the items. The items must be scrutinized to appraise whether or not they measure their respective objectives, are unbiased in relation to women and minority groups, and differentiate between groups of masters and nonmasters of the objectives (item discrimination). In addition, they must be free of structural flaws that could cue or confuse the students.

This type of item analysis is unnecessary and, in fact, undesirable for domain-referenced test items. The use of item statistics for refining and selecting the items would theoretically destroy the defining character of the test, thereby weakening the interpretability of the domain score. Furthermore, given the precision of most of the strategies that are used to generate the item domain, the need to assess item–objective congruence or search for flaws in the items seems questionable.

## 6. Item Selection

Mastery test items are selected nonrandomly based on their congruence with the objectives and their sensitivity to instructional treatments. The item selection criteria recently proffered by Berk (1980c) emphasize clearly the primary importance of congruence and the secondary importance of statistical item properties.

As indicated previously, the items in a domain-referenced test are sampled randomly from the item domain. This assures that they are representative and congruent with the domain.

## 7. Parallel Forms Assumption

The assumption about parallel forms of a criterion-referenced test is related to (a) how the item sample that comprises one test form and the samples that comprise alternate forms are generated, and (b) the characteristics of the item domain from which those samples are generated.

When items are written from objectives-based specifications, it is possible to develop two or more item samples for the same objectives and domain. Frequently, those samples are constructed systematically to contain content and to yield means, variances, and item intercorrelations identical to the first sample. Item samples or alternate test forms with those properties are said to be classically parallel or equivalent to the first form. This statistical equivalence imposes restrictions on the domain; it requires that the content or set of behaviors being measured by the items be relatively homogeneous and, therefore, that the items in the domain possess similar difficulty levels.

Since domain-referenced item samples can be drawn randomly from an item domain, they are said to be randomly parallel. No specific statistical properties apply to these test forms nor is there any condition imposed that limits the variability of item difficulty levels in the domain. When the test maker cannot actually build test forms by randomly sampling from the domain, these forms and their characteristics can be "assumed."

## 8. Standard Setting

More than 20 different methods for setting performance standards have been recommended in the literature. Despite several extensive reviews of these methods, standard setting is still the stickiest technical topic. Perhaps the simplest framework for understanding the various methods is a bilevel classification (Berk 1980d). The first level partitions the methods into two major categories based on their assumptions about the acquisition of the underlying trait or ability: state models and continuum models. The second level classifies the methods according to whether they are based purely on judgment or incorporate both judgmental and empirical information: judgmental methods and judgmental–empirical methods/models.

## 8.1 State Models

State models assume that mastery or true-score performance is an all-or-nothing state; the standard is set at 100 percent. Deviations from this true state are presumed attributable to "intrusion" (false mastery) and/or "omission" (false nonmastery) errors. After a consideration of these errors, the standard is adjusted to values less than 100 percent. The judgmental–empirical models employ decision rules to identify the cutoff score that minimizes expected loss due to classification errors. These rules require judgments in designating the loss ratio.

## 8.2 Continuum Models

Continuum models assume that mastery is a continuously distributed ability that can be viewed as an interval on a continuum, that is, an area at the upper end of the continuum circumscribes the boundaries for mastery. This conceptualization appears to fit the design and intent of most criterion-referenced tests. It is therefore not surprising that the bulk of the research has concentrated on continuum models.

Although it was inevitable that the experts on criterion-referenced testing would not agree on a "best method" for setting standards, there is consensus on one issue—all of the methods involve some form of human judgment. A completely objective, scientifically precise method does not exist. Regardless of how complex and technically sophisticated a method might be, judgment plays a role in the determination of the cutoff score and/or in the estimation of classification error rates.

## 8.3 Judgmental Methods

These are based on judgments of the probability that competent persons would select particular distractors in each item or would answer each item correctly. The subjectivity of these item content decisions used to arrive at an overall cutoff score has been expressed succinctly as "pulling the probabilities from thin air." This problem is reflected in the variability among judgments within a single method and also across methods.

## 8.4 Judgmental–Empirical Methods

These are based on some type of judgment and actual or simulated data, judgmental data, and/or distribution assumptions. The role of judgment should not be underestimated. That is, the judgmental component usually supplies the foundation for much of the statistical estimation of probabilities of correct classification decisions and false mastery/false nonmastery decision errors.

The judgmental–empirical methods differ according to other characteristics as well: (a) their overall purpose; (b) the definition of the criterion variable; (c) a consideration of utilities; (d) the statistical sophistication; and (e) their practicability. Perhaps the most important initial distinction pertains to their purpose. Only the criterion groups and contrasting groups approaches are intended to select a cutoff score. All of the remaining methods presume that a standard already exists on a criterion or latent variable. Subsequently, this standard is translated into a cutoff score for the test, and decision error rates based on various assumptions are estimated. In some cases, those rates can be used to adjust the cutoff. The decision–theoretic models are not techniques for setting standards or optimizing mastery decisions; they are techniques for minimizing the consequences of measurement and sampling errors once the true cutoff has already been chosen.

## 8.5 Application of the Methods

Although a domain-referenced test is not designed expressly for mastery–nonmastery decision making, a cutting score may be set. The choice of a single approach appears to be dependent on the specific test application and several factors related to that application, including political considerations, decision consequences, practical constraints, statistical expertise and resources, and the types of mastery decisions to be made.

A standard *must* be set for the mastery test. The number of cutting scores that need to be selected for a test will differ with the structure of the test and the types of decisions. For objectives-based tests used for individual decisions at the classroom level, cutting scores should be chosen for each item cluster or subtest keyed to an instructional objective. There is nothing implicit in any of the approaches that dictates that the cutting score has to be identical for all subtests. The customary use of one "blanket mastery standard" for all objectives seems inadvisable for the following reasons. First, objectives vary in level of complexity and, therefore, applying the same standard to different objectives will be insensitive to that variability. Second, the difficulty and discrimination indices of items measuring one objective may be quite different from the indices of items measuring other objectives; consequently, it is unrealistic to expect a high proportion of students to obtain the same standard for each objective. Third, since the instruction associated with different objectives is rarely given the same time allotment and attention, performance on some objectives might be noticeably better than the performance on others. Again, this is inconsistent with setting the same standard for all objectives.

If the mastery test happens to be developed as a "minimum competency test" to be used for individual certification decisions at the school level, a single cutting score may be set for the total test rather than for each objective. Decisions regarding graduation and grade-to-grade promotion ordinarily do not require objective-by-objective analysis, although it is possible to specify a certain number of objectives that must be mastered in order to "pass." The information on objective mastery might be employed for follow-up diagnostic purposes along with instructional prescriptions for students who "fail."

## 9. Validity

While the assessment of content validity, criterion-related validity, and construct validity is applicable to both test conceptualizations, the emphases differ markedly. Given the objectives-based specifications of the mastery test, a special review process is necessary in order to determine content validity. This involves an examination of the technical quality and representativeness of the items. Procedures for evaluating item-objective congruence using rating scales and matching tasks have been suggested. It is significant to note that the judgmental and empirical procedures used to establish content validity for the mastery test are quite different from the domain specification strategies used to build in content validity for the domain-referenced test.

In addition to the steps required to ensure content validity, it is also essential to investigate the criterion-related validity and construct validity of the test. The mastery decision framework provides a specific focus for such investigations. The most complex and problematic aspect of this line of inquiry pertains to the definition of the success or mastery criterion. An operational definition must be specified and criterion success and nonsuccess groups of persons need to be identified. The criterion-related validity studies may be concurrent or predictive depending upon how success is defined, for example, success in the current program, or success in the next unit of instruction.

Furthermore, a particular type of construct validity for mastery test scores that deserves special attention is decision validity. It relates to the evidence gathered on the accuracy of mastery–nonmastery classification decisions. That evidence is often expressed as probabilities of correct and incorrect (false mastery and false nonmastery) classifications. Such evidence is crucial in the attempt to justify the selection of the cutting score. When decision validity evidence is not available, it seems pointless even to compute a reliability index. A high reliability index based on an "invalid" or "unjustified" standard, for example, might mean that the mastery test can consistently classify students into the wrong groups. Consistent decision making without accurate decision making has questionable value in criterion-referenced evaluation.

For the domain-referenced test, the tasks employed in developing the test concentrate, for the most part, on building in content validity. The rigor of the domain specifications and their direct link with the test items are the principal features. The effort devoted in the initial stages is designed to pay off with the dividends of descriptive clarity and precise score interpretations.

Another important concern is the construct validity of the scores. Empirically based construct validity studies that employ factor analysis or Guttman scalogram analysis should be conducted. Unfortunately, few such studies have been executed by test makers at the district or state levels.

## 10. Reliability

Similar to the topic of standard setting, the literature is replete with studies and reviews of reliability methods, with more than a dozen methods proposed to date. The types of reliability that are appropriate for mastery and domain-referenced tests are contingent upon the parallel forms assumption, cutting score selection, and the intended uses of the test scores.

Several different approaches to mastery test reliability are indicated according to the usual though not essential assumption of classically parallel test forms, the selection of a cutting score, and the use of the scores for mastery–nonmastery decisions. The classification consistency estimates of $p_o$ or $\kappa$ based on a threshold loss function have been highly recommended. The recent comparisons of various one- and two-administration estimates suggest that Hambleton and Novick's method for estimating $p_o$ and Huynh's method for estimating $p_o$ and $\kappa$ may be especially useful (Berk 1980b). When distinctions among degrees of mastery and nonmastery along the score continuum are desirable, not just the qualitative master–nonmaster classification assumed by the threshold loss function, Livingston's $k^2$ (X, $T_X$) squared-error loss index should be considered.

Since the major purpose of the domain-referenced test is to estimate and to clearly interpret an individual's domain score in terms of a well-defined behavioral domain, point and interval estimation approaches would seem to be most appropriate. When that purpose is viewed in conjunction with the randomly parallel test forms assumption, there appear to be at least two point estimates and two standard errors of measurement for interval estimates that a test maker should consider (see Berk 1980b). In addition, two indices of "dependability" derived from generalizability theory have been proposed which also merit serious attention. One of those indices, $\phi(\lambda)$, is a function of the cutting score $(\lambda)$. When it is desirable to make mastery–nonmastery decisions with a domain-referenced test, a cutting score should be selected and the $\phi(\lambda)$ index could be used as a measure of test score dependability relative to $\lambda$.

## 11. Conclusions

This review of the most salient characteristics of the mastery and domain-referenced approaches to criterion-referenced measurement indicates that each type of test is designed systematicaly to yield scores for particular uses. As in norm-referenced test construction (see *Norm-referenced Assessment*), the selection and estimation of the technical characteristics are governed primarily by the intended interpretation(s) of the test scores and the subsequent decisions based on them.

Ergo, the technical aspects of the development process must be addressed in order to assure meaningful results. The procedures outlined in Table 1 and described in the accompanying text should facilitate the choice of appropriate methodologies in specific applications.

## Bibliography

Berk R A 1980a A comparison of six content domain specification strategies for criterion-referenced tests. *Educ. Technol.* 20: 49–52

Berk R A 1980b A consumers' guide to criterion-referenced test reliability. *J. Educ. Meas.* 17: 323–49

Berk R A (ed.) 1980c *Criterion-Referenced Measurement: The State of the Art.* Johns Hopkins University Press, Baltimore, Maryland

Berk R A 1980d A framework for methodological advances in criterion-referenced testing. *Appl. Psychol. Meas.* 4: 563–73

Berk R A (ed.) 1984 *A Guide to Criterion-Referenced Test Construction and Use.* Johns Hopkins University Press, Baltimore, Maryland

Brown S 1980 *What Do They Know? A Review of Criterion-Referenced Assessment.* Scottish Education Department, Edinburgh

Popham W J 1978 *Criterion-Referenced Measurement.* Prentice-Hall, Englewood Cliffs, New Jersey

Roid G H, Haladyna T M 1981 *A Technology for Test-Item Writing.* Academic Press, New York

# Standardized Tests

**R. M. Moy**

Test standardization is the process of referencing a raw-score scale to stable, verifiable, and meaningful units of measurement. Standardized tests measuring the same ability and referenced to the same scale can then be used interchangeably for the purpose of comparing different examinees taking different tests. The principal problem in any standardization effort is establishing the reference scale. There have been four general bases for such scales: population norm referencing, item domain referencing, criterion referencing, and latent trait modeling. Each of these techniques is presented in greater detail in the sections that follow.

For the standardization process to work, it is crucial that the raw scores themselves are stable, and concerns over test reliability are also central to the standardization problem. In fact, the standardization of test administration procedures, which would figure heavily in computation of test–retest and parallel forms reliabilities, is often referred to when talking about the standardization process. Both this latter concept of standardization and the referencing concept deal with establishing a stable meaning for raw test scores, and both are important for valid standardizations.

In and of themselves, raw test scores do not have inherent meanings. They are only indirect indices of unobservable mental abilities. It is necessary for the test user to link up the scores with external standards of performance so that the scores can be interpreted and used for decision making. Decisions made in terms of raw scores seem arbitrary and lack impact. Knowing a person obtains a score of 75 is not as meaningful as if one can say that the score corresponds to the 30th percentile of all college freshmen or represents 60 percent of some item domain.

Although standards of performance are frequently derived from the distribution of scores in a general population of which the test user's examinees are members—a norm-referenced approach—it is possible to establish other standards independent of any particular test population or set of items. These latter type standards can be developed under a theoretical framework linking up raw scores with a priori conceptions of test performance. Needless to say, the more knowledge and control one has over the testing situation the more useful the standards one can develop.

## 1. Early Efforts at Standardization

Ever since the interest in mental testing began with the work of Galton, Cattell, and Binet in the last part of the nineteenth century, there has been concern over separating the variation in test scores due to differences in mental abilities from that due to differences in measurement conditions. The earliest mental tests were administered on an individual basis, and it was obvious that a person's score could very well be affected by the way the test tasks were administered for each examinee. The problem of possible errors in observation was formally addressed by Spearman in 1904 in an article entitled "'General Intelligence,' Objectively Determined and Measured," where he developed the concept of the reliability coefficient. This led to an increased awareness of the effect of differing methods of test administration on the comparability of test scores across examinees, and the need for standardization of testing procedures.

At the same time, early efforts at determining the relationship of different tests among themselves were investigated through the use of cross-classification tables and Pearson product–moment correlations. It was not entirely clear what relationship test scores had to actual mental abilities, but the use of these techniques helped test constructors to determine if they were on the right track.

Attempts at giving test scales meaning beyond raw-score scales can be found in Binet's establishment of mental-age scores, and Terman's development of an intelligence quotient scale. Binet (1911) linked scores on his tests to the observed performance of normal children from 3 to 13 years of age. Each test consisted of several tasks and task difficulties were linked to mental-age scores if 75 percent of the particular age group could perform the task. Terman (1917) worked from a more theoretical perspective and based his scaling on the assumption that intelligence is normally distributed in the general population. He established the raw-score scale of his Stanford revision of the Binet scale (by manipulating scoring procedures) such that they would produce normally distributed IQs for each age level in a representative sample of children.

Whereas Binet worked with a norm-referenced approach, Terman developed his scale from an a priori conception of how ability is distributed in the population. These two early efforts represent different approaches to the standardization problem, but for the most part the rationales for Binet's and Terman's referencing techniques are basically the same as those carried out today.

## 2. Norm-referenced Standardization

For most cases, standardization refers to the development of test norms—a table of general population percentile ranks associated with each raw score on the test of interest. With such a table, the test user should be better able to interpret the raw score performance of specific individuals. For example, a test which is relatively easy will have less discrimination between adjacent score points at the upper range of scores than for the lower range, and differences in scores in the upper end of the scale will not have as much significance as differences at the lower end. This would not be apparent if raw number right scores were used.

In order for a norm-referenced scale to be widely used, the percentile ranks must be based on a population general enough to allow the test users to make knowledgeable comparisons, and the actual standardizing sample must be large enough to produce stable results. Thus, standardization with respect to distributions of scores is typically done only with testing programs which are well-organized and widely enough established to obtain the appropriate sampling of examinees.

Typically, standardization samples range from 2,000 to 5,000 examinees (as a perusal of test reviews in Buros' *Mental Measurement Yearbooks* will indicate), but with widely used tests, samplings of 50,000 plus are common. Large sample sizes however, do not necessarily mean the standardizations are of high quality, since the samples may still be drawn on ad hoc bases. If test publishers do not provide a description of the sampling plans, as is often the case, their published norms should be carefully evaluated for each particular test use.

Standardizations can be carried out at a local level such as for a school or a city, but national-level standardizations are often needed to make comparisons of examinees with wide differences in educational background (see *Test Norms*). Such standardizations are most feasible in those countries with nationwide testing programs. In countries such as the United States, where the decision to administer tests is made at local levels, it is not possible to obtain truly random standardization samples. If the effects of nonrandom sampling go uncontrolled, the resulting standards are not feasible as stable and verifiable. Scalings based on nonrandom samplings will have varying degrees of approximation to a random sample scaling depending on the relationship that the characteristics of the drawn sample have to the tested ability. For example, scalings based on middle-class Caucasian high-school students in the United States would be quite different from that of a random sample in terms of verbal abilities, but perhaps not so different in terms of blood-pressure readings.

The seriousness of decision-making errors due to nonrandom scalings depends very much on the testing situation. If a single test is being used to compare individuals, as may be the case in achievement testing in a particular school, there will probably be little or no problem making relative decisions about persons' abilities. However, if two test publishers develop two different tests of the same ability and separately use nonrandomly drawn national samples for standardization purposes, a test user comparing two individuals taking different tests may reach the wrong conclusions regarding their relative abilities. For example, this would most likely occur when universities make admission decisions based on different publishers' college entrance exams.

It would seem that two standardized tests of the same ability should yield comparable measurements, but unless this is explicitly demonstrated with research directly comparing the results of the standardized scores for a particular population of interest, the label "standardized" is very misleading. In some cases, all that it really means is that the test has been administered to a large number of persons and that different scores indicate a change in the cumulative frequency distribution of scores among these individuals.

The basic assumption of standardizing a test on a frequency distribution of scores is that a change in percentile ranks corresponds to a true change in the ability of interest. This cannot be proven, but has to be assumed, which brings up another possible source of inconsistency between the standardized scales of two tests of the same ability. Each test constructor simply asserts that his or her particular test measures what it is supposed to measure, but with different test specifications, different item contents, and even test formats, measurement biases may very well affect observed scores and thus the interpretation of a standardized scale (see *Norm-referenced Assessment*).

## 3. Standardization of Measurement Conditions

If the tests do, indeed, measure different types of ability unbeknown to the test constructors, then what has to be done is to introduce stricter standardization of the measurement conditions.

In general, standardization of testing procedures is principally concerned with obtaining comparable test performances between individuals. On the other hand, there are many other factors which cannot be controlled simply because examinees usually only take a test once. Thus, an examinee's true ability is confounded with both the examination time and place as well as any other factors unique to the test situation, such as the test administrator and even the other examinees in the room.

Given the possibilities for mismeasurement of a person's true ability, it may seem that even if the score scale would be standardized on a representative sample from a given population, a person's observed score is unavoidably affected by confounding circumstances still left uncontrolled after reasonable standardization of administration procedures.

A standardized test needs to be robust with respect to these possible sources of score bias. An unreliable test standardized to even the most representative of nationwide samples is useless. To remedy the problem and to develop high-quality measurements, as many sources of unreliability must be either controlled or neutralized. It is possible to run generalizability studies which would systematically look at examinee behavior across these suspected sources of bias and determine if they need to be controlled or if the test needs to be redesigned (see *Generalizability Theory*).

This brings us back to the problem of interpreting the results from two tests developed by different test publishers, but intended to measure the same construct or ability. The situation can be viewed as another instance where a concern for standardization of administration is necessary. In this situation, however, an assertion is put forth that any differences in test form are irrelevant to the rank ordering of individuals. In other words, it should make no difference to the examinees which of the two test forms they receive, since their standardized scores would be identical. Again, a generalizability study can be designed to test the feasibility of this assertion. If significant differences in performance are observed for the same examinees across the two test forms (as would be indicated by significant examinee by test form interactions) a decision has to be made whether to consider the tests as distinctly different, or to redesign the test such that ability is defined by a composite performance over the test forms.

Standardizations based on the distributions of scores in a population are often criticized on the basis that the stability of the percentile units is illusory and that they would have to be redone periodically to maintain their comparability with more current standardization efforts. Due to inevitable educational and social changes, the distribution of abilities of a particular population is unlikely to remain the same, and the amount of differences in ability represented by adjacent points on the raw-score scale will not stay the same either. For standardization efforts involving complicated sampling plans and large samples of examinees, this unstable characteristic is particularly disheartening. The amount of time and effort required to put together a well-planned standardization will often be so high that the norms may even be out of date by the time they get published.

## 4. Domain-referenced Standardization

In order to avoid the inherent instability of population-based standards, domain-referenced scales may be a workable alternative. Instead of depending on the knowledge one has of the examinee population for providing meaning to a raw-score scale, a domain of items is used instead. As long as the domain can be defined and a set of items can be randomly generated from the domain (see Roid and Haladyna 1980 on test generating techniques), the percent correct score, also known as a domain score, can be used as a standard. Theoretically, any test constructor using the same domain and test generation specifications will come up with a test that should yield the same percent correct scores for any individual. With domain scores, one should have a better feel for what the examinee is capable of doing. In contrast, a percentile rank score will change depending on which population the examinee is being compared with.

However, domain scores are not without their problems. The stability of a domain score not only depends on the reliability of a person's score within a test, but also on the adequacy of the particular test's domain sampling.

The use of the domain-referencing approach makes explicit the task of generating parallel test forms. In order for the tests to be parallel and produce stable domain scores, either the number of items sampled must be large or the specifications have to be fairly strict. If the test specifications are strictly defined, the equivalence of the tests should be well-assured, but as the allowable test items become more and more narrowly defined, the utility of the test results will suffer.

Obviously both norm-referenced and domain-referenced standards have their respective advantages and disadvantages, but it does not necessarily follow that one has to choose one method of standardization exclusive of the other. In fact, both can be used simultaneously to produce more meaningful scores than when only one method is used alone.

It should be made clear, at this point, that what has been dealt with so far are methods of standardization for the purpose of giving comparative meanings to points on a test's raw score scale. The goal is to provide some basis for giving these points a standard meaning which can be transferred from test to test so that inter-individual comparisons can be made (see *Domain-referenced Tests*).

### 5. Test Standardization and Criterion-referenced Tests

When test scores are intended to be used for comparing individuals to specified performance standard, standardization takes on a slightly different emphasis. Here, interpretability of adjacent raw-score units is no longer of paramount importance. Instead, scores must be related to instruction decisions. Tests that are designed for making comparisons to a standard are called criterion-referenced tests. The scores of these tests take on their meaning because "they are directly interpretable in terms of specified performance standards" (Glaser and Nitko 1971, p. 653).

Confusion arises between criterion-referenced tests and domain-referenced tests because they both deal with defining domains. However, in the former case, the domain must be related to instructional objectives, and instructional decisions are made based on the examinee's demonstrated knowledge and the designated performance standard.

It is the process of relating scores to this standard that would be called standardization. Instead of relating raw scores to a percentile rank or a percent of items correct, standardization of criterion-referenced tests would then consist of defining a domain of instructionally relevant tasks, the generation of a representative sample of task items, determination of objective performance criteria for scoring the items, and decision making based on the overall observed performance across tasks. If each of these steps is properly carried out the test results are not only directly interpretable, but they are equivalent to the results from other test forms similarly constructed.

Although the results of criterion-referenced tests are more easily interpreted than those from norm-referenced tests, the standardization procedure is much more rigorous. Aside from developing appropriate definitions of task domains which have instructional impact, one has to make sure that scoring procedures and criteria for determining successful completion of a test task are explicit enough that variation in testing conditions, such as different test examiners, different types of examinees, or different test formats, will not affect the test results. Although these same concerns are present in some applications of norm-referenced standards, if relative decisions are made within a group, they are not very crucial. However, they are crucial to all applications of criterion-referenced tests. Also the specifications of performance standards must be explicitly dealt with and create a whole area of needed research and justification.

### 6. Absolute Scaling Through Latent Trait Modeling

One final possibility for the standardization of tests is the use of latent trait models to define an invariant ability scale. This ability scale is assumed to underlie the observed performance of examinees on each test item. Latent trait models specify the relationship between the underlying ability and probability of getting an item correct.

Given enough data and some a priori idea of the abilities of a sample of examinees, one can plot out the observed probabilities of getting an item correct for examinees of a given ability level. The mathematical modeling of the resulting curves, called item characteristic curves, is what is meant by latent trait modeling. The fewer parameters one needs to specify the shape of the curves for all possible items in a test, the more powerful the model.

At the present time models have been proposed using one-, two-, and three-item parameters. If one can assume that the probability of getting an item correct is a function of a single underlying ability, and that all the items in a test measure this same ability, that is, the items are unidimensional, then it is possible to use the latent trait models to develop a scale which remains constant across all groups of examinees and any subset of items. In other words, a scale is developed that is both sample free and item free.

Item unidimensionality is a rather strong assumption, but it enables one to objectively measure persons in constant units pretty much the same way as one would view a scale on a thermometer or a ruler. With all of the other scales developed through norm referencing, domain referencing, or criterion referencing, the units of measurement would vary depending on the test population and the particular items used.

Valid standardization with respect to latent trait modeling is very dependent on the assumption of unidimensionality of items and the adequacy of the particular model chosen to account for examinee test performance. The ability of latent trait models to describe actual test behavior is open to considerable debate, and until more knowledge of and control over the testing process is obtained, the use of the models for standardization purposes will remain an enticing, but illusory alternative.

### 7. Evaluation of Standardizations

Given that the scores from any of the tests mentioned so far are reliable, the quality of a standardization depends very much on procedural issues—the selection of an appropriate basis for standardization, and use of representative, adequate, and appropriate sampling of persons, items, or both. However, deciding whether or not the standardization is adequate for a particular decision-making purpose is still up to the individual test user. The more similar the examinees are to one another in educational background and the greater the similarity in test forms that might be used for different examinees, the less crucial it is that the test user be concerned over the way in which the standardizations were carried out. When the decisions to be made are very important and there are large differences in examinees or tests, the only check that can be done is to carry out a systematic study of the differences and make sure that they are unrelated to the standardized scores.

For example, if a person were to take two standardized test forms of the same ability, his or her standardized scores should remain constant. Generalizability studies across test forms and different groups of examinees should bear out the hypothesis of no test form effect or person by test form interactions. In the event that there are effects which indicate a lack of appropriateness of the standardized scores, an examination of the variance components associated with the test form effects can be used in the calculation of generalizability coefficients to determine if the errors of test form differences are too great for the decisions to be made. This approach can be used for any of the different techniques for coming up with standardized scores. All that is required is that a sample of persons representative of those examinees for whom test decisions are to be made take all forms involved in the standardization.

Unfortunately, test users rarely have the time or resources to carry out such studies routinely. However, it is possible to accumulate evidence over time which will help test publishers and test users to better understand the nature of their tests and standardization groups. One important study that has significant implication for standardization efforts is the Anchor Test Study (Bianchini and Loret 1974) in which eight widely used reading comprehension tests in the United States, developed by different test publishers, were restandardized on a carefully planned stratified random sample representative of the United States' fourth, fifth, and sixth graders. Among the findings were large discrepancies on the order of 10 to 18 points difference in percentile ranks between publishers' norms and the Anchor Test Study norms for some of the tests. Also, if children were classified according to socioeconomic status and race, their standardized scores would vary significantly depending on which publisher's reading test was used. The study points out two things: publishers' norms need to be scrutinized more closely (especially with respect to the guidelines provided by the American Psychological Association's *Standards for Educational and Psychological Tests*), and discrepancies need to be investigated further to draw conclusions about standardizing techniques.

## 8. Summary

So far with the present state of educational testing technology there are no standardized tests in the strict sense that the raw scores can be referenced to an invariant and objective scale. Measurement specialists have been hampered in their efforts to come up with an appropriate standardized scale because of problems in sampling and deficiencies in test construction techniques. What exist now as standardized tests are principally ad hoc attempts at giving meaning to individual raw-score scales. These less than ideal attempts will certainly result in unstable standardizations and test users should, as much as possible, be fully apprised of their deficiencies.

However, despite their shortcomings, it is unwarranted to conclude that all present standardization efforts are useless. The resulting standardized scales may very well be vast improvements over using raw score scales, but it is still necessary for sources of scaling instabilities to be explained and quantified before the test results can be used for specific decision-making purposes.

## Bibliography

American Psychological Association 1974 *Standards for Educational and Psychological Tests*. American Psychological Association, Washington, DC

Bianchini J C, Loret P G 1974 Anchor test study. Final report. ERIC Document Nos. ED 092 634, ED 092 601

Binet A 1911 Nouvelles recherches sur la mesure du niveau intellectuel chez les enfants d'école. *L'Année Psychol.* 17: 145–201

Buros O K (ed.) 1972 *The Seventh Mental Measurements Yearbook*. Gryphon, Highland Park, New Jersey

Glaser R, Nitko A J 1971 Measurement in learning and instruction. In: Thorndike R L (ed.) 1971 *Educational Measurement*, 2nd edn. American Council on Education, Washington, DC

Roid G, Haladyna T 1980 The emergence of an item-writing technology. *Rev. Educ. Res.* 50: 293–314

Spearman C 1904 "General intelligence," objectively determined and measured. *Am. J. Psychol.* 15: 201–93

Terman L M, Lyman G, Ordahl G 1917 *The Stanford Revision and Extension of the Binet–Simon Scale for Measuring Intelligence*. Warwick and York, Baltimore, Maryland

# Minimum Competency Tests

### E. L. Baker and B. H. Choppin

When students are expected to pass a test in order to progress through an educational system, some judgment of their competency is made. Minimum competency testing has more explicit connotations. On the one hand, the emphasis on competency rather than achievement suggests that some practical application is expected as a consequence of mastery of the test, that is, transfer to some real life or later school experience. On the other hand, the term "minimum" communicates that the performance level is adequate rather than excellent. But the minimum competence movement goes well beyond its consequences to individuals, for it may very well be used to convey to the school system the public's requirements for accountability.

Although the possibility of such testing has been widely discussed in other countries, it is only in the

United States that it has been implemented to any serious extent. During the 1970s, many states enacted laws that obliged high-school students to pass competency tests, usually in basic skill areas, before they could receive a high-school diploma—the sign that they had completed secondary education.

> . . . critics of the schools, believers in basic education as the first business of the schools, observers of the decline of scores registered by the National Assessment of Educational Progress, and people aware that textbooks are often written to the ability of students several grade levels below the level of intended use have joined in a public revolt against school failures and have become advocates of minimum competency testing. The news media have strengthened the minimum competency testing movement by giving it national publicity and by spotlighting dismaying news about test scores. The movement gains added force from the general disaffection of the public with many traditional institutions that were formerly above reproach, and citizens are not reluctant to confront educators with their dissatisfaction. (Gray 1980 p. 5)

In clear ways, the entire movement can be traced to the common uses and public reporting of test scores, the credibility that these scores carry, and the judgment of the American public that education must be improved. Implicit in minimum competency rhetoric, and explicit in practice, is the requirement to provide remedial instruction for learners until they can satisfactorily perform on the test itself. Seen in its most generous light, the minimum competency test effort is a benign, but enormously enlarged, version of mastery learning as described by Bloom (1969). However, controversy grows over the appropriateness of the entire practice, the development of the specific measures, and the effects on the ordinary activity of teachers.

## 1. Competency Testing Programs

Minimum competency tests are almost always referenced to objectives that describe the general type of skill the student should be able to demonstrate. Items are assembled to constitute a test of such competency, and a cutoff score or band is set, below which students do not pass. The consequences for individuals who fail vary with the sanctions imposed by the authorities. In some cases (mainly in primary school), failing children are required to repeat a grade. In other cases, failure on the test places the student in a special remedial strand of instruction where he/she receives extra practice in test-taking skills and/or in the content and skills measured on the test. Often students are permitted an unlimited number of trials until they are successful. In other cases, the high-school diploma is withheld and students receive merely a certificate of completion. The management of these sanctions varies from region to region. In some states in the United States, for example, a student must pass the regulation test or he/she will be denied the diploma, whereas in other states individual school districts are permitted to use their own tests, or no tests at all.

## 2. The Tests

The characteristics of the tests actually used naturally vary but some common elements can be discerned. First, the test is almost always a criterion-referenced measure. This means that some form of objective, or outcome statement, has been promulgated about the skills to be measured and some attempt to provide items corresponding to the general objectives has been made. Often, the statement of the objectives follows from the recommendations of a policy group in the school district or state. The policy group may be an elected board of education, or may be an ad hoc task force consisting of parents, teachers, administrators, and other public officials.

In practice, the care devoted to test construction varies greatly. Often, the development of the test items is left to a contractor who provides the test, a technical manual, and sometimes a scoring service to the school authority. In other cases, the test is designed directly by school personnel, with the assistance or review of a technical expert.

A major issue in the development of these tests is the matter of test security, that is, a way to safeguard the test from being seen by teachers or students in advance. The matter of security influences the strategy for developing comparable test forms, and in some cases, only one form of the test is developed. (In light of the repeated opportunities to attempt the test, practice and memory effects are likely to contribute to students' scores when they make multiple attempts.) Security also influences the extent to which the specifications for the test are fully disseminated to interested parties. For example, if test specifications are vague, such as the ability to read prose, teachers and students are not much advanced by having the specifications available. Seeing sample or actual test items is the only way to ensure that instruction, remedial or otherwise, is properly directed towards what is to be tested. Where the specifications are well-defined and strong cues are presented to the teacher and student about appropriate tasks (for instance: "to paraphrase literal facts in consumer awareness information"), then the security of individual tests is less necessary because the specifications facilitate the generation of comparable items, and hence new test forms.

## 3. Criteria

To have confidence in the practical, as opposed to motivational, value of competency tests, certain criteria for test development and implementation need to be observed. First, the specifications for the test must be clear and public, affording all interested parties the opportunity to prepare for the test. Secondly, the test should assess cognitive skills involving transfer, to warrant the emphasis on the test and the belief that a pass has some meaning. Third, standards should be set that provide meaning in terms of the school curriculum rather than only in relation to the competency test itself. Fourth, the competencies and items should attend to issues of cultural bias to promote the fairness of the test. Fifth, because any test is imperfect, decisions about students should be based on broader data than test performance alone. Performance on school work, teachers' judgments, and other information should be considered in making a decision, particularly when denial of certification is the consequence of failure. Last, the test should be used as an opportunity to improve the quality of education. The *minimum* in "minimum competency tests" should have meaning only if the student of the test is to stratify and track students. In successive revisions, higher standards of performance should be expected. Unless attempts are made to focus on the instructional implications of poor test performance, the result of minimum competency testing may be a restricted curriculum for students from poorer or culturally different backgrounds.

Test formats have tended to emphasize responses that permit rapid and efficient scoring and, therefore, items which require the selection of responses from a fixed list have been most frequently adopted. However, these test formats give rise to criticism related to the basic issue of validity. For example, many competency tests with objectives related to student writing use multiple choice proxies of writing, such as editing ability. In some cases, the competency notion has been translated to mean practical, life skills, such as filling out a job application or balancing a check book, but the multiple choice format may not be well suited for this.

## 4. Standards

Another issue concerns the standards used in minimum competency testing (MCT), and the meaning such standards have for the community and for the schools and students. For instance, it appears that the "pass" levels for many tests in the United States have been set at around the normal performance for eighth or ninth grade students (i.e. 14-year olds). The meaning that that particular level has for establishing competency for secondary school graduation, for 18-years olds, is blurred. None of the statistical or arithmetic methods used for establishing standards have escaped without criticism. As with most performance measurement, the number of trials (items) interacts with the reliability of the measure, and in MCT, reliability is especially influenced by where the cut, or dividing, score between pass and fail is placed. Reliability becomes a central issue when one considers the numbers of students taking the test. Because the consequences of passing and failing apply to individuals rather than to groups, it is desirable to minimize the chances of classifying a student incorrectly. However, to raise the reliability of a test to an acceptable level, the number of items necessary for each

competency would be impractical and lead to fatigue and other errors.

A related issue is the type of error the school is prepared to make in setting standards. Schools may wish their errors to be symmetrical, or they may wish to minimize the probability of holding back students who in truth should be passed. Since retention is a direct cost to schools, and passing a student who deserved to fail is an indirect cost to society, the judgment needs to be made carefully.

## 5. Minimum Competency Testing as Educational Policy

Minimum competency testing was developed in the United States more as a result of political pressures than strictly educational considerations. As such it has often been introduced "hastily, chaotically, haphazardly, and ill-advisedly" (Gray 1980). By 1982, MCT programs were in operation, or at an advanced stage of planning, in 42 of the 50 United States.

A number of those authorities who jumped on the bandwagon when it first began to roll are now having to face courtroom challenges from the families of students who failed the test and who feel that the MCT was unfair (biased, discriminatory, unreliable, irrelevant, etc.). Beckham (1980) provides a detailed analysis of the legal situation.

Many experts in the educational field, including a number who have endorsed other testing programs, have expressed considerable unease at the way in which MCT has developed—and the controversy surrounding the topic was aired on nationwide television as a result of a major "clarification hearing" sponsored by the National Institute of Education in 1981.

On the other hand, Bloom (1979) states, in modest terms, the good that MCT might achieve.

> The recent interest in setting academic standards in terms of minimum competency requirements for graduation is a development which may be the basis for insuring that most students reach particular standards of learning at various earlier grade points in the school system. If such standards can be achieved at each target point, this can be one of the more effective methods of insuring that (all the children) do learn more effectively. If such minimum standards can be related to the optimal standards as well as optimal learning conditions, then most children can be brought up to the best that the public educational system can offer.

If MCT is to succeed in these terms, then it needs to be better thought out than many of the schemes currently in operation. Brickell (1978) proposed a key set of questions to be asked and answered as a prerequisite to establishing a coherent policy on minimum competency testing. Even when satisfactory answers to these questions are available, much remains to be done before the positive results described by Bloom can be achieved. The current American emphasis on the legal implications of MCT, and other forms of testing, serve to distract attention from the serious educational issues that MCT has raised.

## Bibliography

Beckham J 1980 *Legal Implications of Minimum Competency Testing.* Phi Delta Kappa, Bloomington, Indiana

Bloom B S 1969 Learning for mastery. *Evaluation Comment* 1: (2)

Bloom B S 1979 *Prejudice and Pride: The Brown Decision after Twenty-five Years.* US Government Printing Office, Washington, DC

Brickell H M 1978 *Let's Talk about Minimum Competency Testing.* Education Commission of the States, Denver, Colorado

Gray D 1980 *Minimum Competency Testing: Guidelines for Policymakers and Citizens.* Council for Basic Education, Washington, DC

Jaeger R M, Tittle C K (eds.) 1980 *Minimum Competency Achievement Testing, Motives, Models, Measures, and Consequences.* McCutchan, Berkeley, California

# External Examinations

## H. G. MacIntosh

Inevitably an article of this length on a topic as wide ranging as external examinations can only deal with general issues in a relatively superficial fashion. In particular, the wealth of illustrations required to illuminate these issues is impracticable and it is essential, therefore, that readers check the relevance and the validity of the comments made by reference to examinations with which they are familiar.

Reference to a dictionary will show the word "external" to mean amongst other things "outside", whilst an examination is a "test" or "enquiry". External examinations are thus tests or enquiries conducted by outsiders, that is to say, by people who are not directly connected with those being tested. This definition, incidentally, says nothing about who is to be tested, how they are to be tested, or for what purposes. Ironically, in view of recent developments, the original impetus to create external examinations was an egalitarian one stemming as it did from a desire to remove nepotism and patronage as a basis for selection, often into government service, and to extend the range and numbers of those from whom the selection took place. External examinations were also designed to smooth out disadvantages arising from uneven distribution of resources whether physical, human, or financial. The examinations (mainly oral) conducted by the Imperial Chinese Civil Service and those for selection for grammar schools in the United Kingdom—the 11+ (largely written)—provide two good illustrations of this intention.

Over time, the operation of external examinations has been characterized by certain features. First, there is the scale of their operation. This is in general substantial, not least because of the trends towards ever larger entries, particularly in the period 1950 to 1980. The examinations are in consequence mainly organized today by large agencies whose revenue comes from the fees of those who take them. The bureaucratic and commercial implications of this particularly in relation to timing and to the range of assessment techniques used are significant.

These agencies fall into a number of different categories, although the distinctions between them are often blurred in reality. Many are directly controlled by government, either central or local as, for example, the *baccalauréat* in France and the *Abitur* in Germany.

Alternatively, the examinations can be conducted through agencies approved or underwritten by the government as, for example, the boards administering the General Certificate of Education (GCE) and the Certificate of Secondary Education (CSE) examinations in the United Kingdom. In 1988 these were both replaced by the General Certificate of Secondary Education (GCSE). The GCE and CSE examinations, incidentally, provided a particularly influential model around the world as a result of the United Kingdom's colonial past; note, for example, the West African Examinations Council (WAEC), the Caribbean Examinations Council (CXC), and the Malaysian Examinations Syndicate (MES). Occasionally, as in Sweden, the government itself is directly involved in the process of examining. Here the National Board of Education (NBE) develops tests which are used as the monitor for teacher assessment of students in schools.

Other agencies are non-profit-making educational corporations such as the Educational Testing Service (ETS) and the Psychological Corporation in the United States. Such bodies act as agents for clients of all kinds in the field of specific examination construction as well as undertaking substantial research and development into testing in general. Then there are the directly commercial testing agencies. These tend to be much more significant in areas such as North America where there is no system of public examinations in schools of the kind that exists at present in Europe and in much of the developing world. Many of these testing agencies as, for example, Harcourt, Brace and World (USA) and the National Foundation for Educational Research/Nelson (UK) now form part of large publishing conglomerates. The tests produced by such agencies are naturally designed to sell but they are usually subject to rigorous standards and the constructors lay great stress upon providing users with information for interpretation. Finally, there are the professional bodies which, as part of the process of maintaining standards, may set their own entrance examinations or more commonly examinations which lead to additional qualifications as the individual moves up the professional ladder. The Institute of Bankers in the United Kingdom provides an illustration of such a body.

A second general feature has been the marked

emphasis placed upon the use of the results of external examinations for the purpose of selection. There are, of course, a whole variety of possible purposes to which such results can be put. These may be briefly summarized as diagnosis, evaluation, guidance, grading, prediction, and selection. The evidence produced from examinations, whatever their nature, necessitates the making of comparisons if they are to be put to use but those comparisons may take one of two basic forms. An individual's performance can either be measured against the performance of a group, for example an age group or a class or another school, or it can be measured against some predetermined standard of mastery. Testing which does the former is called norm-referenced(see *Norm-referenced*), whilst testing which does the latter is called criterion-referenced (see *Criterion-referenced Assessment in Evaluation*). The design models necessary to facilitate these two approaches are markedly different, notably in their capacity to discriminate; in the former, discrimination is essential, indeed central, whilst in the latter it is unnecessary. Failure to distinguish between the possible and the actual usage of the results of external examinations has undoubtedly led to an overemphasis upon a discriminating design model and has made them in consequence unhelpful for diagnostic and evaluative use. The effect of this upon attitudes to external examinations and to assessment in general has been extremely significant.

A third feature has been the relatively limited range of what is actually assessed in external examinations. This is the result both of their origins and of the scale of their operations. The original egalitarian thrust was in reality extremely limited, extending as it did the opportunities hitherto limited to the privileged and wealthy to the slightly less privileged and slightly less wealthy, or in class terms from the aristocracy to the middle class. The range of opportunities opened up by external examinations was also restricted and the major emphasis was placed upon academic competencies and/ or subject-based achievement. This emphasis still continues today. The result is an academic cocoon which envelopes most external examinations and ensures that they concern themselves either with testing achievement in relation to specific subjects or specific areas of the curriculum or with the testing of those aptitudes deemed appropriate for success in higher education. More often than not the parameters of what is to be tested are marked out by the examining agencies by means of prescribed syllabi. In general, countries which have retained external examinations at the terminal school-leaving age, as in the United Kingdom, have concentrated upon testing subject achievement. Those which have no such examinations, as, for example, the United States, have in general made use of aptitude tests of which the Scholastic Aptitude Test (SAT) developed by ETS provides a good example.

Two notable exceptions to the academic domination of external examinations are to be found in the areas of industrial and trade testing and commercial examinations (particularly office skills). It is, however, significant that an institution such as the City and Guilds of London Institute (CGLI) which was founded in 1878 is still regarded as a world leader in the field of industrial examinations. This owes nearly as much to the relative scarcity of expertise in this area as it does to the quality of the CGLI's examinations.

The scale of operations carried out by the majority of the agencies currently conducting external examinations is extensive and this has been used by them as a reason for severely curtailing their range of testing techniques and for restricting the timing of their examinations. Written terminal tests remain the norm and oral and practical testing and assessment spread over time continue to be little used except in relatively small-scale experiments. Moreover, since knowledge is both easier and cheaper to test than concepts, skills, personal characteristics, and attitudes, most external examinations emphasize the former and neglect the latter. They are also slow to respond to change and to encourage innovation.

Consideration of the three features which have been expanded in the preceding paragraphs permits an operational rather than a dictionary definition of external examinations to be made. It suggests that a very large majority of present-day external examinations are norm-referenced, terminal, written tests designed for those in full-time education. They tend to be unsympathetic to group work and to interdisciplinary curricula and are primarily concerned with the measurement of knowledge and/or aptitudes which are deemed relevant to further academic studies.

Support for such a definition which some might regard as unfair and overstated is to be found in the arguments which are frequently put forward in defence of external examinations. These state that such examinations motivate student learning; they check whether or not the stated aims of specific courses of study have been realized; they give the community at large a reliable yardstick against which to measure the effectiveness of knowledge; they raise the status of subjects in schools; they provide a key qualification for school leavers which is of value to a wide range of employers; and they identify those likely to benefit from further full-time education.

The picture presented in this account has made, directly and indirectly, major criticisms of external examinations. If these are justified then the development of substantial opposition to the continuance of external examinations might be expected. This is indeed the case, particularly in developed countries in Europe, North America, and Australasia where alternatives mainly in the shape of teacher-moderated assessment are being explored and introduced.

Future directions are, however, far from clear. On the one hand there is growing concern throughout the world about the effectiveness of the educational system in general and of the comprehensive school in particular. This has caused governments to look more closely at possible approaches to monitoring the effectiveness of the system. One such approach could be a closely supervised system of external examinations either nationally controlled or nationally underwritten. There have been a number of recent developments in this direction. In the United States there is the National Assessment of Educational Progress (NAEP) programme with its marked impact upon the development of statewide minimum competency programmes. In the United Kingdom there has been the establishment of the Assessment of Performance Unit (APU) and a programme of public examination reform carefully orchestrated by the government. The Australians have considered the possibilities of establishing something similar to the APU but have not pursued it, whilst in Sweden a government sponsored research study into a possible programme of national assessment is currently under way.

On the other hand there are a number of factors, worldwide in their impact, although particularly relevant for developed countries, which argue for the abolition of external examinations and their replacement by more broadly based forms of assessment. Such assessment would make use in particular of those who by definition are excluded from implementing external examinations—the teachers of those being assessed. The two major factors here are the continued development of the comprehensive school and the growth of youth unemployment which is unlikely ever to go away. The first of these has questioned the external examination system designed to test the academic and hence the minority, whilst the latter by removing the "meal-ticket" value of the external certificate has started to erode, for the first time, public confidence in the system.

The trends described in the previous paragraphs have accelerated in the 1980s, but the paradox still remains: substantial public support for an external system which is increasingly seen to be inadequate in terms of the information it provides, the evidence it uses, and the ways in which it reports results. With an increasing stress in the secondary curriculum upon breaking down subject barriers, upon greater student autonomy in relation to learning and upon a wider range of contexts, concepts and skills, this mismatch can only widen.

It remains in consequence far from easy to see where the future lies, particularly in the light of renewed world interest in national curricula and national assessment, even in predominantly federal countries like Australia.

The only thing one can say with certainty is that there is no single satisfactory world solution. On current evidence there seem to be two main possibilities as far as the future of external examinations are concerned. First, the increased use of "mixed economy" systems which combine with varying emphases external, usually terminal, examinations with internal in-course teacher assessment. The new GCSE in Britain, with its requirement in all subjects for 20 percent internally assessed coursework, provides a good example. With a virtually universal shift to criterion referencing and to more natural uses of assessment, the part played by internal assessment is likely to increase, although as the British National Assessment proposals underline, public opinion will still continue to demand some form of external monitoring. In some countries, as for example The Netherlands, this has led to greater use of centrally constructed tests, prepared in this case by the National Institute for Education Measurement (CITO) for use in schools. In others like Australia, it has led to the creation of new organizations such as the Victorian Curriculum and Assessment Board (VCAB), or the Board of Secondary School Studies (BOSSS) in Queensland, which is largely concerned with accreditation and validation.

The second possibility is the replacement of external examinations by records of achievement or profiles, which are locally developed upon national guidelines. Alone amongst current initiatives, these records with their stress upon ipsative- or self-referencing provide the possibility of integrating the formative and summative functions of assessment within a system where the tension is constructive rather than destructive. Their introduction will require very significant changes in attitude by employers and higher education to their current selection and admission policies, as well as a large scale programme of pre-, and in-service teacher training. In many countries, particularly in the developing world, it is doubtful whether the necessary political will or societal support will be forthcoming for such actions. What is certain, however, is that external examinations as currently constructed and operated are increasingly inadequate to meet current needs, whether as national monitoring instruments or as devices for admission and selection, or as vehicles for helping young people and those who teach them to learn more about themselves and their needs. Reconstruction, whether gradual or speedy, partial or wholesale, is thus inevitable.

# Differential Test Batteries and Omnibus Tests

## R. Sumner

A set of tests applied to produce information for prognostic or diagnostic purposes may be referred to as a battery of tests. An ad-hoc battery may be composed of ability and attainment tests, personality questionnaires, interest inventories, attitude or motivation scales, and even physiological tests, such as reaction time. Each test should be chosen because it relates to a particular aspect of a criterion, such as selection for specialized occupational training. A test, in this context, may contribute relevant information (a) independently of any other test, and (b) in combination with results from other tests in the set.

## 1. Differential Test Batteries

An ad-hoc assemblage of varied instruments would not be called a differential test battery. These are customarily more coherent in several ways and typically have been developed and produced by a publisher coordinating a team of authors working to a defined brief. The tests in a differential battery have a common structure; for example, a specified sequence of levels corresponding to age groups, and a unified scheme for expressing scores derived from the raw score (number of items correct) obtained by a person taking the tests. The derived score scheme is the key feature of differential testing because it enables the comparison of scores from the constituent tests to be made on scales with the same metric.

Whilst the administration of a battery of tests can be quite complicated, the interpretation of the differences between tests is undoubtedly complex. For this reason the supply and use of this type of battery is (customarily) restricted to people who have followed a recognized advanced course of training in psychometrics or the particular battery it is wished to use.

The tests in a battery each yield a raw score for every person tested; in turn, the raw scores are transformed to derived scale points. These scores express a person's actual performance as more or less accurate estimates of true performance on attributes represented by the items in the tests. Technically, test reliability governs the amount of error likely to inhere in an estimate. It is well-known that naive or badly trained testers accept obtained scores at face value. In differential interpretation, ignoring the likely errors inherent in scores which are compared could mislead those concerned and even result in tragic consequences.

## 2. Score Profiles and Differences

A common method for displaying scores is "the profile". An individual's profile considered in isolation from other pertinent data has little interpretive validity. For instance, someone's raw scores on three 50-item tests might be (A) 10, (B) 40, and (C) 15 respectively. If the tests represented (A)—mechanical, (B)—clerical, and (C)—mathematical aptitudes a naive interpretation would be that the person would succeed in clerical training but fail an engineering course. The difference between the extreme scores is (B) minus (A); i.e. $40 - 10 = 30$ points. But there would be errors of measurement for both tests. Assuming each test has a standard error of measurement (i.e., of obtained score) of 4, "confidence bands" of one standard error give a maximum likely difference of $(40 + 4)$ minus $(10 - 4)$; i.e. 38 points and a minimum of $(40 - 4)$ minus $(10 + 4)$, i.e. 22 points. Hence, over a range of 38 the error band takes up 16 points whilst the minimum difference between bands is 22 points. This oversimplified example illustrates that the error associated with a difference score is disproportionately higher than the error of the original scales.

Standardizing test score to the normal curve adds interpretive power to separate tests and differential batteries especially.

Thus normalized scales representative of defined populations allow subpopulation means to be compared with those for the parent population. Any individual's standardized scores can then be interpreted in relation to the means and differences for appropriate reference groups (and the appropriate standard errors). For example, a person may score near the average for adult males but lie only at the 10th percentile for computer operators.

Reputable publishers provide this type of data in manuals for differential test batteries. The technical data should, preferably, include tables of intercorrelations between the constituent tests for a variety of populations; e.g., school pupils, adults with college qualifications, migrant or ethnic minorities. The reliability of the difference between any pair of scores can then be estimated from the formula

$$r \text{ difference } (A - B) = \frac{r_A + r_B - 2r_{AB}}{2 - 2r_{AB}}$$

when $r_A$ and $r_B$ are the test reliability coefficients and $r_{AB}$ is the correlation between tests $A$ and $B$. Clearly, in a battery of, say, eight tests there are $7 + 6 + 5 + 4 + 3 + 2 + 1$ pairs of comparisons, or 28 in all. The complexity of profile interpretation is now apparent, as is the desirability of using constituent tests with only moderate to zero, or even negative, intercorrelations.

Score profiles are often plotted as points on a chart upon which the tests are listed in order. For some batteries, a division of the standardized score scale into categories is used (i.e. nine divisions, called "stanines"; 10 divisions "stens"; 100 divisions "percentiles"). The instructions should require that the standard error band is shown for each score recorded.

The common practice of joining successive profile score points with straight lines is potentially misleading in emphasizing differences between tests recorded adjacently whilst neglecting the more widely spaced results. Such profile charts are popular for matching individuals with criterion groups (e.g. computer programmers, vehicle mechanics).

Another matching technique utilizes prediction equations derived from the multiple correlation of several tests with a measure of the relevant criterion (e.g. job success as rated by superiors). The differential weights derived are applied subsequently to the scores obtained by a person taking the battery to indicate degree of match with criterion.

Standardized norm profiles for specific groups (such as successful system designers, ageing adults with dementia, or adolescent dyslexics, etc.) are sometimes given in the manual for a test battery. Users of differential batteries should (a) study critically the validation data given in publishers' manuals, (b) regard their own interpretations of results as conditional (i.e. probabilistic) rather than conclusive, and (c) seek salient evidence to complement test scores.

## 3. Omnibus Tests

Like differential test batteries, omnibus tests also aim at comprehensive coverage of a broad field. The items may be organized into subtests similar in structure to a test battery, but whereas battery subtests are generally scored so as to develop a profile of performance, all components of an omnibus test are combined together and a single total score is produced. Although the mixture of skills and content means that it is virtually impossible to give meaning to particular score values, the omnibus test may nevertheless be useful for ranking candidates or for relating overall performance to previously established norms.

In recent years, the increasing influence of technology on developing and scoring tests has led to the virtual disappearance of omnibus tests, and their replacement by test batteries, even when the statistical evidence for the viability of particular subscores is weak.

# Testing Domains of Knowledge, Ability, and Interest

## Reading Comprehension Assessment

### E. P. Haller

Reading comprehension is one of the most frequently tested academic skills in United States schools. Its impact can be seen in newspaper accounts of reading test results and political debates. Because reading tests are an important resource for decision makers, the instruments used to assess reading comprehension skills deserve careful evaluation. This article reviews the traditional approach to reading comprehension assessment and discusses some of the confounding factors prompting the current search for more effective measures.

## 1. Early Approaches to Reading Assessment

Reading comprehension tests were developed in the early years of this century to evaluate student achievement. Test booklets were usually composed of short passages of one or two paragraphs followed by three or four multiple-choice questions. The average grade level of reading comprehension was calculated on student answers.

Results of these tests were used to evaluate not only student achievement but also the effectiveness of instructional approach. In addition, tests results became a resource for curriculum planning. These tests are still widely used in many school districts and the results remain the primary measure of student performance, instructional effectiveness, and curriculum planning.

Although the standardized reading comprehension tests are among the most influential and most widely used assessment instruments (Valencia and Pearson 1987), other measures of reading comprehension are particularly important in everyday instruction in the classroom. These include observations of the classroom teacher (perhaps a much underestimated source). Classroom teachers observe strengths and weaknesses of readers and then are able to shape instruction to meet reader needs.

The basal reading program provides the fundamental instructional reading materials and the basal tests which are part of the program and are constructed to match these materials. If the classroom instruction follows the instructional directives in the basal program, these tests can provide the classroom practitioner with another useful assessment tool.

Another measure of reading comprehension is the cloze procedure (Taylor 1953). In this test, words are deleted at regular intervals in a reading selection. The usual intervals are every fifth word. Although this test procedure is somewhat more controversial, research has shown the cloze technique to be an effective measure of reading comprehension.

During the 1960s, dissatisfaction with the traditional approach to reading instruction and assessment provoked further research. Under the influence of behaviorism, reading comprehension had been viewed as a collection of discrete mental skills that form a hierarchy of mental behaviors. These skills were taught by adjusting instruction to the individual's level of mastery. This approach embodies a criterion or goal assessment rather than a set of norms determined by children's performance at a particular grade level. Since students usually learn what they are taught, this change in instructional philosophy raised the question of the validity of a traditional standardized assessment of reading comprehension.

## 2. Cognitively-based Reading Assessment

As a result of research findings from the 1970s and 1980s, researchers grew dissatisfied with the skill approach to the reading comprehension process. Influenced by observations such as Vygotsky's (1962) studies of the interdependency of language and thought, researchers began to explore and compare observable reading behaviors and self-reported reading activities of good and poor comprehenders. Their studies found skilled comprehenders to be active participants in the construction of comprehension. These readers would establish purposes for the reading task, monitor the level of understanding activity and initiate appropriate compensating strategies when comprehension faltered. This self-management of the cognitive abilities is sometimes referred to as *metacognition*. A meta-analysis of 20 intervention studies using metacognitive approaches showed substantial improvement among students who received instruction in use of metacognitive activities to facilitate reading comprehension (Haller et al. 1988).

One impact of metacognitive research has been an emphasis on the capacity of the reader to guide the comprehension process. This shift to a more process-oriented framework (Haertel and Walberg 1981) in studying the comprehension process has caused some professionals to begin to rethink the adequacy of the traditional reading comprehension test.

One concern is the use of short paragraphs as the principal measure of reading comprehension. Short paragraph testing may rely more on short-term memory faculties while longer reading selections may require more metacognitive activity. If this is so, then short paragraph testing may not reflect sufficiently the metacognitive aspect of comprehension formation. In addition, short paragraphs are not representative of school reading selections, as most classroom assignments are longer than one paragraph. This mismatch can affect the ecological validity of the assessment (Valencia and Pearson 1988).

Other investigations comparing skilled and less skilled comprehenders found reader knowledge to be an important factor in comprehension formation. In these studies, the influence of knowledge components such as vocabulary, background information, and knowledge of organizational features were found to determine comprehension of written information. This determination is important when considering the norming of the standardized reading comprehension test. If the normed population and the population to be evaluated do not share similar knowledge, estimates of comprehensibility would be spurious for the group to be evaluated.

Research in metacognition and reader knowledge shows the importance of appropriate mental activity and suitable prior knowledge in shaping readers' understanding. Improved understanding of reading comprehension not only makes possible improved instruction, but also suggests a need to rethink testing techniques. Some confounding factors presented by this new body of research are discussed below.

One factor relates to the difference in reader knowledge and the use of multiple-choice questions. Knowledge components such as vocabulary and background information may provide some students with enough knowledge to recognize the correct multiple-choice answer without reading the paragraph.

Another factor concerns the validity of the traditional standardized reading test due to its high correlation with intelligence tests (Jacobs and Paris 1987). This may be due in part to the high correlation between the score on the vocabulary section of the IQ test and the total IQ test score, and the role of vocabulary as a significant informational component in the formation of comprehension during the reading process. Vocabulary is such a powerful knowledge component in the formation of understanding of written information that some educators have suggested that at the junior high-school level each subject area should have its own reading comprehension test.

Finally, the last confounding factor is the motivational component of purpose. Purpose not only serves a motivational function but it also provides a focus and directional component that enhances the reading process. Research has shown that skilled comprehenders are more apt to initiate purpose and goals than less skilled comprehenders.

These are a few of the concerns regarding the standardized reading comprehension tests. However, it should be kept in mind that all tools have limitations and, if weaknesses are recognized, wise choices can be made and results can be interpreted more meaningfully. Perhaps the best approach is not to rely on one testing instrument but on an assortment of testing techniques in an effort to achieve a more complete assessment of reading comprehension.

## Bibliography

Haertel G D, Walberg H J 1981 Ability and learning: A theoretical synthesis. *Educ. Psychol.* 1: 241–52

Haller E P, Child D A, Walberg H J 1988 Can comprehension be taught? A quantitative synthesis of "metacognitive" studies. *Educ. Researcher* 17(9): 5–8

Jacobs J E, Paris S G 1987 Children's metacognition about reading: Issues in definition, measurement, and instruction. *Educ. Psychol.* 22: 255–78

Taylor W L 1953 "Cloze procedure": A new tool for measuring readability. *Journalism Q.* 30: 415–33

Valencia S W, Pearson P D 1987 Reading assessment: Time for a change. *Read. Teach.* 40: 726–32

Valencia S W, Pearson P D 1988 Principles for classroom comprehension assessment. *Remed. Spec. Educ.* 9(1): 26–35

Vygotsky L S 1962 *Thought and Language*. MIT Press, Cambridge, Massachusetts

# Assessing Communication Skills

## J. W. Oller Jr.

The assessment of communication skills is approached from three points of view. First, the several abilities judged to constitute communication skills are examined; then the different tasks that may be defined as communication tests are considered; and finally, populations to be tested are taken into account.

## 1. Abilities

Canale and Swain have proposed dividing communicative competence into three subordinate capacities: (a) grammatical competence including "knowledge of lexical items and rules of morphology, syntax, semantics, and phonology"; (b) sociolinguistic competence subsuming sociocultural rules of use and rules of discourse; and (c) strategic competence which is believed to come into play in order to "compensate for breakdowns in communication." It is not entirely clear yet how the subcomponents of discourse rules and sociocultural rules are to be differentiated from each other or from semantics, presently subsumed under grammatical competence.

Other authors have proposed somewhat different divisions of communicative competence. Moreover, it has been demonstrated that the number of noncontradictory possibilities is limited only by the imagination of the theorists.

Investigations of the schema or grammatical systems underlying event structures, stories, and narratives promise to contribute important insights.

## 2. Communication Tests

Determining what should count as a test of communication skills is at least as difficult as determining how to characterize communication skills in the first place. Even to say which tests are not measures of communication skills is no simple matter. Where, for instance, does strategic competence leave off in order for intelligence to take over? Where does knowledge of lexicon, or of semantics, or of the rules of discourse, give way to the sort of knowledge that is supposedly assessed by achievement tests? In other words, is it possible to distinguish clearly between what can loosely be defined as the ability to know (presumably, intelligence), the acquisition of knowledge (usually referred to as achievement), and the ability to acquire or communicate knowledge (say, communicative competence, or language proficiency)?

Moreover, if storage, retrieval, and transfer of information must all be included in the scope of communicative competence, how will affect be excluded? Recently, Brewer and Lichtenstein (1980) have suggested that affective factors should be incorporated into the grammatical descriptions (or schema) of stories. Thus, perhaps theories of communicative competence will have to be expanded to include such elements as personality and emotion, to say nothing of imagination. Otherwise, how will the valuation of goals, plans, and conflicts, not to mention such crucial elements as need-to-know, interest, suspense, surprise, and resolution be accounted for? It seems that many heretofore neglected aspects of communication will have to be taken into account in any truly adequate theoretical perspective. Because of these considerations, the complexity of assessing communication skills becomes more apparent as does its importance to educational endeavors.

Traditionally, two broad classes of tests were distinguished. Tests consisting of discrete-point items involving such tasks as phonological discrimination, synonym matching, surface morphology, and so on, were conceived to measure just one element at a time from a given inventory of elements. By contrast, integrative tests, for example, dictation, composition, cloze, question answering, oral interview, and so on, were believed to assess ability to use many elements and components more or less simultaneously. More recently, a subclass of pragmatic tests has been distinguished within the broader class of integrative tests. These tests must meet two naturalness constraints: (a) they must require the mapping of sequences of elements of discourse into meaning structures, and (b) they must press the examinees to do this under normal time pressure (Oller 1979). Although pragmatic tests may be holistic or analytic in orientation, it is doubtful that they can ever be "discrete-point tests" in the sense of the earlier theorizing by Lado (1961) and others. (For further examples of specific testing techniques, see Cohen 1981, Oller 1979, and Valette 1977; and for a most up-to-date account of the overall theoretical problem, see Bachman 1989.)

## 3. Populations

No doubt the majority of work in the assessment of communication skills has involved mainstream monolingual populations, especially studies of literacy. The data samples in this paradigm have quite naturally included the broad spectrum from the early grades upward. However, in the early 1980s theoretical advances were made largely as a result of developments in educational linguistics and particularly in foreign or second language testing. These secondary populations of bilinguals must be considered normal in spite of the fact that they display certain idiosyncratic tendencies due to the influences of distinct native language backgrounds, and other variables.

Extraordinary populations, whether gifted or deficient, are also of interest. A special subclass within extraordinary populations are persons who happen to be multilingual or in some cases semilingual. With regard to the assessment of children with communicative disorders, there is some research (Damico and Oller 1980) showing that criteria aimed at functional effects of utterances are superior to criteria which focus more exclusively on surface morphology and syntax (this is not to say that the latter should be neglected). In regard to diagnosing disorders in children who are acquiring more than one language, again the research shows a significant superiority of meaning-oriented criteria over surface criteria. This research is consistent with findings employing other populations as well.

## Bibliography

Bachman L F 1989 *Fundamental Considerations in Language Testing*. Addison-Wesley, Reading, Pennsylvania
Brewer W F, Lichtenstein E H 1980 Event schemas, story schemas, and story grammars. Technical Report No. 197. Educational Resources Information Center (ERIC) document No. ED 199 668. In: Baddeley A, Long J (eds.) 1981

*Attention and Performance IX*. Erlbaum, Hillsdale, New Jersey

Cohen A D 1981 *Testing Language Ability in the Classroom.* Newbury House, Rowley, Massachusetts

Damico J, Oller J W 1980 Pragmatic versus morphological/ syntactic criteria for language referrals. *Language, Speech, and Hearing Services in Schools* 11: 85–94

Lado R 1961 *Language Testing: The Construction and Use of Foreign Language Tests: A Teacher's Book.* McGraw-Hill, New York

Oller J W 1979 *Language Tests at School: A Pragmatic Approach.* Longman, London

Valette R M 1977 *Modern Language Testing: A Handbook,* 2nd edn. Harcourt, Brace, Jovanovich, New York

# Essay Examinations

E. S. Quellmalz

Since the time of Aristotle, educators have recognized the value of extended discourse for assessing students' understanding and for interpreting their academic and personal experiences. Oral examinations predominated for centuries, and continue today, as a test format preferred in educational contexts where intensive individual assessment is desirable and possible. Essay examinations, too, require students to express and elaborate their knowledge and viewpoints, but, unlike oral examinations, do not permit the examiner and examinee to interact and clarify the students' responses. Essay exams can represent both the accuracy and sophistication with which students use subject matter information and strategies; they can also document the clarity and coherence of students' manipulation of discourse structures (exposition, persuasion) and sentence-level conventions (syntax, punctuation).

Despite the rich cross-section of students' subject matter expertise and writing competence that essay exams can provide, they are often criticized as being unreliable and costly. Considering the extensive use of essay exams to inform educators about students' progress through and out of an educational system, there is remarkably little empirical research that addresses issues in essay examination methodology, particularly on techniques for improving their technical quality.

This article summarizes prevailing practices briefly, but will focus on methodological problems and potential solutions documented by empirical research. Many of the points derive from the expanding bodies of literature on test design, the comparability of essay exams and objective tests, and also the relatively recent research on methodological issues involved in the assessment of writing as a distinct communication skills domain.

## 1. Prevalence of Essay Examinations

Essay examinations are widely used in school systems throughout the world. They are given during school terms to monitor the development of subject matter and writing skill, at the end of courses and schooling levels to certify achievement, and as entrance exams to determine qualifications for admission to a higher level. In the recent past, however, the economic and methodological problems plaguing essay examination procedures have prompted some school systems to abandon the essay as a test format in favor of shorter, more economically scored objective tests. In the United States, for example, test publishers have conducted numerous studies in order to document the comparability of multiple-choice test results with scores from essay exams. For tests of writing, high correlations between objective test total scores and global essay scores were used as evidence to support the substitution of multiple-choice tests for essay exams. The dominance of this psychometric logic and methodology over the strong theoretical, but empirically unverified arguments of subject matter specialists resulted in the virtual elimination of essay examinations in large-scale assessment in the United States. In many other countries, multiple-choice tests have become widely used at both elementary- and secondary-school levels.

The prevalence of multiple-choice testing at all levels of schooling in the United States has been increasingly criticized. A recent report by the National Assessment of Educational Progress (NAEP) warned that students' ability to engage in disciplined thought and to express it in coherent, supported discourse is seriously deficient (NAEP 1981). The report attributes the problem to an overemphasis on low-level recognition responses to curriculum materials as well as in tests. Researchers are challenging the construct validity of multiple-choice questions for measuring subject matter and, especially, writing-skill development. They urge a return to essays and other constructed response test formats that will stimulate students to use higher-level reasoning processes as they formulate extended discourse, solve complex problems, or apply subject matter concepts and principles.

Increasingly, the concern of these researchers is supported by empirical research. In writing assessment, for example, studies are beginning to reveal weak relationships between subskill scores on multiple-choice tests and ratings of the quality with which students use those skills in their essays (Quellmalz et al. 1982). As researchers look to essays and other performance measures for valid and reliable representations of levels of competence, however, they question seriously many current essay examination practices.

## 2. Purposes of Essay Examinations

### 2.1 Functions

Essay tasks are intended to measure the quality or status of subject matter and writing ability. Since "quality" and "status" imply standards of judgment, the question arises "in comparison to what?" Evaluation literature frequently distinguishes between comparisons of individuals to each other (norm-referenced testing) and comparisons of individuals to standards of subject matter achievement (criterion- or domain-referenced testing). Norm-referenced tests permit identification of the best students within a particular pool; domain-referenced tests describe the level of subject matter mastery. Current evaluation thinking suggests that a well-constructed test can serve both functions. Students can be placed on a competence continuum that will permit monitoring and certifying of their level of development, and that will also allow comparing them normatively to the progress of other populations of students on the same skills continuum.

### 2.2 Goals

An important issue in the design of essay examinations is the rationale underlying selection of the skills to be assessed and taught. These skills presumably derive from information about the level of subject matter knowledge or writing skill required for students to function in their immediate and future school, work, and home environments. However, claims for the "ecological validity" of competencies and goals often lack empirical verification.

In some countries, the goal levels set for subject matter achievement or writing skill may vary for students of different ability or socioeconomic levels. Similarly, the skills required for entrance to advanced training may vary according to the population the trade school or university serves. In the United States, with its goal of universal schooling and literacy, many school systems have set minimum competency standards in the three basic skills areas of reading, writing, and mathematics. In some schools, these are survival-level skills that can be demonstrated in a single paragraph; in other schools (and other countries), the levels of performance and writing assignments are more ambitious. Subject matter goals, too, may vary from the simple recall of important facts, to the application of complex strategies and principles. Approaches to setting achievement standards have ranged from arbitrary decisions to careful analyses of future academic and job requirements. Seldom, however, have standards been empirically validated on actual criterion groups (Bush 1977).

Critical components of essay examination methodology are the precise definition of (a) the skills to be assessed; (b) the essay problem assignment; and (c) the scoring criteria. When schools use the same essay exam to assess both students' grasp of a specialized subject matter, and also their ability to use their knowledge to construct an organized essay, subject matter performance is often confounded with writing ability. A promising approach to this problem has been the use of test specifications to define important features of an exam's design, scoring, and interpretation (see Sect. 3).

## 3. Structure of Essay Assignments

### 3.1 Skill Specification

The most basic rule of measurement is that the skill to be measured must be sufficiently defined so that it can be assessed reliably. Essay exams have been repeatedly criticized for their lack of objectivity. To address this problem, the first step in formulating test specifications is to define the skill(s) assessed. Skill specification is generally considered to include definition of the content and behavior. In subject matter essay exams, the content would be facts, concepts, and principles (such as osmosis or taxation). The behavior would reference not just the observable behavior "write," but the procedures, strategies, and solution routines the student was to apply to the content. For example, "The student will write an essay comparing the economic causes of the revolutionary and civil wars." In tests of writing ability, the focus is not on content points covered, but on the discourse features of the requested essay, for example, whether the composition is a well-formed example of narrative or expository writing.

### 3.2 Components of the Writing Assignment

When assessments gather samples of students' written production, a series of issues arise regarding the structure of the assignments used to prompt the writing. The intent of test specifications is both to describe what is being assessed in relation to the problems or assignments previously set and the kind of response that is expected, and also to provide item-writing guidelines for generating additional homogeneous essay tasks. In subject matter essay exams, the specification would describe the range of ways the problem could be presented to students in the essay question. For example, how much and what kind of information about the topic is given to the student? Is the structure of the question sufficiently precise to elicit all desired concepts? Also, what level of interpretation is requested? Are students asked, for instance, to summarize, compare, analyze, or evaluate subject matter content? Does the assignment inform students of the scoring criteria (Ingenkamp 1977)?

In tests of writing ability, the structures of assignments have varied considerably. At one end of the continuum, essay tasks are described as "topics." As long as the topics are familiar, distinctions may not be made between terse prompts such as "Lost?" which could cue quite varied discourse structures, and "Convince the school board to change the dress code," which more clearly directs students' treatment of discourse mode, topic, and audience. Underlying the assumed comparability of vague, unstructured prompts is a view of writing as an undifferentiated construct—a skill that can be equally demonstrated in response to any one of a myriad writing tasks.

In contrast to this undifferentiated approach to designing writing assignments, a more detailed method has been developed. This is a result of studies of those factors in the writing task that cue students to produce essays that differ substantially in structure and style. Critics of the kinds of writing assignments typically presented in classroom and assessment tasks contend that most assignments do not present full rhetorical contexts that sufficiently inform students about the writing purpose, topic, audience, writers' role, and intended criteria for judging the essays (Britton et al. 1975). Recent research suggests that different rhetorical purposes (to express, persuade, inform) place different cognitive demands on the writer and, consequently, students write differentially well when addressing different rhetorical aims and audiences (Quellmalz et al. 1982). Also, since the actual content or "topic" of the writing assignment is not the main issue in writing assessment, research is exploring ways of using pictures, other media, or reading passages to provide students with enough information about the topic so that they will be free to concentrate on structuring their essays. In some countries it is usual to deal with this problem by permitting a choice of topics.

A final, seldom studied, feature of essay assignments is the time allotted for planning, writing, and at least reviewing, if not revising, the essay. The amount of time scheduled for essay writing varies widely across countries and clearly can support or constrain students' chances to demonstrate their competence.

In sum, current test theory and research supports the advisability of structuring essay examination prompts that clearly specify the aim, topic, audience, writers' role, and evaluative criteria and that permit sufficient time for students to engage in all aspects of the writing process.

## 4. Scoring Criteria and Rating Scale Formats

The criteria used to judge essay examinations operationally define which features of content and test structure constitute a "good," or at least a "competent," response. To be credible, criteria should not reflect the preferences of only a few individuals, but should represent standards endorsed by a community of professionals knowledgeable about the subject matter. Moreover, these criteria should refer to those features of content and written expression amenable to instructional intervention. For example, the dimensions of "depth," "flavor," and "creativity" may enhance the quality of the essay, but a growing number of educators contend that it is neither logical nor fair to hold students accountable for subject matter or writing expertise that the schools cannot demonstrate that they can teach, and, therefore, should not test.

Criteria used to evaluate student content and written expression vary along a number of dimensions: (a) from qualitative value judgments to quantitative counts of information and text features; (b) from global reactions to analytic judgments; (c) from comprehensive attention to a range of concepts and text features to isolated focus on particular information or text features; (d) from vague guidelines to replicable precise definitions.

Generally, readers' reactions to students' essays involve three level of judgments: (a) subjective, global impressions of overall quality; (b) analytic judgments about component test features; (c) a holistic quality judgment combining subjective impressions with judgments about the quality of the combination of text elements. In general-impression scoring, a rater reads an essay once and assigns it a quality score. General-impression ratings are global, heavily qualitative, and based on vague guidelines that may not reference component text features nor their differential weighting or importance.

The most quantitative, detailed, and replicable scales are analytic rating scales where readers assign several scores for various features of the essay. Analytic scales vary considerably in the range of content, rhetorical, structural, and syntactic elements referenced and in the relative weights of these elements. For example, in an attempt to be comprehensive, the Diederich Expository Scale was derived from factor analyses of "good" essay elements cited by many raters. It presents nine subscales ranging from content ("ideas") to sentence-level mechanics ("spelling"). In contrast, other analytic text analysis schemes such as T-unit analyses or counts of cohesive ties focus on isolated components of the written piece. Some analytic scales rely heavily on several scores or "error counts" for readily spotted factual details or sentence-level mechanical essay features such as grammar and punctuation, yet give little attention to the relationships among concepts or features of the discourse structure, such as organization or elaboration. Holistic rating scales, where readers assign a single score, often combine characteristics of both general-impression and analytic approaches. Holistic schemes vary widely in the range of text elements contributing to each score point and the specificity with which score levels are defined (Ingenkamp 1977, Quellmalz 1980).

Since the focus, specificity, and objectivity of criteria informing impressionistic, holistic, or analytic approaches may vary considerably, an examination program should weigh carefully the nature of the criteria selected and their underlying rationale. Otherwise, the program may find that the criteria do not mesh well with aims of the assessment and instructional program, and do not provide a useful status report and/or diagnostic feedback. For example, studies of alternative scoring schemes for evaluating writing competence have shown that seemingly compatible rating schemes may, upon application, result in quite different classifications of the same set of essays.

The need for explicit criteria is also apparent for

scoring subject matter essay exams. Students commonly complain about the ambiguous subjective criteria used for subject matter essay exams in classroom assessments. Certainly, when the results of large-scale achievement exams have serious consequences for students (e.g., exit, selection, certification, or graduation), explicit, public, and rational scoring keys are imperative.

## 5. Rating Procedures

When large numbers of papers must be scored by a pool of readers, an assessment program must ensure that evaluation criteria are uniformly interpreted and applied. Such standardization involves both the formulation of explicit criteria and procedures for training raters. In the United States, rater training follows a fairly standard procedure. Following a brief introduction to the rating scale, readers begin to practice applying criteria to a set of papers representing the test sample. A trainer leads discussion of the features of each paper that result in the paper's classification to a particular grade. Training time varies according to the number of separate scores recorded for each paper and according to the clarity of the criteria. The rigor of the procedures used to decide if acceptable rater agreement levels have been attained at the end of training vary from a show of hands to pilot tests requiring independent scoring of essays. In many countries, subject matter examinations are scored by raters with subject matter expertise, but who receive little or no formal training. Failure to conduct any structured training or to check on prior agreement levels may increase the risk of unreliable scoring.

On exams of writing ability in the United States, training times reported for holistic and primary trait sessions have averaged 2 to 4 hours; analytic scales with five to eight subscales range from 4 to 8 hours. Trained raters can assign a holistic or primary trait score to a student's paper in from 30 seconds to $1\frac{1}{2}$ minutes, while the rating time required to assign five to eight separate analytic scores ranges from four to five minutes for multiparagraph essays and from two to four minutes for paragraphs.

Once independent scoring begins, some large-scale writing assessments attempt to maintain rater agreement, and prevent rater drift, by periodically conducting agreement checks on common papers. Discrepant ratings may be discussed with master readers, by the entire group, or may be referenced to written feedback sheets explaining the rationale for "expert scores" (Quellmalz 1980). An alternative procedure for resolving discrepancies is to adjudicate them with a third reading by a different rater.

In many assessment programs, the procedures for establishing and maintaining scoring standards vary dramatically, particularly for subject matter exams. There may be only one reader per paper. Readers may or may not receive a written scoring guide, and training on its

use. In the United States, however, written examinations for admission to advanced university campuses or professional schools are read by two trained raters. In countries using essay exams for high-school or university admission, or for certification, an individual's score may vary; a problem attributable in part to imprecise criteria and less rigorous rating methodology (Spencer 1979).

## 6. Reliability and Validity of Essay Examinations

### 6.1 Reliability

The reliability of an examination program depends on the degree to which it eliminates measurement error. Four potential sources of error (or score fluctuation), identifed for examinations of writing ability, but applying as well to tests of subject matter skill, are: (a) the writer-within-subject individual differences; (b) the assignment variations in item or task content; (c) between-rater fluctuations; (d) within-rater instability.

To avoid within-subject error, achievement testing programs attempt to determine the reliability of students' performance by gathering performance on a pool of homogeneous items or assignments. Since essay writing requires at least 20 or 30 minutes, it is often logistically difficult to have students write many essays in an examination. Studies of the consistency of student performance across a series of essays often report low reliabilities for a single essay. However, analyses of the stability of student writing performance across several essays have also been confounded by the failure to limit essay task structure variability to differences in topic. Often the several essays differ in discourse mode as well and therefore do not represent homogeneous task or item requirements. Designing comparable essay assignments using the features discussed for specifying task structures is a promising method for reducing error variance due to the assignment. To reduce error associated with individual variability, most writing assessment experts recommend collecting essays on at least two parallel assignments. Similarly, the reliability of subject matter essay exams increases when scores on several essays are combined (Spencer 1979).

The most prevalent issue concerning reliability in essay examinations is that of interrater agreement. Statistical indices of agreement levels include coefficient alpha, generalizability coefficients, point biserial correlations, and simple percentages of agreement. In the United States, competency testing programs try to report agreement levels of at least 80 percent, and/or generalizability coefficients of at least 0.60. The most effective method of reducing interrater variability is to provide training on clearly specified criteria. To reduce error due to within-rater score fluctuations over time (rater drift) due to reader fatigue and/or carelessness, some form of interspersed check procedure seems helpful (Quellmalz 1980). Although a few studies report that readers tend to get more lenient or more harsh as rating progresses, few assessment programs routinely monitor this problem by comparing early and late scored essays.

With recent advances in computer technology, research is seeking ways to eliminate the cost and variability of human rating by devising programs for machine scoring of essays. However, computer scoring is still plagued by the computer's limitations to counting and pattern matching. To date, these matching and counting functions have been used mostly to count total numbers of words and words per sentence, types of punctuation, spelling errors, and to relate these frequencies to human ratings of overall essay quality. Counts of prepositions and "to be" verbs predict stylistic problems such as overuse of complex sentence structures or inactive verbs, while counts of cohesive ties relate to essay coherence. Page reports some success for use of the computer to score subject matter essays by having the computer count the frequency of key content terms. The basic programming problem, however, is to find commands that will recognize when commas or cohesive ties or subject matter facts are used appropriately. This current limitation and the logistical and economic problems of typing essays into the computer relegate computerized scoring for large-scale competency testing to the future (see *Computer Scoring of Essays*).

In order for a large-scale assessment to make generalizations about stability and level of students' competency, it is important that the design of the assignments, the number of assignments (items), and the scoring procedures show that irrelevant sources of score fluctuation have been controlled, and that the essay ratings represent reliable samples of students' writing competence.

## 6.2 Validity

The validity of an examination derives from evidence that the test accurately and dependably measures the specified skill(s). Evidence for the validity for an exam may take several forms. One form focuses on the test content (i.e., the items or essay assignments) and gathers judgments of subject matter experts that the items or essay tasks have content, face, or descriptive validity, that the experts judge the objectives or skills defined to be important and representative subject matter competencies, and that the items, problems, or writing assignments will elicit these skills.

Other forms of validity focus on test performance to examine (a) whether the scores are comparable to scores on other tests of the same skills (concurrent validity); (b) if the score levels predict future success (predictive validity); and (c) if the performance pattern appears to measure the underlying trait (construct validity).

In the United States, test specifications are often used to describe how the skill is defined and the rules for generating the items or assignments. The specifications serve as a reference for subject matter experts' judgments of the exam's content validity. Unfortunately, judgments of content validity for essay exams tend to refer to test objectives and assignments, and there is no consideration of the rating criteria. Equally unverified is whether experts judge that the essay assignments and criteria will distinguish among levels of skill development.

The most common methods of attempting to establish the validity of essay exams have been comparisons of scores to "related" measures. In the case of tests of writing ability, the "other" measures chosen as criterion variables are often reading tests, multiple-choice tests, or class grades (which themselves are often suspect). Several recent studies have found very low correlations between representations of writing-skill constructs. Even relating essay examination scores to grades on other essay exams may be technically questionable if the criteria for the two assignments differ. Recent research has documented how superficially similar rating scales can rank the same set of essays quite differently.

Studies of the predictive validity of essays face the same definitional problem of picking an appropriate criterion variable. Although many United States studies of the predictive validity of norm-referenced tests of writing ability found high correlations with future university success, it is unlikely that writing skills were as much the cause as other more general abilities.

The heart of a test's validity is whether it measures the underlying skill construct, that is, whether it taps the hypothesized mental store of information and strategies. Conventional factor analytic techniques used to establish construct validity are being replaced by facet analyses and multitrait–multimethod (MT-MM) analyses. A recent study using MT-MM to examine the factor structure underlying multiple-choice subscores and essay and paragraph ratings confirmed that essays provided more distinct information about hypothesized writing traits than did the objective test scores (Quellmalz et al. 1982). More studies using such techniques might elaborate our understanding of skill constructs.

## 7. Summary

The complexity of designing valid essay examination programs dramatically illustrates the more general problem educators face in integrating testing and instruction. Systematically conceptualized, designed, and validated tests require careful descriptions of objectives and their rationale, the structure of the assessment task, the scoring criteria and procedures, and evidence that the results are consistent, accurate, and predictive.

## Bibliography

Britton J, Burgess T, Martin N, McLeod A, Rosen H 1975 *The Development of Writing Abilities (11–18)*. Macmillan, London

Bush P 1977 Comparability of grading standards in public examinations in England and Wales: Methods and problems.

In: Ottobre F M (ed.) 1977 *Criteria for Awarding School Leaving Certificates: An International Discussion.* Pergamon, Oxford, pp. 14–28

Coffman W E 1971 Essay exams. In: Thorndike R L (ed.) 1971 *Educational Measurement*, 2nd edn. American Council on Education, Washington, DC

Cooper C R, Odell L (eds.) 1977 *Evaluating Writing: Describing, Measuring, Judging.* State University of New York at Buffalo, Buffalo, New York

Ingenkamp K 1977 *Educational Assessment.* National Foundation for Educational Research, Slough

National Assessment of Educational Progress 1981 *Reading, Thinking, and Writing.* Educational Commission of the States, Denver, Colorado

Quellmalz E S 1980 *Problems in Stabilizing the Judgment Process.* University of California at Los Angeles Center for the Study of Evaluation (Technical Report No. 136) Los Angeles, California

Quellmalz E S, Capell F, Chou C 1982 Effects of discourse and response mode on the measurement of writing competence. *J. Educ. Meas.* 19(4): 241–58

Spencer B 1979 The assessment of English: What is needed? In: Dockrell W B (ed.) 1979 *National Surveys of Achievement.* Scottish Education Department, Edinburgh, pp. 84–96

# Vocabulary Measures

**K. K. Block**

Research related to development and use of vocabulary measures is scattered across a broad range of educational and psychological periodicals. A recent, comprehensive, computer-based literature review located articles with "vocabulary," or "word meaning," in their title in such disparate periodicals as the *Elementary School Journal*, the *Educational Researcher*, and the *Journal of Verbal Learning and Verbal Behavior*, journals varying greatly in type and breadth of audience. Ideas of major importance to this topic have been published and discussed in a number of countries including Canada, the Netherlands, the United Kingdom and the United States.

Vocabulary development and the measurement of vocabulary are international topics. They have been given sustained attention by individuals who are both researchers and practitioners. Developments in cognitive psychology also promise a deeper understanding of the classical measurement and instructional problems described here.

## 1. Purposes of Vocabulary Measures

Vocabulary measures are developed to serve three different educational purposes.

Firstly, measures are developed to have gatekeeping functions: to "select-in" the individual who knows the vocabulary, or meets a certain vocabulary level required in a later job, or task. Conversely, these gatekeeping measures act to "select-out" those who don't know the vocabulary, or meet the standard. Another form of gatekeeping occurs when vocabulary is measured as part of the database for a psychological diagnosis. Psychological diagnosis of students affects educational placement decisions. This gatekeeping function may generally be referred to as measurement for placement purposes.

The second form of measurement is measurement for instructional purposes: to determine who knows what words and what word-learning skills, so that needed words, or skills, can be taught. A familiar example is found in school language classes, where vocabulary lists and vocabulary word skills are explicit curriculum objectives.

A third type of vocabulary measure is taken to discriminate among students: to find out who knows how much currently (achievement) and who will eventually excel (ability). It is generally known that school students differ widely in amount and kind of vocabulary knowledge. This third form of measure is often developed by assuming that, although amount of vocabulary knowledge might differ widely among students, the special learning processes which lead some students to acquire far more vocabulary than others are the real source of differences among students. A familiar educational version of this measurement problem are methods for measuring verbal IQ, found on various standardized IQ tests. When general IQ is interpreted as ability to learn, a high verbal IQ is thought to be responsible for increased knowledge, especially the knowledge of vocabulary words.

Each of the above measurement problems has its own set of technical requirements. Research has advanced technology and understanding to different degrees on each type of measurement problem. In time, new knowledge important for one problem can advance work on another, since these problems are in fact interdependent. It can be concluded that cognitive process measurement provides a fresh approach to at least the second two measurement objectives.

## 2. Measuring for Placement

Within educational settings, a professional psychologist or an educational clinician will measure vocabulary to enable informed educational placement decisions to be made, including the identification of candidates for remedial instruction. Vocabulary very often is only one informational component in a selection and placement decision. These decisions are most often based on the outcomes of a battery of tests. Although it can be documented what tests comprise these batteries (Goh et al. 1981) it cannot be determined how important or what kind of a role the vocabulary measure plays, per se. This measure is not used independently: whether or not the measure is taken and how it is interpreted diagnostically is dependent upon scores obtained on other tests.

Within the assessment practices of educational clinicians there are tacit theories about etiology and nature of reading and language disorders. Vocabulary scores can be used to support these theories, or they could be disregarded if the weight of the evidence is contrary to the usual interpretation of a vocabulary score. It is currently impossible to sketch out in any detailed way the role vocabulary measures play in clinical educational diagnosis and placement. Research is needed to document not only what tests are used and why, but also to examine the tester's reasoning. As a model for this work experimental studies of the educational diagnostic process could be used in the manner of the Johnson et al. (1981) study of cognition in medical diagnosis.

## 3. Measuring for Instruction

To determine whether or not a student knows the meaning of a specific vocabulary word, one must define what is meant by knowledge (a content problem) and/or what ought to be demonstrated, as a result of knowledge possession (a performance problem). Both approaches to vocabulary testing have appeared in the literature.

### 3.1 Performance Approach

The earliest papers on diagnostic testing of vocabulary were written by Cronbach (1942, 1943). Cronbach felt the knowledge of a word is multifaceted and he wrote that, if a student could "define" a word, such behavior would indicate mastery of a generalization. If a student could "recognize an illustration," this behavior would indicate that the word can be applied to situations to which it is appropriate (what Cronbach called "mastery of application"). If the student could recall the different meanings the word may have in different contexts, this would indicate knowledge of breadth of meaning. If the student could apply the word correctly to possible situations, even unfamiliar ones, and recognize inapplicability in situations where it does not apply, then this student would have shown precision in the mastery of the word meaning. If the student could use the term in thinking and in discourse, the meaning of the word would thus be available (availability of meaning).

Cronbach then considered types of test items—recall items, multiple choice, matching to select a correct definition, synonym, or example; and examined how well each type of item would work to test each type of knowledge he had identified. He found many weaknesses, concluding that traditional item formats do not provide really valid techniques for determining whether a student does or does not know a word, and the various senses in which he or she does or does not. He favored an interview technique, in which students could be asked several questions about a word. In a later paper, Cronbach (1943) developed a test format for precision of meaning, which is identical to item design procedures used in tests of concept acquisition.

Cronbach's conclusions about traditional item formats were based on logical analysis, not data. Later work in Pittsburgh showed that with careful distractor generation (based on research and good intuitive judgments) satisfactory concurrent validity (about 0.90) can be obtained between multiple choice and definition stating. Test–retest reliability was low (0.56) in this work because the students were given lists of the words that they had missed before they were retested. At retest, predictably perhaps, they chose another distractor, something referred to as a "lose-shift" phenomenon. Content validity was assessed by attempts to predict, on the basis of a preinstructional constructed definition, which multiple-choice distractor should be selected, for both correctly defined and incorrectly defined words. The consistency between multiple choice and constructed definition was found to be 0.68. It was thus shown that the multiple-choice test, when designed on the basis of good hypotheses and data on meaning confusions could, in fact, be technically adequate. However, drawing conclusions about knowledge based on performance alone might not be conceptually adequate.

### 3.2 Content Approach

Carroll (1964) examined the relationship between words, meaning, and concepts. The impact of this paper, so far as the measurement of vocabulary knowledge is concerned, was that it defined vocabulary knowledge to be knowledge in the same structural form as concepts. This implied that vocabulary can be tested as concepts are tested, with the classification of examples and nonexamples. Classification was also the behavior measured by Cronbach's test for precision of meaning (Cronbach 1943). A word definition can be considered a concept by definition (a defined concept, Gagné 1977), and a universe of examples and nonexamples can be generated by using it similarly to procedures for teaching and testing concepts (Markle and Tiemann 1970, Merrill and Tennyson 1977).

In the concept literature, the nature of the relationships between concepts (e.g., superordinate, subordinate, coordinate, etc.) is always considered when teaching a domain of related concepts. In developmental and experimental psychology, an approach to defining word meaning, called semantic features theory, has been developed through studies of experimental tasks involving comparisons and contrasts of related words and families of words. It holds that word meaning is a bundle of semantic features that serves to differentiate the target word from other words. These "other words" can of course be the super-, sub-, coordinate words in a hierarchical domain, yielding a set of features that could be summarized in a definition. For example, the meaning of the word "bird" is derived from its contrast to a superordinate category, "animal" (a bird is a type of animal), its contrast to a subordinate category term (the class of birds contains robins), and its contrast to a coordinate category term (a comparison of bird to dog yields differences in terms of the typical medium of movement, air versus land, and so forth). The properties, "a type of," "containment of," and "medium of movement" are some of the semantic features that define the word, bird. A definition based on these features might be: "a type of animal moving through the air".

It must be noted that there is no "essential" set of features which comprise a given word's meaning, because a word's meaning according to semantic features theory, is derived from the word-to-word comparisons inherent in experimental tasks. Therefore, it cannot necessarily be inferred that features elicited in an experimental task are those same features needed to correctly perform educational tasks. To determine featural content for educational tasks (that is, to define word meaning essential for success in school), the informational requirements of those tasks would need to be analyzed. These analyses would afford a more complete specification of meaning features to be considered when testing for instructional purposes. Rarely, of course, is the test developer afforded this time. A dictionary definition, as proposed by Carroll, is probably a satisfactory solution to defining the meaning content of a word. In principle, the definition is supposed to capture the invariant features, however widely the specific features vary from task to task. The diagnostic tester must be acutely sensitive to the relation of what meaning information was taught, or encountered in natural experiences, and what is required on the test (Markle 1975, Martin and Olson 1971).

### 3.3 Cognitive Approach (Content and Performance)

Research by van Daalen-Kapteijns and Elshout-Mohr (1981) in Amsterdam has also documented important differences in vocabulary cognitive processes, specifically those which allow learning new vocabulary words from sentence contexts. From an analysis of "think aloud" protocols, they studied the execution of two processes: model utilization (ways a provisional representation of meaning changed as a function of new information) and decontextualization (the depth of the inference drawn about the target word from sentence information). They found high and low verbal subjects (differentiated on the basis of verbal comprehension) to be significantly different in learning process scores (model use and decontextualization) as well as in learning product score (statement of the definition). The fact that definition quality appeared to be affected by a given student's ability to use meaning information analytically, permits traditional measures of vocabulary knowledge, such as stating definitions to be related to nontraditional information processing measures revealed in think aloud protocols. The Amsterdam work is completely consistent with earlier conclusions about classification tests and degree of concept understanding.

Measurement for instructional purposes might soon be reformulated to capture the competence underlying performance. The Amsterdam work suggests the competence of high verbal students is made possible by a well-structured knowledge representation, where knowledge representation is a construct defined in cognitive science research. This organization of knowledge allows them to manipulate conceptual information more analytically than low verbals who seem to use concepts holistically. Because of the interdependence of the knowledge structure, and its uses, tests which tap it will provide prescriptions both for content (what new words, etc.) and learning process (how to learn each new word).

### 4. Measures to Discriminate Among Students

Traditionally, students are differentiated in terms of amount they currently know (achievement) or in terms of how much they are expected to acquire (aptitude or ability). There has always been a discomforting vagueness in representations of the relationship between achievement and ability. Ability is responsible for achievement: the more ability, the higher the achievement and vice versa. But how does this happen? How is ability responsible for achievement? For a while, many persons were satisfied with the notion that a measure of verbal ability was composed of verbal knowledge (knowing words and information) plus general IQ, or "g." People have felt it was the general IQ, or "g," which was responsible, probably, for greater learning (achievement) by the high ability student. However, it ought to be possible to discern, in a deeper way, how greater degrees of knowledge come about through learning. The van Daalen-Kapteijns and Elshout-Mohr (1981) work has pioneered such a possibility for the subject area of vocabulary. Their theory of acquisition of words from context specifies cognitive learning processes that are qualitatively different for students of high and low verbal ability. They are the first researchers to demonstrate that students differentiated mainly on the basis of knowledge products (quantity of vocabulary knowledge) can also be differentiated on the basis of processes which operate on knowledge. A coherent theory of individual differences between students in vocabulary knowledge and ability is on the verge of being formulated.

### Bibliography

Carroll J B 1964 Words, meanings and concepts. *Harvard Educ. Rev.* 34: 178–202

Cronbach L J 1942 An analysis of techniques for diagnostic testing. *J. Educ. Res.* 36: 206–17

Cronbach L J 1943 Measuring knowledge of precise word meaning. *J. Educ. Res.* 36: 528–34

Gagné R M 1977 *The Conditions of Learning*, 3rd edn. Holt, Rinehart and Winston, New York

Goh D S, Teslow J, Fuller G B 1981 The practice of psychological assessment among school psychologists. *Professional Psychol.* 12: 696–706

Johnson P E, Duran A S, Hasserbrock F, Moller J, Priesuta M, Feltovich P, Swanson D 1981 Expertise and error in diagnostic reasoning. *Cognit. Sci.* 5: 235–83

Markle S M 1975 They teach concepts, don't they? *Educ. Res.* 4: 3–9

Markle S M, Tiemann P W 1970 Conceptual learning and instructional design. *Br. J. Educ. Technol.* 1: 52–62

Martin C, Olson D 1971 Variety of exemplars versus linguistic contexts in concept attainment in young children. *Dev. Psychol.* 5: 13–17

Merrill M D, Tennyson R D 1977 *Teaching Concepts: An Instructional Design Guide.* Educational Technology Publications, Englewood Cliffs, New Jersey

van Daalen-Kapteijns M M, Elshout-Mohr M 1981 The acquisition of word meanings as a cognitive learning process. *J. Verb. Learn. Verb. Behav.* 20: 386–99

# Foreign Language Performance Tests

**R. L. Jones**

In the literature of human measurement a distinction is frequently made between a knowledge test (sometimes referred to as a "paper-and-pencil" test) and a performance test. The difference between the two should be obvious from the respective names. A knowledge test measures the amount of information an examinee possesses about a given topic. The format is often multiple choice, but can also be true–false, matching, fill-in, short answer, and essay. Subjects such as history, mathematics, literature, chemistry, psychology, and so on, lend themselves well to knowledge tests. A performance test is generally used only if there is a requirement to demonstrate proficiency in a specific task which cannot be measured by a knowledge test, for example, musical ability, artistic skills, public speaking, and so on. The two tests that are required in most countries to obtain a driver's license represent the knowledge and performance tests very well. First, candidates must demonstrate that they "know" the traffic regulations, road safety, and something about the function of the automobile. Then they must "perform" satisfactorily behind the wheel. Both tests must be passed in order for the license to be issued.

Knowledge tests have been the standard in most second language programs for the past several decades. A typical language knowledge test isolates parts of the language and asks the examinee to make additions, deletions, changes, and so on, for example write in (or select from a set of alternatives) the correct suffix for a verb or adjective, change a sentence from the present to the past tense, or rewrite a sentence with a new subject. It could be argued that in all of these tasks some degree of language performance is taking place, but not the same kind of performance that is typical of a spontaneous communication situation. These kinds of tests are often useful for classroom placement, assigning grades, motivation, and so on, but their correlation with real language ability is questionable. They provide useful information, but they do not necessarily show how well the examinee can coordinate all facets of communication in a given situation. In order for a test to predict task-oriented proficiency, it must in some way simulate samples of the task or tasks. The test must be as direct as possible, and the examinee must use the language in a manner similar to that which would be required on the job. For this reason language performance tests have become more popular in recent years. There is an increasing need to provide predictive information about how well the examinee will perform in a real-life situation.

Some language teachers hesitate to use performance tests because of the time and expense involved, and because of the subjective nature of administration and scoring. It is true that in order to gain the realism associated with a performance test, it is necessary to pay a certain price. It does require more human effort to evaluate the language performance of each individual examinee. However, it is not necessary to sacrifice reliability. If certain procedures are followed, a performance test can achieve a high degree of test and scorer reliability. The following steps can be useful in developing a valid, reliable, and efficient language performance test. It must be kept in mind, however, that whenever human judgment is involved in any kind of measurement, the chance for variation from judge to judge exists. Consistency among the judges depends mainly on their sensitivity to the criteria which have been established for the test.

## 1. Job Analysis

A careful study of all requirements associated with the job must first be done. Let it be assumed, for example, that the job in question is that of a graduate teaching assistant in the history department of an American university. Candidates must first of all have a good understanding of the subject matter they will be teaching. They must also be able to organize the material and present it clearly in class. Finally, they must be able to establish a good working relationship with their students.

## 2. Determination of Language Tasks

The next step is to decide how language proficiency relates to the job. What should be the level of proficiency that is required and which of the specific language skills (speaking, listening, reading, writing) are necessary? This step really determines the nature of the test. It might be the case that language proficiency is important for only a few of the tasks required in the job. Some positions would assume a high degree of proficiency in all skills, while in other cases only one or two of the skills might be important. The main objective in this step is to match the test with the position. In the case of the position for graduate teaching assistant discussed in Sect. 1, it would be assumed that all candidates should have the necessary vocabulary to teach the subject, and that the pronunciation would be sufficiently comprehensible that students would have little problem understanding them in class. Furthermore, they would need to be able to understand questions that students typically ask in class. In some cases it might be required that candidates understand regional differences in pronunciation and even other foreign students.

## 3. Elicitation Techniques

Language samples can be elicited in a variety of ways, but will usually involve either a natural conversation (interview technique) or role play (simulation). For example, if prospective graduate teaching assistants are being tested for the history position, the interviewer may first engage in a structured conversation with each candidate about the subject matter that is taught. This would give information about pronunciation, vocabulary, structure, and fluency. The interviewer might then simulate a classroom situation in which a few typical students are asked to listen to a "minilecture" and ask some questions. This would provide valuable information about the candidate's ability to perform in a real situation.

## 4. Scoring System

In most cases some kind of checklist or rating scale is used. The checklist outlines the critical performance factors that are to be observed, for instance, pronunciation, vocabulary, grammar, fluency, comprehension, naturalness, sociolinguistic ability, and so on. The factors should be weighted according to their importance in the task. Although some factors might have equal value, others might be considered more or less critical. These weightings should reflect the decisions made in Sect. 2 concerning the type and degree of proficiency needed for the position. The rating scale is used to determine the final rating of the examinee's performance. It can be a dichotomous scale, that is, either pass or fail, or it can be a scale with several degrees. It can be based on a general overall impression of the examinee, or it can be the result of a carefully calculated score.

## 5. Development of Training Materials

Because a performance test does not exist on paper, as does, for instance, a grammar or reading comprehension test, it is vitally important that everyone involved in the administration or scoring of such a test be thoroughly trained. Human judgment can be a relative matter, but if a person is trained to match his or her observations against well-understood criteria, judgments can become quite precise. Such is the case with judges who evaluate the performance of figure skaters or divers. They look for certain cues and determine a rating accordingly. Training material for language performance testing should dwell on the administration of the test (elicitation techniques, examiner–examinee rapport, efficiency, etc.) and scoring. Typically, persons being trained would have the opportunity to observe a number of tests, either live or by video recording. Important procedures would be pointed out. As part of the training material, a staged test illustrating incorrect procedures can be very helpful. In order to develop a feeling for the scoring procedure, the trainees can listen to a series of recorded tests at various levels. First they would simply listen to tests of predetermined levels, in order to develop an awareness of what the criteria are. Then they would be asked to score some recorded tests to see how close their ratings match the accepted standard.

In conclusion, it should be emphasized that a performance test does not have to be a long, complex, and involved procedure. Indeed it should be as simple as it possibly can, as long as it provides the necessary information. The test needed to determine if a candidate is qualified to work as a hotel clerk does not need to be as comprehensive as one which will determine if a foreign medical doctor should be allowed to practice. Each need will be different, and thus no two tests will be alike. If designed, administered, and scored according to the steps outlined here, a language performance test can be a very useful tool in making decisions about the placement of candidates according to language ability.

## Bibliography

Jones R L 1979 Performance testing of second language proficiency. In: Brière E J, Hinofotis F (eds.) 1979 *Concepts in Language Testing* . TESOL, Washington, DC, pp. 50–57
Ryan D G, Frederiksen N Performance tests of educational achievement. In: Lindquist E F (ed.) *Educational Measurement*. American Council on Education, Washington, DC, pp. 483–92
Wesche M 1981 Communicative testing in a second language. *Can. Mod. Lang. Rev.* 37: 551–71

# Models of Intelligence

## J. E. Gustafsson

Research on the structure of intelligence has sought to determine the answers to two basic questions, namely: (a) how many dimensions are needed to describe individual differences in cognitive abilities? and (b) what are the interrelationships among the dimensions of ability? During the first six decades of the twentieth century these questions were investigated by several groups of researchers, each presenting competing models of the structure of intelligence. Among these, one line of distinction goes between models which postulate a general factor of intelligence (e.g., Burt 1949, Spearman 1904; Vernon 1950), and models which do not allow for a general factor (e.g., Cattell 1971, Guilford 1967, Thurstone 1938). Another line of distinction goes between hierarchical models (e.g., Burt 1949, Horn and Cattell 1966, Vernon 1950) and models in which all dimensions are ascribed equal generality (e.g., Guilford 1967, Thurstone 1938).

It has proved difficult to secure evidence that firmly establishes one of these models as the superior one. This led Sternberg (1981 p. 143) to conclude that the factor analytic approach has ". . .failed because it has been too successful in supporting, or at least in failing to disconfirm, too many alternative models of intelligence". However, one purpose of this article is to present some research which provides at least a tentative resolution of the problems of choice of model.

In parallel with the research on the structure of intelligence an entire industry has developed which specializes in producing and using psychological tests of cognitive abilities for purposes of diagnosis, classification, and selection of individuals within a vast array of institutions, such as schools, hospitals, the armed forces, and industry. The relationship between research and application is not simple, however, and another purpose of the present article is to discuss some of the relationships between the more theoretically oriented work on models of intelligence on the one hand, and the more practically oriented work aiming to develop instruments to measure intelligence on the other.

## 1. One or Many Dimensions of Intelligence?

Building upon work conducted by Galton and Pearson in the late nineteenth century, Spearman (1904) suggested the first, rather crude, analytical techniques for investigating the rank of a matrix of correlations and, on the basis of empirical studies of several sets of variables, he concluded that "all branches of intellectual activity have in common one fundamental function (or group of functions), whereas the remaining or specific elements of the activity seem in every case to be wholly different from that in all the others" (Spearman 1904 p. 284). These results were formalized in the two-factor theory of intelligence, which states that performance on a task is affected by two factors only, the $g$-factor, which is common to all tasks, and the $s$-factor which is unique to each task.

In his empirical work Spearman used small samples of variables and subjects and often found a very good fit between the observational data and the model. However, there were also deviations. In some cases it was found that the $s$-factors were correlated, thus giving rise to group-factors. It was found that the model broke down when tests that were "too similar" were included in a battery of tests, again because of a correlation between the $s$-factors. These facts were readily admitted by Spearman, but they came to cause great problems for his theory when other researchers tested and rejected it (e.g., Kelly 1928).

At about the same time that Spearman published his first results on the two-factor theory, Binet and Simon (1905) published the first intelligence test. As is well-known, this test differed from previous mental tests in that it contained quite complex items, and in that it used a very varied set of items. This test proved to be more useful in practical applications, and it set a model for several generations of tests of general mental ability.

The contributions of Spearman and Binet appeared close in time so it might be thought that the Spearman model provided a theoretical basis for the Binet and Simon test. However, in spite of the fact that for both these researchers a single, general, mental ability was the focus of interest, the simultaneous appearance of their work seems to be a coincidence. They were in fact highly critical of one another: Binet did not approve of the statistical nature of Spearman's work, and Spearman argued that Binet's conception of the total score on the test as an average of several abilities was theoretically indefensible. Spearman sympathized, however, with the basic idea of "throwing many miscellaneous tests into a single pool" (Spearman 1927 p. 84) and he admitted that "Our g is, in fact, really obtained by this practice, with rough–much too rough–approximation" (Spearman 1927 p. 84).

The fundamental difference between the positions of Spearman and Binet is that while Spearman thought of $g$ as a dimension of individual differences in its own right, Binet regarded general intelligence as being composed of several partly independent characteristics. Thus, Binet saw the test score as reflecting a mean of several different abilities, while Spearman saw the test score as reflecting a unitary dimension. These two basic positions concerning the nature of general intelligence can be identified in many controversies within the field of intelligence.

Binet's work had the strongest impact on practice (Carroll 1982), however, and during the first decades of the twentieth century a large number of tests were developed. In parallel, statistical methods for test and item analysis were developed and the testing technique was accommodated to allow group testing as well. As Carroll pointed out, these early tests "employed a rather wide array and variety of tasks involving the understanding and manipulation of verbal and nonverbal materials and problems" (Carroll 1982 p. 36) but during the 1920s tests started to appear that purported to measure somewhat independent dimensions of ability (Carroll 1982 p. 35).

However, it was not until improved factor-analytic techniques were available that viable multidimensional alternatives to Spearman's theory could be formulated. Through a generalization of the Spearman method, Thurstone (1931, 1935) extended factor analysis to encompass multiple common factors, and developed computational techniques which made it feasible to apply the method with large numbers of tests.

Thurstone (1938) applied multiple factor analysis to a test battery of 38 tests, many of which were newly developed, and found about a dozen factors, each of which accounted for performance on a subset of the factors in the battery. There was no sign of a general factor.

Most factors identified by Thurstone (1938) were replicated several times by Thurstone and his colleagues (e.g., Thurstone and Thurstone 1941) and it was possible to set up a list of six or seven easily replicable primary mental abilities (PMAs), such as: Verbal Comprehension (V), involved in understanding of language and frequently found in tests such as reading, verbal analogies, and vocabulary; Word Fluency (W), affecting the fluent production of language, and measurable by tests such as rhyming or naming words in a given category; Induction (I), measured by tests requiring the subjects to find a rule in complex material; Space (S), found in manipulation of geometric or spatial relations; Perceptual Speed (P), reflected in quick and accurate grasping of visual details; and Number (N), involved in quick and accurate arithmetic computations.

In further studies conducted during the 1940s and 1950s by Thurstone and others the list of factorially identified primary abilities was considerably extended, partly by demonstrations that several of the original PMAs were differentiable into more narrow factors, and partly by extensions into new domains, such as perception (Thurstone 1944), language (Carroll 1941) and number (Coombs 1941).

The influence of the multiple factor approach on test construction and test use is clearly seen from about 1940 onwards, in that a considerable number of "multifactor" batteries were published [e.g., the Science Research Associates (SRA) Primary Mental Abilities (PMA) battery by Thurstone and Thurstone (1949–1965) and the Differential Aptitude Test (DAT) by Bennett et al. (1947–1975)]. These batteries contain homogeneous subtests to measure different specific abilities, and they yield profiles of scores, which may be used for purposes of diagnosis, guidance, and counselling, as well as for purposes of prediction and selection. Frequently, however, the subtest scores are also aggregated into subtotal and total scores, to represent broader areas of competence.

It would seem, however, that the multifactor batteries have not fared very well in evaluations of their ability to provide differential prediction of achievements in areas that should require different profiles of abilities (e.g., Thorndike 1986). On the basis of analyses of validity coefficients for the Differential Aptitude Test and six other multitest batteries, McNemar (1964) concluded: "Aside from tests of numerical ability having differential value for predicting school grades in math, it seems safe to conclude that the worth of the multitest batteries as differential predictors of achievement in school has not been demonstrated." In a similar vein, Carroll speculated ". . .that a large part of whatever predictive validity the DAT and other multiple aptitude batteries have is attributable to an underlying general factor that enters into the various subtests. . ." (Carroll 1982 pp. 83–84).

The rapid proliferation of mental abilities produced by Thurstone and his followers made it necessary to bring order to the multitude of factors and from the 1950s onwards much effort has been devoted to this task. An example of this is the work by French and his colleagues (French 1951, French et al. 1963, Ekstrom et al. 1976) who reviewed the research, trying to determine which factors were distinct and cross-identified in several studies.

The Guilford (1967) "Structure of Intellect" (SI) model may be seen as another attempt to organize the factor-analytic findings, and to develop guidelines for further test development and research. In the SI model each test and factor is uniquely identified as a combination of levels on three facets (operations, content, and products). Guilford argued that each of the PMAs could be mapped onto the SI model, and that the model provides the guidelines necessary for constructing tests so that the other cells in the model may be factorially identified. However, as a consequence of the assumption that the factors are orthogonal the levels on all three facets must be identified, and a very large number of abilities must be assumed. Thus, instead of solving the problem of achieving a parsimonious description of abilities it would seem that the SI model has contributed further to the problem of proliferation of abilities.

## 2. The Hierarchical Approach

Ever since multiple factor analysis was invented by Thurstone it has been the dominating form of factor analysis, and it may be argued that this particular kind of factor analysis bears a large part of the responsibility for the proliferation of factors (Undheim 1981). However, still another way to solve the problem of the multitude of factors is to allow the factors to be correlated, and then analyse the correlations among the factors with factor-analytic methods to obtain higher-order factors. Such higher-order analyses yield hierarchical models, in which factors at lower levels are subsumed under factors at higher levels. Thurstone and Thurstone (1941) conducted such an analysis of the intercorrelation among six PMAS and they did, indeed, find a general factor in the second-order analysis, which factor was most highly loaded by the *I*-factor.

A more elaborate hierarchical model has been developed by Catell and Horn (e.g., Cattell 1963, Horn 1968, Horn and Cattell 1966). The two dimensions of most central importance in this model are fluid intelligence (*Gf*) and crystallized intelligence (*Gc*), and the whole theory is often referred to as *Gc–Gf* theory. Both these dimensions reflect the capacity for abstraction, concept formation, and perception and eduction of relations. The *Gc* dimension, however, is thought to reflect individual differences associated with systematic cultural influences, and is central in tasks of a verbal–conceptual nature. The *Gf* dimension in contrast reflects effects of biological and neurological factors, and factors such as incidental learning, and this dimension is most strongly shown in tasks that are either new or very familiar to the examinees.

In the early formulation of *Gc–Gf* theory Horn and Cattell (1966) identified some three or four additional second-order factors, such as General Speediness (*Gs*), General Fluency (*Gr*), and General Visualization (*Gv*). In later research reported by Horn and collaborators (e.g., Horn 1980, Horn 1986, Horn and Stankov 1982, Stankov and Horn 1980) the list of second-order factors has, however, been considerably expanded, and a hierarchical model based on levels of functions has been proposed. Cattell (1971) likewise has proposed an elaborate theory in hierarchical terms of the organization of abilities.

While hierarchical models have not been widely used in research in the United States, such models have had a strong position in research in the United Kingdom following Spearman. One contributor of such a model is Burt (1949), who also made contributions to the development of factor analysis. The most influential model was, however, proposed by Vernon (1950, 1961) ". . . as a hypothetical integration of all the factorial investigations that have been carried out" (Vernon 1961 p. 26).

In the Vernon model, factors of at least three degrees of generality are identified: the general factor, major group-factors, and minor group-factors. Among the major group-factors Vernon distinguishes between verbal–numerical–educational (*v:ed*) and spatial–practical–mechanical–physical (*k:m*) ability. The *v:ed* factor subdivides into minor group-factors, such as verbal and number factors, reading, spelling, linguistic, and clerical abilities, and also into fluency and divergent thinking abilities. The *k:m* factor subdivides too and this complex includes minor group-factors such as perceptual, physical, psychomotor, spatial, and mechanical factors. At the level below the minor group-factors the tests would be found but ". . . there is ample evidence to support the view that group-factors are almost infinitely sub-

divisible, depending only on the degree of detail to which the analysis is carried" (Vernon 1961 p. 26).

The Vernon model thus represents the most influential hierarchical model from the United Kingdom tradition of research while the Cattell–Horn model represents the most elaborate and influential of the hierarchical models developed within United States research. There are obvious similarities between these models, but there are also differences: The Cattell–Horn model lacks the *g*-factor which has such a prominent place in the Vernon model, and there are only two broad group-factors in the Vernon model, while there are several broad abilities in addition to *Gf* and *Gc* in the Cattell–Horn model.

## 3. Studies Comparing Hierarchical Models

In a series of recently conducted studies these competing hierarchical models have been compared empirically (Gustafsson 1984, 1987, Undheim 1981, Undheim and Gustafsson 1987). In these studies confirmatory higher-order factor-analytic techniques [Linear Structural Relationships Analysis (LISREL), Jöreskog and Sörbom 1981] were used to test hypotheses about the arrangement of factors at different levels within a hierarchical model. In brief summary the results were as follows:

(a) At the first-order level very good support was obtained for the primary factors (e.g., *V*, *I*, *S*, *P*, *N*, . . . ) in the Thurstone and Guilford traditions, and it seems that these are easily identifiable as soon as a sufficient number of tests measuring the factor are included in the battery.

(b) At the second-order level very good support was obtained for the broad factors proposed within the framework of the Cattell–Horn model, and in two or more studies the factors, *Gf*, *Gc*, *Gv*, *Gs*, and *Gr* have clearly been identified.

(c) At the third-order level a general factor has been obtained. What is most interesting, however, is the fact that all the studies have shown that there is a loading of unity of *Gf* in the *g*-factor, which implies that *Gf* is equivalent with the *g*-factor.

This latter result implies that *Gf* for reasons of parsimony should be lifted above, as it were, the other broad factors identified by Cattell and Horn, and that these other factors should be purged of their *g*-variance. This would leave a *Gc*-residual (*Gc'*) which seems to be more or less identical with the major group-factor that Vernon labels *v:ed*; and it would leave a *Gv*-residual (*Gv'*) that is very similar indeed to the *k:m* factor in the Vernon model. Thus, the fact that *Gf* is identical with *g* in a sense resolves the conflict between the hierarchical models proposed by Vernon and by Cattell–Horn. Since the hierarchical model includes the primary abilities identified in the Thurstone tradition as well, it does in a sense unify several previous models that have been viewed as being quite incompatible. It must be stressed, though, that the *g*-factor identified within this model is quite different from what is obtained by most current measures of general mental ability. While the former would be derived mainly from nonverbal reasoning tests, many IQ tests have such a strong verbal bias that they should probably best be considered measures of *Gc*.

It is interesting to consider the implications of this hierarchical model for the measurement of intelligence. It has already been concluded that throughout the history of mental testing, measures have been obtained of a rather loosely defined general mental ability, either through use of IQ tests of the Binet type, or through creation of composites of scores on homogeneous tests. Throughout most of the history of mental testing specific abilities have been measured as well, as is done with the multifactor batteries. The hierarchical model includes both broad and narrow abilities so both these practices would, in a general sense, be compatible with such a model of the structure of abilities. However, it would seem that the hierarchical model of abilities also carries much more far-reaching implications for the measurement of general and specific abilities, and in the remainder of this article these implications will be described in general and nontechnical terms.

## 4. Measurement of General and Specific Abilities

With the exception of Spearman very few researchers seem to have regarded general ability as anything but an aggregate of those quite different abilities that are important for school achievement. Horn (1986), for example, argued strongly against the concept of general intelligence on the ground that the conglomerate measures used to identify it cannot represent a functional unity. However, the fact that *g* and *Gf* have been shown to be equivalent implies that the *g*-factor may be identified "not only as the first, unrotated centroid or principal factor axis factor or as the inevitable summit factor after successive higher order analyses—but as a general dimension uniquely identified through simple structure" (Undheim 1981 pp. 251–52). Since dimensions identified under the criterion of simple structure fulfil rather stringent criteria of invariance, this implies that the general factor of intelligence can be "objectively determined and measured". How best to measure *g* and other abilities still remains to be determined however.

From the hierarchical model it follows that the observed variance obtained on any test is due to a set of orthogonal factors of varying breadth. For example, of the variance in the scores on a spatial visualization (*Vz*) test 35 percent may be due to the *g*-factor; 15 percent to *Gv'* (the residual in *Gv* which remains after *g* has been partialled out); 15 percent to *Vz'* (the residual visualization primary after *g* and *Gv'* have been partialled out), 15 percent to a test specific factor, and the remainder random error variance.

While the relative size of the contributions from these sources of variance may be influenced to a certain

extent, it is quite inconceivable that any one of them could be brought up to 100 percent within a homogeneous test. This illustrates the fundamental principle that "no test measures a single factor" (Vernon 1961 p. 133); each and every intellectual performance measure is affected by several sources of influence of different degrees of generality, and it is even theoretically impossible to achieve a truly "univocal" measure of a single specific ability.

From this line of reasoning it also follows that when the aim is to obtain measures of the broader abilities (i.e., *g* and the second-order abilities in the Cattell–Horn model) a single homogeneous test is unlikely to suffice, since the scores to a rather large extent will be influenced by narrow factors. The Raven Progressive Matrices Test is frequently cited as a good measure of the *g*-factor, and upon the suggestion of Spearman it was indeed constructed to be such a measure. However, studies (e.g., Gustafsson 1987) indicate that only some 55 percent of the variance in this test is due to the *g*-factor. This implies that the test measures the *g*-factor with a reliability of 0.55, which for most theoretical and practical purposes is too low to be acceptable.

It would thus seem that the only way to estimate broad abilities is to combine information from several tests. Optimally this is done through an estimation procedure which takes into account the differential relationships between the tests and the broad abilities. Simple versions of such procedures were developed in the early twentieth century (Spearman 1927), but they have only rarely been used in practical applications, and there is a need to develop new procedures which take advantage of the advances within the statistical and computational fields.

From the fact that any observed measure represents a composite of abilities it also follows that to identify uniquely a specific ability it is necessary to partial out the effects of the more general abilities. This in turn implies that even if only a certain specific ability is in the focus of interest it is necessary to administer several tests, in order to allow estimation of the general and specific dimensions of ability.

## 5. Conclusion

The hierarchical model of ability supports the measurement of general mental ability as well as identification of specific abilities. However, in previous psychometric work it seems that general mental ability has been conceived of as a conglomerate or as an average of several more narrowly defined abilities, while in the hierarchical model the general factor is uniquely identified through the principle of simple structure as an ability in its own right.

From the hierarchical model it also follows that in all those measurement situations where the purpose is to identify any particular ability, it is necessary to use multiple measures, and to adopt a multivariate psychometric model. In the late 1980s, multivariate models of measurement (Wittman 1988) are only at a crude stage of development. It may be noted, however, that throughout the history of psychometrics "many of the advances, even in 'pure' statistics, were occasioned by the technological requirements of the mental ability testing movement" (Carroll 1982 p. 43). It may be hoped, therefore, that the progress in the description of the hierarchical structure of ability will cause a rapid development of multivariate psychometric models.

## Bibliography

Bennet G K, Seashore H G, Wesman A G 1947–1975 *Differential Aptitude Tests*. Psychological Corporation, New York

Binet A, Simon T 1905 Méthodes nouvelles pour le diagnostic du niveau intellectuel des anormaux. *L'Année Psychol.* 11: 191–244

Burt C L 1949 The structure of the mind: A review of the results of factor analysis. *Br. J. Educ. Psychol.* 19: 100–11, 176–99

Carroll J B 1941 A factor analysis of verbal abilities. *Psychometrika* 6: 279–307

Carroll J B 1982 The measurement of intelligence. In: Sternberg R J (ed.) 1982 *Handbook of Human Intelligence*. Cambridge University Press, Cambridge, pp. 29–120

Cattell R B 1963 Theory of fluid and crystallized intelligence: A critical experiment. *J. Educ. Psychol.* 54: 1–22

Cattell R B 1971 *Abilities: Their Structure, Growth and Action*. Houghton-Mifflin, Boston, Massachusetts

Coombs C H 1941 A factorial study of number ability. *Psychometrika* 6: 161–89

Ekstrom R B, French J W, Harman H H 1976 *Kit of Factor-referenced Cognitive Tests*. Educational Testing Service, Princeton, New Jersey

French J W 1951 The descriptions of aptitude and achievement tests in terms of rotated factors. *Psychometric Monogr.* No. 5

French J W, Ekstrom R B, Price L A 1963 *Kit of Reference Tests for Cognitive Factors*. Educational Testing Service, Princeton, New Jersey

Guilford J P 1967 *The Nature of Human Intelligence*. McGraw-Hill, New York

Gustafsson J E 1984 A unifying model for the structure of intellectual abilities. *Intelligence* 8: 179–203

Gustafsson J E 1987 Hierarchical models of individual differences in cognitive abilities. In: Sternberg R J (ed.) 1987 *Advances in the Psychology of Human Intelligence*, Vol. 4. Erlbaum, Hillsdale, New Jersey

Horn J L 1968 Organization of abilities and the development of intelligence. *Psychol. Rev.* 79: 242–59

Horn J L 1980 Concepts of intellect in relation to learning and adult development. *Intelligence* 4: 285–317

Horn J L 1986 Intellectual ability concepts. In: Sternberg R J (ed.) 1986 *Advances in the Psychology of Human Intelligence*, Vol. 3. Erlbaum, Hillsdale, New Jersey, pp. 35–78

Horn J L, Cattell R B 1966 Refinement and test of the theory of fluid and crystallized intelligence. *J. Educ. Psychol.* 57: 253–70

Horn J L, Stankov L 1982 Auditory and visual factors of intelligence. *Intelligence* 6: 165–85

Jöreskog K G, Sörbom D 1981 LISREL V: *Analysis of Linear Structural Relationships by Maximum Likelihood and Least Squares Methods*. Research report 81–8, Department of Statistics, University of Uppsala, Uppsala

Kelley T L 1928 *Crossroads in the Mind of Man: A Study of Differentiable Mental Abilities*. World Books, Yonkers-on-Hudson, New York

McNemar Q 1964 Lost: Our intelligence. Why? *Am. Psychol.* 19: 871–82

Spearman C 1904 General intelligence objectively determined and measured. *Am. J. Psychol.* 15: 210–93

Spearman C 1927 *The Abilities of Man*. Macmillan, London

Stankov L, Horn J L 1980 Human abilities revealed through auditory tests. *J. Educ. Psychol.* 72: 21–44

Sternberg R J 1981 Nothing fails like success: The search for an intelligent paradigm for studying intelligence. *J. Educ. Psychol.* 73: 142–55

Thorndike R L 1986 After 80 years of G is testing going to H? Paper presented at the annual meeting of the American Educational Research Association, San Francisco

Thurstone L L 1931 Multiple factor analysis. *Psychol. Rev.* 38: 406–27

Thurstone L L 1935 *The Vectors of the Mind*. Chicago University Press, Chicago, Illinois

Thurstone L L 1938 Primary mental abilities. *Psychometric Monogr.* No. 1

Thurstone L L 1944 *A Factorial Study of Perception*. Chicago University Press, Chicago, Illinois

Thurstone L L, Thurstone T G 1941 Factorial studies of intelligence. *Psychometric Monogr.* No. 2

Thurstone L L, Thurstone T G 1949–1965 *Primary Mental Abilities*. Science Research Associates (SRA), Chicago, Illinois

Undheim J O 1981 On intelligence IV: Toward a restoration of general intelligence. *Scand. J. Psychol.* 22: 251–65

Undheim J O, Gustafsson J E 1987 The hierarchical organization of cognitive abilities: Restoring general intelligence through the use of linear structural relations. *Multivariate Behav. Res.* 22: 149–71

Vernon P E 1950 *The Structure of Human Abilities*. Methuen, London

Vernon P E 1961 *The Structure of Human Abilities*, 2nd edn. Methuen, London

Wittman W W 1988 Multivariate reliability theory: Principles of symmetry and successful validation strategies. In: Nesselroade J R, Cattell R (eds.) *Handbook of Multivariate Experimental Psychology*, 2nd edn. Plenum, New York

# Cognitive Style

## D. J. Satterly

Cognition includes the processes of perception, thinking, reasoning, understanding, problem solving, and remembering. Studies of cognitive style originated in attempts to understand individual differences in these processes which might account for the wide variation in outcome among children and adults ostensibly faced with the same task or demands. There is no universally agreed definition of cognitive style but most researchers have emphasized three features: styles are intellectual characteristics of individuals; they describe processes which are relatively stable over time; and intraindividual stabilities are consistent across tasks having similar requirements.

The concept of cognitive style differs from others used to explain the range of intellectual differences. Unlike intelligence (which refers specifically to differences in the effectiveness with which individuals perform mental tasks), cognitive styles attempt to describe differences in the ways in which children and adults think and learn. There is general agreement that a comprehensive description of the range and variety of approaches in cognition requires the use of a number of styles each of which, preferably, supplies information which is independent of that supplied by others.

The emphasis of cognitive styles on individual consistencies ensures overlap with personality. For example, the dimension of reflection–impulsivity (see below), refers to the tendency to evaluate answers to questions and solutions to problems before commitment (reflection) as opposed to the tendency to respond rapidly with the first response that appears reasonable (impulsivity). Correlations have been found between field independence style, the individual's sense of personal identity, and the formation of social relationships.

Styles also differ in the extent to which they resemble ability constructs. Field independence tests correlate quite highly with performance on intelligence tests and are similar to abilities, whereas tests of tendency to proceed serially or holistically do not imply that one represents more effective cognition than the other.

Various methods have been used to study cognitive styles. The typical paradigm has been to develop criteria for the classification of individuals (usually a "test"), to examine the consistency with which these individual differences appear in relevant tasks, and then to examine the relationship between cognitive style tests and scores on tests of other characteristics. This programme of research activity has been more extensive for certain styles (e.g. field independence, reflection–impulsivity) than for others (levelling–sharpening, tolerance of ambiguity).

The chief features of some of the most extensively researched cognitive styles are described below. Their potential in assessment is to complement the information provided by ability and aptitude tests about an individual's cognitive make-up. Ability tests assess the performance or level of skill of individuals in well-defined subject areas; aptitude tests indicate the probability with which new material will be learned, whilst cognitive style tests assess their typical approach or ways of learning and thinking in a variety of tasks. For example, field dependence or psychological differentiation (style a) is measured by two tests. The first (embedded figures) measures the extent to which children and adults can extract simple shapes embedded in more complex figures, and the second (rod and frame test) measures how well subjects can maintain an appreciation of the position of the vertical against conflicting cues. Both are interpreted as distinguishing those subjects who are analytic in perception and thought from those whose approach is more global (less differentiated). By these means teachers and others can identify pupils whose style is congruent with the demands of the task (for example, field independence or analytic style has been implicated in logical thinking) and those for whom special assistance is required to encourage a more analytic approach.

Other examples of the use of tests of style in measurement and classification can be given. Reflection vs. impulsivity (style b) describes ways in which a child typically approaches a task unless instructed to behave differently. It is measured using the matching familiar figures test in which respondents are presented with a series of items which require them to select from a group of six highly similar pictures the one which corresponds exactly with a standard. A score is derived from the number of errors made and mean length of solution time, thus contrasting reflective with impulsive behaviour. Knowledge of these tendencies alerts teachers and others to possible sources of error in learning and to a need to encourage reflection where it is appropriate to the task but contrary to the child's preferred approach, or to encourage speedier information processing where this is advantageous to performing the task in hand. Convergent thinkers (style c) need special help and encouragement to make them think in a divergent way as is required when generating a number of different answers in "creative" tasks. Similarly, the successful solution of a variety of spatial tasks is often aided by the use of visual imagery codes. Pupils identified as high in verbal but low in visual coding (style e) may require special teaching procedures which will go unrecognized by the teacher who is unaware of the possible existence of the sensory modality preferences of children.

Areas of particular interest to educators include the educational implications of styles and their origins and development. Research has documented the relationship of styles to performance in schools and higher education institutions and has involved the testing of specific hypotheses about the ways in which pupils of contrasting styles learn (Witkin et al. 1977, Kogan 1971). Genetic factors, child-rearing practices, degree of parental authority, social relationships, and specialization in schools have been suggested as contributing to the origin and development of styles. However, few consistent empirical relationships between styles and educational progress have been demonstrated. The research has helped increase the awareness of teachers and others of the many ways in which the cognitive characteristics of individuals differ, but the nature of the relationships among the various styles is far from clear (Goldstein and Blackman 1978).

Chief features of the 10 styles most extensively studied are:

(a) Field independence vs. field dependence. The tendency to be analytic in perception and thought versus the tendency towards global appraisal. Field independent children are superior in maths and science, field dependent children find it easier to form social relationships.

(b) Reflection vs. impulsivity. The tendency to evaluate potential responses versus the tendency to respond quickly with the first "reasonable" answer to come to mind. Reflectives make fewer errors, for example, in reading.

(c) Convergence vs. divergence. A bias towards effectiveness in tasks demanding a single correct answer versus performance in tasks where a number of different responses are required. This style appears to distinguish maths/science from arts students.

(d) Levelling vs. sharpening. The tendency during perception and in memory to minimize differences between stimuli versus the tendency to be sensitive to them.

(e) Verbalizers vs. visualizers: preference for sensory modality. The relative reliance on visual, verbal, or kinesthetic modes of adjustment to the world. "Verbalizers" prefer to store information in verbal codes, "visualizers" in images.

(f) Serialist vs. holist. Contrasts a linear, sequential approach in problem solving with one which attempts to deal with the whole problem.

(g) Confidence vs. caution. A risk-taking dimension in which a chance is taken to increase the likelihood of success versus an approach in which caution is exercised to reduce the risk of failure.

(h) Conceptual style. The type of class concept formed among disparate stimuli.

(i) Category width. Consistency of cognitive range. The tendency to include a wide range of instances in a category or concept group versus a tendency to exclude those which deviate from a central tendency.

(j) Cognitive complexity. The tendency to use multidimensional constructs when organizing environmental stimuli versus a preference for the use of simpler constructs. This dimension seems to be more domain specific than other cognitive styles investigated. A person could use complex concepts when understanding scientific subjects, for example, and simple ones when dealing with political issues.

## Bibliography

Coop R H, Siegel I E 1971 Cognitive style: Implications for learning and instruction. *Psychol. Sch.* 8: 152–61

Goldstein K M, Blackman S 1978 *Cognitive Style: Five Approaches and Relevant Research.* Wiley, New York

Kogan N 1971 Educational implications of cognitive styles. In: Lesser G S (ed.) 1971 *Psychology and Educational Practice.* Scott, Foresman, Glenview, Illinois

Messick S et al. 1976 *Individuality in Learning.* Jossey-Bass, San Francisco, California

Witkin H A, Moore C A, Goodenough D R, Cox P W 1977 Field-dependent and field-independent cognitive styles and their educational implications. *Rev. Educ. Res.* 47: 1–64

# Verbal Reasoning Tests

## C. Whetton

In the United Kingdom, group intelligence tests which are largely verbal in content and used in an educational context are often referred to as verbal reasoning tests. These tests consist of a variety of item types, typically including similes, antonyms, analogies, codes, and anagrams. Verbal reasoning tests are usually objective, requiring a mixture of completion and multiple-choice responses, and are tests of power rather than speed. They are generally designed to provide an overall measure of scholastic ability without having a specific curriculum content. Although to some extent they measure the ability to follow written instructions, they principally assess both inferential and deductive skills. The tests are highly reliable and are relatively good predictors of subsequent academic performance.

There is no generally agreed definition of what verbal reasoning tests should comprise or what they measure. The common thread that runs through tests of this type is that they provide an assessment of school progress without being dependent on a particular curriculum. It is therefore possible to compare pupils in different schools and different school systems. The tests are perhaps best seen as the inheritors of one historical tradition of intelligence assessment which predominated in the United Kingdom for many years from the early work of Spearman (1927) through to the hierarchical model of intelligence of Vernon (1950). This can be contrasted with the American view which stresses the diverse nature of intelligence as a group of separate but intercorrelated factors.

Spearman's view of the structure of intelligence was that all questions had some variance due to a general intelligence factor "g" and some variance specific to that question. Questions which had a high proportion of variance due to "g" should be concerned not with the content of the question but with the abstract expression of relationships. This was designated the "eduction of relations and correlates". Eduction of relations corresponds to the inference of a general rule from specific instances whereas eduction of correlates corresponds to the deduction of a specific instance from another instance and a given general rule. The influence of this view of intelligence can be seen in many of the item types used in verbal reasoning tests.

Vernon's hierarchical model of intelligence proposed that the general intelligence factor "g" could be first divided into two major group factors, a verbal–educational factor ($v{:}ed$) and a spatial–mechanical–practical ($k{:}m$) factor. These could then be further subdivided into minor group factors. Verbal reasoning tests can be seen as measures of the $v{:}ed$ group factor and hence to be poorer indicators of educational attainments which have spatial or practical requirements.

Finally, in terms of Cattell's (1963) theory of intelligence, verbal reasoning tests should be classed amongst those measures which reflect "crystallized general intelligence", that is that they draw in the main on a person's acquired knowledge and skills, especially those from a school context. This is in contrast to "fluid general intelligence" which calls upon little formalized learning content but needs the ability to see complex relationships. They cannot therefore be seen as being culture-fair tests and should ideally be used only with a homogeneous population with common language and educational experience.

Verbal reasoning tests typically include a variety of item types mainly concerned with the production of, use of, and relationships between words. In some cases they also include items which require the manipulation of letters or numbers. Although there are many possible classifications, the items can be divided into five broad overlapping categories according to the types of operation required in the question: vocabulary items, relationships, sentences, reasoning, and symbol manipulation.

(a) *Vocabulary items*. This is a category concerned with the assessment of vocabulary through requiring the production of words and understanding of their meanings. A large proportion of the items in a verbal reasoning test measure the vocabulary of the testee directly or indirectly. Although the question types do not apparently require "eduction" this has gone on at an earlier stage when the meanings of words have been "educed" from everyday speech. Vocabulary forms an important part of most individual intelligence tests and is one of the best predictors of overall score in these batteries. Examples are:

(i) Underline the word in the brackets which means the same as the word in capitals.

ANCIENT
(time, ruin, old, history, grandmother)

(ii) Underline two words, one from each bracket, which can be combined to make one longer word.

(elm, pine, ash)   (apple, orange, grape)

(iii) Write one letter in the brackets to complete both words.

LEA(  )NEE

(b) *Relationships*. This category is concerned with the relationships between words. In some cases the relationship must be educed from the question (e.g., verbal analogies) but in others the relationship should have been educed from the context of the words in general usage (e.g., opposites). The relationships may extend to more than two words, as in questions where some concept must be formed of a group of words. Examples are:

(i) Underline the word in brackets which completes the sentence in the most sensible way.

Carpenter is to saw as painter is to
(paint, brush, hammer).

(ii) Underline two words, one from each bracket, which have opposite or nearly opposite meanings.

(positive, letter, addition)
(plus, number, negative)

(iii) Underline the word which does not belong with the others.

(expensive, bargain, cheap, small, dear)

(c) *Sentences*. This category of question is concerned with the use of words within sentences and hence the understanding of the structures of language. Again the emphasis is on the crystallized aspects of intelligence, those depending on education and cultural usage. Examples are:

(i) Underline the two words which must change places to make the sentence sensible.

They hotel their cases and left the packed.

(ii) Put these scrambled words into order and write the correct sentence in full.

LIKE CATS MEAT FISH AND

(d) *Reasoning*. This type of question comes closer to the "eduction" principle and also to the apparent meaning of "verbal reasoning". These questions require reasoning and are expressed in a verbal context. They may have the form of logical syllogisms or be more informally expressed. Examples are:

(i) All seagulls eat fish.
Pigeons do not eat fish.

If both these statements are true, which of the following is also true?

Pigeons are not seagulls.
Pigeons are seagulls.
Fish eat pigeons.

(ii) Mary is fatter than Celia. Jenny is thinner than Celia. Who is the thinnest?

(e) *Symbol manipulation*. In this final group of items are those concerned with the manipulation of figures and letters regarded as symbols. For these questions the eduction of relationships generally does not depend on vocabulary. Although the production of a word may be required, these can be viewed simply as collections of letters which form the more important elements of the question. Other items are concerned solely with the manipulation of numbers or letters without requiring the production of words. This type of item is loaded most heavily with Cattell's fluid general intelligence factor, having little informational content but requiring the ability to see relationships. It also corresponds most closely to Spearman's principle of eduction. Examples are:

(i) Complete the third pair of words in the same way as the other two pairs.

band, ban; song, son; tear, (    )

(ii) Write a word in the brackets so that the three words on the right of the sign ** go together in the same way as the three words on the left.

RUT (TAP) APE ** FAR (    ) OWL

(iii) Complete the series in the most sensible way.

CP, DP, EQ, FQ, GR, (    ), (    )

(iv) Use three of the numbers on the left to make up the number you are given, using the signs in the brackets correctly.

2, 3, 6, 10, 12      19 = (    +      -    )

These examples serve to emphasize that verbal reasoning tests are essentially group intelligence tests with a distinct verbal content. They are therefore open to the many criticisms that have been made of tests of this type and of the concept of intelligence. They provide only a single global score which gives a very limited view of a person's abilities. This can be contrasted to the much more complete view provided by a multiple abilities battery designed to assess a wider range of intelligence factors.

Verbal reasoning tests are, however, highly reliable [for tests of 85 items, internal consistency (KR20) reliabilities are customarily of the order of 0.95] and good predictors of further academic attainment (for example, correlations with school examination results two years later are usually above 0.7). For this reason they were commonly viewed as indicating capacity to learn and were widely used in the United Kingdom as part of the process for selecting children at the age of 11 for a separate academic education in grammar schools (the 11+ test). This view of verbal reasoning tests as measures of capacity to learn has declined and they are better regarded as measures of reasoning which reflect the person's experiences up to the time of testing, not as providing a fixed potential.

## Bibliography

Cattell R B 1963 Theory of fluid and crystalized intelligence: A critical experiment. *J. Educ. Psychol.* 54: 1–22
Spearman C E 1927 *The Abilities of Man: Their Nature and Measurement.* Macmillan, London
Vernon P E 1950 *The Structure of Human Abilities.* Wiley, London

# Learning Ability Tests

## S. Hegarty

Learning ability tests seek to measure the ability to respond to instruction and so are measures of potential rather than achievement. By contrast with intelligence tests, where the emphasis is on performance, they seek information on the processes underlying performance. They are particularly relevant to the assessment of outgroups whose learning opportunities are diminished or are different from the mainstream, for example, students who are culturally disadvantaged or come from ethnic minorities.

## 1. Reasons for Using the Notion of Learning Ability

Learning ability does not lend itself readily to precise measurement but there are several reasons why investigators have sought to construct tests based on learning ability. A major consideration is that the use of such tests avoids some of the problems associated with intelligence testing. The emphasis in the latter is on the measurement of performance rather than the processes that underlie it. This emphasis is reversed in tests of lear which set out explicitly to gather information on these processes. Moreover, tests of learning ability need not rely to the same extent as intelligence tests on materials that are specific to a given culture. This is because of the teaching element they incorporate. Test items can be based on quite unfamiliar material if preliminary teaching is based on it. Intelligence tests have less scope in this respect since they rarely involve explicit teaching and are obliged to assume a far larger core of common experience; test items must be based on relatively familiar material which will inevitably be drawn from the majority culture.

A related point is that tests of learning ability make it possible to equate to some extent the amount of relevant learning experience. This is achieved by ensuring that as far as possible the test tasks are unfamiliar ones. Any inadvertent differential familiarity with the materials can be reduced in this way since all the children are given practice on them, and have their misunderstandings corrected, before the test proper begins.

There is evidence to suggest that tests of learning ability can discriminate between children with uniformly low IQ scores. In other words, low IQ does not define a homogeneous group with respect to learning ability.

Jensen (1963) reports a study conducted in California where tests of learning ability were administered to three groups of children with low, average, and high IQ. Children with average and high IQs returned average and high learning ability scores. Quite a different picture emerged from the children with low IQ: their learning ability scores were not uniformly low and indeed spanned the whole range of scores obtained. Some had very low scores but others obtained scores that exceeded the mean scores of the high IQ group.

The relationship to conventional academic requirements may be noted. Learning ability is clearly associated with school work. Whatever else they seek to achieve, teachers want children to respond to teaching and to learn. In this sense the ability to learn is fundamental. Tests based on it provide a sample of the child's learning behaviour, leading to a measure of the ability to profit from teaching. There is evidence—outlined below—to suggest that for certain groups of children, tests of learning ability are better predictors of school achievement than are intelligence tests.

## 2. The Nature of Learning Ability

While the notion of learning ability is intuitively a familiar and useful one there are considerable difficulties in giving a formal account of it. First, there is the frequent confusion with intelligence. Intelligence and learning ability are sometimes thought to be synonymous. While this is clearly erroneous it is difficult to specify the relationship between them. Then, there are those who argue that it is not a satisfactory construct either because the various uses do not cohere or because it can only be measured indirectly. A third area of difficulty stems from evidence bearing on the relationship between learning ability and achievement, and on the extent to which learning ability can be "taught". Thus, Jensen and Rohwer (1965) found in a paired-associate learning task where children had to link pairs of pictures, that performance improved when they were taught to construct a sentence containing the names of the two pictures in a pair the first time each pair was presented.

The amount of empirical work based on the concept of learning ability is limited so that any theoretical account must at the present be tentative. This is not to say that the construct is invalidated or that the difficulties outlined make it impossible to articulate a coherent account of it. A first broad distinction can be made between the learning involved in the initial processing of data and in their subsequent transformation. This corresponds to White's (1965) distinction between associative and cognitive abilities and to Jensen's separation of level I and level II abilities. The first of these has to do with the registering and elementary processing of data, as in rote learning and paired-associate learning. The second refers to the subsequent more sophisticated processing and transformation of perceptual input that occurs in activities like abstracting similarities, reasoning, and manipulating numbers.

Beyond this basic division conceptualizations diverge and there is no general agreement on how learning ability should be defined. Different studies have defined it in various ways. This is illustrated in the following section where the test materials used imply tasks of concept formation, number seriation, paired-associate learning, and auditory rote learning. As further empirical work is carried out it should be possible to delineate the nature of learning ability and its relationship to other concepts more clearly.

## 3. Tests Based on Learning Ability

The number of tests available which are based on the notion of learning ability is limited. Hegarty and Lucas (1978) describe eight widely varying examples. These range from assessment practices within Soviet defectology based on "teaching experiments" and Feuerstein's "instrumental enrichment" work with disadvantaged immigrants in Israel to Jensen's work with Mexican–American children. Three examples will be described here based respectively on the work of Budoff, Hegarty, and Henning.

Budoff's work is set in the context of the frequent academic failure of disadvantaged children in America—"children from poor and/or non-white homes tend to score at below-average levels on tests which purport to measure intelligence" (Babad and Budoff 1974). This was attributed to various factors but in particular to the difficulty these children have with the required problem-solving strategies. They may be able to reason adequately but their experiences tend not to prepare them for the demands of middle-class schools and middle-class tests.

In order to obtain a more realistic and less biased picture of these children's abilities, Budoff developed a learning potential procedure based on a process-oriented conceptualization of intelligence. The emphasis is on *how* problems are solved and on the child's ability to improve performance on tasks following a systematic learning experience. The tasks used are reasoning problems, administered in a test–train–test sequence. The child is taught how to solve the problems by employing a suitable strategy.

Budoff has used three kinds of learning task to carry out his assessment programme: an altered version of Kohs Block Designs (Budoff 1969), Raven's Progressive Matrices, and the Series Learning Potential Test. The first two of these need not be described here since what is novel is the way in which they are used. This can be described equally well in the case of the third set of materials. The series learning potential test is a group test for use with younger children. It involves completing a series of pictures or geometric forms, arranged in a pattern in which the figures change systematically. Each item consists of a horizontal row of cells containing stimulus figures. One cell is left blank. The subject must

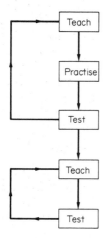

**Figure 1**
Model for NFER test of learning ability

identify, from a set of multiple choices on the right, the picture which best completes the series. Four concepts may vary in a series: semantic content (meaningful or geometric figures), size, colour, and orientation. The concepts may vary symmetrically or asymmetrically and the blank space may be placed in any part of the series.

The National Foundation for Educational Research (NFER) test of learning ability described by Hegarty (1978) offers a second example. This was developed in the context of underachievement by children from ethnic minorities in the United Kingdom. This underachievement was compounded with the fact that existing tests were considered to be unsuitable for many of these children because of their culture specificity.

The aim of the NFER test is to assess the child's ability to respond to structured teaching and so benefit from instruction. The test materials are designed in terms of the model shown in Fig. 1. The child is first taught a simple task by demonstration and then given practice on related material until the instructions have been understood. Testing follows, with each test trial preceded by further practical teaching. This procedure enables one to dispense entirely with verbal instructions—an important requirement when testing children who may have a limited competence in the tester's language. It also helps equate to a certain extent the amount of relevant prior learning experience. The battery comprises five subtests covering different aspects of the ability to learn: paired-associate learning; auditory rote learning; concept formation; number seriation; and the grasp of relationships.

The test is intended for use primarily with children from ethnic minority backgrounds where the use of other tests is unreliable. In validation studies with such children the tests predicted well to subsequent school attainment. It was compared with the Wechsler Intelligence Scale for Children (WISC) in one such study and

was found to predict school performance after 12 months significantly better than the latter.

An example of a rather different kind is provided by Henning's Learning Ability Profile. This is intended for use with adults of average education though the complexity of the items varies considerably. It seeks to be a learning tool as well as an assessment instrument: the person taking the test is given feedback on every response he or she makes; and responses must continue—in a multiple-choice mode—until the correct answer is achieved, the final score reflecting the number of incorrect responses made.

The Learning Ability Profile has been tried on groups of varying educational, socioeconomic, and cultural backgrounds. There were "no significant differences among racial groups, males and females, and between persons in their occupational prime years and persons 50 years of age and older" (Henning 1975). The claim to provide a measure that is impervious to cultural differences has resulted in the Profile being used in education, industry, and government in North America.

In summary, learning ability tests offer an alternative mode of psychometric investigation that can be used to replace or supplement other forms of assessment. Their use is particularly relevant when dealing with those who are culturally deprived or come from ethnic minorities. A good deal of further work, both theoretical and empirical, is needed before the full potential of learning ability tests can be realized or their use be well-established.

## Bibliography

Babad E, Budoff M 1974 A manual for the series learning potential test. Mimeograph, Research Institute for Education Problems, Cambridge, Massachusetts

Budoff M 1969 Learning potential: A supplementary procedure for assessing the ability to reason. *Semin. Psychiatry* 1: 278–90

Cronbach L 1969 *Essentials of Psychological Testing.* Harper and Row, New York

Feuerstein R 1980 *Instrumental Enrichment: An Intervention Program for Cognitive Modifiability.* University Park Press, Baltimore, Maryland

Hegarty S 1978 *Manual for the NFER Test of Learning Ability (Individual Form).* National Foundation for Educational Research (NFER), Slough

Hegarty S, Lucas D 1978 *Able to Learn? The Pursuit of Culture-fair Assessment.* National Foundation for Educational Research (NFER), Slough

Henning M 1975 *Learning Ability Profile (LAP): A Culture Fair Assessment Instrument.* Falcon/Whittaker, Albuquerque, New Mexico

Jensen A R 1963 Learning ability in retarded, average and gifted children. *Merrill-Palmer Q.* 9: 123–40

Jensen A R, Rohwer W D 1965 Syntactical mediation of serial and paired-associate learning as a function of age. *Child Dev.* 36: 601–08

White S 1965 Evidence for a hierarchical arrangement of learning processes. In: Lipsitt L P, Spiker C (eds.) 1965 *Advances in Child Development and Behavior*, Vol. 2. Academic Press, New York

# Culture-free Tests

## S. Hegarty

Culture-free tests are independent of cultural context and scores on them should not in any measure reflect access to specific cultural experience, knowledge, or values.

### 1. Relationship to Culture-fair Assessment

Culture-free tests should not be confused with culture-fair tests. A continuum can be imagined from tests which are highly specific to given situations and relevant only in these situations to tests which are wholly non-specific in this way. Tests which come toward the latter end of the continuum are "culture reduced", and more likely to be culture fair, but it is only in the limit that they could be styled culture free.

Conventional tests comprise items which are never quite void of cultural content or reference. "How many centimetres in a metre?" is less culture specific than "What is the capital of Scotland?" and "How much is seven times five?" less so than either. All make some cultural reference however and imply a context outside of which they are meaningless. Since scores on such tests will reflect the degree of familiarity with these contexts, such tests should not be described as culture free, but rather culture reduced or culture fair as appropriate.

### 2. Physiological and Perceptual Measures

These considerations do not apply in the same way to measures based on laboratory techniques such as choice reaction time and evoked electrical potentials of the brain. There is no reason in principle to suppose that such measures would be subject to cultural variation, and if reliable psychometric information could be obtained from them it could be taken as culture free. In a review of relevant laboratory studies, however, Jensen (1980) concluded that while laboratory methods of mental measurement showed small but reliable correlations with conventional IQ scores they were virtually useless for any practical purposes. They were unlikely to offer alternatives to conventional psychometric tests.

Further developments along these lines have come from current research work based on the notion of inspection time. In the study of perception, visual stimuli are presented very briefly in a controlled manner by means of a device known as a tachistoscope. When this is done in such a way that the image does not enter the subject's short-term memory, the period of time required to discriminate reliably between stimuli is known as inspection time (Vickers et al. 1972). A number of studies have examined the correlations between inspection time and various measures of intelligence, vocabulary, and spatial ability. In a review of these studies, Brand and Deary (1982) report a median correlation of −0.80 between inspection time and general intelligence for young adults covering a wide IQ range. While this research is in its infancy it offers the prospect of an empirical psychometric measurement which is both culture free and of practical use.

### Bibliography

Brand C, Deary I 1982. Intelligence and "inspection time". In: Eysenck H (ed.) *A Model for Intelligence*. Springer, Berlin
Jensen A R 1980 *Bias in Mental Testing*. Methuen, London
Vickers D, Nettelbeck T, Willson R J 1972 Perceptual indices of performance: The measurement of "inspection time" and "noise" in the visual system. *Perception* 1: 263–95

# Vocational Aptitude

## C. K. Tittle

Measures of vocational aptitude are distinguished from other tests of developed abilities by their assumptions about the test taker's prior experiences and the use of the test scores. Achievement measures are linked to defined educational curricula and experiences, and measures of general ability (intelligence tests) are composed of heterogeneous item types that are considered least related to directed learning experiences. Between these two ends of a continuum are the vocational aptitude measures. They are more homogeneous in item content than measures of general ability and are designed to predict student performance in specific, vocationally related areas such as clerical, mechanical, art, or music. It is important to recognize the continuous nature of this classification, especially if experiences of particular groups differ from those of the general sample upon which the vocational prediction measure is developed. What is apparently an aptitude or developed ability measure for some students may be closer to an achievement measure for others.

Although many measures of vocational aptitude have been constructed, they have been empirically based in their development, with extensive reliance on analyses of correlations between tests. Aptitude measures show little connection to psychological theories. To date, aptitude measures have been limited to cognitive and some psychomotor measures, with little attention to the social or interpersonal competencies that often are important components of on-the-job performance.

## 1. Uses in Educational Settings

Vocational aptitude measures have two main uses in educational settings: (a) early in the secondary-school years, to select students or assist students to select specific vocational programs such as shop or business; and (b) at any stage in secondary school, to encourage students to explore vocations in which their aptitude scores, interests, and experiences suggest they might be successful. Each use suggests the type of validity evidence required to interpret test scores. The first use emphasizes the prediction of how well the student will perform in a specific vocational training program or later occupational placement. The second, counseling use, includes the comparison of the student's scores with those of individuals who have been successful in a training program or occupation. Differential validity evidence is needed when there is more than one aptitude measure and two or more vocational or occupational (criterion) groups are considered at the same time. That is, evidence is needed that the measures discriminate among profiles or scores for successful workers or trainees in different occupations.

Studies of aptitude measures used in school or work settings have focused on differences in average scores between groups in occupational courses or occupations (employment). There is some evidence supporting this differentiation, but typically there is extensive overlap in score distributions making prediction for individuals weak. This is particularly true of multiple test batteries used in schools. Usually a composite score (verbal plus numerical measures) is the best predictor of academic performance, limiting the usefulness of the multiple test batteries. There is some evidence that the tests provide differentiation of occupational group membership over the long term, particularly for high–low level occupations, but the tests are not predictive (over a long time) of success within an occupation.

Aptitude measures also provide part of the information used for admissions to some postsecondary institutions and to professional schools, for example, law and medicine. In selection testing for professional schools, academic abilities (verbal and numerical measures), sometimes supplemented by highly specialized tests, are used. The validity evidence is usually correlational, between test and professional school grades. There is little evidence of the validity of these test scores in predicting performance on the job. In one of the few studies of professional school grades and work performance, medical school grades were not related to later performance.

Aptitude measures may also be part of large-scale vocational–guidance assessment batteries (developed abilities' measures, interests, and plans) taken by students at the end of secondary school. Similar selection and classification or counseling uses of these measures

are found in military and industrial settings. The following sections provide information on the background and theory underlying approaches to vocational aptitude measures, give examples of these measures, and identify current areas of research.

## 2. Background

The origins of aptitude measures are in the development of the study of individual differences. This is usually said to have begun with the observation of differences in recording of times of stellar transits in 1796 at the Greenwich Observatory (Dunnette 1976). A major step was taken by Sir Francis Galton, with the publication of *Hereditary Genius* in 1869. This publication included the beginning of a system for classifying individuals according to their abilities, the idea that human abilities were distributed according to the normal probability curve, and the procedure of expressing the relative standing of individuals in a standard score. These early abilities of reaction times and measures of vision and hearing, were shown to be unrelated to learning in educational settings. In 1905 Alfred Binet published the first Binet Test, a metrical scale of intelligence. His tasks were similar to the ones children would be asked to do in day-to-day learning such as to identify familiar objects, name the months in order, and define abstract words. In 1916 the Stanford–Binet Test was published by Terman in the United States and widespread research activity began on the measurement of human abilities. Dunnette (1976) points out that Binet studied carefully the behavior of school learning that he wanted to predict. However, this approach has been less used in the study of vocational aptitude measures that are intended to predict human work performance in organizations.

Several events contributed to a growing interest in measuring vocational aptitudes (Anastasi 1982). There was an increasing recognition of variation within individuals in the tasks on intelligence tests. There was some attempt to provide scores on similar sets of items within intelligence tests, but the tests were not designed to yield reliable scores on subsets of items and the items tended to be very heterogeneous. Analyses also showed that most general intelligence tests were heavily weighted with verbal comprehension. Other areas, such as mechanical abilities, were not included, with the exception of some of the performance or nonlanguage scales. Another impetus came from the development of career counseling in psychology, as well as the use of tests by the military and industry.

The movement from a test of scholastic or academic ability (intelligence) to tests of specific abilities was heavily dependent on the application of a statistical technique, factor analysis, to the examination of the correlations among different tests. Theories of the organization of abilities, including those we call aptitudes, have evolved from factor-analytic studies. Procedural differences in factor analysis, and the dependence of results on the particular combination of tests used in each study, have contributed to the development of different models of how abilities are organized.

Factor analysis is intended to simplify observed data, the correlations among tests, by reducing the number of variables or dimensions necessary to account for the correlations. A "factor" is described by the correlation (the weight) of each test with the hypothetical dimension (the factor). If six tests are taken and the scores correlated, and if there are two factors or dimensions which can account for the variance among the tests, then the factors can be described by looking at the items in the tests with the highest weight on each factor. Thus, one factor may have high weights for tests of vocabulary and reading, and might be labeled a verbal factor. The second factor might be weighted with tests requiring facility with numbers, and would be characterized or described as a numerical factor.

The first theory, proposed by Spearman, has been labeled the two-factor theory. It originally stated that all intellectual activities shared a single common factor, "g," or general factor, as well as specifics or "s" factors (Anastasi 1982). Later modifications included group factors, such as arithmetic or mechanical. Some American theorists described multiple factor theories, using only group factors. Thurstone was prominent among these theorists, proposing a set of group factors called the primary mental abilities. The factors were verbal comprehension, word fluency, number, space, associative memory, perceptual speed, and induction (general reasoning). A three-dimensional model of the "structure of intellect" was proposed by Guilford (1967). In Guilford's model, abilities or traits are organized on three dimensions: operations, what the respondent does; contents, the nature of the materials on which operations are performed; and products, the form in which information is processed by the respondent. The model includes 120 cells or potential factors.

An alternative, hierarchical theory of the organization of abilities has been proposed, principally by British psychologists such as Vernon (1961). Vernon's model specifies Spearman's "g" factor at the top of a pyramid, next two broad group factors (verbal–educational and practical–mechanical), followed by minor group factors and, at the bottom, specific factors. The minor group factors are such tests as verbal and number under the verbal–educational major group factor, and mechanical information, spatial, and psychomotor under the practical major group factor.

In practice, most of the tests constructed as vocational aptitude measures follow the multiple-factor approach, although most provide for scoring or developing composite scores that have the effect of using at least part of the hierarchical theory.

## 3. Multiple Test Batteries

There are a number of multiple aptitude batteries used in schools in the United States that illustrate the current state of the art. These batteries and their tests are identified here to provide an idea of their scope. Specific evaluations of these batteries and individual aptitude tests will be found in Buros (1978).

The Thurstone Tests of Primary Mental Abilities have already been mentioned. The 1962 revision has scores for five factors—verbal meaning, number facility, reasoning, perceptual speed, and spatial relations. A widely used battery is the Differential Aptitude Tests (DAT), designed primarily for educational and vocational counseling in secondary schools. Eight scores are obtained: verbal reasoning, numerical ability, abstract reasoning, clerical speed and accuracy, mechanical reasoning, space relations, spelling, and language usage. The tests show predictive validity with high school course grades, but ". . . the results are somewhat less encouraging with regard to differential prediction . . . there is evidence of a large general factor underlying performance in all academic work" (Anastasi 1982 p. 378). An index of scholastic aptitude (verbal reasoning plus numerical ability) is therefore provided. Fewer data are available on vocational criteria.

The United States Employment Service developed the General Aptitude Test Battery (GATB) which is used in the United States by state employment offices and has been made available as a model or starting point for the development of aptitude batteries in other countries. Twelve tests yield nine factor scores: verbal aptitude (vocabulary); numerical aptitude (computation and arithmetic reasoning tests); spatial aptitude; general learning ability (composite of verbal, numerical, and spatial aptitudes); form perception; clerical perception; motor coordination; finger dexterity; and manual dexterity.

The Armed Services Vocational Aptitude Battery (ASVAB) is the most widely used aptitude battery in United States high schools. Six composite scores are made available in high school reports: verbal ability; clerical ability/perceptual speed; analytic, quantitative ability/mathematics; mechanical ability; trade technical; and academic ability (Wilfong 1980). One of the criticisms of the Armed Services Vocational Aptitude Battery has been that some tests are apparently sex linked in experience, particularly shop information and automotive information. They would thus provide little indication of the ability of girls to learn information in these or related areas and are likely to be misleading if considered or thought of as predictors of performance in vocational courses. The assumption of common prior experiences of groups for whom any vocational aptitude test is appropriate should therefore be checked throughout the test development process and in separate validity studies.

## 4. Special Aptitude Tests

There are a number of tests of vocational aptitude that are not included in the multifactor test batteries, either because of time constraints or special requirements for administration. These include such measures as those in the psychomotor, mechanical reasoning, and music areas. Such tests may be useful for individual students who evidence an interest in one of these areas. Counselors may administer special aptitude measures on an individual basis as part of exploring the relationship of developed abilities and interests in a particular vocation.

## 5. Research Areas

Research on vocational aptitudes has several areas of development. One area is influenced by technology— developments in computer-based testing (adaptive testing), computer-based test interpretation reports, and computer-based guidance systems. Adaptive testing, also called tailored testing, offers the possibility of more efficient and accurate measurement. Computer test interpretations can be based on the integration of information from a number of sources, measures of developed abilities, expressed or inventoried interests, and course grades, to provide comprehensive career guidance to students or adults (see Anastasi 1982 pp. 453–54). Aptitude measures may also be part of computer-based guidance systems (analyses and descriptions are given by Katz and Shatkin 1980, and Shatkin 1980).

Another area which will affect vocational aptitude measures is research on cognitive abilities that is linked with experimental cognitive psychology. Some studies in cognitive psychology examine interventions (training) that may affect test performance. Such studies may eventually provide models for the adaptation of vocational education programs to learners with different "aptitudes" or cognitive skills. Alternatively, successful completion of simulated, short-term or partial training programs may be both more valid and defensible as selection procedures for vocational programs.

Social issues in the United States have also affected the use of vocational aptitude tests in educational settings. Regulations for programs receiving federal aid have required equal access to educational programs and the elimination of discrimination against women and minorities. School programs have been developed that give students sample experiences in many vocational areas, so vocational choices of all students can be based on first-hand experiences. Users of vocational aptitude tests need to be concerned with the evidence (construct validity) for test interpretation and the outcomes (possible adverse impact on groups) of test use (Messick 1980), both in vocational guidance and selection into vocational programs.

## Bibliography

Anastasi A 1982 *Psychological Testing*, 5th edn. Macmillan, New York

Buros O K (ed.) 1978 *The Eighth Mental Measurements Yearbook*. Buros Institute of Mental Measurements, Lincoln, Nebraska

Dunnette M D 1976 Aptitudes, abilities and skills. In: Dunnette M D (ed.) 1976 *Handbook of Industrial and Organizational Psychology*. Rand McNally, Chicago, Illinois

Guilford J P 1967 *The Nature of Human Intelligence*. McGraw-Hill, New York

Katz M R, Shatkin L 1980 *Computer-assisted Guidance: Concepts and Practices RR-80-1*. Educational Testing Service, Princeton, New Jersey

Messick S 1980 Test validity and the ethics of assessment. *Am. Psychol.* 35: 1012–27

Shatkin L 1980 *Computer-assisted Guidance: Description of Systems RR-80-23*. Educational Testing Service, Princeton, New Jersey

Vernon P E 1961 *The Structure of Human Abilities*, 2nd edn. Methuen, London

Wilfong H D 1980 ASVAB Technical Supplement to the High School Counselor's Guide. Directorate of Testing, United States Military Enlistment Processing Command, Fort Sheridan, Illinois

# Vocational Interest Measures

## C. K. Tittle

It is readily observed that there are individual differences in the interests or preferences of persons for vocations. Definitions of interests have focused on activities for which an individual has a liking or disliking, or a tendency to do or to avoid. Operationally, interests have been designated as vocational or educational, although items with the same specific activities might be found on either an occupational or educational interest measure. Interests are distinguished from measures of developed abilities (achievements or aptitudes) which assess competence or skill. In mathematics, for example, the distinction would be in assessing competence or skill in mathematics, as contrasted to a preference for or liking to do mathematical problems. Interest measures are not intended to predict whether an individual will do well or be successful in an occupation. Interest measures are assumed to be relevant to vocational satisfaction—the satisfaction with one's work activities and environment.

Measures of vocational interests typically have not been theoretically or conceptually based. They have been developed by assembling groups of items, in some instances general activities, in others work-setting-derived activities, and in others occupational titles, and constructing scales based on one of two procedures. The first procedure results in occupational (or empirical criterion) scales. These scales are based on the empirically determined relationship between the interests (response patterns) expressed by the taker of the interest inventory and those of individuals who express satisfaction with their employment in an occupation or who have entered a college major, such as secondary-school teacher. The scales thus constructed reflect people similarity.

For some inventories there is a different first step in such scale construction. The scales must first discriminate between the occupational group and a general reference group composed of individuals from a broad sampling of occupations. Separate reference groups of females and males have been used in the construction of occupational scales for men and women. (The utility of general reference groups based on gender in occupational-scale construction has been questioned in research studies in recent years.)

The second procedure results in scales called basic interest or homogeneous scales. They are based more typically on activity similarity. That is, groups of items are formed into scales on the basis of internal criteria, some form of clustering items. The ideas of the test constructor, sorting by judges, intercorrelations of items and item-scale score correlations, and factor analysis are all procedures that are used for constructing homogeneous scales.

The reliance on empirical criterion groups and internal criteria to form scales for interest measures continues today. A review of the test development manuals for current instruments typically does not yield a theoretical rationale or discussion of the sources of the items as samples from a well-defined domain of work activities, environments, or set of psychological constructs. The disjunction between general theories of psychology and research on interest measures remains. The historical influence of trait and factor views from the study of individual differences and personality (psychodynamic) theories are evident, bound by the idea of matching the person and the job. But there is little direct concern with the relationship between personal and environmental characteristics. Interest measures have been built around the likes and dislikes of the person alone and the link between measured interests and job satisfaction remains a central problem for interest measurement methodology.

Since there is little theoretical work to shed light on the development and use of vocational interest measures, the sections which follow focus on selected topics in which there is continuing research and then consider the uses of vocational interest measures in relation to recent developments in counseling in educational settings.

## 1. Research

The topics of continuing research interest are: classification schemes relevant for vocational interest inventories; the number of independent dimensions of interests; and the effects of taking an interest inventory (a part of validity).

### 1.1 Classification Schemes

Occupational classifications have been used to group scores on vocational interest inventories and/or to relate scores to groups or clusters of occupations. The need for classification systems is based on the limited number of basic interest areas assessed in inventories (from 6 to about 30) and occupational scales (as many as 160). Classification systems permit the linking of basic interests or occupational scales to clusters of occupations. For example, some 600 occupations are coded, clustered, and linked to 25 job families in the American College Testing Program (1977) Career Planning Program. (The 600 occupations comprise the occupations in which 95 percent of American workers are employed.)

Holland (1976) provides examples of classification systems in three broad categories, those that organize occupations according to prestige and socioeconomic levels, job content, and/or worker characteristics. Sociological prestige systems have not been used with interest inventories, although levels based on educational requirements and level of responsibility have (Roe 1956). Two prominent systems that emphasize job content are those of the United States Census and the Dictionary of Occupational Titles (DOT). Worker characteristics are also part of the Dictionary of Occupational Titles. The Worker Traits Arrangement groups jobs, ". . . according to kind of work, as well as some combination of worker traits, such as educational development, vocational preparation, aptitudes, interests, temperaments, and physical demands" (Holland 1976 p. 526).

Systems that have been derived from psychological analyses of individuals and the results of factor analyses of interest measures have more widespread use in assigning summary codes or general occupational themes to interest inventory occupational or basic interest scales. These classifications are then used to provide a link to the Dictionary of Occupational Titles or other occupational descriptions. Roe (1956) suggested a classification system that incorporated both levels (based on the educational and responsibility requirements of jobs) and groups (similar to factors derived from analyses of interest measures). The eight groups she proposed are: service, business contact, organization, technology, outdoor, science, general cultural, and arts and entertainment. Holland (1976 p. 530) lists the factors from early factor studies that appear similar to Roe's groups. He has also proposed a six-category system that is intended to serve as a typology of personality and occupations (Roe's categories are given in parentheses): social (service), enterprising (business contact), conventional (organization), realistic (technology, outdoor), intellectual (science), and artistic (arts and entertainment, general cultural).

### 1.2 Number of Dimensions

The number of dimensions or structure of interests is of concern both in counseling and in test development. The structure imposed on scores, as in the classification systems, facilitates interpretation and focusing discussions with students. The structure also provides part of the framework for decision making in the test development process.

A statistical procedure, factor analysis, is used to examine the number of dimensions. Factor analysis provides a means to simplify observed data, the correlations among occupational scales or basic interest scores, by reducing the number of variables or dimensions necessary to account for the observed correlations. A "factor" is described by the correlation (the weight) of each score with the hypothetical dimension (the factor). If 30 basic interest scales are administered, does each scale represent a unique dimension or are there fewer dimensions than scales? For example, if there are eight factors or dimensions which can account for the variance among the 30 scales, then the factors can be described by looking at the items in the scales with the highest weight on each factor. For example, scales labeled as mathematics, physical science, and engineering might have high weights on one dimension. Examination of the items might lead to labeling the factor as logical. The emphasis in the items in the three scales is on activities requiring logical thought, problem solving, and quantitative reasoning (Jackson 1977).

Procedural differences exist in factor analyses as well as differences in the use of types of items (forced choice items resulting in ipsative scores versus choice among a set of alternatives resulting in normative or group interpreted scores). Also, results of factor analyses are dependent on the particular set of tests used in each study. All of these differences combine to make generalizations about the number of underlying dimensions or structure of interests problematic.

Holland (1976) suggests that there are four to eight dimensions of interests and that these have a characteristic order (fall in a circular order) in a two-dimensional space. Some studies have suggested that the two-dimensional space may not fit all data (Lunneborg 1981 pp. 41–43) and that there may be additional factors related to satisfaction in work environments. With respect to the question of additional factors, Jackson (1977) found 10 factors in an analysis of 34 basic interest scales. The 34 scales include what Jackson calls work roles and work styles. Eight factors are based on measures of work roles (activities relevant to occupations such as law). Two factors are based on measures of work style (preference for certain kinds of work environments such as an environment with job security). The eight worker role factors appear to overlap with Roe's groups (given in parentheses): helping (service), enterprising (business contact), conventional (organization), practical (technology, outdoor), inquiry and logical (science), communicative (general cultural), and expressive (arts and entertainment).

The two worker-style factors, socialized and assertive, are not found in Roe's groups. The socialized factor has high weights for scales labeled accountability, job security, stamina, and planfulness. The assertive factor has high weights for scales labeled independence, dominant leadership, and interpersonal confidence. Thus

these two dimensions appear to tap a different facet of the work environment than the job-activity focus found in the work-role scales. The work-style dimensions appear more directly oriented to personality characteristics as they function in the work environment.

Further research should lead to a greater understanding of the number of dimensions in interest inventories and the relationship of measured interests to work environments. Evaluations of many interest inventories available in English will be found in Mitchell (1985).

### 1.3 Effects of Taking an Interest Inventory

Several developments have focused attention on what happens to individuals as a result of taking an interest inventory. One development has been the social concern over the effects of taking any psychological measure. Messick (1980) has placed this social concern within an expanded view of validity, arguing that both evidence for and the consequences of test interpretation and test use are of concern in test validity. Another important development was the examination of interest inventories for their fairness (or lack thereof) for women. The concern arises from the data on sex segregation in occupations and earning differences within occupations. To what extent do interest inventories contribute to maintaining these differences?

Studies which have examined the accuracy of classification for occupations or college majors suggest that interest inventories provide "hit rates" or group membership predictions of about 40 percent when using six groups. Expressed interests (asking persons what occupation they plan to enter) typically do as well as "inventoried" interests in classification studies. These studies provide information for test interpretation, but do not provide data on the *use* of the test results by students. Studies of effects (actions taken based on receiving inventory results such as trying out new career-related activities or considering more occupations) do not show great differences among inventories. Neither do they show strong evidence of increases in outcome measures such as number of occupations considered, whether traditional or nontraditional for either females or males, or pursuit of occupational information. Both of these outcomes are relevant when the goal in using the inventory is career exploration. These studies suggest that greater attention should be given to the design and evaluation of instructional materials to be used with interest measures to improve the use of test results. The most interpretable studies are likely to be those which ascertain the student's goal in taking an inventory and tailor both treatment and outcome measures for groups of students with the same goals.

## 2. Counseling Developments and Interest Measures

Several developments in counseling have affected the use of vocational interest measures. These include an emphasis on career development, career exploration, and the career decision-making process. In large part this development has as its goal an increase in the career options individuals explore, since students typically consider only a small number of occupations. In the United States, sex fairness in the development and use of interest inventories has been another area of influence. Computer availability has also had an influence by providing test interpretations for interest inventories. An even greater impact may occur with computer-assisted (interactive) guidance systems.

## 2.1 Career Development and Exploration

The purpose of vocational counseling has changed from an emphasis on trait matching (the people-similarities approach mentioned earlier) to one of viewing career development as part of the process of developing and implementing a self-concept. This has led to the examination of the process by which individuals make career plans and choices. Within this framework, the use of career interest inventories for expanding choice and furthering exploration of career alternatives has been emphasized. This has resulted in a greater emphasis on identifying basic interest areas (the activities-similarities approach). Basic interest areas are then linked to clusters of occupations. The exploration of occupations, through print and vocationally relevant experiences can then be examined in studies of effects. Super and Hall (1978 pp. 340–50) discuss the nature of career exploration in detail and identify other behavioral measures of exploration.

## 2.2 Sex Fairness

The sex fairness of vocational interest measures has been debated and studied intensively since the early 1970s. The issues were defined, discussed, and researched, resulting in the *Guidelines for Assessment of Sex Bias and Sex Fairness in Career Interest Inventories* (Diamond 1975, Tittle and Zytowski 1978). The *Guidelines* range from a recommendation to use the same form of an interest inventory for men and women to technical considerations of using same sex or combined sex scales and norms. The *Guidelines* have influenced the development and revision of interest inventories in the United States since their publication.

## 2.3 Computer Interpretation and Guidance Systems

Computer interpretations of vocational interest measures are now available for several widely used instruments. In the use of test results by counselors, the counselor may have knowledge about student attainments and preferences gained in a variety of settings or interviews. In such a situation, the interpretation of test results is placed in the context of this knowledge. In computer reports, the interpretation is usually limited to the information provided only by the test results. Another aspect of computer interpretations is that interpretation of results for students with the same scores

will be standard, since the computer interpretation is developed by using a fixed set of decision rules. These rules are based on "cutting scores" to which verbal interpretations are attached. For example, any student at or above the 90th percentile in an interest area may be said to have a "very high interest"; students from the 70th to the 89th percentiles may be said to have a "moderately high interest"; and so on.

Computer-assisted guidance systems (CAG) are a different application of technology to counseling and guidance. These systems typically include some assessment of interests, aptitudes, and attainments of the user, as well as information for occupations, including work environments, names of potential employers, and where to find additional information. Katz and Shatkin (1980) describe the major concepts underlying several computer-assisted guidance systems as a concern for the user's understanding, competence, and opportunities for satisfaction in vocations. That is, there is less emphasis on trait matching for success or membership in specific occupations for prediction and differential validity. Thus some computer-assisted guidance systems focus on helping with the career decision-making process without necessarily dictating the content of the decisions. In this aspect they reflect the career development and exploration emphasis that is influencing the use of career interest inventories.

In summary, vocational interest inventories have a history in educational use since the early 1900s. The use and interpretation of interest measures has reflected the dominant views in psychology since that time. Interest measures reflect a mix of purposes and uses, from the trait matching and prediction emphasis, to encouraging career exploration and the process of using information in career related decision making. Issues of sex fairness and the need for a better understanding of the career choice process for women are also affecting the use of these measures.

## 3. Interest Measures in Evaluation

Interest measures are frequently used as part of the "treatment" in educational and job-related training programs. For example, cooperative education programs in secondary and post-secondary institutions typically have career awareness and career development objectives or goals. In such programs computer-based guidance systems and/or interest measures are often part of the intervention, that is, they constitute a component of the program. In evaluation studies of such programs, measures of the development of career decision-making skills, career maturity, and certainty of career choices may be sought. This is a developing area of research which includes attempts to measure student perceptions of needs in relation to the career decision-making process, certainty of career choice, and feelings of self-efficacy or confidence in tasks and behaviours related to career decision-making (e.g., Taylor and Betz 1983). These areas are often assessed by a series of items pre and post the programs/courses with goals of career development.

## Bibliography

American College Testing Program 1977 *Handbook for the ACT Career Planning Program 1977 Edition*. American College Testing Program, Iowa City, Iowa

Diamond E E (ed.) 1975 *Issues of Sex Bias and Sex Fairness in Career Interest Measurement*. National Institute of Education, Washington, DC

Holland J L 1976 Vocational preferences. In: Dunnette M D (ed.) 1976 *Handbook of Industrial and Organizational Psychology*. Rand McNally, Chicago, Illinois

Jackson D N 1977 *Jackson Vocational Interest Survey Manual*. Research Psychologists Press, Port Huron, Michigan

Katz M R, Shatkin L 1980 *Computer-assisted Guidance: Concepts and Practices RR-80-1*. Educational Testing Service, Princeton, New Jersey

Lunneborg P W 1981 *The Vocational Interest Inventory Manual*. Western Psychological Services, Los Angeles, California

Messick S 1980 Test validity and the ethics of assessment. *Am. Psychol.* 35: 1012–27

Mitchell J V, Jr (ed.) 1985 *The Ninth Mental Measurement Yearbook*. University of Nebraska Press, Lincoln, Nebraska

Roe A 1956 *The Psychology of Occupations*. Wiley, New York

Super D E, Hall D T 1978 Career development: Exploration and planning. *Annu. Rev. Psychol.* 29: 333–72

Taylor K M, Betz N E 1983 Applications of self-efficacy theory to the understanding and treatment of career indecision. *J. Vocat. Behav.* 22: 63–81

Tittle C K, Zytowski D G (eds.) 1978 *Sex-fair Interest Measurement: Research and Implications*. National Institute of Education, Washington, DC

**Part 7**

# Research Methodology

# Part 7

# Research Methodology

## Introduction

Research methodology for evaluation studies poses significant challenges. Rather than addressing neat, theoretically grounded questions, evaluators may have to ferret out program goals, describe program implementation, and assess multiple outcomes, often at scattered sites where different versions of the program are administered to nonequivalent groups of children. Data may be collected using dozens of different instruments from students, teachers, parents, and administrators. Field conditions very often preclude the random assignment of children to treatment and control groups; the need for quick turnaround to inform pressing decisions often makes longitudinal designs impractical; limited resources and testing time force compromises in study instrumentation; and it may not even be clear what questions the evaluation should attempt to answer. Simple description may be at least as important as statistical generalization, but if the right data are not collected, the descriptions may be distorted and incomplete. The topic of evaluation research methodology is further complicated by the plurality of philosophies, perspectives, and approaches found in evaluation research.

Part 7 of the *Encyclopedia* surveys the major approaches and issues in evaluation Research Methodology. Both quantitative and qualitative research paradigms are represented. It begins with a section of seven articles on Basic Principles of Design and Analysis in Evaluation Research, followed by four articles on Issues in the Design of Quantitative Evaluation Studies and three articles on Issues in Qualitative Evaluation Research.

Part 7(a) begins with an article entitled *A Twenty Year Perspective on Evaluation Study Design*. This article describes experimental, quasi-experimental, survey, and naturalistic evaluation designs for assessing the efficacy of educational programs in field settings. Sources of invalidity affecting these designs are reviewed. Because many educational programs are complex, the use of quasi-experimental designs supplemented by surveys and naturalistic inquiries is recommended. Small, simple quasi-experiments and observational studies can be used to model and replicate program components, illuminating their roles in the more comprehensive program context, and serving to strengthen causal inferences.

The discussion next turns to *Experimental Design*, broadly conceived. Issues in the selection and use of experimental and quasi-experimental designs are discussed further, with a more formal definition of true experiments and an explanation of their advantage with respect to causal inference. The strong internal validity of true experimental designs may come at the cost of lower external validity, which is one reason why the evaluator may turn instead to quasi-experimental designs. Several examples are given of these designs, illustrating the possible threats to validity presented earlier. Methods of assuring adequate statistical power are described, especially in the context of analysis of variance and analysis of covariance. Finally, the importance is emphasized of adequately describing the experimental subjects, the setting, and the treatment.

A third article provides an interesting introduction to *Statistical Analysis in Educational Research*, relating a fictitious account of two teachers formulating and testing hypotheses with the aid of a headmaster who is schooled in statistics. Using concrete examples and a minimum of mathematical formalism, the article explains the basic ideas of experiments, hypothesis testing, the importance of replication, contingency table analysis, correlation, and regression. The discussion then turns to larger, more formal studies, and it is shown that the same principles apply.

From a statistical perspective, education data are hierarchically organized. Students are nested within classrooms, classrooms within schools, and schools within larger educational authorities. This organization gives rise to multilevel data. Special methods for such data are addressed in the next article, on *Multilevel Analysis*. Rapid progress is being made in the development of statistical models and estimation methods for such data, and a number of important papers on this subject have appeared in the past few years. After defining and explaining the problem of multilevel analysis, the article reviews different approaches, beginning with the early idea that the problem was to choose the proper level of analysis for the question posed, and moving to modern approaches for estimating parameters at two or more levels simultaneously. The interpretation of grouping effects, conditions for pooling data, problems in significance testing, advances in model estimation, and other analytical issues are addressed.

The next article in this section offers a thorough treatment of *Regression Analysis*, including simple linear regression, multiple linear regression, polynomial regression, and other models. The assumptions and mathematical basis of these models and of least squares estimation are described. This article also brings analysis of variance into the regression framework, and discusses several more specialized topics.

The series of general design and analysis articles turns next to a discussion of *Triangulation*, which is the bringing to bear of multiple perspectives or data sources to better understand the phenomenon under study. Clearly, triangulation is important to both quantitative and qualitative evaluation research, but it is most closely identified with qualitative methods. Four types of triangulation are distinguished, including multiple data sources, investigators, theories, and research methodologies. These may be combined in "multiple triangulation."

The final article in Part 7(a) continues the theme of multiple data sources with a discussion of *Data Banks and Data Archives*, including the importance and utility of these information resources. The major data banks and archives in the United Kingdom and the United States are described, with specific information on access. Technical problems of documentation, coding, data entry, and file building are also discussed. The data obtained from large-scale evaluation studies are a valuable resource for secondary analysis. Data archiving may substantially increase the benefits from such data-collection efforts beyond their original purposes.

The four articles in Part 7(b), Issues in the Design of Quantitative Evaluation Studies, cover sample design, cross-sectional survey studies, longitudinal research methods, and the measurement of change. The first article, on *Sample Design*, emphasizes the importance of careful sampling in evaluation studies. Probability and non-probability samples are described and illustrated for experimental and survey studies. This article offers an introduction to several issues treated in greater depth in the three subsequent articles.

Evaluators often make use of cross-sectional surveys to collect information on attitudes, attainments, school conditions, or other matters. The article on *Cross-sectional Survey Studies* provides a thorough grounding in this important research method. The article emphasizes the trade-off between cost and precision, and the importance of designing a survey with a specific set of purposes in mind. Methods of population definition are discussed, followed by a consideration of sampling techniques including simple random sampling, stratified sampling, systematic, and multistage sampling. Next, questionnaires and other data collection strategies are briefly discussed. The article then turns to sources of error in surveys, including sampling errors for complex sample designs versus simple random samples. Finally, problems of causal inference are considered, and the article concludes with some examples highlighting the usefulness of cross-sectional surveys.

The article on *Longitudinal Research Methods* complements and extends the treatment of cross-sectional surveys. It begins by citing major longitudinal studies in Europe and the United States, and illustrates the kinds of questions that can only be addressed using data collected at multiple points in time. Alternative designs are presented, including simultaneous cross-sectional studies, trend studies, time series studies, intervention studies, and panel studies. The discussion then turns to various threats to internal and external validity for longitudinal studies, including the high cost of this form of research, and the vicissitudes of research support. The analysis of longitudinal data also poses special challenges, including the measurement of change, which often involves vertical equating of different tests. Growth curve approaches to the measurement of individual change are reviewed, and the article concludes with a description of explanatory and causal analysis for longitudinal data.

The last of the four articles in Part 7(b), entitled *Measuring Change: The Difference Score and Beyond* examines the measurement of individual change. A two-phase strategy is set forth, in which estimation of growth for individuals is followed by the analysis of interindividual differences in growth, which may be related to other variables or individual characteristics. The discussion of measuring individual change begins with the use of difference scores, which provide unbiased estimates of individual growth, but which may be unreliable because two waves of data (e.g., pretest and posttest) are not sufficient for accurate estimation of growth trajectories, and also because high reliability requires both the accurate measurement of individual growth and of variation in the amount of growth by different individuals. Alternative approaches, including estimated true-score gains and residualized gain scores, are also discussed. In the second part of this article, methods for measuring change with multiwave data are described and explained, and a third section of the article provides an overview of recent estimation methods and statistical software.

The three articles that comprise Part 7(c) are primarily concerned with qualitative research methods and address observation techniques, case study methods, and analysis of evidence in humanistic studies. The first of these articles, on *Observation Techniques*, begins by surveying and organizing this broad area. Elements common to these techniques include purpose, operational definition, training of observers, the focus, setting, and unit of time, the schedule of the observations taken, and methods of recording, processing, and analyzing the data collected. Several types of observation systems are described and illustrated, and guidelines are provided for selecting an observation instrument.

Ethnographic, evaluative, and educational *Case Study Methods* are described and discussed in the next article, together with brief treatments of case studies in action research, and teachers as researchers. The article then describes some of the major steps in case study research including negotiating access, carrying out field work, organizing the records obtained, and reporting. The epistemology of ethics of case studies are also addressed.

The final article, on *Analysis of Evidence in Humanistic Studies*, provides an extensive treatment of qualitative inquiry methods. The framework adopted divides a qualitative research study into four interacting stages of design, data collection, data analysis, and summary and integration. The discussion focuses on the third stage of data analysis, especially components of data reduction, matrix display, and conclusion drawing and verification. Detailed, practical advice is given and illustrated by an actual research example where the influence of evaluators' politics and philosophies on the evaluations they undertook and the manner in which they approached them is investigated. The article illustrates a qualitative research design and conceptual framework, and discusses methods of data collection, reduction, and analysis, including matrix display, conclusion drawing and verifying, and tactics for deriving meaning. Finally, methods for confirmation, summary, and integration of findings are presented.

# Basic Principles of Design and Analysis in Evaluation Research

## A Twenty-year Perspective on Evaluation Study Design[1]

### J. Benson and W. B. Michael

It has been more than 20 years since the Elementary and Secondary Education Act (ESEA) was enacted by Congress. The Act provided massive amounts of federal funds for the improvement of education. For the field of evaluation, two important aspects of the Act were that all programs receiving ESEA funds under Titles I and III be evaluated and that a report be forwarded to an agency of the federal government. Many of the personnel in local education agencies were not prepared to evaluate the programs because of a lack of training in program evaluation. Indeed, as the discipline of program evaluation was in its infancy, few educators were trained in its techniques.

In this circumstance, many of the early evaluation designs drew from the experimental designs employed in psychology. As Stufflebeam (1971) pointed out, experimental designs have had substantial utility for evaluating the attainment of goals or objectives of comprehensive ongoing programs involving measurable products (summative or terminal evaluation), but only minor usefulness for evaluating the process components underlying the development and implementation of programs (formative evaluation). It is clear why early evaluation studies failed to detect program effects through using traditional experimental designs that assume a fixed treatment and that focus more on program impact than on program strategies and implementation. Evaluators have learned over the past 20 years that many contextual factors such as social and political forces do influence programs and that true experimental designs are not so useful in detecting and studying these important extraneous factors as are other types of designs (Cronbach 1982 pp. 26–30).

The three major objectives of this article are: (a) to indicate the purposes of evaluation design; (b) to describe four types of designs used most often in program evaluation (experimental, quasi-experimental, survey, and naturalistic); and (c) to identify sources of invalidity in designs that may compromise the accuracy of inferences regarding program effectiveness. Special emphasis is placed upon the use of quasi-experimental designs that are especially appropriate in evaluating the effectiveness of evaluation programs in field settings.

## 1. Purposes of Evaluation Design

The twofold purpose of design in evaluation or research is to provide a framework for planning and conducting a study. In the context of program evaluation, two major components of design include: (a) specification of exactly what information is needed to answer substantive questions regarding the effectiveness of the program; and (b) determination of an optimal strategy or plan through which to obtain descriptive, exploratory, or explanatory information that will permit accurate inferences concerning possible causal relationships between the treatment or treatments employed and observable outcomes. In addition, Cronbach (1982 Chap. 1) has suggested that the design should anticipate the primary audience of the final report concerning program effectiveness such that methods and analyses conform to their level of understanding and informational needs.

## 2. Four Basic Types of Evaluation Design

### 2.1 Overview

The procedures employed to obtain evaluation information have been classified into four design types: (a) experimental; (b) quasi-experimental; (c) survey; and (d) naturalistic. As mentioned previously, early evaluation designs were essentially experimental. It was soon discovered, however, that experimental designs were frequently not flexible enough to encompass all

1 This article was originally published in the *International Journal of Educational Research*, Vol. 11, No. 1. It appears here with permission from Pergamon Press plc © 1987.

aspects of a particular program operating in a field setting. Thus, adaptations of these designs were developed and termed quasi-experimental. In addition, educational programs, which were often new or innovative, were implemented at many sites involving a large number of participants. In these situations, survey designs, which were borrowed from sociology, were used to obtain descriptions of how programs operated as well as information regarding who was affected. More recently, naturalistic studies have been introduced to provide detailed information to decision makers. A variation on the previously cited designs that has received attention in the past (Reichardt and Cook 1979) and that is being revitalized (Cronbach 1982) is to combine quasi-experimental or experimental designs with naturalistic designs in order to evaluate more effectively both the implementation and the impact of the program.

## 3. Experimental Designs

Used to study cause and effect relationships, the true experimental design is considered the most useful one to demonstrate program impact if conditions of randomization in selection of participating units and in the assignment of treatments can be met (Boruch and Wortman 1979). This design is differentiated from others by the fact that the evaluation units have been assigned to the treatment and control conditions at random. Evaluation units can be individuals, groups of individuals, institutions, regions, states, or even nations. The program under evaluation is usually defined as the treatment condition. The control condition may be a traditional, neutral, or placebo treatment or no treatment at all. The key element is that the units to be evaluated have been either randomly selected or assigned at least to one treatment and to one control condition. The study is then implemented, and one or more criterion measures are administered after the treatment (and sometimes before the treatment). Finally, differences between the treated and control groups are compared to determine the relative effectiveness of the competing conditions.

### 3.1 Campbell and Stanley's Three True-experimental Designs

Campbell and Stanley (1966) identified three true experimental designs which they termed: (a) the pretest–posttest control group design (Design 4); (b) the Solomon four-group design (Design 5); and (c) the posttest-only control group design (Design 6). Campbell and Stanley presented a list of threats to the validity of inferences regarding cause and effect that could be formulated from the outcomes arising from use of these three designs as well as of several quasi-experimental ones. As Design 5 is actually a combination of Design 4 and Design 6, these two designs are detailed first.

If $E$ and $C$, respectively, represent experimental and control units, $R$ stands for random selection of units and assignment of treatment (or lack of treatment) to

the units, 01 and 03 constitute pretest, administered to the $E$ and $C$ units, respectively, $X$ portrays the treatment, and 02 and 04 indicate the posttests given to the $E$ and $C$ units, respectively, the paradigm describing Design 4 is as follows:

$$
\begin{array}{lllll}
E & R & 01 & X & 02 \\
C & R & 03 & & 04.
\end{array}
$$

In the instance of Design 6, the pretest is absent so that it will not react with the treatment. If 05 and 06 stand for the posttest taken by participants in the $E$ and $C$ units, respectively, and if all other letters remain the same as for Design 4, the paradigm representing Design 6 is as follows:

$$
\begin{array}{llll}
E & R & X & 05 \\
C & R & & 06.
\end{array}
$$

The composite of Design 4 and Design 6 yields Design 5, one of the most powerful designs available for controlling threats to the validity of a cause and effect inference by ruling out alternative hypotheses of potential causation. It is diagrammed as follows:

$$
\begin{array}{lllll}
E & R & 01 & X & 02 \\
C & R & 03 & & 04 \\
E & R & & X & 05 \\
C & R & & & 06.
\end{array}
$$

It is interesting to note that a $2 \times 2$ table can be established in which one margin indicates absence versus presence of treatment (No $X$ versus $X$) and the other margin indicates omission versus administration of the pretest (No Pretest versus Pretest). As in a factorial design, this table can be used to ascertain whether an interaction effect exists between pretesting and the treatment. The absence of any significant interaction effect between the pretest and treatment in a pilot study would indicate that Design 4 probably could be used quite effectively.

These three experimental designs are characterized by control of most extraneous variables thought to affect the outcomes of a program. In addition to an experimental unit that receives the treatment or intervention experience, a control unit provides a baseline from which to judge the impact of the treatment.

### 3.2 Limitations of the Three True-experimental Designs

Although experimental designs are very powerful, they are often difficult to apply in field studies, as programs (treatments) frequently are implemented differentially at each locale where socio–political factors may interact with the treatment in a way not controllable by the design. When these factors are identified, they are often hard to measure. Evaluating the impact of a program using an experimental design is best employed after the program has been fully implemented and pilot tested. Even then, employing an experimental design in which nearly all extraneous variables except the treatment have been controlled may result in the program being so sterile that it is ungeneralizable. Even with randomization there may be compensatory efforts on the part of members in the control unit or resentment or defeatism that can lead to reduced motivation and effort.

### 3.3 Advantages Inherent in Replication with Small Experimental Studies

Small experimental investigations run on separate aspects of a complex program and constitute practical alternatives to determining the effectiveness of selected aspects of a treatment in diverse settings. Each aspect of the program, if it is multifaceted, can comprise an experimental study. For example, a matrix approach to smaller experimental studies is possible where each layer of the program is evaluated by type of unit or participant. This approach allows one to determine for which type of unit or participant which aspect or aspects of the program are most effective. Saxe and Fine (1979) have illustrated how multiple studies within an evaluation can be designed.

## 4. Quasi-experimental Designs

Because experimental designs have been well documented in the psychological literature, the focus of this presentation is directed toward more recent quasi-experimental designs and naturalistic forms of inquiry. The purpose of a quasi-experimental design is to approximate a true experimental design, typically in field settings where control or manipulation of only some of the relevant variables is possible (Isaac and Michael 1981). The distinguishing feature of the quasi-experimental design is that the evaluation units have not been randomly selected and often have not been randomly assigned to treatment conditions. This situation can occur, for example, in compensatory education programs where all eligible evaluation units are mandated to receive the innovative program. In this case, it is not possible to use randomization, as such a procedure would be highly disruptive to existing units or intact groups. In this situation, many threats to the validity of a causal inference between one or more treatments in several outcomes can be expected to be present. Thus, somewhat less confidence can be placed in the evaluation of findings from the use of quasi-experimental designs than from the employment of true experimental designs. In comparison with the true experimental designs, quasi-experimental ones, however, offer greater flexibility for field settings and sometimes afford greater potential for generalizability of results in realistic day-to-day environments. It is often possible to "patch up" quasi-experimental designs when difficulties begin to occur. For example, a proxy pretest or multiple pretest indicators can be introduced to reduce a potential selection bias or to correct for it.

### 4.1 Two Major Types of Quasi-experimental Design

Campbell and Stanley (1966) and Cook and Campbell (1979) have reported two major types of quasi-experimental procedures: (a) nonequivalent control-group designs; and (b) interrupted time-series designs. Each of these two major methods is broken down into specific sets or subclasses of designs. For the nonequivalent control-group situation, Cook and Campbell (1979) have proposed 11 subdesigns, and for the interrupted time-series paradigm they have offered six subdesigns. Mention should be made of the fact that in a quasi-experimental design the terms *nonequivalent control group* and *comparison group* have been substituted for the term *control group* employed in true experimental designs.

### 4.2 An Illustrative Paradigm for Each of the Two Major Types of Quasi-experimental Design

By far, the most common quasi-experimental design has been what Campbell and Stanley (1966) have termed the nonequivalent control-group design (Design 10) and which Cook and Campbell (1979) have identified as the untreated control-group design with pretest and posttest. This design, which does not involve random selection of participating units, can be represented by the following paradigm, the symbols of which have been previously defined:

$$E \qquad 01 \quad X \quad 02$$
$$\text{-----------------------}$$
$$C \qquad 03 \qquad 04$$

The broken line in the diagram separating the two groups indicates that no formal means such as randomization has been employed to assure the equivalence of the units; in other words, a potential selection bias could exist. In this design, it is assumed, although not always correctly, that the treatment is assigned randomly to one or the other of the two units. The greatest threats to the validity of this design are sources of error—namely, differential selection, differential statistical regression, instrumentation, the interaction of selection with maturation (the presence of differential growth rates in the two units during the treatment period), the interaction of selection and history, the interaction of pretesting with the treatment, and the interaction of selection (group differences) with the treatment.

Within the context of the interrupted time-series design, one of the most promising ones is that of the multiple time-series design described by Campbell and Stanley (1966) as Design 14 and by Cook and Campbell (1979) as the interrupted time-series with a non-equivalent no-treatment control group time-series. This design is quite similar to the previous one except for the fact that several pretest and several posttest measures are present. This design may be diagrammed as follows:

$$E\ 0\ 0\ 0...0\ X\ 0\ 0\ 0...0$$
$$\text{-----------------------}$$
$$C\ 0\ 0\ 0...0 \qquad 0\ 0\ 0...0$$

This particular design affords the advantage of establishing fairly reliable baseline data in the pretest observations and of indicating through several posttests sustained effects of the treatment. Such a design can be quite useful in evaluating the long-term effects of psychotherapy or various forms of educational intervention. A plot of the regression lines (often broken) of the 0 measures for *E* and *C* units against a sequence of time points corresponding to each of the 0 symbols may reveal that after the application of the treatment a substantial separation between regression lines exists if the treatment has been effective. The main threats to the validity of the design would be history, instrumentation if it immediately follows the treatment, the interaction of the testing at various periods with the treatment, and the interaction of selection (dissimiliarity in the groups) with the treatment.

### 4.3 Ex Post-facto Design

A form of quasi-experimental design that is frequently employed but not recommended has been the ex post facto one assigned by Campbell and Stanley (1966) the name of static-group comparison and classified by them as Design 3. In this design, data have been obtained for a treatment and comparison group after the treatment has occurred. For example, an evaluator might wish to determine the benefits of a college education by comparing competencies of a group of college graduates with a group of noncollege graduates in the same community. Frequently, efforts are made to match the groups after the treatment variable has occurred. This design may be diagrammed as follows:

```
E    X    02
- - - - - - - - - -
C         04
```

The static-group comparison procedure contains virtually every possible threat to the validity of any inference regarding a causal relationship between the treatment and an outcome. At best, the method might hold some promise for exploratory research or initial hypothesis formulation.

### 4.4 Changing Conditions in a Field Setting

Research in field settings typically involves a changing or evolving program (treatment). Thus, quasi-experimental designs need to be flexible and adaptable to the situation. The program may have been developed with the view that modifications will be introduced progressively as feedback from intermediate evaluations becomes available. In another situation the program may change because of contextual forces such as social or political pressures arising in conjunction with preliminary outcomes. In any event the design needs to be fluid, not static, to provide an appropriate framework for conducting an ongoing evaluation during the formative stages of program development as well as a summative evaluation of program impact.

### 4.5 Suggestions for Selecting a Comparison Group in the Absence of Randomization

Wolf (1984) has provided several useful suggestions for selecting a comparison group when randomization is not possible. First, one might be able to use a cohort from a previous or later year that was not affected by a change in the population or environment from one year to the next. A limitation is that data necessary for the evaluation may not have been recorded for the cohort group of interest.

A second approach is to utilize a neighboring institution as a comparison group. Two advantages are that program imitation is not so likely to take place as in the instance of an institution located in a foreign setting and that data gathering can occur concurrently in both groups. A disadvantage is that the groups may not be comparable on all dimensions. Moreover, the comparison unit may choose to withdraw at a critical data gathering time if appropriate incentives are not built into the study.

A third strategy is that when a standardized instrument is used, norm group data reported in the technical manual can be utilized for comparison purposes. This procedure can be quite risky, however, as the norm group may not be similar to the one being evaluated. In many evaluation situations, the purpose of a program is to aid some extreme group either advantaged or disadvantaged. The subjects in these extreme groups often are not well represented (if they are represented at all) in most norm samples.

### 4.6 Replication of Evaluation Studies

Wolf (1984 p. 147) has pointed out that replication studies can improve the validity of quasi-experimental designs. Using different cohorts to study program impact would eliminate the difficulty imposed by carryover effects (positive or negative transfer effects) often encountered in counter-balanced experimental designs involving cognitive processes. Building replications into designs allows programs to be studied over longer periods of time and thus enhances the probability that any potential effect of a program can be detected. The concept of using replications in quasi-experimental studies is similar to that found in carrying out multiple small-scale experimental investigations discussed earlier, in that multiple studies conducted at various levels or layers of a program represent separate replications. Thus, both approaches can strengthen the extent to which the effectiveness of treatments can be generalized (Saxe and Fine 1979).

## 5. Survey Designs

Survey designs were developed to afford an efficient method of collecting descriptive data regarding: (a) the characteristics of existing populations; (b) current practices, conditions, or needs; and (c) preliminary information for generating research questions (Isaac and Michael 1981 p. 46). Surveys are frequently used in sociology, political science, business, and education to gather systematically factual information necessary for policy decisions.

Survey designs proceed first by identifying the population of interest. Next, the objectives are clarified and a questionnaire (structured or unstructured) is developed and field tested. A relevant sample is selected, and the questionnaire is administered to its members by mail or telephone or in person. The results are then tabulated in a descriptive fashion (i.e., as in reporting means, frequencies, percentages, or cross-tabulations). Because the nature of the survey is basically descriptive, inferential statistics are usually not appropriate for summarizing the data obtained from the survey design. In addition, survey data often are used in subsequent ex post facto designs discussed previously.

Documentation regarding the response rate also is an important consideration in survey studies. Although survey designs afford an efficient and relatively inexpensive method of gathering data among large populations, the response rate is considered a severe limitation. If the rate is low, the data may not provide representative and accurate indicators of the perceptions of a population. Formulas have been developed to determine the minimum proportion of respondents required to be confident that the sample provides a relevant and accurate representation of the population (Aiken, 1981).

Questionnaires used in survey designs can be developed to measure status variables (what exists) as well as constructs (hypothesized concepts) related to attitudes, beliefs, or opinions. When constructs are measured by a survey some evidence of their validity must be addressed. A questionnaire may be highly structured or loosely structured as in a personal interview. Details on constructing questionnaires along with the advantages and disadvantages can be found in Ary et al. (1985) and in Isaac and Michael (1981).

Survey designs have been criticized on the grounds that an attempt to standardize the questionnaire for all respondents may result in items that often are too superficial in the coverage of complex issues. In addition, survey designs frequently miss contextual issues that lead to a respondent's marking a particular alternative. To overcome these limitations, case studies or naturalistic designs have been adopted to be more responsive to the varied informational needs of decision makers.

## 6. Naturalistic Designs

A major criticism of the three previous design strategies discussed up to this point is their failure to capture the context in which programs operate. In field settings, it is crucial to understand a contextual situation surrounding the program to be evaluated. The context, which includes types of participants, locales, and different occasions, can interact with the program in unique ways.

Thus, a thorough understanding and documentation of the context in which the program is to function is usually as necessary as the product or outcome information obtained at the conclusion of the program. During the last 20 years, evaluators have become aware that social and political forces can do as much to shape and to alter program effects as can the program itself.

Several educators and evaluators have advocated that ethnographic or naturalistic designs be adopted for use in educational research and evaluations (Lincoln and Guba 1985, Patton 1980). These designs grew out of the need to study phenomena as they naturally occur in the field. Naturalistic designs draw heavily from the ethnographic techniques of anthropologists. The goal of a naturalistic/ethnographic study is to understand the phenomena being observed. Naturalistic designs, like ethnographies, imply a methodological approach with specific procedures, techniques, and methods of analysis. Lincoln and Guba (1985) have described naturalistic inquiry as a major paradigm shift in research orientations. They have illustrated how the naturalistic paradigm differs from the positivist paradigm in five areas (axioms): (a) there are multiple realities; (b) it is impossible to separate the researcher from that being researched; (c) only hypotheses about individual realities are possible; (d) it is impossible to separate cause and effect relationships because of their simultaneous interaction; and (e) inquiring is value-bound. Thus, naturalistic designs differ on several basic points from positivist designs (experimental, quasi-experimental, or survey). The subjectivity that the researcher/evaluator brings to a study is openly confronted in naturalistic designs.

Naturalistic designs provide in-depth investigations of individuals, groups, or institutions as they naturally occur. A major feature of this design has been the use of a human instrument (the observer) to collect, filter, and organize the incoming data. Naturalistic inquiry differs from surveys and experimental/quasi-experimental designs in that usually a relatively small number of units is studied over a relatively large number of variables and conditions (Isaac and Michael 1981). In the past, naturalistic approaches were thought to be useful as background information in planning an evaluation, in monitoring program implementation, or in giving meaning to statistical data. Lincoln and Guba (1985) and Skrtic (1985) have suggested that naturalistic methodologies are more than supportive designs for the more quantitatively oriented evaluation and research investigations. In fact, these writers have maintained that naturalistic inquiry affords a sufficient methodology to be the only one used in an evaluation study.

In establishing naturalistic designs as a different methodological approach unto itself, Lincoln and Guba (1985 Chap. 9) have developed guidelines for conducting a naturalistic study. The basic design differs from the positivist perspective in that it evolves during the course of the study; it is not established prior to the study. Some elements of the design, however, can and must be prespecified such as: (a) establishing the focus of the study; (b) determining the site(s) of data collection and instrumentation; (c) planning successive phases of the study; and (d) establishing the trustworthiness of the data. The concept of trustworthiness is similar to what Campbell and Stanley (1966) have termed validity. Guba (1981) proposed a different terminology under the general heading trustworthiness that he has perceived is more nearly appropriate for naturalistic designs. A meaningful naturalistic study should have *credibility* (internal validity), *transferability* (external validity), *dependability* (reliability), and *confirmability* (objectivity). Lincoln and Guba (1985) have suggested several techniques for implementing (Chap. 10) and for establishing the trustworthiness of the study (Chap. 11).

To date, there have been relatively few published investigations employing true ethnographic or naturalistic designs in educational evaluations. In one such study, Skrtic (1985) reported on the implementation of *The Education for All Handicapped Children Act* in rural school districts. This study is important for three reasons. First, it represents the first national, multisite evaluation using the naturalistic inquiry methods espoused by Lincoln and Guba (1985). Second, it takes a design strategy thought to be useful in studying a few evaluation units in-depth and extends it to a national study where many evaluation units are investigated exhaustively. Third, some of the difficulties in employing naturalistic methods are discussed from the standpoint of both practical field problems and the more theoretical issues of establishing the trustworthiness of

the data. This latter aspect is critical for making naturalistic designs more useful and acceptable to the practicing evaluator than are alternative design strategies. Until this methodology is tested further, its utility as a descriptive or explanatory technique should be used very cautiously.

## 7. Sources of Invalidity for Experimental and Quasi-experimental Designs

### 7.1 Contributions of Campbell and Stanley

The landmark work by Campbell and Stanley (1966) in identifying threats to the accuracy of causal inferences between treatments and outcomes in experimental and quasi-experimental designs alerted researchers in the social and behavioral sciences to two major areas of concern regarding the validity of their designs. The focus of their work was on the internal and external validity of experimental and quasi-experimental designs. Internal validity refers to the confidence one has that the findings in a given study or experiment are attributable to the treatment alone. Internal validity is strengthened when rival hypotheses that might account for an observed relationship between treatment and outcome can be eliminated from consideration. External validity refers to the generalizability of the findings to other populations, settings, and occasions. Thus internal validity issues are concerned with whether a cause and effect relationship exists between the independent and dependent studied, whereas external val-

*Table 1*
Threats to the Validity of Designs*

| Threats | Features |
| --- | --- |
| (1) Statistical conclusion validity | Was the study sensitive enough to detect whether the variables covary? |
| (a) Low statistical power | Type II error increases when alpha is set low and sample is small; also refers to some statistical tests. |
| (b) Violated statistical assumptions | All assumptions must be known and tested when necessary. |
| (c) Error rate | Increases, unless adjustments are made with the number of mean differences possible to test on multiple dependent variables. |
| (d) Reliability of measures | Low reliability indicates high standard errors which can be a problem with various inferential statistics. |
| (e) Reliability of treatment implementation | Treatments need to be implemented in the same way from person to person, site to site, and across time. |
| (f) Random irrelevancies in setting | Environmental effects which may cause or interact with treatment effects. |
| (g) Random heterogeneity of respondents | Certain characteristics in subjects may be correlated with dependent variables. |
| (2) Internal validity | Was the study sensitive enough to detect a causal relationship? |
| (a) History | Event external to treatment which may affect dependent variable. |
| (b) Maturation | Biological and psychological changes in subjects which will affect their responses. |

*Table 1*
Threats to the Validity of Designs* (*continued*)

| Threats | Features |
|---|---|
| (c) Testing | Effects of pretest may alter responses on posttest regardless of treatment. |
| (d) Instrumentation | Changes in instrumentation, raters, or observers (calibration difficulties). |
| (e) Statistical regression | Extreme scores tend to move to middle on posttesting regardless of treatment. |
| (f) Selection | Differences in subjects prior to treatment. |
| (g) Mortality | Differential loss of subjects during study. |
| (h) Interaction of selection with maturation, history, and testing | Some other characteristic of subjects is mistaken for treatment effect on posttesting; differential effects in selection factors. |
| (i) Ambiguity about direction of causality | In studies conducted at one point in time, problem of inferring the direction of causality. |
| (j) Diffusion/imitation of treatments | Treatment group members share the conditions of their treatment with each other or attempt to copy the treatment. |
| (k) Compensatory equalization of treatments | It is decided that everyone in experimental or comparison group receive the treatment that provides desirable goods and services. |
| (l) Demoralization of respondents | Members of group not receiving treatment perceive they are inferior and give up. |
| (3) Construct validity of cause and effects | Which theoretical or latent variables are actually being studied? |
| (a) Inadequate explication of constructs | Poor definition of constructs. |
| (b) Mono-operation bias | Measurement of single dependent variable. |
| (c) Mono-method bias | Measurement of dependent variable in only one way. |
| (d) Hypothesis-guessing | Subjects try to guess researchers' hypothesis and act in a way that they think the researcher wants them to act. |
| (e) Evaluation apprehension | Faking well to make results look good. |
| (f) Experimenter expectancies | Experimenters may bias study by their expectations when entering into study and during study. |
| (g) Confounding constructs and levels of constructs | All levels of a construct are not fully implemented along a continuum, they may appear to be weak or nonexistent. |
| (h) Interaction of different treatments | Subjects are a part of other treatments rather than of an intended one. |
| (i) Interaction of testing and treatment | Testing may facilitate or inhibit treatment influences. |
| (j) Restricted generalizability | The extent to which a construct can be generalized from one study to another. |
| (4) External validity | Can the cause and effect noted in the study be generalized across individuals, settings, and occasions? |
| (a) Interaction of selection and treatment | Ability to generalize the treatment to persons beyond the group studied. |
| (b) Interaction of setting and treatment | Ability to generalize the treatment to settings beyond the one studied. |
| (c) Interaction of history and treatment | Ability to generalize the treatment to other times (past and future) beyond the one studied. |

* Adapted from Cook and Campbell, 1979.
1 = evaluation methods

idity issues are concerned with the extent to which observed cause and effect relationships can be generalized from one study to another reflecting different types of persons in varied settings across numerous occasions. Designs are sought that will minimize the influence of extraneous factors that might confound the effect of the treatment.

### 7.2 Extensions by Campbell and Cook

More recently, Cook and Campbell (1979) have extended the work on the validity of designs to include two additional areas of concern as well as to refine and extend the original internal and external validity categories. In dealing with internal validity issues, a researcher is first interested in determining whether certain independent and dependent variables demonstrate a quantitative relationship. Because the basis of a relationship depends upon statistical evidence, the term *statistical conclusion validity* was introduced. Once a relationship is established between certain variables, it is then of interest to determine whether the relationship is causal. Ascertaining whether a causal relationship exists between a measure of a treatment (the *independent variable*) and an outcome (the *dependent variable*) is the central issue of *internal validity*. The researcher needs to be able to demonstrate that the causality between the variables is a function of some manipulation, not a function of chance or of one or more extraneous variables. Once a relationship has been identified between the independent and dependent variables in association with a possible causal hypothesis on the basis of eliminating several rival alternative hypotheses, the researcher needs to be fairly certain that the theoretical (latent) constructs that represent the observed (manifest) variables are correct. Cook and Campbell (1979) have called this step the establishment of the *construct validity of causes or effects*. They have pointed out that the mere labeling of operationally defined observed variables is not sufficient to establish the link to a theoretical construct. Verifying construct validity is a highly complex process. Once the observed variables representing a cause and effect relationship have been determined not to be limited to a particular or specific operational definition but can be extended to a more generalized abstract term, construct validity has been established. Then, it is of interest to ascertain to what other persons, settings, and occasions the causal relationship can be extended. This latter issue is one of *external validity*.

These four areas of validity are not grounded in theory so much as they are centered around the practical issues an evaluator or researcher must address in eliminating rival hypotheses and factors that may interfere with the particular hypotheses and variables of interest. The separate areas addressed under each of the four forms of validity were developed from the practical experiences of Cook and Campbell (1979) and their colleagues in developing and implementing various designs in field settings. The four forms of validity and the separate areas covered under each have been summarized in Table 1.

For the three true experimental designs, the two quasi-experimental designs, and the ex post facto design described earlier, threats to their validity were cited. Additional information regarding what is meant by the kinds of threats to internal and external validity previously mentioned for these designs is set forth in the second column of Table 1.

### 7.3 Need for Smaller Studies in Diverse Settings

It is obvious that all possible threats under each of the four categories of validity cannot be controlled in any one study and that a single study would not be sufficient to determine cause and effect relationships associated with the impact of an educational program. This argument suggests the need for smaller and more carefully controlled studies to be conducted in the evaluation of instructional programs.

A second argument for smaller more controlled studies has been the general finding that programs instituted in the social and behavioral sciences tend to have only a small to moderate impact. This situation stems from the fact that programs, which are often complex, are implemented differentially in various settings and are influenced by a host of political and social contexts.

Given these constraints, smaller studies aimed at eliminating bias (internal validity concerns) and random error (statistical conclusion validity concerns) appear imperative, especially with new or innovative educational programs. Once a program has been field tested and has been found to have a probable effect, controlled studies are needed to determine what constructs are operating in the cause and effect network (construct validity regarding cause and effect concerns) and to ascertain in what settings, for which populations, and over what occasions (external validity concerns) the observed and theoretical relationships apply.

### 7.4 Objections to Validity Distinctions

Objections to validity distinctions offered by Cook and Campbell (1979 p. 85) have been raised. For example, why should issues of internal validity have superiority over those of external validity? For that matter, why should any one form of validity have priority over another? These questions can be answered only by the researcher for a given research–evaluation situation. For the case in which information is needed to aid a policy decision, perhaps issues of external validity should supercede those of internal validity. Cronbach (1982) has made this point very convincingly. However, in the case in which a new innovative program is developed, the outcome of interest is whether the program is effective. In this situation, internal validity should take priority over external validity concerns. Finally, there could be a situation in which information on both the effectiveness of an educational program and assistance with a policy decision is the expected outcome. In this case, multiple studies aimed at controlling as many threats in all four validity areas should be designed and initiated.

It is apparent that the meaningful conduct of evaluation studies concerning the effectiveness of educational programs in field settings requires substantial modifications in the true experimental designs employed in psychology. Use of quasi-experimental designs in combination with surveys and naturalistic inquiry affords an opportunity to replicate in simple studies selected aspects of a complex program. An information base can be acquired to permit a generalized inference of promising causal connections between treatments and observable changes in program outcomes for participating units in diverse settings.

## Bibliography

Aiken L R 1981 Proportion of returns in survey research. *Educ. Psychol. Meas.* 41: 1033–38

Ary D, Jacobs L C, Razavieh A 1985 *Introduction to Research in Education*, 3rd edn. Holt, New York

Boruch R F, Wortman P M 1979 Implications of education evaluation for evaluation policy. In: Berliner D C (ed.) *Review of Research in Education*, Vol. 7. American Educational Research Association, Washington, DC, pp. 309–61

Campbell D T, Stanley J C 1966 *Experimental and Quasi-experimental Designs for Research*. Rand McNally, Chicago

Cook T D, Campbell D T 1979 *Quasi-experimentation: Design and Analysis Issues for Field Settings.* Rand McNally, Chicago, Illinois

Cronbach L J 1982 *Designing Evaluations of Educational and Social Programs.* Jossey-Bass, San Francisco

Guba E G 1981 Criteria for assessing the trustworthiness of naturalistic inquiries. *Educ. Commun. Technol. J.* 29: 75–91

Isaac S, Michael W B 1981 *Handbook in Research and Evaluation*, 2nd edn. EDITS, San Diego, California

Lincoln Y S, Guba E G 1985 *Naturalistic Inquiry.* Sage, Beverly Hills, California

Patton M Q 1980 *Qualitative Evaluation Methods.* Sage, Beverly Hills, California

Reichardt C, Cook T 1979 Beyond qualitative versus quantitative methods. In: Cook T, Reichardt C (eds.) 1979 *Qualitative and Quantitative Methods in Evaluation Research.* Research Progress Series in Evaluation, Vol. 1, Sage, Beverly Hills, California, pp. 7–32

Saxe L, Fine M 1979 Expanding our view of control groups in evaluations: In: Datta L, Perloff R (eds.) *Improving Evaluations.* Sage, Beverly Hills, California, pp. 61–69

Skrtic T 1985 Doing naturalistic research into educational organizations. In: Lincoln Y S (ed.) 1985 *Organizational Theory and Inquiry: The Paradigm Revolution.* Sage, Beverly Hills, California, pp. 185–220

Stufflebeam D L 1971 The use of experimental design in educational evaluation. *J. Educ. Meas.* 8: 267–74

Wolf R M 1984 *Evaluation in Education: Foundations of Competency Assessment and Program Review*, 2nd edn. Praeger, New York

# Experimental Design

## R. Tate

Experimental design attempts to ensure valid causal inferences from randomized experiments conducted within practical constraints of available resources and time. This design process must first consider whether an experiment is, in fact, feasible. If so, the design process continues and attempts are made to anticipate possible threats to the validity of conclusions and to eliminate or minimize those threats. It should be noted that there is another, more narrow, methodological literature often labeled "experimental design" which is concerned with the associated statistical design and analysis. Important concepts in this statistical literature are included as one component in the broader framework considered here with respect to experimental design.

## 1. The Experiment

A "true" or randomized experiment is defined as an inquiry in which experimental units have been randomly assigned to different experimental treatments. A sense of the versatility of the experiment is offered by consideration of each of the elements in this definition. An "inquiry" might be a research study to improve theoretical understanding or an evaluation seeking a pragmatic comparison of different instructional programs. Such inquiries can be conducted either in laboratory settings or in real "field" settings. The experimental "unit" is usually the focus of the inquiry. Thus, in studies of variables influencing the behavior and achievement of individual students, the unit would be the student, while the class would be the appropriate unit in studies of class-level variables on average class outcomes. In other words, an experiment can be used to understand phenomena at any level of the educational hierarchy. The experimental "treatments" may be different levels of a single theoretical construct or variable, for example "degree of structure in instruction," or they may be several instructional programs which differ on many dimensions. Often, one of the treatments is a "control" treatment, that is, a group with no implemented treatment at all. Finally, the random assignment of subjects ("subjects" will be used for "units" hereafter for concreteness) to treatments will result in experimental groups associated with each of the treatments.

An experiment can also be defined as an inquiry in which there are one or more active treatment variables or factors. An active variable is one which has been manipulated in the inquiry, where "manipulation" consists of the random assignment of subjects to different levels of the variable. This definition illustrates that a study may have more than one treatment variable, each variable having multiple treatment levels. For example, an investigator may wish to consider simultaneously the variable "degree of structure" having the three levels of low, medium, and high structure and a second variable "feedback to student" with two levels of "daily feedback" and "no feedback." The subjects would be randomly assigned to each of the resulting six treatment combinations of low structure/daily feedback, and so on. The simultaneous consideration of multiple treatment variables allows the identification and description of interactions between the variables.

The goal of an experiment is causal inference. "Causation," in this context, is defined in a commonsense fashion; if a treatment variable is manipulated or changed while holding constant all other possible determinants of the outcome of interest, and there is a subsequent change in the outcome, then it is said that there is a causal relationship between the manipulated variable and the outcome. There is no implication that the manipulated variable is the only cause of the outcome, only that it is one of probably many causes. It should be noted that use of the concept of causation is sometimes challenged, with some arguing that the concept is "prescientific." There should be little difficulty, however, with the relatively narrow definition used here, a definition which is compatible with utilitarian inquiry seeking understanding of those variables which can be manipulated in the attempt to improve society.

Typical outcomes or dependent variables of interest in educational inquiry which focuses on the individual student include academic achievement, attitudes, traits, self-perceptions, and job performance. The analysis of outcome data for individuals almost always describes the treatment effect on the central tendency (often the mean) of the outcome; it is also usually of interest to determine any effects on the variability and the shape of the distribution of the outcome variable. When the unit is some aggregate like the class or the school, the investigator will be interested in within-aggregate characteristics like the mean or variability of an individual-level outcome or the correlation between several variables within each class or school. The study of the aggregates may also consider various global outcomes like measures of group or organizational harmony and efficiency.

The experiment, when it is feasible, is a particularly efficacious mode of inquiry for causal inference. This is due to the random assignment of subjects to treatments. Generally, outcome differences across different treatment groups can be the result of two factors—differences in the attributes of the subjects in the different groups and the differential effects of the various treatments. Random assignment creates treatment groups which are initially comparable (in a probabilistic sense) on all subject attributes; it can then be concluded in an experiment that any final outcome differences are due

to the treatment effects alone, assuming that other possible threats to validity to be discussed below have been controlled.

## 2. Threats to Validity

The design of an experiment should ensure adequate validity or truthfulness of conclusions. Cook and Campbell (1979), restructuring somewhat the classical discussion of Campbell and Stanley (1963), have identified four different validities which may be pertinent. These are associated with different aspects of the general experimental goal of concluding that a causal relationship between treatment and outcome constructs does or does not exist in specified populations of units, settings, and times. This conclusion will typically be based on the observed relationship between experimental operationalizations of the constructs of interest for a sample of units, settings, and times. The different validities, then, refer to the following component questions leading to the general conclusion (validity type given in parentheses): (a) Does an empirical relationship between the operationalized variables exist in the population (statistical conclusion validity)? (b) If the relationship exists, is it causal (internal validity)? (c) Can the relationship between the operationalized variables be generalized to the treatment and outcome constructs of interest? (construct validity of cause and effect)? (d) Can the sample relationship be generalized to or across the populations of units, settings, and times of interest (external validity)?

Design can be viewed, in part, as the process of anticipating different possible threats to the validity of conclusions and seeking study procedures which will eliminate or minimize those threats. Some of the many common threats which have been discussed in detail by Campbell and Stanley (1963), Cook and Campbell (1979), and others will now be briefly considered.

### 2.1 Statistical Conclusion Validity

The statistical conclusion about the presence or absence of a relationship in the population is often based on statistical hypothesis testing. Statistical conclusion validity results, then, from the use of the appropriate test procedure with acceptable error probabilities. The probability of a false rejection of the null hypothesis of no relationship in the population, that is, the significance level, must be set before the test is conducted, with values of 0.01 or 0.05 usually being considered acceptable. A second error probability is the probability of failing to reject the null hypothesis when it is false. Alternatively, the power of the test defined as the probability of correctly rejecting a false null hypothesis can be considered. For a given significance level and effect size (i.e., strength of relationship), it is possible to determine the sample size required to produce an acceptable power.

The "fail to reject" decision from a test can sometimes be taken further. If the test has adequate power (say 0.90) for the "threshold" effect size defining an effect of practical importance, then a "fail to reject" outcome results in confidence that a practically important relationship does not exist in the population. That is, adequate power allows a decision to "accept," for all practical purposes, the null hypothesis.

Inadequate power is one of the most common threats to statistical conclusion validity when the researcher wishes to be able to detect an effect of practical importance. If the power for the threshold effect size is low, then it is, of course, incorrect to interpret "fail to reject" as implying there is no relationship of practical importance. There are many possible reasons for low power; these reasons and some approaches for ensuring adequate power are discussed in Sect. 4. Another threat is the use of an inappropriate statistical procedure. For example, if important assumptions of the procedure being used are violated by the study data, then the actual error rates may be different from the nominal rates set for the study. Statistical analysis procedures will be discussed briefly in Sect. 5.

### 2.2 Internal Validity

The threats to validity of a conclusion that final outcome differences in a study are due to the treatment effect would consist of any other reasonable explanations for the outcome differences. For example, as indicated in Sect. 1, the primary purpose of random assignment of subjects to treatments is to control the "selection" threat to internal validity, that is, the threat that final outcome differences may simply reflect initial group attribute differences. Randomization also controls some other threats to internal validity. First, once the selection threat is controlled, then a series of threats based on interaction with selection are also controlled. For example, different maturation rates for initially different groups (i.e., the selection × maturation interaction) are not a threat in an experiment. Also, since initial selection is not based on a prescore (e.g., to create "highs" and "lows"), statistical regression to the mean is not a problem.

Cook and Campbell (1979) point out, however, that random assignment may often aggravate other threats to internal validity. Treatment-related attrition and atypical behavior on the part of subjects are two threats which are often due to the differences in desirability typically found across different treatments in an experiment. Subject attrition which is related to the treatment variable may mean the initially comparable groups are no longer comparable at the end of the study; the resulting group attribute differences then represent an alternative explanation for any final outcome differences. Atypical behavior might include either "compensatory rivalry" (the "underdog" trying harder) or "resentful demoralization" on the part of subjects in the less desirable treatments or control groups.

### 2.3 Construct Validity of Causes and Effects

It is important that the treatment and outcome constructs of interest are adequately fitted by the oper-

ational manipulations and measures actually used. Construct validity is questioned when there is a "possibility that the operations which are meant to represent a particular cause or effect construct can be construed in terms of more than one construct" (Cook and Campbell 1979 p. 59). Consider a possible study of the effect of "degree of structure" which randomly assigns students to different treatments based on varying structure. If other instructional variables, such as amount of time devoted to helping individuals or amount of diagnostic testing, are also inadvertently varied across the treatments, there will be a question about the "real" reason for any final outcome differences. Threats to construct validity would consist of any reasons for an operation either underrepresenting all of the aspects of a construct or overrepresenting a construct by including irrelevant aspects. For example, since it can be argued that a construct is seldom precisely represented by a single operation, a "mono-operation bias" may result unless multiple operations are used to define both treatment and outcome.

### 2.4 External Validity

External validity refers to the validity of the generalization of study results to explicit or implicit target populations of subjects, settings, and times. The validity of such generalizations depends, of course, on the degree to which the samples of persons, settings, and times used in the study are representative of the populations of interest. Formal random sampling procedures (e.g., simple random, stratified random, and cluster sampling) and the associated statistical inferential procedures are available and, if used, allow precise statements about the probability of any degree of nonrepresentativeness due to chance.

For many research and evaluation studies, however, the assessment of external validity is not so formal and precise (e.g., Bracht and Glass 1968). Often, sampling is not directly from the ultimate target population of interest, but rather from some subpopulation which is accessible to the investigator. This distinction between accessible and target populations means that external validity must then be concerned with the validity of two inferential leaps, one from the sample to the accessible population, and the other from the accessible population to the target population. If the sample is the result of a formal random sampling procedure, then precise statements can be made about the validity of the first inferential leap. Sample size is a critical factor here, as with statistical conclusion validity, with larger sample sizes resulting in an increased confidence in sample representativeness. The validity of the second inference, generalizing from the accessible population to the target population, also depends on representativeness. However, this is not ensured by the use of a formal sampling procedure, but must be demonstrated by adequate similarity between the two populations on all characteristics which might be important contextual variables for the relationship of interest.

A judgment of external validity is also required when a researcher wishes to generalize across different populations or subpopulations. For example, a goal may be to demonstrate that a certain treatment effect is found in both boys and girls and across several grade levels. Of course, such a generalization also implies the researcher must be able to generalize separately to each of the individual subpopulations.

External validity is threatened when there is a combination of two factors: (a) a question about representativeness of the sample, and (b) a possibility of interaction between treatment and subjects, settings, or times. The first factor is present when representativeness has not been ensured through use of an appropriate sampling procedure and/or demonstrated through empirical comparisons. The second factor, interaction, refers to the possibility that the effect of a treatment may vary across the different persons, settings, and times comprising the target population. Thus, any treatment effect found in some ill-defined portion of the target population may not be the same as the effect of interest in the total population. Since in most cases, adequate theory or empirical evidence which convincingly argues against such interaction does not exist, a serious question about representativeness is all that is needed to conclude that external validity has not been demonstrated.

## 3. The Decision to Use an Experiment

The decision concerning which mode of inquiry to use for a planned causal study involves three questions: (a) Which of the available modes of inquiry, including the experimental, are feasible? (b) What can be achieved with each of the feasible modes under the constraints of allowed resources and time? (c) Which mode is best for the purposes of the inquiry? Consider, first, two of the possible alternative approaches for a quantitative causal inquiry. One alternative is a quasi-experimental approach (Cook and Campbell 1979) in which there is a treatment intervention but no assumption of random assignment of subjects to treatments. One variation of this approach is the "nonequivalent group" design in which treatments are introduced to existing groups. Another variation is the "interrupted time series" design involving assessment of a treatment effect with a series of measures before and after introduction of the treatment. Second, when there is no treatment intervention, that is, in correlational or natural-setting studies, path analysis allows an investigator to determine whether a hypothesized causal model is consistent with observed empirical correlations.

The question of the feasibility of an experiment for the planned inquiry depends in large part on the feasibility of random assignment of the subjects to different treatments. First, many individual attribute variables such as sex, race, age, IQ, personality traits, and so on cannot be experimentally manipulated. Researchers in sociology of education, for example, are often interested

in the effects of individual and family attributes, and must use techniques like path analysis in their search for causal models. Also, high levels of variables like pain, fear, and stress could not be included in experiments for obvious ethical reasons, and controversial programs concerning, say, sex education or training in political protest, may not be allowed in some communities for political reasons. Thus, the experiment is not, by definition, an option when manipulation of the treatment variable is not technically, ethically, or politically feasible.

Another aspect of feasibility is whether it is possible in practice to obtain permission to randomly assign subjects. In laboratory settings, this is usually not difficult, since only the agreement of each volunteer subject is necessary, and volunteers understand before the experiment that assignment to different treatments will be involved. In field settings, however, the same task is often much more difficult. When it is desired to study individuals, such as students or teachers, in their "everyday" work or study environment, it is necessary to obtain permission from both administrative "gatekeepers" of the environment of interest and the subjects themselves. Gatekeepers may often be reluctant to grant such permission because of their concern about possible inconvenience and disruption of work, or their doubts about the value of the treatments being studied. If the gatekeepers do perceive a proposed treatment as being valuable, they may object to the random assignment of some teachers and students to control groups or less desirable treatments. Finally, even if the gatekeepers do permit access to the teachers and students, the potential subjects themselves may choose not to participate for the same reasons given above.

An experiment, if feasible, is usually superior to the alternatives for controlling certain critical threats to internal validity (i.e., the validity of causal inference). This is, of course, an important consideration when conducting a causal inquiry. Random assignment in an experiment does not guarantee correct causal conclusions, but it usually does result in fewer assumptions being required for a causal inference. For example, "selection" is a critical threat for the nonequivalent group design because of the use of intact groups. The investigator must therefore attempt to explicitly model all of the important group differences to allow the necessary statistical adjustments, and there is usually some question about the assumption that the causal modeling is appropriate. Selection (or, in causal modeling terminology, misspecification) is also a serious threat to causal inferences from path analysis in correlational studies. "History" is a potential threat in the interrupted time series design, and it is necessary to assume (with adequate empirical support) that the introduction of the treatment did not coincide with some other event which could have been the real reason for change in the outcome. Both of these threats, selection and history, are controlled by the random assignment in an experiment.

The degree of intervention associated with the different modes of inquiry ranges from the strong intervention of the experiment to the weak or nonexistent intervention in a correlational study. This variation may have important implications. There may be situations, especially in field settings, where overt intervention may distort or change the setting and the behavior of subjects from those of interest (as with, for example, the resentful demoralization or compensatory rivalry mentioned in Sect. 2). Also, since a greater degree of intervention may often take more time to plan and implement and may therefore cost more, the choice of inquiry mode may be partially constrained by available resources and time. Thus, it may be said that the experiment is superior for causal inquiry, other things being equal, but of course the "other things" in the qualification are often not equal.

Since the difficulty of obtaining permission for random assignment often depends on the setting, it is perhaps best to consider the laboratory versus field decision simultaneously with the inquiry mode decision. The dominant factor in selecting the setting is often external validity. If (a) the target setting for the inquiry is a real field setting, (b) the setting is viewed as important in influencing the phenomena of interest, and (c) it is not feasible to design a laboratory setting to adequately simulate the field setting, then a field setting is clearly needed for acceptable external validity. For example, the basic premise in research on "contextual effects" in the school setting is that context is an important determinant of individual teacher or student behavior; such research would thus usually require field research in school settings. On the other hand, many instructional treatments are designed for efficiently teaching specific topics to small groups of students and often might best be studied in laboratory settings.

The laboratory versus field decision also has other implications. For example, the greater control of irrelevant factors which is allowed in the laboratory setting would provide, for the same sample size, greater statistical power than would be found in the relatively "noisy" field setting, thus improving statistical conclusion validity. The tighter control on the implementation of treatments in the laboratory would also contribute to construct validity. Finally, the arrangement for and implementation of studies in field settings, especially when there are multiple widespread sites, will often be more time consuming and costly than a laboratory study.

The interaction of the laboratory versus field decision with the inquiry mode decision can be illustrated with a situation where both the laboratory and the field settings may be viable options for an inquiry. Depending on the circumstances, the choice may be difficult. Assume, for example, the gatekeepers for the field setting of interest will allow a treatment intervention but not random assignment. The investigator is then faced with the choice between a laboratory experiment or a field quasi-experiment. Some of the factors involved

in such a choice would include the extent to which the laboratory setting simulates the target setting, the comparability of intact groups available in the field setting, the potential for systematic attrition and atypical behavior in each of the settings, the resources and time required to conduct the inquiry in each setting, and the relative importance of the different validities for the study.

In summary, there is no suggestion here that an experimental approach, assuming it is feasible, should always be used. Rather, the choice of the optimal approach should involve an estimation of the validities of conclusions which could be obtained under each of the feasible alternatives. The different inquiry modes and settings typically offer different strengths and weaknesses, and the final choice will be the setting/mode combination which best fits the purpose of the inquiry.

## 4. Design of the Experiment

The "decision to use an experiment" and the "design of the experiment" may at first appear to be two separate steps in the conduct of an inquiry. As indicated in the previous section, however, the choice of a mode of inquiry implies at least a partial design for each of several approaches to predict the relative strengths and weaknesses of each. The current section, then, is concerned with the continuation and refinement of the design process already underway, assuming that an experiment is to be used.

Design is concerned with anticipating and eliminating or minimizing important threats to validity within the constraints of available resources and time. It is not possible here to discuss design considerations associated with all of the many possible validity threats, but the process can be illustrated with several of the more common design concerns. First, different approaches to ensuring adequate statistical power will be discussed. Relatively more space is devoted to this topic, not because it is logically more important than other topics, but because it has proven to be more amenable to quantification and elaboration and has been considered extensively in the literature. Next, the internal validity threat of treatment-related attrition of subjects will be discussed. Finally, the importance of detailed descriptive information for validity will be emphasized.

### 4.1 Power

Consider a simple experiment with two treatments. The treatment effect size is defined here as the difference in the outcome means for the two populations associated with the treatments. As indicated in Sect. 2, the investigator can define a threshold value of the effect size which represents a difference of practical or scientific importance. Once the level of significance is specified, there are two remaining parameters which influence the power of the hypothesis test (in this case, a t-test) to detect an effect equal to the threshold value. One is the sample size, $n$; an increase in $n$, other things being equal, results in an increase in power. The second is the error variability, often represented with the standard error of estimate. For the simple two-group t-test, this is just the estimated standard deviation of the outcome variable, Y, for each of the two populations. It can also be understood by reference to the analysis model which underlies the test of interest, a model which expresses Y as a function of one or more independent variables. (The model for the t-test consists simply of a single "dummy" variable representing the active treatment variable.) The error variability, then, is the variability of Y which is not explained by the independent variables in the model. Since error variability can also be viewed as background noise in which the treatment effect is embedded, increasing error variability makes it more difficult to detect the effect, that is, it decreases the power.

The most direct route to ensuring adequate power for a test is simply to determine and use the sample size required for a power of, say, 0.90 to detect the threshold effect size. This is easily accomplished with available tables (e.g., Cohen 1977) and adequate resources. An estimate of the anticipated size of the standard error of estimate is required, but otherwise the determination is straightforward. Unfortunately, the required sample size for an analysis model consisting of just the active treatment variable(s) can often be larger than study resources will allow. Also, even if the required $n$ would be allowed by the study budget, most investigators would still be interested in improving the efficiency of the inquiry to achieve the same power with smaller $n$ and less cost.

The key to improving the efficiency of a test lies in the control of and reduction of the error variability. There are two general approaches to this goal. Consider, first, the different contributors to error for an analysis model containing just the active treatment variables. The error variability is due to measurement error in Y, the inherent variability associated with the target populations of subjects and settings, and variability due to extraneous study factors such as undesired variation in treatment implementation or the occurrence of atypical events during the study. Two obvious ways to improve efficiency, then, would be to improve the reliability of the Y measure and to minimize extraneous factors operating in the study. Also, the investigator may choose to use subject and/or setting subpopulations which are more homogeneous than the target populations. The increase in power associated with this last approach, however, would be accompanied by a threat to external validity of the study.

The second basic approach to error reduction attacks the problem of population heterogeneity, not by using a more homogeneous subpopulation, but by expanding the analysis model to include one or more attribute variables which are related to the outcome variable. The addition of such "control" variables to the model already containing the active treatment variables will result in an increase of the Y variability which is explained by the model and a corresponding decrease in the unexplained or error variability. Randomized block designs and analysis of covariance (ANCOVA) designs are two main variations on this theme which have been developed in the experimental statistical design literature (e.g., Kirk 1968, Myers 1979, Neter and Wasserman 1974, Winer 1971).

The randomized block design can be illustrated with a simple experiment involving one active treatment variable with $k$ levels. If there is large variability of ability in the population of students of interest and a strong relationship between Y and ability, then the investigator may elect to block on ability. The sample of students would be ranked on ability and grouped into homogeneous blocks of size $k$ based on this ranking. Then, the $k$ students in each block would be randomly assigned, one to each of the $k$ treatment levels. Randomization within the blocks is often referred to as a restriction in randomization. The associated analysis model consists of two independent variables, the treatment variable and the categorical blocking variable, with the addition of the blocking variable resulting in the desired reduction in error variability.

A blocking variable is most effective when subjects within blocks are very homogeneous and there is great heterogeneity between blocks. Since the blocking variable is a categorical variable, it can be formed in many different ways. In addition to using a ranking on a single interval variable (as in the example above), blocks can also be created by combining several interval, ordinal, or nominal variables. Another way to create blocks is to expose each subject to each of the $k$ treatments, considering each individual subject to be a block. This repeated measures design may be said to permit each subject to "act as his/her own control," and can provide very efficient tests; it should only be used, however, when there is confidence that there is no "carry-over" effect from treatment to treatment.

Analysis of covariance is similar to a randomized block design in that it reduces error variability and increases power by adding one or more control variables (called covariates or concomitant variables) to the analysis model. It is also different, however, in several important aspects. Analysis of covariance does not involve any initial restriction on randomization like that in randomized block designs. That is, subjects are randomly assigned to the different treatment levels without regard to covariate values. Also, ANCOVA assumes the covariate is an interval rather than categorical variable; thus, it is necessary to properly specify the functional nature of the relationship between Y and the covariate (i.e., whether it is linear or nonlinear). It is assumed that the covariates are measured before implementation of the treatments or, if not, that they have not been affected by the treatments. In addition to increasing power, ANCOVA also allows an adjustment of outcome differences to compensate for any initial group differences resulting from the random assignment.

When a potential control variable is an interval variable, the investigator may chose to use it either as a covariate or to create a blocking variable. Since (a) analogous randomized block and ANCOVA designs provide roughly the same power for typical Y–control variable correlations, (b) both designs in their classical form have similar assumptions (e.g., that there is no interaction between the treatment and control variables), and (c) both can be modified to handle violations of these assumptions (see Sect. 5), it makes little difference for these considerations which design is used. One possible basis for a choice between the two would lie in the assumed measurement level of the control variable. If the investigator does not wish to be concerned about the nature of the functional relationship between the outcome and control variables, the randomized block design would be chosen. On the other hand, use of an ANCOVA will allow an explicit description of the Y–covariate relationship, a description which may be of interest in its own right when nonlinear relationships are discovered. A second basis of choice is that the decision to use the randomized block design must be made before the start of the study because of the required restriction in randomization. In contrast, the decision to use an ANCOVA can be made at any time during or after the study, as long as appropriate covariate measures are available.

In summary, there are many approaches to the improvement of the power of a test. The goal usually is to provide acceptable power for detecting the threshold effect size. However, it should be noted that even when this goal cannot be realized because of limited resources and a small sample size, continuation of the inquiry is still legitimate as long as the limitations are recognized. In this situation, the investigator is gambling that the real effect size is sufficiently greater than the threshold value so that there is a good chance of detecting it. Also, it must be recognized that the "fail to reject" conclusion in this case offers little information about whether an effect of practical importance really exists.

Finally, the above discussion assumes that hypothesis testing is the inferential mode being used to make decisions about the presence or absence of a relationship in the population. Interval estimation can also be used with (or instead of) hypothesis testing to describe the treatment effects. All of the above discussion also applies to interval estimation, except the criterion is, instead of adequate power, the desired maximum width of the confidence intervals on treatment contrasts.

### 4.2 Treatment-related Attrition

Even when initial comparability of treatment groups has been achieved through random assignment, the presence of treatment-related attrition of the subjects can result in groups which are no longer comparable at the end of the study, a nonequivalence which may be the real reason for any outcome differences. One important facet of the attack on this problem is the avoidance of any unnecessary burden, inconvenience,

or frustration for subjects which may result in their leaving the study. For example, efforts to work within the schedule of each subject or to provide necessary transportation may pay off in reduced attrition. It is more difficult to avoid differences in the desirability of different treatments in a study, differences which are probably the major reason for treatment-related attrition. This may be especially true for control groups which do not have the benefit of any treatment at all. One possible way to improve the retention of subjects in control groups and less desirable treatment groups is to promise that these subjects may have the superior treatment at some later date.

When some attrition does occur in a study, it is important to gather the necessary information to determine if it is related to the treatments. Thus, each subject leaving the study could be asked, in a nonthreatening way, for the reason. Also, the extent to which attrition is treatment-related can be described quantitatively. The attrition rate and various subject attribute variables can be tested as a function of the treatment variable during and at the end of the study.

The investigator should plan a back-up analysis when there is a possibility that treatment-related attrition will occur. The logical backup for an experiment consists of the various analyses associated with the nonequivalent group design for quasi-experimental inquiry. Since these analyses depend on adequate quantitative modeling of the ways in which the groups differ, the investigator anticipating attrition should always attempt to collect relevant subject attribute data before the study starts. Even if there is some question about the precise nature of final group differences in the presence of treatment-related attrition, it is still sometimes possible to draw conclusions if the general direction of those differences is known. Consider, for example, a simple treatment group versus control group comparison; if (a) it is clear that there has been systematic attrition and that the final control group is generally more able and motivated than the treatment group, and (b) the mean achievement for the treatment group is still higher than that for the control group, then there is little question about the superiority of the treatment group even though the exact degree of superiority cannot be determined.

### 4.3 Description for Validity

Detailed descriptions of subjects, treatments, and settings are a critical element in establishing the validity of conclusions from a study. The description of subject attributes provides a basis for establishing external validity, making covariate adjustments to improve power, determining if any attrition is treatment related, and conducting quasi-experimental analyses if necessary. Detailed description of each treatment as implemented is important for construct validity. It is of little value to know precisely the size of a treatment effect without knowing precisely what treatment was responsible for the effect. And, of course, it is not uncommon for a treatment as implemented to be very different from the treatment as planned. Description of the setting is valuable for external validity, with pertinent aspects including physical dimensions such as lighting and noise level and organizational characteristics like school discipline policy and grading procedures. Finally, the interaction of subjects with the treatments should be described in the search for unanticipated treatment effects. Such process description will also often provide important clues when the treatments are not working as expected.

In summary, the design of an experiment may include the considerations briefly discussed here plus many others. Design is further complicated by the possibility that attempts to minimize one threat to validity may simultaneously aggravate another threat. For example, the use of extensive observation and measurement to provide the detailed description suggested above may, because of associated distraction of the subjects, drastically alter the setting from the one of interest. Clearly, the optimal design of an inquiry can be a complex and subjective task, a process not easily represented by mechanical formulas or guidelines.

## 5. Statistical Analysis of Data

The appropriate analysis model for an experiment can often be found in the traditional analysis of variance (ANOVA) and analysis of covariance (ANCOVA) literature (e.g., Kirk 1968, Myers 1979, Winer 1971). There are many models and associated considerations of potential interest; only some can be mentioned here. For example, completely randomized ANOVA models like one-way ANOVA (for a single treatment variable) or a $k$-way factorial design (for $k$ treatment variables) may be used when it is not necessary to include control variables. When control variables are required to ensure adequate power, many variations of the randomized block design and ANCOVA are available. Block designs may include multiple blocking variables, and when the numbers of treatment variables and levels increase, there are incomplete block and fractional replication designs which provide efficient tests with blocks of reasonable size. ANCOVA models can also be elaborated by including multiple treatment variables and multiple covariates.

The simplicity of computations for these models will depend on the pattern of cell sizes in the design. All fixed effects ANOVA and ANCOVA models are special cases of the general linear model (e.g., Neter and Wasserman 1974). In general, it is not feasible to compute general linear model results by hand. However, the computational procedure simplifies drastically for ANOVA designs with only one factor or factorial designs with equal or unequal but proportional cell sizes, producing the simple computational equations found in standard ANOVA texts. On the other hand, when a factorial ANOVA/ANCOVA design has unequal and disproportionate cell sizes, the factors of the resulting "nonorthogonal" design are correlated, and the general

computerized procedure for the linear model must be used for an exact solution.

It is not uncommon to find that the assumptions associated with standard analyses are violated for the study data at hand. Fortunately, there is evidence that significance tests are relatively robust to the violation of some assumptions. For example, moderate violations of the homogeneity of variance and normality assumptions in the presence of approximately equal cell sizes can usually be tolerated. In contrast, other violations may be more critical, requiring adjustments or use of a different analysis technique. Thus, drastic violations of the homogeneity and normality assumptions may require the consideration of transformations of the outcome variable or the use of an alternative analysis like generalized least squares or a nonparametric procedure. As another example, there may be evidence of the existence of an interaction between a treatment variable and a control variable, a violation of an important assumption in both the standard randomized block design with a cell size of one and the ANCOVA design. Interaction terms must then be added to the analysis model, using either a generalized randomized block design with cell size larger than one or a general linear model representation of ANCOVA. It should be noted that this last model no longer produces an ANCOVA in the conventional sense, but is identical to the aptitude–treatment–interaction (ATI) model mentioned briefly below. It may also be found in ANCOVA that the relationship between Y and the covariate is nonlinear, another violation of the standard analysis. Again, a general linear model with added polynomial terms would allow adequate fit of the model to study data.

There are some designs of interest in educational research and evaluation which are not fitted precisely by standard ANOVA/ANCOVA models. For example, ATI research attempts to identify and describe interactions between active instructional treatment variables and student aptitudes. An ATI analysis model would typically consist of a categorical treatment variable, one or more interval aptitude variables, and the necessary interaction terms. Another nonstandard design is one with interval treatment variables such as amount of study time allowed in class or the number of homework problems required. A general linear model with any required polynomial or interaction variables would allow the estimation of a multidimensional "response surface" describing the treatment effects.

Finally, there are sometimes multiple outcomes of interest in a study. Often, the investigator will simply conduct multiple analyses, one for each of the outcome variables. If the number of outcomes is relatively large, however, the investigator will be confronted with an inflation of error rate due to the many tests and a cumbersome and complex description based on numerous results. In this situation, the multivariate general linear model (e.g., Timm 1975) may be used. Multivariate global hypotheses and simultaneous inference procedures provide the necessary control of error rates and confidence levels, while the associated generalized discriminant analysis may provide a more parsimonious description of the effect in terms of derived optimal variates.

## Bibliography

Bracht G, Glass G 1968 The external validity of experiments. *Am. Educ. Res. J.* 5: 437–74

Campbell D T, Stanley J C 1963 *Experimental and Quasi-experimental Designs for Research.* Rand McNally, Chicago, Illinois

Cohen J 1977 *Statistical Power Analysis for the Behavioral Sciences*, rev. edn. Academic Press, New York

Cook T D, Campbell D T 1979 *Quasi-experimentation: Design and Analysis Issues for Field Settings.* Rand McNally, Chicago, Illinois

Kerlinger F N 1973 *Foundations of Behavioral Research,* 2nd. edn. Holt, Rinehart, and Winston, New York

Kirk R E 1968 *Experimental Design: Procedures for the Behavioral Sciences.* Brooks/Cole, Belmont, California

Myers J L 1979 *Fundamentals of Experimental Design,* 3rd edn. Allyn and Bacon, Boston, Massachusetts

Neter J, Wasserman W 1974 *Applied Linear Statistical Models: Regression, Analysis of Variance, and Experimental Designs.* Irwin, Homewood, Illinois

Phillips D C 1981 Toward an evaluation of the experiment in educational contexts. *Educ. Res. AERA* 10: 13–20

Timm N H 1975 *Multivariate Analysis with Applications in Education and Psychology.* Brooks/Cole, Monterey, California

Winer B 1971 *Statistical Principles in Experimental Design.* McGraw-Hill, New York

# Statistical Analysis in Educational Research

## G. F. Peaker

This article is a fictitious account of the happenings in a school in which two teachers became interested in improving their teaching and the work of the school and sought to check whether the things that they did were effective in increasing the learning of their students. Fortunately, the headmaster of the school had taken a degree in mathematics, and had read courses in statistics, in the days before the ready availability of calculators and computers and was well-able to give advice on some of the statistical issues that were raised. In this account the methods and procedures of elementary statistics are considered in a way in which the principles of statistics are advanced for consideration and the calculations are reduced to a minimum in an attempt to make clear the statistical principles involved. The statistical principles which are commonly applied in educational research are presented in a form that, hopefully, persons who like the two teachers in the article have not undertaken courses in statistics or educational research methods, can follow and understand.

## 1. Experiments

Miss Brown, who taught one of two parallel classes in the school, had given a good deal of thought to improving the presentation of part of the curriculum through the use of some visual aids that she had devised. The headmaster was mildly impressed, but being old enough to have lived through many tides of fashion, said that he would like some cogent evidence that the new method was really an improvement. Miss Green who took the other parallel class, was more doubtful, but was willing to take part in an experiment to see whether the claims for the new method had solid support. They agreed that, during a trial period of six weeks, Miss Brown would use the new method with her class while Miss Green covered the same field with her class in the customary way. At the end of the period the progress made in the field by the two classes would be assessed, and the results compared. But how could they be compared, and what sort of result would be convincing? They turned to the headmaster for advice.

The headmaster pointed out to Miss Green and Miss Brown that the existence of the two parallel classes was a fortunate circumstance, because an implication of the word "parallel" used in this sense was that if the numbers in the two classes were equal every Brown child could be a matched pair with a Green child of roughly the same ability and general standing. Consequently in the assessment of progress it would be possible to compare each of these pairs so that, at any rate roughly, like could be compared with like. But what if the numbers were not equal? What if Miss Brown had two more children than Miss Green? In that case two children in the middle of Miss Brown's class could be left out of the pairing, without bias to the results.

The headmaster went on to explain that if at the end of the agreed period the assessment was made, and that it turned out that in 19 of the 30 pairs the Brown child had made more progress, that in 9 cases, the Green child had done so, and that there were two ties, this would be 19 to 9. What were they to conclude? Was this result evidence of real superiority on the part of the Brown method, or was it a chance result that could easily be reversed on another occasion?

Some light on this could be gained by considering a case where they had no doubt that chance was at work. The tossing of coins would provide such a case. If they tossed 30 coins repeatedly in a box the average number of heads would fluctuate round 15, drawing closer to it as the number of times the box was shaken increased. This is a very easy, though rather noisy, experiment to make, and sceptical readers must perform it for themselves. They will find, if they persist, that on about two occasions in three the score does not depart from 15 all by more than three, and that on about 19 occasions out of 20 it does not depart by more than six. The general rule is that the odds are about 19 to 1 against a departure by more than the square root of the number of coins, and about 2 to 1 against the departure by more than half this number.

The headmaster continued to explain to Miss Green and Miss Brown that if they ignored the ties, they would have a departure of five from the even balance of 14 each. The square root of 28 is 5.3, so that the departure would be almost equal to the square root, and they would have therefore rather strong evidence that something more than chance had been at work. If they had 24 to 4 instead of 19 to 9 the departure would have been practically double the square root, and the evidence would have been very strong indeed. The headmaster explained that this was perhaps the simplest instance of the general rule that a result would be convincing to the extent that it exceeded its own standard error, a term used to describe the variability of a measure over repeated sampling. In this case the standard error was half the square root of the number of matched pairs, and the departure from the even balance was about double this amount. The odds against this being a chance result were about 19 to 1. The odds against a chance departure of three or more standard errors would be very large indeed.

The headmaster now suggested that if the circumstances were such that each child could be given a reliable test the experiment would be more sensitive. When they had merely said that the Brown child had done better than the Green, or vice versa, they were ignoring the question of how much better? And it was plainly possible that if they could assess this it might tip the balance more, or less, towards Miss Brown. Before long Miss Green and Miss Brown had agreed to develop an appropriate test and give it to both their classes at the end of the experimental period of six weeks, but

they wondered whether they could analyse the results without buying a calculator and learning how to use it.

The headmaster explained to them that they could do all the calculations necessary on the chalkboard, if they used some simple statistical techniques. It was perhaps fortunate that in each of their classrooms there were 30 desks arranged in five rows and six columns and at the beginning of the school year the students had been assigned to their seats in an alphabetical order. Of course, if the students had not been arranged in seats in this way, or had not been seated in alphabetical order, they could still have proceeded to analyse the test scores they had collected by using procedures that would have the same effect. However, in this case, because the students had been randomly assigned to their seats the procedures suggested were sound. If each student in Miss Green's class was matched with a student in Miss Brown's class according to where they sat in the classroom, and if for each pair of matched students the score for a Green student was subtracted from the score for a Brown student, the results could be set out on the chalkboard as shown in Table 1.

In Table 1, the 30 differences have been set out in six columns and five rows. Altogether the 30 pairs have given Miss Brown's class a total superiority of 56 or an average superiority of 1.87 per pair. To see how convincing this result would be, it must be compared with its standard error. This can be found by looking at the row of ranges at the foot of the table. The range is the difference between the highest and the lowest entry in each column. To find the standard deviation, or scale, of the differences, it is necessary to divide the average range by the range factor for groups of five, which is 2.33. The total of the six ranges is 53, and dividing 53 by six times 2.33 gives 3.8 as the standard deviation or scale. To obtain the standard error, the scale 3.8 is divided by the square root of the number of pairs, which is 30 in this case, producing 0.69. So the average superiority of the Brown method is given by the average

**Table 1**
Results of experiment for matched pairs of students. Scores recorded are Brown student minus Green student

| Classroom rows | | Classroom columns | | | | | | |
| --- | --- | --- | --- | --- | --- | --- | --- | --- |
| | | A | B | C | D | E | F | Total |
| Scores | 1 | 2 | −2 | 8 | 4 | −1 | −3 | 8 |
| | 2 | −3 | 4 | 10 | 10 | −5 | 0 | 16 |
| | 3 | 6 | 2 | 2 | 2 | −1 | 1 | 12 |
| | 4 | 5 | 4 | −1 | −1 | 4 | 4 | 15 |
| | 5 | 2 | −1 | 0 | 2 | 1 | 1 | 5 |
| Total | | 12 | 7 | 19 | 17 | −2 | 3 | 56 |
| Average | | 2.4 | 1.4 | 3.8 | 3.4 | −0.4 | 0.6 | 11.2 |
| Positive entries | | 4 | 3 | 3 | 4 | 2 | 3 | 19 |
| Negative entries | | 1 | 2 | 1 | 1 | 3 | 1 | 9 |
| Range in column | | 9 | 6 | 11 | 11 | 9 | 7 | 53 |

score plus or minus the standard error: $1.87 \pm 0.69$. The estimate is 2.7 times its standard error. This is stronger than the evidence from merely counting the signs, as would be expected, since more information has been used (Hartley 1950, David 1951).

The headmaster explained that although this use of the range was not included in many statistical textbooks, provided the items were in a random order the standard deviation, or scale, could always be obtained with enough accuracy, and the minimum of arithmetic, by the use of ranges. The range factors—that is, the factors by which the average range should be divided to give the standard deviation—are 2.04, 2.33, and 2.53 for batches of four, five, and six respectively. For larger batches the method would be less accurate, but could be used to give a check on the usual working by summing squares. The factor is 3.09 for batches of 10, and roughly four, five, and six in batches of 25, 100, and 500, and the procedures described are the basis for analysis of variance.

## 2. Replication of Experiments

The headmaster then explained, with some hesitation, that the apparent superiority of the new method could have nothing to do with the method as such, but might merely represent the fact that Miss Brown could be a better teacher than Miss Green, in the enthusiasm of her new discovery. And might it not be the case that the parallelism of the classes was to some extent a delusion, and the matching very imperfect? These were substantial objections, but they had to be considered before any very firm conclusions could be reached. They amounted to saying that one small experiment could not by itself be very convincing. The answer was replication—that is the repetition of the experiment, preferably under different conditions. To secure the most appropriate variation of the conditions was the object of experimental design. While more could be said about this, it must be noted that any replication was better than none, and that progress need not be delayed because the circumstances were not propitious for a good experimental design.

The advantage of replication can be seen by looking at the columns in Table 1. No single column by itself was particularly convincing. Apart from the fact that one of them (E) gave the palm to Green and not to Brown it would be quite easy to get four heads in five tosses of a coin. But when the six columns were aggregated the evidence was seen to be stronger. In the same way the evidence might be greatly strengthened by a sixfold repetition of the experiment. Or of course, it might be wiped out. Consequently, if three or four other schools could be found who were willing to try the experiment there was a better prospect of reaching firm conclusions. The prospect would be enhanced if the schools differed widely in their circumstances. Common sense suggests, and large-scale surveys have confirmed, that a child's school achievement must be affected by a very large number of varying circumstances, which are called variables for short. By comparing matched groups in the same school it has been possible to get rid of interschool variation, since only one school has been involved. This could be seen to be both a strength and a weakness. It would strengthen the evidence for that school, but it provided weak grounds for generalizing to the other schools. If there was a plan to bring in more schools, should these be as like the first school as possible, or as unlike?

There were arguments on both sides. If the evidence from the first school was rather weak it would perhaps be better to try the experiment again in other schools that were like it, in the hope of getting stronger evidence for this kind of school. If the first evidence was rather strong there would be grounds for thinking that it should not be repeated in other schools of the same kind, and in this case it would be better to widen the range of reference and generalization by seeking rather different schools for the replication. In practice, of course, the question could be settled by the fact that there were only three or four schools that were in communication with the first and willing to repeat the experiment. It would be a mistake to reject the proffered assistance of these volunteers in the hope of getting a better experimental design. But if there were a choice the strength of the initial evidence would be a useful guide in making it.

Matching the children had done something to reduce the clouding variation within each school, and matching the teachers would do more. The headmaster explained that the clouding variation was the variation in the factors that were left out of account, and therefore tended to blur the results of the experiment. But the matching of teachers could only occur through good fortune, since the organization of the school could hardly be upset to produce it. Here there was a real clash between what was desirable as a matter of school policy and what was desirable for experimental design. Teachers were more likely to work effectively with methods they believed in. On the other hand if the better teachers were all on one side then the apparently greater success of a new method might merely be evidence of this, and not evidence that the new method was intrinsically better than the old. Another insidious possibility was what is known (from the name of the works where it was first noted) as the Hawthorne effect. Merely taking part in an experiment tended to increase the zeal of those concerned. This had a well-known parallel in medicine, where patients given placebos and patients given treatment alike made better progress than those who were left untreated. The fact that experiments generated enthusiasm was itself a strong argument in their favour, even if nothing else were gained. Holidays do people good, even though after the holiday they return to their starting point.

Some light could be obtained by considering whether there were marked differences in the results from different schools taking part, and if so whether these could be linked with known circumstances. But what would be considered as marked differences? As in the case of the single school the thing to look at is the standard error. The results above showed that the average superiority of the Brown method came out at $1.87 \pm 0.69$. Since standard errors could be added by Pythagoras' theorem, the standard error of a difference would be the root mean square of the standard errors of the items. If the standard error were the same in a second school the standard error of the difference would be 0.98, so that differences would not be remarkable until they exceeded two. If there were several schools in the experiment, it would be possible to look at the range instead of at the separate differences.

With four, six, and ten schools the critical factors were 3.6, 4.0, and 4.5. That is, if with four schools the difference between the highest and the lowest Brown superiority exceeded 3.6 times the average standard error it would be useful to look for something to account for this, which it would not be with a smaller range. If the range were not excessive it might be concluded that the new method was successful to about the same extent in all the schools, and that this would make it rather improbable that its apparent superiority was illusory and really reflected only differences between teachers.

## 3. Repeated Surveys and Contingency Tables

The next time Miss Green and Miss Brown met with the headmaster to discuss the experiment that Miss Brown had planned to undertake, Miss Green suggested that the major factor that influenced the performance of the students in her class appeared to be parental attitudes towards encouraging higher school achievement. As a consequence she argued there was more to be gained from persuading parents to adopt more encouraging attitudes than from undertaking the proposed experiment. Miss Brown, however, suggested that common sense and general experience would seem to indicate that a higher level of performance at school would produce more favourable parental attitudes and to her the effect that Miss Green had proposed would appear to operate in the opposite direction. Under these circumstances it was more desirable for her to undertake the proposed experiment and in this way raise the level of achievement of the students in her class, and as a consequence improve the attitudes of the parents towards their children's schooling and towards the school. The headmaster saw quickly that it was necessary for him to explain some of the problems that were likely to arise when data were collected in a nonexperimental study, and since data were not available, he made up some data so that they could together discuss what might happen if at the beginning of the year they set out to measure not only student achievement for all students in the school but also to assess parental attitudes. Of course it was clear that to throw some light on this perplexing question it would be necessary to carry out a repeated study for all students in the school

*Table 2*

Results of surveys of parental attitudes and school achievement

|  |  | Second survey | | | | |
| --- | --- | --- | --- | --- | --- | --- |
|  |  | ++ | +− | −+ | −− | Total |
| First | ++ | 170 | 5 | 4 | 1 | 180 |
| survey | +− | 58 | 11 | 2 | 3 | 74 |
|  | −+ | 3 | 2 | 10 | 42 | 57 |
|  | −− | 1 | 4 | 3 | 172 | 180 |
| Total |  | 232 | 22 | 19 | 218 | 491 |

Numbers changing:
Steadies—363, Crossers—122, Double crossers—6

12 months later. Without the repeated study there would be no chance of teasing out whether parental encouragement had led to higher achievement or whether higher achievement had influenced parental attitudes.

The results that the headmaster used in their discussion of this problem are recorded in Table 2. In the table the first sign ($+$ or $-$) relates to parental attitudes and the second sign to student achievement. A positive sign is associated with an encouraging attitude, or an above average level of achievement, and a negative sign a neutral or negative attitude and an average or below average level of achievement. The rows are associated with the first survey and the columns are associated with the second survey carried out a year later. There were data for both occasions for 491 of the 521 students in the school. By adding the entries on the leading diagonal in the table the number of students for whom there had been no changes in sign would be obtained. There were 363 such students who could be described as "steadies". By adding together the entries on the other diagonal, it can be seen that there were six cases in which both parental attitudes and achievement had changed signs. Thus there were six "double-crossers". From the addition of the entries in the eight remaining cells of the table it can be noted that there were 122 cases where one sign had changed. These students have been referred to as the "crossers". The information contained in Table 2 could be seen more readily if the table were rewritten with the entries in the diagonals removed as in Table 3.

The rows and the columns have been labelled as convergent or divergent according to whether the crossing brings parent and child closer together or further apart. There were 106 cases of convergence and only 16 cases of divergence. Furthermore, there were 100 $(58 + 42)$ cases where the child followed the parent and only 6 $(3 + 3)$ cases where the parent followed the child. Thus, the headmaster explained, if these numbers had been obtained there would be strong prima facie evidence in favour of the view that it was the attitudes that produced the achievement rather than vice-versa. If the figures in the table were reversed, a strong case would

**Table 3**
Crossers in the results of survey

| | | Second survey | | | | Total | Category |
|---|---|---|---|---|---|---|---|
| | | ++ | +− | −+ | −− | | |
| First survey | ++ | | 5 | 4 | | 9 | Divergent |
| | +− | 58 | | | 3 | 61 | Convergent |
| | −+ | 3 | | | 42 | 45 | Convergent |
| | −− | | 4 | 3 | | 7 | Divergent |
| Total | | 61 | 9 | 7 | 45 | 122 | |
| Category | | Convergent | Divergent | Divergent | Convergent | | |

exist for a reversal of the interpretation, while if the number of divergent cases was very large neither interpretation would suffice. However, it would be necessary to count the number of divergent cases, if only to be satisfied that the number was small.

## 4. Correlation

The headmaster explained that for the purposes of simplification, a comparison had been made with both attitudes and achievement reduced to variables with two values only. It would, however, have been preferable to use data in which attitudes and achievement had been assessed along an interval scale. If the data had been in interval form it would have been necessary to use correlation coefficients. But the statistical principles associated with the use of correlation coefficients could be well-illustrated by using data assessed in two nominal categories (+ or −) instead of being measured along an interval scale. With two categories, the tetrachoric correlation coefficient could be employed to express the relationship between the two variables.

In Table 2 the data in the right hand column giving the totals for the categories used in the first survey could be set out in a two-by-two contingency table as shown on the left-hand side of Table 4. Likewise the totals for the categories used in the second survey, obtained from the final row of Table 2 could also be set out in a two-

by-two contingency table, as shown on the right-hand side of Table 4.

From the two halves of Table 4, a tetrachoric correlation coefficient can be obtained. The calculation of the tetrachoric correlation is complex, but tables and an ABAC are readily available which permit the values to be read off very quickly. For the first survey the correlation is 0.67 and for the second 0.96.

The headmaster went on to show that four other correlation coefficients could be derived from Table 2:

(a) Parents in the first survey with parents in the second survey = 0.99.

(b) Children in the first survey with children in the second survey = 0.75.

(c) Parents in the first survey with children in the second survey = 0.98.

(d) Parents in the second survey with children in the first survey = 0.67.

The contingency tables used for the calculations of these correlation coefficients have been recorded in Table 5. They were obtained by combining the appropriate rows and columns in Table 2.

If the correlation coefficients were all collected together and set out in a table as in Table 6, the patterns amongst the correlations would become clearer and would reveal the relationships that were argued to exist from Table 2.

**Table 4**
Contingency tables for results of first and second surveys

| First survey | | Parent | | Totals | Second survey | | Parent | | Totals |
|---|---|---|---|---|---|---|---|---|---|
| | | + | − | | | | + | − | |
| Child | + | 180 | 57 | 237 | Child | + | 232 | 19 | 251 |
| | − | 74 | 180 | 254 | | − | 22 | 218 | 240 |
| Totals | | 254 | 237 | 491 | Totals | | 254 | 237 | 491 |

**Table 5**
Combined tables for calculation of tetrachoric correlation coefficients

| | | Parent second survey ($P_2$) | | | | | Child second survey ($C_2$) | | |
|---|---|---|---|---|---|---|---|---|---|
| $r = 0.99$ | | + | − | Total | $r = 0.75$ | | + | − | Total |
| Parents first ($P_1$) survey | + | 244 | 10 | 254 | Child first ($C_1$) survey | + | 187 | 50 | 237 |
| | − | 10 | 227 | 237 | | − | 64 | 190 | 254 |
| Total | | 254 | 237 | 491 | Total | | 251 | 240 | 491 |
| | | Child second survey ($C_2$) | | | | | Parent second survey ($P_2$) | | |
| $r = 0.98$ | | + | − | Total | $r = 0.67$ | | + | − | Total |
| Parent first ($P_1$) survey | + | 234 | 20 | 254 | Child first ($C_1$) survey | + | 180 | 57 | 237 |
| | − | 17 | 220 | 237 | | − | 74 | 180 | 254 |
| Total | | 251 | 240 | 491 | Total | | 254 | 237 | 491 |

The headmaster then explained that the following conclusions could be drawn from Table 6.

(a) Correlation $P_1 P_2$ (0.99) is greater than correlation $C_1 C_2$ (0.75), that is, children shift more than their parents.

(b) Correlation $P_2 C_2$ (0.96) is greater than correlation $P_1 C_1$ (0.67), that is, the shift among parents is more towards agreement.

(c) Correlation $P_1 C_2$ (0.98) is greater than correlation $P_2 C_1$ (0.67), this suggests that children move towards their parents rather than parents moving towards their children.

At this point in the discussion Miss Brown who had been following the argument very carefully said that she was very uneasy about drawing the final inference from the difference between the correlation coefficients, and the discussion was adjourned until a later occasion while Miss Brown sought to consult her nephew David who was undertaking research into statistical procedures (Rogosa 1980).

**Table 6**
Summary of correlations

| | $P_1$ | $P_2$ | $C_1$ | $C_2$ |
|---|---|---|---|---|
| $P_1$ | 1 | 0.99 | 0.67 | 0.98 |
| $P_2$ | 0.99 | 1 | 0.67 | 0.96 |
| $C_1$ | 0.67 | 0.67 | 1 | 0.75 |
| $C_2$ | 0.98 | 0.96 | 0.75 | 1 |

## 5. Simple Regression and Analysis of Covariance

On the next occasion when Miss Green and Miss Brown met with the headmaster to discuss the study that Miss Brown had planned, Miss Green raised the question of how their previous discussions would be modified if the data they had used for both attitudes and achievement had been measured along an interval scale, and how the procedures would change if additional factors were introduced. She suggested to the headmaster that perhaps it would be better to undertake the study in several schools instead of using students from only one school. The headmaster did not wish to be drawn away from a discussion about the experimental study, but quickly saw the relevance of the issues being raised. In his reply, which we now quote, he made reference back to the design of the experimental study.

When we have parallel classes matching, it is the natural procedure to give each side of an experiment a fair chance. How can we replace it in the case where parallel classes do not exist? The inquiries that would be needed to match children in different schools would be too extensive to be practicable, unless the circumstances are very favourable. It will usually be easier to replace them by giving each child in the experiment an initial and a final assessment in the subject matter. The exact form of these two assessments, examinations, or tests will need careful discussion among the teachers concerned, but this will not be a waste of time, since it will do much to clarify what it is hoped that the children will learn during the progress of the experiment.

When the final test has been given, the success of the experiment can be judged by plotting the final marks vertically against the initial marks horizontally. We can use colour to distinguish the methods that are being compared; let us say red for the new method and blue for the old. We can distinguish schools by indicating the position of a pupil by a distinct shape for each school, such as circles, triangles, clubs, hearts, spades, and diamonds. These will be enough to cover the case where six schools are taking part, with three on the side of the new method and three on the other side. Let us suppose that on the average there are 30 pupils in each of the six classes. If so, our diagram will include 180 points or markers, of which 90 will be red and 90 blue, while there will be 30 or thereabouts for each of the six shapes. The 180 points or markers will make a roughly elliptical cloud.

There will be two smaller clouds, coloured red and blue, and six little ones, each distinguished by the characteristic shape of its points. The clouds will be elliptical because, if the tests have been well-chosen, the abler and more knowledgeable children will tend to do rather better in both the initial and the final test, and the less able and less knowledgeable rather worse. The greater this tendency the slimmer the elliptical shapes.

We can now find the average increase in the final test that corresponds to unit increase in the initial test. We can do this by dividing the paper into eight (say) vertical strips and drawing a short horizontal line across each strip in a position such that half the points in the strip are above the horizontal and half below. We then mark the middle of each horizontal line and draw a line through all these eight points. This is the regression line. It tells us what is the average score on the final test corresponding to any given score on the initial test. It also tells us, and this is what we want to know, whether the red children have on the whole been more successful than the blue. This will be the case if the points above the line are preponderantly red, and the points below preponderantly blue.

Miss Brown was clearly interested in the possibility of analysing data from six schools, and she sought clarification at this point. "What do you mean by preponderantly?" she asked, "How much preponderance is needed for evidence in favour of red?".
The headmaster replied,

To answer this question with the least amount of arithmetic, we can merely count the red points above and below the line. With 90 points the even break would be with 45 above and 45 below. The square root of 90 is 9.5, so that if we have 55 or more red points above the line, and therefore 35 or fewer below the line we have firm evidence in favour of the new method. But 50 above and 40 below would be only rather weak evidence. As a check we can carry out the complementary count on the blue points. This should give the reverse result, since, if we have drawn the regression line properly, there will be about as many points (red and blue) above it as below.

By making similar counts and calculations for each of the six schools individually we can find whether there is any evidence of marked differences between the success of the two methods in different schools. If there is little difference it is more likely that the new method will be equally successful in other schools. If there is a great deal of difference the interesting question is why?

The procedure that the headmaster described, he said, was a simple form of the analysis of covariance, just as in the earlier discussion he had described a simple form of the analysis of variance. He went on to say that while it would be easy to undertake such an analysis

using a programmable calculator or a computer, there was still a great deal to be gained from actually plotting the evidence on paper and taking a good look at it. Moreover, the test which was available for examining data in this way, of measuring the departure from the even break against the square root of the number of cases involved, was a very simple one to apply.

## 6. *Multiple Regression Analysis*

Miss Green, who at this point considered that the headmaster had not fully answered the question that she had asked, once again raised the issue of examining data for more than two variables, and also commented that the sizes of classes were less than 30 in most of the neighbouring schools and in his discussions the headmaster had only considered cases in which the classes were equal in size with 30 students. The headmaster took up these two points as he continued with the discussion.

If you have taken care to draw a probability sample and have obtained numerous measures from its members, it would clearly be wasteful to stop short of a full analysis of the results. However, a salient feature of the results will be that the variables are all intercorrelated, so that each blurs the effect of the others. For example, consider the question of the effect of the size of the teacher's class. It is very hard to believe that, if other things were equal, merely adding several more children to the class will improve the average achievement. Yet most surveys show mild positive simple correlations between the average size of class in school and the average achievement for that school. But this can hardly be the whole story. The result has only to be stated to arouse the conjecture that there must be various favourable circumstances, associated with large classes, to explain a result that would otherwise be incredible. But what can these circumstances be?

To answer such questions we need multiple regression analysis, which discloses what is left of a simple correlation when the effects of other correlated variables are removed. This is only one of several forms of multivariate analysis, but it is perhaps the most generally useful.

Until the advent of the electronic computer the sheer weight of the arithmetic made extensive applications impracticable. This difficulty has now been overcome, owing to the extreme rapidity with which computers can do arithmetic, and particularly the kind of arithmetic needed here, which consists only of the repeated application of the same short series of steps. Work that would be intolerably tedious and lengthy to do by hand can be done by the computer in a few minutes or even seconds. None the less, if you are to make a sensible use of the computer output you must understand the nature of the process. However, the computations are sufficiently complex to leave for a discussion at another time. It is perhaps more important for us to consider the interpretation of the results.

The first step in the interpretation is easy. We are entitled to say that the variables that have not survived the regression are irrelevant, on the evidence of the sample, though even here we have to keep in mind that some of them might have survived on the evidence of another sample, so that it is important to have a proper estimate of sampling error. For some of the variables, however, the difficult question of cause and effect may arise. For example, are the attitude variables mere proxies for more fundamental attitudes that we ought to have measured but have not? If there is a causal relation, in which sense does it work? For example, does parental encouragement produce better achievement in school, or does better achievement in school produce more parental encouragement? The analysis can show the existence and the strength of a relation, but cannot tell us how or why in what sense it works. For this we must rely on our general experience of parents, teachers, children, and schools. Consequently we have a sort of double sieve. Some explanations compatible with the analysis may not be compatible without judgment from our general experience; on the other hand some explanations compatible with our general experience may not be compatible with the analysis. Those that are compatible with both have a higher probability than they had before the surveys were carried out. This double sieving is the ordinary way of scientific progress.

The question of cause and effect is a great deal simpler if a sound experiment has been carried out. However, in educational research there are very severe ethical restrictions upon experiment. Thus in education it is rarely justifiable to apply the method of artificial randomization to control for unknown factors that might influence the results, as has been so successful in agricultural and industrial work. In our earlier discussion you were teaching parallel classes, which can in fact be regarded as an example of artificial randomization, since in this context the word "parallel" implies the random allocation of students to classes. The subsequent matching of the students is an example of the use of what are called, in the technical language of factorial experiments, randomized blocks, each block being a pair of students in this case. "Blocking" in the language of the design of experiments corresponds to "stratification" in survey design. In each case the object is to get as much of the variation as possible between the blocks or strata, in order to reduce the sampling fluctuation.

The use of parallel classes in the experiment that you are planning eliminates the wide range of ability and background between the children from the uncertainty in the comparison of the two methods. But cases like this, where randomization already exists, are in the nature of fortunate accidents. To apply artificial randomization in other cases would generally result in the disruption of school organization, to an extent that would make the game not worth the candle. We can be the more confident about this when we remember that the distribution of relationships, like that of characteristics, exists only in a framework of specific populations, and that inferences derived from the experimental testing of several treatments are restricted to the population included in the experimental design. In general, we cannot solve simultaneously all the problems of measurement, representation, and control; we have to compromise and do the best we can, and in educational work this compromise will only rarely include the devices of artificial randomization.

## 7. The Scale of Inquiry

So far in the discussions that they had had, the headmaster and Miss Green and Miss Brown had discussed the small-scale experimental study in only one, or at most six schools that the enterprising teacher could carry out to test the ideas that had emerged from experience and reflection. The headmaster explained that

such small-scale experiments could be among the most useful. Successful innovation in teaching method was more likely to begin in the classroom than elsewhere. Only rudimentary experimental design was needed, and, if the experiment was successful, a simple statistical test of the kind discussed would provide prima facie evidence of this. While it would be a mistake to attach great weight to the results of one small experiment it would always be possible to replicate what looked like a successful experiment to see whether the success was repeated.

Nevertheless, he pointed out as he continued, there were a very large number of different influences interacting to advance or retard a student's learning in very complicated ways. It was plain that there might be a great number of factors influencing a student's school achievement that might never have been thought of. Quite a large number had been thought of, and some of them had been measured, but even so there remained a formidable problem of trying to disentangle them and estimate their several effects. Broadly speaking, there were two ways of tackling this problem. The first was to try to set up an experimental situation in which it was reasonable to hope for success in balancing all the variables but two, and then to observe the effect of one of these two on the other. This is called a bivariate experiment. The second was to measure the other variables instead of attempting to balance them. This is called a multivariate experiment. In the first case there was a criterion variable and a predictor variable, and observations could be made of the effect of the predictor on the criterion. In the second case there was again a criterion variable, but now there were several predictors, and the object was to estimate what the effect of each would be if it acted in isolation. In the first case the other variables could be controlled by the experimental design. In the second case each predictor could be taken in turn and controlled statistically.

Whether a variable would be regarded as a predictor or a criterion depended upon what was being attempted. The same variable could play both parts although not of course simultaneously. A variable could be considered as a criterion when an attempt was being made to estimate the influence of other variables on it. When an attempt was made to estimate its influence on other variables it would be called a predictor. Predictors are sometimes spoken of as independent variables, and criteria as dependent variables. While both usages were well-recognized, neither was totally satisfactory. Independent variables did not need to be independent in the statistical sense, and predictors often did not predict in the everyday sense of making a forecast about the future.

In planning a study in educational research a choice must be made between undertaking a simple experiment in the classroom setting and replicating the experiment in other classrooms or schools if it proved to be successful, or undertaking a large-scale inquiry in a random sample of schools. In a simple experiment it was only possible to investigate two variables at a time. In a large-scale inquiry it was possible to examine the effects of many factors simultaneously. Large-scale inquiries had two advantages that could be set against the much greater flexibility and intimacy of small-scale work. First, they could be carried out with random samples of students, parents, teachers, and schools, and greater generality could be claimed from the findings. Secondly, the numbers could be made large enough to stand multivariate analysis so that much more could be done in the way of disentangling the effects of the different variables. However, these advantages were bought dearly at the expense of both flexibility and intimacy. The sacrifice of intimacy and flexibility that was entailed by large-scale work would only be justified if there was a compensating advantage of representativeness. The only sure way of obtaining this compensating advantage, would be to apply probability sampling to a large and important population, such as the population of children aged 14 in all the government schools of a country. The main point that distinguished this form of sampling from others, such as selecting the sample by expert judgment or by the "quota" method, was that only with probability sampling could the accuracy of the estimates be found from the material evidence of the sample itself.

At this stage in the discussion Miss Green and Miss Brown asked the headmaster further questions on probability sampling. But since this topic was well-removed from the topic under discussion of planning the experiment, he offered to find an essay that he had written many years before on probability sampling and pass it to them so that they could read about the subject at their leisure. The text of this essay follows.

## 8. Probability Sampling

The essence of probability sampling is that every member of the population to be sampled should have a specifiable, nonzero chance of appearing in the sample. To ensure this requires a good deal of careful organization, which is totally absent, for example, from the methods by which members of the public are frequently chosen for television interviews. It is a consoling reflection that some of the sillier statements made in such interviews are likely to arise from the fact that the idle and the exhibitionist have an unduly large chance of being selected for interview.

Humankind has acquired enough knowledge of the world to invest in a considerable technology that often produces dramatic effects. All this knowledge has been acquired from samples, since only minute portions of space and time have ever been scrutinized. This suggests that nature tends to offer fair samples for inspection, and that the problem of fairness cannot therefore be very important. But this is altogether too easy. It ignores the immense amount of experience that has gone into the recognition of natural kinds and the invention of manufacturing processes so that in the upshot one bit of copper wire is very like another bit. Furthermore, it

ignores the fact that in classical physics the only concern is with averages reckoned over enormous numbers of unit particles. But in educational research concern is with the unit—the individual boy or girl, or man or woman—and not merely with the aggregate or population.

Fairness in the sample can be secured by giving every member of the population a specifiable chance of appearing in it. The accuracy of representation depends upon the size of the sample, and the size is given not by the number of members in the sample, but by the number of independent selections that have been made.

Suppose it is desirable to obtain a fair and reasonably accurate sample of the boys and girls in some specified population. Let the population be specified as the population, in January 1984, of boys and girls in the last year of primary education in England. In principle, though plainly not in practice, the simplest way of doing this would be to write the name of every pupil in the population on a ping pong ball and then whirl the balls in an enormous churn, as in the Irish sweep, and take the names on the winning balls as the sample. If there were $N$ balls altogether, and $n$ were selected, every member of the population would have a specifiable chance ($n/N$) of being selected.

This is plainly impracticable. The churning process could be replaced by the use of random numbers, which are, so to speak, prechurned, but the labour of collecting the relevant names from all the primary-school registers in England would be enormous. None the less there are several practicable methods by which a close approximation to this simple, single stage, sampling could be made. But since these methods would take some time to describe, and are unlikely to be used, they need not be gone into.

A method that has been used in practice is to select the boys and girls by specifying a date, and taking those whose birthdays fall on this date. This is quite different in principle, since only one independent choice, namely the choice of the date, is made. The selection is not a probability sample, but a subpopulation. It is not the case that every boy and girl in the full population has a specifiable nonzero chance of entering the sample. The chance is zero for all except those born on the given date. However, it is reasonable to think that the subpopulation will be like the general population in those respects that do not depend on the date. But there are some important respects, such as the age of entering and leaving school, and of taking examinations, in which children born in March differ from those born in October. This could be overcome by taking several birthdays, spread uniformly round the year—for example, the first of every month. This would, of course, produce a very large sample, but large samples are needed for some purposes. Another way of obtaining a large simple sample is to take one child in 10 in the relevant population in every school, making the selection not by birthdays but by the use of random numbers or some other lottery process. For example, a number not exceeding 10 could be allotted to each school. A school that drew the number eight would take the eighth, eighteenth, twenty-eighth, and so on, name on the registers for its sample. It is to be noted that while this process would be fair over all schools the results might look unfair in particular schools. According to the starting number allocated to the school the school sample might be untypically good, about right, or untypically bad. It would be, and has been, fatal to the fairness of the whole sample if the schools that drew numbers rejected them, on the grounds that they were unfair to the school, and chose for themselves more typical samples.

So far the simplest types of sampling have been looked at, where the selection is made directly in terms of the final unit, in this case the child. This single stage sampling is only suitable for very large enquiries which can bear the weight of corresponding with and carrying out the work in every school in the country. For enquiries on a smaller scale two-stage sampling is needed. The two stages are first the selection of schools and secondly, the selection within selected schools. The preliminary selection of schools has two advantages. In the first place it greatly reduces the amount of field work. Secondly, it gives more information about schools as such. These are the advantages of complex sampling. The price to be paid for them is that a complex sample has to be larger, in terms of the number of boys and girls, than a simple sample of the same accuracy. The reason for this is that students, parents, and teachers in the same school tend to resemble one another more than they resemble students, parents, and teachers in other schools, just as apples on the same tree tend to resemble one another more than they resemble apples on other trees, particularly if the trees are of different kinds. The point about "different kinds" can be overcome by stratification—that is, by sampling the kinds separately. Thus in sampling secondary schools, the draw is made after a preliminary separation into comprehensive, grammar, modern, technical, and other types, and into boys, girls, and mixed. This ensures that the sample estimates are not blurred by the differences between types. The practice has been to make a further stratification by region, though this is not very important, since regional differences (in contrast to neighbourhood differences) are generally small. It is to be noted that in a complex sample of the two-stage type the number of independent choices is the number of schools. A student's chance of selection is conditional upon whether or not the school attended is selected in the first instance. This makes no difference to the method of making the estimates. In each case the sample can be treated as though it were the population if the chances of selection have been everywhere the same, while compensating weights are needed if the chances have been unequal from one class to another. It does, however, make a difference to the method of estimating error, which is equally important. It should be noted that sampling errors are not mistakes; they are fluctuations or wanderings, as in "knight

errant", or "we have erred and strayed like lost sheep". They represent the average variation between one sample and another when the same method of drawing the sample is used in each case. The point about probability sampling, as distinct from other forms of sampling, is that these errors can be estimated. A sample chosen by expert judgment, or a quota sample, as used in some forms of public opinion polls, may be an excellent sample or may not; in either case the extent of its departure from representativeness cannot be ascertained from the internal evidence of the sample itself. With a probability sample this can be done.

The rules for estimating standard errors for single-stage samples are simple and well-known. For complex samples they are much more complicated, and for the multivariate analysis of complex samples it is not practicable to estimate the reliability directly. It is, however, possible to obtain reasonably satisfactory estimates of error by subsampling. For example, if a quantity, such as a correlation coefficient or a regression coefficient is calculated first from the whole sample and then from a half sample, the difference between the two estimates is itself an estimate of the error in the whole sample estimate. By comparing a large number of such estimates with the corresponding estimates calculated as though the sample were a simple sample, the design effect can be obtained, which is the ratio of the size of the complex sample to that of a simple sample with the same reliability. In splitting off the half sample the full complexity of the complex design must be followed. Thus if the complex sample is a stratified sample of schools, half the schools in each stratum must be taken for the half sample, for example by taking every alternate school. The size of the design effect increases with the number of children taken from each school. Experience has shown that a good rough preliminary rule for estimating, in two-stage stratified sampling, is to assume that about 10 percent of the variation lies between schools and 90 percent between students within schools. This enables preliminary estimates to be made for any allocation of the sample, either of the standard errors or of the simple equivalent sample. Thus if a sample of 2,000 students comes from 100 schools the simple equivalent sample would be 690, while if the 2,000 were drawn from 200 schools instead of 100 the simple equivalent sample would be 1,050. This can be extended to three-stage sampling, in which the first stage is to draw local authorities, the second to draw schools within selected authorities, and the third to draw students within selected schools. In this case about 3 percent of the variation lies between authorities, about 7 percent between schools within authorities, and the remainder between students within schools. A sample of 2,000 students from 100 schools in 20 local authority areas gives a simple equivalent sample of 380 pupils, but if the 100 schools came from only five areas the simple equivalent sample would fall to 140.

In sampling, the key is "probability". In sampling schools, parents, teachers, and students "probability" is used in the same restricted sense as in games of chance. Each member of a specified population is given a specifiable, nonzero, chance of being drawn in the sample, and other chances, such as that of a particular error of estimate exceeding a certain size, are calculated by the rules of combinatorial algebra, or by resorting to approximations, when the algebra becomes too complicated to be manageable.

By applying the rules to the evidence given by past experience, it is possible to determine the size of sample that is needed if the results obtained are not to be vitiated by uncertainty. Then by applying the rules to the new evidence it is possible to see whether the posterior estimate confirms the prior estimate of the magnitude of the sampling fluctuation.

## 9. Statistical Inference

When Miss Green and Miss Brown returned to talk to the headmaster after they had read his essay on sampling, the head drew attention to the key word "probability" in the last paragraph. He said

In all educational research, there is another important aspect of probability. In this sense it is more akin to "credibility". This sense is not only much wider. It is also much vaguer, since our judgment of credibility often depends upon a great range of imperfectly remembered experience. This accounts for the facts that each of us has his own system of credibilities, and that the systems often agree but sometimes do not. For this reason different persons may draw different conclusions from the same evidence, which gives scope for the legal profession.

Both kinds of probability deserve due respect, and failure to recognize this is responsible for some needless disputes between champions of teacher opinion and partisans of educational research.

Research results depend on both kinds of probability, and probability changes when the evidence changes. If all we know of Smith is that he is an Englishman the probability that his right eye is blue is about a half. But this probability is completely changed if we now learn that his left eye is blue.

The champions of "objectivity" sometimes tend to overlook the fact that our inferences about other people begin with introspection, memory, and testimony. Their opponents, on the other hand, tend to underrate the extent to which these inferences can be strengthened by observing regularities of behaviour. To strike a good balance needs temperate judgment.

Regularities of behaviour can be observed intimately, on a small scale, by teachers in their classrooms. They can also be observed, less intimately but on a much larger scale, by sampling whole populations. In the first case the scale may be extended by subsequent replication. In the second the broad generalizations may be refined by later work. Thus there is a part for everyone to play, and, while it is plain that we know very little about the immense variety of human nature, it is reasonable to hope that if we apply ourselves to the task we may learn more.

The headmaster went on to explain that as the study of a particular research question progressed it would be possible to plan a more detailed investigation to test specific relationships. In such a study a decision is commonly required as to whether an observed relationship could be ascribed to *sampling error* or whether it could be argued with confidence that it was the result of an experimental condition. The statistical techniques involved in making inferences of this kind are referred to as *tests of statistical significance*, and the procedures employed are known as *significance testing*. Sometimes such tests can be applied between the estimates made for independent samples, or between the estimates obtained under different conditions with the same sample. Sometimes, however, a test of significance is used to examine the difference between the estimate made for a single sample and a fixed value.

### 9.1 Hypothesis Testing

Consider the situation where previously established theory has led to the design of an experiment which uses an *experimental group* and a *control group*. Measurements are made on both groups. Since a treatment is applied to the experimental group, and the treatment is absent from the control group, it can be assumed that any significant difference between the two groups can be ascribed with confidence to the application of the treatment and not to other causes. If $\bar{X}_t$ is the estimate of the population mean $\mu_t$ for the treatment group and $\bar{X}_c$ the estimate for the population mean $\mu_c$ for the control group, the trial hypothesis may be advanced for testing that no difference exists between $\mu_t$ and $\mu_c$. This *null hypothesis* may be written

$$H_0 : \mu_t - \mu_c = 0$$

It is, however, also necessary to specify an *alternative hypothesis* which is to be accepted if the null hypothesis is rejected by the testing procedures employed. An appropriate alternative hypothesis may be written.

$$H_1 : \mu_t - \mu_c \neq 0$$

The logical steps that are applied by the investigator in significance testing are:

(a) the null hypothesis is assumed to be true, this involves the population values $\mu_t$ and $\mu_c$;

(b) the empirical data are examined, and the difference between the observed mean values $(\bar{X}_t - \bar{X}_c)$ is obtained;

(c) the question is asked, what is the probability of observing a difference equal to or greater than the one obtained by drawing samples at random from the populations involved, when it is assumed that the null hypothesis is true?;

(d) if this probability is small, the investigator may be led to reject the null hypothesis; if the probability is not small, then it must be accepted that the observed difference could be accounted for by sampling variations; and

| | Truth | |
|---|---|---|
| Decision | $H_0$ is true | $H_1$ is true |
| Accept $H_1$ | $\alpha$ | Correct decision |
| Accept $H_0$ | Correct decision | $\beta$ |

**Figure 1**
The two types of error

(e) if the null hypothesis is rejected, then the alternative hypothesis may be accepted, which implies that the observed difference is a result of the application of the treatment.

At this point in the discussion Miss Green, who had been following the argument very closely, asked whether there was also a chance that the alternative hypothesis was true even though the null hypothesis was accepted. The head agreed that it was clearly possible to have two types of error.

### 9.2 Type I and Type II Errors

If the alternative hypothesis $H_1$ is accepted when the null hypothesis $H_0$ is true, the error is referred to as a *Type I error*. However, it is also possible that the null hypothesis $H_0$ might be accepted when the alternative hypothesis $H_1$ is true. This error is known as *Type II error*. The total situation is represented diagrammatically in Fig. 1. In the cases where we accept $H_1$ and $H_1$ is true or we accept $H_0$ and $H_0$ is true, a correct decision has been made. However, there is a probability of accepting $H_1$ when $H_0$ is true, given by $\alpha$, and a probability of accepting $H_0$ when $H_1$ is true given by $\beta$.

### 9.3 Levels of Significance

In discussing hypothesis testing above, it was assumed that $H_0$ was true, and since the probability of observing a difference equal to or greater than the one obtained was small the alternative hypothesis had been accepted. Commonly a level of significance of either 0.05 or 0.01 is adopted for this probability, which is indicated in Fig. 1 by $\alpha$. If the observed probability is less than the chosen value of $\alpha$, namely 0.05 or 0.01, then the null hypothesis is rejected, and, in general practice, this decision is made without reference to the Type II error of probability $\beta$. However, the danger of applying too stringent a test associated with the error of Type I, or too small a value of probability $\alpha$, is that the value of $\beta$ can become large. In advanced work in statistics the levels of significance of both $\alpha$ and $\beta$ are examined and the power of the testing procedure is considered for samples of different sizes and differences between population mean values of different magnitudes.

Miss Brown, who was more concerned with establishing that the treatment applied in the experiment that she wished to conduct was beneficial than with those situations where there was no difference between mean values and the null hypothesis was true, asked whether it was possible to make allowance for the fact that the mean value of the experimental group was expected to exceed the mean value for the control group. The head replied that, if she had confidence in her treatment, then it would be advantageous to use a *one-sided test* or *one-tailed test* instead of a *two-sided test* or *two-tailed test*.

### 9.4 Directional and Nondirectional Tests

If an investigator wished to examine and choose between the null hypothesis $H_0: \mu_t - \mu_c = 0$, and the alternative hypothesis $H_1: \mu_t - \mu_c = 0$, there is no implication that the treatment group mean $\mu_t$ is greater than the control group mean $\mu_c$. The statistical test used is a two-sided or two-tailed, or *nondirectional test*. If the 5 percent probability level is employed in testing for significance, then 2.5 percent probability is associated with $\mu_t - \mu_c > 0$, and 2.5 percent probability is associated with $\mu_t - \mu_c < 0$. With these probabilities the difference between the means must exceed 1.96 times the standard error of the difference for significant error to be present. This nondirectional test is appropriate where there is concern for the absolute magnitude of the difference between the mean values for the treatment and control groups, without regard for the sign of the difference. However, it is possible to hypothesize the direction of the difference, for example $H_1: \mu_t - \mu_c > 0$, namely where the difference is positive in sign because the nature of the treatment leads to a greater treatment mean value $\mu_t$ being expected. Under these circumstances the null hypothesis can be reformulated to become $H_0: \mu_t - \mu_c \leq 0$ and the 5 percent probability is assigned in one direction and a one-sided or one-tailed test is employed. Here the treatment mean must exceed the control mean by 1.64 times the standard error of the difference for a significant effect to be reported. The use of a *directional test* leads to smaller differences between mean values being reported as significant, provided that the difference is in the expected direction. If the treatment mean value is significantly greater than the control mean value, the null hypothesis is rejected and the alternative hypothesis is accepted.

## 10. Conclusion

The head, in concluding the discussion, pointed out that the use of probabilities in *statistical inference* demanded different approaches according to the level of expectation for the differences being tested, that arose from substantial theories. Where much was known about the introduction of a treatment and where a value in dollars could be assigned both to the costs of implementation, as well as to the benefits derived from the gains associated with the treatment, then statistical *decision theory*, that provided a guide for choosing an effective decision-rule, should be employed. Failure to take account of such costs could lead to disastrous errors in practice. Thus it would not be merely a question as to whether Miss Brown's treatment was superior, but rather an issue of what the cost benefits associated with its use were when weighed against the costs of implementation, that should determine whether a decision was made to proceed with the introduction of the treatment on a widespread basis. Advanced procedures of statistical inference sought to take these matters into account. On the other hand it could be argued that in the field of education, since each teacher commonly has to decide what actions he or she should take, personal probabilities should be taken into account. If *personal probabilities* were taken into consideration then a Bayesian approach should be employed.

## Bibliography

David H A 1951 Further applications of range to the analysis of variance. *Biometrika* 38: 393–409

Ferguson G A 1976 *Statistical Analysis in Psychology and Education*, 4th edn. McGraw-Hill, New York

Guilford J P 1954 *Psychometric Methods*, 2nd edn. McGraw-Hill, New York

Hartley H O 1950 The use of range in analysis of variance. *Biometrika* 37: 271–80

Hays W L 1963 *Statistics for Psychologists*. Holt, Rinehart, and Winston, New York

Kish L 1965 *Survey Sampling*. Wiley, New York

Rogosa D 1980 A critique of cross-lagged correlation. *Psychol. Bull.* 88: 245–58

Thorndike R L (ed.) 1971 *Educational Measurement*, 2nd edn. American Council on Education, Washington, DC

# Multilevel Analysis

## J. P. Keeves and N. Sellin

Many investigations into educational problems are concerned with two basic types of variables, namely, measures of the properties of individual students, and measures of the properties of groups of students. This occurs because students are customarily brought together into classes for the purposes of instruction by teachers; because classes are grouped together in schools; and schools are linked together into larger units, such as school districts, for administrative purposes. Problems arise in the analysis of data collected at two or more levels as a consequence of the fact that it is rarely possible to assign students randomly to treatment or control groups in an experimental study, or to allocate the groups by random selection to receive the treatment or stand as the control. In addition, naturally occurring groups of students are found, in general, to contain members who are more like each other than they are like the members of other groups. The clustering of students with similar characteristics into groups means that unless it can be shown that the groups do not differ significantly from each other it is inappropriate to pool students from different groups into a combined group for the purposes of analysis. The problems that occur in the analysis of the data do not arise only because it has been necessary to sample first schools or classrooms and then to sample students within schools or classrooms, but also because the characteristics of the students commonly influence the treatments they receive in the groups (Keeves and Lewis 1983).

In truly experimental studies, where random allocation of students to treatment and control groups has taken place, analysis of variance and covariance procedures can be employed. However, since random assignment can rarely be fully carried out, in both quasi-experimental studies and those in which data are collected from natural situations, statistical control must be exercised in the analysis of data through regression and related procedures in order to examine the effects of both individual and group level variables. Formerly the issue associated with the appropriate level of analysis was considered to be influenced largely by the nature of the research questions to which answers were sought, for example, whether the problem was concerned with individual students or with classroom groups, as well as by the level at which sampling had taken place and at which generalization to other situations was sought. More recently it has become apparent that a multilevel analysis strategy is required if appropriate answers are to be obtained. Many aspects of this problem have been addressed by Burstein. In addition, they have been admirably treated by Finn (1974) in the analysis of data from rigorous experimental studies, where unequal numbers of students are clustered in treatment and control groups. These issues were examined further by Cronbach (1976). However, it is becoming increasingly apparent that strategies of multi-level analysis are required for the effective examination of data collected in schools and classrooms. This article seeks to expose the nature of these analytical problems, and to develop a multilevel approach to analysis for the examination of such data, where regression and related statistical procedures are involved.

## 1. Levels of Analysis

Since the publication of the article by Robinson (1950) on the problems associated with ecological correlations and the making of inferences about the behaviour of individuals from data analysed at the group level, there has been a general awareness that consideration had to be given to the appropriate level of analysis to be employed in data in which correlation and regression coefficients were reported. Three different levels of analysis have been available, and the question has been which of these three levels should be employed [a detailed discussion of the terms employed and the principles involved can be found elsewhere].

## 1.1 Between Students Overall

In this level of analysis the data from different groups are pooled and a single analysis is carried out between all students in the total sample. In symbols a regression analysis of this type with two predictor variables can be stated as follows

$$Y_{ij} = b_0 + b_1 X_{ij} + b_2 G_{ij} + \varepsilon_{ij} \tag{1}$$

where $Y_{ij}$ is the criterion variable, $X_{ij}$ is a student predictor variable, $G_{ij}$ is a group predictor variable $(G_j)$, $j = 1, \ldots, J$ for groups, $i = 1, \ldots, n_j$ for students within groups, $N = \Sigma_{j=1}^{J} n_j$ for the total number of students, and $\varepsilon_{ij}$ is the random error.

It should be noted that the group variable $G_j$ has been disaggregated to the student level. This type of analysis was used exclusively in the First International Mathematics Study (Husén 1967), and has been widely used in many investigations during the past two decades.

## 1.2 Between Groups

In this type of analysis data are aggregated by group, and the mean value for each group forms the criterion variable. Likewise, the student data for each predictor variable are aggregated by group, and group data for a group level predictor variable need not be disaggregated. In symbols a regression analysis of this type with two predictor variables can be stated as follows:

$$Y_{.j} = c_0 + c_1 X_{.j} + c_2 G_j + \alpha_j \tag{2}$$

where $Y_{.j}$ is the mean value of the criterion variable $(Y_{ij})$ for group $j$, $X_{.j}$ is the mean value for the predictor variable $(X_{ij})$ for group $j$, $G_j$ is a group predictor variable, and $\alpha_j$ is the random error.

This level of analysis was used together with the between students overall analysis in the examination of the data collected in the International Association for the Evaluation of Educational Achievement (IEA) Six Subject Study (Peaker 1975), and has been relatively widely used in other investigations.

## 1.3 Between Students Within Groups

In this type of analysis the measures for each student are subtracted from the group mean and thus the deviation values from the group mean are employed. Moreover, the data for all groups are pooled for a combined analysis. It is clearly not possible to include group level variables in such analyses. In symbols a regression analysis of this type with two predictor variables can be stated as follows:

$$(Y_{ij} - Y_{.j}) = w_1(X_{1ij} - X_{1.j}) + w_2(X_{2ij} - X_{2.j}) + \delta ij \tag{3}$$

where $X_{1ij}$ and $X_{2ij}$ are two student predictor variables and the remaining symbols are defined above.

This type of analysis together with the between groups type of analysis were used in the examination of the data collected in the Plowden National Survey in England (Peaker 1967).

## 1.4 Contextual Analysis

A fourth mode of analysis is sometimes employed that examines the contextual effects of a student level variable. In this mode of analysis the criterion variable at the student level is regressed on both a student level predictor variable and a variable which involves the mean values of that student predictor variable, which has been aggregated by groups and then disaggregated for analysis to the student level. In symbols a regression analysis of this type can be stated as follows:

$$Y_{ij} = b_0 + b_1 X_{ij} + b_2 X_{.j} + \varepsilon_{ij} \tag{4}$$

where the symbols employed are as previously defined with $X_{.j}$ being the contextual variable.

Analyses using the first three models have been undertaken by Larkin and Keeves (1984) in a study of the effects of class size on achievement. Differences were recorded in the magnitudes of the regression coefficients obtained for the same measure analysed at the three different levels of analysis. These differences, in general, were not inconsistent with an intuitive understanding of classroom processes and it was argued that with careful interpretation of the evidence, meaningful results were obtainable at each level. This view is contrary to the view that the differences arise at different levels of aggregation because of specification error (Cooley et al. 1981). There is no doubt that errors in the specification of the models used at different levels will give rise to erroneous results. Nevertheless, it is also possible that differences in model specification may be appropriate at different levels, according to the differences in the research questions being examined, and may give rise to different estimates of effect. This does not necessarily involve specification error. As Cooley et al. (1981) correctly point out, the differences are a consequence of grouping effects, when factors influencing group membership are related to one of the variables involved in the analysis.

Aitkin and Longford have all examined in some detail the results of analyses employing all four models outlined above. They dismiss the fourth mode of analysis because there is no reliable interpretation of a context effect "since it can be arbitrarily large or small". Moreover they state, "It will be found quite generally that the standard errors of individual level variables aggregated to the school level are very large, when the individual level variables are also included" (Aitkin and Longford 1986 p. 12).

## 2. Grouping Effects

The divergent and sometimes contradictory results that arise in regression and correlation analyses conducted at different levels stem from the effects of grouping. Sellin (1986) has examined the factors which determine grouping effects for both simple and complex regression models in ordinary least squares regression analysis. He has shown that the cross-level differences between the regression coefficients obtained in analyses at the three different levels are essentially due to one factor, namely the differences between individual level and aggregate level variances of individual level predictors. In comparing model (1) with model (3), it should be noted that the calculation of deviation scores for analyses using model (3) automatically reduces the variances of both the criterion and the predictor variables. In comparing model (1) with model (2) the results established by Sellin apply to analyses that use not only individual-related predictors, but also to more complex analyses that employ both individual-related predictors and group-related predictors. Since the group level variances are necessarily smaller than their individual level counterparts, because of the loss of information associated with the calculation of the group means, a strong case must be argued before the aggregation of data to the group level takes place. Moreover, it cannot always be argued that aggregation implies improved measurement of group characteristics and that the estimate of the group level effect is to be preferred, since this would assume that within-group variance of student measures was error variance. For example, in obtaining measures of classroom climate, such an assumption would mean that the differences in the perceptions of different students were essentially error. If such a view could be explicitly defended then the group level analysis would be appropriate, but the choice between the student and group level use of a variable should be made in advance and a comparison of the estimates of effect at the two different levels would not be made.

It is of interest to examine the relationship associated with the difference between an aggregated group level regression coefficient and the corresponding student level regression coefficient namely $(c_1 - b_1)$ when expressed in the symbols of Eqns. (1,2), and the between-group variance expressed as a fraction of the total variance. The grouping effect is sometimes referred to as "aggregation bias" and the use of this term is probably not inappropriate. In Fig. 1 this relationship is illustrated in a sketched diagram that shows how aggregation bias will generally tend to change as the proportion of between-group variance to total variance changes.

It will be seen that when the between-group variance is small compared with the total between-student variance then the aggregation bias is small. This corresponds to random grouping. However, the aggregation bias increases as the proportion of variance associated with between-group variance increases to reach a maximum value but falls again to zero as the proportion approaches 1.0. Peaker (1975 p. 120) has shown, using data from the IEA Six Subject Study, conducted in 13 countries, in three subject areas, and at three grade levels, that this proportion is commonly of the order of 20 percent. Consequently in most studies undertaken in different parts of the world the existence of such bias must be expected.

For those 12 countries that tested in science at the 14-year-old level in 1970, the average bias for the standardized partial regression coefficients when science achievement was regressed on an index of socioeconomic status at the between-school and student levels of analysis was 0.28. The average proportion of the school variance to the total student variance for science achievement test scores for those 12 countries was 0.21. Generally speaking, the regression coefficients doubled in size from student to school levels of analysis. The average size of the clusters was 24 students per school, and the average values of the design effects were for correlation coefficients $-2.6$ and for regression coefficients $-1.7$. This would imply intraclass correlation coefficients for the correlations of 0.07, and for the regression coefficients of 0.03. While these measures of clustering are not large they can be associated with quite substantial proportions of between-school variance to total between-student variance and substantial aggregation bias. Since clustering has such important consequences for the estimates of regression coefficients when aggregated data are used, it would seem important that further work should be done to assess the extent of clustering associated with particular predictor and criterion variables in different situations in the analysis of data.

In addition, it would seem very dubious to undertake the disaggregation of a variable from the group level to the individual student level unless it could be argued convincingly that the measure obtained at the group level applied equally to each individual student in the group. For example, it would not be inappropriate to disaggregate the variable, size of class, from the group level to the individual student level in analysis, but measures of teacher–student contact, which involved classroom practices and that influenced individual students in different ways, probably could not be mean-

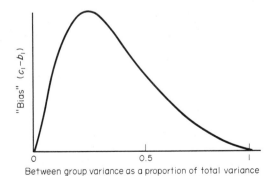

*Figure 1*
Relationship between aggregation bias and proportion of group variance to total variance

ingfully disaggregated for student level analyses. It would seem necessary for teacher–student contact to be assessed at the student level and the information related in analysis to each student involved. However, the disaggregation of data does not lead directly to a loss of information in the way that the aggregation of data does, and as for consequence does not introduce bias into the analysis. Nonetheless, both aggregation and disaggregation require careful justification, and the comparison of the coefficients obtained from different levels of analysis would appear to make little sense.

## 3. The Framework of Multilevel Analysis

The discussion in the previous section leads to the conclusion that for data collected at more than one level, for example the student and school levels, an analyst must consider the desirability of examining the data at both levels in a way that the two analyses are complementary with the separate components of variance at the two levels being partitioned and subjected to analysis. In this treatment of multilevel analysis the formulation advanced by Mason et al. (1983) has been followed. The data are collected at two levels: the student or micro level and the group or macro level.

The micro level equation may be stated:

$$Y_{ij} = b_{0j} + b_{1j} X_{1ij} + b_{2j} X_{2ij} + \varepsilon_{ij} \tag{5}$$

where $Y_{ij}$ is the criterion variable, $X_{1ij}$ and $X_{2ij}$ are two student predictor variables, and $\varepsilon_{ij}$ is random error at the micro level.

At the macro level the equations may be stated:

$$b_{0j} = c_{00} + c_{01} G_{1j} + \alpha_{0j} \tag{6}$$

$$b_{1j} = c_{10} + c_{11} G_{1j} + \alpha_{1j} \tag{7}$$

$$b_{2j} = c_{20} + c_{21} G_{1j} + \alpha_{2j} \tag{8}$$

where $G_{1j}$ is the macro level or group predictor variable and $\alpha_{kj}$ is random error at the macro level for $k = 0, 1, 2$.

These equations are written with the usual assumptions associated with the rank condition, and with the error terms at the micro level independent of the errors at the macro level. Equations (6) to (8) represent the effects of the macro level predictor variable ($G_1$) on the three parameters of the micro level model and it is assumed that once the systematic component associated with this variable has been removed from $b_0$, $b_1$, and $b_2$ the resulting variability is strictly random.

A single equation can be stated for the multilevel model by substituting Eqns. (6) to (8) in Eqn. (5).

$$Y_{ij} = c_{00} + c_{01} G_{1j} + c_{10} X_{1ij} + c_{11} X_{1ij} G_{1j}$$
$$+ c_{20} X_{2ij} + c_{21} X_{2ij} G_{ij} +$$
$$[\alpha_{1j} X_{1ij} + \alpha_{2j} X_{2ij} + \alpha_{0j} + \varepsilon_{ij}] \tag{9}$$

The term in brackets represents a combination of random effects of the micro level variables, namely $\alpha_{1j} X_{1ij}$

and $\alpha_{2j} X_{2ij}$, and random error components, namely $\alpha_{0j}$ and $\varepsilon_{ij}$. The random coefficients associated with $X_{1ij}$ and $X_{2ij}$ require special statistical treatment that will be discussed below in connection with the hierarchical linear model (HLM). If, however, $\alpha_{1j} = \alpha_{2j} = 0$ is assumed, Eqn. (9) reduces to a regression model that has no unusual estimation or computational problems.

## 4. Conditions for Pooling Data

In research situations where groups from the primary sampling unit and students within groups are studied with or without sampling at a second stage, consideration must be given as to whether it is appropriate to pool data across groups. If, however, sampling has occurred at the individual student level the problems associated with the pooling of data are clearly less acute, since some of the effects of grouping have been reduced by random sampling procedures.

Pedhazur (1982) has argued that the critical issues to consider in the pooling of data for analysis at the between-students overall level or the between-students-within-groups level as stated in Eqns. (1, 3) above are:

> . . . such an analysis is valid only after it has been established: (1) the $b$'s are not significantly different from each other (the $b$'s are homogeneous); and (2) there are no significant differences among the intercepts of the separate groups. In short, when $r_t$ or $b_t$ is calculated it is assumed that a single regression equation fits the data of all groups. (Pedhazur 1982 p. 537)

Four possible situations arise which influence the analyses. It should be noted that the $b_{0j}$ and $b_{1j}$ coefficients in Eqn. (5) are considered to be random variables whose variability can be examined and tested using the error variance associated with the micro level measures. These situations are:

*Case 1.* Both the $b_{0j}$ and $b_{1j}$ coefficients are not significantly different from each other.

*Case 2.* The $b_{0j}$ coefficients are significantly different, but the $b_{1j}$ coefficients are not.

*Case 3.* The $b_{0j}$ coefficients are not significantly different, but the $b_{1j}$ coefficients are.

*Case 4.* Both the $b_{0j}$ and $b_{1j}$ coefficients are significantly different from each other.

These four situations can be shown in a $2 \times 2$ contingency table (see Table 1).

(a) *Case 1.* In this case there are no significant differences between the $b_{0j}$ and $b_{1j}$ coefficients. Since there are not significant differences between groups, and since the $b_{0j}$ coefficients do not differ, analyses at the between-group level are inappropriate. Moreover the analyses can be carried out by pooling the student data and using the between-students overall model since the $b_{1j}$ coefficients are equal.

(b) *Case 2.* In this case there are significant differences between $b_{0j}$ coeffficients and hence between groups.

**Table 1**
Contingency table for coefficients $b_{0j}$ and $b_{1j}$

| $b_{0j}$ and $b_{1j}$ | not significantly different | significantly different |
|---|---|---|
| not significantly different | Case 1 | Case 2 |
| significantly different | Case 3 | Case 4 |

However, there are no significant differences between the $b_{1j}$ coefficients and under these circumstances it is appropriate to pool the data in a between-students-within-groups analysis and obtain an estimate of the $b_1$ coefficient. Thus a pooled between-students-within-groups analysis can be conducted as well as a between-groups analysis as suggested by Cronbach and Webb (1975). It has been proposed by Wiley (1976) that the effect of the student level variable can be included in the between-groups analysis as indicated in the following equation:

$$Y_{.j} - b_1 X_{.j} = c_0 + c_1 G_j + \alpha_j \tag{10}$$

Equation (10) is appropriate if it can be assumed that the effects of $X$ and $Y$ operate at the within-group level and that $b_1$ represents the appropriate estimate for the effects of $X$ on $Y$. However Eqn. (10) corresponds to a model that does not specify the effects of $X$ on $G$ or $G$ on $X$.

(c) *Case 3*. In this case there are no significant differences between the $b_{0j}$ coefficients and under these circumstances a between-groups analysis is inappropriate. However, since there are significant differences between the $b_{1j}$ coefficients it is inappropriate to pool the data at the micro or between-student level and separate analyses for each group should be carried out. Macro level analyses of the $b_{1j}$ coefficients could also be carried out.

(d) *Case 4*. In this case there are significant differences between the $b_{0j}$ coefficients and the $b_{1j}$ coefficients and under these circumstances a full multilevel analysis should be undertaken.

In educational research, where the investigation of differences between schools and classrooms is of primary interest, it would seem that Case 4 would be the situation occurring most frequently in practice. It is, however, unsafe to test simply for statistical significance. Specht and Warren (1976 p. 60) have warned against unwarranted recognition of differences which are small and although statistically significant are substantively slight. This advice should be heeded if trivial analyses are to be avoided when very large samples are employed.

For simplicity, and without loss of generality, the data for variables at the individual level are commonly subtracted from the corresponding group mean values.

Thus deviation scores are employed in the analysis at this level, and the micro level equation may be stated:

$$(Y_{ij} - Y_{.j}) = b_{1j}(X_{1ij} - X_{1.j}) + b_{2j}(X_{2ij} - X_{2.j}) + \varepsilon_{ij} \tag{11}$$

It should be noted that the intercept term $b_{0j}$ is no longer included in the equation. However, this does not prevent a multilevel analysis being carried out. It should also be recognized that while deviation scores have been calculated, the scores have not been standardized, so that metric or unstandardized coefficients are employed which can be compared across groups in the analyses.

## 5. Testing for Significant Differences

Before proceeding to consider the hierarchical linear model it is necessary to obtain the variance components at the micro and macro levels and test the multilevel data for significance. A series of regression analyses at different levels can be undertaken in which the criterion is regressed on one or more predictors using ordinary least squares regression analysis. In the analysis at the group level the aggregated measures are weighted by the number of students within each group. This maintains the orthogonality of the analyses at the different levels. The results of such a series of analyses are given in Table 2.

In analysis 1 at the between-students overall level, the total variance is partitioned into a sum of squares due to regression and a residual sum of squares and the effects of regression are tested for significance. In analysis 2, the regression analysis has been carried out at the between-groups level with a group level predictor $G_1$. In the analysis 3, the regression analysis has been carried out at the pooled-between-students-within-groups level. In this manner the total variance can be seen to have been partioned into a between-groups component and a between-students-within-groups component. In analysis 4, the regression analysis is carried out at the unpooled-between-students-within-groups level. In analysis 5, using the results of analysis 3 and analysis 4, a test is applied to determine whether the slopes of the within-group regression lines differ significantly from each other or from a common slope that could be fitted. In analysis 6, a test is applied to determine whether the variation between the slopes of the regression lines is due to a group level variable. The different variance components and the corresponding degrees of freedom, together with the statistical tests are given. An example of this analysis of variance components is given by Keeves and Larkin (1986). For simplicity, this discussion has been presented for only one predictor variable, but could be readily extended for two or more predictor variables at the different levels, although analyses 3 and 4 should be carried out with the same regressors. The tests applied are similar to those used for homogeneity of variance in analysis of covariance (Ferguson 1966 pp. 337–48). Consideration

**Table 2**
Partitioning of variance in regression analyses with the criterion regressed on the predictors

| Level of Analysis | Sum of Squares | $df$[a] | Mean Square | F-Ratio |
|---|---|---|---|---|
| **Between students overall ($Y_{ij}$)** | | | | |
| Due to Regression on $X_1$ | $t_1$ | 1 | $t_1$ | $\dfrac{t(N-2)}{T}$ |
| Residual | $T_1$ | $N-2$ | $T_1/(N-2)$ | |
| Total | $t_1 + T_1 = t_2 + T_2 + t_3 + T_3$ | $N-1$ | | |
| **Between groups ($Y_{.j}$)** | | | | |
| Due to Regression on $G_i$ | $t_2$ | 1 | $t_2$ | $\dfrac{t_2(J-2)}{T_2}$ |
| Residual | $T_2$ | $J-2$ | $T_2/(J-2)$ | |
| Total | $t_2 + T_2$ | $J-1$ | | |
| **Pooled between students within groups ($Y_{ij} - Y_{.j}$)** | | | | |
| Due to Regression on $X_1$ | $t_3$ | 1 | $t_3$ | $\dfrac{t_3(N-J-3)}{T_3}$ |
| Residual | $T_3$ | $N-J-3$ | $T_3/(N-J-3)$ | |
| Total | $t_3 + T_3$ | $N-J-1$ | | |
| **Unpooled between students within groups ($Y_{ij} - Y_{.j}$)** | | | | |
| Due to Regression on $X_1$ | $t_4$ | $J$ | $(t_4-t_3)/(J-1)$ | $\dfrac{(t_4-t_3)(N-2J-2)}{T_4(J-1)}$ |
| Residual | $T_4$ | $N-2J-2$ | $T_4/(N-2J-2)$ | |
| Total | $t_4 + T_4 = t_3 + T_3$ | $N-J-2$ | | |
| **Testing for Significance of differences between $b_{ij}$s** | | | | |
| Unpooled – Pooled SS | $t_4 - t_3$ | $J-1$ | $(t_4-t_3)/(J-1)$ | $\dfrac{(t_4-t_3)(N-2J-2)}{T_4(J-1)}$ |
| Residual | $T_4$ | $N-2J-2$ | $T_4/(N-2J-2)$ | |
| **$b_{ij}$s regressed on $G_1$** | | | | |
| Due to Regression on $G_1$ | $v_1$ | 1 | $v_1$ | $\dfrac{v_1(J-2)}{V_1}$ |
| Residual | $V_1$ | $J-2$ | $V_1/(J-2)$ | |
| Total | $v_1 + V_1$ | $J-1$ | | |

a degrees of freedom, i.e., the number of values that are free to vary, given the number of constraints imposed on the data. The interrelations between the number of degrees of freedom in different analyses in this Table should be noted.

should not only be given to the statistical significance of the tests applied but also to the proportion of the total variance associated with the various components of variance so that trivial effects are not given unwarranted recognition.

In Case 2 where the tests applied in analysis 2 indicate both significant and substantial effects, but where the tests applied in analysis 5 do not, a pooled-between-students-within-groups analysis can be employed to estimate the common regression slope across groups and the components of variance due to the significant student level variables removed before a more detailed between groups analysis is undertaken. This is the group level analysis employed by Wiley (1976) and also illustrated with simulated data by Tate and Wongbundhit (1983). However, it is Cases 3 and 4 discussed above that are of particular interest in school and classroom studies, where significant and substantial differences are detected between groups in the regression slopes since these results are associated with effects that research into educational problems must seek to explain.

## 6. Hierarchical Linear Models (HLM)

The task facing educational research workers which is of vital importance in the study of classrooms, schools, and school districts, as well as in cross-national studies of educational achievement, is the development of appropriate procedures for the analysis of multilevel data. The general framework for such procedures is that of multiple regression, with the outcome variables regressed on variables which measure student as well as teacher, classroom, and school characteristics. The procedures must take into consideration the nesting of students within classrooms, and possibly classrooms within schools, and make full provision for the clustering or grouping effects of the micro units within the macro units. In order to ensure generality of findings it is customary for random sampling of both the macro units and the micro units to take place. Thus, where such sampling has occurred, the effects at both micro and macro level should be regarded as "random" rather than "fixed" effects. The general class of models which have been developed for the analysis of multilevel data has become known as "hierarchical linear models" (HLM), although such terms as "variance components analysis models" and "multilevel models" have been used. At the time of writing this field was passing through a stage of rapid development, and in this article the different approaches are presented, and the issues which have been raised are briefly discussed.

A major problem, as can readily be envisaged, is not only that of formulating the analyses to be carried out but also the inversion of large and complex matrices. As a consequence three different algorithms have been developed with different computing routines and with different analytical strategies. These strategies are:

(a) a general EM algorithm (Mason et al. 1983),

(b) a Fisher scoring algorithm (Aitkin and Longford 1986), and

(c) a generalized least squares algorithm (Goldstein 1986a, Goldstein 1986b).

Each approach is discussed below.

### 6.1 The General EM Algorithm

This approach involves a two stage process. In the first stage a criterion variable at the micro level is regressed on a micro level predictor variables. At the second stage the regression coefficients from the micro stage, including the intercept terms, where meaningful, are regressed on the macro level predictor variables. The major difficulty in this strategy is that the estimation of the regression slopes is associated with considerable error. The issue in the macro level analysis is that of separating the variability in the regression coefficients into their "real" and "random error" components. Mason et al. (1983) developed a restricted maximum likelihood Bayesian estimation procedure, and Raudenbush and Bryk (1986) have extended and applied this procedure to the re-analysis of the data from the 1982 follow-up of the *High School and Beyond Study*. The major problem that Raudenbush and Bryk consider is the error variance in the estimation of the regression coefficients. Since the sampling precision of these regression coefficients varies across units of different sizes and with different extent of variation in the micro level predictor variables, the basic assumptions of ordinary least squares regression analysis would have been violated. Raudenbush and Bryk proposed that the variability in these regression coefficients should be divided into two components, namely, variance due to sampling and the variance of the parameter itself. Following the partitioning of the variance of these regression coefficients into the sampling and parameter components, the parameter variance is estimated as accurately as possible. This permits the macro level effects to be more accurately estimated from an analysis using the parameter component of the variance.

A Bayesian estimation procedure is employed to obtain values of the micro level regression coefficients with reduced error variance, that is, the sum of the parameter variance and the sampling variance. These weights are obtained by an iterative process in which the initial estimate of each micro level regression coefficient is compared with the mean value of these coefficients. Outlier values which are unreliable are successively weighted down and the group coefficient is weighted down more until convergence is obtained. The procedure "shrinks" these micro level regression coefficients and reduces the variance of the estimates prior to the macro level analysis. Since the micro level regression coefficients have been estimated more accurately, the estimates of the effects of the school level variables on these coefficients might be expected to be stronger. While this procedure is computationally complex, it is relatively straightforward conceptually and can be applied where specific models for micro level and macro level effects are being examined.

This approach to hierarchical linear modelling involves two major assumptions, namely, (a) the criterion variable at the micro level is normally distributed, and (b) the regression coefficients obtained from the analysis at the micro level are normally distributed. The first assumption is generally satisfied when achievement tests are used as criterion measures. However, the second assumption could be more problematic, since little experience has been gained from the examination of the distributions of such coefficients. The other assumptions that are necessary do not differ from those required for ordinary least squares (OLS) regression analyses, which have been found to be generally robust. Indeed it might be asked whether OLS regression analysis could be employed. If the condition of homogeneity of the variances of the micro level regression coefficients is satisfied then it might be expected that the use of OLS regression analyses would yield similar results. One problem encountered in the analysis of the micro level regression coefficients is that the intercept terms ($b_{0j}$), which are obtained when scaled predictor variables are used, for example, a pretest score of achievement, have no clear meaning since the position of the axis to obtain the intercept is arbitrary. The situation is simplified if, as Raudenbush and Bryk (1986) propose, the within-group data for the micro level analyses are centred around the group mean values of the micro level variables. Where significant differences exist between the group means of the micro level criterion variable, then a macro level analysis using these group means would appear to be necessary, but allowance cannot readily be made for the effects of the student level predictor variables in the analyses at the group level.

## 6.2 The Fisher Scoring Algorithm

Aitkin and Longford (1986) have reported on the use of the Fisher scoring algorithm in the context of statistical modelling problems connected with British school effectiveness studies. The Fisher scoring algorithm provides maximum likelihood estimates and standard errors for the regression coefficients and group parameter effects of the model:

$$Y_{ij} = b_0 + b_1 X_{ij} + d_j + \varepsilon_{ij} \tag{12}$$

where the symbols are defined as in Eqn. (1) except that $d_j$ are the school or group effects assumed to be a random sample from distribution $N(0, \sigma_I^2)$, and $\sigma_I^2$ is the group parameter variance.

It should be noted that this model is in many ways equivalent to the inclusion of a dummy variable for each group and the fitting of a single intercept and regression coefficient for the total set of data. Group level predictor variables that explain the variation in the estimates of $d_j$ can subsequently be sought. However, the micro level regression coefficients are assumed not to vary, and this

strategy would appear to be a variation of Case 2 rather than a true HLM analysis required by Case 4.

In fitting the model, weights are employed that are estimated from the variance component estimates. As with the previous procedure which used the general EM algorithm, because the within-group observations are correlated, a coefficient for the ratio of the parameter variance to the sum of the parameter variance and the sampling variance is obtained from the estimates of the parameter variance and the sampling variance. The weights are a maximum when the estimates of the parameter variance are zero, and reduce to zero when the parameter variance is large compared to the sampling variance. This model can be extended to include additional "fixed effect" micro level predictor variables. Aitkin and Longford (1986 p. 16) note:

> school level variables cannot reduce the pupil level component since these variables are constant within school. The failure to distinguish between pupil and school variance components has led in the past to attempts to "increase $R^2$" by including school level variables in individual level regressions. When the school variance component is zero or very small such attempts are bound to be fruitless, when it is appreciable, a serious overstatement of significance of such variables is almost inevitable, because the standard errors of the parameter estimates for such variables are seriously understated by individual level regressions.

While certain points are well made, it has long been recognized that simple random sample estimates of error are inappropriate for the testing of such estimates of not only regression coefficients but also mean values, correlation coefficients and multiple $R$'s. More appropriate procedures are widely used. The variability in the micro level regression slopes across groups would seem to be an issue of greater consequence.

Consequently, Aitkin and Longford (1986 p. 19) extended their model to include a term in the equation to account for variation in the regression slopes.

$$Y_{ij} = b_0 + b_1 X_{ij} + d_j + f_j X_{ij} + \varepsilon_{ij} \tag{13}$$

Where $b_0$ and $b_1$ are the mean intercept and regression slope and $d_j$ and $f_j$ are the random intercept and slope for group $j$, and where $d_j$ and $f_j$ are not assumed to be independent of each other.

The data which they examined provided an example where one school had a markedly different slope to the others after appropriate adjustments had been made as a result of this analysis. This was a finding of considerable interest.

The general strategies of analysis that they advanced have been employed in the re-analysis of the data obtained in the study of *Teaching Style and Pupil Progress* (Aitkin, Anderson, and Hinde 1981; Aitkin, Bennett and Hesketh 1981). The existence of substantial intraclass correlations for the mean score estimates of clustering effects ranging from 0.17 in English and 0.35 in reading indicated the need to undertake a multilevel analytical approach.

Aitkin and Longford (1986 p. 23) also make the

valuable point that the clustering effects are not simply a consequence of the sampling design but result from the inherent nature of the grouping of students with similar characteristics within schools.

### 6.3 Generalized Least Squares Algorithm

Goldstein (1986a) employed the statistical model presented in Eqn. (9) which included an interaction term associated with a micro level predictor variable and a macro level predictor, in order to analyse multilevel data. Moreover, he recognized that if such an approach were adopted then the number of levels involved in an analysis was not necessarily limited to two. In this way the groupings of students within classrooms, classrooms within schools and schools within districts could all be taken into account in a single analysis. The overall variance of the criterion variable was partitioned into components for each level in the ensuing analysis, hence the term "variance component model" was used.

Goldstein proposed that iterative generalized least squares procedures should be employed to obtain estimates of the parameters of the model associated with both "fixed" and "random" coefficients. Like the two other procedures described above generalized least squares weighted the data according to the accuracy of the estimates at the group level. Goldstein argued that this analytic strategy could also be applied to models for time-related data, with a set of measurements for each individual on a particular variable at different ages or time points. Moreover, there is no requirement that the measurements at each time point should involve the same variable. This approach would appear to be a very powerful and highly flexible one for the efficiency analysis of data gathered in educational research. In addition, the use of generalized least squares, while yielding estimates equivalent to maximum likelihood estimates in cases with normal errors, also provides efficient estimates for other distributions. The application of this approach to a range of analyses of educational data is awaited.

## 7. Some Analytical Issues

De Leeuw and Keft (1986) have considered many of the recent developments discussed in this article and have raised several analytical issues. In addition they have undertaken the analysis of the same data set using four different approaches: (a) ordinary least squares regression analysis using the two stage estimation procedure represented by Eqns. (5, 6) to (8), (b) ordinary least squares regression analysis using a one state estimation procedure represented by Eqn. (9), (c) weighted least squares with Swamy weights, and (d) weighted least squares with maximum likelihood weights.

### 7.1 Random or Fixed Variables

Many studies have been undertaken that have paid insufficient attention to whether or not the regression coefficients from the micro level analysis should be regarded as random variables or as fixed coefficients. Not only should the nature of the sampling process be taken into consideration, but as Tate and Wongbundhit (1983) have argued: (a) the micro level regression coefficients can reflect particular policies and strategies associated with the groups, (b) they are also influenced by unspecified factors associated with the groups, (c) these disturbance factors are commonly considered as giving rise to random variability and, (d) failure to specify these coefficients as random variables annuls attempts that might be made to adjust for such error. It should be noted that ordinary least squares regression analysis treats these regression coefficients as fixed, when there is clearly a very strong case to consider such measures as random variables.

A further question is concerned with whether or not the micro level and macro level predictor variables should be considered as random regressors or fixed regressors. De Leeuw and Kreft (1986) acknowledge that the models they have employed regard the predictor variables as fixed regressors, when random variables are probably involved. They argue for the development of procedures that deal with both mixed regressor models and fully random regressor models.

### 7.2 Estimation Procedures

The two important aspects of any consideration of estimation procedures are whether the estimates of the parameters are unbiased and whether the estimates of error are efficient. There are, however, further questions as to whether the sampling distributions of the estimates of error are known so that significance tests can be applied. It should be recognized that jackknifing strategies are always available for the estimation of errors in complex models. Their use is not uncommon in educational research where ordinary least squares regression procedures are employed, and where allowance has to be made for the effects of clustering. Moreover, ordinary least squares is known to be robust for the data that are obtained in the examination of educational research problems.

(a) *Least squares estimation.* Ordinary least squares regression procedures are widely used in educational research and have been employed in multilevel analysis. For example, Larkin and Keeves (1984) have used least squares regression analysis without weighting, arguing that the appropriate weights which might have been used would be given by the numbers of cases in each group involved in the analysis at the micro level. Consequently, the use of weighted least squares regression analysis (Chatterjee and Price 1977), would have contaminated the analysis with respect to the variable of interest, namely class size. Under these circumstances it was considered inappropriate to weight the data. While the estimation of parameters by ordinary least squares produces unbiased estimates, the estimation of errors of these estimates is inefficient. Clearly in analysis the most efficient estimation procedures available should be employed. However, De Leeuw and Kreft

(1986 p. 72) contend that "the weighted estimate will generally improve on the unweighted estimates, although this is by no means certain".

(b) *Weighted least squares.* De Leeuw and Kreft (1986) argue that the weighted least squares estimate has the same asymptotic distribution as the unweighted separate equation estimate. However, since the weighted estimates are generally more efficient and thus improve on the unweighted estimates at least with relatively small numbers of groups and group sizes the use of weighted estimates is to be preferred.

(c) *Separate or single equation estimation.* There is little doubt that separate equation analyses are easier to interpret and to understand and are less likely to be contaminated by problems of multicollinearity than are single equation analyses. However, both approaches lead to unbiased estimates.

(d) *Maximum likelihood or weighted least squares estimation.* In general, maximum likelihood estimation procedures lead to smaller estimates of error and are thus more efficient, although in the example presented by De Leeuw and Kreft (1986) the gains were slight. It must be recognized, however, that the use of maximum likelihood procedures in general requires that the variables included in the analysis are normally distributed.

(e) *Generalized least squares.* Although generalized least squares is an analytic strategy that was advanced more than 50 years ago, and has been treated by Johnston (1972), it would appear that the variance estimates obtained are not distributed as a chi-square distribution and no proper methods are available to provide confidence limits about the values predicted by regression analysis.

### 7.3 Contextual Effects

A common problem in educational research is concerned with the assessment of school and classroom climates. Measures of climate are obtained from the views and perceptions of students with respect to the situations that they experience. While it is recognized that individuals within a particular group will view a common situation differently and that their different perceptions will influence differentially their behaviour, there is expected to be a high degree of commonality within the group with respect to their views of the situation which they jointly experience. Thus the variability in individual perceptions can also be regarded as error in the measurement of a shared climate. Under such circumstances it might be expected that there would be regularity both within and between groups with regard to the influence of perceptions on behaviour. This expectation can be tested empirically by the analysis of data at the micro level of analysis using Eqn. (5) and by examining whether the differences between regression slopes ($b_{1j}$) across groups are significant. If there are significant effects of the perceptions of climate on the criterion as assessed by the regression coefficients at the micro level of analysis, but nonsignificant or trivial differences between the regression slopes, then a common slope can be estimated using Eqn. (3) through a pooled between-individuals-within-groups regression analysis. This common slope, it is argued, not only applies to all individuals within their particular groups, but must also logically apply across groups. There is no reason to expect that the group effects differ in any way from the individual effects. Any such differences that have been previously reported are an artefact of analysis using grouped data and must be regarded as aggregation bias. As a consequence, before undertaking any analysis at the group level to examine the effects of group level variables on the criterion measure a partial adjustment has been proposed by Wiley (1976) and presented in Eqn. (10).

If significant differences exist in the values of $b_{1j}$ from the micro level analysis using Eqn. (5), it would seem important to examine why such differences existed using a strategy of multilevel or HLM analysis. Only when an answer was known to that question could the group mean values or the micro level equation intercepts ($b_{0j}$) be examined. It would seem essential to adjust at least in part each group mean value of the criterion measure as in Eqn. (10) in those situations where intercepts ($b_{0j}$) have no identifiable meaning. The equation for this partial adjustment can be stated as follows:

$$Y._j - b_{1j} X_1._j = c_0 + c_1 G_j + \alpha_j \qquad (14)$$

where $b_{1j}$ represents the micro level regression slopes for variable $X_{1ij}$ as in Eqn. (5).

This equation involves the adjustment of the outcome mean values for each group by specific within group effects, using the same logic as in Eqn. (10) with $b_1$ replaced by $b_{1j}$.

No adjustment of this type has been reported. It would seem that the use of an iterative approach such as that employed in partial least squares path analysis would provide an appropriate analytical strategy to undertake adjustments of this type based on micro and macro levels of analysis.

## 8. Conclusion

Multilevel analysis is a field where a number of highly significant papers have recently been published. Much has been accomplished towards the solution of a critical problem in the analysis of educational research data in the short period of time since Mason et al. (1983) suggested to research workers in the social sciences that the problem might be addressed using multilevel analysis procedures. De Leeuw and Kreft (1986 p. 79) conclude with the following statement:

> Our first and foremost recommendation is that if one uses contextual analysis, or slopes as outcomes analysis, then one should try to specify the statistical model as completely as possible. This does not necessarily mean that one must adopt the specification we have investigated here. In fact, we believe that our model, although certainly a step ahead, is not quite general enough. It must be generalized in such a way that it can deal with recursive models, in which there are several dependent variables and the regressors are random.

Moreover, for many school career analysis situations it must have provisions for incorporating categorical variables. These seem to be developments that are needed from the modeling point of view.

Recently, Wong and Mason (1985) have also developed a hierarchical logistic regression model for multilevel analysis where a categorical criterion variable is employed. We must await with interest the applications of these principles and procedures not in simulation studies but in the detailed analysis of the extensive bodies of data in educational research that are multilevel in nature and that are concerned with real problems.

## Bibliography

Aitkin M, Anderson D, Hinde J 1981 Statistical modelling of data on teaching styles. *J. Royal Stat. Soc.* A, 144: 419–61

Aitkin M, Bennett N, Hesketh J 1981 Teaching style and pupil progress: A re-analysis. *Br. J. Educ. Psychol.* 51(2): 170–86

Aitkin M A, Longford N 1986 Statistical modelling issues in school effectiveness studies. *J. Royal Stat. Soc.* A, 149(1): 1–26

Chatterjee S, Price B 1977 *Regression Analysis By Example.* Wiley, New York, Chap. 5

Cooley W W, Bond L, Mao B-J 1981 Analyzing multilevel data. In: Berk R (ed.) 1981 *Educational Evaluation Methodology: The State of the Art.* Johns Hopkins University Press, Baltimore, Maryland

Cronbach L J 1976 *Research on Classrooms and Schools: Formulation of Questions, Design, and Analysis*, Occasional Paper of the Stanford Evaluation Consortium. Stanford University, California

Cronbach L J, Webb N 1975 Between-class and within-class effects in a reported aptitude × treatment interaction: Re-analysis of a study by G. L. Anderson. *J. Educ. Psychol.* 67: 717–24

De Leeuew J, Kreft I 1986 Random coefficient models for multilevel analysis. *J. Educ. Stat.* 11(1): 57–85

Ferguson G A 1966 *Statistical Analysis in Psychology and Education.* McGraw Hill, New York

Finn J D 1974 *A General Model for Multivariate Analysis.* Holt, Rinehart and Winston, New York

Goldstein H 1986a Multilevel mixed linear model analysis using iterative generalized least squares. *Biometrika* 73(1): 43–56

Goldstein H 1986b Statistical modelling of longitudinal data. *Ann. Hum. Biol.* 13: 129–42

Husén T (ed.) 1967 *International Study of Achievement in Mathematics*, 2 Vols. Almqvist and Wiksell, Stockholm

Johnston J 1972 *Econometric Methods*, 2nd edn. McGraw Hill, New York

Keeves J P, Larkin A I 1986 The context of academic motivation. *Int. J. Educ. Res.* 10(2): 205–14

Keeves J P, Lewis R 1983 Data analysis in natural classroom settings. *Aust. J. Educ.* 27(3): 274–87

Larkin A I, Keeves J P 1984 *The Class Size Question: A Study at Different Levels of Analysis.* Australian Council for Educational Research (ACER), Hawthorn, Victoria

Mason W M, Wong G Y, Entwisle B 1983 Contextual analysis through the multilevel linear model. In: Leinhardt S (ed.) 1983 *Sociological Methodology 1983–84.* Jossey-Bass, San Francisco, California

Peaker G F 1967 The regression analyses of the national survey. In: Central Advisory Council for Education 1967 *Children and Their Primary Schools: A Report of the Central Advisory Council for Education*, (Plowden Report), Vol. 2, Appendix 4. Her Majesty's Stationery Office, London

Peaker G F 1975 *International Series in Evaluation*, Vol. 8: An Empirical Study of Education in Twenty-One Countries. Almqvist and Wiksell, Stockholm

Pedhazur E J 1982 *Multiple Regression in Behavioral Research.* Holt, Rinehart and Winston, New York

Raudenbush S, Bryk A S 1986 A hierarchical model for studying school effects. *Soc. Educ.* 59: 1–17

Robinson W S 1950 Ecological correlations and the behavior of individuals. *Am. Sociol. Rev.* 15: 351–57

Sellin N 1986 On Aggregation Bias in Educational Research. Paper presented to the 28th IEA General Assembly, Stockholm

Specht D A, Warren R D 1976 Comparing causal models. In: Heise D R (ed.) 1976 *Sociological Methodology 1976.* Jossey-Bass, San Francisco, California

Tate R L, Wongbundhit Y 1983 Random versus nonrandom coefficients models for multivariate analysis. *J. Educ. Stat.* 8(2): 103–20

Wiley D E 1976 Another hour, another day: Quantity of schooling, a potent path for policy. In: Sewell W H, Hauser R M, Featherman E L (eds.) 1986 *Schooling and Achievement in American Society.* Academic Press, New York

Wong G Y, Mason W M 1985 The hierarchical logistic regression model for multivariate analysis. *J. Am. Stat. Assoc.* 80: 513–24

# Regression Analysis

## M. M. Tatsuoka

Regression analysis refers to a broad class of statistical techniques that are designed to study the relationship between a criterion (or dependent) variable, $Y$, and one or more predictor (or independent) variables, $X_1, X_2, \ldots, X_p$. The means by which such study is effected is a regression equation, which is an equation of the general form

$$\hat{Y} = f(X_1, X_2, \ldots, X_p) \tag{1}$$

where the circumflex on the $Y$ denotes that what is represented by the function of the $X$'s is a "predicted"

or "modeled" $Y$-value rather than one that is actually observed.

The function $f(\ )$ may, at one extreme, be a simple linear function of a single predictor (i.e., $b_0 + b_1 X$). At the other extreme it may be a complicated weighted sum of several predictors raised to various powers and include also products of two or more predictors (e.g., $b_0 + b_1 X_1 + b_2 X_2 + b_3 X_1^2 + b_4 X_1 X_2 + b_5 X_1 X_2^2$). The terms may even include transcendental functions such as $\log X_j$, $e^{aX_j}$, and so forth. However, such a term may be defined as a separate predictor, and the task of determining the combining weights (or regression coefficients) will become more involved but no new principle will have to be invoked.

What is the general principle involved in determining the regression coefficients? It is desirable that the modeled $Y$-values, $\hat{Y}_i$ (where $i$ represents the $i$-th individual in the sample), should "be as close as possible" to their actually observed counterparts $Y_i$. More specifically, "closeness" can be defined so as to mean small total (or average) squared discrepancies between $Y_i$ and $\hat{Y}_i$. That is, the quantity

$$Q = \sum_{i=1}^{N} (Y_i - \hat{Y}_i)^2 \equiv \sum_{i=1}^{N} e_i^2 \qquad (2)$$

can be defined as the "loss function," which is to be minimized by appropriate choice of the regression-coefficient values. (Here $N$ is the sample size, and $e_i$ is simply another symbol for $Y_i - \hat{Y}_i$, known as "error" or "lack of fit" of the $i$-th observation to the model.) This is the famous least-squares principle.

Of course, invoking the least-squares principle, by itself, does not completely solve the problem of determining the regression coefficients. Before that, a decision must be made on what particular functional form to adopt for $f(\ )$; that is, the regression model must be chosen. Until this choice is made, the very task of minimizing the loss function is ill-defined. For instance, the minimum $Q$ attainable by adopting the class of linear functions $f(X) = b_0 + b_1 X$ as the regression model and determining the optimal $b_0$ and $b_1$ values will, in general, be "undercut" if one allows a quadratic function $f(X) = b_0' + b_1' X + b_2' X^2$ as a candidate and determines the optimal values of $b_0'$, $b_1'$, and $b_2'$. Thus, the choice of a type of regression model is the crucial first step before one can even apply the least-squares principle.

Ideally, there should be some theoretical grounds for making this choice. A substantive theory in the field of research should dictate whether to adopt, say, a linear, quadratic, or exponential regression model. Unfortunately, it is seldom the case in behavioral science that there is a substantive theory precise enough to specify a particular type of regression model. It is thus frequently necessary to proceed by trial-and-error. In this case, the decision is guided by another principle of scientific endeavor: the canon of parsimony, which holds that a more complicated model should not be used when a simpler one will suffice.

In the context of choosing a regression model, this usually means that a linear model should be tried first, and only if this proves not to yield an "adequate" fit should a sequence of more complicated models be tried successively. A crucial point here is how to decide whether the fit offered by a given regression model is adequate or not. One way is to test whether or not a significant decrease would be obtained in the loss function $Q$ if one were to go from the simpler to the more complicated model. Only if the decrease $Q_1 - Q_2$ (say) is significantly greater than zero would there be jus-

tification for using the second model. To ignore this and jump suddenly to a complicated, well-fitting model would be to commit the error of "overfitting" the sample at hand. An excellent fit may be obtained to the current dataset, but this would more likely than not incur a drastic drop in the extent of fit in a future sample from the same population, when an attempt is made to replicate (cross-validate) the finding or utilize the regression equation.

What was said above concerning the choice of a class of regression models holds equally well with regard to the number of predictor variables to include. Even when the mathematical form of a model is fixed, say to a multiple linear regression form, the fit can generally be improved by adding more and more predictor variables. But the more that is added, the less likely it will be that the extent of fit achieved in the sample at hand will hold up in future samples. Hence, a predictor variable should not be added to an existing multiple regression equation unless the addition results in a significant decrease in the loss function $Q$—or, as is shown below—a significant increase in the squared multiple correlation coefficient.

In the forgoing, nothing was said about the purposes of regression analysis, since it was assumed that the reader was familiar with at least the simplest (or most practical) of the purposes served; namely the prediction of such things as college or job performance for the screening or guidance of candidates. However, regression analysis is coming more and more to be used for a purpose that has traditionally been served by analysis of variance (ANOVA) and analysis of covariance (ANCOVA). This usage will be discussed below after a description of several models, their properties, and some problems inherent in regression analysis.

It should also be pointed out here that a regression model, properly speaking, requires the values of the independent variable(s) to be fixed by the researcher. Examples would be ages of the subjects to be used, dosages of a drug to be administered, and so on. This is in counterdistinction to the correlation model, in which dependent and independent variables alike are random variables, whose values are "brought along" by the subjects sampled—for example, course grades and pretest scores; height and weight. Most of the techniques of regression analysis are applicable equally to the regression and correlation situation, although some differences in significance tests and so on do exist. This article will speak for the most part in the language of the regression model; this allows one to refer to groups defined by values of the independent variable(s), and hence to subgroup means of $Y$.

## 1. Models, Properties, and Problems

### 1.1 Simple Linear Regression

The simplest regression model takes the form of a single-predictor linear equation,

$$\hat{Y} = b_0 + b_1 X \qquad (3)$$

where the constants are determined, as mentioned earlier, so as to minimize the loss function $Q = \Sigma(Y - \hat{Y})^2$. The results turn out to be

$$b_1 = \Sigma x_i y_i / \Sigma x_i^2 \tag{4}$$

and

$$b_0 = \overline{Y} - b_1 \overline{X} \tag{5}$$

(Here $x_i = X_i - \overline{X}$ and $y_i = Y_i - \overline{Y}$ are deviations from the means.) $b_1$ is called the coefficient of regression of $Y$ on $X$—or, simply, the "regression coefficient"—while $b_0$ is the $Y$-intercept. These constants are unbiased estimates of the corresponding population constants $\beta$, and $\beta_0$.

When $b_1$ and $b_0$ as defined by Eqns. (4) and (5) are substituted back into the expression for $Q$ with $\hat{Y}$ replaced by $b_0 + b_1 X$, after doing some algebra, the following is obtained:

$$Q_{min} = \Sigma y^2 - (\Sigma xy)^2 / \Sigma x^2 \tag{6}$$

This is called the residual sum of squares of $Y$, denoted $SS_{res}$. Factoring out $\Sigma y^2$ in the right-hand expression yields

$$SS_{res} = (\Sigma y^2)[1 - (\Sigma xy)^2 / (\Sigma x^2 \Sigma y^2)] \tag{7}$$

The reader may recognize the fraction in the brackets to be equal to the square of the product–moment correlation coefficient $r_{xy}$. Thus,

$$SS_{res} = (\Sigma y^2)(1 - r_{xy}^2) \tag{8}$$

Recalling that $SS_{res}$ is another symbol for $Q_{min}$, the minimum value of the loss function that can be achieved for the given regression model by using the optimal $b_0$ and $b_1$, it can be seen that the larger $r_{xy}$ is in absolute value, the smaller $Q_{min}$ is. (Of course $0 \leq |r_{xy}| \leq 1$, as the reader probably knows.)

Equation (8) may also be written as $SS_{res} = \Sigma y^2 - r_{xy}^2 \Sigma y^2$, and it may further be shown that

$$r_{xy}^2 \Sigma y^2 = \sum_{i=1}^{N} (Y_i - \overline{Y})^2 \tag{9}$$

which is called the sum of squares due to linear regression, symbolized $SS_{lin.\,reg.}$. It therefore follows that

$$r_{xy}^2 = SS_{lin.\,reg.} / SS_{tot} \tag{10}$$

where $SS_{tot}$ has been written for $\Sigma y^2$ (since this is the total sum of squares of ANOVA). This is the mathematical formulation of the well-known statement that "the squared correlation is the proportion of the variability of the dependent variable that is associated with its linear regression on the independent variable."

The reader may recall that the $t$ statistic for testing the significance of a correlation coefficient is $t = r(N - 2)^{\frac{1}{2}} / (1 - r^2)^{\frac{1}{2}}$, which follows a $t$ distribution with $N - 2$ degrees of freedom when the null hypothesis is true. The square of this statistic, which may be rearranged slightly to read

$$F = \frac{r^2 / 1}{(1 - r^2)/(N - 2)} \tag{11}$$

follows an $F$ distribution with 1 and $N - 2$ degrees of freedom. Substituting for $r^2$ and $1 - r^2$ from Eqns. (10) and (8), respectively, the following is obtained:

$$F = \frac{SS_{lin.\,reg.}/1}{SS_{res}/(N - 2)} \tag{12}$$

or, upon rewriting the numerator and denominator as mean squares,

$$F = \frac{MS_{lin.\,reg.}}{MS_{res}} \tag{13}$$

which bears an obvious resemblance with the customary $F$ ratio in one-way ANOVA: $F = MS_b / MS_w$.

## 1.2 Multiple Linear Regression

One way in which the simple linear regression Eqn. (3) can be complexified by one step is to add a second predictor variable to get

$$\hat{Y} = b_0 + b_1 X_1 + b_2 X_2 \tag{14}$$

The constants $b_0$, $b_1$, and $b_2$ are again determined by minimizing $Q = \Sigma(Y - \hat{Y})^2$ with $\hat{Y}$ replaced by the second member of Eqn. (14). Setting the appropriate partial derivatives equal to zero results in the equations,

$$(\Sigma x_1^2)b_1 + (\Sigma x_1 x_2)b_2 = \Sigma x_1 y \tag{15}$$

$$(\Sigma x_2 x_1)b_1 + (\Sigma x_2^2)b_2 = \Sigma x_2 y \tag{16}$$

and

$$b_0 = \overline{Y} - b_1 \overline{X}_1 - b_2 \overline{X}_2 \tag{17}$$

The first two of these equations, called the normal equations, may be written in a compact form by defining the sum-of-squares-and-cross-products (SSCP) matrix of the predictor variables,

$$S_{xx} = \begin{bmatrix} \Sigma x_1^2 & \Sigma x_1 x_2 \\ \Sigma x_2 x_1 & \Sigma x_2^2 \end{bmatrix} \tag{18}$$

the vector of regression coefficients (more precisely, partial regression coefficients),

$$b = \begin{bmatrix} b_1 \\ b_2 \end{bmatrix} \tag{19}$$

and the vector of sums of cross products (SCP) between predictors and criterion,

$$S_{xy} = \begin{bmatrix} \Sigma x_1 y \\ \Sigma x_2 y \end{bmatrix} \tag{20}$$

The normal equations then become

$$S_{xx} b = S_{xy} \tag{21}$$

which may be solved to yield

$$b = S_{xx}^{-1} S_{xy} \tag{22}$$

(provided that $S_{xx}$ is nonsingular). The similarity between this and Eqn. (4) for the one-predictor case is evident—especially if the latter is deliberately rewritten in the form

$$b_1 = (\Sigma x^2)^{-1}(\Sigma xy) \tag{23}$$

Those who are not familiar with matrix algebra may either simply follow the formal analogy with the one-predictor situation described in the previous subsection or refer to a reference such as Green (1976) or to the matrix-algebra chapter in any of several multivariate analysis texts (e.g., Tatsuoka 1971).

If Eqn. (14) is generalized to

$$\hat{Y} = b_0 + b_1 X_1 + b_2 X_2 + \ldots + b_p X_p \tag{24}$$

one has only to define a larger SSCP matrix (with $p$ rows and $p$ columns) $S_{xx}$ and larger ($p$-dimensioned) vectors $\mathbf{b}$ and $S_{xy}$ to go into Eqn. (21). The equation for the $Y$-intercept $b_0$ is not worth rewriting in matrix notation. The general case can be simply written as

$$b_0 = \overline{Y} - b_1 \overline{X}_1 - b_2 \overline{X}_2 - \ldots - b_p \overline{X}_p \tag{25}$$

The index which measures how well (or poorly) a multiple linear regression model fits a given set of observations—that is, how small the minimum value of $Q$ can be made by choosing regression coefficients and intercepts that satisfy Eqns. (21) and (25)—is defined as the product–moment correlation coefficient $r_{Y\hat{Y}}$ between the observed and modeled criterion scores $Y$ and $\hat{Y}$. This is called the multiple correlation coefficient and is symbolized as $R_{y \cdot 123 \ldots p}$ (or simply $R$ if the context makes it clear what the criterion and predictor variables are). $R$ may be computed by actually determining each person's "predicted" (i.e., modeled) $Y$ score, $\hat{Y}_i$, from Eqn. (24) and correlating it with the observed $Y$ score, $Y_i$. This, however, would be extremely tedious to do, and in practice one of several algebraically equivalent formulas is used that gives the same result. One of these is $R^2 = S'_{xy}\mathbf{b}/\Sigma y^2$, where $S'_{xy}$ (or $S_{yx}$) is the transpose of $S_{xy}$—that is, a row vector with the same elements as the $S_{xy}$ defined before. Nevertheless, it is important to keep in mind that $R = r_{Y\hat{Y}}$.

A test of the null hypothesis that the population multiple correlation coefficient is zero may be carried out by using an $F$ statistic that is a direct generalization of that displayed in Eqn. (11) for the one-predictor case;

$$F = \frac{R^2/p}{(1 - R^2)/(N - p - 1)} \tag{26}$$

which follows an $F$ distribution with $p$ and $N - p - 1$ degrees of freedom under the null hypothesis.

A more important test, in view of the earlier admonition against proceeding to a more complicated regression model than warranted by the data, is one that allows a test to be carried out to determine whether the addition of a new predictor results in a significant decrease of the loss function. This may now be restated in terms of an increase in the squared correlation coefficient, by using the relation between $Q_{\min}$ (i.e., $SS_{res}$)

and $r^2$ given by Eqn. (8) and its multiple-predictor extension. For if the residual $SS$ using one predictor $X_1$ is denoted by $SS_{res(1)}$ and that using two predictors, $X_1$ and $X_2$, by $SS_{res(2)}$ then the decrease in $Q$, $SS_{res(1)} - SS_{res(2)}$, is, by Eqn. (8) and its two-predictor extension, equivalent to $(\Sigma y^2)(R^2 - r^2)$. Hence, the $F$ statistic for testing the significance of the increase from $r^2$ to $R^2$ is

$$F = \frac{(R^2 - r^2)/1}{(1 - R^2)/(N - 3)} \tag{27}$$

The divisor, 1, in the numerator is the difference, 2–1, between the numbers of predictors; the $N - 3$ dividing the denominator is $N - p - 1$ with $p = 2$. The degrees of freedom of this $F$ statistic are 1 and $N - 3$. More generally, the statistic for testing the significance of the increase in $R^2$ (or the "incremental $R^2$" as it is often called) in going from a $p$-predictor model to a $(p + 1)$-predictor model is

$$F = \frac{(R^2_{p+1} - R^2_p)/1}{(1 - R^2_{p+1})/(N - p - 2)} \tag{28}$$

which has an $F$ distribution (under the null hypothesis) with 1 and $N - p - 2$ degrees of freedom.

The incremental $R^2$ is sometimes used in the reverse (then called the decremental $R^2$) as a measure of how much the predictability of the criterion decreases when a particular predictor variable is removed from a multiple regression equation. This was called the "usefulness" of that predictor by Darlington (1968) in an article that compares the advantages and disadvantages of several measures of the relative importance of each predictor variable in predicting or "expanding" the criterion. The best known of such measures is, of course, the standardized regression weight $b_j^*$ (or "beta weight") associated with each variable, which is related to the corresponding raw-score regression weight $b_j$ by the equation $b_j^* = (s_j/s_y)b_j$ where $s_j$ and $s_y$ are the standard deviations of $X_j$ and $Y$, respectively. However, Darlington points out several drawbacks of the beta weight as a measure of each variable's contribution to the predictability of the criterion.

## 1.3 Polynomial Regression

Another way in which the simple linear Eqn. (3) may be complexified is to add, successively, a term in $X^2$, $X^3$, and so on, while holding the number of actual predictor variables to one. Such a regression equation is called a polynomial regression equation of degree $m$, when $X^m$ is the highest degree term involved. The effect of adding higher degree terms is to enable the modeling of datasets in which the $Y$ means corresponding to the distinct values of $X$ trace curves of more and more complicated forms.

Once again, it cannot be overemphasized that the mistake should never be made of overfitting the data at hand by using a polynomial equation of a degree higher than warranted. In fact, it can be seen without too much difficulty that, if there are $K$ distinct values of $X$ in the dataset (and hence at most $K$ distinct $Y$-means), the subgroup $Y$ means $\overline{Y}_1, \overline{Y}_2, \ldots, \overline{Y}_K$ can be fitted perfectly by a polynomial regression equation of degree $K - 1$. (This is because the number of constants whose values can be chosen in a polynomial equation of degree $K - 1$ is $K$, which is the number of $Y$-means to be fitted.) Clearly such a fit is spurious and would never begin to hold up in a subsequent sample.

The determination of the regression coefficients and the successive significance testing may be done by precisely the same methods that were described for multiple linear regression in the preceding subsection. This should not be difficult to see, because in a cubic regression equation (for instance) the successive powers $X$, $X^2$, and $X^3$ may be regarded as three different predictor variables, $X_1$, $X_2$, and $X_3$, respectively. Thus, the SSCP matrix for the normal equations may be written by the simple device of starting out with the SSCP matrix appropriate to the three-predictor linear model case, then moving the subscripts upwards to the position of exponents, and finally using the rule of exponents $(x^m x^n = x^{m+n})$. The SSCP matrix then becomes

$$\mathbf{S}_{xx} = \begin{bmatrix} \Sigma x^2 & \Sigma x^3 & \Sigma x^4 \\ \Sigma x^3 & \Sigma x^4 & \Sigma x^5 \\ \Sigma x^4 & \Sigma x^5 & \Sigma x^6 \end{bmatrix} \tag{29}$$

Similarly, the predictor-criterion SCP vector $\mathbf{S}_{xy}$ becomes

$$\mathbf{S}_{xy} = \begin{bmatrix} \Sigma xy \\ \Sigma x^2 y \\ \Sigma x^3 y \end{bmatrix} \tag{30}$$

With $\mathbf{S}_{xx}$ and $\mathbf{S}_{xy}$ thus constructed, the normal equations [Eqn. (21)] are written and solved in exactly the same way as before.

The multiple correlation coefficient, defined as $R = r_{Y\hat{Y}}$ in the context of multiple linear regression, can be used in conjunction with polynomial regression equations just as well. Hence, it can be computed as $R = \mathbf{S}'_{xy}\mathbf{b}/y^2$ with the newly defined $\mathbf{S}_{xy}$ and $\mathbf{b}$ solved from the redefined normal equations.

The significance tests, both for a given multiple correlation coefficient itself and for the residual from the polynomial regression equation of a given degree, can likewise be conducted in the ways described in the previous subsection. For the former the $F$ statistic given in Eqn. (26) is used, where the $p$ used for the number of predictors may be replaced by $m$ to denote the degree of the polynomial. Similarly, for testing, if it is warranted to go from an $m$-th degree equation to an $(m + 1)$-th, Eqn. (28) may be used, again with $p$ replaced by $m$.

Although the forgoing significance tests are generally adequate and commonly used, there is one troublesome thing about them. This is that, in using these formulas, it is tacitly being assumed that the residual sum of squares, $(1 - R^2)\Sigma y^2$ or $(1 - R^2_{m+1})\Sigma y^2$ as the case may be, is attributable to "pure sampling error." This would

be true if it was known that the degree of the regression equation entertained at any given stage is indeed the correct population model (in which case there would be no need to conduct a significance test). Otherwise, $SS_{res}$ would be an overestimate of pure sampling error, since it would include also a portion due to regression of $Y$ on a higher degree term of $X$. For this and other reasons, it is often advisable to use an alternative approach to constructing and testing polynomial regression equations, which is known as the method of orthogonal polynomials. Very briefly, this approach uses a sequence of polynomials $P_1(X), P_2(X), P_3(X)$, and so on, instead of pure powers of $X$ as the terms of the regression equation. Thus, for example, a cubic regression equation would be written as $\hat{Y} = a_0 + a_1 P_1(X) + a_2 P_2(X) + a_3 P_3(X)$.

For situations when the values that $X$ can take are equally spaced (and hence can, by a suitable linear transformation, be transformed into $1, 2, \ldots, K$) and each of these $X$ values is taken by the same number of cases, there is a specific sequence of orthogonal polynomials $P_1(X), P_2(X), \ldots, P_{K-1}(X)$ for each $K$. These were originally derived by R. A. Fisher, and tables of their values are available in many textbooks on experimental design (see, e.g., Winer 1971). As explained in these books, orthogonal polynomials have the important property that, for each $K$ their values for $X = 1, 2, \ldots, K$ sum to 0. Hence, the polynomial values may be used as coefficients of a contrast among the subgroup means of $Y$. For example, with $K = 5$ and $j = 1$,

$$\hat{\psi}_1 = P_1(1)\overline{Y}_1 + P_1(2)\overline{Y}_2 + \ldots + P_1(5)\overline{Y}_5 \tag{31}$$

is a contrast of the five subgroup means of $Y$ "attributable" to the first-degree polynomial, $P_1(X)$.

A further important property is that, associated with each contrast $\hat{\psi}_j$ for any given $K$, there is a sum of squares $SS(\hat{\psi}_j)$, with one degree of freedom, that constitutes an additive component of the between-groups sum of squares in the following sense:

$$SS(\hat{\psi}_1) + SS(\hat{\psi}_2) + \ldots + SS(\hat{\psi}_{K-1}) = SS_b \tag{32}$$

Moreover, the partial sums of these $SS(\hat{\psi}_j)$'s are related to the $SS$ due to regressions of successive degrees:

$$SS(\hat{\psi}_1) = r^2\Sigma y^2 = SS_{\text{lin. reg.}} \tag{33}$$

$$SS(\hat{\psi}_1) + SS(\hat{\psi}_2) = R^2_2\Sigma y^2 = SS_{\text{quad. reg.}} \tag{34}$$

$$SS(\hat{\psi}_1) + SS(\hat{\psi}_2) + SS(\hat{\psi}_3) = R^2_3\Sigma y^2 = SS_{\text{cubic reg.}} \tag{35}$$

and so forth. (Here each $R_m = r_{Y\hat{Y}m}$ is the correlation of $Y$ with the $m$-th degree regression.)

Consequently, the question of whether or not the $m$-th degree regression equation is "adequate" for modeling the $K$ subgroup means of $Y$ may be tested by

$$F = \frac{\left[SS_b - \sum_{j=1}^{m} SS(\hat{\psi}_j)\right] / (K - 1 - m)}{MS_w} \tag{36}$$

with $K - 1 - m$ and $N - K$ degrees of freedom. If this is significant, it is possible to proceed to the $(m + 1)$-th degree equation; if not, it can be concluded that the $m$-th degree equation is adequate.

### 1.4 Multiple Nonlinear Regression

This combines the complexities of multiple-linear and polynomial regression models. That is, higher degree terms of each of several predictors, and possibly products among two or more predictors, constitute the terms of the regression equation. Geometrically, this would represent a curved surface or "hypersurface." Such an equation can again be treated like a multiple linear regression, with each term regarded as a separate predictor. Hence, nothing new in the way of determining the regression coefficients, computing multiple correlation coefficients, and conducting significance tests needs to be added.

However, the presence of product terms (which could go beyond the simple $X_1X_2$ type and include such monstrosities as $X_1^2X_2X_3$) does introduce a considerable difference in interpretation. To illustrate the point, the simplest case will be examined:

$$\hat{Y} = b_0 + b_1X_1 + b_2X_2 + b_3X_1X_2 \qquad (37)$$

By collecting the last two terms, this may be rewritten as

$$\hat{Y} = b_0 + b_1X_1 + (b_2 + b_3X_1)X_2 \qquad (38)$$

which somewhat resembles a multiple linear regression equation with two predictors $X_1$ and $X_2$, except that the coefficient of $X_2$ is not a constant but is itself a linear function of $X_1$. What this means is that the effect of $X_2$ on the criterion $Y$ depends on the value of $X_1$. Assuming $b_3 > 0$, it can be seen that the larger $X_1$ is, the larger the coefficient $b_2 + b_3X_1$ of $X_2$ becomes, hence the greater the effect of $X_2$ on $Y$. This, as the reader may have recognized, is what is known as interaction in ANOVA. The effects of the two independent variables are not simply additive, but are exerted jointly—each enhancing the effect of the other.

## 2. ANOVA and Multiple Regression

Since the mid-1960s or so, the writings of Darlington (1968), Kerlinger and Pedhazur (1973), Cohen and Cohen (1975), and others, have done much to popularize, in the behavioral and social sciences, the use of multiple regression analysis in situations where analysis of variance has traditionally been the main if not the sole analytic tool. This has been hailed by many as a recent innovation, but in point of fact some early writings of R. A. Fisher indicate that he invented ANOVA as a computational tool to get around the intractable computational difficulties, in the precomputer era, that arose when multiple regression was applied to designed experiments—that is, when the independent variables were qualitative variables (such as different fertilizers,

different varieties of corn, etc.) that were manipulated by the experimenter.

The nature of the difficulty is not hard to see even in the case of one-way designs with qualitative independent variables having a large number of "levels"—for example, five or six different instructional methods for teaching some subject matter. Since there is no a priori ordering to the different teaching methods, it will not do to define a variable called "method," denoted $X$, give it the values $1, 2, 3, \ldots, 6$ (say), and use it as the independent variable in a simple linear regression analysis. Rather a technique has to be used known as "coding," of which there are several varieties.

Perhaps the most widely used type is that known as "dummy variable coding." Suppose there are $K$ categories ($K$ different teaching methods, $K$ different religions, etc.) to the independent variable. $K - 1$ dummy variables $X_1, X_2, \ldots, X_{K-1}$ are then introduced and values assigned to members of the different categories as follows:

> $X_1 = 1$ and $X_2 = X_3 = \ldots = X_{K-1} = 0$
> for Category 1 members;
>
> $X_2 = 1$ and $X_1 = X_3 = \ldots = X_{K-1} = 0$
> for Category 2 members:
>
> .
> .
> .
>
> $X_{K-1} = 1$ and $X_1 = X_2 = \ldots = X_{K-2} = 0$
> for Category $K - 1$ members;
>
> $X_1 = X_2 = X_3 = \ldots = X_{K-1} = 0$
> for Category $K$ members.

A multiple (linear) regression analysis of the criterion variable $Y$ (a suitable measure of achievement in the subject matter, observed on the entire sample) is then carried out. The test of significance of the multiple correlation coefficient thus obtained gives results identical to those given by the familiar $F$ = test of ANOVA;

$$F = \frac{R^2/(K - 1)}{(1 - R^2)/(N - K)} = \frac{MS_b}{MS_w} \qquad (39)$$

where the first ratio comes from Eqn. (26) with $p$ replaced by $K - 1$. The curious reader will no doubt wonder why this should be so. Why do two techniques so seemingly different as multiple regression and ANOVA yield identical results?

Before answering this question, it is useful to look at how the technique of coding is extended to designs involving two or more factors. For specificity, suppose it is desirable to handle a $3 \times 4$ factorial-design ANOVA by the multiple regression approach via dummy-variable coding. Two dummy variables $U_1$ and $U_2$ (say) would be used for coding the three categories of factor A, and three dummy variables $X_1, X_2,$ and $X_3$ for the four levels of B. How is the interaction A $\times$ B expressed? The reasoning introduced in Sect. 1.4 has simply to be applied so that the product of two variables represents an interaction between them. It is thus necessary to form all possible products between one of the $U$'s and one of the $X$'s—that is, $U_1X_1, U_1X_2, U_1X_3, \ldots, U_2X_3$ and treat these as six additional predictor variables. There would therefore be a total of $2 + 3 + 6 = 11$ "dummy" predictor variables in the multiple-regression version of the $3 \times 4$ ANOVA problem. It is easy to see that the number of predictor variables increases rapidly with the complexity of the design; so it is not surprising that Fisher should have striven, and succeeded, in inventing the alternative computational routines of ANOVA. Without the benefit of a computer, the solution of the normal equations (21) is a formidable task even when $p = 4$ or 5.

Returning now to the question of identity of the results obtained by the usual ANOVA method and the multiple-regression approach, just outlined, it can be recalled that a set of $K$ group means of $Y$, $\overline{Y}_1, \overline{Y}_2, \ldots, \overline{Y}_K$ can be perfectly fitted by a poly-nomial regression equation of degree $K - 1$. Hence, as pointed out earlier, the sum of squares $R_{K-1}^2 \Sigma y^2$ due to the regression equation of degree $K - 1$ is equal to $SS_b$, since $\Sigma n_k(\hat{Y} - \overline{Y})^2 = \Sigma n_k(\overline{Y}_k - \overline{Y})^2$ when $\hat{Y} = \overline{Y}_k$ for each group. It therefore follows that $(1 - R_{k-1}^2)\Sigma y^2 = SS_w$, and hence that Eqn. (26) becomes

$$F = \frac{R^2/(K-1)}{(1-R^2)/(N-K)} = \frac{MS_b}{MS_w} \tag{40}$$

which is the customary $F$-test of ANOVA.

Consequently, in order to show that the same holds for the multiple correlation of $Y$ with the $K - 1$ dummy variables $X_1, X_2, \ldots, X_{K-1}$ introduced above, it need only be shown that

$$R_{Y \cdot X_1 X_2 \ldots X_{K-1}} = R_{Y \cdot X X^2 X^3 \ldots X^{K-1}} \tag{41}$$

Although a general proof of this relation requires some background in linear algebra, it is a simple matter to verify that it holds for, say $K = 3$.

It stands to reason (and it can be proved both algebraically and geometrically) that the criterion vari-able $Y$ has the same multiple correlation with $X_1$ and $X_2$ as it does with $X$ and $X^2$. This reasoning can be extended to the general case of $K - 1$ dummy variables for $K$ groups. Each dummy variable may be shown to be a linear function of $X, X^2, \ldots, X^{K-1}$ where $X$ may be given the values $0, 1, \ldots, K-1$ (or $1, 2, \ldots, K$ or any $K$ distinct values for that matter) for members of the $K$ groups, respectively. Hence $Y$ has the same multiple correlation with $X_1, X_2, \ldots, X_{K-1}$ as it does with $X, X^2, \ldots, X^{K-1}$, and since it is already known that $r_{Y \cdot \hat{Y}_{K-1}}^2 \Sigma y^2 = SS_b$, it follows that the significance test of $R_{Y - X_1 X_2 \ldots X_{K-1}}$ is equivalent to the $F$ test $MS_b/MS_w$ of ANOVA.

Two other coding systems that are often used are effect coding and contrast coding. In the former, which is a special case of the latter, all members of a particular group (usually the $K$th) are given the value $-1$ in all the $K - 1$ coding variables, while members of one and only one of the other groups are given a $+1$ on each coding variable in turn, members of all other groups getting 0's. Thus, for instance, with $K = 4$:

| | | | |
|---|---|---|---|
| 1 | 0 | 0 | for Group-1 members |
| 0 | 1 | 0 | for Group-2 members |
| 0 | 0 | 1 | for Group-3 members |
| $-1$ | $-1$ | $-1$ | for Group-4 members. |

Note that the columns here constitute the coding vari-ables. This system has the advantage that the resulting regression coefficients $b_1, b_2, \ldots, b_{K-1}$ represent the successive treatment effects $\overline{Y}_1 - \overline{Y}, \overline{Y}_2 - \overline{Y}, \ldots, \overline{Y}_{K-1} - \overline{Y}$ (assuming that members of Group $j$ got the 1 on the $j$-th coding variable).

In the more general contrast coding system, it is usual to use—as the values of each coding variable for the several groups—any set of numbers that add up to zero, with the further condition that no column (listing the values for one coding variable) be a linear combination of the other columns. Thus, the first three columns below qualify as values for a set of contrast coding variables, but the last three columns do not, because VI = IV + V.

| | I | II | III | IV | V | VI |
|---|---|---|---|---|---|---|
| Group 1: | 3 | 0 | 0 | 1 | 0 | 1 |
| Group 2: | $-1$ | 2 | 0 | $-1$ | 1 | 0 |
| Group 3: | $-1$ | $-1$ | 1 | $-1$ | 0 | $-1$ |
| Group 4: | $-1$ | $-1$ | $-1$ | 1 | $-1$ | 0 |

Each contrast coding variable asks a specific question. For example, I above asks whether $\overline{Y}_1$ differs sig-nificantly from the average of $\overline{Y}_2$, $\overline{Y}_3$, and $\overline{Y}_4$; II asks whether $\overline{Y}_2$ differs significantly from the average of $\overline{Y}_3$ and $\overline{Y}_4$. When the contrasts further satisfy the condition of orthogonality—that is, when the products of corresponding values of any pair of coding variables sum to zero (as do those in the set I, II, III)— the resulting analysis has an interesting property. Namely the coding variables are then uncorrelated among them-selves, and hence the squared multiple $R$ is the sum of the squares of the zero-order $r$'s of the several coding variables with the criterion:

$$R_{Y \cdot 12 \ldots (K-1)}^2 = r_{Y1}^2 + r_{Y2}^2 + \ldots + r_{Y,K-1}^2$$

### 2.1 Advantages of the Multiple Regression Approach

The advantages of the multiple regression approach to ANOVA are implicit in the above discussions. The main advantage is that, with a judicious choice of coding variables, it is possible to dispense with the two-stage procedure of carrying out "global" significance tests and then going on to more specific, "fine-grained" sig-nificance tests that address specific issues, and go directly to the latter.

Another advantage is that a mixture of quantitative and categorical variables can be used as the independent variables in multiple regression whereas in ANOVA the independent variables must all be categorical or delib-erately categorized (e.g., "high," "medium," "low" in mechanical aptitude), thus resulting in a loss of infor-mation.

Also, there is a greater flexibility available to the researcher in the order in which the independent variables are entered into the analysis. Since, at each stage, the significance of the increase in $R^2$ is tested, this corresponds to asking whether or not the later entered variable affects the criterion over and above the effects associated with the earlier entered variables.

Finally, and somewhat ironically, the "simplified" computational routines that Fisher developed in the precomputer days for ANOVA are mixed blessings at best in the computer age. Multiple regression offers a unified approach that dispenses with having to use specific formulas for specific designs.

An approach that further formalizes, generalizes, and routinizes the multiple regression approach is called the general linear model approach. This avoids (at least initially) an explicit coding of members of different subclasses by using coding variables and, instead, utilizes what is called the design matrix to specify the structural equation of the design being used. The interested reader is referred to treatises by Bock (1975), Finn (1974), and to a brief, introductory booklet by Tatsuoka (1975).

## 3. Concluding Remarks

Space limitations have precluded the discussion of several ancillary but nevertheless noteworthy topics in the forgoing. Cursory mention will therefore be made of some of them here, and the reader will be referred to suitable sources.

### 3.1 Correction for Shrinkage

One consequence of using the least-squares principle in determining the regression coefficients (more precisely, estimating the population regression coefficients) and the multiple correlation coefficient is that the latter is necessarily "inflated" for what can reasonably be expected as the correlation $r_{Y\hat{Y}}$ when the equation is used in a subsequent sample. A correction is therefore called for, and one that is commonly used is Wherry's shrinkage formula,

$$R_w^2 = 1 - \frac{N-1}{N-p}(1-R^2) \qquad (42)$$

where $N$ is the sample size, $p$ the number of predictor variables, and $R$ and $R_w$ are the observed and "corrected" (or deflated) multiple-$R$, respectively.

This formula, however, is not the most appropriate one, for it is actually an estimate of what the population $R^2$ would be if the regression coefficients were optimized in the population as a whole. A better shrinkage formula is that developed by Stein (1960), which reads

$$R_s^2 = 1 - \frac{N-1}{N-p-1}\frac{N-2}{N-p-2}\frac{N+1}{N}(1-R^2) \qquad (43)$$

What this equation gives is an estimate of the cross-validated $r_{Y\hat{Y}}^2$ in the population, using the sample-based

regression equation. It therefore is closer to what is being looked for, that is the $r_{Y\hat{Y}}^2$ in a subsequent sample, using the current regression equation.

### 3.2 Alternative Predictor-weighting Schemes

By the same token as the sample $R^2$ is an overestimate of the population $R^2$ and the cross-validated $r_{Y\hat{Y}}^2$ in the population, the observed regression coefficients $b_j$ or $b_j^*$, as the case may be, are extremely unstable from one sample to the next. Several authors have therefore proposed alternative weighting schemes, the most recent of which is Wainer's (1976) unit-weight system, which holds that not much predictive power is lost by simply giving every standardized predictor a weight of one. While this has considerable intuitive appeal, some cautions against uncritical acceptance of the proposal are given by Laughlin (1978) and by Pruzek and Frederick (1978), to which Wainer (1978) responds in defence.

### 3.3 Ridge Regression

A different problem occurs when one predictor has a high multiple correlation with some of the others. In this situation the sample SSCP matrix $\mathbf{S}_{xx}$—or correlation matrix $\mathbf{R}_{xx}$ if the standardized predictors are being used—becomes close to singular, and the solution of the normal equations for $\mathbf{b}$ or $\mathbf{b}^*$ becomes extremely inaccurate. One method designed to cope with this problem (often called the problem of multicollinearity) is known as ridge regression, and it consists essentially of modifying the correlation matrix by subtracting a suitable constant from the diagonal elements. Marquardt and Snee (1975) present a good exposition of this method.

### 3.4 Applications

Applications of multiple regression analysis in educational research—especially those of the "technological" variety designed for practical prediction purposes—are too numerous even to think of reviewing in the limited space available. A highly selective, minuscule set of abstracts of some of the more innovative and research-oriented applications is given here, and the reader is referred to other sources of research examples.

An often cited and early example of the "ANOVA qua multiple regression" type of research is Cronbach's (1968) reanalysis of Wallach and Kogan's (1965) study of creativity in young children. The original researchers did a $2 \times 2$ ANOVA for each sex separately, using dichotomies on indices labeled "intelligence" and "creativity" as the independent variables and measures of social interaction and confidence in schoolwork as the criteria. Cronbach used the sequential multiple regression approach entering intelligence [renamed "achievement" ($A$) to avoid "surplus connotations"] and creativity [likewise renamed "flexibility" ($F$)] first and then adding sex ($S$), $AS$, $FS$, and $AFS$, testing the incremental $R^2$ each time. Outcomes that contradicted Wallach and

Kogan's original results were that a significant $A \times F$ interaction was found on several dependent variables while the $A \times S$, $F \times S$, and $A \times F \times S$ interactions were in general nonsignificant.

In a study of the effects of classroom social climate on learning, Anderson (1970) included quadratic and product terms of the predictors, using samples at random from about 110 high-school physics classes. The criteria were posttest–pretest gain scores on a physics achievement test, a test on understanding science, and two other tests. Treating males and females separately, a total of eight multiple regression equations were constructed, entering IQ, LEI (learning environment inventory), IQ $\times$ LEI, $(IQ)^2$ and $(LEI)^2$ sequentially as predictors in each case. Not surprisingly, the IQ $\times$ LEI interaction was found significant in many cases, but the detailed graphical presentations of the resulting response surfaces are well worth careful study.

Another ingenious study relating environmental forces to cognitive development was that by Marjoribanks (1972), who was interested also in the possible effects of ethnic background (Canadian Indians, French Canadians, Jews, southern Italians, and WASPs). Specifically, eight "environmental variables" ($P$) (press for achievement, press for intellectuality, press for independence, etc.) plus ethnicity ($E$) served as the independent variables, and four subtests (verbal, number, spatial, and reasoning) of the SRA Primary Mental Abilities Test constituted the dependent variables. The main results for the verbal subtest (which was the most highly affected by the independent variables) was that $R^2_{V \cdot P_1 P_2 \ldots P_8 E_1 E_2 \ldots E_4} = 0.61$ while $R^2_{V \cdot P_1 P_2 \ldots P_8} = 0.50$ and $R^2_{V \cdot E_1 E_2 \ldots E_4} = 0.45$. (Note that there are eight variables in the environmental press set, since each is a quantitative variable in its own right, while there are four coding variables for the five ethnic groups.) From these three $R^2$ values, it may be inferred that the proportion of variability in verbal ability attributable to environmental press alone is $0.61 - 0.45 = 0.16$, while that attributable to ethnicity alone is $0.61 - 0.50 = 0.11$. This subtraction of squared multiple $R$'s is in the same spirit as that of incremental (or decremental) $R^2$'s, described above. Note, however, that the differencing is here done for sets of variables (the eight environmental variables as a set, and the four ethnic variables as a set) rather than individual variables. The systematic study of the separate effects of single sets of independent variables and the joint effects of two or more sets, when the independent variables fall into natural clusters as they do here, was called commonality analysis by Mayeske and his co-workers (1969) who used it as a prominent tool in a reanalysis of the well-known Coleman Report (*Equality of Educational Opportunity* 1966).

More than one study in the area of detection and correction of salary inequalities (between the sexes, among ethnic groups, etc.) have used multiple regression as their main analytic tool.

Birnbaum (1979), however, argues that it is fallacious to conclude, on the basis of a regression analysis of salary on merit (as measured by the typical indices of number of journal articles and other publications, ratings of teaching, years of experience, etc.), that discrimination exists whenever the actual salaries ($Y$) for a minority group fall short of the predicted salaries ($\hat{Y}$) based on the regression equation for the majority group (e.g., white males). He contends that the opposite regression—that of merit on salary—should also be considered. Group bias should be inferred only if a particular group is shown to have a lower mean salary holding merit constant and to have higher mean merit holding salary constant. An equitable system is proposed in which part of the salary increase is based on merit alone while another part is based on both merit and current salary in a compensatory manner (i.e., with current salary fixed, a person with greater merit gets a larger raise, whereas with merit fixed, a person with lower current salary gets a larger raise).

Besides Kerlinger and Pedhazur (1973) and Cohen and Cohen (1975), the following are excellent sources for discussions of illustrative research studies using regression analysis—and, in the second case, related techniques such as canonical correlation, covariance structure analysis, factor analysis, and path analysis: Pedhazur (1982) and Kerlinger (1977).

### 3.5 Computer Programs

No account of regression analysis would be complete without some mention of the available computer programs. Briefly, all the well-known computer packages such as BMD, BMDP, OSIRIS, SAS, and SPSS include one or more multiple regression and/or general linear model programs. A package that is not typically implemented at a computer center but requires one's own typing in the FORTRAN file is the package included in Cooley and Lohnes' textbook (1971). In addition, a stand-alone program for the general linear model, called MULTIVARIANCE, is available from International Educational Resources, Inc.

Each of these programs has its advantages and disadvantages, so it is not feasible to rate them from "best" to "least desirable." One thing that all these programs have in common is the stepwise multiple regression (Draper and Smith 1966) capability—something that was implicit through all the forgoing discussions but never explicitly mentioned; that is, adding predictors one at a time so that the incremental $R^2$ at each step is as large as possible and terminates the adding when the resulting incremental $R^2$ is not significant at a prescribed level. A related procedure is that of adding the independent variables successively in a predetermined order—not necessarily that which will maximize the incremental $R^2$—having to do with some sort of priority ordering either chronological or theoretical. It will be recalled that all the research examples alluded to, utilized this procedure.

Finally, it is almost trite to say that, with the increasing availability and popularity of microcomputers, one should become cognizant of the availability and efficiency of software capable of carrying out multiple regression and other statistical analysis that is proper to or compatible with each machine. A short-range economy may prove to be a long-term waste unless a brand is carefully selected to match its capabilities with a person's needs and plans.

## Bibliography

Anderson G J 1970 Effects of classroom social climate on individual learning. *Am. Educ. Res. J.* 7: 135–52

Birnbaum M H 1979 Procedures for the detection and correction of salary inequities. In: Pezzullo T R, Brittingham B F (eds.) 1979 *Salary Equity: Detecting Sex Bias in Salaries Among College and University Professors*. Lexington Books, Lexington, Massachusetts, pp. 121–44

Bock R D 1975 *Multivariate Statistical Methods in Behavioral Research*. McGraw-Hill, New York

Cohen J, Cohen P 1975 *Applied Multiple Regression/Correlation Analysis for the Behavioral Sciences*. Erlbaum, Hillsdale, New Jersey

Coleman J S, Campbell E Q, Hobson C J, McPartland J, Mood A M, Weinfeld F D, York R L 1966 *Equality of Educational Opportunity*. United States Government Printing Office, Washington, DC

Cooley W W, Lohnes P R 1971 *Multivariate Data Analysis*. Wiley, New York

Cronbach L J 1968 Intelligence? Creativity? A parsimonious reinterpretation of the Wallach–Kogan data. *Am. Educ. Res. J.* 5(4): 491–511

Darlington R B 1968 Multiple regression in psychological research and practice. *Psychol. Bull.* 69: 161–82

Draper N R, Smith H 1966 *Applied Regression Analysis*. Wiley, New York

Finn J D 1974 *A General Model for Multivariate Analysis*. Holt, Rinehart and Winston, New York

Green P E 1976 *Mathematical Tools for Applied Multivariate Analysis*. Academic Press, New York

Kerlinger F N 1977 *Behavioral Research: A Conceptual Approach*. Holt, Rinehart and Winston, New York

Kerlinger F N, Pedhazur E J 1973 *Multiple Regression in Behavioral Research*. Holt, Rinehart and Winston, New York

Laughlin J E 1978 Comments on "Estimating coefficients in linear models: It don't make no nevermind". *Psychol. Bull.* 85: 247–53

Marjoribanks K 1972 Ethnic and environmental influences on mental abilities. *Am. J. Sociol.* 78: 323–37

Marquardt D W, Snee R D 1975 Ridge regression in practice. *Am. Statistician* 29: 3–20

Mayeske G W et al. 1969 *A Study of Our Nation's Schools*. United States Office of Education, Washington, DC

Pedhazur E J 1982 *Multiple Regression in Behavioral Research: Explanation and Prediction*, 2nd edn. Holt, Rinehart and Winston, New York

Pruzek R M, Frederick B C 1978 Weighting predictors in linear models: Alternatives to least squares and limitations of equal weights. *Psychol. Bull.* 85: 254–66

Stein C 1960 Multiple regression. In: Olkin I, Ghurye S G, Hoeffding W, Madow W G, Mann H B (eds.) 1960 *Contributions to Probability and Statistics: Essays in Honor of Harold Hotelling*. Stanford University Press, Palo Alto, California, pp. 424–43

Tatsuoka M M 1971 *Multivariate Analysis: Techniques for Educational and Psychological Research*. Wiley, New York

Tatsuoka M M 1975 *The General Linear Model: A "New" Trend in Analysis of Variance*. Institute for Personality and Ability Testing, Champaign, Illinois

Wainer H 1976 Estimating coefficients in linear models: It don't make no nevermind. *Psychol. Bull.* 83: 213–17

Wainer H 1978 On the sensitivity of regression and regressors. *Psychol. Bull.* 85: 267–73

Wallach M, Kogan N 1965 *Modes of Thinking in Young Children: A Study of the Creativity–Intelligence Distinction*. Holt, Rinehart and Winston, New York

Winer B J 1971 *Statistical Principles in Experimental Design*, 2nd edn. McGraw-Hill, New York

# Triangulation

## N. K. Denzin

Triangulation is the application and combination of several research methodologies in the study of the same phenomenon. The diverse methods and measures which are combined should relate in some specified way to the theoretical constructs under examination. The use of multiple methods in an investigation so as to overcome the weaknesses or biases of a single method taken by itself is sometimes called multiple operationalism. The insistence on a multiple operational orientation in the social sciences is commonly associated in the field of psychology with the work of Donald T. Campbell and his associates (Brewer and Collins 1981).

Two outgrowths of Campbell's works have included the multitrait–multimethod matrix technique (Campbell and Fiske 1959) and the invention of the cross-lagged panel correlational technique (Pelz and Andrews 1964). The use of multiple measures and methods so as to overcome the inherent weaknesses of single measurement instruments, has, however, a long history in the physical sciences. The concept of triangulation, as in the action of making a triangle, may be traced to the Greeks and the origins of modern mathematics.

## 1. The Need for Triangulation

The social sciences rely, in varying degrees, on the following research methods: social surveys, experiments and quasiexperiments, participant observation, interviewing, case study and life history constructions, and unobtrusive methods (Denzin 1978). Each of these methods have built-in weaknesses which range from an inability to enter realistically the subject's life-world in experiments and surveys, to the problems of reflecting change and process in unobtrusive methods, the controlling of rival interpretive factors in participant observation and life histories, or an excessive reliance on paper and pencil techniques in surveys and interviewing.

The realities to which sociological methods are fitted are not fixed. The social world is socially constructed, and its meanings, to the observer and those observed, is constantly changing. As a consequence, no single research method will ever capture all of the changing features of the social world under study. Each research method implies a different interpretation of the world and suggests different lines of action the observer may take towards the research process. The meanings of methods are constantly changing, and each investigator brings different interpretations to bear upon the very research methods that are utilized.

For those reasons, the most fruitful search for sound interpretations of the real world must rely upon triangulation strategies. Interpretations which are built upon triangulation are certain to be stronger than those which rest on the more constricted framework of a single method.

## 2. The Hermeneutics of Interpretation

What is sought in triangulation is an interpretation of the phenomenon at hand that illuminates and reveals the subject matter in a thickly contextualized manner. A triangulated interpretation reflects the phenomenon as a process that is relational and interactive. The interpretation engulfs the subject matter, incorporating all of the understandings the researcher's diverse methods reveal about the phenomenon.

A hermeneutic interpretation does not remove the investigators from the subject matter of study but rather places them directly in the circle of interpretation.

While it is commonplace in the social sciences to place the investigator outside the interpretive process, hence asking the research methods to produce the interpretation that is sought, the hermeneutic interpretation dictates that "what is decisive is not to get out of the circle [of interpretation] but to come into it the right way" (Heidegger 1962 p. 195). Triangulation is the appropriate way of entering the circle of interpretation. The researcher is part of the interpretation.

## 3. Types of Triangulation

While it is commonly assumed that triangulation is the use of multiple methods in the study of the same phenomenon, this is only one form of the strategy. There are four basic types of triangulation. Data triangulation, involving time, space, and persons is the first type. Investigator triangulation consists of the use of multiple, rather than single observers. Theory triangulation consists of using more than one theoretical scheme in the interpretation of the phenomenon. Methodological triangulation, using more than one method, may consist of within-method or between-method strategies. Multiple triangulation exists when the researcher combines in one investigation multiple observers, theoretical perspectives, sources of data, and methodologies (Denzin 1978 p. 304).

## 4. A Case of Multiple Triangulation

The social sciences must move beyond investigations that triangulate only by data source, or by research method. Multiple triangulation must become the goal and aim of these disciplines. There are, however, few outstanding illustrations of this commitment. Perhaps Thomas and Znaniecki's publication, *The Polish Peasant in Europe and America* (1918, 1919, 1920) remains the classic in the social sciences.

This five-volume work, which sought to build a social psychology within the nascent field of sociology, utilized personal, historical, religious, and economic documents from and about Polish society, as it was disintegrating and undergoing transition prior to the First World War. The work consists of five documentary volumes which offer a study of the social organization and evolution of the peasant primary groups (family and community) under the influence of industrialization and immigration to America and Germany. Volumes 1 and 2 study the peasant family, the Polish marriage and class system, economic life, religious attitudes, and include correspondence between members of six family groups. Volume 3 is the autobiography of a peasant immigrant. Volume 4 examines the dissolution of primary groups in Poland and Volume 5 is based on studies of the Polish immigrant in America.

Thomas and Znaniecki's investigation used triangulated data, investigators, theories, and methods. Life histories, autobiographies, and family letters were at the core of their study, yet, in an unparalleled fashion, the research utilized participant observation, interviews, quasicomparative experiments on a grand scale, unobtrusive methods (letters), and surveys. Theoretically, the work wove its way (often implicitly) through the theories of Freud, James, Marx, Spencer, Durkheim, Mauss, Weber, Tonnies, Simmel, Hegel, Mead, Cooley, and Comte.

This study, still a classic and in need of reinterpretation, illustrates the scope and volume that multiple triangulation may assume. Smaller in size, but illustrative and pivotal in importance, stands Geertz's (1972) study on the "Balinese Cockfight." This investigation, based on description and interpretation, also triangulated data, investigators, theory, and methods.

## 5. Problems in Designing Multiple-triangulated Investigations

There are at least four basic problems to be confronted in such research. These are: (a) locating a common subject of analysis to which multiple methods, observers, and theories can be applied; (b) reconciling discrepant findings and interpretations; (c) novelty, or the location of a problem that has not been investigated before; (d) restrictions of time and money.

The location of a common subject of analysis can only be resolved through a clear understanding of the question the investigator wishes to answer. Divergent and discrepant findings are to be expected, for each inspection of the phenomenon is likely to yield different pictures, images, and findings.

These differences are not to be ignored, but should be reported so that future investigators can build upon such observations. Novel or new problems are often, upon inspection, not new, but merely manifestations of familiar topics previously examined from different perspectives and questions. Restrictions of time and money are the least problematic, for if investigators are thoroughly committed to understanding a problem area they will persist in examining it, even under difficult circumstances.

Triangulation is the preferred line of research in the social sciences. By combining multiple observers, theories, methods, and data sources, social scientists can begin to overcome the intrinsic bias that is bound to come from single-method, single-observer, single-theory investigations.

## Bibliography

Brewer M B, Collins B E 1981 *Scientific Inquiry and the Social Sciences: A Volume in Honor of Donald T. Campbell.* Jossey-Bass, San Francisco, California

Campbell D T, Fiske D W 1959 Convergent and discriminant validation by the multitrait–multimethod matrix. *Psychol. Bull.* 56: 81–105

Denzin N K 1989 *The Research Act: A Theoretical Introduction to Sociological Methods*, 3rd edn. Prentice Hall, Englewood Cliffs, New Jersey

Fielding N G, Fielding J L 1986 *Linking Data.* Sage, Beverly Hills, California

Geertz C 1972 Deep play: Notes on the Balinese cockfight. *Daedalus* 101: 1–37

Heidegger M 1962 *Being and Time.* Harper, New York

Lincoln Y S, Guba E G 1985 *Naturalistic Inquiry.* Sage, Beverly Hills, California

Patton M Q 1980 *Qualitative Evaluation Methods.* Sage, Beverly Hills, California

Pelz D C, Andrews F M 1964 Detecting causal priorities in panel study data. *Am. Sociol. Rev.* 29: 836–48

Silverman D 1985 *Qualitative Methodology and Sociology.* Gower, Brookfield, Vermont

Thomas W I, Znaniecki F 1918, 1919, 1920 *The Polish Peasant in Europe and America: Monograph of an Immigrant Group.* Gorham Press, Boston, Massachusetts

# Data Banks and Data Archives

### J. Anderson and M. J. Rosier

Research data are arranged in data sets, defined as organized collections of related data. The term data bank is commonly used to refer to a collection of related data sets, often associated with a single research project or survey. The quantity of data in most data sets or data banks usually necessitates the use of computerized retrieval systems with data stored in machine-readable form. Data archives are places where machine-readable data, such as those contained in data sets, are stored, preserved, and catalogued for access and use by others. Increasingly, educational researchers are making use of data held in data archives to answer questions, for example, about the achievement, attitudes, or attributes of students and schools, or to compare their data with other data collected at a different time or in a different place.

## 1. Data Banks in the Social Sciences

Although the concept of an educational data bank may conjure up visions of vast amounts of information being kept on file about schools, teachers, and students and thus may be thought of as depersonalizing education, there are reasons that may be advanced for maintaining such data banks.

The collection of research data, particularly large longitudinal studies or studies conducted nationwide or across countries, is expensive. The possibility that such data may be used by other research workers, for secondary analysis or for providing benchmarks to enable comparisons at some time in the future, helps to justify the expenditure. There is also a certain obligation on the part of researchers to ensure that collections of data, especially if funded by public monies, are made available as soon as possible to colleagues in the wider research community. This represents an extension of the current practice of the evaluation of the quality of scientific work by means of peer review and thus may lead to better educational research. The analysis of a data set by secondary analysts asking different questions and using a variety of models and statistical techniques should lead to a more robust interpretation of the data, particularly where initial analyses were conducted under severe time constraints imposed by the sponsoring agencies.

The archiving of data and their use by others may also reduce the need to interrupt schools and other educational institutions, which may in turn enhance the response by institutions on occasions when data are collected in the future. This applies particularly to the use of archived data sets for the training of research workers who wish to concentrate their efforts on developing a repertoire of statistical techniques rather than on data collection. Part of the justification for establishing the Social Science Research Council (SSRC) Survey Archive in the United Kingdom was that survey data are "a valuable resource in terms of both human effort and cash funds, and ought, therefore, to be protected and utilized so that the gain in knowledge that each individual effort represents is not needlessly dissipated, nor needlessly replicated".

One of the pioneering data banks in education was prepared for Project TALENT (Tiedeman 1972). Other well-known data banks have been associated with the cross-national studies conducted by the International Association for the Evaluation of Educational Achievement (IEA): the IEA Mathematics Data Bank (Wolf 1967) and the IEA Six-subject Data Bank (Schwille and Marshall 1975, Walker 1976). The IEA Six-subject Data Bank, for instance, holds data collected from approximately 250,000 students, 50,000 teachers, and 10,000 schools in 21 countries as part of six international surveys of achievement in science, reading comprehension, literature, civic education, and French and English as foreign languages. In each of the surveys, student achievement data, as well as information about students' home and socioeconomic backgrounds, attitudes, and interests, together with information from teachers and schools, were gathered by testing students age 10 years, 14 years, or in the last year or pre-university year of schooling. The data bank is lodged in data archives in Sweden (Institute of International Education, University of Stockholm) and in the United States (Inter-University Consortium for Political and Social Research, Ann Arbor, Michigan), as well as in other repositories at research centres and universities in Australia, the United Kingdom, Canada, Japan, and New Zealand. The rich IEA data banks have been accessed by research workers from many countries (Postlethwaite and Lewy 1979).

For preparing data for lodgment in a data bank as well as for accessing them once there, the computer is a vital research tool. However, even though physically smaller and ever more powerful computers are constantly being developed, not even today's largest computer could store in its central processing unit (CPU) more than a small fraction of, say, an IEA data bank. A data bank must usually be held in supplementary storage, such as on magnetic disc or tape. Data arranged in data files are stored as small magnetized dots on the iron oxide surface of the disc or tape. Reading heads, reading across the surfaces of a disc (random access) or sequentially through a tape (sequential access), are able to retrieve particular data as requested by users and return these to the CPU. In this way computers permit the storing of vast quantities of data in compact form for subsequent analysis by the research workers who gathered the data originally or by other researchers engaged in secondary analysis of the data.

The establishment of data banks in the social sciences has been paralleled by the development of refined statistical software packages which facilitate the researcher's task of accessing and analysing data. Most computer installations have integrated packages of programs for the management and analyses of social science data: for example, the Statistical Package for the Social Sciences, commonly known as SPSS (Nie et al. 1975),

and OSIRIS (Institute for Social Research 1981). The major packages usually have the facility to access data sets prepared by the use of other packages.

## 2. Data Documentation

Before any use can be made of a particular data set, such as, say, the science survey data set for 10-year-olds in Italy held in the IEA Data Bank, it is necessary to have adequate documentation to enable the data to be interpreted.

The documentation requirements are of two kinds. First, there is general documentation providing information about the study for which the data were collected; and, second, there is specific documentation describing the format or layout of the machine-readable data. The central requirement is the adequacy of the documentation rather than the particular conventions adopted. The total documentation for any data set would normally contain:

(a) identifying information (e.g. title of study, investigator(s), abstract, related publications);

(b) background information (e.g. describing the context within which the study was conducted);

(c) details of design and sampling (of which greater detail may be included in a report cited in the bibliography);

(d) data gathering information (including test instruments and how these were administered); and

(e) information about data organization (e.g. coding of responses and how the response data are stored in the data set).

All or part of this documentation may be located with the data on the computer in machine-readable form. Again, the crucial issue is the availability of this information, rather than how it is stored.

## 3. Data Organization

In educational research a data set typically comprises measures obtained for a sample of cases. The case, which is the basic unit of analysis, may be some larger unit such as a class of students or a school. Measures might include, for instance, personal characteristics, demographic data, and achievement scores, in which event each case would contain these groups of variables, and the ordering of the variables would be exactly the same for all cases.

When data are being prepared in a form ready for analysis, all variables for each case are organized into a data file. Three steps are involved: coding, entering data, and file building. At the same time a codebook is usually prepared, containing information about the coding scheme adopted for all variables and their location on the data file.

## 3.1 Coding the Data

In entering data into the computer it is usual to code the information collected for each case by assigning symbols to each item on the completed instrument(s). Alphabetic and special characters are generally to be avoided in coding the data, since the computer is able to process numerical data more efficiently. The practice of using multiple codes for a single item, which would involve making several punches in a single column of a card, should also be avoided since many statistical software packages cannot handle this format.

To illustrate the assigning of symbols to items, respondents' names are often coded 001, 002, 003 . . . while sex might be coded as 1 (male), 2 (female). Coding is thus seen to result in compact storage and, in the case of personal data, helps to preserve confidentiality. Accompanying documentation must clearly indicate the meaning of all assigned codes (though names of respondents or schools are not displayed) and this information is commonly included in a codebook.

For open-ended questionnaire items coding must frequently follow the data collection. An example of an item involving both pre- and post-coding is illustrated in the following:

> Do you speak a language other than English? Yes? No?
> If so, which main one? .................................

Upon examination of responses, a decision may be made to group the languages elicited in the second question: for example, as North European, South European, and Other. Consequently, a single digit could be used to code responses to both questions as follows:

1—English only
2—English and North European
3—English and South European
4—English and other

There are several good texts (e.g. Johnson 1977) that provide details of coding schemes.

Where possible, the coding of the data should preserve the information contained in the original responses, provided that the requirements of anonymity are observed. For example, a variable measuring school size should be coded in terms of the actual enrolments, allowing the investigator or secondary analyst to group the numbers as desired (e.g. less than 600, 601–800, 801–1,000, more than 1,000). Similarly, if the study includes a test, the responses to each test item should be individually coded. Optionally, the data set may contain in addition certain derived scores, such as totals or subscores for groups of items, provided the accompanying documentation details how the derived scores were obtained.

Where respondents fail to answer, or respond "inapplicable" or "don't know", such responses should also be given specific code values. Many of the statistical software packages allow up to three values to be des-

ignated as missing and thus it is possible to distinguish between these particular instances of missing data and yet at the same time to process them similarly in any analysis (for example, by excluding all such cases in analyses). If, for instance, two digits have been used to code a given variable, then the following codes could be reserved as missing value codes:

97—Inapplicable
98—Don't know
99—Omitted (or not ascertained)

For some analysis packages, problems may occur if missing responses are represented by blanks or spaces on the data file, instead of by alphanumeric symbols.

## 3.2 Data Entry and File Building

Once the data are coded, they may then be entered into the computer. This is commonly accomplished by punching the data on to 80-column cards, or by using response formats that can be optically scanned by a computer-linked device, or by keying directly via a terminal (key-to-disc). Where there is more than one card per respondent (or case), it is usual to identify each record with the case and card number, a useful precaution with cards in the event of dropping them. Supposing each case extended over two cards, an arrangement such as that illustrated in Fig. 1 might be used.

The first stage in building a data file is to merge these cards into a single record, which means that the identification data on each card need to be included once only on each record. As the cards are merged, a "sort-and-merge" check is usually made to ensure that the number of cases in the data file corresponds to the number of cases in the study and that for each case there is the same number of cards. Other kinds of checks attempt to identify the presence of "wild" code values (values outside the range specified for the variable), resulting from miskeying or mispunching.

When the originally coded data on the data file are assembled, and corrected as necessary, a common practice is to create a range of secondary variables from

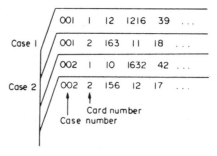

**Figure 1**
Arrangement for identifying records where each case extends over two cards

particular original or primary variables. For example, a variable to measure socioeconomic level may be a composite formed from variables measuring occupation, education, and income. The procedures adopted in forming such secondary variables always need to be fully documented.

### 3.3 Preparing the Codebook

The preparation of a codebook is an essential part of preparing the data file, since the codebook contains details about the characteristics of each variable and its location on the file. The following features are included for each variable in most codebooks:

(a) Variable identification: Each variable is identified by a number or a set of alphanumeric characters. For example, the SPSS system uses a set of alphanumeric characters with a maximum length of eight characters.

(b) Variable name: In general, the variable identification is linked to a variable name or label. Variables to be used in an analysis are usually selected by means of the variable identification, while the printout may give both the variable identification and the variable name in order to improve readability.

(c) Location: The location of each variable within a given record on a data file must be specified in terms of the numbers of the columns it spans, which is equivalent to giving the number of the first column of the entry for the variable and the width of the entry (the number of columns occupied by the entry).

(d) Format: The format of the variables should be specified in terms of the number of decimal places present or implicit in the data for the variable.

(e) Missing data code(s): Where code values have been assigned to missing responses, these should be specified.

(f) Item text: It is also useful to include with each item the actual text of the item used to solicit the data for each variable, even if such information is available in accompanying documentation.

(g) Code values: For each variable with a defined set of code values, the values should be given together with the responses to which they are assigned.

(h) Notes: It is often useful to add notes providing further information about a variable, especially for warnings about problems associated with the data for a given variable.

If the codebook is prepared in machine-readable form, access to data in a data file and statistical analyses of the data are greatly facilitated. Computer software is available for preparing and generating codebooks at most data archives. Software (written in FORTRAN) is also available (Anderson 1981) for reading machine-readable codebooks. This program extracts the information that defines and describes the full data set or any desired subset of the data, and then, in conjunction with SPSS, it generates SPSS data-definition control cards. Output from the program simply requires the insertion of SPSS task-definition or procedure cards and data analysis can immediately commence. Because the codebook is accessed directly, accuracy is ensured in locating all variables, variable labels, format specifications, missing data values, and value labels. This procedure avoids both the tediousness and susceptibility to error of the manual assembly of control cards.

## 4. Documenting Data Sets for Lodgment in Data Archives

The following description of a national study exemplifies the type of documentation necessary for a data set to be lodged in a data archive. The document was prepared under the kind of cost and time constraints which normally apply in research studies.

The Second IEA Mathematics Study (Rosier 1980a) collected information in Australia in 1978 from large samples of students in two target populations: 13-year-old students and Year 12 mathematics students. Information was also collected from mathematics teachers and school principals. The main report of the study made comparisons between the 1978 data and those collected in 1964 for the First IEA Mathematics Study (Husén 1967, Keeves 1968).

The data files from the IEA data bank for the First IEA Mathematics Study were reorganized to bring them into a form compatible with the files for the Second IEA Mathematics Study. Thus the second study included secondary analysis on the data from the first study. The data from the second study and the reorganized data from the first study were both set up using the OSIRIS system, which includes a machine-readable dictionary linked to the set of data. There were 12 data files altogether: separate files for students, teachers, and schools, for the two population levels, and for the two studies (1964 and 1978).

It was decided to present the documentation describing the data for the second study as a technical report in a microfiche format that could be reproduced by photocopying rather than in a machine-readable format (Rosier 1980b). The microfiche format was more economical in terms of the resources available for the study, and had the additional advantage that copies of administrative documents and the testing instruments could be included in the same volume. In particular, the mathematics test items for this study included diagrams, and so could not have been included in a normal machine-readable format.

The same technical document also included the codebooks for the reorganized data files from the first study, but excluded details of sampling and administration which had been reported earlier. The technical document contained the following sections:

(a) Section 1: Introduction, including reference to the main publications of the study and acknowledgment of the persons associated with its conduct.

(b) Section 2: Sampling of schools and students for each of the two populations.

(c) Section 3: Administrative procedures involved in liaison with education departments, and school coordinators, and in the conduct of the testing in schools.

(d) Section 4: Preparation of data for analysis including coding and punching procedures, and details of the stages following in building the data files for the second study and in reorganizing the data files from the first study.

(e) Appendix 1: Copies of the main administrative documents used in contacting schools and conducting the testing in schools.

(f) Appendix 2: Copies of the testing instruments, including the responses of the first case in each file and the code values assigned to these responses.

(g) Codebooks: The codebook for each of the 12 files contained:

(i) description of variable types and names,
(ii) variable list containing coding details for each variable,
(iii) variable location, and
(iv) sample data, giving the value for each variable for the first five cases on each file.

## 5. Access to Data Archives

Major data archives have already been established for the social sciences. The archives collect data sets, often reorganizing the data files and documentation before making them available to other users. The archives also provide a range of services to distribute information about the nature and availability of the data sets, and to assist researchers in accessing them.

Two major archives are the SSRC (Social Science Research Council) Survey Archive, and the Inter-university Consortium for Political and Social Research (ICPSR). The former is the national repository of social science data in the United Kingdom. Established in 1967, its brief is "to collect and preserve machine-readable data relating to social and economic affairs from academic, commercial, and governmental sources and to make that data available for secondary analysis". This archive is located at the University of Essex, Colchester, Essex C04 35Q, England.

The latter archive, the ICPSR, is based at the University of Michigan, and is a major source of archived data sets for universities and other institutions in the United States. The ICPSR also maintains links with universities and national bodies in other countries, such as the SSRC Survey Archive in the United Kingdom, and provides reciprocal borrowing rights. It is located at the Institute for Social Research, University of Michigan, Ann Arbor, Michigan 48106, United States.

The archives produce catalogues describing the data sets that may be borrowed. Researchers normally gain access to the data sets by using the formal channels that have been established between the archives and the institutions participating in the system. Data sets are usually supplied on magnetic tapes according to specified technical formats. Documentation in the form of codebooks and test instruments is usually supplied at a nominal cost.

Two international bodies have been established to promote the development and use of data archives. The International Association of Social Science Information Services and Technology (IASSIST) was established in 1976. The International Federation of Data Organizations (IFDO) was started in 1977.

## 6. Some Issues

Although much progress has been made in establishing good data archives, more work is needed before the level of data archiving can be regarded as satisfactory. Three issues affect future developments.

### 6.1 Obtaining Data Sets

One of the major problems faced by archives is the difficulty in obtaining data sets. Even where data sets are identified and located, there may be problems in obtaining them for inclusion in the archives. Some researchers are still wary of releasing their data for examination by other persons. Progress in this area will depend largely on a spirit of cooperation between the original researchers and the secondary analysts. One avenue is to encourage the joint authorship by the primary and secondary researchers of publications arising from secondary analysis. At the least, the original researchers should be offered the opportunity to make rejoinders in publications which include the results of secondary analysis.

Frequently, there are certain conditions governing access to particular data sets. The SSRC Survey Archive, for instance, has three access categories: (a) unconditional access, (b) access conditional on the depositor being informed of the request, and (c) access conditional on the prior consent of the depositor being obtained. The researcher requesting access to archived data is usually required to sign an undertaking to protect the anonymity of individuals and of institutions supplying the data, to acknowledge indebtedness to the original data collectors and to the archive, and to furnish to the archive any publications resulting from use of the data.

Some funding agencies are now making it a condition of their grants that any data collected under the grant should be lodged in appropriate data archives. However, the grants should also be large enough so that the researcher has sufficient resources to build good data sets supported by adequate documentation.

## 6.2 Adequate Documentation

The usefulness of a data set depends largely on the adequacy of the documentation which describes details of the collection of the data and characteristics of the data. Good documentation is necessary if for no other reason than that it reduces the costs of secondary analysis by increasing the efficiency with which data can be accessed.

For example, good documentation may include a listing of the data for the first few cases on each file. When the secondary analyst first reads an archived file, it is then possible to compare the results from the archived file with the documented listing to ensure that all the data are present, and that the data files correspond to those submitted by the original researcher. In the same way, the codebook entries for each variable should contain a statement about the number of cases (frequency) associated with each code value. The secondary analyst should be able to reproduce these frequencies from the archived data set. As further assistance to the secondary analyst, the set of data collection instruments could be reproduced with the original responses and the associated coding for one case—say, the first case.

## 6.3 Level of Aggregation of Data

Data are most useful to secondary analysts when they are stored at a minimal level of aggregation (the microlevel). This means that the original responses to questionnaire or test items are retained in a coded form on the data file. The secondary analyst then has the option of changing the level of aggregation, for example by deriving total test scores from a set of test items, or by deriving a mean school score from the data for students in a given school. If only the aggregated data (total or mean scores) are provided, the option of conducting analyses at the individual level is no longer available. Of course, steps must be taken to ensure that access to

microlevel data does not enable conditions of anonymity or confidentiality to be breached.

## Bibliography

Anderson J 1981 *Machine-readable Codebooks*. Flinders University of South Australia, Adelaide

Husén T (ed.) 1967 *International Study of Achievement in Mathematics: A Comparison of Twelve Countries*. Almqvist and Wiksell, Stockholm

Institute for Social Research 1981 OSIRIS *IV User's Manual*, 7th edn. Institute for Social Research, University of Michigan, Ann Arbor, Michigan

Johnson M C 1977 *A Review of Research Methods in Education*. Rand McNally, Chicago, Illinois

Keeves J P 1968 *Variation in Mathematics Education in Australia*. Australian Council for Educational Research, Hawthorn, Victoria

Nie N H, Hull C H, Jenkins J G, Steinbrenner K, Bent D H 1975 SPSS *Statistical Package for the Social Sciences*, 2nd edn. McGraw-Hill, New York

Postlethwaite T N, Lewy A 1979 *Annotated Bibliography of IEA Publications (1962–1978)*. International Association for the Evaluation of Educational Achievement (IEA), University of Stockholm, Stockholm, Sweden

Rosier M J 1980a *Changes in Secondary School Mathematics in Australia 1964 to 1978*. Australian Council for Educational Research, Hawthorn, Victoria

Rosier M J 1980b *Sampling, Administration and Data Preparation for the Second IEA Mathematics Study in Australia*. Australian Council for Educational Research, Hawthorn, Victoria

Schwille J, Marshall S 1975 *The IEA Six-subject Data Bank: A General Introduction*. University of Stockholm, Stockholm

Tiedeman D V 1972 *Project TALENT Data Bank: A Handbook*. American Institutes for Research, Project TALENT. Palo Alto, California

Walker D A 1976 *The IEA Six-subject Survey: An Empirical Study of Education in Twenty-one Countries*. Almqvist and Wiksell, Stockholm

Wolf R M 1967 *Data Bank Manual: International Project for the Evaluation of Educational Achievement, Phase I: International Study of Achievement in Mathematics: A Comparison of Twelve Countries*. Almqvist and Wiksell, Uppsala

# Issues in the Design of Quantitative Evaluation Studies

## Sample Design[1]

### K. N. Ross

Sampling in evaluation research is generally conducted in order to permit the detailed study of part, rather than the whole, of a population. The information derived from the resulting sample is customarily employed to develop useful generalizations about the population. These generalizations may be in the form of estimates of one or more characteristics associated with the population, or they may be concerned with estimates of the strength of relationships between characteristics within the population.

Provided that scientific sampling procedures are used, the selection of a sample often provides many advantages compared with a complete coverage of the population: reduced costs associated with gathering and analyzing the data, reduced requirements for trained personnel to conduct the fieldwork, improved speed in most aspects of data manipulation and summarization, and greater accuracy due to the possibility of more intense supervision of fieldwork and data preparation operations.

The evaluation research situations in which sampling is used may be divided into three broad categories: (a) experiments in which the introduction of treatment variables occurs according to a prearranged experimental design and all extraneous variables are either controlled or randomized; (b) surveys in which all members of a defined target population have a known non zero probability of selection into the sample; and (c) investigations in which data are collected without either the randomization of experiments or the probability sampling of surveys.

Experiments are strong with respect to internal validity because they are concerned with the question of whether a true measure of the effect of a treatment variable has been obtained for the subjects in the experiment. Surveys, on the other hand, are strong with respect to external validity because they are concerned with the question of whether the findings obtained for the subjects in the survey may be generalized to a wider population. Investigations are weak with respect to both internal and external validity and their use is due mainly to convenience or low cost.

### 1. Populations: Desired, Defined, and Excluded

In any evaluation study it is important to have a precise description of the population of elements (persons, organizations, objects, and so on) that is to form the focus of the study. In most evaluation studies this population will be a finite one that consists of elements which conform to some designated set of specifications. These specifications provide clear guidance as to which elements are to be included in the population and which are to be excluded.

In order to prepare a suitable description of a population it is essential to distinguish between the population for which the results are ideally required, the desired target population, and the population which is actually studied, the defined target population. An ideal situation, in which the researcher has complete control over the research environment, would lead to both of these populations containing the same elements. However, in most evaluation studies some differences arise due, for example, to: (a) non coverage—the population description may accidentally omit some elements because the researcher has no knowledge of their existence; (b) lack of resources—the researcher may intentionally exclude some elements from the population description because the costs of their inclusion in data gathering operations would be prohibitive; or (c) an ageing population description—the population description may have been prepared at an earlier date and therefore it includes some elements which have ceased to exist.

The defined target population provides an operational definition which may be used to guide the construction

1 This article was originally published in the *International Journal of Educational Research*, Vol. 11, No. 1. It appears here with permission from Pergamon Press plc © 1987.

of a list of population elements, or a sampling frame from which the sample may be drawn. The elements that are excluded from the desired target population in order to form the defined target population are referred to as the excluded population. For example, during a cross-national study of science achievement carried out in 1970 by the International Association for the Evaluation of Educational Achievement (IEA), one of the desired target populations was described in the following way:

> All students aged 14.00–14.11 years at the time of testing. This was the last point in most of the school systems in IEA where 100 percent of an age group were still in compulsory schooling. (Comber and Keeves 1973 p. 10)

In Australia it was decided that, for certain administrative reasons, the study would be conducted only within the six states of Australia and not within the smaller Australian territories. It was also decided that only students in those school grade levels which contained the majority of 14-year-old students would be included in the study. The desired IEA target population was therefore reformulated in order to obtain the following defined Australian target population:
All students aged 14.00–14.11 on 1 August 1970 in the following Australian states and secondary school grades:

| | |
|---|---|
| New South Wales | Forms 1, 2, and 3 |
| Victoria | Forms 1, 2, 3, and 4 |
| Queensland | Grades 8, 9, and 10 |
| South Australia | Years 1, 2, and 3 |
| West Australia | Years 1, 2, and 3 |
| Tasmania | Years 1, 2, 3, and 4 |

The numbers of students in the desired IEA target population, the defined Australian target population, and the excluded population have been presented in Table 1. For Australia overall, the excluded population represented less than four percent of the desired target population.

## 2. Sampling Frames

The selection of a sample from a defined target population requires the construction of a sampling frame. The sampling frame is commonly prepared in the form of a physical list of population elements, although it may also consist of rather unusual listings, such as directories or maps which display less obvious linkages between individual list entries and population elements. A well constructed sampling frame allows the researcher to "take hold" of the defined target population without the need to worry about contamination of the listing with incorrect entries or entries which represent elements associated with the excluded population.

In practical evaluation studies the sampling frame incorporates a great deal more structure than one would expect to find in a simple list of elements. For example, in a series of large-scale evaluation studies carried out in 21 countries during the 1970s (Peaker 1975), sampling frames were constructed which listed schools according to a number of stratification variables: size (number of students), program (for example, comprehensive or selective), region (for example, urban or rural), and sex composition (single sex or coeducational). The use of these stratification variables in the construction of the sampling frames was due, in part, to the need to present research results for sample data that had been drawn from particular strata within the sampling frame.

## 3. Representativeness

The notion of representativeness is a frequently used and often misunderstood notion in evaluation research. A sample is often described as being "representative" if certain known percentage frequency distributions of element characteristics within the sample data are similar to the corresponding distributions within the whole population.

The population characteristics selected for these comparisons are referred to as *marker variables*. These variables are usually selected from among important

*Table 1*
The numbers of Australian students in the desired IEA target population and the defined Australian target population

| Location | Desired IEA target population | Defined Australian target population | Excluded population |
|---|---|---|---|
| *States* | | | |
| New South Wales | 78,163 | 76,317 | 1,846 |
| Victoria | 62,573 | 62,030 | 543 |
| Queensland | 33,046 | 31,839 | 1,207 |
| South Australia | 22,381 | 21,632 | 749 |
| West Australia | 19,128 | 18,708 | 420 |
| Tasmania | 7,868 | 7,789 | 79 |
| *Other Territories* | 3,427 | 0 | 3,427 |
| Total | 226,586 | 218,315 | 8,271 |

demographic variables that are not related to the conduct of the evaluation. Unfortunately there are no objective rules for deciding either which variables should be nominated as marker variables, or the degree of similarity required between percentage frequency distributions for a sample to be judged as "representative" of the population.

It is important to note that a high degree of "representativeness" in a set of sample data refers specifically to the marker variables selected for analysis. It does not refer to other variables assessed by the sample data and therefore does not necessarily guarantee that the sample data will provide accurate estimates for all element characteristics. The assessment of the accuracy of sample data can only be discussed meaningfully with reference to the value of the mean square error, calculated separately, for particular sample estimates (Ross 1978).

The most popular marker variables in the field of education have commonly been demographic factors associated with students (sex, age, socio-economic status, and so on) and schools (type of school, school location, school size, and so on). For example, in a series of evaluation studies carried out in the United States during the early 1970s, Wolf (1977) selected the following marker variables: sex of student, father's occupation, father's education, and mother's education. These variables were selected because their percentage frequency distributions could be obtained for the population from tabulations of census data prepared by the United States Bureau of the Census.

## 4. Probability Samples and Nonprobability Samples

The use of samples in evaluation research is usually followed by the calculation of sample estimates with the aim of either estimating the values of population parameters from sample statistics, or testing statistical hypotheses about population parameters. These two aims require that the researcher has some knowledge of the accuracy of the values of sample statistics as estimates of the relevant population parameters. The accuracy of these estimates may generally be derived from statistical theory provided that probability sampling has been employed. Probability sampling requires that each member of the defined target population has a known, and nonzero, chance of being selected into the sample.

In contrast, the stability of sample estimates based on nonprobability sampling cannot be discovered from the internal evidence of a single sample. That is, it is not possible to determine whether a nonprobability sample is likely to provide very accurate or very inaccurate estimates of population parameters. Consequently, these types of samples are not appropriate for dealing objectively with issues concerning either the estimation of population parameters, or the testing of hypotheses in evaluation research.

The use of nonprobability samples in evaluation research is sometimes carried out with the (usually implied) justification that estimates derived from the sample may be linked to some hypothetical universe of elements rather than to a real population. This justification may lead to research results which are not meaningful if the gap between the hypothetical universe and any relevant real population is too large.

In some circumstances, a well-planned probability sample design can be turned accidentally into a nonprobability sample design if some degree of subjective judgement is exercised at any stage during the execution of the sample design. Researchers may fall into this trap through a lack of control of field operations at the final stage of a multistage sample design. The most common example of this in educational settings occurs when the researcher goes to great lengths in drawing a probability sample of schools, and then leaves it to the initiative of teaching staff in the sampled schools to select a "random" sample of students or classes.

## 5. Types of Nonprobability Samples

There are three main types of nonprobability samples: judgement, convenience, and quota samples. These approaches to sampling have in common the characteristic that the elements in the target population have an unknown chance of being selected into the sample. It is always wise to treat the research results arising from these types of sample design as suggesting statistical characteristics about the population, rather than as providing population estimates with specifiable confidence limits.

### 5.1 Judgement Sampling

The process of judgement, or *purposive*, sampling is based on the assumption that the researcher is able to select elements which represent a "typical" sample from the appropriate target population. The quality of sample selected by using this approach depends on the accuracy of subjective interpretations of what constitutes a typical sample.

It is extremely difficult to obtain meaningful results from a judgement sample because, generally speaking, no two experts will agree upon the exact composition of a typical sample. Therefore, in the absence of an external criterion, there is no way in which the research results obtained from one judgement sample can be judged as being more accurate than the research results obtained from another.

### 5.2 Convenience Sampling

A sample of convenience is the terminology used to describe a sample in which elements have been selected from the target population on the basis of their accessibility or convenience to the researcher. Convenience samples are sometimes referred to as "accidental" samples because elements may be drawn into the sample simply because they just happen to be situated, spatially or administratively, near to where the researcher is conducting the data collection.

The main assumption associated with convenience sampling is that the members of the target population do not vary according to accessibility or convenience. That is, that there would be no difference in the research results obtained from a random sample, a nearby sample, a cooperative sample, or a sample gathered in some inaccessible part of the population.

As for judgement sampling, there is no way in which the researcher may check the precision of one sample of convenience against another. Indeed. The critics of this approach argue that, for many research situations, readily accessible elements within the target population will differ significantly from less accessible elements. They therefore conclude that the use of convenience sampling may introduce a substantial degree of bias into sample estimates of population parameters.

### 5.3 Quota Sampling

Quota sampling is a frequently used type of non-probability sampling. It is sometimes misleadingly assumed to be accurate because the numbers of elements are drawn from various target population strata in proportion to the size of these strata.

While quota sampling places fairly tight restrictions on the number of sample elements per stratum, there is often little or no control exercised over the procedures used to select elements within these strata. For example, either judgement or convenience sampling may be used in any or all of the strata. Therefore, the superficial appearance of accuracy associated with proportionate representation of strata should be considered in the light that there is no way of checking either the accuracy of estimates obtained for any one stratum, or the accuracy of overall estimates of population characteristics obtained by combining individual stratum estimates.

## 6. Types of Probability Samples

There are many ways in which a probability sample may be drawn from a population. The method that is most commonly described in textbooks is simple random sampling. This method is rarely used in practical evaluation research situations because: (a) the selection and measurement of individual population elements is often too expensive; and (b) certain complexities may be introduced intentionally into the sample design in order to address more appropriately the objectives and administrative constraints associated with the evaluation. The complexities most often employed in evaluation research include the use of stratification techniques, cluster sampling, and multiple stages of selection.

### 6.1 Simple Random Sampling

The selection of a simple random sample is usually carried out according to a set of mechanical instructions which guarantees the random nature of the selection procedure. For example, Kish (1965) provides the following operational definition in order to describe procedures for the selection of a simple random sample of elements without replacement from a finite population of elements.

> From a table of random digits select with equal probability $n$ different selection numbers, corresponding to $n$ of the $N$ listing numbers of the population elements. The $n$ listings selected from the list, on which each of the $N$ population elements is represented separately by exactly one listing, must identify uniquely $n$ different elements (Kish 1965 pp. 36–7).

Simple random sampling, as described in this definition, results in an equal probability of selection for all elements in the population. This characteristic, called *epsem* sampling (equal probability of selection method), is not restricted solely to this type of sample design. For example, equal probability of selection can result from either the use of equal probabilities of selection throughout the various stages of a multistage sample design, or from the employment of varying probabilities that compensate for each other through the several stages of a multistage sample design. Epsem sampling is widely applied in evaluation research because it usually leads to self-weighting samples in which the simple arithmetic mean obtained from the sample data is an unbiased estimate of the population mean.

### 6.2 Stratified Sampling

The technique of stratification is often employed in the preparation of sample designs for evaluation research because it generally provides increased accuracy in sample estimates without leading to substantial increases in costs. Stratification does not imply any departure from probability sampling, it simply requires that the population be divided into subpopulations called strata and that the probability sampling be conducted independently within each stratum. The sample estimates of population parameters are then obtained by combining the information from each stratum.

In some evaluation studies stratification is used for reasons other than obtaining gains in sampling accuracy. For example, strata may be formed in order to employ different sampling procedures within strata, or because the subpopulations defined by the strata are designated as separate domains of study.

Variables used to stratify populations in education generally describe demographic aspects concerning schools (for example, location, size, and program) and students (for example, age, sex, grade level, and socio-economic status).

Stratified sampling may result in either proportionate or disproportionate sample designs. In a proportionate sample design the number of observations in the total sample is allocated among the strata of the population in proportion to the relative number of elements in each stratum of the population. That is, a stratum containing a given percentage of the elements in the population would be represented by the same percentage of the total number of sample elements. In situations where the elements are selected with equal probability within strata, this type of sample design results in epsem sampling and self-weighting sample estimates of population parameters.

In contrast, a disproportionate stratified sample design is associated with the use of different probabilities of selection, or sampling fractions, within the various population strata. This can sometimes occur when the sample is designed to achieve greater overall accuracy than proportionate stratification by using *optimum allocation* (Kish 1965 p. 92). More commonly, in educational settings, disproportionate sampling is used in order to ensure that the accuracy of sample estimates obtained for stratum parameters is sufficiently high to be able to make meaningful comparisons between strata.

The sample estimates derived from a disproportionate sample design are generally prepared with the assistance of "weighting factors". These factors, represented either by the reciprocals of the sampling fractions or by a set of numbers proportional to them, are employed in order to prevent inequalities in selection probabilities from causing the introduction of bias into sample estimates of population parameters. The reciprocals of the sampling fractions, called "raising factors", refer to the number of elements in the population represented by a sample element (Ross 1978).

The weighting factors are usually calculated so as to ensure that the sum of the weighting factors over all elements in the sample is equal to the sample size. This ensures that the readers of evaluation reports are not confused by differences between actual and weighted sample sizes.

### 6.3 Cluster Sampling

A population of elements can usually be thought of as a hierarchy of different sized groups or *clusters* of sampling elements. These groups may vary in size and nature. For example, a population of school students may be grouped into a number of classrooms, or it may be grouped into a number of schools. A cluster sample of students may then be selected from this population by selecting clusters of students as classroom or school groups rather than individually, as would occur when using a simple random sample design.

The use of cluster sampling in evaluation research is sometimes undertaken as an alternative to simple random sampling in order to reduce research costs for a given sample size. For example, a cluster sample consisting of the selection of 10 classes, each containing around 20 students, would generally lead to smaller data collection costs compared with a simple random sample of 200 students. The reduced costs occur because the simple random sample may require the researcher to collect data from as many as 200 schools.

Cluster sampling does not prevent the application of probability sampling techniques. This may be demonstrated by examining several ways in which cluster samples may be drawn from a population of students. To illustrate, consider an hypothetical population, described in Fig. 1, of 24 students distributed among six classrooms (with four students per class) and three schools (with two classes per school). A simple random sample of four students drawn without replacement from this population would result in an epsem sample with each element having a probability of selection, $p$, equal to 1/6 (Kish 1965 p. 40). A range of cluster samples, listed below with their associated $p$ values, may also be drawn in a manner which results in epsem samples.

(a) Randomly select one class, then include all students in this class in the sample ($p = 1/6 \times 1/1 = 1/6$).

(b) Randomly select two classes, then select a random sample of two students from within these classes ($p = 2/6 \times 2/4 = 1/6$).

(c) Randomly select two schools, then select a random sample of one class from within these schools, then select a random sample of two students from within these classes ($p = 2/3 \times 1/2 \times 2/4 = 1/6$).

### 7. The Accuracy of Estimates Obtained from Probability Samples

The degree of accuracy associated with a sample estimate derived from any one probability sample may be judged by the difference between the estimate and the value of the population parameter which is being estimated. In most situations the value of the population parameter is not known and therefore the actual accuracy of an individual sample estimate cannot be cal-

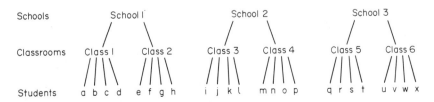

**Figure 1**
Hypothetical population of 24 students

culated in absolute terms. Instead, through a knowledge of the behavior of estimates derived from all possible samples which can be drawn from the population by using the same sample design, it is possible to estimate the probable accuracy of the obtained sample estimate.

## 7.1 Mean Square Error

Consider a probability sample of $n$ elements which is used to calculate the sample mean, $\bar{x}$, as an estimate of the population mean, $\bar{X}$. If an infinite set of samples of size $n$ were drawn independently from this population and the sample mean calculated for each sample, then the average of the resulting sampling distribution of sample means, the expected value of $\bar{x}$, could be denoted by $E(\bar{x})$.

The accuracy of the sample statistic, $\bar{x}$, as an estimator of the population parameter, $\bar{X}$, may be summarized in terms of the mean square error (MSE). The MSE is defined as the average of the square of the deviations of all possible sample estimates from the value being estimated (Hansen et al. 1960).

$$\begin{aligned} \text{MSE } (\bar{x}) &= E(\bar{x} - \bar{X})^2 \\ &= E(\bar{x} - E(\bar{x}))^2 + (E(\bar{x}) - \bar{X})^2 \\ &= \text{Variance of } \bar{x} + (\text{Bias of } \bar{x})^2 \end{aligned}$$

A sample design is unbiased if $E(\bar{x}) = \bar{X}$. It is important to remember that "bias" is not a property of a single sample, but of the entire sampling distribution, and that it belongs neither to the selection, nor to the estimation procedure alone, but to both jointly.

For most well designed samples in education the sampling bias is usually very small—tending towards zero with increasing sample size. The accuracy of sample estimates is therefore generally assessed in terms of the variance of $\bar{x}$, denoted var($\bar{x}$), which quantifies the sampling stability of the values of $\bar{x}$ around their expected value $E(\bar{x})$.

## 7.2 The Accuracy of Individual Sample Estimates

In educational settings the researcher is usually dealing with a single sample of data and not with all possible samples from a population. The variance of sample estimates as a measure of sampling accuracy cannot therefore be calculated exactly. Fortunately, for many probability sample designs, statistical theory may be used to derive formulae which provide estimates of the variance based on the internal evidence of a single sample of data.

For a simple random sample of $n$ elements drawn without replacement from a population of $N$ elements, the variance of the sample mean may be estimated from a single sample of data by using the following formula:

$$\text{var}(\bar{x}) = \frac{N - n}{N} \frac{s^2}{n}$$

where $s^2$ is the usual sample estimate of the variance of the element values in the population (Kish 1965 p. 41).

For sufficiently large values of $N$, the value of the

finite population correction, $(N - n)/N$, tends toward unity. The variance of the sample mean in this situation may be estimated to be equal to $s^2/n$.

The sampling distribution of the sample mean is approximately normally distributed for many educational sampling situations. This approximation improves with increased sample size even though the distribution of elements in the parent population may be far from normal. This characteristic of sampling distributions is known as the *central limit theorem* and it occurs not only for the sample mean but also for most estimators commonly used to describe survey research results (Kish 1965).

From a knowledge of the properties of the normal distribution we know that we can be "68 percent confident" that the range $\bar{x} \pm \text{SE}(\bar{x})$ includes the population mean, where $\bar{x}$ is the sample mean obtained from a single sample and $\text{SE}(\bar{x})$, often called the standard error, is the square root of var($\bar{x}$). Similarly the range $\bar{x} \pm 1.96 \text{ SE}(\bar{x})$ will include the population mean with 95 percent confidence.

While the above discussion has concentrated mostly on sample means derived from simple random samples, the same approach may be used to set up confidence limits for many other population values derived from various types of sample designs. For example, confidence limits may be calculated for complex statistics such as correlation coefficients, regression coefficients, multiple correlation coefficients, and so on (Ross 1978).

## 7.3 Comparison of the Accuracy of Probability Samples

The accuracy of probability samples is usually compared by considering the variances associated with a particular sample estimate for a given sample size. This comparison has, in recent years, been based on the recommendation put forward by Kish (1965) that the simple random sample design should be used as a standard for quantifying the accuracy of a variety of probability sample designs which incorporate such complexities as stratification and clustering. Kish (1965 p. 162) introduced the term *deff* (design effect) to describe the ratio of the variance of the sample mean for a complex sample design, denoted c, to the variance of a simple random sample, denoted srs, of the same size. That is,

$$deff = \frac{\text{var}(\bar{x}_c)}{\text{var}(\bar{x}_{srs})}.$$

For many complex sample designs that are commonly used in evaluation research the values of *deff* for sample means, and multivariate statistics, such as correlation coefficients and regression coefficients, are greater than unity (Ross 1978). Consequently, the accuracy of sample estimates in these studies may be grossly overestimated if formulae based on simple random sampling assumptions are used to calculate sampling errors.

The potential for arriving at false conclusions in evaluation research by using incorrect sampling error calculations has been demonstrated in a study carried out by Ross (1976). This study showed that it was highly misleading to assume that sample size was, in itself, an adequate indicator of the sampling accuracy associated with complex sample designs. For example, Ross (1976 p. 40) demonstrated that a two-stage cluster sample of 150 students (that was selected by randomly selecting six classes followed by the random selection of 25 students within these classes) had the sampling accuracy for sample means as would a simple random sample of 20 students.

### 7.4 Error Estimation Procedures for Complex Probability Samples

The computational formulae required to estimate the variance of descriptive statistics, such as sample means, are widely available for a wide range of probability sample designs which incorporate such complexities as stratification and cluster sampling (Kish 1965). However, in the case of more complex analytical statistics, such as correlation coefficients and regression coefficients, the required formulae are not readily available for sample designs which depart from the model of simple random sampling. These formulae are either enormously complicated or, ultimately, they prove resistant to mathematical analysis (Frankel 1971).

Due to the lack of suitable sampling error formulae for analytical statistics, researchers have sometimes tended to accept estimates based on formulae which assume that data have been gathered by using simple random sampling assumptions. This course of action may lead to erroneous evaluation conclusions because results described as "significant" may in reality be well within the bounds of random error (Ross 1978).

In the absence of suitable formulae, a variety of empirical techniques have emerged in recent years which provide "approximate variances that appear satisfactory for practical purposes" (Kish 1978 p. 20). These techniques may be divided into two broad categories: Random Subsample Replication and Taylor's Series Approximations.

In Random Subsample Replication a total sample of data is divided into two or more independent subsamples, each subsample following the overall sample design but being smaller in size. Then "a distribution of outcomes for a parameter being estimated is generated by each subsample. The differences observed among the subsample results are then analysed to obtain an improved estimate of the parameter, as well as a confidence assessment for that estimate" (Finifter 1972 p. 114). The main approaches in using this technique have been Independent Replication (Deming 1960), Jackknifing (Tukey 1958), and Balanced Repeated Replication (McCarthy 1966). The use of Taylor's Series Approximations is often described as a more direct method of variance estimation than the three approaches described above. In the absence of an exact formula for the variance, Taylor's Series is used to approximate a numerical value of the first few terms of

a series expansion of the variance formula. A number of computer programs have been prepared in order to carry out the extensive numerical calculations required for this approach (Wilson 1983).

## 8. Sample Design for Two-stage Cluster Samples

The two-stage cluster sample is probably the most commonly used sample design in educational research. This design is generally employed by selecting either schools or classes at the first stage of sampling, followed by the selection of either clusters of students within schools or clusters of students within classes at the second stage. In many evaluation studies the two-stage cluster design is preferred because this design offers an opportunity for the researcher to conduct analyses at higher levels of data aggregation. For example, the selection of students within classes at the second stage of sampling would, provided there were sufficient numbers of classes and numbers of students selected within classes, permit analyses to be carried out at the "between-student" level (by using data describing individual students) and also the "between-class" level (by using data based on class mean scores).

### 8.1 The Design Effect for Two-stage Cluster Samples

The value of the *design effect* (Kish 1965 p. 257) for the two-stage cluster sample design depends, for a given number of clusters and a given cluster size, on the value of the coefficient of intraclass correlation. That is,

$$deff = \frac{\text{var}(\bar{x}_\text{c})}{\text{var}(\bar{x}_\text{srs})} = 1 + (b - 1)\,roh$$

where $\text{var}(\bar{x}_\text{c})$ is the variance of the sample means for the two-stage cluster sample design, $b$ is the size of the selected clusters, and *roh* is the coefficient of intraclass correlation.

The coefficient of intraclass correlation, often referred to as *roh*, provides a measure of the degree of homogeneity within clusters. In educational settings the notion of homogeneity within clusters may be observed in the tendency of student characteristics to be more homogeneous within schools, or classes, than would be the case if students were assigned to schools, or classes, at random. This homogeneity may be due to common selective factors (for example, residential zoning of schools), or to joint exposure to the same external influences (for example, teachers and school programs), or to mutual interaction (for example, peer group pressure), or some combination of these.

### 8.2 The Effective Sample Size for Two-stage Cluster Samples

The *effective sample size* (Kish 1965 p. 259) for a given two-stage cluster sample is equal to the size of the simple random sample which has a level of sampling accuracy, as measured by the variance of the sample mean, which is equal to the sampling accuracy of the given two-stage cluster sample. A little algebra may be used to demonstrate that the actual size, $n_c$, and the effective sample size, $n^*$, for a two-stage cluster sample are related to the design effect associated with that sample in the following manner (Ross 1978 pp. 137–138),

$$n_c = n^* \times deff.$$

From previous discussion, *deff* is replaced in this formula by an expression which is a function of the cluster size and the coefficient of intraclass correlation. That is,

$$n_c = n^* \times (1 + (b - 1)roh).$$

For example, consider a two-stage cluster sample based on a sample of 10 schools followed by the selection of 20 students per school. In addition, consider a student characteristic (for example, a test score or attitude scale score) for which the value of the coefficient of intraclass correlation is equal to 0.1. This value of *roh* would be typical for clusters of students selected randomly from within secondary schools in Australia (Ross 1983). In this situation, the above formula simplifies to the following expression,

$$200 = n^* \times (1 + (20 - 1)\,0.1).$$

Solving this equation for $n^*$ gives a value of 69 for the value of the equivalent sample size. That is, given the value of 0.1 for *roh*, a two-stage cluster sample of size 200 that is selected by sampling 10 schools followed by sampling 20 students per school would have sampling accuracy equivalent to a simple random sample of 69 students.

For a given population of students, the value of *roh* tends to be higher for clusters based on classes rather than clusters based on schools. Ross (1978) has obtained values of *roh* as high as 0.5 for mathematics test scores based on classes within Australian secondary schools. Using this value of *roh* in the above example provides an effective sample size of only 19 students!

### 8.3 Sample Design Tables

Sample design tables are often prepared for well-designed evaluation studies in which it is intended to employ two-stage cluster sampling. These tables present a range of sample design options, each designed to have a prespecified level of sampling accuracy. A hypothetical example has been presented in the following discussion in order to illustrate the sequence of calculations and decisions involved in the preparation of these tables.

Consider an evaluation study in which test items are administered to a two-stage cluster sample of students with the aim of estimating the percentage of students in the population that are able to obtain correct answers. In addition, assume that a sampling accuracy constraint has been placed on the design of the study so as to ensure that the sample estimate of the percentage of

students providing the correct answer, $p$, will provide $p \pm 5$ percent as 95 percent confidence limits for the value of the percentage in the population.

For reasonably large samples it is possible to assume normality of the distribution of sample estimates (Kish 1965 pp. 13–14) and therefore confidence limits of $p \pm 5$ percent are approximately equivalent to an error range of plus or minus two standard errors of $p$. Consequently, the error constraint placed on the study means that one standard error of $p$ needs to be less than or equal to 2.5 percent.

Consider a simple random sample of $n^*$ students selected from this population in order to calculate values of $p$. Statistical theory may be employed to show that, for large populations, the variance of the sample estimate of $p$ as an estimate of the population value may be calculated by using the following formula (Kish 1965 p. 46),

$$var(p) = \frac{p(100 - p)}{n^* - 1}.$$

The maximum value of $p(100 - p)$ occurs for $p = 50$. Therefore, in order to ensure that we could satisfy the error constraints described above, the following inequality would need to be valid,

$$(2.5)^2 \geq \frac{50(100 - 50)}{n^* - 1}.$$

That is, the size of the simple random sample, $n^*$, would have to be greater than or equal to about 400 students in order to obtain 95 percent confidence limits of $p \pm 5$ percent.

Now consider the size of a two-stage cluster sample design which would provide equivalent sampling accuracy to a simple random sample of 400 students. The design of this cluster sample would require knowledge of the numbers of primary sampling units (for example, schools or classes) and the numbers of secondary sampling units (students) which would be required.

From previous discussion, the relationship between the size of the cluster sample, $n_c$, which has the same accuracy as a simple random sample of size $n^* = 400$ may be written in the following fashion. This expression is often described as a "planning equation" because it may be used to explore sample design options for two-stage cluster samples.

$$n_c = 400 \times (1 + (b - 1)roh).$$

The value of $n_c$ is equal to the product of the number of primary sampling units, $a$, and the number of secondary sampling units selected from each primary sampling unit, $b$. Substituting for $n_c$ in this formula, and then transposing provides an expression for $a$ in terms of $b$ and *roh*. That is,

$$a = \frac{400}{b} \times (1 + (b - 1)\,roh).$$

**Table 2**
Sample design table for two-stage cluster samples with sampling accuracy equal to a simple random sample of 400

| Cluster size | $roh = 0.1$ | | | $roh = 0.2$ | | | $roh = 0.4$ | | |
|---|---|---|---|---|---|---|---|---|---|
| $b$ | *deff* | $n_c$ | $a$ | *deff* | $n_c$ | $a$ | *deff* | $n_c$ | $a$ |
| 1 | 1.0 | 400 | 400 | 1.0 | 400 | 400 | 1.0 | 400 | 400 |
| 2 | 1.1 | 440 | 220 | 1.2 | 480 | 240 | 1.4 | 560 | 280 |
| 5 | 1.4 | 560 | 112 | 1.8 | 720 | 144 | 2.6 | 1,040 | 208 |
| 10 | 1.9 | 760 | 76 | 2.8 | 1,120 | 112 | 4.6 | 1,840 | 184 |
| 15 | 2.4 | 960 | 64 | 3.8 | 1,530 | 102 | 6.6 | 2,640 | 176 |
| 20 | 2.9 | 1,160 | 58 | 4.8 | 1,920 | 96 | 8.6 | 3,440 | 172 |
| 30 | 3.9 | 1,560 | 52 | 6.8 | 2,730 | 91 | 12.6 | 5,040 | 168 |
| 40 | 4.9 | 1,960 | 49 | 8.8 | 3,520 | 88 | 16.6 | 6,640 | 166 |
| 50 | 5.9 | 2,400 | 48 | 10.8 | 4,350 | 87 | 20.6 | 8,250 | 165 |

As an example, consider $roh = 0.1$, and $b = 20$. Then,

$$a = \frac{400}{20} \times (1 + (20 - 1)\,0.1)$$
$$= 58.$$

That is, for $roh = 0.1$, a two-stage cluster sample of 1,160 students (consisting of the selection of 58 primary sampling units followed by the selection of clusters of 20 students) would have sampling accuracy equivalent to a simple random sample of 400 students.

In Table 2, the planning equation has been employed to list sets of values for $a$, $b$, *deff*, and $n_c$ which describe a group of two-stage cluster sample designs that have sampling accuracy equivalent to a simple random sample of 400 students. Three sets of sample designs have been listed in the table, corresponding to *roh* values of 0.1, 0.2, and 0.4. In a study of school systems in 10 developed countries, Ross (1983 p. 54) has shown that values of *roh* in this range are typical for achievement test scores obtained from clusters of students within schools.

The most striking feature of Table 2 is the rapidly diminishing effect that increasing $b$, the cluster size, has on $a$, the number of clusters that are to be selected. This is particularly noticeable when the cluster size reaches 10 to 15 students.

Consider, for example, two sample designs applied in a situation where a value of $roh = 0.4$ may be assumed: (a) a total sample of 2,640 students obtained by selecting 15 students per cluster from 176 clusters; and (b) a total sample of 8,250 students obtained by selecting 50 students per cluster from 165 clusters. From Table 2, it may be observed that both of these sample designs have sampling accuracy equivalent to a simple random sample of 400 students.

While these two sample designs have equivalent sampling accuracy, there is a striking difference between each design in terms of total sample size. However, the magnitude of this difference is not reflected proportionately in the difference between the number of clusters selected.

This result illustrates an important point for the planning of evaluation studies that seek to make stable estimates of population characteristics, namely that the sampling accuracy levels of two-stage cluster sample designs, for cluster sizes of 10 or more, tend to be greatly influenced by small changes in the number of clusters that are selected at the first stage of sampling, and relatively less influenced by small changes in the size of the selected clusters.

The main use of sample design tables like the one presented in Table 2 is to permit the evaluator to choose, for a given value of *roh*, one sample design from among a list of equally accurate sample design options. The final choice between equally accurate options is usually guided by cost factors, or data analysis strategies, or a combination of both of these.

For example, the cost of collecting data by using "group administration" of tests, questionnaires, and so on usually depends more on the number of selected schools than on the number of students surveyed within each selected school. This occurs because the use of this methodology usually leads to higher marginal costs associated with travel to many schools, compared with the marginal costs of increasing the number of students surveyed within each selected school. In contrast, the cost of collecting data by using "individual administration" of one-to-one tests, interviews, and so on, may often depend more on the total sample size than on the number of selected schools.

The choice of a sample design option may also depend upon the data analysis strategies that are being employed in the evaluation. For example, analyses may be planned at both the "between-student" and "between-school" levels of analysis. In order to conduct analyses at the between-school level, data obtained from individual students may need to be aggregated to obtain data files consisting of school records based on student mean scores. This type of analysis generally requires that sufficient students be selected per school to ensure that stable estimates are able to be made for individual schools. In addition, it generally requires that sufficient students and schools are available at each level of analysis so as to ensure that meaningful results may be obtained.

## 9. Sample Design and Experimental Approaches to Evaluation

One of the most simple, and most popular, experimental designs employed in evaluation studies is concerned with the use of *treatment* and *control* groups followed by a comparison of mean scores for the criterion variable. For example, the researcher may wish to examine the difference in the mean mathematics test scores for a treatment group of students exposed to an innovative program of mathematics instruction compared with a control group of students exposed to a traditional program of instruction.

In conducting the experiment it would be likely that the researcher would note some difference between the treatment group mean $(\bar{x}_1)$ and the control group mean $(\bar{x}_2)$. The important question, however, is whether this difference is sufficiently large to justify the conclusion that the means associated with the relevant parent populations are different.

A statistical procedure that is often used for checking this conclusion is the well known *t*-test for the significance of the difference between two means obtained for independent samples (Ferguson 1966 p. 167). The *t*-test employs the ratio of the difference in sample means $(\bar{x}_1 - \bar{x}_2)$ to the standard error of the difference in sample means $(s_d)$. This ratio has, assuming equal parent population variances, a distribution of *t* with $n_1 + n_2 - 2$ degrees of freedom.

The method used to estimate the value of $s_d$ in this ratio depends on the nature of the sampling and management of the experiment. For example, consider a study in which the students selected to participate in the study were: (a) assigned randomly and individually to the two experimental groups; and (b) responded to the experimental conditions independently of each other for the duration of the experiment. In this case $s_d$ would be estimated as the square root of the sum of the variances of the group means. The appropriate estimate of the *t* ratio for this experimental design would then be (Ferguson 1966 p. 167):

$$t = (\bar{x}_1 - \bar{x}_2)/\sqrt{(s^2/n_1 + s^2/n_2)}.$$

In order to simplify calculations, we may assume that the sample sizes for treatment and control groups are the same $(n_1 = n_2 = n)$, and also that the between-student standard deviations of student scores are the same $(s_1 = s_2 = s)$.

Under these simplifying assumptions the value of $s_d$ would be $s\sqrt{2/n}$, and the corresponding estimate of *t*

would be:

$$t_{\text{srs}} = (\bar{x}_1 - \bar{x}_2)/(s\sqrt{2}/n).$$

The "srs" subscript associated with the *t* ratio in the formula given above refers to the use of simple random sampling in the selection and allocation of the students to the experimental conditions. This estimate is quite different from the value which would be obtained if cluster sampling of intact groups had been employed in the selection and allocation of students. For example, consider a study in which the students selected to participate in the study were: (a) assigned randomly as intact class groups to the two experimental conditions; and (b) responded to the experimental conditions as intact class groups. In this case $s_d$ should be estimated by using a design effect factor in order to account for the degree of clustering associated with the use of intact class groups. The value of $s_d$ in the estimate of the *t* ratio would be:

$$s\sqrt{(2.deff/n)},$$

and the corresponding estimate of *t* ratio would be:

$$t_{\text{cluster}} = (\bar{x}_1 - \bar{x}_2)/(s\sqrt{(2.deff/n)}).$$

The vast majority of program evaluations in education are administered according to the "cluster" design described above. However, the data analyses for these studies often proceeds by using the "srs" formula to estimate the *t* ratio. In these situations the value of the *t* ratio may be over-estimated by a factor of $\sqrt{deff}$. The impact of this erroneous approach to the estimation of the *t* ratio leads to the possibility that the differences in mean scores between the experimental groups could be mistakenly interpreted as being statistically significant.

It is a sobering exercise to examine the magnitude of the influence of a design effect factor on the calculation of the *t* ratio. For example, Ross (1978) has shown that the intraclass correlation coefficient for mathematics test scores obtained from students in intact class groups in Australian secondary schools can be as high as 0.57. Using this value of *roh*, the value of *deff*, assuming a class size of 20, may be estimated from the formula relating the design effect to the intraclass correlation coefficient. That is,

$$deff = 1 + (20-1)\,0.57 = 11.83.$$

The adjustment factor for the estimated *t* ratio in this example would be the square root of 11.83. The *t* ratio would therefore need to be 3.43 times larger than the estimate of the *t* ratio obtained without taking account of the clustering effects associated with intact class groups.

The implications of this example for applications of *Analysis of Variance* techniques may be considered by noting that the *F* ratio is equal to the square of the *t* ratio in situations where only two experimental groups are employed (Ferguson 1966, p. 293). In this situation the adjustment factor for the *F* ratio would be equal to *deff*. That is, the value of the $F$ ratio which would emerge by applying statistical procedures appropriate for "srs" designs to a cluster design would need to be divided by 11.83.

The application of this kind of adjustment to many published evaluation studies would undoubtedly lead to observed differences between control and treatment groups being within the boundaries of chance fluctuation.

A number of authors (for example, Glass and Stanley 1970, Page 1975, Cronbach 1976, Hopkins 1982) have suggested that significance tests based on individual-level analyses may be unacceptable in studies which employ intact class groups as the units of sampling and experimentation. In particular, Glass and Stanley (1970) put forward a strong argument for using class means as the units of analysis in these types of studies; whereas Hopkins (1982) demonstrates skillfully that choice of the correct linear model will, under some assumptions, permit analyses to be carried out using students as the units of analysis.

The Glass and Stanley argument represents a worst case view of the example presented above concerning the use of the design effect to adjust $t$ and $F$ values. It is a worst case view because it would be similar to assuming a value of 1.0 for the intraclass correlation coefficient, which in turn would give a value of *deff* equal to the size of the class groups. That is, the observed value of $t$ and $F$ would need to be adjusted by 4.47 and 20, respectively.

## 10. Evaluation Designs when Sampling is not Possible

The key difficulty in dealing with the findings of an evaluation study that is not based on a probability sample drawn from a defined target population is that the researcher may be unable to assess accurately the confidence which can be attributed to generalizations that extend beyond the sample to some wide-ranging population of interest.

This situation can occur in evaluation studies where sampling is not possible due to administrative, political, or ethical constraints. For example, consider an evaluation of a government program designed to assist all students attending schools below a certain percentile cut-off point on an objective indicator of poverty. The withholding of the benefits of the program from an eligible student may, in some settings, be prohibited by law. In this situation the whole of the target population for whom the program was intended would form the treatment group for the program and there would be no possibility of selecting a comparable control group.

Many of the initial Title I evaluation designs prepared for the United States Office of Education faced this problem (Tallmadge and Wood 1976). The approach taken in these evaluations was generally either to use a benchmark population in order to provide a norm-referenced metric for gains made by the treatment group, or to form an approximate control group by sampling from a non-equivalent population and then employing regression adjustment in order to make comparisons (Gay 1980).

The norm-referenced design has involved the pre-testing and posttesting of students participating in the program, followed by a comparison of the gains made by these students in terms of percentile equivalents on standardized tests. In this situation a kind of surrogate control group is established through comparison of student gains with a set of norms obtained for an appropriate age-related or grade-related reference group. The regression-adjustment design has involved the comparison of predicted posttest scores with actual posttest scores. The prediction of posttest scores in this model has generally been based on correlations between pre-test and posttest scores and has been applied to results obtained from the treatment group of students participating in the program and an approximate control group of students sampled from just above the cut-off point set for the program. The effectiveness of the program has then been considered by investigating the degree to which the program participants were doing better than expected.

## 11. Conclusion

The discussion of sampling presented in this chapter has reviewed the characteristics of the types of probability and non-probability samples that are commonly used in evaluation studies in education. In addition, it has examined some of the implications of employing complex sample designs which depart markedly from the traditional model of simple random sampling.

This discussion incorporates two key messages which need to be remembered during the construction of sampling plans for evaluation studies.

The first message is that *sample size* is only one component of sample design and therefore the degree of accuracy associated with the results obtained from a sample should not be judged soley by the size of the sample. Consequently, small well-designed samples may provide more accurate information than large poorly-designed samples. For example: (a) a large sample selected by using non-probability sampling methods could result in large levels of bias because only readily accessible elements have been selected while important but less accessible elements have been overlooked; or (b) a large sample based on the technique of cluster sampling, for a population in which the size of the intraclass correlation coefficient was substantial, could lead to the effective sample size being extremely small compared with the actual sample size.

The second message is that good samples do not occur by accident, nor are they readily available in the sampling sections of standard textbooks on evaluation methodology. Rather, good samples are designed in the sense that they are planned to provide an optimal degree of sampling precision within the limitations posed by the administrative, cost, and analysis constraints that are placed on the particular evaluation studies in which they are to be used. Therefore, the sample design adopted for an evaluation study should represent the conclusion of an iterative process in which the final design is chosen from among the options described in a set of sample design tables that have been prepared, discussed, modified, and fine-tuned to the needs of the study.

## Bibliography

Comber L C, Keeves J P 1973 *Science Education in Nineteen Countries.* Wiley, New York

Cronbach L J 1976 *Research on Classrooms and Schools: Formulation of Questions, Design and Analysis.* Stanford University, Stanford, California

Deming W E 1960 *Sample Design in Business Research.* Wiley, New York

Ferguson G A 1966 *Statistical Analysis in Psychology and Education*, 2nd edn. McGraw Hill, New York (3rd edn. 1971)

Finifter B M 1972 The generation of confidence: Evaluating research findings by random subsample replication. In: Costner H L (ed.) 1972 *Sociological Methodology.* Jossey-Bass, San Francisco, California, pp 112–175

Frankel M R 1971 *Inference from Survey Samples: An Empirical Investigation.* Institute for Social Research, Ann Arbor, Michigan

Gay L R 1980 *Educational Evaluation and Measurement: Competencies for Analysis and Application.* Merrill, Columbus, Ohio

Glass G V, Stanley J S 1970 *Statistical Methods in Educat-ion and Psychology.* Prentice Hall, Englewood Cliffs, New Jersey

Hansen M H, Hurwitz W N, Madow W G 1960 *Sample Survey Methods and Theory*, Wiley, New York

Hopkins K D 1982 The unit of analysis: Group means versus individual observations. *Am Educ. Res. J.* 19: 5–18

Kish L 1965 *Survey Sampling.* Wiley, New York

Kish L 1978 On the future of survey sampling. In: Namboodiri N K (ed.) 1978 *Survey Sampling and Measurement.* Academic Press, New York

McCarthy P J 1966 *Replication: An Approach to the Analysis of Data from Complex Surveys.* United States National Center for Health Statistics, Washington, DC

Page E B 1975 Statistically recapturing the richness within the classroom. *Psychol. Sch.* 12: 339–44

Peaker G F 1975 *An Empirical Study of Education in Twenty-one Countries: A Technical Report.* Wiley, New York

Ross K N 1976 *Searching for Uncertainty: An Empirical Investigation of Sampling Errors in Educational Survey Research*, ACER Occasional Paper No. 9. Australian Council for Educational Research, Hawthorn, Victoria

Ross K N 1978 Sample design for educational survey research. *Eval. Educ.* 2: 105–95

Ross K N 1983 *Social Area Indicators of Educational Need.* Australian Council for Educational Research, Hawthorn, Victoria

Tallmadge G K, Wood C T 1976 *User's Guide: ESEA Title 1 Evaluation and Reporting System.* RMC Research Corporation, Mountain View, California

Tukey J W 1958 Bias and confidence in not-quite large samples (Abstract). *Annals of Mathematical Statistics* 29: 614

Wilson M 1983 *Adventures in Uncertainty,* ACER Occasional paper No. 17. Australian Council for Educational Research, Hawthorn, Victoria

Wolf R M 1977 *Achievement in America.* Teachers College Press, New York

# Cross-sectional Survey Studies

**D. A. Walker and P. M. Burnhill**

No single definition of a survey is completely satisfactory. There are many different types of survey, but in general they all attempt to obtain measurements from a sample of individuals selected from a predefined finite population in their natural setting. In many instances the individuals are people, but they might be, for example, books in a library. In the cross-sectional type of survey, with which this article is concerned, the measurements are obtained at or about a particular time, and for the most part the purpose is to describe situations and estimate frequencies rather than to establish causal patterns. In a longitudinal survey, on the other hand, measurements of the same individual are made at intervals over a period of time which may cover several years. Although the techniques of survey methods have been largely developed outside the field of education it is possible to highlight the main issues arising in surveys by illustrations drawn from educational surveys. These issues include the definition of the population to be surveyed, the methods of collecting the data, techniques of sampling, the basis for making inferences from the sample to the population, and the control and measurement of the various errors that arise in every survey.

The two central concepts in survey design are cost and error, and account must be taken of each in planning a survey. What follows is only a brief guide to these concepts. The literature on survey design is large, but a study of at least part of it will repay anyone proposing to use survey methods. Some of the literature covers a wide range of topics (e.g., Moser and Kalton 1971), some is especially suitable for the nonmathematical reader (e.g., Hoinville et al. 1978, Kalton 1983, Stuart 1976, Sudman 1976), while some provides more technical details (e.g., Kish 1965, O'Muircheartaigh and Payne 1977, Ross 1978). The book by O'Muircheartaigh and Payne is one of the few general books on survey analyses of samples from finite populations.

## 1. Purposes of Surveys

A survey may be largely descriptive in purpose, the findings consisting mainly of statements of the values of the variable measured. For example, the purpose of the first Scottish Mental Survey in 1932 was to ascertain the distribution of intelligence among children in Scottish schools who were born in 1921. The published results showed that the scatter of intelligence quotients was greater than had been expected, and that it was greater among boys than among girls. The Australian Studies in School Performance (Bourke and Keeves 1977) were designed to "estimate for Australia the number of children who were failing to attain the basic skills of literacy and numeracy as assessed by the tests of reading, writing, and numeration and to specify relationships between other factors . . . and the attainment of competence".

On the other hand, a survey may be conducted to test hypotheses arising from studies of smaller, selected groups and to seek explanations for relationships that have been found, or are expected to be found, between variables. For example, it had been observed in the United Kingdom that there was a negative correlation between intelligence test score and size of family. This gave rise to the fear that the national average of intelligence might be falling. The second Scottish Mental Survey (Scottish Council for Research in Education 1949) was therefore conducted to test this hypothesis, and the opportunity was taken to measure a number of sociological variables with a view to examining the interrelationships between these and test scores.

The researcher intending to conduct a survey must be very clear about the purpose the survey is intended to serve. The purpose will determine the population to be surveyed, the variables to be included, and the methods of obtaining the data. The international surveys conducted by the International Association for the Evaluation of Educational Achievement (IEA) (Husén 1967, Peaker 1975) were not intended to provide "league tables" of national achievement, but to relate these achievements to a variety of variables describing the characteristics of the national groups. In this way, it was hoped, the participating countries would be able to ascertain what changes in their systems would benefit their students. The surveys were then designed with these purposes in mind.

## 2. The Population to be Surveyed

The researcher must also be clear on the population to be surveyed and the nature of the units composing that population if the findings are to have the intended generality; the intended or target population should be defined. There must also be some means of identifying and locating units (or members) of the population in order that a sample may be selected and then surveyed.

The problem of defining the population can be especially difficult when interest is in the upper reaches of the secondary school. The dividing line between "secondary" and "tertiary" education can be arbitrary and often corresponds with institutional divisions in the type of education: academic/general or technical/vocational. Students in both sectors may be studying science and mathematics to the same standard, and may belong to the same birth cohort. A population of interest defined carefully in the planning stages will greatly facilitate the drawing of conclusions.

There may be more than one way in which a target population can be defined. It might be all children in a given area born in a particular year. An alternative target population could be all children in that area at a particular stage in the school system. This is a different population, though there may be a large overlap, and findings from one population will not necessarily apply to the other. It should also be understood that the target population applies to a specified unit of interest. A population of students has a corresponding population of teachers who teach them, but that group of teachers is not necessarily representative of the body of teachers.

To select a sample, a listing or frame of the target population is required; if none exists, a means of constructing the whole or part of this sampling frame has to be found. Deficiencies in the sampling frame can severely undermine the best laid sample designs. In almost all studies of children of school age it may be appropriate to define an excluded population. This may be quite a small group (e.g., the mentally handicapped) or involve a substantial proportion of an age group (e.g., those who have already left school). However, there are other excluded subgroups who cannot be so easily identified. Lists constructed in schools may omit truants or those absent through illness, and school registers can be out of date and so effectively exclude some students. Defects in the sampling frame limit inference in much the same ways as the other errors of noncoverage discussed later.

## 3. Techniques of Survey Sampling

A population census is a survey. Often a population census will involve the whole of a specified population: the sampling fraction is 100 percent. Similarly, in education it is possible to approach a complete population. In the Scottish Mental Surveys over 90 percent of the two populations, which numbered 85,000 and 70,800, were tested, and in the Scottish Scholastic Survey of 1953 about 95 percent of the population of 76,000 took the tests. Whether such a heavy burden of testing, correction, and analysis with its accompanying costs is justifiable depends on the purposes of the survey, but in many cases the information required does not have to be completely accurate: some error is allowable as long as the extent of the error can be estimated. In these cases only a sample of the target population need be involved.

How then should a sample be selected and what is meant by accurate information? Accurate estimates are defined as having small bias and small variable error. If the researcher has extensive knowledge of the population it may well be that a judgment sample, that is, one selected in the light of the previous knowledge of the population, may give more precise estimates than would a sample of the same size drawn at random. However, there is no way of knowing whether greater precision has been achieved and the estimates may be biased. The same objection applies to a quota sample, again because of the lack of random selection of the sample members which quota sampling may provide. Randomization methods in sampling offer protection against bias in the selection of the sample members. A random method of selection gives each of the units in the population a known chance or probability, of selection, hence the term probability sampling, which is commonly used to distinguish it from nonrandom methods. Moreover, because the probability of selection is known, not only does random sampling protect against bias, it also enables the researcher to estimate from the sample data the extent of the error due to sampling.

In practice, the degree of randomness is often restricted by refinements of the sampling process. One such refinement is stratification. In most countries schools vary in size. If a sample of schools were selected completely at random it might be that the sample would contain an excessive proportion of large (or small) schools, and thus would not be adequately representative of the population of schools. The population of schools could be divided into subpopulations or strata according to the number of pupils enrolled, and the sample then selected from the strata in such a way that the different strata are adequately represented. Stratification by size can be accompanied by stratification by other variables, for example the religious affiliation of the school.

Systematic sampling is an administratively easy way of sampling which can also offer some degree of implicit stratification. For example, if the task is to select a 10 percent sample of students from within a school, this may be done on the basis of the school's registers of students. Suppose that the students have been streamed by ability into different classes and that a register is kept of each class. Then every 10th student may be selected from a list of the classes; the starting point being chosen at random. In this way the students from each class are represented in the sample in roughly the desired proportions of ability, that is, there has been some stratification. Care has to be taken that the register list has not been prepared in such a way that the sampling interval has special properties; for example if the list contained boys and girls in alternating positions then selecting every 10th student would produce a highly unrepresentative sample.

It may be very costly to prepare a complete listing or sampling frame, especially in a large country. Recourse may then be had to multistage sampling. For example, in the United States a possible sampling scheme would be to select a random sample of states (the primary sampling units) and within each of these a random sample of school districts. These in turn could provide a random sample of schools and these in turn a random sample of students. The advantage of this method is the saving in costs, since detailed information is not required about units not selected. Multistage sampling of this type was used in some of the countries taking part in the IEA investigations.

One form of multistage sampling which warrants separate mention is cluster sampling, which occurs when all members of the selected primary sampling units are included in the sample. This has advantages and disadvantages which can best be illustrated by an example. The 10-year-old children who were to be the population surveyed in the second Scottish Scholastic Survey were known to be in about 2,600 schools. A simple random sample would have involved correspondence with and entry to most, if not all, of these schools. It was therefore decided that the primary sampling unit would be the school and that all 10-year-olds in the selected schools would be tested. This involved only 169 schools with corresponding economies in cost. The disadvantage was that the estimates of mean score obtained from the sample were much less precise than those which would have been obtained from a simple random sample of the same size. In fact, the 5,000 pupils tested provided the precision that would have been available from about 670 pupils selected in a completely random fashion (Scottish Council for Research in Education 1968). This is due to the resemblances within clusters (in this case schools) which detract from the independence which simple random sampling entails. This point is taken up again in the section on errors.

A refinement which has been widely used in the IEA surveys is to select schools with probability proportional to size, and then to select a sample of students within these schools with probability inversely proportional to size. The net effect is that all students have the same chance of selection, but the number in each school is kept reasonably small and the cluster effect is reduced. It is, however, essential that the selection within schools be random, and precise instructions must be given as to how this is done. In the Six Subject Study carried out by the IEA in 1970 and 1971, the average number of students tested in each school was 26 (Peaker 1975).

These are examples of complex sampling, which when properly used may increase the efficiency and decrease the cost of a survey.

## 4. Methods of Collecting Data

In educational research the usual method of collecting data is through tests and self-completion questionnaires, though interviewing has also been used. Access to the school system has long been a privilege of the researcher, but it is subject to the school authorities being satisfied that the project is worthwhile, has been adequately planned, and will not throw too heavy a burden on students and teachers. Interviewing may be carried out by teachers, psychologists, health visitors, social workers, or by specially trained interviewers. The use of professionals can be especially valuable in obtaining data on family and social backgrounds.

A useful development has been the use of postal surveys, where the questionnaires are distributed and collected through the postal system, thus giving access to a wider sample of the population than could be reached at the same cost by other methods. This method has been successfully used in the Scottish National School Leaver Survey (Gray et al. 1982, Raffe 1984).

## 5. The Pretest and the Pilot Survey

The need for pretesting the items in tests and questionnaires is already well-known but must be stressed. Designing tests and questionnaires is not easy and demands thought and systematic testing. Each item should be tried out on a reasonably large number of students from a roughly equivalent population. This gives the opportunity to detect and remove ambiguities, to ascertain the range of possible responses, especially to items which are open ended and will require coding or will be changed to closed items in the final survey, and to ensure that the items are yielding the information desired.

When the requisite number of items has been obtained and a draft test or questionnaire constructed, it is very desirable if not essential that a pilot run (sometimes called a dry run) be organized, again with an equivalent group, to test the final form and all the procedures that will be followed in the main survey, including any follow-ups to ensure that measurements are obtained from as many as possible of those selected. The pilot run also gives an opportunity to learn what the results of the main survey are likely to be. It is worthwhile devoting say one-tenth of the resources available for a survey to mounting a pilot run and thus avoiding expensive mistakes in the main survey.

## 6. Sources of Error

It is a truism that the findings of almost all surveys are subject to errors, but it is important that the source of error be identified and as far as possible quantified, so that the researcher may be able to state how accurate are the findings. The errors may be variable or systematic and may arise from nonobservation, from the mode of measurement, or may be attributable to sampling.

### 6.1 Errors of Nonobservation

The extent to which membership of the achieved sample falls short of the target sample, arises from several sources. If the data defining the population have been derived from material collected some time previously, changes may have occurred by the time the actual survey takes place. In some cases it will be possible to make the necessary adjustments during the survey. A greater difficulty is likely to be nonresponse, the most extreme form being unit nonresponse (for example, refusal to cooperate) and the less extreme being missing data or item nonresponse (where items or questions in tests or questionnaires have produced no reply). The threat of nonresponse is that respondents and nonrespondents are not alike, and inferences based solely on replies from respondents will be biased. One method of dealing with direct refusals and those "away from school" is for the researcher, when selecting the sample, to draw a second sample as a reserve list, members of which can be invited to serve if one of the original sample refuses. The difficulty here is that the sample is then no longer a straightforward probability sample and the threat of bias remains. Where refusal rates are high, as was the case in some of the countries taking part in the IEA surveys, this will create problems. Methods of post-stratifying, that is weighting subgroups differentially, may lead to a reduction of this bias. Where the problem is item nonresponse it may be possible to fill some of the gaps from other sources or by making certain assumptions. Algorithms for this missing data problem include "mean value", "cold deck," "hot deck", and "nearest neighbour" replacement.

### 6.2 Errors of Measurement

These arise from a variety of sources. If the tests or questionnaires are poorly designed the questions may be misunderstood. If the data are collected by interviewers, for example where psychologists administer individual tests, a certain amount of the variance of scores is attributable to differences between testers. If items are of open-ended type, where responses have to be coded, errors of coding occur. Methods of reducing these errors are in some cases obvious, but in others not easy to design or employ. Separate measurement of response variance is not generally possible: instead the response variance inflates the estimated sampling variance.

### 6.3 Sampling Errors

These are, in principle, quantifiable where the sample is a probability sample. The standard error of a statistic is a measure of the discrepancy between the value estimated in the sample and the mean value that would be obtained from a very large number of such samples. Assuming unbiased sampling methods, the latter is equivalent to the "true" value in the population. The size of a standard error depends partly on the size of the sample but also on the sample design. Unfortunately, too few of the authors of statistical packages pay sufficient attention to the effect of sample design on the estimation of standard errors. In fact, most packages compute the standard error as though the design were simple random sampling from an infinite population. Since in practice many surveys are based on selection without replacement from finite populations and may make use of stratification and multistage sampling, these computed estimates of the standard errors will be biased.

Reference was made earlier to the variety of sampling schemes. Stratification was used to make the samples more representative of the population in the expectation that this would lead to greater precision in estimation. The change in precision is measured by the design effect, which is the ratio of the sampling variance produced by the complex sample design to that which would be produced by a simple random sample of the same size. An alternative form of the same definition is the ratio of the number of sampling units in the complex sample to the number required in a simple random sample to produce the same standard error. If the design effect is less than 1 there has been a gain in precision, and this is usually the effect of stratification. Multistage or cluster sampling on the other hand produces design effects greater than 1. The loss of precision has to be weighed against the financial and administrative savings effected by the complex design.

The point has already been made that this feature of cluster sampling arises from the fact that resemblances within clusters are greater than resemblances outside clusters. One measure of the within-cluster homogeneity is the intraclass correlation (*roh*) and there is an approximate relationship between design effect and *roh*. It is expressed in the equation

$$\text{design effect} = 1 + (m - 1)roh$$

where $m$ is the average number of units in a cluster. The important point to note here is the influence of $m$. Even for low values of *roh*, say 0.1, small clusters of size 11 produce a design effect of 2, but clusters of size 51 produce a design effect of 6. It is therefore advisable to reduce as far as possible the size of clusters even if that involves increasing their number. For higher value of *roh*, where there is a high degree of within-cluster homogeneity, it is all the more important to select a large number of clusters. Gains in precision are, however, achieved at extra financial cost.

The formulas for the standard errors of simple statistics such as means and totals are known for complex designs but are more complicated than for simple random sample designs. The formulas for the standard errors of other statistics, for example regression coefficients, are problematic for data from complex designs and in some cases are not known. One way round this difficulty is to make use of generalized but approximate estimators of the sampling variance which implicitly take into account the sample design employed and may be used for any statistic. In the simple replicated estimator the sample is divided into a number of subsamples (called replicates), each of equivalent design. The statistic of interest is then calculated for each replicate, and the variation in the value of the statistic across the replicates is used to estimate the standard error. A related technique called the Tukey–Quenouille jack-

knife procedure was used in the Australian Studies in School Performance (Bourke and Keeves 1977) and the IEA Six Subject Survey (Peaker 1975).

To sum up, methods of reducing errors in the findings of surveys range from the careful construction and pretesting of tests and questionnaires, through the selection of appropriate sampling designs, to the elimination as far as possible of response errors and coding errors and the use of the appropriate methods of estimating sampling errors.

## 7. Analysis and Interpretation of Survey Data

In this section reference is made to two (possibly related) debates about the analysis of survey data. The first concerns the relevance of survey design in the analysis—does design matter? The second concerns the search for causation—is causal inference possible in cross-sectional survey data?

Cross-sectional surveys are often thought of as descriptive in purpose, and in general the findings usually include point estimates of totals, means, and so on. Measures of association between two or more variables may also be computed. If these statistics have been derived from probability samples then the population values and the standard errors can be estimated from the sample data by employing the probabilities of selection alone. This school of inference is called the randomization or design-based school and is predominant among survey samplers. An alternative approach taken is to propose a probability model to represent the structure in the population, and to derive the random mechanism used in making the leap from sample to population from this probability model. A useful discussion of design-based versus model-based inference is contained in Smith (1976). The default option is to ignore the design and the structure in the popoulation, and to assume implicitly that the data were drawn from an infinite population by simple random sampling: this can, for reasons stated earlier, result in misleading conclusions but is the approach adopted in most standard statistical packages and hence in much published work.

Attempts to establish causation on the basis of empirical data are fraught with problems. Many of these reside in the substantive field in question, but there are several of a methodological nature and some relate to cross-sectional surveys in particular. Consider the assessment of the effects of different teaching strategies on pupil performance. In a true experiment pupils would be assigned randomly to the different treatments. Generally, survey data consists of observations made in natural settings where no attempt has been made to exercise experimental control. It should then be recognized that the allocation of pupils to teaching strategies was not random but was the result of some unknown, and not simple random, mechanism and that this threat of selection bias undermines strict causal inference. Because X (the teaching strategy) and Y (reading achievement) are highly correlated it does not follow that X causes Y (or that Y causes X). A third (confounding) factor may be at work. Causal interpretation consists of the specification of the order of causation, derived from theory or from presumed time ordering, and the attempt to control statistically the influence of confounding factors. Such problems are the subject for other articles in this Handbook. Suffice it to say that in cross-sectional surveys measurements are taken at, or about, one particular time. Establishing the order of causation is not straightforward. To overcome this difficulty questions of a retrospective nature are sometimes asked in surveys, but these are subject to errors of recall, and these errors may themselves be associated with the other variables.

When interpreting survey data, the researchers should take care to state the population to which they wish to generalize, indicate the means by which they make the inference, and respect the reader by suggesting the threats to the inference and by providing the means by which these threats may be evaluated.

There is also much to be said for the judicious combination of experimental method with the cross-sectional survey. The strength of the experimental method lies in the testing and measurement of an effect; methods of sample selection used in cross-sectional surveys provide a basis for generalizing the results of the experiment beyond the sample.

## 8. The Usefulness of Cross-sectional Surveys, with Examples

The preceding sections may have given the impression that cross-sectional surveys are so hazardous and prone to errors of execution and interpretation that their use can hardly be justified. This is not the case and many successful and useful cross-sectional surveys have been carried out.

Consideration of the value and usefulness of surveys involves an appraisal of the purposes to be served by the survey and an assessment of the design and execution of the survey, that is, of the credibility of the survey's findings. The more important the purpose of the survey the higher the standard demanded of the survey design, and hence the higher the cost. The purposes to which the survey method has been put in the field of education are many and vary along several dimensions. A small-scale one-off exploratory survey, requiring little in the way of resources, may be sufficient to stimulate hypothesis generation. A large-scale continuous survey may be necessary to secure evidence in major policy decision making. There have also been large-scale one-off surveys of great importance in educational research, one of the most notable being that conducted in the United States under Section 402 of the 1964 Civil Rights Act, which provided the basis of a report (Coleman et al. 1966) to the President and to Congress on racial equality of educational opportunity. While the survey was of major policy importance, the analysis of this survey has contributed to academic argument on the effectiveness of schools.

Reference has already been made to the Australian Studies in School Performance, which covered all states and territories and schools of all types at both primary and secondary school levels. The sampling procedures incorporated stratification, cluster selection, and weighting, and the jackknife procedure was used to calculate the sampling errors of the estimates of performance. The results and details of the techniques are described in the three volumes published by the Australian Government Publishing Service in 1976 and 1977.

Reference has also been made to the Scottish Mental and Scholastic Surveys, reports on which have been published by the Scottish Council for Research in Education. The Scottish Education Department and the Centre for Educational Sociology in the University of Edinburgh have been successful in mounting a regular series of National School Leaver Surveys despite the lack of a sampling frame. Their postal questionnaires have enjoyed a high response rate (86 percent) and through stratification have achieved design effects of 0.6.

The second volume of the Plowden Report (Central Advisory Council 1967) gives detailed information on a number of surveys carried out in England and Wales. These include the 1964 survey of parents of school children, surveys of standards in reading conducted between 1958 and 1964, and the first report of the National Child Development Study, 1958 cohort.

In the United States a programme for the National Assessment of Educational Progress has since 1969 covered science, writing (composition), mathematics, music, literature, social studies, art, reading, and career and occupational development. A series of reports has been published and a bimonthly newsletter is circulated from the office in Princeton, New Jersey. Most states also have their own assessment programmes which involve cross-sectional surveys.

The International Association for the Evaluation of Educational Achievement (IEA) has published a series of International Studies in Evaluation, describing cross-sectional surveys of science, reading comprehension, literature, civic education, and English and French as foreign languages.

A large number of surveys are also conducted by, or on behalf of, governments in order that statistical accounts of the education system are available.

## 9. A Concluding Remark

A distinction was made earlier between surveys that were descriptive in purpose and those that were analytical; both requiring inference to a predefined target population—the latter involving some degree of causal explanation. In practice, there should be no such clear dichotomy. Attempts to provide adequate descriptions necessarily require categorizations which invoke theoretical constructs and invite causal interpretation. However, these interpretations can never be of better quality than the data on which they are based. Considerations of theory and purpose should motivate attention to all aspects of data generation by survey method.

## Bibliography

Bourke S F, Keeves J P 1977 *Australian Studies in School Performance,* Vol. 3. Australian Government Publishing Service, Canberra

Central Advisory Council for Education (England) 1967 *Children and their Primary Schools,* Vol. 2: *Research and Surveys.* (Plowden Report.) Her Majesty's Stationery Office (HMSO), London

Coleman J S et al. 1966 *Equality of Educational Opportunity.* Office of Education, United States Department of Health, Education and Welfare, Washington, DC

Gray J M, McPherson A F, Raffe D (eds.) 1982 *Reconstructions of Secondary Education: Theory, Myth and Practice Since the War.* Routledge and Kegan Paul, London

Hoinville G, Jowell R, Airey C, Brook L, Courtenay, G, Hedges B, Kalton G, Marton-Williams J, Walker D, Wood D 1978 *Survey Research Practice.* Heinemann, London

Husén T (ed.) 1967 *International Study of Achievement in Mathematics: A Comparison of Twelve Countries.* Almqvist and Wiksell, Stockholm

Kalton G 1983 *Introduction to Survey Sampling.* Sage, Beverly Hills, California

Kish L 1965 *Survey Sampling.* Wiley, New York

Moser C A, Kalton G 1971 *Survey Methods in Social Investigation.* Heinemann, London

National Assessment of Educational Progress *Newsletters.* Princeton, New Jersey

O'Muircheartaigh C A, Payne C (eds.) 1977 *The Analysis of Survey Data.* Wiley, New York

Peaker G F 1975 *An Empirical Study of Education in Twenty-one Countries: A Technical Report.* Almqvist and Wiksell, Stockholm

Raffe D (ed.) *Fourteen to Eighteen.* The changing Pattern of Schooling in Scotland. Aberdeen University Press, Aberdeen

Ross K N 1978 Sample design for educational survey research. *Eval. Educ.* 2(2): 105–95

Scottish Council for Research in Education 1949 *The Trend of Scottish Intelligence: A Comparison of the 1947 and 1932 Surveys of the Intelligence of Eleven-year-old Pupils.* University of London Press, London

Scottish Council for Research in Education 1968 *Rising Standards in Scottish Primary Schools 1953–63: Attainments of 10-year-olds in English and Arithmetic.* University of London Press, London

Smith T M F 1976 The foundations of survey sampling: A review. *J. Roy. Stat. Soc. (A)* 139: 183–204

Stuart A 1976 *Basic Ideas of Scientific Sampling.* 2nd ed. Griffin, London

Sudman S 1976 *Applied Sampling.* Academic Press, New York

# Longitudinal Research Methods

## J. P. Keeves

Longitudinal research studies, that is, investigations conducted over time, are of growing importance in the social and the behavioural sciences and, in particular, in the field of education. In the past investigations conducted over time have been relatively rare, although some important studies have been undertaken. In Sweden, the Malmo study conducted by Husén and his colleagues has been in progress for nearly 60 years. Data were initially collected in 1928 and many reports from this study have been published (Husén 1969, Fägerlind 1975). In the United Kingdom, two major series of studies have been conducted. The first investigation was started shortly after the Second World War, when all children born in one week in March 1946 formed the sample and detailed medical records as well as information on their educational development were collected (Douglas 1964). The second investigation is the ongoing National Child Development Study which was started 12 years later with a sample of all children born in the United Kingdom during the first week of March 1958 (Davie et al. 1972, Fogelman 1983, Butler and Golding 1986). In the United States, there have been at least eight major longitudinal studies that have investigated well-defined samples of children and that have sought to obtain a large variety of measurements on different characteristics of human development: these particular studies have been reviewed by Bloom (1964) in a study titled *Stability and Change in Human Characteristics.*

In all these studies, which have collected data at many points in time, significant problems have inevitably been encountered in maintaining contact or tracing the members of the chosen samples. As a consequence these investigations are sometimes referred to as "tracer studies". This name emphasizes the strategies that are employed for preventing bias which would distort the findings of an investigation as a consequence of substantial losses over time from the sample. In recent years there has been an increased interest in the problems associated with the design of longitudinal research studies and the strategies used in the analysis of the data collected, as well as with the sources of bias that could invalidate the findings. This work has led to significant advances in the methodology associated with such investigations, particularly in the areas of design and analysis. Educational research is concerned with the processes of change, and the study of change requires that observations are made for at least two points in time. While it is possible to describe the practice of education by means of a cross-sectional study undertaken at a single point in time, it is necessary to conduct investigations which are longitudinal in nature in order both to describe and explain the influence of educative processes on the constancy and change of related events. Thus the methods of longitudinal research are central to the empirical study of education, whether there is concern for individuals, classrooms, schools, social subgroups, or educational systems. Although there are substantial problems associated with the investigation of change (see, for example, Cronbach and Furby 1970), the importance to education cannot be denied of providing a detailed description of patterns of stability and change and a coherent explanation of how and why change has occurred or failed to occur. This article is concerned with the methods of longitudinal research and addresses the problems associated with the investigation of both stability and change. It is important to recognize that, while longitudinal methods are frequently contrasted with cross-sectional methods, a detailed comparison between the two methods is largely inappropriate because constancy and change can only be examined through repeated observation which is the key characteristic of the longitudinal method.

## 1. Explaining Stability and Change

Three major systems of influence can be identified in the field of education which affect stability and change in human development (see Baltes and Nesselroade 1979). Using these systems an explanation or causal analysis of human development can be attempted. While educational research is commonly concerned with the investigation of educational processes at the classroom, school, social subgroup or systemic levels, it is necessary to recognise that the investigation of stability and change in human development must be carried out at the individual level at which the three systems of influence operate. The three sets of influences on human development have their origins in: (a) biological factors, (b) environmental factors, and (c) planned learning experiences or interventions. These three sets of influences interact with each other in significant ways. In particular, since each individual has the opportunity to choose, at least to some degree, whether or not a response will be made to both environmental and intervention influence, and given that such choices may in part be biologically determined, the nature and extent of interactions between the three sets of influences are highly complex. The nature of these three types of influence warrants further consideration.

(a) *Biological influences.* These refer to those determinants that show a strong correlation with chronological age both across historical periods and across a wide range of individuals from different social groups. Development under these influences is ontogenetic and age graded. Normative age-related developments should be seen as largely biological in origin.

(b) *Environmental influences.* These refer to non-biologically based determinants of development that have a pervading effect on those individuals experiencing a particular environment. Bloom (1964) has considered the meaning of the term "environment" and has suggested that it refers to:

> ... the conditions, forces and external stimuli which impinge on the individual. These may be physical, social, as well as intellectual forces and conditions. We conceive of a range of environments from the most immediate social interactions to the more remote cultural and institutional forces. We regard the environment as providing a network of forces and factors which surround, engulf and play on the individual. (Bloom 1964 p. 187)

The environment as conceived by Bloom is the total stimulus situation, both latent and actual, that interacts, or is capable of interacting, with the individual. Thus while individuals will experience common environments, significant variations will occur as individuals interact with their environments. As a consequence invariant sequences of development will not occur. Development under environmental influences will be largely non-normative, although common patterns will occur in so far as common environment is experienced.

(c) *Intervention influences.* These include those planned learning experiences provided by a wide range of educational institutions that are deliberately designed and form the educative process. They differ in kind from the pervasive influences of the environment, in so far as they are designed for a particular stage of development and are directed towards highly specific outcomes. The effects of planned learning experiences are assessed in terms of the achievement of particular outcomes rather than in terms of normative and non-normative development. Whereas biological and environmental influences may result in either stability or change in specific characteristics, intervention influences, if successfully administered, lead to change. Constancy in characterisics involves lack of success in the administration of the intervention.

The interaction between these three types of influence gives rise to analytical problems when attempts are made to identify the effects of particular influences over time. The administration of an intervention under experimental conditions, in which subjects have been randomly assigned to treatment groups and control groups, provides the most appropriate methodology for the investigation of the effects of an intervention, in so far as the cause of change can be identified. However, in many situations within which educational research is conducted, either it is not physically possible to undertake random allocation to treatment or control groups, or alternatively, randomization and the application of the intervention so affects the educational process that significant distortion from the natural setting occurs. In addition, it must be recognized that even where random assignment to treatment and control groups takes place, prior experiences, as well as genetic and environmental influences, can so interact with the administration of the intervention that the nature of the intervention might be changed significantly by these prior and concurrent influences. Some interactions of this type are amenable to analysis where the models being examined can be derived from theoretical considerations (Campbell and Stanley 1963). However, other interactions, more particularly those between biological and environmental influences would not at this time appear to be always amenable to rigorous analysis.

A specific problem which arises involves the confounding of biological age-graded effects and environmental non-age-graded effects as a result of a changing environment across the different time periods or age levels at which biological influences are being investigated. Moreover, in so far as some environmental influences may be age related, a similar confounding can arise between different classes of environmental effects. Attempts to unravel such interactions have given rise to specific designs in the conduct of longitudinal investigations. It will be evident from the above comments that while investigation at different points of time is the key characteristic of longitudinal research, from which it gains its strength, the use of different time points gives rise to certain problems in the conduct of longitudinal studies and the subsequent analysis of the data collected.

## 2. The Status of Time in Longitudinal Research

Baltes and Nesselroade (1979 p. 2) have stated that "the study of phenomena in their time-related constancy and change is the aim of longitudinal methodology". Furthermore, where repeated observations are made of individuals or groups in order to describe or explain both stability and change, time acts not only as the logical link between the repeated observations, but also as a variable that is a characteristic of the individuals or groups.

Thus the use of time in longitudinal research studies takes place in two distinct ways. First, time is used as a subject characteristic. Second, time is used as a design characteristic (von Eye 1985). Examples of the first usage occur when chronological age is employed as the basis for the selection of an individual or a group for study, or when the members of an age cohort are studied at successive intervals during their life span. In addition, in retrospective studies events that occurred at particular times in the life of an individual are not only readily identified, but also have spatial significance. A major limitation on the use of time in this way is that it is not a manipulable variable and subjects cannot be randomly assigned to different time values. The second use of time is as a design characteristic, which occurs in learning studies, when the extent of learning is measured after successive time periods. Fortunately, in this use of time in a longitudinal study, time is an alterable variable and the effects of time are amenable to analysis. The strength of time in longitudinal studies as a design characteristic arises from the role played by time in the underlying substantive theory. Increasingly, there is recognition that the effects of environmental and intervention influences are time related, in so far as exposure

to the environment or to the intervention has significant consequences for the magnitudes of measurable outcomes. Nevertheless, length of exposure is only one of many factors: for example, the intensity of exposure, or the nature and intensity of opposing forces can influence educational outcomes. Thus the effects of time are commonly concealed by the effects of these alternative forces.

Time is not only a continuous variable, but equal time intervals are also readily determined. In addition, in many situations a starting point at which time is zero can be identified. Thus it is possible to collect data in the form of a time series and to examine the constancy or change in particular characteristics with respect to time as recorded on an interval scale. Moreover, because time is a continuous variable, which is measured on an interval scale, it is commonly possible to investigate time samples of behaviour in order to study and compare practices which occur under different conditions. In the investigation of classroom behaviour extensive use is made of time samples in order to compare the practices of different teachers, or the effects of different teaching and learning conditions on student behaviours.

Perhaps the most significant characteristic of time lies in its relationship to causal influence, since earlier events influence later events but not vice-versa. Thus while it cannot be assumed that measurements made on a variable obtained at an initial point in time can be causally related to an outcome measure obtained at a later time, it is clear that unless the appropriate time sequence exists it is not possible to argue logically for a possible causal relationsip. The *possibility* of investigating causal relationships between variables measured at different points in time is the important contribution that longitudinal research methods have made to the exploration of causal explanations based on theory and the testing of path models and structural equation models, and this has led to the increased emphasis on longitudinal research in education during the 1970s.

## 3. Types of Longitudinal Research

Inferences concerning the nature and extent of change over time and the factors influencing change are, in general, obtained from five design strategies (Kessler and Greenberg 1981 pp. 2–3): simultaneous cross-sectional studies, trend studies, time series studies, intervention studies, and panel studies.

### 3.1 Simultaneous Cross-sectional Studies

Within this strategy, two or more related cross-sectional studies are conducted at the same point in time with different age groups being sampled by each cross-sectional study. The same predictor and criterion variables are observed for each age sample. Moreover, the age samples are each drawn from the same larger population. However, each sample is drawn independently

*Table 1*
Simultaneous cross-sectional data matrix[a]

| Age group | Sample | Time point | Observed variables |
|-----------|--------|-----------|--------------------|
| $A_1$ | $S_1$ | $T_1$ | $V_1, V_2, V_3 \cdots\cdots V_e$ |
| $A_2$ | $S_2$ | $T_1$ | $V_1, V_2, V_3 \cdots\cdots V_e$ |
| .. | .. | .. | .. |
| .. | .. | .. | .. |
| .. | .. | .. | .. |
| $A_m$ | $S_m$ | $T_1$ | $V_1, V_2, V_3 \cdots\cdots V_e$ |

a Source: von Eye 1985 p. 3141

of the other. Table 1 describes the data matrix for the simultaneous cross-sectional design where there are $m$ groups of subjects ($=m$ age samples) which are observed with respect to $e$ variables (see von Eye 1985 p. 3141). The longitudinal dimension in the design of studies of this type is achieved by consideration of the different chronological ages associated with the independent samples. This design has been employed in the studies carried out by the International Association for the Evaluation of Educational Achievement (IEA). However, only two of the many reports issued by IEA have made significant use of the longitudinal element in this design (Comber and Keeves 1973, Carroll 1975). Because in these studies three age groups, the 10-year-old, the 14-year-old, and the terminal secondary-school levels, were tested, it was not possible to employ identical tests at each age level. However, overlapping tests were administered and standardized procedures were employed to bring the achievement outcomes to a common scale. This design has also been employed in the Australian Studies in School Performance (Keeves et al. 1978) and in the National Assessment of Educational Progress in the United States (Tyler 1985). In these two studies comparisons across age levels, which involved the longitudinal component of the design, employed in the main individual items or small clusters of items that were common to the different age groups tested. The scaling and measurement issues associated with such comparison will be considered in Sect. 5. As von Eye (1985) has pointed out, this design is both simple and economical to execute and, since only one point in time is involved, the confounding effects of environmental influences are reduced and the effects of intervention influences such as retention differences across countries (Comber and Keeves 1973) and years spent in foreign language learning (Carroll 1975) are more clearly evident. Nevertheless, there are some specific deficiencies in this type of design which arise from the fact that only one time point is employed (von Eye 1985 p. 3141). The conclusions which can be derived from this design are only valid under the following assumptions: (a) the age samples have been drawn from the same common population; and (b) the factors influencing change in the criterion variables and their effects have remained constant across the time span during which

the different age samples have been exposed to those factors.

### 3.2 Trend Studies

Within this strategy, two or more related cross-sectional studies are conducted with identical age groups at points of time that are sequential. Similar sampling procedures are employed at each time, so that sound comparisons can be drawn over time, and identical or related measures are employed on each occasion. Perhaps the strongest and most widely discussed set of trend data has been associated with the scores on the Verbal and Quantitative Scholastic Achievement Tests in the United States (Donlon 1984). To obtain these sets of data common test items were employed across occasions, so that the data could be accurately chained from one occasion to the next. Widespread debate has taken place in attempts to explain the highly significant decline in Scholastic Aptitude Test (SAT) scores and the more recent rise that has occurred. However, while many competing explanations have been advanced, none has gained clear support over the others.

In Table 2 the data matrix associated with trend studies is presented. It illustrates that at successive points in time new samples are drawn. In addition, the age group under survey remains constant and the same variables are observed, so that constancy and change in characteristics of interest in the changing populations can be examined. Further examples of research studies which have investigated trends in educational achievement are those carried out by the Assessment of Performance Unit (APU) in England and Wales (Black et al. 1984), the Australian Studies in Student Performance (ASSP) in Australia (Bourke et al. 1981), and the National Assessment of Educational Progress (NAEP) in the United States (Tyler 1985). Two sets of problems arise in such studies. First, there are the problems of the meaningfulness and validity of achievement test items in circumstances where the curriculum of the schools is changing and new curricular emphases are evolving. These problems can be allowed for in part by the removal of obsolete test items and their replacement with new and more appropriate items. Nevertheless, uncertainties remain as to whether the reduced number of test items that are common across occasions are equally valid for successive samples of students over

*Table 2*
Trend data matrix

| Age group | Sample | Time point | Observed variables |
|-----------|--------|-----------|--------------------|
| $A_1$ | $S_1$ | $T_1$ | $V_1, V_2, V_3 \cdots\cdots V_e$ |
| $A_1$ | $S_2$ | $T_2$ | $V_1, V_2, V_3 \cdots\cdots V_e$ |
| .. | .. | .. | .. |
| .. | .. | .. | .. |
| .. | .. | .. | .. |
| $A_1$ | $S_m$ | $T_m$ | $V_1, V_2, V_3 \cdots\cdots V_e$ |

time, in order to provide a trend that could be used to guide future curriculum planning and educational practice. A second set of problems is concerned with the statistical procedures that are employed to scale a constantly changing sample of test items to obtain a reliable measure of educational achievement. While latent trait scaling techniques have been developed in recent years (Morgan 1982, Spearritt 1982, Donlon 1984), which could be employed for this purpose, the issue remains as to whether with a changing curriculum a single latent trait can be considered to exist that covers an area of the school curriculum and that remains unchanged across time.

The major shortcoming of the trend studies referred to above has been that they were not designed initially in such a way as to permit any trends which might have been detected to be explained through the use of biological, environmental, or intervention variables. A study which has been conducted by the International Association for the Evaluation in Educational Achievement in ten countries in the curriculum field of science in 1970 and 1984 provides a major attempt to examine the possibility of undertaking a trend study in which change in educational achievement across time might be accounted for by changing educational influences.

### 3.3 Time Series Studies

This type of longitudinal study has its origins in developmental psychology over a hundred years ago. A very large number of such studies have been reported from many parts of the world. Bloom (1964) undertook an integrative work to examine stability and change in human characteristics which sought to draw from the major studies which had been reported in the United States the patterns of growth associated with physical and intellectual characteristics. These longitudinal studies assume that human development is a continuous process which can be meaningfully examined by a series of "snapshots" recorded at appropriate points in time. They do not necessarily involve equal time intervals between successive observational points. Development can be examined in a valid way through the use of the continuous time scale which has strong metric properties. In Table 3 the research data matrix for such longitudinal studies has been recorded, from which it will be

*Table 3*
Time series data matrix

| Age group | Sample | Time point | Observed variables |
|-----------|--------|-----------|--------------------|
| $A_1$ | $S_1$ | $T_1$ | $V_1, V_2, V_3 \cdots\cdots\cdots V_e$ |
| $A_2$ | $S_1$ | $T_2$ | $V_1, V_2, V_3 \cdots\cdots\cdots V_e$ |
| .. | .. | .. | .. |
| .. | .. | .. | .. |
| .. | .. | .. | .. |
| $A_m$ | $S_1$ | $T_m$ | $V_1, V_2, V_3 \cdots\cdots\cdots V_e$ |

seen that the same sample is followed at successive time points with corresponding increases in the age of the group under survey. Information is collected on a wide range of variables relevant to the aspect of human development being investigated.

Von Eye (1985) has drawn attention to five advantages which this type of design has over the simultaneous cross-sectional design and the trend design referred to above. First, it is possible to identify intra-individual constancy or change directly, thereby reducing the confounding that arises from changing environmental circumstances, since repeated observations are made of the same subjects. Von Eye (1985 p. 3142) states that evidence supporting this advantage has been found repeatedly in the differences in the growth curves obtained from time series longitudinal designs compared with those obtained from simultaneous cross-sectional designs. Second, by observing more than one individual or one group of individuals, differences between individuals or groups in the intra-individual sequences of development become clear. This enables homogeneity or variability in development to be examined between individuals or groups. Third, since each group of individuals possesses characteristics that are used to identify individuals as members of the group, the time series design permits the constancy or change in the dimensions characterizing membership of a class to be examined through the investigation of relationships associated with such characteristics both within classes as well as between classes. The two further advantages of the time series design involve the identification of time related influences on development. Since this design does not include the examination of the effects of time-specific interventions on development, only those influences that occur naturally over time are involved. The fourth advantage is associated with the study of linkages between such influences and intra-individual or intra-group constancy or change in particular characteristics. Finally, the fifth advantage is concerned with the investigation of relationships between time-based influences on interindividual and intergroup constancy or change in specific characteristics.

The conduct of time series studies is expensive since it is commonly very costly to maintain contact with a significant number of sample members over an extended period of time, and sample losses can give rise to substantial distortions of observed relationships. A further problem is that a limited sequence of observations, either through starting with an age group at some time after birth, or through premature limitation of the observation sequence might mean that critical information is not available to reveal either a coherent pattern of development or to identify the effects of factors that influence development.

The costs associated with the conduct of prospective time series studies have led many research workers to employ a retrospective time series design in which a sample is selected and the members of the sample are invited to recall events in their lives at particular times or when they were at specific ages. Retrospective studies suffer from two major shortcomings. First, the sample selected is necessarily biased, because only those who have survived are available for interrogation, and the losses through death, migration, and residential mobility might distort in significant ways the relationships that are derived from the data. Secondly, the recall by subjects of events that took place at earlier stages in their lives can also be distorted either deliberately or unintentionally, because in changing circumstances individuals prefer to present a favourable view of their past lives.

The report of the study of the development of talent in young people reported by Bloom (1985) presents striking findings of how 120 young men and women who reached the highest levels of accomplishment in their chosen fields as Olympic swimmers, world-class tennis players, concert pianists, sculptors, research mathematicians, and research neurologists, were influenced by their homes and educative processes. This study made use of the retrospective time series design, but inevitably was unable to include those who aspired towards such goals, but did not achieve them.

### 3.4 Intervention Studies

Intervention studies involve a variation of the time series design, but differ with respect to the insertion of a planned learning experience or intervention at a selected time or across a period of time in the lives of individuals. Such intervention designs may involve the selection of probability samples, the random allocation of subjects or groups to treatments, the administration of experimental and control treatments, the monitoring of treatment conditions, and the use of immediate and delayed posttests. In Table 4 the data matrix for a simple intervention design has been presented. There are of course a large number of variations on the basic design shown in Table 4 that might have been employed and Kratochwill (1978 pp.34–35) presents the range of design variations for single-subject and multiple-subject time series investigations.

In the design in Table 4 the samples associated with both the experimental and control groups remain constant throughout the investigation. Initial data on sets

of predictor and criterion variables are obtained at time $T_1$ when all subjects are at age $A_1$. Between times $T_1$ and $T_2$ the treatment conditions are administered to the experimental group and no treatment is given to the control group. At time $T_2$, when subjects are at age $A_2$, immediate posttests are given to both the experimental and the control groups and again at time $T_m$ delayed posttests are given to both the experimental and the control groups. Many studies have employed the intervention design in the field of educational research. Important studies to use this design have been the Ypsilanti Perry Pre-School Project conducted by the High/Scope Educational Research Foundation and reported by Weikart and his colleagues (Schweinhart and Weikart 1980, Weikart 1984) to evaluate Head Start Programs in the United States; the Sustaining Effects Study concerned with the evaluation of Title I Programs for educational disadvantage in the United States (Carter 1984); and the Mount Druitt Study supported by the Bernard Van Leer Foundation, a study which involved the evaluation of early childhood intervention programs in disadvantaged schools in Sydney, Australia (Braithwaite 1983). There are many problems associated with the analysis of data from such studies, since few major investigations of this type are able to allocate subjects randomly to experimental and control groups, or to constrain the administration of the intervention or treatment, so that characteristics of the experimental group do not influence the nature of the treatment applied. Thus biological and environmental influences can interact with intervention influences to such a degree in intervention studies that the assumptions associated with analysis of variance or analysis of covariance techniques are not sustained, and these procedures cannot always be safely used in the analysis of the data collected through intervention designs. Greater use has been made during recent years of structural equation models to tease out the complex interrelationships which exist within the bodies of data collected in such studies. In spite of these analytical problems, it must be recognized that through the administration of a treatment to an experimental group and the withholding of a treatment from a control group, it is possible to make stronger inferences about the influence of factors associated with such intervention designs than could be achieved from studies in natural settings.

**Table 4**
Intervention data matrix

| Age | Experimental group | Control group | Sample | Time point | Observed variables |
|-----|-----|-----|-----|-----|-----|
| $A_1$ | $E_1$ | $C_1$ | $S_1$ | $T_1$ | $V_1, V_2, V_3 \cdots\cdots\cdots V_e$ |
| | Treatment | No Treatment | | | |
| $A_2$ | $E_1$ | $C_1$ | $S_1$ | $T_2$ | $V_1, V_2, V_3 \cdots\cdots\cdots V_e$ |
| $A_m$ | $E_1$ | $C_1$ | $S_1$ | $T_m$ | $V_1, V_2, V_3 \cdots\cdots\cdots V_e$ |

### 3.5 Panel Studies

In trend studies relationships associated with time of measurement are examined while the age of the group under investigation is held constant. In simultaneous cross-sectional studies, the time of measurement is held constant and the age of the group being surveyed is allowed to vary, while in the time series design a single cohort is selected and the time of measurement and the age of the cohort are allowed to covary together. All three designs have their shortcomings, in so far as effects associated with time of measurement, age of group being investigated, and the cohort chosen cannot be completely separated from each other. This has led to the development of panel studies in which an attempt is made to unravel the effects of factors associated with age, time of measurement, or cohort.

Schaie (1965) has advanced a general model for the study of longitudinal bodies of data that combines the three aspects of time, namely, cohort $(C)$, time of measurement $(T)$ and age $(A)$. In this model, a measure obtained on variable $V$ is a function of cohort, time of measurement and age, that is, $V = f(C, T, A)$. This function includes the interactions between the three aspects of time, $C \times T$, $T \times A$, $C \times A$, and $C \times T \times A$. In Fig. 1, the design of a panel study in which the ages of five-year cohorts which are measured at five-year intervals has been presented. The entries recorded in each column correspond to the simultaneous cross-sectional design. The entries in the constant age diagonals correspond to the trend design, and entries in each row correspond to the time series design. In time-sequential analyses, chronological age $(A)$ and time of measurement $(T)$ are combined. In such studies at least three cohorts have to be measured in one investigation (see rectangular boxed data points for years of measurement of 1995 and 2000). In this way complete data are obtained for two time points, 1995 and 2000, and two age levels, 10 years and 15 years, so that an $A \times T$ interaction can be tested. However, the cohort factor

$(C)$ is confounded with age and time of measurement. A similar problem arises in a cohort-sequential analysis in which chronological age and cohort are considered as independent factors. In this case three separate time points are required for the collection of data (see diamond boxed data points for years of measurement 1980, 1985, and 1990). Here the 1980 and 1985 cohorts are being investigated at ages of 0 years and 5 years, and the $A \times C$ interaction can be tested, but it follows that time of measurement is confounded. In a similar way the cross-sectional analysis permits the study of the $C \times T$ interaction, but three age levels have to be investigated (see square box for the 1990 and 1995 cohorts, which are surveyed in years 2005 and 2010). Here the age factor is confounded with cohort and time of measurement.

Schaie (1965) considered that age factors were primarily concerned with biological influences associated with ontogenetic development, and that cohort factors involved environmental influences which operated prior to the first time point of an investigation. The time factors were considered to involve environmental effects which were common to all subjects being studied. The interaction effects arose from interactions between the environmental factors and genetic factors. However, if the assumption of a common population was violated then cohort factors could include genetic differences between cohorts together with the more commonly accepted environmental differences.

Baltes et al. (1979) have proposed a modified version of Schaie's General Developmental Model which is presented in Fig. 2. The figure shows the birth cohorts at five-year intervals from 1980 to 2010 for ages 0 to 30 years and at times of measurement from 1980 to 2040. The simple designs, namely, the simultaneous cross-sectional, conducted in year 2010, the trend, for age 30 years, and the time series for the 2010 cohort are shown in Fig. 2(a). A second strategy is presented in Fig. 2(b), where simultaneous cross-sectional sequences, trend sequences and time series sequences are shown. Each

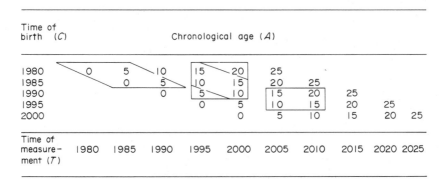

**Figure 1**
Panel design showing ages of five-year cohorts measured at five-year intervals[a]

a Source: adapted from Schaie (1965 p. 23)

**Age in years**

| Cohort | 0 | 5 | 10 | 15 | 20 | 25 | 30 |
|---|---|---|---|---|---|---|---|
| | | | | | | | SC |
| 1980 | 1980 | 1985 | 1990 | 1995 | 2000 | 2005 | 2010 |
| 1985 | 1985 | 1990 | 1995 | 2000 | 2005 | 2010 | 2015 |
| 1990 | 1990 | 1995 | 2000 | 2005 | 2010 | 2015 | 2020 |
| 1995 | 1995 | 2000 | 2005 | 2010 | 2015 | 2020 | 2025 |
| 2000 | 2000 | 2005 | 2010 | 2015 | 2020 | 2025 | 2030 |
| 2005 | 2005 | 2010 | 2015 | 2020 | 2025 | 2030 | 2035 |
| 2010 | TS  2010 | 2015 | 2020 | 2025 | 2030 | 2035 | 2040 |
| | | | | | | | TR |

(a)

**Age in years**

| Cohort | 0 | 5 | 10 | 15 | 20 | 25 | 30 |
|---|---|---|---|---|---|---|---|
| | | | | | | SCS | |
| 1980 | 1980 | 1985 | 1990 | 1995 | 2000 | 2005 | 2010 |
| 1985 | 1985 | 1990 | 1995 | 2000 | 2005 | 2010 | 2015 |
| 1990 | 1990 | 1995 | 2000 | 2005 | 2010 | 2015 | 2020 |
| 1995 | 1995 | 2000 | 2005 | 2010 | 2015 | 2020 | 2025 |
| 2000 | 2000 | 2005 | 2010 | 2015 | 2020 | 2025 | 2030 |
| 2005 | 2005 | 2010 | 2015 | 2020 | 2025 | 2030 | 2035 |
| 2010 | TSS  2010 | 2015 | 2020 | 2025 | 2030 | 2035 | 2040 |
| | | | | | | TRS | |

(b)

*Figure 2*
(a) A modified version of Schaie's General Developmental Model illustrating simultaneous cross-sectional (SC, diagonal band), trend (TR, upright rectangle) and time series (TS, horizontal band) designs
(b) Simultaneous cross-sectional sequences (SCS), trend sequences (TRS) and time series sequences (TSS) design strategies

a Based on Baltes et al. 1979 p. 64   b Cell entries refer to dates of measurement

involves a replication of a basic design illustrated in Fig. 2(a). The simultaneous cross-sectional sequence involves the collection of replicated information on each age group, while the time series sequences involve the examination of two cohorts.

Whereas the basic designs were considered to be primarily descriptive in nature, the sequence designs were seen by Schaie (1965) also to permit explanation. The distinction between description and explanation is recognized as an important one. Nevertheless, it is clearly not possible to test all three factors, cohort, age, and time of measurement in the one analysis. Nor is it possible to examine the three way interaction, however, extensive the data collection might be. The explanatory analysis of data would seem to involve rather more than the investigation of the three factors and their two-way interactions. The construction of structural equation models from theory and the testing of the models using data that permits the examination of cohort related influences, age-related influences, and time of measurement would appear to be necessary. Where the same

cohort is involved in the collection of data at different time points, the different time points can be incorporated into the model. However, the explanation of trends and relationships exhibited across simultaneous cross-sectional studies would appear to demand new analytical strategies. As increasingly large bodies of data become available, for example in the Sustaining Effects Study (Carter 1984), the reduction with age in the magnitude of such influences as the effects of school factors on achievement in a simultaneous cross-sectional study clearly warrants more thorough investigation.

In the field of education, relatively few panel studies have been undertaken over time periods that are long enough for age and cohort effects to be distinguished. The Plowden Follow-up Study (Peaker 1971, Marjoribanks 1975) was an important study that involved three grade groups which were investigated on two occasions. Moreover, Peaker (1971) was the first educational research worker to use path analysis as a technique for the examination of longitudinal data using causal models. Subsequently, Marjoribanks (1975) undertook a further examination of the same body of data using more elaborate path models. Another study of interest has been the Australian Studies of School Performance (Keeves et al. 1978) in which two parallel groups of students aged 10 and 14 years were initially tested in 1975, and were traced and followed from 1978 to 1984 with detailed information obtained on their career expectations and their transition from education into the workforce (Williams et al. 1980, 1981). Matching cohorts are available from a repeated testing program which was conducted in 1980 and the samples are being followed.

## 4. Validity Issues in Longitudinal Studies

The complex nature of longitudinal studies makes them particularly vulnerable to uncontrolled factors that can threaten their experimental validity. Like other empirical investigations longitudinal studies can yield meaningful results only in so far as the measurements recorded and the data analysed are both valid and reliable, and the samples employed are both randomly generated and remain representative of the populations from which they were derived. Without the maintenance of these essential conditions sound generalizations cannot be made beyond the particular groups under investigation. While the pattern of results associated with both the descriptive and explanatory analyses of data from nonrepresentative samples could appear informative, unless these findings were generalizable beyond the situation in which the data were generated, the effort involved in collecting and analysing the data would be largely wasted. Kratochwill (1978) has identified two classes of validity, internal and external validity, and has listed the different types of threat that are likely to occur in longitudinal studies and which arise from these two sources. Internal validity is concerned with the degree of certainty with which measurements associated with the predictor or explanatory variables are capable of accounting for the observed constancy and change in the criterion variables. It will be evident that high levels of reliability and validity of the predictor variables are necessary preconditions for the interpretation and explanation of time-related observations. External validity refers to the manner and extent to which the findings from the analyses carried out could be generalized to different situations beyond those in which the specific body of data was collected. Kratochwill (1978 p. 11) notes that the quest for both high internal and external validities can operate against each other. The requirement to obtain a high level of internal validity can demand the exercising of tight experimental controls on the collection of data which might so distort the natural setting in which development occurs that the external validity of the investigation was threatened. Fortunately the development and testing of causal models derived from theory and the exercising of statistical controls that are consistent with the structure of these models have greatly reduced the demand for rigid

experimental designs, so that random allocation to experimental and control groups and the administration of treatment conditions according to rigid specifications is no longer considered to be as important as it was in former decades.

### 4.1 Threats to Internal Validity

In longitudinal studies where time plays a key role, consideration must be given at the design stage to the temporal order in which data are gathered on predictor variables with respect to the criterion measures. There are, however, other less obvious threats to internal validity which arise from the conduct of an investigation over an extended period of time.

(a) *History*. Events that are unrelated to a predictor variable but that take place at the same time may be undetected, but may give rise to change in the criterion variable. Alternatively events which have occurred at an earlier time may have influenced both the predictor variable and at a later time the criterion variable. Such threats to validity are reduced if some control is exerted both over the manipulation of the predictor variable through planned intervention, and over the time at which the intervention is administered with respect to other factors believed or known to influence development.

(b) *Maturation*. Changes within subjects of a physical or psychological nature due to maturation may occur over time and may also influence performance on the criterion variables. Such changes may remain undetected and thus may confound findings that could be ascribed to other causes. As with historical influences these threats to validity are reduced by an effective design and by attention being given to the collection of appropriate data.

(c) *Practice effects in testing*. If similar or identical tests are employed at successive points in time in the collection of data in longitudinal studies, the performance of subjects may increase due to practice effects. These effects may influence the performance of some subjects to a greater extent than others, and thus a confounding occurs in the data collected on the criterion measures.

(d) *Reliability of instruments*. Some measurements of developmental changes such as those associated with physical growth, can be obtained with a high degree of reliability, while other measurements, such as those associated with attitudes and values, commonly have a substantially lower level of reliability. In longitudinal studies, where not only a range of instruments but also many observers must be used at different points in time, it is desirable to ensure that both standardization of instruments and thorough training of observers take place not only to reduce random error but also systematic error or bias in the measurements made over time.

(e) *Multiple intervention interference*. Any investigation intrudes to some extent on the lives of individuals and longitudinal studies are particularly vulnerable in this regard. It is possible that individuals are affected differentially either positively or negatively by investigation, especially where intervention has occurred. In addition, delayed effects produced on some criterion measures may be falsely ascribed to a later treatment when the effect was caused by an earlier treatment.

(f) *Instability in the subject being measured.* In studies of teaching behaviour, errors of measurement not only arise from the unreliability of observation, but also as a consequence of instability in the behaviour of both teachers and students. Certain aspects of teacher behaviour are time related, being dependent on the time of day, the day of the week, or the month of the school year. Under these circumstances what might be either natural variation or systematic variation in behaviour, might be viewed as a consequence of intervention and in turn as mediating between the intervention and the criterion measures of student performance.

(g) *Changes in the composition of samples.* One of the major problems in the conduct of a longitudinal study is the loss from samples over time. It is highly likely that such losses could introduce substantial bias, since those subjects who are lost from a study are commonly the more mobile, frequently of high or low rather than average socioeconomic status, or involve those who are less highly motivated to take part in such a study. While it is commonly possible in a longitudinal study to present information on the characteristics of subjects who have been lost from the study, and it is sometimes possible to weight the data used in the analyses to correct in part for such bias, in general, such losses have an unknown confounding influence on the findings.

(h) *Reactive interventions.* In longitudinal studies it is not uncommon for the research worker to become aware of events in the lives of individuals that cannot be ignored or left without some action. Under such circumstances, although prejudicial to the results of an investigation, the research worker is frequently required to intervene and thus confound or contaminate all subsequent measurements made on predictor and criterion variables.

(i) *The use of natural groups.* It is rarely possible in longitudinal studies in educational research to randomly assign subjects to experimental and control groups, and it is commonly necessary to employ natural groups in an investigation. These natural groups may differ from the outset with respect to the predictor variables used in the study, and in addition the groups might react differently in ways that would influence the nature of the treatments administered to them. Both the initial differences between the natural groups and the consequent variations introduced in the treatments administered to them may confound the results of a study.

Some types of longitudinal study are more vulnerable to these threats to internal validity than are others. While the simultaneous cross-sectional design suffers from severe limitations in the nature of the information

that can be derived from it, this design has the advantage that it does not involve the conduct of a study over an extended period, and is not subjected to the threats to interval validity that clearly exist for more complex designs.

## 4.2 Threats to External Validity

Educational research is a field of investigatory activity that is evolving over time as new tactics and strategies for research are developed and as new procedures for the analysis of data are introduced. Even though a well-designed and controlled investigation might have been planned, there is the risk that during the conduct of the study, the procedures employed will be challenged in the light of new knowledge and new understandings. Alternatively, new analytical procedures might become available that could have been employed if a different design had been used or if different information had been collected. As a consequence the conduct of a longitudinal study and the analysis of the data collected that were beyond challenge at the time of its conception might be seriously threatened at the time of its completion Pedhazur's (1982) questioning of the validity of the data analyses for the IEA Six Subject Study involved a challenge of this kind.

(a) *Population validity.* Educational policies and practice are subject to constant change, both as new knowledge becomes available and as responses occur to political pressures. Longitudinal studies require time to conduct, to analyse the data collected, and to report the findings. As a consequence both of the inevitable timelag and the politicization of the field of education, it has been argued that when the findings of major longitudinal studies in the field of education were released, the characteristics of the population and the circumstances under which the studies were conducted had changed to such an extent that the findings were no longer valid or relevant. The Sustaining Effects Study in the United States (Carter 1984) suffered this fate. Nevertheless, it must be recognized that while superficial changes are commonly experienced in education, there is a natural conservatism of the teaching profession and in the community that enables the findings of research to maintain their validity for longer periods than are generally acknowledged. Furthermore, the findings from studies conducted in many different parts of the world support the view that there is some universality across populations, across countries, and across time. It is nevertheless necessary to establish the ecological validity of research conducted at different times and in different settings so that the relevance beyond a particular setting and at a particular time is accepted. There are many threats to ecological validity; the discussion which follows is derived from that presented by Kratochwill (1978) and is based on the work of Bracht and Glass (1968).

(b) *Explicit statement of treatment conditions.* The validity of research findings and their applicability to other situations depend on a detailed knowledge of the treatment conditions. This requires that a complete and specific description of the predictor variables and the treatment conditions under which the longitudinal investigation was carried out are provided, so that readers and reviewers of the research findings are able to assess the extent to which the findings can be generalized to other situations. The widely used techniques of meta-analysis assist in the combining of the results from similar studies to obtain more general findings.

(c) *Multiple intervention interference.* In the discussion above of threats to internal validity it was pointed out that multiple interventions might confound the findings obtained from a particular longitudinal study. Likewise multiple interventions might be expected to increase the difficulty with which results from such studies might be compared with the findings from investigations where only a single intervention was administered. Similar problems arise in the extent to which the findings from multiple intervention studies might be generalized to other settings.

(d) *Hawthorne effect.* When subjects are aware that they are taking part in a long-term investigation, it would seem that their behaviour, particularly in the longer term aspects, might be significantly affected. Such behaviour might be influenced in ways that are either favourable or unfavourable to the investigation. Moreover, different subjects might respond in different ways.

(e) *Use of appropriate criterion variables.* In longitudinal studies where biological, environmental, and intervention influences are being investigated, there is a risk that a particular criterion variable will be employed that is not sensitive to the different influences that are present. Consequently, it is common in longitudinal studies to employ a battery of criterion variables in the expectation that the range of outcomes which arise from the different influences will be covered. Thus, in general, longitudinal studies are multivariate in nature, and analytical procedures have to be employed in the examination of the data that will take into consideration the many criterion measures on which information has been obtained. Nevertheless, it must be recognized that longitudinal studies, by their nature, must be thoroughly planned in advance and thus lack flexibility to handle unexpected outcomes.

(f) *The effects of critical events on individuals.* Not only is development influenced by biological, environmental, and intervention factors, but critical events in the lives of individual subjects, such as a road accident, or a breakup of the family, may have significant effects on a subject's development. In longitudinal studies conducted over a period of time, the probability of the occurrence of a critical event is significantly greater than in other types of studies, and such events which occur naturally in the lives of substantial numbers of people, serve to distort the data collected. Furthermore, since they are unique, although relatively common events, they are difficult to allow for in the analysis of data and could confound the findings derived from a study.

(g) *The effects of historical events on groups.* In a similar manner, events of an historical nature can affect in significant ways the development of groups. Political unrest and natural disasters can occur during the conduct of a longitudinal study under such circumstances as to confound the effects of an intervention or to affect differentially certain subgroups involved in the investigation and thus distort the overall validity of the study and prevent its findings being generalized to other settings.

(h) *The effects of publication.* Longitudinal studies must maintain support from funding agencies, and this requires them to publish interim reports of their findings. The effects of publication are commonly to make the subjects of an investigation more conscious of their involvement and more aware of the nature of the study. Publication of results can prove damaging to a study if the findings are controversial and attract widespread publicity. Not only is it possible that the subjects of the investigation might distort the information that they provide on occasions subsequent to the release of findings, but some subjects might withdraw from further participation in the investigation. Some longitudinal studies have sought to use the publicity gained in the media to maintain the involvement of the subjects in the study. However, this approach carries with it the significant risk of reducing the validity of the information collected.

Perhaps the greatest threat to the validity of longitudinal studies in educational research, is the magnitude of the task of conducting such a study. In order to sustain an investigation over many years, immense commitments in the form of highly skilled personnel and financial resources are required. Changes in the personnel involved in the conduct of a longitudinal study can be prejudicial to the administration and the rigour with which the investigation is carried out. This poses a major threat to the validity of a study. Likewise the high costs of longitudinal research can result in fluctuations in the financial support provided over time, with the consequent need to change in significant ways both the nature of a study and its conduct in order to contain costs. This can damage substantially the validity of the findings of longitudinal research studies.

## 5. Analysis of Longitudinal Research Data

The analysis of the data collected in a longitudinal research study has two primary aims: descriptive analysis and explanatory analysis. However, before any analyses can be undertaken attention must be given to the problems of measuring attributes on appropriate scales.

### 5.1 Measurement of Change

The particular problem encountered in educational research studies that employ a longitudinal design is that it is commonly inappropriate to use the same instrument across different age groups and at different points in time. The procedures employed for equating the measurements obtained using two different instruments by bringing the scores to a common scale require either that (a) the two instruments are administered to a common sample, or (b) the two instruments contain common components or common items when administered to different samples. Three procedures are employed to bring these scores to a common scale.

(a) *Linear scaling*. In this procedure it is assumed that both the test items and the persons tested represent appropriate samples in the measurement of an underlying trait that is normally distributed with respect to both test items and persons. The scores are standardized, commonly to a mean of zero and a standard deviation of one, and the line of equivalence is used to equate one set of scores with the other. Figure 3(a) illustrates the use of this procedure (see Thorndike 1971 p. 569).

(b) *Equipercentile scaling*. In this procedure it is similarly assumed that both the test items and the persons tested represent appropriate samples for the measurement of an underlying trait. In using this procedure cumulative frequency distributions are calculated, the scores obtained at equal percentile points for each test, and a line of equivalence is plotted (see Thorndike 1971 p. 571). Figure 3(b) illustrates the use of this procedure which has the advantage over the linear scaling procedure that no assumptions need be made with respect to the shape of the distributions.

(c) *Latent trait measurement*. It is also possible to employ models based on the assumption of an unobservable, but underlying latent trait which exhibits a relationship with age, for example, as represented by a logistic function. One-parameter, two-parameter (Birnbaum 1968) and three-parameter (Lord 1980) models have been developed. The one-parameter model relates to either item difficulty or person ability. The two-parameter model allows for variability in item discrimination and the three-parameter model also allows for guessing in multiple-choice items where several

alternative responses are provided. Goldstein and Blinkhorn (1977) have questioned the use of latent trait procedures in the development of a common scale of measurement over time particularly in educational research, because of the problems of finding sensible interpretations of any results from such models for other than narrowly defined psychological attributes. Linear scaling was used by Comber and Keeves (1973) in the development of an international scale for achievement in science across 10-year-old, 14-year-old and terminal secondary-school age groups. A variation of the equipercentile scaling technique was used in the scaling of Scholastic Aptitude Test (SAT) scores over time in the United States (Donlon 1984) and latent trait measurement procedures using a modified three-parameter model have been employed in the scaling of scores in the National Assessment of Educational Progress (NAEP) in the United States (Beaton 1987, Bock et al. 1982). However, Sontag (1983) has provided evidence to support the use of the one-parameter model in the scaling of achievement test scores.

### 5.2 Univariate Models of Change

Statistical time series models have been used to describe a great variety of patterns of change in which measurements have been related to age or to another time scale. Goldstein (1979) has listed procedures for the fitting of growth curves to individual records. The most widely used model assumes that relative rate of change in size decreases proportionately to increases in size. Thus where size is very small the relative growth rate is high, but the actual growth rate is low because of small size. However, as size increases the growth rate increases, and when size approaches the final size, the relative and actual growth rates slow down.

The equation for rate of growth is expressed in the following form:

$$\frac{k}{y}\frac{dy}{dt} = b(k - y) \tag{1}$$

where $b$ is a constant, and $k$ is the final size (a constant).

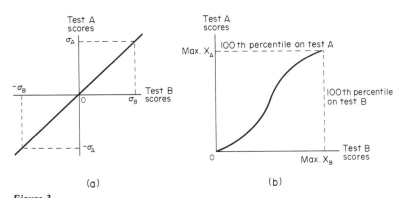

*Figure 3*
(a) Line of equivalence for linear scaling
(b) Line of equivalence for equipercentile scaling

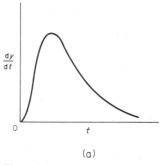
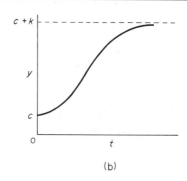

**Figure 4**
(a) Curve for rate of growth
(b) Curve for growth

The equation for the growth curve is given by the logistic function:

$$y = c + \frac{k}{1 + e^{a - bt}} \qquad (2)$$

where $a$ is a constant, and $y = c$ is the value of the lower asymptote and $y = c + k$ is the value of the upper asymptote.

The curves for rate of growth and growth are shown in Fig. 4(a) and 4(b) respectively.

An alternative model for the measurement of growth is provided by the Gompertz curve in which the relative rate of change in size decreases exponentially with time, and thus in equally small intervals of time there are equal proportional decreases in relative growth rate.

The equation for rate of growth is expressed in the following form:

$$\frac{1}{y} \frac{dy}{dt} = b\, e^{a - bt} \qquad (3)$$

where $a$ and $b$ are constants, and the equation for growth is given by:

$$y = k \exp[-\exp(a - bt)] \qquad (4)$$

Although research workers in the fields of child and adolescent development have considered the use of other types of curves, the logistic and the Gompertz curves have found most extensive use, including the combining of curves across different age ranges. Burt (1937) found, for example, that the growth in the height of girls from birth to 18 years could be represented by the sum of three logistic curves.

More powerful mathematical models are likely to become useful in the analysis of data in educational research as the accuracy of measurement increases and thus the quality of the data included in the analysis increases. Overviews of the mathematical methods and statistical procedures which might be used to describe change in longitudinal research studies have been provided by Goldstein (1979), Nesselroade and Baltes (1979), and Coleman (1981).

### 5.3 Multivariate Models of Change

In longitudinal research, the costs of carrying out the processes of data collection and maintaining contact with the sample under survey are so great that, in general, there is little to be gained by collecting data on only one criterion measure. As a consequence data are commonly available on a wide range of characteristics rather than on an isolated variable. Under these circumstances multivariate procedures of analysis are widely used in longitudinal research studies. This has also led to the use of techniques in an exploratory way to condense the large bodies of data and to examine for change more simplified data structures. Techniques that are widely used include exploratory factor analysis, multidimensional scaling, cluster analysis, and configural frequency analysis. Variation in the factor patterns or cluster patterns over time are taken to indicate change and development, while stability in factor and cluster patterns over time would seem to imply the measurement of a dimension that is unaffected by environment or biological influences.

### 5.4 Explanatory and Causal Analysis

In empirical research in education two strategies are available for the investigation of causal relationships, and in general, both involve the use of longitudinal designs. First, in experimental studies in which subjects are randomly selected from a population and are randomly assigned to experimental and control groups multivariate analysis of variance techniques are appropriate. Such studies which do not demand the collection of data at two points in time are rare in the investigation of educational processes. Secondly, in intervention studies where some degree of randomization in the allocation of subjects to treatments has been achieved, it may be possible to use multivariate analysis of covariance techniques in the examination of data. However, it is necessary to establish that antecedent conditions are unrelated both logically and empirically to the application of the intervention before covariance procedures can be used. Moreover, since time and time-related factors cannot be manipulated under experimental conditions and applied as interventions or treatments, in studies where more than one time-related variable is being investigated, analysis of variance and covariance techniques cannot be employed because such effects remain confounded.

A variety of techniques are, however, available for the examination of data to provide explanation in terms of causal relationships. These techniques make full use of the time relationships which are present in longitudinal designs. The analytical procedures which are employed require the development of causal models from prior research studies and established theory, and the testing of these models for fit using the available data. Among the procedures now available which are capable of analysing complex bodies of scaled data are Linear Structural Relations Analysis (LISREL) and Partial Least Squares Path Analysis (PLS). For the examination of less complex bodies of qualitative and categorical data log-linear modelling and configural frequency analysis techniques are gaining acceptance. The use of these explanatory analytical procedures requires that the longitudinal study should be designed with a clearly stated theoretical formulation from which causal hypotheses and causal models involving structural relationships between variables are developed for testing. These hypotheses and models are tested and accepted as plausible explanations of the available evidence or are rejected. The incorporation of accepted models into substantive theory that is coherent and is useful for further exploration is seen as the outcome of enquiry. Longitudinal research has an important role to play in this regard within the field of educational research.

## Bibliography

Baltes P B, Cornelius S M, Nesselroade J R 1979 Cohort effects in developmental psychology. In: Nesselroade J R, Baltes P B 1979 *Longitudinal Research in the Study of Behavior and Development*. Academic Press, New York

Baltes P B, Nesselroade J R 1979 History and rationale of longitudinal research. In: Nesselroade J R, Baltes P B 1979 *Longitudinal Research in the Study of Behavior and Development*. Academic Press, New York, pp. 1–39

Beaton A E 1987 Implementing the New Design: The NAEP 1983–84 Technical Report. National Assessment of Educational Progress/Educational Testing Service, Princeton, New Jersey

Birnbaum A 1968 Some latent trait models and their use in inferring an examinee's ability. In: Lord F M, Novick M R (eds.) 1968 *Statistical Theory in Mental Test Scores*. Addison-Wesley, Reading, Massachusetts

Black P, Harlen W, Orgee A 1984 *Standard of Performance—Expectation and Reality*, Assessment of Performance Unit (APU), Occasional Paper 3. Department of Education and Science, London

Bloom B S 1964 *Stability and Change in Human Characteristics*. Wiley, New York

Bloom B S (ed.) 1985 *Developing Talent in Young People*. Ballantine, New York

Bock R D, Mislevy R, Woodson C 1982 The next stage in educational assessment. *Educ. Res.* AERA 11(3): 4–11

Bourke S F, Mills J M, Stanyon J, Holzer F 1981 *Performance in Literacy and Numeracy: 1980*. Australian Government Publishing Service for the Australian Education Council, Canberra

Bracht G H, Glass G V 1968 The external validity of experiments. *Am. Educ. Res. J.* 5: 437–74

Braithwaite J 1983 *Explorations in Early Childhood Education*. Australian Council for Educational Research, Hawthorn, Victoria

Burt C B 1937 *The Backward Child*. University of London Press, London

Butler N R, Golding J (eds.) 1986 *From Birth to Five: A Study of the Health and Behaviour of Britain's Five Year Olds*. Pergamon, Oxford

Campbell D T, Stanley J C 1963 Experimental and quasi-experimental designs for research on teaching. In: Gage N L (ed.) 1963 *Handbook of Research on Teaching*. Rand McNally, Chicago, Illinois

Carroll J B 1975 *The Teaching of French as a Foreign Language in Eight Countries*. Wiley, New York

Carter L F 1984 The sustaining effects study of compensatory and elementary education. *Educ. Res.* 13(7): 4–13

Coleman J S 1981 *Longitudinal Data Analysis*. Basic Books, New York

Comber L C, Keeves J P 1973 *Science Education in Nineteen Countries: An Empirical Study*. Wiley, New York

Cronbach L J, Furby L 1970 How we should measure change: Or should we? *Psychol. Bull.* 74(1): 68–80

Davie R, Butler N, Goldstein H 1972 *From Birth to Seven: A Report of the National Child Development Study*. Longman, London

Donlon T F 1984 *The College Board Technical Handbook for the Scholastic Aptitude Test and Achievement Tests*. College Entrance Examination Board, New York

Douglas J W B 1964 *The Home and the School*. MacGibbon and Kee, London

Fägerlind I 1975 *Formal Education and Adult Earnings: A Longitudinal Study on the Economic Benefits of Education*. Almqvist and Wiksell, Stockholm

Fogelman K (ed.) 1983 *Growing Up in Great Britain: Collected Papers from the National Child Development Study*. Macmillan, London

Goldstein H 1979 *The Design and Analysis of Longitudinal Studies. Their Role in the Measurement of Change*. Academic Press, New York

Goldstein H, Blinkhorn S 1977 Monitoring educational standards: An inappropriate model. *Bull. Br. Psychol. Soc.* 30: 309–11

Husén T 1969 *Talent, Opportunity and Career*. Almqvist and Wiksell, Stockholm

Keeves J P, Matthews J K, Bourke S F 1978 *Educating for Literacy and Numeracy*. Australian Council for Educational Research, Hawthorn, Victoria

Kessler R C, Greenberg D F 1981 *Linear Panel Analysis: Models of Quantitative Change*. Academic Press, New York

Kratochwill T R (ed.) 1978 *Single Subject Research. Strategies for Evaluating Change*. Academic Press, New York

Lord F M 1980 *Applications of Item Response Theory to Practical Testing Problems*. Erlbaum, Hillsdale, New Jersey

Marjoribanks K 1975 Cognitive performance: A model for analysis. *Aust. J. Educ.* 19(2): 156–66

Morgan G 1982 The use of the Rasch latent trait measurement model in the equating of Scholastic Aptitude Tests. In: Spearritt D (ed.) 1982 *The Improvement of Measurement in Education and Psychology.* Australian Council for Educational Research, Hawthorn, Victoria

Nesselroade J R, Baltes P B 1979 *Longitudinal Research in the Study of Behavior and Development.* Academic Press, New York

Peaker G F 1971 *The Plowden Children Four Years Later.* National Foundation for Educational Research, Slough

Pedhazur E J 1982 *Multiple Regression in Behavioral Research. Explanation and Prediction,* 2nd edn. Holt, Rinehart and Winston, New York

Schaie K W 1965 A general model for the study of developmental problems. *Psychol. Bull.* 64: 92–107

Schweinhart L J, Weikart D P 1980 *Young Children Grow Up: The Effects of the Perry Preschool Program on Youths through Age Fourteen.* High Scope Press, Ypsilanti, Michigan

Sontag L M 1983 Vertical equating methods: A comparative study of their efficacy. Ph.D. thesis, Teachers College, Columbia University, New York

Spearritt D (ed.) 1982 *The Improvement of Measurement in Education and Psychology.* Australian Council for Educational Research, Hawthorn, Victoria

Thorndike R L (ed.) 1971 *Educational Measurement,* 2nd edn. American Council on Education, Washington, DC

Tyler R W 1985 National Assessment of Educational Progress (NAEP). In: Husén T, Postlethwaite T N (eds.) 1985 *The International Encyclopedia of Education.* Pergamon, Oxford, Vol. 6, pp. 3478–80

von Eye A 1985 Longitudinal research methods. In: Husén T, Postlethwaite T N (eds.) 1985 *The International Encyclopedia of Education.* Pergamon, Oxford, Vol. 5, pp. 3140–52

Weikart D P (ed.) 1984 *Changed Lives: The Effects of the Perry Preschool Program on Youths through Age Nineteen.* High Scope Press, Ypsilanti, Michigan

Williams T R, Clancy J, Batten M, Girling-Butcher S 1980 *School Work and Career: 17 Year Olds in Australia.* Australian Council for Educational Research, Hawthorn, Victoria

Williams T R, Batten M, Girling-Butcher S, Clancy J 1981 *School and Work in Prospect: 14 Year Olds in Australia.* Australian Council for Educational Research, Hawthorn, Victoria

# Measuring Change: The Difference Score and Beyond

## J. B. Willett

Questions about individual growth are crucially important in research on education. After all, the very purpose of education is to foster learning, to bring about changes in individual attitude, achievement, and value. For instance, when academic learning is being examined, we might ask, for each child: Does his or her achievement change over time? Does it increase or decrease? Does it grow at a steady rate, or does it level out after one or two years? These are questions about the way that the individual child is changing over time. They are questions about *within-individual growth*; questions in which *time is the predictor* (Willett and Singer 1989).

In most empirical studies, the investigation of *within-individual growth* is usually only a *first phase*: a phase that logically precedes the investigation of how the within-individual changes differ from one person to the next. Frequently, it is the *second-phase* questions about *inter-individual differences in growth* that have the greatest empirical importance. These are questions about the way in which individual learning is related, over children, to background, training, and environment. Do certain categories of child grow in different ways? Are girls more likely to show rapid increases, or decreases, in their achievement than boys? Do children who are trained in different ways enjoy different growth patterns?

Despite the obvious importance of these questions, influential methodologists have argued fallaciously for many years that within-individual change cannot be measured well. In fact, the traditional case against the measurement of change has been articulated so strongly that many empirical researchers simply refuse to measure individual change at all.

But why has the measurement of change been considered so difficult? The principle reason is that, for many years, methodologists have labored under a simple misconception. They have insisted on viewing change in a very restricted way. They have conceptualized it solely as an increment, as the difference between before and after. Every child has been regarded as having acquired a quantum of achievement, say, in the time between pre- and postmeasurement and, traditionally, investigators have only been concerned with the size of the acquired "chunk". This failure to conceptualize individual growth and change as a *continuous process of development over time* has hamstrung the creation of decent statistical methods for measuring change.

The myth that individual change cannot be measured adequately has been a serious stumbling block to the empirical evaluation of learning. Rather than simply throwing their hands up in despair, methodologists ought to have admitted the educational importance of questions about growth and asked: What do we need to do in order to measure change? Can individual growth be measured adequately, or even well? Is it possible to distinguish among children on the basis of their growth? And if so, how?

In the last decade, methodologists have begun to answer these questions. They have concluded that, if change is to be measured well, researchers must move beyond the limitations of the pre/post (or *two-wave*)

design. Individual development is a continuous process that can only be measured adequately when it has been observed for extended periods of time. Thus, good change measurement must be based on the collection of longitudinal (or *multiwave*) data. Methodologists have shown that, when multiwave designs replace two-wave designs, the problems that seemed to plague the measurement of change simply disappear.

This article chronicles competing methodologies that have been used for measuring change, detailing how traditional two-wave methods have been superseded by improved multiwave methods, and dealing with a number of problems that have beset change measurement for many years. Finally, it looks at the more recent, longitudinal methods, and argues that such methods are capable of providing an accurate measure of growth.

## 1. Measuring Change with Two Waves of Data

Traditionally, researchers observed the status (the achievement, say, or the attitude) of each sampled child at the beginning and end of their study in order to obtain a *two-wave growth record* for each child. In the first phase of the statistical analysis, a measure of change that summarized the growth of each child was constructed from the growth records. The measures of individual change obtained were then used in subsequent regression or correlational analyses to investigate how individual growth was related, over children, to selected covariates of substantive interest to the researcher. This latter phase has been called *the investigation of systematic interindividual differences in growth* (Rogosa and Willett 1985).

The question then arises as to how the within-individual growth summaries should be computed when only two waves of data have been collected for each child? The simplest and most intuitively pleasing two-wave measure of change is easily obtained by subtracting the initial observed status from the final observed status for each child. Such a measure is known as a *difference*, *change*, or *gain score*. Although highly favored originally, in recent years the difference score has been misguidedly perceived as unreliable, invalid, and unfair, prompting methodologists to promote a coterie of other two-wave measures of change, including at least two *regression-based estimators of true change* and several types of *residual change score*. These latter strategies have been attacked in their turn as inadequate and the two-wave measurement of change has been superseded by conceptually superior and statistically more powerful multiwave methods.

Because much of the distress surrounding the measurement of change has centered on the psychometric concept of reliability, the following sections begin with a discussion of the intrinsic fallibility of empirical measurement and then present a brief outline of the difference score and its modified forms.

### 1.1 The Fallibility of Empirical Measurement

When a child's achievement is assessed by a test or rating instrument, a combination of his or her *true capability* and whatever *random error* happens to accompany the measurement is recorded. If the random error is large, then the child's *observed capability* may be quite different from its underlying true value. Similarly, when growth is being investigated, it is not the fallible *observed changes* that are of key interest but the underlying *true changes*. Measures of observed change simply provide a fallible lens through which the hidden nature of true change may be discerned.

Typically, methodologists have been content to assume that *observed status* is simply the *sum of true status and random measurement error*: $X_{ip} = \xi_p(t_i) + \varepsilon_{ip}$, where $t_i$ is the time of the $i^{th}$ occasion of measurement, and subscript $p$ indicates the person in the population that is being represented. The symbol $\xi$ denotes true status, and the parenthetical inclusion of $t_i$ indicates that it is changing with time. The measurement errors $\varepsilon_{ip}$ are often assumed to be drawn randomly and independently from identical normal distributions.

The fallibility of a measuring instrument is often summarized by its *reliability*. Because of the influence of measurement error, when duplicate sets of measurements on the same individuals are compared they will never be *exactly* congruent. If the duplication is very poor then the measure being evaluated is considered *unreliable*. On the other hand, duplicated measurements usually do show *some* level of congruence. This tendency toward consistency over duplicated measurements is called *reliability*.

Reliability and measurement error are causally related. If the random errors of measurement are large and haphazard, then the measurement of a trait will be inconsistent on replication and reliability will be low. If measurement error is diminishingly small, then reliability will be high. There is an important need for all measurement to be reliable. An unreliable measure may give a very different value of the same trait on replication of the measurement, and therefore any ordering of individuals within a group will differ from measurement to measurement.

Nevertheless, because of the way that reliability is defined—as a ratio of the interindividual variation in true and observed scores—caution must be exercised when reliability coefficients are interpreted. Low reliability, for instance, may be caused either by large measurement error variation or by a low level of true score heterogeneity among members of the population being sampled. One cannot judge from the magnitude of reliability alone whether excessive measurement error variation or a lack of interindividual true variation has reduced reliability. This confounding of error and true-score variation makes the interpretation of reliability particularly slippery, especially when individual change is being measured.

## 1.2 The Difference Score

The observed pretest and posttest measurements of a child's status (obtained at times $t_1$ and $t_2$) are $X_{1p} = \xi_p(t_1) + \varepsilon_{1p}$ and $X_{2p} = \xi_p(t_2) + \varepsilon_{2p}$ and therefore the difference score for the $p^{\text{th}}$ child is $D_p = X_{2p} - X_{1p}$. The observed difference score for each child can be expressed as the sum of the underlying true change, $\Delta_p = \xi_p(t_2) - \xi_p(t_1)$, and the difference between the two measurement errors, $(\varepsilon_{2p} - \varepsilon_{1p})$. In a growth study, true change, and not observed change, is the key focus of interest.

Statistically speaking, the observed difference score is a fairly reasonable commodity. It is intuitively appealing, easy to compute, and an unbiased estimator of the underlying true change. Despite these advantages, the difference score has been criticized so resoundingly over the years that it has been largely abandoned as a measure of within-individual change. It has been condemned for both its purported unreliability, and its correlation with initial status (Linn and Slinde 1977). Recently, however, these deficiencies, discussed below, have been shown to be largely imaginary (Rogosa et al. 1982, Rogosa and Willett 1983, 1985, Willett 1988).

### 1.2.1 The purported unreliability of the difference score

One argument against the difference score holds that it is always unreliable; another that the difference score cannot be both reliable and valid simultaneously. In general, neither of the claims is correct. The misconceptions have arisen from misinterpretation of the observed pretest–posttest correlation as an index of construct validity in expressions for the reliability of the difference score (Rogosa et al. 1982, Willett 1988). In fact, in perfectly ordinary situations, the reliability of the difference score can be quite respectable (Rogosa and Willett 1983). In fact, when differences in growth from one person to the next are large, the reliability of the difference score can be *greater* than the reliabilities of the constituent pretest and posttest scores (Willett 1988).

Even if the difference score *were* always unreliable, however, this would not necessarily be a problem. Low difference-score reliability does not unilaterally imply that within-individual change has been measured imprecisely. Low reliability often occurs in practice because almost everyone in the sample is growing at about the same rate. So even though the 20 points (say) that every child has grown can be accurately measured, different children cannot be distinguished by their growth, and the difference score appears unreliable. This problem of interpretation does not call the difference score itself into question—we know quite precisely that everyone has grown by 20 points—but it does reveal a fundamental flaw in the concept of reliability as an indicator of measurement quality.

### 1.2.2 Correlation of the difference score with initial status

The difference score has also been roundly condemned for at least three other reasons, all of which originate in critics' misunderstanding of the association between it and pretest status (Linn and Slinde 1977, Plewis 1985).

First, some critics claim that *any* measure of change that is not independent of initial status must be unfair because it gives "an advantage to persons with certain values of the pretest scores" (Linn and Slinde 1977 p. 125). This argument is illogical: why *should* growth and status be unrelated? How can an unbiased estimate be unfair? The intimate connection between growth and status is an inevitable consequence of history. Those who are growing most rapidly will automatically have a higher level of status when subsequently compared with those who are growing more slowly.

Second, numerous investigators have estimated the correlation between growth and initial status over persons (see, for instance, Bloom 1964) and have worried because their findings disagree. Some find the correlation to be positive, some zero, and some strongly negative. This concern again begs the question as to why a single value for this correlation should be expected. Providing all children are not growing perfectly parallel, the correlation between growth and initial status will differ as different occasions are chosen for the pretest measurement (Rogosa and Willett 1985). Unless some very important occasion can be declared substantively to be *the* initial time, there is no way that there can be a unique answer to the question: What is the correlation between growth and initial status? Researchers should *expect* to disagree.

Third, the difference score has been criticized because its correlation with the pretest is thought to be always negative. In reality this claim is false (see Thorndike 1966), but even if it were true, it would not provide grounds for dismissing the difference score. Those that condemn the difference score in this way have usually committed one of two mistakes. They have either caused the negative correlation themselves by "standardizing" the pretest and posttest scores to the same standard deviation before computing the difference score (an ill-advised process that destroys much valid growth information), or they are being confused by the vagueness of statistical estimation.

In this latter case, the *population correlation of true initial status and true change* is often estimated by the *sample correlation of observed initial status with the observed difference score*. Unfortunately, because the pretest measurement errors appear (with opposite sign) in the difference score, this estimator is badly negatively biased and often turns out to be negative even though the underlying true correlation is positive. However, an unbiased estimate of within-individual change—the difference score—should not be rejected simply because a common estimator of the association between true change and true initial status is biased [and anyway, this latter bias is easily corrected, (see Willett 1988)].

## 1.3 Weighted Estimators of True Change

Even though the difference score is not the outcast that many critics claim, modifications of it have been proposed to better estimate true change: Webster and Bereiter's (1963) *reliability-weighted measure of change*, and Lord's (1956) regression-based *estimated true change*. These modified estimators improve the measurement of within-individual change by trading off unbiasedness for a reduction in mean-squared error.

Under very broad assumptions, the modified measures are simply weighted linear combinations of the observed-difference score for the particular child and the average observed-difference score over the entire group, with weights that depend on the reliability of the difference score. Essentially, the weighting scheme places emphasis on those aspects of the growth measurement that are the most trustworthy: favoring the difference score when it is reliable but, otherwise, setting each child's growth equal to the average growth for everyone when there is little real interindividual variation in growth to be detected. Even though the modified scores are unquestionably better estimates of within-individual true change, they are usually perfectly correlated with the corresponding difference scores and have identical reliabilities. Therefore, parallel investigations of interindividual differences in growth using any of these scores usually lead to identical conclusions.

### 1.4 Residual Change Scores

Motivated by a desire to create change measures that were uncorrelated with pretest score, the *residual change score*—obtained by estimating residuals from the population regression of true final status on true initial status—was proposed. Much energy has been dissipated in the psychometric literature as authors have detailed the properties of the many estimators of residual change, and considerable controversy has been aroused. Methodologists disagree as to exactly what is being estimated, how well it is being estimated and how it can be interpreted. In addition to the many technical and practical problems that arise in the practical application of residual change scores, there also remain unresolved issues of logic and substance (Rogosa et al. 1982, Rogosa and Willett 1985, Willett 1988). Consequently, these scores have been largely discredited as measures of change.

### 1.5 Investigating Systematic Interindividual Differences in Growth with Two Waves of Data

Once a measure of change has been computed for each person in the sample, the relationship between growth and other background variables can be investigated by the ordinary methods of correlation and regression. For instance, to find out if changes in achievement are related to gender, pre/post differences in test score could be correlated with a dummy variable representing gender.

Unfortunately, while straightforward, this rudimentary second-phase strategy is flawed. The difference score is a fallible measure of growth that contains both true change and measurement error. This latter random "noise" attenuates the second-phase findings, and the sample correlations obtained underestimate the true relationship between growth and the covariates.

This problem can only be avoided by correcting the findings of the second-phase analysis for the fallibility of the difference score. Such disattenuation requires that additional empirical information be gathered, usually in the form of an external estimate of the reliability of the difference score. However, because the disattenuation is very sensitive to minor fluctuations in the size of the reliability estimate, and because the quality of these estimates is often very dubious, there exists the very real possiblity of major imperfection.

If the difference score is avoided and Lord's (1956) estimate of true change used instead, information in addition to the pre/post measurement is still required so that the estimate of true change can be constructed in the first place. In fact, regardless of the measure of change adopted, if second-phase findings are to be successful then information in addition to the pre/post measurement is always required. This emphasizes a fundamental weakness of the pre/post design. Two waves of data do not contain sufficient information for measuring change. For an accurate measurement, multiwave data are needed.

### 2. Measuring Change with Multiwave Data

Taking a "snapshot" of achievement before and after is not the best way to reveal the intricacies of a child's progress. Achievement may be changing smoothly over time with some complex and substantively interesting trajectory, but pre/post measurement will be unable to reveal the details of that trajectory. Indeed, when just two waves of data are available, only the simplest possible growth curve—a straight line—can be used to represent the trajectory. Just as any self-respecting data analysts would deride a regression fit to two datapoints, so should they mistrust a two-wave measure of change.

To characterize individual growth adequately, a longitudinal perspective must be adopted. Achievement, attitude, or whatever, must be examined carefully over time. Each child's observed growth record—a temporally ordered discrete series of fallible measurements—must be systematically assembled.

Preliminary analyses of the observed growth records are aided by the plotting, for each child, of empirical growth-trajectories: graphs of observed status displayed against time with some type of fitted or sketched trendline included on the graph. Given a collection of such plots, questions of within-individual growth and interindividual differences in growth can easily be explored. For the former, separate inspection of each of the plots may indicate whether each child's growth is linear, or whether it is curvilinear. For the latter, visually observed comparisons across children may reveal systematic differences between this group and that.

Corresponding to the exploratory inspection and comparison of empirical growth-trajectory plots, a more formal multiwave analysis of growth requires that two types of statistical model be defined: a model to represent within-individual growth, and a model to represent interindividual differences in growth. The adoption of carefully chosen models permits individual growth to be characterized and summarized with greater validity. There is the real possibility, for instance, that theories of psychological or linguistic development may suggest an appropriate functional form for within-individual growth, say. Subsequent analyses could then capitalize on this informed choice, and the quality of the research findings would be enhanced.

Some types of growth may, for instance, be theoretically constrained to rise to a ceiling. Then, by entertaining a growth model that includes an *asymptote*, not only can hypotheses about the shape of the within-individual growth be tested but also specific features of that growth can be associated with variation over persons in background, training, and environment. For example, some background characteristics may be related to the ultimate limits on growth (the asymptotes), while others may be related to the instantaneous rates of growth. When substantive theory informs model choice, an arena of richer research questions can be accessed.

### 2.1 A Model for Within-Individual Growth

It is the underlying true growth trajectory of each person that is of critical interest. The multiple entries in the observed growth record are simply a fallible lens through which the true growth is perceived. When a mathematical model is selected to represent growth, it is the underlying true growth—the functional form of $\xi_p(t)$—that is being represented.

There are an infinite number of mathematical models that could be used to represent growth. Some are simple, like the straight line, whereas others, like the negative-exponential and quadratic curves, are more complex. It is even possible to join several models together, creating a sort of piecewise individual growth function. In the previous article, *Longitudinal Research Methods*, J P Keeves discusses several mathematical models commonly used to represent nonlinear individual growth.

Once a within-individual growth model has been picked, everyone's growth is assumed to have this same generic shape, with particular people being distinguished by the values of various constants—the within-individual growth parameters—that appear in the mathematical function. Different growth models have different numbers of growth parameters. The straight-line growth model, for instance, has two: status at some arbitrary initial time (the *intercept*), and rate of growth (the *slope*):

$$\xi_p(t) = \xi_p(t^*) + \theta_p(t - t^*) \qquad (1)$$

where the intercept $\xi_p(t^*)$ is the status of the $p^{th}$ person at an arbitrarily selected time $t^*$ (which could represent, for instance, the time at which that person entered the study), and the slope $\theta_p$ is the rate at which true status is growing. If the slope is positive, then true status is increasing with time; if it is negative, then true status is decreasing with time.

Provided the choice of growth model is valid, the within-individual growth parameters completely specify each person's growth. Consequently, these parameters are usually estimated during analysis, the estimates providing an empirical summary of within-individual change. For instance, under the straight-line model, estimates of the within-individual slopes provide a ready and effective measure of change for each person.

Growth models are usually picked so that the growth parameters are rationally interpretable in terms of the underlying growth process, but sometimes well-fitting polynomials are adopted as approximations. Largely for reasons of parsimony, the linear and quadratic functions have become the most popular of these. A straight line, for instance, provides an uncomplicated summary of growth when only a small part of the lifespan is being studied or when the observed growth records contain only a few timepoints.

### 2.2 A Model for Interindividual Differences in Growth

Interindividual differences in growth occur when the growth parameters differ from person to person. For instance, if children's within-individual growth in achievement has been represented by a straight line, then any possible pattern of interindividual differences can be attributed solely to differences in intercept and slope among children.

Once a suitable growth model has been chosen, vague questions about differences in growth from child to child can be replaced by more refined questions about interindividual variation in the growth parameters. By adopting an appropriate growth model, the research question is focused more meaningfully on the hypothesized attributes of the underlying growth process.

For instance, the growth parameters may differ from child to child in a way that is systematically related to some background characteristic, $\omega_p$, such as gender, socioeconomic status, type of enrichment program, language spoken in the home, and so forth. Then, under a straight-line growth model, the investigator might ask: Is there a systematic relationship between the within-individual growth rates and the covariate? Is growth in achievement related to gender, to socioeconomic status, to enrichment program?

One of these hypothesized interindividual relationships might be represented by the following simple linear regression model:

$$\theta_p = \beta_0 + \beta_{\theta\omega}\omega_p + \text{error} \qquad (2)$$

(see Rogosa and Willett 1985). In this model, the interindividual regression slope $\beta_{\theta\omega}$ summarizes the linear population relationship between the individual rates of true growth and the covariate. If people with larger values of the covariate grow more rapidly, then $\beta_{\theta\omega}$ will be positive; if smaller values of $\omega_p$ correspond to more rapid rates of true growth then $\beta_{\theta\omega}$ will be negative. A nonzero value of $\beta_{\theta\omega}$, or of the corresponding correlation coefficient $\rho_{\theta\omega}$, indicates that the covariate is a predictor of linear growth. One or both of these interindividual parameters, $\beta_{\theta\omega}$ or $\rho_{\theta\omega}$, is usually estimated in the second phase of a growth study.

One of the main advantages of a longitudinal perspective is that the investigator is not limited solely to the simple within- and interindividual models presented here. Substantively valid curvilinear functions can be used to model within-individual growth, and sophisticated multiple regression models can be used to relate interindividual differences in growth parameters to several covariates simultaneously. Systematic interindividual variation in the rate parameter of the negative-exponential growth model, or in the acceleration parameter of the quadratic growth model, can be examined. A new world for measuring growth, far from the pre/post design, has been revealed.

## 3. Doing the Statistical Analyses

In any growth investigation, models corresponding to Eqns. (1) and (2) would be fitted using the multiwave observed growth records gathered during data collection. Below several appropriate data-analytic strategies are outlined, ranging from a simple regression-based exploratory approach that can be implemented with most statistical packages to the more sophisticated use of empirical Bayes estimation and customized software.

The within-individual growth models can easily be fitted to the observed growth records by ordinary least-squares (OLS) regression analysis: one fitted growth trajectory per person. Then, under the straight-line model, the estimated slopes are measures of the observed rate of change for each person and can be used directly in subsequent second-phase correlation or regression analysis. This strategy is straightforward, and the OLS growth rates provide more precise measurement of change than was possible with the difference score.

Due to the idiosyncracies of measurement, some people may have empirical growth records whose entries are highly ordered and whose corresponding empirical growth trajectories are very smooth. Other people may have more erratic growth records. Consequently, the precision (*standard errors*) of the first-phase growth parameter estimation will differ from person to person.

The second-phase analyses can be improved (made asymptotically efficient) if *weighted least-squares regression analysis* is used to estimate the interindividual model in Eqn. (2) with weights that depend upon the standard errors of the first-round individual growth parameter estimates. With suitable chosen weights, for instance, the more precise individual growth-rates (those with the smallest standard errors) will play a more important role in the second-phase analyses. Willett (1988) presents an appropriate expression for the weights.

All of the analyses will automatically be improved if the first-phase estimation is made more precise. In practice, this is easily achieved by collecting more waves of data on each person in the sample. The standard errors of fitted growth-rates, for instance, decrease dramatically as extra waves of data are added. It is for this reason alone that multiwave designs provide much more reliable methods for measuring change. Ultimately, the researcher has total control over the quality of his or her findings, and can simply continue to "add waves" to the design until some desired level of precision is reached (see Willett, in press).

A more sophisticated technique involves estimating the within- and interindividual growth models simultaneously by Bayesian methods. Methodology for analyzing growth has been advancing very rapidly. Currently, the most sophisticated estimation methods—and also a proprietary piece of computer software called Hierarchical Linear Modeling (HLM)—have been provided by Bryk and Raudenbush (1987). In HLM, parameter estimates similar to those obtained above by weighted least-squares are used as "start values" for the iterative analyses.

## Bibliography

Bloom B S 1964 *Stability and Change in Human Characteristics*. Wiley, New York

Bryk A S, Raudenbush S W 1987 Application of hierarchical linear models to assessing change. *Psychol. Bull.* 101: 147–58

Linn R L, Slinde J A 1977 The determination of the significance of change between pre- and posttesting periods. *Rev. Educ. Res.* 47: 121–50

Lord F M 1956 The measurement of growth. *Educ. Psychol. Meas.* 16: 421–37

Plewis I 1985 *Analysing Change: Measurement and Explanation Using Longitudinal Data*. Wiley, New York

Rogosa D R, Brandt D, Zimowski M 1982 A growth curve approach to the measurement of change. *Psychol. Bull.* 92: 726–48

Rogosa D R, Willett J B 1983 Demonstrating the reliability of the difference score in the measurement of change. *J. Educ. Meas.* 20: 335–43

Rogosa D R, Willett J B 1985 Understanding correlates of change by modeling individual differences in growth. *Psychometrika* 50: 203–28

Thorndike R L 1966 Intellectual status and intellectual growth. *J. Educ. Psychol.* 57: 121–27

Webster H, Bereiter C 1963 The reliability of changes measured by mental test scores. In: Harris C W (ed.) 1963 *Problems in Measuring Change*. University of Wisconsin Press, Madison, Wisconsin, pp 39–59

Willett J B 1988 Questions and answers in the measurement of change. In: Rothkopf E Z (ed.) 1988 *Review of Research in Education*, Vol. 15. American Educational Research Association, Washington, DC, pp. 345–422

Willett J B Some results on reliability for the multiwave measurement of change: Implications for empirical design. *Educ. Psychol. Meas.*, in press

Willett J B, Singer J D 1989 Two types of question about time: Methodological issues in the analysis of teacher career path data. *Int. J. Educ. Res.* 13(4): 421–37

# Issues in Qualitative Evaluation Research

## Observation Techniques

### J. A. Stallings and G. G. Mohlman

There are many techniques used to observe and record human behavior and physical environments. These include checklists, rating scales, narrative descriptions, and interactive coding systems. Each of these techniques is appropriate for specific kinds of data to be collected. Each has some advantages and some disadvantages.

### 1. Common Elements

Although the observational techniques differ, there are several elements that all observation systems have:

(a) *A purpose.* The purpose of the observation will guide the selection of the technique to be used. Observations may be used for research on effective teaching; to evaluate teachers' performance; to evaluate a child's social, physical, or cognitive development; or to examine program implementation.

(b) *A set of operational definitions.* Operational definitions guide the observers so that by following the prescribed rules, each observer will assign the same value or category to the event being observed. For example, what must a student be doing to be recorded as "off task?" (Staring? Sleeping? Chatting? Doodling? Waiting?) The operational definition must state explicitly which behaviors are included in being "off task."

(c) *A means to train observers.* To collect reliable observation data, training for observers must be provided. Observers must learn the operational definitions and specific procedures for recording data. Depending upon the complexity of the observation technique, the training period may be a few hours, several days, or several weeks. Observers should be checked for accuracy before they begin collecting data. There are several means to measure observer accuracy. The most often used is to have paired observers record the same event in the natural situation and calculate their interrater agreement or the interrater reliability of observation. Another method is to show observers a precoded videotaped event and compare their recordings to the criterion.

(d) *A focus of observation.* Each observation has a focus phenomenon to be looked at or listened to. This might be a teacher, an aide, a child, materials, activities, or physical facilities.

(e) *A setting.* All observations have a setting. They may be conducted in classrooms, school grounds, hallways, lunch rooms, students' homes, or staff rooms. The observer will go where it is necessary to obtain the data required for the study.

(f) *A unit of time.* Each observation has a specified length: seconds, minutes, hours, or days. Observation data can be collected according to a time sample or a real-time method. To illustrate the difference, consider the coding of interactions between a teacher and a child. Under the time sample method, the observer uses a time piece and only records an interaction, for example, every 10 seconds. The only interaction coded is the one occurring when exactly 10 seconds have passed. Thus, the interactions that occur between the time intervals are not recorded. In a real-time method, every interaction is coded. Another real-time method is the narrative description—everything that is relevant to the purpose is recorded. The issue here is one of interpretation. Do the data collected during the selected coding intervals (for example, one code every five minutes) accurately represent what went on between the coding intervals? Are the intervals spaced so far apart that some important events were not coded by the observer? This issue usually arises when using checklist category systems. If one is counting behaviors only during certain equally spaced intervals, then the target behaviors should be relatively stable ones. In any other case, real-time data are likely to provide a more accurate picture.

(g) *Observation schedule.* All observations need a schedule for gathering the data. This might be a fall pretest and a spring posttest for research purposes. For staff development, weekly or monthly observations may be required, whereas staff evaluation might only occur on a yearly basis.

The time of day for observations must also be established. End-of-the-day teacher and student behavior is likely to appear different from early morning behavior. Monday activities may be different from Tuesday and Wednesday activities. Therefore, to obtain a more stable sample of behavior, the schedule should allow for the same period of time to be observed on several consecutive days at each period of observation. All members of the sample should be observed during a similar time period. For example, if some teachers and students are observed in early September, and others are observed in October, the data will not be comparable since those observed in October will be more acclimatized to school.

(h) *A method to record data.* Observations may be recorded with audiotapes, videotapes, minicomputers, optical scan forms, or paper and pencil. The method of recording will affect how the data are processed.

(i) *A method to process and analyze data.* The events recorded must be processed and categorized systematically in order to draw conclusions from the data. Processing can take several forms. Observation data can be optically scanned, key punched directly from the records, or hand sorted for key words and concepts in narratives. Analysis of observation data usually takes the form of frequency counts, percent of occurrences, scores on rating scales, presence or absence of events, and quality statements.

## 2. Types of Observational Techniques

The following sections will describe some of the purposes, advantages, and disadvantages of several observational techniques.

### 2.1 Checklists

A list of expected behaviors is prepared and every time the behavior occurs during the specified observation time unit, the observer enters a tally mark next to the appropriate category. The time unit is usually in terms of seconds; for example scan the room for 30 seconds and record it; five minutes later, scan the room and record again. Checklists are particularly useful in showing the presence or absence of specific teacher or student behaviors.

Another type of checklist is the seating chart. One way this is used is to code each student by name who is off-task at the time the observation is made. An "S" under the student's name on the chart indicates socializing. "W" indicates waiting, and "U" indicates uninvolved. A check of off-task students is usually made every five minutes throughout the period.

A more sophisticated checklist is the "Snapshot." One mark indicates the activity occurring, the material being used, and with whom the teacher is working.

As shown in Fig. 1, the Snapshot, the classroom activities are listed down the left side of the page, and the materials are listed across the top. The observer records the information in each appropriate space, recording each unique grouping occurring in the classroom. A completed Snapshot documents the number and kind of groupings, the activity and materials of each group, and whether an adult is present.

The letters at the beginning of each row indicate the placement of each category of participants in the classroom: T = teacher; A = aide; O = other adult; I = independent student.

If it is a team-teaching arrangement, both teachers are shown in the activity with the student or students they are working with when the Snapshot is recorded. The 1, S, L, and E in the rows relate to the number of students with whom the teacher is working: 1 = one student; S = 2–8 students; L = 9 to one less than the total group, and E = everyone.

The letters marked in Fig. 1 indicate that the teacher is giving instruction to one student in a workbook. The other students are working alone in workbooks. An aide is doing some classroom management task. Five grids are completed each 45-minute period and each class period is observed three days in a row.

The advantage of the checklist is that observers can be trained to use it rather easily if categories to be checked are discrete and if the operational definitions are clear and not overlapping. The event either is or is not occurring at the time the record is made. Another advantage is that the data can be easily keypunched directly from the records and frequency counts are easily produced. This makes processing and analyzing the data relatively inexpensive.

A disadvantage of the checklist is that only a limited number of preselected events can be recorded. If the list becomes too long (over 20) the observer has a difficult time scanning the list to see whether the event occurred during the specified time frame. The data collected will not provide information about interactions, continuous behavior, or the quality of the events.

### 2.2 Rating Scales

Rating scales require the observer to watch the focus of the observation for a specified period of time. The period of time to observe may vary from five minutes to 60 minutes. At the end of the time, the observer rates the prevalence of certain behaviors during the period on a scale (see Tab. 1).

A good use of the rating scale is to assess high-inference variables such as teacher enthusiasm or student initiative. These types of variables can be evaluated better over a period of continuous time rather than from frequency counts made during short time samples. Similar to the checklists, the rating scales have the advantage of being easily processed and quantified.

A disadvantage of rating scales is the inherent subjectivity of ratings. A summary of the observer's opinion is produced rather than actual observed events. In order to produce usable data, very specific definitions must be made of the attributes of each point of the scales. What one observer rates as high teacher enthusiasm may be rated as moderate enthusiasm by another observer. Therefore, the scale must define how frequent the teacher seems to be enthusiastic as well as what an enthusiastic teacher looks like and sounds like. The training of observers to develop acceptable interrater

## Classroom Snapshot

Material →
Activity ↓

| Activity | | 01 Textbook | 02 Workbook/ Worksheet | 03 Test | 04 Game/ Manipulative material | 05 Machine | 06 Chalkboard | 07 Noncurricular reading | 08 No material |
|---|---|---|---|---|---|---|---|---|---|
| 01 Reading silently | T A O i | I S L E | I S L E | I S L E | I S L E | I S L E | I S L E | I S L E | I S L E |
| 02 Reading aloud | T A O i | I S L E | I S L E | I S L E | I S L E | I S L E | I S L E | I S L E | I S L E |
| 03 Marking assignments | T A O i | I S L E | I S L E | I S L E | I S L E | I S L E | I S L E | I S L E | I S L E |
| 04 Instruction/ explanation | T A O i | I S L E | ● S L E | I S L E | I S L E | I S L E | I S L E | I S L E | I S L E |
| 05 Discussion/ Reviewing assignments | T A O i | I S L E | I S L E | I S L E | I S L E | I S L E | I S L E | I S L E | I S L E |
| 06 Practice drill | T A O i | I S L E | I S L E | I S L E | I S L E | I S L E | I S L E | I S L E | I S L E |
| 07 Written assignments | T A O i | I S L E | I S ● E | I S L E | I S L E | I S L E | I S L E | I S L E | I S L E |
| 08 Taking test quiz | T A O i | I S L E | I S L E | I S L E | I S L E | I S L E | I S L E | I S L E | I S L E |
| 09 Nonmath or nonreading instruction | T A O i | I S L E | I S L E | I S L E | I S L E | I S L E | I S L E | I S L E | I S L E |
| 10 Social inter- action (TAAO) | T A O i | I S L E | I S L E | I S L E | I S L E | I S L E | I S L E | I S L E | I S L E |
| 11 Student uninvolved | T A O i | I S L E | I S L E | I S L E | I S L E | I S L E | I S L E | I S L E | I S L E |
| 12 Being disciplined | T A O i | I S L E | I S L E | I S L E | I S L E | I S L E | I S L E | I S L E | I S L E |
| 13 Classroom manage- ment (TAAO ●) | T A O i | I S L E | I S L E | I S L E | I S L E | I S L E | I S L E | I S L E | I S L E |

**Figure 1**
The Snapshot, a comprehensive classroom observation system[a]

a Source: Stallings and Needels 1978

**Table 1**
Overall emotional-attitudinal climate: Affective categories and Florida Climate Control System (FLACCS) classroom global ratings[a]

Example questions:
(a) Circle the rating which best described the teacher's attitude towards the class:

| Highly positive | Positive most of the time | Neither positive nor negative | Negative occasionally | Highly negative |
|---|---|---|---|---|
| 5 | 4 | 3 | 2 | 1 |

For example, if you felt the teacher's attitude towards the class was *extremely* positive, you would rate this question "5."

(b) Circle the rating that best describes the students in this class:

| Class appears extremely happy and/or satisfied | Most students appear happy and/or satisfied much of the time | About half appear happy and/or satisfied much of the time | Occasionally pupils appear happy and/or satisfied | Class appears extremely unhappy and/or dissatisfied |
|---|---|---|---|---|
| 5 | 4 | 3 | 2 | 1 |

For example, if you felt the class was satisfied most of the time, but not always, you would rate this question "4."

a Source: Soar 1975

reliability is likely to require several days of practice in the classrooms and frequent checking of interrater agreement.

## 2.3 Interactive Coding Systems

An interactive coding system allows an observer to record everything a teacher or a student says or does during a given time span. The time is usually several five-minute intervals spaced evenly throughout a class period.

An interaction system developed by Ned Flanders has been widely used in research. The categories are nonjudgmental and the system is particularly useful in evaluating teacher-led group discussions. The level of the group's involvement, as well as the teacher's questioning and feedback strategies, can be assessed. Statements made by the teacher and students are entered on a matrix. The Flanders categories and codes are well-defined and reasonably easy to memorize and use (see Tab. 2). Seven codes show whether the student is responding to the teacher's question, or initiating a new idea. For example, a T-4 followed by an S-8 and then a T-2 indicates that the teacher asked a question, a student responded, and the teacher praised the student. This kind of information can help teachers see how often they accept, praise, or categorize students. The system can be particularly useful to teachers if they analyze audio- or video-tapes made while they are instructing a class.

An elaboration of the Flanders system has been widely used to identify effective classroom teaching processes and to guide teacher training. Profiles prepared of each teacher's classroom behavior are based upon approximately 900 interactions taken over a three-day period. Recommendations are made to increase or decrease specific behaviors to a criterion level. A second

**Table 2**
Flanders categories for interaction analysis[a]

Teacher talk:
  Response
    (a) Accepts feelings
    (b) Praises or encourages
    (c) Accepts or uses ideas of student
    (d) Asks questions
  Initiation
    (e) Lectures
    (f) Gives directions
    (g) Criticizes or justifies authority
Student talk:
  Response
    (h) Responds
  Initiation
    (i) Initiates conversion
  Other
    (j) Silence or confusion

a Source: Flanders 1970

set of observations at the end of a semester will show the teachers how much they have changed behaviors.

Interaction systems have the advantage of being very objective. The variables are understandable and acceptable to teachers and administrators. Each code is defined so that it is unique. A frequency count is provided for each type of question asked, response given, praise offered, correction given, and instruction provided. Counts are made of organizing statements and behavioral control statements. Specific positive and negative affect statements or actions are also recorded. The frequency counts can then be transformed to percentages of total interactions.

The disadvantage of an interaction coding system is that some of the quality of the interaction is lost. For example, a very good thought-provoking question will be coded as "2" which equals an "open-ended/thought-provoking" question. The data will not show that the level of questioning was truly excellent. Another disadvantage is that the content of the lesson is lost. The data will only show that the appropriate academic subject is being pursued, for example, reading aloud is occurring, but the data will not reveal what is being read. A final disadvantage is that comprehensive interaction systems, such as Stallings', require a five- to seven-day training session to collect data reliably. The data require complicated programming to process. Once the program is developed, however, an advantage is that the optical scan processing is available and is quite efficient in saving time and money.

### 2.4. Narrative Description

This technique involves writing in narrative form everything observed that is relevant to the focus and purpose of the observation. Although some technical terms may be useful and desirable, for the most part, the terms used to describe the observed phenomena are the observer's natural words.

Narrative descriptions can be used for clinical supervision, for individual child observation, or for case studies of individuals or schools. In most cases, the observer is guided to look for specific events. For example, in a beginning-of-the-year classroom management study conducted by Evertson and Emmer (1980), observers were instructed to record teacher statements about rules for behavior penalties, and expectations for quality and quantity of work. They were also asked to record teachers' consistency of carrying out rules and procedures. The narrative descriptions had a clear focus which was guided by the hypotheses and interests of the investigators.

Narratives may also take the form of anecdotal records that describe an episode in specific detail. For example, the episode might be a heated discussion between teachers in a staff meeting or between children in the playground.

Specimen records are another form of narrative description. In this case, all of the behavior of a single individual is recorded over a specified period of time.

The purpose is to record everything the person says or does during that period of time. It is not interpreted or summarized by the observer. Such records kept on a daily or weekly basis help develop case study material. Over time, patterns of behavior are likely to emerge.

Narrative descriptions have several advantages. The context of the observation can be described in a rich and holistic manner. The natural sequence of events is preserved. Unpredicted events can be reported. Qualitative statements can be made, for example, "The teacher is very warm and loving to the children as she strokes them and sings softly during rest time." None of the quantitative observation instruments could adequately record that kind of incident.

Another advantage is the short training period. Observers do not have to learn complicated coding systems or the definitions for points on rating scales. Their records are usually kept in notebooks or on forms with wide margins and with space left for coding at a later date.

Evertson et al. (1980) have described the process of building a good research team for classroom observation. Observers must practice writing what they see, keeping the purpose of the observations clearly in mind. There may be some difficulty in getting two observers to describe the same event in the same way. The activities in classrooms often happen simultaneously and the phenomena selected to record may be different for different observers. Developing consistency in gathering the original narrative data may require considerable paired practice in classrooms.

A major disadvantage lies in the processing of narrative data. Many pages of handwritten text must be read, categories selected, and narratives coded for key words and concepts before the data can be summarized. This can be a time-consuming and costly process if the sample is very large. Narrative descriptions that are well-focused such as those collected by Evertson and Emmer are less difficult to code because many categories are preselected. This still allows for other categories to emerge from the data.

### 3. Selecting an Observation Instrument

The purpose of the observation must guide the selection of the instrument. What are the questions? If a teacher is to be evaluated for carrying out a specific lesson plan, then a clinical narrative description approach is most likely required. If a researcher is trying to learn about a large array of effective teaching strategies in a large sample, a comprehensive coding system may be required. If the teachers wish to learn more about which students are off-task during specific activities, a checklist may be most appropriate.

Any observation system used must be checked for validity to see whether it is indeed collecting the data it expects to collect, for example, the variable "students show initiative and are self-motivated." How do students look? What do they do or say that indicates self-motivation? Does the operational definition of this variable have good face validity?

Another important point to consider is whether observers can be trained to gather the data accurately. Here, it is helpful to have a criterion for correctness as well as reports of interrater agreement.

The stability of the behavior must also be considered. Teachers may be consistent in their manner of asking questions and providing feedback from one day to another in the same subject. However, they may alter this approach in a different subject. Or, the teacher may use a very dictatorial approach to classroom management in September and a more democratic one in November. The observation system should be sensitive enough to reflect these differences.

*Bibliography*

Borich G D, Madden S K 1977 *Evaluating Classroom Instruction: A Sourcebook of Instruments.* Addison-Wesley, Reading, Massachusetts

Boyer E G, Simon A, Karafin G R (eds.) 1973 *Measures of Maturation: An Anthology of Early Childhood Observation Instruments.* Research for Better Schools, Philadelphia, Pennsylvania

Brandt R M 1972 *Studying Behavior in Natural Settings.* Holt, Rinehart and Winston, New York

Evertson C, Emmer E 1980 *Effective Management at the Beginning of the School Year in Junior High Classes.* Research and Development Center for Teacher Education, University of Texas, Austin, Texas

Evertson C, Emmer E, Clements B 1980 *Report of the Methodology, Rationale, and Instrumentation of the Junior High Classrooms Organization Study.* Research and Development Center for Teacher Education, University of Texas, Austin, Texas

Flanders N A 1970 *Analyzing Teacher Behavior.* Addison-Wesley, Reading, Massachusetts

Kowalski J P S 1978 *Evaluating Teacher Performance.* Educational Research Service, Arlington, Virginia

Simon A, Boyer E G 1967 *Mirrors for Behavior: An Anthology of Classroom Observation Instruments.* Research for Better Schools, Philadelphia, Pennsylvania

Soar R S 1975 Follow through classroom process measurement and pupil growth (1970–71). Final Report. Educational Research Service, Arlington, Virginia. ERIC Document No. ED 106 297

Stallings J A 1977 *Learning to Look: A Handbook on Classroom Observation and Teaching Methods.* Wadsworth, Belmont, California

Stallings J A, Needels M 1978 *Secondary Observation Instrument.* SRI International, Menlo Park, California

# Case Study Methods

## L. Stenhouse

Case study methods involve the collection and recording of data about a case or cases, and the preparation of a report or a presentation of the case. The collection of data on site is termed "fieldwork", and it involves: (a) generally, participant or nonparticipant observation and interviewing; (b) probably, the collection of documentary evidence and descriptive statistics, and the administration of tests or questionnaires; and (c) possibly, the use of photography, motion pictures, or videotape recording.

Sometimes, particularly in evaluation research, which is commissioned to evaluate a specific case, the case itself is regarded as of sufficient interest to merit investigation. However, case study does not preclude an interest in generalization, and many researchers seek theories that will penetrate the varying conditions of action, or applications founded on the comparison of case with case. Generalization and application are matters for judgment rather than for calculation, and the task of case study is to produce ordered reports of experience which invite judgment and offer evidence to which judgment can appeal. In this, case study resembles history, and, like history, its appeal to judgment often demands the representation or quotation of persons. This element of naturalistic presentation or portrayal raises in case study ethical problems regarding the use of data identifiably associated with living persons.

This article does not cover the case study of individual subjects in psychology, narrative historical studies of individual schools, or documentary films of cases.

## 1. Case Study and the Psychostatistical Paradigm

The psychostatistical paradigm of educational research is expressed in field experiments and surveys based on sampling. It is founded on the insight that to draw a sample from a population randomly rather than by judgment permits the use of the mathematics of probability to estimate the reliability and validity of results obtained in the sample. This entails the expression of observations as quantitative indices. The paradigm is elegant, but in practice many educational problems involve such a complex interaction of variables that they elude quantitative techniques which reduce disparate observed phenomena to the homogeneity of traits or types. This suggests the need for analyses based on close observation.

Case study may be seen as a response to this need for a return to close natural observation, or as a reaction against the positivist epistemology implied in the psychostatistical paradigm. Case study methods are often described as naturalistic, qualitative, descriptive, responsive, interpretative, hermeneutic, or idiographic by way of contrast to the abstracted, quantitative, nomothetic approach of psychostatistical methods that strip observation to indices. However, quantitative indices are often used in case study, though generally descriptively and in a subordinate role, and there is some scope for the use of single-case experimental designs.

## 2. Styles of Case Study

Although case study methods are in flux, for the purpose of exposition it is worth describing four broad styles of work. The first of these, ethnography, is located within the social sciences. The others, evaluation, educational case study, and action research, are closely related to educational action and are differently modulated derivations from the curriculum movement.

### 2.1 Ethnographic Case Study

In ethnography, a single case is studied in depth by participant observation supported by interview, after the manner of cultural or social anthropology, which concentrates on the understanding of human societies and cultures, particularly through the observation and interpretation of inter-personal relations in the context of an emphasis on custom and institutions. Some would restrict the term ethnography to those studies conceived within the theoretical framework of cultural anthropology. However, the term is also generally applied to case studies conducted in the neoethnographic tradition of the Chicago school of sociologists and their successors, and set within sociological, rather than anthropological, theory. Of ethnographic case study it may be said that it calls into question the apparent understandings of the actors in the case and offers from the outsider's standpoint explanations that emphasize causal or structural patterns of which participants in the case are unaware. It does not generally relate directly to the practical needs of the actors in the case, though it may affect their perception and hence the tacit grounding of their actions. Examples of the use of such methods have been reported by Hargreaves (1967), Wolcott (1967), and Peshkin (1978).

### 2.2 Evaluative Case Study

In evaluative case studies a single case or a collection of cases is studied in depth with the purpose of providing educational actors or decision makers (administrators, teachers, parents, pupils, etc.) with information that will help them to judge the merit and worth of policies, programmes, or institutions. Case study styles of evaluation developed in the curriculum movement and examples of such research have been reported by Stake and Gjerde (1974) and MacDonald (1981).

Evaluative case studies are caught in the time scale of the programmes they are evaluating and the decisions they are informing and this has led to the development of "condensed fieldwork", in which interview typically dominates participant observation, since the latter is essentially a long-term, in-depth technique. In evaluation, the case to be evaluated is commonly a pro-

gramme or policy expressed in a number of institutions or settings and the evaluator is thus concerned with multiple case studies in a number of sites: hence multisite case study (Stake and Easley 1978).

### 2.3 Educational Case Study

Many researchers using case study methods are concerned neither with social theory nor with evaluative judgment, but rather with the understanding of educational action. They may adopt a strategy close to that of the ethnographer (Smith and Keith 1971) or close to that of the evaluator (Hamilton 1977). They are concerned to enrich the thinking and discourse of educators either by the development of educational theory or by the refinement of prudence through the systematic and reflective documentation of experience.

It seems likely that multisite approaches will have an increasing part to play in educational case study (Stenhouse 1982).

### 2.4 Case Study in Action Research

Action research is concerned with contributing to the development of the case or cases under study by feedback of information which can guide revision and refinement of the action. In the curriculum movement, action research was extensively used in research and development projects to produce curricular specifications and materials. When teaching strategies were important in the development, teachers were heavily involved in developing their own teaching through self case study.

## 3. Teacher as Researcher

A significant development in the field of educational case study is the teacher-as-researcher movement. In evaluative case study, this has led to school self-evaluation within the framework of the accountability movement. In educational case study, practising teachers have produced studies of their own classrooms or schools, mainly in unpublished research degree dissertations. Such case studies present particular problems and advantages because of the status of the observer as a responsible participant. The teacher action research movement has gathered pace in England and Wales and Australia in particular, and is also beginning to evoke considerable interest in Scandinavia.

## 4. The Conduct of Case Studies

The conduct of case studies falls naturally into four phases: selecting cases and negotiating access, fieldwork, the organization of records, and the writing of a report.

### 4.1 Selecting Cases and Negotiating Access

Most single case studies are opportunistic: a matter of seeing interest in a case to which one has access.

However, each case studied adds to the collection of cases, and ideally the choice of case should be made bearing in mind its relation to the corpus of cases available. In multisite case study, the collection of cases should cover the range of variables judged to be the most important in relation to the theme of the study.

A high proportion of case-study workers cite the advice offered by Glaser and Strauss (1967 p. 55):

> By maximizing or minimizing differences among comparative groups, the sociologist can control the theoretical relevance of his data collection. Comparing as many differences and similarities in data as possible tends to force the analyst to generate categories, their properties, and their inter-relations as he tries to understand his data.

Random sampling is only applicable where case studies conducted within a sample run alongside quantitative methods deployed within the psychostatistical paradigm. Normally the external validity of case study hinges on judgmental comparison or the generation of theory rather than on calculations that premise randomness.

Once a case is selected, it is necessary to negotiate access. In educational research this process is complicated by the hierarchical structure of accountability. The researcher may need to negotiate with the administrative authority before approaching an institution, with the head of the institution before approaching staff, with staff before approaching pupils. At each stage there is danger that the fieldworker might be seen as sponsored by the higher authority with consequent risks of distortion of data. It is crucial that access to data is not conceded to authorities in return for access to the case, thus exposing the subjects of study and influencing their responses.

### 4.2 Fieldwork

Fieldwork is that process of evoking, gathering, and organizing information which takes place on, or in close proximity to, the site of the events or phenomena being studied. This definition is intended to cover not simply the work done on site, but also that done during evenings and weekends that are intervals within a period of on-site study. Fieldwork includes: collecting and evoking documents; observing; and measuring or collecting statistics.

(a) *Collecting and evoking documents.* "It is," wrote the Webbs (1897), "a peculiarity of human, and especially of social, action that it secretes records of facts, not with any view to affording material for the investigator, but as data for the future guidance of the organisms themselves." Such documents as log books, minutes and school timetables, letters, and memos are, for many research purposes, invaluable. Also valuable, though more subject to distorting influences, are statements for audiences, such as brochures addressed to parents or school magazines.

In addition to such records, written testimony may be available in the form of diaries, autobiographies, memoirs, and letters, though these are relatively uncommon in educational case studies. However, such documents may be evoked by the researcher: in particular, participants may be asked to keep diaries or engage in correspondence.

It is also possible that there will be visual records such as architects' plans or photographs of school classes or perhaps even films or videotapes about an institution such as a school or college.

Documents are readily collected as a rule, do not raise problems of record keeping for the researcher, are not usually so prolific in an educational setting as to overburden the researcher, and are subject to well-established canons of critical appraisal which have been worked out by historians.

(b) *Observing.* By observing is meant perceiving appearances, events, or behaviour (including speech). The observer may be fully participant, that is, filling an available role in the social setting under observation; aspirant participant, that is, seeking to achieve acceptance in an unusual participant role such as researcher; nonparticipant, that is, seeking to minimize participant interaction with those observed; or covert, that is, hidden from those observed by such a device as a one-way screen. Fully participant observation can itself be covert if the research interest of the observer is screened from those observed, though this limits the observer's capacity to engage in direct inquiry.

Close and thoughtful observation of others is always an important and intensive feature of participant observation, and this includes, as an important element, observation of speech in natural settings.

Observation clearly calls for some kind of recording, and the field notebook is the classic form. But it is not easy to keep a good record. Taking notes during observation is generally intrusive, and field notes are usually written up from memory as soon as possible after the event. Clear indications are desirable to distinguish paraphrase from quotation. Sometimes photography can be used either as a record or as a stimulus for writing. A trained memory is at a premium.

As fieldwork becomes more condensed, the participant observer role is attenuated, and observation becomes located within a study where the main weight is carried by interviewing. Observation often provides cues for the agenda of interview or follows from remarks made by an interviewer. The crucial issue in such fieldwork is whether to trust observation over interview or interview over observation. In some cases one is clearly more reliable than the other: in other cases the matter is contentious. It is clear, however, that, as fieldwork becomes condensed, influence based on observation becomes more precarious because of the observer's limited acquaintance with the site.

(c) *Interviewing.* Observation of speech behaviour shades across into interview, as the spoken transaction becomes initiated and managed by the researcher, who becomes the audience for what is spoken. Many participant observers try to keep interviewing as informal and as close to observation as possible, making their interviews many and short and conducting them in informal settings—walking along a corridor or driving in a car, for example. One problem of such interviews is their recording. Most often they are recorded from memory in a notebook at the earliest opportunity.

As fieldwork becomes more interview based and less observation based, interviews tend to become more formal. For example, they are often arranged by appointment. Generally, however, interviews are not structured by a schedule, though the interviewer will commonly have an agenda in mind. Early questions are usually broadly framed, later questions tend to be more focused. The style of an interviewer is largely a matter of personality. The aim is to establish a relaxed conversation—whether it be relatively formal or relatively informal. Learning to listen well is important.

Seating arrangements are significant. To sit side-by-side or obliquely facing one another is, as it were, to look out on the world together, a good position for a collaborative interview. Face-to-face seating favours interrogation. However, the effects of seating interact with the styles of the persons involved.

How to record an interview is a matter of contention. Some feel that tape recording is more intrusive than note taking, others take the opposite view. Formally, it is clear that tape recording provides the most reliable record, though with the disadvantage that tape recordings are themselves not easy to use as sources for later work. If time and resources allow, tapes are generally transcribed. Where limited resources make this impossible, a good procedure is to play the tape through and make notes on pages ruled into three columns: one column contains the tape recorder counter number, the second contains a running index of content, and the third is devoted to verbatim quotations.

The process of interviewing and recording the interview creates a "document" in the sense that historians use that word. At the extreme of participant observation, interpretation in the field is at a premium: the extreme of interviewing produces a document for subsequent critical interpretation at leisure.

(d) *Measuring or collecting statistics.* Many are involved in case study as a reaction against the psychostatistical paradigm, and have regarded case study as qualitative. However, the contrast is not between quantitative and qualitative, but between samples and cases (Stenhouse 1982).

Thus the emphasis in statistical applications would be on the description of the case and its comparison with other cases rather than on statistical inference based on sampling. A reading of Ball (1981) will show how far case study has gone in the use of indices. There is plenty of room for development and work on social indicators, on unobtrusive measures, and on exploratory data analysis, where relevant.

## 4.3 Organization of Records

As a result of the processes described above, it is now possible to imagine the researcher having a substantial collection of documents, observer's notes, interview transcripts, statistics, and the like. Perhaps these materials extend to 1,000 pages or more. The task may be to write up the case or to write across a number of cases of which this is one. This raw material produced by case study may be termed the "case record" (Stenhouse 1982).

Experience shows that case studies are inclined to falter at this point. In particular, social scientists used to handling data reduced by quantitative techniques find the sheer bulk of the record daunting, though historians commonly deal with the problem in yet more acute form.

Two strategies are: progressive reduction of the record and indexing. Progressive reduction selects from the record a smaller record, perhaps photocopied, and then further reduces that by weeding. It is important to take notes during such reduction so that the relation of the reduced record is kept in mind. The alternative, indexing, also requires note taking and a gradual build-up of an interpretation, but the indexing of the record allows selection without actual pruning. Marginal colour codings can also be useful.

It is good practice to make two copies of the record if possible, one to stand as primary source, the other to use as a working copy.

## 4.4 Reporting and Writing a Report

There is not really enough experience of the problem of writing up this kind of material in educational research. For present purposes a good starting point is to consider the use of narrative, portrayal, vignette, and analysis.

Narrative reporting has two great strengths: directness and subtlety. Its directness comes partly from the familiarity of its conventions to readers, and partly because the narrative form constrains the author from presenting his or her own logic in the teeth of resistance from the story. Its subtlety lies in a capacity to convey ambiguity concerning cause and effect by selecting information that invites the reader to speculate about alternative interpretations.

Portrayal reporting is an attempt to preserve some of the qualities of narrative in descriptive writing that lacks a natural story line. As in documentary film, characters, incidents, and descriptions of an environment in which they are set are juxtaposed to provide a portrayal which is interpretative of the case as a whole.

Vignette reporting has the status of a sketch compared to a fully worked picture. The selection of the subject of a vignette is an interpretative act, for a vignette crystallizes some important aspect of a case. Commonly a vignette is used to concretize an analysis by relating an incident or offering a snapshot of a person or a place.

Analysis reporting debates its points explicitly, wherever possible reviewing evidence. Most often the conceptual framework is contributed by its author and draws on the social sciences. Though cruder than narrative, it is more explicit. Whereas the words of narrative are crowded with connotations and derivations, those of analysis tend to be starker and denotive in the light of their definitions. Analysis favours the search for precision in terminology and in theory.

Interesting problems in the reporting of case study research are set by multisite case study. Stake and Easley in *Case Studies in Science Education* (1978) offer in one volume portrayals of each case and in another an overview which attempts to look across the cases. It could be argued that the overview is too concerned to generalize as opposed to contrast, but there is a lack of examples of attempts to use contrast to highlight variables.

## 5. Case Study Theory and Explanation

Case study is pitched between science and history, and the role of theory and the nature of explanation is debatable. Polar positions can be illustrated by quotation. Popper speaks for the scientific pole:

A scientist, whether theorist or experimenter, puts forward statements, or systems of statements, and tests them step by step. In the field of the empirical sciences, more particularly, he constructs hypotheses, or systems of theories, and tests them against experience by observation and experiment. (1959 p. 27)

Gardiner speaks for the historical pole:

We do explain human actions in terms of reaction to environment. But we also explain human actions in terms of thoughts, desires, and plans. We may believe that it is in principle possible to give a full causal explanation of why people think, desire, or plan the things they do in terms of their past experience or training or perhaps in terms of the working of their bodies. But, even if the latter proposition is true, it still does not follow that explanation in terms of thoughts and desires has been rendered superfluous, or that it has been "reduced" to cause–effect explanation. (1961 p. 139)

Between these two poles lies theory in the social sciences.

Glaser and Strauss (1967) characterized case study methods as generative of theory grounded in the study of the case rather than as capable of testing theory, and their position has been very influential among researchers. However, their reserve must be related to the weakness of theory in the social sciences, since strong theory can readily be falsified or shown to be paradoxical on the basis of a single case.

Case study workers with a strong interest in theory have generally been attracted by phenomenology and symbolic interactionism which stress the status of experience and of meaning, as contrasted with the residual behaviourism of much social theory. Recently some case studies have been set within Marxist theory (Willis 1977).

Case study in educational research might reasonably be thought of as giving priority to educational practice as compared to social theory, and this issue has divided

researchers. Marxist standpoints are attractive as offering a dialectical resolution of this conflict in the concept of praxis, which in Marxist theory expresses the problem of the unity of theory and practice.

Habermas, who has a central concern with this problem, also builds on Vico:

Vico retains the Aristotelian distinction between science and prudence, episteme and phronesis: while science aims at "eternal truths", making statements about what is always and necessarily so, practical prudence is only concerned with the "probable". Vico shows how this latter procedure precisely because it makes less theoretical claims, brings greater certainty in practice. (Habermas 1971 p. 45)

If educational case study appeals to the experience of participation and consequently tends towards the vernacular because it recognizes "the task of entering into the consciousness and the conviction of citizens prepared to act" (Habermas 1971 p. 75), then both its theoretical basis and its contribution to theory are likely to continue to be the subject of lively debate.

## 6. Ethics and Educational Case Study

The problem of ethics particular to case study arises principally because of the portrayal of persons or institutions in forms that subject them to the possibility of recognition. There are social scientists who take the view that ethical considerations of this sort should not normally be allowed to block the pursuit of truth and there are also researchers who place ethical considerations in the context of accountability and the "right to know". Judging by the statements of the ethics committees of various associations of social and psychological scientists, those who take a hard line are in a minority.

However, there is a basic dispute as to whether data gathered about people are to be regarded as owned by them and hence to a high degree open to their control or whether they are owned by the researchers who have gathered the data and subject only to their ethical principles.

Various procedures are used by those who believe the data in principle belong to the subjects in order to negotiate contracts for the conduct of case study and clearance of data gathered. It has become evident that subjects cannot always see clearly the implications of their consent and many workers thus feel that, though contract may be necessary, it does not exempt the researcher from further ethical considerations.

It might be thought a reasonable principle that no data be used in such a way as to threaten disadvantage to the persons portrayed, but this is difficult to interpret both in terms of anticipation of risk and in terms of what counts as a recognizable disadvantage.

In educational case study where the purpose of the research is to improve educational practice and hence the lot of children and the professionalism of teachers, there is at least some room for a consideration of the responsibility of subjects to take some risks on professional grounds.

What is clear is that no researcher should embark on research by case study methods without a thoughtful review of ethical problems and a study of the relevant literature.

## Bibliography

Ball S J 1981 *Beachside Comprehensive: A Case-study of Secondary Schooling*. Cambridge University Press, Cambridge

Gardiner P 1961 *The Nature of Historical Explanation*. Oxford University Press, London

Glaser B G, Strauss A L 1967 *The Discovery of Grounded Theory: Strategies for Qualitative Research*. Aldine Press, Chicago, Illinois

Habermas J 1971 *Theorie und Praxis*. Suhrkamp, Frankfurt

Hamilton D 1977 *In Search of Structure: Essays from a New Scottish Open-plan Primary School*. Hodder and Stoughton, London

Hargreaves D H 1967 *Social Relations in a Secondary School*. Routledge and Kegan Paul, London

MacDonald B 1981 *The Experience of Innovation*. CARE, University of East Anglia, Norwich

Peshkin A 1978 *Growing Up American: Schooling and the Survival of Community*. University of Chicago Press, Chicago, Illinois

Popper K R 1959 *The Logic of Scientific Discovery*. Hutchinson, London

Smith L M, Keith P M 1971 *Anatomy of Educational Innovation: An Organizational Analysis of an Elementary School*. Wiley, New York

Stake R E, Easley J 1978 *Case Studies in Science Education*. CIRCE, University of Illinois, Urbana, Illinois

Stake R E, Gjerde C 1974 *An Evaluation of T. City*. American Educational Research Association (AERA) Monograph Series in Curriculum Evaluation No 7. Rand McNally, Chicago, Illinois

Stenhouse L 1982 *Papers on Case-study Research in Education*. CARE, University of East Anglia, Norwich

Webb S, Webb B 1897 *Industrial Democracy*. Longmans Green, London

Willis P E 1977 *Learning to Labour: How Working Class Kids get Working Class Jobs*. Saxon House, Farnborough

Wolcott H F 1967 *A Kwakiutl Village and School*. Holt, Rinehart and Winston, New York

# Analysis of Evidence in Humanistic Studies

**S. Sowden and J. P. Keeves**

Much of the evidence available about educational processes is collected in the form of published documents, transcripts of interviews, observations of practice, field notes, tape recordings of oral presentations, and written statements. Such data that are qualitative in nature are of considerable value. They are rich, personal, close to the real world, and contain a depth of meaning that more abstract forms of evidence lack. Nevertheless, substantial difficulties arise in educational research in the collection and use of data in this form. While bodies of evidence of this kind can provide an understanding of educational phenomena and enable individuals to develop their own personal interpretations of the educational situations in which they work, there are significant problems involved in the assimilation of the evidence into the corpus of knowledge about education and its processes. The collection of such data is labour intensive, lasting sometimes many years. Furthermore, the analysis of the data is time consuming and sometimes very difficult because the evidence has been collected without a recognizable structure. Commonly, sampling has not been employed, and if representative or random sampling were attempted it has been abandoned as rich data became available from other sources. As a consequence the important question of the generalizability of the findings cannot be considered. Furthermore, in general, the procedures by which the evidence has been analysed have not been reported or discussed.

Miles and Huberman (1984) have addressed these issues in an important publication entitled *Qualitative Data Analysis: A Sourcebook of New Methods*. They are specifically concerned with the generalizability of the findings derived from qualitative research and with the replicability of analyses of qualitative data. They have advanced canons for the examination of evidence collected in naturalistic research investigations that increase the consistency and robustness of the findings. Their proposals cut across the several areas of knowledge that contribute to humanistic research in education, namely the disciplines of sociology, history, law, political science, linguistics, psychology, and anthropology.

Miles and Huberman advance systematic procedures for the drawing of conclusions, testing the conclusions for consistency and coherence, and indeed simplifying the tasks of analysing large bodies of qualitative data. They argue that in the reporting of research it is essential for the researcher to accept the responsibility of being accountable, and to present clearly a statement on the analytical procedures employed. However, such a strategy demands that there should be consensus about the appropriateness and strength of the particular procedures which have been used. Their practical sourcebook is a highly significant contribution of educational research. This article draws extensively on their work and illustrates their strategy through the discussion of an application to a research study in education concerned with some factors influencing the conduct of evaluation studies.

The philosophical and epistemological foundations of Miles and Huberman's work have been subjected to criticism by Donmoyer (1985, 1986), to which Huberman and Miles (1986) have replied. It is not necessary to address these issues in this article. However, this article endorses the view that neither the scientific nor the humanistic research perspectives have a unique advantage and that there is an epistemological unity in educational research. Furthermore, we recognize that the hardline distinctions that are commonly made between quantitative and qualitative research methods are largely artificial. The difference between quantitative and qualitative data lies in the level of abstraction and the extent of simplification since, as Kaplan (1964 p. 207) has argued, "quantities are of qualities", and the claim that one method is antithetical or alternative to the other is misconceived. In addition, it is necessary to consider the view that all inquiry into educational questions is at least to some extent value-laden. Kaplan (1964 pp. 374–86) has examined the several ways in which values play a part in inquiry. There are implications for the replicability of the results of inquiry where another investigator with different values conducts a similar inquiry. Kaplan (1964 p. 387) has also suggested that the only way to avoid subjective relativism in inquiry is to "face the valuations and to introduce them as explicitly stated, specific and sufficiently concretized value premises". The problem is not whether values are involved in inquiry and whether it is possible to gain access to "reality" independently of values, but "how they are to be empirically grounded". This article presents procedures for building the findings of humanistic research studies on empirical evidence through the systematic analysis of qualitative data.

## 1. Strategies of Analysis

The approach to data analysis using these procedures is characterized by strategies that employ both deduction and induction. These procedures are deductive insofar as some orientating constructs—informed by the prior knowledge, the experience, and the values of the investigator—have been put forward and operationalized and matched to a body of field data. This has the advantage of focusing and reducing the data that could be collected. Induction is employed insofar as the gathered data are used to modify and rebuild the original constructs. While deduction and induction are distinct and separate concepts, the difference between the deductive process and the inductive process becomes blurred when it is recognized that the conception of the orientating constructs which were used in the process of deduction were themselves a product of induction (Miles and Huberman 1984 p. 134). The interaction between deductive and inductive processes in the strategy of research where investigation is grounded in empirical evidence and the real world, is a key characteristic of the procedures proposed by Miles and Huberman (1984).

There are four major stages in this strategy of research into educational problems, namely: (a) design of investigation, (b) collection of data, (c) analysis of data, and (d) summarizing and integrating the findings. This article is primarily concerned with the third of these stages, the analysis of data. However, insofar as analysis is dependent on design, collection, and integration, an account must be provided of these three other stages and of their influence and dependence on the analysis of data. Miles and Huberman (1984 pp. 21–23) have identified three key components of data analysis, namely: (a) data reduction, (b) matrix display and examination, and (c) conclusion drawing and verification. This article will explore in some depth these three components of data analysis. Following Miles and Huberman (1984 p. 23), an interactive model is presented of the way in which the four stages of a research strategy interact with the three key components of data analysis listed above. In Fig. 1 the four stages and the three key components of data analysis form an interactive and cyclical process. As the research worker progresses through the four stages it is necessary for consideration to be given continuously to the analysis of the data and to the reduction, display, and conclusion drawing and verification components. The whole process is iterative as well as being interactive in a way that only successive iterations permit.

It is important to recognize that this model does not differ greatly from a model that could be constructed to represent the strategy employed in quantitative research in education. The major difference is that quantitative research commonly starts with a stronger knowledge base, and tends to proceed sequentially in well-defined stages, rather than in the interactive or iterative way that is characteristic of qualitative research, which is more fluid and has a weaker knowledge base. This article seeks to elucidate the components of the model being advanced for the analysis of qualitative evidence, so that studies conducted within this context can be more effectively audited.

## 2. A Research Example

The research study employed in this article to illustrate the use of the procedures advanced by Miles and Huberman (1984) was associated with an investigation into the influence of research workers' views of evaluation (e.g., their views of the politics of evaluation and their philosophical orientations) and the influence of factors in the research situation on the types of evaluation studies that the evaluators undertook and the manner in which they conducted an evaluation. While much has been written about educational evaluation and many different models and approaches to evaluation have been advanced, at the time the study was planned, no previous research was known that examined the factors influencing the way particular evaluators conducted their evaluation studies.

Thus the investigation had little on which it could draw in opening up this area of inquiry. A qualitative exploratory study appeared to be the desirable design,

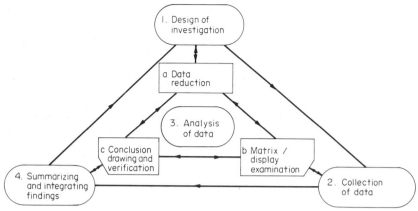

**Figure 1**
An interactive model of qualitative data analysis

although if the scope of investigation had been restricted a more quantitative approach might have been attempted, particularly if an already existing instrument to measure views of evaluation had been employed. Fifteen evaluators were selected as a representative sample of research workers and other persons engaged in evaluation studies. Each evaluator was asked to identify two evaluation studies that he or she had conducted, for which research reports were available and for which the clients would be willing to be interviewed regarding the conduct of the evaluation study. Thus the raw data comprised 30 reports of evaluation studies, the tape recordings of 30 interviews with the clients who had commissioned each of the 30 reports, and tape recordings with each of the 15 evaluators on two occasions. In addition, the research worker accumulated field notes associated with each evaluator and with each evaluation study. Moreover, since reports on both the views of each evaluator and the conduct of each evaluation were prepared and sent to each evaluator for confirmation, correspondence with each evaluator was assembled. This investigation can be seen to have involved case studies of 15 evaluators, each of whom had undertaken two evaluation studies. Thus the research investigation was one that involved a multisite case study strategy.

This strategy of investigation, the multisite case study approach, is being used increasingly in the field of educational research. Sometimes such an investigation is conducted together with a quantitative study, and the qualitative multisite case studies are carried out to complement the more quantitative work. However, sometimes in educational research only one case is investigated, and where this occurs it is common to examine the changes that occur over time and the two or more occasions provide replications of the initial case. Thus a research situation is developed that is akin to the multisite case study approach, with each occasion being considered equivalent to a separate site for the

case study. This present investigation through the use of two occasions for each evaluator included certain features of this alternative strategy.

## 3. The Design of Investigations

The conventional views of both quantitative and qualitative investigations in education are that the former, the quantitative investigation, involves a highly structured approach while the latter, the qualitative investigation, involves a minimal amount of prestructuring and a very loose design. On the one hand, quantitative research is seen to involve an identified theoretical perspective, the use of standardized instruments, the testing of prespecified aspects of a conceptual framework, and a high degree of abstraction from the real world. On the other hand, qualitative research is seen to be building theory from observations of the real world, to be loosely structured, and to be very open-ended with respect to the collection of data. It is not surprising that neither description is appropriate. Most quantitative research workers in education are more flexible than is suggested above. Likewise most investigators engaged in qualitative research now work somewhere between these two extremes. Qualitative research workers also recognize that a conceptual framework, at least in rudimentary form, has commonly been employed to guide an investigation, and that with little effort previous research could be found that would account conceptually for the phenomenon under investigation, even if it could not be classed as an established theory. It is this conceptual framework that serves to focus and restrict the collection of data as well as to guide the reduction and analysis of the evidence collected.

A conceptual framework serves to describe and explain the major facets of an investigation. It identifies the key factors and the assumed relationships between them. It is not essential that such relationships should be causal. They may simply involve sequences which occur over time, or alternatively there may merely be a pattern in the events or between the factors being observed. If such patterns or time sequences in relationships or causal connections are not assumed to be present, then it is unlikely that the factors being investigated will hold much interest for the research worker. The conceptual framework commonly attempts to state in graphical or narrative form these factors and the relationships between them. Use is made of this conceptual framework in the design of the study. First, it identifies who and what will be examined. Second, it postulates relationships between the persons and the factors being investigated. Such presumed relationships can influence the order in which information is assembled and the type of information collected, as well as the extent of detail obtained.

The conceptual framework also provides a map for the research worker of the field being investigated. Miles and Huberman (1984 p. 33) have made several suggestions with regard to developing a conceptual framework:

(a) use a graphical rather than a narrative format;

(b) expect to revise successively the framework;

(c) encourage each research worker in a team to develop a separate framework, and compare the different versions;

(d) avoid a global level of generality that is not specific enough to provide focus and identify bounds, and is not so general that it cannot be proved wrong; and

(e) use prior theorizing and previous empirical research to test the framework.

Once the framework has been developed it can be used for formulating specific research questions. The process of deduction is commonly involved. Many research workers engated in qualitative studies reject this step. However, the development of their ideas, while latent and implicit, commonly uses similar processes. Such investigators should be challenged to make as explicit as possible their thought processes. The research questions advanced for a study will require successive refinements. Priorities will need to be proposed, and the number of questions to which answers are being sought will need to be reduced to a manageable size. It is important to ensure that all field workers in a multisite study are familiar with the research questions being investigated, and that during an extended study both the chief investigator and the field workers keep the research questions under review.

Once the research questions have been identified, the collection of data must be influenced by identifying cases to be studied. Some form of sampling is generally involved. One of the great dangers in qualitative research is to sample too many cases. The number of cases is limited both by the amount of data that can be

processed and by the costs involved. It would seem from experience that 15–20 cases is the maximum amount of evidence that one person can work with for a detailed qualitative analysis. Where more cases have been involved in studies, it is not unusual for much of the available information to be cast aside and only evidence from up to 15–20 cases to be used, at least in the detailed reporting of the study. Furthermore, with more than 15–20 cases quantitative methods can be readily employed, through the use of contingency table analysis and the Fisher Exact Test. Other quantitative statistical procedures can be used with numbers of cases in excess of 30.

Even with up to 15 cases some basis for sampling of cases must be employed, whether the cases are typical, exemplar, random, extreme, innovative, or simply the most accessible. The extent to which the findings can be generalized beyond the single case depends on the basis upon which the cases were selected and the relationship between the selected cases and a wider population. It is important to recognize that sampling can occur of settings, events, and processes as well as of people. In the long term the major constraints on the number of cases to be studied are those of time and cost. Balance must be achieved between the research questions, time, cost, the complexity of the investigation, the number of research workers available to assist, and the number of cases selected.

The extent to which instrumentation is employed likewise depends on the research questions being asked, the number of research workers engaged in the data collection phase, and the level of clarity of the conceptual framework. Arguments can be advanced for both little or no prior instrumentation and for detailed instrumentation. However, failure to develop a conceptual framework or to identify appropriate research questions or to construct suitable instruments should not be justified on the grounds of lack of time or lack of effort. Advanced planning usually pays.

## 4. The Conceptual Framework: An Example

A conceptual framework for the investigation is shown in Fig. 2. The key actors in this situation under investigation are the evaluator and the client. Of primary importance to the investigation are the evaluator's views of evaluation. These include the evaluator's research perspectives, views about the politics of evaluation, and views of the role of evaluation in relation to policy. In addition, there are research situation factors, which subdivide into external factors and internal factors. The external factors in the research situation involve the nature of the programme being evaluated, the political climate, and the concerns of the different stakeholders in the evaluation. The internal factors in the research situation include those factors directly related to the evaluator, such as the institutional position of the evaluator and of the team members with whom the evaluator works. These two sets of factors—namely the evalua-

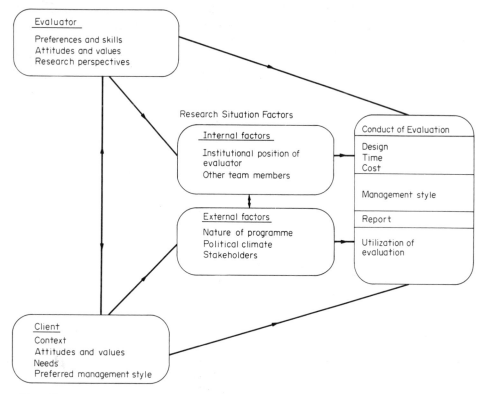

**Figure 2**
Conceptual framework for investigation

tor's views of evaluation and the research situation factors—influence not only each other but, more importantly, the conduct of the evaluation. Likewise, the views of the client interact with those of the evaluator to influence the conduct of the evaluation.

The conduct of evaluation includes the design of the study, how the study is managed, (e.g., who controls the direction of the evaluation and the strategies used by the evaluator to share this control), as well as the nature of the report. A further important element in the conduct of the evaluation is the likely utilization of the evaluation. The nature and extent of utilization of the findings of the evaluation arise from a complex interaction between the characteristics of the evaluator, the internal and external research situation factors, and the characteristics of the client.

In this study the key research question was concerned with the influence of the evaluator's views of evaluation and the research situation factors on the conduct of the evaluation. However, there were a substantial number of subsidiary questions, the answers to which were considered to assist with an understanding of the key question. The employment of arrows in Fig. 2 indicates not only time sequences in events which take place during the course of an evaluation, but also causal influences between the different factors in the con-

ceptual framework. There were, in addition, certain patterns or relationships which were likely to be revealed by the study, such as those between the research perspective preferences of the client and the evaluator. It was agreed that an evaluator with particular characteristics was likely to attract work from a particular client, and a client was likely to choose an evaluator where their research perspectives were consistent with each other. These different possible relationships gave rise to a series of research questions that were assigned a lower level of priority in the investigation.

The number of evaluators to be investigated was set at 15. A representative sample of evaluators was chosen from persons in different geographical locations who were known to have different contexts, namely academic research situations, independent research organizations, governmental authorities, and commercial organizations. The selection of evaluators also sought to ensure that scientific, humanistic, and critical social science perspectives, as well as both male and female perspectives were represented. In addition, the evaluators were encouraged to select evaluation studies that were typical of their work, but which at the same time covered a range of different types of evaluations that they had conducted.

## 5. Data Collection

Miles and Huberman (1984) have argued that the preliminary analysis of data should proceed concurrently with the collection of data so that the phase of data collection merges with that of data analysis. There are two important reasons for this. First, there is the very real danger, in a study in which qualitative data are collected, of assembling such a huge amount of evidence that the analysis becomes an overwhelming task which not only jeopardizes the completion of the work associated with the analysis phase of the investigation, and in some cases has been known to lead to the termination of a study, but more commonly reduces the quality of the work carried out. A second advantage of undertaking the analysis concurrently with the collection of data is both that gaps in the data become apparent, and new hypotheses and relationships emerge before it is too late to collect relevant data. In addition, an understanding of the evidence, which commonly takes time to grow, benefits from the longer period available. Sometimes ongoing analysis permits the preparation of an interim report that is reassuring for the client and facilitates the flow of funding for the study.

It is of value to prepare an overall tabular plan for the collection of data to show which items of data are going to be obtained through each particular stage in the inquiry. To some extent such a table serves also as a checklist to ensure that each item of information required for the investigation will be collected in the most appropriate way.

It is also important to maintain detailed documentary records of the data collected and Miles and Huberman (1984 pp. 50–51) suggest the use of the following forms:

(a) *A contact summary form.* This should be used to record the information associated with each contact made in the collection of data, such as an interview with an evaluator or client. In addition, this form would also record memoranda and information of importance to the study which should be noted as they arise.

(b) *A document summary form.* This should be employed to maintain a concise record of all documents which are obtained such as newspaper articles, correspondence, agendas and minutes of meetings that provide background information of relevance to the investigation. The documents are often bulky and must be filed separately. However, a file summary which indicates clearly the relevance of the document to the investigation as well as the location of the document is of considerable assistance as the volume of such material grows during the course of the study.

(c) *Field notes.* These should be compiled daily, if possible, on a standard form and inserted in a looseleaf folder to record information of relevance to the investigation. Such notes are additional to an in interview schedule, observation schedule, or tape recording of an interview and serve to record key items of information that are obtained or observed independently of the interview or observation period. Commonly these field notes can contain reflective remarks that arise from watching a situation or talking to people linked to the evaluator or the client. A distinction must be made between the raw field notes, which are rough scribblings and jottings, and the permanent notes that could be read by any reviewer of the work. The permanent notes are more than a sum of the raw notes. They contain reflections and commentary on issues that emerge from a consideration of the raw notes.

(d) *Memos.* These are an important additional source of ideas. Field work and coding are absorbing tasks. However, the very intensity of these stages of an investigation frequently gives rise to new and original ideas, which if not recorded in some way as they occur are lost. The most effective procedure is to have available a standard memorandum form on which these ideas can be recorded as they arise. Probably some sifting of such memoranda is required at a later stage, if a large number are produced. Of particular importance among the memos that are written are ones relating to propositions or relationships to be examined in the course of the investigation.

(e) *Data accounting sheets.* These are an essential documentary record of progress on a particular question. If possible the data collected should be related as closely as possible to the major research questions, or if this is not possible, to the areas of the investigation linked to the research questions. On the data accounting sheet a record should be maintained of whether or not a particular source of data relevant to a research question or an area of inquiry has been collected.

## 6. Analysis of Data

The analysis of the data collected in a study passes through three interrelated stages, namely, data reduction, data display, and conclusion drawing and verification. As already mentioned in an earlier section of this article, in qualitative research these stages are not sequential, but form part of an iterative process. Nevertheless, unless the stages are seen as separate there is the danger that they can merge to such an extent that the tasks associated with each are not examined or adequately planned. Each of these three stages will be considered in turn.

### 6.1 Data Reduction

The primary task in data reduction is that of coding the interview record, the observation record or the document. To code evidence obtained by these data collection procedures two approaches are available: the use of key words, or a numerical classification system, which may or may not involve a taxonomy. The development of a taxonomy requires considerable effort in advance of the coding, as well as a detailed understanding of the field. The use of key words has greater flexibility on the surface, but is likely to become complex and confusing unless careful initial planning has occurred. A pilot run through a reduced sample of the evidence, or preferably a pilot study with perhaps three to six cases, should be carried out in order to develop the key words or the taxonomy. The major danger in the development of a numerical coding system or a key word system is that the system will lack the structure necessary to use it systematically in the detailed examination of data. A further relevant aspect is the identification of important quotes that could be used in the reporting of the study. It is common in presenting the findings of an investigation based on the use of qualitative data to rely on telling quotes to make an important point and to convince the reader of the report. The process of data reduction should include a starring of codes or key words so that appropriate quotes related to a particular idea or relationship can be readily identified.

One of the most difficult items of evidence to summarize, that arises in the processing of qualitative data, is the taped interview. The use of a tape recording of an interview permits the interviewer to conduct the interview in a relatively relaxed way, without concern that key points will be lost. There is, however, always the danger that the interviewee will withhold comment because a permanent record is being made. In addition to this, the reduction of the data held on a tape recording poses substantial problems. At one time when taped interview records were less commonly used, it was possible to recommend that each interview record should be typed and hard copy obtained. Today this involves a prohibitive cost for most investigations and procedures have to be employed that will minimize cost and yet achieve effective coding of the available evidence. The procedures adopted in the research study being used to illustrate this approach to the analysis of qualitative data are described below.

In this study, taped interviews with evaluators and clients were coded using the following method.

(a) While listening to a tape, a summary of each point made by the interviewee was recorded. These summaries involved paraphrasing responses and were sometimes accompanied by transcriptions of relevant quotations.

(b) A set of key words was developed from the first six interviews that could be used to summarize and reduce further the evidence held. The structure for the key word system was built around the structure of the interview, which had been planned in advance.

(c) In order to access the information held both on tape and in the point-to-point summaries, a key word was placed in the left-hand margin of the pages of the summary to provide a reference to the content of each point made in the interview.

(d) In order to access quickly the source material on a tape, the tape counter numbers giving that section of the tape within which each point was made were recorded in a second column adjacent to each key word.

(e) Once an interview was coded in the above way, a summary of the themes occurring in the interview was made. The summary was built around the planned structure of the interview. Separate summaries were prepared for each of the two interviews with the valuators and for each of the interviews with the clients.

(f) The four interview summaries associated with each evaluator were examined for inconsistencies, and systematic checks with the tape recording were made to confirm or resolve the inconsistencies.

(g) A summary of the views and perspectives of each evaluator was prepared and returned to the valuator with a request to confirm the record that had been obtained and where necessary to resolve observed inconsistencies. In this way each evaluator was provided with an opportunity to verify information that was being carried foward to the next stage in the process of analysis. This sequence of steps, while time consuming and laborious, ensured that the research worker had assimilated thoroughly the views of each evaluator, and in the processes of condensation and assimilation had not, in an unwarranted way, distorted the evidence provided by an evaluator or a client.

It is important to note that the research worker was not limited to using the information contained in the summary that had been verified by the evaluator. However, the confirmation given by the evaluator, or in rare cases the correction provided, was further evidence that in summarizing the tape recordings significant distortion of the data had not occurred.

In addition, to provide a further check on the reliability of the coding procedures employed, a second person coded a sample of 12 taped interviews with evaluators and clients using the methods outlined above. Ten-minute sections of the taped interviews for each of the two interviews with four evaluators, and for one interview with a client of each of the four evaluators, were used. This involved the recoding of 120 minutes of taped interviews. The reliability of the coding procedures was estimated using the following formula.

$$\text{Reliability} = \frac{\text{Number of agreements}}{\text{Total number of agreements and disagreements}}$$

A level of intercoder reliability of 80 percent was sought. The criteria for agreement were that each of the following three conditions had to be met: (a) the same section of a taped interview was considered to represent a point; (b) for each point summarized, the same key word, selected from the final listing of key words was used by both coders; and (c) the two summaries of each point had the same meaning.

### 6.2 Matrix Display and Examination

The use of a matrix display is a valuable procedure for summarizing information so that patterns are evident in a form that can subsequently be used in the presentation of results. Success in the use of a matrix display lies not in whether a "true" or "correct" matrix has been developed, but in whether the use of a matrix display has served the function of providing answers to a research question being asked. Miles and Huberman (1984 pp. 211–12) have listed the key features of a matrix display as well as a set of rules for matrix construction.

The key features of a matrix display are concerned with choices made during the design of a matrix that are associated with ways of partitioning the data.

(a) The first feature relates to whether the matrix has a descriptive or explanatory purpose, and whether an attempt is being made to lay out the data in a manner that might reveal a pattern in the data, or in a way that shows why things happen.

(b) The matrix can be constructed to show relationships within a single case or across cases involved in a study.

(c) The matrix consists of rows and columns and can be constructed in such a way that the categories employed in the rows and columns are ordered or nonordered. Once the development of a matrix has proceeded beyond the initial stages of describing the evidence, it would seem likely that some ordering of categories would be required.

(d) A special case of ordering the information contained in the rows and columns is associated with time ordering. Time sequences are involved in temporal flow, causal chains, or cycles of events.

(e) Sometimes a matrix is constructed with the categories of a particular variable along one axis, or with social units along an axis as is common in educational investigations, where the units commonly used are: students, classrooms, schools, school districts, state systems, and a national system.

(f) The most commonly used matrix is the two-way grid. However, it is sometimes necessary to construct a three-way or four-way matrix, although they are hard to use and present. A three-way matrix can be shown diagrammatically by subdividing each column in a parallel fashion, and a four-way matrix can also be shown diagrammatically by subdividing each row in a similar manner. The pattern involved in the data is usually lost, by using more than a four-way matrix. Greater clarity can be gained by breaking the data down into submatrices.

(g) Furthermore, a choice is available with respect to what is recorded in each cell. Commonly an identifying code is recorded that refers to each case, but sometimes direct quotes or extracts from field notes can be recorded.

(h) Finally, if the set of key words has been carefully developed or if the taxonomy associated with numerical coding is appropriate, then these coding systems are naturally associated with the categories that are employed in matrix displays.

Miles and Huberman (1984, p. 212) advanced nine rules of thumb for the building of matrix displays:

(a) keep each display on one large sheet;

(b) restrict the number of categories used in each row or column to the range 5 to 15;

(c) plan to use a preliminary form of a matrix display and to revise it several times before constructing a final form;

(d) encourage members of the research team to develop alternative ways of displaying data in a matrix;

(e) transpose rows and columns where appropriate;

(f) collapse the categories of a complex matrix, since a reduced form will sometimes reveal clearer patterns;

(g) be prepared to add new rows and new columns at all times;

(h) maintain fine-grained rows and columns so that important differences in the data can be shown; and

(i) remember that a particular research question may require a series of matrix displays and be ready to try additional forms.

The development of appropriate matrix displays is an art in research that is acquired with practice and with increased depth of understanding of the issues involved. Miles and Huberman (1984 pp. 212–13) also suggest certain rules of thumb for recording entries in a matrix display so that detail is not lost and yet patterns that exist in the data emerge. In addition, they propose rules for examining a matrix display. It is important to recognize that the tasks of summarizing and of entry of data into a matrix display serve to make the investigator thoroughly familiar with the data, so that some interrelationships between factors operating in the data are held in mind and new relationships emerge. The development of a matrix display thus serves several purposes of familiarization, testing of relationships, providing a basis for speculation on new relationships, and a form of presentation of findings to the reader of a report. Ultimately the purpose of matrix display is the identification of a pattern and the provision of an explanation.

### 6.3 A Research Example of Matrix Display

In the study of evaluators described above there were four sources of data, which included two interviews with each evaluator, one interview with each client, and the evaluation reports. In this research the analysis was divided into three parts. The first part was concerned with the evaluator's views of evaluation; the second was concerned with the conduct of evaluation and the factors influencing conduct, and considered both research situation factors and the views held by an evaluator; while the third part involved cross-case comparisons. In relation to the second and third parts of the analysis the data from each of the above four sources had to be initially analysed together for each evaluator so that relevant information could be combined from the different sources. As a consequence one set of matrix displays involved each evaluator as a separate case, and another set of matrix displays involved cross-case comparisons. It was not desirable to develop a display that kept each source of information in a separate cell, although it was possible that the views of clients would differ in systematic ways from the views of evaluators, or that reports would consistently reveal different perspectives from those advanced by evaluators at interviews. Thus a letter code could be used to indicate the source of an item of information, and a number to indicate the evaluator involved.

The first part of the analysis was concerned with each evaluator's views of evaluation which included views on the nature of educational research. As a consequence, a series of two-way matrix displays was developed, one for each evaluator to examine evidence concerned with the evaluators' views of evaluation and the epis-

temologies that they endorsed. In Fig. 3 the structure of a matrix display which was used to examine evidence of the epistemologies endorsed by the 15 evaluators is given. The vertical entries in this display indicate the source of evidence that could be used to classify or type each evaluator according to his or her epistemological approach. The horizontal entries in the matrix display include three salient and distinguishing features of both the scientific and naturalistic epistemological approaches to evaluation. Other approaches, such as a critical social science approach, had to be allowed for. Entries for each evaluator can be placed under the appropriate column headings. The completed matrix displays permitted the researcher to classify or type the epistemological approaches preferred by evaluators. The matrix display was started after the first of the two interviews with the evaluators in order to check whether an adequate representation of the different views of educational research was being obtained. If gross imbalances had been observed, it might have been necessary to add further evaluators to the study so that an adequate range of views had been sampled.

Figure 4 records the matrix display that was constructed for evaluators so that evidence could be examined on the consistency of the views of each evaluator with respect to epistemology and evaluation models. In this matrix display, the horizontal axis provides for the classification of epistemological approaches preferred by evaluators, while the vertical axis classifies the views evaluators expressed about evaluation models. The cat-

| Epistemology | Scientific | | | Interpretative / Naturalistic | | | Other |
|---|---|---|---|---|---|---|---|
| Evaluator and source of information | Value – free inquiry | Explanation by inquiry | Empirical general – ization | Value – laden inquiry | Under – stand – ing by inquiry | Interpre – tative inquiry in context | Critical social science approach |
| A  Interview 1<br>Interview 2<br>Report | | | | | | | |
| B  Interview 1<br>Interview 2<br>Report | | | | | | | |
| C  Interview 1<br>Interview 2<br>Report | | | | | | | |
| D  Interview 1<br>Interview 2<br>Report | | | | | | | |

*Figure 3*
Matrix display of epistemological views of evaluators

| Epistemology | Scientific | | | Interpretative / Naturalistic | | | Other |
|---|---|---|---|---|---|---|---|
| Evaluation models | Quasi – experi – mental | Non – experi – mental | Inter – vention | Non – inter – vention | Ethno – graphic | Partic – ipatory | Critical social science |
| Goal based | | | | | | | |
| Eclectic | | | | | | | |
| Utility focused | | | | | | | |
| Interpretative | | | | | | | |
| Participatory | | | | | | | |
| Critical self – reflection | | | | | | | |

**Figure 4**
Matrix display of relationship between epistemology and evaluation models

egories used on this latter axis emerged from an analysis of the previous matrix displays of evaluators' views of evaluation models. The categories of epistemological preferences used on the horizontal axis were developed from the analyses considered in the matrix display in Fig. 3. In Fig. 4, the evaluators were located in appropriate cells, with notes on justifications given by evaluators for what might seem to be inconsistent positions on the two axes. In studying the consistency between the views evaluators expressed about evaluation and the way evaluators conducted their studies, it was possible to locate the evaluation and the way evaluators conducted their studies, it was possible to locate the evaluation studies conducted by the evaluators in these cells. This provided an indication as to whether the views expressed by evaluators had an influence on the design of the studies they undertook.

Information on the views of each evaluator came primarily from the first of the two interviews with each evaluator. The other two sources, namely the second of the two interviews with the evaluator, and the evaluation reports, were sometimes used. Information from these different sources did not necessarily provide consistent evidence. Consequently, a report was sent to each evaluator on the researcher's interpretations of the evaluator's views to obtain confirmation that the researcher had recorded the dominant views of each evaluator.

It will be apparent to the reader that the preferred epistemological approach expressed by an evaluator may not be that underlying a methodological approach adopted by that evaluator in a particular evaluation study. In such cases, it was of interest to investigate factors in the research situation which were influential in the choice of the approach. In the conceptual framework informing the research, one external factor in the research situation postulated as influencing the conduct of an evaluation was the client's preference. This preference might account for the situation where an evaluator employed a methodological approach at variance with the epistemological preference expressed by the evaluator. However, it is also reasonable to assume that a client would be attracted to, and in turn attract, an evaluator with similar preferences. Consequently, one research question in this investigation was the extent to which the preferences of the evaluator interacted with the preferences of the client and were subsequently related to the nature of the evaluation conducted. An examination of this question would require three matrix displays. One matrix display would examine the relationship between the epistemological preferences of the 15 evaluators and the preferred approaches of the 30 clients. A second would investigate the relationship between the epistemological preferences of the 15 evaluators and the methodological approaches adopted by the evaluators in the 30 studies, while the third would investigate the relationship between the approach preferred by each of the 30 clients and the approach adopted in each of the 30 studies. These three matrix displays involved cross-case analyses along the three dimensions: epistemological preferences of evaluators, preferred approaches of clients, and the actual approaches adopted in the studies. Some of the cases illustrated interesting interactions, and where no methodological preference was expressed by a client, the evaluator was found to adopt a methodological approach that was consistent with that evaluator's preferred epistemological stance.

### 6.4 Conclusion Drawing and Verifying

The crucial stage in the analysis of the data is the drawing of conclusions and the verification of the conclusions. Miles and Huberman (1984 pp. 215–31) have identified 12 tactics for deriving meaning from evidence. The important issue at this stage in the analysis of the data is not one of whether meaning can be found in the evidence available, however chaotic the evidence might seem, but rather whether or not the conclusion is soundly drawn from the evidence available. The checks that can be applied in the drawing of conclusions are whether the results can be presented in a meaningful way to the reader of a research report and whether another person analysing the same body of evidence would draw the same conclusions. In addition, there is the important question as to whether the research worker is entitled to claim generality for the conclusions beyond the particular body of data that was collected. While the tactics for the deriving of conclusions differ from those of verifying meaning, eliminating possible bias, and confirming the generality of the findings, it is evident that the processes of derivation and verification are interrelated.

### 6.5 Tactics for Deriving Meaning

(a) *Counting.* In qualitative research there is a tendency to reject counting the number of instances for which a relationship is observed or an event occurs. However, to ignore a count is to overlook the most obvious data. Whether so simple a test should be applied to verify that a pattern was unlikely to occur by chance could become more controversial, particularly if little could be said about the nature and quality of the sample.

(b) *Noting patterns and themes.* Commonly in textual reports or matrix displays recurring patterns of results are quickly seen. A real danger is that of not remaining open to evidence that disconfirms the pattern.

(c) *Imputing plausibility.* Once a particular result or a specific pattern of results has been observed, there is commonly a need on the part of the investigator to consider the plausibility of the result or pattern. The question is asked as to whether the result "makes good sense". There is a very real danger that once a result has been observed, justification will be found and plausibility will be imputed, and the finding will be accepted without further checking.

(d) *Clustering.* Qualitative research lends itself to classifying and clustering events and people into groups. The use of matrix displays greatly facilitates simple clustering. It should be recognized that the outlier or exceptional case can help to provide an understanding of the manner in which a naturally occurring cluster is formed. As a consequence both the outliers and the typical cases should be studied in detail.

(e) *Using metaphors.* At the analysis stage of an investigation and prior to the reporting of results it can be of considerable value for the qualitative researcher to think about the available evidence in terms of metaphors. The use of analogies and metaphorical thinking provides not only a means for writing a report in an interesting and lively way, but also provides a valuable tactic for seeing through a morass of detail in order to detect new and different perspectives. There is of course the danger for the research worker of developing an analogue ahead of the evidence and failing to test the underlying idea or relationship adequately against the data, and "premature closure" of this kind should be avoided. The wisest approach is to seek opportunities to discuss ideas both formally and informally in order to test out such ideas with both colleagues and critics.

(f) *Splitting categories.* In the planning of the coding and the analysis of the data, categories can be formed that collect a very high proportion of the cases. Classification schemes that fail to discriminate between cases serve little useful purpose. Efforts should be made in such circumstances to use the available evidence, as well as further data that might be obtained to subdivide the category and the associated cases into groups that could add meaning to the analyses and lead to the detection of an important relationship.

(g) *Combining categories.* The converse to splitting categories is also important. Where there are too few cases in certain categories, these categories serve little purpose in the task of cross-classification. If categories can be combined so that the distribution of cases across categories is more balanced, then it is more likely that meaningful patterns and relationships will be observed.

(h) *Compositing.* It is common to include in a study factors that are either conditionally related or have elements in common. There is a danger that the use of too many factors that have fine distinctions between them will lead to loss of meaning. The solution is to combine factors and the categories within those factors by procedures of union of sets of elements or the intersection of sets of elements in order to form new factors that have greater meaning.

(i) *Noting relations.* An important step in the analysis of evidence is to examine factors that vary directly (i.e., both increase) or indirectly (i.e., one increases while the other decreases) together. The large amount of evidence which is collected in a qualitative study makes the identification of such relationships extremely difficult. Nevertheless, if the number of likely relationships could be restricted on logical grounds then a systematic search is likely to yield valuable results.

(j) *Finding mediating factors.* It is not uncommon for factors at the beginning and the end of a chain to be found to be related, such as the preference an evaluator has for a particular methodological approach, and the type of approach used in an evaluation. This particular relationship, while of interest, provides little understanding of the influence of factors that mediate between the two linked concepts. The search for mediating factors might lead to an examination of preferences of the client which could be shown to provide the link in a chain of evidence.

(k) *Building a logical chain of evidence.* The preceding tactic was concerned with searching for a factor that mediated within a logical chain, and this tactic began the development of a related chain of factors such that the prior members of the chain were related in a logical way to the subsequent members of the chain. For example, to extend the chain which was commenced above where it was suggested that the preferences of the client operated as a mediating factor, could lead to the inclusion of external factors, such as the type of program being evaluated, the political climate, and the interests of the stakeholders, as further possible links in a logical chain.

(l) *Constructing a causal chain.* A causal chain of factors should not only involve a logical sequence as was sought in the preceding two tactics, but should also involve a temporal sequence. Since earlier events influence later events and not vice versa, the construction of a causal chain must of necessity be governed by a strict time sequence between the operation of the factors in the chain. The evidence collected in a qualitative study might provide tentative support for the existence of mediating factors, logical chains, and causal chains and indicate whether a link between adjacent factors is present. However, to proceed beyond a tentative link requires the employment of related theory, rather than the observation of evidence collected from a natural setting and linked in a meaningful way in the concluding stages of an investigation. The approach advanced here is that of induction from the evidence, rather than deduction from theory, although as suggested earlier these processes may not be formally distinguishable in the search for meaning within a study that makes extensive use of qualitative data.

## 7. Confirming Findings

The dangers associated with the pondering over large bodies of qualitative data are that while striking relationships may be suggested which are strong in analogy and clearly presented using metaphor, they run the risk of being incomplete, inadequate, and possibly wrong. Another investigator examining the same body of evidence, but without perhaps the same extent of total immersion in the data, may be unable to detect the relationships reported. Alternatively, a research worker investigating the same or similar cases may advance radically different findings. Similar problems arise in studies that employ quantitative methods. However, researchers using qualitative methods have, in general, not addressed the question of how to ensure that their findings are replicable and robust, and how to convince other researchers that the tactics they have employed

are sound in these respects. Miles and Huberman (1984 p. 230) have identified some of the common sources of error in developing conclusions from qualitative data. They include:

(a) the holistic fallacy, which involves ignoring the outlier cases and erratic strands so that events are interpreted as more patterned and with greater congruence than they actually possess;

(b) elite bias, which involves giving greater credence to the opinions of high status, articulate respondents than to lower status, less articulate ones; and

(c) "going native", which involves accepting the perceptions and explanations of events advanced by the respondents being studied without bringing scholarship and experience in investigation to bear on the work of inquiry.

Miles and Huberman (1984 p. 231–43) have advanced 12 tactics that are useful in qualitative research for confirming findings.

(a) *Checking the investigation for representativeness.* This tactic seeks to avoid the pitfalls of sampling nonrepresentative respondents, observing nonrepresentative events, and drawing inference from nonrepresentative processes. Nonetheless, it must be recognized that the exceptional case can sometimes reveal more than can be seen from the uniformity of all the representative cases. These dangers are overcome by: searching deliberately for contrasting cases, sorting the cases into categories in a systematic way, sampling randomly from within a total universe, and increasing the number of cases being studied.

(b) *Checking for researcher effects.* This tactic seeks to diminish in every way possible the influence that the intrusion of an investigator into the situation being studied may have. It is important to recognize that not only may the researcher influence the situation being investigated, but the situation may also have an effect on the perceptions of the researcher in ways that may introduce bias. These problems may be avoided by: spending more time at the site of the investigation, using unobtrusive observation procedures, coopting the assistance of an informant to report on the effects of the researcher on the situation being studied, making sure that misinformation about the investigation does not contaminate the research, undertaking interviews off the site in order to examine the effects the place of interview may have, reducing emphasis on the role of the investigator, guarding against identifiable sources of bias (e.g., the holistic fallacy, elite bias, and going native), avoiding undue concern for individuals by thinking conceptually, trying to sense if deliberate attempts are being made to mislead, keeping research questions in mind, discussing field notes with an experienced researcher, and avoiding the effects on the respondent of knowledge about the issues being investigated.

(c) *Triangulation.* This involves a range of procedures

that the research worker can use to increase the strength of observation. There are four types of triangulation: methodological triangulation which involves the use of more than one method to obtain evidence; theory triangulation which involves the use of more than one theoretical perspective in the interpretation of phenomena; investigator triangulation which involves the use of more than one observer; and data triangulation which involves replication of the investigation in time, in location, or with another sample of persons. The use of more than one method of triangulation is both costly and time consuming. However, if the issues under investigation are of sufficient importance then the costs of time and money are no doubt worth the increased strength of the findings provided by extensive triangulation.

(d) *Weighting the evidence.* This is a tactic that can be employed to make allowance for the fact that some data are stronger and other data are more suspect. In order to employ differential weighting of evidence, it is necessary to identify clearly the assessed strength of the data, preferably at the time of collection. This would involve the keeping of a running log on data quality issues and the preparation of a clear summary of information on the relative quality of different items of evidence. There are significant dangers involved in the weighting of data unless it is undertaken on well-argued and rational grounds.

(e) *Making contrasts and comparisons.* This is a sound tactic for drawing conclusions and presenting results. In qualitative research contrasts can be made between persons, cases, groups, roles, activities, and sites. However, it is important that the units being compared or contrasted should be identified in some way that is not directly related to the data to be used in the comparisons. Moreover, it is necessary to recognize in advance the extent of a difference that is worthy of consideration.

(f) *Examining the outlier case.* This is a tactic that can reveal information which would otherwise remain hidden. The temptation is to ignore the outlier and seek uniformity, yet understanding can result from the search for reasons as to why the extreme case has occurred. Outlier cases are not just exceptional people, but can include atypical situations, unique treatments, uncommon events, and unusual sites. Once these exceptional cases have been identified, the characteristics that make them exceptional should be investigated and an explanation as to why the exception has arisen should be sought.

(g) *Using the exceptional case to account for regularity.* This is the complementary side of identifying, examining, and explaining the outlier. The exceptional case should be seen as not only telling much about itself but also telling something about the group from which it was drawn.

(h) *Searching for a spurious relationship.* This tactic is often rewarding. While two factors might be seen to be related in a way that could be interpreted as causal, establishing the existence of a third factor which influenced both commonly leads to a rejection of the causal nature of the observed relationship.

(i) *Replicating a finding.* Conducting a further separate study or providing an opportunity for an independent investigator to re-examine the available evidence is an important tactic in research, where generality is sought. As indicated above, the exceptional case or the outlier can be of considerable value. However, it is also important to distinguish between those cases where regularities are present and where a nomothetic dimension exists, and those cases which are unique and where an idiographic dimension is involved.

(j) *Checking out rival explanations.* This is an important step in developing full understanding. While it is important to search for a reasoned explanation of an event or problematic situation, it is also necessary to advance alternative explanations and if possible to resolve between the two or more explanations that have been proposed. Evidence that would help determine which of two alternative explanations was more coherent must be considered to be critical. A greater contribution to understanding is achieved by a resolution between two rival explanations than by merely confirming a well-held explanation or established result. However, confirmation is in itself of consequence.

(k) *Looking for negative evidence.* This is a useful tactic since it extends the approaches of examining outlier cases, using the exceptional case, and testing out a rival explanation. The search for evidence that could disconfirm an established result can provide opportunities for the development of understanding, whether or not the pursuit of negative evidence is successful. The failure to find negative evidence after a deliberate search does not and cannot establish the "truth" of a result. However, it does increase the probability that the original result is sound.

(l) *Getting feedback from respondents.* This can provide understanding of both the events being studied and the interpretation or explanation provided for the events. This tactic involves confronting respondents with emerging theoretical explanations of events and inviting them to report on the validity of the explanations with respect to their knowledge and understanding. The purpose is not one of counting heads to indicate support or rejection of a particular explanation, but rather to obtain additional evidence, to provide new insights, and to learn more about the problematic situation under investigation. Only if the procedures of participant verification are carefully and deliberately planned, with key findings clearly presented, together with coherent interpretations of the findings will the participants be able to contribute in a meaningful way.

## 8. Summarizing and Integrating the Findings

Whereas standard procedures have been developed for the writing of theses, research reports, and journal articles that record the conduct and present the findings of quantitative research conducted from a scientific perspective, in the reporting of qualitative or naturalistic research appropriate procedures have not been developed. The dangers are that while an increasing amount of empirical research using qualitative data is being carried out, either it is not being reported or it is being reported in such a way that the research cannot be audited and the conclusions cannot be verified (see, for example, the influential Australian report by Connell et al. 1982). This gives rise to the anomalous situation that while in research using qualitative data the evidence is rich and detailed, the very richness and detail of the data collected prevent presentation in a coherent form that would lead to acceptance of the findings as a contribution to scholarly inquiry.

There are few agreed-upon procedures or established conventions for the reporting of research based on qualitative data. As a consequence, the quality of such research cannot be verified, because information on the methods employed is lacking. Furthermore, because of the detail in the data, the reports that are prepared are lengthy and time consuming to read, and as a result the findings from such studies are quickly lost in the growing volume of published research.

There are two important aspects of reporting research which is based on qualitative data. The first involves the presentation of the findings of the research, the second involves reporting on the methods that were employed in the conduct of the research. Research in education, irrespective of the nature of the data collected, is part of the ongoing work of contributing to and building a body of knowledge about educational processes as well as providing guidance for policy making and practice. Thus any specific piece of research will make contributions, first to theory about educational processes, second to educational practice, and third to the planning of further investigatory activity. It would seem important that, if possible, each of these three aspects should be addressed in the preparation of a report. Nonetheless, the reader of a research report is initially interested in grasping the key findings of the investigation, before examining other aspects relating to theory, practice, and further inquiry.

Two tactics can be suggested to assist in the presentation of the findings of research based on qualitative data. After the development of a logical sequence or alternatively a causal chain of factors, it can be of value to present this information in diagrammatic form where a path diagram is used to portray the relationships. The path diagram possesses the characteristics of a model in a form that assists comprehension of both the known constructs and their interrelations, and gives rise to the generation of further constructs and relationships that might be examined. A second tactic that is of value in the presentation of results is the formulation of propositions. These propositions can enter into a report in two ways. First, in the opening chapters where a conceptual framework is discussed, propositions can be advanced that can guide the collection of data and the analysis of data, in a similar way to research questions. Furthermore, in the drawing of conclusions attention can again turn to the propositions stated at the beginning of a study and they can be examined or tested with the evidence available. An alternative approach involves the developing of a set of propositions using inductive processes and based upon the conclusions that are drawn from the analysis of evidence. In this use the propositions serve to summarize the findings in a form that can be readily comprehended by the reader and tested in subsequent investigations. They provide a clear and concise focus for both the reporter and the reader to use in identifying what a particular investigation has shown.

A second important task involved in the reporting of an investigation that makes use of qualitative data is the provision of a clear and concise account of how the data were analysed. Guba and Lincoln (1981) refer to the provision of this type of information as an "audit trail". The idea is that another investigator should be able to follow step by step the audit trail to verify the procedures employed in the analysis of the data. Miles and Huberman (1984 pp. 244–45) have developed a documentation form for use by research workers in education who are working with qualitative data to record the procedures used to analyse the data. A separate form is employed for each specific research question. The researcher is required to summarize on the form "what the analysis of the research question was designed to do". The researcher also records on the form the procedural steps taken, the decision rules employed, and the operations of analysis involved in the examination of data with respect to the specific research questions. The form requires at the end a summary of what the analysis found. The amount of detail included on a form will be determined by the nature of the analyses carried out. Miles and Huberman (1984 p. 247) indicate that for the detailed examination of a research question, commonly seven or eight steps are involved and each step or episode requires approximately a page in order to summarize the information. They also suggest that the forms should be completed concurrently with the conduct of the analyses. The use of the documentation form will also indicate to the research worker the extent and manner in which the analytical techniques are employed on a specific analytical task. Where too great a reliance is made on a very limited number of analytical techniques the researcher should deliberately seek to increase the range of procedures employed. Miles and Huberman indicate that the completion of the standard form requires something of the order of 20 percent of the time necessary to analyse the data with respect to a particular research question. While these audit procedures are time consuming, they form part of a deliberate attempt to develop standard procedures for the analysis of qualitative data on which consensus might be achieved.

## Bibliography

Connell R W, Ashenden D J, Kessler S, Dowsett G W 1982 *Making the Difference.* Allen and Unwin, Sydney

Donmoyer R 1985 The rescue from relativism: Two failed attempts and an alternative strategy. *Educ. Res.* 14(10): 13–20

Donmoyer R 1986 The problem of language in empirical research: A rejoinder to Miles and Huberman. *Educ. Res.* 15(3): 26–27

Guba E G, Lincoln Y S 1981 *Effectiveness Evaluation.* Jossey Bass, San Francisco, California

Huberman A M, Miles M B 1986 Concepts and methods in qualitative research: A reply to Donmoyer. *Educ. Res.* 15(3): 25–26

Kaplan A 1964 *The Conduct of Inquiry.* Chandler, San Francisco, California

Miles M B, Huberman A M 1984 *Qualitative Data Analysis: A Sourcebook of New Methods.* Sage, Beverly Hills, California

**Part 8**

# Educational Policy and Planning

# Part 8

# Educational Policy and Planning

## Introduction

Evaluation is something of a hybrid. It begins with methods of inquiry developed to advance generalizable, theoretically grounded knowledge, and adapts them to address finite, practical questions about the improvement and success of specific programs and policies. This adaptation requires the evaluator to deal with programs and policies in real-world contexts, as they are actually implemented, and not as theoretical abstractions. The evaluator's responsibility extends beyond the generation of knowledge to communicating that knowledge effectively so that it can be put to use.

This last Part of the *Encyclopedia* is divided into two sections: Evaluation Research, Decision Making, Social Policy, and Planning; and Dissemination and Utilization of Evaluation Research.

The first section opens with an article on *Social Theory and Educational Research*. The author briefly summarizes the evolution of social theory and emergence of multiple disciplinary perspectives in the analysis of educational problems, and then contrasts the social and natural sciences in terms of their spheres of inquiry, epistemologies, and canons of evidence and generalization. Recent changes in social theory as applied to educational problems include new conceptions of the nature of the human agent, of language, of social action, and of hermeneutics. These changes may point the way toward a synthesis of positivist, or scientific, approaches with more naturalistic modes of inquiry. Developments which may point the way toward such a synthesis include statistical methods for treating nonrecursive, multilevel systems, inquiries into metacognition, and changes in theories of social action. The article concludes that as the findings and generalizations of the social sciences find application in education, they may find greater acceptance in society at large.

The next three articles examine *Educational Research and Policy Making, Legitimatory Research*, and *Policy-oriented Research*. The article on *Educational Research and Policy*

*Making* begins by distinguishing two constituencies for educational research: first, teachers and school administrators; and second, educational policy makers. Focusing on the application of research in the policy arena, the article goes on to compare the settings and cultures of policy making versus research, and reviews seven different models or concepts of research utilization in the social sciences.

The article on *Legitimatory Research* offers a useful and provocative analysis of research undertaken to strengthen and maintain existing bureaucratic structures, or to support policies and practices operating within a system. Such research is often conducted by the organization itself, or if externally commissioned, under close scrutiny and supervision. It often takes the form of evaluations, and is generally reported only in summary form, being intended primarily for use by senior officials within the system.

The third article, on *Policy-oriented Research* examines the proper and constructive use of evaluation research to inform educational policy. It contrasts policy-oriented and basic research along a number of dimensions, locating the fundamental distinction in their contrasting purposes and functions. It then discusses policy analysis as a field of study, and describes four categories of policy-oriented studies, including surveys, experimental studies, development studies, and evaluation studies. The basic-policy research distinction is analyzed in some detail, and implications are drawn for the further development of policy analysis as a field of inquiry.

The section then turns to the question of applications of evaluation research to policy and planning, beginning with an article on *Policy Analysis*, which considers the social context and institutions through which policy-oriented studies come to have their effect. It traces the emergence of schools of public policy in the United States, and of the profession of policy analyst. The author distinguishes policy analysts from academic researchers in terms of their interdisciplinary training and perspective, their focus on the viability of alternative actions from the perspective of decision makers, and the institutions by which they are employed. Through policy analysts, research can influence policy much more directly than models of "percolation"," knowledge creep", or gradual diffusion would suggest. Policy analysts are also contrasted with policy intellectuals who are further removed from decision makers, writing for specialized journals and formulating the broader arguments and positions that over time influence the creation of new policy alternatives.

Another perspective on the application of evaluation research is given by the next article, on *Planning the Quality of Education*. Here, the information needs of actors at different levels of the educational system, and the sources of that information, are analyzed and compared. The discussion treats decision makers at four broad levels by way of illustration: teachers and parents, school principals, state and provincial officials, and national officials. At successively higher levels, different kinds of absolute and comparative information become relevant, and the information must be contextualized in different ways. The article draws attention to the pitfalls of interpreting data at any level without regard to the relevant characteristics of those pupils, classes, schools, or localities from which the data were obtained.

The article on *Educational System Assessment and Planning Models* focuses on the highest level of aggregation discussed in the preceding article, with a practical introduction to tools and resources for long-term planning at the national level. Major models and simulation systems are cited and briefly reviewed, as are major planning efforts by international organizations. The article traces the evolution of these models from simple predictions of the size of future student cohorts through sophisticated models based on labor-force requirements, culminating in dynamic models in which the effects of alternative courses of action can be played out through time.

The last six articles of the *Encyclopedia* examine the Dissemination and Utilization of Evaluation Research, beginning with a general introduction to *Knowledge Diffusion in Education*. This article considers the creation of educational knowledge and elaborates on the seven modes of knowledge utilization mentioned earlier in the article on educational research and policy making. Additional models of knowledge dissemination and utilization, which were developed from systematic studies of a number of different fields are then presented. The various approaches are located on a continuum from a research, development, and diffusion orientation at one pole to a problem solving orientation at the other. Finally, some practical approaches to planned diffusion are discussed, and implications are drawn.

The next article, *Dissemination of Educational Research*, takes a more global perspective on the existing knowledge infrastructure. After defining the problem of dissemination in terms of reaching different audiences and presenting information intelligibly, the article distinguishes between the more and the less developed nations of the world, and discusses dissemination within each of these two broad communities. Problems including dissemination across language barriers are also discussed.

The third article, on *Knowledge Utilization*, begins with a consideration of knowledge utilization as an area of study, and describes the major research traditions that underlie most contemporary work. It then goes on to describe available conceptual frameworks, methodology, and practice. The conceptual frameworks presented all express the need for some kind of knowledge transformation to bridge the gap between the formulation of a practical problem and the structure of a research problem. Knowledge use is interpretive, socially constrained, systemic, and transactive. Methodological problems in research on knowledge utilization include defining what is meant by use, selecting an appropriate unit of analysis, and collecting reliable and valid information. Given the complexity of the phenomenon, it is not surprising that few clear findings have emerged from a search for single causes or factors. The article concludes with a discussion of how knowledge is applied, and some of the factors that influence the impact and application of research findings. Theoretical, conceptual, and methodological issues have been clarified, but there is as yet no systematic social science of knowledge utilization.

The fourth article, on *Reporting Evaluations of Learning Outcomes*, focuses on the reporting and interpretation of student learning in ways that are maximally useful for different audiences. The focus is on the reporting of school learning as reflected in test scores and other forms of assessment. Three principles are discussed. First, reports of learning outcomes should indicate what has been learned, and what of the expected learning has not taken place, rather than focusing on abstract quantification of individual differences. Second, direct demonstrations of learning are preferable to indirect indicators of learning. Third, users should be given as much information as possible, but in no more detail than can be assimilated and used. These guidelines are illustrated in discussions of reports on student learning for teachers and parents, for school principles, for school districts, and for state, regional, and national agencies.

Evaluative information is more broadly defined in the fifth article, *The Information Side of Evaluation for Local School Improvement*, to include substantially more than test scores. It encompasses multiple domains (personal, instructional, institutional, societal), multiple sources (teachers, students, administrators, parents), and multiple methods (survey, interview, participant observation, historical, archival). Comprehensive collection of quality information is treated as part of ongoing school improvement. This article also discusses briefly the complex problems of data aggregation in hierarchical school organizations.

The final article, on *Reporting the Results of Evaluation Studies*, takes a different perspective, describing the variety of formats and methods of communication between the evaluation staff and clients. These include both formal written reports and informal reporting processes. Several types of reports are described, including progress reports, interim reports, final reports, and executive summaries. Reporting is treated as an ongoing process throughout the duration of the evaluation, not simply as the preparation of a final report at the end.

# Evaluation Research, Decision Making, Social Policy, and Planning

## Social Theory and Educational Research

### J. P. Keeves

For much of the 100 years that have lapsed since the field of empirical research in education was first established, there was a stereotyped view that the research worker, trained in the discipline of psychology was well placed to prescribe for pedagogical practice the "do's" and "don'ts" which could be derived from the laws of generalizations of psychological theory. The audiences for the counsel of the educational research worker and psychologist were practising classroom teachers who sought to improve both student learning and the efficiency of their daily work (Jackson and Kiesler 1977). It is perhaps not surprising that this view should have been advanced at a time when psychology was developing as a science and when empirical research in education was being established as a systematic activity. However, with the growth of the field of educational research after the Second World War, and more particularly as a result of the injection of substantial funds for educational research in the 1960s, scholars from disciplines other than psychology became active in the investigation of educational problems. These scholars came, in the main, from the social science disciplines of sociology, political science, economics, demography, anthropology, and linguistics. They brought with them different perspectives and they frequently saw educational problems in terms of social theory.

The dominant view of social processes in the 1960s was that of structural functionalism, which was a perspective where the influence of Parsons in the United States had been highly significant. Parsons interpreted the social theories of European scholars of the nineteenth and early twentieth centuries, including Durkheim, Weber and Pareto, and to a lesser degree Marx. In addition, he developed the functionalist conception of sociology. Although his writings were complex, his ideas had considerable appeal and influence. From this perspective educational inquiry could no longer be seen as a field where psychological principles only would be applied. For example, Feinberg has argued that the appropriate perspective for educational inquiry is that of social reproduction, since:

Education is best understood by recognizing that one of the functions of any society is that of maintaining intergenerational continuity—that is, of maintaining its identity as a society across generations and even in the context of many possible and significant changes, and that it is the activity and institution of education, both formal and informal, that carries on this function. (Feinberg 1983 p. 6)

While these views involving an emphasis in educational research on social theory were not new, since they were shared with Plato, Marx, and Dewey, they have had a growing influence on the conduct of inquiry into educational problems.

Nonetheless, from the 1970s functionalism as an approach to research in the social sciences has been under siege. The perspectives provided by positivism and the scientific approach, which underpinned both functionalism and an alternative but related approach of naturalism, were based on the strategies of inquiry of the natural sciences, particularly the biological sciences. They were strongly challenged as being inappropriate for inquiry in the social sciences and for educational research. An alternative approach has emerged with a humanistic perspective. In addition critical theory has become established and has sought not only to understand the relations between value, interest, action, and power, but also to change society. These new approaches have also advanced new research perspectives and methodologies including those of ethnomethodology, ethnography, symbolic interactionism, historical materialism, action research, participatory research, cultural anthropology, social phenomenology, dramaturgical sociology, as well as critical social science. Since the mid-1970s the many alternative approaches to the study of society and to research in the field of education have generated both conflict and confusion, as they have competed against one another for scholarly acceptance.

The recent debate that has taken place in the 1980s with respect to both educational and social science research has been concerned with the merits and demerits of quantitative or qualitative research, with issues of the value-free or value-laden nature of investigation in the social sciences, and with the roles of understanding (*Verstehen*) as contrasted with explanation (*Erklären*). The view has been advanced that the humanistic and scientific approaches should be seen as complementary to one another rather than in direct opposition. However, important theoretical developments took place during the early 1980s that have clarified the nature of social research and as a result the nature of social research. These developments, as exemplified in the writings of Giddens (1984), are leading to a unification of the alternative views of social science and educational research. The advancement of a coherent approach to investigation in these fields, that recognizes the shortcomings of structural functionalism, and makes provision for the key ideas contained in the many different research strategies which have been proposed since the mid-1970s, is an important and in many ways exciting development. Before considering these changes in the field of social theory it is necessary to examine three aspects of the differences which are said to exist between investigation in the social and natural sciences.

## 1. The Social and the Natural Sciences

Three aspects of inquiry in the social and natural sciences are of particular interest. Firstly, there is concern for the nature of the worlds of inquiry. Secondly, there is concern for the epistemological origins of inquiry. Thirdly, there is concern for the nature of the generalizations that can be made within the two approaches to inquiry of the scientific and humanistic research traditions.

### 1.1 The Worlds of Inquiry

Popper and Eccles (1977) have distinguished between three worlds of inquiry. The entities of the real world are World 1. The products of the human mind that are built into a corpus of knowledge form World 3. World 3 contains within it propositional knowledge. The important point is that World 3 objects acquire a reality of their own. There is in addition, however, a world of individual mental states, which comprises the states of consciousness and psychological dispositions as well as the unconscious states of individuals. Popper and Eccles refer to this as World 2. Contained within World 2 is personal knowledge. Educational research in the area of metacognition seeks to map certain aspects of this personal knowledge, recognizing that it is heavily overlaid by the mental state of each individual. Personal knowledge about education and society is acquired in part from experience and in part from corporate bodies of knowledge, commonly presented in propositional form. Inquiry conducted from the humanistic perspective contributes very directly to personal knowledge through the interpretations it provides of social and educational processes. Information obtained through these strategies is presented in such a way as to appeal to

individual readers. In so far as it is commonly concerned with motives and expressed reasons this information can interact readily with existing personal knowledge. It seeks to build directly new personal knowledge for each individual. Subsequently, it may prove possible to develop theory from this personal knowledge and transfer ideas to a corporate body of propositional knowledge concerned with causal explanation which resides in World 3. It should be noted that World 3 also contains works of art, music, and literary writings that are parts of the world of shared knowledge.

The body of propositional knowledge that has been assembled by the natural sciences can be used to transform the real world through technology. Moreover, it has been the marked success of research and development strategies in the physical and biological sciences acting through technology that has enhanced the standing of both scientific research and technological development not only in the field of scholarly inquiry but also in daily life. Furthermore, it has been the apparent failure of the social and behavioural sciences, and of educational inquiry to use their findings through technology and strategies of research, development, and dissemination that has led to disillusionment and a serious questioning of the relevance of educational and social science research.

Figure 1 presents in diagrammatic form some of the relationships that exist between these three worlds of inquiry, and technology.

From the perspectives of both functionalism and naturalism there are no essential differences between inquiry in the natural sciences and in the social sciences. Both fields of inquiry are considered to be involved in the development of a shared body of knowledge about the real world. The real world is knowable through direct observation or through the use of instrumentation, and the research worker seeks to eliminate personal values from the observations made and the measurements recorded by complex instruments. However, since the

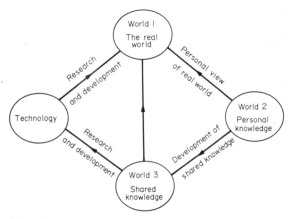

*Figure 1*
The worlds of inquiry

mid-1970s, the approaches of both functionalism and naturalism have been questioned, in educational and social science research.

## 1.2 Epistemological Origins of Inquiry

Recently our understanding of the epistemological origins of knowledge that is developed within both the scientific and humanistic perspectives has changed. It is argued that no longer can these two approaches be seen to be substantially different. Furthermore, it is acknowledged that both scientific and social science research workers are influenced by their previous knowledge and theories which guide what they observe and record from the real world. In neither field is it possible to contend that the real world can be apprehended independently of our previous knowledge and theories of the world. Thus Quinean philosophy argues that either field of inquiry belongs to the same coherent "web of belief" (Quine and Ullian 1970). While the extent to which a personal view of the real world is permitted to intrude on inquiry may differ between different fields of investigation, the differences that occur are ones of degree and not of kind.

Furthermore, while the extent to which abstraction occurs, and the extent to which measurement is employed, may differ between the two fields, both quality and quantity are misconceived if they are considered to be alternatives and antithetical to one another and are employed to differentiate between the two fields (Kaplan 1964 p. 207). Thus it is argued that there is a unity of inquiry, in social science and educational research, derived from the epistemological basis of inquiry whatever approach is taken, namely, the scientific perspective or the humanistic perspective. Furthermore, the methods that are employed in both the sciences and the social sciences are determined by the problem in need of resolution. The goal of inquiry is to develop answers to the questions being investigated and to solve problems.

## 1.3 Laws and Generalizations

The success of the natural sciences would appear to arise from the capacity of inquiry to advance generalizations that possess a universality which entitles them to be classified as laws. In this respect the social sciences have not experienced the same degree of success. However, it is necessary to recognize that the laws of science are not absolute truths which are established after the facts have been obtained. They have initially been developed from theory which has a role in the process of determining what the facts are. In these matters the generalizations of science do not differ from those of the social sciences. However, the major findings of science are concerned with relationships where a very large number of elementary units is involved. Such relationships are essentially probabilistic statements, where the probability of a statement holding in any particular situation is unity not because of inherent certainty but because with very large numbers the probabilities are extremely close to 1.0. In the social sciences the situations being investigated rarely involve such very large numbers of elementary units so that probabilities of 1.0 could not be expected. However, since the early 1970s social science research workers have learnt to work with probabilities of less than unity, and computers have become available so that a large enough number of cases can be investigated for stable estimates of probabilities to be recorded.

In addition, developments in statistical analysis in the mid-1980s have made it possible for statistical control to be exercised in order to make allowance for the many factors that operate in any particular situation in educational and social science investigations. The differences between the natural and the social sciences lie not in the approaches to investigation but in the large number of factors over which some control must be exercised in the social sciences and in education. The differences between the natural sciences and the social sciences are not essentially differences in kind but rather differences in degree.

There are, however, differences between the social sciences and the natural sciences that have come to light in research on social theory conducted in the mid-1980s. These differences do not arise from the epistemological foundations of research, where an essential unity exists. However, it is recognized that the universality of the laws of science is in marked contrast to the limited nature of the generalizations that can be established in the social sciences. These developments in social theory are considered in the next section.

## 2. Recent Changes in Social Theory

Giddens in an unpublished address given at the University of Melbourne in August 1986, has identified four areas of social theory where important developments have emerged which, if recognized, help to resolve the conflicts that have arisen between the alternative approaches to research in the social sciences and education.

## 2.1 The Nature of the Human Agent

It must be acknowledged that in social science and educational research the individual person, with his or her unique personal knowledge that constitutes World 2, has a very different role in the study of problems in society and education from the role played by the individual in the investigation of phenomena in the natural sciences. However, the widely held view during the years when functionalism dominated inquiry in the social sciences was that human beings, in the main, did not understand why they behaved as they did and that the purpose of the social sciences was to investigate and to explain the behaviour of groups of human beings. In the famous sociological study of suicide by Durkheim, it was found that suicide rates remained constant across years within particular countries, but differed significantly between countries. This finding was used to argue that social causes were required to explain the factors that lead individuals to kill themselves. Likewise, in the educational field, it is found that retention rates at the terminal year of schooling not only differ between countries, between school types, between social class groups, and between schools, but also remain remarkably constant across years within any particular group. Clearly, different students are involved in deciding whether to leave school or remain to Year 12 each year, yet a surprising degree of regularity is observed between schools and other groups over time. On the surface it would appear that sociological factors should be invoked to provide an explanation of such data, and that an account in terms of purely psychological principles would be inadequate.

This oversimplified view, which is quite commonly advanced in explanations of social class differences in educational outcomes and practices has been largely discredited. Individuals cannot be regarded as passive units in the analysis of evidence from a sociological perspective or even as neutral subjects in psychological research. Human beings must be considered rather as active agents, who know what they are doing in most situations and are making conscious decisions with regard to their actions. In this respect they differ in significant ways from animals, which are the units of much biological research concerned with the effects of environmental and ecological forces. It must also be acknowledged that not only do most individuals know what they are doing most of the time but, as those philosophers influenced by Wittgenstein have shown, they have, and can provide, reasons for their decisions. Human beings are not just puppets operated within a social system by social forces. What happens to them in society is at least to some extent the consequence of deliberate efforts by the individuals to make it happen. From the perspective of naturalism there would be a search for the underlying causes for both group and individual behaviour. However, a new perspective of human agency is emerging that seeks to investigate both the reasons and intentions of individuals as agents as well as those institutional and social phenomena that influence individuals independently of their own volition.

As an example of these newer perspectives, Giddens (1984) has reexamined the findings which Willis (1977) reported in his study of working-class boys at school in a poor district of Birmingham. Willis treats the boys as actors who have a considerable tacit and discursive knowledge of the school and social environment of which they are a part. The behaviour of the boys is influenced by the knowledge that they will take up unskilled and unrewarding jobs when they leave. As a consequence, they develop rebellious attitudes towards the authority system of the school that are consistent with the attitudes they will develop toward authority in the workplace and on the shop floor, and which they

learn from their parents and older friends. They employ humour, banter, and aggressive sarcasm in a single-minded way to challenge and test authority. They are purposeful agents in their social activities exploring the intended and unintended consequences of their actions. Thus the behaviour of individual agents is influenced by the large social setting and constrained by the smaller cultural setting of which they are part. However, such agents know what they are doing and can provide an account of their actions.

It is necessary to recognize that much of what is known to human agents is not known in the form of reasoned argument. A high level of skill is required to be an effective member of society, but many of the skills developed cannot be readily stated, since language is extremely complicated. The fact that much knowledge is tacit does not mean that it does not influence the actions of an individual. This, in part, renders inaccessible some of the reasons for the decisions that an individual makes, but it also provides a new perspective with respect to language.

### 2.2 The Nature of Language

In the 1980s there have been significant advances in both philosophy and social theory with respect to the use of language. The traditional view of language and its relationship to human activity has been that language is a medium used by human beings to describe things. From this perspective language is a symbol system that enables us to communicate with each other and to generate a description of the world in which we live. Wittgenstein in his earlier writings accepted this view that language is a medium of description and to a considerable extent, reflected what the world is like. Subsequently Wittgenstein proposed radical changes to this view. He has argued that language is all the things you do with language. In daily life, language is used to get things done in a social context in which actions must be taken in conjunction with other human beings. The consequence of this new understanding of language is that the written text and the spoken word have no essence of their own. They can only be interpreted within the context of the practical actions involved where language is a form of social activity.

The change in emphasis and understanding of the nature of language is all the more important when it is recognized that in everyday life the use of language commonly occurs at a tacit level. Day to day actions are taken through a form of language that presumes a great deal more than is actually said. Furthermore, those things that are not said must necessarily be done. Language is a substitute for action, and action replaces the things that cannot be said. When viewed from this perspective, language has a very different role from that where it is used merely for descriptive purposes. This changing view of language is related to the examination and study of meaning which will be discussed in a later section of this article. It also leads to a changing view of the nature of social action.

## 2.3 The Nature of Social Action

During the last 100 years many different views of the nature of social inquiry have been held, including the perspectives of Marxism and pragmatism. However, those research workers who were conducting inquiry in the social sciences within the perspectives of functionalism or naturalism sought universal generalizations about the social world. Knowledge of these generalizations would allow the introduction of change for the betterment of society. These views were particularly strongly held in the field of educational research. The research, development, and dissemination model was seen to apply both in the field of education as well as the other social sciences, and this model was considered to operate in much the same way as technology generated by the natural sciences was seen to provide control and to permit change of the natural world. The dream of some research workers in the social sciences was that by obtaining knowledge about the processes of human society, it would be possible to control the social world. They sought to provide a social technology and to engage in social engineering that paralleled the scientific technology of the nineteenth century. Because of the success of inquiry in the physical and biological sciences this has been the dominant view in most discussions about the practical implications of the social sciences, and it is this approach that has been involved in the accusations by administrators, politicians, and natural scientists of the paucity of practical results arising from educational and social science research. Furthermore, it is the view that seeks to identify tangible evidence of the applications of educational and social science research in practice.

In the mid-1950s it was possible to answer the critics of educational and social science research with proposals for both increased funding and significant expansion of research activity. In addition, it was commonly claimed that with increased resources and effort both important generalizations and significant practical applications would emerge. Today, we are coming to recognize that such a view was simplistic and naive. However, there is no doubt that the increased resources for educational research, in particular, transformed this area of inquiry in the period of 20 years from the early 1960s to the early 1980s. An immense body of knowledge about educational and social processes was assembled that is only now being assimilated in a purposeful and meaningful way. Nevertheless, it is also apparent that few universal generalizations have emerged that can be directly applied to benefit either educational practice or the operation of society.

Giddens (1984) argues that we have failed to understand in an adequate way the nature of social action in the context of a new social theory. He contends that the technological view of the application of social science research is grossly inadequate, and that there is a sense in which such a view has seriously underestimated the practical impact of research in education and the social sciences on the world in which we live.

In the quest for universal generalizations in the study of educational processes and in social research we have failed to recognize the existence of World 2 and the role of human agents in society. Furthermore, Giddens (1984) argues that we have misunderstood the nature of the relationships associated with language as a form of practical action or praxis. In the study of educational problems and societal processes, human beings as a group do not remain as passive subjects of inquiry. They comprehend the debate which arises during the formulation of ideas, and they not only assimilate these ideas but they also accommodate to them and are changed. Thus as we have indicated in Fig. 1, World 3, the world of shared ideas, interacts with World 2, the world of personal knowledge, to such an extent that the views and perceptions of World 1, the world of real things, held by human agents, are changed. Since the real world is itself unknowable without these views and perceptions which are held by human beings, and thus the very foundations of our knowledge are without certainty, we are confronted with a situation in which generalizations are advanced, but their existence has been generated from the social theories held by research workers.

It is clear that Popper and Eccles (1977) are concerned with these same issues, approaching these problems from the perspective of the natural scientist. However, the problems are of greater magnitude in the social sciences because, as recent developments in social theory have proposed, human beings act as social agents. Furthermore, universal schooling and widespread higher education have, during recent decades, greatly facilitated the dissemination of advances in social theory through paperback publication, journal articles, and the mass media. As a consequence the rate of change of social and educational processes has been significantly increased.

An example drawn from the field of education is informative of how such processes work. In the years following the Second World War, initially in the United States, scales of socioeconomic status (SES) were developed and it was soon shown convincingly that there was a clearly identifiable relationship between the SES level of the home and achievement of children at school. Research of this kind was repeated in the United Kingdom and the general relationship confirmed. Soon this relationship was found to have a generality that was sustained in most developed countries, although variations were detected in some less developed countries. It was clear that where large random samples of students were drawn from age populations in which all children in an age group were still at school, this general relationship was observed. It was argued that children from homes of low socioeconomic status were educationally deprived and compensatory programmes to overcome educational disadvantage were needed. However, when the recipients of such programmes learnt of the purposes of these compensatory programmes and the emergent theory concerned with cultural and social deprivation, they resented these perspectives and the labels which were attached. Consequently, the emphasis of the programmes was changed. There was concern for equity rather than equality, since the recipients of the programmes commonly did not wish to be equal, but rather to share more fully in the rewards of society on their own terms. While the general relationships recorded several decades ago remain, the social theory has changed and the nature and administration of such programmes have been modified in significant ways.

Keeves (1986) has reviewed these changes in programmes for educational disadvantage in Australia. There is no doubt that social theory has had a significant influence on the establishment of such programmes of social action. However, in the process of introducing these programmes the views of the recipients have changed both the nature of the programmes and the underlying social theory associated with these aspects of social reality. Similar accounts could be given of the changes that have occurred in the fields of equal opportunity according to sex, and multiculturalism in those societies where significant variation in ethnic mix occurs. These are fields where the world of educational inquiry interacts with that of sociology and social inquiry.

There are important reasons why it is not possible to point to a substantial number of universal generalizations which have been generated by educational and social science research. When, from a study of human action, new ideas and concepts emerge which explain a social process in a clearer way than members of society are themselves able to provide, these ideas are appropriated by those members of society and incorporated back into their social lives. Sometimes these ideas have the effect of changing social life, and sometimes the effect of changing the nature of the ideas and concepts of social theory. It is not the case that the initial views and generalizations associated with the educational and social processes were necessarily wrong, but rather that the ideas were so powerful that they changed both the social processes as well as perceptions of them. The original ideas were not trivial or of little consequence but, as a result of their formulation and dissemination by the social scientist, society itself was changed. However, the impact of new ideas and theories in the social sciences depends upon how human agents assimilate and accommodate to these new ideas and theories, and this view leads us to consider a changing approach to hermeneutic inquiry.

## 2.4 The Nature of the Double Hermeneutic

The hermeneutic approach to inquiry in education and the social sciences has long been established in continental Europe. It involves the study of meaning and comprises the theory and practice of interpretation and understanding in the different social contexts in which human beings live and work. It has developed from many different facets of scholarly inquiry in the social sciences, and its goal is that of understanding (*Verstehen*) in the study of human conduct within a social context. Moreover, this approach recognizes that in order to obtain meaning with respect to how and why humans act it is necessary for an investigator to enter into dialogue with the human agents. Furthermore, the changing view of language extends the range of hermeneutic inquiry to include the use of language in daily life at the tacit level as well as at the discursive level. Thus, inquiry may be concerned with the meaning of action for which language is a substitute. However, the changes that have occurred in social theory with respect to the nature of social action and the influence of ideas and social theory on personal knowledge require further changes in the hermeneutic approach to inquiry.

Giddens (1984) argues that a double hermeneutic is involved. There is not only the frame of meaning provided by individuals as they view the real world, or the interaction between World 2 and World 1 as shown in Fig. 1. There is also a second frame of meaning provided by the same individuals as they view the world of shared meaning and assimilate the ideas and concepts developed by social scientists. In Fig. 1 this would require an arrow from World 3 to World 2. Thus, an investigation of the meanings given by lay persons to both the events of the real world and the ideas and concepts of the social sciences is necessary. In the situation discussed earlier, where there was concern for equality of educational opportunity, the social scientists and educational research workers involved employed such phrases as "educationally disadvantaged" and "culturally deprived" as metalanguage terms to describe human agents in specific situations. However, those human agents saw the context in which they lived very differently. They did not regard themselves as deprived or disadvantaged, but rather lacking the power to obtain social justice. As a consequence they sought greater equity in their treatment by those in power, and greater empowerment and thus greater control over their own lives. The intersection of the two frames of meaning generated a change both in the ideas employed in relation to equality or equity in society as well as a change in praxis and the administration of the programmes. In the past, hermeneutic inquiry has explored the meaning of social reality from one direction only. There is, however, a double hermeneutic involved and the meaning must be examined from two different perspectives, since the ideas and concepts of the social sciences circulate back into the world in which they were developed and become part of the processes of observing and describing the world.

## 2.5 Summary

The four changes outlined above help to map out a new approach to social theory in which there are possibilities of a synthesis taking place across the many apparently conflicting alternative theoretical and methodological perspectives that have been advanced since the mid-1970s. In addition, it is evident that this emerging synthesis carries across the wide range of disciplines that comprise the field of the social sciences and the humanities. Because education has a key role in the processes of social reproduction, the four areas of change–namely, the nature of the human agent, the nature of language, the nature of social action, and the nature of the double hermeneutic–are all closely related to educational processes. Consequently, the domain of educational sociology and the activity of educational research assume within this new perspective an even more central position than they have previously held. Nonetheless, it must be acknowledged that the ideas and changes discussed in this article are presented from the perspective of sociology and social theory. No consideration has so far been given to human learning and the processes by which it occurs. It is clear that the contribution of learning to social reproduction cannot be overlooked, and that the viewpoint of psychology cannot be ignored. In the main, psychological research workers have adopted a positivist perspective. Whether this perspective can be maintained in view of the changes to social theory is uncertain. The changes described above with respect to the nature of the human agent provide human beings with greater autonomy than has commonly been granted to them by existing psychological theories.

Giddens (1984) has developed a "theory of structuration" that incorporates and extends some of the ideas presented in this article, in which he has attempted to overcome many of the unwanted and unwarranted dualisms that have arisen between earlier social theories. Giddens accepts the Parsonian view that the problem of order in the social world is the central problem confronting social theory, but a strictly deterministic perspective is necessarily rejected in a conception which grants human agents greater autonomy. Thus, a stochastic perspective would appear to be required to permit causal relationships to be examined in situations where strict determinism must be abandoned. Since the late 1960s social science and educational research have advanced in directions that would permit such a perspective to be maintained not only in theory but also from the standpoint of systematic investigation. Whether or not Gidden's theory of structuration would permit the investigation of causal relationships from this perspective is not clear. However, it is evident that the forced dualism between the quantitative and qualitative approaches to inquiry is being rejected in the social sciences. This leaves the way clear for an alternative to be advanced that unifies the divergent approaches that exist in educational and social science research.

## 3. Towards the Future

If we accept the changes outlined above, then it is possible to consider where social science and educational inquiry might proceed in the future. If these changes are rejected in whole or in part we are forced back to the situation of conflict and confusion that has beset investigation in this area since the mid-1970s. The emergent synthesis that Giddens has advanced would seem to draw strength from its potential to resolve conflict and from its capacity to account for the unresolved issues that have confronted philosophers and social theorists during recent decades. Several signposts which point the way ahead for future research and inquiry can be advanced.

### 3.1 Nonrecursive Systems

Most of the causal models that have been employed to examine in probabilistic or stochastic terms the influence of individual and group variables on educational outcomes have been recursive models that have made no allowances for interactive effects. If human agents are influenced by forces in their environment and in turn interact with and change the environment, then a recursive model is inappropriate. Until recently it has been difficult to examine and estimate the parameters of nonrecursive models. However, it is now possible in particular circumstances to develop and test by a variety of analytical techniques causal models that include such interaction effects, provided an instrumental variable can be identified and the model is fully specified. The techniques that have been employed in educational research include indirect regression analysis (Hauser 1973, Larkin and Keeves 1984), or two-stage least squares regression analysis when included in partial least squares path analysis (Sellin 1986). The increased availability of appropriate computer programs is likely to lead to increased use of this type of analysis, and the possibility of investigating the magnitudes of relationships associated with reciprocal effects involving human agents must be welcomed.

### 3.2 Multilevel Analysis

The concept of a human agent acting within a specified context that involves both individual level as well as group level factors has been difficult to investigate. This has been a result of:

(a) the known effects of aggregation bias;

(b) the conceptual problems of disaggregation of data from the group level to the individual level;

(c) the ecological fallacy associated with analysis undertaken at the group level when inferences at the individual level are required; and

(d) the lack of meaning and instability of estimates of contextual effects in individual level analysis using an aggregated variable.

Recently in both social science and educational research, work has been undertaken to investigate strategies of multilevel analysis that would permit individual level effects to be disentangled from group level effects. The long-term prospects of this development are highly promising and the implications for the sociology of education where both sociological and psychological factors are being examined is considerable.

### 3.3 Inquiries into Metacognition

During recent years investigations have been conducted in the area of metacognition. A great deal more needs to be known about how the concepts and theories of the social sciences modify the personal knowledge of individuals and how such personal knowledge not only influences individual action but in turn changes social concepts and theory. This is now a potentially fruitful field of inquiry with consequences in the longer term for educational practice, particularly if allowance can be made for the autonomy of the individual when engaged in learning.

### 3.4 Studies of Social Action

Gidden's (1984) review of changes in theories of social action helps to account for the paradox as to why social science and educational research have appeared so unrewarding for those who have invested both time and resources in this enterprise. In order to provide support for Gidden's ideas, it would seem desirable that a series of case studies in different disciplinary areas should be undertaken to show how the theories developed in the different disciplines have had a substantial influence on the operation of modern society and the daily lives of human agents. The field of education and, in particular, the sociology of education is a potentially rich one for such investigation since the striking phenomena of the past 100 years have been the development of universal primary education, the moves towards a high level of participation in secondary education, the expansion of tertiary education, and the recent emergence of lifelong or recurrent education. These developments have their origins in changes in social theory. In turn, these developments have led to marked advances in social theory itself. Connell (1980) has documented this development, but the interpretation of this remarkable story in terms of Gidden's ideas remains.

## 4. Conclusion

The apparent failure of social science and educational research to produce universal generalizations should not be overemphasized. The application of the technique of meta-analysis is starting to bear fruit and the past few years have seen an assimilation of findings from disparate sources and the assembling of a substantial body of knowledge about educational processes in particular.

Nevertheless, Giddens has argued that the emergence of new ideas and relationships in the fields of the social sciences and education is commonly accompanied by the widespread acceptance of those ideas by human agents in society, and that the ideas are brought back into the praxis of everyday life and have the effect of changing society. Thus, contrary to common belief, the concepts of the social sciences have helped in a highly significant way to restructure society, and consequently to change the circumstances under which the general relationships were established. Thus generalizations which are reported in the fields of education and the social sciences must be considered to be less immutable and to lack the permanence of generalizations reported in the natural sciences. In the late 1980s, we live in a world which is undergoing great social change, much of which has resulted probably not from scientific research and the accompanying technological development, but from research in the social sciences and a greater understanding of the social and educational processes which have served to reshape the world they have sought both to interpret and explain.

### Bibliography

Connell W F 1980 *A History of Education in the Twentieth Century World*. Teachers College Press, New York

Feinberg W 1983 *Understanding Education. Toward a Reconstruction of Educational Inquiry*. Cambridge University Press, Cambridge

Giddens A 1984 *The Constitution of Society*. Polity Press, Cambridge and Blackwell, Oxford

Hauser R M 1973 *Sociological Background and Educational Performance*. American Sociological Association, Washington, DC

Jackson P W, Kieslar S B 1977 Fundamental research in education. *Educ. Res.* 6(8): 13–18

Kaplan A 1964 *The Conduct of Inquiry*. Chandler, San Francisco, California

Keeves J P 1986 *Equitable Opportunities in Australian Education*. Victorian Government Printer, Melbourne

Larkin A I, Keeves J P 1984 *The Class Size Question: A Study at Different Levels of Analysis*. Australian Council for Educational Research (ACER), Hawthorn, Victoria

Popper K R, Eccles J C 1977 *The Self and Its Brain*. Routledge and Kegan Paul, London

Quine W V O, Ullian J S 1970 *The Web of Belief*. Random House, New York

Sellin N 1986 Partial least squares analysis. *Int. J. Educ. Res.* 10(2): 189–200

Willis P 1977 *Learning to Labour*. Saxon House, Farnborough

# Educational Research and Policy Making

## T. Husén

Educational research has two constituencies of practitioners: (a) teachers and school administrators, and (b) policy makers in education. Classroom practitioners expect educational research to help them improve the planning and execution of teaching. At the turn of the century the emerging psychology with its empirical and experimental methods was expected to provide guidelines for educational practice by identifying the facts and laws of learning, and by providing an understanding of individual development, and individual differences. In his *Talks to Teachers on Psychology* (1899) William James underlined that education being an art and not a science could not deduce schemes and methods of teaching for direct classroom application out of psychology. "An intermediary inventive mind must make the application, by using its originality." In order to bridge the gap between theory and practice, James tried over and over again to make his presentation of psychology less technical. In the preface to his book which appeared several years after the lectures were given for the first time he says:

> I have found by experience that what my hearers seem least to relish is analytical technicality, and what they most care for is concrete practical application. So I have gradually weeded out the former, and left the latter reduced; and now, that I have at least written out the lectures, they contain a minimum of what is deemed 'scientific' psychology and are practical and popular in the extreme.

In general, there is a similar relationship between research and practice in policy making. For a long time this relationship was, by both partners involved, conceived of in a rather simplistic way. Policy makers wanted research that primarily addressed their pressing problems within the framework of their perceptions of the world of education. They wanted findings that could be more or less directly applied to issues and problems under their consideration. Researchers conceived of their role as expert problem solvers who advised policy makers what to do.

The problem of how research in education is related to policy making was hardly studied before the 1960s. However, after this date, resources given to educational research grew markedly. Governments and private foundations within a period of a decade massively increased the funds for research in education, most of which was conducted by behavioral scientists. Hopes grew correspondingly high about what research might achieve in broadening the knowledge base for educational practice. Research was expected to provide recipes for the successful solution to classroom problems. Policy makers expected educational research to help them in the planning and execution of reforms that would improve the quality of a nation's schools. Typically, the enormous increase of funds for educational research under the provisions of the Elementary and Secondary Education Act passed by the United States Congress in 1965 was part of a big package of legislation on compensatory education being in its turn part of the Great Society program (Husén 1979).

In the 1960s the research and development (R & D) model which had been developed in science and technology was extended to the fields of education and social welfare. The model assumes a linear relationship between fundamental research, applied research, development of a prototype, its mass production, and dissemination in the field. The high hopes easily led to

frustrations. Researchers began to be accused of coming up with "findings" which were "useless" to practitioners, be they school teachers or administrators, in schools or governments. There was a growing demand for "relevance."

The simplistic model of "linear" or "direct" application does not work in education for two main reasons. In the first place, education is like other areas in the social realm imbued with values. Educational research deals with a reality which is perceived differently depending upon ideological convictions and values held by both practitioner and researcher. The way a problem is conceptualized, how it is empirically studied and analyzed, and how the findings from studies are interpreted often depends very much on tacit or overt value assumptions. One typical example is research on bilingual education, the extent to which a minority child in a country with a main language should have an opportunity to be instructed in his or her mother tongue. Secondly, and often overlooked, are the widely different conditions under which researchers and policy makers operate. Studies of these conditions began in the 1970s.

The value problem in educational research has begun to be analyzed by educational philosophers. It is highlighted by the controversy between logical positivism or neopositivism which has dominated the social science scene since the 1940s and critical philosophies of various brands. The former takes the social reality educational research deals with as a fact and takes for granted that research can advance "objectively" valid statements about that reality. The role of the researcher vis-à-vis the policy maker is that of a technician: he or she provides the instrument or the expertise that policy makers and practitioners "use" in framing and implementing their plans and policies. The latter type of philosophy sees critical studies as a means of changing society and thereby more or less explicitly allows value premises to enter into the research process.

In the following, the different conditions under which policy makers and researchers operate will be analyzed and the differences in ethos which guide endeavors in the respective categories will be described. After that, various research utilization models will be dealt with.

## 1. The Setting for Policy Making

Tensions between researchers and policy makers depend on certain constraints under which policy is shaped and implemented. Some of these have been discussed by Levin (1978).

Policy makers are primarily or even exclusively interested in research that addresses problems which are on their agenda. This means that what researchers conceive as fundamental research which bears no or only a very remote relationship to the issues of the day is of little or no interest, if change in political regime or administration can mean a rearrangement of issues. For instance, the issues of private schools, educational vouchers, and busing have taken on quite a different importance under the Reagan than under the Carter administration in the United States. In Europe after the Second World War the central issue in many countries was to what extent the structure of the mandatory school should be comprehensive with regard to intake of students and programs. In countries like Sweden, England and Wales, and the Federal Republic of Germany many studies pertaining to the pedagogical and social aspects of comprehensiveness have been conducted and have been referred to extensively in the policy debate. In England the 1944 Education Act with its provisions for tripartite, secondary education in grammar, technical, and modern schools, and the selection for grammar school (the so-called 11+ examination) became an issue of the first order and gave rise to a large body of research on methods of selection and their effects. The issue of equality of educational opportunity has been a major one in Europe and the United States since the 1950s and recently in many developing countries as well. It has consequently inspired a large volume of research (Husén 1975).

Politicians have party allegiances which influence not only what they regard as relevant, innocuous, or even dangerous research but also their willingness to take research findings into account. Research, even if it addresses itself to a major issue on the political agenda, can be discarded or even rejected by one side in a political controversy if it does not support its views. Politicians, in the same way as court advocates, tend to select the evidence which they interpret as supporting their views.

Policy makers have their particular time horizon which in a parliamentary democracy tends to be rather narrow and determined not only by regular general elections but also by the flow of policy decisions. Research which takes years to complete cannot be considered if the policy maker's timetable requires the outcomes of a research project or program to be available "here and now." Research findings have to be made available in time for the decisions that by necessity have to be taken, irrespective of the nature of the "knowledge base" on which the decision maker stands. He or she needs immediate access to findings. This is a dilemma which planners and policy makers in a government agency continuously have to face. On the one hand, strategic planning with a relatively broad time perspective goes on. On the other hand, operational decision making is a continuous process which cannot wait for specially commissioned research to produce "relevant facts" of a rather simple, straightforward nature. This had led many administrators involved in policy making to demand that research should be strictly decision or policy oriented and address problems "in the field" only.

Policy makers are concerned only with policies in a particular area of their own experience as politicians or administrators. They therefore tend to disregard the connections with other areas. Educational policies have been advanced in order to solve what basically are problems in the larger social context. For example, in the United States in the mid-1960s compensatory education programs with enormous federal funds were made available to local schools. The intention was to "break the poverty cycle" by providing better education and thereby enhancing the employability of the economically disadvantaged (Husén 1979).

Policy makers are in most cases not familiar with educational research or social science research in general. In particular, they are not familiar with the language researchers use in communicating with each other, a language that ideally serves precision in presenting theories and methods, but by laypersons is often perceived as empty jargon. The problem then is to disseminate research findings in such a way that they can be understood by "ordinary people."

## 2. The Setting for Research

Researchers operate under conditions that in several respects differ from those under which people of practical affairs in politics and administration operate. There are differences of background, social values, and institutional settings.

Researchers in education have traditionally been performing their tasks at teacher-training institutions, most frequently at universities. As a result of growing government involvement, research units have more recently been established by public agencies as instruments of planning and evaluation. Researchers conduct their work according to paradigms to which they have become socialized during their graduate studies. They are in the first place anxious to preserve their autonomy as researchers from interferences by politicians or administrators. Secondly, their allegiance is more to fundamental or conclusion-oriented research than to applied or decision-oriented research. Thirdly, and as a consequence of this orientation, they pay much more attention to how their research is received by their peers in the national or international community of scholars in their field of specialization than by their customers in public agencies. This means among other things that once a technical report has been submitted, the researcher tends to lose interest in what happens to his or her findings.

Researchers are much less constrained than policy makers with regard to what problems they can tackle, what kind of critical language they can employ, and, not least, how much time they can use in completing a study. An investigation by the Dutch Foundation for Educational Research (Kallen et al. 1982) found that the great majority of projects financed by the Foundation lagged behind the timetable agreed upon for their completion. In order to conduct an empirical field study properly several years are required. The relevant literature on the "state of the art" has to be reviewed, methods have to be developed, data have to be collected in the field, data have to be processed and analyzed, sufficient time has to be allowed for writing the report, and finally, it takes some time for critical reviews in scholarly journals to appear. This is a process which typically takes about four to six years. Thus, the researcher has a different time horizon to that of the policy maker, both in terms of how much time he or she can allow for a study but also in terms of how his or her study fits into the ongoing research in the field. He or she perceives the study as an often humble contribution to an increasingly growing body of knowledge in a particular problem area.

Status in the research system depends upon the reputation that crystallizes from the continuously ongoing review of a researcher's work by colleagues inside or outside his or her own institution. Whereas in an administrative agency status depends on seniority and position in the organizational hierarchy, it is in the long run the quality of a person's research and the recognition of this that determines the reputation in the scholarly community to which the researcher relates himself or herself.

## 3. Disjunctions between Researchers and Policy Makers

The differences in settings and in value orientation between policy makers and educational researchers constitute what could be referred to as different kinds of ethos. It is even possible to speak of "two cultures." The research customers, the politicians, and/or the administrators/planners in a public agency, are by necessity pragmatists. They regard research almost entirely as an instrument for achieving a certain policy or for use in planning or implementing certain administrative goals. They want research to be focused on priority areas of current politics.

University-based researchers are brought up in the tradition of "imperial, authoritative, and independent" Research with a capital R. In order to discharge properly what they regard as their task, academics tend to take an independent and critical attitude, not least toward government. They tend to guard anxiously their academic autonomy.

These differences in value orientation and outlook tend to influence the relationship between the policy maker and the researcher all the way from the initiation of a research project to the interpretation of its findings. The "researchworthiness" of a proposed study is assessed differently. The policy maker looks at its relevance for the issues on the agenda, whereas the researcher in the first place tends to assess it on the basis of "research-immanent" criteria, to what extent the proposed research can contribute to fundamental knowledge. The researcher wants to initiate studies without any particular considerations to the applicability of the findings and with the purpose of extending the frontiers of fundamental knowledge.

The fact that education by necessity deals with values anchored in various ideologies easily brings educational research into the turmoil of political controversy. Most regimes and administrations in power tend to perceive social science research with suspicion because of its critical nature. Those who want to preserve the status quo often tend to regard research as subversive radicalism. It is, however, in the nature of research to be in a literal sense "radical," that is to say, to go to the root (Latin *radix*).

The close relationship between education and certain political and social philosophies has made it tempting for social scientists to become ideological evangelists. This has had an adverse effect on their credibility. The common denominator of what is understood by "academic ethos" is critical inquiry that does not spare partisan doctrines, not even the ones of the party to which the researcher belongs.

In the 1960s, social science and behavioral research on an unprecedented scale began to be supported by the government in countries such as the United States, Sweden, the United Kingdom, and the Federal Republic of Germany. Social scientists began to have a strong appeal and provided the arguments liberal politicians needed in favor of programs in education and social welfare. The liberals had a strong confidence in what social science could achieve. This meant that economists, sociologists, and psychologists were commissioned to conduct research that was part of the implementation of various programs in education (Aaron 1978). At the same time there was a quest for evaluation of these programs and increasingly a component of evaluation was included in planning them.

Soon discrepancies between expectations and actual research performances began to be aired and led to demands for accountability. There have since the early 1970s been indications of a decreasing credibility on the part of policy makers vis-à-vis researchers. Expert testimonies on major policy issues have been seen as inconclusive and inconsistent. James Coleman's 1966 survey of equality of educational opportunity was interpreted to support desegregation in the public schools of the United States (Coleman 1966). His subsequent studies of busing were interpreted as providing counter-evidence. Policy makers want, as President Truman once expressed it in talking about his economic advisors, "one-handed" advice and are not happy with "on the one hand—on the other hand." Furthermore, the credibility gap has been widened by allegations of ideologically imbued professional advice. In some countries social scientists working in education have been accused of "Leftist leanings" and subversive intentions. Political preferences among social scientists have even led to the establishment of research institutions with different political orientations, such as Brookings Institution and the American Enterprise Institute in the United States.

There are some inherent difficulties for educational research to prove its usefulness. The committee which at the end of the 1970s evaluated the National Institute of Education pointed out that improvements in the learning and the behavior of students as a result of research endeavors are difficult to demonstrate. The committee gave three main reasons for this: (a) a low level of sophistication in the social sciences in comparison with the physical sciences does not allow it "the luxury of predictable results"; (b) problems of bringing about and measuring changes in human learning and behavior are "vastly more complex" than those in the field of technological change; (c) the need for improvement in education is so great that expectations on educational R & D have been set much higher than is possible to achieve.

The crucial problem behind many of the frustrations felt by customers of educational research is that research cannot provide answers to the value questions with which social issues, including those in education, are imbued. This means that research even of the highest quality and "relevance" can only provide partial information that has to be integrated with experience and human judgment. The Australian Minister of Education (Shellard 1979) quoted Gene Glass as saying that there is more knowledge stored in the nervous systems of 10 excellent teachers about how to manage classroom learning than what an average teacher could distill from all existing educational research journals.

Implied in what has been said so far are three major reasons for a "disjunction" between policy making and research.

Research does not "fit" a particular situation. It might not at a given point in time be related to any political issue. Women's equal rights were for a long time a dead issue. But when they became an issue, they rapidly began to spur an enormous amount of research. But research addressing itself to issues on the agenda might come up with evidence that is out of phase with the policy-making process. As pointed out above, policy makers, like advocates, want to use research in order to support or legitimize a "prefabricated position." Often the situation occurs whereby research findings are in contradiction with or at least do not support the policy that a decision-making body or an agency wants to take or has already taken.

Research findings are from the policy maker's point of view not particularly conclusive. Furthermore, it is in the nature of the research process that in order to make a public issue "researchable" the overall problem has to be broken down into parts that more readily lend themselves to focused investigations.

A third major reason for the disjunctions between researchers and policy makers is ineffective dissemination. Research findings do not by themselves reach decision makers and practitioners. Researchers seek recognition in the first place among their peers. They place high premium on reports that can enhance their academic reputation and tend to look with skepticism upon popularization. It has been suggested that this problem can be dealt with by middlepersons who can serve in the role of "research brokers" or policy analysts and can communicate to practitioners what appears to be relevant to them. A particular type of research broker is the one who conducts meta-analyses of research, that is to say, reviews critically the existing research in a particular field in order to come up with relatively valid conclusions from the entire body of research.

## 4. Models of Research Utilization

The way research, in particular social science research, is "utilized" in educational policy making, in general has been studied in the first place by political scientists. Important contributions to the conceptualization have been made by Weiss (1979, 1980) and to the empirical study of the problem by both her and Caplan (1976).

In the first place, Weiss points out that "decisions" on policies or policy actions are not taken in the orderly and rational way that many think, namely that individuals authorized to decide sit down and ponder various options, consider relevant facts, and choose one of the options. Policies are decided upon in a much more diffuse way. What occurs is a complicated dynamic interaction between various interest groups, where by means of arguments advanced by them, administrative considerations, and, not least, the inertia in the system, guidelines for action begin to emerge. The best way to characterize this process is to talk about "decision accretion."

Not least researchers have been caught in rational and "knowledge-driven" models of how research findings relate to policy making. Research findings rather "percolate" through public opinion to policy makers. Instead of the latter taking into consideration particular studies, they tend to be influenced by the total body of research in a particular field. Findings usually do not reach those in positions of influence via scientific and technical reports but to a large extent via the popular press and other mass media. A body of notions that forms a *commune bonum* of "what research has to say" is built up via diverse channels of popularization. Theoretical conceptions and specific findings are "trickling" or "percolating" down and begin to influence enlightened public opinion and, in the last run, public policy.

Weiss (1979) distinguishes between seven different "models" or concepts of research utilization in the social sciences. The first model is the research and development (R & D) model which has dominated the picture of how research in the physical sciences is utilized. It is a "linear" process from basic research via applied research and development to application of new technology. There was a time in the 1960s and early 1970s when the R & D model was expected to apply in education by the development of programmed instruction and material for individualized teaching. Weiss points out that its applicability in the social sciences is heavily limited, since knowledge in this field does not readily lend itself to "conversion into replicable technologies, either material or social."

The second model is the problem-solving one, where results from a particular research project are expected to be used directly in a pending decision-making situation.

The process can schematically be described as follows: identification of missing knowledge → acquisition of research information either by conducting a specific study or by reviewing the existing body of research → interpretation of research findings in the context given policy options → decision about policy to pursue.

This is the classical "philosopher-king" conception. Researchers are supposed to provide the knowledge and wisdom from which policy makers can derive guidelines for action. Researchers, not least in Continental Europe, for a long time liked to think of themselves as the ones who communicated to policy makers what "research has to say" about various issues. The problem-solving model often tacitly assumes consensus about goals. But social scientists often do not agree among themselves about the goals of certain actions, nor are they in agreement with the policy makers.

The third model is the interactive model which assumes "a disorderly set of interconnections and back-and-forthness" and an ongoing dialogue between researchers and policy makers.

The fourth model is the political one. Research findings are used as ammunition to defend a standpoint. An issue, after having been debated for quite some time in a controversial climate, leads to entrenched positions that will not be changed by new evidence. A frequent case is that policy makers in power have already made their decision before they commission research that will legitimize the policy for which they have opted.

The fifth model is the tactical one, whereby a controversial problem is "buried" in research as a defense against taking a decision at the present moment.

The sixth model is the "enlightenment" one, which according to Weiss is the one through which "social science research most frequently enters the policy arena." Research tends to influence policy in a much more subtle way than is suggested by the word "utilization," which implies more or less direct use according to the first model. In the enlightenment model research "permeates" the policy process, not by specific projects but by its "generalizations and orientations percolating through informed publics and coming to shape the way in which people think about social issues." Furthermore, without reference to any specific piece of evidence, research can sensitize policy makers to new issues, help to redefine old ones, and turn "nonproblems into policy problems." Empirical evidence appears to support this model. In a study where she was interviewing 155 policy makers in Washington, DC, Weiss found that 57 percent of them felt that they "used" research but only 7 percent could point to a specific project or study that had had an influence.

The seventh model in Weiss's taxonomy, finally, is referred to as "research-as-part-of-the-intellectual-enterprise-of-society" (research-oriented) model. Social science research together with other intellectual inputs, such as philosophy, history, journalism, and so on, contribute to widening the horizon for the debate on certain issues and to reformulating the problems.

## 5. Overcoming Disjunctions

The conclusion from analyses and studies of the relationships between research and educational policy making is that the former has an influence in the long run but not usually in the short term following specific projects at specific points in time. The impact of research is exercised by the total body of information and the conceptualization of issues that research produces. It does not yield "products" in the same way as research in the physical sciences. In spite of misgivings about research as "useless" to practitioners and allegations that it contributes little or nothing to policies and practice, research in the social sciences tends to "creep" into policy deliberations. The "linear" R & D model of research utilization derived from science and technology does not apply in the field of social sciences relevant to educational issues. Nor does the problem-solving model which presupposes either value-free issues or consensus about the values implied.

Research "percolates" into the policy-making process and the notion that research can contribute is integrated into the overall perspective that policy makers apply on a particular issue. Research contributes to the enlightenment of those who prepare decisions which usually are not "taken" at a given point in time but are rather accretions (Husén and Kogan 1984).

## Bibliography

Aaron J H 1978 *Politics and the Professors: The Great Society in Perspective.* Brookings Institution, Washington, DC

Caplan N 1976 Social research and national policy: What gets used by whom, for what purposes, and with what effects? *Int. Soc. Sci. J.* 28: 187–94

Coleman J S et al. 1966 *Equality of Educational Opportunity.* United States Department of Health, Education and Welfare, Washington, DC

Cronbach L J, Suppes P (eds.) 1969 *Research for Tomorrow's Schools: Disciplined Inquiry for Education: Report.* Macmillan, New York

Dutch Foundation for Educational Research 1978 *Programming Educational Research: A Framework for the Programming of Research Within the Context of the Objectives of the Foundation for Educational Research in the Netherlands.* Stichting voor Onderzoek van het Onderwijs (SVO), Dutch Foundation for Educational Research, Staatsuitgeverij, 's-Gravenhage

Her Majesty's Stationery Office (HMSO) 1971 *The Organisation and Management of Government R and D* (The Rothschild Report). Her Majesty's Stationery Office, London

Husén T 1968 Educational research and the state. In: Wall W D, Husén T (eds.) 1968 *Educational Research and Policymaking.* National Foundation for Educational Research, Slough

Husén T 1975 *Social Influences on Educational Attainment: Research Perspectives on Educational Equality.* Organisation for Economic Co-operation and Development (OECD), Paris

Husén T 1979 Evaluating compensatory education. *Proceedings of the National Academy of Education,* Vol. 6. National Academy of Education, Washington, DC

Husén T, Boalt G 1968 *Educational Research and Educational Change: The Case of Sweden*. Almqvist and Wiksell, Stockholm

Husén T, Kogan M (eds.) 1984 *Educational Research and Policy: How Do They Relate?* Pergamon, Oxford

James W 1899 *Talks to Teachers on Psychology: And to Students on Some of the Life's Ideals*. Longmans, Green, London

Kallen D, Kosse G B, Wagenar H C (eds.) 1982 *Social Science Research and Public Policy Making: A Re-appraisal*. National Foundation for Educational Research–Nelson, London

Kogan M (ed.) 1974 *The Politics of Education: Edward Boyle and Anthony Crosland in Conversation with Maurice Kogan*. Penguin, Harmondsworth

Kogan M, Korman N, Henkel M 1980 *Government's Commissioning of Research: A Case Study*. Department of Government, Brunel University, Uxbridge

Levin H M 1978 Why isn't educational research more useful? *Prospects* 8(2): 157–66

Lindblom C E, Cohen D K 1979 *Usable Knowledge: Social Science and Social Problem Solving*. Yale University Press, New Haven, Connecticut

Rein M 1980 Methodology for the study of the interplay between social science and social policy. *Int. Soc. Sci. J.* 32: 361–68

Rule J B 1978 *Insight and Social Betterment: A Preface to Applied School Science*. Oxford University Press, London

Shellard J S (ed.) 1979 *Educational Research for Policy Making in Australia*. Australian Council for Educational Research, Hawthorn, Victoria

Suppes P (ed.) 1978 *Impact of Research on Education: Some Case Studies: Summaries*. National Academy of Education, Washington, DC

United States Office of Education 1969 *Educational Research and Development in the United States*. United States Government Printing Office, Washington, DC

Weiss C H 1979 The many meanings of research utilization. *Public Admin. Rev.* Sept.–Oct.

Weiss C H 1980 Knowledge creep and decision accretion. *Knowledge: Creation, Diffusion, Utilization* 1: 381–404

# Legitimatory Research

**J. P. Keeves**

The rapidly growing interest in policy-oriented research has led to the need to distinguish between those programmes of research that are associated with the generation of change, and those that serve to maintain and consolidate existing situations. Educational organizations hold considerable power over the lives of the individuals within them, and it is not surprising that in education there should be a strong reciprocal relationship between power and knowledge. Power on the one hand controls the use and flow of knowledge. On the other hand knowledge is used to support existing arrangements for the exercising of power. Legitimatory research is that type of research which is undertaken to strengthen and maintain existing power structures in educational systems as well as the policies and practices operating within those systems. The term "legitimatory" is used because the research is conducted with the express purpose of legitimating existing arrangements for the exercising of power from the perspectives of the institution supporting the research and controlling the release of the findings.

## 1. Policy-oriented Research

Investigations in the field of education are increasingly being planned with a strong policy orientation. The purpose of such research is to provide information for decision making with respect to educational policy and practice. Administrators and politicians recognize the usefulness of evidence to which they can add their own value judgments before embarking on a course of action that involves the development and implementation of new policy. When research into an educational problem is designed, conducted, and reported with the specific aim of providing information for the making of policy, or for monitoring the implementation of policy, or for examining the effects of existing policy, then the term "policy-oriented research" is used. Research of this type in the field of education is becoming more common as politicians and administrators seek and achieve greater control over the allocation of the funds available for research and evaluation studies. Consequently it is not surprising that Weiss (1979), in a classification of ways in which social science research might be utilized, has identified a political approach and a tactical approach that are related to the legitimatory research discussed in this article. Husén (1984), however, argues that Weiss's seven models may be merged into only two major ones, and that the political and tactical approaches are best combined. It is this combined model that we would refer to as a legitimatory approach to research utilization. In addition, Suchman (1970) has listed the possible misuses of evaluation, which correspond to a legitimatory approach to evaluative research. The growing incidence of such research has led to this more detailed examination of its nature and purpose.

There are types of policy-oriented research in education that have been developed with the particular purpose of introducing change. They combine investigation, educational development and, in general, the promotion of social change. Two important types of research in this area are known as "action research" and "participatory research". In participatory research, for example, the researcher with specialized knowledge and training commonly joins people in the workplace, and together they undertake an investigation which seeks primarily to improve education and, through education, to improve the lives of those people involved.

It is clear that people undertaking this type of policy-oriented research are not neutral in the value judgments which they bring to the conduct of an investigation. Thus, in participatory research in particular, there is a commitment to the processes of change in order to benefit and sometimes emancipate those engaged in the investigation.

It is possible for research to be carried out with the specific purpose of preventing change or obtaining evidence to support an existing institution or to maintain an existing policy. The systematic collection of educational statistics on the numbers of schools of different kinds; the numbers of enrolled students, teachers, and ancillary staff; as well as the average numbers of students in daily attendance; can be seen as a simple example of this type of legitimatory research. Commonly, although this information is collected and tabulated, it is generally published in part and not in a form that would permit the evidence being used against the educational organizations involved. The data are held and used in situations and in ways that would support the organization and would not permit the organization to be challenged.

This type of research that is frequently neither conspicuous nor publicized is commonly undertaken within large educational bureaucracies that have not only the necessary resources to support such research, but also the responsibility to maintain an educational system. Since, in general, such investigations are carried out to legitimate existing policies and practices, the term "legitimatory research" is appropriate. The findings from research conducted within this perspective are commonly not released as a scholarly publication. They remain as "in house" reports that are summarized in a few pages for administrators and policy makers to read.

An example arising from the compilation of educational statistics may contribute to an understanding of how this type of research activity operates. If the information on the average numbers of students by age in daily attendance in some educational systems were examined by critics, they would probably note a very high level of absenteeism at age levels near the end of compulsory schooling. Since it is generally not in the interests of schools and school systems that disruptive students should be present in classrooms, it is considered preferable that this information should not be released, even though it is relevant in a significant way to educational and social problems related to juvenile delinquency. In addition, such absenteeism might be perceived to be a consequence of inadequate teaching or of irrelevant curricula.

In some countries, this type of research has very limited visibility, although it is relatively widespread and obtains regular funding, at the expense of more impartial and scholarly work. Within most large educational organizations, such as universities, local educational authorities, national and state offices of education and indeed within teacher unions, there are research units that seek to maintain existing policies and support established institutions. The research conducted within these units is often of a legitimatory nature. A very wide variety of investigatory activity is involved. It may range from the examination of pass rates and studies of prediction of success in universities, to the monitoring of standards of educational achievement in state and national systems, or studies of teacher stress by teacher unions. The findings from such investigations are only released and widely publicized when it is of value politically to use the information available to sustain existing policies and practices.

Giddens has discussed certain aspects of the dissemination of research findings. He suggests that an investigation can be undertaken from perspectives where:

> . . . the new knowledge or information is used to sustain existing circumstances. This may, of course, happen even where the theories or findings concerned could, if utilized in certain ways, modify what they describe. The selective appropriation of social science material by the powerful, for example, can turn that material to ends quite other than those that might be served if they were widely disseminated. (Giddens 1984 p. 342)

This article discusses the characteristics of research carried out within this perspective. It is also concerned with the nature of the process of legitimation. In addition, it considers an example of legitimatory research, and examines the functions of research in the legitimatory process.

## 2. Power and Knowledge

Legitimation is a social process. Power and authority are not, in general, assigned or transmitted at a single point in time to an educational organization, or an individual within an organization, but are acquired gradually over time. Power and authority can never be taken for granted. They are constantly being challenged and exposed to competing claims. Consequently, legitimation becomes a continuously operating process. Without legitimation, power and authority are insecure and impermanent.

The concept of legitimation owes much to the writings of Weber, who was concerned with belief in a legitimate order:

> Action, especially social action which involves social relationships, may be oriented by the actors to a *belief* (*Vorstellung*) in the existence of a "legitimate order". The probability that action will actually empirically be so oriented will be called the "validity" (*Geltung*) of the order in question. (Henderson and Parsons 1947 p. 124)

In addition, the writings of Habermas (1975) have sounded a warning about the legitimacy crisis faced by public administration. This work has supported an attack on established views of institutional governance, particularly in the field of education.

The link between these ideas and the development and use of knowledge was made by Berger and Luckmann (1967 p. 110). They saw legitimation as a "second-order" process that operated on the "first order" ideas and relationships concerning society and social institutions in such a way as to develop new meanings that would make this knowledge "objectively available and subjectively plausible". In this sense it validates institutionalized knowledge and an institutional order. Thus it is possible to speak not only of the legitimation of a social institution but also of the legitimation of knowledge through the production of new knowledge.

Research is concerned with organized and systematic activities which are designed to produce knowledge. Consequently legitimatory research involves the compilation of new knowledge that will strengthen a social institution and will validate institutionalized knowledge. In the field of education, research can contribute in a significant way to the legitimation of social institutions and to the support of educational organizations and their policies, programmes, and practices. However, educational research is a pursuit that is itself in need of validation, and the support for research provided by educational organizations serves to legitimate research as an activity. Thus educational institutions both validate and are validated by educational research. The dependence of research on educational organizations for financial and operational support, as well as the contribution of research towards maintaining the educational organizations pose certain problems for educational research. Consequently, research that is undertaken at the request of, and with financial support from, an educational organization in order to support the continuance and to maintain the operation of that organization as well as its existing policies and practices, can appropriately be referred to as "legitimatory research".

## 3. Characteristics of Legitimatory Research

Relatively few studies have been carried out to examine the processes and characteristics of legitimatory research. Although it has had a long-standing presence in many educational organizations, it has only been with the emergence of the field of policy-oriented research that its nature and function have become clear. Some characteristics of legitimatory research and the processes through which such research is conducted are considered below.

The characteristics of legitimatory research are as follows:

(a) The *problem* to be investigated arises from existing policies and practices within an educational organization. This, of course, is not unique to legitimatory research.

(b) The major *aim* of the research is to maintain the existing structure of an educational organization, and the continuance of its existing policies and practices.

(c) Legitimatory research is generally *conducted* by people with competence in research who are employed by the educational organization, so that the organization maintains control over the entire investigation.

(d) In general, the focus of the research is on the *operation* of the organization, on the activities of the people within it, or on the characteristics of those who seek entry into the organization.

(e) Central to the operation of legitimatory research is its role in providing information in a concise form for the senior educational administrators in order to *consolidate their position of power* within an organization.

(f) The release of the findings of the research is, in general, *controlled* by a senior administrator to occur at a time to optimize the impact that the findings might have on the legitimation of a particular policy or practice.

(g) It is rare for the findings of legitimatory research to be *published* in a form that would enable both the methods of investigation and the inferences drawn from the research to be examined critically and challenged. The reports are commonly only circulated in summary form on the grounds that the likely readers are interested only in the main conclusions of the investigation, and would not be interested in examining the available evidence in any detail.

(h) Where the investigation is undertaken by research workers who are outside the day-to-day operation of the organization, a *steering committee* is commonly set up to exercise control over the conduct of the investigation.

(i) If the research workers are external to the organization, problems may arise over the publication of the reports of a study. Lynn and Jay (1982 pp. 97–99) draw a distinction between the *suppression of a research report* and the making of a decision not to publish it. In addition, they list the steps that can be taken to discredit research reports and so prevent their publication.

(j) Frequently, legitimatory research is conducted under the guise of an *evaluation study*, since the need for evaluation is widely acknowledged on the grounds of accountability, yet what is being sought is information to sustain a programme or policy in its existing form.

To illustrate these characteristics of legitimatory research an example is provided below.

## 4. A Study of Staffing and Resources: An Example

In this example, where an independent research organization was commissioned to work with eight educational organizations, some of the problems that can arise in a legitimatory research study were encountered.

The major expenditure in Australian schooling, as

with other countries, is on the salaries of teachers, which commonly comprise between 75 and 80 percent of the total budget allocated to the provision of education in schools. Since education in Australia is a responsibility of the states and not of the commonwealth or federal government, the proportion of the total state budgets allocated to education in schools is high, generally of the order of 30 percent. Overall, a little under 6 percent of gross domestic product (GDP) is spent on education in Australia. Clearly the total expenditure on the salaries of the teaching service is a matter of considerable significance.

Following a long period of militancy by the teacher unions in Australia during the late 1960s and early 1970s directed towards decreasing class sizes, funds were made available for marked reductions in student–teacher ratios and thus class sizes. As could be anticipated, this was accompanied by a very substantial increase in the costs of education that had to be provided at the expense of other activities conducted by the state governments. The ministers of education within New Zealand and each of the Australian state and commonwealth governments, together with their advisers, who are the senior administrators in their educational bureaucracies, meet regularly as members of the Australian Education Council to develop common policies for the conduct of education in their regions. The ministers of education and, to a lesser extent, the directors-general of education recognized that if they were to pursue policies for the broad general development of their regions as well as for the general growth of education, it would be necessary to contain the pressure from the teacher unions for further reductions in class sizes. Thus they were placed in a position of seeking to maintain current policies and practices, and the existing structures of their organizations, without becoming committed to policy changes that would involve a further reduction in student–teacher ratios and class sizes.

As a first step, a review of previous research into class size was commissioned (Lafleur et al. 1974). This review found that little research work had been carried out in Australia, and there were inconclusive findings with regard to the effects of class size on achievement and attitude. However, it should be noted that in Australia the First International Mathematics Study conducted by the International Association for the Evaluation of Educational Achievement (IEA) in 1964, and the First IEA Science Study in 1970 had found relationships which indicated that, at the 13- and 14-year-old levels respectively, the larger the classes the higher the average levels of achievement of the students. These relationships remained significant even after other relevant factors on which data were collected had been taken into account. Although it was difficult to account for these findings, they left much to be explained with regard to the sustained demand for further reductions in class sizes.

In 1978, the results of the meta-analysis by Glass and Smith (1978) into the relationships between class size and achievement were published. The findings from this study had received widespread publicity and were hailed with acclaim by the teacher unions. More recently, the criticisms of the work of Glass and Smith that have been made by Slavin (1984a, 1984b) have thrown doubt on the findings of a meaningful relationship between class size and achievement. However, for a period of several years the work of Glass and Smith was accepted as authoritative throughout Australia and New Zealand and gradual reductions in class size took place.

The Australian Education Council, at its meeting in early 1978, expressed interest in the complex questions associated with student–teacher ratios and class sizes and commissioned a study into these problems which would be undertaken in collaboration with the staff of the research branches of the education departments in each of the regions. This study became known as the "Staffing and Resources Study". The initial reports of the work of Glass and Smith had a significant impact on the planning of this study. It was argued by some that further investigations of a non-experimental kind to examine relationships between class size and achievement were of doubtful value. Nevertheless, it was considered that if a study of teaching behaviour could be undertaken which would examine relationships between such behaviours and class size it would be relevant. However, the main thrust of the study would be to examine policies and practices at the level of school systems and schools.

The ministers of education sought a study that would examine the costs of education and, in particular, relationships involving the contribution of reductions in class size to the costs and to the benefits, if any, in terms of achievement outcomes and students' and teachers' attitudes. Immediately after work on this study into a highly sensitive area was authorized, pressures were mounted to distort the study and its design so that only peripheral issues would be investigated. Thus the ministers and some of the senior administrators sought a study which would legitimate existing policies. However, the forces for change in Australian education, such as the teacher unions, and some staff at the middle and lower management levels in the bureaucracies sought to modify the plans for the study so that it would generate change. The research workers who were members of an independent educational research organization and who had accepted responsibility for the conduct of the study, were not fully aware at the time the study was commissioned of the tensions that were likely to develop in the study. These tensions were a result of the conflict between the forces of conservatism that sought a legitimatory research study, and innovative educational practitioners who sought to alter the design of the investigation and the conduct of research in ways that focused on the need for change and the directions in which change should proceed.

The legitimatory nature of this study which was carried out at the request of the ministers of education, who were responsible for eight educational systems, led to sustained attacks on the study from both inside and outside these eight systems. While the senior administrators within the eight systems were willing for a detailed examination of policies and practices to be carried out within each system by their own staff, some were unwilling for this information to be made available to the other systems or to external investigators who would be comparing and contrasting the operations of the eight systems. Moreover, in one system a teacher union prevented the undertaking of a survey of schools in that system.

In due course carefully written reports were prepared and published. The reports covered the following areas: (a) a review of policies in the eight systems (McKenzie and Keeves 1982), (b) a survey of practices in 600 schools (Ainley 1982), (c) a report on critical issues associated with practices in 15 schools that were innovative in their organizational structures (Sturman 1982), (d) a study of relationships between class size, teacher and student behaviour and educational outcomes of achievement and attitudes (Larkin and Keeves 1984), and (e) an executive summary report of the first three volumes listed above (Ainley et al. 1982). In reviewing the study several years after its completion, it was found that some changes flowed from the study. However, the changes introduced were towards an increase in the efficiency of each system rather than educational reform. By and large, the reports of the study were made to serve the purpose of reducing the rate of change in the eight systems.

Several implications may be drawn from this study for the conduct of legitimatory research into a major policy area.

(a) If the issues being investigated are in conflict with the *policies of the teacher unions*, moves are made to block the conduct of a study.

(b) If the issues examined by the study challenge aspects of the *operation of the bureaucracies*, then ways are found to distort the conduct of the study.

(c) Legitimatory research is susceptible to interference from administrators and others who wish to *control the investigation*.

(d) The *findings of legitimatory research* will only be used by senior administrators and politicians at times and in ways that will achieve their previously determined purposes.

(e) Major research studies frequently take *several years* to bring to a satisfactory conclusion. During that time both the political and administrative officials who proposed the study may have been replaced and new officials may see issues from very different political perspectives.

(f) Legitimatory research exists because politicians and senior administrators need *evidence to support and legitimate* their policies and the educational organizations in which they work. The findings from such research are used only if they can be directed towards these ends.

## 5. Conclusion

It is common for legitimatory research to lead only to a summary report which does not permit an adequate examination of the conduct of the investigation on which the findings are based. As a consequence, although research of a legitimatory nature is relatively widespread within educational bureaucracies, little has been written about this type of research. More detailed analyses of its characteristics and its influence are urgently needed.

## Bibliography

Ainley J G 1982 *Six Hundred Schools: A Study of Resources in Australian and New Zealand Government Schools.* Australian Council for Educational Research (ACER), Hawthorn, Victoria

Ainley J G, Keeves J P, McKenzie P A, Sturman A 1982 *Resource Allocation in the Government Schools of Australia and New Zealand.* Australian Council for Educational Research (ACER), Hawthorn, Victoria

Berger P L, Luckmann T 1967 *The Social Construction of Reality.* Penguin, London

Giddens A 1984 *The Constitution of Society.* Polity Press, Cambridge and Blackwell, Oxford

Glass G V, Smith M L 1978 *Meta-Analysis of Research on the Relationship of Class Size and Achievement.* Far West Laboratory for Educational Research and Development, San Francisco, California

Habermas J 1975 *Legitimation Crises.* Beacon Press, Boston, Massachusetts

Henderson A M, Parsons T 1947 *Max Weber: The Theory of Social and Economic Organization.* Free Press, New York and Oxford University Press, Oxford

Husén T 1984 Issues and their background. In: Husén T, Kogan M (eds.) 1984 *Educational Research and Policy: How Do They Relate?* Pergamon, Oxford, pp. 14–20

Lafleur C D, Sumner R J, Witton E 1974 *Class Size Survey.* Australian Government Publishing Service, Canberra

Larkin A I, Keeves J P 1984 *The Class Size Question: A Study at Different Levels of Analysis.* Australian Council for Educational Research (ACER), Hawthorn, Victoria

Lynn J, Jay A 1982 *Yes Minister. The Diaries of a Cabinet Minister by the Rt. Hon. James Hacker MP.* Vol. 2. British Broadcasting Corporation, London

McKenzie P A, Keeves J P 1982 *Eight Education Systems: Resource Allocation Policies in the Government School System of Australia and New Zealand.* Australian Council for Educational Research (ACER), Hawthorn, Victoria

Slavin R E 1984a Meta-analyses in education: How has it been used? *Educ. Res. AERA* 13 (8): 6–15

Slavin R E 1984b a rejoinder to Carlberg et al. *Educ. Res. AERA* 13 (8): 24–27

Sturman A 1982 *Patterns of School Organization: Resources and Responses in Sixteen Schools*, Australian Council for Education Research (ACER), Hawthorn, Victoria

Suchman E A 1970 Action for what? A critique of evaluative research. In: O'Toole R (ed.) 1970 *The Organization, Management and Tactics of Social Research.* Schenkman, Cambridge, Massachusetts

Weiss C 1979 The many meanings of research utilization. *Public Admin. Rev.* 39: 426–31

# Policy-oriented Research

## J. D. Nisbet

Policy-oriented research is best defined in terms of its instrumental function rather than by the topics of study. When research in education is designed, managed, and reported with the specific purpose of informing policy decisions or assisting or monitoring their implementation, the term "policy-oriented" is used to distinguish this approach from "fundamental" research which is primarily designed to extend the frontiers of knowledge. This definition of policy-oriented research may be extended to include evaluation. It may also be applied to research which is closely tied to educational practice as well as policy.

In this approach, educational issues which are of current concern are accepted as priority topics for research. The function of this research is to provide an information base for decision making; administrators, politicians, or teachers then add the necessary value judgments, supposedly so that policy and practice are firmly based on empirical evidence from experiment and survey. The implicit model in this perception of the relation of research to policy is that the task of research is to establish the "facts", which are then used to inform judgment. This instrumental view of the function of research, however, is limited, and it makes naive and simplistic assumptions about how policy and practice are determined. If adopted uncritically, the emphasis on relevance constrains inquiry within the limits of existing policy and risks a trivialization of research. But with a clearer understanding of the function of research and with enlightened administration of research funding, the present trend towards policy-oriented studies could enable research to make a more effective contribution to educational practice.

## 1. Definitions

The definition of policy-oriented research is usually expressed by contrasting it with fundamental research. A variety of terms can be used to express the contrast: applied versus basic or pure research, policy-oriented versus curiosity-oriented studies, work directed towards decision or action versus work directed towards knowledge or theory. Less charitably, "relevant" research may be contrasted with "academic" research. Whichever terms are used, they carry value judgments which can be misleading if they are not made explicit. The distinction between pure and applied research in education is itself misleading. "From one point of view, *all* educational research is applied research, designed to bring about changes in the way education is carried on, rather than simply to add to our existing stock of knowledge" (Taylor 1973). Defined narrowly, policy-oriented research is research which has direct application to current issues in educational policy or practice.

A wider definition (and, to anticipate the argument of this analysis, a better one) is that policy-oriented research consists of careful, systematic attempts to understand the educational process, and through understanding to improve its efficiency. However, as this definition could apply to all forms of educational research, its main virtue is that it blurs these misleading distinctions among various kinds of research.

Listing the processes involved (see Sect. 3) is one way of defining. Policy-oriented research includes survey work or any comparable data gathering which enables policy makers or practitioners to base their decisions on evidence rather than prejudice or guesswork. Thus policy-oriented studies include the search for solutions to pressing educational or social problems, identifying and resolving the problems involved in implementing policy decisions, monitoring and evaluating initiatives in educational practice, and experimental studies to compare alternative educational methods. They also include policy studies and retrospective analyses of past policy, the purpose of which is to help make better policy decisions in the future.

Thus, the essential distinction between policy-oriented and other forms of educational research is in terms of purpose, rather than in choice of subject or method. Since the perception of educational issues as being of current concern is subject to volatile, popular fashions, an aspect of children's learning may be regarded as a theoretical issue this year but a topic for policy-oriented research next year. The end products of policy-oriented research are decisions or recommendations for action. The products of fundamental research are contributions to knowledge, understanding, or theory. Since decisions and action necessarily imply the adoption of some theory or interpretation, and theory likewise has long-term implications for action, the distinction between the two categories is not as sharp as is sometimes assumed. Though policy-oriented research usually operates within the context of accepted theory, and does not aim to modify theory, it may do so incidentally. Similarly, fundamental research does not aim to affect practice, but it may do so indirectly. Policy-oriented research is responsive, whereas fundamental research is autonomous.

Autonomous educational research, which does not have to be accountable in the sense of producing useful or usable findings, runs the risk of pursuing topics which are of interest only to other researchers. In its extreme, it is concerned with attacking other people's theories or findings, irrespective of whether the points at issue are of any importance outside the research sphere. Responsive research, designed as a response to a practical need, is no less likely to raise and illuminate fundamental issues, and there is the added bonus that it can be useful at the same time. It runs the risk of being left behind by the rapid course of events, since by the time results are available the problem which they were designed to answer is liable to have changed, or to be no longer seen as important.

Since responsive research operates within the context of existing policy or practice, it is limited in its generalizability, but it is more likely to have an impact on the specific policy or practice for which it is designed. The impact of this kind of research, however, is incremental rather than radical. It is for reasons such as this that those who provide funds for research projects in education are likely to favour, or even to demand, a policy orientation. Policy-oriented research modifies (and hopefully improves) the existing situation, protecting it from running into trouble by identifying or anticipating problems. It may, however, challenge established policy by demonstrating its impracticability, and may even develop or explore alternative policies. But it is essentially concerned with movement from a present situation, and therefore it obliges researchers to relate their work to "reality", usually in the form of empirical studies or field work.

## 2. Trends

Although pressure towards policy-related work has become more extreme since the early 1970s, many of the early educational research studies had a strong practical orientation. Binet's work, for example, which laid the foundations of psychometry, began with the problem of early identification of slow-learning children. The work of Thorndike and others in the 1920s on the psychology of the elementary-school curriculum aimed to influence educational policy and classroom practice. The "scientific movement" in educational research envisaged the creation of a science of education based on experimentation, which could then be used to improve decision making at all levels, from the day-to-day practice of the teacher in the classroom to the long-term planning of educational provision, resources, and training. Large-scale national studies such as the Eight-year Study in the 1930s (to test the feasibility of accreditation of schools) and the international programme of research on examinations also in this period, were directed to produce practical recommendations for improvement of the system. But the distinction between practical and theoretical research was not stressed at this time. The two kinds of inquiry were seen as complementary, and since there was practically no direct public finance involved, the conduct of research was left wholly to the academic researchers whose salaries were paid by universities and colleges. Even the national councils for educational research founded in this period (in Scotland, Australia, and New Zealand in the 1930s and England later) prided themselves on producing results useful to teachers as well as works of scholarship.

The growth of research in the years after 1950 can be divided into four phases: 1955–65, the beginning of publicly financed research on a substantial scale; 1965–70, a period of massive expansion; 1970–75, the growth of accountability; and from 1975, a trend towards central control of research.

The first phase was initiated by awareness that educational research could make a significant contribution to policy and practice. The social sciences had come of age and their potential value was recognized. (Perhaps it was merely that administrators found themselves at a disadvantage in controversies if they could not produce empirical evidence to support their decisions or express their policies in the context of social science concepts which were becoming more widely accepted.) In Sweden, the linking of research to policy began in the late 1940s. In the early 1960s, in the United States and the United Kingdom (and subsequently in many other countries), formal institutional structures were created for channelling public funds into educational research and development, particularly for curriculum development and for intervention programmes. As a result, between 1964 and 1969, expenditure on research in education in the United Kingdom multiplied tenfold; in the United States, expenditure doubled in each year from 1964 through 1967. The increase in funding soon led to a demand for accountability, and for a greater say in how the funds were to be spent. In 1970 in the United Kingdom, politicians demanded that research policy in education "had to move from a basis of patronage—the rather passive support of ideas which were essentially other people's related to problems which were often of other people's choosing—to a basis of commission . . . the active initiation by the Department [of Education] on problems of its own choosing, within a procedure and timetable which were relevant to its needs".

Perhaps too much had been expected, or promised, and disillusionment was allied with suspicion of "academic drift", in which preoccupations with theories were being given priority over pressing practical issues. In the United Kingdom this trend was most evident, expressed in the crude customer–contractor principle of the 1971 Rothschild Report: "The customer says what he wants; the contractor (the researcher) does it if he can; and the customer pays." This method of deciding how research should be funded was widely challenged at the time. A policy statement by the United Kingdom Social Science Research Council argued: "It is not so much a matter of an ordered hierarchy of priorities, as a process of grasping at opportunities presented by an almost accidental coagulation of interest among a group of able research workers around a chosen problem in order to shift a frontier of knowledge forward." But the idea of "an almost accidental coagulation", however accurate as a description of the research process, could not survive the energy crisis of 1973 and the economic constraints of the years which followed. The need to cut back expenditure made decisions on priorities inevitable, and increasingly these decisions were made by central government. Now research which is not linked to policy is at risk of being seen as a dispensable luxury, and researchers have to be ready to tackle major policy issues as legitimate topics for inquiry, and sometimes even as the only topics worth studying.

Thus, to quote from a review of developments in eight countries,

> Across the world, educational research is now an integral part of modern administrative procedure. Increased investment in research has led to . . . a concern that the conduct, organisation, and funding of research should be directed towards maximising its effect on policy and practice. The major questions to which answers are still sought are, What forms of research should have priority? and, Who is to decide? (Nisbet 1981).

## 3. Utilization

The analysis of policy has become an academic study of growing importance in recent years. Weiss (1977), reviewing the contribution of social research to public policy, allots to research only a limited influence in decision making: its more important effect is indirect and long-term through "a gradual accumulation of research results", shaping the context within which these decisions are made. Thus research is only one of many inputs to policy making, one contribution to a complicated process in which there are many other competing forces. The policy maker seeks to establish a policy which is acceptable to those with power to influence its implementation. Their concern is not so much a matter of being "right" (for there are different "right" solutions, depending on one's values) but rather of reconciling divergent views in a solution which is seen as "fair" by a maximum number of those affected by it. It is therefore impossible to describe a policy as correct, except in relative terms as correct for some stated aims or values. Since the aims and values of all those with some access to power are bound to be in conflict, it is not possible to find policies which are correct for everyone.

In this amorphous process of policy making, there are several functions which research can perform. First, insofar as information conveys power, research strengthens the hand of any group which can produce research findings to support its preferred viewpoint. (Even to describe assertions as "research" strengthens their impact, until the speaker is challenged for "evidence": the scientific model is implicit throughout this interaction.) Administrators commission policy-oriented research to strengthen their hand against the many pressure groups in the policy-making arena. In the view of the administrators, pressure groups are those who seek to further their own policies, whereas administrators see themselves as neutral to the policy they implement. Information thus weakens the power of those who play on ignorance or twist facts to suit their private ends. This however assumes that research is value free, or at least that research makes explicit the values on which it is based.

A second function for research is to ensure that action will achieve what is intended by a policy. For this purpose, research is used to work out the details of how to implement decisions, by identifying obstacles, including the opinions and attitudes of those who are likely to oppose implementation of a policy, and perhaps testing out solutions to overcome these obstacles in trials with pilot groups. There are other functions which Weiss (1977) also identifies: for example, the use of research to legitimate policies which have already been decided, or to procrastinate by offering research as an alternative to action, and similar improper uses against which the researcher should guard.

The underlying assumptions in this view of policy-oriented research are considered in the next section. Accepting for the moment this view of research, a range of types of research can be listed which fall within the scope of policy-oriented studies.

(a) *Surveys to gather relevant "facts" as a database for decision.* In the United Kingdom, for example, every major educational report since the 1950s has been accompanied by a research programme: the 1960 Crowther Report and the 1963 Newsom Report on secondary education, the 1963 Robbins Report on higher education, the 1967 Plowden Report on primary education, the 1976 Warnock Report on handicapped children, and so on. The American practice has been to commission an expert or team of experts to produce independent reports which are made available for public debate and which help to create a favourable climate for decision.

(b) *Experimental studies to resolve controversies.* For example, are open-plan schools better than traditional buildings? Is class size related to educational achievement? Since issues like these cannot readily be resolved by laboratory experiments, they usually involve surveys of existing practice, and therefore overlap with (a), but they are more narrowly focused and specify the hypotheses they are designed to test.

(c) *Development studies for implementing policies.* The introduction of an innovation accepted as desirable, such as a new examination procedure or computer-assisted learning, requires pilot studies to establish feasibility and identify likely obstacles to success.

(d) *Evaluation studies.* Whereas (c) is a monitoring of institutions to provide guidance for future decisions, the traditional use of evaluation is a retrospective review of past decisions: Did it work? How could it have been improved? The distinction between (c) and (d) however, is not clear, since formative evaluation falls more readily into category (c).

In all four types, the most valuable research design is one which focuses on analysis of problems, rather than simply seeking to supply answers to questions. There are of course some who still hold the unrealistic expectation that research should provide ready-made incontrovertible solutions. In 1976, for example, the Secretary of the English Department of Education and Science complained: "It is exceptional to find a piece of research that really hits the nail on the head and tells you pretty clearly what is wrong or what should be done." Weiss (1977) describes this as the "linear model" of research utilization and criticizes its "instrumental naivete". The sequence is: "A problem exists; information or understanding is lacking; research provides the missing knowledge; a solution is reached." There are relatively few situations in which this model can be applied. The essential feature of policy-oriented research is that it is designed to contribute towards a solution either by producing recommendations for action, describing as fully as possible the complexity of implications and complications, or by establishing conceptual frameworks which enable decisions to be made with fuller insight and understanding.

The belief that educational decisions can be guided by the results of scientific inquiry carries with it the corollary that the value of research can be judged by evidence of its impact, or at least by evidence that it has clear implications for action. Good research on this interpretation is research which influences (or can influence) policy or practice. Is there evidence that education is any better as a result of research? There has been no shortage of sceptics, even in the 1950s. In 1955, for example, Lamke wrote that if research over the past three years in medicine, agriculture, physics, or chemistry were wiped out, our lives would be changed materially; "but if research on teacher personnel over the same three years were to vanish, educators and education would continue much as usual" (Nisbet and Broadfoot 1980 p. 14). If research, after all its vast expenditures, has not resulted in visible improvement in the educational system, then either the system is at fault (or the teachers are to blame) for being unable to make use of the findings, or the money is being spent wrongly and the research itself is faulty. (There is, of course, another explanation, that this view of how research affects the system is over-simple.) Sometimes there has been the suspicion that the only ones who have derived benefit from the investment in educational research and development are the researchers themselves. Being isolated from the practical realities of the "outside world", as it was termed, they diverted public money to academic interests of their own instead of to the problems which required solutions. The solution adopted was to take the decisions on research priorities out of the hands of the researchers and put them in the hands of the administrators. Since research could not give direction to policy, then the influence should be reversed and policy makers should be given control of research, allowing policy priorities to determine the choice and design of research. If those who are in contact with the "real world" take over the management of research, so the assumption goes, impact will be improved, relevance will be greater, and the risk of wasted money will be avoided.

Consequently, decisions on research priorities are now often made by those who are not themselves directly involved in research. This mode of working is familiar to the economist, the engineer, and the agricultural specialist but less common in legal and medical matters. The administrator who controls research funds now expects to be involved in the initial decisions on the topic of inquiry, the time scale, the personnel required, the design, and of course the cost. When the project is funded, there will be continuing interest (or interference, as it may appear) in monitoring what is being done through an advisory committee (sometimes a steering committee) and regular reporting. Tighter control may sometimes be imposed by "stepped funding" in which funds for each stage are conditional on approval of a report on the previous one (an impossible procedure to operate without year-long delays between the stages). The mode of reporting and arrangements for publishing and discussing the findings may also be specified in the contract (though the more common complaint is that research sponsors fail to set aside money, time, or staff for diffusion). The contract may require surrender of copyright to the sponsors and acceptance of their right to veto should they find the results not to their liking.

It is difficult to stand against these pressures. Not only can sponsors withhold funds: even the access to schools is usually made conditional on approval of the research project as a whole and the research instruments in detail. Thus policy-oriented research can become wholly directed and censored by people who are not themselves researchers and who have a vested interest in the outcomes. The researcher is put in the position of servant to the policy maker. Clearly, the dangers here are that criticism of a policy is not likely to be encouraged; that important issues are organized out of debate; and that researchers, obliged to undertake studies which they do not see as most urgent, most interesting, or most promising, will work less intensively and move on when they can to other less restrictive fields of study. Fortunately, many of those responsible for the funding of research projects are aware of these dangers. The picture above of the research slave is a caricature, though each element in it has been experienced by those who undertake commissioned research. In most countries, as yet, the relationship between researchers and the providers of funds for research is quite close, both sides understanding the requirements and constraints of the other (as will be shown in the concluding Sect. 5).

## 4. Analysis

The contrast between policy-oriented and fundamental research in education derives partly from the field of science. The long-standing debate over the relative value of pure and applied science mirrors many of the arguments discussed here. Pressure for more applied studies in educational research reflects the positivist belief that, in education as in science, there are solutions to problems, existing somewhere or other but hidden at present because the information or the techniques or the resources to discover them are lacking. Though seldom explicitly stated, the positivist assumption appears in policies for research funding and in the disillusionment if results are disappointing.

This kind of assumption underlies the early history of educational research when there was no public funding. Educational research had its origins, as pointed out above, in the "scientific movement" in education which was in its hey-day during the first 40 years of this century. By research, a science of education would be established, an organized body of empirical evidence from which would be derived theories and principles refined and tested by experiment. From such a science, it would be possible to derive answers to problems, or at least to develop methods to discover answers. The scientific movement treated education as unproblematic. It assumed that the state of "being an educated person" was not a matter for discussion, that there were "best methods" of teaching and learning, and that these methods could be identified by experiment. What is the optimum time to be devoted to spelling? At what age should a foreign language be taught? Which typeface is most legible? Some of these questions have straight answers; others do not. The position is tenable in areas where "the processes and outcomes of inquiry are independent of their social and historical context" (Becher and Kogan 1980 p. 93). There are issues of this kind in education, and not all of them are merely concerned with miniscule detail. Where there is consensus on values, where decisions on aims are relatively non-controversial, the researcher's task is "to pursue generalisations about the most effective means of achieving desired goals" (Broadfoot and Nisbet 1981 p. 116). It is here that research is most readily policy oriented and has its most evident impact.

> In topics where there is a general consensus on values, research findings seem to be particularly effective: they are readily incorporated into policy or action. But when basic assumptions are challenged, then research . . . is treated merely as one more pressure group with vested interests. (Broadfoot and Nisbet 1981 p. 117)

In contrast, there are topics

> . . . in which there can be no possibility of maintaining that the processes and outcomes can be separated from, or evaluated outside, their social and historical context. Here . . . knowledge depends on the development of a refined judgment rather than on incontrovertible demonstration. (Becher and Kogan 1980 p. 93)

This is the relativist end of the continuum.

> A positivist perspective makes two assumptions. First, that there is a fixed and unchanging reality based on constant relationships which is amenable to scientifically modelled, objective research. Second, that the formulation of the research question itself is part of an objective process. The relativist rejection of this position . . . emphasises the problematic nature of education itself. (Broadfoot 1979 p. 127).

The distinction may be illustrated using an applied science like engineering. The design and improvement of pyramids, canals, engines, or central heating raise issues which can be decided by scientific inquiry. The decisions, however, are not always infallible when the context changes, and what is needed is a new insight rather than an incremental modification. Berlyne (Dockrell and Hamilton 1980 p. 8) illustrates the point by relating the response of an imaginary advisory committee in 1810, just before the beginning of the railway age, asked to forecast the development of the transport system. "One thing", the committee concluded, "has stood the test of time over several thousand years: the horse has come to stay. Authorities as diverse as Genghis Khan, Dick Turpin, Julius Caesar, and Buffalo Bill, all agree on one thing from long experience, that there is no better way of getting from one place to another than on a horse."

This illustrates the weakness of the criterion of "relevance". Relevance in educational research is liable to mean finding results which are capable of being implemented within the existing system. Hence, if the direction of research is assigned to those whose interest (in both senses of the word) is in the existing system, there is a risk that they may choose only those new ideas or findings which leave their prejudices undisturbed, resulting in innovation without change. This was what Rousseau had in mind in 1762 when he wrote: "People are always telling me to make practical suggestions. You might as well tell me to suggest improvements which can be incorporated with the wrong methods at present in use."

The pressure towards "relevance" may thus operate in a reactionary way. This has led some radical reformers to reject all "contamination" from working within the system, even opposing attempts to ameliorate present conditions, because this is to patch over the cracks, to bolster a system which should be brought to collapse. No administrator can adopt such a standpoint. Administration is committed to incrementalism: if not to piecemeal change, at least to that degree of reform which is demonstrably achievable. Consequently, it is argued, researchers must be given guidance or direction from those who face directly the problem of the "real" world, to avoid the risk of producing work which cannot be exploited.

Difficulties involved in policy-oriented research can be categorized under three types of explanation, adapted from Caplan et al.'s (1975) explanations of the nonutilization of research in policy formation.

The "knowledge-specific" explanation attributes the difficulty of relating research to policy to the kind of information which is provided by research because of its methodology. This is too narrow and limited to be of direct value to policy makers. Research tackles problems by focusing on selected aspects, eliminating other factors in order to achieve generalizable conclusions. Policy has to make decisions in a given context.

The "two-communities" explanation contrasts the different worlds of the researcher and the policy maker. These two worlds have different and even conflicting values, different reward systems, and even different languages.

The "policy-maker constraint" explanation emphasizes the pressures for immediate and acceptable decisions in the formulation of policy. Information for decision making is usually required sooner than research can provide it. Consequently, attempts are made to predict future relevance. Since the framework within which such predictions are made is the current position, itself the product of historical factors, these lists of priority topics are liable to come up with yesterday's problems, especially if they are compiled on the advice of senior members of the education profession. They are almost certain to be out-of-date by the time that research can be mounted to deal with them. Policy makers also have to ensure that their decisions are acceptable, and so they must take account of factors outside the traditional realm of research, including political feasibility. Research findings may appear to be unrealistically impractical. The point can be illustrated by the story of the traveller who asked a local the way to a neighbouring village. "Well, if I were you", was the reply, "I wouldn't start from here." This is how the policy maker often sees the advice of the researcher.

Policy-oriented research tends to rely on a rational analysis model for solving social problems. This model assumes a sequence of stages: establish the facts, specify the objectives, define the problem, canvass a range of solutions, work out the implications of each solution, make a choice, communicate the decision, and plan its implementation. Cronbach et al. (1980 pp. 94–95) criticize this process of rational decision making applied to educational issues.

All the strings are in the hands of the decision maker . . . Rationalism is dangerously close to totalitarianism . . . Concentrating information and, therefore, power in the hands of control management is seen as the sovereign remedy at some moments in history, yet, at those very times, some observers of the system have warned that the "efficiency" so achieved is illusory. The larger the role of experts in governance, the more difficult it becomes for ordinary citizens to give direction to action. When information is closely held, what reaches the public is filtered so that it supports policies that the authorities favour. Insofar as information is a source of power, evaluations carried out to inform a policy maker have a disenfranchising effect. An open society becomes a closed society when only the officials know what is going on.

The closed circle of research restricted to questions which are relevant to currently accepted procedures may thus become an obstacle to radical reform. This argument can also be applied generally in the field of science. According to Kuhn (1970), a major part of scientific research is directed towards solving routine problems in which a dominant paradigm is applied, thus supporting or reinforcing established theories; and this proceeds until a scientific revolution overthrows

accepted beliefs, only to establish a new orthodoxy which then dominates the pattern of research. Thus research, which is commonly regarded as a force for change, may often operate as a restrictive or reactionary influence. In education, if research is confined to processes in the existing system or to problems as defined by current policy, it will result only in marginal change. Indeed,

. . . by reinforcing the importance of the framework of thought which identifies certain aspects as 'problems', legitimating their priority in the agenda of concern, it has a stabilising effect which discourages alternative perspectives. Challenging interpretations are seen as less relevant . . . are less likely to be funded, and less likely to be accepted by editors for publication, and if published, less likely to be read or quoted. (Broadfoot and Nisbet 1981 p. 119)

In a complementary way, the indirect, long-term influence of fundamental research is to create the theoretical context in which day-to-day issues are perceived, to write an agenda of concern. New concepts or structures or theories are introduced and gradually absorbed into popular thought and discussion, until they become a new climate of opinion, variously described as a "prevailing view" (Cronbach and Suppes 1969), "a cumulative altering of conceptions of human behaviour" (Getzels), "ideas in good currency" (Schön), "sensitizing" (Taylor), or "a gradual accumulation of research results which can lead to far-reaching changes in the way people and governments address their problems" (Weiss 1977). Administrators and politicians respond to the "resonance" of research findings. Often these research findings have been filtered, are out-of-date and highly popularized. As Keynes observed in the field of economics: "Practical men who believe themselves to be quite exempt from any intellectual influence, are usually the slaves of some defunct economist."

## 5. Implications

Thus two functions of research can be distinguished: one long-term, creating or changing the prevailing view; the other more immediate, working out the routine problems within the context of the current prevailing view. These are the basic and policy-oriented styles of research, but the distinction between them is not as sharp as has been suggested. The applied sciences have often contributed as much to pure science as they have received from it.

Academic status tends to be accorded to those who make contributions to pure science. They are the aristocrats of research, a small elite who provide the model to which many aspire. Why should a lesser status be given to the proletariat workers who are prepared to have their research skills used as an instrument of management and control, to identify stress points so that policy and practice may be trimmed accordingly? Research of this kind can be a powerful weapon of reform, testing out new ideas, modifying or rejecting them if they are at fault, and if the evidence shows them to be feasible, establishing their credibility all the more widely and quickly. This style of research attracts funds; it is difficult in a time of financial constraint and accountability to justify the expenditure of public funds on any other kind of research in education. Since failure is immediately evident, it can be used to remedy the past weaknesses of educational research and improve its techniques. The results are more likely to have impact and thus to create in the long-term a favourable climate of opinion as to the value of educational research.

The danger of this line of action is of accepting a purely technocratic role for research, creating an elite group of researchers in alliance with bureaucrats to manage the system. Though at first sight this is an attractive role for the researcher, it is potentially divisive, since it divides the researcher and his or her powerful partner from the teaching profession and the public. An alternative style of research is the "teachers as researchers" movement, or "action research". This is a school-based form of research, in which teachers are encouraged to apply the techniques of research to their own practical work. The teachers define the problems to be researched and they investigate and reflect on their own practice. This style of research also has its risks. It could merely aggravate the present situation, if teachers were to study only what is of immediate concern to them. It could then restrict research even further within the limits of inflexible classroom traditions and narrow professional perspectives. But it could also lead out of the constraints in which educational research is now caught.

> It may be that the very act of teachers addressing their own classroom problems from a research perspective will be the most fertile soil for educational research to grow in. Fundamental research can grow from modest questioning. Collaborative research can be developed in quite a different way, retaining its democratic devolvement of responsibility so as to prevent the emergence of an elite group of researchers in alliance with those responsible for management and control. If it can be developed so as to provide teachers (and administrators and parents and all those concerned with education) with the means of improving their own understanding, then its effect will be to put educational studies into a questioning framework. To do this, it must go beyond "routine problems", and be concerned instead with the parameters used for thinking about education, redefining issues, and restructuring perceptions. This is no small task, but one well worth attempting. (Broadfoot and Nisbet 1981 p. 121)

This interactionist model for educational research applies also to the relation of research to policy. The association of policy, administration, and research can be developed in such a way that each illuminates the others. Cronbach et al. (1980), quoting Elmore and Caplan, argue for an intermediate structure between research and application, "some institutional means of arguing about the policy relevance of ambiguous results". Cronbach suggests a "collegial group", rather like an advisory council. However, this bridging element could readily be created by a change in the relationships

of researchers to their various partners in the educational enterprise. The 1975 Annual Report of the Scottish Council for Research in Education (Simon and Taylor 1981 p. 171) describes a procedure of "negotiated research", in preference to a customer merely specifying his or her requirements on the Rothschild model. The negotiation of a research commission is developed out of an extended discussion of what is sought and what can be offered, in which (ideally) researchers and customers each accept the other's contribution to the proposal. This Cronbach describes as a "context of accommodation" rather than a "context of command" (1980 pp. 83–84); and with specific reference to evaluation, he argues for the research worker to "learn to serve in a context of accommodation and not dream idly of serving a Platonic guardian" (p. 100). A balance needs to be found between the autonomous and responsive modes of research in education.

If policy-oriented studies can be implemented in this enlightened way, educational research stands to gain from its closer association with both policy and practice. "Two worlds of educational research may be distinguished, the practical and the theoretical, pure and applied; but we are more likely to have a balanced attitude if we can have a foot in both worlds" (Simon and Taylor 1981 p. 175). The contributions of research to policy, to practice, and to theory are not easily reconciled, but the research enterprise in education would suffer if any one of these three is regarded as of lesser importance.

## Bibliography

Becher T, Kogan M 1980 *Process and Structure in Higher Education.* Heinemann, London

Broadfoot P M 1979 Educational research through the looking glass. *Scottish Educ. Rev.* 11: 133–42

Broadfoot P M, Nisbet J 1981 The impact of research on educational studies. *Br. J. Educ. Stud.* 29: 115–22

Caplan N S, Morrison A, Stambaugh R J 1975 *The Use of Social Science Knowledge in Policy Decisions at the National Level: A Report to Respondents.* University of Michigan, Ann Arbor, Michigan

Cronbach L J, Suppes P (eds.) 1969 *Research for Tomorrow's Schools: Disciplined Inquiry for Education.* Macmillan, New York

Cronbach L J et al. 1980 *Toward Reform of Program Evaluation.* Jossey-Bass, San Francisco, California

Dockrell W B, Hamilton D (eds.) 1980 *Rethinking Educational Research.* Hodder and Stoughton, London

Husén T, Boalt G 1968 *Educational Research and Educational Change: The Case of Sweden.* Wiley, New York

Husén T, Kogan M (eds.) 1984 *Educational Research and Policy: How Do They Relate?* Pergamon, Oxford

Kogan M 1974 *The Politics of Education.* Penguin, Harmondsworth

Kuhn T S 1970 *The Structure of Scientific Revolutions,* 2nd edn. Chicago University Press, Chicago, Illinois

Nisbet J D 1981 The impact of research on policy and practice in education. *Int. Rev. Educ.* 27: 101–04

Nisbet J D, Broadfoot P M 1980 *The Impact of Research on Policy and Practice in Education.* Aberdeen University Press, Aberdeen

Simon B, Taylor W (eds.) 1981 *Education in the Eighties: The Central Issues.* Batsford, London

Suppes P (ed.) 1978 *Impact of Research on Education: Some Case Studies.* National Academy of Education, Washington, DC

Taylor W (ed.) 1973 *Research Perspectives in Education.* Routledge and Kegan Paul, London

Weiss C H (ed.) 1977 *Using Social Research in Public Policy Making.* Heath, Lexington, Massachusetts

# Policy Analysis[1]

## M. Trow

Husén (1984) has argued that the relation of research to policy is far more complex, far more indirect than it formerly appeared. Drawing on the informed writings of Weiss (1979) and Kogan et al. (1980) among others, and from rich experience, he dismisses as irrelevant, at least to the field of education, two classical models of the application of research to policy that Weiss lists among seven different models of concepts of research utilization: the "linear" model, which leads neatly from basic knowledge to applied research to development to application, and the "problem-solving" model, in which research is done to fill in certain bodies of knowledge needed to make a decision among policy alternatives. These are dismissed on the grounds that they simply do not even roughly describe what happens in the real world. The remaining models are merged into two. One is an "enlightenment" or "percolation" model, in which research somehow (and just how is of greatest interest) influences policy indirectly, by entering into the consciousness of the actors and shaping the terms of their discussion about policy alternatives. The second, the "political model," refers to the intentional use of research by political decision makers to strengthen an argument, to justify positions already taken, or to avoid making or having to make unpopular decisions by burying the controversial problem in research.

Of these two models, the first or "percolation" model is the more interesting, since it is the way through which research actually has an influence on policy, rather than merely being used to justify or avoid making decisions. Moreover, the percolation model and its mechanisms and processes are so subtle that they challenge study and reflection.

## 1. Researchers and Policy Analysts

The decade since the mid-1970s has seen in the United States, and to some extent elsewhere, the emergence of a profession, that of the policy analyst, whose training, habits of mind, and conditions of work are expressly designed to narrow the gap between the researcher and the policy maker and to bring systematic knowledge to bear more directly, more quickly, and more relevantly on the issues of public policy. This article attempts to compare and contrast the researcher and the policy analyst to see how this breed of staff analyst/researcher, inside as well as outside government, may affect the ways in which research comes to bear on policy. The comparison is not intended to be invidious, that is, there is no implication that the invention of policy analysis has in any way solved the problems of the relation of research to policy that Husén, Weiss, and others have identified. But it may be of interest to see how this emerging profession affects that process, and how it generates new problems—intellectual, political, and moral—as it solves some of the old.

Policy analysis developed as a formal discipline in the mid-1970s through the coming together of a number of strands of work and thought in the social sciences. These included operations research developed during the Second World War on a strongly mathematical basis for improving the efficiency of military operations—the deployment of submarines, bombing raids, and convoy management. Added to this were new forms of microeconomics developed in the 1950s and 1960s; the long-standing tradition of work in public administration; the newer and increasingly strong strain of behaviorism in the political sciences; organizational theory; certain lines of applied sociology and social psychology; and the emerging interest in the role of law in public policy. Graduate schools of public policy were established in a number of leading American universities around 1970. Twelve leading universities now have genuine graduate schools of public policy; there are literally hundreds of others which offer programs which include some measure of policy analysis in their schools of management, public administration, or business administration. To the mix of social science and law, some schools have added scientists, engineers, and others interested in public policy problems. These graduate schools for the most part offer a 2-year postgraduate professional degree, ordinarily the Master of Public Policy. Their graduates go directly into public service at national, state, or local levels, or get jobs in think-

---

1 This is an edited version of the article, "Researchers, policy analysts, and policy intellectuals", by Martin Trow which was published in *Educational Research and Policy: How Do They Relate?* (1984) edited by T Husén and M Kogan. It appears here with permission from Pergamon Press plc © 1984.

tanks or private agencies concerned with public issues—for example, organizations concerned with the preservation of the environment, with education, overseas trade, and so forth. These latter "private" organizations, however, are directly involved for the most part in public policy—indeed, much of what they do is to try to influence public policy, so the conditions of work for public policy analysts in them resemble those of analysts who enter governmental service itself.

There are several aspects of the training of policy analysts that need to be emphasized. As must already be clear, the training of the policy analyst is intensely inter-disciplinary. This is required first because of the diverse nature of its intellectual antecedents; the field itself reflects the coming together of diverse currents in what Lasswell (Lerner and Lasswell 1951) called the "policy sciences". But more important, the training has to be interdisciplinary because that is the way the problems present themselves to decision makers. Real decisions, as we all know, do not respect the boundaries of the academic disciplines: they always have political, economic, and organizational components; they may well also have legal, educational, biological, or other technical implications as well.

Perhaps the most important distinguishing characteristic of policy analysts as contrasted with academic research social scientists is that they are trained, indeed required, to see and to formulate problems from the perspectives not of the academic disciplines, but of the decision makers. In their work, they accept the constraints and values of decision makers—the political pressures on them, the political feasibility of a proposal, its financial costs, the legal context within which it will operate, the difficulties of implementing it, of shaping organizations, and of recruiting, training, and motivating people to work in the service of its purposes. They are, if effectively trained, sensitive to the costs and benefits of programs, to the trade-offs in any decision, and to the alternative advantages of government and the market in achieving social purposes. In a word, they try to see problems from the perspective of the decision maker, but with a set of intellectual, analytical, and research tools that the politician or senior civil servant may not possess. They are, and are trained to be, the researchers in government at the elbow of the decision makers, or if not in government, then serving the "government in opposition" or some think-tank or interest group which hopes to staff the next administration or agency on the next swing of the political pendulum. Of course, not all policy analysts are "researchers," as the university conceives of research. But what they do, bringing ideas and information to bear on social "problems" in a search for "solutions," is the kind of "research" that has the most direct influence on public policy.

By contrast, the faculty members of schools of public policy are not, for the most part, like the students that they train; the former are almost without exception academics with PhDs, trained in and drawn from the social science disciplines, specialists originally who have a particular interest in public policy, and who do research on policy issues, but not on the whole like the research that their students will be doing in their government or quasi-government jobs. The faculty members of these schools are for the most part what Wilson (1981 p. 36) has called "policy intellectuals," while their students are policy analysts—the staff people and bureaucrats serving their policy-oriented clients in and out of governments. The relationship of the policy intellectual in the university to the policy analyst in government bears on the issue of "knowledge creep" and "research percolation" that Husen and Weiss speak of, and to which this article will return.

Let us look at some of the characteristics of "researchers" as Husén describes them, and at some of the "disjunctions" between research and policy that the nature of the researcher in the university gives rise to. The field of policy analysis and the new profession of policy analyst were, one might say, invented precisely to meet the need of policy makers for analysis and research carried out within the same constraints that the policy maker experiences. Policy analysis thus aims to narrow those "disjunctions" between research and policy of which Husén speaks. He describes three conditions under which researchers work that are different for policy analysts:

(a) Researchers are usually performing their tasks at . . . universities. . . . They tend to conduct their research according to the paradigms to which they have become socialized by their graduate studies. Their achievements are subjected to peer reviews which they regard as more important than assessments made by the customers in a public agency. (Husén 1984, p. 10)

Analysts, by contrast, work for the most part in government or in shadow governmental agencies, or in large private business organizations. The paradigms of research that they acquire in graduate school emphasize the importance of serving the client, of defining or clarifying the nature of the problem, or identifying the policy options available, of evaluating those alternatives in terms of their cost, probable effectiveness, political feasibility, ease of implementation, and the like—the same criteria which the decision maker would use in planning and choosing a course of action. The analyst is trained then to make recommendations among the action alternatives that have been identified, supporting the recommendations made with appropriate arguments and evidence.

Much, perhaps most, of what such analysts do is not published, is not reviewed by peers, and will almost certainly appear, if at all, in greatly modified form, either anonymously or under someone else's name. The analyst's reputation will be made *not* in an academic setting, but in his or her agency, and more importantly among the small but active community of analysts in government agencies, on legislative staffs, in think-tanks, and special interest organizations who know of the analyst's work and its quality. Incidentally, it is in that arena of discussion and assessment—the analyst's analog to the scholar's "invisible college"—that we need to look for the mechanisms of information "drift" and "creep," and for the processes of percolation through which research and evidence come to influence policy.

> (b) Researchers operate at a high level of training and specialization, which means that they tend to isolate a "slice" of a problem area that can be more readily handled than more complicated global problems. (Husén 1984 p. 10)

By contrast, analysts are trained to be as interdisciplinary as possible, to follow the requirements of a problem in their choice of ideas, theories, and research methods, rather than to allow the theories and methods of their discipline select and shape their problems. This is not wholly successful, in part because their teachers in these schools are not themselves equally familiar with the variety of research methods and perspectives across disciplinary lines, and because their students, the fledgling analysts, inevitably come to be more familiar and comfortable with some kinds of analysis rather than others. Nevertheless the requirement that they see problems as to the policy makers would were they analysts, requires analysts to transcend the constraints of a single discipline and to tackle problems as wholes rather than by "slices."

> (c) Researchers are much less constrained than policy makers in terms of what problems they can tackle, what kind of critical language they can employ and how much time they have . . . at their disposal to complete a study. (Husén 1984 p. 10)

Analysts, by contrast, ordinarily are assigned their studies, or do them within circumscribed policy areas. That does not wholly preclude their exercise of discretion; and indeed, they may exercise very important amounts of initiative in how they formulate their problems, and in the range of responses to the problems they consider (Meltsner 1976 pp. 81–114). From the researcher's perspective, the captive analyst is merely "a hired gun" doing what he or she is told by political or bureaucratic superiors. But from the perspective of the analyst, discretion, even within the constraints of a given policy problem or area, may be very considerable. How to control air pollution in a given area, for example, allows a variety of regulatory solutions, from setting standards for allowable emissions for different kinds of plants and industries to setting charges on pollutants requiring polluters to pay for each unit of pollutant emitted. The issues are political, technical, economic, legal, and normative—and they are not always decided a priori by political or administrative decision makers.

It is true that analysts are ordinarily held to a closer time frame than are academic researchers; it is not unusual for students to become accustomed to doing analyses of various policy problems, drawing upon the best available data, research, and advice, within 48 or 72 hours, exercises designed to prepare them for the fierce time pressures of legislative hearings or the negotiations that accompany the writing and revision of legislation. Other exercises allow them a week, and a major piece of research equivalent to a master's essay will take up to six months. Time constraints on the job also vary; analysts become skillful in knowing who has been working on a given problem area, and where published or unpublished research or data on the issue can be found. For the analyst, knowledgeable people are a central research resource, and the telephone is part of the student's equipment alongside computers and the library.

As analysts develop the skill of rapidly bringing ideas to bear on data, and data on ideas, they become heavily dependent upon existing statistics and on research done by others. They are often skillful, and even bold, in drawing analogies between findings in different areas of social life, allowing them thus to use the findings of research in one area for informing decisions in another. These analysts cannot often meet the scholar's standards of depth and thoroughness in their research—for example, in the review of the research literature, or in the critical evaluation of the findings of relevant research. Yet working under time and other pressures in the political milieu, the analysts know that the alternative to what they are doing is not a major university-based research project, but more commonly the impressions, anecdotes, and general wisdom of a staff conference. Their own reports, which include discussions of alternative lines of action based on data regarding their comparative costs and benefits, must they believe, be better than an unsystematic discussion among friends and advisers.

Policy analysts in government as we have described them have some of the characteristics of researchers, but are more narrowly constrained by their bureaucratic roles. They also have some of the characteristics of Kogan's middle-men, professionals who serve a liaison function (Kogan et al. 1980 pp. 36–38), though they are more active and ready to take research initiatives than the term "middle-man" implies. But they also are not infrequently the decision makers themselves.

## 2. An Example from the Field of Education

One almost always talks about research *influencing* decision makers—and if the researcher is a university social scientist then the decision maker is almost certainly someone a distance away with his or her own concerns, political commitments, interests, and prejudices. But the policy analyst has the advantage of acting within the bureaucracy to make or directly affect a myriad of administrative decisions that rarely get into the newspapers, are not debated by politicians or on floors of legislatures, but nevertheless have very large consequences.

One illustration comes from the University of California, half of whose budget—the half which pays the operating costs of the University, faculty salaries, and the like—comes from the State of California. The preparation of the University's budget and its incorporation into the governor's budget is a complicated procedure. Very substantial parts of the University's budget are governed by formulas, relating, for example, support levels to enrollment levels, that have been negotiated over the years between the budget analysts in the central administration of the University and their counterparts in the State Department of Finance. These formulas, essentially bureaucratic treaties, are mutual understandings which give the university a greater degree of fiscal security and predictability than one would ever guess from reading the newspapers, which almost never report these matters, but only the visible debates in the legislature and speeches by the governor.

The formulas, of course, do not cover all contingencies, especially in an institution as fluid and diverse as the University of California with so many different sources of energy and initiative creating new programs, facilities, and claims on public funds all the time. Claims for resources, old and new, are argued out or negotiated annually between the University analysts and the State Department of Finance analysts; they speak each other's language, and often have been trained in the same graduate schools and departments, not infrequently in Berkeley's School of Public Policy. In these negotiations, "good arguments" by the University are rewarded; that is, requests for additional support funds that are supported by a good bureaucratic argument are often accepted, and new activities are built into the governor's budget. The arguments made for these programs are the arguments of analysts, often based on analogies with existing state-funded activities, and backed by data showing the actual nature of the activity and its costs. For example, the University wants the State to revise the formula allocating funds for the replacement of scientific equipment used in teaching; it wants more generous provision for teaching assistants; it wants the State to assume the costs of certain athletic facilities; it wants the State to support remedial courses for underprepared students; and so on. In support of these claims the University analysts do research on the actual useful life of laboratory instruments in different scientific departments and on how that record compares with the life of instruments in other universities and in commercial labs; it studies the use and distribution of teaching assistants in the University and how their work contributes to the instructional program; it studies who uses the athletic facilities and for what purposes; and so on. These are not matters of high principle; there exists a broad area of value consensus between the negotiators, but the quality of the research backing those claims is crucial to whether they are accepted, and indeed whether they ought to be accepted. The sums of money that are allocated in these ways are in the aggregate very large. There are many areas of public life in which civil servants exercise wide discretion in decision making, though they are often wise enough to deny that they are in fact making policy or decisions,

but merely "implementing" them. Nevertheless, when we reflect on the influence of research on policy, we should not neglect the realm of bureaucratic and technocratic decision making in the public sector where researcher and decision maker come together in the person of the policy analyst. University-based researches need to be reminded that not all research has to percolate down through a complex network of relationships to enter another complex process of "decision accretion"; some research has access to decision makers quickly and directly, and is done for and by them.

The newly emergent field of policy analysis seems to be thriving in the United States, at least in a modest way, even in the face of budget cuts and hiring freezes in the federal and in many state and local governments. Policy analysts are in demand whether public expenditures are rising or falling; the problems posed to government by budgetary constraints are even more severe than those posed by expansion and the proliferation of public programs and services. With all the cuts, most governments are not reducing the absolute level of public expenditures on social services, but merely reducing their rates of growth. In any event, public life is becoming increasingly more complex and there is no shortage of work for policy analysts.

## 3. Four Problems Facing the Policy Analyst

It should not be thought that the emergence of policy analysis, and of the infrastructure of graduate schools, journals, professional associations and meetings which give it definition and self-consciousness, solve all the problems of the relation of research to policy. For if policy analysts solve some of those problems, they also create new ones. This section outlines four such problems in the realm of policy analysis as currently practiced, though this does not imply that there are only four. These are all problems which in significant ways affect the quality of the analyst's work and his or her influence on policy and decision making.

First, and this is problem that the analyst shares with academic research in education, policy analysis makes relatively little use of ethnographic research methods, the method of direct observation of customary behavior and informal conversation. One consequence of this is that the policy analyst is a captive of existing and usually official statistics; where those statistics are wrong or misleading, and inadequate also. By contrast, university researchers are more likely to question the quality of research data, though it is likely that they rarely question the quality of official statistics.

Second, the outcome of public policy analysis, its reports and recommendations, is affected not only by the analyst's own preferences and biases and those of the client, but also by how the analyst bounds the problem, the phenomena and variables that will be taken into account. These boundaries are sharply constrained by the analyst's position within the bureaucratic work setting, more so than for the university-based researcher.

Third, for every policy analyst outside the university there is tension between the needs and requirements of the client, on one hand, and their own professional commitments to intellectual honesty, to the searching out of negative evidence, and to their freedom to speak and publish what is known or has been learnt, on the other. Bureaucratic research settings put severe strains on those scholarly and professional values. Indeed, the moral issue of how policy analysts deal with dual loyalty to their professional identity as analysts and to their political masters and clients is at the heart of policy analysis and not, as moral issues often are, at the margins.

Finally, there is the relation between policy analysts and policy intellectuals which bears on the nature of communication and persuasion in the political arena, and more broadly on the processes of "decision accretion" through enlightenment and the percolation of research findings, ideas, and assumptions in the decision-making process.

## 4. Policy Intellectuals and Policy Analysts

In his paper identifying several models of connections between research and policy, Husén (1984) is drawn to the enlightenment or "percolation" model. He quotes Weiss to describe research as permeating the policy making process, entering the policy arena not through specific findings or recommendations, but by its "generalizations and orientations percolating through informed publics in coming to shape the way in which people think about social issues" (Weiss 1979).

There is, I think, broad agreement that much of the impact of research on policy (I would say all) occurs in this subtle, difficult-to-measure way. But is this not at variance with the image of the policy analyst directly at the policy maker's elbow, preparing papers and reports at his or her request, speaking to issues and problems that the policy maker will be facing even if not yet recognizing their character or the available options? This image of the policy analyst is in fact compatible with the metaphor of the "percolation" of research, and of the notion of research entering into the general debate and discussion about an issue going on among interested publics, an ongoing debate that crystallizes into policy at a moment when a political actor chooses to place it on the agenda for action and not merely discussion. The analyst in government cannot often do basic research or long-range studies; he or she is to a large extent a consumer and adapter of research, part of the attentive audience for research, and among the most active participants in the critical discussion about the issue and the literature that grows up around it. In the United States, analysts who are educated at schools of public policy are especially trained to take part in that discussion because their teachers and their teachers' peers in other policy schools and professional and academic departments do the research and comment on the research of others in such journals as *The Public Interest, Policy Analysts, Public Choice, Policy Studies Journal*, and *The Journal of Policy Analysis and Management* among others. These university-based writers and researchers, some of whom teach in the schools of public policy, are what Wilson calls "policy intellectuals." And his view of their influence on policy is not far from that of Weiss and Husén's notion of the percolation model. Reviewing the role of policy intellectuals over the past decade, Wilson observes that

> If the influence of intellectuals was not to be found in the details of policy, it was nonetheless real, albeit indirect. Intellectuals provided the conceptual language, the ruling paradigms, the empirical examples . . . that became the accepted assumptions for those in charge of making policy. Intellectuals framed, and to a large degree conducted, the debates about whether this language and these paradigms were correct. The most influential intellectuals were those who managed to link a concept or a theory to the practical needs and ideological dispositions of political activists and governmental officials. (Wilson 1981 p. 36)

Wilson goes further than most of us in downplaying the role of research per se as against the power of the arguments of skillful intellectuals.

> At any given moment in history, an influential idea—and thus an influential intellectual—is one that provides a persuasive simplification of some policy question that is consistent with a particular mix of core values then held by the political elite . . . Clarifying and making persuasive those ideas is largely a matter of argument and the careful use of analogies; rarely . . . does this process involve matters of proof and evidence of the sort that is, in their scholarly, as opposed to their public lives, supposed to be the particular skill and obligation of the intellectual in the university. (Wilson 1981 p. 36)

The role of the policy intellectual in policy debates, independent of his or her research, is of great importance and deserves to be studied more closely. The influence of such informed discussion and argument will, I think, vary in different policy fields. But of special interest is the combined effect of policy intellectuals based in the universities and the policy analysts whom they have trained, or who were trained to read them, to understand them, and to use their arguments in the preparation of their reports for decision makers in government. These staff papers, reports, and memoranda give the policy intellectuals' ideas and work access, in ways that the intellectuals themselves do not always have, to the committee rooms and governmental conversations where decisions are made.

## 5. Policy Analysts Versus Interest Groups

The structure of government in the United States, both in Washington and in the state capitals, is changing, becoming even more open and responsive than it has been to vocal, well-organized special interest groups, less to vocal, well-organized special interest groups, and less and less managed by traditional elites. In the field of education, states Murphy,

> State policy systems, no longer the captive of state education establishments, are now far more accessible to interest groups and open to public view. The adoption of a large number of policy reforms reflects a new responsiveness on the part of state government to these groups.
>
> Within government, the most important change is the heavy involvement of legislators and governors in educational matters. Spurred on by worries about money, school quality, and social issues (e.g., integration), general state government has used its new staff and expertise to challenge education professionals and to remove education from its privileged perch "above politics."
>
> There's a different cast of participants outside government as well . . . Some of the new lobbies promote equality, representing such interests as urban areas, the poor, blacks, Hispanics, the disadvantaged, the handicapped, girls. Reform of state school finance laws has been promoted for the past decade by a network of scholars, foundation executives, lawyers, government officials, community organizers, and citizen groups. Other groups work for efficiency and effectiveness, lobbying for comprehensive planning, improved budgeting, accountability laws, standards for graduation, competency tests for students and teachers. More recently, some of these groups have been promoting tax limitation measures and controls on expenditures. Still other lobbies promote "the public interest." (Murphy 1981 p. 128)

All this energy and activity (in part a consequence of mass higher education) generates an extraordinary level of noise, demands, charges and counter-charges, court actions, and so forth. Pressures of every kind are felt by legislators, elected officials, and their staffs. Policy analysts inside government provide some counterweight, some degree of stability, predictability, and rationality through their professional patterns of response to these pressures and demands. This is not to say that the political activists and their pressure groups are not often successful. But how a government agency responds to organized political pressure may well be shaped by the anonymous analysts in the executive and legislative staffs and agencies. And it is through them that a large or at least a different, set of ideas comes into play in these discussions, and these ideas at their best are less narrow and parochial, more likely to be illuminated by historical and comparative perspectives and by the ongoing discussion that policy intellectuals carry on among themselves in the professional journals.

The structure of politics, the character of the policy areas in which discussions and debate about policies are carried on, are quite different in, for example, Sweden then they are in the United States. Careful studies of actual policy formulation and implementation in specific areas must illuminate the patterns of "social interaction" that more often than not are the major determinants of outcomes in the policy arena. In these increasingly complex networks of social interaction, the relations between policy analysts in government and policy intellectuals in the university are of large and growing importance in the United States, with close analogues in Sweden and other western societies.

## 6. Conclusion: Research and the Rhetoric of Politics

It is natural that members of the research community are concerned that the research they do provides true and illuminating accounts of the institutions and processes that they study. Some researchers are also interested in whether research has any influence on the shaping of policy and the making of decisions, and if it does, how it enters the decision process and affects the outcomes of those decisions.

But it may be useful, and not wholly subversive of the research itself, to reflect that the policy research has value independent of its truth or quality or its influence on policy. That is because social research is one of the ways in which political discussions are carried on in democratic societies, a way that is supportive of liberal democratic politics. Political argument is increasingly conducted in the language of research and analysis; concepts like "cost-benefit" and "trade-off" have found their way into the daily language of politicians and bureaucrats. Moreover, social research and democratic politics have some close affinities. For one thing, like democratic politics, social research is a process not of assertion or demonstration, but of persuasion. Moreover, it is a form of persuasion that appeals to reason and evidence rather than to supernatural authority, or tradition, or the charisma of an individual, or the authority of a legal order. The appeal to research findings is very far from the coercive domination of others by force or threat, and equally far from political manipulations which depend on the exploitation of a differential of knowledge and awareness between manipulator and the manipulated. The appeal to "research findings" is the appeal to the authority of reason, to a rationality that connects means and ends in ways that are consistent with strongly held social values. Max Weber has said that the contribution of sociology to politics is not to affirm ultimate ends, but to help clarifiy, if possible to "make transparent," the connections between means and ends so that choices can be made in greater awareness of the consistency of the means chosen with the ends intended. Insofar as social science attempts to do that, it becomes part of the persuasive mechanism of politics, rooting politics, at least in part, in persuasion based on an appeal to reason and knowledge. It need not weaken professional concern for the quality and truth of research to suggest that social research makes its largest contribution to liberal society not through its findings, but by its steady affirmation of the relevance of reason and knowledge to the politics of democracy.

## Bibliography

Husén T 1984 Issues and their background. In: Husén T, Kogan M (eds.) 1984 *Educational Research and Policy: How do They Relate?* Pergamon, Oxford pp. 1–36

Kogan M, Korman N, Henkel M 1980 *Government's Commissioning of Research: A Case Study.* Department of Government, Brunel University, Uxbridge

Lerner D, Lasswell H (eds.) 1951 *The Policy Sciences.* Stanford

University Press, Stanford, California

Meltsner A J 1976 *Policy Analysts in the Bureaucracy.* University of California Press, Berkeley, California

Murphy J T 1981 The paradox of state government reform. *Public Interest* 64: 124–39

Weiss C H 1979 The many meanings of research utilization. *Pub. Admin. Review* 39: 426–31

Wilson J Q 1981 Policy intellectuals and "public policy". *Public Interest* 64: 31–46

# Planning the Quality of Education[1]

## K. N. Ross and T. N. Postlethwaite

This article explores the types of information that may be employed to guide decisions about the quality of education, and presents some approaches for reporting this information in formats that are appropriate for the various levels at which decisions are made. In recent years, educational planning has often been focused on a limited range of activities concerned with forecasting numbers of students, teachers, and support staff, and predicting the demand for, and location of, supporting plant and equipment which is likely to be required by an education system at any one point in time (Lewin 1988). All this work provides excellent information for guiding decision making concerning the quantity, but unfortunately often provides very little input concerning the quality, of education. This is indeed an unfortunate situation, because ministries and departments of education in most countries are charged with the responsibility of making informed decisions in both of these domains.

In addition to this problem, there is often a lack of understanding within educational planning agencies that the collection and management of useful research information about the quality of education requires an acknowledgement that planning decisions in this domain need to be made at various organization levels (Tyler 1986).

For the purposes of illustration, four broad levels of decision making in education are described: (a) parent and teacher decision making concerning a particular student, (b) school-principal decision making concerning a particular school, (c) official state or provincial decision making concerning a particular group of schools, and (d) official national decision making concerning all a nation's schools.

## 1. Information for Different Levels of Planning

Education, as delivered through formal and nonformal schooling, typically comprises an enterprise designed to facilitate an individual's or a group's cognitive, affective, psychomotor and social learning. Those responsible for

successful outcomes in these areas include parents, teachers, school principals, state and provincial officials, and national officials.

These persons need to monitor various educational processes and outcomes and, with the assistance of appropriate information, make decisions—tomorrow, next week, next month, next year or in a few years' time—which will influence the education of those in their charge. However, the types of decisions these people have to make and, therefore, the type of information they require is often quite different.

### 1.1 Teachers and Parents

Teachers and parents need to gather and share information concerning the nature of the educational behaviours (knowledge, skills and values) that have been taught, the extent to which these have been learned by the child, and the contexts in which the child has demonstrated these behaviours with either competence or difficulty.

In some circumstances this information will describe student performance on individual test items or particular tasks. However, care needs to be taken to ensure that any single item or task provides a stable and representative sample of a defined behaviour across suitable areas of content and context. Generally, it will be necessary to employ a group of items or tasks in order to be able to make reliable statements concerning a defined behaviour for a particular child.

The information needs to be expressed in a manner which avoids technical and educational jargon in order to permit a clear agenda for teacher and parent action to be prepared. This agenda can only address effectively the child's learning strengths and weaknesses in situations where teachers and parents both understand, and agree to, the nature of the child's educational requirements.

### 1.2 School Principals

School principals seldom need to have information about the educational behaviours of individual children.

[1] This article was originally published in *Prospects* XVIII, No. 3. It appears here with permission from UNESCO © 1988.

When this kind of information is required, the principal can consult with the appropriate teacher. However, principals often need to be informed about the progress of learning for each class in the school. Information expressed at the classroom level is more suitable for assisting with decisions concerning the deployment of school resources to ensure that all classes achieve the school's educational goals which have been set by the principal, teachers, and parents (Tyler 1986 p. 109).

In addition, the principal needs to have information on how well the school is performing in comparison with other similar schools. This is especially important in respect of "core" educational goals which are also valued by these similar schools. Principals can use this information to review the school's goals, set priorities among these goals, and focus a whole-school effort on improving the school's learning environment in ways which are relevant to the students' aptitudes, interests, and home circumstances.

### 1.3 State and Provincial Officials

State and provincial officials do not require information as detailed as that required by school principals because they are far removed from both the daily operations of schools and the daily responsibilities of parents, teachers, and principals. The broader role required of these officials, be they administrators, coordinators or supervisors, demands that they should make decisions only after having examined information which is sufficient to establish the existence of problems serious enough, or opportunities great enough, to warrant a considerable commitment of their time and state, or provincial resources.

Information appropriate in this context should be presented in such a manner as to help officials to employ planning approaches that will provide large groups of schools with the expertise and resources required to set up and evaluate their educational programmes, and then, guided by the results of the evaluations, to adopt procedures that will improve their effectiveness.

To assist planning decisions in this area there is also a need for a periodic and independent appraisal of student progress with respect to the agreed goals of schools within the state or province. This would entail an "audit" of a sample of the agreed goals and, if some major discrepancy were noticed between school-level information and state-level information, a more detailed investigation could be undertaken. These audits require care because appraisal of a school calls for the support of students, teachers, parents, and the school principal. This support will not be forthcoming if the collection of information takes up too much student time, results in major disruptions to the school programme, costs too much, or does not provide reliable, valid, and useful results.

### 1.4 National Officials

National officials require less detailed information than do state or provincial officials. These officials do not work with individual children or classes, and they are unlikely to concern themselves with the affairs of an individual school or a small group of schools. Rather, their role is to make broad policy decisions concerning the linkages between the legislated directives of past and present governments, and the plans and resources required to attend to these directives. These decisions are expected to have impact across whole or large parts of school systems and therefore, because of the conservative inertia of educational institutions and the high costs of initiating system-wide change, a great deal of accurate information about students and schools needs to be collected at the system level.

National officials must have access to information that will identify long-term trends in their education system's capacity to assist all students to make progress towards achieving a high standard of physical, social, and cognitive development. In some circumstances these trends will call for intervention in what is seen as an emerging and widespread problem of the inability of students to achieve success in a specific section of the curriculum. In other circumstances, the focus will be on the curriculum itself because it may be seen as being in need of revision and restructuring in order to take account of recent research and/or new social and economic conditions. For most school systems, decisions concerning these matters are grounded in comparative data for various demographic groups within the society and therefore the system-wide information will need to be expressed according to breakdowns associated with, for example, gender, ethnicity, and socioeconomic factors.

### 2. Mechanisms for Providing Information

In many countries a great deal of the information required for the various levels of decision making is already available in the form of large-scale datasets obtained from national and international surveys of educational achievement. Some examples are: the Australian Studies in School Performance Project in Australia (Bourke et al. 1981), the Assessment of performance Unit (APU) in England (Gipps and Goldstein 1983), National Assessment of Educational Progress in the United State (NAEP 1986); the Indonesian 6th, 9th, and 12th Grade Surveys (Jiyono and Suryadi 1982), the International Association for the Evaluation of Educational Achievement (IEA) surveys in some 40 countries (Pelgrum and Warries 1986).

The data associated with large-scale surveys usually contain useful benchmarks of student performance on at least some of a nation's agreed educational goals. In addition, many of the so-called independent variables used in these surveys often provide important descriptive information which may be of use to state and national officials.

It is important to note that care needs to be exercised when employing survey data to ensure that the sample designs were drawn up and executed in a scientifically valid fashion. Those surveys that neglect to provide a clear description of the target population, the objective procedures used to select the sample, the stratification decisions, the stages and units of multistage sampling, the procedures used to minimize the dangers of bias through nonresponse, the size of the designed and achieved samples, and the magnitude of the sampling errors, should be treated with great caution.

Another important source of information may be found in data gathered as part of a national examination system. These data can be provided at many levels of aggregation, for example, as average school scores and as average scores for groups of schools serving communities with similar socioeconomic characteristics.

If neither survey data, nor examination data are available, then school systems may be faced with the design of their own performance monitoring procedures. A recent example of this has been the state-wide testing procedures adopted by the State of California in the United States (Los Angeles Times 1987).

## 3. Examples of the Information to be Provided

A tentative list is presented below of the kinds of questions that might be asked at the four planning levels described above. In association with each of these levels a hypothetical table of results has been presented in order to illustrate how information might be assembled and displayed in order to provide appropriate responses to the questions.

### 3.1 Teacher's Questions

A teacher may want to know his or her students' achievements on specific subdimensions of mother tongue, mathematics, and science.

The subdimensions considered for each of the three subject areas would depend on the curricular components that have been taught within the teacher's class. For example, the first sub-dimension in the mother tongue area could be spelling; the second could be reading comprehension required for understanding simple instructions; the third, reading comprehension required for making inferences; the fourth, creative writing, and so on. In the mathematics area the subdimensions could be estimation, arithmetic calculations, elementary equations, and so on. In the science area

the subdimensions could be the solar system, differences between plants and animals, properties of metals, and so on. Generally, for any reasonable level of reliability in judging a student's capacity to have mastered a domain associated with a subdimension, it would be necessary to have at least eight to ten items (Morgan 1979).

If there are six subdimensions, numbered 1 to 6, and a total score, for each of the three curricular areas, and 10 items have been used to assess each subdimension, then a hypothetical table of results for a particular class might be displayed as in Table 1. For the sake of illustration, only four students have been included. The results listed in this table would enable the teacher of this class to discern a number of interesting performance patterns, both within the profiles of individual students and among the profiles of all students in the class. The teacher would need to digest this information and then, in association with parents and colleagues, formulate a plan of action for individual students and for the whole class.

From the hypothetical results presented in Table 1, the teacher can see that all students have performed quite well on all subdimensions associated with science. The teacher and students would be very satisfied with their performance in this area of the curriculum.

Table 1 shows that all students, except for student A, performed reasonably well on the mathematics subdimensions. However, student A performed extremely well for the other two areas. On the basis of these results the teacher may suggest that this student should concentrate his or her efforts a little more on mathematics in order to obtain a better and more balanced performance across all three areas.

An unusual pattern of results has emerged for the mother tongue. All students have performed reasonably well, except on subdimension 3. The teacher would need to reflect upon the factors which may have prevented effective learning in this area. Some of these factors could be: (a) that insufficient class time was allocated to learning the material associated with this subdimension, (b) that the students were confused by the way in which the teacher explained the material, (c) that the textbook devoted insufficient space to the material, (d) that no applied examples or homework was given to consolidate the learning of the material, (e) that the material covered for this subdimension was unusually complex

**Table 1**
Hypothetical table of results for a class

| Student | Mother tongue | | | | | | | Mathematics | | | | | | | Science | | | | | | |
|---|---|---|---|---|---|---|---|---|---|---|---|---|---|---|---|---|---|---|---|---|---|
| | 1 | 2 | 3 | 4 | 5 | 6 | Total | 1 | 2 | 3 | 4 | 5 | 6 | Total | 1 | 2 | 3 | 4 | 5 | 6 | Total |
| A | 9 | 10 | 4 | 9 | 10 | 10 | 52 | 4 | 5 | 5 | 3 | 7 | 5 | 29 | 9 | 10 | 9 | 10 | 9 | 10 | 57 |
| B | 9 | 8 | 1 | 8 | 9 | 10 | 45 | 9 | 7 | 8 | 9 | 7 | 7 | 47 | 8 | 8 | 9 | 9 | 9 | 8 | 51 |
| C | 9 | 7 | 3 | 8 | 9 | 9 | 45 | 8 | 7 | 9 | 8 | 7 | 7 | 46 | 8 | 10 | 8 | 9 | 8 | 8 | 51 |
| D | 9 | 9 | 2 | 9 | 8 | 9 | 46 | 8 | 7 | 9 | 7 | 7 | 7 | 45 | 8 | 9 | 10 | 8 | 9 | 9 | 53 |

relative to the other four subdimensions, and (f) that the material was presented in a fashion which was not relevant to the students' interests and backgrounds.

## 3.2 School Principal's Questions

A school principal may wish to know what subdimensions of which subject areas and at which grade levels is his or her school doing well or poorly in comparison with other similar schools and all schools in his or her district.

In order to address this kind of question, the school principal needs one or more points of comparison: a relative measure of performance which will focus on the performance level of his or her school with respect to other similar schools, and an absolute measure of performance which will provide information concerning the amount of the agreed curriculum which has been mastered by the students.

A relative measure of performance could be estimated by comparing the school's performance with other similar schools within the same school system. The term *similar* here refers to other schools serving students from the same kind of socioeconomic background, having the same standard of staff and equipment, and teaching the same curriculum. The comparisons between these schools could be carried out using breakdown variables which define important groups of students within the schools in terms of gender, ethnicity, year level, and so on. One of the important benefits associated with a relative comparison of schools is that it may be possible to learn from the teaching methods and educational environments of other schools that serve similar communities but are more productive in terms of student learning outcomes.

An absolute measure of performance could be estimated by using preset levels of achievement which indicate several broad bands of performance for the whole school. For example, if 75 percent or more of the students at a particular grade level master the material associated with a specific subdimension, then the performance for this class level is said to be "good". If the percentage of students mastering the material is between 50 and 75 percent then this is defined as "moderate", and below 50 percent is designated as "poor". Each of these three levels of performance would lead to different actions being required of the principal. For example, a poor performance level may require a major redeployment of school resources and effort in order to improve student learning, whereas a good performance level may require the principal to limit his or her activities to providing positive feedback to students and teachers in the form of encouragement.

Table 2, a hypothetical table of the mean and student standard deviation of raw total scores, has been presented for the mother tongue, mathematics, and science. These results show the relative, but not the absolute, performance of school Y compared with other similar schools, and compared with all schools in the same state. The results suggest that a different kind of response is required of the school principal for each of the three curriculum areas. The scores in this table would need to be expressed in the form of "mastery" levels in order to make statements about absolute levels of performance.

In the mother tongue, school Y performed poorly relative to other similar schools, and poorly relative to all other schools in the same state. This situation would warrant a review of the school's mother tongue educational programme with a view to improving the performance of the students. The review might begin by visiting some of the other similar schools to try and find out what features of their programme appear to be

*Table 2*

Hypothetical results for a relative comparison of a school with other similar schools and all schools in the same state

| Schools | Mother tongue | | Mathematics | | Science | |
|---|---|---|---|---|---|---|
| | Mean | Standard deviation | Mean | Standard deviation | Mean | Standard deviation |
| *School Y* | | | | | | |
| Males | 40.6 | 2.1 | 45.8 | 2.4 | 50.3 | 4.4 |
| Females | 41.3 | 2.2 | 33.4 | 2.3 | 49.7 | 4.5 |
| Total | 40.7 | 2.5 | 39.5 | 4.4 | 50.0 | 4.5 |
| *Similar schools* | | | | | | |
| Males | 55.4 | 2.4 | 40.1 | 2.7 | 50.1 | 2.2 |
| Females | 53.0 | 2.3 | 39.2 | 2.2 | 49.2 | 2.1 |
| Total | 54.2 | 2.4 | 39.6 | 2.8 | 49.5 | 2.2 |
| *All schools* | | | | | | |
| Males | 54.1 | 2.3 | 39.0 | 2.6 | 57.3 | 2.1 |
| Females | 51.9 | 2.2 | 38.1 | 2.3 | 56.2 | 2.2 |
| Total | 53.1 | 2.3 | 38.5 | 2.7 | 56.7 | 2.3 |

resulting in a better learning environment for their students.

The scores for mathematics show that school Y is performing about as well as other similar schools and also marginally better than other schools in the same state. However, when these mathematics results are broken down by gender, it becomes apparent that, for school Y, there are unusually large performance differences between males and females. The magnitude of these differences exceeds substantially the differences noted for similar schools and other schools in the same school district. This result would warrant a detailed investigation of the learning environments and opportunities that are being provided for female students within the school. The extremely high mathematics performance displayed by the male students suggests that some excellent mathematics programmes are available within the school, and that action should be taken to ensure that female students are able to benefit from this high-quality teaching.

The mean total scores for science indicate that the school is performing poorly with respect to all other schools in the same state, but about as well as other similar schools. A pattern of results like this could be associated with a major difference in school science resources between, on the one hand, school Y and other similar schools, and, on the other hand, all other schools in the same district. In this situation it may not be easy for the principal to improve the learning environment for science in the school because the main reason for these differences might be the availability of expensive laboratory facilities, which represents a factor beyond the principal's control. Furthermore, an important issue associated with the pattern of standard deviation scores in science would need to be addressed by the school principal because the variation between student scores in the school is extraordinarily high when compared with similar schools and other schools in the same state. This result would require an investigation to find out why, within the same school, there is such a high variation in student performance.

The discussion presented above addressed the school principal's question in terms of relative performance. In order to consider the question from an absolute perspective the performance of the school would need to be expressed as a table reporting the percentages of students achieving mastery in the three curricular areas. The principal could then use the previously described benchmarks of poor, moderate, and good to analyse the school's performance. The setting of percentage mastery levels for these three categories would need to be carried out in association with the most experienced classroom teachers.

### 3.3 State Official's Questions

A state official may want to know which schools and/or groups of schools in his or her state are performing well or poorly.

State officials are mainly interested in the efficient deployment of state-wide resources so that all schools for which they are responsible have an opportunity to optimize the quality of their educational environments. In some instances, these resources may consist of staff, plant and/or equipment, whereas in other instances less tangible resources may consist of information and ideas that facilitate educational improvements without requiring substantial financial inputs. An example of a successful deployment of the latter type of resource would be found in situations where teacher-constructed curricular materials that have been shown to improve learning are shared as part of a pool of teaching aids.

In Table 3 hypothetical results that would address the information needs of school district officials have been presented. For the sake of illustration, only four schools in the district have been included. These results list the overall performance of each school in the three subject areas described above and then provide a composite score, for example, by using a summation of scores for each area.

The task of the state official in examining these data is to look for patterns of results which might suggest an opportunity for the state to target resources in a more effective and efficient manner. For example, at the individual school level it can be seen that, according to the levels of the composite scores, the overall performance of each school listed in Table 3 is quite similar. However, from an observation of the subject scores it may be noted that each school has both strengths and

*Table 3*
Hypothetical results for all schools in a state

| Schools | Mother tongue | | Mathematics | | Science | | Composite score | |
|---------|------|-----------|------|-----------|------|-----------|------|-----------|
| | Mean | Standard deviation | Mean | Standard deviation | Mean | Standard deviation | Mean | Standard deviation |
| 1 | 40.7 | 2.5 | 50.3 | 2.4 | 59.4 | 2.5 | 51.6 | 2.6 |
| 2 | 42.3 | 2.2 | 52.8 | 2.5 | 59.2 | 2.5 | 51.2 | 2.3 |
| 3 | 58.3 | 2.6 | 22.2 | 2.7 | 42.6 | 2.3 | 50.9 | 2.4 |
| 4 | 58.1 | 2.2 | 26.3 | 2.1 | 44.3 | 2.0 | 50.2 | 2.2 |
| State | 53.1 | 2.3 | 38.5 | 2.7 | 56.7 | 2.3 | 50.8 | 2.5 |

weaknesses. Probably of more importance is the appearance of two internally homogeneous clusters of schools, the first containing schools (1 and 2) having poor performance in the mother tongue and excellent performance in mathematics and science, and the second containing schools (3 and 4) having excellent performance in the mother tongue and poor performance in mathematics and science. The existence of these two clusters should prompt a more detailed investigation of why these clusters exist. For example, can the existence of the clusters be explained in terms of differences in student backgrounds, teacher's qualifications, curricular emphases, and so on?

A further question that comes to mind is to ponder whether the mother-tongue teachers in the first cluster could profit by experiencing direct observation of the mother-tongue programmes of schools in the second cluster; and, vice versa, whether the science and mathematics teachers in the second cluster would learn something by observation of equivalent programmes of schools in the first cluster.

Where important patterns exist in school scores, like the clusters described above, it may be important for state officials to seek supplementary information from local sources concerning the special circumstances of the schools in each cluster. An interesting example of this occurred during the 1970s in Indonesia where it was found that the English-language scores of students in certain schools in Bali were several standard deviations above the scores that could be expected of the most able students in the country. These results were explained following the discovery that the schools were located close to golf courses frequented by English-speaking tourists, and that after school hours, and at weekends, many of the students spent a great deal of time practising their English conversational skills while working at the golf course.

### 3.4 National Official's Question

A national official may want to know what major factors are associated with differences between schools in his or her country, and whether these differences are evident in terms of spatial differentiation (for example, provincial differences, urban/rural differences, and so on), or in terms of demographic descriptors (for example, ethnic status, socioeconomic status, and so on).

The national official's task in addressing this many-faceted question commences with decisions concerning the key indicators to be used in order to judge the performance of the education system. In the past many countries have employed "coarse" performance indicators concerned with enrolment rates and graduation rates. However, more recently, there has been greater interest in highly specific indicators concerned with such matters as attendance rates, retentivity rates, student achievement levels, and discipline problems. Murnane (1987) notes the emergence of this trend in the United States where, although enrolment data had been collected at the national level from 1867, there was no data collected at the national level to assess what students learned in school until 100 years later.

### 3.5 Spatial Differentiation and Demographic Descriptors

Table 4 presents a hypothetical set of results in order to consider the patterns of student achievement across the nation according to two variables that describe spatial differentiation: state location and urban/rural setting. A similar table could be prepared to show demographic variables by displaying student achievement according to several classifications of variables concerned with ethnic and socioeconomic status. It is these kinds of tables that provide essential information

*Table 4*
Hypothetical table of results in urban and rural areas for each state and the nation

| Province | Mother tongue | | Mathematics | | Science | | Composite score | |
|---|---|---|---|---|---|---|---|---|
| | Mean | Standard deviation | Mean | Standard deviation | Mean | Standard deviation | Mean | Standard deviation |
| *State 1* | | | | | | | | |
| Urban | 36.7 | 2.5 | 33.3 | 2.4 | 37.4 | 2.5 | 42.6 | 2.6 |
| Rural | 41.3 | 2.2 | 40.8 | 2.5 | 43.2 | 2.5 | 49.2 | 2.3 |
| Total | 39.0 | 2.8 | 37.1 | 2.7 | 40.3 | 2.9 | 45.9 | 2.9 |
| *State 25* | | | | | | | | |
| Urban | 45.8 | 2.1 | 45.3 | 2.4 | 47.7 | 2.4 | 53.7 | 2.2 |
| Rural | 45.7 | 2.2 | 45.1 | 2.6 | 47.6 | 2.4 | 53.5 | 2.3 |
| Total | 45.8 | 2.3 | 45.2 | 2.7 | 47.7 | 2.4 | 53.6 | 2.3 |
| *Nation* | | | | | | | | |
| Urban | 43.6 | 2.3 | 43.1 | 2.6 | 45.5 | 2.6 | 51.5 | 2.4 |
| Rural | 43.5 | 2.4 | 42.9 | 2.8 | 45.4 | 2.6 | 51.3 | 2.5 |
| Total | 43.6 | 2.5 | 43.0 | 2.9 | 45.5 | 2.6 | 51.4 | 2.5 |

when national officials attempt to devise long-term educational planning strategies.

The results in Table 4 indicate that, at the national level, there are negligible differences between urban and rural areas in all three subjects. In addition, the overall performances of students in State 25 is quite good, being generally a little more than two score points above the national level, both for the total state figures and also for urban and rural areas. State 1, on the other hand, displays overall performance figures which are substantially lower than the national average. In addition, within State 1 there are large variations in student performance between urban and rural areas.

The evidence presented in Table 4 would provide grounds for a thorough review of educational provision in State 1. The national official would probably commence such a review by proposing a comparison of the educational environments provided for students in States 1 and 25. Some relevant questions to consider would be those concerned with differences between these two states in terms of teacher quality, school buildings, curriculum and, importantly, the socioeconomic background of the students.

### 3.6 Factors Associated with Differences between Schools

The circumstances of schools should always be taken into consideration before making decisions concerning their performance as educational institutions. That is, the output of schools, as measured by the amount of learning experienced by students, should be considered in association with the quality of student intake and the prevailing social and physical environment within which schools operate. If schools are judged solely by the average achievement scores of their students, then many schools that are doing an extremely effective job, given their circumstances, may be misjudged as being ineffective and vice versa.

For example, consider a school that has overcrowded and inadequate buildings, has very few textbooks, has limited access to cultural experiences for its students because of isolation, and has many students from very poor and illiterate families. It would be extremely unfair to judge this school as performing poorly if it was found that the average literacy score of its students was slightly below the national average. In fact, after taking account of the school's circumstances, it would probably be considered that the school has performed admirably.

The circumstances of schools may be described in terms of two broad classifications of variables that are sometimes labelled as malleable and nonmalleable. The nonmalleable variables are those that influence the outcomes of schooling, but are not, in the short term, readily amenable to manipulation by those decision makers responsible for the management of the education system. Some examples of these kinds of variables would be the socioeconomic circumstances of students' home backgrounds, the geographical environment of the school, and the distance of the school community from various educational and cultural facilities. The malleable variables are those that influence the outcomes of schooling and, in the short term, may be manipulated by decision makers. Some examples of these would be textbook provision, teacher inservice training programmes, homework requirements, school staffing, school curricula, and so on.

The national official, being unable to influence the nonmalleable variables in the short term, is most likely to pose the following two questions: What are the differences between schools in terms of their output, after taking into account school circumstances as measured by the nonmalleable variables? Which of the malleable variables are most influential in assisting schools to become more effective?

One approach to providing answers to these two questions would be to begin by using a between-schools regression analysis with the nonmalleable variables as predictor variables and mean student achievement scores as the criterion variable. The resulting regression equation could be used to create a measure of school output which has been statistically adjusted for the circumstances of the school, as measured by the nonmalleable variables. It should be noted here that the calculation of adjusted scores requires a great deal of care with respect to using data aggregated to the school level (see Keeves and Sellin 1988).

This adjusted output measure would be equal to the school residual score calculated by subtracting the expected, or predicted, student mean achievement score, obtained from the regression equation, from the actual mean student achievement score. A large positive residual score would indicate that a school was performing efficiently because it was doing "better than expected" after taking account of the nonmalleable variables. Similarly, a large negative residual score would mean that a school was performing inefficiently because it was doing "worse than expected" after taking account of the nonmalleable variables. It is important to note that, generally, some degree of "confounding", or "overlapping", tends to occur between malleable and nonmalleable variables in most educational environments. Consequently, there may be a tendency to overadjust for the nonmalleable circumstances when forming the residual scores by using regression analysis. Fortunately, this statistical artefact tends to result in conservative estimates of the residuals and accordingly increases the confidence by which schools with large residual scores may be classified as being either efficient or inefficient.

Following these analyses, a sample of very efficient schools could then be compared with a sample of very inefficient schools in terms of their differences with respect to the malleable variables. The comparison of these two groups of schools would address the second of the questions presented above.

In some situations it may be deemed important to conduct a test of statistical significance between the two groups with respect to an important malleable variable.

Care should be taken with this procedure in order to ensure that the test incorporates an allowance for the sampling of intact groups of students. This matter, in association with a method for calculating an appropriate allowance, has been discussed by Ross (1987).

Consider, for example, a situation where the major difference between the two groups of schools was concerned with library provision (Fuller's 1987 review of school effects in Third World countries notes that library size and activity contributes consistently towards improved learning outcomes). In this situation the national official would need to launch an investigation, probably of a qualitative nature, to find out why this had occurred. The reason for the situation might be linked to any, all, or none of the following possibilities. Perhaps there were problems associated with the distribution of library books. Perhaps some schools were able to obtain more books than other schools. Perhaps the books incorporated a cultural bias which resulted in their rejection by certain schools which served particular ethnic communities. Perhaps a simple clerical error had resulted in some schools not receiving their books.

Unfortunately, in most educational settings the differences between the two groups of schools will probably be associated not just with one clear malleable variable as described above. Rather, there will probably be a range of interrelated variables which will need to be grouped according to the different actions that need to be taken and the costs of these actions. Some actions may be inexpensive and easy to implement (for example, correcting the clerical error which interfered with the distribution of the books) while other actions may be expensive and difficult to implement (for example, purchasing new books for each school and ensuring that they fit the cultural requirements of the local community).

When all actions are grouped and costed, they may be presented to key decision makers for consideration. At this stage, a prioritization process will probably be required in order to enable those actions that are selected for implementation to be manageable within a country's budgetary and political situation. For example, some actions which involve large expenditures may need to be deferred until better economic conditions prevail, while other actions, which focus on complex ethnic and cultural issues, may require lengthy preliminary negotiations with community leaders before implementation commences.

## 4. Conclusion

This article has presented a rationale, and some hypothetical examples, for considering the different levels of decision making within education systems and the ways in which relevant information may be gathered and displayed in a manner that will assist with decision making.

There are many low-cost opportunities for fruitful sharing of information across decision-making levels provided that sufficient prior thought is given to the nature and presentation of the information that is collected. For example, the regular data collections conducted by teachers and school principals about their own schools can sometimes be coordinated among a cluster of schools in order to provide information that is also of interest to state or national officials. Similarly, by including some supplementary data collections, large-scale surveys of educational achievement can report their results in a form required by national or state officials and in a form that assists teachers and school principals.

The discussion presented in this article concerning the notion of comparing school performance after adjusting each school's output for the quality of its input is not a new idea for educational researchers. However, it is a relatively novel concept for most parents and, surprisingly, it is an idea that is often bypassed during "informed" discussion of schools and their reputations for excellence. The school mean test scores for large school systems in the United States which are regularly reported in the mass media, with little interpretive comment, represent excellent examples of the dangers associated with this approach (Los Angeles Times 1987).

In conclusion, the issues that have been canvassed in this article have implications for future changes in the ways in which educational planners are trained. In particular, the current tendency to provide intensive training in quantitative techniques needs to be supplemented by experience in linking these techniques to decision making requirements concerning the quality of education at all levels of education systems.

## Bibliography

Bourke S F, Mills J M, Stanyon J, Holzer F 1981 *Performance in Literacy and Numeracy: 1980*. Australian Government Publishing Service, Canberra

Fuller B 1987 What school factors raise achievement in the Third World? *Rev. Educ. Res.* 57: 255–77

Gipps C, Goldstein H 1983 *Monitoring Children: An Evaluation of the Assessment of Performance Unit*. Heinemann, London

Jiyono, Suryadi A 1982 The planning, sampling, and some preliminary results of the Indonesian 9th grade survey. *Eval. Educ.* 6: 5–30

Keeves J P, Sellin N 1988 Multilevel Analysis. In: Keeves J P (ed.) 1988 *Educational Research, Methodology, and Measurement: An International Handbook*. Pergamon, Oxford, pp. 689–700

Lewin K 1988 Educational planning for scientific and technological development. In: Husén T, Postlethwaite T N (eds.) 1988 *The International Encyclopedia of Education, Supplement 1*. Pergamon, Oxford, pp. 671–79

Morgan G 1979 *A Criterion-referenced Measurement Model with Corrections for Guessing and Carelessness*, Occasional Paper, No. 13. Australian Council for Educational Research, Hawthorn, Victoria

Murnane R J 1987 Improving education indicators and economic indicators: The same problems? *Educ. Eval. and Policy Analysis.* 9: 101–16

*National Assessment of Educational Progress* (NAEP) 1986 *The Reading Report Card: Progress Toward Excellence in Our Schools.* NAEP, Princeton, New Jersey

Pelgrum H, Warries E (eds.) 1986 *International Association for the Evaluation of Educational Achievement (IEA)'86:* *Activities, Institutions, and People.* IEA, Enschede, Netherlands

Ross K N 1987 Sample design. *Int. J. Educ. Res.* 11: 57–75

Los Angeles Times (Metro Supplement) 1987 Los Angeles school achievement test scores. 8 November pp. 1–2.

Tyler R W 1986 Changing concepts of educational evaluation. *Int. J. Educ. Res.* 10: 1–113

# Educational System Assessment and Planning Models

R. G. Davis

The methodology of planning is fitted to two major types of models designed to accomplish the main tasks of planning: the heuristic and the algorithmic models. *Heuristic* models are applied to the first task of planning: the exploration of problems, needs, issues, and values, and the development and statement of ends, purposes, and plan goals. *Algorithmic* models are designed to accomplish the two main technical tasks of planning: (a) the analysis of current and past internal states of the school system and the demographic, social, policial, and economic context variables that affect education and the school system; and (b) the forecasting of possible and desirable states of school system based on the identification of key internal (system) and external (societal) variables, the analysis of the relationships and trends among these variables, and the estimation of the parameter values that will shape the forecast.

Value and goal analysis, data analysis and estimation, and forecasting are the three main tasks in educational planning, and methodological requirements derive from these tasks. Without the analysis of goals and values, plan analysis is purposeless; without the analysis of past and present facts and data, planning is only fortuitously relevant to reality.

Similar models and methods serve in all three educational planning settings: (a) systems (economic, social, political, school) planning; (b) institutional (mainly university) planning; and (c) program/project planning, where a *program* is a set of education activities with defined objectives within an institutional context, and a *project* is a freestanding, limited-term set of activities (Davis 1966, Davis 1980).

The United Nations, United Nations Educational, Scientific and Cultural Organization (UNESCO), International Institute for Educational Planning (IIEP), and Organization for Economic Cooperation and Development (OECD) in Europe, Africa, Asia, and Latin America led the way in systems planning (OECD 1965, UNESCO 1974), with later work from Harvard/CSED and Stanford International Development Education Committee (SIDEC) in the period 1962–1980.

In institutional planning Hopkins and Massy (1981) at Stanford, the Resource Requirements Prediction Model (Hussain 1971), Judy's work (1969) on the CAMPUS model, and the work done at the National Center for Higher Education Management Systems (NCHEMS) laid the foundations for university planning.

CAMPUS and the Resource Requirements Prediction Model (RRPM) were large-scale systems simulation models that forecast enrollments using demographic and economic targets, enrollment flow rates and input norms (student–teacher and student–space ratios) to derive input requirements, costs, budgetary allocations, and financial requirements plans. Similar models developed in Europe in this period included MSAR in Portugal, HIS in the Federal Republic of Germany, and TUSS in the Netherlands.

Project planning went forward in many settings. While the work in program planning was usually done by university educators and not planners, the work in project planning was done by training specialists from the Peace Corps, International Labour Organization (ILO) or United Nations International Children's Emergency Fund (UNICEF) working in on-site, nonformal education/training projects, or by economists working on project evaluation in government agencies (Roemer and Stern 1975, ETS 1979) and in hundreds of technical papers prepared by and for World Bank, United States Agency for International Development (USAID), UN staff or their consultants.

## 1. Toward the Current State of the Art

### 1.1 First Stages of Systems Level Planning

School systems planning began in earnest in countries newly emerging politically and developing economically in the post-Second World War period. Planning models and methods were designed to fit international goals that prescribed education as a universal right of all; literacy and basic education for adults; primary education for children, middle and secondary schooling where possible; and the delivery of schooling through a national, centralized, and standardized school system based mainly on European colonial models. The planning models and methods were straightforward.

(a) Assess (in census or survey) the number in the age-eligible populations and project these numbers into future years, as plan targets (early plans had few goal statements).

(b) On a pro rata or per student basis, derive the main inputs required to provide schooling, with teachers estimated on the basis of a student–teacher ratio, physical space requirements on the basis of a student–space ratio, and a small added allocation for materials and "other education inputs."

(c) Estimate costs by multiplying student load by per student input costs; estimate budgets and allocations, then project expenditures and financial resources required for future years.

Plan targets were derived from population projections, and costs and allocations from system input norms and unit cost formulas. Forty years later, in the current state of the art, comprehensive modeling systems, though better designed, and written in more advanced programming languages like TURBO-PASCAL or Q, are founded on the same basic demographic and enrollment models, using rates calculated with the same basic algorithms.

*1.2 Stage Two: Systems Flow Dynamics and Output Measures*

The early models simply set age-eligible populations as entrant targets, without planning for sufficient input resources to provide adequate services to ensure promotion and graduation. The result was non-promotion, dropout, and no real output. To monitor real output, planners applied enrollment flow data and rates. At a later stage, the rates were built into matrices of transition coefficients in Markov process models used to estimate and project enrollment flows and graduates.

The models provided estimates of flows, wastage, and true enrollment burden; input requirements and costs; clearer measures of systems throughput and output; a more precise basis for estimating effectiveness and efficiency and for matching output requirements to target attainment. Policy makers could now assess school output, or the lack of it, and analyze weaknesses at least in aggregate and average terms, and thus begin to deal with educational "quality."

*1.3 Stage Three: External Targets: Labor Force Planning*

The use of labor force requirements as educational systems targets was woven out of several developmental strands: concern with economic growth in developing countries; creation of national and sectoral planning offices and mid-term, cyclic planning in developing countries, for example, India's First Five Year Plan in 1954; emphasis on output and cost efficiency; and development of "modern sector" industries requiring workers trained in costly and highly specialized education/training programs and institutions.

The labor force models in the basic planning repertoire were simple (Parnes 1962, OECD 1970):

(a) Economic growth (GNP), forecast by sectors and/or industries, was taken from the national plan or separately projected.

(b) Productivity, that is, product per worker, was forecast by sector/industry based on past trends and assumptions about changes in markets, investments, technology and other influences on economic growth. Estimates were based on "comparative" or "historical" analysis, experience, and guesses.

(c) Dividing the projected product (a) by projected product per worker (b) yields (c) the numbers of workers employed by industry.

(d) Within industries, workers were classified by occupation using comparative or historical experience, assumptions about technology, scale, investment, and organizational complexity.

(e) Occupations were related to education/training, and the numbers of educated and trained people required to meet the new growth targets and replace worker retirements and deaths were estimated. In the projections, education levels were almost always raised for future years.

(f) The "supply" (the number of completers of various levels and kinds of education/training) was forecast and compared to labor force requirements forecasts. The resulting surplus or deficit data provided the education targets for the plan.

*1.4 Stage Four: Planning for Differentiated Education Training*

Labor force requirements, expressed as occupations related to specific education/training outputs, focused attention on the planning of differentiated programs for professional, technical, and occupational training. Within formal schooling, occupational education specialists dominated program planning, at first with little concern for labor force requirements plans. Later, however, program plans were connected to systems labor force plans. Outside the formal school system, the planning of on-the-job training, apprenticeship, extension, and "nonformal" education developed. The planning of training programs and projects has its own methodology: from job description to task analysis, to learning objectives, content, and sequence, instructional strategies (level of simulation, sequence of material, practice and reinforcement, generalization, test, and feedback), instruction, input analysis, and costing. To this should be added project evaluation which covers the testing of performance and cost-benefit analysis or analysis of internal rate of return on the project.

*1.5 Stage Five: Methods for Supplementing Labor Force Planning*

The accuracy and reliability of labor force forecasting have been widely challenged by academics and policy makers, and just as widely practiced, with only a few refinements added over the years. Input–output tables, plant level data and staffing tables, population service ratios, demand/supply interaction analysis and adjustment, shift and share ratios and models have helped to sharpen labor force estimates, but the same crude models and methods are still used. Labor force planning, although plagued by small errors, can help educators avoid large mistakes. Rate of return analysis, the other economics-based planning approach favored by economists for its simplicity, has rarely served in real planning situations for guiding educational plans and policies at the systems level, but has been useful for economic evaluation at the project level.

### 1.6 Stage Six: Comprehensive Systems Models

Comprehensive systems models, in mathematical program form, with rate of return in the objective function, and population intake targets, enrollment output targets, and resource and budgetary constraints linked to activity levels by input/output technological coefficients have been designed and proposed for systems planning (Bowles 1969, Schiefelbein and Davis 1974). Impressive in form, and only moderately deceptive if used to simulate alternative policies rather than to calculate a single optimal outcome, large program models were little used in actual planning, and serve primarily to show the main linkages of school "systems": goals to system output, output to enrollment flow, flow to inputs and technology, inputs and technology to resources, resources to costs, costs to budget allocations, and allocations to resources and revenues.

### 1.7 Summation of Planning Experience: Second World War to Late 1980s

These generalizations can be made about developments in planning methodology over the 40 years since the Second World War:

Most advances in the state of the art of planning models and methods came out of field work and operations in planning tied to technical assistance projects and development activity, rather than from academic research or formal field research.

As yet, no comprehensive model covering both heuristic and algorithmic applications and covering all three main tasks of planning (goal setting, data analysis, and projection) applied in all three settings (systems, institution, and project planning) has been developed or applied. Planners work mainly with sets of small component models and methods.

The models and method of planning are more effective in dealing with analysis and projection than with ends, purposes, values, and goals in planning. Plans deal better with how school systems work than with the end-purposes of education.

There is more data than information and more information than there are users who can understand and apply it. More time is spent processing data than analyzing it, and there is more analysis of information than there is use of it in management and decision making in education.

## 2. The Current Stage: Interactive Planning Models

The large systems simulation models mentioned earlier have evolved into matrix-based modeling systems based on mainframe computers, and then into spreadsheet modeling programs on personal computers, where packages such as LOTUS, Javelin, and IFPS offer a repertoire of accessible models and methods for the main technical tasks of systems or institutional planning. These tasks include analysis of time series data and trends and projection of key variables (population, enrollment, instructional activities, inputs, and revenues).

Models in the form of *templates* to be used for recurring planning tasks can be designed in general form. Later the data from actual schools can be inserted in order to run the model. In the United States, the National Center for Higher Education Management Systems has developed a series of templates on LOTUS that are useful, when adapted to specific institutional needs, for the standard planning tasks: enrollment forecasting, input requirements estimates, costing, and financial planning. Typical templates for systems planning are the POPEX model used for forecasting school entrants, the Economics in Curriculum Choice (ECC) model for school program costing (Nazareth 1986), and scores of other examples used in World Bank, technical assistance agencies, and planning offices. The design and use of special purpose models or templates for ad hoc planning task applications is one form of current planning model development. The applications of small computer models to school planning are too wide and varied to list and many of them are unreported, for example, linear or goal programming applied to scheduling, resource management, and allocations. The Productivity Analysis Support System (PASS), an optimization-based decision support system used to monitor the relative efficiency and effectiveness of 25 Texas school districts in meeting targeted output levels, is an example of one of the larger applied efforts (Bessent et al. 1986).

The second major development is that task components are assembled into modeling system frameworks using different programming languages (e.g., TURBO-PASCAL, Q, REAL BASIC, C . . .), and varying plan tasks can then be called up and related within the modeling system shell. Research Triangle Institute (RTI) and Harvard have developed, applied, and tested the HOST/PETS interactive modeling shell in Central America and Egypt. The development of large simulation models, with multiple components and policy game dimensions has gone on for several years at Utrecht (Klabbers 1985).

Both the small model applications on spreadsheets and the larger modeling shells have advantages and disadvantages for planners. The programmed shell or system is elegant and conserves computer capacity, since it builds in only functions that are to be used, and it is designed to perform sets of related tasks. In contrast, small applications and templates are simpler, easier to understand, easier to adapt to fit new or changing tasks, and easier to teach and communicate to users. Given the central role of communication in social planning, the simpler models are easier to communicate and easier to understand and they stimulate more interaction with users during the design phase.

### 2.1 Feeding the Model: Data management and Information Systems

Forecasting frameworks, whether of a special purpose or more general kind, are supported by many different computer program packages. These include packages for data analysis, information storage, retrieval, and use. Small relational database packages for use with structured, quantitative information serve well for smaller planning models on personal computers. Hierarchical databases such as FOCUS or RAMIS serve large computers. SPIRES and NOTEBOOK are excellent text-handling databases, used more by planners to store and process supporting documentation. Database programs go on toward advanced systems for prototyping, where information systems experts and the decision makers who will use the system work cooperatively from the outset to develop the system through the stages preceding final use.

The personal computer and program packages used in planning (spreadsheets, database systems, project management systems, time series analysis, forecasting, and packages of general statistical methods) have put planning within reach of most managers and helped to take the mystery out of information technology (Bloomfield and Updegrove 1981b, McNeish 1982).

### 2.2 Behind the State of the Art: Simplicity

The methods of educational planning have become simpler. As a result, the planning process is more open socially to the participation of decision makers policy makers, and managers; and also to an important group that has heretofore been excluded from the inner councils, the presumed beneficiaries of educational plans: teachers, students, and citizens who must use school services and pay for them. The planning process has grown more dynamic and immediate as simpler, interactive modeling processes encourage direct intervention and continuous change. The models are better served with data and information for use in the modeling process, which permits many different views of the system and the key variables. It is simpler to test hypotheses, using "what-if" changes. The modeling systems permit projection out to the future, as well as tracing back from future goals to the intermediate steps and current status requirements, using the target and goal-seeking tracebacks in the packages. In short, it is more difficult to make a major mistake by developing a plan with only one view of the future. The multiple views of the future may also be in error, but the odds are reduced and the important gain is that learning results from the very process of considering alternative views. The significant development is not in the technology itself,

but in the enhanced learning it supports through increased participation and communication in the process of planning and in the number, breadth, and depth of alternatives that can be considered.

Even with these new developments in technology, it is no easier than it ever has been to deal with values and with social, political, and cultural ends and purposes of education. Heuristic modeling helps in exploring complex issues, probing assumptions and values, and designing frameworks for choice, but not in making wise choices. Heuristic models are valuable in developing, articulating, and systematizing plan goals, but not in evaluating them, much less in determining their worth to many different groups with competing values.

### 2.3 Goal Analysis and Heuristic Modeling: The State of the Art

Heuristic models help planners deal with the most important, and at the same time most intractable, elements of educational planning:

(a) The identification of the values of those who plan and those for whom they plan, and the statement of these values in a mutually acceptable structure of plan ends, purposes, and goals.

(b) The exploration of complex situations in order to clarify and order the values and goals, the issues and problems, and the needs of the participant beneficaries.

(c) The analysis of the present and past in order to project the future—a central problem for social planning, where the models and methods of time series analysis provide no means for formulating the basic assumptions on which a projection essentially rests.

(d) The analysis of the educational process in qualitative terms, in order to trace educational outputs/ outcomes to antecedent interventions and inputs. Models based on dynamic programming DYNAMO on large computers and Stella for personal computers, are promising but not yet widely used (Clauset and Gaynor 1982).

For the problems of dealing with new and complex issues and for identifying underlying values, and for developing plan goal structures, the following heuristic approaches have proven useful:

(a) Galileo is a communications factor-analysis methodology for mapping value positions and distances on issues of concern to planners and their clients (Woelfel and Fink 1980).

(b) The American Association of State Colleges and Universities has developed a 10-stage paradigmatic structure, which tracks past trends into the future, and analyzes their cross-impacts on sectors of an institution or school system. The AASCU paradigm goes out into the future, posits goals, and traces back required steps to reach the goals. It develops scenarios (consistent and integrated descriptions of the future), traces constraints on future attainment of goals, and identifies organizational units that will be responsible for future actions.

(c) The K–J Method (Kawaikita 1980) is an inquiry system for exploring and classifying complex issues in a new problem area. It helps in tracing fundamental relationships among key variables, and is a more powerful heuristic version of computer-based "Outliners" or "Idea Generator" packages.

(d) Delphi offers two variants: Delphi Exercise and Policy Delphi. Delphi Exercise is a way of forecasting future events that are based on the pooled opinions (consensus) of experts. Policy Delphi is a structure for articulating varying and sometimes conflicting points of view on issues and values that underlie a problem.

Although many heuristic models and paradigms are useful in planning practice, the four listed above are illustrative of the tasks to which heuristics can be applied in planning. No model can take the uncertainty out of future forecasts, deal in quantitative terms with value differences, or articulate and harmonize conflicting goals. Heuristics help however, not only in identifying and dealing with value differences but in reminding planners that these differences exist and that the analytic methods of planners, and the planners themselves, are limited and fallible.

Artificial intelligence (AI) and expert systems, which are heuristic procedures for systematizing rules of thumb for dealing with unsystematic situations, problems, and issues, are thought to be the future direction for social analysis and planning. If the past is a guide, AI will solve some problems, leave some problems unsolved, and create some new and unsolvable problems. Its significance lies in its future promise. It points the planner toward the future. The future is the planner's domain.

## Bibliography

Bessent A, Bessent E W, Clark C T, Elam J E 1986 A microcomputer-based productivity support system for increasing the managerial efficiency of operating units. In: Andriole S (ed.) *Microcomputer Decision Support Systems: Design, Implementation, and Evaluation.* QED Information Systems, Wellesley, Massachusetts

Bloomfield S D, Updegrove D A 1981a A modeling system for higher education. *Decis. Sci.* 12(2): 310–21

Bloomfield S D, Updegrove D A 1981b Modeling for insight, not numbers. In: Wilson J (ed.) *New Directions for Higher Education.* Jossey-Bass, San Francisco, California, pp. 93–104

Bowles S 1969 *Planning Educational Systems for Economic Growth.* Harvard University Press, Cambridge, Massachusetts

Chesswas J D 1969 *Methodologies of Educational Planning for Developing Countries.* UNESCO, International Institute for Educational Planning, Paris

Clauset K H, Gaynor A K 1982 A systems perspective on effective schools. *Educ. Leadership* 40: 54–59

Davis R G 1966 *Planning Human Resource Development.* Rand McNally, Chicago, Illinois

Davis R G 1980 *Planning Education for Development: Educational Models and Schemata*, Vols. 1 and 2. Harvard Center for Studies in Education and Development, Cambridge, Massachusetts

Educational Testing Service (ETS) 1979 *A Manual for the Analysis of Costs and Outcomes in Nonformal Education.* ETS, Princeton, New Jersey

Hopkins D S P, Massy W F 1981 *Planning Models for Colleges and Universities.* Stanford University Press, Stanford, California

Hussain K 1971 *A Resource Requirements Prediction Model.* (RRPM-1), National Center for Higher Education Management Systems, Boulder, Colorado

Judy R W 1969 Systems analysis for efficient resource allocation. In: *Higher Education: Development and Implementation of CAMPUS*, Report to Conference on Management Information System (MIS). Washington

Kawaikita J 1980 *The Original KJ Method.* Kawaikita Research Institute, Tokyo

Klabbers B 1985 Instruments for planning and policy formation. *Simulat. Games* 16(2): 135–60

McNeish M F 1982 Selecting a modeling system. EDUCOM *Bull.* 17(3): 37–41

Nazareth A 1986 The economics in curriculum choice (ECC) model. *Educ. Planning* 5(3): 34–40

Organization for Economic Cooperation and Development 1970 *Occupational and Educational Structures of the Labor Force and Levels of Economic Development.* OECD, Paris

Parnes H 1962 *Forecasting Educational Needs for Economic and Social Development.* Organization for Economic Cooperation and Development, Paris

Roemer M, Stern J J 1975 *The Appraisal of Development Projects.* Praeger, New York

Schiefelbein E, Davis R G 1974 *Development of Educational Planning Models and Application in the Chilean School Reform.* Lexington Books, Lexington, Kentucky

Tinbergen J, Bos H C 1965 *Econometric Models of Education: Some Applications.* Organization for Economic Cooperation and Development Technical Report. OECD, Paris

Woelfel J, Fink E L 1980 *The Measurement of Communication Processes: Galileo Theory and Method.* Academic Press, New York

# Dissemination and Utilization of Evaluation Research

## Knowledge Diffusion in Education

### J. P. Keeves

This article is concerned with the transmission of knowledge about education from those who are involved in research and development to those who must employ that knowledge in their daily work. Just as knowledge in many fields of human endeavour has increased greatly, so too, in education as a consequence of the very significant growth in expenditure on research and development since the early 1960s, has there been a substantial increase in the knowledge about the educational processes for diffusion or dissemination to all those who have use for such knowledge. However, as Huberman and his colleagues have pointed out (Huberman et al. 1981), it is evident that the dissemination of knowledge in education is far more complex and far less manageable than in other fields which would superficially appear similar, such as agriculture or public health.

Related to the increase in knowledge in education and in other fields, there has been widespread recognition of a need for research and investigation into the processes of transmission of knowledge. While diffusion research is emerging as an area of study which is attracting research workers from several disciplines in an attempt to form a single integrated body of concepts and generalizations about the diffusion process, it is important to recognize that the overall area is still very fragmented because of the wide range of disparate elements associated with the creation and utilization of knowledge in different fields of endeavour. One important source of this fragmentation is associated with the different disciplinary perspectives from which the knowledge under consideration has been created. Rogers and Shoemaker (1971) classified the 2,750 items in their diffusion bibliography in seven major and seven minor disciplinary traditions, but they noted that a transfer of ideas was taking place across disciplines in many of the studies under survey. From this review Rogers and Shoemaker were able to revise previous work on the identification of factors which affected the rate of adoption of an innovation. They noted that adoption was not the only outcome, since in reality rejection was also likely to occur; that evaluation of innovations took place either

formally or informally at all stages; and that even after adoption had occurred, further evaluation might lead to subsequent rejection. In addition they noted four stages in the innovation–decision process which are as follows: (a) knowledge—the individual is exposed to the innovation's existence and gains some understanding of how it functions; (b) persuasion—the individual forms a favourable or unfavourable attitude towards the innovation; (c) decision—the individual engages in activities which lead to a decision to adopt or reject the innovation; and (d) confirmation—the individual seeks reinforcement for the innovation–decision which has been made, but a previous decision may be reversed if conflicting information about the innovation is received (Rogers and Shoemaker 1971 p. 103).

From research into the diffusion process there has started to emerge a conceptual paradigm related to the transmission of knowledge that is relevant to many disciplines. Since most social scientists, including educators, are interested in social change, the broad area of diffusion research offers a convenient framework within which to develop such understandings, because a general approach to diffusion has something to offer each discipline. It is necessary before examining the processes of transmission of knowledge in the field of education to consider first the particular characteristics of both the creation and utilization of knowledge in education and how these relate to the processes of diffusion.

## 1. Creation of Educational Knowledge

It is important to recognize that in the field of education, by and large, the body of knowledge that has the most profound influence on policy and practice is derived not from research or from scholarly analysis but from the accumulated wisdom of teachers and administrators working in schools and administrative units throughout the world. Systematic and cumulative research and development in education is a relatively recent phenomenon, commencing only during the twentieth century and only gaining sufficient strength to make a substantial contribution on a worldwide basis during the late 1960s and the 1970s. It has, however, been possible to document the impact of research and development on education through a series of case studies which establish beyond doubt the contribution that research has made during this century to educational policy and practice (Suppes 1978).

Educational research and development yield outcomes that are of three distinct types. Rich (1977), from a study of the use of social science information by administrators in the United States, found it of value to differentiate between the instrumental and the conceptual utilization of knowledge: between what he termed knowledge for action and knowledge for understanding. Likewise, Fullan (1980) has suggested that there are two main types of knowledge available for use. The first refers to knowledge that can be applied to a particular problem and is derived from a specific research study or from a collection of studies. The second refers to cumulative knowledge.

From these perspectives it can be seen that there is firstly knowledge together with the use of knowledge in the field of education, which has been derived from research and study in education, that is associated with principles, broad conceptions, and fundamental paradigms, and that provides a basis for an understanding of the educational process. It must be recognized that such knowledge which is largely of a theoretical nature, is nevertheless important, even if it does not appear to have any immediate application. Contrary to common belief, one of the major outcomes of the very substantial investment in educational research that has taken place since the early 1970s has been the gradual assembling of a considerable body of knowledge about schools and how they function that is only now being built into a coherent conceptual framework.

Secondly, there are findings arising from educational research that have direct applications in educational policy and practice. Nevertheless, it is rare for an individual research study to yield findings that can be used alone to change either policy or practice. The complexity of most educational activities and of the settings in which such activities are carried out will restrict the applicability of the findings derived from a single investigation. However, if several similar studies have been undertaken in a variety of situations, there frequently emerges a more general finding that gains are to be made through the implementation of a new policy or practice.

A third and important type of outcome of educational research and development is the preparation of a tangible product that incorporates the findings of research and has a direct use in schools and classrooms. The marked increase in research and development that occurred in many parts of the world during the late 1960s and the 1970s resulted in the production of a number of educational materials for classroom use, each of which was derived from a particular body of research. The acceptance of these materials varied according to the quality of the research, the quality of the materials, and, in particular, the extent to which the ideas underlying the development of the materials were disseminated to the teachers using particular materials in their classrooms.

These three types of outcome of educational research and development, concerned with principle and paradigm, with policy and practice, and with products that have immediate and direct application in schools are different in kind. They are also associated with different types of utilization and with different approaches to diffusion and dissemination.

## 2. Utilization of Educational Research

As a consequence of the increased body of research-based knowledge in education it has become clearer how such knowledge might be used in the making of policies, the development of practice, and the introduction of tangible products. Weiss (1979) has identified seven ways of utilization of social science research, and all seven approaches would seem to apply in the field of education. What is envisaged is a classification of type of knowledge or product combined with an approach to utilization in the form of a two-way matrix with the three types of knowledge along one axis and the seven approaches to utilization along the other. While not all cells of this matrix will be associated with a specific application, this systemization of the creation of knowledge with the utilization of knowledge would appear to be an appropriate framework within which to consider in detail the mediating process of diffusion or transmission. Moreover, it would seem likely that certain models of the diffusion process will relate to either specific categories of creation of knowledge, or categories of utilization of knowledge, or possibly to a specific cell within the creation–utilization classificatory grid. The seven approaches to utilization of knowledge are considered below.

(a) *Knowledge-driven approach.* Underlying this approach is the view that basic research reveals some findings that have direct application in practice. While this approach would seem highly applicable in the fields of the natural and medical sciences, it is less relevant to education. However, the findings relating to the teaching of subtraction and division have influenced the methods of instruction used in schools in both the United Kingdom and the United States. They provide clear examples of how specific knowledge can be applied in the field of education.

(b) *Problem-solving approach.* In educational policy and practice, a commonly held view of research utilization envisages research as providing empirical evidence and conclusions to help to solve a particular policy problem. In this approach the problem exists and is identified and a decision has to be made to solve the problem, but information and understanding are lacking on how the problem might be solved. Under these circumstances it is appropriate to recognize that research could provide the missing knowledge and understanding.

(c) *Interactive approach*. In this approach neither the researcher involved in the creation of knowledge, nor the practitioner with a problem to be solved, work independently of the other. They interact with one another in a manner that involves both a search for knowledge as well as a solution to a problem. Sometimes the necessary knowledge is obtained through a search for and reconceptualization of findings already available and sometimes the need to obtain an appropriate solution leads to a substantial programme of research and development. The creation of new knowledge, however, is only one component of an interactive process that also involves the utilization of knowledge.

(d) *Enlightenment approach*. Probably the most common way in which knowledge derived from educational research is used for policy making or practice is through the cumulative effects from a substantial number of research studies each of which contributes to a change in thinking about certain educational questions. In this approach there is no assumption that decision makers or practitioners seek out research-based knowledge to assist them, but rather they are influenced by an enlightenment that has come to them as a result of the cumulative findings derived from research, often without an awareness of the origins of the knowledge.

(e) *Political approach*. Recognition that policy and practice are influenced by an accumulated body of research findings has led many educational policy makers and practitioners to resolve to make certain changes, and then to seek legitimation from research. This can occur through a search in the research literature to find support for the proposed change; a task that is not as difficult as would seem at first because of the often contradictory nature of the results of research studies in the same area. Alternatively, it can occur through the commissioning of research, particularly of an evaluative kind, to find evidence to legitimate a decision that has already been made but perhaps not been publicly or explicitly stated. Some of the research in recent years into open-plan schooling was of this kind.

(f) *Tactical approach*. Related to the political approach is a tactical approach where certain decisions which were made have subsequently come under challenge. In these circumstances it is a common ploy to commission research as a delaying action to enable the new policy or practice to become more thoroughly established. The implications of the findings of the research may have to be faced at a later stage.

(g) *Research-oriented approach*. Underlying this approach to the utilization of research-based knowledge is the view that the process of inquiry is of value in itself. It is assumed that if policy makers and practitioners are directly engaged in the research enterprise they will not only facilitate the utilization of research findings but they will also promote wider diffusion and acceptance of research-based knowledge. This approach

emphasizes the unity of the three components of creation, diffusion, and utilization of knowledge rather than the distinctiveness of each component process. In part this is an underlying theme in action research and in the teachers as researchers or the teachers as evaluators movements that were advocated in the early twentieth century and which have gained acceptance once more in recent years.

## 3. The Diffusion Process

The theoretical framework that has helped to guide much of the thinking about the diffusion process in education, although of relatively recent development, has come to be called the "classical diffusion model". A detailed statement of this model is provided by Rogers and Shoemaker (1971). The four main elements of this model are: (a) an innovation defined as an idea perceived as new by an individual, (b) is communicated through certain channels, (c) over a sustained period of time, (d) among the members of a social system. This classical model in one form or another is still the most popular for the study of diffusion or for an understanding and use of the diffusion process. There are many other models that differ in their degree of comprehensiveness, such as the suggestion made by Hood (1973) that there are three models for the study of change in education: the organizational improvement model, the extension network model, and the research, development, and marketing model. However, the most extensive treatment of models of the diffusion process has been undertaken by Havelock and his colleagues and their models provide a sound basis for the consideration of the transmission or dissemination of knowledge in education. In this article the models developed by Havelock will be described in some detail, because with these models it is possible to investigate the diffusion process in education in a coherent way. In addition, it is possible to consider the planning of a range of services for the transmission of knowledge in education in terms of various combinations of the Havelock models. It is also important to note the interrelations between the Havelock models and the various categories of knowledge creation and utilization considered in the previous sections of this article.

## 4. The Havelock Models

In the mid-1960s, Havelock undertook a major review of the literature in the diverse fields of medicine, agriculture, industrial technology, and education and, in 1970, a national survey of school districts in the United States, to learn what research workers and practitioners said about the processes of dissemination and utilization of knowledge from research. From the review he concluded that there were three existing perspectives or models which described the transmission of knowledge from the research centres to the user.

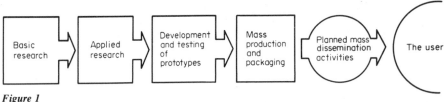

**Figure 1**
The research, development, and diffusion model
Source: Havelock R G 1971

### 4.1 Research, Development, and Diffusion Model

In this model it was assumed that there was a rational and orderly sequence from basic research, to applied research, to the development and testing of a prototype, the preparation and packaging of a product, and the planned dissemination to the user (Havelock 1971). This model is presented diagrammatically in Fig. 1. In it, the user is seen to play a relatively passive role. While this model gained wide acceptance in the 1960s, experience would appear to indicate that it involves a gross oversimplification of the manner in which knowledge about education and the products of research actually spread. It should be noted that the model relates directly to one of the approaches to utilization of knowledge advanced by Weiss (1979).

### 4.2 Social Interaction Model

This second perspective is seen to apply widely in the spread of knowledge both in agriculture and in medicine. In this model individuals are seen as interacting with colleagues within a reference group or through membership of an association, and these colleagues influence whether or not the individuals accept the research findings and the practices advocated, or adopt particular products. Informal personal contacts within the reference group provide the opportunity for the transmission of ideas. This model is portrayed in Fig. 2. Some educational innovations spread in this way, but the operation is dependent on the leaders of the reference groups and associations gaining access to the necessary information from research sources.

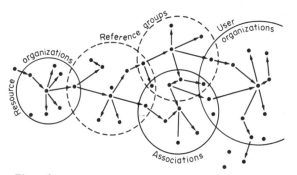

**Figure 2**
The social interaction model
Source: Havelock R G 1971

### 4.3 Problem-solving Model

A third approach, that is widely accepted as applying in education, is the problem-solving model. Again it relates to one of the categories of knowledge utilization advanced by Weiss (1979). In this model each user identifies a need, diagnoses a problem, undertakes a search for a solution, and tries possible alternative solutions to the problem. In education, this model would appear to be particularly applicable to the solving of organizational problems. Consultation with a research worker or person outside the system engaged in solving a problem is not necessarily part of the process, and when one is consulted it is customary for a nondirective or advisory role to be adopted. This approach involves an emphasis on a local initiative and the development of a local solution that in all probability would not apply in another setting. The nature of this problem-solving model is shown in Fig. 3.

### 4.4 Linkage Model

Subsequently, Havelock (1973) attempted to combine the best documented features of each of the previous models in order to account for a two-way flow of information between the source and the user. This led to the development of a fourth model, which is presented in simplified form in Fig. 4. The user and the resource system are involved in a reciprocal and collaborative interaction, and each reacts to assimilate the ideas that the other can provide. Thus there is a linkage established between the two systems and the model is known as the linkage model. An important component of the linkage model is the presence of a linkage medium, since direct face-to-face contact is rarely possible in educational work between the users and the resource system. It should be noted that the linkage model has three major components; the resource system, the linkage medium, and the user system. Within the user system are the schools, their teachers and students, the parents of the students, the regional and state education boards or authorities, and the administrative staff serving those boards or authorities. The linkage medium comprises the linkage agents, linkage instruments, and linkage institutions. The linkage institutions include the colleges of education and teachers' colleges, curriculum centres, inservice education centres, teachers' centres and resource centres, and the regional offices or district offices as these institutions are variously called in different parts of the world. The linkage agents are, in

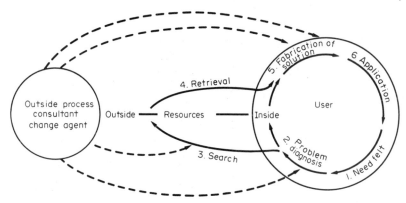

**Figure 3**
The problem-solver model

Source: Havelock R G 1971

the main, the persons who work within the linkage institutions, and include college lecturers, education officers, advisory officers, school district officers, supervisory and inspectorial officers, and curriculum consultants. The linkage instruments consist of published reports, journals, video programmes, pamphlets, and the like. All three components are used in one way or another for the two-way communication between the two systems. There remains the resource system which necessarily includes the research institutions, the universities, and their research centres, curriculum development centres, and other research and development centres. It is important to recognize that in the linkage model there is not just a one-way transmission of information from the resource system to the user system. There is in addition a necessary transmission of information from the user system to the resource system. Without this communication of issues and needs for research and development, the resource system would be operating largely in a vacuum. Huberman et al.

(1981) have examined the operation of the linkage model in terms of knowledge transfer theory and organizational theories. They have emphasized that very few real-world knowledge transfer situations involve only one resource system and only one user, and the linkage paradigm presented above must be enlarged to provide for these complexities. In addition they suggest that the term "network" must be employed to refer to relations among individuals, and the term "interorganizational arrangements" to refer to the more formal relations that must necessarily be established between organizations or institutions. Not only are networks and interorganizational arrangements built up among the members of a resource system and among the members of a user system, but they must also be built up between the user system, the linkage agents and linkage organizations, and between these agents and organizations and the resource system. Huberman et al. (1981) have begun to explore the nature of the transactions that occur between and within these systems.

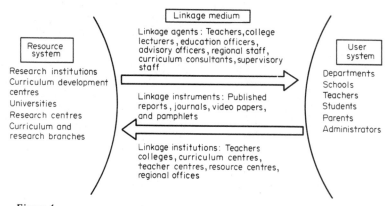

**Figure 4**
The linkage model

Source: Havelock R G 1971

## 4.5 A Study of the Linkage Model

Owen (1979) has carried out a significant study to investigate the applicability of the linkage model to the adoption and implementation of the Australian Science Education Project materials by Australian secondary schools. The research undertaken by Owen has found that elements of all three models: the research, development, and diffusion model; the problem-solving model; and the social interaction model operate in a complex way within the linkage model in a manner that is consistent with the perspective advanced by Havelock (1973). The contribution made by Owen has been not only to identify in the Australian setting the characteristics of the user system but also to investigate the dimensions of the linkage medium. The user system was viewed by Owen in terms of five characteristics: knowledge of research findings; openness to innovation and change; interaction with other users, and with the linkage medium; organization within the user unit, so that resources available are effectively displayed; and cooperation within the user unit, so that individual users share with each other experiences gained during the introduction of the innovation. In addition, Owen identified four linkage mechanisms which were associated with a high level of adoption and maintenance of an innovation. These were: participation within the research and development enterprise; contact with the charge agent; engagement in relevant teacher education programmes; and the examination of appropriate dissemination material. Adoption and effective utilization of innovative practices in the Australian setting appeared to require not only possession of a high degree of several of the user characteristics, but also the effective operation of several of the linkage mechanisms. Possession of one characteristic alone by a user, or the operation of one mechanism alone within the linkage medium was not enough.

Owen did not investigate directly how the resource system could act most effectively in the diffusion and dissemination of its research findings and products. However, the account that he has provided of the way in which and the degree to which one innovation spread across Australia gives some picture of how a resource system should operate to ensure that maximum gains are made in the use of findings and products of educational research and development. Nevertheless, it is clear that a one-way flow from the resource system to the user system is not considered an appropriate or effective account of the processes of dissemination or diffusion of the products of research and development in education. Furthermore, the chance interactions within a social network or interorganizational arrangement as envisaged within the social interaction model, or the passive wait for the users to identify a need as envisaged in the problem-solving model are clearly not efficient approaches to the diffusion and utilization of knowledge in education. Nevertheless, there are situations operating in practice in which Owen and his colleagues have

been able to show that one of the three component models is operating largely in isolation and without interplay with either of the other two models as is envisaged within the linkage model. Hence all four models are required to give a complete account of the real-world situation.

## 5. Approaches to Planned Diffusion

There is no single method or procedure which alone can be recommended to carry out the effective transmission of useful knowledge in education. Rather there would seem to be many approaches that should be used when and where they are considered appropriate. It is clearly necessary to identify different approaches and promote and develop their use in ways judged to be most effective. Nevertheless, it is important to recognize that not only should the resource system be planning to ensure that the maximum benefits flow from its research and development work, but the user system should also be planning to ensure that it receives maximum benefit from the research and development work that is carried out. This latter is accomplished both by ensuring that knowledge is disseminated in appropriate ways as well as by ensuring that the research being undertaken takes cognizance of the perceived needs of the users.

Thompson (1981) in an account of the programmes sponsored by the National Institute of Education in the United States, saw these dissemination programmes lying along a continuum from the Educational Resources Information Centre (ERIC) at one end to local problem-solving work at the other. This view of dissemination may be extended to suggest that most dissemination activities in education may be considered to lie along a similar continuum ranging from a research, development, and diffusion orientation at one end to an orientation towards problem solving at the school and classroom levels at the other. While this view is perhaps an oversimplified one, the two orientations do take cognizance of the perspectives of the resource system and the user system respectively. Thus to consider diffusion programmes and activities as lying along a continuum is helpful in ordering thinking about such programmes. This framework, the diffusion continuum, which is represented in Fig. 5, may be used to give a brief account of the major types of formal programmes or planned activities that are operating in the transmission of knowledge about education. It must be recognized that there are informal activities which occur as well to assist in the diffusion of knowledge. These are covered, in the main, by the social interaction model where it operates at an informal level. This model can, however, be used in a more deliberate way through the establishment of networks among individuals.

## 5.1 Programs of Publication

Perhaps the most obvious form of dissemination of information is through planned programmes of pub-

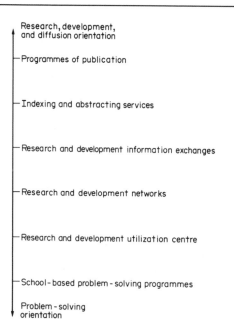

Research, development,
and diffusion orientation

Programmes of publication

Indexing and abstracting services

Research and development information exchanges

Research and development networks

Research and development utilization centre

School-based problem-solving programmes

Problem-solving
orientation

**Figure 5**
The diffusion continuum

lication in the form of books, research monographs, journals, microfiche documents, summary reports, and newsletters. The major problems encountered are associated with the need to write for different audiences. Reports providing full technical detail are necessary in order for an assessment to be made of the quality of the research, but such reports are largely incomprehensible to practising teachers and administrators. On the other hand, summary reports can receive widespread publicity, but be based on poor quality work that is effectively concealed by skilful writing and lack of detail. It is important to note that while some of the costs of production of publications can be reduced through the increased use of technology in typesetting and preparation, the overall costs of printing and distribution might be expected to rise to such an extent that much important material may become lost or buried through lack of resources for publication.

## 5.2 Indexing and Abstracting Services

A second approach to dissemination is the systematic compilation of an index and the provision of an abstracting service in the field of education. In the late 1970s and early 1980s significant steps were taken through the introduction of new technology to improve both the quality of such services and their accessibility. Access can now be provided to indexing and abstracting services by means of computer-based systems across countries linked by satellite, through microfiche copies of reports, and through videographic procedures. It must be recognized, however, that such systems based on advanced technology are costly to install.

## 5.3 Research and Development Information Exchanges

Both the profusion and diffuseness of much of the reporting in the field of educational research makes it difficult for individual users to select directly from the publications available, or through an abstracting service, the more general ideas that could influence their thinking on specific issues, or that could assist with the solving of particular problems. However, there are increasing numbers of newsletters and similar publications which provide both summaries of research that is reported more fully elsewhere, as well as discussions of current problems and issues. At the present time the programmes and activities in this area and the information available are perhaps too far towards the research, development, and diffusion end of the continuum in Fig. 5. They do not present as fully information on the problems being encountered by schools that would be helpful to the research system in its thinking about research studies which might be planned and conducted. Moreover, there is a need for such exchanges to promote the widespread adoption of validated innovations as opposed to simply disseminating information from research or from the evaluation of particular programmes.

## 5.4 Research and Development Networks

The establishment of research and development networks is based on the assumption that the exchange of information can take place in ways other than those provided by printed documents. In the main, networks rely on social interaction between individuals, and operate at an informal level. The functions of the networks are: (a) to select, synthesize, and interpret the findings of educational research for practitioners in the schools and for policy makers, (b) to identify validated innovations and to spread information about such practices, (c) to provide information to consumers on products together with evidence of their effectiveness, (d) through discussion and debate to communicate the needs of practitioners and policy makers to research workers, and (e) to collect information on the experiences of practitioners and to add this information to the accumulated body of knowledge about education. In general, networks are loosely structured and rely on informal contacts and the social interaction between members of the network to achieve the goals set within the network, rather than through the adoption of clearly defined policies and programmes. It is, however, possible for change agents to be appointed to develop such networks and so to fulfil a mission to effect the widespread adoption of particular innovations or products rather than to merely supply information regarding new practices and policies.

## 5.5 Research and Development Utilization Centres

From the time of the setting up of the Schools Council in the United Kingdom in the mid-1960s there has been an increase in the establishment and growth of a range of centres and units, both in that country and more recently elsewhere, whose activities are directed towards: (a) the enhancement of problem-solving capabilities, (b) the supply of appropriate research and development resources, (c) the promotion of an awareness of the existence and nature of problems, and (d) the stimulation and motivation of personnel within schools and districts to meet the conditions necessary for change and innovation. In general, the centres which have been established are of two types, differing in the extent to which they focus on more specific but widely occurring problems, or on more general issues relating to the common problems of schools and teachers in an area. The former more specific problems are catered for in resource centres, which commonly provide services and facilities to assist with the resolution and treatment of particular problems. The latter more general problems are catered for in teachers' centres that have far greater flexibility of operation in order to meet the specific needs of the teachers and school administrators served by the centres. Since many of the centres that have been established are self-governing, there has been marked variation in their stated aims and the ways in which they function. As a consequence, the impression is often gained of an amorphous collection of small centres and units serving many different purposes. Nevertheless, since such centres are located more at the problem-solving end of the continuum presented in Fig. 5 than at the research, development, and diffusion end it is not surprising that such differences in purpose and function should appear since, in the main, these research and development utilization centres have been set up to help solve the problems of a specific group of educational practitioners, rather than to fulfil a highly specified role or to promote a highly specific programme or product.

### 5.6 School-based Problem-solving Programmes

During the 1970s there was an increased emphasis and a widespread acceptance in many parts of the world of school-based evaluation programmes. Stemming from this work the practice has developed of examining specific problems of a curricular or organizational kind within schools without conducting a full-scale evaluation exercise. There is clearly a growing interest in the identification and analysis of specific problems in schools, together with attempts to find solutions to those problems. The effectiveness of such programmes may, in part, depend on their capacity to draw on the knowledge and expertise available from research and development enterprises. While there may be little cause to doubt that a great deal of value is being achieved by such programmes, there would sometimes appear to be a lack of appropriate structures and strategies by which guidance and assistance could be obtained from resource systems to provide the knowledge and understanding which can be derived from research and development in education.

## 6. Some Issues in Dissemination in Education

The models of the diffusion process advanced above expose some of the weaknesses in current dissemination programmes. The research, development, and diffusion approach is deficient in so far as it assumes relatively passive consumers and a linear sequence of activities. The problem-solving perspective has limitations as a strategy in so far as it involves responding only to local initiatives, and makes no provision for the planning and promotion of change through the dissemination of knowledge about improved practice. The social interaction approach pays little attention to the nature of the knowledge or innovation to be diffused or to how implementation takes place after adoption. The linkage perspective, in so far as it combines the most appropriate features of the three earlier models is the most useful. It permits a diagnosis of need and a planned organization of the resources whether in the form of knowledge or innovatory practice and product, to ensure their relevance to the user. However, as Raizen (1979) has pointed out, unless those responsible for the implementation of proposed changes are involved at an early stage in the process of identification of the problem, and in the consideration of alternative strategies for its solution, it is unlikely that effective implementation will occur after the adoption of a proposed improvement. It is clear that future research in the field of diffusion needs to focus on the implementation process and the subsequent history of an innovation once it has been introduced. In the planning of strategies for widespread programmes of diffusion it would appear important to give full consideration to the range of alternatives that lie along the continuum extending from research, development, and diffusion at one extreme to specific problem-solving programmes at the other. However, it is necessary to recognize the need for full cooperation between the individuals and agencies involved, rather than to depend on programmes originating solely from the resource system or from a centralized bureaucracy.

Furthermore, recognition must also be given to the need to provide information in forms that are appropriate to the specific audience receiving the information. In addition, it is necessary to acknowledge both the difficulty and the importance of combining and condensing the information available so that a coherent and consistent message is presented. Following a decade or more of intensive research and development in the field of education during the 1970s, the major task in the diffusion of knowledge is the finding of ways of synthesizing the evidence that is available and presenting the findings in a manner that is meaningful to audiences who conduct school systems and who implement change in systems, schools, and classrooms. Following the synthesis of the evidence available, the next major development would appear to be the formation of dissemination centres in which linkage agents would work to promote educational policies and practices that would incorporate the best of what is known from research about the educational process.

## Bibliography

Fullan M 1980 An R & D prospectus for educational reform. In: Mack D P, Ellis W E (eds.) 1980 *Interorganizational Arrangements for Collaborative Efforts: Commissioned Papers.* Northwest Regional Educational Laboratory, Portland, Oregon, pp. 29–48

Havelock R G 1971 The utilisation of educational research and development. *Br. J. Educ. Technol.* 2: 84–98

Havelock R G (ed.) 1973 *Planning for Innovation through Dissemination and Utilization of Knowledge.* Center for Research and Utilization of Scientific Knowledge, Ann Arbor, Michigan

Hood P D 1973 How research and development on educational roles and institutional structures can facilitate communication. *J. Res. Dev. Educ.* 6(4): 96–113

Huberman A M, Levinson N S, Havelock R G, Cox P L 1981 Interorganizational arrangements: An approach to educational practice improvement. *Knowledge: Creation, Diffusion, Utilization* 3: 5–22

Husén T, Kogan M (eds.) 1984 *Educational Research and Policy: How do they Relate?* Pergamon, Oxford

Kosse G B (ed.) 1982 *Social Science Research and Public Policy Making.* NFER-Nelson, Windsor

Owen J M 1979 The Australian Science Education Project: A study of factors affecting its adoption and implementation in schools. Doctoral Thesis, Monash University, Monash

Raizen S A 1979 Dissemination programs at the National Institute of Education: 1974–1979. *Knowledge: Creation, Diffusion, Utilization* 1: 259–92

Rich R F 1977 Uses of social science information by federal bureaucrats: Knowledge for action versus knowledge for understanding. In: Weiss C H (ed.) 1977 *Using Social Research in Public Policy Making.* Heath, Lexington, Massachusetts, pp. 199–211

Rogers E M, Shoemaker F F 1971 *Communication of Innovations: A Cross-cultural Approach,* 2nd edn. Free Press, New York

Suppes P (ed.) 1978 *Impact of Research on Education: Some Case Studies.* National Academy of Education, Washington, DC

Thompson C L 1981 Dissemination at the National Institute of Education: Contending ideas about research, practice and the federal role. Paper presented at the 1981 Annual Meeting of the American Educational Research Association, Los Angeles, California

Weiss C H 1979 The many meanings of research utilization. *Public Admin. Rev.* 39: 426–31

# Dissemination of Educational Research

**K. King**

Dissemination will be considered here as the process whereby research results reach different audiences. In the case of educational research findings it is useful to think of at least three possible audiences that may be the objects of the dissemination process: (a) other researchers; (b) practitioners in the schools, colleges, and other parts of the education system; and (c) policy makers, including politicians, responsible for decisions about education at the national or local levels. It will also be valuable conceptually to look at dissemination in a North–South perspective, since there are many concerns about the present structures of dissemination, and the extent to which these are influenced by the relative power of Northern industrialized nations over the majority of less industrialized, developing countries of the South.

In both North and South, there are similarities between the relative difficulty of dissemination to the different audiences mentioned above. By far the easiest of the three is the dissemination of research results from the original researcher to other researchers; much more difficulty arises when trying to spread new educational findings to practitioners, whether school teachers, teacher trainers, or adult educators. Finally, the greatest difficulty is for new and important research to reach policy makers and politicians in Ministries of Education and regional or local councils. In part these differences are explained by the fact that for many researchers their preferred audience is other researchers. Their

first inclination is the presentation of results in learned journals, or in specialist conferences of other researchers. The language of these communications is usually the technical language of their particular field. All this is to be expected, given that researchers seek recognition and eventual promotion in their professions by this first form of dissemination. The transfer of their findings to practitioners is normally left to the educational weekly newspapers, or if some research is particularly topical, it can be disseminated by the more serious daily papers. This question of topicality is equally important for dissemination into the policy process. Occasionally, independent research results are coincidentally to hand when a particular educational crisis sparks public and political attention, but there is little likelihood of the bulk of educational research being disseminated to the decision-making level. The principal obstacle to dissemination both with practitioners and policy makers is that the technical language of research is not accessible to those audiences and in addition, the task of "translating" research language into a commonsense summary is seldom undertaken. One way around this problem of poor dissemination from individual researchers to government bodies has been for the government agency itself to sponsor research on themes which it feels are important; as a corollary, an increasing amount of attention is given by some researchers to "policy research"—conducting research quite deliberately on issues upon which government can be expected to review policy options backed by research. It is possible to see three important dimensions in the dissemination of research in the North and in the South.

## 1. Research Dissemination in the North

In many ways this is the most active of the three dimensions. Researchers in the North are supported by the apparatus necessary to research communication. Journals both general and specialized are abundant and they appear with regularity. Copies of new research articles are readily available either from the original scholars or from data banks on educational research. Reprographic facilities are almost everywhere taken for granted and university and research libraries are committed to acquiring current books and periodicals. Despite this developed infrastructure for dissemination in the North, language remains a major barrier to the flow of information between industrialized countries. There is, for example, much more rapid diffusion amongst anglophone Canada, the United Kingdom, Ireland, and the United States than there is amongst Japan, the Soviet Union, France, the Federal Republic of Germany, Scandinavia, or Spain. To a limited extent, the language barrier can be overcome by multilingual data banks, and by the existence of small international networks of researchers in the North who meet on a disciplinary basis, and act as informal translators of research across language groups.

As far as dissemination to practitioners and policy makers in the North is concerned, it is again the case that many channels are available and open for the flow of research communication. Policy research centres and contracted research aid this process, as does the existence of research funding which frequently builds support to dissemination into the educational research grant itself.

## 2. Dissemination in the South

This covers dissemination of research within a particular developing country on the one hand, and from one country to another across the South. Both within and across countries of the South, there are major problems of research dissemination with all three types of audiences under discussion. In addition to many of the difficulties experienced in the North, notably language barriers, there are a series of dissemination obstacles which make the situation qualitatively different in many, but by no means all, of the developing countries of the South. Dissemination within the nation itself is often hindered by the absence or irregularity of scholarly journals, infrequent professional meetings, and the relatively small size and consequent isolation of some research communities. In some countries, the educational research community is extremely small, but this does not necessarily make it any more likely that research will be satisfactorily disseminated than where there are large numbers of competing research findings.

It seems that some kind of critical mass is almost essential to afford researchers an audience to address in the first instance.

At the regional level or across continents, the situation is in general worse. Even within the same language group, there is not necessarily much research dissemination at all amongst anglophone East, West, Central, or Southern Africa, nor even much amongst neighbouring countries in East or West Africa. Indeed, without funding for regional meetings on a regular basis and the frequent interchange of national journals, the present very weak South–South dissemination cannot rapidly improve.

The very strength of the dissemination process in the North interferes with the improvement of dissemination in the South. Although scholars in the South may wish to have their findings read locally and regionally, their own local journals are frequently less regular, and less likely to be purchased by the national and university libraries than international journals in the field. Hence, many researchers prefer Northern journals for their findings and it is thus sometimes the case that research is disseminated from South to South via a journal of international standing in a Northern capital.

This seems certainly not to be the case as far as much of Spanish-speaking Latin America is concerned. Research is communicated through some journals across the continent and this is aided by an organization of Spanish language research summaries (*Resumenes Analiticos*). There is a widely based concern in the region with the dissemination of educational research, and an interest in exploring ways that researchers can communicate with both policy makers and practitioners.

The pattern is different again in South and Southeast Asia. In some countries, the existence of strongly centralized government research centres brings the research process much nearer to the decision-making process. There remains, however, a problem for university-based research to gain recognition in this situation.

Finally, on this South–South dimension, it has to be acknowledged that some countries, for example India, have a very large local research production, and many hundreds of educational journals. These may well have some direct policy impact within the country itself but there seems to be very little dissemination of Indian research findings in education to audiences outside India, either in the North, or to other anglophone countries in the South.

## 3. Dissemination between the North and the South

As a result of the long-standing patterns of communication between metropolis and colony during the colonial period, and their continuation after formal independence from the colonial empires, whole sections of the world look Northwards not only to disseminate their findings, but also to select the kind of research to undertake in the first place. Such is the influence of Northern university research centres, their links to funding, and to the dissemination infrastructure, that new research themes and findings are disseminated rapidly and effectively. A powerful channel for their dissemination North–South has been the presence of very large numbers of developing country scholars in Northern universities since the early 1950s. Long-term doctoral training in the North has predisposed Southern scholars to work on topics and methodologies of interest in the North, and also to the reproduction (or dissemination) of these results in their own universities. The corollary of this has been very significant numbers of Northern scholars doing research in the Third World, often with more adequate funding than those they worked amongst. In many cases, the natural outlet for such Northern research upon the South has been Northern journals, or the bilateral and multilateral agencies concerned with education in developing countries. As a consequence both of the South–North movement of Third World scholars and the North–South movement of Northern scholars, the comparative advantage of dissemination via the industrialized countries has been strengthened. To some extent, therefore, the research dissemination situation is an analogue of the larger pattern of Northern dominance in information processing, storage, and communication.

It should be noted, however, that there have been some critical influences in research which have flowed from the South to the North. These would include insights into the conduct of participatory and action research, in which Latin America has been a particularly powerful disseminator Northwards of methodology and approaches. Another example would be methodologies for literacy, with Freire being only one of many sources of inspiration. Together, these do a little to correct the balance of Northern influence on the South. But although small in scope, some of these Southern successes in dissemination may also be instrumental in suggesting ways in which the research community can reach and involve practitioners, particularly teachers, in the research process. Collaborative research with teachers is of course by no means a Southern monopoly, but it does suggest some new ways of altering some aspects of educational research from being a specialist activity of the professional researcher to being also a part-time enthusiasm of the practising teacher. In this situation, the task of research dissemination is greatly altered, and collaborative research with teachers becomes the counterpart of the policy research mode with decision makers. Both, in different ways, reduce significantly the gap between the researchers and two of the principal audiences.

## Bibliography

Husén T, Kogan M (eds.) 1984 *Education Research and Policy: How Do They Relate?* Pergamon, Oxford

Myers R 1981 *Connecting Worlds of Research.* International Development Research Centre, Ottawa, Ontario

Nisbet J, Broadfoot P 1980 *The Impact of Research on Policy and Practice in Education.* Aberdeen University Press, Aberdeen

# Knowledge Utilization

**W. Dunn, B. Holzner, and G. Zaltman**

The study of knowledge utilization is a product of the historic rise in reflective awareness of the importance of scientific and professional knowledge in contemporary societies. Scholarly and practical interest in knowledge utilization has grown apace with changes in modern social organization characterized in terms of the post-industrial (Bell 1973) or knowledge society (Machlup 1980). The ascendance of this new form of social organization, marked by the explosive growth of knowledge industries which will soon account for more than 50 percent of the total measured economic activity of many societies, has done much to stimulate the growth of an emergent interdisciplinary social science of knowledge utilization.

## 1. A New Problematic

The core problematic of this emergent interdisciplinary field is best stated as a question: What must we examine in order to understand and shape applications of scientific and professional knowledge to problems of social practice? Although this question bears a surface resemblance to problems addressed by evaluators in education, agriculture, health, and other domains of social practice, the study of knowledge utilization involves a significant shift in the aims of the social sciences. While practical applications of scientific and professional knowledge clearly provide the rationale for evaluation research and other specialties within the applied social sciences, contributors to the applied social sciences have traditionally largely confined their investigations to the social and cognitive conditions under which scientific and technical knowledge is *produced* (see, for example, Campbell 1977). By contrast, an emerging social science of knowledge applications aims at creating theories, methods, and substantive findings which improve our comprehension of the effects of social and cognitive factors on the *application* of knowledge in contexts of social practice (see Dunn and Holzner 1988).

## 2. Multidisciplinary Sources

This emergent field has practical as well as academic sources, drawing in part on earlier programmatic appeals for a sociology of the social consequences of the basic and applied sciences, as represented by the work of Merton (1973), and Lazarsfeld et al. (1975). Recently, Holzner (1978) and Holzner and Marx (1979) have called for a classical sociology of knowledge "turned upside down," a new field of sociological inquiry, which addresses the effects of social arrangements on the application of science and other forms of knowledge. Convergent programs have emerged in the economics of knowledge applications (Machlup 1980) and in proposals for a sociology of applied scientific validity focusing on program evaluation and other policy sciences (Campbell 1987).

Apart from its origins in academic sociology and economics, this emergent field has also been informed by earlier policy-oriented appeals in Europe and the United States to link science to the achievement of social and economic goals, for example, Huxley's *Scientific Research and Social Needs* (1934), Bernal's *The Social Function of Science* (1939), and Bush's *Science: The Endless Frontier* (1944). In line with these practical proposals is the tradition of action research, as exemplified by the contributions of Kurt Lewin, the "practical theorist" (see Marrow 1969). The tradition of action research is closely associated with recent developments in the epistemology of professional practice (e.g., Schön 1983) and with efforts to link processes of knowledge application to theories and strategies of planned social change (e.g., Havelock 1969, Zaltman 1979, Glaser et al. 1983).

Given these multiple origins, it is evident that the field of knowledge applications is less a division of sociology, per se, than it is an interdisciplinary applied social science, or what Havelock (1969 p. 1) had earlier called a "science of knowledge utilization". As such, the field includes but transcends sociology, encompassing theory and research by economists (e.g., Machlup 1980), psychologists (e.g., Campbell 1988), social psychologists (e.g., Caplan 1979), political scientists (e.g., Rich 1981), information scientists (e.g., Kochen 1975), and specialists in action-oriented fields including planned social change, social marketing, social research and development, and the communication of innovations (see, for example, Rothman 1980, Rogers and Kincaid 1981, Zaltman 1983).

Multidisciplinary literature published over the last 25 years has been reviewed periodically by contributors to the field, including Rogers and Shoemaker (1971), Havelock (1969), Dunn and Holzner (1982), Glaser et al. (1983), Zhang (1986), and Dunn and Holzner (1988). Allowing for overlap among the works cited in these reviews, and recognizing the exclusion of government reports and scholarly works published in languages other than English, the published literature will probably have reached 10,000 items by 1990. New contributions to this literature are frequently published in two main scholarly journals: *Knowledge: Creation, Diffusion, Utilization* and *Knowledge in Society: The International Journal of Knowledge Transfer*. The latter is explicitly international in scope.

## 3. Conceptualization

Thus far, there has been no comprehensive synthesis of the conceptual content of this large and expanding body of literature. Although recent syntheses in specialized areas such as education (e.g., Huberman 1987) and science impact assessment (e.g., Dunn and Holzner 1987) mark a step in this direction, it is difficult to construct from such efforts a clear vision of the conceptual content of the field as a whole. Nevertheless, it is useful to view published work in the field in terms of four broadly accepted theses as described below.

### 3.1 Subjectivity

The subjectivity thesis holds that scientific and professional knowledge, however well-warranted on logical and empirical grounds, is subjectively construed by individual and collective actors. These subjective constructions are products of competing sets of organized assumptions, standards, or criteria employed to assess knowledge claims. The organization of these sets has been discussed in the topological and structural vocabularies of "cognitive maps", "schemata", or "frames of reference" (see, for example, Holzner and Fisher 1979). In turn, the content of these organized sets has been described in terms of "reality tests", "truth tests", and "utility tests" (see, for example, Weiss and Bucuvalas 1980). The thesis of subjectivity, which has nothing to do with the doctrine of epistemological relativism, was cogently stated by Machlup (1980 p. 108), whose five classes of knowledge are based on the criterion of "the subjective meaning of the known to the *knower*" (emphasis original).

### 3.2 Corrigibility

The corrigibility thesis holds that scientific and professional knowledge, whether directed toward understanding or toward action, may be improved. The improvement of knowledge has been viewed in many ways, for example, as a process involving empirical and conceptual problem solving (Laudan 1977), rational consensus (Habermas 1975), epistemological evolution (Campbell 1988), or reflective social learning in contexts of professional practice (Schön 1983). In each case, however, scientific and professional knowledge is viewed as corrigible by virtue of non-arbitrary standards of assessment which, when applied to competing knowledge claims, permit judgments about their comparative evidential merit. Theses of corrigibility and subjectivity are the normative and descriptive sides of the same coin.

### 3.3 Sociality

The thesis of sociality holds that the production, transfer, and utilization of scientific and professional knowledge are social processes. The sociality thesis affirms that the application of scientific and professional knowledge is influenced by social arrangements which are structured according to power, wealth, privilege, class, and status. There is ample evidence that the structure of social arrangements—societies, governments, communities, organizations—affects the production, transfer and utilization of scientific and professional knowledge (see, for example, Rich 1981). Available evidence also shows that variations in social, political, and organizational structures affect, and in turn are affected by, the subjective interpretation and epistemological justification of knowledge claims (see, for example, Weiss and Bucuvalas 1980, Dunn 1982, Campbell 1987). Altogether, theses of sociality, corrigibility, and subjectivity affirm that processes of knowledge application may be viewed, simultaneously and legitimately, from standpoints which are "external" as well as "internal" to the process of scientific and professional inquiry.

### 3.4 Complexity

The complexity thesis holds that knowledge-related stages, phases, or functions are interdependent in their properties and effects. Thus, for example, Rothman (1980) views social research and development as a set of interdependent phases, the properties and effects of which interact through time, while Holzner and Marx (1979) see what they call the social system of knowledge as a socially constrained configuration of interdependent knowledge functions ranging from knowledge mandating and knowledge production to knowledge distribution and knowledge utilization. The complexity thesis punctuates the importance of viewing knowledge-related functions and their products as an interdependent system of elements with properties that are at once subjective, corrigible, and social.

These four theses may be investigated with a range of conceptual tools available for analyzing processes of knowledge creation, transfer, and utilization (Holzner 1983). These conceptual tools permit analyses of the functions and structure of knowledge systems and the processes by which knowledge is constructed in practice settings.

Knowledge-related activities are differentially distributed in society and often occur in highly specialized social frameworks. As the economist Machlup (1963, 1969, 1980, 1982) has shown, it is fruitful to view a society from the point of view of the structured distribution of knowledge-related activity. This aspect of a social system is called the social knowledge system, which encompasses a complex array of institutions, organizations, social roles, and positions. The social structure of knowledge systems is related in complex ways to the creation and use of knowledge, limited by a society's moral culture and sense of identity (Robertson and Holzner 1980). Processes of knowledge creation, transfer, and utilization are interdependent, although such interdependence is not always beneficial—as illustrated by the vigorous utilization of Lysenko's "findings" by the Communist Party of the Soviet Union and the resulting constraints for Soviet biology at the time.

The diffuse (nonspecialized) knowledge systems of simple societies have been replaced in the advanced industrial countries by highly specialized and often formally institutionalized structures. In complex modern knowledge systems, the scientific community and the science-based professions, while they constitute the core, do not exhaust the system (Knorr-Cetina and Mulkay 1983, Elias et al. 1982, Merton 1973).

Knowledge systems can be analyzed in terms of knowledge functions, institutional domains, and frameworks for knowledge, as well as in terms of the centrality or peripherality of system components or "regions". The major knowledge functions can be described under the following five headings:

(a) producing knowledge, for example, in scientific research and scholarship;

(b) organizing and structuring knowledge as in the construction of theories, but also of texts, curricula, and information systems;

(c) distributing knowledge, for example, through journals, electronic networks, or linkage agents;

(d) storing knowledge in archives as well as in the memory of individuals and collectivities; and

(e) using knowledge, with varying kinds of feedback relations to any of the other functions.

The analytical distinctiveness but empirical interpenetration of activities and structures serving these functions is emphasized in the fourth section of this article.

Major institutional domains, such as agriculture, education, medicine, or other domains of public policy may evolve into specialized social knowledge systems of their own. The established professions are good examples (Freidson 1986), as are scientific specialties in the natural and social sciences (Dunn et al. 1987, Holzner et al. 1987).

Finally, the distinction between center and periphery (Shils 1975) points to the fact that these systems are not only differentiated, but also ordered along a dimension of higher and lower degrees of prestige, influence, and, in some instances, formal authority. Further, the regions of the knowledge system are variously limited or peripheral to the center of political power.

The knowledge system constitutes a society's most important resource for a collective learning capacity. Societies, like individuals, live in a reality which is often harsh and dangerous, but they can only come to terms with their realities by what they learn about them, that is, with the manner in which they socially construct what is taken to be real.

This raises the question of the definition of knowledge. It is undeniably true that different societies, regions within one knowledge sytem, and different historical epochs exhibit vast differences in what is taken to be valid knowledge. Is the student of knowledge utilization therefore to conclude that "knowledge" is whatever is socially taken to be knowledge? The answer is no. There needs to be a critical assessment of knowledge. Throughout history there has been a quest for valid knowledge which has recently been vastly accelerated. Such validity was at times established on the basis of traditional authority. or religious revelation, or the dictates of conscience, or rationally guided empirical inquiry, or formal, logical, or mathematical calculation, or in still other ways. It is quite clear that not all such modes of validation of knowledge claims are of equal merit. Indeed, we are living in the context of an historical process striving for ever more "adequate" knowledge claims.

Yet there is not now and will never be a single algorithm for the determination of ultimate knowledge. This position, which is that of a constructivist and evolutionary epistemology (see Campbell 1988), accentuates the importance of certain conceptual tools for the analysis of processes within and across regions of the knowledge system. They are the concepts' frame of reference, reality tests, theories-in-use, and situated rationality.

A frame of reference is the structure of assumptions and implicit or explicit decision rules in inquiry which provides the framework for the construction of meanings. It provides a perspective that focuses attention, but it also sets boundaries for what is to be considered the field of relevant information (Weiss and Bucuvalas 1980).

Reality tests are important components of frames of reference. In knowledge-use studies and practice, it is of crucial importance to discover empirically in what ways knowledge claims are scrutinized and on what grounds they are accepted or rejected.

The concept of theories-in-use will be dealt with especially in the section on knowledge-utilization practice. It refers to the working theories of practitioners that, embedded in their frames of reference, actually guide their actions. The surfacing of these often tacit theories and their formalization and critique is an important tool in knowledge-utilization practice.

Situated rationality refers to the fact that actors often attempt to proceed rationally within their frames of reference, even as they are tied into situations which pose for them certain more or less inescapable predicaments.

## 4. Methodology

Empirical research on knowledge utilization has been variously criticized by the research community itself (Weiss 1977, Dunn 1986a, 1986b). This section of the article is primarily a description of the methodology employed in a large sample of knowledge-utilization studies scrutinized in a multi-year project supported by the United States National Institute of Education (Dunn and Holzner 1982).

A key decision in knowledge-utilization research is the selection of an appropriate unit of analysis. In studying the impact of knowledge use on collective decisions it is often essential to obtain data about a respondent's relationship with other individuals. Aggregations of individual responses may provide an inaccurate or actually misleading picture. However, in the actual set of empirical studies almost all dealt with individuals as units of analysis. For example, questionnaires are often used to assess the concerns of individual users and nonusers about the implementation of particular educational innovations.

Available studies reflect a diversity of research designs ranging from case studies and cross-sectional analyses to quasi-experiments conducted in representative contexts of practice. Some case studies are based on prior theory, while others are not. A few knowledge-use studies are based on quasi-experimental designs, including real-time field experiments where research-based ideas, suggestions, or recommendations are actively introduced into practice settings. Cross-sectional or longitudinal studies exploring factors affecting the utilization of research include research on the sources of information used by congressional staff members and studies of the uses of social science research by federal, state, and local policy makers.

The prevailing method for obtaining data in knowledge-use studies is the self-administered questionnaire. The use of content analysis, naturalistic observation, and interview schedules is relatively rare, while few studies are qualitative in the specific sense that they seek to capture the underlying contextual meanings attached to knowledge and its uses. Knowledge-use studies, while they can be based heavily on the use of questionnaires whose reliability may be readily assessed, are frequently based on procedures with unknown or unreported reliability and validity. Given that knowledge-use studies are intimately related to the assessment of cognitive (subjective) properties of many kinds, the absence of information about the reliability of procedures and the validity of constructs represents a serious unresolved problem of most research in the field.

A central problem of knowledge-use studies is defining what is meant by use. The most widely used definition in the field is one that distinguishes between conceptual and instrumental uses of knowledge (Weiss 1977). Generally, conceptual use refers to changes in the way the users think about problems, while instrumental use refers to changes in behavior, especially changes that are relevant to decision making. While many unresolved difficulties continue to plague this twofold distinction (Dunn 1983a), many knowledge-use studies continue to employ it. Instrumental use, for example, tends to imply that respondents are single decision makers, notwithstanding the collective or systemic nature of organizational decision making. Given these and related difficulties it is striking that most studies define use in primarily instrumental terms, with the remainder stressing uses that are conceptual (Weiss and Bucuvalas 1980), symbolic, or affective (Anderson et al. 1981).

Available research yields little consistent empirical support for claims that particular classes of factors—economic, political, social, organizational, behavioral, attitudinal—affect the creation, diffusion, and utilization of knowledge in decisive and practically significant ways. There are many reasons for the inconsistency or instability of research findings, many of which stem from conceptual and methodological problems documented by Weiss (1977), Miles (1981), Dunn and Holzner (1982), Huberman and Miles (1982), and Lindquist (1988). The most important of these problems are reviewed below.

## 4.1 The Problem of Criteria

In terms of what criteria should knowlege use be defined? Answers to this basic question assume a variety of forms. Knowledge use may be viewed as principally conceptual, defined and measured in terms of mental processes of various kinds, and it may be represented and measured in terms of overt behavior. The distinction between conceptual and instrumental use, while it provided an initial focus for early studies, conceals a number of important dimensions according to which knowledge and its uses may be classified and measured. Instrumentally focused definitions of use, for example, generally neglect properties related to the expected benefits, purposes, and underlying assumptions of knowledge and its uses. Even those studies based on a conceptual definition of use often focus on surface properties of knowledge, taking for granted the meaning of knowledge, research, or information.

## 4.2 The Multiattribute Problem

Why does knowledge vary in perceived relevance, adequacy, and cogency? This question calls attention to the fundamentally interpretive character of processes of knowledge use. Processes of knowledge use are structured by the ways that policy makers, practitioners, and social scientists anticipate or predict events, such anticipation being a function of collective and individual reference frames and of the coordinative social contexts in which they are established, maintained, and changed. The specification of these subjectively meaningful contexts is frequently a product of the meanings of researchers, and not of those to whom such categories are applied. What is needed are procedures for identifying criteria actually employed to assess knowledge, as distinguished from criteria that are imposed on research contexts by investigators.

## 4.3 The Transactional Problem

How can knowledge transactions be conceptualized and measured? Research on individual frames of reference, while important for mapping the meanings surrounding processes of knowledge use, does not necessarily deal with the distribution of various reality tests or with changes in the structure of individual and collective frames of reference over time. A recognition of the contextual, relational, and generative properties of knowledge use has prompted many researchers to discard the terms interaction, exchange, and transfer, replacing these with the concept of transaction. While research on communication networks recognizes the importance of distinguishing contextual and referential meanings (Rogers and Kincaid 1981, Lievrouw 1988), it has been difficult to preserve subjectively meaningful dimensions of knowledge transactions.

## 5. Knowledge Practice

Practice refers to processes whereby data are given meanings that pass certain reality tests and are incorporated into a frame of reference, consequently reinforcing or changing existing beliefs and/or behaviors. For example, at an individual level a set of research results may be interpreted as supporting court-mandated school busing. Reality tests applied by the individual may certify this meaning as being both socially and technically valid. This may reinforce the individual's assumptions and decision rules about the merits of court-ordered school busing. Such reinforcement may be expressed through more vigorous social actions on the part of the individual whose sociopolitical beliefs have now been heightened.

## 5.1 Knowledge Application in Relation to Production and Dissemination

Traditionally, social processes related to knowledge production have been studied relatively independently of the social processes of dissemination and knowledge application. More recent thinking is taking a somewhat different perspective (Zaltman 1983). This perspective suggests that knowledge production, dissemination, and application are interactive in nature or, more accurately, that they are not separable constructs. Knowledge production occurs during application and dissemination. Similarly knowledge dissemination may occur during its production and application. To borrow a metaphor from statistics, rather than focusing on so-called "main" effects it may be more helpful to concentrate on so-called "interaction" effects. A kind of dialectic may also characterize the three processes. That is, while substantial pressures encourage the production of knowledge, equally powerful, though less well-understood, pressures "forbid" the production and dissemination of knowledge, keeping significant social events "hidden" and hence difficult to study or inform others about (Nelkin 1982, Westrum 1982, Peters and Ceci 1982). Also, while there is significant motivation to apply knowledge there are equally significant and prevalent motivations to prevent knowledge application or to even disavow the presence of knowledge. Thus, while it is conceptually convenient to separate the different knowledge functions, it is also necessary to remember that they commingle to the degree that one process may contain the others.

## 5.2 Theories-in-Use and Frames of Reference

The assumptions, expectations, and decision rules which constitute frames of reference set the context for ideas guiding action. Such sets of ideas represent theories which individuals as well as complex social units such as government bureaucracies use in dealing with their internal and external environments. These causal maps or theories have been labelled theories-in-use (Schön 1983). This concept has developed in the context of knowledge applications (Zaltman 1979, 1983).

Research findings concerning the impact of theories-in-use on knowledge practice include the well-documented finding that knowledge developed without consideration of theories-in-use among practitioners is unlikely to pass their reality tests (Rogers and Shoemaker 1971). Research about the value of prevention in mental health, if conducted with an understanding of the dominant curative orientation of mental health practitioners, is more likely to be accepted than the same research ideas developed without this sensitivity to practitioner theories-in-use. Moreover, when practitioners are actively involved in the development of knowledge as "reverse consultants" the resulting research is generally judged by all parties to be of higher technical quality and greater relevance to practice. Finally, the more that practitioners share researcher frames of reference about the conduct of research, the more likely that research will be accepted independently of the researcher's sensitivity to practitioner concerns. Thus, shared frames of reference with respect to knowledge-production issues affect knowledge applications.

The more consonant a set of research findings are with practitioners' theories-in-use the more likely their acceptance and application. The more divergent these findings are the more likely they are to be rejected or to be adapted in a way the originators of the research would themselves reject. These processes of knowledge rejection and knowledge adaptation have received considerable attention. They pertain not only to practitioners' behaviors but to the behaviors of agents active in knowledge production and dissemination systems. Knowledge which is perceived as surprising—as contrary to expectations—is likely to be rejected even if the surprise is in a positive direction. Frames of reference establish a kind of intellectual and social "comfort zone" and an item of information whose meaning could cause an agency to operate outside this comfort zone will tend to be rejected. This is partially described by the notion of group think (Boje and Murningham 1982). Group dynamics often present evidence which runs contrary to an existing or emerging consensus. Individuals and groups will often stop short of the point in their information-acquisition activities at which they might encounter information falling outside their comfort zones and which might require a major alteration in their theories-in-use. This is reflected by the term "half-knowledge" (Lazarsfeld cited in Marin 1981): enough is known about a situation for the organization to realize that there is a possibility that were more known, a difficult decision or action may be required. The notion of hidden events is also relevant here (Westrum 1982). A hidden event is a social phenomenon whose existence is either seriously doubted or simply not known about at all. Events may be hidden for several reasons: fear of ridicule keeps individuals from reporting phenomena and hence multiple experiences of the event go uncorrelated; arrogance with respect to evidence, for example, "If it existed I'd know about it"; misclassification (Greaves 1980); the absence of and/or the inability of accepted methodology to study the event (Charman 1979); restricted or "forbidden" access to information collection and application opportunities (Nelkin 1982); and so forth.

The meanings assigned to data by those who originate or create them may not be congruent with the meanings assigned or developed by those who disseminate and apply the data. More precisely, the meanings which are enacted by users of a research report may be at substantial variance with the meanings disseminators felt they were conveying. Moreover, both disseminators and users may have interpretations which are not shared by knowledge producers. Data are assimilated into frames of reference in ways which are biased toward reinforcing existing theories-in-use (Nisbett and Ross 1980). These tendencies have been observed not only at the level of the individual but among informal groups and formal organizations as well. The mechanisms whereby this occurs cannot be treated here. The important point is that a given set of statistics or a given verbal reporting of an event can give rise to very different "productions" of knowledge. These productions may be so divergent that the stake-holder group originating the data, when observing practitioners' behaviors based on the latter group's assigned meaning of these data, would conclude that a very different set of data were being acted upon. Of course practitioners often do agree with meanings assigned by producers and disseminators. However, the social realities of the context of application might require giving greater or lesser emphasis to certain concepts or sets and omitting some concepts altogether while adding yet others. In effect, a somewhat different theory is required and hence developed even if unwittingly by practitioners as a result of the realities of the implementation context.

## 5.3 Planned Social Change

A second major approach for viewing knowledge-use practices utilizes planned social-change concepts (Havelock 1969, Zaltman 1979, Rothman 1980, Cernada 1982, Glaser 1981). This approach argues that new information may result in new social constructions or interpretations which are innovations. These innovations may exist only as ideas or as practices and products. If these innovations pass the reality tests applied by key stakeholders and are adopted they may result in changes in the structure and functioning of social systems. Thus the application of knowledge may result in social change.

If knowledge "products" can be regarded as innovations resulting in social change then strategies for promoting product innovations such as medical drugs, solar energy technology, and instructional tools might be usefully applied to achieve more complete dissemination and use of other types of innovations such as scientific research intended for use by research scientists or practice innovations intended for other practitioners (Fine 1981, Larsen 1982). This is consistent with the view of knowledge practice as transactional and knowledge as a social construct. That is, the field of planned social change considers the diffusion of innovations as exchange processes between different communities which may have different frames of reference. Thus there is an emphasis on researcher understanding of the needs and requirements of potential users prior to the production of knowledge and in the design of knowledge products. The communication behaviors of potential users as well as their adoption decision processes are considered in the design of dissemination strategies. The role of linking agents (Havelock et al. 1973) and linking systems (Holzner 1983) become central concepts when knowledge use is viewed as planned social change. Moreover, formal management information systems assume greater prominence as user-initiated linking systems within this view of knowledge applications.

## 6. Conclusions

Until recently the study of knowledge utilization has not been consciously shaped by theory and research in the sociology, economics, and psychology of knowledge or, more broadly, by a basic interdisciplinary social science that seeks to examine practical applications of scientific and professional knowledge. Instead, the field of knowledge use has been mainly oriented towards the translation of social science knowledge into guidelines for the improvement of practice. While this applied research orientation has created greater sensitivity to the costs and benefits of the social sciences, it has contributed little to the resolution of basic theoretical, conceptual, and methodological issues. Such issues are high on the agenda of an emergent interdisciplinary social science of knowledge utilization.

## Bibliography

Anderson C, Ciarlo J A, Brodie S 1981 Measuring evaluation: Induced change in mental health programs. In: Ciarlo J A (ed.) 1981 *Utilization Evaluation: Concepts and Measurement Techniques*. Sage, Beverly Hills, California pp. 97–123

Bell D 1973 *The Coming of Post-industrial Society: A Venture in Social Forecasting*. Basic Books, New York

Boje O M, Murnighan J K 1982 Group confidence pressures in iterative decisions. *Manage. Sci.* 28(10): 1187–96

Campbell D T 1977 *Descriptive Epistemology: Psychological, Sociological and Evolutionary*. Preliminary Draft of the William James Lectures. Harvard University, Cambridge, Massachusetts

Campbell D T 1987 Guidelines for monitoring the scientific competence of preventive intervention research centers: An exercise in the sociology of scientific validity. *Knowledge: Creation, Diffusion, Utilization* 8: 389–430

Campbell D T 1988 *Methodology and Epistemology for Social Science: Selected Papers*, E S Overman (ed.). University of Chicago Press, Chicago, Illinois

Caplan N S 1979 The two-communities theory and knowledge utilization. *Am. Behav. Sci.* 22: 459–70

Cernada G P 1982 *Knowledge into Action: A Guide to Research Utilization*. Baywood, Farmingdale, New York

Charman W N 1979 Ball lightning. *Phys. Rep.* 54: 261–306

Ciarlo J A (ed.) 1981 *Utilizing Evaluation: Concepts and Measurement Techniques*. Sage, Beverly Hills, California

Dunn W N 1980 The two-communities metaphor and models of knowledge use: An exploratory case survey. *Knowledge: Creation, Diffusion, Utilization* 1(4): 515–36

Dunn W N 1981 If knowledge utilization is the problem, what is the solution? Work Paper KU-109. Program for the Study of Knowledge Use, University of Pittsburgh, Pittsburgh, Pennsylvania

Dunn W N 1982 Reforms as arguments. *Knowledge: Creation, Diffusion, Utilization* 3(3): 293–326

Dunn W N 1983a Measuring knowledge use. *Knowledge: Creation, Diffusion, Utilization* 5: 120–33

Dunn W N 1983b Qualitative methodology. *Knowledge: Creation, Diffusion, Utilization* 4(4): 590–97

Dunn W N 1986a Evaluating the effects of policy analysis: Toward a theory of applications. In: Nagel S S (ed.) 1986 *Research in Public Policy Analysis and Management*, Vol. 3, JAI Press, Greenwich, Connecticut, pp. 193–210

Dunn W N 1986b Studying knowledge use: A profile of procedures and issues. In: Beal G M, Dissanayake W, Konoshima S (eds.) *Knowledge Generation, Exchange, and Utilization*. Westview Press, Boulder, Colorado, pp. 345–69

Dunn W N, Ginsberg A 1986 A sociocognitive network approach to organizational analysis. *Hum. Rel.* 39: 955–75

Dunn W N, Holzner B 1982 *Methodological Research on Knowledge Use and School Improvement*, Final Report. US Department of Education, Washington, DC

Dunn W N, Holzner B 1987 Introduction: Toward knowledge systems accounting. *Knowledge: Creation, Diffusion, Utilization* 9: 163–7

Dunn W N, Holzner B, Shahidullah M, Hegedus A M 1987 The architecture of knowledge systems: Toward policy-relevant science impact indicators. *Knowledge: Creation, Diffusion, Utilization* 9: 205–32

Dunn W N, Holzner B 1988 Knowledge in society: Anatomy of an emergent field. *Knowledge in Society: The International Journal of Knowledge Transfer* 1(1): 3–26

Elias N, Martins H, Whitley R (eds.) 1982 *Scientific Establishments and Hierarchies*, Sociology of the Sciences Yearbook, Vol. 6. Reidel, Dordrecht

Fine S H 1981 *The Marketing of Ideas and Social Issues*. Praeger, New York

Freidson E 1986 *Professional Powers: A Study of the Institutionalization of Formal Knowledge*. University of Chicago Press, Chicago, Illinois

Glaser E 1981 *Knowledge Transfer Strategies*. Paper presented at Conference on Knowledge Use. University of Pittsburgh, Pittsburgh, Pennsylvania

Glaser E M, Abelson H H, Garrison K N 1983 *Putting Knowledge to Use: Facilitating the Diffusion of Knowledge and the Implementation of Planned Change*. Jossey-Bass, San Francisco, California

Greaves G B 1980 Multiple personality. 165 years after Mary Reynolds. *J. Nervous and Ment. Disease* 168: 577–96

Habermas J 1975 *Legitimation crisis.* Beacon Press, Boston, Massachusetts

Havelock R G 1969 *Planning for Innovation through Dissemination and Utilization of Knowledge.* Center for Research on Utilization of Scientific Knowledge, Institute for Social Research. University of Michigan, Ann Arbor, Michigan

Havelock R G, Havelock M C, Markowitz E A 1973 *Educational Innovation in the US,* Vol. 1: *The National Survey: The Substance and the Process.* Center for Research on Utilization of Scientific Knowledge, University of Michigan, Ann Arbor, Michigan

Holzner B 1978 The sociology of applied knowledge. *Sociol. Symp.* 21: 8–19

Holzner B 1983 Social processes and knowledge synthesis. In: Ward S A, Reed L J (eds.) 1983 *Knowledge Structure and Use: Implications for Synthesis and Interpretation.* Temple University Press, Philadelphia, Pennsylvania

Holzner B, Dunn W N, Shahidullah M 1987 An accounting scheme for designing science impact indicators: The knowledge system perspective. *Knowledge: Creation, Diffusion, Utilization* 9(2): 173–204

Holzner B, Fisher E 1979 Knowledge in use: Considerations in the sociology of knowledge applications. *Knowledge: Creation, Diffusion, Utilization* 1(2): 219–44

Holzner B, Marx J H 1979 *Knowledge Application: The Knowledge System in Society.* Allyn and Bacon, Boston, Massachusetts

Huberman M 1987 Steps towards an integrated model of research utilization. *Knowledge: Creation, Diffusion, Utilization* 8(4): 586–611

Huberman M, Miles M 1982 Drawing valid meaning from qualitative data: Some techniques of data reduction and display. Paper prepared for a symposium on Advances in the Analysis of Qualitative Data. Annual Meeting of the American Educational Research Association, New York, March 1982. American Educational Research Association, Washington, DC

Knorr K D, Krohn R, Whitley R (eds.) 1981 *The Social Process of Scientific Investigation,* Sociology of the Sciences Yearbook 4 (1980). Reidel, Dordrecht

Knorr-Cetina K D, Mulkay M 1983 *Science Observed.* Sage, Beverly Hills, California

Kochen M (ed.) 1975 *Information for Action: From Knowledge to Wisdom.* Academic Press, New York

Larsen J 1982 *Information Utilization and Nonutilization.* American Institutes for Research in the Behavioral Sciences, Washington, DC

Laudan L 1977 *Progress and Its Problems: Toward a Theory of Scientific Growth.* University of California Press, Berkeley, California

Lazarsfeld P F, Reitz J G, Pasanella A K 1975 *An Introduction to Applied Sociology.* Elsevier, New York

Lehming R, Kane M (eds.) 1981 *Improving Schools: Using What we Know.* Sage, Beverly Hills, California

Lievrouw L 1988 Four programs of research in scientific communication. *Knowledge in Society: The International Journal of Knowledge Transfer* 1(2): 6–22

Lindquist E A 1988 What do decision models tell us about information use? *Knowledge in Society: The International Journal of Knowledge Transfer* 1(2): 86–111

Machlup F 1963 *Essays on Economic Semantics.* Prentice-Hall, Englewood Cliffs, New Jersey

Machlup F 1969 If matter could talk. In: Morgenbesser S, Suppes P, White M (eds.) 1969 *Philosophy, Science and Method: Essays in Honor of Ernest Nagel.* St. Martin's Press, New York, pp. 286–305

Machlup F 1980 *Knowledge: Its Creation, Distribution, and Economic Significance,* Vol. 1: *Knowledge and Knowledge Production.* Princeton University Press, Princeton, New Jersey

Machlup F 1982 *Knowledge: Its Creation, Distribution, and Economic Significance.* Vol. 2: *The Branches of Learning.* Princeton University Press, Princeton, New Jersey

MacRae D 1988 Professional knowledge for policy discourse: Argumentation versus reasoned selection of proposals. *Knowledge in Society: The International Journal of Knowledge Transfer* 1(2): 6–24

Marin B 1981 *Knowledge: Creation, Diffusion, Utilization.* Sage, Beverly Hills, California

Marrow A J 1969 *The Practical Theorist: The Life and Work of Kurt Lewin.* Basic Books, New York

Merton R K 1973 *The Sociology of Science: Theoretical and Empirical Investigations.* University of Chicago Press, Chicago, Illinois

Miles M B 1981 Mapping the common properties of schools. In: Lehming R, Kane M T (eds.) 1981 *Improving Schools: What We Know.* Sage, Beverly Hills, California, pp. 42–114

National Institute of Education 1973 *Building Capacity for Renewal and Reform.* National Institute of Education, Washington, DC

Nelkin D 1982 Forbidden research: Limits to inquiry in the social sciences. In: Beauchamp T L, Faden R (eds.) 1982 *Ethical Issues in Social Science Research.* Johns Hopkins University Press, Baltimore, Maryland

Nisbett R E, Ross L 1980 *Human Inference: Strategies and Shortcomings of Social Judgment.* Prentice-Hall, Englewood Cliffs, New Jersey

Peters D P, Ceci S J 1982 Peer-review practices of psychological journals: The fate of published articles, submitted again. *Behav. and Brain Sci.* 5: 187–95

Remmling G W 1967 *Road to Suspicion: A Study of Modern Mentality and the Sociology of Knowledge.* Appleton-Century-Crofts, New York

Rich R F 1981 *Social Science Information and Public Policymaking: The Interaction Between Bureaucratic Politics and the Use of Survey Data.* Jossey-Bass, San Francisco, California

Robertson R, Holzner B (eds.) 1980 *Identity and Authority: Explorations in the Theory of Society.* St. Martin's Press, New York

Rogers E M, Kincaid D L 1981 *Communication Networks: Toward a New Paradigm for Research.* Free Press, New York

Rogers E M, Shoemaker F F 1971 *Communication of Innovation: A Cross-Cultural Approach,* 2nd edn. Free Press, New York

Rothman J 1980 *Using Research in Organizations: A Guide to Successful Application.* Sage, Beverly Hills, California

Schön D A 1983 *The Reflective Practitioner.* Basic Books, New York

Shils E A 1975 *Center and Periphery: Essays in Macrosociology.* University of Chicago Press, Chicago, Illinois

Snow C P 1959 *The Two Cultures and the Scientific Revolution.* Cambridge University Press, Cambridge

Spiegel-Rösing I, de Solla Price D 1977 *Science, Technology and Society: Cross-disciplinary Perspectives.* Sage, London

Sundquist J 1978 Research brokerage: The weak link. In:

Lynn L (ed.) 1978 *Knowledge and Policy: The Uncertain Connection*. National Academy of Science, Washington, DC, pp. 126–44

Weiss C H (ed.) 1977 *Using Social Research in Public Policy Making*. Heath, Lexington, Massachusetts

Weiss C H, Bucuvalas M J 1980 Truth tests and utility tests: Decision makers' frames of reference for social science. *Am. Sociol. Rev.* 45: 302–12

Westrum R 1982 Social intelligence about hidden events. *Knowledge: Creation, Diffusion, Utilization* 3: 381–400

Zaltman G 1979 Knowledge utilization as planned social change. *Knowledge: Creation, Diffusion, Utilization* 1: 82–105

Zaltman G 1983 Theory-in-use among change agents. In: Seidman E (ed.) 1983 *Handbook of Social Intervention*. Sage, Beverly Hills, California, pp. 289–312

Zhang X 1986 The core scholars and literature in studies of knowledge use: A citation analysis. Unpublished manuscript. Department of Sociology, University of Pittsburgh, Pittsburgh, Pennsylvania

# Reporting Evaluations of Learning Outcomes[1]

## R. W. Tyler

Most reports of educational evaluations are not understood by laypeople and are widely misinterpreted. In fact, they are not generally understood by teachers and administrators, and, as a result, the information that could provide a basis for improving the educational program or institution is not communicated. Basic to this failure of communication are several practices devised by psychometrists and adapted without careful consideration by those engaged in educational evaluation.

### 1. Shortcoming in Current Reporting Procedures

Psychometrists, seeking to measure aspects or factors of the psyche, focus on the appraisal of characteristics of the person rather than on what the person has learned. They hypothesize the existence of abilities, aptitudes, or other factors within the individual, and seek to devise ways of identifying and measuring these characteristics. The teacher, on the other hand, is expected to help students of many different backgrounds and with various observable characteristics learn what the schools try to teach, such as, to read, write, compute, explain natural phenomena, become interested in intellectual activities and aesthetic objects, perceive things in new perspectives, and so forth. The teacher's task is to help children learn these things as effectively as possible. What the teacher really wants to know from the results of an educational evaluation are the answers to such questions as: What have the students learned? Where are they having difficulty in learning? The teacher is interested in knowing about those hypothetical abilities, aptitudes, and other factors assumed to be within the individual only when they are shown to be causal variables that can be altered by the teacher so as to improve student learning. Otherwise, the report of test results in terms of individual characteristics is not used by the teacher or is misinterpreted as in using aptitude test results to justify the practice of not encouraging students whose scores are low to try to learn.

The focus on individual characteristics leads psychometrists to treat test results as indicators of factors rather than direct evidence of learning. This leads to the prevailing practice of reporting test results in abstract numbers, such as numerical scores, without explaining the concrete referents from which the scores are derived. An even greater source of misinterpretation arises from translating "raw" scores into grade equivalents, or percentiles which have the appearance of clarity, but, in fact, are interpretations of hypothetical referents that are often different from the actual situation.

As an example, the results of standardized tests in the elementary school subjects are usually reported in grade equivalents obtained by translating the raw scores into a scale which is constructed by assuming that the mean of the scores made by students taking the test, who were at the beginning of the first grade, represents the grade equivalent of 1.0. Then, the mean of the scores obtained by students at the beginning of the second grade is called 2.0, and so on, through to the last grade of the elementary school. It is also assumed that the mean scores will progress linearly from grade to grade. For example, it is assumed that the mean scores for students in the middle of the school year will be one half of the difference between the mean scores for the beginning of the next grade and the mean for the beginning of this grade. To illustrate: if the mean score of the students taking a standardized arithmetic test at the beginning of the second grade is 62 and the mean score for students taking the test at the beginning of the third grade is 68, then a score of 65 is assumed to be the mean score that would be attained by students who take the test in the middle of the school year.

Students with the same score often show very different patterns of test performance. They may have answered correctly items that are taught in later grades and failed to answer correctly items that are taught in earlier grades. Teachers obtain no informa-

---

1   This article was originally published in the *International Journal of Educational Research*, Vol. 10 No. 1. It appears here with permission from Pergamon Press plc © 1986.

tion from a grade equivalent score about what the student has learned and with what learning tasks he has difficulty. Parents and other laypeople assume that a child whose grade equivalent is 3.2 should, if properly placed, be in the third grade, not realizing the child may already have mastered many of the things taught in grade 3, while failing to answer correctly items that are taught in other grades.

In high school subjects, the usual practice is to report standardized achievement test results in terms of percentile ranks, based on a hypothetical normal distribution in which all of the scores obtained from the norming administration of the test are placed. A review of typical standardized tests indicates that the items in a test that deals with things taught in any particular school represent only a fraction of what that school is teaching. This is due to the fact that high school courses vary from school to school in the particular content taught. In the construction of a test for national use, the test makers examine textbooks and available curriculum guides to identify topics that are common to many of the books and guides. Test items are then constructed for these common topics. The topics that are not common, however, are more numerous than those for which test items are written. Hence, the report, for example, that the mean of the scores that the student of teacher A obtained on the test was at the 40th percentile of the norming population gives no dependable indication of what these students have learned nor even how well they have learned what they have been taught.

## 2. Suggested Improvements for Reporting Results of School Learning

It is, of course, necessary to use abstract numbers in studies that seek to identify hypothetical variables that are not directly observable, since their form and extent of functioning must be estimated from observed differences in individual behavior. However, the results of school learning can be much more directly defined, identified, and described in meaningful terms that are relatively concrete.

In reading, for example, learning to comprehend reading material is commonly defined in terms that are easily understood. In the primary grades, comprehension behavior is often defined as reading aloud accurately, or telling in one's own words what the selection says, or doing what the printed directions tell one to do. In the middle grades the definition of "comprehend" takes into account that reading at that level involves getting information from the printed page.

The definition of the reading material which the student is expected to comprehend is also easily understood. In the primary grades the reading material usually includes children's stories, newspaper items, directions for assembling and using toys and games. If a test in reading for children in the primary grades has been constructed by sampling the kinds of comprehension

and the several kinds of reading material, the results can be reported in terms of what the children comprehend: fairy tales, newspaper items, directions for toys and games. If desired, the test could sample several levels of complexity in the reading materials, such as range of vocabulary and complexity of syntax. Then results can be reported in terms of the levels of complexity of the reading materials that each child comprehended. Concrete examples of each level can be included in the report so that the user can make his or her own judgment of what the levels of complexity mean. To take an example in arithmetic, the definition of "computation" with whole numbers is often given as: adding, subtracting, multiplying and dividing with whole numbers; and the content and contexts in which the elementary school child is expected to use computation is often defined as: planning, personal, and group activities in which quantities are estimated, making retail purchases, estimating sales taxes on purchases, and measuring familiar objects and areas.

Levels of complexity in computation behavior are usually defined by increasing numbers of digits in the numbers involved in the computation. Most arithmetic courses do not categorize contents and contexts in terms of difficulty or levels of complexity for children learning to compute. Hence, if a test in arithmetic has been constructed by sampling the kinds of computation and the several contents and contexts in which the students can be expected to use computation with whole numbers, the results can be reported in terms of what kinds of computation they performed accurately— addition, subtraction, multiplication and division— and in which contexts they solved the computational exercises accurately. If desired, the test could sample computation with one-digit numbers, with two-digit numbers and with numbers of three or more digits. The results could then be reported in these terms representing levels of complexity for children learning to compute.

As an example from another subject and at the high school level, the field of high school biology is typical. One of the major objectives for this subject as presented in curriculum guides is to understand and explain in scientific terms common phenomena of plants and animals. The behavior, understanding and explaining in scientific terms, is often defined as the student perceiving a biological phenomenon as involving relevant scientific concepts and principles and using them appropriately in his or her explanation. In most biology courses, there are from 20 to 40 concepts used and from 50 to 70 principles presented. The presentations in textbooks and laboratory exercises include several phenomena involving each of the concepts and principles. Students are expected to generalize from these examples and to understand and explain many other biological phenomena encountered in their environment.

An evaluation of student learning in relation to this objective should include test situations in which the student encounters biological phenomena and seeks to explain them in scientific terms. The results of such a test can be reported in terms of the use of each concept and principle if each one has been reliably sampled in the test exercises. More commonly, the concepts and principles will be grouped into classes, each of which is reliably sampled. In that case, the results can be reported in terms of the proportion of the test exercises in each class in which the concepts and principles were appropriately used in the explanations. If desired, the phenomena could be classified into levels of complexity and results reported in terms of the proportion of exercises appropriately explained for each level of complexity.

An evaluation of the products of learning furnishes a somewhat different example of the reporting of results. In evaluating the written work of students, several criteria are usually used, such as clarity, logical organization, and coherence, and each paper is appraised in terms of each criterion. Furthermore, to reduce individual idiosyncrasy in assessment, one or more examples of each level of the criterion are established by a panel of judges and used as a standard to guide all the appraisals. The prevailing practice has been to report the mean levels for each group of students. This furnishes little information of use to teachers, parents, school administrators, and others. A more useful report would present an example of each level for each criterion and state the percentage of the group whose written work was judged to be at that level. To illustrate: in class X, 15 percent of the students' writing was judged to be in the top level in clarity, 60 percent in the middle level in clarity, and 25 percent in the low level in clarity, and so on with the other criteria. By presenting concrete examples of products, parents and other laypeople can understand more clearly what schools are teaching and students are expected to learn than abstract scores can ever provide.

The above examples are by no means exhaustive. They are presented only to illustrate certain major guidelines in reporting the results of an educational evaluation. The first of these is to report results that tell what has been learned and what of the expected learning has not taken place. To report these things there should have been clear definitions of what students are expected to learn. From these definitions, suggestions are obtained about useful terms for reporting the results. Second, since an educational evaluation is focused on what students have learned, one should avoid the use of indicators wherever more direct assessment of the learning can be made, and avoid abstract numbers in reporting wherever what students have learned can be reported more concretely. This reduces the dependence upon untested assumptions in deriving a score. Third, one should present the users of the results with as much information as can be obtained from the evaluation, but in no more detail than they can use. This guideline requires considerable elaboration to suggest its practical employment.

## 3. Reports for Different Users

### 3.1 Reports for Teachers and Parents

The teacher or parent who works with individual students can use information about each individual whose learning he or she is guiding. Hence, reports of an evaluation for the teacher or parent should not only indicate which children have learned what they have been taught but also the particular kinds of learned behavior with what content and in what contexts they demonstrated effectiveness, and what difficulties were evidenced.

For a general report to parents, this information needs to be presented clearly but in nontechnical terms. The purpose is two-fold: to give parents information about the particular things the child is expected to learn, and information about what the child is learning and where difficulties are being encountered. Most parents have not understood the test scores that have been reported, and this has led to misinterpretations that have often hampered constructive efforts of the home.

Some test users have reported the results item by item but this item analysis commonly leads to another misunderstanding. The item analysis reports the number or percentage of test takers who responded to the item in a particular way, usually the percentage who answered the item correctly. However, a single item is rarely, if ever, a representative sample of a defined behavior, or a defined content, or a defined context. Teachers often treat item analyses as though the response to an item indicated probable responses to the kind of behavior that item represents. To draw any dependable inference about a kind of behavior requires information from enough appropriate items to evaluate a representative sample of that behavior. Failing to understand this, some teachers modify their educational efforts to deal with what they thought they could infer from the item analysis.

The reliability of the item analysis is based on estimates of the variability among students responding to the item; it is not an estimate of the variation among items that could be constructed to represent a kind of behavior that can be estimated from actually giving a sample of such exercises to the students.

### 3.2 Reports for School Principals

The principal of a school does not usually need to have information about the learning of an individual child. When that is needed on occasion, the teacher can be asked to supply it. The principal needs to know about the progress of learning in each classroom so that assistance can be provided where needed. For example, the principal is usually expected to take the leadership in developing educational goals for each year. These goals should be established after reviewing the educational achievements of the past year, then the school's teaching staff deliberate on goals for the next year which are substantially beyond the achievements of the past year but seem to the teachers to be obtainable for the next year. The review of the results of the last educational evaluation will reveal the objectives that were not reached by most students and other indications of problems that need correction and for which the plan for next year represents a substantial improvement over the past year.

For the purposes of setting annual goals, the educational evaluation results can be helpfully expressed in terms of the proportion of the class group who reached or exceeded the goals set for that year. As an example, consider an elementary school enrolling children from homes in which the parents have had little education and where the opportunities to develop and apply what is learned in school are limited. At the end of the third grade, most children from middle-class homes have learned the mechanics of reading, that is they can get the plain-sense meaning of written material that deals with content and contexts with which they are familiar. However, in the school in the inner city, the educational evaluation showed that only 25 percent of the children at the end of the third grade could read and comprehend this simple material.

After staff discussion and deliberation the goal in reading set for the third grade the following year was for 35 percent of the students to reach this standard. Thus, reporting results in terms of the percentage of students reaching accepted and defined standards, provided the principal and all the school staff with the information needed to set annual goals and to monitor progress toward them. Reporting the percentage of students exhibiting behavior that intefers with school learning can also be useful in goal setting and monitoring. For example, the percentage of students who were absent 5 days, 10 days, 15 days and 20 days in a term furnishes information helpful in setting goals representing improved attendance.

### 3.3 Reports for School Districts

Most local school districts include a number of schools. The district personnel do not need data from an educational evaluation that is as detailed as that needed by the principal of each school. The officers of the district—administrators, coordinators, supervisors, resource persons, and so on—cannot perform the daily functions of teachers, principals, and parents. They must depend on the persons in the local schools to perform these functions. Persons from the district office can stimulate the efforts of the teachers and principals in the schools, they can assist and train local personnel in goal setting, monitoring, and revising goals and plans, they can provide other kinds of assistance, but they cannot take the place of the local school personnel nor depend on their authority to get compliance with their ideas.

To furnish assistance in depth, district personnel need to identify problems serious enough, or opportunities great enough, to justify a considerable commitment of their time. The results of evaluations should indicate what proportion of the students in the local school are attaining the learning objectives and what proportion are having difficulties. The district personnel may ask for breakdowns in these proportions in terms of student demography or sex, or other variables thought to have a causal connection to student achievement. The district personnel also need to know the evidence used by the local school staff in setting the annual goals. However, district personnel do not usually need data on individual students nor even on particular classrooms within the school. The school is the basic unit for monitoring and reporting. Further breakdowns may be needed to guide the appropriate inquiries of the district.

Periodically, the district office needs an appraisal of learning that is independent of the evaluations carried on by personnel in the local school. This is necessary to assure the validity of the data submitted by the school. A few principals may not be able to resist the temptation to doctor results so that their schools will look good. The periodic independent appraisal has the same function in relation to local evaluations that an independent financial audit has to the accounts and accounting activities of an institution. As in the financial audit, only a sample of checks are made and if they are not in harmony with the results presented by the local school personnel, a further investigation is undertaken to obtain valid results at the level of detail required.

There are technical problems in conducting an independent appraisal that utilizes a limited amount of students' time, requires modest expenditures, and obtains valid and reliable samples of the various kinds of learning objectives from reliable samples of students from each local school. If only a fraction of the important objectives are sampled, local teachers interpret them as the only ones. So they focus their teaching efforts on these few objectives and neglect the others. If only a fraction of the students are sampled, the reliability of the results may be too low and the reason some students are not tested is not easily explained to the local school staff and parents. An answer to these technical problems is a process often called matrix sampling, as the allocation of test exercises to particular students is often done by making a matrix chart with individual students in the one axis and the test exercises on the other. By the use of matrix sampling, the reliability of the test exercises as representative samples of the learned behavior applied to representative samples of relevant content in representative samples of appropriate context, does not need to be reduced. All of the test exercises constructed for use in making evaluations useful to the local school are presented to the students, but no one student responds to all the exercises. If the completion of all the test exercises would require five hours for one student to do them all, the test can be broken into five subtests each taking an hour of the student's time. One-fifth of the students is given one subtest, another fifth of the students is given a second subtest, and so on. Every student completes test results for the equivalent of one-fifth of all the students in the school.

The results of this independent appraisal can be reported in terms of each kind of educational objective, and the proportion of the students in each school who made expected progress in attaining the objective, and the proportion having difficulty. As with other tests, where representative samples of different levels of behavior are obtained, these can be reported in terms of the percent of the students reaching or exceeding each level. The report of these results can be compared with the results submitted by each school. Where there are serious discrepancies, inquiries should be undertaken to seek to obtain more dependable data.

### 3.4 Reports for State, Regional and National Agencies

Reports of educational evaluation results that are useful to state agencies, regional organizations, and state and national policy makers need to be even less detailed than those for school district personnel. State, regional, and national groups do not work directly with individual children and they need no more information about the child's educational progress and problems than does the Surgeon General of the United States need to know about the health progress and problems of an individual child. The responsibility for working directly with individual children on their educational progress and problems is that of the teacher and parent.

It is helpful for policy development as well as for state oversight in education to know what children in their area of jurisdiction are learning, what learning is expected of these children at various stages of their development, what progress they are making and what problems they are encountering. Since the answers to these questions are thought to vary in relation to demographic factors, the questions need to be asked in relation to each major demographic factor. What can the results of evaluation contribute to answering these questions?

In the United States, the constitutional responsibility for public education is left to the government of each state. Most states delegate a great deal of this responsibility to local school districts. Although many of the states have adopted courses of study, none of them defines in clear terms the behavior that students are expected to learn. The courses of study usually specify subjects to be taught, sometimes topics to be covered, but no definition is clearly given as to what students are to learn in these subjects or about these topics. These actual definitions are usually developed by individual teachers although there is increasing agreement among educators that the teaching staff of a school needs to work as a team to define and agree on the definition of what students are to learn in different subjects and at different levels of their development.

Although in practice, individual teachers or local schools define learning objectives, there is a good deal of consensus among the educated public on the definition of what students should learn in the public elementary and secondary schools. This was documented in the experience of the United States in getting agreement on the learning objectives to be appraised in the National Assessment of Educational Progress (NAEP). In developing an evaluation program to inform policy makers and the public in a state or region, the procedure followed in developing the NAEP is a practicable one. It is also possible to gain a more informed consensus by arranging for discussion groups to discuss at some length the issues of desirable learning goals and to bring together for further discussion and deliberation the reports of the conclusions reached in many smaller discussion groups. One way of doing this is to invite public participants through invitations to many local groups, such as church groups, labor groups, Chambers of Commerce, service clubs, and hobby groups. When the self-selected members come together in a large auditorium, they are presented with an explanation of the project. Then the large group is broken up into discussion groups with about 20 people in each group. Each discussion group is moderated by a person who participated in three brief training sessions. The discussions are directed by a discussion guide who raises the major issues as questions to be discussed and deliberated, and tentative conclusions are reached. The discussion groups usually meet in three or four two-hour sessions. Each discussion group prepares a report of its recommendations which are reproduced for all participants. Then a final meeting is held with the members of all the groups. At this final meeting consensus is sought on the recommendations as they are revised and reformulated to satisfy most participants. This is a time-consuming procedure but it has developed a clearer understanding of what schools are expected to do, and thus furnishes a basis for guiding an evaluation and reporting results.

The report of the results of assessments should take into account what the policy makers understand to be the things students are expected to learn. The reports can help further to clarify the meaning of these expectations by presenting an exercise or two that was used to appraise this kind of learning. Where it is appropriate, the report should present examples of different levels of skill, or complexity, or breadth of learning, and for each giving the percent of particular groups who performed at that level or breadth. Where possible, the degree of progress can be reported in terms of the proportion in previous years who performed at that level or breadth. The proportion of students who demonstrated difficulties in performance can be an additional kind of information where this result is obtained from other responses and is not simply the proportion who did not perform at the reported level. Where the learning is thought to be influenced by certain demographic factors, the proportions should be reported for each demographic group for which there was a representative sample taking the test.

### 4. Concluding Remarks

These examples are not complete; they are presented

only as illustrations of efforts to report the results of educational evaluation in terms that are understood by the users as concrete evidence about the learning of clearly defined behavior. From the need for detailed reports by those who work with individual students to the need by policy makers for reports of learning achievements on a large scale, one can select the data and report the results so as to be responsive as far as possible to the kinds of questions different groups are asking.

*Bibliography*

Tyler R W 1942 General statement on evaluation. *J. Educ. Res.* 35: 492–501

Tyler R W 1949 *Basic Principles of Curriculum and Instruction.* University of Chicago Press, Chicago, Illinois

Tyler R W 1951 The functions of measurement in improving instruction. In: Lindquist E F (ed.) 1951 *Educational Measurement.* American Council of Education, Washington, DC, pp. 47–67

Tyler R W 1983 Educational assessment, standards, and quality: Can we have one without the others. *Educational Measurement: Issues and Practice.* 2(2): 14–15, 21–23

Tyler R W 1983 A rationale for program evaluation. In: Madaus G F, Scriven M, Stufflebeam D L (eds.) 1983 *Evaluation Models: Viewpoints on Educational and Human Services Evaluation.* Kluwer-Nijhoff, Boston, Massachusetts, pp. 67–78

# The Information Side of Evaluation for Local School Improvement[1]

## K. A. Sirotnik

The theory and practice of "evaluation" for educational settings—particularly public schools—are undergoing a number of interesting transformations in the rapidly accelerating "information society" in which we live. Added to this is a sociopolitical context in which: (a) more accountability pressures and demands from federal and state levels are being laid at the doorsteps of districts and schools; and (b) fewer large-scale school improvement programs are being supported and funded federally than was the case in the 1960s and 1970s.

One transformation resulting from the combination of these forces is that the object of traditional evaluation designs is changing, from a focus on programmatic intervention to a focus on schooling itself. In other words, the "program" for evaluative focus is now the ongoing constellation of daily activities and outcomes constituting the program of the local school. This suggests the need for a considerable variety of information designed to facilitate any number of evaluative purposes from appraising the impact of specific programmatic interventions, to informing organizational and instructional planning and development activities, to, perhaps most importantly, monitoring the periodic health of the school work and learning environment. Since the processes of collecting, storing, retrieving, analyzing, and reporting multiple forms of information are no longer particularly problematic (at least from a technological point of view), district- and school-based comprehensive information systems are becoming one significant vehicle whereby evaluation can be reconceptualized specifically for local school improvement. (See, for example, Bank and Williams 1987, Burstein 1984, Cooley and Bickel 1986, Hathaway 1984, Idstein 1987, McNamara 1980, Sirotnik 1984a, Sirotnik and Burstein 1987).

This article covers three main issues: (a) information domains (the "what"), information sources (the "who"), and methods for collecting information (the "how"); (b) the aggregation of information and concerns regarding the appropriate unit of analysis; and (c) practical details regarding the quality of data collection procedures. The article concludes with some views on how the process of collecting information needs to fit into a wider commitment to inquiry and school renewal.

## 1. Collecting Information: What, from Whom, and How?

When conceptualizing, defining, and collecting information about what goes on in schools the key word is *multi*—multicontent, multisource, and multimethod. In *A Study of Schooling* (Goodlad 1984), a heuristic was developed that helped to map out the schooling terrain (see Fig. 1). Although more could be invented, the four domains—personal (or individual), instructional (or classroom), institutional (or school), and societal (or schooling in general)—proved adequate in encompassing most of the information that schools and districts could possibly collect. The data sources listed are, of course, only illustrative of the many that could be relevant; administrators, district staff, and other community constituencies might be important additional sources of information.

Figure 1, underrepresents the complexity of the whole. However more recently this figure has been augmented and refined in several ways (see Sirotnik 1984, Sirotnik and Burstein 1983). First (see Fig. 2), a substantive facet has been added that makes explicit the potential information inherent in the *circumstances*, *activities* (processes), and *meanings* in and of the school

1 This article was originally published in the *International Journal of Educational Research*, Vol. 11, No. 1. It appears here with permission from Pergamon Press plc © 1987.

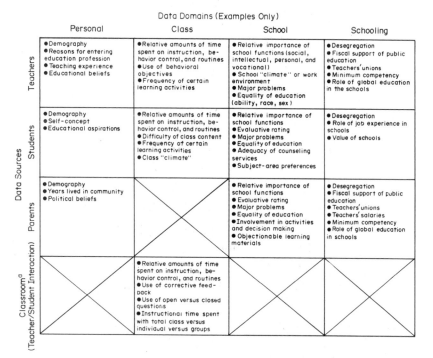

**Figure 1**
The schooling terrain: map one

[a] Data were collected on this data source through observation. For the purposes of this conceptualization, observers are being treated not as a data source, but as part of the data collection *method*, just as questionnaire and/or interview methods were used in collecting data from teachers, students, and parents

setting. The circumstances of schooling constitute the array of structures, situations, and physical features in the school setting—the "givens" at any point in time. Age and conditions of the school facility, community demography, size of the school (for example, number of students), teacher–student ratio, teacher turnover, student transiency, duration of current principalship, daily schedule (for example, period structure at the secondary level), student tracking policies, materials and resources, and so on are just a few of the circumstances that vary from school to school.

The activities are the ongoing and dynamic behaviors and processes that constitute the practice of schooling. These are the activity components of organizational and curricular commonplaces (Goodlad et al. 1979) such as instructional practices, learning activities, decision-making, communications, evaluation, and so forth, at all levels of the schooling process (see Fig. 3). These commonplaces cut across the potential data sources and data domains in Fig. 2.

What are not captured just by the circumstances and activities of the educational setting are the meanings that people infer from and bring to bear upon the setting. One sizeable chunk of these meanings is the constellation of "orientations"—sentiments (feelings),

opinions, attitudes, beliefs, and values—that interact with the circumstances and activities of schooling. For example, the effectiveness of administrative-staff communication mechanisms may interact with staff perceptions of the school work environment and staff attitudes and beliefs regarding the exercise of authority. Classroom management techniques may depend upon teacher beliefs like "The student should be seen and not heard" versus a more egalitarian stance on student participation. The allocation of teaching resources to different content areas will depend on opinions regarding the most important function of schooling (for example, academic versus vocational schooling). Another sizeable chunk of meanings derived from one way meaning is attached to the teaching–learning act. A domain of tasks are sampled that are believed to define learning objectives, and then students' performance on this sample of tasks is appraised. This is called an achievement test. The point is that such performance measures are just one more class of indicators by which educational meaning is construed.

Thus, the setting can be characterized, things happen in it, and people attempt to make sense out of it. Using the terms loosely, one might refer to the circumstances as the "factual" information, information that, if sys-

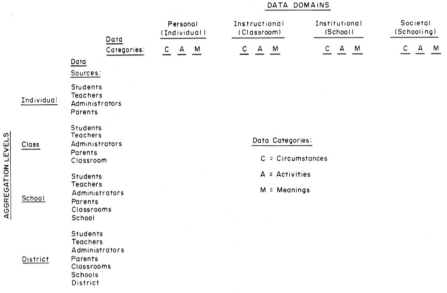

**Figure 2**
The schooling terrain: map two

tematically recorded, could be determined through document and archive review; activities such as "observational" information (one would admit to this category of information the perceptions not only of trained observers but all participants in the setting); and meanings such as "phenomenological" information with the understanding that methods for gathering it are not restricted to those ordinarily used in the phenomenological tradition.

A second necessary refinement of Fig. 1 is achieved through the addition of an aggregation facet. This is not meant to be an analytical gimmick; rather, it is to suggest the fact that data collected at, or aggregated to, different levels may mean different things (Burstein 1980,

| Schooling Commonplaces | Cultural/Ecological Dimension | | |
|---|---|---|---|
| | Circumstances | Activities | Meanings |
| Physical Environment | | | |
| Human Resources | | | |
| Material Resources | | | |
| Curriculum[a] | | Information Grid | |
| Organization | | | |
| Communication | | Survey Questionnaire | |
| Problem-solving/ | | Interview | |
| Decision-making | | Observation | |
| Leadership | | Case Study | |
| Issues/Problems | | Document/Archive Review | |
| Controls/Restraints | | | |
| Expectations | | | |
| Climate | | | |
| Evaluation | | | |

**Figure 3**
The schooling terrain: map three

[a]Curriculum is to be interpreted broadly and should include at least these additional commonplaces (see Goodlad et al. 1979): Goals/objectives; content; instructional materials; classroom activities; teaching strategies; assessment; time; space; and grouping

Cronbach et al. 1976, Sirotnik 1980). In other words, information gathered at one level of the educational enterprise (for example student perceptions of classroom learning environments) can be aggregated to create information (not necessarily at the same level) at other levels of the system (for example, a classroom measure of discipline and control or, perhaps at the school level, an indicator of policy regarding order and discipline).

A third complication of the foregoing maps of schooling terrain is the addition of the necessary time facet (Fig. 4) denoting that much of the information in Figs. 1–3 is not static. Even in Fig. 4, it is necessary to chop out some time segment; for example, the usual K–12 (Kindergarten through year 12) elementary and secondary educational time frame is represented with the potential for preschool and postsecondary information. Different inquiry purposes will, of course, suggest different points of entry and departure in this continuum of schooling. The point is, however, that a comprehensive information system must be capable of the *longitudinal* study of schooling.

Finally, in keeping with this multicontent, multisource, multilevel conception of information, is a multimethod perspective on the appropriate forms of information collection. This necessarily implies a multiparadigmatic perspective on what constitutes appropriate knowledge. Using the concepts of *convergent validity* (Campbell and Fiske 1959) from the more quantitative tradition, and *triangulation* (Denzin 1978) from the more qualitative tradition, demands that much of the information suggested in Figs. 1–4 can and should be collected in different ways. Various methods include, but are not limited to, survey questionnaire, interview,

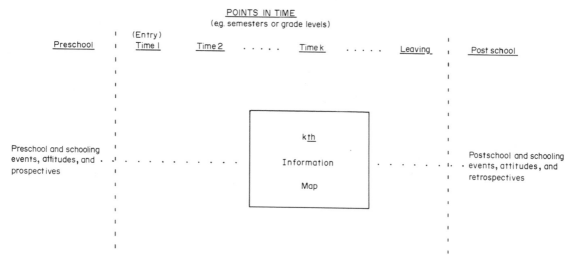

**Figure 4**
The schooling terrain: map four

observation, case study, and historical analysis and document/archive review. The choice of methods, as usual, depends on such matters as how well-understood are the constructs in question, time and resources available for data collection, analysis, and interpretation, volume of information desired, and so forth.

Moreover, various compendiums of constructs, items, and data collection devices exist (e.g. Nowakowski et al. 1984, Sirotnik 1984b). However, the reader should be careful to avoid collecting information simply because it is there. Information is a key ingredient to making an inquiry rigorous and systematic, i.e., using relevant data to inform staff dialogue, facilitate decision-making, guide actions, and provide a descriptive context for evaluations. However, information does not drive an inquiry. Rather, a viable inquiry process continually suggests the kind of information likely to be useful to augment, stimulate, and sustain the effort. Information fuels the engine of inquiry but does not automatically determine the direction of travel.

## 2. Multilevel Issues

Even a cursory glance at Figs. 1–4 will reveal a latent, multilevel morass of information likely to frighten the bravest of data analysts. Indeed, the quantitative treatment of information gathered at and/or aggregated to two or more levels (e.g., individual, class, grade, school, district, etc.), with the intent of exploring multivariate relationships in the data, has only recently been taken seriously by some methodologists unwilling to put aside the conceptual and analytical issues buried in multilevel information. These issues, broadly conceived, fall into either measurement or statistical categories of concerns. A brief outline of these is given below using a rather simple, illustrative example.

Suppose it was of interest to assess the classroom learning environment construct "teacher concern" in a secondary school; students in each class would respond to items like "This teacher cares about me as a person" on, say, a five-point Likert scale of agreement. Following typical internal consistency analyses—factor analyses and/or item-total correlations and alpha analyses—each student would receive a total score on a culled set of "teacher concern" items. Suppose, further, that the relationship between "teacher concern" and a measure of class achievement was the object of statistical investigation at this school.

In this case, several routes might be taken by data analysts depending upon how naïve or sophisticated (and/or daring) they might be. At the naïve end, correlational analyses will be conducted across all students regardless of class membership—a *total* analysis. Sharper analysts will remember intact class warnings from their design courses and they might decide that the class is really the unit of analysis, give the "class scores" equal to the means of the student scores, and perform the correlational analysis on these class measures—a *between* (class) analysis. Towards the more sophisticated end, the analyst will be concerned about the variance within classes on the measures as well and might conduct a number of correlational analyses for each class separately—*within* (class) analyses; additionally, if the results warrant it, these analyses might be "averaged" for interpretive purposes—a *pooled within* analysis. Finally, the sophisticated analyst will recognize the conceptual and empirical value in exploring both within and between analyses simultaneously—a *multilevel* analysis.

The basic dilemma is that each of these analytical approaches can yield quite different results (see Knapp 1977, for the basic bivariate case); so what is the appropriate unit of analysis? The basic resolution, of course, is that it depends on the question(s) being investigated and what one believes is being measured. Moreover, given the multilevel nature of schooling phenomena, it is unlikely that any single-level analysis will ever be adequate, and furthermore, given the lack of working theoretical models of schooling, it is likely that the empirical consequences of multilevel analyses will need to be investigated. It should be noted, incidentally, that the statistical consequences of multilevel analyses can be quite complex, especially when these analyses are conducted longitudinally.

Another issue of central importance to psychometric analysis is that of measurement. Three highly interrelated subcategories of concerns arise in this respect: construct–indicator match, alternative indices of group level constructs, and analytic decisions in scale construction.

First, following the example above, what is being measured by the item "My teacher cares about me as a person"? Is it something about the individual student respondent or, when responses are aggregated (e.g., using the mean), something about the students as a group, something about the teacher, something about the class, all of the above, some of the above, or none of the above? We can either make a decision by fiat or, preferably, we can look at the empirical consequences of several possibilities. For example, thinking about the aggregate response as an indicator of a teacher or class construct, we would want to investigate the variance (and correlates thereof) of this aggregate across classes—a *between* analysis. If, rather, we viewed the data as representing individual perceptions contextualized by classroom experience, then we would be apt to investigate item response variance *within* classes. It would be hard to decontextualize these data and justify a total analysis. Parenthetically, the grammatical form of the item in this example is important, but tends to make little difference in items of this nature; that is, even an item like "This teacher cares about *us* as *people*" exhibits far more within class than between class variation (Sirotnik 1980, Sirotnik et al. 1980). It should be added that construct–indicator issues pertain not only to the scaling of items but also to "stand alone" questions such as age, socioeconomic status (SES), teacher experience, and so on (see Burstein 1980). The SES of students within a class, for example, may measure their families' learning resources; aggregated to the class level, however, SES may be a proxy for ethnicity or school tracking policies.

Second, aggregating from the individual to group level usually takes the form of computing the arithmetic average. This makes sense if we are looking for some kind of group level indicator that is conceived as an additive constant in each individual response. If, however, we are seeking to measure, say, group consensus, asymmetry, independent–dependent variable relationship, or the like, then aggregates such as the variance, percentage above a given cutoff point, or a within group

regression coefficient may be more useful. There is no redeeming value in using the mean just because of its analytical ease.

Third, and intimately tied to the above concerns, is the question of how to go about analyses at the psychometric stage of scale development. In the above example, it was inferred that factor analyses or alpha coefficients were computed across individuals regardless of class membership. This is how most people compute them, although it is ill-advised given the above argument, which suggests that between class and within class correlation matrices should be the ones that are analysed. It is also quite likely that the factor–structure, item–total correlations, and so on, will vary depending upon which matrix is analysed; that is, the very same set of items may behave quite differently and measure different constructs depending upon the level of analysis.

In sum, if we are to contextualize our evaluative inquiries into schooling with information of the types discussed above, and if we are not to ignore the multilevel nature of schooling, then we are forced into coping with the often sticky measurement and statistical issues in multilevel analyses. The interested reader will want to first read a few overview articles (for example, Knapp 1982, Sirotnik and Burstein 1985) and then consult some of the more technical references in these reports.

## 3. Collecting Information: Problems and Possibilities

Traditional experimental design and evaluation research literature quite correctly warned of the problems to be encountered when attempting to model laboratory research in field settings. Threats to interpreting independent–dependent variable relationships, to generalizability, to construct validity, and to statistical sensitivity—due largely to the inability to randomize subjects to treatment conditions, the systematic loss of subjects, the passage of time, imperfect treatment interventions, and the like—have given rise to a body of work attempting to compensate for these problems through better design and analysis (see, for example, Bentler 1980, Cook and Campbell 1979, Muthen and Joreskog 1983, among others).

Better design and analysis, however, cannot compensate for bad data arising out of faulty information collection procedures. This issue has recently been highlighted by Burstein et al. (1985) in the specific context of evaluating programmatic interventions. However, data collection faults—such as burdening respondents with time consuming paper and pencil surveys or interviews, asking overly sensitive questions, personality clashes between data collectors and respondents, inappropriate and/or inconsistent timing of data collection, inconsistent changes in instrumentation, data sources, data collection settings, and/or data collector approaches in gathering ostensibly the same information, and so forth—are equally disastrous for inquiry using comprehensive information systems of the type being described here. This is especially the case if a primary focus of the school-based inquiry has to do with monitoring the total school program over time. Three issues deserve special emphasis in the evaluative context suggested above: information overload, sensitivity of information, and the timing of data collection.

## 3.1 Information Overload

In a major research project, *A Study of Schooling*, over 800 survey responses were collected from teachers, 350 from students, and 275 from parents at the secondary level. Similar amounts of information were collected at the elementary level. Additionally, principals and teachers were interviewed for approximately one hour, and classes were observed for entire periods (or days) on three separate occasions. For typical schools in and around major cities, collecting this amount of information required approximately four highly trained data collectors working 18 days at senior high schools, three working 18 days at junior high schools, and four working 13 days at elementary schools. Surveying of students required two (sometimes three) class periods at the secondary level and three (sometimes four) sessions (about 35–40 minutes) at the elementary level. The teacher survey took from one and a half to three hours to complete. This volume of information served well for research purposes, but it would be far too great for schools trying to develop ongoing, multipurpose (but purposeful) appraisal systems.

There is a growing literature on the effect of "respondent burden" on the quality of information gathered (for example, Frankel and Sharp 1980). Large enough increases in the volume, frequency, or duration of data collection impact unfavorably upon the reliability and validity of the information due to missing data, respondent fatigue and loss of attention, uncooperativeness, and so on. To illustrate, in a project which involved working with a high school staff developing an information system, a significant increase in missing data became apparent after 100–150 items in a student survey (Sirotnik and Burstein 1987). It also became clear that the burden was not only on respondents, but also on the "gatekeepers" of those respondents—teachers, principals, and district administrators upset about the time being drained from the school program.

However, there are, of course, some useful designs and analytical tools for alleviating some of the burden. For example, not everything has to be collected from everyone; for certain purposes, information can be gathered from a sample of respondents, a sample of questions, or samples of both (as in matrix sampling). The virtues of matrix sampling to estimate score distribution parameters of scaled sets of items for sufficiently large respondent samples (for example district level, school level, and perhaps grade levels in large enough schools) are now well known (see Sirotnik and Wellington 1977). For single survey items where the information is primarily useful at aggregated levels (for schoolwide eval-

uation and planning activities, for example), ordinary respondent sampling is adequate. It is possible to further decrease burden over time by sampling different respondents on each occasion, although some overlap will be necessary for correlational studies. If careful longitudinal work is to be carried out, a small but representative respondent cohort would be useful.

Technology can also play an alleviating role. There is more than enough power in desk-top microcomputers to automate the paper/pencil part of information collected for ongoing systems of the type described here. Software could be developed that would contain the entire set of surveys and survey questions and would record and store the responses of students, teachers, and so on. Respondents would sit down, enter their name (or pre-assigned ID code), respond to questions as prompted, be branched as necessary to different course contents, and be referenced to specific classes or periods. Questionnaires would not need to be conducted in one sitting (assuming situational effects can be minimized); respondents could return another time and pick up where they left off. Moreover, in the event of some items being omitted, respondents could be prompted to complete them (or indicate their wish not to answer them). Ordinarily cumbersome data management problems then become trivial: completed response protocols are now stored and are ready for analysis automatically; multiple samplings of the same students that occurs at the secondary level in different periods can be easily managed by prompting them only once for demographic and schoolwide information while prompting them repeatedly for information pertaining to each class in which they were sampled, and so forth. Technology not only holds some promise for relieving much of the burden in data collection, but also holds the same for data analysis. In fact, students are an excellent resource for performing the data analysis tasks, and the data analysis tasks become an excellent "hands-on" learning experience for students in mathematics, statistics, and computer science classes.

However, methodology and technology are only tools in the hands of, one hopes, sensible and sensitive people. The real key to relieving the burden of information-based appraisal systems lies in a viable inquiry process at district and building levels that allows for participatory deliberation and judicious selection of relevant information for mutually endorsed purposes.

## 3.2 Sensitivity of Information

In this "age of information," the issue of sensitive information goes well beyond the usual issues, for example personal items (age, religion, ethnicity, and so on), upsetting items (nuclear war, pending personnel decisions, and so on), embarrassing items (sexual behaviour, number of hours watching TV versus reading the latest in educational research and practice), and so forth. Certainly, this aspect of information sensitivity is important and must be contended with when constructing, testing, and using information-gathering devices.

Use and abuse issues in using comprehensive information systems, however, will emerge as even more important concerns (Sirotnik 1984c). The Orwellian reality of computer technology significantly exacerbates the ever-present problems of information security and respondent confidentiality. Anonymity and confidentiality have traditionally been handled by eliminating identification codes or establishing trust. Computerizing the entire process makes it easy to keep track of respondents. Linking teacher responses to those of their students in their classrooms, or linking students' responses one year with their responses the next, are necessary data management tasks if certain correlational or longitudinal analyses are to be done. These tasks, of course, require a "dictionary" that links names to ID (identification) numbers.

It may well be that the future holds a climate of increasing distrust and that analyses requiring respondent confidentiality will be a thing of the past. It may be that the most promising strategy is to involve people in significant ways in the conceptualization, development, and use of their own information system.

### 3.3 Timing the Collection of Information

Scheduling is a major consideration in collecting information in schools, not only because of potential confounding and error effects due to missing or tardy baseline data, too few observations over time, unsystematic time sampling, and so forth, but also because no time ever seems to be the right time to schedule a major data collection.

It is unlikely that an information-based, comprehensive appraisal system could collect large amounts of data more than once per academic year. However, many data collection activities are ongoing by definition: accumulating attendance and dropout rates, achievement assessment that is referenced to instructional continuums, and so on. Additionally, specialized surveys or interviews for special circumstances will occur on an as-needed basis (for example a drug abuse survey, a parent survey on a pending school closure, and so on); and specific evaluations of programmatic interventions will probably require additional assessments in accord with the evaluation design. General "audits" of the school's circumstances, activities, and meanings, however, might be done, say, between the 10th and 20th week of the first or second semester, depending on what the need is for the information.

### 4. Conclusion

This article has noted the importance of seeing the collection and use of information as *part* of a larger commitment to self-examination—individually and collaboratively—on the part of those seriously concerned with schools (administrators, teachers, students, and parents, for example). Many of the problems above can

be largely overcome as the idea, value, and use of information become "cultural regularities" of schooling (Sarasson 1971).

This view of collaborative, informed inquiry is as "methodological" as the quantitative and qualitative methods endorsed above. Information-based appraisal systems will not become a cultural regularity of schooling until *critical discourse* becomes a way of organizational life in schools (Sirotnik and Oakes 1986). This means a commitment to rigorous and sustained inquiry by the relevant stakeholders around such generic questions as: What goes on here in the name of educational goals, curricular emphasis, principal leadership, assessment of effectiveness, and so on? How did it come to be that way? Whose interests are being served by the way things are? Is this the way we want it? What other information do we have, or need to get, to help inform our deliberations? What are we going to do about all this, and how are we going to monitor it?

It is this kind of organizational and professional context that the collection, analysis, interpretation, and use of comprehensive information can play a major role in evaluation for local school improvement..

## Bibliography

Babbie E R 1983 *The Practice of Social Research*. Wadsworth, Belmont, California

Bank A, Williams R C 1987 Creating an ISS . . .. In: Bank A, Williams R C (eds.) 1987 *Information Systems and School Improvement: Inventing the Future*. Teachers College Press, New York

Bentler P M 1980 Multivariate analysis with latent variables: Causal modeling. *Annu. Rev. Psychol.* 31: 419–56

Burstein L 1980 The analysis of multilevel data in educational research and evaluation. *Rev. Res. Educ.* 8: 158–233

Burstein L 1984 The use of existing databases in program evaluation and school improvement. *Educ. Eval. Pol. Anal.* 6: 307–18

Burstein L, Freeman H E, Rossi P H (eds.) 1985 *Collecting Evaluation Data: Problems and Solutions*. Sage, Beverly Hills, California

Burstein L, Freeman H E, Sirotnik K A, Delandshere G, Hollis M 1985 Data collection: The Achilles heel of evaluation research. *Sociol. Meth. Res.* 14: 65–80

Campbell D T, Fiske D W 1959 Convergent and discriminant validation by the multitrait–multimethod matrix. *Psychol. Bull.* 56: 81–105

Cook T D, Campbell D T 1979 *Quasi-experimentation: Design and Analysis Issues for Field Settings*. Rand McNally, Chicago, Illinois

Cooley W W, Bickel W E 1986 *Decision-oriented Educational Research*. Kluwer-Nijhoff, Boston, Massachusetts

Cronbach L J, Deken J E, Webb N 1976 *Research on Classrooms and Schools: Formulation of Questions, Design, and Analysis*. Occasional Paper of the Stanford Evaluation Consortium, Stanford University, Stanford, California

Denzin N K 1978 *The Research Act: A Theoretical Introduction to Sociological Methods*, 2nd edn. McGraw Hill, New York

Frankel J, Sharp L 1980 *Measurement of Respondent Burden: Summary of Study Design and Early Findings*. Bureau of Social Science Research, Washington, DC

Goodlad J I 1984 *A Place Called School: Prospects for the Future*. McGraw Hill, New York

Goodlad J I, Klein M F, Tye K A 1979 The domains of curriculum and their study. In: Goodlad J I et al. (eds.) 1979 *Curriculum Inquiry*. McGraw Hill, New York

Hathaway W E 1984 *Evolution, Nature, Uses and Issues in the Creation of Local School District Comprehensive Information Systems*. Paper presented at the conference of the American Educational Research Association. ERIC Document No. ED 244377

Idstein P 1987 We'll create the future, but may keep it a secret. In: Bank A, Williams R C (eds.) 1987 *Information and School Improvement: Inventing the Future*. Teachers College Press, New York

Knapp T R 1977 The unit-of-analysis problem in applications of simple correlation analysis to educational research. *J. Educ. Stat.* 2: 171–86

Knapp T R 1982 The unit and the context of the analysis for research in educational administration. *Educ. Admin. Q.* 18: 1–13

McNamara T C 1980 *Ongoing Documentation Systems*. Paper presented at the conference of the American Educational Research Association.

Muthen B, Joreskog K G 1983 Selectivity problems in quasi-experimental studies. *Eval. Rev.* 7: 139–74

Nowakowski J, Bunda M A, Working R, Bernacki G, Harrington P 1984 *A Handbook of Educational Variables: A Guide to Evaluation*. Kluwer-Nijhoff, Boston, Massachusetts

Sarason S B 1971 *The Culture of the School and the Problem of Change*. Allyn and Bacon, Boston, Massachusetts

Sirotnik K A 1980 Psychometric implications of the unit-of-analysis problem (with examples from the measurement of organizational climate). *J. Educ. Meas.* 17: 245–82

Sirotnik K A 1984a An outcome-free conception of schooling: Implications for school-based inquiry and information systems. *Educ. Eval. Pol. Anal.* 6: 227–39

Sirotnik K A 1984b *Principles and Practice of Contextual Appraisal for Schools*. Laboratory in School and Community Education, University of California Los Angeles, California

Sirotnik K A 1984c *Using versus Being Used by School Information Systems*. Paper presented at the conference of the American Educational Research Association, ERIC Document No. ED 263117

Sirotnik K A, Burstein L 1983 *Methodological Issues in Studying the Effectiveness of Schooling: Recent Developments and Lingering Concerns*. Paper presented at the American Educational Research Association.

Sirotnik K A, Burstein L 1985 Measurement and statistical issues in multilevel research on schooling. *Educ. Admin. Q.* 21: 169–85

Sirotnik K A, Burstein L 1987 Making sense out of comprehensive school-based information systems: An exploratory study. In Bank A, Williams R C (eds.) 1987 *Information Systems and School Improvement: Inventing the Future*. Teachers College Press, New York

Sirotnik K A, Oakes J 1986 Critical inquiry for school renewal: Liberating theory and practice. In: Sirotnik K A, Oakes J (eds.) 1986 *Critical Perspectives on the Organization and Improvement of Schooling*. Kluwer-Nijhoff, Boston, Massachusetts, pp. 3–93

Sirotnik K A, Wellington R 1977 Incidence sampling: An integrated theory for "matrix sampling". *J. Educ. Meas.* 14: 343–99

Sirotnik K A, Nides M A, Engstrom G A 1980 Some methodological issues in developing measures of classroom learning environment: A report of work in progress *Stud. Educ. Eval.* 6: 279–89

# Reporting the Results of Evaluation Studies[1]

## A. H. Passow

One of the most important stages in the conduct of evaluation studies is the reporting process. The major purposes of evaluation, purposes which are not mutually exclusive, include: (a) contributing to decisions about program installation, program continuation, and/or program modification; (b) obtaining evidence to rally support either for or in opposition to a program; and (c) contributing to the understanding of basic psychological, social, or other processes (Anderson and Ball 1978). The fulfillment of these purposes depends to a large extent on the nature and quality of the reporting process. Adequate and appropriate communication of findings and recommendations to various relevant individuals and groups will determine how effective the decision-making processes will be.

The operant phrase is *the reporting process* which is intended to indicate that more than the preparation of a final report is involved. Rather, there must be communication to various groups and individuals throughout the evaluation process using a variety of communication means. Some reporting is in the form of formal reports, other reporting may be quite informal, depending on the nature and intent of the communication. The organization or agency which initiates and pays for the study will want a formal report. The individuals and groups who are involved in the decisions regarding the program will require various kinds of communications, including a report on the findings and the recommendations for future action. Individuals and groups who are supplying information will want feedback. Thus, as Anderson and Ball (1978 p. 93) observe: "It is rather obvious that program evaluation cannot be carried out without some communication among the agents in the process—funding organization, program director, program participants, evaluation staff, and the

1   This article was originally published in the *International Journal of Educational Research*, Vol. 11, No. 1. It appears here with permission from Pergamon Press plc © 1987.

communities and institutions within which the program is being developed or assessed."

The evaluators need to determine at the outset what the elements of the communication network are in a particular setting: who needs to be informed about what, who needs to be involved at what points and how, and who needs what information in order to participate in decisions about the program as well as to implement and effect these decisions. Communication, of course, is not simply a one-way avenue from the evaluators to the clients; unless there is two-way communication, the reporting and the outcomes are likely to be limited.

It is essential that the evaluators keep the program staff and others involved in the program informed, providing sufficient information so that there will be an adequate understanding of what the evaluation is all about without invalidating the findings by biasing the participants. Sufficient information is that which will reduce the anxieties of those involved, secure the needed cooperation in the data-gathering process without biasing the data, and establish trust and confidence in the findings and recommendations. Adequate information is essential to build a sound relationship between the program participants and the evaluators so that all aspects of the evaluation process can be facilitated. Taking Scriven's (1967) concept of formative and summative evaluation as a guide, the reporting can also be thought of as related to in-process (formative) and final (summative) communication.

## 1. Reporting/Communicating in an Evaluation Study

A look at an evaluation study conducted over a two-year period will illustrate the reporting/communicating process. The description focuses on the reporting and communicating and is not a complete account of the study.

With declining enrollments a school system found it necessary to close one of its two junior high schools (grades 7 and 8—ages 12 and 13) and consolidate the students into one building. The recommendation to take this action was made by the district's Superintendent of Schools who coupled it with the proposal that the new school should be a middle school, rather than a junior high school, with a philosophy, program, structure, staffing, and functioning appropriate to a middle school. Other details of the proposal included the following recommendations:

(a) A middle school should be organized to include all of the district's seventh and eighth graders, however, only the seventh graders should be involved in the first year, and both seventh and eight graders should be enrolled beginning with the second year.

(b) Instruction in the basic academic subjects: English, Social Studies, Mathematics, and Science. These should be provided four days a week rather than the traditional five days a week. In addition, a wide variety of so-called "mods," or ten-week mini-courses should be provided on the fifth day. The four-day academic and one-day mod program was to be scheduled over a six-day cycle.

(c) The students should be organized into four teams of approximately 100 pupils in which the basic academic subjects should be taught by a team of four teachers.

(d) More attention should be paid to the range of characteristics and needs of this age group, including additional guidance.

As the Superintendent's proposal was discussed at the formal Board of Education meetings, in the community and in the news media, support for and opposition to the plan began to develop. Those opposed to the new design appeared to focus on features which they considered to represent a move away from concern for high academic standards and for provisions for students of high ability and performance. Those in favor of the new middle school plan saw it as being more responsive to the entire student body through provisions for teams, electives, and new program offerings, such as the computer laboratory. After considerable discussion in a variety of forums, a decision was made to proceed with the new program, but the vote by the Board of Education was not a unanimous one. Even though there appeared to be general support for the plan as perceived by the Superintendent and the Board of Education members, many issues continued to arouse concern among parents, teachers, other members of the school community, and the Board members themselves. Among the most controversial issues were the four-day academic schedule, the mod program, heterogeneous grouping, scheduling, and provisions for gifted students.

As approved by the Board of Education, the Superintendent's plan was accepted with two provisions: (a) that there be an evaluation conducted by an external agency or group, and (b) that accelerated classes in English and Mathematics be organized after the first 10 weeks of school. Four elevation teams submitted competitive proposals for undertaking the evaluation. The successful team's proposal was for a two-year evaluation study, focusing on the seventh grade during the first year, and the seventh and eighth grades during the second year, after both grades had been admitted and the two-year middle school program was functioning fully. The evaluation team consisted of two university professors and 7 doctoral students the first year and 10 the second year.

Using the mandate of the Board of Education for a comprehensive evaluation of the new middle school for guidance, the evaluation team developed its procedures for gathering data. The major sources of information were teachers and administrative staff (both central office and building), interviews, and questionnaires; student interviews, questionnaires, and test data; parent interviews and questionnaires; documents from the

Board of Education and the central office related to the middle school; and observations in the classrooms and the school.

During initial meetings with members of staff, the evaluators described the purpose of the study and how it was to be conducted and assured the staff that the study was concentrated on the school as a unit and that individual staff members were not being evaluated. At these initial meetings, it was also pointed out that teacher concerns, reactions, and recommendations would be an important input and would be reflected in the instruments used and the procedures followed in gathering and analyzing the data. Aside from formal faculty meetings at which the evaluators reported on the purpose of the study and how it was to be conducted, the evaluators always spent time communicating informally with staff members in the faculty room each time they were at the school. These informal meetings provided opportunities for the staff members to inquire about what was going on, to make suggestions about the procedures and the data being collected, and to discuss matters raised by their colleagues, or the evaluators. These informal sessions proved invaluable in establishing relationships and mutual trust, and helped the evaluators to understand the data being collected. They were an important part of the informal reporting process.

The basic focus of the study was on the instructional program, the staff, operational policies, and their impact on pupil performance and perceptions. Each of the classrooms in the school was observed on at least one occasion by different members of the evaluation team to obtain a broad picture of the instructional processes. In addition to the observations, interviews were conducted with teachers, students, parents, administrators (including department chairpersons and team leaders), board members, and other members of the community. The interviews provided the basic data from which the questionnaires were constructed. Standard procedures were used in developing, pretesting, revising, and conducting the surveys for all of the groups studied.

During the first year, two sets of interviews were conducted with a small sample of individuals who were selected to represent a broad spectrum of opinions of people who were most knowledgeable about the range of issues involved in the policy decision. These persons were identified on the basis of documents with an effort made to include both individuals who had been outspoken in favor of and others who had been equally outspoken in opposition to the decision for a middle school. These individuals were interviewed again in the fall and in the late spring. The second interview schedule was designed to elicit the reactions of the interviewees once the program was well under way and focused on issues which had been identified in the first interviews.

In October, most of the teachers responded to a form with questions dealing with perceived positive aspects of the new middle school program, concerns related to the program, and suggestions for change. After the responses were analyzed, meetings were conducted with each of the four teacher teams to report the findings and to discuss and confirm them. An in-depth comprehensive questionnaire was then designed, using the preliminary survey and the team meeting discussions as its foundation. This questionnaire included items dealing with middle school goals, instructional programs, instructional strategies, teaching styles, administration, school and district policies, ability grouping, decision-making input, scheduling, the academic program, the mod/minicourse program, pupil personnel services, testing, and so on. The questionnaire consisted of three parts: (a) 149 items dealing with attitudes and perceptions concerning various aspects of the program, (b) 30 items dealing with levels of satisfaction for each program area, and (c) 10 demographic items. The responses were analyzed for the staff as a whole, for each of the four teams, and for teachers not assigned to a team or assigned to more than one team. These findings were reported to and discussed by the teachers.

Several questionnaires were administered to the students during the year. In order to assess the transition from the elementary schools to the middle school, a questionnaire was administered to all seventh graders after two months in the school. A standard articulation survey form was modified with the assistance of the guidance counselors and the principal. Students were asked to respond to questions about adjustment to school routines, the curriculum, the teachers and teaching, peer relationships, and feelings about the program generally. These data were analyzed for the seventh grade group as a whole as well as by sex, by team, and by sending elementary school. When the data were compiled, the findings were reported to the faculty, with special attention given to aspects which were perceived as problematic by the students.

At the beginning of each 10-week period, students selected the mod/minicourse electives in which they wished to participate. A questionnaire was designed to elicit student reactions to the mod/minicourse program in general as well as evaluative judgments of each elective in which the student participated during the 10-week period. Students who participated in more than one mod elective (the majority) completed a separate evaluation for each mod. These questionnaires were analyzed at the end of each 10-week period and a computer printout was provided for the teacher of each mod. This report on the student responses to a mod/minicourse was provided for each teacher at the end of each 10-week period. In addition, there were a number of items on the middle school student questionnaire administered toward the end of the school year which elicited student responses to the mod/minicourse program overall.

A middle school student questionnaire was designed to study the perceptions of the students regarding their academic and social self-concepts as well as their opinions regarding the middle school, its teachers and teaching, and the mod/minicourse program. A 103-item questionnaire also contained a section with 48 "curricular areas" aimed at securing student judgment about the middle school experience in general and specific aspects in particular. These questionnaires were analyzed for the total group as well as by sex, by team, and by sending elementary school.

Two tests, the Metropolitan Achievement Test and the Otis–Lennon Mental Ability Test, were administered as part of the district's regular testing program. For this study, the reading and mathematics scores of the Metropolitan Achievement Test were examined together with the mental ability or IQ scores from the Otis–Lennon Test. The seventh grade student's sixth and seventh grade test scores as well as the eighth grade students' (i.e., those a year ahead and still in the junior high school setting) seventh grade scores on the same achievement and mental ability tests were presented in the form of Stanine Scores. In addition, these same scores were presented as Stanine Bivariate Distributions, with the achievement scores examined in relation to the measured ability. Thirdly, the seventh and eighth graders' reading and mathematics scores were presented in total population mean Stanine Scores for comparison. These test data were analyzed to answer the questions as to how the seventh grade middle school students were doing compared to eighth grade when they were seventh graders and how students were performing in relation to their ability.

A study was also undertaken to determine the amount of student involvement in the learning activities, that is, the time-on-task. This study aimed at determining whether students were more "on task" in some subjects than in others and whether "on task" behavior occurred more frequently at the beginning or at the end of the class period, if either. "On task" behavior was compared in regular classes and mod/minicourses. Educational activities (lecture, discussion, small group work, individual work, and the like) and organizational settings (working independently, in small groups, or in whole class) were examined as well in relation to time-on-task. All of the regular classes and a sample of the mod/minicourse classes were observed over a two-day span.

Finally, a questionnaire was designed to obtain the opinions and perceptions of the parents most closely associated with the middle school program. All seventh grade parents were included, together with a sample of sixth grade parents from each of the five elementary schools. In addition, all members of the Middle School Committee, an advisory group, were sent the Parent Study Questionnaire. The 87-item instrument sought parents' opinions about all aspects of the middle school program and the school's functioning. The questionnaire also included a demographic section with questions about family background and history, and contact with the school. Space was provided for any additional comments. These data were analyzed for the parent group as a whole, by whether they had children in seventh and/or sixth grade, by sending elementary school, and by the team to which their seventh grade child had been assigned.

Two final reports were prepared: one was an executive summary which summarized all of the findings in relatively nontechnical terms and provided a set of 11 recommendations which were aimed at building on the strengths of the program during its first year and at addressing the observed weaknesses and problems. The second report was really a combination final report and technical report in the sense that it contained all of the data analyses for all of the surveys—more than would usually go into a final report.

The executive summary and final report were the basis for a meeting with the Board of Education members and the chief administrators which was scheduled some three weeks after they had received them and had time to study them. A large number of copies of the executive summary were then made available to the public, with copies of the final report placed in the public libraries and school offices as well as the central office. A public meeting was then held, at which the evaluators summarized the findings and recommendations briefly and then responded to questions from those parents in attendance. Finally, the evaluators met with the central administrators, the building administrator, and the middle school staff on a number of occasions to discuss the findings and recommendations and help plan the second year of the school's operation during which the school would have its full student complement of seventh and eighth-graders.

In conducting the second-year evaluation of the implementation, the focus was once again on the question of how well the school was working in terms of student outcomes as well as the quality of life at the school. In appraising the latter, the evaluators were concerned with whether a climate for learning had been created which nurtured both cognitive and affective growth for a very special group of young adolescents. The school had become a single unit housing all of the district's seventh and eighth graders with a complete middle school staff and a single administration. One of the factors which influenced data collection and the interpretation of the results was the knowledge of impending program changes required by the state education department, changes which were to be implemented in the fall of the following year. Some features of the original middle school program would have to be modified to meet the state's new mandates. Consequently, the evaluators paid particular attention to perceptions concerning how the mandated changes would influence the philosophy on which the middle school program was based as well as elements of the program's operations.

Almost all of the same studies were repeated: student adjustment to the middle school, student perceptions of the middle school experience, student assessment of the mod/minicourse program (which had been modified considerably based on evaluator recommendations), reading and mathematics achievement, time-on-task observations, teacher perceptions and opinions, and parent and community survey. While the same studies were conducted, the same instruments were not used. The questionnaires were revised to take into account the fact that there were now seventh and eighth graders in the school, that the number of teachers had increased because of the two-grade complement, that program changes had occurred, and so on. Individual interviews were conducted with all of the teachers and administrators and these provided the basis for the teacher questionnaire. Frequent visits to the school by evaluation team members provided many informal contacts with school and district personnel, and made possible observations of the day-to-day activities in the school.

Analyses of the student responses on the questionnaire were done for the total group, by seventh and eighth grade team assignments, by sex, and by sending-school. The teacher interviews provided the basis for developing a questionnaire which was analyzed in terms of total staff response, grades taught (i.e., seventh grade, eighth grade, or both), and by years of service at the middle school (i.e., one or two years). The parent questionnaire was designed to obtain the opinions of all parents whose children were enrolled in the school. Except for five items, the same parent survey was used for parents of both grades. Where anchor items were used from the previous year, comparisons were presented. The data were presented by means for the first year, means for seventh grade parents for the second year, means for eighth grade parents for the second year, and totals for both grades for the second year.

Interim reports were presented to the staff and administrative personnel as findings became available. In addition, an executive summary and final report were prepared and presentations made to the Board of Education and school administrators at a closed meeting, to the public at an open Board meeting, and to the staff and administrators after the executive summary and full final report had been made available earlier, as in the first year. Ten recommendations were included in the second-year final report.

## 2. Reports and the Reporting Process

As can be seen from the above illustration of a two-year evaluation study, reporting is an ongoing process, not simply a final report which is issued at the end of a study. Since the major purpose of evaluation is to assist decision-makers in making decisions based on better information, communication/reporting is an integral part of the evaluation process throughout. A good deal of reporting, particularly that which occurs early on is fairly informal. An evaluator must ascertain the information needs of the different audiences who are involved and use various means of communicating to those audiences. Progress, or in-process reporting will be quite different from summative or final reporting.

Progress reports, as Wolf (1984) points out "usually include a relatively short summary of activities engaged in during a particular time period, a preview of upcoming activities, a statement of problems encountered and/or resolved and, possibly a brief statement of preliminary findings" (pp. 200–201). Progress reports are used to keep those involved in the program informed about the way the evaluation is proceeding, to provide a check on the accuracy of data being collected and its interpretation, and to provide an indication of additional information needed and how it can be collected. Interim findings can sometimes be used by decision-makers to initiate program changes, as part of the formative evaluation process.

The final report includes the results of the study, the conclusions drawn from the findings about the program, and recommendations regarding the future of the program. The final report may also include an executive summary, and a technical report, or these may be separate documents. The executive summary is usually a relatively short, concise document which summarizes the major findings, the conclusions, and the recommendations which emerge. The executive summary is written in nontechnical language for wide dissemination to individuals who need to be informed but want only the essence of the findings and recommendations, not the details on which the conclusions and recommendations are based. The technical report may be issued as a separate report or as an appendix in the final report. The technical report contains the tables, the statistical analyses, and even the data-collecting instruments and procedures. As the name implies, this report discusses technical aspects and problems of the evaluation which have been encountered which are usually not of great interest to a wide audience even though they may be fascinating to the evaluator. There will be some audiences or members of some audiences who will want to see the data and statistical analyses and these should be provided in the technical report.

The full evaluation report or final report is the document which fleshes out the executive summary, providing more details regarding the findings, conclusions, and recommendations for future action without providing the tables and statistical analyses or discussions about problems encountered. The full final report includes descriptions of the program and its implementation, the evaluation procedures and processes, the concerns and issues identified and studied, the findings, the conclusions, and the recommendations. The final report should contain sufficient information to respond to the concerns and issues of the audiences and provide enough information so that the judgments on which the recommendations are based are clear. Wolf (1984) draws a distinction "between judgments about the worth of an educational course, program, or curriculum and judgments about future action" (p. 186). Both kinds of judgments need to be dealt with in the final report and sufficient information needs to be presented for the audiences to understand both. Judgments about the value of an educational program should be based on the data collected and its analysis. Judgments about future action, on the other hand, may be more subjective, more political, and may take into account forces and factors which go beyond the data. Thus, as Wolf (1984) cautions: "Since the evaluation worker will be going beyond the bounds of the kinds of conclusions that are made in conventional studies, it is important that judgments of worth be clearly separated from the rest of the material in an evaluation report" (p. 187). Guba and Lincoln (1981) argue that "the reaching of judgments and recommendations is a matter for interaction between the evaluator and the several audiences; the report should, however, highlight the judgments and recommendations that need to be made and provide the basic information from which they can jointly be fashioned by the evaluator and the audience" (p. 365).

A draft of the executive summary and the final report should be made available for discussion with some of the key individuals involved in the program being evaluated prior to the preparation and presentation of the final version. Making available the report draft enables the evaluator to find out whether the team has obtained accurate data. Are the data accurate and complete? Have the data been correctly interpreted? Are there conditions or factors which are important which might mitigate or alter the findings or the recommendations? Making a draft of a report available also avoids the element of surprise when the final report is presented so that policy makers and those responsible for the program are not faced with the unexpected when confronted with a final document in public. It must be stressed that providing a draft of a report is not for the purpose of negotiations and alterations but rather for discussions about the completeness and accuracy of the data, the correctness of the interpretation, and consideration of factors which might affect implementation. Some recommendations emerge not directly from the data and findings but rather from the experience and values of the evaluators who presumably bring an expertise and competence which extends beyond the concerns and issues raised by those responsible for the program.

Finally, there is another kind of report, one prepared for the media. While this may be a news release, it is an important document. An evaluation report may be a lengthy, complicated document which a news reporter may skim for its attention-catching phrases. If the evaluation report is one to which the public should have or would want to have access, it is better to prepare a public information document which correctly summarizes the findings, conclusions, and recommendations—briefly, succinctly, and accurately—for use by those who write or report the news.

The life-span value of evaluation reports vary with the nature of the program being studied. In a sense, if evaluation is for the purpose of helping decision makers make better or better informed decisions about a program—its installation, continuation, or modification—then whether and when a report becomes obsolescent will depend on whether and how the recommendations for future action have been implemented, whether and how the conditions affecting the program change, whether and how the values of the audience change, and so on. Evaluation reports become obsolete and this is an aspect of a study which must be recognized by both the evaluators who prepare reports and those responsible for programs who use those reports.

It is important that evaluators bear in mind that it is a reporting process to which they must attend throughout the conduct of an evaluation study, not simply the preparation of a final report.

## Bibliography

Anderson S B, Ball S 1978 *The Profession and Practice of Program Evaluation.* Jossey-Bass, San Francisco, California

Guba E G, Lincoln Y S 1981 *Effective Evaluation: Improving the Usefulness of Evaluation Results through Responsive and Naturalistic Approaches.* Jossey-Bass, San Francisco, California

Wolf R M 1984 *Evaluation in Education: Foundations of Competency Assessment and Program Review*, 2nd edn. Praeger, New York

Scriven M 1967 The methodology of evaluation. In: Tyler R W (ed.) 1967 *Perspectives of Curriculum Evaluation.* Rand McNally, Chicago, Illinois

# Contributors Index

Contributors are listed in alphabetical order together with their affiliations. Titles of articles which they have authored follow in alphabetical order, along with the respective page numbers. Where articles are co-authored, this has been indicated by an asterisk preceding the article title.

†deceased

† deceased

# Name Index

The Name Index has been compiled so that the reader can proceed either directly to the page where an author's work is cited, or to the reference itself in the bibliography. For each name, the page numbers for the bibliographic citation are given first, followed by the page number(s) in parentheses where that reference is cited in text. Where a name is referred to only in text, and not in the bibliography, the page number appears only in parentheses.

The accuracy of the spelling of authors' names has been affected by the use of different initials by some authors, or a different spelling of their name in different papers or review articles (sometimes this may arise from a transliteration process), and by those journals which give only one initial to each author.

# Subject Index

The Subject Index has been compiled as a guide to the reader who is interested in locating all the references to a particular subject area within the Encyclopedia. Entries may have up to three levels of heading. Where the page numbers appear in bold italic type, this indicates a substantive discussion of the topic. Every effort has been made to index as comprehensively as possible and to standardize the terms used in the index. Given the diverse nature of the field and the varied use of terms throughout the international community, synonyms and foreign language terms have been included with appropriate cross-references. As a further aid to the reader, cross-references have also been given to terms of related interest.